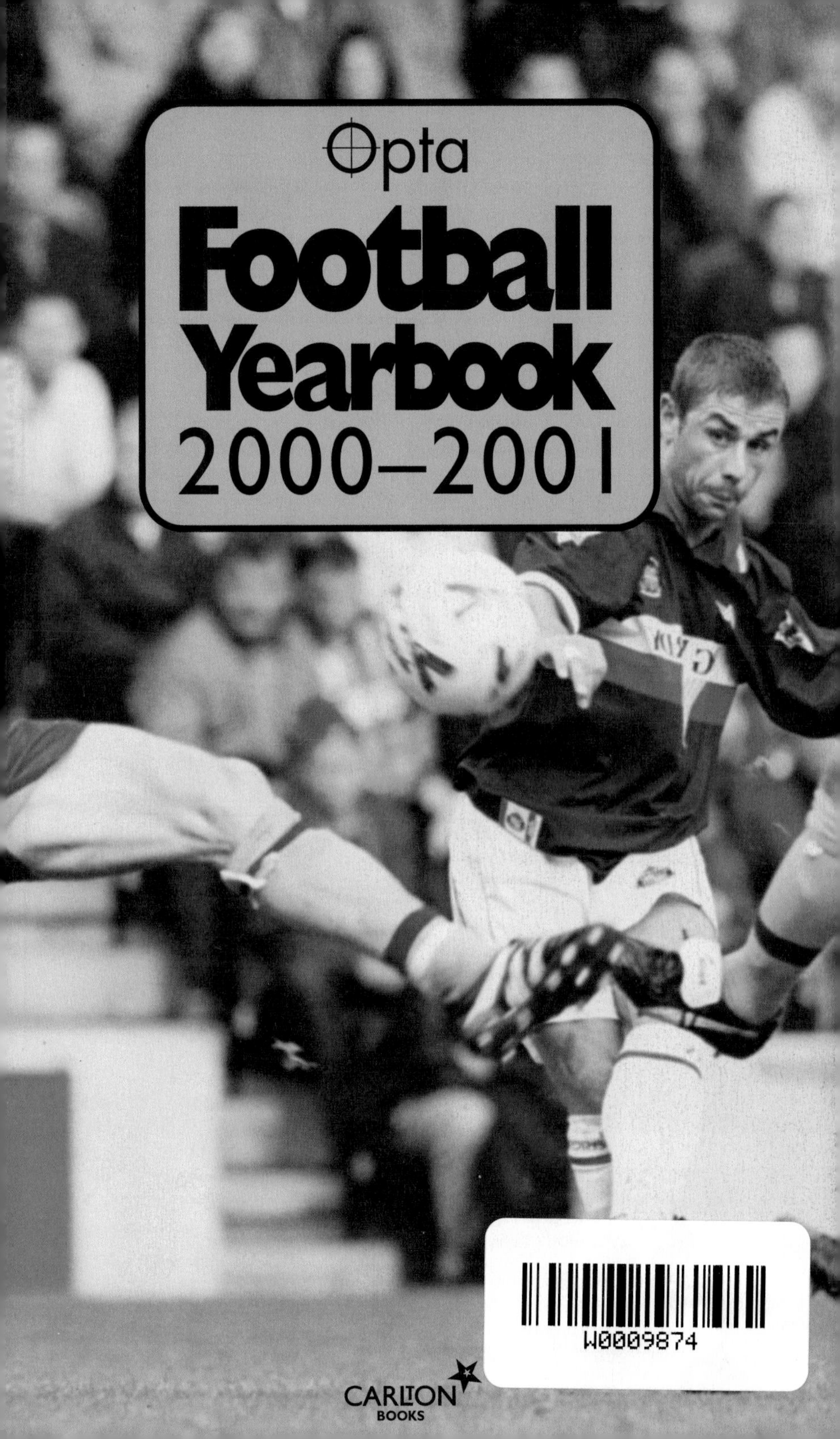
Opta
Football
Yearbook
2000–2001
W0009874
CARLTON
BOOKS

CONTENTS

Foreword by Howard Wilkinson

Preface by Terry Venables

1 INTRODUCTION 11

2 THE TEAMS 29

Introduction	29	Middlesbrough	184
Arsenal	30	Newcastle United	198
Aston Villa	44	Sheffield Wednesday	212
Bradford City	58	Southampton	226
Chelsea	72	Sunderland	240
Coventry City	86	Tottenham Hotspur	254
Derby County	100	Watford	268
Everton	114	West Ham United	282
Leeds United	128	Wimbledon	296
Leicester City	142	Charlton Athletic	310
Liverpool	156	Ipswich Town	318
Manchester United	170	Manchester City	326

3 THE PLAYERS 335

Pen portraits and Opta statistics for every player who took to the pitch in a Premiership match in 1999–2000 and profiles of players to watch in the coming season.

4 COMPARATIVE TABLES 607

The Teams	608	Teams of the season	660
The Players	634	Referees	672
The Index	654		

FA Premier League Fixture List 2000–2001 678

FOREWORD BY HOWARD WILKINSON

Football was a very different game when I signed for my hometown club Sheffield Wednesday back in June 1962.

There were no revolving advertising hoardings, no "technical areas" for coaching staff, no all-seater stadia and a goalkeeper could pick up a backpass – then hold the ball for more than six seconds.

And above all, statistics on the game – beyond the scoreline and match attendance figure – were about as rare as my goals!

The idea of every kick being filmed, monitored and recorded, then stored in a computer database, would have been like something out of a science fiction "B" movie.

These days, performance statistics for players and teams are compiled on a simply phenomenal scale. There is no hiding place for players anymore. If you want to find out who has committed the most fouls in the league over the course of the season, you can.

Some people in the game hide behind the notion that statistics can be used to prove different sides of the same argument, or that they can be misleading. Certainly, I'm not the sort of "statto" that swears by tables of figures. But I do believe stats can be used very effectively to motivate players, as do many of the top coaches in the game.

A player likes to know he has the highest pass completion rate at his club, or that he wins the most tackles. Someone who's not cutting the mustard statistically won't like it one bit and the shrewd coach can use those stats to help the player raise his game.

I speak to all the top managers regularly and I can tell you that many of them are very interested in the Opta stats. They receive Manager's Reports on every league game their team plays. And they may ask to see stats from their forthcoming opponents and hope to identify weaknesses.

Liverpool boss Gerard Houllier and West Ham's Harry Redknapp, for example, are managers who always use the stats to help with training and motivation, while David O'Leary usually has a copy of the 1999–2000 Opta Yearbook to hand in his office at Elland Road.

I and other League Managers' Association (LMA) committee members Alan Curbishley and Dave Bassett went to Opta's offices to give our input to their new OSCA system of analysis. The data that can be collected by the company has increased dramatically with this new system and the technology used is certainly impressive.

The media's appetite for the stats has grown, too, as you will see elsewhere in this book. Suddenly coaches have to be careful what they say. If they criticise a referee for being the most "whistle-happy" in the Premiership, they are not just risking an FA misconduct charge. Opta will have the stats at their fingertips to either prove or disprove the manager's words – and there will probably be no shortage of newspapers and websites wanting to print the stats.

Healthy scepticism of this type of work will and should always exist. I remember an interesting moment in the 1999–2000 season when Chelsea chairman Ken Bates accused Leicester City of being a "kick-

"There is no hiding place for players anymore"

and-rush" side. Opta produced stats to show that, in fact, Chelsea had attempted more long passes than any other side in the Premiership.

Doubters would immediately say that a measured long pass from Frank Leboeuf is rather different to an optimistic punt forward in the hope that a pacy forward will latch on to it – but opinions will always differ.

If I had been then-Leicester manager Martin O'Neill, I would have used the stats to fire up my players. Knowing how shrewd Martin is, he probably did.

With Opta's statistics having such a massive impact on the domestic game, it's hardly surprising that the company has continued to nurture into the media-friendly force it is now. Demand for stats in all sports is growing, like it or not. Pick up any national newspaper in mid-season and you will see no end of tables and numbers in the sports section. They wouldn't bother printing the stats if there was no demand for them.

There's no shortage of stats in the coming pages and there's something in the book for everyone. The stats allow you to directly compare your team with the other 19 in the league and look at the facts for any player who featured in the 1999–2000 Premiership season. These are things you can't access in any other book, anywhere in the world.

So if you've ever heard of Opta and wondered what all the fuss was about, you're about to find out.

PREFACE BY TERRY VENABLES

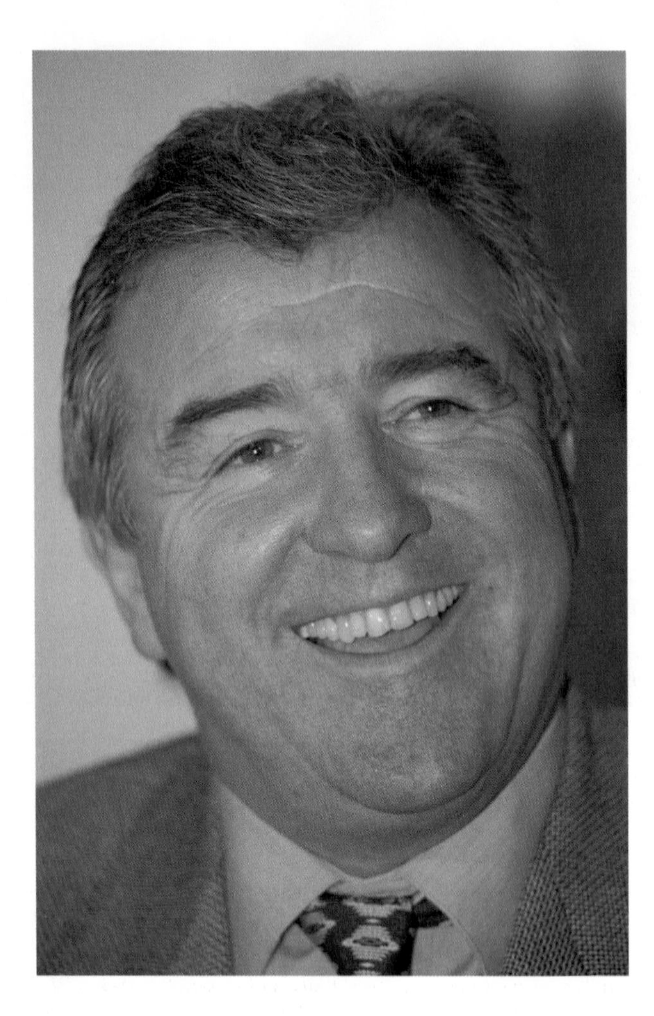

Back in my coaching days, I have to admit I was always a bit sceptical of the value of statistics in football. Sitting in the dug-out watching the action was enough to tell me most of what I needed to know about players' performances.

I didn't need to look at a table of figures to know that Gary Lineker was a lethal finisher!

But my experiences with the media have opened my eyes to how compelling football statistics can be for the spectator. It's hardly surprising the newspapers in this country use Opta stats in such depth when they can stoke up such intense debate.

It's no secret that I'm a big Alan Shearer fan. I respect his decision to quit the international stage, but I still believe England will miss him. Some of the stick he took in the press when I was the England boss was unbelievable. There were times when he wasn't finding the net as often as he would have liked, but the press seemed totally to overlook his overall importance to the squad.

Then he smashed home that goal in Euro 96 against Switzerland, played leading roles in the wins over Scotland and Holland and scored against Germany. All of a sudden he was a national hero again.

So I had a sense of déjà vu when I read the criticism of Shearer throughout 1999–2000 – and the calls in certain sections of the media for the skipper to be dropped by Kevin Keegan before the recent Euro 2000 tournament.

I read the Opta statistics ahead of the qualifiers against Luxembourg and Poland with interest. There's no doubting the fact that the stats were damning. And the figures in the *London Evening Standard* showed what was undeniable given Shearer's strained relations with Ruud Gullit: the skipper was going through a bad patch.

So I managed more than a wry smile when he blasted a hat-trick against

Luxembourg and five for Newcastle against Sheffield Wednesday.

With the right service, Shearer still has what it takes. Look again at those goals he grabbed in Euro 96. Gary Neville's cross for his header against Scotland, the pin-point corner against Germany. Bobby Robson saw that, changed the Toon's tactics and hey presto: Shearer finished the season with 23 Premiership goals.

Everyone knows that stats don't tell the full story; people will always rightly make up their own minds based on what they see. But the stats add a very interesting dimension to the debate.

Another England stalwart, goalkeeper David Seaman, was closely monitored by the statisticians in 1999–2000.

Now there's no doubt in my mind that "Safe Hands" is one of the best 'keepers England has ever had. His displays in Euro 96, particularly against Scotland, will always live in the minds of all those fans watching. And any Arsenal fan will tell you what a fantastic shot-stopper he's been over the years.

I'm not in the least bit surprised that Kevin Keegan chose to stick with him in Euro 2000 – I would have done the same thing. Seaman's experience at the top level makes him one of the first names on the teamsheet and when Keegan gave young Richard Wright his chance in the friendly in Malta, you could see how experience is a commodity you just can't buy. Wright will go on to be a top 'keeper, but he would be the first to admit that nerves got to him that day.

Seaman attracted criticism because of his age. The stats showed that he kept out the lowest percentage of shots faced of any goalie in the Premiership.

That's quite a stat, and one that certainly raised my eyebrows.

No-one reading this is pretending that all of the 'keepers above him in the charts are better than England's number one. But before Opta came along, stats like that simply didn't exist.

The expectations of fans watching a big match on TV have evolved over the years. My old pal Jimmy Hill pioneered the idea of a panel of experts at half-time – then went on to be one of the first people on the panel every week. That idea changed the whole shape of football coverage in this country, but now fans want more than just opinion. They expect to see detailed analysis, a bit of proof. They want to see the facts for themselves. How many shots on target did each side have? Who had the most possession, corners, fouls?

There's a thirst for information these days. And that thirst comes from the media as well as the fans.

But you have to put the stats in their proper context. You might look at David Batty's pass completion rate in this book and see it's better than Dennis Bergkamp's. But you have to remember the different types of passes they are attempting. It's never enough to take the data on face value – you have to assess the stats in relation to what actually happens on the pitch.

After every England game, I write a column in the *News of the World* about the team's performance. Every time, my column is accompanied by the Opta stats on every England player. The stats are vital to the coverage of the match in my view. How many times have you looked at the stats and thought: "That's interesting". I know I have, many times.

They might not change my mind about a player or a team – but they certainly give us all food for thought.

That's why this book is so fascinating to football fans everywhere. We all have our views on players and teams, but football is about more than just opinions. It's easy to analyse performances with your eyes, but Opta introduce a real sense of objectivity to the analysis.

And that, quite simply, makes their work essential reading for football fans everywhere.

FILA
Dr
Marten

HOW IS PLAYER PERFORMANCE MEASURED?

Opta developed the system of analysis in conjunction with former England coach Don Howe. The original manual system has been replaced by a custom-built, PC-based video analysis system called OSCA, which has cut the time required to analyse a game and dramatically increased the amount and type of data that is collected.

There are more than 200 distinct actions and outcomes for players that range from different kinds of shots and passes, to tackles and blocks and from different kinds of fouls and yellow cards to saves made by the goalkeeper. Every close season, the list of actions is discussed to determine the value of each element and then new categories may be added acccordingly.

OSCA allows a specially-trained person to watch a match on video through a PC and using the unique software, to click on icons to record each action performed by every single player on the ball, their fouls and discipline and also to monitor key decisions made by the officials. The new system will be in place for the start of the 2000–01 Premiership season.

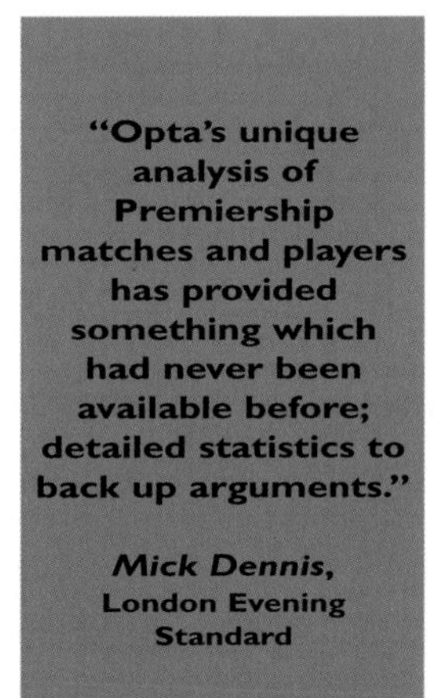
"Opta's unique analysis of Premiership matches and players has provided something which had never been available before; detailed statistics to back up arguments."

Mick Dennis,
London Evening Standard

Opta receive the referee's copy of the video on the morning after a game and then begin the analysis. An analyst takes several hours to complete a full match, depending on the flow of the game and the number of contentious decisions.

Once the game is analysed, the data is downloaded into a database from which Opta journalists are able to provide information in many diverse ways.

Managers' Reports are created for each match and sent to a number of key personnel at the Premiership clubs involved, including managers, directors and coaching staff.

In addition, many clubs request further details on player positions at set-pieces, moves leading to goalscoring opportunities, or where free-kicks are conceded or won, for both their own teams and forthcoming opposition.

Referees' Reports are produced identifying key decisions (including commendable and controversial) made in each match, details of goals and disciplinary issues. These are sent to Referees' Officer Philip Don.

The data that is collected is then downloaded from the database into a spreadsheet, from which all of the media requirements for player profiles, match reports and key information about the Premiership can be provided.

The analysis is checked by the operations manager and key information such as cards issued is checked with the official Referees' Reports. Opta also produce a video highlighting disputed goals and the FA Premier League's goal committee rules on them within 48 hours. This system replaces the previous controversial goal committee, which only previously convened roughly every six months. Any differences are checked and the database is updated by Opta's operations team if necessary with the correct information.

The system of analysis is under constant review. Opta hope to be able to develop passing matrices which will show the areas of a pitch where the player makers his passes and also identify which player he seeks out most regularly.

Plus information on whether shots are right-footed, left-footed or headers will also be logged. This should allow comparisons to show where players' strengths and weaknesses lie.

And the play leading up to key incidents such as goals will be monitored to calculate the number and type of passes.

Opta are currently working with the League Managers' Association to enhance the analysis even further and modify the data output that is produced to increase its value to people within the game.

Then, in turn, this should provide the media with even more information with which to inform, provoke and entertain its demanding audience.

THE OPTA PORTFOLIO

Head to Head CARLING OPTA

Paolo Di Canio v Robbie Keane

1999-2000 Premiership Stats Only

Player Head-to-Head
West Ham United programme
22 April 2000

www.planetfootball.com

Special reserves

Wenger's depleted Gunners refuse to down-play FA Cup

BIG MATCH STATISTICS

Team Head-to-Head
London Evening Standard
19 January 2000

Opta's back catalogue of Premiership statistics is growing all the time and because of the inherent versatility of the database used to store and compile the statistics, the raw data can be presented in a wide variety of media-friendly ways.

Whether it is on an individual match, season-long or season-on-season basis, Opta's system of analysis allows statistics to be tailored depending on their clients' different needs.

The full range of Opta's statistics can now be found in the "Optamizer" section of planetfootball's comprehensive website (www.planetfootball.com). The site provided regularly updated statistics on every player in the 1999-2000 Carling Premiership, Nationwide leagues and Scottish Premier League.

There are also team tables comparing key areas of performance such as passing, shooting, discipline and tackling, statistical features, match previews and match reports highlighting trends that may prove useful to those people who come to the site to make use of its links to SurreySports online betting service.

One of the most popular statistical services provided on the Planet Football site is Opta's Team of the Week. Opta analysts watch every kick of every Premiership game, awarding plus or minus scores for every action, making their Team of the Week the most objective around. In fact, Opta now compile regional as well as national teams of the week, all based on objective analysis.

The various Teams of the Week are used in a host of regional newspapers. The national Team of the Week can also be seen in the *Sunday Mirror* and on the BBC's website, BBC Online.

As well as the Team of the Week, Opta produce a weekly Index of player form showing their top 50 players. The Index has certainly proved controversial and many a debate has been sparked by the weekly rankings. Based on a six-game rolling average, the Index can be seen in a variety of regional newspapers and it is also carried weekly in the *News of the World* and the *Sunday Mirror*.

Discipline, or the lack of it, is always a hot issue. While data on bookings and yellow cards is freely available to the media, only Opta provide accurate data on fouls. Their discipline tables take a number of forms including team, player and referee tables. All these rankings are based on Opta's own disciplinary points system and are a popular weekly feature in a variety of regional and national newspapers.

Of course, many of Opta's clients require a more in-depth service. Opta cover every match played in the Premiership and also monitor many European and international matches. Opta's statistical match reports are a

THE OPTA PORTFOLIO

CARLING OPTA STATS

GOALKEEPERS | DEFENDERS | MIDFIELD

ATTACKING MIDFIELD | STRIKERS | FOUL PLAY

The Opta Index
News of the World
21 May 2000

Splat Stats
Daily Star
29 April 2000

58 DAILY STAR, Saturday, April 29, 2000

Off the ball

Dons on downer

7 The number of games struggling Wimbledon have lost on the trot – more than any other Premiership team this season.

6 Own goals scored by Southampton players this season, more than any other Premiership side.

13 Hat-tricks scored in the Premiership this season.

2,237 passes made by Second Division champions Preston's Graham Alexander – more than any other player in the country.

Phillips in late show

12 of Sunderland striker Kevin Phillips' goals have come in the last 15 minutes of Premiership matches.

16 The number of times champions Manchester United have scored three or more goals in the Premiership on the way to their sixth title in eight seasons.

5 goalkeepers used by West Ham in the Premiership this season – more than any other top-flight club.

23 Clean sheets kept by Second Division Preston in the League, the most in the country.

Kevin Phillips

CARLING OPTA

Scholes on the mark

9 Premiership goals scored by Manchester United's Paul Scholes, more than any other English midfielder.

5 The run of unbeaten games for First Division Nottingham Forest, the longest unbeaten run City Ground boss David Platt has enjoyed as a manager either at Forest or Serie A side Sampdoria.

35% Of French striker Thierry Henry's goals for Arsenal have come in Europe.

162 Mark Schwarzer, the goalkeeper who has made the most saves.

WIN tickets to watch Leeds v Everton

Team of the Week,
Team Tables & Index
Sunday Mirror

popular feature of many regional newspapers, and for big games they can also be seen in many national and international newspapers.

A host of top club magazines including Arsenal, Chelsea, Leeds, Liverpool and Manchester United also use Opta's comprehensive match statistics in their own match report sections.

Teletext take their post-match service a step further. Opta provide them with a 60-page review of the weekend's fixtures, which takes a look at individual player as well as team performance from the various clubs.

For those clients who do not have room for a full statistical match report, Opta provide a "quick stat" service. Monitoring shots on and off target, corners, fouls, offsides, yellow and red cards, quick stats are used by a wide variety of clients including *The Mirror*, *The Sun*, *The Guardian* and Teletext.

Opta's statistical expertise is not limited to post-match analysis, though. One of the most popular services the official player performance statisticians provide is their pre-match head-to-head material. Comparing rival players' statistics has proved a big hit, and Opta's head-to-head profiles were featured in around 100 regional newspapers and 76 match day programmes during the 1999-2000 season.

Also popular are Opta's "random numbers" or "splat stats". These are used by a variety of clients including the BBC and BSKYB to highlight quirky aspects of player and team performance. You can see a selection of these statistics running along the bottom of many of the pages in this book.

The regional and national press often pick up Opta's own statistical features. And they are a popular part of many websites too. The planetfootball website has an entire section devoted to Opta features while Virgin Net and BBC Online also carry regular statistically-based features.

While their special features are very popular, Opta are often called on to provide statistics to accompany breaking news on an ad hoc basis. If a big transfer story breaks, Opta will invariably be asked to provide the statistics to prove the player's worth. If one player claims to be better than another, Opta will be asked to prove or disprove their claims and if a manager is appointed or sacked, Opta will usually be asked to provide statistics on his past achievements.

In fact, such is Opta's reputation that many clients now approach them for football-related information that they might be able to find elsewhere. They come to Opta because of the company's growing reputation as THE authoritative voice of football statistics.

THE OPTA INDEX

The Opta Index is basically a form guide. When a match is analysed, each player's actions are recorded. For each of these actions, a player earns or loses points – for example, a goal is worth up to 575 points, whereas a short pass in a player's own half earns only six points and a foul costs a player 45 points.

Over the course of a game, a player will accumulate a total number of points to give him a Game Score. This can be used to compare his performance with other players and the player with the most points in the game is nominated as Opta's man of the match.

The Index, which has featured in many newspapers and on television, uses these Game Scores to provide a form guide which is calculated over a period encompassing the previous six FA Carling Premiership matches. You can see an example in the table below, which features Arsenal's Dennis Bergkamp.

Each player's points from the last six games are added to give him a total, which is then divided by the number of minutes played and then multiplied by 90 (minutes), to give him an average score per game played. This is his Index Score.

These Index Scores can then be used to compare players' performances over those six games, with the player who has the highest average being the most in-form player.

The players are then divided by the position that they play – goalkeepers, defenders, midfielders, attacking midfielders and attackers – to create a series of tables providing an at-a-glance guide to current Premiership player form.

The following week, when Arsenal play again, Bergkamp's score will change as the Manchester United match drops out of the last six and is replaced with his score against the Gunners' next opponents.

Opta also produce a Season Index. This shows each player's average score across every game they have played during the 1999–2000 Premiership season and this is the figure which is featured in tables throughout this book particularly pages 654–659.

DENNIS BERGKAMP

OPPOSITION	MINS PLAYED	OPTA GAME SCORE
v Manchester United	90	1,112
v Everton	90	1,258
v Coventry City	90	1,473
v Southampton	0	0
v Sunderland	90	1,515
v West Ham	71	1,611
TOTAL	431	6,969

Opta Index Score 6,969/431 x 90(mins) = 1,455

WHO USES THIS INFORMATION?

The data gathered by Opta's team of highly-trained analysts is extremely valuable to a range of different audiences.

● THE PROFESSIONALS

A report on each match is sent directly to the participating teams 24 hours after the game, usually to the manager or coach, but also to other personnel within the club.

Many find the information extremely valuable and each club decides how best to use the data supplied to them. Some clubs use it to identify weaknesses in aspects of players' performances; others use the data to set targets. Opta are currently working with the League Managers Association to enhance the system of analysis and the data that is produced to increase its value to people within the game.

● THE BETTING INDUSTRY

Spread-betting has become more commonplace over the last few years as the amount of data collected "live" has increased. Opta monitor the performances of players in live televised matches, supplying the ongoing information so that the bookies can adjust the spread if necessary during the course of the event.

Opta also conduct post-match measurement and adjudication. Key incidents such as timing or distances that goals are scored from can be assessed – or Opta's analysts can be called upon to settle any disputes between the betting industry and its customers.

● THE MEDIA

The demand for information and analysis of football has increased dramatically over the last few years. There is huge coverage of football in all national newspapers after games, as well as comment and news every day throughout the week. And, not only are there television channels dedicated to sport, but the first channel focusing on a single club has been introduced and is likely to be followed by others.

There are also pages to fill in matchday programmes; regional newspapers look to provide in-depth information to readers on their local clubs; and Internet sites meet the demand for FA Carling Premiership football from a worldwide audience.

Football has never been more high profile and Opta offer the media information to satisfy the demand from their customers. Material requested ranges from previews to match reviews where it is possible to see just how and where a game was won or lost. In addition, Opta data can be used to back-up stories or to dispel media myths.

● GAMES

Opta's statistics are used by many clients to run interactive fantasy games in their publication or medium.

● THE LAW

Opta's data and expertise have been used in several cases where a dispute between players and associations or other organisations exists.

OPTA CLIENTS 1999–2000 SEASON

NATIONAL NEWSPAPERS

The Sun, The Times, The Daily Telegraph, The Express, The Mirror, The Sunday Times, The Observer, The Sunday Express, The Star, News of the World, The Sunday Mirror

REGIONAL NEWSPAPERS

London Evening Standard, North Eastern Evening Gazette, Coventry Evening Telegraph, Sheffield Star, Leicester Evening Mercury

MATCHDAY PROGRAMMES

TV STATIONS

Sky Sports – Soccer Saturday, Goals on Sunday, Soccer AM, TWI

MISCELLANEOUS

Virgin Net, BBC Online, ITV Teletext, Sports Interactive, AOL

MAGAZINES

Four Four Two, MOTD, Man Utd, Leeds, Chelsea, Arsenal, Liverpool

THE BETTING INDUSTRY

Surrey Sports, City Index, Sporting Index

SHEARER TORTURE

Harry Harris
CHIEF FOOTBALL WRITER
ALAN HAS TO BE DROPPED

The Mirror
25 August 1999

The case against Shearer
PREMIERSHIP STATISTICS
Skipper's stats don't add up

London Evening Standard
1 September 1999

What a difference a year makes! Defeat in the 1999 FA Cup final by Manchester United had capped a depressing season for Alan Shearer. He had scored just 14 league goals, with six of those coming from the penalty spot and this was the second time he had come away from Wembley with a loser's medal.

The Newcastle United and England captain found himself heading into the new season with critics questioning his commitment as well as his ability to perform at the top level, following a number of serious injuries.

His strained relationship with manager Ruud Gullit was a continual source of debate in the media and matters came to a head when he was dropped by the Dutchman for the Tyne and Wear derby with bitter rivals Sunderland.

It was clearly a case of "this Toon ain't big enough for the both of us" and only a matter of time before one or other of the club's larger-than-life personalities was forced out. With Shearer a legend in his own lifetime on Tyneside, there was only ever going to be one winner.

Gullit left to be replaced by Bobby Robson and it was if a cloud had been lifted from the club. The team had earned just one point from their opening six matches, but eased away from the relegation zone over the course of the next few months and Shearer finished the season with 23 league goals – his highest tally in a black and white shirt.

Those first few weeks of the season, though, must have been torture for the England skipper. The style of the team was clearly not suited to him, while his on-field demeanour was that of a very unhappy player. Uriah Rennie sent him off in the first match of the season against Aston Villa for persistent foul play, as Shearer allowed his frustration to affect his game. Questions were raised about his fitness, his form and his commitment and his place in the England team was hard to justify, given the form of his rivals.

In the run up to the crucial Euro 2000 qualifying games against Luxembourg and Poland, Opta statistics were first used by *The Mirror* to compare Shearer's performances with those of other potential England strikers. At the time, Kevin Phillips had already scored three goals, as had Aston Villa's Dion Dublin. Emile Heskey had scored two from two shots and Andy Cole had helped Manchester United win the Treble in the previous campaign. In fact, the only England contender Shearer was outperforming was his former Blackburn team-mate Chris Sutton, who was having an equally torrid time from the press, following his £10 million move to Chelsea.

The *London Evening Standard* then published Shearer's statistics for the current and previous season, showing the decline in his performances and how unfavourably he compared with his Premiership peers.

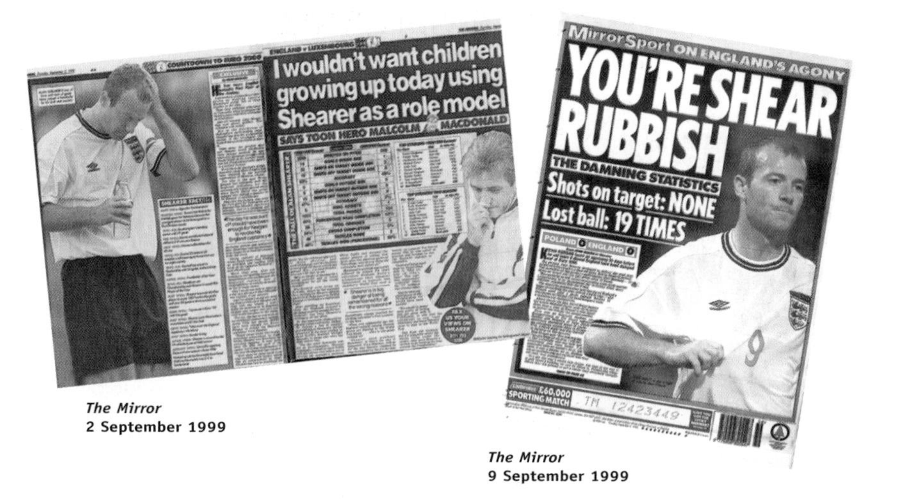
COUNTDOWN TO EURO 2000

I wouldn't want children growing up today using Shearer as a role model

SAYS TOON HERO MALCOLM MACDONALD

MirrorSport ON ENGLAND'S AGONY

YOU'RE SHEAR RUBBISH

THE DAMNING STATISTICS

Shots on target: NONE

Lost ball: 19 TIMES

POLAND 0 ENGLAND 0

£60,000 SPORTING MATCH

The Mirror
2 September 1999

The Mirror
9 September 1999

While England coach Kevin Keegan stood up for the man he made the most expensive signing in British football, ex-Newcastle hero Malcolm MacDonald fiercely criticised Shearer in *The Mirror*, with the paper using Opta's statistics to back up some of his arguments.

Shearer seemed to ram the words of his critics firmly back down their throats, scoring a hat-trick as England thrashed Luxembourg 6–0.

Gordon Strachan was moved to comment in *The Observer* on Shearer's performance and on the statistics. He quite rightly pointed out the inadequacies of Shearer's Newcastle team-mates in providing the right kind of service to their skipper, venturing that the previous day's performance had shown what good approach play meant to Shearer.

However, the wolves were not about to let their grip loosen and a disappointing England display against Poland provided more ammunition for the critics' cause. The skipper was vilified for failing to fire in a single shot on target and invariably wasting possession when he received it. *The Mirror* summed up their feelings with the headline "You're Shear rubbish".

The 0–0 scoreline meant that England had to wait and hope that Sweden could beat Poland, so that Keegan's men would have another chance to qualify in a play off.

Shearer returned to his club, clearly wondering what he had done to deserve all this criticism, but rather than folding under the pressure, he found salvation in the shape of new manager Robson.

The Magpies strolled out in their first home game under Robson's control and trounced Sheffield Wednesday 8–0 to record their first win of the season. Shearer grabbed five goals for himself and the club and their skipper rarely looked back.

Despite FA Cup disappointment at Wembley for the third year in a row – this time in the semi-final – Shearer finished the season as part of a side that seem to be heading back in the right direction.

All the criticism clearly took its toll though. On 26 February, ironically following the return match against Sheffield Wednesday, Shearer announced that he would retire from international football after the Euro 2000 tournament. The criticism turned to tributes and the polls about who should play for England instead of Shearer, became votes on who could possibly replace one of England's all-time great forwards.

Cynics would suggest that Shearer knew that his performances at the very top level could no longer justify his automatic selection, but supporters accepted that he wanted to devote more time to his family and his beloved Newcastle United, where he is expected to eventually step up into a coaching role. Whatever the truth, there is no doubt that Shearer is one of the finest strikers ever to play for England, where his international goalscoring statistics rank alongside the best in the modern game.

THE FOREIGN LEGION

THE EXPRESS SPORT

WALKER CUP TRIUMPH FOR BATTLING BRITAIN

The foreign legion who are killing our game

NEED SOME CASH FROM YOUR PENSION FUND NEST EGG?

EXPRESS SPECIAL SURVEY: Only England's golden oldies appear to fit the bill for Keegan's midfield requirements

Rusty Gazza is still best bet

LET US PRAY

Invasion ruining our game

HOW THE MIDFIELD PLAYERS COMPARED ON SATURDAY

SHADED PLAYERS ENGLISH QUALIFIED

Di Canio backing kid Cole to fire up an England revival

SPORT SCOPE

The Express
13 September 1999

The fall out from England's disappointing 0–0 draw in Warsaw with Poland, which left Kevin Keegan's side relying on Sweden beating the Poles for his side to qualify for Euro 2000, rumbled on for weeks after the game.

One of the most crucial aspects of England's poor performance had been identified as the lack of creativity in the team's midfield.

The media seized upon this issue, blaming the number of foreign imports being brought into the Premiership for restricting the development of young English talent.

Even at this point, some pundits believed that the fading talent of Paul Gascoigne was still England's best bet for success. Others ventured that youngsters like Joe Cole were the answer, despite his tender years and lack of first-team Premiership football with West Ham.

The Express asked Opta to look at the performances of English players versus their foreign counterparts over the course of one weekend. Opta's analysis spelt out the problems only too clearly.

The lack of options was highlighted by the fact that Paul Gascoigne was indeed the best performing midfield player on that particular weekend. Dennis Wise was ranked second and he did get his chance to impress with England later in the season.

However, the majority of top talent on show did not qualify to play for England. From Emmanuel Petit and Patrick Vieira at Arsenal, to Walid Badir at Wimbledon, 44% of all starting midfield players plying their trade for Premiership clubs were foreigners.

In addition, players like Graeme Le Saux and Jason Euell were played out of position in midfield, while others like Jody Morris, Lee Hendrie and Nicky Butt were playing ahead of first-choice picks such as Didier Deschamps, George Boateng and Roy Keane, who would consign them to the bench for most of the campaign.

Although players such as Steven Gerrard, Kieron Dyer and Joe Cole have emerged and are knocking on the door of the England squad, they are the exceptions.

Chelsea fielded the first-ever team in English football history without a British player in the starting line up, when they met Southampton at The Dell. Stephen Hughes left Arsenal for Everton because of a lack of first-team outings and Muzzy Izzet chose Turkey ahead of England, as Keegan ignored the Leicester player's good form.

With more foreign signings on the cards, Keegan's prophecy that the next England manager will be watching Nationwide Division One football to complete his squad may soon be a reality.

ENGLAND EXPECTS

Here's the team Kev should have picked to face Poland

and there's NO MARTYN NO NEVILLE NO ADAMS NO KEOWN NO PEARCE NO BATTY NO SCHOLES NO MACCA NO FOWLER NO SHEARER

Keegan pledges to back his flops

News of the World
12 September 1999

One of the football fan's favourite pastimes is picking their own team. This is particularly true when it comes to the national team, when everyone seems to have an opinion on who should be playing for England.

Each time a national squad is announced, Opta Index publish an England XI based on the players who are showing the best form over a defined period. The unique Index ranking system provides a starting point for discussion, bringing underrated players to the fore who might not ordinarily be considered, as well as the established stars at high profile clubs.

After the disappointing 0–0 draw with Poland in the Euro 2000 qualifiers which left England relying on Sweden to do them a favour, the *News of the World* asked Opta to select the in-form players who should have played in that match.

They then asked respected pundit Ron Atkinson to comment on these players versus the starting XI selected from Kevin Keegan's Warsaw pack.

David Beckham was the only player to make both line-ups, although players like Tony Adams, Gary Neville and Paul Scholes had not played sufficient Premiership football to qualify for the Opta team and Steve McManaman was playing abroad at Real Madrid.

Interesting selections included Emile Heskey, who later established himself against Argentina, Andy Cole, who was on the shortlist for the player of the year awards and youngsters like Danny Mills and Jonathon Woodgate, alongside veterans like Tim Flowers and Nigel Winterburn. Strangely, one of Opta's selections was at Euro 2000 playing for another team. Muzzy Izzet had a fantastic season, but after being ignored by Keegan, the Leicester midfielder decided to play for Turkey.

The *News of the World* asked: "Can statistics be trusted and is this information good enough to pick a national team?"

Atkinson answered: "Knowing which players are on top of their game is handy for any manager, but it is not a foolproof way of selecting a team. Having said that, it is interesting to see that the Opta team has thrown up a few players who have not had a look-in for Keegan's international line-ups."

This synopsis illustrates perfectly how Opta's statistics provide greater understanding of the game as long as they are used in context. They can illustrate strengths and weaknesses of a performance, but need to be applied with reference to the real game.

WIDE BOY OR MIDDLE MAN?

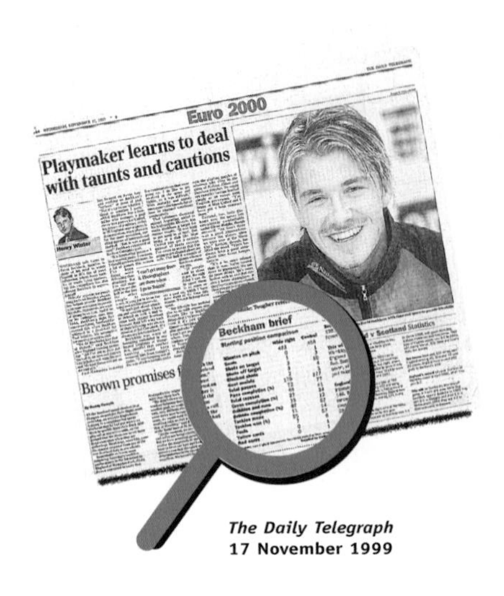

Euro 2000

Playmaker learns to deal with taunts and cautions

Beckham brief

The Daily Telegraph
17 November 1999

England verdict: Lack of room for the wide men – but there's room for improvement in midfield

Lost on a wing back and prayer

Beckham better as an outsider

The Observer
27 February 2000
Design © Graphic News

The 1999–2000 campaign was a very eventful one for David Beckham. He was voted second in the FIFA World Player of the Year, helped United to the Premiership title and played in Euro 2000 for England.

However, he was constantly in the news for his off-field activities and, after a training ground bust-up with Alex Ferguson, found himself dropped for the crucial Premiership match against Leeds.

He also had his trademark highlighted hair shorn off, scored a couple of cracking free-kicks and once again finished as the most prolific creator of goals in the top flight of the English League.

Debate also raged about Beckham's best position on the pitch. While Ferguson clearly sees Beckham as a wide player, due to his high-quality crossing ability, England's lack of a creative central midfielder has generated calls for the United player to be used in the middle of the park.

The central midfield role is not a new one for Beckham at international level. Glenn Hoddle used him in the middle on several occasions and *The Daily Telegraph* featured Opta's exclusive statistics alongside an interview with Beckham by Henry Winter in advance of the play-off second leg against Scotland.

Once England had qualified, England's preparations for Euro 2000 began with a friendly against Argentina. The debate came to the fore once again and *The Observer* ran a feature after the game comparing Beckham's performances against Scotland and versus Argentina.

The quality of his crossing would seem to back the decision to play Beckham wide, but for England the statistics painted a different picture. A central role gave him the licence to get more involved and he proved far more effective, too.

Beckham fired in almost twice as many efforts at goal when playing centrally, although his accuracy was quite poor in both positions.

While he had two assists to his name from wide positions and just one when inside, his passing accuracy since the World Cup was marginally higher when playing centrally. He also made almost a hundred passes more in total.

And, perhaps most intriguingly, Beckham still managed to fire almost as many crosses and corners when playing centrally, recording a better completion rate than when playing wide.

So, with Kevin Keegan looking for the right blend, Beckham may get the chance to play the starring role, taking centre stage rather than standing in the wings.

NOT-SO-ABLE SEAMAN

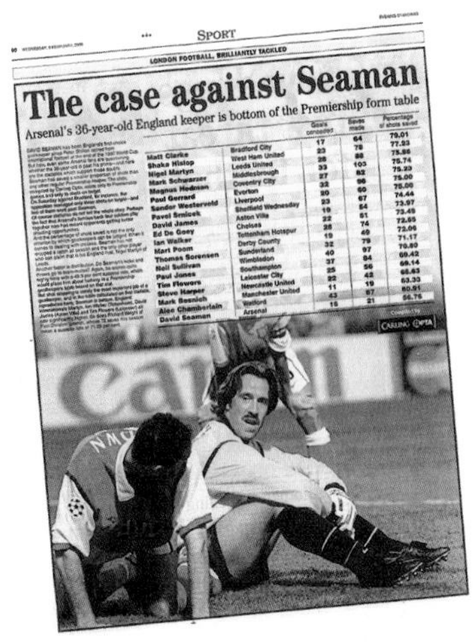

SPORT

LONDON FOOTBALL, BRILLIANTLY TACKLED

The case against Seaman

Arsenal's 36-year-old England keeper is bottom of the Premiership form table

		Goals conceded	Saves made	Percentage of shots saved
Matt Clarke	Bradford City	17	64	79.01
Shaka Hislop	West Ham United	23	78	77.23
Nigel Martyn	Leeds United	28	88	75.86
Mark Schwarzer	Middlesbrough	33	103	75.74
Magnus Hedman	Coventry City	27	82	75.23
Paul Gerrard	Everton	32	96	75.00
Sander Westerveld	Liverpool	20	60	75.00
Pavel Srnicek	Sheffield Wednesday	23	67	74.44
David James	Aston Villa	19	54	73.97
Ed De Goey	Chelsea	22	61	73.49
Ian Walker	Tottenham Hotspur	28	74	72.65
Mart Poom	Derby County	19	49	72.06
Thomas Sorensen	Sunderland	32	79	71.17
Neil Sullivan	Wimbledon	40	97	70.80
Paul Jones	Southampton	37	84	69.42
Tim Flowers	Leicester City	25	56	69.14
Steve Harper	Newcastle United	22	42	68.63
Mark Bosnich	Manchester United	11	19	63.33
Alec Chamberlain	Watford	43	67	60.91
David Seaman	Arsenal	15	21	56.76

Compiled by CARLING OPTA

London Evening Standard
9 February 2000

THE MIRROR, Saturday May 20, 2000

CARLING OPTA PREMIERSHIP STATS, 1999-2000

Q Can you name the worst shot-stopper in the top flight?

A ENGLAND'S NUMBER ONE

ARSENAL keeper David Seaman had the poorest saves-to-shots ratio in the Premiership this season.

The Mirror
20 May 2000

The Arsenal defence, with David Seaman behind them, has become a legend in its own lifetime. In the 1998–99 season, the Gunners conceded just 17 goals – a Premiership record – but it was clear that Arsene Wenger would have to rebuild his famed rearguard as age began to take its toll.

Wenger seemed to have the ideal deputy for Seaman with Alex Manninger waiting in the wings and when the England 'keeper was injured in a pre-season friendly against Monaco, the young Austrian stepped into the breach.

Manninger played the first nine Premiership games and helped Arsenal to third place in the league and three unbeaten games in the Champions League, before Seaman recovered for the trip to West Ham.

Arsenal were beaten at Upton Park and then lost two crucial Champions League games at Wembley. Barcelona fired four goals past Seaman, while Gabriel Batistuta netted with Fiorentina's sole attempt on target.

The Batistuta goal eliminated the Gunners and brought back memories of Ryan Giggs's FA Cup semi-final replay winner, when Seaman appeared to go down early and allow the opponent to fire into the net above him.

The Gunners continued to pick up league points, but Seaman's performances were unconvincing. At White Hart Lane, Spurs hit just two attempts on target, but both of them beat Seaman and the Gunners lost 2–1.

People questioned whether Seaman was past his best and, after a poor run that saw Arsenal slip out of contention in the Premiership, the media began to notice the poor performances.

Opta supplied the *London Evening Standard* with a shot-stopping ranking of first-choice Premiership goalkeepers. David Seaman featured at the bottom of the list, saving just 56.76% of shots on target that he faced.

The statistics became a major talking point with TV and the national press debating Seaman's position while Opta discussed the statistic live on talkSPORT.

The situation was exacerbated by the fact that Manninger recorded a better saves-to-shots ratio and performed well when substituting for the England number one. Wenger, though, stuck by Seaman and the Yorkshireman did repay that faith by making some crucial saves as Arsenal made their way through to the final of the UEFA Cup.

He also kept his place as England's number one in Euro 2000.

ON ME "'EAD" SON

HEADY DAYS FOR BERGKAMP

Dennis puts Arsenal on nodding terms with a new tactic in the chase for the Champions League

The Mirror
28 February 2000

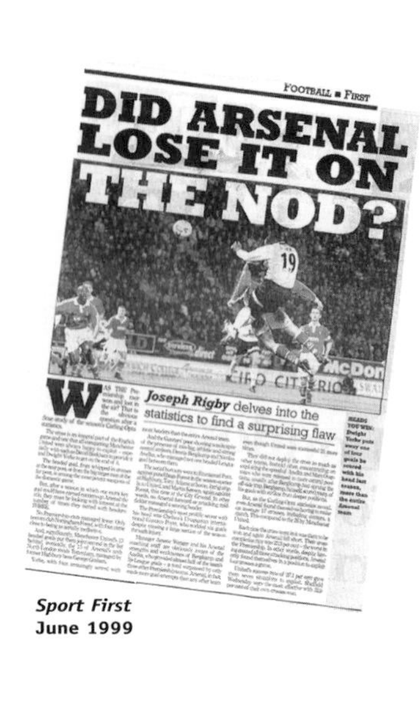
DID ARSENAL LOSE IT ON THE NOD?

Joseph Rigby delves into the statistics to find a surprising flaw

Sport First
June 1999

In the highly competitive world of Premiership football, the difference between success and failure is sometimes obvious. The Champions are often the top scorers or have the best defence and those who are relegated usually concede more than the teams above them or struggle to find the net.

There is usually a combination of factors, but occasionally it is possible to point to one particular flaw that has a marked impact on the final outcome.

Arsenal finished second behind Manchester United in the 1998–99 season by just one point, despite setting a Premiership record, conceding just 17 goals in 38 games. The Red Devils won the title by virtue of the fact that they scored 21 more goals than the Gunners, despite Arsene Wenger's side firing in more shots over the course of the campaign than any other team and 43 more than United. So why were the Gunners outscored?

The statistics showed that Arsenal had registered the worst crossing accuracy in the Premiership at just 24%, but this was hardly a reflection on the quality of Marc Overmars and Ray Parlour. The reason for such a poor return was that Arsenal rarely attempted headers. Nicolas Anelka, Dennis Bergkamp and later Nwankwo Kanu all preferred the ball to feet.

The absence of such an attacking weapon was clear. Arsenal scored just three headed goals in the entire season out of their tally of 59 strikes. That represented just 5% of the total – the lowest ratio in the league. *Sport First* asked Opta to look into areas where the league title may have been won and lost and the headed goals factor was the clearest issue.

The 1999–2000 title win was more clear cut, with Manchester United finishing 18 points clear of the Gunners, but the headed goals factor came into play once more. Dwight Yorke scored more headers than any other top-flight player, nodding home eight times in his tally of 20 goals.

In contrast, the Gunners scored just five headers and Dennis Bergkamp's nod against Southampton at Highbury was the first headed Premiership goal by an Arsenal striker since Christopher Wreh in April 1998 – some 22 months earlier. Opta supplied one of its popular "splat" stats to *The Mirror* and a table of the top headed goalscorers in the Premiership which they used alongside their match report of the game as an interesting footnote to the contest.

RED DEVILS IN DISGUISE

SPORT
Are they really Red Devils?
WE REVEAL THE TRUTH ABOUT MANCHESTER UNITED: PAGE 86

SPORT
United are such goody-goodies
Believe it or not, they're the best behaved team in the Premiership
The Dirty Dozen
The League of Gentlemen

London Evening Standard
16 February 2000

"They seem to think that because they are Manchester United you are not allowed to kick them, but we harassed and got among them and they didn't like it."

That was the opinion of England captain Alan Shearer, speaking after his Newcastle side had beaten the Premiership Champions 3–0, in a game dominated by continual baiting and harassment of the match officials by United players.

Three of Sir Alex Ferguson's side's bookings that day were for dissent, and Roy Keane was sent off for two bookable offences, the first of which was for arguing with referee Stephen Lodge.

Two weeks prior to the Newcastle game, the Red Devils were hosting Middlesbrough at Old Trafford, when Bryan Robson's side were awarded a penalty.

Incensed United players ran up to referee Andy D'Urso, complaining bitterly about the decision, and hounding him so much that he was forced to retreat, almost running backwards to avoid contact with the irate players.

If Shearer's comments are true, and the way to get a result against United is to "get among them", then not many teams tried hard enough, with the Champions losing just three matches and scoring 97 goals on their way to the title.

Despite the incidents at St James's Park and Old Trafford, United finished the season with fewer bookings than anyone else, and also conceded the fewest fouls.

United were penalised for a foul challenge every 8.26 minutes on average, compared to every 5.46 minutes for Leeds, who committed more fouls than any other Premiership side.

It was not just the United team as a whole, but also the individual players who were consistently staying on the right side of the law, with the 1999–2000 Champions not having one player among the worst individual offenders.

Under the Opta points system, one point is awarded for a foul, three for a yellow card, and six for a sending-off.

The Manchester United player with the most points in 1999–2000 was Roy Keane, but he is way down in 64th place compared to the rest of the Premiership.

Ironically, Shearer appears in the top 10, while for United only Keane, Jaap Stam and David Beckham feature in the top 100 dirtiest players.

Many will still feel that the best team in the country receive more leniency from referees than others, but the statistics show that over a 38-game period, Manchester United were the cleanest team in the top flight.

FOX HUNTING

London Evening Standard
2 February 2000

LONDON FOOTBALL, BRILLIANTLY TACKLED

Sorry, Ken . . . but your team play the most long passes in the Premiership

	LONG PASSES	% ACCURACY
Chelsea	2159	59
Man United	2033	60
Newcastle	1968	60
Liverpool	1862	61
Sunderland	1756	56
Aston Villa	1752	51
Arsenal	1717	61
Everton	1692	47
Watford	1688	44
Sheff Wed	1645	53
Derby County	1638	51
Leicester	1626	53
Coventry	1622	52
Leeds United	1599	54
Wimbledon	1568	45
West Ham	1556	58
Southampton	1554	47
Bradford	1488	48
Tottenham	1337	58
Middlesbrough	1296	54

(Premier League statistics only)

Compiled by CARLING OPTA

KEN BATES sparked a bitter row with Leicester on the eve of the FA Cup clash between the sides when he accused Martin O'Neill's team of playing kick-and-rush football.

O'Neill called the Chelsea chairman a cretin and said: "If we kick the ball more than 25 yards it is not the right ball but when Chelsea's world-class players do that, it is deemed beautiful. You just can't win."

Well, Ken, it's Chelsea, not Leicester, who favour the long ball.

Our exclusive tables, supplied by Carling Opta, show Chelsea have hit more long passes than any other team in the Premiership this season. Opta regard a long pass as greater than 15 yards.

That might leave O'Neill with a satisfied grin on his face but, of course, that's not the whole picture. A long, accurate pass is rather different to hoofing the ball forward and Chelsea players find a team-mate with nearly two-thirds of their long passes.

They are also pretty accurate with their short passes, trailing only Manchester United and Arsenal in the table.

Leicester, in contrast, are below half way in each of the tables. They complete just over half of their long passes and 73 per cent of their short passes.

But it is Watford and Wimbledon, perhaps predictably, who are in the bottom two of the short passes table.

	SHORT PASSES	% ACCURACY
Man United	8551	84
Arsenal	8134	76
Chelsea	7742	79
Newcastle	7564	78
Liverpool	7333	77
Everton	6883	75
Sheff Wed	6348	75
West Ham	6316	77
Aston Villa	6306	73
Sunderland	6206	73
Coventry	6126	74
Tottenham	6109	72
Leeds United	6091	75
Leicester	5881	73
Derby County	5824	72
Middlesbrough	5486	73
Bradford	5364	71
Southampton	5332	71
Watford	5164	65
Wimbledon	5082	64

(Premier League statistics only)

Carling Opta are the official statisticians for the Premiership. Using a scoring system devised by former England coach Don Howe, they evaluate every kick, pass, shot save and throw in every Premiership game

"Leicester pack their goal, play kick-and-rush, hope to snatch a breakaway goal and if all else fails, rely on penalties after extra time."

That was Chelsea chairman Ken Bates's verdict on his club's FA Cup fifth round opponents and it echoed the opinion of Arsene Wenger, whose Arsenal side had crashed out to the Foxes in the previous round.

Martin O'Neill was unsurprisingly upset by such remarks, seeing them as nothing more than sour grapes on Wenger's part and hypocritical asides from Bates. He pointed out: "If we (Leicester) kick the ball more than 25 yards it is not the right ball, but when Chelsea's world-class players do that, it is deemed beautiful. You just can't win."

After John Gregory had added his voice to the debate, criticising Leicester for the way they played in the goalless first leg of the Worthington Cup semi-final, O'Neill, his tongue firmly in cheek, used the Villa manager's own words in his programme notes for the second leg, promising that his team would "...do their very best to cross the half-way line and win the game before a penalty shoot-out is needed." The Foxes beat Villa 1–0 with a goal from Matt Elliott.

Opta produced a series of statistical tables which proved that, while Leicester played their fair share of long passes, they were some way behind the kick-and-rush kings of the Premiership – Chelsea!

Of course the fact that Chelsea played more long passes than any other team only tells half the story. After all there's a difference between an aimless hoof and a pinpoint crossfield pass.

The Blues actually completed a higher percentage of all passes over 25 yards than most other Premiership teams, a fact which suggests that they did not just play the percentage pass.

This suspicion is confirmed by the fact that Wimbledon and Watford, both of whom tended to resort to the long ball, completed the lowest percentage of attempted long passes over the season.

As for Leicester, they completed a lower percentage of their long passes than Chelsea, but were some way ahead of the likes of Watford and Wimbledon. However, the fact that only six other teams made fewer short passes than the Foxes suggests that they are one of the Premiership's more direct sides.

Whether that made them unattractive to watch is open to debate. At least they won a trophy in the 1999–2000 season which is more than can be said for some of their more "cultured" rivals.

MAKING EMILE OUT OF IT?

DAILY STAR, Saturday, April 8, 2000 67

FOUL GUY NOT FALL GUY

Heskey's top target

■ by MATT D'ARCY

BATTERED and bruised striker Emile Heskey was last night revealed as the Premiership's most-fouled footballer.

Kop boss Gerard Houllier says that proves his £11m record signing doesn't deserve the fall guy label pinned on him by Villa chief John Gregory.

Carling Opta statistics show Heskey has been fouled 82 times this season – more than any other player in the game.

Three weeks ago Gregory accused the powerful striker of being a "cheat who falls over too easily, conning referees."

However, Houllier says statistics prove that the only way defenders can stop Heskey in full flight is by fouling him.

Catch

"I'm not surprised that he is the most fouled player because Jamie Redknapp told me that when he was with the England squad nobody could catch Emile fairly," recalled the Liverpool boss.

"He would just turn and go and nobody could catch him. And since he came here we have seen for ourselves that he is very difficult to stop because he is not only strong and powerful he is also penetrating, direct and very quick.

"What John Gregory said was unfair, but that's John, he just likes to talk. Last season at Villa Park, Stan Collymore badly tackled Michael Owen, got sent off and John said Michael is a baby-faced assassin. I couldn't believe it."

Houllier's side are at home to Tottenham tomorrow, and he couldn't be happier with Heskey's contribution in his first month at Anfield.

The England striker did not score until late on in his fifth match, last Saturday's 3-0 win at Coventry.

"But Houllier declared: "He has settled much better than we believed he would.

"He has played five games, we've picked up 11 points and he has been extremely important in our attacking moves.

"He has been involved directly or indirectly in five of the eight goals we've scored in those five games and that's not too bad by any standards.

"But I measure him more by his contribution to the team than by his goals and I am more than happy with what he has contributed so far."

This will be 22-year-old Heskey's 11th game in six weeks. But Houllier, who rested 20-year-old Owen two weeks ago against Newcastle, leaves 19-year-old Steven Gerrard out of the squad against Spurs, joining Fowler, Redknapp and Steve Staunton on the sidelines.

NOBBLED

TOP TEN fouled players:
82: Emile Heskey (Liverpool).
81: David Ginola (Spurs).
78: Niall Quinn (Sunderland).
63: Don Hutchison (Everton), Hamilton Ricard (Middlesbrough).
62: Harry Kewell (Leeds).
60: Trevor Sinclair (West Ham).
58: Patrick Vieira (Arsenal).
57: Alan Shearer (Newcastle).
56: Kevin Phillips (Sunderland).

IN IT FOR KICKS: Heskey is the most-fouled Premiership player

GRAHAM: Wrong to hit out

Saint George

GEORGE GRAHAM is ready to keep his mouth shut if ref Stephen Lodge upsets him at Anfield tomorrow.

The under-fire Spurs boss lashed out at first-season Premiership ref Alan Wiley on Monday and landed himself in trouble with the FA.

"I thought he started very nervously and then deteriorated into pure incompetence," said Graham, following the 3-2 home defeat by Middlesbrough.

Peers

But yesterday the tough-talking Scot admitted he may have overstepped the mark. "Perhaps I shouldn't have spoken out so much and made it public," he said. "I still think he gave an extremely nervous performance, probably because he was in front of his peers.

"The Premiership referees' officer Philip Don was watching, plus another official from the Referees' Association."

Daily Star
8 April 2000

It was quite a season for Emile Heskey. The burly striker impressed everyone on his first start for England against Argentina in February, won a Worthington Cup winners' medal with Leicester four days later and sealed a dream move to boyhood heroes Liverpool in March.

But the season did not pass without controversy for the £11 million striker, who came in for strong criticism from some quarters for his on-pitch conduct.

The general crux of his opponents' arguments was that, despite his strong, physical frame, Heskey went to ground too easily. His biggest detractor was Aston Villa manager John Gregory, whose comments about the Liverpool forward prompted a vehement defence from Gerard Houllier using Opta's exclusive player statistics.

Heskey faced Villa in his second game for the Reds, the match ending 0–0 after strike partner Michael Owen thumped a first-half penalty against the bar. But an incident in the 70th minute, when Heskey went down heavily on the edge of the area under Ugo Ehiogu's challenge, led Gregory to brand the former Fox "a cheat", and to comment: "I see Emile brought his skates with him from Leicester."

Heskey felt Gregory's remarks were unfair and responded by saying: "Every time I play against Aston Villa he's [Gregory] got something to say."

Houllier defended his player further in an interview with *The Daily Star*, citing Opta's statistic that Heskey was the most fouled player in the Premiership, with opponents unable to cope with the striker's turn of pace.

The burly target man finished the season as the most sinned against player in the top flight, winning Leicester and Liverpool a combined total of 100 free-kicks, just ahead of David Ginola – a player who has suffered widespread accusations of "simulation" on the football pitch.

No-one drew more fouls in the final third of the pitch than Heskey. He was illegally challenged 38 times in the danger zone and won three penalties in the process – only Kevin Phillips and Andy Campbell were awarded more spot-kicks for fouls against them.

Whether you concur with Gregory or Houllier on the subject of Heskey, the significant fact is that the Liverpool attacker wins plenty of free-kicks in dangerous areas. Patrick Berger scored direct from set-pieces three times last term, while no team notched more strikes from outside the area than the Reds. And with Heskey leading the line, that could have massive implications for Liverpool's opponents in 2000–01.

CARLING
CHAMPION

THE TEAMS

Each club that participated in the 1999–2000 Carling Premiership season has its own section within this part of the book. The sections are in alphabetical order from Arsenal through to Wimbledon and then following that, the promoted clubs.

You will find:

- important details about each club, highlighting key personnel and contact details;
- a review of the season;
- a full breakdown of appearances, goalscorers and disciplinary issues;
- a profile of the manager;
- a graph charting the league position across the course of the season;
- charts that show how, when and where each team scored or conceded their goals as well as who netted for and against each side.
- a full breakdown of each player's performance;
- Index scores for the top players at each club and Opta's nomination for their player of the season;
- the top performers at each club across a series of key categories;
- a match report on one of the best performances during the season.

After this, you can find key details on the three sides who were promoted to the Premiership from the Nationwide League Division One and who will feature in the forthcoming 2000–01 season.

For Charlton Athletic, Ipswich Town and Manchester City

You will find:

- important details about each club, highlighting key personnel and contact details;
- a review of the season;
- a full breakdown of appearances and goalscorers;
- a profile of the manager;
- a graph charting the league position across the course of the season;
- charts that show how, when and where each team scored or conceded their goals as well as who netted for and against each side.

Dreamcast

ARSENAL

ADDRESS

Avenell Rd, Highbury, London N5 1BU

CONTACT NUMBERS

Telephone: 020 7704 4000
Fax: 020 7704 4001
Ticket Office: 020 7704 4040
Ticket Information: 020 7704 4242
GunnersLine: 09064 744000
The Gunners Shop: 020 7704 4120
e-mail: enquiries@arsenal.co.uk
Website: www.arsenal.co.uk

KEY PERSONNEL

Chairman: P D Hill-Wood
Vice-Chairman: D B Dein
Directors: Sir Roger Gibbs
C E B L Carr, D D Fiszman
K J Friar, R Carr
Club Secretary: D Miles
Manager: Arsene Wenger

SPONSORS

SEGA

FANZINES

The Gooner
Up The Arse
Highbury High

COLOURS

Home: Red shirts with white sleeves, white shorts and red stockings
Away: Yellow shirts with blue shorts and stockings

NICKNAME

The Gunners

HONOURS

League Champions: 1930–31, 1932–33, 1933–34, 1934–35, 1937–38, 1947–48, 1952–53, 1970–71, 1988–89, 1990–91, 1997–98
FA Cup: 1930, 1936, 1950, 1971, 1979, 1993, 1998
League Cup: 1987, 1993
European Cup Winners' Cup: 1994
Fairs Cup: 1970

RECORD GOALSCORER

Cliff Bastin – 150 league goals, 1930–47

BIGGEST WIN

12–0 v Loughborough Town – Division Two, 12 March 1900

BIGGEST DEFEAT

0–8 v Loughborough Town – Division Two, 12 December 1896

SEASON REVIEW

Like the Leeds team of the late 1960s and early 1970s, Arsene Wenger's Arsenal are gradually earning the reputation as the "nearly men" of English football. Runners-up to Manchester United for the second season in succession, knocked out of both domestic cup competitions on penalties and beaten in another shoot-out in the UEFA Cup final, it is safe to say that the Gunners had more than their fair share of disappointments in season 1999–2000.

They started the campaign minus Nicolas Anelka but with Thierry Henry and Davor Suker added to the ranks. Nwankwo Kanu inspired them to a 2–1 Charity Shield success over Manchester United, and wins over Leicester and Derby County, together with a point away to Sunderland, put them up among the league's early front-runners.

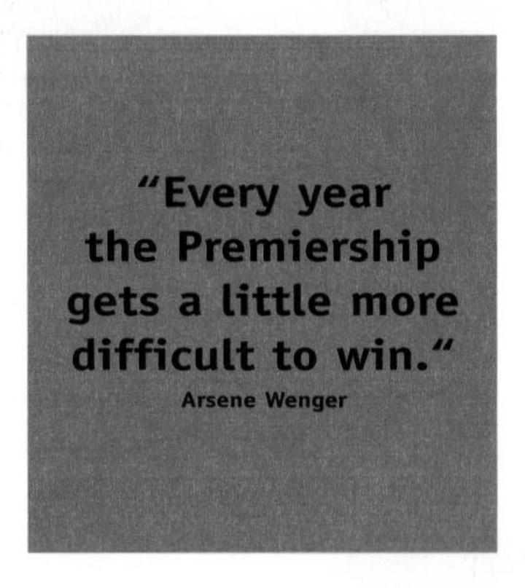

"Every year the Premiership gets a little more difficult to win."
Arsene Wenger

The visit of Champions Manchester United to Highbury on 22 August was billed as an early title decider, and while that might have been a little premature, there was certainly more than a hint of things to come when Roy Keane grabbed two goals to cancel out Fredrik Ljungberg's earlier effort and earn the Red Devils a 2–1 win.

That match was followed by a 2–0 success over Bradford City, a game that was notable mainly for the profligacy of Thierry Henry. A £10.5 million pound signing from Juventus, Henry had struggled to come to terms with his switch from winger to striker and his finishing bore the signs of a player short on confidence in front of goal.

In fact, as in the previous season, the entire Arsenal team were struggling to convert chances into goals. They attempted more shots than any other club in the top flight over the campaign, but their overall goals-to-shots ratio of 12% fell some way short of the 19% that Manchester United registered.

Another area of concern was discipline. Other teams had more players sent off in the 1999–2000 season, but no one attracted more criticism than Arsenal. The low point came at Upton Park when Patrick Vieira was sent off and reacted by spitting at Neil Ruddock, who had rushed to join in the ensuing melée. Vieira subsequently "involved himself" with a policeman in the players' tunnel.

The upshot of this was a six-game ban and a £45,000 fine. Injuries to key players including captain Tony Adams and Emmanuel Petit had already disrupted Arsene Wenger's plans: Vieira's ban merely exacerbated his problems.

At the turn of the year, Arsenal had lost five games – four of them away. By the end of the season they had lost seven times on their Premiership travels including defeats at West Ham, Coventry, Bradford and Middlesbrough – grounds where Manchester United had won easily.

There was the suspicion in these games that players like Petit and Marc Overmars, who had both been linked with high-profile moves abroad, were not giving their all. Equally worrying was the form of the defence. Shorn of the inspirational Adams for large chunks of the season, the back-line looked strangely vulnerable.

David Seaman took much of the blame for this. He kept just five clean sheets and registered the lowest saves-to-shots ratio of any other regular Premiership goalkeeper. Alex Manninger, who had started the season because of an injury to Seaman, actually managed the same number of shut-outs and had a better saves-to-shots ratio, but was still deemed too inconsistent to take the number one

7 Arsenal won more matches after going behind

SEASON REVIEW

jersey from the England man.

Arsene Wenger insisted that the increasing fragility of his defence was a team problem and not one limited purely to his back-line, but it would be a major surprise if he did not bring in new defensive blood before the start of the 2000–01 season.

The Champions League did not prove as much of a distraction domestically as it had to Chelsea, but it was still a miserable affair for the Gunners. While their away form proved a problem in the Premiership, the reverse was true in the Champions League. Draws away to Fiorentina and Barcelona were not enough to progress beyond the first group stage, as both of the return games at their adopted home Wembley were lost. Minnows AIK Solna were beaten twice, but Arsenal finished third and sadly found themselves relegated to the UEFA Cup.

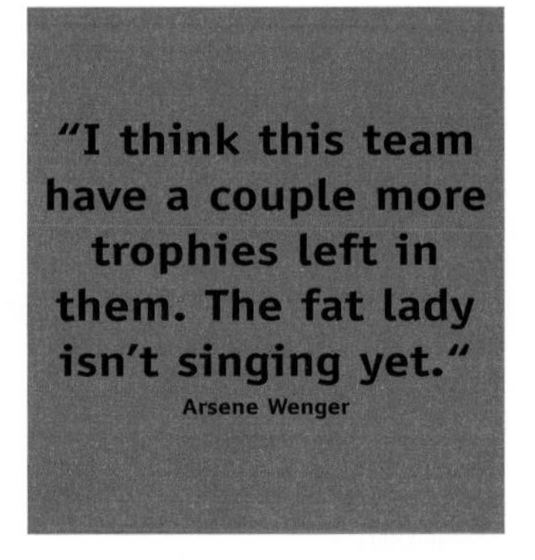

"I think this team have a couple more trophies left in them. The fat lady isn't singing yet."
Arsene Wenger

The Gunners were considerably better away from Wembley, beating Nantes, Deportivo La Coruña, Werder Bremen and Lens at Highbury and losing just once away (to Deportivo) en route to a UEFA Cup final date with Galatasaray in Copenhagen.

That match was lost on penalties, a fact that came as no surprise. After beating Blackpool in the third round, Arsenal had gone out of the FA Cup in a fourth round replay – on penalties. They also lost in the Worthington Cup, going out at Middlesbrough – on penalties. With vital misses from the spot away to Fiorentina in the Champions League and a further two failures in the Premiership, Arsenal's record from the spot in 1999–2000 read: "Taken 20, missed 10", giving them an appalling success rate of just 50%.

Despite their cup disappointments, the team did put together a good run in the league, winning eight games in a row between 19 March and 5 May. Thierry Henry, who had looked so poor earlier in the season, was the catalyst behind this run. The Frenchman scored in seven consecutive league games to equal the Premiership record jointly held by Mark Stein and Alan Shearer, and will break that record if he scores in his first appearance in the 2000–01 season.

While their run came too late to catch Manchester United, it was enough to take them into second spot and guarantee Arsenal a place in the 2000–01 Champions League. With Wembley no longer an option, the team are likely to play their home games at Highbury.

In the Premiership they will have to improve on two things: their away record and, most importantly, their squad. A record points difference of 18 proves that Arsenal are now a long way behind their main rivals. While few would dispute that their preferred starting XI is a match for Sir Alex Ferguson's first-choice team, there is no doubt that Manchester United's squad has greater quality in depth.

Arsene Wenger has learned from bitter past experience that his squad is not strong enough to cover for the loss of key players like Adams, Petit and Vieira. With older members of the Highbury playing staff gradually being replaced by new imports and even more games on the cards in 2000–01, the canny Frenchman must strengthen his squad or Arsenal may once again have to resign themselves to being second best.

While that would be a significant achievement for the majority of other Premiership teams, for a club of Arsenal's size and ambition it would represent yet another anti-climax.

than any other team in the Premiership

ARSENAL

DATE	OPPONENT	SCORE	ATT.	ADAMS	BARRETT	BERGKAMP	BLACK	BOA MORTE	COLE	DIXON	GRAY	GRIMANDI	HENRY	HUGHES	KANU
7.8.99	Leicester H	2–1*	38,026	–	–	89^{1}	–	–	–	90	–	90□	s45	–	90
10.8.99	Derby Co A	2–1	25,901	–	–	90^{1}	–	s5	–	90	–	–	85□	–	75
14.8.99	Sunderland A	0–0	41,680	–	–	45	–	s45	–	90□	–	–	90	–	90
22.8.99	Man Utd H	1–2	38,147	–	–	90	–	–	–	90	–	–	77	–	70
25.8.99	Bradford H	2–0	38,073	–	–	67	–	–	–	–	–	90	61	–	78^{1}
28.8.99	Liverpool A	0–2	44,886	90	–	90	–	–	–	90	–	–	90□	–	–
11.9.99	Aston Villa H	3–1	38,093	90	–	76	–	–	–	90	–	90□	s8	–	$s14^{1}$
18.9.99	Southampton A	1–0	15,242	90	–	90	–	–	–	90	–	90□	$s19^{1}$	–	71
25.9.99	Watford H	1–0	38,127	90	–	s16	–	–	–	–	–	–	74	–	88^{1}
3.10.99	West Ham A	1–2	26,009	90	–	90□	–	–	–	–	–	90□	71□	–	s19
16.10.99	Everton H	4–1	38,042	90	–	69	–	–	–	90^{1}	–	90	–	–	$s21^{1}$
23.10.99	Chelsea A	3–2	34,958	90	–	–	–	–	–	90□	–	–	s28	–	90^{3}
30.10.99	Newcastle H	0–0	38,106	90	–	s45	–	–	–	–	–	90	45	–	–
7.11.99	Tottenham A	1–2	36,085	90	–	90□	–	–	–	90□	–	s12	–	–	72
20.11.99	Middlesbro H	5–1	38,082	90□	–	74^{2}	–	–	–	71	–	51	–	–	90
28.11.99	Derby Co H	2–1	37,964	90	–	63□	–	–	–	–	–	90□	73^{2}	–	s27
4.12.99	Leicester A	3–0*	20,495	90	s1	–	–	–	–	90	–	90^{1}□	89	s26	90
18.12.99	Wimbledon H	1–1	38,052	–	–	–	–	–	–	90	–	90	90^{1}	–	90
26.12.99	Coventry A	2–3	22,757	90	–	–	–	–	–	90	–	60□	90□	–	90
28.12.99	Leeds Utd H	2–0	38,096	90	–	–	–	–	–	–	–	90	74^{1}	–	90□
3.1.00	Sheff Wed A	1–1	26,155	90	–	–	–	–	–	–	–	90	90	–	71
15.1.00	Sunderland H	4–1	38,039	–	s7	–	–	–	–	90	–	–	83^{2}	–	–
24.1.00	Man Utd A	1–1	58,293	–	–	–	–	–	–	90	–	90□	90	70	–
5.2.00	Bradford A	1–2	18,276	–	–	s22	–	–	–	90	–	90	90^{1}□	–	–
13.2.00	Liverpool H	0–1	38,098	–	–	59	–	–	–	90	–	90	90	–	–
26.2.00	Southampton H	3–1	38,044	90	–	70^{1}□	–	–	–	90	–	–	–	–	90
5.3.00	Aston Villa A	1–1	36,930	–	–	45	–	–	–	90^{1}	–	50	90	–	90
12.3.00	Middlesbro A	1–2	34,244	–	–	$s30^{1}$	–	–	–	–	–	90	90	–	90
19.3.00	Tottenham H	2–1*	38,131	90□	–	–	–	–	–	90	–	85■	76^{1}	–	90□
26.3.00	Coventry H	3–0	38,027	–	–	68	–	–	–	90	–	90^{1}	75^{1}	–	$s22^{1}$
1.4.00	Wimbledon A	3–1	25,858	–	–	74	–	–	–	90	–	90	$s24^{1}$	–	66^{2}
16.4.00	Leeds Utd A	4–0	39,307	90	–	67□	–	–	–	90	–	–	74^{1}	–	$s23^{1}$
23.4.00	Watford A	3–2	19,670	–	–	90□	–	–	–	–	–	90	90^{2}	–	–
29.4.00	Everton A	1–0	35,919	90	–	69	s4	–	–	90	–	90	–	–	90
2.5.00	West Ham H	2–1	38,092	90	–	90	–	–	–	56	–	90	–	–	90
6.5.00	Chelsea H	2–1	38,119	90	–	68	–	–	–	90	–	90	90^{2}□	–	s22
9.5.00	Sheff Wed H	3–3	37,271	–	–	s45	–	–	–	90^{1}	–	90	90^{1}	–	90
14.5.00	Newcastle A	2–4	36,450	–	–	–	–	–	90	–	s19	–	–	–	71^{1}

□ Yellow card, ■ Red card, s Substitute, 90^{2} Goals scored

*including one own goal

1999–2000 PREMIERSHIP APPEARANCES

KEOWN	LJUNGBERG	LUZHNY	McGOVERN	MALZ	MANNINGER	OVERMARS	PARLOUR	PETIT	SEAMAN	SILVINHO	SUKER	UPSON	VERNAZZA	VIEIRA	VIVAS	WESTON	WINTERBURN	TOTAL
90	45	–	–	–	90	s26	64	90	–	s1□	–	–	–	90	–	–	90	990
90□	–	s15	–	–	90	–	21	90[1]	–	s69	–	90	–	90	–	–	90	990
90	s51	–	–	–	90	–	90	39	–	90	–	90□	–	90□	–	–	–	990
90	90[1]	–	–	–	90	s20	90□	–	–	90	s13	90	–	90	–	–	–	990
90	90	–	–	–	90	s29	90	–	–	90	s23	s12	–	90[1]□	90	–	–	990
90□	90□	–	–	–	90	64	75	–	–	s15	s26	–	–	90□	–	–	90	990
90	–	–	–	–	90	82	90	–	–	s21	69[2]	–	–	90	–	–	90□	990
90	45	s6	–	–	90	84	s45	–	–	–	–	–	–	90	–	–	90□	990
90	67	90	–	–	90	90	90	–	–	90	s23	–	–	90	s2	–	–	990
90□	90	71	–	–	–	s19	–	–	90	90	90[1]	–	–	86■	–	–	–	986
90	s14	–	–	–	–	65	76	–	90	s25	90[2]	–	–	90	–	–	90	990
90	62	–	–	–	–	89	90	65□	90	90	90□	–	s1	–	s25□	–	–	990
65□	90	90	–	–	–	s30	–	–	90	60	90	s25	–	90	–	–	90	990
89■	54■	–	–	–	–	90	–	78□	90	–	s18□	–	–	90[1]□	–	–	90	953
–	90	–	–	–	–	90[3]	90	90	90	–	s16	s39	–	–	s19	–	90	990
–	–	90	–	s9	90	81	90	90	–	–	s17□	90	–	–	–	–	90	990
–	–	–	–	–	90	90[1]	–	90	–	64	–	13	–	–	s77	–	90	990
–	90	90	–	–	90	90	–	90□	–	90	s17	–	–	–	–	–	73	990
90	90[1]	–	–	–	–	90	–	90	90	–	s30[1]	–	–	–	–	–	90	990
–	90[1]□	90	–	–	–	90□	–	88	90	90	s16	–	–	90	–	–	s2	990
–	90	90□	–	–	–	27	–	90[1]	90	90	s19	–	–	90	–	–	s63	990
90	31	90	–	s59	–	–	90	90	90	90	90[2]	–	–	90	–	–	–	990
90	90[1]	–	–	s20	–	–	90	90	90	23	–	–	–	90	–	–	s67	990
90	90	–	–	68	–	–	90	90	90	–	90	–	–	–	–	–	90	990
90	77	s13	–	–	–	s45	90□	45	90	90	s31	–	–	90	–	–	–	990
90	90[2]	–	–	–	–	s20	90	90	90	90	–	–	–	90□	–	–	–	990
90	–	s40	–	–	–	s45	90	73□	90	90	–	–	–	90	–	–	s17	990
–	60	90	–	–	s45	–	79	90	45	90	s11	–	–	90	–	–	90□	990
–	s34	90	–	–	90	56	90□	–	–	90	–	–	–	90	–	–	s14	985
–	s15	90	–	–	–	80	90	90	90	–	s10	–	–	90□	–	–	90	990
90	–	43■	–	–	–	44	90	s46	90	90	–	–	–	90	–	–	s16	943
90[1]	90	–	–	–	–	s16[1]	90	82□	90	90□	–	–	–	90□	–	–	s8	990
90□	–	90	–	–	–	64	90[1]	90	90	s26	–	–	–	90□	–	–	90	990
90	–	–	–	–	–	86[1]	90	80	90	90□	–	–	–	s21	–	–	s10	990
–	–	90□	–	–	–	90[1]	90	s34[1]	90	90	–	–	–	90□	–	–	–	990
–	–	s14	–	–	–	45	90	76	90	90	–	–	–	90	–	–	s45	990
90	–	90	–	–	–	90	45	–	90	s28[1]	–	–	–	90	–	–	62	990
90	–	90	s23	90[1]	90	–	45	–	–	s45	90□	–	90	–	–	67	90	990

THE MANAGER

ARSENE WENGER

For 18 other Premiership teams, runners-up spot in the Premiership and a place in the UEFA Cup final would be deemed a highly-successful season, but Arsene Wenger will still reflect on what could have been in 1999–2000.

It was not all disappointing, with one encouraging sign for Wenger being the excellent form of £10.5m signing Thierry Henry, who replaced "Super Nic" Anelka as Highbury's top striker. But Arsenal's French boss now faces his biggest challenge yet in trying to cope with replacing the famous defence who, collectively, are nearing the end of their careers.

Wenger guided Monaco to the French title in 1988 and joined Arsenal after a spell in Japan with Grampus Eight, and the Gunners' manager has been linked with the Japanese national team for the 2002 World Cup.

The Frenchman guided the Gunners to the Premier League and FA Cup "Double" in 1998, and was justly presented with the Manager of the Year award that season.

Such is Wenger's reputation in the game that he has also been linked with the Real Madrid and Barcelona posts, but Arsenal fans will want him to stay, as arguably the most astute manager in the Premiership will be as keen as ever to bring the 2000–01 title back to north London.

LEAGUE POSITION

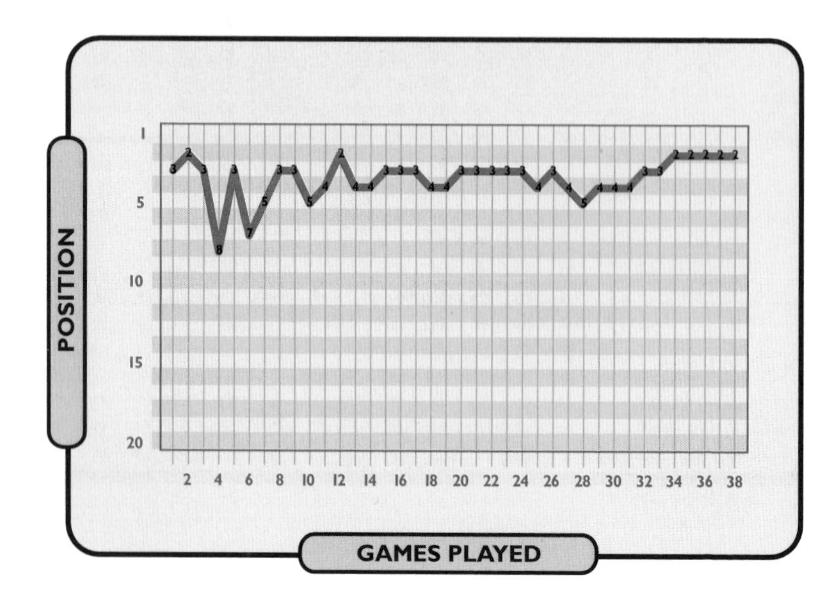

THE GOALS

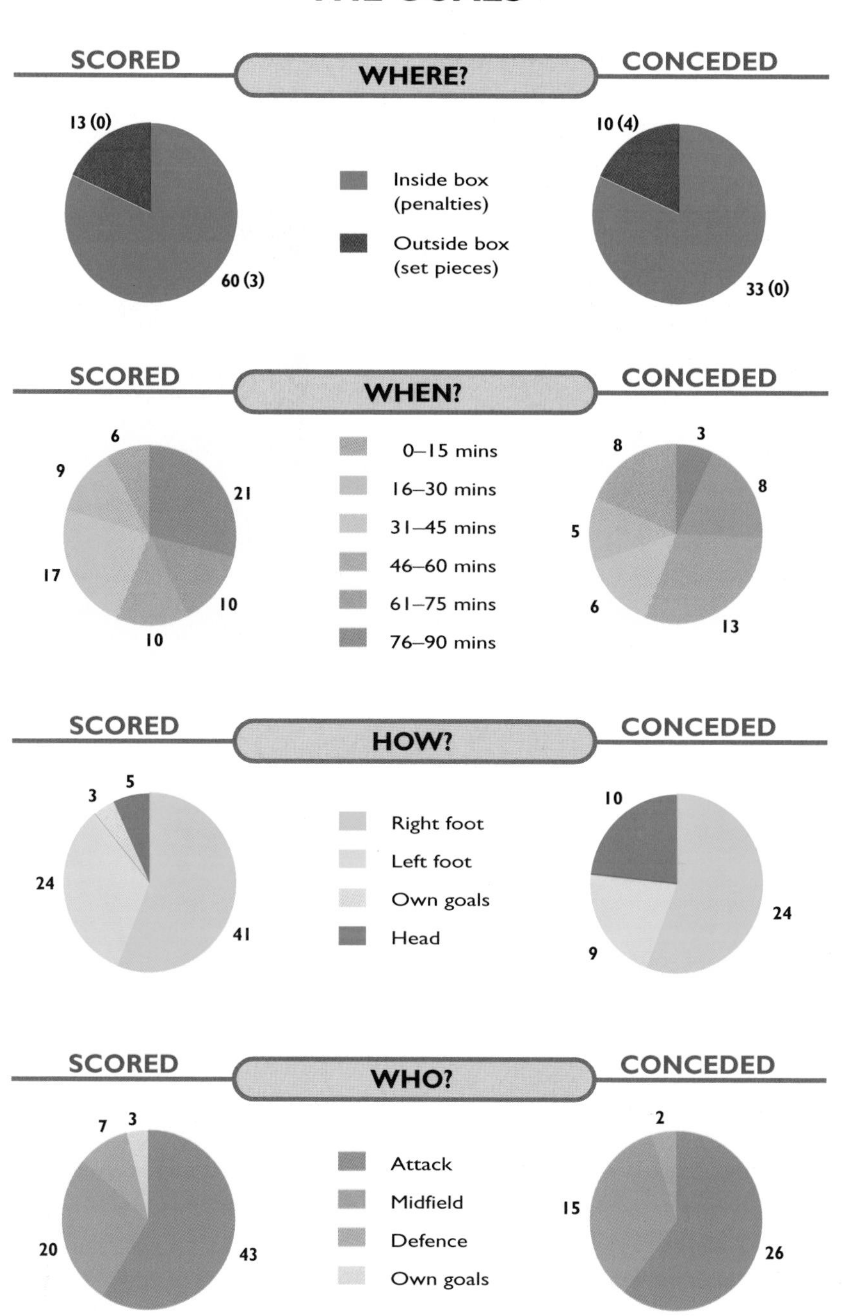

15 minutes than any other side

ARSENAL

	ADAMS	BARRETT	BERGKAMP	BLACK	BOA MORTE	COLE	DIXON	GRAY	GRIMANDI	HENRY	HUGHES	KANU	KEOWN
APPEARANCES													
Start	21	0	23	0	0	1	28	0	27	26	1	24	27
Sub	0	2	5	1	2	0	0	1	1	5	1	7	0
Minutes on pitch	1890	8	1881	4	50	90	2467	19	2328	2251	96	2160	2404
GOAL ATTEMPTS													
Goals	0	0	6	0	0	0	3	0	2	17	0	12	1
Shots on target	7	0	39	0	1	1	7	1	7	51	0	34	3
Shots off target	4	0	25	0	1	1	10	0	9	41	0	45	5
Shooting accuracy	64%	0%	61%	0%	50%	50%	41%	100%	44%	55%	0%	43%	38%
PASSING													
Goal assists	1	0	9	0	0	0	1	0	1	8	1	4	0
Long passes	264	0	101	1	1	7	332	0	370	73	4	149	250
Short passes	600	1	678	1	22	27	840	6	916	759	41	886	749
PASS COMPLETION													
Own half %	84%	0%	79%	50%	75%	74%	86%	100%	84%	74%	93%	87%	87%
Opposition half %	65%	100%	61%	0%	53%	67%	69%	50%	68%	62%	76%	66%	65%
CROSSING													
Total crosses	4	0	50	0	1	1	86	0	18	96	4	29	12
Cross completion %	100%	0%	22%	0%	100%	0%	30%	0%	44%	29%	50%	21%	75%
DRIBBLING													
Dribbles & runs	43	0	112	1	3	4	64	1	39	150	5	151	35
Dribble completion %	88%	0%	65%	0%	0%	25%	88%	100%	90%	65%	80%	64%	91%
DEFENDING													
Tackles made	73	0	22	0	3	6	60	0	88	23	0	31	47
Tackles won %	60%	0%	73%	0%	67%	33%	47%	0%	61%	65%	0%	48%	70%
Blocks	31	0	5	0	0	1	28	0	32	1	0	0	51
Clearances	172	0	0	0	0	2	57	0	118	10	1	4	332
Interceptions	33	0	4	0	1	0	11	0	18	3	0	1	31
DISCIPLINE													
Fouls	25	0	35	0	5	2	18	1	46	54	2	35	38
Offside	3	2	14	0	0	0	2	0	2	42	0	14	0
Yellow cards	2	0	6	0	0	0	3	0	8	6	0	2	5
Red cards	0	0	0	0	0	0	0	0	1	0	0	0	1

GOALKEEPER NAME	START/ (SUB)	TIME ON PITCH	GOALS CONCEDED	MINS/GOALS CONCEDED	SAVES MADE	SAVES/ SHOTS
MANNINGER	14(1)	1305	16	82	29	64%
SEAMAN	24	2115	27	78	43	61%

PLAYERS' STATISTICS

LJUNGBERG	LUZHNY	MALZ	MCGOVERN	OVERMARS	PARLOUR	PETIT	SILVINHO	SUKER	UPSON	VERNAZZA	VIEIRA	VIVAS	WESTON	WINTERBURN	TOTAL	RANK
22	16	2	0	22	29	24	23	8	5	1	29	1	1	19		
4	5	3	1	9	1	2	8	14	3	1	1	4	0	9		
1815	1462	246	23	1927	2430	2056	2177	969	449	91	2627	213	67	1907		
6	0	1	0	7	1	3	1	8	0	0	2	0	0	0	73*	2nd
24	3	2	0	29	12	12	6	31	1	0	7	0	0	2	280	1st
14	1	5	0	32	22	19	6	16	3	0	22	0	0	1	282	2nd
63%	75%	29%	0%	48%	35%	39%	50%	66%	25%	0%	24%	0%	0%	67%	50%	4th
2	1	1	0	8	2	7	3	1	0	0	3	2	0	0	55	2nd
112	235	21	7	110	174	308	185	82	28	6	313	15	8	224	3380	5th
668	480	92	6	621	932	982	891	314	127	33	1260	79	24	835	12870	2nd
81%	86%	84%	86%	76%	82%	84%	81%	79%	84%	69%	86%	77%	96%	80%	83%	2nd
67%	64%	72%	50%	71%	69%	67%	67%	65%	65%	57%	74%	72%	57%	75%	68%	4th
39	44	7	0	98	78	134	90	42	4	1	13	14	0	57	922	2nd
28%	27%	57%	0%	29%	22%	31%	26%	33%	50%	100%	62%	50%	0%	30%	30%	9th
128	35	6	0	169	123	60	106	47	1	1	99	8	0	53	1444	1st
67%	86%	83%	0%	72%	67%	78%	70%	70%	100%	100%	78%	88%	0%	83%	72%	20th
80	56	2	0	24	72	94	103	10	8	4	130	8	1	99	1044	7th
68%	50%	50%	0%	54%	58%	61%	52%	80%	63%	50%	68%	88%	0%	52%	59%	1st
10	23	3	1	3	5	24	19	4	5	0	21	4	0	21	292	20th
21	83	4	1	5	29	54	67	5	51	1	81	12	1	53	1178	20th
10	12	1	0	6	9	15	17	3	1	0	19	3	0	15	214	16th
25	10	6	1	8	45	29	32	13	7	3	63	8	1	21	534	14th
4	0	0	0	10	9	0	5	17	0	0	1	0	0	1	126	11th
2	2	0	0	1	3	5	3	4	1	0	9	1	0	3	66	9th
1	1	0	0	0	0	0	0	0	0	0	1	0	0	0	5	=3rd

*Including three own goals

CROSSES CAUGHT	CROSSES PUNCHED	CROSSES NOT CLAIMED	CATCH SUCCESS	THROWS/ SHORT KICKS	% COMPLETION	LONG KICKS	% COMPLETION
20	9	0	100%	101	93%	313	42%
28	11	0	100%	106	94%	674	40%

PLAYER OF THE SEASON

PLAYER	INDEX SCORE
THIERRY HENRY	1,133
Emmanuel Petit	1,122
Patrick Vieira	973
Silvinho	961
Tony Adams	949
Martin Keown	885
Lee Dixon	821
Gilles Grimandi	756
Ray Parlour	740
David Seaman	294

Thierry Henry had his doubters in his early Arsenal days, but the young French striker quickly adapted to Premiership life and it was his firepower which helped the Gunners clinch their place in the Champions League.

Henry, who was a prodigy of Arsene Wenger's at Monaco, finished the season in record-breaking fashion, scoring in seven consecutive league games – equalling the Premiership record. Despite playing most of his career as a wide man, Wenger converted him to a more central striking role at Arsenal and they certainly reaped the rewards. His 17 Premiership goals helped him achieve an average Index score of 1,133 in his first season in English football – and helped to fill the void left by Nicolas Anelka.

The 1998–99 player of the season Emmanuel Petit was ranked just behind his fellow-countryman with an Index score of 1,122. The mercurial midfielder scored three goals and laid on seven more for team-mates as the Gunners claimed the coveted 1999–2000 Premiership's runners-up spot.

Patrick Vieira made it a Gallic trio at the top of Arsenal's player ratings with an average of 973 points. He won 88 tackles which proved to be the third-highest total in the Premiership, although the red card he received at West Ham held his points total back.

Another new face, Silvinho, also made his mark in the 1999–2000 season, ousting Nigel Winterburn from the left-back spot and earning an average of 961 points per game.

Two players missing from the Arsenal top 10 are Dennis Bergkamp and Marc Overmars. Neither player was able to qualify due to an insufficient number of minutes played, and without their presence Arsenal struggled to link properly as a side.

Only later on in the season, when both players returned to the team, did the Gunners hit top form, losing only one of their last 10 league matches.

100% David Seaman was the only regular

FIVE OF THE BEST

After losing at Middlesbrough in March, the Gunners slipped to fifth place in the Premiership, and it looked as if 1999–2000 was to be Arsene Wenger's worst season at Highbury. But a typical late surge in form and eight successive victories meant that Arsenal won the race for second place comfortably, ensuring another campaign in the Champions League.

TOP GOALSCORERS

	GOALS	GOALS/SHOTS
THIERRY HENRY	17	18%
Nwankwo Kanu	12	15%
Davor Suker	8	17%
Marc Overmars	7	11%
Fredrik Ljungberg	6	16%

Thierry Henry was undoubtedly the biggest Highbury success story in 1999–2000, scoring 17 league goals and also leading the way in the accuracy stakes. The Frenchman has been successfully converted from a winger to a centre-forward and scored at least once in each of his last seven league appearances. Dennis Bergkamp is notable by his absence from the top scorers, but fellow-frontmen Kanu and Davor Suker notched 20 goals between them, the Croatian scoring with 17% of his efforts.

Arsenal's passing has brought them many plaudits in recent seasons, but it suffered slightly in 1999–2000. Patrick Vieira and Emmanuel Petit were not as accurate as Roy Keane and Paul Scholes but the younger Frenchman was still as involved as ever. Petit had a mixed campaign but still created seven goals for the Gunners. Lee Dixon and Nigel Winterburn were as busy as always, proving that there is still plenty of life in those ageing limbs.

TOP PASSERS

	SUCC PASSES	COMPLETION
PATRICK VIEIRA	1,234	78%
Gilles Grimandi	977	76%
Emmanuel Petit	939	73%
Lee Dixon	889	76%
Nigel Winterburn	819	77%

TOP TACKLERS

	WON	SUCCESS
PATRICK VIEIRA	88	68%
Emmanuel Petit	57	61%
Fredrik Ljungberg	54	68%
Gilles Grimandi	54	61%
Silvinho	54	52%

The sight of Patrick Vieira bearing down on an opponent is a magnificent one, and the World Cup winner made 88 tackles for Arsenal in 1999–2000, winning 68% of them. That was over 30 more than any other colleague, although a host of Gunners slid into more than 50 challenges. Newcomer Silvinho had made the left-back slot his own by the season's end and he finished with 54 tackles, the same amount as the much-improved Gilles Grimandi.

Patrick Vieira was the bad boy of London N5 for the second season running, racking up nine yellow cards and a much-publicised sending-off in a game with West Ham. The incident saw Vieira hit with a six-game ban, but in fairness, he was far better-behaved than in 1998–99. Two other Frenchmen, Grimandi and Henry, follow Vieira, the latter having committed 54 fouls in his first season at Highbury.

DISCIPLINE

	POINTS	FOULS & CARDS
PATRICK VIEIRA	96	63F, 9Y, 1R
Gilles Grimandi	76	46F, 8Y, 1R
Thierry Henry	72	54F, 6Y, 0R
Martin Keown	59	38F, 5Y, 1R
Ray Parlour	54	45F, 3Y, 0R

ACTION	ADAMS	DIXON	HENRY	KANU	KEOWN	LJUNGBERG	OVERMARS	PARLOUR	PETIT	SEAMAN	SILVINHO	SUKER	VERNAZZA	VIVAS	TOTAL	CHELSEA
Time On Pitch	90	90	28	90	90	62	89	90	65	90	90	90	1	25	990	990
GOALS																
Goal	–	–	–	3	–	–	–	–	–	–	–	–	–	–	3	2
Shot on target	–	1	–	–	–	–	1	–	–	–	–	–	–	–	2	2
Shot off target	–		–	2	–	1	2	1	–	–	–	–	–	–	6	2
Blocked shot	–	1	–	–	–	–	1	–	–	–	–	1	1	–	4	3
Own goal	–	–	–	–	–	–	–	–	–	–	–	–	–	–	–	–
PASSES																
Pass to own player	24	26	4	20	22	12	17	34	19	–	27	18	1	10	234	228
Pass to opposition	6	11	5	18	1	5	8	12	4	–	17	8	1	4	100	101
Cross to own player	1	1	–	1	–	–	1	–	–	–	–	–	–	1	5	6
Cross to opposition player	–	1	–	–	1	3	3	–	–	–	1	3	–	–	12	10
Goal assist	–	–	–	–	–	–	2	–	–	–	–	–	–	–	2	2
Pass completion %	81%	69%	44%	54%	92%	60%	65%	74%	83%	0%	60%	62%	50%	73%	68%	68%
TACKLES & CLEARANCES																
Tackle	2	1	1	2	–	4	–	3	1	–	6	1	–	–	21	29
Clearances, blocks and interceptions	17	7	1	1	34	3	3	17	9	–	7	1	–	1	101	113
DRIBBLES & RUNS																
Dribble ball retained	7	5	1	9	2	5	8	6	1	–	8	3	–	1	56	43
Dribbles ball lost	–	–	–	3	–	4	3	1	1	–	–	4	–	1	17	6
Dribble success %	100%	100%	100%	75%	100%	56%	73%	86%	50%	0%	100%	43%	0%	50%	77%	88%
DISCIPLINE																
Fouls	1	2	2	–	2	1	–	3	1	–	1	2	–	3	18	15
Penalty conceded	–	–	–	–	–	–	–	–	–	–	–	–	–	–	–	–
Free kick – offside	–	–	–	–	–	–	–	–	–	–	–	–	–	–	–	3
Yellow cards	–	1	–	–	–	–	–	–	1	–	–	1	–	1	4	4
Red cards	–	–	–	–	–	–	–	–	–	–	–	–	–	–	–	–
GOALKEEPERS																
Distribution to own player	–	–	–	–	–	–	–	–	–	14	–	–	–	–	14	15
Distribution to opposition player	–	–	–	–	–	–	–	–	–	20	–	–	–	–	20	23
Goalkeeper distribution %	0%	0%	0%	0%	0%	0%	0%	0%	0%	41%	0%	0%	0%	0%	41%	39%
Save	–	–	–	–	–	–	–	–	–	2	–	–	–	–	2	2
Ball caught	–	–	–	–	–	–	–	–	–	1	–	–	–	–	1	1
Ball dropped	–	–	–	–	–	–	–	–	–	–	–	–	–	–	–	–
Goal conceded	–	–	–	–	–	–	–	–	–	2	–	–	–	–	2	3

71% Chelsea conceded a higher percentage of

Arsenal went into this clash in fourth place in the table, but had already been defeated in three of their opening 11 Premiership games – just one loss fewer than they recorded during the entire 1998–99 season. Consequently, Arsene Wenger announced that his side could not afford any more defeats if they were to regain the title.

But for much of the game, the Gunners struggled to get into their stride against a combative Chelsea team and had to rely on an heroic late show by Kanu which put the Blues' forlorn title hopes up the creek.

This fixture has traditionally had its fair share of unsavoury incidents and it was clear that the players were fired up from the whistle, as Lee Dixon was booked for a petulant kick at Graeme Le Saux after just two minutes.

While both sides completed a well below-par 68% of their passes during the match, it was Gianluca Vialli's team that seemed the more incisive and they created the better of the game's early chances. Tore Andre Flo had a shot blocked by Martin Keown after six minutes, before Chris Sutton missed a good headed opportunity on 13.

The opening goal came in the 39th minute when a Dan Petrescu cross eluded Martin Keown and Dixon to find Flo, who expertly headed past David Seaman into the back of the net. Chelsea's Romanian then provided the finishing touch to a Le Saux cross seven minutes into the second half to leave the Gunners trailing 2–0 and sinking to defeat in the pouring rain.

But Arsenal managed to rally well after Petrescu's goal, winning 66% of their challenges – 25 percentage points greater than Chelsea. Dixon had a shot saved by Ed De Goey after a clever free-kick by Davor Suker on 56 minutes. But the Croatian was less thoughtful seven minutes later when he chose to shoot from a narrow angle, rather than set up the unmarked Kanu.

The Nigerian grabbed his first goal on 75 minutes, controlling a speculative shot by Marc Overmars in the area before eluding Marcel Desailly and Frank Leboeuf to shoot past De Goey.

The same Arsenal combination then beat Chelsea's big Dutch 'keeper just eight minutes later. Overmars skipped past Leboeuf before drilling a low cross to Kanu. The ex-Inter player managed to control the ball and get past Desailly with a single flick before firing a rasping drive into the back of the net.

His work still not finished, Kanu blocked an attempted clearance by Albert Ferrer and picked up the ball out near the corner flag. He side-stepped De Goey's rash challenge before sending a powerful shot past the Blues' two French centre-backs and into the roof of the net from a virtually impossible angle right out on the goal line.

By the final whistle, Wenger's side had fired in 15 shots, six more than the Blues. Kanu attempted 12 dribbles and runs, more than any other player on the pitch, found a team-mate with 20 of his passes and showed exemplary finishing, scoring with each of his three shots on target to finish with an Opta points score of 1,981.

goals to strikers than any other team

ASTON VILLA

ADDRESS

Villa Park, Trinity Road,
Birmingham B6 6HE

CONTACT NUMBERS

Contact Numbers
Telephone: 0121 327 2299
Fax: 0121 322 2107
Commercial: 0121 327 5399
Ticket Office: 0121 327 5353
Club Call: 09068 121148
Villa Village Superstore:
0121 327 2800
e-mail: postmaster@astonvilla-fc.co.uk
Website: www.astonvilla-fc.co.uk

KEY PERSONNEL

Chairman: H D Ellis
President: J A Alderson
Directors: S M Stride
M J Ansell, D M Owen
A J Hales
Club Secretary: S M Stride
Manager: John Gregory

SPONSORS

1999–2000 LDV
2000–2001 NTL

FANZINES

Heroes And Villans
The Holy Trinity

COLOURS

Home: Claret and sky blue
stripes, claret shorts, claret
stockings with sky blue band
Away: Turquoise shirts with
black panel, black shorts,
turquoise stockings

NICKNAME

The Villans

HONOURS

League Champions: 1893–94,
1895–96, 1896–97, 1898–99,
1899–00, 1909–10, 1980–81
Division Two Champions:
1937–38, 1959–60
Division Three Champions: 1971–72
FA Cup: 1887, 1895,
1897, 1905, 1913, 1920, 1957
League Cup: 1961,
1975, 1977, 1994, 1996
European Cup : 1982
European Super Cup: 1982
World Club Championship 1982

RECORD GOALSCORER

Harry Hampton –
215 league goals, 1904–15

BIGGEST WIN

12–2 v Accrington Stanley –
Division One, 12 March 1892

BIGGEST DEFEAT

1–8 v Blackburn Rovers –
FA Cup 3rd Round, 16 February 1889

SEASON REVIEW

As in 1998–99, Aston Villa enjoyed a season of two halves in 1999–2000. Unlike the previous campaign, though, 1999–2000 started badly and got better, ending – albeit unsuccessfully – with a place in the FA Cup final.

Pre-season brought two major new signings to Villa Park: David James from Liverpool and George Boateng from Coventry City. But neither player sparked the imagination of the Birmingham public who, even after seeing their side record an opening-day victory at St James's Park, did not turn out at home games. Crowds failed to top the 30,000 mark in the first two months of the 1999–2000 season.

Part of the blame for this was felt to lie with John Gregory's tactics. Villa were in second place after six games, but their matches had been largely uninspiring affairs, won or lost by the odd goal.

> **"Any Premiership manager is one defeat away from a crisis."**
> **John Gregory**

Unlike his team, Gregory himself was providing the media with plenty to talk about. The Villa manager was no stranger to controversy during the course of the season and he started his one-man campaign against referees early with a stinging attack on Jeff Winter for his performance as fourth official in the game against Newcastle.

That cost him £2,000 – but he was undeterred, attacking both David Elleray and Winter again for their performances in Villa's defeats at Arsenal and Leicester. Rob Harris was next, earning criticism for sending off Steve Staunton of Liverpool in a 0–0 draw at Villa Park, while Elleray came in for his second earbashing of the season after awarding Sunderland a controversial penalty in the narrow 2–1 defeat at the Stadium of Light.

Gregory was himself the subject of criticism, as his team faded away to drop out of the top 10 by the end of October. Ugo Ehiogu called Villa's poor home attendances "depressing", at the same time muttering about his own misgivings over the direction the club was going in.

Gregory's rather insensitive handling of the Stan Collymore situation did no one at the club, least of all Collymore, any good; and even the signing of skilful Benito Carbone from Sheffield Wednesday did little to lift the veil of gloom descending over Villa Park.

Worthington Cup victories over Chester City and an under-strength Manchester United side raised spirits slightly, but a £32,000 fine for Gregory, this time for criticising Uriah Rennie's performance in the season opener, sent morale crashing again.

A rather public falling-out with Ehiogu and a sequence of results that brought no wins in nine league games saw the media vultures circling hungrily over Villa Park. Gregory had been handed a 28-day touchline ban for threatening to "punch the fourth official's lights out" at the Leicester match, and when Villa lost 2–1 to Coventry courtesy of a goal from Robbie Keane – a player for whom Gregory had refused to pay £6.5 million earlier in the season – all eyes turned to Doug Ellis.

To the chairman's credit, he stuck by his manager and was rewarded with an upturn in form. Southampton were trounced in the Worthington Cup fourth round and, although Villa lost to Newcastle, the team's performances were improving.

The luck that seemed to have deserted them for much of the first half of the season was certainly on their side in the cup competitions. First "lucky losers" Darlington were pulled out of the bag in the draw for the third round of the FA Cup. Then, despite losing to West Ham in a

37% of Aston Villa's goals were headers

SEASON REVIEW

penalty shoot-out in the fifth round of the Worthington Cup, the team were given a reprieve when it was announced that West Ham's Emmanuel Omoyinmi, who had come on as a substitute, had been ineligible to appear in that competition.

The match was replayed, and Villa's win was made all the sweeter by Gregory's candid admission that he had nearly made the mistake of playing Carbone, who was himself ineligible.

In the league, Villa were on a run that was to take in 12 unbeaten games and lift them to sixth in the league. There were some problems with Carbone, who hinted that he might leave the club in the summer, but on the pitch the little Italian was in magnificent form, developing a great understanding with Player of the Season Paul Merson that was to yield plenty of goals.

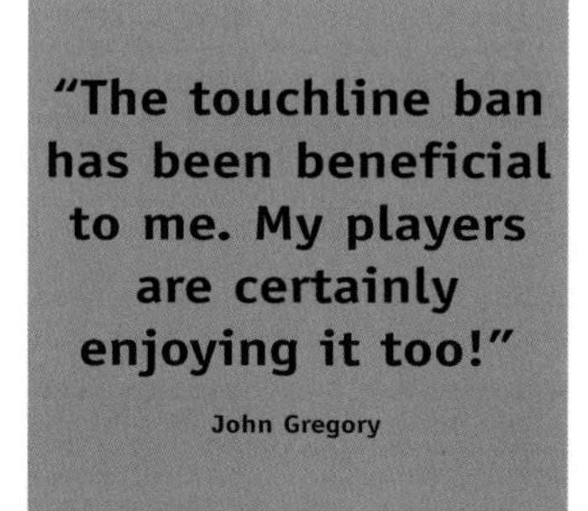

"The touchline ban has been beneficial to me. My players are certainly enjoying it too!"

John Gregory

Of more concern was an injury sustained by Dion Dublin against Sheffield Wednesday that left the striker with a broken neck, though remarkably he made a comeback just three months later.

Stan Collymore left the club, bringing another unhappy chapter in his eventful career to a close. Ironically, the club who took him off Villa's hands – Leicester City – eliminated Villa from the Worthington Cup soon afterwards.

There was to be better news in the FA Cup, where Southampton, Leeds and Everton were all eliminated on the way to a semi-final date with Bolton Wanderers. Unfortunately, the game at Everton was soured by Carbone's sending-off and Gregory's subsequent attack on referee Dermot Gallagher, who was accused of failing to "engage his brain".

The continuing contract wrangles with Carbone failed to impact on the team's performance on the pitch and although their unbeaten run came to an end against Southampton, they did not lose in the league again until the final day of the 1999–2000 season.

Attendances had picked up and the voices of discontent that had been raised against Gregory earlier in the season were a distant memory.

A place in the FA Cup final was assured with a penalty shoot-out victory over Bolton Wanderers; David James, who had been in fine form, was the hero of the hour, conceding just one spot-kick.

The former Liverpool man, who earned a recall to the England squad, was less fortunate in the final, dropping the ball to allow Roberto Di Matteo to score the only goal of the game in a 1–0 victory for Chelsea.

That defeat left Gregory and his team looking to the Intertoto Cup as their only route into Europe in 2000–01.

Gregory expressed some doubts about the wisdom of entering the competition, but, as Doug Ellis pointed out, a club of Villa's size needs European competition.

If they can repeat the consistency they showed in the second half of the 1999–2000 season, there is no reason why the Villa team cannot succeed both at home and abroad.

Much depends on Gregory's ability to convince key members of his squad like Gareth Southgate, Ugo Ehiogu and the outspoken Julian Joachim that the club is capable of competing for major honours.

The signing of Belgian striker Luc Nilis proves that Gregory is serious about bringing more players of international quality to Villa Park.

But the club will need to add some silverware to their trophy cabinet before the doubters are convinced of their ability to become a Premiership force.

– the highest ratio in the division

ASTON VILLA

DATE	OPPONENT	SCORE	ATT.	BARRY	BEWERS	BOATENG	CALDERWOOD	CARBONE	CUTLER	DELANEY	DRAPER	DUBLIN	EHIOGU
7.8.99	Newcastle A	1–0	36,600	–	–	56	87	–	–	90□	–	90	90□
11.8.99	Everton H	3–0	30,337	–	–	57	90	–	–	90	–	62^{1}	90□
16.8.99	West Ham H	2–2	26,250	–	–	45	90	–	–	90	–	90^{2}	90
21.8.99	Chelsea A	0–1	35,071	–	–	–	76	–	–	90	s1	90	90
24.8.99	Watford A	1–0	19,161	–	–	s10□	90	–	–	90^{1}	–	90	90
28.8.99	Middlesbro H	1–0	28,728	–	–	s23	90	–	–	90	–	90^{1}	67
11.9.99	Arsenal A	1–3	38,093	–	–	–	90	–	–	90□	–	71	90□
18.9.99	Bradford H	1–0	28,083	90□	–	84□	–	–	–	–	–	90^{1}	90
25.9.99	Leicester A	1–3	19,917	90	–	90	s24	–	–	s27	–	90^{1}	90
2.10.99	Liverpool H	0–0	39,217	90□	–	67□	–	–	–	90	–	90	90
18.10.99	Sunderland A	1–2	41,045	90	–	84	90	–	–	90□	–	90^{1}	–
23.10.99	Wimbledon H	1–1	27,160	90□	–	75	90	90	–	90	–	90^{1}	–
30.10.99	Man Utd A	0–3	55,211	90□	–	55	90	76	–	90	–	90	–
6.11.99	Southampton H	0–1	26,474	90	–	s9	90	90	–	90	–	90	–
22.11.99	Coventry A	1–2	20,184	–	–	90□	90	–	–	75	–	90^{1}	–
27.11.99	Everton A	0–0	34,750	90	–	90	90□	s24	–	–	–	90	–
4.12.99	Newcastle H	0–1	34,531	90	–	90□	90	s38	–	90□	–	52	–
18.12.99	Sheff Wed H	2–1	23,885	90	–	90	s4	81	–	–	–	86	90
26.12.99	Derby Co A	2–0	33,222	90	–	90^{1}	–	56	–	–	–	–	90
29.12.99	Tottenham H	1–1	39,217	90	–	90	–	66	–	–	–	–	90
3.1.00	Leeds Utd A	2–1	40,027	90	–	90□	–	80□	–	–	–	–	90
15.1.00	West Ham A	1–1	24,237	90	–	79	s11	79	–	–	–	–	90
22.1.00	Chelsea H	0–0	33,704	90	–	90	–	90	–	s30	–	–	90
5.2.00	Watford H	4–0	27,647	90	–	71	90	90	–	90	–	–	90
14.2.00	Middlesbro A	4–0*	31,571	90	–	73	–	90^{1}	s7	90	–	–	90
26.2.00	Bradford A	1–1	18,276	90	–	90□	–	90	–	90	–	–	90
5.3.00	Arsenal H	1–1	36,930	90	–	–	–	–	–	90	–	–	90
11.3.00	Coventry H	1–0	33,177	90	–	90	–	90	–	90	–	–	90^{1}□
15.3.00	Liverpool A	0–0	43,615	90□	–	90	–	90	–	90	–	–	90
18.3.00	Southampton A	0–2	15,218	90	–	90	–	90	–	–	–	–	90□
25.3.00	Derby Co H	2–0	28,613	90	–	90^{1}	–	80^{1}	–	90	–	s10	90
5.4.00	Sheff Wed A	1–0	18,136	90	–	–	–	–	–	45	–	90	90
9.4.00	Leeds Utd H	1–0	33,889	90	–	90	–	60	–	–	–	s30	90
15.4.00	Tottenham A	4–2	35,304	90	s1	90□	–	90^{1}	–	s43	–	90^{2}	90
22.4.00	Leicester H	2–2	31,229	90	–	90□	–	90	–	–	–	80	90
29.4.00	Sunderland H	1–1	33,949	90^{1}□	–	90	–	90	–	90	–	s29	90
6.5.00	Wimbledon A	2–2	19,188	90	–	–	–	90	–	90□	–	80^{1}□	90
14.5.00	Man Utd H	0–1	39,217	90	–	81	–	60	–	90□	–	90	90

□ Yellow card, ■ Red card, s Substitute, 90^{2} Goals scored

*including one own goal

1999–2000 PREMIERSHIP APPEARANCES

ENCKELMAN	GHRAYIB	HENDRIE	JAMES	JOACHIM	MERSON	SAMUEL	SOUTHGATE	STONE	TAYLOR	THOMPSON	VASSELL	WALKER	WATSON	WRIGHT	TOTAL
–	–	s34	90	90[1]	–	–	90	s3	90	90□	–	–	–	90	990
–	–	s33	90	90[1]	s28	–	90	s22	90[1]	68	–	–	–	90□	990
–	–	s45	90	90	–	–	90	s2	90	88	–	–	–	90□	990
–	–	90□	90	90	s20	–	90	s13	90□	70□	–	–	–	90	990
–	–	90	90	90	80	–	90	–	90□	–	–	–	–	90	990
–	–	90	90	78	90	–	90	–	90	–	s12	–	–	90	990
s39	–	62	51	90[1]	90□	–	90	–	90□	s28	s19	–	–	90	990
90	–	90	–	64	s35	–	90	s6	90	55	s26	–	90	–	990
90	–	90□	–	90	–	–	65■	–	90	66	–	–	63□	–	965
90	–	80	–	90	s23	–	90	s10	90	90□	–	–	–	–	990
–	–	90	90	–	s35	–	90	s6	90□	90□	55	–	–	–	990
–	s12	90	90	–	s15	–	90	–	78	90	–	–	–	–	990
–	–	90	90	–	s14	–	90	s35	90	72	–	–	–	s18	990
–	s9	–	90	–	81	–	90	90	–	81□	–	–	–	90	990
–	–	90□	90	75	–	–	90	90	90□	–	s15	–	s15	90	990
–	–	90□	90	66	–	–	90	–	90□	–	–	–	90□	90□	990
–	–	9	90	90	s17	–	90	–	90	s64□	–	–	–	90□	990
–	–	–	90	s51	90[1]	–	90	–	90[1]□	–	s9	–	90	39	990
–	–	–	90	90	75	–	90	s15□	90[1]	–	s34	–	90	90	990
–	–	–	90	90	90	–	90	s16	90[1]□	–	s24	–	90	74	990
–	–	–	90	90	90□	–	90[2]	90	–	–	s10□	–	90□	90	990
–	–	–	90	90	90	–	90	90	90[1]	–	s11	–	–	90	990
–	–	–	90	45	90	–	90	s27	90	–	s18	–	60	90	990
–	–	s6	90	64	84[2]	s19	–	90[1]	–	–	–	s26[1]	–	90	990
–	–	s27	83	90[2]	63	–	90	90	s17	–	–	–	–	90	990
90	–	s13	–	90	77[1]	–	90	24	s66	–	–	–	–	90	990
90	–	s9	–	90	90	–	90	90	90	–	–	81[1]	–	90	990
90	–	–	–	86	79	–	90	s11	90	–	–	s4	–	90□	990
90	–	s31	–	88	59	–	52	90	s38	–	–	s2	–	90	990
90	–	69	–	s28	90	s21	–	62	90	s9	–	–	90	81	990
–	–	s15	90	61	90	90	–	s29	75	–	–	–	–	90	990
–	s26	90□	90	s35	–	90	–	s45	–	90[1]	–	55	90	64	990
–	s39	67	90	90[1]	90	90□	–	–	–	s23	–	–	90	51	990
–	–	–	90	–	90	90□	–	–	–	90□	–	–	46	90[1]	990
–	–	s18□	90	s10	90[1]	90	–	–	–	72[1]	–	–	90□	90	990
–	87	s13	90	61	90	s3	90	–	–	77	–	–	–	–	990
–	–	90[1]	90	s10	90	s25	90	–	–	90	–	–	–	65	990
90	–	65	–	s30	90	–	90	–	s25	s9	–	–	–	90	990

THE MANAGER

JOHN GREGORY

A sixth-placed finish in the Premiership, the semi-finals of the Worthington Cup and runners-up in the FA Cup, plus the possibility of UEFA Cup football through the Intertoto Cup, made it an excellent season for Aston Villa.

But for manager John Gregory it was the most testing time of his managerial career, after being a whisker away from the sack earlier in the campaign.

Gregory's first relationship with Villa was as a player, and he also enjoyed spells with Derby County, QPR, Brighton and Northampton, winning six England caps.

His managerial career began at Portsmouth in January 1989 before he moved to Plymouth in February 1990, where he lasted just five months.

He took charge of a struggling Wycombe Wanderers side in October 1996, and in his first season steered them clear of relegation by eight points.

Gregory was appointed Villa boss in February 1998, and at the start of the 1998–99 season made club history when his side were unbeaten in their first 12 Premiership matches.

With Villa having enjoyed a successful 1999–2000, Gregory will now be looking to build on the firm foundations he has laid during his time at the club.

LEAGUE POSITION

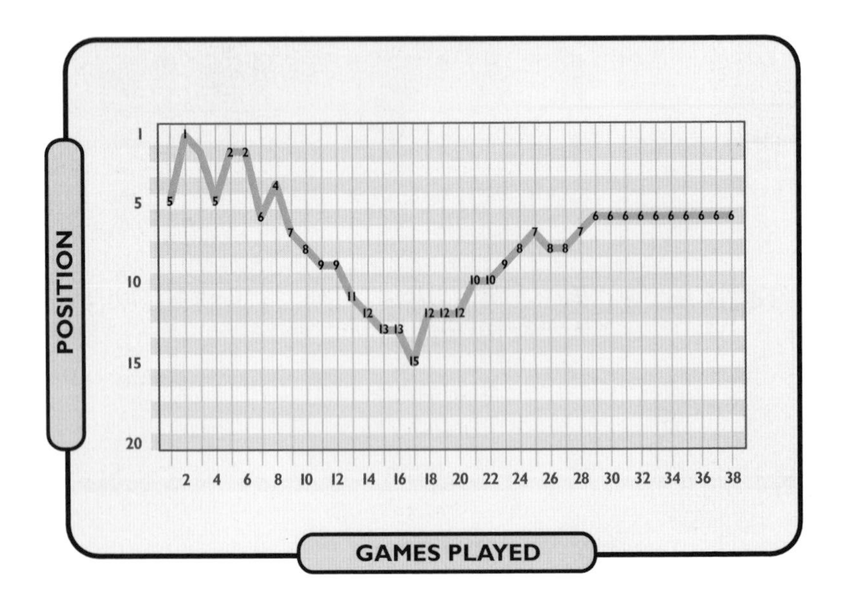

4 Villa conceded the fewest goals

THE GOALS

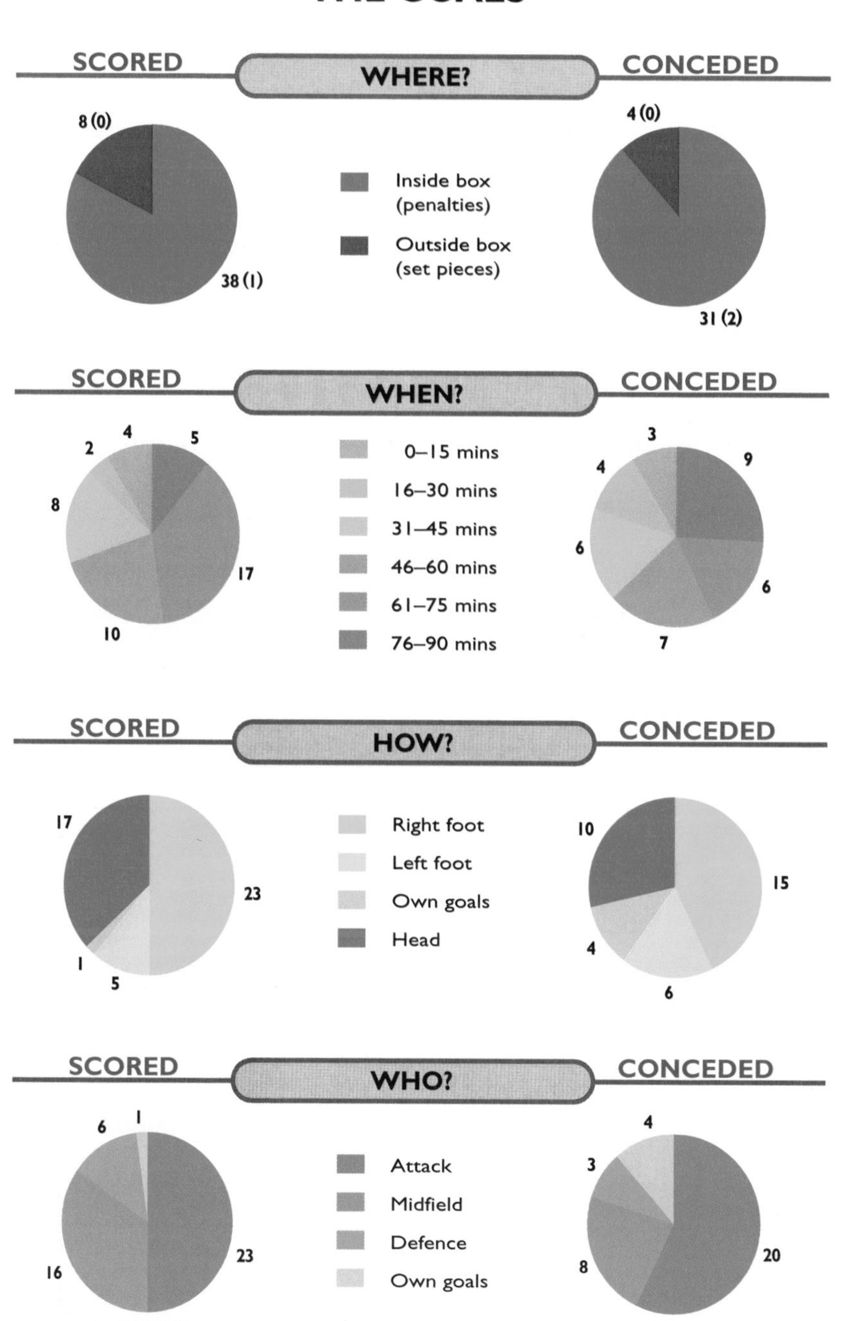

from shots struck outside the area in the Premiership

ASTON VILLA

	BARRY	BEWERS	BOATENG	CALDERWOOD	CARBONE	DELANEY	DRAPER	DUBLIN	EHIOGU	GHRAYIB
APPEARANCES										
Start	30	0	30	15	22	25	0	23	31	1
Sub	0	1	3	3	2	3	1	3	0	4
Minutes on pitch	2700	1	2489	1372	1870	2290	1	2030	2767	173
GOAL ATTEMPTS										
Goals	1	0	2	0	3	1	0	12	1	0
Shots on target	5	0	11	1	23	2	0	22	7	0
Shots off target	9	0	14	2	28	2	0	41	14	0
Shooting accuracy	36%	0%	44%	33%	45%	50%	0%	35%	33%	0%
PASSING										
Goal assists	1	0	0	0	5	2	0	4	0	0
Long passes	457	0	251	105	103	199	0	71	268	13
Short passes	733	1	849	284	654	686	4	667	633	46
PASS COMPLETION										
Own half %	68%	0%	86%	86%	75%	73%	0%	80%	74%	61%
Opposition half %	57%	0%	68%	56%	60%	60%	100%	62%	51%	61%
CROSSING										
Total crosses	50	0	36	1	56	73	0	5	6	8
Cross completion %	28%	0%	19%	0%	30%	30%	0%	60%	33%	25%
DRIBBLING										
Dribbles & runs	86	0	90	13	109	99	0	22	32	9
Dribble completion %	94%	0%	80%	92%	57%	82%	0%	86%	97%	56%
DEFENDING										
Tackles made	74	0	126	26	50	125	0	23	81	4
Tackles won %	58%	0%	56%	58%	44%	39%	0%	48%	44%	50%
Blocks	53	0	11	15	0	35	0	6	58	6
Clearances	226	0	53	158	2	107	0	31	332	4
Interceptions	13	0	20	14	7	19	0	10	15	1
DISCIPLINE										
Fouls	37	0	58	14	36	21	0	48	53	5
Offside	1	0	1	0	65	2	0	12	2	0
Yellow cards	6	0	9	1	1	6	0	1	5	0
Red cards	0	0	0	0	0	0	0	0	0	0

GOALKEEPER NAME	START/ (SUB)	TIME ON PITCH	GOALS CONCEDED	MINS/GOALS CONCEDED	SAVES MADE	SAVES/ SHOTS
CUTLER	0(1)	7	0	0	0	0%
ENCKLEMAN	9(1)	849	9	94	32	78%
JAMES	29	2564	26	99	76	75%

PLAYERS' STATISTICS

HENDRIE	JOACHIM	MERSON	SAMUEL	SOUTHGATE	STONE	TAYLOR	THOMPSON	VASSELL	WALKER	WATSON	WRIGHT	TOTAL	RANK
18	27	24	5	31	10	25	16	1	2	13	31		
11	6	8	4	0	14	4	5	10	3	1	1		
1676	2382	2225	518	2727	1046	2369	1412	233	168	1084	2642		
1	6	5	0	2	1	5	2	0	2	0	1	46*	=13th
8	23	16	0	3	5	9	8	1	2	3	4	153	18th
11	16	26	0	6	5	10	11	3	1	6	4	209	9th
42%	59%	38%	0%	33%	50%	47%	42%	25%	67%	33%	50%	42%	19th
0	5	8	0	1	2	0	2	2	0	2	5	39	=8th
153	35	254	59	406	101	105	170	7	3	166	367	3293	7th
707	516	833	109	531	372	784	519	83	53	303	825	10192	13th
82%	66%	80%	73%	78%	78%	83%	82%	89%	75%	57%	71%	77%	16th
70%	65%	68%	61%	51%	71%	70%	64%	65%	55%	51%	63%	63%	14th
48	28	196	2	7	47	9	93	2	2	36	95	800	8th
33%	32%	38%	100%	29%	36%	22%	25%	50%	0%	28%	34%	32%	5th
103	81	114	4	34	44	28	53	26	5	57	49	1058	10th
81%	69%	75%	100%	94%	84%	79%	79%	65%	60%	74%	96%	79%	6th
44	39	31	11	88	38	109	35	8	1	34	57	1005	12th
45%	51%	48%	73%	57%	58%	55%	54%	63%	0%	59%	37%	51%	15th
10	2	2	13	68	10	19	6	0	1	9	28	352	18th
25	0	15	27	346	20	74	22	0	0	37	109	1616	10th
19	8	9	2	35	7	37	11	5	0	5	19	257	10th
25	35	22	8	33	28	44	23	7	3	12	15	528	15th
10	34	8	0	0	4	5	1	6	5	1	4	161	4th
6	0	2	2	0	1	8	7	1	0	4	5	65	10th
0	0	0	0	1	0	0	0	0	0	0	0	1	=17th

*Including one own goal

CROSSES CAUGHT	CROSSES PUNCHED	CROSSES NOT CLAIMED	CATCH SUCCESS	THROWS/ SHORT KICKS	% COMPLETION	LONG KICKS	% COMPLETION
0	0	0	0%	0	0%	4	75%
18	4	1	95%	26	88%	216	31%
58	20	10	85%	80	81%	818	38%

PLAYER OF THE SEASON

PLAYER	INDEX SCORE
MARK DELANEY	849
Paul Merson	845
Gareth Southgate	817
Ian Taylor	780
George Boateng	753
Dion Dublin	749
Alan Wright	705
Gareth Barry	693
Ugo Ehiogu	676
David James	660

A sixth-placed finish and an FA Cup final for Villa were their reward for the season, bringing with them the possibility of a run in Europe in 2000–01.

John Gregory built his Villa side on a strong defence and they conceded the third fewest goals in the Premiership during the 1999–2000 season.

Top of the Opta Index was the Welsh right wing-back Mark Delaney with 849 points. The former Cardiff City man scored one and made two for the Villans, while in defence he made 125 tackles and 107 clearances. He would appear to have a very exciting future at Villa Park after such a terrific season

Behind Delaney in the ratings was Paul Merson, who has been enjoying a new lease of life in the West Midlands. The former England man was instrumental as a playmaker for John Gregory's side, with five goals and eight assists during the course of the campaign.

Gareth Southgate remained one of Villa's most consistent performers. He was the second highest-placed player during the 1998–99 season and was third in 1999–2000 with 817 points. The England defender was the lynchpin of the Villa back-line which conceded just 35 goals in the Premiership. He made a total of 346 clearances at the back and even chipped in with a couple of rare goals.

Midfield duo Ian Taylor and George Boateng combined tough tackling with goals from the middle of the park to support the attack, while striker Dion Dublin overcame a horrific injury during the season to finish with an average of 749 points and end the season as Villa's top scorer. Teenager Gareth Barry enjoyed another steady season, culminating in a call-up to England's Euro 2000 squad.

Goalkeeper David James also made it into the top 10 after keeping 12 clean sheets in the league. This form led to him earning a recall to the England squad, but he will want to forget his costly error at Wembley which literally handed the FA Cup to Chelsea.

10 No goalkeeper dropped crosses on

FIVE OF THE BEST

A dismal autumn saw Aston Villa plummet down the Premiership as manager John Gregory faced the prospect of the sack. But a spirited revival saw the team return to top form and lose just two of their last 21 league games. A mixture of English grit and the flair of men such as Benito Carbone meant that the progress made under Gregory was not undone.

TOP GOALSCORERS

	GOALS	GOALS/SHOTS
DION DUBLIN	12	19%
Julian Joachim	6	15%
Ian Taylor	5	26%
Paul Merson	5	12%
Benito Carbone	3	6%

The season's most spectacular injury occurred when Dion Dublin clattered into Gerald Sibon and broke a bone in his neck. He was forced to undergo a serious operation and was absent from the Villa team for three months, yet he still finished as the leading marksman at Villa Park. Scoring was a considerable problem for the team, with Julian Joachim the second-highest scorer, albeit with just six goals. Benito Carbone's wage demands look extravagant when you consider he scored with just 6% of his efforts.

Villa's passing often avoided the midfield and subsequently they made fewer passes than any other team in the top six. Former Coventry star George Boateng was the slickest man at the club, along with his central colleague Ian Taylor. Surprisingly, Paul Merson was the most inaccurate of the midfield trio, with just 69% of his passes finding a man in claret and blue. Last season's top man Alan Wright falls to second, but is still one of the most consistent passers at the Midlands club.

TOP PASSERS

	SUCC PASSES	COMPLETION
GEORGE BOATENG	812	74%
Alan Wright	787	66%
Paul Merson	755	69%
Gareth Barry	730	61%
Ian Taylor	658	74%

TOP TACKLERS

	WON	SUCCESS
GEORGE BOATENG	71	56%
Ian Taylor	60	55%
Gareth Southgate	50	57%
Mark Delaney	49	39%
Gareth Barry	43	58%

John Gregory attributed much of the club's recovery to the form of George Boateng in the Villa engine room, and the Dutchman made more tackles than any of his team-mates. His partnership with Ian Taylor was a strong base on which the Midlanders built. Gareth Southgate was his usual imperious self at the back, while two younger defenders, Mark Delaney and Gareth Barry, were more than able to hold their own, the latter now securing a place in the England squad.

Aston Villa were again one of the fairest teams in the Premiership in 1999–2000, collecting just one red card all season, Gareth Southgate being ordered from the field in the derby clash with Leicester. George Boateng was the nearest the club had to an *enfant terrible*, with nine yellow cards. Popular central defender Ugo Ehiogu and Ian Taylor were joint second, but in truth Villa were a club with few disciplinary problems to worry about.

DISCIPLINE

	POINTS	FOULS & CARDS
GEORGE BOATENG	85	58F, 9Y, 0R
Ugo Ehiogu	68	53F, 5Y, 0R
Ian Taylor	68	44F, 8Y, 0R
Gareth Barry	55	37F, 6Y, 0R
Dion Dublin	51	48F, 1Y, 0R

ACTION	BARRY	BEWERS	BOATENG	CARBONE	DELANEY	DUBLIN	EHIOGU	JAMES	MERSON	SAMUEL	THOMPSON	WATSON	WRIGHT	TOTAL	TOTTENHAM
Time On Pitch	90	1	90	90	43	90	90	90	90	90	90	46	90	990	990
GOALS															
Goal	–	–	–	1	–	2	–	–	–	–	–	–	1	4	2
Shot on target	–	–	–	1	–	–	–	–	1	–	1	–	–	3	5
Shot off target	–	–	–	–	–	–	–	–	1	–	–	–	–	1	6
Blocked shot	–	–	–	–	–	–	–	–	–	–	–	–	–	–	1
Own goal	–	–	–	–	–	–	–	–	–	–	–	–	–	–	–
PASSES															
Pass to own player	23	–	22	21	7	21	18	–	32	19	29	16	19	227	308
Pass to opposition	13	1	8	15	5	9	7	–	7	6	13	7	24	115	130
Cross to own player	–	–	1	1	1	–	–	–	3	–	–	–	–	6	8
Cross to opposition player	–	–	1	1	–	–	–	–	–	–	–	1	2	5	11
Goal assist	–	–	–	1	–	2	–	–	–	–	–	–	–	3	2
Pass completion %	64%	0%	72%	59%	62%	72%	72%	0%	83%	76%	69%	67%	42%	66%	69%
TACKLES & CLEARANCES															
Tackle	1	–	1	3	4	–	4	–	2	2	2	2	2	23	17
Clearances, blocks and interceptions	12	–	–	–	–	1	11	–	–	10	–	3	4	41	37
DRIBBLES & RUNS															
Dribble ball retained	3	–	1	2	1	–	–	–	5	–	2	3	2	19	26
Dribble ball lost	–	–	–	–	–	–	–	–	–	–	1	–	–	1	2
Dribble success %	100%	0%	100%	100%	100%	0%	0%	0%	100%	0%	67%	100%	100%	95%	93%
DISCIPLINE															
Fouls	2	–	3	3	1	5	1	–	–	1	2	1	–	19	14
Penalty conceded	–	–	–	–	–	–	–	–	–	–	–	–	–	–	1
Free kick – offside	–	–	–	4	–	–	–	–	–	–	–	–	–	4	4
Yellow cards	–	–	1	–	–	–	–	–	–	1	1	–	–	3	4
Red cards	–	–	–	–	–	–	–	–	–	–	–	–	–	–	–
GOALKEEPERS															
Distribution to own player	–	–	–	–	–	–	–	7	–	–	–	–	–	7	24
Distribution to opposition player	–	–	–	–	–	–	–	27	–	–	–	–	–	27	16
Goalkeeper distribution%	0%	0%	0%	0%	0%	0%	0%	21%	0%	0%	0%	0%	0%	21%	60%
Save	–	–	–	–	–	–	–	5	–	–	–	–	–	5	3
Ball caught	–	–	–	–	–	–	–	2	–	–	–	–	–	2	1
Ball dropped	–	–	–	–	–	–	–	1	–	–	–	–	–	1	
Goal conceded	–	–	–	–	–	–	–	2	–	–	–	–	–	2	4

76 Benito Carbone was flagged offside

Two of the perennial "nearly teams" clashed at White Hart Lane in this fixture, as Villa put on a brilliant second-half display, turning the game completely around in a breathtaking 12-minute spell to earn an unlikely three points.

Both sides looked edgy in the opening exchanges, but as soon as David Ginola started getting more of the ball, the home team started to take control. Predictably they took the lead through the creative industry of the Frenchman after 17 minutes. Ginola played a classy one-two with Mauricio Taricco, and then the 33-year old crossed with pinpoint accuracy to the unmarked Steffen Iversen, who headed home.

Tottenham were superb in the first 45 minutes, with Ginola pulling the strings all over the park, and they should have made it 2–0 when Chris Armstrong was sent clean through on goal. But he misjudged his lob, playing it into the grateful arms of Villa goalkeeper David James. The much-maligned forward almost made amends minutes later when his overhead kick bounced off the top of the bar.

Two minutes after the break Tottenham did get the second goal that their play had deserved. Stephen Carr played a long ball over the top and the lively Armstrong knocked the ball past the onrushing James and finished from a tight angle. It appeared that Tottenham and Armstrong were finding their form – a perfect tonic for manager George Graham, who was in hospital suffering with rheumatoid arthritis.

But then Dion Dublin – in only his fifth game back since breaking his neck – led one of the most spectacular comebacks of the season. The big target man won a penalty just after the hour when his volley hit Iversen's arm and the former Coventry striker coolly dispatched the kick himself, sending Walker the wrong way.

The visiting defenders began to put the shackles on Ginola, effectively killing off the threat from the home side as Villa started to play some flowing football of their own. Young defender Gareth Barry made 12 clearances, blocks and interceptions – more than any other player – to help turn the tide of the game in the Midlanders' favour.

Spurs' chief tormentor was Benito Carbone, who twisted and turned on the wing before whipping in a cross after 69 minutes for Dublin to smash the ball home with a spectacular overhead kick – a brave manoeuvre with suitable reward.

Dublin returned the compliment within a minute, cushioning a header back to Carbone, who lashed the ball over Walker from the edge of the area and into the top corner. That stunning strike was bettered four minutes later with a carbon copy lay-off by Dublin and a volley by Alan Wright that screamed into the net.

Dublin won the penalty that got the Villans back in the game, scored with both his shots and created the other two goals making his personal comeback as sweet as his team's.

Both teams managed to fire seven shots on target, but Villa showed the value of good finishing.

more times than any other player

asics
JCT600

BRADFORD CITY

ADDRESS

The Bradford & Bingley Stadium,
Valley Parade, Bradford,
West Yorkshire BD8 7DY

CONTACT NUMBERS

Telephone: 01274 773355
Fax: 01274 773356
Ticket Office: 01274 770022
Club Call: 09068 888640
Bantam Leisure (Shop): 01274 770012
e-mail: bradfordcityfc@compuserve.com
Website: www.bradfordcityfc.co.uk

KEY PERSONNEL

Chairman: G Richmond
Club President: J Tordoff
Vice-Chairman: D Thompson FCA
Managing Director: S Harvey
Directors: D Richmond
E Richmond, T Goddard
M Richmond, J Rhodes
Prof. D Rhodes OBE
Club Secretary: J Pollard
Manager: Paul Jewell

SPONSORS

JCT 600

FANZINES

City Gent

COLOURS

Home: Claret and amber
shirts, claret shorts
and amber stockings
Away: All white with
claret and amber trim

NICKNAME

The Bantams

HONOURS

Division Two Champions: 1907–08
Division Three Champions: 1984–85
Division Three (North) Champions:
1928–29
FA Cup: 1911

RECORD GOALSCORER

Bobby Campbell – 121 league goals,
1981–84, 1984–86

BIGGEST WIN

11–1 v Rotherham United –
Division Three (North),
25 August 1928

BIGGEST DEFEAT

1–9 v Colchester United – Division
Four, 30 December 1961

SEASON REVIEW

Just as Alan Hansen got it wrong in 1996 when he wrote off Manchester United with the words "You don't win anything with kids", so Rodney Marsh committed a footballing *faux pas* when he stated that if Bradford stayed up in 1999–2000 he would have his head shaved at Valley Parade.

For long periods of the season Marsh's mane looked safer than Bradford City. When the heat was on, though, the Bantams rose to the occasion, sealing an amazing last-day escape with a 1–0 victory over Champions League-chasing Liverpool.

The scorer that day was David Wetherall, one of several veterans at the club who brought their very considerable experience to bear on the battle against the drop. Wetherall and Gunnar Halle were both signed from Leeds, Dean Saunders was brought in from Benfica and Neil Redfearn from Charlton to join the likes of Stuart McCall, John Dreyer, Wayne Jacobs and Peter Beagrie in the roll-call of over-30s at Valley Parade.

"I'll pick up some fish and chips on the way home and then – in the nicest possible way – I shall stick two fingers up at all our critics."

Paul Jewell

Saunders proved an instant success, scoring the goal that gave Bradford an opening-day victory at Middlesbrough, and while fellow veteran John Dreyer put the ball in his own net in the next game – a 1–1 draw with Sheffield Wednesday – 10th position after their first two games represented a better start than many pundits had predicted.

After that, though, the team lost their next three games, dropping into the bottom four, which they left just once in the rest of the season.

Scoring proved a major problem – only Wimbledon managed fewer shots on target than Bradford and only Watford finished with fewer goals – but life was also uncomfortably busy for the defence, who were forced into more blocks and clearances than any other Premiership side during the campaign.

Having said that, they never stopped working. Relegation rivals Sheffield Wednesday and Wimbledon were often accused of lacking spirit, but that allegation was rarely levelled at a Bradford City side who fought tooth and nail to preserve their Premiership status.

Vital victories over better teams such as Arsenal, Liverpool and Sunderland were earned by dint of work-rate and dour defending; qualities embodied in the likes of Dean Windass, who, despite his role as a striker, made 165 tackles, clearances, blocks and interceptions to help his defence.

That fighting spirit was less evident in knockout competition. After scraping past Reading on away goals in the second round of the Worthington Cup, Bradford were beaten by Yorkshire rivals Barnsley in the third round; a depressing defeat. But nothing compared to the embarrassment of a 3–1 fourth-round FA Cup defeat at the hands of Second Division Gillingham.

Back in the league with the team struggling to score, some supporters even began to question Paul Jewell's credentials as a manager. They found it hard to understand how he could let Isaiah Rankin and Lee Mills go out on loan when the side was finding life so difficult in front of goal in the top flight.

The failure of foreign imports Bruno Rodriguez and later Jorge Cadete to make an impression did nothing to allay fears that Bradford did not have the firepower needed to stay up.

Unlike the three clubs which finished below them, though, Bradford stayed disciplined at the back, conceding fewer goals than Wimbledon, Sheffield

561 David Wetherall made the highest

SEASON REVIEW

Wednesday or Watford, and it was this that ultimately kept them up.

When Gary Walsh was injured, Matt Clarke stepped in and let no one down, and when Clarke was out Aidan Davison proved a capable replacement. With Wetherall and the outstanding young prospect Andy O'Brien in front of them, Bradford's various goalkeepers – while still having to earn their money – were never worked as hard as those of their relegation rivals.

Critics might argue that in any other season Bradford would have gone down. No team has ever stayed in the Premiership with a lower points tally. But that would be harsh on a side which defied the predictions of virtually everyone but the most optimistic of their own die-hard fans.

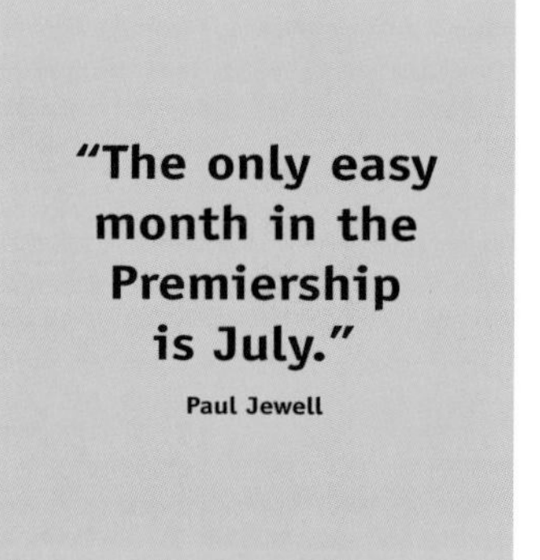

"The only easy month in the Premiership is July."
Paul Jewell

Only after Sunderland were beaten at the Stadium of Light did the media start to consider that Bradford might survive the drop. When Wimbledon were beaten 3–0 in one of the most important games of the season to take Bradford out of the bottom three, people began to talk seriously of survival.

Even then, Wimbledon were favourites to stay up – their goal difference was still superior and on paper they had the easier games left.

When Wimbledon picked up a late point against Aston Villa on the same day as Bradford were being beaten 3–0 at Filbert Street, the Bantams were plunged back into the bottom three. As their final game was against Liverpool and Wimbledon had an easier-looking fixture against a Southampton side who had nothing left to play for, the obituaries were already being written for Bradford.

Whatever happened to the Dons, Bradford knew that they had to win their game to stand any chance of survival. Fittingly, it was Player of the Season David Wetherall who scored what has been described as the most important goal in the club's history. When news of a 2–0 defeat for Wimbledon was confirmed, the unlikely great escape was complete.

Wimbledon had lost out to a side which embodied all the qualities which they themselves had once been famous for, namely hard work, determination and a willingness to take anyone on.

Players like Jamie Lawrence and Peter Beagrie might have made the headlines for their hairstyles and somersaults, but when it came to football they were deadly serious about survival. With the inspirational Stuart McCall leading by example from midfield, no-one was allowed to consider relegation.

Bradford's transfer coffers are unlikely to be as full as those of many of their fellow Premiership incumbents – a fact that will make it hard for them to strengthen their squad.

They will have to wheel and deal to get players who will improve the squad and give them the chance to consolidate the Bantams' place in the top flight in the way that both Derby County and Leicester City have done in recent seasons.

If they can maintain the superb spirit at Valley Parade, Bradford can approach what is likely to be another season of struggle with plenty of confidence. They will certainly be able to afford themselves a wry smile before their first home game of the campaign.

It is strongly rumoured that the 2000–01 season will kick off at Valley Parade with some very special pre-match entertainment, as Rodney Marsh has his head shaved. It is unlikely that the Sky TV pundit will be as quick to write off the battling Bantams again.

BRADFORD CITY

DATE	OPPONENT	SCORE	ATT.	BEAGRIE	BLAKE	CADETE	CLARKE	DAVISON	DREYER	GRANT	HALLE	JACOBS	LAWREN
7.8.99	Middlesbro A	1–0	33,762	90□	–	–	–	–	90	–	90□	90	–
14.8.99	Sheff Wed H	1–1	18,276	90^1□	–	–	–	–	90	–	90	90	61
21.8.99	Watford A	0–1	15,564	90	–	–	–	–	90□	s18	90	90□	60
25.8.99	Arsenal A	0–2	38,073	90	s27	–	–	–	90□	–	45	90	63
28.8.99	West Ham H	0–3	17,926	90	s37	–	–	–	90	–	90□	90	–
12.9.99	Tottenham H	1–1	18,143	90	s45	–	–	–	–	–	90	66	–
18.9.99	Aston Villa A	0–1	28,083	90	–	–	–	–	–	–	90	–	–
25.9.99	Derby Co A	1–0*	31,035	76	78	–	–	–	–	–	90	s28	–
2.10.99	Sunderland H	0–4	18,204	90□	90	–	–	–	–	–	90	–	–
16.10.99	Wimbledon A	2–3	10,029	–	90	–	–	–	–	–	90	90	–
23.10.99	Leicester H	3–1	17,655	–	90^1	–	–	–	–	–	90	–	s6
1.11.99	Liverpool A	1–3	40,483	–	90	–	90	–	–	–	68	–	s22
6.11.99	Coventry H	1–1	17,587	s50	83	–	90	–	–	–	58□	–	s32□
20.11.99	Leeds Utd A	1–2	39,937	78	s26	–	90	–	–	–	90	–	90
28.11.99	Chelsea A	0–1	31,591	90	s22	–	90	–	–	–	90	–	90
4.12.99	Middlesbro H	1–1	17,708	86	90	–	90	–	–	–	s64	–	90
18.12.99	Newcastle H	2–0	18,286	s12	–	–	90	–	–	–	90	–	90□
26.12.99	Man Utd A	0–4	55,188	s35	s9	–	90	–	–	–	90□	–	55
28.12.99	Everton H	0–0	18,276	s27	s15	–	90	–	–	–	90	–	–
3.1.00	Southampton A	0–1	15,027	90	s31	–	90	–	–	–	59	–	90
8.1.00	Chelsea H	1–1	18,276	s28	90	–	90	–	–	–	90	–	–
15.1.00	Sheff Wed A	0–2	24,682	60	90	–	90	–	–	–	90	–	90
22.1.00	Watford H	3–2	16,864	90^1	–	–	75	s15	–	–	90	90	90
5.2.00	Arsenal H	2–1	18,276	90	–	–	–	90□	s1	–	90	90	90
12.2.00	West Ham A	4–5	25,417	90^1	–	–	–	90	–	–	90	90	90^2
26.2.00	Aston Villa H	1–1	18,276	90	s22	s15	–	90	–	–	90	90	68
4.3.00	Tottenham A	1–1	35,472	90	–	s10	–	90	s13	–	90□	90□	90^1
12.3.00	Leeds Utd H	1–2	18,276	90^1	s24	s24	–	–	–	–	66	90□	90□
18.3.00	Coventry A	0–4	19,201	90	s45	s70	–	90	–	–	45	75	90
25.3.00	Man Utd H	0–4	18,276	90	s20	70	90	–	–	–	58	90	90
1.4.00	Newcastle A	0–2	36,572	90	s24	s20	90	–	70	–	90□	90	–
8.4.00	Southampton H	1–2	17,439	90□	90^1	63	90	–	–	–	90□	90	–
15.4.00	Everton A	0–4	30,646	90	90	–	90	–	s24	–	90	66	–
21.4.00	Derby Co H	4–4	18,276	90^1	90	–	90	–	90□	–	90□	77	–
24.4.00	Sunderland A	1–0	40,628	89	86	–	90	–	90^1	–	90	90	–
30.4.00	Wimbledon H	3–0	18,276	90^2	67	–	90	–	90	–	90	90	–
6.5.00	Leicester A	0–3	21,103	72□	90	–	90	–	60	–	90	10	s30
14.5.00	Liverpool H	1–0	18,276	81	–	–	90	–	90□	–	90	s9	90

□ Yellow card, ■ Red card, s Substitute, 90^2 Goals scored

*including one own goal

1999–2000 PREMIERSHIP APPEARANCES

McCALL	MILLS	MYERS	O'BRIEN	RANKIN	REDFEARN	RODRIGUEZ	SAUNDERS	SHARPE	SOUTHALL	WALSH	WESTWOOD	WETHERALL	WHALLEY	WINDASS	TOTAL
–	90	–	90	–	90□	–	s8[1]	–	–	90	–	90	90	82	990
–	90	–	–	–	90	–	s29	–	–	90	–	90□	90	90	990
–	90	–	–	–	72	–	s30	–	–	90	–	90	90	90	990
s45	–	–	90	–	–	–	90	–	–	90	–	90□	90	90	990
90	s45	–	45	–	s26	–	53	–	–	90	–	90	90	64	990
90[1]□	90	s24	90	–	–	s13	77	–	–	90	–	90	90	45	990
90□	45	90	90	–	–	s45	90	–	–	90	–	90	90	90	990
90	90	33■	90	–	–	–	62	–	–	90	s14	90	90	s12	933
90	90	90	90	–	–	–	90	–	–	90	–	90	–	90□	990
90	90[1]	–	90	–	90	–	s32	58	–	90	–	90	–	90[1]	990
90	90[1]	–	90	–	90[1]	–	84	90	–	90	–	90	–	90	990
90	90	–	90	s12	78□	–	90	90	–	–	–	90□	–	90[1]□	990
90	90[1]	–	90	s7	90□	–	40	90	–	–	–	90	–	90	990
90□	90□	s12	90	–	64	–	–	90□	–	–	–	90	–	90[1]□	990
–	89	90	90	s1	90	–	–	–	–	–	–	90	68	90	990
90	90[1]	90	90	–	90□	–	–	s4	–	–	–	90	–	26	990
90	90	90	90	–	–	–	90[1]□	78	–	–	–	90[1]	–	90	990
90	90	81	90	–	81□	–	s9	90	–	–	–	90	–	90	990
90□	90	63	90	–	90□	–	90	90	–	–	–	90□	–	75	990
90	70	s45	90	–	s20	–	90	45	–	–	–	90	–	90	990
90	90[1]	90	90	–	90	–	90	–	–	–	–	90	–	62	990
72	s30	90	90	–	90	–	90	–	–	–	–	90	–	s18	990
90	–	–	90[1]	–	s13	–	89	–	–	–	s1	90	77[1]	90	990
90	–	–	90	–	–	–	90[1]	–	–	–	–	90	90	89[1]	990
90	–	–	90□	–	–	–	90	–	–	–	–	90	90	90[1]	990
90	–	–	90	–	–	–	90	–	–	–	–	90	75	90[1]	990
90	–	–	90	–	–	–	80	–	–	–	–	90	77	90	990
90	–	–	90	–	–	–	90	–	90	–	–	90□	66	90□	990
90□	–	–	90	–	–	–	90	s15	–	–	–	90	20	90□	990
90	–	–	90	–	–	–	90	s32	–	–	–	90	–	90	990
90	–	–	90	–	–	–	90	66	–	–	–	90	–	90	990
90	–	–	90	s27	–	–	–	90	–	–	–	90	–	90	990
90	–	–	90□	s32	–	–	58	90	–	–	–	90□	–	90	990
90	–	–	90	s13	–	–	s19	–	–	–	71□	90	–	90[3]□	990
90	–	–	90	s7	–	–	83	s1	–	–	s4	90□	–	90	990
90	–	–	90	–	–	–	90	–	–	–	s23	90	–	90[1]	990
90□	–	–	90	s18	–	–	90	s80	–	–	–	90	–	90	990
90	–	–	90	s12	–	–	78	90	–	–	–	90[1]	–	90	990

THE MANAGER

PAUL JEWELL

Few outside Bradford fancied the Bantams' chances of surviving longer than a season in the Premiership, but under the guidance of 35-year-old Paul Jewell they did just that.

Already the toast of the town after guiding City to the Premiership in his first full season in charge, Jewell's reputation has now soared after completing the seemingly-impossible task of keeping Bradford in the top flight.

Jewell originally shone at Valley Parade as a player, making more than 300 appearances for the Yorkshire side, and turned the club's fortunes around in 1998–99 by guiding them to automatic promotion to the Premiership.

Many saw 1999–2000 as a season of 38 "cup finals", but thanks to Jewell and chairman Geoffrey Richmond the Bantams have at least another 38 to come.

The fact that 14 of the 25 players fielded by Bradford also featured for the Bantams in Division One proves not only how tight the purse-strings are at Valley Parade, but also Jewell's ability to get the best from his players.

It was a big shock to all Bantams fans when Jewell resigned in June to take up the manager's post at Sheffield Wednesday.

LEAGUE POSITION

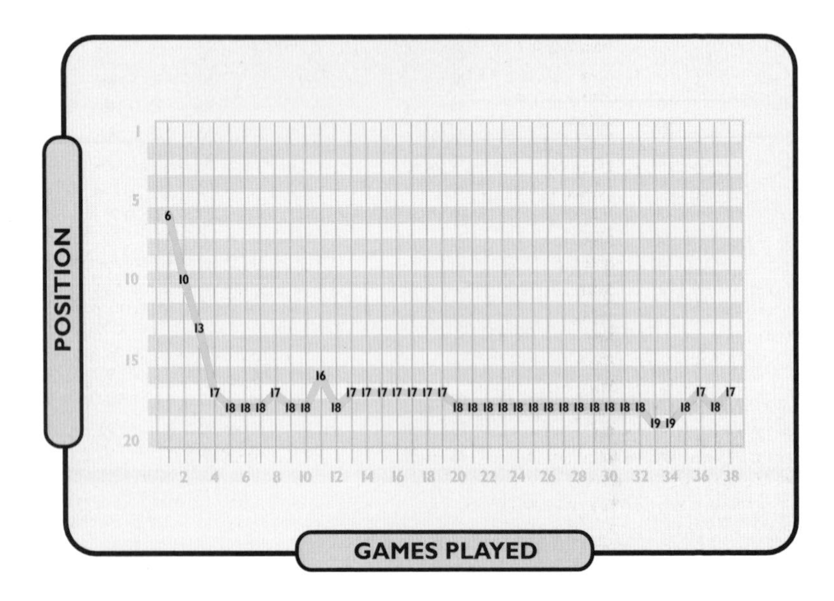

9 Bradford City conceded the most goals

THE GOALS

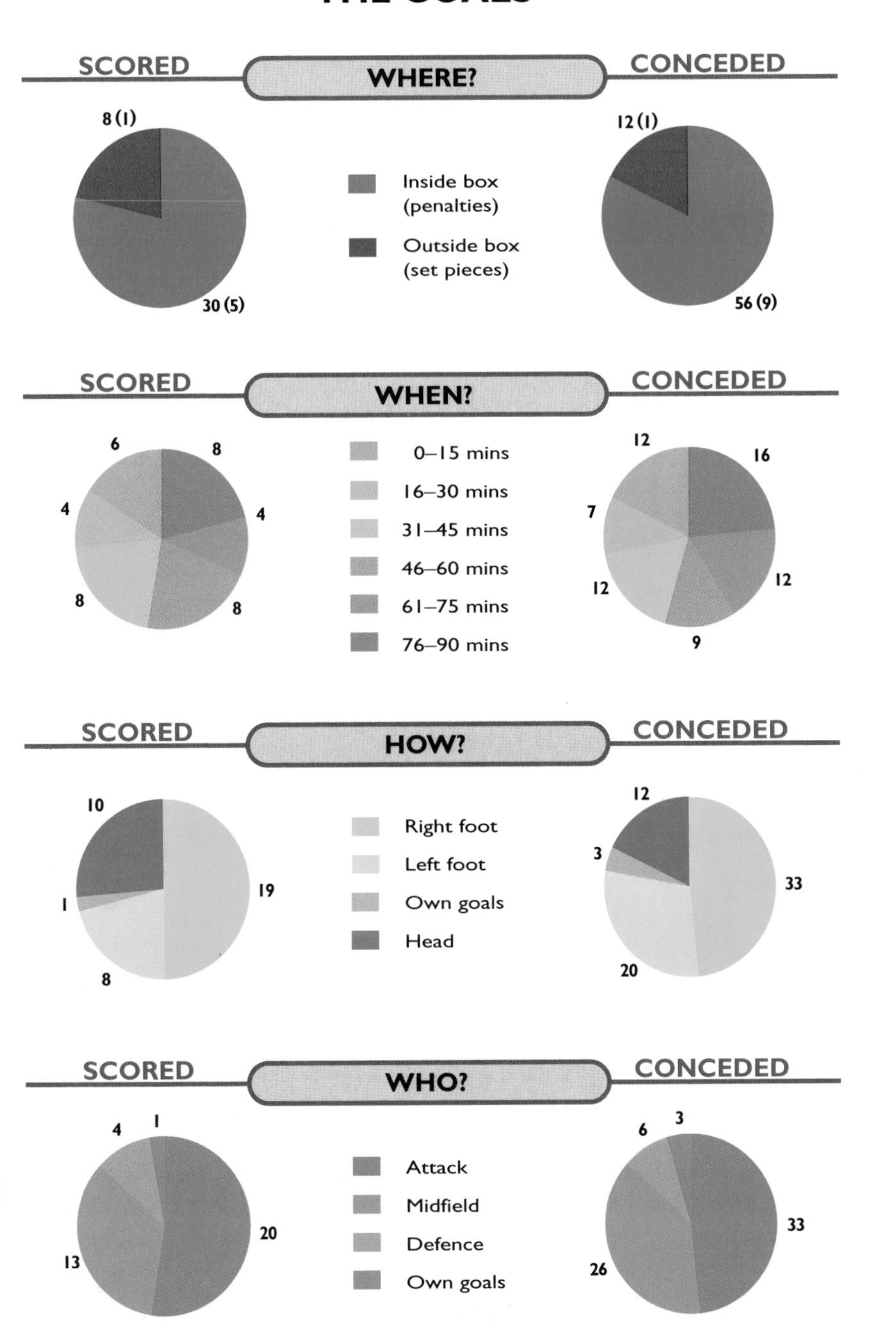

from the penalty spot in the Premiership

BRADFORD CITY

	BEAGRIE	BLAKE	CADETE	DREYER	GRANT	HALLE	JACOBS	LAWRENCE	McCALL	MILLS
APPEARANCES										
Start	30	15	2	11	0	37	22	19	33	19
Sub	5	13	5	3	1	1	2	4	1	2
Minutes on pitch	2764	1651	272	978	18	3163	1861	1657	2997	1719
GOAL ATTEMPTS										
Goals	7	2	0	1	0	0	0	3	1	5
Shots on target	19	13	2	2	0	3	1	7	4	18
Shots off target	27	11	0	4	0	5	1	5	4	22
Shooting accuracy	41%	54%	100%	33%	0%	38%	50%	58%	50%	45%
PASSING										
Goal assists	5	1	0	1	0	4	0	0	2	3
Long passes	274	81	8	100	1	292	261	68	398	45
Short passes	741	463	71	193	4	658	554	380	1061	519
PASS COMPLETION										
Own half %	74%	76%	93%	75%	50%	71%	74%	60%	79%	76%
Opposition half %	53%	62%	43%	52%	67%	58%	63%	47%	68%	60%
CROSSING										
Total crosses	284	56	5	4	0	56	31	19	23	9
Cross completion %	32%	23%	20%	50%	0%	20%	16%	21%	39%	33%
DRIBBLING										
Dribbles & runs	212	82	8	5	1	87	23	73	35	54
Dribble completion %	67%	74%	63%	60%	0%	82%	83%	75%	94%	76%
DEFENDING										
Tackles made	135	32	4	38	0	106	63	63	137	27
Tackles won %	39%	66%	25%	55%	0%	50%	51%	48%	53%	63%
Blocks	17	6	1	18	0	63	21	14	48	1
Clearances	42	9	1	115	0	193	123	44	111	14
Interceptions	8	7	0	6	0	26	11	6	45	3
DISCIPLINE										
Fouls	55	12	3	19	0	55	10	24	51	21
Offside	5	14	3	1	0	3	0	0	0	20
Yellow cards	5	0	0	4	0	8	3	3	6	1
Red cards	0	0	0	0	0	0	0	0	0	0

GOALKEEPER NAME	START/ (SUB)	TIME ON PITCH	GOALS CONCEDED	MINS/GOALS CONCEDED	SAVES MADE	SAVES/ SHOTS
CLARKE	21	1875	36	52	91	72%
DAVISON	5(1)	465	13	36	22	63%
SOUTHALL	1	90	2	45	3	60%
WALSH	11	990	17	58	58	77%

For more information visit our website:

PLAYERS' STATISTICS

	MYERS	O'BRIEN	RANKIN	REDFEARN	RODRIGUEZ	SAUNDERS	SHARPE	WESTWOOD	WETHERALL	WHALLEY	WINDASS	TOTAL	RANK
	10	36	0	14	0	28	13	1	38	16	36		
	3	0	9	3	2	6	5	4	0	0	2		
	888	3195	129	1254	58	2451	1189	113	3420	1283	3083		
	0	1	0	1	0	3	0	0	2	1	10	38*	=18th
	0	3	1	6	0	21	3	0	11	3	34	151	19th
	3	3	4	17	0	35	1	0	15	4	38	199	14th
	0%	50%	20%	26%	0%	38%	75%	0%	42%	43%	47%	43%	17th
	0	0	0	0	0	2	1	0	2	1	2	24	19th
	105	293	5	104	0	82	155	9	237	84	253	2855	18th
	230	496	28	398	14	665	318	20	591	481	902	8787	18th
	71%	71%	67%	88%	0%	85%	71%	69%	73%	85%	85%	76%	17th
	54%	49%	67%	63%	67%	66%	52%	46%	47%	67%	66%	59%	17th
	16	10	0	18	0	42	58	0	9	19	49	708	=14th
	25%	50%	0%	22%	0%	14%	22%	0%	33%	47%	22%	27%	16th
	31	34	5	26	2	87	30	1	26	16	59	897	17th
	77%	79%	40%	69%	50%	68%	73%	100%	100%	88%	73%	74%	15th
	29	128	2	45	1	19	32	2	89	49	73	1074	5th
	52%	57%	100%	56%	0%	47%	47%	0%	64%	45%	59%	52%	9th
	19	126	0	8	0	1	15	2	124	8	25	517	1st
	75	395	0	32	0	9	51	9	561	25	58	1887	1st
	15	52	0	20	0	11	14	1	42	11	9	287	4th
	13	30	6	43	1	41	13	3	56	4	72	535	13th
	1	0	1	2	2	44	2	0	1	1	20	120	=14th
	0	2	0	6	0	1	1	1	7	0	6	55	14th
	1	0	0	0	0	0	0	0	0	0	0	1	=17th

*Including one own goal

CROSSES CAUGHT	CROSSES PUNCHED	CROSSES NOT CLAIMED	CATCH SUCCESS	THROWS/ SHORT KICKS	% COMPLETION	LONG KICKS	% COMPLETION
40	23	1	98%	65	77%	771	42%
14	5	0	100%	9	78%	177	34%
0	0	0	0%	1	100%	28	36%
31	7	1	97%	30	90%	380	34%

PLAYER OF THE SEASON

PLAYER	INDEX SCORE
DAVID WETHERALL	968
Andrew O'Brien	882
Peter Beagrie	856
Matt Clarke	843
Dean Windass	801
Stuart McCall	783
Wayne Jacobs	742
Lee Mills	705*
Gunnar Halle	683
Dean Saunders	548

All players played 75 minutes in at least 19 matches except those marked * who played just 17 games.

Bradford's great escape on the last day of the campaign earned them another season in the top flight, and many put this down to the team spirit and battling qualities Paul Jewell had instilled into his side.

No player could have epitomised this more than centre-back David Wetherall. The former Leeds man may be best remembered for his last-day goal which earned them victory over Liverpool, but it was his defensive ability which really stood out.

Wetherall made a massive 561 clearances during the course of the season – more than any other Premiership player. He also saved the Bantams on four occasions with goal-line clearances. The big defender amassed an average of 968 points, making him Bradford's top player.

He was closely followed in the rankings by fellow-defender Andrew O'Brien, who recorded an average of 882 points. Like Wetherall, O'Brien made a large number of clearances throughout the course of the season as he appeared in all but two of the Bantams' league games.

Experienced winger Peter Beagrie enjoyed his return to top-flight football with an Index score of 856 points. The tricky winger scored seven goals and created five as he proved to be an integral link player between the Bantams' defence and attack.

Two other heroes of the promotion campaign, Wayne Jacobs and Lee Mills, produced some consistent displays, while 'keeper Matt Clarke made the number one spot his own with some fine performances. He kept three clean sheets in the last four games, which helped earn Bradford the points that kept them afloat.

Dean Windass finished the season as top scorer, netting a crucial 10 goals in the survival battle. And experience was certainly an important factor for Bradford with veterans such as Stuart McCall, Gunnar Halle and Dean Saunders all finding themselves ranked among Bradford's top 10 players.

126 Andy O' Brien made more defensive

FIVE OF THE BEST

No-one gave them a chance, and when Everton trounced Bradford City 4–0 with five games to go Paul Jewell's plucky side looked doomed. But three wins and a draw meant the Bantams can look forward to another season at the highest level. Something that will not survive is pundit Rodney Marsh's hair.

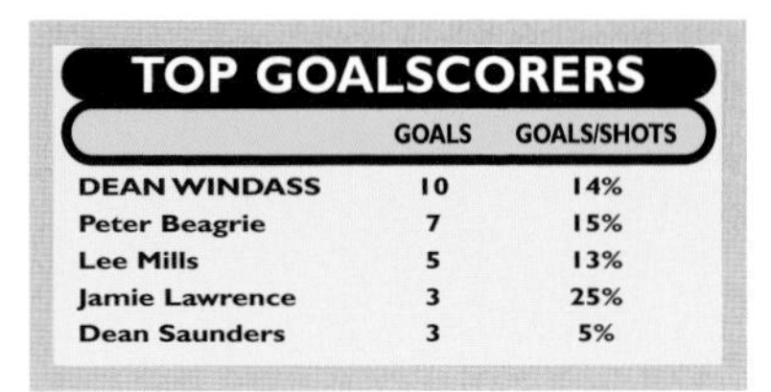

TOP GOALSCORERS

	GOALS	GOALS/SHOTS
DEAN WINDASS	10	14%
Peter Beagrie	7	15%
Lee Mills	5	13%
Jamie Lawrence	3	25%
Dean Saunders	3	5%

Dean Windass featured in every game in 1999–2000 and finished as the club's top scorer with 10 goals. Acrobatic winger Peter Beagrie, who registered seven league goals including two in the vital 2–0 win against Wimbledon in April, followed him. Goals were hard to come by for the Bantams, though, and fans were bemused when Lee Mills and Isaiah Rankin were allowed to go out on loan. Mills scored with 13% of his shots, including a spell of four in seven games before Christmas.

Stuart McCall returned to Valley Parade and helped the team reach the Premiership, and his vast experience helped steady the ship. He was one of only 24 players in the top flight to make more than 1,000 successful passes, and the only player in the City squad to push him for accuracy was burly striker Dean Windass. Another veteran player, Gunnar Halle, was a steady influence, though one fears the team will need considerable strengthening before 2000–01 kicks off.

TOP PASSERS

	SUCC PASSES	COMPLETION
STUART McCALL	1,042	71%
Dean Windass	806	70%
Gunnar Halle	591	62%
Peter Beagrie	576	57%
Wayne Jacobs	544	67%

TOP TACKLERS

	WON	SUCCESS
ANDREW O'BRIEN	73	57%
Stuart McCall	73	53%
David Wetherall	57	64%
Gunnar Halle	53	50%
Peter Beagrie	53	39%

Fledgling central defender Andrew O'Brien adapted to life at the highest level with admirable ease, making 73 successful tackles. Stuart McCall made the same amount of winning challenges, but his success overall was lower. Final-day hero David Wetherall was third and his stout play at the back, allied to some memorably important goals, ensured that the club record signing was certainly value for money.

Bradford were the cleanest of the three promoted teams, suffering just one red card when Andy Myers was dismissed at Derby. Fiery Dean Windass finished as the Bradford bad boy, largely due to the 72 fouls he conceded. In fact, only six players in the Premiership were penalised more often than the well-travelled striker. The five highest-placed men in the discipline table have a total age of 165 years, proving that they are older but not necessarily wiser.

DISCIPLINE

	POINTS	FOULS & CARDS
DEAN WINDASS	90	72F, 6Y, 0R
Gunnar Halle	79	55F, 8Y, 0R
David Wetherall	77	56F, 7Y, 0R
Peter Beagrie	70	55F, 5Y, 0R
Stuart McCall	69	51F, 6Y, 0R

blocks than any other Premiership player

ACTION	BEAGRIE	CLARKE	DREYER	HALLE	JACOBS	LAWRENCE	McCALL	O'BRIEN	RANKIN	SAUNDERS	SHARPE	WETHERALL	WINDASS	TOTAL	LIVERPOOL
Time On Pitch	81	90	90	90	9	90	90	90	12	78	90	90	90	990	990
GOALS															
Goal	–	–	–	–	–	–	–	–	–	–	–	1	–	1	–
Shot on target	–	–	–	–	–	–	–	–	–	–	–	–	3	3	3
Shot off target	–	–	–	–	–	–	–	–	1	–	–	–	1	2	3
Blocked shot	–	–	–	–	–	–	1	–	–	2	–	–	1	4	14
Own goal	–	–	–	–	–	–	–	–	–	–	–	–	–	–	–
PASSES															
Pass to own player	13	–	14	21	–	11	31	7	–	16	14	12	17	156	344
Pass to opposition	13	–	10	9	1	15	9	10	–	8	8	1	13	97	124
Cross to own player	2	–	–	–	–	–	–	–	–	–	–	–	–	2	11
Cross to opposition player	2	–	–	3	–	–	–	–	–	–	2	1	1	9	16
Goal assist	–	–	–	1	–	–	–	–	–	–	–	–	–	1	–
Pass completion %	50%	0%	58%	65%	0%	42%	78%	41%	0%	67%	58%	86%	55%	60%	72%
TACKLES & CLEARANCES															
Tackle	3	–	4	2	1	10	3	3	–	3	2	4	4	39	20
Clearances, blocks and interceptions	2	–	9	11	4	1	5	15	–	1	5	17	3	73	38
DRIBBLES & RUNS															
Dribble ball retained	5	–	–	3	–	4	1	–	–	2	–	–	2	17	19
Dribble ball lost	–	–	–	–	–	2	–	–	–	–	–	–	–	2	2
Dribble Success %	100%	0%	0%	100%	0%	67%	100%	0%	0%	100%	0%	0%	100%	89%	90%
DISCIPLINE															
Fouls	–	–	3	1	–	1	2	–	3	2	1	3	3	19	12
Penalty conceded	–	–	–	–	–	–	–	–	–	–	–	–	–	–	–
Free kick – offside	–	–	–	–	–	–	–	–	–	1	–	–	1	2	2
Yellow cards	–	–	1	–	–	–	–	–	–	–	–	–	–	1	2
Red cards	–	–	–	–	–	–	–	–	–	–	–	–	–	–	–
GOALKEEPERS															
Distribution to own player	–	16	–	–	–	–	–	–	–	–	–	–	–	16	24
Distribution to opposition player	–	18	–	–	–	–	–	–	–	–	–	–	–	18	9
Goalkeeper distribution %	0%	47%	0%	0%	0%	0%	0%	0%	0%	0%	0%	0%	0%	47%	73%
Save	–	3	–	–	–	–	–	–	–	–	–	–	–	3	3
Ball caught	–	2	–	–	–	–	–	–	–	–	–	–	–	2	2
Ball dropped	–	–	–	–	–	–	–	–	–	–	–	–	–	–	–
Goal conceded	–	–	–	–	–	–	–	–	–	–	–	–	–	–	1

11 Bradford players cleared more shots off the

After their heroic performances during the 1998–1999 campaign saw Bradford beat the odds to gain promotion from Division One, most pundits wrote the Bantams off as mere cannon-fodder for the Premiership big boys. But City went into their final game against Liverpool knowing that survival was within their grasp.

14 May 2000
1–0
BRADFORD CITY
vs.
LIVERPOOL

Few outside Valley Parade fancied the Bantams' chances. But since gaining promotion, Jewell's team had rarely been overawed by their supposed betters, and got off to the best possible start in this crucial encounter.

David Wetherall opened the scoring with a powerful header from Gunnar Halle's free-kick after just 12 minutes to send the home fans into raptures.

For the rest of the half, the Valley Parade crowd lived in fear of a comeback from Gerard Houllier's team. But Liverpool were never allowed to settle into their rhythm by a Bradford team that displayed a gritty, physical side to their game. They made 39 challenges over the 90 minutes – 19 more than the Reds.

And on the stroke of half-time, as false rumours of a goal by the Saints against Wimbledon passed around the crowd, the supporters' fears were almost realised. Owen used his lightning pace to elude the Bradford defence and round 'keeper Matt Clarke. But as he fired in his shot, the back-tracking Halle stuck out a leg to divert the ball narrowly wide of the goal.

It was a moment that was indicative of the way the second half would go, with Liverpool bombing forward in search of an equaliser. Houllier's team fired in 20 shots, but saw a staggering 14 of them blocked by a Bradford player, as the home side's determination looked increasingly likely to ensure their survival.

As news that Southampton had actually taken the lead against the Dons early in the second half filtered through, a party atmosphere ensued, with fans urging their fellow-supporters to "Stand up if you're staying up". And Isaiah Rankin and Dean Windass both had scoring chances to turn Valley Parade into a real carnival venue. But neither player was able to convert the opportunities that came their way.

Unfortunately for Jewell's side, Liverpool continued to press forward to the end, the Bantams only managing a passing accuracy rating of 60% – 12 percentage points lower than the visitors.

But with Wetherall marshalling the back-line, Bradford were able to hold on to their slender lead. The former Leeds centre-back made 17 crucial clearances, blocks and interceptions – more than any other player on the pitch. And he also showed great composure with his distribution, finding a team-mate with 92% of his passes, to earn an Opta Index score of 1,148 points and the man of the match award.

When Wimbledon conceded a second goal, the fans knew that only a complete collapse by their side could prevent them from staying up. And with the defence standing firm, Bradford were able to hold out until the final whistle to complete one of the most unlikely survival stories in Premiership history and ensure another season among the big boys.

line than those from any other side

Mitre
ULTIMAX

CHELSEA

ADDRESS

Stamford Bridge, Fulham Road,
London SW6 1HS

CONTACT NUMBERS

Telephone: 020 7385 5545
Fax: 020 7381 4831
Ticket Office: 020 7386 7799
Club Call: 09068 121159
Chelsea Megastore: 020 7565 1490
Website: www.chelseafc.co.uk

KEY PERSONNEL

Chairman: K W Bates
Directors: C Hutchinson
Ms Y S Todd, M Russell
Assistant Club Secretary: C Lait
Manager: Gianluca Vialli

SPONSORS

Autoglass

FANZINES

The Chelsea Independent
Cockney Rebel
Curious Blue
Matthew Harding's Blue & White Army

COLOURS

Home: Blue shirts, blue shorts
and white stockings
Away: All yellow or all white

NICKNAME

The Blues

HONOURS

League Champions: 1954–55
Division Two Champions:
1983–84, 1988–89
FA Cup: 1970, 1997, 2000
League Cup: 1965, 1998
European Cup Winners' Cup: 1971,
1998
UEFA Super Cup Winners: 1998

RECORD GOALSCORER

Bobby Tambling –
164 league goals, 1958–70

BIGGEST WIN

9–2 v Glossop NE – Division Two,
1 September 1906

BIGGEST DEFEAT

1–8 v Wolverhampton Wanderers –
Division One, 26 September 1953

SEASON REVIEW

Chelsea played more games than any other club in 1999–2000, yet they nearly finished the season with nothing to show for their efforts. Happily for Blues fans, the FA Cup was secured with a 1–0 victory over Aston Villa in the last-ever final to be played beneath the Twin Towers, in the club's 61st game of an arduous season.

Among the pre-season favourites for the title, particularly with the addition of Didier Deschamps and £10 million striker Chris Sutton to their squad, Chelsea came out of the starting blocks impressively, hitting top spot on the opening day with a 4–0 victory over promoted Sunderland. They followed that up with an easy 3–0 win over Skonto Riga in the qualifying round for the Champions League, assuring qualification with a 0–0 draw in the away leg.

> **"We've come to a crucial time in the future of the club. The club is healthy, rich and very well organised. We've got to make sure the football side is the same."**
>
> Gianluca Vialli

Unfortunately, that is where Chelsea's main problem began. Their performances in Europe's premier club competition were quite at odds with their stuttering form in the league. After playing out an enthralling draw with Italian Champions AC Milan at Stamford Bridge, they were beaten 1–0 by basement boys Watford, a result that saw many commentators question the commitment of the club's cosmopolitan foreign legion to the Chelsea cause.

After losing to Hertha Berlin in Germany, Chelsea went unbeaten for the remainder of the first group stage – recording a brilliant 5–0 victory over Galatasaray in Istanbul in the process – and started the second stage well with victory over Feyenoord and a battling 0–0 draw in Rome's Olympic Stadium.

But although they achieved a remarkable 5–0 Premiership victory over Manchester United during that time, they won just two other league games in a 10-game spell that spanned three months.

Part of the problem lay upfront. Gianfranco Zola failed to find the target in the Premiership for eight months after scoring on the opening day of the season, and the much-maligned Sutton finished the season with a paltry haul of one league goal from 10 shots on target.

While Manchester United managed to score four or more goals 10 times in the Premiership, Chelsea – for all their pressure – managed the feat just three times, scoring 43 fewer goals than the Champions and finishing with the fifth worst goals-to-shots ratio in the Premiership.

By the time they had lost their sixth game of the season, a 2–0 home defeat by Leeds, Chelsea were in 10th position, 17 points behind the leaders and in real danger of falling apart at the seams.

The criticism that they received after the Leeds game seemed to spur them on, though. While Frank Leboeuf moaned to the media about the treatment handed out to French players by referees and English players, his team-mates buckled down to a run that lifted them back into the top five.

George Weah was recruited on loan from AC Milan and made an immediate impact scoring on his debut against Tottenham. And while they stabilised in the league, Chelsea continued to make progress on two fronts in cup competition.

Qualification from the second group stage of the Champions League was assured despite defeats at the hands of Lazio and Marseille. The team had gone out of the Worthington Cup early when a shadow side was defeated 1–0 by Huddersfield in the third round, but comfortable victories over Hull City, Nottingham Forest, Leicester City and

16 Ed De Goey kept more clean sheets

SEASON REVIEW

Gillingham ensured them an FA Cup semi-final date with Newcastle United.

Their opponents in the Champions League quarter-finals were tournament favourites Barcelona, a team whose line-up looked even more exotic than Chelsea's. But they proved no match for Vialli's men, who put in a sparkling display of attacking football to take a 3–1 lead into the second leg at the Nou Camp.

The mood in the Chelsea camp was understandably buoyant going into the FA Cup semi-final four days later where, despite being second-best to Newcastle for long periods of the match, Gustavo Poyet buried two of just six goal attempts that the team managed all match to take them to the final.

Back in the heat of the Champions League, though, Luis Figo's strike in the first leg at Stamford Bridge proved to be the decisive moment of the tie. Trailing 2–1 with seven minutes to go in the second leg, Chelsea allowed substitute Dani to steal in for Barcelona's third and take the tie into extra-time. The Catalan side scored twice more to win the game 5–1 and the tie 6–4 on aggregate.

The need to win the FA Cup became all the more pressing because, as hard as the team had tried to rescue their Premiership campaign, a top three spot proved beyond them.

With Liverpool doing enough to secure fourth place, Chelsea's only route into Europe was via the FA Cup or through a potentially disruptive Intertoto Cup campaign in the summer.

The final proved a disappointing affair with few clear-cut chances, let alone memorable moments, but Chelsea secured victory with a goal from Roberto Di Matteo. That was a deserved reward for a team that took its fair share of criticism. Fielding the first all-non-British side in English football history at Southampton on Boxing Day was seen by many as the beginning of the end for English international football, but Chelsea received little credit for bringing players like Jon Harley and Jody Morris through the youth ranks.

"We should've done better at places like Derby, Watford and Sheffield Wednesday, but then you'd be more up for stepping out with Claudia Schiffer than your next-door neighbour."

Gianluca Vialli

For all the accusations that their overseas players "weren't up for it", Chelsea came through a gruelling season with a trophy, were seven minutes away from the semi-finals of the Champions League and finished fifth in the Premiership. That is not the record of a team lacking motivation.

They may have had their problems going forward, but Chelsea were determined enough at the back to record the second best defensive record in the FA Carling Premiership and saw goalkeeper Ed De Goey keep a total of 27 out of 28 clean sheets in all competitions, setting a club record in the process.

The need for a striker capable of scoring 20 or more goals a season was one that Vialli moved quickly to solve at the end of the campaign when he signed the prolific Jimmy Floyd Hasselbaink from Atletico Madrid.

On their day, Chelsea are more than a match for any team in Europe, let alone the Premiership.

But no Chelsea player scored more than 10 league goals in 1999–2000, a fact that contributed heavily to their failure to secure a lucrative place in the 2000–01 Champions League.

With the addition of Hasselbaink to their ranks, the Blues will start the 2000–01 season as many people's favourites to wrestle the Premiership crown from Manchester United's grasp.

than any other Premiership goalkeeper

CHELSEA

DATE	OPPONENT	SCORE	ATT.	AMBROSETTI	BABAYARO	CUDICINI	DALLA BONA	DE GOEY	DESAILLY	DESCHAMPS	DI MATTEO	FERRER	FLO
7.8.99	Sunderland H	4–0	34,831	–	s10	–	–	90	90	90	s4	90	$s17^{1}$
14.8.99	Leicester A	2–2*	21,068	–	90□	–	–	90	–	–	–	90□	90
21.8.99	Aston Villa H	1–0*	35,071	s3	90	–	–	90	90	–	–	90	s14
28.8.99	Wimbledon A	1–0	22,167	s10	90	–	–	90	90	88	–	90	67
11.9.99	Newcastle H	1–0	35,092	–	90	–	–	90	90	–	–	90□	s22
18.9.99	Watford A	0–1	21,244	90	–	–	–	90	90	90	–	90	61
25.9.99	Middlesbro A	1–0	34,183	70	s20	–	–	90	90□	89□	–	–	s20
3.10.99	Man Utd H	5–0*	34,909	–	90	–	–	90	–	90□	–	90	s21
16.10.99	Liverpool A	0–1	44,826	–	90	–	–	90	74■	90	–	90	s22
23.10.99	Arsenal H	2–3	34,958	–	90	–	–	90	90	90□	–	90	70^{1}
30.10.99	Derby Co A	1–3	28,614	64	90	–	–	90	–	s37	90	90	–
7.11.99	West Ham H	0–0	34,935	s22	90	–	–	90	90	90	–	90	90
20.11.99	Everton A	1–1	38,225	2	90	–	–	90	90	90	s88	81□	90^{1}
28.11.99	Bradford H	1–0	31,591	–	90	–	–	90	90	90□	–	90	90^{1}
4.12.99	Sunderland A	1–4	41,377	–	90□	–	–	90	45	–	–	–	90
19.12.99	Leeds Utd H	0–2	35,106	–	–	–	–	90	45	90	90□	90	58
26.12.99	Southampton A	2–1	15,232	75	90□	–	–	90	–	90□	90	90□	90^{2}
29.12.99	Sheff Wed H	3–0	32,938	82	90	–	–	90	–	23	90	–	82^{1}
4.1.00	Coventry A	2–2	20,164	–	90	–	–	90	90	78	85□	90	90^{2}
8.1.00	Bradford A	1–1	18,276	–	90	–	–	90	–	90	s33	90	90
12.1.00	Tottenham H	1–0	34,969	–	–	–	–	90	–	–	90	–	56
15.1.00	Leicester H	1–1	35,063	s45	–	–	–	90	–	45	90	65	s25
22.1.00	Aston Villa A	0–0	33,704	–	–	–	–	90	–	90	–	–	s16
5.2.00	Tottenham A	1–0	36,041	–	–	–	–	90	90	90	–	–	s13
12.2.00	Wimbledon H	3–1	34,826	–	–	–	–	90	–	71	–	–	s19
26.2.00	Watford H	2–1	34,928	–	–	–	–	90	90^{1}	90	–	s32	90
4.3.00	Newcastle A	1–0	36,448	–	90	–	–	90	–	–	48	90	s18
11.3.00	Everton H	1–1	35,113	–	90	–	–	90	–	–	90	90	s45
18.3.00	West Ham A	0–0	26,041	–	90	–	–	90	90	90	s8	90	82□
25.3.00	Southampton H	1–1*	34,956	s4	–	–	–	90	90	–	–	90	–
1.4.00	Leeds Utd A	1–0	40,162	–	90	–	–	90	–	–	90	90	–
12.4.00	Coventry H	2–1*	32,316	s41	–	–	s35	90	–	–	55	–	49
15.4.00	Sheff Wed A	0–1	21,743	70	90	–	s45	90□	90□	s45	–	–	s20
22.4.00	Middlesbro H	1–1	34,467	90	–	–	–	90	90	61	–	–	s29
24.4.00	Man Utd A	2–3	61,593	45	–	–	–	90	–	45	–	–	90
29.4.00	Liverpool H	2–0	34,957	–	45	–	–	90	90	–	90^{1}	–	–
6.5.00	Arsenal A	1–2	38,119	–	–	–	–	90	90	s30	90	–	90
14.5.00	Derby Co H	4–0	35,084	s26	90	90	–	–	56	90	90^{1}□	32	90^{1}

□ Yellow card, ■ Red card, s Substitute, 90^{2} Goals scored

*including one own goal

1999–2000 PREMIERSHIP APPEARANCES

GOLDBAEK	HARLEY	HOGH	LAMBOURDE	LE SAUX	LEBOEUF	MELCHIOT	MORRIS	PETRESCU	POYET	SUTTON	TERRY	THOME	WEAH	WISE	WOLLEASTON	ZOLA	TOTAL
–	–	–	–	90□	90	–	–	86	80[2]	73	–	–	–	90	–	90[1]	990
s67	–	90	–	23	90	–	–	90□	90□	s21	–	–	–	90[1]□	–	69	990
s14	–	–	–	–	90□	–	90	76	90□	76□	–	–	–	90	–	87	990
–	–	–	–	–	90□	–	s2	80[1]	90	s23	–	–	–	90□	–	90	990
45	–	–	–	57	90[1]□	–	90	s45	s33	68	–	–	–	90□	–	90	990
61	–	90	–	90□	–	–	90	s29	–	90□	–	–	–	–	–	s29	990
–	–	–	90[1]	90	90	–	s1	90□	–	90□	–	–	–	90	–	70	990
–	–	90	–	s12	90	–	s25[1]	78	90[2]	90[1]	–	–	–	65□	–	69	990
–	–	–	s16□	s26	64□	–	–	74	90	90□	–	–	–	87■	–	68	971
–	–	–	–	53□	90	–	–	90[1]	s37	90□	–	–	–	90□	–	s20	990
–	s26	33	s57□	–	53[1]	–	90	–	90	90	–	–	–	–	–	90	990
–	–	–	–	–	90□	–	90	90	90□	–	–	–	–	–	–	68	990
–	–	s9	–	–	57■	–	90	51	–	90□	–	–	–	–	–	s39	957
s61	–	90	–	–	–	–	90	29	90	–	–	–	–	–	–	90	990
s45	45□	90	90	–	–	–	90	–	90[1]	–	s45	–	–	77	s13	90	990
–	90	s19	–	–	68■	–	–	s26	90	90	–	–	–	90□	–	s32	968
–	s15	–	–	–	90□	–	s3	87	90	–	–	90	–	–	–	–	990
–	–	–	90	–	90□	–	s8[1]	90	90	–	–	90	–	s67[1]	–	s8	990
–	–	–	–	–	–	–	s12	s16	74	s5	–	90	–	90	–	90	990
–	–	–	–	–	–	–	s6	90[1]	84	68	90	90	–	57	–	s22	990
–	90	–	90	–	90	–	–	90	56	s34	90	90	s34[1]	90□	–	–	990
–	90	–	–	–	90	–	–	45	s45	–	–	90	90	90[1]	–	90	990
–	90	s37	90	–	53	–	90	–	74	74	–	90	90	90	–	s16	990
–	90	–	90[1]	–	–	–	s5	85	90□	77	–	90	90	90	–	–	990
–	90	–	90	–	90	–	s19[1]	63	90[1]	71	–	90	90[1]	90	–	s27	990
–	90[1]	–	58	–	–	–	90□	90	90	–	–	90	–	–	–	90	990
–	–	–	–	–	90	–	90	s42	90[1]	72	–	90	–	90	–	90	990
–	72	–	–	–	90	–	90	–	s18	90	–	90	–	90[1]	–	45	990
–	–	–	–	–	90	–	82□	65	s25	s8	–	–	–	90	–	90	990
–	90	–	–	–	–	–	90	90	s16	74	–	90	90	90	–	86	990
–	88[1]	–	s2	–	90	–	90□	–	–	90□	–	90	90	90	–	–	990
–	90	–	–	–	90	–	90	90	49	–	–	90	s41	90	–	90[1]	990
–	–	–	90	–	–	–	45	45	90	90	–	90	90	–	–	–	990
–	s18	–	90	–	–	72	s29	–	90[1]	90	–	90	–	90	–	61	990
–	s45	–	90□	–	90	90	s45	73[1]	–	s17	–	90	–	90	–	90[1]	990
–	90	–	–	–	90	90	70□	–	s45	s9	–	s20	81[1]	90	–	90	990
–	–	–	90	–	40	90	60	–	s30[1]□	–	–	s50□	90	90	–	60	990
–	–	–	–	–	90	s58	–	–	64[1]	–	s34	–	–	90	–	90[1]	990

THE MANAGER

GIANLUCA VIALLI

Such has been the transition for Chelsea over the past few years that Blues fans will be a little disappointed to have won only the FA Cup, but in Gianluca Vialli they have a talented manager.

He is a former world record transfer, and as a player won four European trophies, two Italian Championships, four Italian Cups and one FA Cup – and scored 16 goals in 59 appearances for the national team.

Vialli, Ruud Gullit's first Chelsea signing, took over from the Dutchman as manager in February 1998 – and Chelsea are now recognised as one of the best teams in England.

This is a credit to the bald-headed Italian, whose ability has not gone unnoticed in his homeland, where he has been linked with some top managerial posts.

Ken Bates will be keen to hang on to his man, though, as the disappointment of 1999–2000 only goes to show the level of expectancy and belief around Stamford Bridge that the former Juventus and Sampdoria legend has helped to instil.

Vialli is sure to continue to be on the lookout for top-class players, and will hope to have a squad capable of threatening Manchester United's dominance by winning Chelsea their first Championship in 46 years.

LEAGUE POSITION

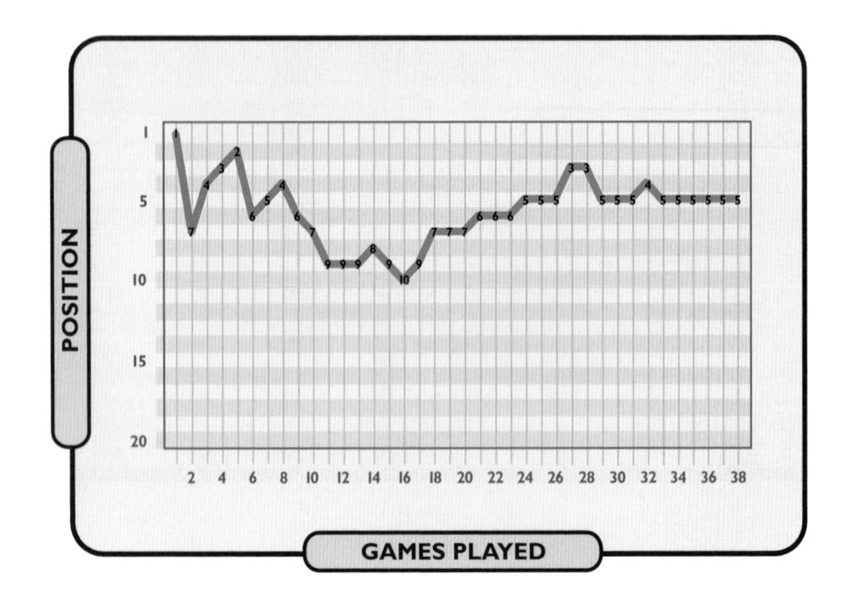

THE GOALS

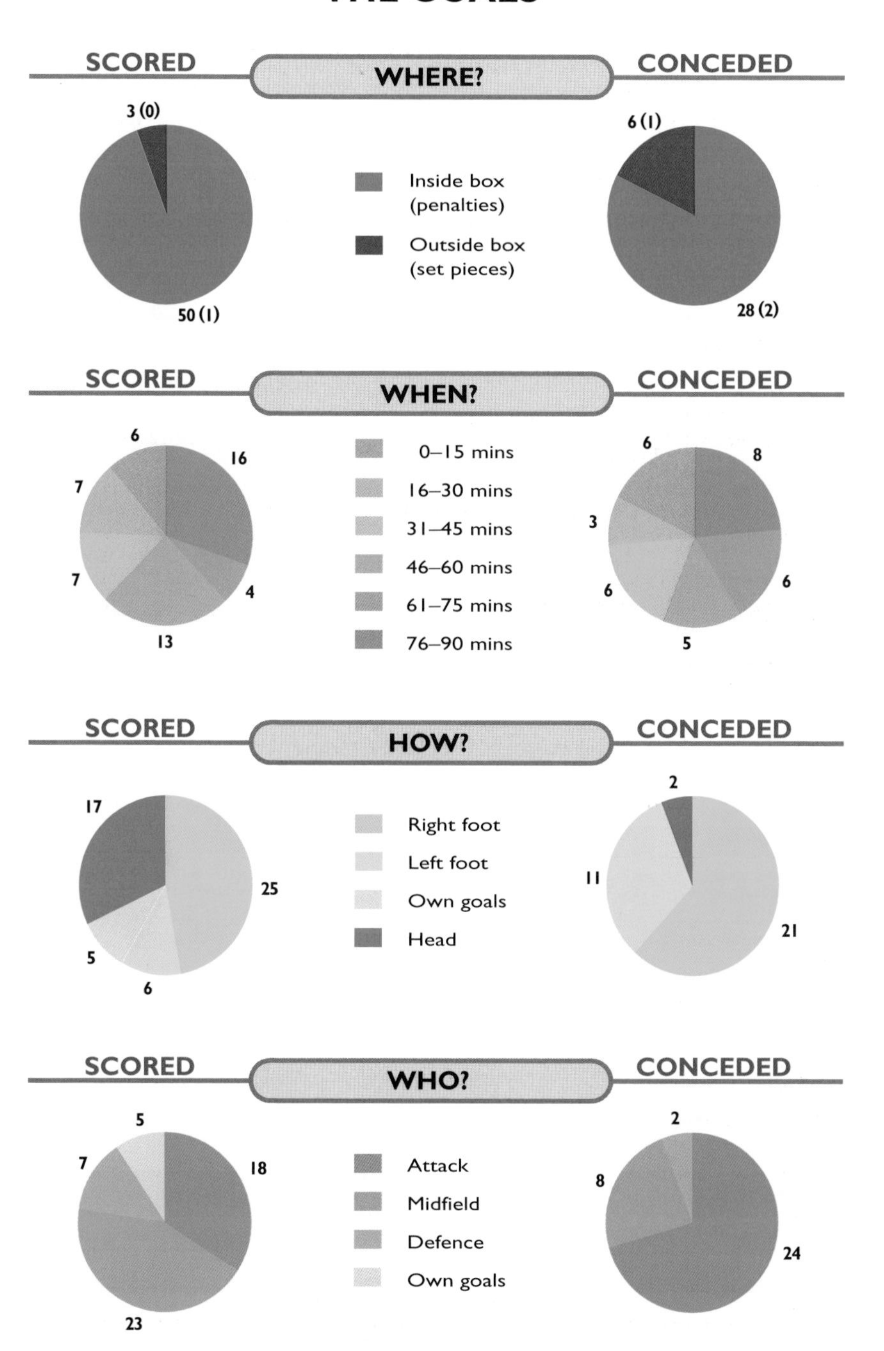

– the lowest ratio of any Premiership club

CHELSEA

	AMBROSETTI	BABAYARO	DALLA BONA	DESAILLY	DESCHAMPS	DI MATTEO	FERRER	FLO	GOLDBAEK	HARLEY	HOGH
APPEARANCES											
Start	9	23	0	23	24	14	24	20	2	13	6
Sub	7	2	2	0	3	4	1	14	4	4	3
Minutes on pitch	739	2055	80	1930	2052	1311	2100	1906	293	1209	548
GOAL ATTEMPTS											
Goals	0	0	0	1	0	2	0	10	0	2	0
Shots on target	4	1	1	1	5	11	2	34	4	5	0
Shots off target	8	5	0	2	15	11	2	28	5	8	1
Shooting accuracy	33%	17%	100%	33%	25%	50%	50%	55%	44%	38%	0%
PASSING											
Goal assists	0	0	0	0	1	2	3	1	0	0	1
Long passes	61	250	11	267	283	145	316	56	21	141	51
Short passes	188	804	37	646	1044	543	733	628	115	375	171
PASS COMPLETION											
Own half %	85%	87%	73%	88%	88%	81%	85%	79%	85%	62%	91%
Opposition half %	67%	72%	67%	77%	73%	74%	67%	65%	78%	56%	71%
CROSSING											
Total crosses	76	53	1	8	40	40	62	29	11	52	1
Cross completion %	22%	28%	0%	75%	25%	30%	35%	41%	9%	25%	100%
DRIBBLING											
Dribbles & runs	49	56	2	31	57	57	86	86	14	77	10
Dribble completion %	80%	93%	100%	97%	93%	75%	90%	72%	93%	73%	100%
DEFENDING											
Tackles made	16	53	4	63	96	40	85	13	13	43	19
Tackles won %	94%	47%	50%	48%	61%	63%	55%	23%	38%	53%	63%
Blocks	3	29	1	44	9	17	31	2	0	17	9
Clearances	2	119	0	193	67	11	139	13	5	23	64
Interceptions	0	17	0	22	25	8	31	2	1	14	1
DISCIPLINE											
Fouls	10	32	2	20	52	19	25	38	3	13	7
Offside	5	3	0	0	1	0	0	35	0	0	0
Yellow cards	0	3	0	2	5	3	4	1	0	1	0
Red cards	0	0	0	1	0	0	0	0	0	0	0

GOALKEEPER NAME	START/ (SUB)	TIME ON PITCH	GOALS CONCEDED	MINS/GOALS CONCEDED	SAVES MADE	SAVES/ SHOTS
CUDICINI	1	90	0	0	4	100%
DE GOEY	37	3330	34	98	96	74%

PLAYERS' STATISTICS

LAMBOURDE	LE SAUX	LEBOEUF	MELCHIOT	MORRIS	PETRESCU	POYET	SUTTON	TERRY	THOME	WEAH	WISE	WOLLEASTEN	ZOLA	TOTAL	RANK
12	6	28	4	19	24	25	21	2	18	9	29	0	25		
3	2	0	1	11	5	8	7	2	2	2	1	1	8		
1123	441	2315	400	1762	1995	2350	1850	259	1690	876	2603	13	2226		
2	0	2	0	3	4	10	1	0	0	3	4	0	4	53*	9th
4	0	6	0	10	14	31	10	2	2	10	15	0	30	202	7th
1	1	7	1	9	14	44	22	2	5	10	14	1	29	245	5th
80%	0%	46%	0%	53%	50%	41%	31%	50%	29%	50%	52%	0%	51%	45%	14th
0	2	0	1	2	5	5	2	0	1	3	5	0	9	43	=5th
167	42	582	45	210	143	179	74	42	304	54	409	1	130	3984	2nd
434	138	708	176	676	714	975	686	77	541	268	1186	3	880	12746	3rd
77%	80%	82%	83%	85%	83%	81%	81%	86%	78%	70%	87%	100%	82%	83%	3rd
63%	64%	56%	79%	70%	74%	70%	59%	60%	55%	57%	75%	50%	72%	68%	3rd
18	22	8	7	17	63	24	7	0	19	4	166	1	139	869	5th
39%	41%	63%	43%	35%	49%	38%	29%	0%	42%	0%	31%	0%	31%	33%	4th
43	26	57	25	32	87	55	22	7	46	47	79	2	118	1171	8th
93%	69%	93%	72%	78%	80%	87%	64%	71%	93%	74%	89%	100%	66%	82%	1st
56	23	91	10	46	49	60	24	6	60	11	95	1	20	998	13th
57%	52%	58%	50%	57%	49%	50%	58%	50%	45%	82%	57%	0%	45%	55%	4th
20	2	57	8	13	9	20	8	5	57	4	15	0	2	382	12th
67	20	209	7	21	34	70	21	20	187	8	37	0	4	1354	18th
8	1	29	1	3	21	10	5	5	12	0	22	0	1	239	12th
37	9	30	6	41	9	42	78	1	33	14	62	0	11	596	3rd
0	2	0	0	1	15	12	16	0	0	31	5	0	30	156	5th
3	3	7	0	4	2	5	7	0	1	0	7	0	0	59	12th
0	0	2	0	0	0	0	0	0	0	0	1	0	0	4	=5th

*Including five own goals

ROSSES AUGHT	CROSSES PUNCHED	CROSSES NOT CLAIMED	CATCH SUCCESS	THROWS/ SHORT KICKS	% COMPLETION	LONG KICKS	% COMPLETION
1	1	0	100%	8	88%	17	71%
53	41	4	93%	249	88%	987	47%

PLAYER OF THE SEASON

PLAYER	INDEX SCORE
GUSTAVO POYET	1,043
Albert Ferrer	979
Dennis Wise	968
Gianfranco Zola	960*
Didier Deschamps	932
Marcel Desailly	889
Frank Leboeuf	858
Celestine Babayaro	848
Emerson Thome	817**
Ed De Goey	655

All players played 75 minutes in at least 19 matches except those marked ** who played 18 games and those marked * who played 17 games.

Gustavo Poyet had promised great things at Chelsea for each of the past two seasons but his progress was cruelly cut short by injury on each occasion. However, a relatively injury-free campaign in season 1999–2000 saw him stamp his authority on the Chelsea side.

Uruguayan international Poyet scored an average of 1,043 points in the Opta Index, with his goalscoring contribution from midfield vital given the poor strike rate of Chelsea's front men.

Poyet was the Blues' joint top scorer with 10 goals. He also claimed five assists and made 1,154 passes as Chelsea claimed fifth spot in the table. The free-scoring midfielder also fired a crucial brace at Wembley to send Chelsea into the FA Cup final and put them on their way to European competition next season.

Spanish full-back Albert Ferrer came second to Poyet in the Index with an average of 979 points. The former Barcelona man made 1,049 passes, creating three goals in the process. He also made 139 clearances and won 55% of the tackles he attempted – higher than average for a Premiership defender.

Dennis Wise earned himself an England recall with his form this season and he led by example on the park for Chelsea. The tenacious midfielder scored four goals, created five and made just under 1,600 passes, helping himself to an Index score of 968 points. He was closely followed by Gianfranco Zola, who created more goals than any other Chelsea player.

World Cup-winning trio Didier Deschamps, Marcel Desailly and Frank Leboeuf all find themselves in the top 10, while record-breaking 'keeper Ed De Goey also makes it.

Dutch stopper De Goey kept more clean sheets than any other Premiership 'keeper in 1999–2000 and in the process broke the club record for the number of clean sheets in league and cup.

Manager Gianluca Vialli will be pleased that two of his new signings – Deschamps and Emerson Thome – made their way into the top 10.

2 Chelsea conceded the fewest headed

FIVE OF THE BEST

Chelsea dished out a warning to the other Premiership sides on the opening day of the 1999–2000 season with a 4–0 demolition of Sunderland. The Blues never got going in the league, though, and limped home in fifth place. Their successes were largely confined to the FA Cup and an extended run in the Champions League.

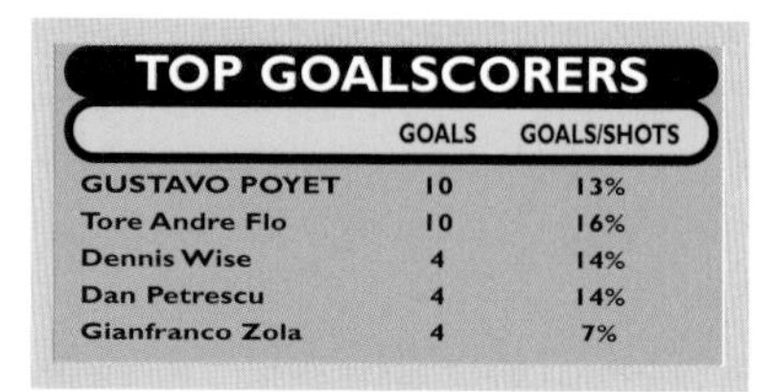

TOP GOALSCORERS

	GOALS	GOALS/SHOTS
GUSTAVO POYET	10	13%
Tore Andre Flo	10	16%
Dennis Wise	4	14%
Dan Petrescu	4	14%
Gianfranco Zola	4	7%

Gianluca Vialli spent £10 million during summer 1999 on the man he hoped would give Chelsea a cutting edge. But Chris Sutton struggled immediately and eventually scored just one league goal. The Pensioners had to rely on Uruguayan midfielder Gustavo Poyet again, and he obliged with 10 goals. Tore Andre Flo was the most deadly striker at Stamford Bridge, but nearly half of his strikes came in the Champions League. Even Zola suffered a barren season, with just 7% of his attempts rippling the net.

The 1999–2000 season was one of Dennis Wise's finest for Chelsea, and the Player of the Year nominee made 1,264 successful passes for the Blues, with only five players making more than that. Didier Deschamps, accused famously by Eric Cantona of being a mere "water-carrier", was just as accurate as Wise, and so was Nigerian defender Celestine Babayaro, although he blotted his copybook by failing to return to west London after the African Nations Cup for a considerable period.

TOP PASSERS

	SUCC PASSES	COMPLETION
DENNIS WISE	1,264	79%
Didier Deschamps	1,042	79%
Frank Leboeuf	900	70%
Celestine Babayaro	829	79%
Gustavo Poyet	827	72%

TOP TACKLERS

	WON	SUCCESS
DIDIER DESCHAMPS	59	61%
Dennis Wise	54	57%
Frank Leboeuf	53	58%
Albert Ferrer	47	55%
Bernard Lambourde	32	57%

Didier Deschamps suffered a lot of criticism from Chelsea fans in 1999–2000, but he was the best tackler in the team which was fourth best in that category. His style was less noticeable than that of Wise or Roy Keane, but the stats prove that he got the job done with the minimum amount of fuss. Frank Leboeuf was another much-maligned player, but he ended the campaign as the third best ball-winner at the club.

Chris Sutton must have hoped to top end-of-season charts when he moved to Stamford Bridge, but unfortunately for the striker he only excelled in conceding free-kicks and collecting yellow cards. The usual suspects, Dennis Wise and Frank Leboeuf, feature as well, though Wise was sent off just once in 1999–2000, a marked improvement on recent years. Didier Deschamps and Gustavo Poyet complete the cosmopolitan top five.

DISCIPLINE

	POINTS	FOULS & CARDS
CHRIS SUTTON	99	78F, 7Y, 0R
Dennis Wise	89	62F, 7Y, 1R
Didier Deschamps	67	52F, 5Y, 0R
Frank Leboeuf	63	30F, 7Y, 2R
Gustavo Poyet	57	42F, 5Y, 0R

goals for the second season in a row

ACTION	BABAYARO	DE GOEY	DESCHAMPS	FERRER	FLO	HOGH	LE SAUX	LEBOEUF	MORRIS	PETRESCU	POYET	SUTTON	WISE	ZOLA	TOTAL	MAN UTD
Time On Pitch	90	90	90	90	21	90	12	90	25	78	90	90	65	69	990	922
GOALS																
Goal	–	–	–	–	–	–	–	–	1	–	2	1	–	–	4	–
Shot on target	–	–	–	–	–	–	–	1	–	2	1	–	–	–	4	1
Shot off target	–	–	1	–	–	–	–	–	–	–	1	1	–	1	4	1
Blocked shot	–	–	1	–	–	–	–	–	–	–	–	–	–	1	2	2
Own goal	–	–	–	–	–	–	–	–	–	–	–	–	–	–	–	1
PASSES																
Pass to own player	57	–	78	69	6	46	3	63	13	33	55	24	50	27	524	377
Pass to opposition	10	–	8	13	3	2	–	12	1	12	10	16	7	3	97	94
Cross to own player	–	–	–	2	–	–	–	–	–	2	–	–	–	1	5	5
Cross to opposition player	1	–	2	2	–	–	2	–	1	1	–	–	2	3	14	10
Goal assist	–	–	–	1	–	–	1	–	–	1	–	–	–	–	3	–
Pass completion %	84%	0%	89%	83%	67%	96%	67%	84%	87%	73%	85%	60%	85%	82%	83%	79%
TACKLES & CLEARANCES																
Tackle	3	–	11	2	1	5	–	8	2	4	4	3	7	1	51	37
Clearances, blocks and interceptions	6	–	10	9	–	22	–	10	–	6	1	1	6	–	71	63
DRIBBLES & RUNS																
Dribble ball retained	2	–	4	4	1	–	1	–	–	3	–	–	2	–	17	10
Dribble ball lost	–	–	–	1	–	–	–	–	–	2	–	1	–	–	4	8
Dribble success %	100%	0%	100%	80%	100%	0%	100%	0%	0%	60%	0%	0%	100%	0%	81%	56%
DISCIPLINE																
Fouls	–	–	1	1	1	1	1	–	1	–	1	4	3	–	14	17
Penalty conceded	–	–	–	–	–	–	–	–	–	–	–	–	–	–	–	–
Free kick – offside	–	–	–	–	–	–	1	–	–	–	–	1	–	2	4	2
Yellow cards	–	–	1	–	–	–	–	–	–	–	–	–	1	–	2	1
Red cards	–	–	–	–	–	–	–	–	–	–	–	–	–	–	–	1
GOALKEEPERS																
Distribution to own player	–	26	–	–	–	–	–	–	–	–	–	–	–	–	26	24
Distribution to opposition player	–	8	–	–	–	–	–	–	–	–	–	–	–	–	8	20
Goalkeeper distribution %	0%	76%	0%	0%	0%	0%	0%	0%	0%	0%	0%	0%	0%	0%	76%	55%
Save	–	1	–	–	–	–	–	–	–	–	–	–	–	–	1	4
Ball caught	–	5	–	–	–	–	–	–	–	–	–	–	–	–	5	2
Ball dropped	–	–	–	–	–	–	–	–	–	–	–	–	–	–	–	–
Goal conceded	–	–	–	–	–	–	–	–	–	–	–	–	–	–	–	5

17 Chelsea kept more clean

Manchester United had not lost in the Premiership since 19 December 1998 and were being tipped to sweep all before them once again, prior to their televised visit to Stamford Bridge. By 5.45pm that afternoon, the Champions had been thrashed – and the nation had sat up and taken notice of Gianluca Vialli's team

It took the Blues just 28 seconds to draw blood and accident-prone 'keeper Massimo Taibi – dubbed "the blind Venetian" – was again at the heart of the action. Dan Petrescu crossed and the Italian rushed off his line, only to collide with Denis Irwin as Gustavo Poyet stole in to head home.

Chelsea doubled their lead 15 minutes later, when Albert Ferrer played an almost identical cross and Chris Sutton rose to head over the stranded Taibi. The second goal had the Champions rattled as Chelsea started to make Alex Ferguson's side look ordinary. Mickael Silvestre, in particular, made a string of mistakes at the back and was tormented by Gianfranco Zola.

United are a team never to be written off, but their chances of a comeback were made even tougher when Nicky Butt's petulance saw him sent off after 22 minutes. Butt lashed out at Dennis Wise following the Chelsea midfielder's high challenge and referee Dermot Gallagher booked Wise and sent Butt off.

The second half saw United fired up, but ultimately even more frustrated, as they were forced to chase the shadows of a Chelsea side exuding confidence. Paul Scholes – who had escaped a booking in the first half for a late challenge on Sutton – went in with both feet on Petrescu and this time saw yellow. The resulting free-kick let Celestine Babayaro in to calmly lay the ball to Frank Leboeuf. The World Cup winner's low shot was parried into the path of Poyet and the Uruguayan made no mistake, as a comfortable victory was becoming a rout.

Vialli's men started to play some excellent football with short, crisp interchanges and recorded a superb passing accuracy of 83%. Five minutes later it paid off as Silvestre was guilty of being caught in possession on the left and Zola nipped in to drive a low cross into the area. Henning Berg, under pressure from Sutton, slid the ball into his own net as Taibi looked on in despair.

If that was the icing on the cake, then there was still a cherry to go on top thanks to the three substitutes. Tore Andre Flo and Graeme Le Saux combined before the Englishman played a delightful pass across the area. As United's despondent defence watched, Jody Morris stole in to hammer the ball through Taibi's legs and complete a five star performance.

This result equalled United's worst defeat in the Premiership and it was Chelsea's biggest ever win over the Manchester side. The Blues fired in 12 shots – eight on target – and kept United's efforts on goal to just two attempts, with a solitary effort testing Ed De Goey.

This turned out to be Taibi's fourth and final league game for United – having conceded 11 goals in his brief stint – and he was loaned to Reggina where he battled against relegation all season.

sheets than any other side

SUBARU
SUBARU

COVENTRY CITY

ADDRESS

Highfield Road Stadium,
King Richard Street, Coventry CV2 4FW

CONTACT NUMBERS

Telephone: 024 7623 4000
Fax: 024 7623 4099
Ticket Office: 024 7623 4020
Club Call: 09068 121166
Superstore: 024 7623 4030
e-mail: info@ccfc.co.uk
Website: www.ccfc.co.uk

KEY PERSONNEL

President: Geoffrey Robinson MP
Chairman: B A Richardson
Deputy Chairman: M C McGinnity
Directors: A M Jepson
J F W Reason, D A Higgs
Miss B Price, G P Hover
Club Secretary: G P Hover
Manager: Gordon Strachan

SPONSORS

Subaru

FANZINES

Peeping Tom
Gary Mabbutt's Knee
Twist And Shout

COLOURS

Home: Sky blue shirts with navy panels, sky blue shorts with navy panels and sky blue stockings with navy trim
Away: White shirts with black panels and red trim, black shorts, white stockings with black trim

NICKNAME

The Sky Blues

HONOURS

Division Two Champions: 1966–67
Division Three Champions: 1963–64
Division Three (South) Champions: 1935–36
FA Cup: 1987

RECORD GOALSCORER

Clarrie Bourton –
171 league goals, 1931–37

BIGGEST WIN

9–0 v Bristol City – Division Three (South), 28 April 1934

BIGGEST DEFEAT

2–10 v Norwich City – Division Three (South), 15 March 1930

SEASON REVIEW

One statistic stands out above all others in Coventry City's 1999–2000 Premiership campaign: the club's failure to win a single away game. At Highfield Road the team were a match for anyone – only two sides, Manchester United and Arsenal, won more home games – but no team in the country, let alone the Premiership, suffered as much on their travels.

Manager Gordon Strachan was at a loss to explain the reasons for his team's Jekyll and Hyde behaviour. Having been part of the Leeds team which went the entire 1992–93 season without winning away the experience was nothing new, but improving that record in 1999–2000 must be Strachan's main task if he is to turn his team into a top 10 side.

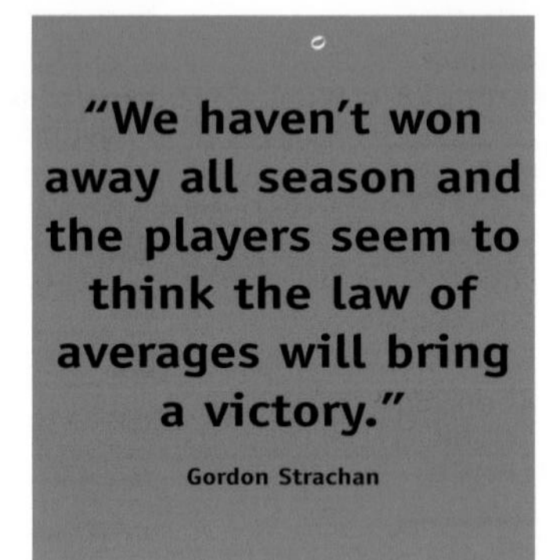

"We haven't won away all season and the players seem to think the law of averages will bring a victory."
Gordon Strachan

Strangely for a team that played so well at home, Coventry started the season with a narrow 1–0 defeat at the hands of Southampton at Highfield Road. Darren Huckerby, who had had a poor match, departed the club soon after, joining Leeds for a fee in the region of £5.5 million. With fellow-crowd favourite George Boateng already sold to Aston Villa in the close season, the club needed to convince supporters that it was more than just a shop window for richer teams.

Moroccan duo Moustapha Hadji and Youssef Chippo had joined in the summer, but Strachan's most audacious signing came once the season was under way. Arsenal, Aston Villa, Manchester United and Tottenham were all known to be admirers of Robbie Keane, but while the others dithered and tried to force Wolves into lowering their asking price, Strachan swooped with a successful £6.5 million bid which took Keane to Coventry – and made the Irish youngster the most costly teenager in English football history.

His impact was immediate. Coventry had followed their opening-day defeat with a 1–0 loss at Leicester and a draw at Wimbledon, but on his debut against Derby Keane scored twice to earn his new side a 2–0 victory. He followed that with an assist for John Aloisi in the 2–1 defeat by Manchester United, to make it clear that he was a good investment.

The Sky Blues' overall form was disappointing, though. In the league they followed a useful draw away to Sunderland with defeats by Leeds and Tottenham, and were turfed out of the Worthington Cup by eventual finalists Tranmere Rovers, who handed out a 5–1 drubbing in the first leg that proved too big a deficit for Coventry to overcome in a second leg which they won 3–1.

City's cosmopolitan midfield set-up was undoubtedly talented, but needed a ball-winner, and Strachan moved to sign Carlton Palmer from Nottingham Forest. The former England man proved to be a great signing. His arrival kick-started the club's best spell of the season, as they went on a run that saw them lose just two of their next 13 Premiership games and progress to the fifth round of the FA Cup.

Palmer's superb performances as anchorman freed up the likes of Chippo, Hadji and Gary McAllister to attack the opposition, and it is noticeable that 11 of the 20 Premiership goals scored during Palmer's first 13 league appearances came from midfielders.

In total, 47% of all Coventry's goals came from midfield, the highest proportion in the Premiership. McAllister, who deservedly finished the season as the Sky Blues' Player of the Year, was the highest-scoring midfielder in the top flight with 11 goals in total – a superb effort.

Palmer succumbed to injury at the turn

11 Gary McAllister was the highest-scoring

SEASON REVIEW

of the year, and suddenly results took a turn for the worse. Coventry had picked up their only away win of the season with the lanky ball-winner in the side (a 3–1 FA Cup third round victory at Norwich) and even though they failed to break their jinx in the Premiership they did manage hard-fought draws at Sheffield Wednesday, Bradford, Southampton and Derby when he was in midfield.

At home they were sensational. High-flying Arsenal and Sunderland were beaten, while Chelsea were held to a draw. Belgian loan star Cedric Roussel was particularly impressive in these games, giving the likes of Tony Adams and Marcel Desailly such a torrid time that Gordon Strachan signed the burly youngster permanently.

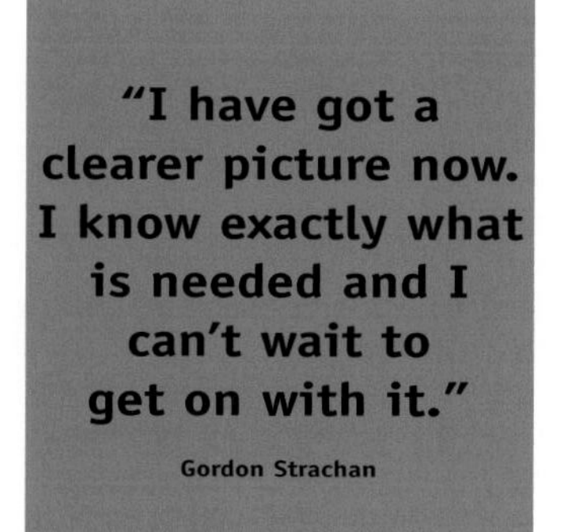

"I have got a clearer picture now. I know exactly what is needed and I can't wait to get on with it."
Gordon Strachan

Roussel's partnership with Robbie Keane, together with McAllister and Palmer's hold on midfield and the unpredictable skills of Chippo and Hadji, made for a good combination that briefly threatened to carry Coventry all the way to Wembley's Twin Towers.

After they had beaten Norwich in the third round of the FA Cup they trounced giant-killing Burnley 3–0 and were leading runaway First Division leaders Charlton 2–0 before succumbing to one of the fight-backs of the year, as the London side ran out 3–2 winners at Highfield Road.

Soon after that defeat Palmer was injured, and without him the team resumed their lightweight look, slumping to defeat in nine of their last 13 games.

There were still some bright moments. On the pitch, Bradford and Sheffield Wednesday both fell to heavy defeats at Highfield Road, while off it Colin Hendry and Ysrael Zuniga were added to the squad as Strachan sought to strengthen his hand.

Steve Ogrizovic waved goodbye to the club after 601 appearances in goal and the youth team put in a good display to reach the Youth Cup final for the second successive season.

The club had dropped into the bottom four at the end of September, but their home form was enough to take them clear of the relegation zone well before the end of the season. That said, the campaign must go down as one of under-achievement.

The team that made Highfield Road into a fortress were too easily rolled over on their travels; a problem which, if left unresolved, could once again prove costly in 2000–01.

Had the Sky Blues managed even half as many points away from home as they did at Highfield Road, they would have finished the season in the top 10.

If they had matched their home record away, they would have finished in second place in the Premiership and also qualified for the Champions League!

The departure of their inspirational skipper McAllister on a free transfer to Liverpool at the end of the season is bound to leave Coventry with a big hole to fill in their team.

Strachan claims that he has a clear picture of what is needed to bring success to Highfield Road, but privately the need to replace McAllister and his side's failure to win away must be worrying him.

His ability to solve both problems could hold the key to Coventry's progress in 2000–01. The club has some highly gifted players, but the squad needs to be improved if City are to move up the Premiership ladder.

Whether there is money in the coffers to improve the playing staff or whether Strachan will have to wheel and deal once more, remains to be seen.

COVENTRY CITY

DATE	OPPONENT	SCORE	ATT.	ALOISI	BETTS	BREEN	BURROWS	CHIPPO	EDWORTHY	EUSTACE	FROGGATT	GUSTAFSSON	HADJI	M.HALL	P.HALL	HE
7.8.99	Southampton H	0–1	19,915	s20	–	–	90	77	90	–	s13	–	90	–	–	90
11.8.99	Leicester A	0–1	19,196	s13	–	–	70■	90□	90	–	77□	–	90	–	–	90
14.8.99	Wimbledon A	1–1	10,635	90□	–	90	90	90□	–	–	s14	–	76	–	–	90
21.8.99	Derby Co H	2–0	17,685	s4	–	–	90	90□	90	–	s31	–	86	–	–	90
25.8.99	Man Utd H	1–2	22,024	$s20^1$	–	84	–	90	90	–	90□	–	70	–	–	90
29.8.99	Sunderland A	1–1	39,427	83	–	90	–	88■	90	–	90□	–	76	–	–	90
11.9.99	Leeds Utd H	3–4	21,532	45^1	–	–	–	90^1	90	–	75	–	90□	s45	–	90
19.9.99	Tottenham A	2–3	35,224	–	–	–	83	90^1	90	–	59	–	90□	s31	s7	9
25.9.99	West Ham H	1–0	19,993	–	–	–	–	61□	90□	–	–	–	90^1	90	–	9
2.10.99	Everton A	1–1	34,839	–	–	–	–	90	90□	–	–	–	90	90□	–	90
16.10.99	Newcastle H	4–1	23,031	–	–	–	–	90□	72□	–	s18	–	90^1	90	–	90
23.10.99	Sheff Wed A	0–0	23,296	–	–	–	–	18	–	–	90	–	90	90	–	9
31.10.99	Watford H	4–0	21,700	–	–	–	–	–	–	–	90^1□	–	90^1	90	–	9
6.11.99	Bradford A	1–1	17,587	–	–	–	–	90	–	–	90□	–	90	90	–	9
22.11.99	Aston Villa H	2–1	20,184	–	–	90	s1	89	–	–	–	–	90	90	–	90
27.11.99	Leicester H	0–1	22,021	–	–	90	45	90	–	–	s45	–	90	–	–	9
4.12.99	Southampton A	0–0	15,168	–	–	90	–	90□	–	–	90	–	90	–	–	9
18.12.99	Liverpool A	0–2	44,024	–	–	90□	–	90	–	–	90	–	74	–	–	9
26.12.99	Arsenal H	3–2	22,757	–	–	90	–	89	–	–	90	s1	90^1	–	–	90
4.1.00	Chelsea H	2–2	20,164	–	–	90	–	90	–	–	90	–	90□	–	–	90
15.1.00	Wimbledon H	2–0	19,012	–	–	90	–	–	–	90	90	–	–	–	–	9
22.1.00	Derby Co A	0–0	28,381	–	–	90	–	–	–	81	90	s9	–	–	–	9
5.2.00	Man Utd A	2–3	61,380	–	–	90	–	–	–	80	90	90	–	–	–	9
12.2.00	Sunderland H	3–2	22,101	–	–	90	–	85	–	90□	10	90	90^1	–	–	9
19.2.00	Middlesbro A	0–2	32,798	–	–	s22	68	90	–	s22	–	68	90□	–	–	9
26.2.00	Tottenham H	0–1	23,077	–	–	90	90	90	–	90	–	–	90	–	–	9
5.3.00	Leeds Utd A	0–3	38,710	–	–	90	90	90	–	90	–	–	–	–	–	9
11.3.00	Aston Villa A	0–1	33,177	–	–	–	s16	90	–	74	90	90	90□	–	–	9
15.3.00	Everton H	1–0	18,518	–	–	–	90	90	–	81	–	90	90	–	–	9
18.3.00	Bradford H	4–0	19,201	–	–	–	–	90	–	90^1	–	90	90	–	–	9
26.3.00	Arsenal A	0–3	38,027	–	–	–	–	90□	–	90	90	63□	71	–	–	–
1.4.00	Liverpool H	0–3	23,098	–	–	–	–	90	–	67	90	–	90	–	–	–
12.4.00	Chelsea A	1–2	32,316	–	–	–	s12	90	–	–	90	–	78	–	–	9
15.4.00	Middlesbro H	2–1*	19,345	–	–	90□	64	s26	–	90□	90	–	90	–	–	9
22.4.00	West Ham A	0–5	24,719	–	s17	90	90	–	–	90	–	–	–	–	–	9
29.4.00	Newcastle A	0–2	36,408	–	s1	90	–	90	–	s25	–	–	90	–	–	9
6.5.00	Sheff Wed H	4–1	19,921	–	–	90	–	88□	–	s2	–	–	90^1	–	–	–
14.5.00	Watford A	0–1	18,977	–	–	90	–	90□	–	–	–	s45	90	–	–	9

□ Yellow card, ■ Red card, s Substitute, 90^2 Goals scored

*including one own goal

1999–2000 PREMIERSHIP APPEARANCES

HENDRY	HUCKERBY	KEANE	KONJIC	MCALLISTER	MCSHEFFREY	NORMANN	OGRIZOVIC	PALMER	QUINN	ROUSSEL	SHAW	STRACHAN	TELFER	WHELAN	WILLIAMS	ZUNIGA	TOTAL
–	70	–	–	90	–	–	–	–	–	–	90	–	90	90	90	–	990
–	–	–	–	90	–	–	–	–	–	–	90	–	90	90	90	–	970
–	–	–	–	90[1]	–	–	–	–	–	–	90	–	90	90	90	–	990
–	–	84[2]	–	90	–	–	–	–	–	–	90	s6	59	90	90□	–	990
–	–	90	s6	90	–	–	–	–	–	–	90	–	s56	34	90	–	990
–	–	90[1]	–	90	s7	–	–	–	–	–	90	–	s14	–	90	–	988
–	–	90	–	90[1]□	s15	–	–	–	75□	–	90	s15	–	–	90	–	990
–	–	90[1]	90□	90	–	–	–	–	–	–	90□	–	–	–	90	–	990
–	–	90	90	84	s6	–	–	90□	–	–	90	–	90	–	s29	–	990
–	–	90	57	90[1]	–	–	–	90	–	–	90	–	90	–	s33	–	990
–	–	90[1]	–	85	–	–	–	90[1]□	–	s5	90	–	90	–	90[1]	–	990
–	–	90	–	90	–	–	–	90	–	s72	90	–	90	–	90□	–	990
–	–	90[1]	–	90[1]	–	–	–	90	–	90	90	–	90	–	90	–	990
–	–	90	–	90[1]	–	–	–	90	–	–	90	–	90	–	90	–	990
–	–	90[1]	–	90	–	–	–	90	–	87[1]	–	–	90□	s3	90	–	990
–	–	90□	–	90	–	–	–	90□	–	35	–	–	90	s55□	90□	–	990
–	–	90	–	90	–	–	–	90	–	64	–	–	90	s26□	90	–	990
–	–	90□	–	90	–	s16	–	90	–	s20	–	–	90	70	90	–	990
–	–	81[1]	–	90[1]	–	–	–	90	–	90	–	–	90	s9	90	–	990
–	–	90[1]	–	90	–	–	–	90	–	87[1]	–	–	90	s3	90	–	990
–	–	90[1]	–	90[1]	–	s9	–	90	–	81	–	–	90	90	90	–	990
–	–	90	–	90	–	–	–	–	s13	90	–	77	90	90	90	–	990
–	–	90	–	90	–	–	–	90	–	90[2]	90	–	s10	–	90	–	990
–	–	90[1]	–	90	–	s5	–	–	s80	90[1]	90	–	–	–	–	–	990
–	–	90	–	90	–	–	–	90□	s14	76	90□	–	–	–	90	–	990
–	–	90□	–	90	–	s9	–	–	s45	–	90	–	–	81	45	–	990
90	–	–	–	90	–	s30	–	–	45	90	s45	–	–	90	–	60	990
90	–	45	–	90	–	–	–	–	–	90□	90	–	–	s45	–	–	990
90	–	–	–	90[1]	–	–	–	–	–	90	90	–	–	90	–	s9	990
90	–	–	–	45	–	–	–	–	90□	77[1]	90□	–	s45	90[1]	–	s13[1]	990
90	–	–	–	90	–	s19	90	–	–	90	90	–	s27	90	–	–	990
90	–	57	–	90	–	–	90	–	s23	90	90	–	90	s33□	–	–	990
90	–	90	–	90[1]	–	–	–	–	90	–	90	–	90	77	–	s13	990
90	–	90[1]	–	90	–	–	–	–	–	–	–	–	90	90	–	–	990
57	–	90	–	90	–	45	–	–	73	s45	s33	–	90	90	–	–	990
–	–	85	–	90□	–	–	–	–	–	65	90	–	90	89	90□	s5	990
–	–	90	–	90[2]	–	–	90	–	–	–	90	–	90	90	90	90[1]	990
–	–	90	–	90	–	s44	–	–	s12	–	90	–	90□	90	45	34	990

THE MANAGER

GORDON STRACHAN

Coventry City manager Gordon Strachan is never without an opinion, but even he was lost for words when asked if he could explain his team's fantastic home form, yet their inability to win away all season.

As a player, the flame-haired Scot had tremendous success, winning two Scottish Championships, three Scottish Cups and the European Cup Winners' Cup with Aberdeen, under the management of Alex Ferguson.

He won the FA Cup with Manchester United in 1985 and the 1991–92 Championship with Leeds United.

Strachan is also the only player to have won both Scottish and English Footballer of the Year awards, gaining the accolades in 1980 and 1992 respectively.

Strachan was appointed as Ron Atkinson's assistant at Highfield Road in March 1995, before taking over from him in November 1996, and under him the Sky Blues have had the potential to become a top-10 team.

So respected and recognised is Strachan that it has even been suggested that he could take over from Sir Alex Ferguson as the next manager of Manchester United – and praise does not come much higher than that.

LEAGUE POSITION

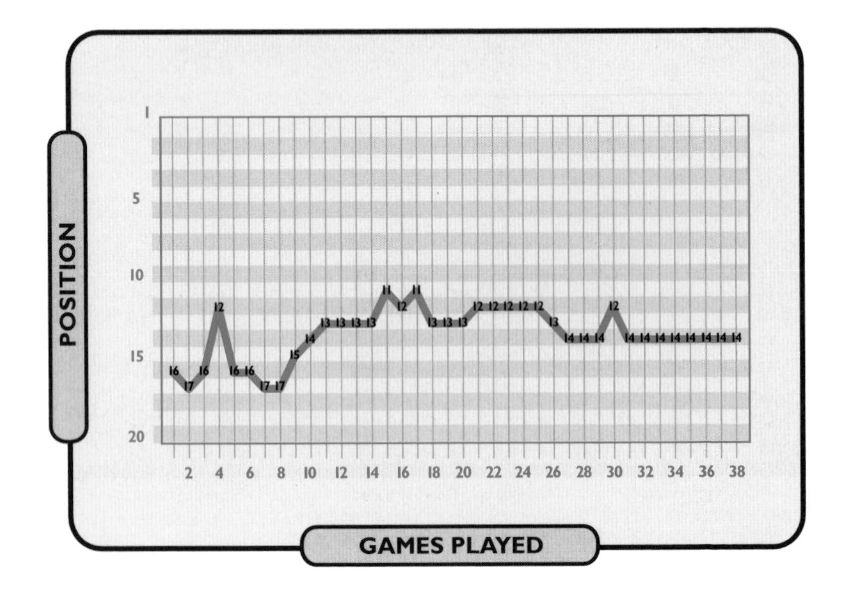

THE GOALS

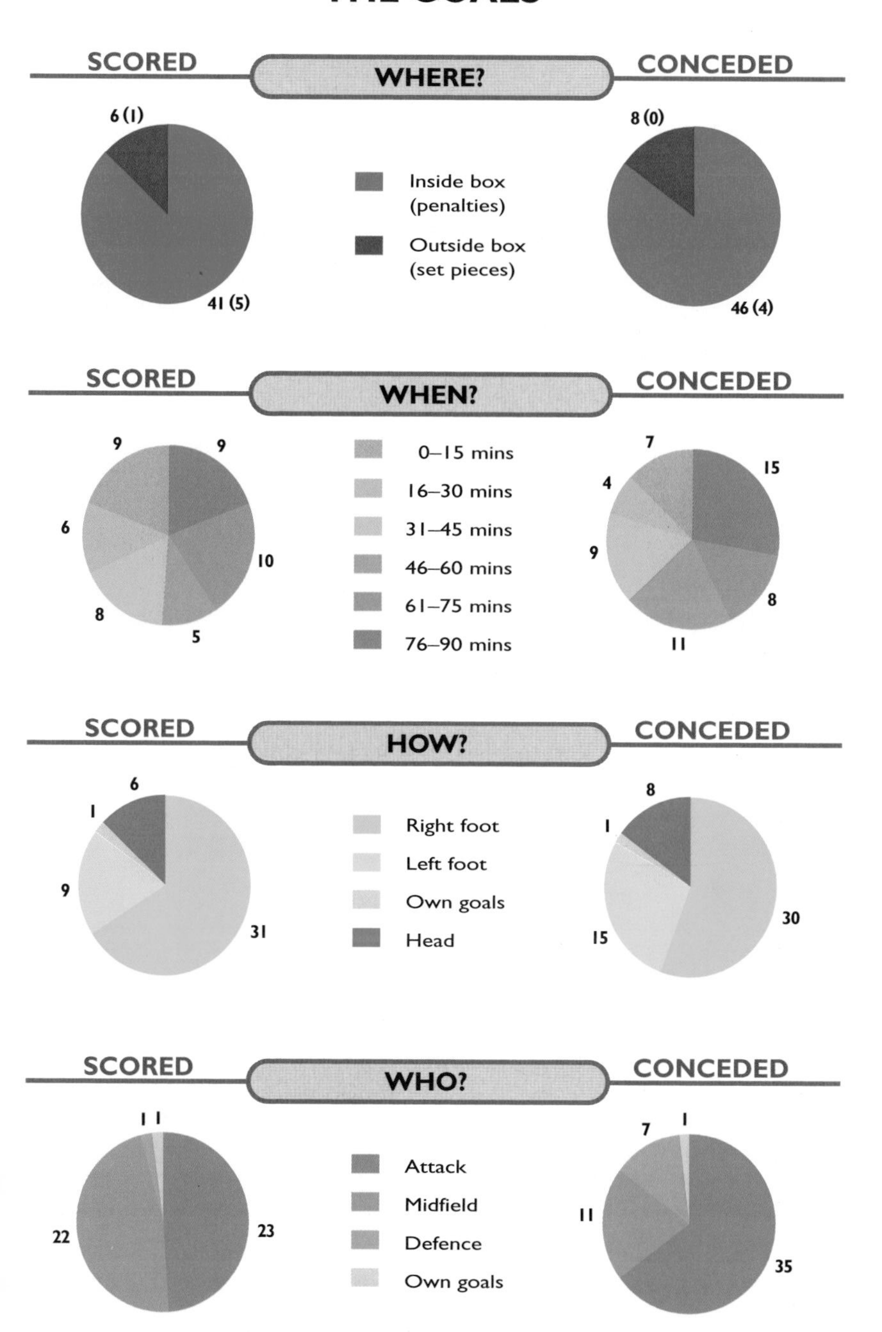

– the highest ratio in the Premiership

COVENTRY CITY

	ALOISI	BETTS	BREEN	BURROWS	CHIPPO	EDWORTHY	EUSTACE	FROGGATT	GUSTAFSSON	HADJI	HALL M	HALL P	HENDRY
APPEARANCES													
Start	3	0	20	12	32	10	13	21	7	33	7	0	9
Sub	4	2	1	3	1	0	3	5	3	0	2	1	0
Minutes on pitch	275	18	1816	989	2781	882	1152	1872	636	2871	706	7	777
GOAL ATTEMPTS													
Goals	2	0	0	0	2	0	1	1	0	6	0	0	0
Shots on target	5	0	2	0	17	1	8	4	1	34	0	0	0
Shots off target	4	0	5	0	14	1	6	5	0	44	2	0	0
Shooting accuracy	56%	0%	29%	0%	55%	50%	57%	44%	100%	44%	0%	0%	0%
PASSING													
Goal assists	0	0	0	0	3	1	0	2	0	7	0	0	0
Long passes	2	2	192	141	183	61	106	172	118	183	58	0	109
Short passes	76	20	436	324	981	288	383	555	181	1081	161	0	173
PASS COMPLETION													
Own half %	76%	78%	77%	85%	82%	87%	81%	72%	71%	74%	84%	0%	72%
Opposition half %	63%	92%	55%	63%	69%	71%	65%	62%	60%	62%	58%	0%	43%
CROSSING													
Total crosses	1	0	13	36	40	16	15	82	13	65	19	0	0
Cross completion %	0%	0%	38%	36%	23%	25%	27%	22%	38%	20%	11%	0%	0%
DRIBBLING													
Dribbles & runs	5	2	30	20	162	26	30	121	11	177	31	0	5
Dribble completion %	60%	100%	93%	80%	77%	85%	90%	74%	91%	70%	94%	0%	80%
DEFENDING													
Tackles made	2	0	35	27	147	30	41	61	32	52	18	0	36
Tackles won %	100%	0%	49%	56%	49%	60%	63%	33%	53%	46%	44%	0%	47%
Blocks	0	0	42	10	25	13	8	12	5	13	12	0	24
Clearances	0	0	158	55	54	90	18	49	15	37	57	0	59
Interceptions	1	0	8	4	18	10	8	13	3	17	14	0	4
DISCIPLINE													
Fouls	4	0	28	13	68	10	30	21	7	41	12	1	9
Offside	4	0	1	0	8	0	2	1	0	21	0	0	1
Yellow cards	1	0	2	0	9	3	2	5	1	5	1	0	0
Red cards	0	0	0	1	1	0	0	0	0	0	0	0	0

GOALKEEPER NAME	START/ (SUB)	TIME ON PITCH	GOALS CONCEDED	MINS/GOALS CONCEDED	SAVES MADE	SAVES/ SHOTS
HEDMAN	35	3150	47	67	136	74%
OGRIZOVIC	3	270	7	39	18	72%

PLAYERS' STATISTICS

HUCKERBY	KEANE	KONJIC	MCALLISTER	MCSHEFFREY	NORMANN	PALMER	QUINN	ROUSSEL	SHAW	STRACHAN	TELFER	WHELAN	WILLIAMS	ZUNIGA	TOTAL	RANK
1	31	3	38	0	1	15	5	18	27	1	25	19	26	3		
0	0	1	0	3	7	0	6	4	2	2	5	7	2	4		
70	2692	243	3364	28	177	1350	560	1614	2508	98	2371	1785	2312	224		
0	12	0	11	0	0	1	0	6	0	0	0	1	1	2	47*	12th
0	34	0	27	0	1	3	0	17	0	1	3	16	1	4	179	11th
0	22	1	26	0	1	6	2	26	0	1	7	24	7	0	204	=11th
0%	61%	0%	51%	0%	50%	33%	0%	40%	0%	50%	30%	40%	13%	100%	47%	9th
0	4	0	4	0	0	0	0	6	0	0	0	2	0	0	29	15th
0	91	13	448	0	11	103	83	49	179	11	402	69	423	11	3220	12th
15	757	43	1372	13	63	479	216	561	519	39	809	664	605	69	10883	8th
100%	83%	100%	84%	100%	74%	80%	81%	70%	83%	82%	79%	79%	82%	65%	80%	9th
58%	69%	50%	67%	67%	62%	63%	62%	59%	64%	71%	60%	63%	47%	56%	63%	13th
6	31	0	207	1	6	6	8	7	11	0	89	25	9	1	708	=14th
0%	29%	0%	26%	0%	0%	67%	13%	14%	45%	0%	34%	20%	0%	0%	26%	18th
3	194	2	94	4	12	34	19	35	17	3	61	63	26	5	1192	7th
100%	66%	100%	88%	25%	67%	85%	95%	89%	94%	100%	82%	67%	92%	80%	77%	9th
2	17	12	92	1	6	70	27	15	54	3	58	40	97	6	982	15th
50%	47%	75%	51%	0%	100%	60%	63%	33%	59%	67%	55%	43%	59%	67%	53%	8th
0	1	6	30	0	1	8	10	4	64	1	31	3	48	1	372	13th
0	4	58	76	1	1	55	24	8	270	4	96	10	318	0	1536	15th
1	11	8	31	0	1	20	7	3	18	2	17	2	41	0	263	9th
1	34	5	24	0	1	27	5	29	28	0	14	34	31	1	479	18th
3	26	0	1	1	0	0	0	29	0	0	3	34	1	7	143	6th
0	3	1	2	0	0	4	2	1	3	0	2	3	4	0	54	15th
0	0	0	0	0	0	0	0	0	0	0	0	0	0	0	2	16th

*Including one own goal

ROSSES AUGHT	CROSSES PUNCHED	CROSSES NOT CLAIMED	CATCH SUCCESS	THROWS/ SHORT KICKS	% COMPLETION	LONG KICKS	% COMPLETION
62	13	6	91%	130	94%	1121	36%
1	2	0	100%	12	92%	124	61%

PLAYER OF THE SEASON

PLAYER	INDEX SCORE
GARY McALLISTER	971
Paul Williams	957
Moustapha Hadji	821
Robbie Keane	812
Youssef Chippo	791
Paul Telfer	753
Magnus Hedman	739
Richard Shaw	697
Steve Froggatt	608
Gary Breen	555

Scottish veteran Gary McAllister proved that age is no obstacle as he enjoyed one of his best seasons to date with Coventry in the Premiership.

Skipper McAllister was an ever-present for Coventry and ended the season as the league's highest-scoring midfielder with 11 goals. He was the Sky Blues' second highest scorer and also had four goal assists as he earned an average of 971 points in the Opta Season Index. The experienced Scot's superb performances impressed so much that he earned himself a move to Merseyside giants Liverpool for the 2000–01 season.

The 1998–99 Player of the Season, Paul Williams, performed well again on the Index, earning 957 points. The big defender missed much of the latter part of the season through injury but his consistent performances earlier on in the campaign led to him coming second in the Coventry rankings thanks to 318 clearances and 97 tackles.

Moroccan Moustapha Hadji recorded more goal assists than any other Coventry player as he earned the third highest points average over the season. The North African found himself on the score-sheet six times as he made a promising impact in his first season in English football.

Gordon Strachan made a big investment when he took Robbie Keane from neighbours Wolves to Highfield Road. Other clubs baulked at the asking price, but the £6 million does not look so extravagant given that the Irishman ended the campaign as the club's leading scorer, Keane's 12 goals from 56 shots earning him an average of 812 points.

Consistent performances from the likes of Youssef Chippo, Paul Telfer and Richard Shaw earned them places in Coventry's top 10 of the season while Swedish 'keeper Magnus Hedman enhanced his growing reputation with an average of 739 points in the Opta Index. And big Gary Breen completes the top 10, thanks to his average points score of 555 across the season.

FIVE OF THE BEST

Coventry became the first team since Leeds in 1992–93 to complete a Premiership season without an away win, but luckily for the Sky Blues they won 12 times at home to finish 14th. Indeed, some of their performances at Highfield Road were scintillating, with the introduction of such talent as Moustapha Hadji, Youssef Chippo and Robbie Keane.

TOP GOALSCORERS

	GOALS	GOALS/SHOTS
ROBBIE KEANE	12	21%
Gary McAllister	11	21%
Cedric Roussel	6	14%
Moustapha Hadji	6	8%
Ysrael Zuniga	2	50%

While John Gregory hesitated about buying Robbie Keane from Wolves, Gordon Strachan nipped in and took him to Warwickshire. The little Irishman responded admirably, slamming home 12 league goals for City, and finished as the sixth most accurate striker in the Premiership. Balding veteran Gary McAllister also had an immense campaign, with 21% of his shots hitting the back of the net. This form has given the former Scotland captain the chance of one last move to Liverpool.

Coventry had one of the most consistent midfields in the Premiership, with the work-rate of McAllister allied to the skill and invention of the two Moroccans. Chippo finished as the most accurate passer at the club, with the skipper just behind on 72%. Hadji was the least precise of the trio, but his searching distribution saw him end with seven assists and six league goals as he enjoyed an impressive introduction to the Premiership.

TOP PASSERS

	SUCC PASSES	COMPLETION
GARY McALLISTER	1,318	72%
Youssef Chippo	845	73%
Paul Telfer	806	67%
Moustapha Hadji	792	63%
Paul Williams	677	66%

TOP TACKLERS

	WON	SUCCESS
YOUSSEF CHIPPO	72	49%
Paul Williams	57	59%
Gary McAllister	47	51%
Carlton Palmer	42	60%
Richard Shaw	32	59%

Youssef Chippo was the lesser-known half of Gordon Strachan's Moroccan swoop, but he proved to City fans over the season that he was a midfield dynamo. He won 72 tackles, more than anyone at the club, although the most successful tackler was gangly veteran Carlton Palmer. The former England international was a valuable addition to the squad. Seasoned professionals Richard Shaw and Paul Williams are also in the top five.

Coventry were the fourth-cleanest team in the Premiership in 1999–2000, but Chippo still managed to rack up a considerable disciplinary points total. Only 10 players committed as many fouls, and he also got red-carded at the Stadium of Light in August. His countryman Hadji is tucked in behind him, but was not nearly as combative. The fiery Robbie Keane is here alongside erstwhile strike-partner Noel Whelan, a man whose long-term future at Highfield Road is in some doubt.

DISCIPLINE

	POINTS	FOULS & CARDS
YOUSSEF CHIPPO	101	68F, 9Y, 1R
Moustapha Hadji	56	41F, 5Y, 0R
Noel Whelan	43	34F, 3Y, 0R
Robbie Keane	43	34F, 3Y, 0R
Paul Williams	43	31F, 4Y, 0R

than any other Premiership team

ACTION	BREEN	CHIPPO	FROGGATT	GUSTAFSSON	HADJI	HEDMAN	KEANE	McALLISTER	PALMER	ROUSSEL	TELFER	WHELAN	WILLIAMS	TOTAL	ARSENAL
Time On Pitch	90	89	90	1	90	90	81	90	90	90	90	9	90	990	990
GOALS															
Goal	–	–	–	–	1	–	1	1	–	–	–	–	–	3	2
Shot on target	–	1	–	–	1	–	–	–	–	1	–	–	–	3	8
Shot off target	–	–	–	–	1	–	2	–	–	–	–	1	–	4	4
Blocked shot	–	–	–	–	1	–	–	1	–	–	–	–	–	2	5
Own goal	–	–	–	–	–	–	–	–	–	–	–	–	–	–	–
PASSES															
Pass to own player	16	26	23	1	16	–	18	32	29	17	26	2	31	237	260
Pass to opposition	6	8	12	–	16	–	11	14	7	8	15	3	22	122	121
Cross to own player	1	–	–	–	–	–	2	–	–	1	2	–	–	6	10
Cross to opposition player	–	3	–	–	3	–	–	6	–	1	2	–	2	17	25
Goal assist	–	–	–	–	–	–	–	1	–	2	–	–	–	3	1
Pass completion %	74%	70%	66%	100%	46%	0%	65%	62%	81%	69%	62%	40%	56%	64%	65%
TACKLES & CLEARANCES															
Tackle	3	2	3	–	2	–	2	5	7	2	–	–	2	28	26
Clearances, blocks and interceptions	10	1	6	–	3	–	–	4	6	–	4	–	5	39	38
DRIBBLES & RUNS															
Dribble ball retained	1	5	4	–	8	–	5	4	2	1	3	1	1	35	33
Dribble ball lost	–	2	1	–	2	–	2	1	–	–	–	–	–	8	7
Dribble success %	100%	71%	80%	0%	80%	0%	71%	80%	100%	100%	100%	100%	100%	81%	83%
DISCIPLINE															
Fouls	1	4	1	–	–	–	2	1	2	1	1	–	2	15	14
Penalty conceded	–	–	–	–	–	–	–	–	–	–	–	–	–	–	–
Free kick – offside	–	1	–	–	–	–	1	–	–	2	–	–	–	4	2
Yellow cards	–	–	–	–	–	–	–	–	–	–	–	–	–	–	2
Red cards	–	–	–	–	–	–	–	–	–	–	–	–	–	–	–
GOALKEEPERS															
Distribution to own player	–	–	–	–	–	15	–	–	–	–	–	–	–	15	17
Distribution to opposition player	–	–	–	–	–	28	–	–	–	–	–	–	–	28	18
Goalkeeper distribution %	0%	0%	0%	0%	0%	35%	0%	0%	0%	0%	0%	0%	0%	35%	49%
Save	–	–	–	–	–	8	–	–	–	–	–	–	–	8	3
Ball caught	–	–	–	–	–	1	–	–	–	–	–	–	–	1	1
Ball dropped	–	–	–	–	–	1	–	–	–	–	–	–	–	1	–
Goal conceded	–	–	–	–	–	2	–	–	–	–	–	–	–	2	3

0 Coventry were the only team in all four divisions

While Coventry managed to go the entire season without winning a single game away from home, their form at Highfield Road provided their fans with some of the most exciting football the Sky Blues have produced in many years, with some inspirational displays from players such as Robbie Keane, Moustapha Hadji and Youssef Chippo.

All these players certainly had their part to play in the match against Arsenal on Boxing Day, as Gordon Strachan's side delivered a series of sucker punches to knock Arsene Wenger's high-fliers for six. With Carlton Palmer, playing the 500th league game of his career, Arsenal were never allowed to settle into their normal rhythm. The former England international made seven tackles, more than any other Coventry player.

McAllister was also playing in one of his career's milestone games, as it was his 100th appearance for the Sky Blues. And the former Scotland captain was the first to find the back of the net, when his speculative drive from well outside the area was deflected by Martin Keown past David Seaman after just seven minutes.

With all the attacking talent on display for Arsenal, Strachan's players could not rest on their slender lead, a point that was highlighted when Kanu nearly put the impressive Fredrik Ljungberg clean through on 36 minutes.

But once they had managed to gain possession, the Sky Blues certainly made it count. After 40 minutes, Hadji received an excellent through-ball from McAllister on the edge of the Arsenal penalty area. He controlled before unleashing a breathtaking curler that clipped the inside of the post on its way into the net to give his side a 2–0 lead at half-time.

But Arsenal came right back into the game at the start of the second half. Thierry Henry, Tony Adams and Ljungberg all wasted good scoring opportunities before the Swedish international fired the Gunners back into the game after 68 minutes. His compatriot Magnus Hedman could only parry Ljungberg's first close-range effort and the midfielder made no mistake with his second attempt.

The fear at Highfield Road was becoming clearly visible among the home supporters as the Gunners continued to press forward. But despite Wenger's team firing 10 shots on target over the 90 minutes – four more than Coventry – Strachan's men retained their composure long enough for Keane to re-establish their two-goal advantage on 72 minutes. The young Irish international produced an outrageous flick to leave Seaman stranded as the ball fell agonisingly into the net.

There was still time for Suker to ensure a tense finale with a well-taken goal with three minutes left. But the Sky Blues were not to be denied their victory.

While they failed to reproduce their home form when on their travels, this game at least provided the Coventry faithful with plenty to cheer about. Their outstanding player was McAllister, who found a team-mate with 32 passes – more than any other Sky Blues player – including one to set up Keane's goal. He also scored from his only shot on target to give him an Opta points score of 1,544.

not to win away from home in the league

Mitre
EDS

DERBY COUNTY

ADDRESS

Pride Park Stadium, Pride Park,
Derby DE24 8XL

CONTACT NUMBERS

Telephone: 01332 202202
Fax: 01332 667540
Ticket Office: 01332 209209
Ticket Line: 09068 332213
Club Call: 09068 121187
Superstore: 01332 209000
e-mail: pressoffice@dcfc.co.uk
Website: www.dcfc.co.uk

KEY PERSONNEL

Chairman: L Pickering
Vice-Chairman: P J Gadsby
Chief Executive: K Loring
Directors: J N Kirkland OBE
R Clarke
Club Secretary: K Pearson ACIS
Manager: Jim Smith

SPONSORS

EDS

FANZINES

Official Magazine:
Rampage

COLOURS

Home: White shirts with black shorts and white stockings
Away: Yellow shirts with blue sleeves, blue shorts and blue stockings

NICKNAME

The Rams

HONOURS

League Champions: 1971–72, 1974–75
Division Two Champions: 1911–12
1914–15, 1968–69, 1986–87
Division Three (North) Champions:
1956–57
FA Cup: 1946

RECORD GOALSCORER

Steve Bloomer – 292 league goals,
1892–1906, 1910–14

BIGGEST WIN

9–0 v Wolverhampton Wanderers –
Division One, 10 January 1891

BIGGEST DEFEAT

2–11 v Everton – FA Cup 1st Round,
1889–90

SEASON REVIEW

The 1999–2000 season was an uncomfortable one for Derby. Used to the security of mid-table, Jim Smith's team were caught up in a relegation dogfight that threatened to end in disaster. The omens in pre-season were not good. Fans' favourite Paulo Wanchope had left the club, Igor Stimac's future was in limbo (he followed Wanchope to West Ham United shortly after the start of the season) and striker Dean Sturridge was once more back on the transfer list.

On paper, a 0–0 draw away to Leeds on the opening day seemed a good result, but despite some good defending Derby rarely threatened to score and their need for a new striker was immediately obvious.

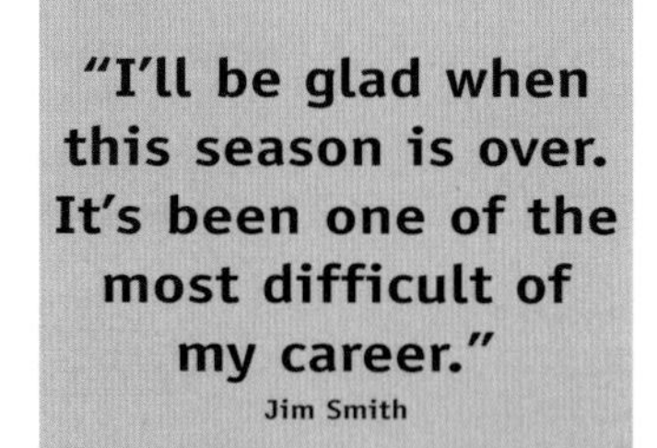

"I'll be glad when this season is over. It's been one of the most difficult of my career."
Jim Smith

Efforts to sign Esteban Fuertes, the second highest scorer in the Argentinean league, were persistently held up by work permit problems and the team staggered to three consecutive league defeats.

Fuertes finally arrived at the end of August, helping the Rams to a 2–0 win at Sheffield Wednesday and scoring the only goal of the game in his home debut against Everton, a performance that prompted Jim Smith to describe his forward as "lucky".

But fortune certainly failed to shine on Derby during September. A deal for Sheffield Wednesday's Benito Carbone fell through because of the striker's reluctance to commit himself to the club beyond the end of the season, while on the pitch the team were in dreadful form.

Back-to-back home defeats by promoted sides Sunderland (who hammered the Rams 5–0) and Bradford saw the club drop into the bottom three. Matters were exacerbated when Lars Bohinen criticised Jim Smith on his website, accusing his manager of lacking tactical nous. Smith reacted by fining Bohinen and putting him on the transfer list. But his promise that Bohinen would never play for the club again proved hollow, as the outspoken Norwegian was selected just days later in the side that beat Swansea 3–1 in the Worthington Cup.

The Bohinen saga was too much for many fans, who were also frustrated by Derby's poor form. When the more vociferous among them were told by the chairman Lionel Pickering to shut up or take their custom to bitter rivals Nottingham Forest, the relationship between the club and its fans reached a new low.

October saw Derby eliminated from the Worthington Cup by Bolton. And spirits were hardly lifted when the team slumped to their lowest position of the season after a lethargic performance at St James's Park saw them lose 2–0 to a rapidly improving Newcastle United side.

The pressure that was mounting in the local press was reflected on the pitch, where a combination of mistimed tackles and desperate challenges was manifesting itself in a disproportionately high number of yellow cards. With 39 bookings by the end of October, the club were the most persistently punished in the Premiership; they were to end the season with the most bookings as well.

This abrasive side to their game was put to good use against Chelsea, though, with two late goals from Rory Delap giving Derby a 3–1 win in a game during which they comprehensively outfought their visitors. That result lifted them out of the bottom three and eased the pressure on the manager and his players.

Unfortunately, November brought successive defeats by Liverpool,

93 Derby earned more yellow cards

SEASON REVIEW

Manchester United and Arsenal that plunged the club back into the relegation zone. Jim Smith was particularly infuriated by the performance of the referees in these three games, feeling that Derby's more "glamorous" opponents had been favoured by the officials.

Against Liverpool, Stefano Eranio had had his leg broken, but Uriah Rennie failed to show a single yellow card to the Merseyside club, while the 2–1 home defeat by Manchester United was notable for Stefan Schnoor's sending-off which Smith claimed had been precipitated by several Manchester United players running 20 yards to remonstrate with referee Mike Reed.

Off the pitch, events took a similiarly depressing turn when Fuertes was deported after his passport was found to be fake. He never returned. Francesco Baiano also departed and Mikkel Beck left the club on loan, but better news came when Georgian wizard Georgi Kinkladze joined on loan from Ajax and Craig Burley arrived from Celtic.

"The problem we've had is that I am never sure what we are going to do in the next game."
Jim Smith

Defeat in the FA Cup by Second Division Burnley merely served to highlight Derby's plight. The club entered the Millennium in the bottom three with just 16 points. Burnley were the ninth club to win at Pride Park and Derby's Premiership record at home read: Played 8, Won 2, Lost 6. There was no doubt that this lack of home form was to blame for their situation, and that the strikers were to blame for a run which had seen the Rams score just seven goals at their own ground.

Smith reacted by signing Belgian hitman Branko Strupar and giving non-league find Malcolm Christie an extended run in the first team. The move worked a treat.

With Strupar scoring the first Premiership goal of the year 2000 with a second-minute strike against Watford and Christie bagging a brace in the 4–1 thrashing of Middlesbrough, Derby started the New Year with an unbeaten run of five matches that saw them climb to 16th place by the end of January.

The team were still a long way from safety, though. Even a 4–0 hammering of relegation rivals Wimbledon was not enough to take them beyond the reach of Bradford, who continued to battle gamely just two points behind the Rams. Successive defeats by Liverpool, Manchester United and Aston Villa did little to improve the situation, but an amazing 4–4 draw with Bradford and a welcome 2–0 victory over Southampton took the Rams six points clear of the drop zone and made the last few games of the season relatively comfortable.

Safety could not disguise the fact that Derby had had a shocking season. Only relegated Watford and Sheffield Wednesday lost as many home games as the Rams, and only Wednesday scored fewer goals at their own ground.

Some hard-earned draws away from home saved the club from relegation. But if significant strides are not made, then Derby might not be as lucky in the 2000–01 season.

Smith is obviously confident that he can take the team back to a position of mid-table comfort, and the Derby board have backed their veteran manager by giving him a two-year extension on his contract.

It remains to be seen whether Smith's players have the necessary desire to justify their manager's faith in their ability. Many of them may well find themselves replaced before or during the course of the 2000–2001 campaign.

than any other Premiership team

DERBY COUNTY

DATE	OPPONENT	SCORE	ATT.	BAIANO	BECK	BOERTIEN	BOHINEN	BORBOKIS	BURLEY	BURTON	CARBONARI	CHRISTIE	DELAP	DORIGO	ELLIOT
7.8.99	Leeds Utd A	0–0	40,118	67	s23	–	–	s13	–	s45	90	–	90□	90□	–
10.8.99	Arsenal H	1–2	25,901	90	79	–	–	s33□	–	s11	79□	–	90^{1}	–	–
14.8.99	Middlesbro H	1–3	24,045	45	45	–	s19□	s45	–	90^{1}□	90□	–	90	–	–
21.8.99	Coventry A	0–2	17,685	–	s61	–	s23	90	–	29□	90	–	90	–	–
25.8.99	Sheff Wed A	2–0	20,943	–	s25	–	71	78	–	–	90	–	90^{1}	–	–
28.8.99	Everton H	1–0	26,550	s45	–	–	45	90	–	–	90□	–	90	–	–
11.9.99	Wimbledon A	2–2	12,282	s20	s37	–	s45	–	–	70	90^{1}	–	45	–	–
18.9.99	Sunderland H	0–5	28,264	s45	45	–	s36	–	–	–	90	–	90□	–	–
25.9.99	Bradford H	0–1	31,035	83□	–	–	–	65	–	–	90	s12	90	90	90
4.10.99	Southampton A	3–3	14,208	–	$s38^{1}$	–	–	s8	–	–	56	–	90^{1}	90	–
16.10.99	Tottenham H	0–1	29,815	s17	90	–	–	82	–	73	–	–	90□	90	–
25.10.99	Newcastle A	0–2	35,614	45	90	–	–	–	–	s33□	–	s45	90	84	–
30.10.99	Chelsea H	3–1	28,614	–	–	–	–	s8	–	90^{1}□	90	–	90^{2}	90	–
6.11.99	Liverpool A	0–2	44,467	–	–	–	–	s69	–	90	90	–	90	90	–
20.11.99	Man Utd H	1–2	33,370	–	–	–	–	74□	–	–	90□	s16	90^{1}	90	–
28.11.99	Arsenal A	1–2	37,964	–	–	–	–	–	–	73	45	–	90□	90□	s45
5.12.99	Leeds Utd H	0–1	29,455	–	–	–	–	–	90	78	90	s12	90	s16	90
18.12.99	Leicester A	1–0	18,581	–	–	–	–	–	90	90□	–	–	90□	90	90
26.12.99	Aston Villa H	0–2	33,222	–	–	–	65	–	90	75	–	s25	–	45	90
28.12.99	West Ham A	1–1	24,998	–	s8	–	90	–	90□	–	90	–	–	–	90
3.1.00	Watford H	2–0	28,072	–	–	–	–	–	90	–	90	–	90	59	90
15.1.00	Middlesbro A	4–1	32,745	–	–	–	60	–	90^{1}	90^{1}	90□	76^{2}	90	–	90
22.1.00	Coventry H	0–0	28,381	–	–	–	90	–	90	81	90	s9	90	–	45
5.2.00	Sheff Wed H	3–3*	30,100	–	–	–	–	–	90^{1}	–	–	90	90	72	90
12.2.00	Everton A	1–2	33,268	–	–	–	–	–	90□	–	–	s45	–	58□	90
26.2.00	Sunderland A	1–1	41,960	–	–	–	–	–	77□	–	90□	$s45^{1}$	90	–	90
4.3.00	Wimbledon H	4–0	28,384	–	–	–	33	–	–	$s19^{1}$	90	87^{1}	90	–	90
11.3.00	Man Utd A	1–3	61,619	–	–	–	–	–	–	–	90	90	90	74□	90
18.3.00	Liverpool H	0–2	33,378	–	–	–	–	–	–	–	79□	90	90	–	90□
25.3.00	Aston Villa A	0–2	28,613	–	–	–	–	–	–	–	90	s29	90	–	61
2.4.00	Leicester H	3–0	25,763	–	–	–	–	–	78^{1}	–	90	–	90^{1}	s37	s8
8.4.00	Watford A	0–0	16,579	–	–	–	–	–	90□	–	90	s12	90	s14	–
15.4.00	West Ham H	1–2	31,202	–	–	–	–	–	90	–	–	s46	90□	89	90
21.4.00	Bradford A	4–4	18,276	–	–	–	–	–	90^{2}□	–	90□	90□	26^{1}■	90	90
24.4.00	Southampton H	2–0	29,403	–	–	s45	–	–	90□	–	–	90^{1}	90	45	–
29.4.00	Tottenham A	1–1	33,044	–	–	s34	–	–	90□	45□	90^{1}□	90□	90	–	–
6.5.00	Newcastle H	0–0	32,724	–	–	–	s32	–	90	90	90□	90	–	90	–
14.5.00	Chelsea A	0–4	35,084	–	–	–	64	–	90	90	–	90	64	90	57

□ Yellow card, ■ Red card, s Substitute, 90^{2} Goals scored

*including one own goal

1999–2000 PREMIERSHIP APPEARANCES

ERANIO	FUERTES	HARPER	HOULT	JACKSON	JOHNSON	KINKLADZE	LAURSEN	MORRIS	MURRAY	NIMNI	POOM	POWELL	PRIOR	RIGGOTT	ROBINSON	SCHNOOR	STRUPAR	STURRIDGE	TOTAL
77□	–	–	–	–	90□	–	90	–	–	–	90	90□	90	–	–	–	–	45	990
90	–	s11	–	–	90	–	90	–	–	–	90	90□	90□	–	–	57	–	–	990
71	–	–	–	–	90	–	90	–	–	–	90	90	90	–	–	s45	–	–	990
67	–	s15□	–	–	90□	–	90□	–	–	–	90	90	90	–	–	–	–	75□	990
s19	65	–	90	–	90	–	90	–	–	–	–	90	90	–	–	90	–	s12[1]	990
s45□	71[1]□	–	90	–	45□	–	90	–	–	–	–	90	90	–	–	90	–	s19	990
90	90□	–	90	–	90[1]	–	90	–	–	–	–	90	90	–	–	53	–	–	990
54	90	s45	90	–	90	–	90	–	–	–	–	90	90	–	–	45	–	–	990
–	37■	s25	90	–	90□	–	–	–	s7	–	–	–	90	–	–	–	–	78	937
–	52	s34	90□	–	90□	–	82[1]□	–	–	–	–	90□	90□	–	–	90□	–	90	990
90□	–	–	90	–	90	–	90	82	s8□	–	–	–	–	–	–	90	–	s8	990
90	–	–	90	–	90	–	90□	57	–	–	–	90□	s6	–	–	90	–	–	990
75	82	–	90	–	90	–	53	s15	–	–	–	90	s37	–	–	90□	–	–	990
21	51	–	90	–	51	–	90	–	–	–	–	90	s39	–	–	90	–	s39	990
–	–	–	–	–	90□	–	90	–	s16	–	90	90	–	–	90□	37■	–	74	937
–	–	–	–	–	90□	s30	90	–	–	60	90	90	90	–	s17	–	–	90[1]	990
–	–	–	–	–	90□	74	63□	–	–	–	90	90	s27□	–	–	–	–	90	990
–	–	–	–	–	90□	–	90	–	–	–	90	90[1]	88□	–	79	s2	s11	–	990
–	–	–	–	–	90	–	90	–	–	–	90	90	90□	–	s15	s45	90□	–	990
–	–	–	–	–	90	–	90□	–	–	–	90	90	90□	–	82	–	–	90[1]□	990
–	–	–	–	–	–	–	90	–	–	68	90	90□	s22	–	s64	s31	90[2]	26	990
–	–	–	–	–	90□	s14	–	–	–	s30□	90	90□	–	–	–	90	–	–	990
–	–	–	–	–	90	s45	90	–	–	–	90	–	–	–	–	90	90	–	990
61	–	–	–	–	90	s29	90	–	–	–	90	–	–	–	–	90	90[1]	s18	990
90	–	–	–	–	90□	90	90	–	–	s32[1]	90	–	90	–	s45	–	45	45	990
90	–	–	–	–	90	89□	90	–	–	–	90	90	–	–	–	s13	45	s1	990
90	–	–	–	–	90	71[1]	90	–	–	–	90	90	–	–	–	s57	–	s3[1]	990
90□	–	–	–	–	90□	90	90	–	–	–	90	–	–	–	–	45	s45[1]	s16	990
90	–	–	–	–	90	90	90	–	–	–	90	85	–	–	–	s11	90	s5	990
88	–	–	–	–	90	90	90	–	–	–	90	90	–	–	–	90□	90	s2	990
–	–	–	–	–	90	53□	90	–	s12	–	90□	90	–	–	–	82□	90	90[1]	990
–	–	–	–	–	90	76	90	–	–	–	90	90	–	–	–	90	90	78	990
–	–	–	–	–	90	–	90	–	–	–	90	90	–	–	s1	44	90	90[1]□	990
–	–	–	–	–	90□	s25	90	–	–	–	90	90	–	–	–	–	65[1]	–	926
–	–	–	–	–	90	89	90	–	s1	–	90	90[1]	–	–	–	90	90	–	990
–	–	–	–	–	90	90	90	–	s11	–	90□	90	–	–	–	40■	–	–	940
–	–	–	–	s1	–	45	89	–	58	–	90	90	–	–	–	90	–	s45	990
–	–	–	–	s26	90	–	90	–	s26	–	90	–	–	s33	–	–	–	90	990

THE MANAGER

JIM SMITH

At times it looked as though Derby's 1999–2000 struggle was taking its toll on manager Jim Smith. He had more than a few harsh words to say about many of the refereeing performances during the Rams' campaign, and described the season as "the most difficult I have experienced", despite nearly 30 years in league management.

Derby County is Smith's 10th managerial port of call, and he also had spells as a player with Sheffield United, Aldershot Town, Halifax Town and Lincoln City.

Smith's first success as a manager came in 1974 when he guided Colchester to promotion from the old Fourth Division, and in 1980 he took Birmingham City into the top flight.

In the mid–1980s Smith guided Oxford United to Third and Second Division Championships, and as manager of Portsmouth in 1992–93 his side came within a single goal of reaching the lofty heights of the Premiership.

He joined Derby in June 1995, and immediately steered them to the top flight in his first season in charge, where they have stayed ever since.

Smith will not want 2000–01 to be a repeat of 1999–2000, however, and will believe that he has a talented enough combination of youth and experience to aim for a top 10 place.

LEAGUE POSITION

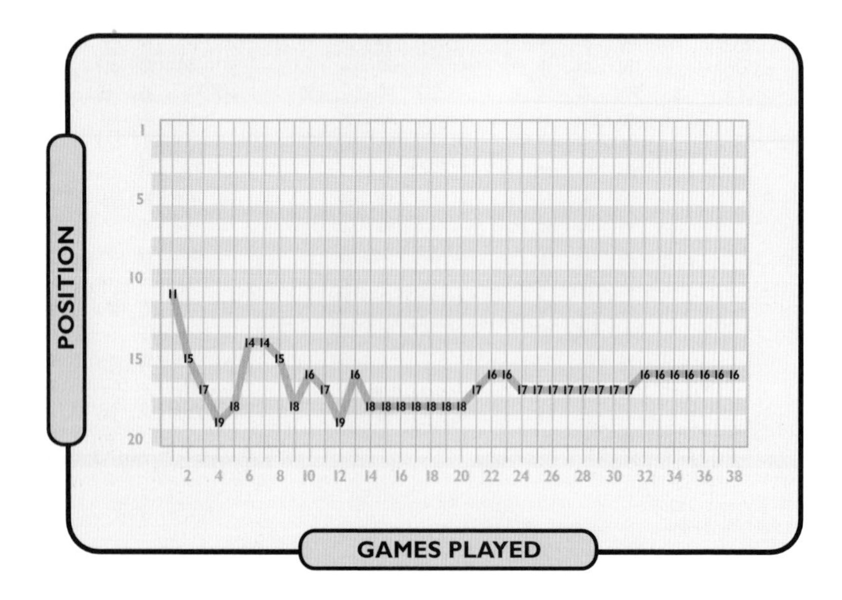

7 Derby scored more last-minute goals than

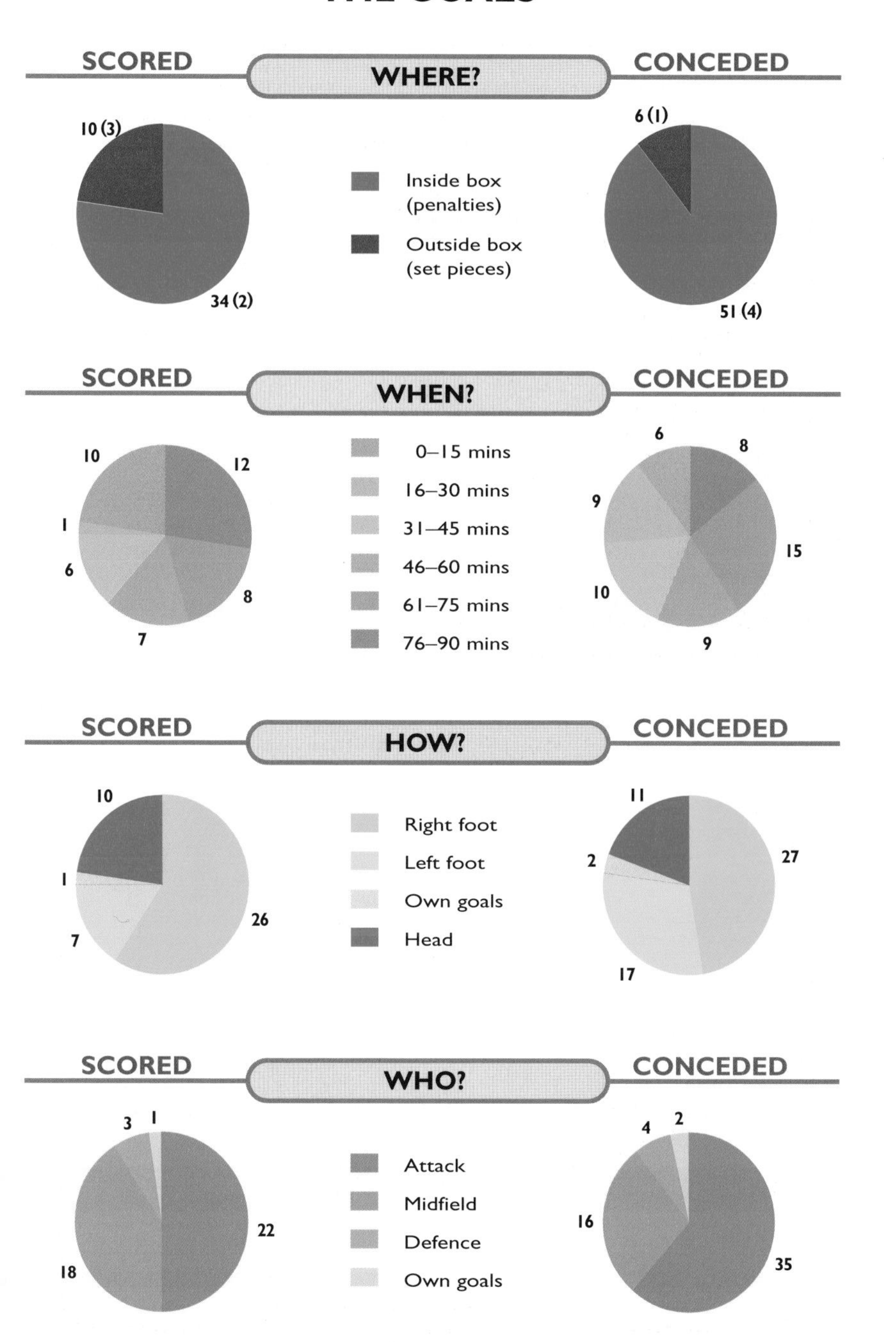
THE GOALS
SCORED
WHERE?
CONCEDED
10 (3)
34 (2)
Inside box (penalties)
Outside box (set pieces)
6 (1)
51 (4)
SCORED
WHEN?
CONCEDED
10
12
1
6
8
7
0–15 mins
16–30 mins
31–45 mins
46–60 mins
61–75 mins
76–90 mins
6
8
9
15
10
9
SCORED
HOW?
CONCEDED
10
1
7
26
Right foot
Left foot
Own goals
Head
11
2
27
17
SCORED
WHO?
CONCEDED
3
1
22
18
Attack
Midfield
Defence
Own goals
4
2
16
35

any of their Premiership rivals

DERBY COUNTY

	BAIANO	BECK	BOERTIEN	BOHINEN	BORBOKIS	BURLEY	BURTON	CARBONARI	CHRISTIE	DELAP	DORIGO	ELLIOTT	ERANIO
APPEARANCES													
Start	5	5	0	8	6	18	15	29	10	34	20	18	17
Sub	4	6	2	5	6	0	4	0	11	0	3	2	2
Minutes on pitch	457	541	79	673	655	1595	1262	2509	1179	2925	1673	1566	1388
GOAL ATTEMPTS													
Goals	0	1	0	0	0	5	4	2	5	8	0	0	0
Shots on target	1	7	0	3	1	11	9	10	20	18	3	3	3
Shots off target	8	8	0	4	4	13	13	15	6	28	1	4	4
Shooting accuracy	11%	47%	0%	43%	20%	46%	41%	40%	77%	39%	75%	43%	43%
PASSING													
Goal assists	2	0	0	1	0	1	1	0	2	4	0	0	0
Long passes	31	12	4	68	56	204	45	403	32	237	186	196	91
Short passes	222	199	22	261	213	454	391	458	215	874	438	356	590
PASS COMPLETION													
Own half %	91%	84%	79%	77%	81%	78%	79%	76%	74%	69%	75%	69%	89%
Opposition half %	67%	62%	58%	67%	66%	60%	58%	49%	58%	57%	65%	49%	72%
CROSSING													
Total crosses	25	2	1	14	58	49	17	19	23	66	54	11	45
Cross completion %	36%	0%	100%	14%	36%	22%	29%	63%	22%	32%	33%	27%	33%
DRIBBLING													
Dribbles & runs	20	16	4	34	40	46	36	30	51	116	45	20	52
Dribble completion %	80%	88%	100%	76%	80%	83%	83%	87%	55%	77%	87%	100%	83%
DEFENDING													
Tackles made	6	11	2	40	22	54	22	95	16	110	56	71	45
Tackles won %	50%	36%	0%	63%	77%	54%	68%	49%	50%	51%	63%	49%	42%
Blocks	0	3	1	2	0	10	3	78	1	50	30	44	7
Clearances	0	3	1	7	32	17	7	297	3	124	85	132	17
Interceptions	1	1	0	4	4	8	5	28	1	27	17	16	8
DISCIPLINE													
Fouls	9	8	1	10	10	24	44	34	22	35	22	18	20
Offside	4	6	0	0	3	2	26	3	19	6	0	2	5
Yellow cards	1	0	0	1	2	7	6	10	2	6	4	1	4
Red cards	0	0	0	0	0	0	0	0	0	1	0	0	0

GOALKEEPER NAME	START/ (SUB)	TIME ON PITCH	GOALS CONCEDED	MINS/GOALS CONCEDED	SAVES MADE	SAVES/ SHOTS
HOULT	10	900	17	53	32	65%
POOM	28	2520	40	63	104	72%

PLAYERS' STATISTICS

FUERTES	HARPER	JACKSON	JOHNSON	KINKLADZE	LAURSEN	MORRIS	MURRAY	NIMNI	POWELL	PRIOR	RIGGOTT	ROBINSON	SCHNOOR	STRUPAR	STURRIDGE	TOTAL	RANK
8	0	0	36	12	36	2	1	2	31	15	0	3	22	13	14		
0	5	2	0	5	0	1	7	2	0	5	1	5	7	2	11		
538	130	27	3156	1090	3167	154	139	190	2785	1479	33	393	1867	1111	1219		
1	0	0	1	1	1	0	0	1	2	0	0	0	0	5	6	44*	17th
3	2	0	5	2	3	1	2	1	12	2	0	0	5	15	17	159	=16th
2	0	0	14	10	5	0	0	3	17	4	1	2	5	19	12	202	13th
60%	100%	0%	26%	17%	38%	100%	100%	25%	41%	33%	0%	0%	50%	44%	59%	44%	15th
0	0	0	4	6	0	0	0	0	1	0	0	0	1	0	0	23	20th
5	5	3	290	87	390	5	16	15	185	113	1	7	216	46	32	2981	16th
142	49	7	960	393	537	31	46	48	933	318	5	103	399	410	308	9382	18th
77%	90%	75%	78%	88%	81%	100%	86%	80%	81%	84%	50%	83%	77%	76%	88%	78%	13th
45%	66%	67%	65%	79%	50%	48%	65%	69%	71%	55%	0%	48%	57%	65%	65%	62%	16th
4	5	0	135	41	28	1	4	5	16	7	0	3	42	11	16	702	=16th
25%	60%	0%	34%	32%	39%	100%	50%	20%	31%	0%	0%	33%	38%	45%	25%	33%	2nd
26	8	0	93	110	33	12	6	11	63	21	0	10	28	18	59	1009	14th
58%	50%	0%	86%	75%	94%	50%	67%	55%	83%	86%	0%	100%	93%	94%	86%	80%	2nd
12	2	0	121	17	81	3	8	2	95	40	2	2	78	7	11	1033	8th
50%	100%	0%	46%	47%	62%	33%	38%	50%	58%	58%	100%	50%	40%	71%	45%	53%	7th
0	0	1	19	2	94	1	0	2	25	30	2	0	42	3	3	453	5th
0	0	1	74	0	261	5	0	2	62	205	5	1	168	5	3	1540	14th
0	0	0	35	2	34	1	0	0	21	24	0	0	13	2	2	254	11th
13	0	0	47	14	30	1	3	7	44	22	0	12	31	19	36	537	12th
11	3	0	0	1	0	0	0	0	1	0	0	10	1	19	12	134	=8th
2	1	0	13	2	5	0	1	1	6	6	0	1	4	1	3	93	1st
1	0	0	0	0	0	0	0	0	0	0	0	0	2	0	0	4	=5th

*Including one own goal

CROSSES CAUGHT	CROSSES PUNCHED	CROSSES NOT CLAIMED	CATCH SUCCESS	THROWS/ SHORT KICKS	% COMPLETION	LONG KICKS	% COMPLETION
24	7	1	96%	67	85%	254	37%
89	20	2	98%	140	90%	827	41%

PLAYER OF THE SEASON

PLAYER	INDEX SCORE
RORY DELAP	901
Horacio Carbonari	843
Mart Poom	783
Tony Dorigo	772*
Stefan Schnoor	741**
Steve Elliott	732**
Darryl Powell	718
Jacob Laursen	698
Craig Burley	670***
Seth Johnson	650

All players played 75 minutes in at least 19 matches except those marked * who played 14 games, ** who played 15 games and *** who played 18 games.

In a disappointing season for the Rams, the only high point was the form of some of their younger players. Rory Delap, who had come down to the east Midlands from Carlisle, excelled for Derby in the variety of positions in which he operated during 1999–2000.

The young Irishman played in defence, midfield and attack as Derby tried to fight off the threat of relegation. Delap scored eight times in the Premiership – making him the Rams' top scorer – and created another four as he became Derby's player of the season, with 901 points in the Opta Season Index for 1999–2000.

The 1998–99 player of the season, Horacio Carbonari, had another consistent season at Pride Park. The accomplished central defender made 291 clearances – more than any other Derby player – and helped himself to two goals as he achieved an average score of 843 points.

Estonian 'keeper Mart Poom saw off competition from Russell Hoult for the number one jersey with a string of fine performances. He claimed more crosses than any other Premiership stopper during the course of the season and his saves-to-shots ratio of 72% matched the average for a Premiership 'keeper. Summer signing from Crewe, Seth Johnson, also made the top 10 and earned an England under-21 call up with his strong midfield displays. He will hope to further enhance his reputation at Pride Park in 2000–01.

Several players were unable to play a full part in the season such as Tony Dorigo, Stefan Schnoor, Steve Elliott and Craig Burley, but they were still able to force their way into the Index along with the longer-standing, reliable performers such as Darryl Powell and Jacob Laursen.

The Rams will be hoping a more settled playing staff will bring a greater consistency next year and that they can avoid the fight for survival at the foot of the Premiership which dominated their 1999–2000 campaign.

13 Seth Johnson earned the joint-highest number

FIVE OF THE BEST

Derby County won just two of their first 12 league games and things did not get too much better for the Rams. Jim Smith's team avoided relegation, but they failed to reach the 40-point total and had to rely on the weakness of other sides. A lack of goals almost cost them dear, and it is something they they will have to rectify in 2000–01.

TOP GOALSCORERS

	GOALS	GOALS/SHOTS
RORY DELAP	8	17%
Dean Sturridge	6	21%
Craig Burley	5	21%
Malcolm Christie	5	19%
Branko Strupar	5	15%

It says something about a season if a club's top scorer is a wing-back, but that was the case with Derby County and Rory Delap. The Irish international is one of the most promising youngsters in the top flight, but he is no centre-forward. The Rams' strikers were relatively accurate in front of goal; it was just that they did not hit enough shots. However, the emergence of Malcolm Christie and the form of midfield warrior Craig Burley should help the team as they try to avoid a repeat of 1999–2000.

Derby's big summer signing of 1999 was Seth Johnson, and the £3 million former Crewe Alexandra man was a rare success. His passing was less accurate than Darryl Powell's or Stefano Eranio's, but he was involved more than them, and he ended the campaign with four assists. The aforementioned Eranio was as silky as always but his season was blighted by injury, a broken leg at Anfield confining him to the sidelines.

TOP PASSERS

	SUCC PASSES	COMPLETION
SETH JOHNSON	862	69%
Darryl Powell	828	74%
Rory Delap	652	59%
Jacob Laursen	606	65%
Stefano Eranio	520	76%

TOP TACKLERS

	WON	SUCCESS
RORY DELAP	56	51%
Seth Johnson	56	46%
Horacio Carbonari	47	49%
Stefan Schnoor	31	40%
Darryl Powell	55	58%

Seth Johnson and Rory Delap were not only classy but gritty as well, both winning 56 tackles in 1999–2000. Argentine Horacio Carbonari was often wildly inconsistent but capable of making some important challenges for the Rams. Another of Jim Smith's foreign imports, German Stefan Schnoor, makes the top five, having won 40% of his tackles. There is a mention, too, for Darryl Powell, whose 58% success rate was well above average for the Premiership.

Struggling teams are often ill-disciplined and it was no surprise that Derby were the third worst-behaved team in the Premiership, picking up more yellow cards than any other side. Stefan Schnoor and Seth Johnson collected 23 between them, with the young English left-footer having to visit the FA for a reprimand. But the only player in the top five with a red card is Delap, who received his marching orders in the remarkable 4–4 draw with Bradford on Good Friday.

DISCIPLINE

	POINTS	FOULS & CARDS
SETH JOHNSON	86	47F, 13Y, 0R
Horacio Carbonari	64	34F, 10Y, 0R
Darryl Powell	62	44F, 6Y, 0R
Deon Burton	62	44F, 6Y, 0R
Rory Delap	59	35F, 6Y, 1R

of yellow cards in the top flight

ACTION	BORBOKIS	BURTON	CARBONARI	DELAP	DORIGO	ERANIO	FUERTES	HOULT	JOHNSON	LAURSEN	MORRIS	POWELL	PRIOR	SCHNOOR	TOTAL	CHELSEA
Time On Pitch	8	90	90	90	90	75	82	90	90	53	15	90	37	90	990	990
GOALS																
Goal	–	1	–	2	–	–	–	–	–	–	–	–	–	–	3	1
Shot on target	–	1	–	1	–	–	–	–	–	–	–	–	–	–	2	3
Shot off target	–	3	–	1	–	–	1	–	–	–	–	–	–	–	5	6
Blocked shot	–	–	1	1	1	3	1	–	–	–	–	–	–	–	7	3
Own goal	–	–	–	–	–	–	–	–	–	–	–	–	–	–	–	–
PASSES																
Pass to own player	4	17	13	17	12	23	9	–	23	10	1	27	5	11	172	266
Pass to opposition	1	17	6	18	5	7	16	–	10	3	1	7	2	7	100	98
Cross to own player	–	1	2	1	–	–	1	–	2	–	–	–	–	1	8	2
Cross to opposition player	1	–	–	–	2	–	1	–	3	–	–	–	–	–	7	14
Goal assist	–	–	–	–	–	–	–	–	–	–	–	–	–	–	–	1
Pass completion %	67%	51%	71%	50%	63%	77%	37%	0%	66%	77%	50%	79%	71%	63%	63%	71%
TACKLES & CLEARANCES																
Tackle	–	2	–	3	2	1	1	–	4	–	–	3	1	3	20	18
Clearances, blocks and Interceptions	1	3	24	7	13	–	–	1	5	9	–	–	4	21	88	75
DRIBBLES & RUNS																
Dribble ball retained	–	2	3	2	1	3	2	–	3	–	1	–	–	3	20	26
Dribble ball lost	–	–	–	–	–	–	–	–	–	–	1	–	–	–	1	
Dribble success %	0%	100%	100%	100%	100%	100%	100%	0%	100%	0%	50%	0%	0%	100%	95%	100%
DISCIPLINE																
Fouls	–	5	–	–	–	4	–	–	1	1	–	–	–	3	14	17
Penalty conceded	–	–	–	–	–	–	–	–	–	–	–	–	–	–	–	–
Free kick – offside	–	1	–	–	–	–	2	–	–	–	–	–	–	–	3	3
Yellow cards	–	1	–	–	–	–	–	–	–	–	–	–	–	1	2	1
Red cards	–	–	–	–	–	–	–	–	–	–	–	–	–	–	–	–
GOALKEEPERS																
Distribution to own player	–	–	–	–	–	–	–	17	–	–	–	–	–	–	17	13
Distribution to opposition player	–	–	–	–	–	–	–	13	–	–	–	–	–	–	13	15
Goalkeeper distribution %	0%	0%	0%	0%	0%	0%	0%	57%	0%	0%	0%	0%	0%	0%	57%	46%
Save	–	–	–	–	–	–	–	3	–	–	–	–	–	–	3	2
Ball caught	–	–	–	–	–	–	–	2	–	–	–	–	–	–	2	1
Ball dropped	–	–	–	–	–	–	–	–	–	–	–	–	–	–	–	–
Goal conceded	–	–	–	–	–	–	–	1	–	–	–	–	–	–	1	3

Going into this game, Derby were one place off the bottom of the Premiership and had won only once in their last eight league and cup games, as well as having collected the worst defensive record in the Premiership at that stage. Few would have predicted a win against high-flying Chelsea.

30 October 1999
3–1
DERBY COUNTY
VS.
CHELSEA

Earlier that month, The Blues had beaten both Manchester United and Galatasaray 5–0 and had just returned from the San Siro, where they had held AC Milan to a 1–1 draw. It was fair to say that the Blues were in good form.

However, Derby opened as the brighter side, with Deon Burton dispossessing Albert Ferrer and testing Ed De Goey in the opening few minutes. That should have served as a warning to the Londoners, as Burton had just returned to the side and was eager to impress.

After seven minutes he did just that. Esteban Fuertes danced into the right side of the area and cut inside Jes Hogh, who only managed to toe the ball back to the edge of the box. The onrushing Burton met the half-clearance with the side of his right foot to steer it past De Goey.

The Blues hit back within three minutes, when Ferrer hit in a deep cross from the right that fell to Frank Leboeuf. The Frenchman controlled the ball before hitting a shot over Russell Hoult into the Derby goal.

But the visitors were not allowed to build on that. Jim Smith's side all worked hard for each other and for the majority of the game it was hard to tell which side were in the Champions League and which were in the relegation zone.

Stefano Eranio was twisting and turning throughout, and almost set up a second goal for the Rams. The former AC Milan player threaded a pass through for Fuertes, who shot over. The Argentinean forced De Goey to collect at his near post soon after, and just before the break Burton crashed a header against the bar after great work from Rory Delap.

Leboeuf – captain in the absence of Marcel Desailly – was withdrawn just before the hour after being given a torrid time by the livewire Burton.

The latter stages saw Derby continue to attack and, just as it looked as if they were going to end up with only a point, they got the second goal that their play had deserved, with 10 minutes remaining.

A poor clearing header fell to Delap and the Irish international controlled the ball on the edge of the area before curling a great shot into the far corner. The game was put beyond doubt in the 88th minute after Lee Morris surged down the right wing and cut inside the Chelsea box. Bernard Lambourde's desperate challenge fell to Delap and the skilful Ram's first-time strike deflected off Lambourde's back and into the net.

The Midlanders' creative play was excellent and they had 17 shots, while Chelsea only managed 13 in the game. At the back, Carbonari played like an old English-style centre-back and put in a performance of solidity and dependability. The Argentinean completed 24 clearances, blocks and interceptions as Chelsea were thwarted time and again.

than those from any other side

one2one

EVERTON

ADDRESS

Goodison Park, Liverpool L4 4EL

CONTACT NUMBERS

Telephone: 0151 330 2200
Fax: 0151 286 9112
Ticket Office: 0151 330 2300
Ticket Line: 09068 121599
Clubcall: 09068 121199
Everton FC Megastore: 0151 330 2030
e-mail: everton@evertonfc.com
Website: www.evertonfc.com

KEY PERSONNEL

Chairman: Sir Phillip Carter CBE
Deputy Chairman: B Kenwright
Directors: K M Tamlin
M J L Abercromby
Lord Grantchester
P Gregg, J Woods
Club Secretary: M J Dunford
Manager: Walter Smith OBE

SPONSORS

One2One

FANZINES

When Skies Are Grey
Speke From The Harbour
Satis?

COLOURS

Home: Blue shirts with white shorts and blue stockings
Away: White shirts, blue shorts and white stockings

NICKNAME

The Toffees

HONOURS

League Champions: 1890–91, 1914–15 1927–28, 1931–32, 1938–39, 1962–63 1969–70, 1984–85, 1986–87
Division Two Champions: 1930–31
FA Cup: 1906, 1933, 1966, 1984, 1995
European Cup Winners' Cup: 1985

RECORD GOALSCORER

William Ralph 'Dixie' Dean – 349 league goals, 1925–37

BIGGEST WIN

9–1 v Manchester City – Division One, 3 September 1906

BIGGEST DEFEAT

4–10 v Tottenham Hotspur – Division One, 11 October 1968

SEASON REVIEW

Given the circumstances in which it started, the 1999–2000 season at Everton must go down as a considerable success. Widely expected to struggle, the Merseyside club eventually finished in 13th place in the Premiership table – just three points outside the top 10.

Such comfort seemed a long way off at the start of the season. Craig Short had departed for Blackburn Rovers, accusing Everton of being a "selling club". And while Kevin Campbell had signed a permanent deal, the names of the players who had left Goodison Park (Olivier Dacourt and Marco Materazzi in particular) seemed to vindicate Short's claims.

Further bad news came when promising young striker Francis Jeffers, unhappy with his wages, requested a transfer. Rather than caving in to the youngster's demands, Walter Smith dropped him from the team for the club's opening game of the season against Manchester United.

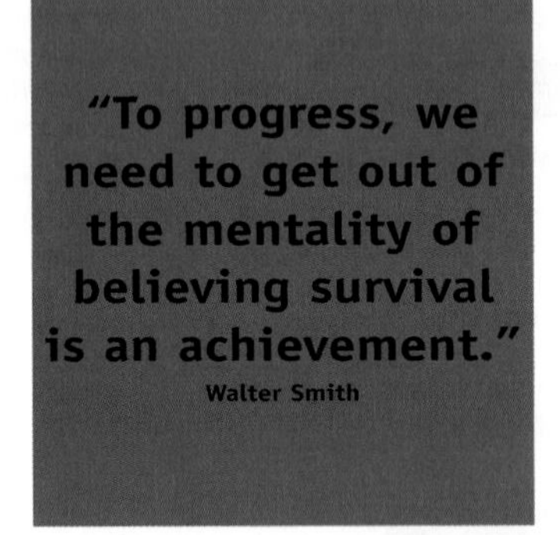

"To progress, we need to get out of the mentality of believing survival is an achievement."
Walter Smith

The match against the Champions was an exciting one. Clearly inferior to their opponents in terms of skill, Everton were nevertheless one of the few teams to match them for work-rate. United dominated for long periods, but the Toffees were heroic in defence and got their reward courtesy of a late Jaap Stam own-goal to earn a 1–1 draw.

After a heart-to-heart meeting with his manager, Jeffers withdrew his transfer request and was restored to the squad for the next game, the visit to Aston Villa; a clash that saw Everton crash 3–0 with John Collins sent off – the first of six Toffees to see red in a campaign where only West Ham had more players dismissed.

More awayday blues followed with a 3–2 loss in a thrilling game at Tottenham, but back at Goodison, the team surged into top gear, smashing a total of eight goals past Southampton and Wimbledon in their next two games. Now fully restored to the side, Jeffers wasted no time in re-establishing his partnership with Kevin Campbell, the pair bagging two goals each.

An early exit from the Worthington Cup at the hands of Second Division Oxford United was sweetened by further progress in the league as the team won all three of its Premiership fixtures. After Sheffield Wednesday were defeated away, unbeaten West Ham were put to the sword at Goodison Park. And then, in a result that delighted their supporters, the team beat Liverpool 1–0 at Anfield to go above their rivals into sixth place in the league.

Coventry scuppered Walter Smith's chances of leading his side to the best start by any Everton team in 20 years with a 1–1 draw at Goodison Park, and their results resumed a more familiar pattern with a run that saw the club failing to win in the next eight games.

Such was the decline that Walter Smith was moved to warn his squad publicly of the dangers of relegation. To their credit the team responded well, winning 3–1 at Watford before returning to Goodison Park on Boxing Day to record an incredible 5–0 victory over high-flying Sunderland.

There was a real air of optimism around the club. Bill Kenwright announced that he had finally acquired a controlling interest in the club, a deal that went through in January when Kenwright paid Peter Johnson £20 million for a 68% stake. Johnson finally left the board in March, bringing to a close what was a very controversial and deeply unhappy chapter in the club's history.

Walter Smith, impressed by the direction the club was going in, signed a new long-

26% Everton were the most clinical team inside the box –

SEASON REVIEW

term contract and although the team failed to win any of their three January Premiership fixtures, the supporters were further buoyed by a good run in the FA Cup. Exeter were the Toffees' first victims falling to a narrow 1–0 defeat at Goodison Park after clinging on bravely for a 0–0 draw at St James's Park. Birmingham City were beaten 2–0 in the fourth round courtesy of two David Unsworth penalties, and Preston North End were also defeated 2–0 to set up a sixth round date with Aston Villa. John Gregory's side proved too strong for Everton on the day, running out 2–1 winners despite having Benito Carbone dismissed.

Off the pitch things also took a turn for the worse as some of Smith's more important squad players were less than happy. Don Hutchison in particular had been angry with the club's new contract offer, calling it a "disgrace". He was relegated to the reserves at precisely the time his club needed him most. Kevin Campbell had picked up an injury that was to keep him out for the rest of the season and, with Francis Jeffers also forced to sit out most of what remained of the campaign, the club were left desperately short of firepower up front.

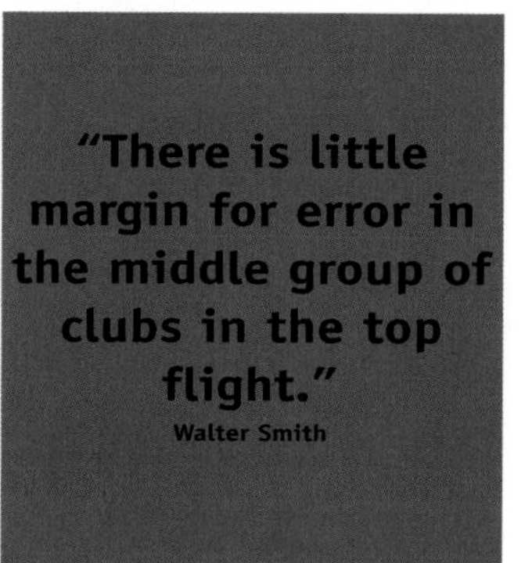

"There is little margin for error in the middle group of clubs in the top flight."
Walter Smith

Free-transfer signing Joe-Max Moore was doing his best to fill the gap, scoring some important goals, while Nick Barmby was also beginning to hit top form. But, although West Ham were beaten 4–0 at Upton Park, the team won just one other game in the absence of their key players, dropping out of contention for a European place as a result.

It was clear to everyone that Everton needed to strengthen, and Mark Hughes and Stephen Hughes were added to the squad to bolster the team during their run-in. Ironically, their home debuts coincided with Everton's first league defeat at Goodison Park all season, as Newcastle United scored twice in the last 10 minutes to win 2–0.

Watford and Bradford both conceded four goals on their visits to Goodison Park, but Everton scored just once more in their final four games.

Nevertheless, only three teams – Manchester United, Arsenal and Newcastle – scored more goals than Everton and although no team was caught offside more often, only United put away a greater percentage of their chances. Even when the goals dried up, few teams worked as hard as the men from Goodison Park, who finished with the second highest number of tackles and the third most interceptions in the Premiership.

With a fully-fit Kevin Campbell, Walter Smith's side might even have managed a top six spot. The shrewd Scotsman will realise that this says as much about the shortcomings of his squad as it does Campbell. Money is still in short supply, and Smith may again lose one or two important members of his squad. But with the backing of a new board he will be permitted to add to his playing staff ahead of 2000–01. A place in Europe, which at times seemed attainable in 1999–2000, will once again be the target.

That in itself is a testament to the fine job Smith has done at Goodison Park. With a board in place who share his ambitions, Everton appear to be on the up. This is not a time for complacency, though. The club has been very close to relegation on several occasions, a situation that is not acceptable to supporters who can still remember two Championships in the last 15 seasons.

more than one in four of their shots found the net

EVERTON

DATE	OPPONENT	SCORE	ATT.	BALL	BARMBY	CADAMARTERI	CAMPBELL	CLELAND	COLLINS	DUNNE	GEMMILL	GERRARD	GOUGH	GRANT	M.H
8.8.99	Man Utd H	1–1*	39,141	–	90	s20	90	–	90□	–	90	90	90□	–	–
11.8.99	Aston Villa A	0–3	30,337	90	90	–	90	–	50■	–	72	90	90	–	–
14.8.99	Tottenham A	2–3	34,539	–	90	s9	90	s17	90	90	73□	90	90	–	–
21.8.99	Southampton H	4–1*	31,755	–	90	s12	90^{1}	–	90	90	s25	90	90^{1}	–	–
25.8.99	Wimbledon H	4–0	32,818	s10	80^{1}	s8	90^{1}□	–	–	90	s4	90	90	–	–
28.8.99	Derby Co A	0–1	26,550	s24	80□	s24	90	–	90	25■	s10	90□	90	–	–
11.9.99	Sheff Wed A	2–0	23,539	–	90^{1}	–	90	–	s12□	–	90^{1}	90	90	–	–
19.9.99	West Ham H	1–0	35,154	s50	90□	–	90	s1	90	90□	s46	90	90	–	–
27.9.99	Liverpool A	1–0	44,802	90□	90	–	90^{1}	–	90	90	–	90	90□	–	–
2.10.99	Coventry H	1–1	34,839	90	45	s45	90	–	90	85□	s5	90	90	–	–
16.10.99	Arsenal A	1–4	38,042	90	90	s12	90	s11	90^{1}	–	78	90	90	–	–
24.10.99	Leeds Utd H	4–4	37,355	79	90	–	90^{2}	–	90	–	27	90	90	–	–
30.10.99	Middlesbro A	1–2	33,916	75	80	s15	90^{1}	–	90□	90	–	90	90	–	–
7.11.99	Newcastle A	1–1	36,164	45	90□	–	90^{1}	90□	90	90□	–	90□	–	–	–
20.11.99	Chelsea H	1–1	38,225	–	90	–	90^{1}	90	–	90	–	90	90	–	–
27.11.99	Aston Villa H	0–0	34,750	–	77	–	90	–	90	90	–	90	90	s13	–
4.12.99	Man Utd A	1–5	55,133	s27	63	–	90	s27	90	63	–	90	90	s10	–
18.12.99	Watford A	3–1	17,346	–	90^{1}	–	90□	69	90	90	–	90□	–	–	–
26.12.99	Sunderland H	5–0	40,017	–	74	–	90^{1}	s16	90	90	–	90	90	–	–
28.12.99	Bradford A	0–0	18,276	–	90	s14□	–	s22	52	90	s16	90	90	–	–
3.1.00	Leicester H	2–2	30,490	–	9	–	90	–	90	–	s81	90	90	–	–
15.1.00	Tottenham H	2–2	36,144	s9	90□	–	90^{1}	–	90	90	–	90	–	–	–
22.1.00	Southampton A	0–2	15,232	s27	90□	–	90	–	90	78	–	7	90	–	–
6.2.00	Wimbledon A	3–0	13,172	90	–	90	90^{2}	–	–	90	–	–	90	–	–
12.2.00	Derby Co H	2–1	33,268	90^{1}□	90	63□	90	–	s27□	90	–	–	90	–	–
26.2.00	West Ham A	4–0	26,025	90	84^{3}	–	90	–	90	–	–	–	90	–	–
4.3.00	Sheff Wed H	1–1	32,020	90	90	–	90	–	90	s14	–	–	–	–	–
11.3.00	Chelsea A	1–1	35,113	–	90□	90^{1}	–	–	90	90	–	90	90□	–	–
15.3.00	Coventry A	0–1	18,518	–	81	s24	–	–	90	90	s9	90	90	–	90
19.3.00	Newcastle H	0–2	32,512	s13	86	s25	–	–	90	s4	–	90	90	–	90□
25.3.00	Sunderland A	1–2	41,934	–	90^{1}	s8	–	–	90	90	–	90	90	–	82
1.4.00	Watford H	4–2	31,960	90	90	–	–	–	90	90	–	90	90	–	90^{1}
8.4.00	Leicester A	1–1	18,705	s6	90	s47	–	–	90	s28	–	90	62	–	–
15.4.00	Bradford H	4–0	30,646	s14	90^{1}	–	–	–	90^{1}	s45	–	90	–	–	80
21.4.00	Liverpool H	0–0	40,052	s6	89	–	–	–	90	90	–	90	–	–	81
29.4.00	Arsenal H	0–1	35,919	s45	90	–	–	–	90	45	–	90	–	–	90
8.5.00	Leeds Utd A	1–1	37,713	90□	90^{1}□	s18	–	–	90	50■	–	90	–	–	72□
14.5.00	Middlesbro H	0–2	34,663	90	90	–	–	–	90	90□	–	90	–	–	90

□ Yellow card, ■ Red card, s Substitute, 90^{2} Goals scored

*including one own goal

1999–2000 PREMIERSHIP APPEARANCES

S. HUGHES	HUTCHISON	JEFFERS	JEVONS	JOHNSON	MILLIGAN	MOORE	MYHRE	PEMBRIDGE	PHELAN	SIMONSEN	UNSWORTH	WARD	WATSON	WEIR	XAVIER	TOTAL
–	85	–	–	–	–	–	–	–	s5	–	90	70	90□	90	–	990
–	90□	s18	–	–	–	–	–	s18	–	–	90	72	–	90	–	950
–	s17	81	–	–	–	–	–	–	–	–	90[2]	73□	–	90	–	990
–	65□	78[1]	–	–	–	–	–	78	–	–	90	s12	–	90	–	990
–	90	82[1]	–	–	–	–	–	86	–	–	90[1]	90	–	90	–	990
–	90□	66	–	–	–	–	–	66	–	–	90	–	–	90	–	925
–	s26	78	–	–	–	–	–	47	–	–	90	64	90	90	s43	990
–	40	89[1]	–	–	–	–	–	–	–	–	44	–	–	90	90	990
–	90	75■	–	–	–	–	–	–	–	–	–	–	–	90	90	975
–	90	90[1]	–	–	–	–	–	–	–	–	–	–	–	90	90	990
–	90	–	–	–	–	–	–	–	–	–	79	–	–	90	90	990
–	90[1]	–	–	s11	–	–	–	s63	–	–	90	–	90	90[1]	–	990
–	90	–	–	s10	–	–	–	90□	–	–	90□	–	–	77■	–	977
–	90	–	–	s45□	–	–	–	90	–	–	90□	–	–	90	–	990
–	90□	90	–	–	–	–	–	90□	–	–	90	–	–	–	90	990
–	90□	90	–	–	–	–	–	90	–	–	90	–	–	90	–	990
–	–	90[1]	–	–	–	–	–	80	–	–	90	–	–	90□	90	990
–	90[1]	–	–	–	–	–	–	90	–	–	90[1]	–	s21	90	90	990
–	90[2]	74[1]	–	–	–	s16	–	90[1]	–	–	90	–	–	90□	–	990
–	90□	90	–	–	–	76	–	90	–	–	90	–	–	90	–	990
–	90[1]	71	–	–	–	s19	–	90□	–	–	90[1]	–	90□	90	–	990
–	90□	82	–	–	–	s8[1]	–	90	–	–	81	–	90□	90	–	990
–	90	90	–	–	–	s12	–	90	–	s83	63□	–	–	90□	–	990
–	84	–	–	–	–	90[1]□	90	90	–	–	90	–	–	90	s6	990
–	90	–	–	–	–	90[1]	90	90	–	–	–	–	–	90	–	990
–	–	–	–	–	–	90[1]	90	90	–	–	90	s6	–	90	90	990
–	–	–	–	–	–	90	90	90	–	–	90	76	–	90[1]	90	990
90	–	–	–	–	–	90	–	90	–	–	–	–	–	90	90	990
70	–	–	–	–	–	66	–	90	–	–	s20	–	–	90	90	990
77	–	–	–	–	–	65	–	90	–	–	90	–	–	90	90	990
90	s8	–	–	–	–	82	–	90	–	–	90	–	–	–	90	990
90[1]	–	–	–	–	–	90[2]	–	90	–	–	–	–	–	–	90	990
84	90[1]	–	–	–	–	43	–	90	–	–	90	–	–	90	90	990
90	90	s10	90	–	–	–	–	90[1]	–	–	45[1]	–	–	90	76	990
90	90	s9	–	–	–	–	–	84	–	–	90	s1	–	90	90	990
45	90	s45	s14	–	–	–	–	76□	–	–	90	–	–	90	90	990
90□	87■	–	–	–	–	–	–	78	–	–	90□	s12	–	90	–	947
90	90	s45	45	–	s45	–	–	–	–	–	90	–	–	45	–	990

THE MANAGER

WALTER SMITH

Everton fans had a rare but very welcome feeling around March and April – they knew their team would not be involved in a relegation battle.

In fact, such has been the turnaround in the club's fortunes since Walter Smith took over in July 1998 that many Evertonians believed that European qualification was possible.

Smith's playing career began at Dundee United in 1966, and after nine years with United he went to Dumbarton before returning to Tannadice for a second spell.

His first taste of management came in 1978 when he was assistant manager to the Scotland youth team.

He was then Jim McLean's right-hand man at Dundee United, was the same to Graeme Souness at Rangers and in 1991 was given the position of Rangers' manager when Souness left for Everton's rivals Liverpool.

Smith was boss at Ibrox from 1991–1998, winning six league titles, three Scottish Cups and three League Cups during what was a hugely successful spell with the Scottish giants.

The Everton manager is in the process of forming an excellent squad of players at the club, but will be keen to continue to add to it in order to be able to compete with the top teams in the Premiership.

LEAGUE POSITION

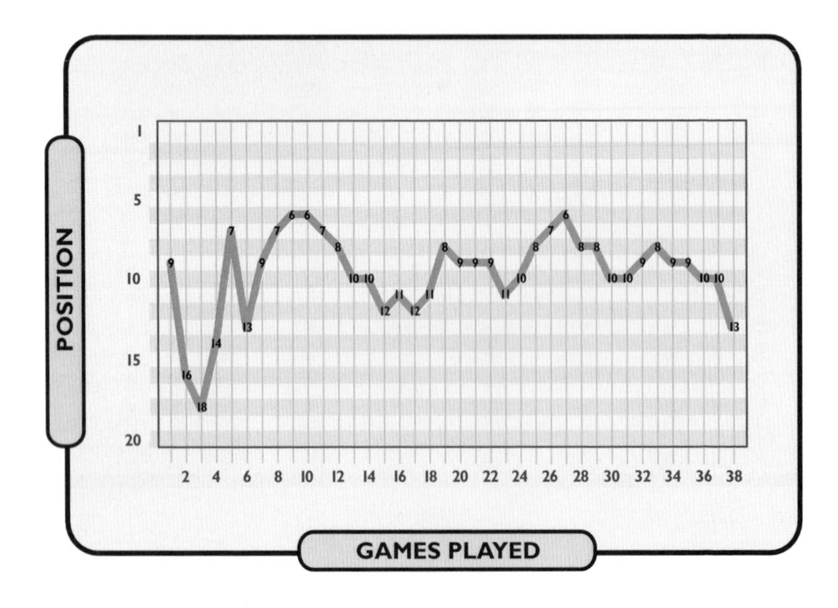

12 Everton scored the joint-most Premiership goals

THE GOALS

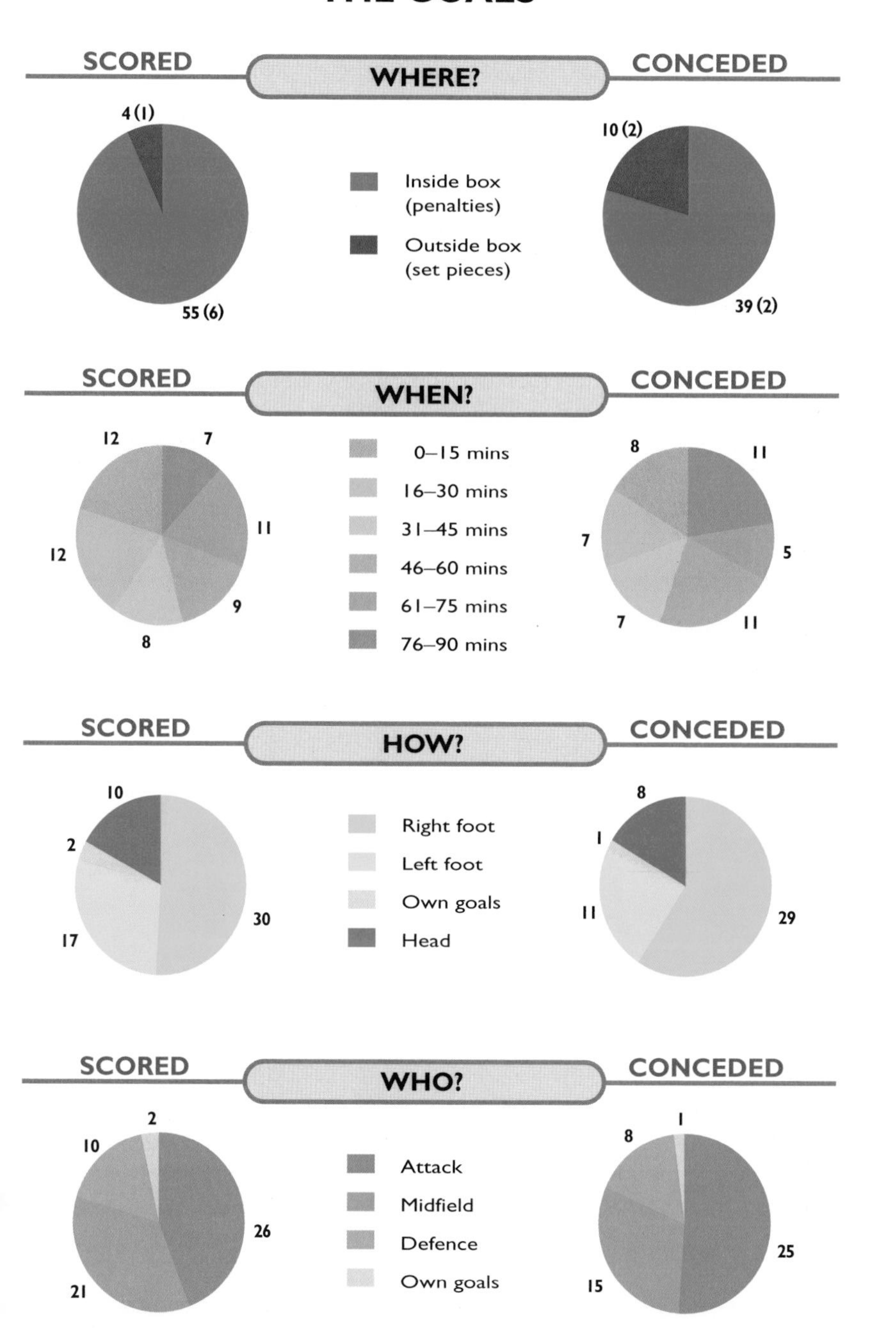

in the opening 15 minutes of matches

EVERTON

	BALL	BARMBY	CADAMARTERI	CAMPBELL	CLELAND	COLLINS	DUNNE	GEMMILL	GOUGH	GRANT	HUGHES M
APPEARANCES											
Start	14	37	3	26	3	33	27	6	29	0	9
Sub	11	0	14	0	6	2	4	8	0	2	0
Minutes on pitch	1420	3098	524	2340	343	2931	2327	626	2582	23	765
GOAL ATTEMPTS											
Goals	1	9	1	12	0	2	0	1	1	0	1
Shots on target	2	25	8	26	0	14	1	1	5	0	5
Shots off target	5	21	3	11	0	29	6	1	2	0	10
Shooting accuracy	29%	54%	73%	70%	0%	33%	14%	50%	71%	0%	33%
PASSING											
Goal assists	0	8	2	7	0	1	0	0	1	0	1
Long passes	180	230	17	67	29	342	305	40	258	2	54
Short passes	380	1207	140	898	111	1382	609	239	879	12	247
PASS COMPLETION											
Own half %	70%	81%	78%	79%	77%	85%	68%	82%	83%	75%	85%
Opposition half %	56%	65%	72%	72%	68%	77%	54%	71%	61%	80%	73%
CROSSING											
Total crosses	23	147	30	10	12	45	36	5	7	0	6
Cross completion %	4%	26%	33%	30%	25%	33%	19%	80%	43%	0%	33%
DRIBBLING											
Dribbles & runs	39	108	54	45	10	102	68	8	20	5	13
Dribble completion %	82%	80%	52%	78%	90%	81%	74%	88%	100%	100%	77%
DEFENDING											
Tackles made	56	94	7	31	8	176	102	20	71	1	8
Tackles won %	54%	49%	57%	65%	38%	61%	48%	40%	68%	0%	63%
Blocks	25	9	1	4	2	30	53	4	60	0	0
Clearances	72	30	0	18	18	38	205	11	352	0	0
Interceptions	9	27	2	7	3	44	28	8	30	0	0
DISCIPLINE											
Fouls	13	25	10	58	3	52	32	8	41	0	39
Offside	0	29	6	64	0	1	0	2	1	0	15
Yellow cards	3	7	2	2	1	4	4	1	3	0	2
Red cards	0	0	0	0	0	1	2	0	0	0	0

GOALKEEPER NAME	START/ (SUB)	TIME ON PITCH	GOALS CONCEDED	MINS/GOALS CONCEDED	SAVES MADE	SAVES/ SHOTS
GERRARD	34	2977	45	66	138	75%
MYHRE	4	360	2	180	12	86%
SIMONSEN	0(1)	83	2	42	4	67%

PLAYERS' STATISTICS

	HUGHES S	HUTCHISON	JEFFERS	JEVONS	JOHNSON	MOORE	MILLIGAN	PEMBRIDGE	PHELAN	UNSWORTH	WARD	WATSON	WEIR	XAVIER	TOTAL	RANK
	11	28	16	2	0	11	0	29	0	32	6	5	35	18		
	0	3	5	1	3	4	1	2	1	1	4	1	0	2		
	906	2482	1443	149	66	927	45	2566	5	2762	476	471	3092	1655		
	1	6	6	0	0	6	0	2	0	6	0	0	2	0	59*	4th
	2	15	23	1	0	11	0	9	0	13	1	0	6	3	171	14th
	6	22	20	2	2	8	1	15	0	11	1	0	12	9	197	15th
	25%	41%	53%	33%	0%	58%	0%	38%	0%	54%	50%	0%	33%	25%	46%	11th
	2	4	6	1	0	1	0	5	0	2	0	0	2	0	43	=5th
	84	282	32	7	6	37	8	209	0	559	30	42	330	144	3295	6th
	339	1232	347	47	19	331	11	1035	2	802	151	88	753	565	11826	6th
	79%	83%	85%	90%	60%	80%	100%	81%	100%	74%	77%	86%	76%	79%	79%	10th
	65%	65%	65%	66%	50%	66%	65%	69%	100%	46%	63%	60%	57%	69%	64%	9th
	18	51	18	3	1	9	7	120	0	69	25	0	18	9	669	19th
	33%	35%	28%	0%	0%	44%	29%	19%	0%	30%	24%	0%	50%	22%	27%	17th
	21	88	56	4	0	28	2	73	1	62	13	0	46	12	879	18th
	76%	66%	66%	100%	0%	68%	50%	86%	0%	97%	77%	0%	93%	83%	78%	8th
	30	81	10	3	0	17	0	84	0	92	18	12	99	67	1089	2nd
	63%	59%	30%	67%	0%	29%	0%	48%	0%	51%	50%	58%	63%	40%	54%	6th
	3	15	2	0	1	3	0	14	0	44	3	7	80	24	384	11th
	3	54	1	0	1	2	0	37	1	234	12	70	356	69	1595	11th
	1	20	4	1	1	0	0	13	0	24	4	7	44	15	293	3rd
	11	69	7	5	1	11	0	43	0	47	10	9	27	33	558	7th
	2	6	37	5	1	7	0	2	0	0	0	0	1	0	179	1st
	1	7	0	0	1	1	0	4	0	4	1	3	3	0	57	13th
	0	1	1	0	0	0	0	0	0	0	0	0	1	0	6	2nd

*Including two own goals

CROSSES CAUGHT	CROSSES PUNCHED	CROSSES NOT CLAIMED	CATCH SUCCESS	THROWS/ SHORT KICKS	% COMPLETION	LONG KICKS	% COMPLETION
54	11	8	87%	129	82%	1048	38%
6	4	0	100%	11	91%	126	33%
2	1	0	100%	2	100%	35	20%

PLAYER OF THE SEASON

PLAYER	INDEX SCORE
JOHN COLLINS	1,105
Richard Gough	970
Don Hutchison	930
David Weir	927
Nick Barmby	895
Kevin Campbell	822
David Unsworth	801
Paul Gerrard	785
Mark Pembridge	718
Abel Xavier	654*

All players played 75 minutes in at least 19 matches except those marked * who played in 18 games.

Walter Smith has put his faith in experience with his Everton side and it paid dividends in 1999–2000 as the Toffees avoided being dragged into a relegation battle as in previous years, finishing comfortably in 13th position.

Scotsman John Collins was the dominant force in the Merseysiders' line-up and was the top-scoring Evertonian in the Opta Season Index with 1,105 points. The former Monaco man attempted more tackles than any other Premiership player during the 1999–2000 season, winning 61% of them.

He also made the most passes in the Everton side, completing 80% – a ratio higher than the average for a Premiership midfielder.

Another old head was behind Collins in the end-of-season Index. Richard Gough belied his years and controlled the Everton backline, earning himself an Index score of 970. The much-travelled Scottish defender made 352 clearances and 71 tackles as he used all his experience to marshal the ever-changing Everton back four.

The performances of Don Hutchison at both club and international level earned him many new admirers during the course of the campaign. His versatility proved to be a great asset as he was able to perform both up front and in midfield. He scored six times and created another four for Everton as he earned an average of 930 points and the Toffees will be keen to resolve his contract dispute.

Nick Barmby finished the season in fine form as he forced his way back into the England reckoning. The former Tottenham and Boro man had the highest number of assists for Everton with eight and was the club's second top scorer with nine goals.

Striker Kevin Campbell suffered from injury in the latter part of the season, but with his 12 strikes and goals-to-shots ratio of 32% he still guaranteed his place in the top 10 players with an average score of 822 points.

FIVE OF THE BEST

While Everton were not pulled into a relegation battle in 1999–2000 a run of just two wins, against Watford and Bradford, in their last 10 games saw them finish a lowly 13th, a poor return for a team with European aspirations. Walter Smith will need to strengthen his paper-thin squad if the Toffees are to make progress in 2000–01.

TOP GOALSCORERS

	GOALS	GOALS/SHOTS
KEVIN CAMPBELL	12	32%
Nick Barmby	9	20%
Joe-Max Moore	6	32%
David Unsworth	6	25%
Don Hutchison	6	16%

Everton had the best goal difference of any team outside the top six, and with the powerful figure of Kevin Campbell up front the team looked dangerous. He scored 12 goals, and finished the campaign with a superb goals-to-shots ratio of 32%, the second best in the Premiership. Unfortunately, his season ended in March with a knee injury and the Toffees subsequently struggled to make an impact. But Nick Barmby chipped in, and the emergence of American Joe-Max Moore will give the fans some hope.

John Collins's future at Goodison Park was less than secure in 1999, but a superb campaign from the Scottish international ensured that his place in the first team is more than solid. Only Roy Keane and Neil Lennon made more successful passes than Collins in the Premiership and his 80% completion rate is far superior to that of his team-mates. Everton were one of only six teams to make in excess of 10,000 true passes, and it was another Scotsman, Don Hutchison, who was just behind his countryman in the top five.

TOP PASSERS

	SUCC PASSES	COMPLETION
JOHN COLLINS	1,379	80%
Don Hutchison	1,049	69%
Nick Barmby	986	69%
Mark Pembridge	910	73%
Richard Gough	853	75%

TOP TACKLERS

	WON	SUCCESS
JOHN COLLINS	107	61%
David Weir	62	63%
Richard Dunne	49	48%
Richard Gough	48	68%
Don Hutchison	48	59%

No player in the Premiership made more tackles than John Collins. The diminutive battler slid into 176 and won an impressive 61% of them. He has fellow-Scotsmen David Weir, Richard Gough and Don Hutchison in the top five, too, proving that the famous thistle can still sting the opposition. It was the ageing Gough who had the best tackle success, an extremely healthy 68%, and it seems that the chiselled stopper still has at least one more season left in him at the top level.

Don Hutchison endured a mixed season at Goodison Park. His prowess at international level made him a respected figure but a contract wrangle saw him dropped for a period after Christmas. His lapse in discipline also cost him dear, as he racked up seven yellow cards and a sending-off at Leeds. Richard Dunne is also in the FA bad books after two red cards in the league and one for the Republic of Ireland. Despite this, Everton still managed to finish halfway up the Opta Fair Play League.

DISCIPLINE

	POINTS	FOULS & CARDS
DON HUTCHISON	96	69F, 7Y, 1R
John Collins	70	52F, 4Y, 1R
Kevin Campbell	64	58F, 2Y, 0R
David Unsworth	59	47F, 4Y, 0R
Richard Dunne	56	32F, 4Y, 2R

than any other Premiership player

ACTION	BARMBY	CAMPBELL	CLELAND	COLLINS	DUNNE	GERRARD	GOUGH	HUTCHISON	JEFFERS	MAX-MOORE	PEMBRIDGE	UNSWORTH	WEIR	TOTAL	SUNDERLAND
Time on pitch	74	90	16	90	90	90	90	90	74	16	90	90	90	990	990
GOALS															
Goal	–	1	–	–	–	–	–	2	1	–	1	–	–	5	–
Shot on target	1	1	–	–	–	–	–	–	–	–	–	–	–	2	2
Shot off target	–	1	–	–	–	–	–	–	2	–	–	–	1	4	4
Blocked shot	1	–	–	1	–	–	–	–	–	–	–	–	–	2	1
Own goal	–	–	–	–	–	–	–	–	–	–	–	–	–	–	–
PASSES															
Pass to own player	17	19	7	27	16	–	26	45	12	5	22	24	17	237	199
Pass to opposition	9	19	3	17	11	–	13	10	6	3	9	21	14	135	150
Cross to own player	–	–	–	–	–	–	–	1	1	–	1	–	–	3	4
Cross to opposition player	1	1	1	–	2	–	–	1	2	–	1	1	–	10	10
Goal assist	–	–	–	–	–	–	1	1	1	–	1	–	–	4	
Pass completion %	63%	49%	64%	61%	55%	0%	68%	81%	64%	63%	71%	52%	55%	63%	56%
TACKLES & CLEARANCES															
Tackle	1	–	1	4	1	–	3	3	–	–	6	6	–	25	19
Clearances, blocks and interceptions	1	1	–	–	3	–	5	4	–	–	1	9	14	38	35
DRIBBLES & RUNS															
Dribble ball retained	–	–	–	1	1	–	–	–	1	1	–	2	1	7	10
Dribble ball lost	1	–	–	–	–	–	–	1	–	–	1	–	–	3	4
Dribble success %	0%	0%	0%	100%	100%	0%	0%	0%	100%	100%	0%	100%	100%	70%	71%
DISCIPLINE															
Fouls	–	2	–	3	–	1	1	1	–	–	1	3	3	15	14
Penalty conceded	–	–	–	–	–	–	–	–	–	–	–	–	–	–	
Free kick – offside	–	2	–	–	–	–	–	–	1	–	–	–	–	3	2
Yellow cards	–	–	–	–	–	–	–	–	–	–	–	–	1	1	2
Red cards	–	–	–	–	–	–	–	–	–	–	–	–	–	–	–
GOALKEEPERS															
Distribution to own player	–	–	–	–	–	15	–	–	–	–	–	–	–	15	17
Distribution to opposition player	–	–	–	–	–	22	–	–	–	–	–	–	–	22	17
Goalkeeper distribution %	0%	0%	0%	0%	0%	41%	0%	0%	0%	0%	0%	0%	0%	41%	50%
Save	–	–	–	–	–	2	–	–	–	–	–	–	–	2	2
Ball caught	–	–	–	–	–	–	–	–	–	–	–	–	–	–	1
Ball dropped	–	–	–	–	–	–	–	–	–	–	–	–	–	–	–
Goal conceded	–	–	–	–	–	–	–	–	–	–	–	–	–	–	5

News that Bill Kenwright's takeover bid for Everton had been accepted came as an early Christmas present for Toffees fans who had long been wishing for a change of direction at Goodison Park. And on Boxing Day the team did their part to boost morale by battering high-flying Sunderland with a devastating display of attacking football.

Although the Black Cats were without Premiership top scorer Kevin Phillips, they were certainly not expected to be trounced by a team that had won only three of their previous eight Premiership home games.

In fact, if anything, Peter Reid's side came out stronger during the game's opening exchanges and won 47% of their challenges over the course of the match. But the Toffees showed throughout the campaign that they only need one chance to punish the opposition, as they scored with an impressive 16% of their shots – the second best strike rate in the division.

And so it proved, when the first real opportunity of the game opened up for Don Hutchison in the 16th minute. Francis Jeffers picked up the ball out on the left wing and drilled a low cross into the box which Mark Pembridge flicked into the path of Hutchison. And the Scottish international calmly placed his first-time shot past Thomas Sorensen.

In the 21st minute, Niall Quinn came close to levelling the scores, only for Paul Gerrard to save well from his powerful header. It was to prove a costly miss, as five minutes later Hutchison doubled the home side's advantage. A John Collins free-kick seemed to have been headed clear by Steve Bould, but the influential Scotland midfielder latched on to the ball, firing a crisp drive that flew into the bottom left-hand corner of the net. And the Toffees kept up the pressure until half-time, with Jeffers converting a wonderful through-ball from Richard Gough.

The Black Cats seemed to have no answer to the quality of the home team's attacking play and failed to get their game back on track. Sunderland were accurate with just 56% of their passes, seven percentage points lower than Everton. And Reid's team fired just two shots on target over the 90 minutes.

Kevin Campbell went close on 61 minutes after some excellent work by Hutchison, but Everton's unrelenting pressure was rewarded just seconds later. Jeffers crossed through a crowd of Sunderland defenders to find Pembridge, who finished well from close range.

Hutchison then sent Nick Barmby clean through on 67 minutes, but the former Tottenham midfielder had his shot expertly saved by Sorensen. However, the Scot's influence on the game continued as he found Campbell in the penalty area five minutes later. And the former Arsenal forward showed great skill in flicking the ball extravagantly past Paul Butler before firing it into the back of the net.

While this was undoubtedly one of the outstanding team performances of 1999–2000, Hutchison's contribution deserves special mention. The former Liverpool midfielder scored with both of his shots and completed 45 passes. He finished with an Opta points score of 2,203.

LEEDS UNITED

ADDRESS

Elland Road, Leeds,
West Yorkshire LS11 0ES

CONTACT NUMBERS

Telephone: 0113 226 6000
Fax: 0113 226 6050
Ticket Office: 0113 292 1000
Club Call: 09068 121180
Club shop: 0113 225 1144
e-mail: football@lufc.co.uk
Website: www.lufc.co.uk

KEY PERSONNEL

President: The Rt Hon
Earl of Harewood KBE LLD
Chairman: P Ridsdale
Managing Director: J Fenn
Directors: A Pearson
D Spencer, A Hudson, I Silvester
Club Secretary: I Silvester
Manager: David O'Leary

SPONSORS

1999 – 2000 Packard Bell
2000 – 2001 Strongbow

FANZINES

The Square Ball
Till the World Stops
We Are Leeds
To Ell And Back

COLOURS

Home: White shirts, shorts
and stockings with yellow
and royal blue trim
Away: Sky blue shirts with
navy band across chest, navy blue
shorts, sky blue stockings

NICKNAME

United

HONOURS

League Champions:
1968–69, 1973–74, 1991–92
Division Two Champions:
1923–24, 1963–64, 1989–90
FA Cup: 1972
League Cup: 1968
Fairs Cup: 1968, 1971

RECORD GOALSCORER

Peter Lorimer – 168 league goals
1965–79, 1983–86

BIGGEST WIN

8–0 v Leicester City – Division One,
7 April 1934

BIGGEST DEFEAT

1–8 v Stoke City –
Division One, 27 August 1934

SEASON REVIEW

David O'Leary's young Leeds side finished third in the 1999–2000 Premiership, qualifying for the UEFA Champions League. The final table does not tell the story of their season, though. The club led the Premiership for long periods of the campaign and there is no doubt that it was Leeds who provided Manchester United with the most sustained challenge for the title.

Their season started on a sour note as prolific marksman Jimmy Floyd Hasselbaink departed for Atletico Madrid in a £12 million move made inevitable by the player's outrageous wage demands. Michael Bridges and Eirik Bakke had been signed in the summer, but neither was thought to be the proven goalscorer that Hasselbaink had shown himself to be.

"It is time to celebrate, reflect and get out the chequebook to give the fans the squad they deserve."
Peter Ridsdale

When a dour Derby side shut Leeds out in a frustrating 0–0 draw on the opening day, the need for a new striker seemed to be of paramount importance. Chairman Peter Ridsdale had assured fans that the money received for Hasselbaink would be ploughed back into the team and he proved to be as good as his word when Leeds signed Darren Huckerby from Coventry City.

On the pitch, Michael Bridges chose a tricky away trip to Southampton to illustrate his goalscoring credentials, netting a brilliant hat-trick that doubled his career tally of Premiership goals and prompted comparisons with Arsenal's Dennis Bergkamp.

If August marked the emergence of Bridges as a force, it also saw the start of another trend that was eventually to undermine Leeds' title challenge. The team lost 2–0 on their visit to Old Trafford, the first of nine defeats against the teams who also finished along with the Whites in the top six at the end of the season.

The team continued to play well, though, underlining their title credentials with five straight wins in September that took them up to second place in the Premiership and into the second round of the UEFA Cup at the expense of Partizan Belgrade of Yugoslavia.

October saw the O'Leary bandwagon pick up even more speed and finished with Leeds sitting proudly at the summit of the Premiership. Lokomotiv Moscow were hammered 4–1 at Elland Road in the second round of the UEFA Cup and a 7–1 aggregate win was wrapped up with a 3–0 win in Russia.

The trip took its toll on the team, though, and they looked lethargic as they slipped to a 2–0 defeat at Wimbledon in the Premiership. The first of a series of off-the-field problems also disrupted O'Leary's plans as Australia invoked FIFA's five-day rule to prevent Harry Kewell from playing against Bradford in the Premiership after he pulled out of a lucrative friendly with Brazil with a conveniently-timed injury.

The Wimbledon defeat saw Manchester United resume control at the top of the table, but wins against Bradford and Southampton took Leeds back ahead of their bitter rivals. Things were less comfortable in the UEFA Cup when Leeds arrived in Russia for their third-round tie against Spartak Moscow, only to find that the temperature had dropped to −15°C, forcing the postponement of the tie.

It was rescheduled for December 2 and the venue shifted to Sofia, but Spartak's officials accused Leeds of attempting to blackmail them into moving the tie to England. Leeds naturally refuted such claims but the affair left a bitter taste in the mouth. When Spartak's coach

94% Nigel Martyn's saves-to-shots ratio

SEASON REVIEW

instructed his players to visualise their opponents as Chechen rebels, the whole episode threatened to degenerate into complete farce.

Leeds sneaked past their eccentric Russian opponents, escaped from Pride Park with a controversial 1–0 win – courtesy of a hotly-disputed penalty – and then brushed aside Port Vale in the third round of the FA Cup.

They were knocked out of the Worthington Cup after a penalty shoot-out with Leicester, but with fixtures coming thick and fast, elimination from one of the domestic competitions proved to be almost a relief to O'Leary's battle-weary team.

> "A lot of people said I shouldn't have taken this job because Leeds were going nowhere. I'd like to talk to those same people now."
>
> David O'Leary

Their one victory over a top-six side came with a 2–0 win against Chelsea and the team went into the the New Year with a one-point lead over Manchester United. Unfortunately, they were unable to capitalise on their nearest rivals' trip to Brazil, losing 2–1 to Aston Villa courtesy of a rare double by Gareth Southgate at Elland Road. The same side put paid to Leeds' FA Cup dream with an exciting 3–2 win at Villa Park.

The club were dragged through the disciplinary mire after an unseemly scuffle with Tottenham in the 1–0 win at Elland Road, but even worse news came with the arrest of Jonathon Woodgate and Lee Bowyer after an incident outside a nightclub. O'Leary stuck by his players, insisting – as he was entitled to – that they were innocent until proven guilty.

The team showed character to put the whole business behind them with a 2–1 victory at Sunderland in which new boy Jason Wilcox impressed, but Manchester United had stepped up a gear and by the time they had beaten Leeds 1–0 at Elland Road, Alex Ferguson's men were six points clear at the top of the table.

Leeds' attention turned to Europe where they beat Roma and Slavia Prague en route to a date with Galatasaray. That semi-final proved to be disastrous in more than just a football sense, as two Leeds fans were murdered before the away leg, leaving an understandably distressed Leeds side to play a game on which their minds were never properly focused.

They lost 2–0 and, even though they managed a 2–2 draw in a return leg, their UEFA Cup run came to a very sad end.

Their Premiership campaign, which had once promised so much, was also threatening to end in disappointment as a series of four successive defeats saw them drop from second to fourth and out of the race for the Champions League spots.

Fortunately for the team, their bad run coincided neatly with Liverpool's slide and, thanks to Leeds old boy David Wetherall, whose goal for Bradford beat Liverpool, they were able to claim third place with a 0–0 draw against West Ham United at Upton Park on the last day of the season.

That, coupled with Harry Kewell's PFA award as Young Player of the Season, brought the campaign to a satisfactory conclusion for the Yorkshiremen.

Leeds had failed to take the big prize, but they had at least secured the chance of a place at Europe's top table, a reward that they undoubtedly merited.

Expectations are high of another successful season in 2000–01. O'Leary has already added more quality to his squad with the signing of Olivier Dacourt and with more big names likely to follow the feisty Frenchman to Elland Road, Leeds' quest for silverware could soon come to a successful end.

LEEDS UNITED

DATE	OPPONENT	SCORE	ATT.	BAKKE	BATTY	BOWYER	BRIDGES	DUBERRY	HAALAND	HARTE	HIDEN
7.8.99	Derby Co H	0–0	40,118	–	90□	90□	90	–	–	90	–
11.8.99	Southampton A	3–0	15,206	s8□	90□	90□	90^{3}	90□	–	90	–
14.8.99	Man Utd A	0–2	55,187	s7	90	90	19	90	–	75	s15
21.8.99	Sunderland H	2–1	39,064	–	90□	90^{1}	58	–	–	90	–
23.8.99	Liverpool H	1–2*	39,703	s22	90	90□	57	–	–	90	–
28.8.99	Tottenham A	2–1	36,012	–	90	90□	45□	90□	–	90^{1}	–
11.9.99	Coventry A	4–3	21,532	–	90	90^{1}	90^{1}	54	–	62^{1}	–
19.9.99	Middlesbro H	2–0	34,122	–	90	90□	52^{1}	–	–	90	–
25.9.99	Newcastle H	3–2	40,192	78	90□	90^{1}	90^{1}	–	s12	90	–
3.10.99	Watford A	2–1	19,677	90	90	–	70^{1}	–	s1	90□	–
16.10.99	Sheff Wed H	2–0	39,437	–	90	90	62□	–	–	–	–
24.10.99	Everton A	4–4	37,355	–	90	90	90^{2}	–	–	90	–
30.10.99	West Ham H	1–0	40,190	–	90	90□	90□	–	–	90^{1}	–
7.11.99	Wimbledon A	0–2	18,747	s29	90	61	–	s45	–	90	–
20.11.99	Bradford H	2–1	39,937	90	90	90□	90	–	–	90^{1}	–
28.11.99	Southampton H	1–0	39,288	s60□	30	90□	90^{1}	–	–	90	–
5.12.99	Derby Co A	1–0	29,455	90□	–	90	90	–	–	90^{1}	–
19.12.99	Chelsea A	2–0	35,106	90	–	85□	48	–	–	90□	–
26.12.99	Leicester H	2–1	40,105	90	–	90^{1}	90^{1}□	–	–	90	–
28.12.99	Arsenal A	0–2	38,096	90	–	79	90□	–	–	90	–
3.1.00	Aston Villa H	1–2	40,027	90	–	–	90	90□	90	90□	–
23.1.00	Sunderland A	2–1	41,947	90□	–	90	75^{1}	90	–	90	–
5.2.00	Liverpool A	1–3	44,793	90	–	90^{1}	s15	90□	–	90□	–
12.2.00	Tottenham H	1–0	40,127	85□	–	90□	–	90	s5	90	–
20.2.00	Man Utd H	0–1	40,160	90	–	90	–	–	–	90	–
26.2.00	Middlesbro A	0–0	34,800	–	–	90	s3	–	90□	90	–
5.3.00	Coventry H	3–0	38,710	90	–	89	80^{1}	–	s45	90	–
12.3.00	Bradford A	2–1	18,276	90	–	90	89^{2}	–	90□	90□	–
19.3.00	Wimbledon H	4–1	39,256	85^{2}	–	–	64	–	90	90^{1}	–
26.3.00	Leicester A	1–2	21,095	90	–	–	71	–	90□	90□	–
1.4.00	Chelsea H	0–1	40,162	90	–	90□	–	–	–	90	–
9.4.00	Aston Villa A	0–1	33,889	90	–	90	60	–	–	90	–
16.4.00	Arsenal H	0–4	39,307	90	–	90□	45	–	90	44■	–
23.4.00	Newcastle A	2–2	36,460	90□	–	s13	80^{1}	90	90□	77□	–
30.4.00	Sheff Wed A	3–0	23,416	69□	–	–	84^{1}	90	s21	–	–
3.5.00	Watford H	3–1	36,324	90	–	90	90^{1}□	90^{1}	–	–	–
8.5.00	Everton H	1–1	37,713	90	–	90	80^{1}	55■	s35	–	–
14.5.00	West Ham A	0–0	26,044	79	–	s11□	29	–	–	–	–

□ Yellow card, ■ Red card, s Substitute, 90^{2} Goals scored

*including one own goal

1999–2000 PREMIERSHIP APPEARANCES

HOPKIN	HUCKERBY	JONES	KELLY	KEWELL	MARTYN	McPHAIL	MILLS	RADEBE	SMITH	WILCOX	WOODGATE	TOTAL
90	–	–	–	90□	90	s38	90	90	52	–	90	990
86	–	s4	–	82	90	–	90□	90	–	–	90	990
s71	90	–	–	83	90	–	90	90	–	–	90	990
90	90	–	–	90	90	–	90[1]	90	s32	–	90	990
68	90	–	–	90	90	–	90□	90	s33	–	90	990
s45	s45	–	s25	90	90	–	65	90□	87[1]■	–	45	987
90□	90[1]	–	s28	90	90	–	90□	90	–	–	s36	990
45	s38	–	s45	90[1]	90	–	90	90	90	–	90	990
–	s17	–	90□	90[1]	90□	–	–	90□	73□	–	90	990
89	s20	–	90	90[1]	90	–	s48	42	90	–	90	990
–	s28	–	90	90□	90	90	90	90	90[2]	–	90	990
–	s23	–	90	90[1]	90	90	–	90	67	–	90[1]	990
–	s32	–	90	90	90	90	–	90	58	–	90	990
s13	90	–	90	90	90	90	–	90	77	–	45	990
–	s14	–	90	–	90	90	–	90	76[1]	–	90	990
–	s29	–	90	90	90	90	90	–	61	–	90	990
–	76	s8	90□	90	90	82	–	90	s14□	–	90	990
–	90	s5	90□	90	90	90[2]	–	90	–	s42	90	990
–	77	–	90	90	90□	90	–	90	–	s13□	90	990
–	–	s11	90□	90□	90	90	–	90	79□	s11	90	990
–	s14	76	90	90[1]	90	–	–	–	76	s14	90	990
–	s15	–	90	90	90	90	–	–	–	90[1]	90	990
–	s15	–	90	90	90	75	–	–	75□	90	90	990
–	s22	90□	90□	68[1]	90	–	–	–	90	90	90	990
–	–	90□	90	90□	90	–	–	90	90	90	90	990
87	s34	–	–	90□	90	–	90□	90	56	90	90	990
–	s10	s1	90	90[1]	90	90	–	90	–	90[1]	45	990
s17	s1	–	90	–	90	73	–	90	90	90	–	990
90	s4	s5	90	86[1]	90	90	–	90	s26	90	–	990
–	s19	–	90	90[1]	90	90	–	90	–	90	90	990
–	s16	–	90	90	90	90	–	90	90□	74	90	990
–	s30	–	90□	90	90	90	–	90	–	90	90	990
–	–	–	90	90	90	90	–	–	90	s45	90	944
–	s10	–	–	90□	90	90	90	90	–	90[1]	–	990
90[1]	s6	90	90	90[1]	90	–	90	90	–	90	–	990
–	80[1]	–	90	90	90	90	90	45	s10	–	s45	990
–	s10	–	90	90	90	90	90	–	–	55	90	955
–	s1	90	90	90	90	90	90□	90	s61	89	90	990

THE MANAGER

DAVID O'LEARY

When Leicester boss Martin O'Neill declined the offer of managing Leeds, David O'Leary was installed as successor to George Graham, and the Irishman has built on the foundations laid by his former mentor.

O'Leary has helped turn his young Leeds team into an exciting side, and their qualification for the 2000–01 Champions League was just reward for a fantastic season.

With more than 500 appearances for Arsenal and 66 Republic of Ireland caps, it is a testament to O'Leary that despite his immense defensive experience and knowledge, Leeds are one of the one of the most attack-minded sides in the country.

The Irishman also showed his maturity during the season when having to guide his young stars through what was a difficult time for everyone connected with Leeds, and the relationship between him and his players has been a major part of their success on the pitch.

Already linked with lucrative sides abroad, O'Leary is fast gaining a reputation and chairman Peter Ridsdale will be more than keen to hang on to his man, as Leeds now have the potential to join the likes of Manchester United, Arsenal and Chelsea in Europe's elite.

LEAGUE POSITION

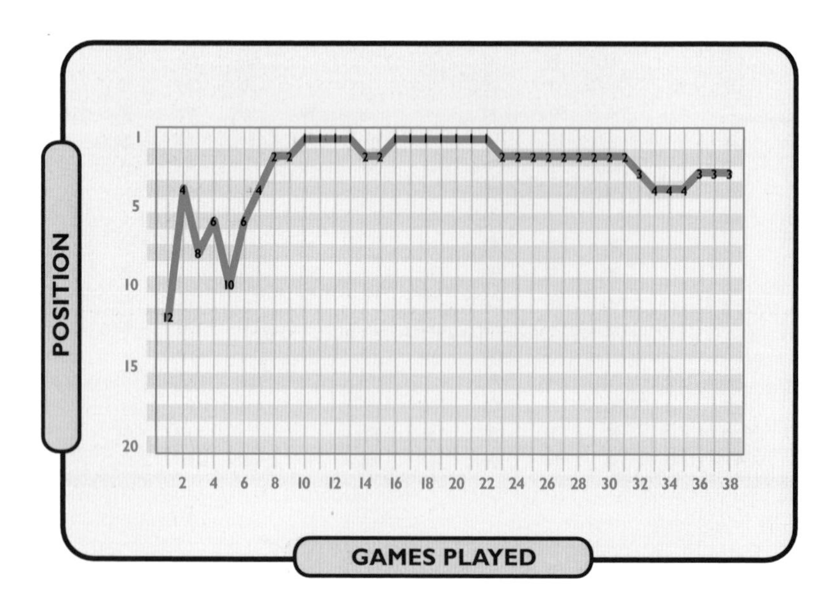

THE GOALS

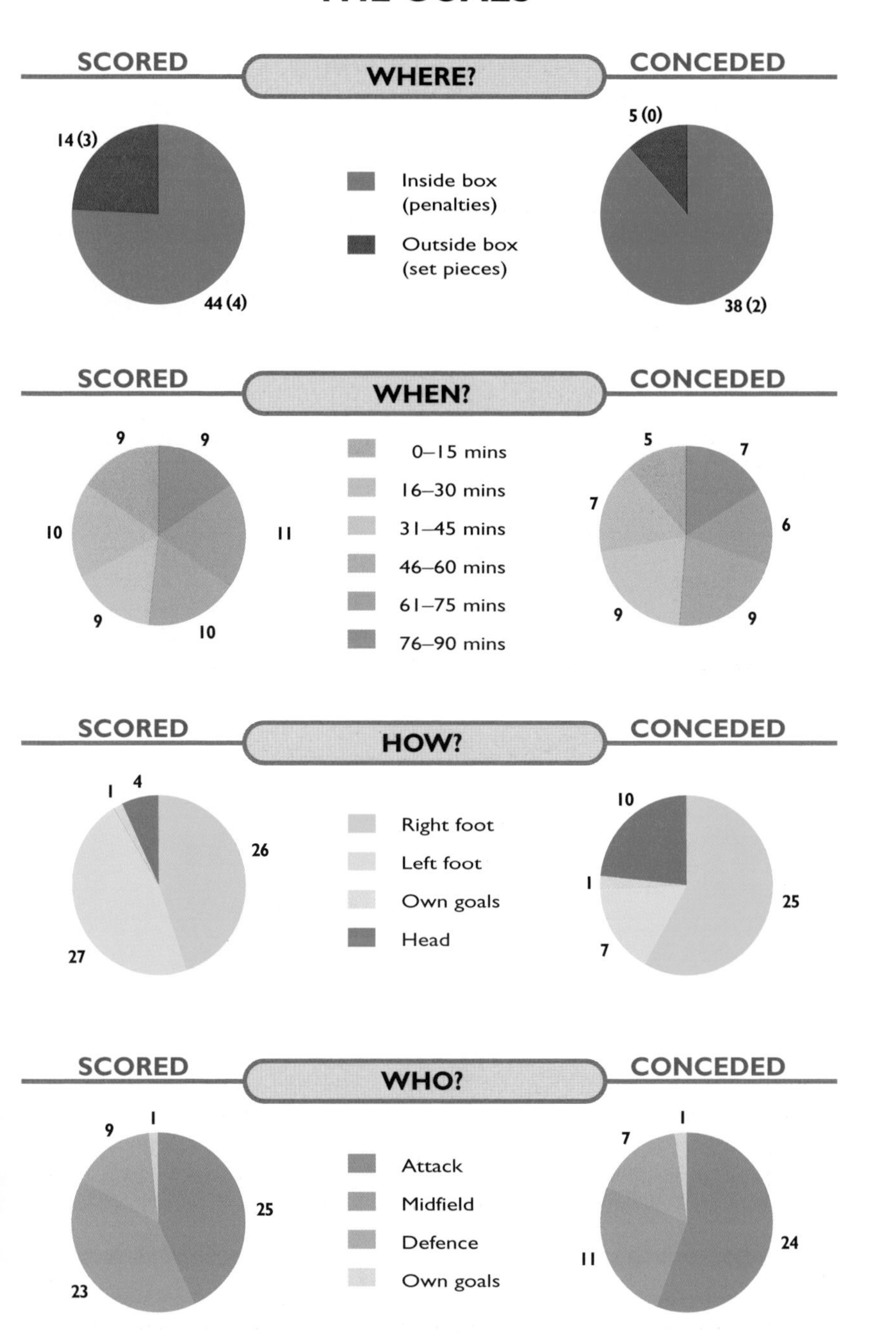

goals than any of their league rivals

LEEDS UNITED

	BAKKE	BATTY	BOWYER	BRIDGES	DUBERRY	HAALAND	HARTE	HIDEN	HOPKIN
APPEARANCES									
Start	24	16	31	32	12	7	33	0	10
Sub	5	0	2	2	1	6	0	1	4
Minutes on pitch	2232	1380	2768	2356	1054	749	2868	15	971
GOAL ATTEMPTS									
Goals	2	0	5	19	1	0	6	0	1
Shots on target	11	2	30	42	1	0	25	0	9
Shots off target	28	6	42	36	2	2	24	0	7
Shooting accuracy	28%	25%	42%	54%	33%	0%	51%	0%	56%
PASSING									
Goal assists	1	3	3	4	0	0	5	0	1
Long passes	235	182	248	83	86	71	584	1	53
Short passes	820	780	798	733	169	188	933	8	331
PASS COMPLETION									
Own half %	75%	91%	82%	71%	67%	73%	75%	100%	84%
Opposition half %	63%	80%	64%	60%	45%	53%	61%	67%	66%
CROSSING									
Total crosses	42	6	48	27	3	8	181	1	27
Cross completion %	19%	33%	17%	22%	100%	38%	33%	0%	30%
DRIBBLING									
Dribbles & runs	96	35	101	114	7	15	97	0	24
Dribble completion %	72%	94%	84%	64%	86%	73%	90%	0%	79%
DEFENDING									
Tackles made	81	67	105	20	34	19	67	2	30
Tackles won %	60%	52%	55%	70%	56%	63%	36%	50%	60%
Blocks	16	9	12	3	22	9	47	1	5
Clearances	37	31	23	3	133	39	154	1	21
Interceptions	15	28	25	4	9	2	13	0	5
DISCIPLINE									
Fouls	52	21	55	65	42	24	33	0	12
Offside	0	0	14	56	0	2	1	0	3
Yellow cards	7	4	13	6	4	4	7	0	1
Red cards	0	0	0	0	1	0	1	0	0

GOALKEEPER NAME	START/ (SUB)	TIME ON PITCH	GOALS CONCEDED	MINS/GOALS CONCEDED	SAVES MADE	SAVES/ SHOTS
MARTYN	38	3420	43	80	144	77%

PLAYERS' STATISTICS

HUCKERBY	JONES	KELLY	KEWELL	McPHAIL	MILLS	RADEBE	SMITH	WILCOX	WOODGATE	TOTAL	RANK
9	5	28	36	23	16	31	20	15	32		
24	6	3	0	1	1	0	6	5	2		
1226	470	2618	3199	2068	1463	2697	1733	1423	2826		
2	0	0	10	2	1	0	4	3	1	58*	5th
15	1	0	43	6	6	1	14	11	3	220	4th
13	5	3	64	12	15	4	16	8	6	293	1st
54%	17%	0%	40%	33%	29%	20%	47%	58%	33%	43%	18th
3	2	0	4	4	1	0	3	2	0	36	11th
18	56	395	147	248	191	241	36	128	228	3231	10th
210	137	707	1093	809	363	660	402	480	610	10231	12th
67%	77%	71%	81%	86%	71%	84%	81%	70%	80%	79%	11th
53%	60%	60%	65%	74%	55%	60%	66%	62%	58%	64%	10th
30	1	62	94	70	27	10	15	119	9	780	10th
30%	0%	23%	23%	31%	30%	80%	13%	34%	44%	29%	12th
119	10	98	336	42	59	34	61	74	41	1365	4th
56%	80%	94%	57%	81%	75%	100%	72%	78%	98%	73%	18th
10	14	59	39	55	64	106	27	29	116	945	18th
40%	71%	56%	51%	53%	48%	60%	41%	62%	56%	54%	5th
0	3	28	8	12	20	74	1	8	80	358	16th
0	6	170	16	23	150	374	5	13	369	1585	12th
4	3	34	15	11	9	49	4	4	33	269	7th
24	15	25	65	24	31	32	57	15	32	626	1st
28	2	0	33	0	1	0	26	2	1	169	3rd
0	2	6	6	0	5	2	5	1	0	75	5th
0	0	0	0	0	0	0	1	0	0	3	=12th

*Including one own goal

CROSSES CAUGHT	CROSSES PUNCHED	CROSSES NOT CLAIMED	CATCH SUCCESS	THROWS/ SHORT KICKS	% COMPLETION	LONG KICKS	% COMPLETION
37	13	2	95%	194	87%	1107	41%

PLAYER OF THE SEASON

PLAYER	INDEX SCORE
LUCAS RADEBE	996
Ian Harte	979
Harry Kewell	919
Jonathon Woodgate	918
Michael Bridges	902
Lee Bowyer	811
Stephen McPhail	764
Nigel Martyn	748
Eirik Bakke	713
Gary Kelly	685

For the second season in succession, South African defender Lucas Radebe came out on top for Leeds in the Opta Season Index. Although the Yorkshire side's youngsters were grabbing all the headlines the strong, consistent performances of Radebe at the back were a huge influence on Leeds' promising season in 1999–2000.

Radebe earned 996 points on average from his displays in the heart of the defence. He made 106 tackles and 374 clearances and his steadying influence was a huge benefit to the more inexperienced players around him, such as Jonathon Woodgate, who once again impressed at the back after winning his first England cap in the summer of 1999.

Irish full-back Ian Harte was close behind Radebe with 979 points. The left-back has become the dead ball specialist for David O'Leary's men. He scored six and created five in the Premiership last season and also managed to fire in 181 crosses.

Unsurprisingly, other Leeds youngsters made a big impression this season and they occupy the majority of the places in the Index.

Harry Kewell earned an average of 919 points for his 10 Premiership goals. He also made 336 dribbles and runs – the second highest total in the Premiership – and completed 66% of his 1,240 passes.

Michael Bridges enjoyed his first season in West Yorkshire, finishing as Leeds' top scorer with 19 Premiership goals. United also never lost a game in which the former Sunderland striker scored.

Lee Bowyer was another who finished well in the Index, and but for his disciplinary record he could have finished with a better score. The midfielder scored five goals and made 105 tackles, but in the process he received 13 yellow cards – the joint-highest total in the Premiership with Seth Johnson of Derby.

Old hand between the sticks, Nigel Martyn, once again produced consistent form, increasing the call for him to be installed as England's number one.

13 Lee Bowyer earned the joint-highest number

FIVE OF THE BEST

When Leeds racked up their 12th win in 14 games on Boxing Day, many must have thought that the Elland Road club were on their way to their first League Championship in eight years, but David O'Leary's young team slowly fell away and finished only third. A place in the Champions League is a just reward for the ever-improving side, though.

TOP GOALSCORERS

	GOALS	GOALS/SHOTS
MICHAEL BRIDGES	19	24%
Harry Kewell	10	9%
Ian Harte	6	12%
Lee Bowyer	5	7%
Alan Smith	4	13%

Eyebrows were raised when Leeds paid £5 million for Sunderland's Michael Bridges during summer 1999, but the young hitman fired home 19 goals for his new employers, with an impressive goals-to-shots ratio of 24%. Young Player of the Year Harry Kewell again wasted a lot of opportunities but scored 10 goals all the same, the majority of which were superb. The one disappointment was that Alan Smith scored just four times, failing to build on his 1998–99 campaign.

Four of the five top passers at Leeds in 1999–2000 were 23 or younger, with the impressive Ian Harte failing to make 1,000 successful passes by just five. His actual pass completion rate was slightly below average, though, and it is the old man of the team, David Batty, who was the slickest ball player. Sadly for the experienced battler, a series of injuries rendered him ineffectual for much of the season.

TOP PASSERS

	SUCC PASSES	COMPLETION
IAN HARTE	995	66%
Harry Kewell	814	66%
Stephen McPhail	811	77%
David Batty	804	84%
Lee Bowyer	719	69%

TOP TACKLERS

	WON	SUCCESS
JONATHON WOODGATE	65	56%
Lucas Radebe	64	60%
Lee Bowyer	58	55%
Eirik Bakke	49	60%
David Batty	35	52%

Jonathon Woodgate ended his 1998–99 season on a high, playing for England in their Euro 2000 qualifying game in Bulgaria. He continued his progress into the new Millennium, making more successful tackles than any other Leeds United player. It was his South African skipper Lucas Radebe who was the most consistent stopper, though, as he won 60% of his challenges. Eirik Bakke won the same amount, but slid into fewer.

In 1998–99, Lee Bowyer was second behind Jimmy Floyd Hasselbaink in the Leeds disciplinary table but, with the Dutchman moving to Atletico Madrid, the fiery Englishman became the worst-behaved man at the club. He collected 13 yellow cards during the season and had to explain his actions to the FA. His team-mates Harry Kewell and Michael Bridges were just behind him, locked with identical records, 65 fouls and six yellow cards apiece.

DISCIPLINE

	POINTS	FOULS & CARDS
LEE BOWYER	94	55F, 13Y, 0R
Harry Kewell	83	65F, 6Y, 0R
Michael Bridges	83	65F, 6Y, 0R
Alan Smith	78	57F, 5Y, 1R
Eirik Bakke	73	52F, 7Y, 0R

of yellow cards in the top flight

ACTION	BAKKE	BOWYER	BRIDGES	HARTE	HUCKERBY	JONES	KELLY	KEWELL	MARTYN	McPHAIL	RADEBE	WILCOX	WOODGATE	TOTAL	CHELSEA
Time on pitch	90	85	48	90	90	5	90	90	90	90	90	42	90	990	968
GOALS															
Goal	–	–	–	–	–	–	–	–	–	2	–	–	–	2	–
Shot on target	–	–	1	–	–	–	–	–	–	–	–	1	–	2	6
Shot off target	2	–	–	–	–	–	1	–	–	–	–	–	1	4	9
Blocked shot	–	–	–	1	–	–	–	–	–	–	–	–	–	1	6
Own goal	–	–	–	–	–	–	–	–	–	–	–	–	–	–	–
PASSES															
Pass to own player	19	13	4	22	4	1	17	17	–	28	16	4	9	154	266
Pass to opposition	9	10	8	20	7	–	17	6	–	9	6	7	4	103	86
Cross to own player	–	1	–	1	1	–	1	–	–	–	–	–	1	5	7
Cross to opposition player	2	–	–	1	1	–	–	3	–	4	–	–	–	11	22
Goal assist	–	1	–	–	–	–	–	–	–	–	–	–	–	1	–
Pass completion %	63%	60%	33%	52%	38%	100%	51%	65%	0%	68%	73%	36%	71%	58%	72%
TACKLES & CLEARANCES															
Tackle	1	3	1	–	3	1	5	2	–	4	1	1	2	24	28
Clearances, blocks and interceptions	16	2	–	13	1	1	20	1	–	8	23	–	19	104	74
DRIBBLES & RUNS															
Dribble ball retained	1	3	–	2	6	–	5	8	–	1	1	–	2	29	39
Dribble ball lost	1	–	–	–	5	–	–	5	–	–	–	1	–	12	9
Dribble success %	50%	100%	0%	100%	55%	0%	100%	62%	0%	100%	100%	0%	100%	71%	81%
DISCIPLINE															
Fouls	3	1	3	1	2	–	–	2	–	2	1	–	3	18	21
Penalty conceded	–	–	–	–	–	–	–	–	–	–	–	–	–	–	–
Free kick – offside	–	–	1	–	1	–	–	–	–	–	–	–	–	2	–
Yellow cards	–	1	–	1	–	–	1	–	–	–	–	–	–	3	2
Red cards	–	–	–	–	–	–	–	–	–	–	–	–	–	–	1
GOALKEEPERS															
Distribution to own player	–	–	–	–	–	–	–	–	17	–	–	–	–	17	10
Distribution to opposition Ppayer	–	–	–	–	–	–	–	–	13	–	–	–	–	13	17
Goalkeeper distribution %	0%	0%	0%	0%	0%	0%	0%	0%	57%	0%	0%	0%	0%	57%	37%
Save	–	–	–	–	–	–	–	–	6	–	–	–	–	6	2
Ball caught	–	–	–	–	–	–	–	–	2	–	–	–	–	2	2
Ball dropped	–	–	–	–	–	–	–	–	–	–	–	–	–	–	–
Goal conceded	–	–	–	–	–	–	–	–	–	–	–	–	–	–	2

106 Leeds fired more shots on target from

With Chelsea stuttering in mid-table, David O'Leary's youthful outfit appeared to have picked exactly the right moment to visit Stamford Bridge. United were second in the Premiership and winning admirers throughout the nation with their free-flowing attacking football. But they were made to exhibit a grittier side to their game against the Blues.

Leeds indicated their willingness to show their physical side as early as the second minute, when Lee Bowyer was booked for a late tackle on Dennis Wise. But the England under-21 international's aggression did little to stem the flow of Chelsea attacks. The home side probed for an opener with Chris Sutton heading narrowly wide from the resulting free-kick. And the former Blackburn striker was presented with another opportunity moments later, but Nigel Martyn dealt with his tame effort easily.

The match continued in this vein for the majority of the first half, with Gianluca Vialli's team pressing forward, only to be chased down by Leeds' hard-working youngsters or denied by the excellent Martyn. Over the 90 minutes, the Blues fired in 21 shots but could only hit the target with six, as they were largely reduced to long-range shooting.

Leeds' only real chance of the first half fell to Michael Bridges but, although his 25-yard shot was firmly-struck and on target, Ed De Goey saved well. The game started to swing United's way at the start of the second half when their constant pressure on the Chelsea midfield began to pay dividends. O'Leary's side won 63% of their challenges and, as Leeds began to wrestle control of the match, the home side began to show their frustration. Ian Harte was booked for a foul on 51 minutes, but it was Chelsea who seemed to lose their cool, and their tackles became more reckless as the game went on. Frank Leboeuf made two bad challenges in quick succession and was booked as his attempts to stop Leeds' attacks became increasingly desperate.

From one free-kick, Harry Kewell stormed forward to the edge of the box, where he showed superb skill to flick the ball over Leboeuf. But as he readied himself to shoot, the Aussie was unfairly crowded off the ball by a horde of Blue shirts. The referee played the advantage and Bowyer was quickest to react, latching on to the ball and crossing for Stephen McPhail to score his first career goal.

Just two minutes later, Leboeuf received his marching orders for a cynical challenge on Kewell. The Frenchman then raised the tension between the sides further with a stamp on the Australian that went unseen by the referee.

With the home side reduced to 10 men O'Leary's team were able to control the remainder of the match, and it was no surprise when they doubled their advantage. Kewell won a free-kick out on the right wing which McPhail curled into the box. The cross-shot eluded everyone, bouncing once before flying into the bottom corner of De Goey's goal.

It capped a splendid performance by the youngster. As well as scoring both his team's goals McPhail also made four tackles and eight clearances, to amass an Opta Index score of 1,780 points.

WALKERS

LEICESTER CITY

ADDRESS

City Stadium, Filbert Street,
Leicester LE2 7FL

CONTACT NUMBERS

Telephone: 0116 291 5000
Fax: 0116 247 0585
Ticket Office: 0116 291 5232
Club Call: 09068 121185
Fox Leisure: 0116 291 5253
Website: www.lcfc.co.uk

KEY PERSONNEL

Chairman: J M Elsom
Directors: Martin George,
Steve Kind FCCA
Club Secretary: Andrew Neville
Manager: Peter Taylor

SPONSORS

Walkers Crisps

FANZINES

The Fox
When You're Smiling
Foxed Off
O'Neill And Pray

COLOURS

Home: Blue shirts, white shorts
and blue stockings
Away: White shirts, blue shorts
and white stockings

NICKNAME

The Foxes

HONOURS

Division Two Champions:
1924–25, 1936–37, 1953–54,
1956–57, 1970–71, 1979–80
League Cup: 1964, 1997, 2000

RECORD GOALSCORER

Arthur Chandler –
259 league goals, 1923–35

BIGGEST WIN

10–0 v Portsmouth – Division One,
20 October 1928

BIGGEST DEFEAT

0–12 (as Leicester Fosse) v
Nottingham Forest – Division One,
21 April 1909

SEASON REVIEW

They were accused of everything from kick-and-run to ticket-touting, from foul play on the pitch to dangerous horseplay off it, but there is no denying the fact that Leicester City enjoyed a hugely successful season in 1999–2000.

Eighth in the Premiership (their best-ever finish), winners of the Worthington Cup and a place in 2000–01's UEFA Cup were more of a reward than any Foxes fan could have dreamed of at the start of the season, especially after the first game when Frank Sinclair kicked off a glut of Premiership own-goals with a late howler that handed Arsenal a 2–1 victory at Highbury.

When the same player put through his own net again to gift his old club Chelsea a 2–2 draw the following week, there were those fans who wondered if anything would ever go right. They need not have worried; after dropping to 16th following a 2–1 defeat by West Ham on 21 August, Leicester steadily climbed to fifth place and were never lower than 13th in the table thereafter.

The early form of midfield duo Neil Lennon and Muzzy Izzet was particularly impressive. Izzet, who had never been much of a goalscorer, suddenly discovered his shooting boots and had notched seven Premiership goals by early October, while Lennon shot to the top of the tackling charts with a series of committed displays alongside his midfield partner.

Izzet's form prompted widespread interest. And with England seemingly reluctant to offer him a chance, Izzet – whose father is Turkish – opted to play his international football for Turkey.

The buoyant mood created by the form of Izzet and co on the pitch was not reflected off it. Accusations of improper conduct regarding tickets for the 1999 Worthington Cup final were still hanging over certain players at the club. A boardroom meeting was convened to discuss this and alleged improprieties concerning links between a construction company, possible plans for a new stadium and chief executive Barrie Pierpoint.

The meeting ended in chaos with Sir Rodney Walker and John Elsom walking out after trading insults with Pierpoint and his allies on the board. This kick-started a dispute that was to rumble on for months threatening to tear the whole club apart. Things eventually resolved themselves, but City had come close to losing their manager, seen plans for a new stadium scrapped, and had players disciplined for their role in the distribution of their Worthington Cup tickets.

> **"People within the game who should know better decided to put the boot in, probably to conceal the real reasons for their failure to overcome us."**
> Martin O'Neill

Amazingly, the team were able to put all this to the back of their minds, and although they wavered in a two-month spell between December and February which saw them go seven league games without a win, their form in cup competitions was beginning to pick up.

After beating Crystal Palace and Grimsby in the second and third rounds respectively of the Worthington Cup, City faced two testing cup ties in the space of four days. First they travelled to non-league Hereford in the FA Cup third round, where they scraped a 0–0 draw. Then they returned to Filbert Street to play Leeds in an ill-tempered Worthington Cup fourth-round clash, which was won by the Foxes on a penalty shoot-out.

Hereford were beaten 2–1 in extra time in the FA Cup replay to set up a clash with cup favourites Arsenal. After drawing 0–0 in another bad-tempered clash at Highbury, City returned to Filbert Street to take on Fulham in the fifth round of the

15 Leicester scored more goals through

SEASON REVIEW

Worthington Cup. In what proved to be one of the most dramatic games of the season, City came back from 2–0 down with five minutes to play to level the game at 2–2. Then, trailing to a Chris Coleman goal in extra time, they levelled the scores again and, just as they had against Leeds, they held their nerve to win a penalty shoot-out.

When Arsenal visited a week later, the Gunners were expected by most people to beat a Leicester side which was without Cottee, Izzet and Lennon, but the Foxes' never-say-die spirit won the day as they resisted everything thrown at them to take the Gunners to a penalty shoot-out.

Man of the Match Tim Flowers had been forced to leave the field with an injury, but Pegguy Arphexad proved a capable deputy and made the saves that took City to their third shoot-out success of the nail-biting season.

"In order to attract top players we have to be near the top six. If we do that, people will realise we are a club worth joining."
Martin O'Neill

The game was not without its repercussions, though. Arsene Wenger derided Leicester for their "negativity", a charge that was picked up by Chelsea chairman Ken Bates ahead of the Foxes' next cup game. The London club won that clash to knock City out of the FA Cup but the manager of Leicester's next cup opponents, John Gregory, was quick to join in the mud-slinging, accusing Leicester of not crossing the half-way line in the 0–0 Worthington Cup semi-final first leg at Villa Park.

Leicester produced the perfect reply, winning the second leg 1–0, and went on to lift the cup with a 2–1 victory over Tranmere Rovers at Wembley courtesy of two trademark Matt Elliott headers. But there was still a feeling within the club that the team was not receiving the credit it deserved.

Leicester did not always complete as many passes as Arsenal or Chelsea and they certainly had fewer goal attempts, but they were resilient and felt that they deserved respect for that, not criticism.

They certainly had good players and one in particular, Emile Heskey, was attracting a lot of interest. Liverpool had been long-term admirers of the powerful striker and it was no surprise when he left for Anfield in an £11 million move.

His replacement Stan Collymore arrived for nothing, but the former Aston Villa man was soon back in the headlines for all the wrong reasons following his antics with a fire extinguisher in the Spanish resort of La Manga, which saw the club quickly ejected from their hotel. However, he scored a hat-trick in the 5–2 victory at Sunderland to answer his critics in the best possible way.

To Leicester's and Collymore's credit, they put the incident behind them, and although Collymore's season ended in misery when he broke his leg in the match with Derby, he looks like being a good signing for the club.

Unfortunately for Collymore and his team-mates, they will be without the inspirational O'Neill in 2000–01. The lure of Celtic proved too difficult for the Leicester manager to resist and he departed for Glasgow soon after the end of the Foxes' campaign.

Peter Taylor was appointed as boss and will try to steer the ship to glory on a fourth front in 2000–01. It remains to be seen whether the new manager can inspire the players to produce the same levels of performance. They will undoubtedly have their critics again, but if season 1999–2000 proved anything, it was that Leicester deserved everyone's respect.

their defenders than any other team

LEICESTER CITY

DATE	OPPONENT	SCORE	ATT.	ARPHEXAD	CAMPBELL	COLLYMORE	COTTEE	DUDFIELD	EADIE	ELLIOTT	FENTON	FLOWERS	GILCHRIS
7.8.99	Arsenal A	1–2	38,026	–	–	–	90^{1}	–	–	90□	–	90	–
11.8.99	Coventry H	1–0	19,196	–	s25	–	90	–	–	90	–	90	s22
14.8.99	Chelsea H	2–2	21,068	–	–	–	72	–	–	90□	–	90	s4
21.8.99	West Ham A	1–2	23,631	–	–	–	90	–	–	90	–	90	s18
24.8.99	Middlesbro A	3–0	33,126	s81	–	–	75^{1}	–	–	90	–	9	–
30.8.99	Watford H	1–0	17,920	90	–	–	86	–	–	90	–	–	–
11.9.99	Sunderland A	0–2	40,105	–	–	–	57	–	–	90	–	90	s19
18.9.99	Liverpool H	2–2	21,623	90	–	–	67^{1}	–	–	90	–	–	s23
25.9.99	Aston Villa H	3–1*	19,917	–	–	–	82^{1}	–	–	90	–	90□	90
3.10.99	Tottenham A	3–2	35,591	–	–	–	90	–	–	90	–	90	68
16.10.99	Southampton H	2–1	19,556	–	–	–	86^{1}	–	–	90	–	90	s13
23.10.99	Bradford A	1–3	17,655	–	–	–	71	–	–	90	–	90	90
30.10.99	Sheff Wed H	3–0	19,046	–	–	–	88^{1}	–	–	90	–	90	s13
6.11.99	Man Utd A	0–2	55,191	–	–	–	78	–	–	90	–	90	–
20.11.99	Wimbledon H	2–1	18,255	–	–	–	90^{2}	–	–	–	–	90	–
27.11.99	Coventry A	1–0	22,021	–	–	–	90	–	–	90	–	90	–
4.12.99	Arsenal H	0–3	20,495	–	–	–	83	–	–	90	–	90	–
18.12.99	Derby Co H	0–1	18,581	–	–	–	s17	–	90	90	–	90	–
26.12.99	Leeds A	1–2	40,105	90	–	–	90^{1}	–	90	90	–	–	65
28.12.99	Newcastle H	1–2	21,225	–	s57	–	60	–	90	90	–	90	90
3.1.00	Everton A	2–2	30,490	s82	s10	–	90	–	90	90^{2}	–	8	–
15.1.00	Chelsea A	1–1	35,063	90	–	–	–	–	90	90	s52□	–	90
22.1.00	West Ham H	1–3	19,019	90	90	–	–	–	90	90	90	–	90
5.2.00	Middlesbro H	2–1**	17,550	–	–	–	–	–	90	90	–	90	90
12.2.00	Watford A	1–1	16,814	–	–	90	90	–	90	90^{1}	–	90	90
5.3.00	Sunderland H	5–2	20,432	–	–	90^{3}	–	–	56	90	–	90	–
11.3.00	Wimbledon A	1–2	14,319	–	–	90	65	–	–	90	–	90	s39
18.3.00	Man Utd H	0–2	22,170	–	–	90	s19	–	82	90	–	90	–
26.3.00	Leeds H	2–1	21,095	–	–	90^{1}□	s24	–	66	90	–	90	s42
2.4.00	Derby Co A	0–3	25,763	90	–	23	–	–	73	90	–	–	s45
8.4.00	Everton H	1–1	18,705	–	–	–	65	s25	–	90	–	90	90
15.4.00	Newcastle A	2–0	36,246	–	–	–	90^{1}	–	–	90	–	90	90
19.4.00	Tottenham H	0–1	19,764	–	–	–	82	–	–	90	–	90	90
22.4.00	Aston Villa A	2–2	31,229	–	–	–	90	s31	–	90^{1}	–	90	90
29.4.00	Southampton A	2–1	15,178	–	–	–	79^{1}	–	s11	90	–	90	90
3.5.00	Liverpool A	2–0	43,456	90	–	–	85^{1}□	–	89	90	–	–	90^{1}
6.5.00	Bradford H	3–0	21,103	90	–	–	90^{1}	–	90	90^{2}	–	–	72
14.5.00	Sheff Wed A	0–4	21,656	90	–	–	70	–	90	90	–	–	45

□ Yellow card, ■ Red card, s Substitute, 90^{2} Goals scored

*including one own goal **including two own goals

1999–2000 PREMIERSHIP APPEARANCES

GOODWIN	GUNNLAUGSSON	GUPPY	HESKEY	IMPEY	IZZET	LENNON	MARSHALL	OAKES	SAVAGE	SINCLAIR	STEWART	TAGGART	THOMAS	WALSH	ZAGORAKIS	TOTAL
–	–	90	43	90	90	90	s47	–	90	90□	–	s72	–	18	–	990
–	–	90	–	90	90^{1}	90□	65□	–	90	90	–	68	–	–	–	990
–	–	90	90^{1}	90	90^{1}	90□	s18	–	90	90	–	86	–	–	–	990
–	–	90	90^{1}	90	90	90	s24	–	66	90□	–	72	–	–	–	990
–	–	90□	90^{2}□	–	90□	90	s15	–	90	90	–	90	–	–	–	990
–	–	90	90□	90	90^{1}□	90□	s4	68	90	90	–	90	–	–	s22	990
–	–	90	90	90	90	90	s33	–	71□	90	–	62■	–	–	–	962
–	–	90	90	60	90^{1}	90	–	s30	90	51■	–	90	–	–	–	951
–	–	90	90	90	90^{1}	90	s8	–	86	90	–	–	–	–	s4	990
–	–	90	90	90	90^{2}	90□	s22	–	90	–	–	90^{1}	–	–	–	990
–	–	90^{1}	90□	90	90	90	s4	–	89□	90	–	77	–	–	s1	990
–	–	90	90	90^{1}	90	90	s35	–	55	90□	–	–	–	s19	–	990
–	–	90	90	90	90	90	–	s2	86	90	–	77^{2}	–	–	s4	990
–	–	90	90	90	90	90	–	–	90	90	–	90	–	s12	–	990
–	–	90	90□	90	–	90	–	90	90	90□	–	90	–	90	–	990
–	–	90	90^{1}	90	90	90	–	–	90	90	–	90□	–	–	–	990
–	–	90	90	68	90	90	s22	s14	76	90	–	90	–	–	s7	990
–	–	–	90	73	90□	–	–	90	90	–	–	90	–	90	90□	990
–	–	–	90	–	90	–	–	90	90	90	–	90	–	–	s25□	990
–	–	–	90	–	33	–	–	–	90□	90	–	90□	s30	–	90^{1}	990
–	–	–	–	–	–	89	–	90	90	90□	–	90	s1	90	80	990
–	53	s37	90	–	–	–	38	90	–	90	–	90^{1}	–	–	90	990
90	57	–	90^{1}	–	–	–	–	–	–	90□	s23	–	s33	–	67	990
–	–	–	–	84	90	90	–	90	90	90	–	90	–	s6	–	990
–	–	–	90	90	–	–	–	90	–	–	–	–	–	90□	90	990
–	–	90	90^{1}□	–	90	90□	–	s34^{1}	90	90	–	90	–	–	–	990
–	–	90	–	90	90	90	s25	–	51	90	–	90^{1}	–	–	–	990
–	–	90	–	–	90	90	s8	71	90	90	–	90	–	–	–	990
–	–	90^{1}	–	–	90	90□	–	90	90	48	–	90	–	–	–	990
–	–	90	–	s17	90	68■	s67	90	90	45	–	90□	–	–	–	968
–	–	90□	–	90	80	90	s45	45	90	–	–	90^{1}□	–	–	s10	990
–	–	90	–	90	–	90	s22	68	82^{1}	90	–	90	–	–	s8	990
–	–	23	–	90	90	–	s8	90	90	90	–	90	–	–	s67	990
–	–	–	–	90	73	90^{1}□	–	59	90	90	–	90□	–	–	s17	990
–	–	90	–	90	90^{1}	90	–	–	90	90	–	36	–	s54□	–	990
–	–	90	–	90	90	90	s5	s1	90□	90	–	–	–	–	–	990
–	–	90	–	72	90	90	–	s8	90	82□	–	–	–	s18	s18	990
–	–	90	–	45	90	90	s20	s45	90	90	–	–	–	s45	–	990

THE MANAGER

MARTIN O'NEILL

"What's the point in giving you the ball when there's a bloody genius on the other wing?"

While Brian Clough may not have rated Martin O'Neill's playing ability that highly, few can doubt that the Irishman is establishing himself as one of the top managers in the game.

The 1999–2000 campaign was O'Neill's most successful in the Premiership, with an impressive eighth-placed finish being backed up by the Foxes' Worthington Cup triumph, which guarantees City a place in the 2000–01 UEFA Cup.

O'Neill joined the Foxes in December 1995, but it is with Wycombe Wanderers that the Ulsterman first made his name. He guided the Chairboys to the Vauxhall Conference title in 1993, and in 1994 promotion from Division Three via the play-offs was achieved. The following year O'Neill's side finished sixth in Division Two to complete a remarkable era for the club.

Few can deny that the Irishman has also done a fantastic job at Filbert Street, keeping them in the top flight for four successive seasons, and helping them qualify for Europe twice in that time. His stock is so high that it seemed only a matter of time before a big club came calling and after turning down Leeds in 1998, O'Neill could not resist the lure of Celtic in 2000.

LEAGUE POSITION

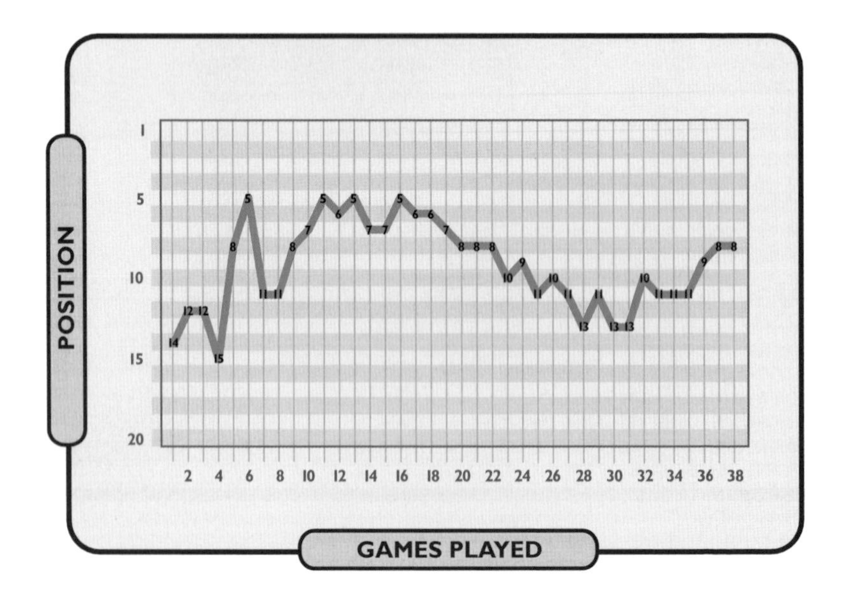

27% of Leicester's goals were scored by defenders

THE GOALS

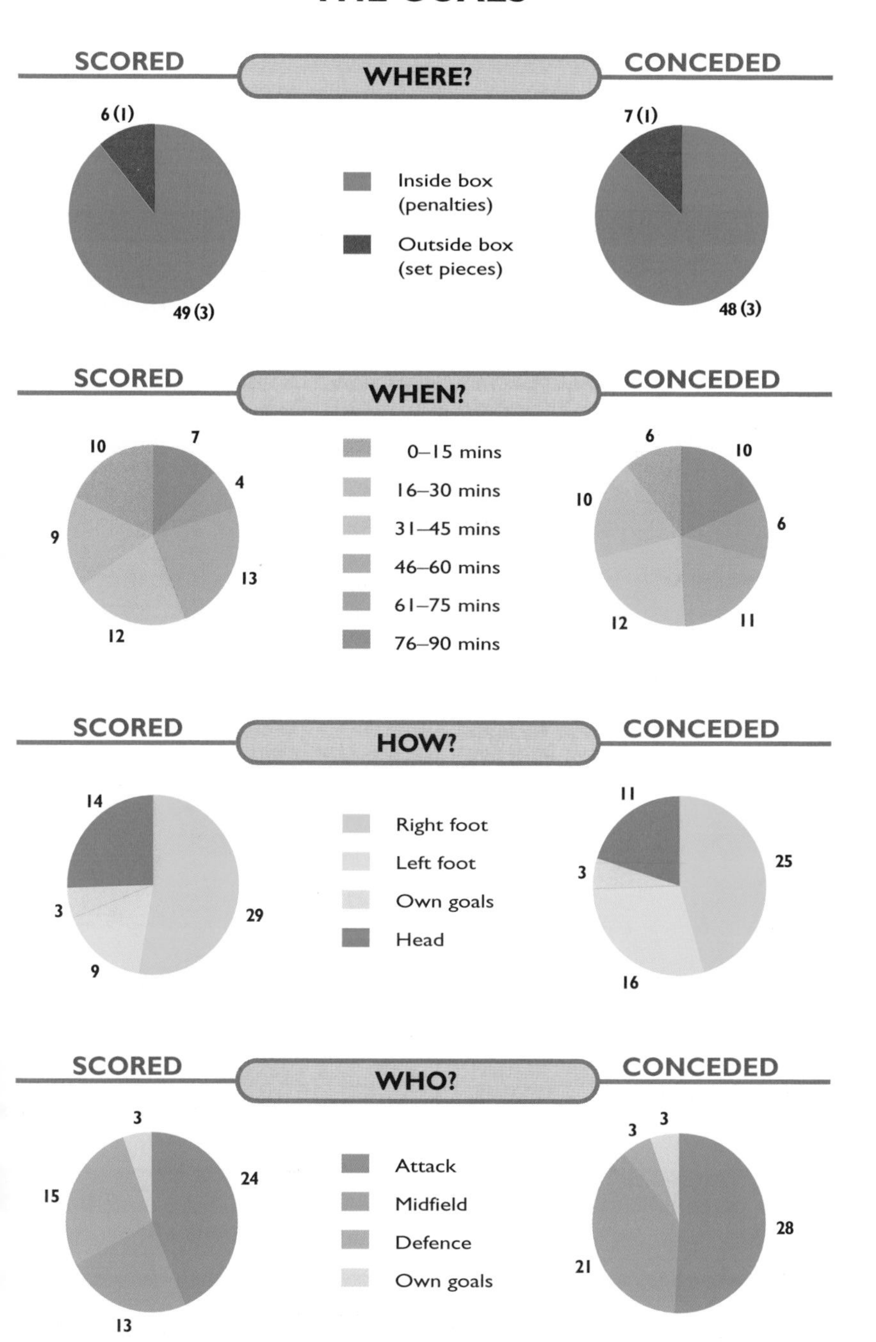

– the highest ratio in the Premiership

LEICESTER CITY

	CAMPBELL	COLLYMORE	COTTEE	DUDFIELD	EADIE	ELLIOTT	FENTON	GILCHRIST	GOODWIN	GUNNLAUGSS	GUPP
APPEARANCES											
Start	1	6	30	0	15	37	1	17	1	2	29
Sub	3	0	3	2	1	0	1	10	0	0	1
Minutes on pitch	182	473	2491	56	1277	3330	142	1658	90	110	2580
GOAL ATTEMPTS											
Goals	0	4	13	0	0	6	0	1	0	0	2
Shots on target	0	11	24	0	9	20	0	1	0	0	5
Shots off target	1	7	16	0	7	26	3	1	0	0	11
Shooting accuracy	0%	61%	60%	0%	56%	43%	0%	50%	0%	0%	31%
PASSING											
Goal assists	1	1	1	0	0	3	1	0	0	0	7
Long passes	3	27	48	0	56	391	19	229	8	3	312
Short passes	40	161	605	7	254	849	44	345	6	28	684
PASS COMPLETION											
Own half %	79%	81%	88%	50%	72%	79%	70%	65%	80%	73%	77%
Opposition half %	63%	63%	74%	75%	64%	63%	55%	59%	33%	72%	58%
CROSSING											
Total crosses	9	4	12	0	37	18	3	6	4	1	255
Cross completion %	11%	25%	33%	0%	32%	33%	0%	33%	25%	0%	35%
DRIBBLING											
Dribbles & runs	12	15	58	4	56	33	8	23	2	7	114
Dribble completion %	75%	47%	66%	75%	86%	97%	88%	96%	100%	86%	72%
DEFENDING											
Tackles made	3	2	7	0	39	73	6	56	3	4	49
Tackles won %	67%	50%	57%	0%	41%	48%	83%	34%	67%	75%	41%
Blocks	1	0	2	0	3	90	0	44	5	0	15
Clearances	1	1	3	0	14	360	3	168	12	0	51
Interceptions	4	0	3	0	3	21	2	12	1	0	7
DISCIPLINE											
Fouls	2	8	28	1	15	54	4	13	0	4	21
Offside	1	9	31	0	4	8	1	0	0	1	5
Yellow cards	0	1	1	0	0	2	1	0	0	0	2
Red cards	0	0	0	0	0	0	0	0	0	0	0

GOALKEEPER NAME	START/ (SUB)	TIME ON PITCH	GOALS CONCEDED	MINS/GOALS CONCEDED	SAVES MADE	SAVES/ SHOTS
ARPHEXAD	9(2)	973	17	57	48	74%
FLOWERS	29	2447	38	64	78	67%

PLAYERS' STATISTICS

HESKEY	IMPEY	IZZET	LENNON	MARSHALL	OAKES	SAVAGE	SINCLAIR	STEWART	TAGGART	THOMAS	WALSH	ZAGORAKIS	TOTAL	RANK
23	28	32	31	2	15	35	34	0	30	0	5	6		
0	1	0	0	19	7	0	0	1	1	3	6	11		
2023	2399	2796	2767	535	1345	3002	2926	23	2620	64	532	690		
7	1	8	1	0	1	1	0	0	6	0	0	1	55*	8th
25	4	24	8	7	2	5	1	0	10	0	0	3	159	=16th
27	8	21	9	8	9	7	3	1	16	1	1	6	189	17th
48%	33%	53%	47%	47%	18%	42%	25%	0%	38%	0%	0%	33%	46%	12th
3	2	3	6	0	3	1	1	0	3	0	0	1	37	10th
44	167	208	310	8	233	231	386	0	355	5	91	68	3202	13th
867	620	1029	1482	185	437	710	636	10	569	14	115	197	9894	14th
80%	74%	83%	90%	79%	80%	74%	78%	100%	73%	50%	67%	76%	79%	12th
65%	66%	71%	79%	63%	59%	60%	56%	63%	52%	67%	45%	60%	65%	8th
41	101	107	54	7	80	50	41	1	16	3	1	28	879	4th
29%	35%	32%	39%	14%	35%	24%	29%	0%	44%	33%	100%	36%	33%	3rd
99	132	124	85	5	41	71	56	2	37	9	7	22	1022	12th
70%	72%	66%	85%	80%	80%	72%	88%	100%	89%	56%	100%	82%	76%	12th
24	67	114	149	5	50	146	121	0	98	4	18	41	1079	4th
58%	58%	68%	70%	40%	58%	53%	55%	0%	52%	25%	50%	54%	56%	3rd
11	17	31	23	1	9	28	79	0	65	1	17	4	447	6th
23	76	62	45	7	20	111	315	0	359	3	88	9	1743	3rd
6	20	31	25	0	5	25	25	0	29	1	4	6	230	14th
46	13	29	32	12	10	44	43	0	46	0	12	7	445	19th
25	2	11	1	9	0	5	1	0	5	0	0	1	120	=14th
5	0	3	7	1	0	4	7	0	5	0	2	2	44	19th
0	0	0	1	0	0	0	1	0	1	0	0	0	3	=12th

*Including three own goals

ROSSES AUGHT	CROSSES PUNCHED	CROSSES NOT CLAIMED	CATCH SUCCESS	THROWS/ SHORT KICKS	% COMPLETION	LONG KICKS	% COMPLETION
18	1	0	100%	40	88%	303	44%
31	19	1	97%	72	90%	816	47%

PLAYER OF THE SEASON

PLAYER	INDEX SCORE
NEIL LENNON	1,177
Muzzy Izzet	1,115
Gerry Taggart	978
Emile Heskey	909
Matt Elliott	908
Frank Sinclair	819
Andrew Impey	739
Robbie Savage	657
Tony Cottee	621
Steve Guppy	620

The Foxes' bargain buy from Crewe, Neil Lennon, once again proved what a shrewd judge of a player Martin O'Neill is by topping the Opta Season Index for Leicester once again.

Lennon saw off the challenge from midfield partner Muzzy Izzet to finish the season with an average points total of 1,177. The tenacious Northern Ireland international will be looking forward to European competition in 2000–01 following more silverware with Leicester in the form of the Worthington Cup.

The former Railwayman enhanced his reputation as one of the best tacklers in the country by winning the second highest number of challenges in the Premiership. He also had an impressive pass completion rate of 83% and was credited with six goal assists.

Izzet was not far behind Lennon with 1,115 points. He made far more of a goalscoring contribution than the Irishman, netting eight times in the league from midfield. He also provided 107 crosses and made 114 tackles as he and Lennon imposed themselves in the middle of the park.

Elsewhere, Leicester's defensive pairing also had a huge influence on the side during the 1999–2000 season. Gerry Taggart and Matt Elliott were the joint-highest scoring defenders from open play in the Premiership with six goals apiece as the Foxes made light of their regular striker shortages.

Taggart made 359 clearances and 98 tackles, while in the attacking third of the pitch he not only scored goals but also contributed three assists.

Elliott can claim similar stats to those of his defensive partner. The Worthington Cup hero made 360 clearances in the league and can also lay claim to three goal assists.

Former striker Emile Heskey registered his average of 909 points before his departure to Liverpool, after netting seven goals for the Foxes helping him become a fixture in the England squad.

33% Tony Cottee had the best

FIVE OF THE BEST

Once again Martin O'Neill defied the critics and gave the fans some very special moments in 1999–2000. A Worthington Cup win and a best-ever Premiership finish of eighth were just rewards for some gritty displays, including a victory at Anfield for a third successive year. O'Neill has left a healthy legacy for incoming Foxes supremo Peter Taylor.

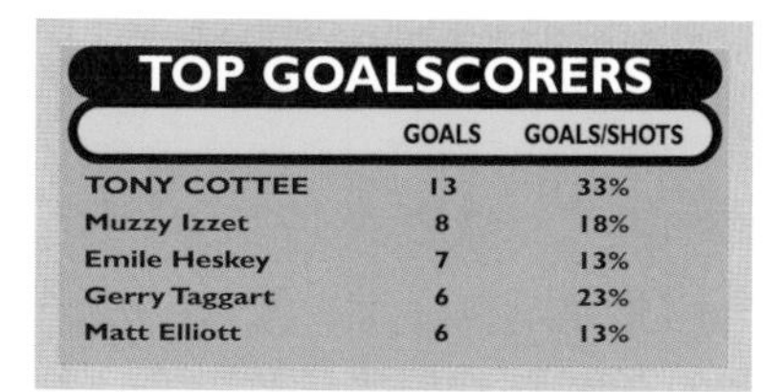

TOP GOALSCORERS

	GOALS	GOALS/SHOTS
TONY COTTEE	13	33%
Muzzy Izzet	8	18%
Emile Heskey	7	13%
Gerry Taggart	6	23%
Matt Elliott	6	13%

The vast majority of the scouts came to the east Midlands to slaver over Emile Heskey, but it was wily veteran Tony Cottee who finished as the club's top scorer. His 13 goals came from just 40 shots, a deadly ratio in any environment. The other supremely accurate Fox was Gerry Taggart, who finished with a goals-to-shots ratio of 23%, his most important strike being the winner at Spurs. His defensive partner Matt Elliott also chipped in with six goals.

Neil Lennon had an immense campaign for Leicester, and finished as the club's premier ball-player for the second season running. Only Roy Keane made more successful passes in the Premiership than the former Crewe player, and Lennon was forced to miss seven games as well. His completion rate was far superior to his team-mates, with only Muzzy Izzet coming anywhere near. Steve Guppy did not enjoy his best season at the club and his passing suffered.

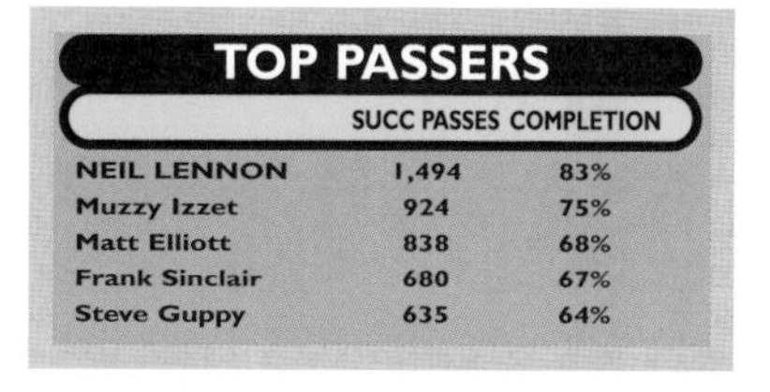

TOP PASSERS

	SUCC PASSES	COMPLETION
NEIL LENNON	1,494	83%
Muzzy Izzet	924	75%
Matt Elliott	838	68%
Frank Sinclair	680	67%
Steve Guppy	635	64%

TOP TACKLERS

	WON	SUCCESS
NEIL LENNON	104	70%
Muzzy Izzet	78	68%
Robbie Savage	78	53%
Frank Sinclair	66	55%
Gerry Taggart	51	52%

Only two players in the Premiership won more than 100 tackles, and Neil Lennon was one of them. He was a powerhouse in the Leicester engine-room, breaking up the opposition's play and being equally constructive. His midfield colleagues, Muzzy Izzet and Robbie Savage, were locked on 78 tackles, with the Turkish player being more successful. The new boss will be keen to keep the three players at the club, as they are one of the most effective units in the Premiership.

Frank Sinclair scored own-goals in consecutive games at the start of the 1999–2000 season, something that left him red-faced and the focus of much attention from the media. He recovered to play a solid role at the back for the Foxes but still finished as the most indisciplined player at the club. Seven yellow cards and one red helped him to 70 Opta points, but only Manchester United were better-behaved than City, and the Foxes have little to worry about in this area.

DISCIPLINE

	POINTS	FOULS & CARDS
FRANK SINCLAIR	70	43F, 7Y, 1R
Gerry Taggart	67	46F, 5Y, 1R
Emile Heskey	61	46F, 5Y, 0R
Matt Elliott	60	54F, 2Y, 0R
Neil Lennon	59	32F, 7Y, 1R

goals-to-shots ratio in the top flight

ACTION	COLLYMORE	EADIE	ELLIOTT	FLOWERS	GUPPY	HESKEY	IZZET	LENNON	OAKES	SAVAGE	SINCLAIR	TAGGART	TOTAL	SUNDERLAND
Time on pitch	90	56	90	90	90	90	90	90	34	90	90	90	990	990
GOALS														
Goal	3	–	–	–	–	1	–	–	1	–	–	–	5	2
Shot on target	1	–	–	–	–	–	–	–	–	–	–	–	1	2
Shot off target	1	–	–	–	1	1	1	–	–	–	–	–	4	5
Blocked shot	1	–	–	–	–	2	–	–	–	–	–	–	3	5
Own goal	–	–	–	–	–	–	–	–	–	–	–	–	–	–
PASSES														
Pass to own player	14	10	28	–	19	24	28	49	7	21	20	19	239	261
Pass to opposition	10	6	6	–	8	12	14	10	3	13	17	23	122	127
Cross to own player	–	1	1	–	2	2	–	1	1	–	–	2	10	10
Cross to opposition player	1	1	1	–	2	5	5	1	1	2	–	1	20	18
Goal assist	–	–	–	–	–	2	–	2	–	–	–	–	4	1
Pass completion %	56%	61%	81%	0%	68%	62%	60%	83%	67%	58%	54%	47%	64%	65%
TACKLES & CLEARANCES														
Tackle	–	3	–	–	2	–	6	3	3	4	5	2	28	20
Clearances, blocks and interceptions	–	1	14	–	–	–	4	3	1	–	11	13	47	41
DRIBBLES & RUNS														
Dribble ball retained	1	4	–	–	–	6	2	1	1	1	–	–	16	11
Dribble ball lost	2	1	–	–	1	3	–	–	–	–	–	–	7	11
Dribble success %	33%	80%	0%	0%	0%	67%	100%	100%	100%	100%	0%	0%	70%	50%
DISCIPLINE														
Fouls	1	1	–	–	–	3	2	3	1	3	1	1	16	16
Penalty conceded	–	–	–	–	–	–	–	–	–	–	–	–	–	
Free kick – offside	1	–	–	–	1	–	–	–	–	–	–	–	2	1
Yellow cards	–	–	–	–	–	1	–	1	–	–	–	–	2	2
Red cards	–	–	–	–	–	–	–	–	–	–	–	–	–	–
GOALKEEPERS														
Distribution to own player	–	–	–	13	–	–	–	–	–	–	–	–	13	16
Distribution to opposition player	–	–	–	15	–	–	–	–	–	–	–	–	15	12
Goalkeeper distribution %	0%	0%	0%	46%	0%	0%	0%	0%	0%	0%	0%	0%	46%	57%
Save	–	–	–	2	–	–	–	–	–	–	–	–	2	1
Ball caught	–	–	–	1	–	–	–	–	–	–	–	–	1	1
Ball dropped	–	–	–	–	–	–	–	–	–	–	–	–	–	–
Goal conceded	–	–	–	2	–	–	–	–	–	–	–	–	2	5

233 Leicester delivered the joint-highest

Prior to this televised game, the News of the World ran stories of Stan Collymore discharging a fire extinguisher at a hotel in Spain and urged Martin O'Neill to sack his latest signing. But the manager stuck by him and for the first time in months, Stan was indeed "The Man" as Leicester trounced high-flying Sunderland.

O'Neill's decision was justified in spectacular style after only 17 minutes. Emile Heskey flicked on a long pass and Collymore smashed the ball into the top corner, illustrating why he is still regarded as one of the English game's most natural talents.

Buoyed by this excellent start, Leicester started to play some of their best football of the season in front of a television audience who, a week earlier, had seen the Foxes grind their way to a Worthington Cup final win.

The second goal came from Heskey and was set up by Neil Lennon. The Irishman won the ball in a 50–50 challenge with Chris Makin and threaded a pass between two defenders for Heskey to run on to and drill past Thomas Sorensen.

It was all too much for Sunderland's assistant manager Bobby Saxton. He was banished from the dug-out by referee Neale Barry after heated comments directed towards the official.

Leicester totally dominated the first half, firing in seven shots, and the home fans struck up an ironic chorus of "Boring, boring Leicester" as the Foxes played some excellent attacking football.

Eight minutes into the second half, though, Sunderland pulled a goal back through a brilliant Kevin Phillips strike. The visitors' most effectual top cat pounced on a low cross to volley home.

Collymore, though, scored his second on the hour and it was almost as spectacular as the first. Neil Lennon played the ball into the area from deep and Collymore craned his neck to direct the ball in from 17 yards. Martin O'Neill's "I told you so" smile was just as wide as Collymore's.

With 15 minutes to go Niall Quinn pulled another goal back for the travelling team – and it was one of his best of the season. The big Irishman brought the ball down with excellent close control, nutmegged Matt Elliott and curled the ball low into the far corner.

With three minutes remaining Collymore completed his hat-trick and claimed the match ball. Heskey broke free down the right and drilled the ball to the far post for the Villa reject to tap in his third.

Substitute Stefan Oakes scored a deflected 25-yard free-kick in injury time to seal a fantastic result for the Filbert Street outfit and prove that on their day, the Foxes can play exciting football.

O'Neill's side hit the target with six shots and scored five times. The star of the show was Collymore, who scored from half of his six goal attempts. His strike partner, Heskey, went on nine dribbles and runs, successfully completing two-thirds of them and ultimately speeding up his move to Liverpool, while in midfield, Lennon was outstanding. The Irish midfielder attempted more passes on the pitch than any other player (59) and was accurate with 83% of his distribution.

Carlsberg

LIVERPOOL

ADDRESS

Anfield Road, Anfield, Liverpool L4 0TH

CONTACT NUMBERS

Telephone: 0151 263 2361
Fax: 0151 260 8813
Ticket Office: 0151 260 8680
Club Call: 09068 121184
Superstore: 0151 263 1760
Website: www.liverpoolfc.net

KEY PERSONNEL

Chairman: D R Moores
Vice-Chairman/President: P B Robinson
Chief Executive: R N Parry BSC, FCA
Directors: J T Cross, N White FSCA
T D Smith, T W Saunders
K E B Clayton FCA, J Burns
Club Secretary: W B Morrison
Manager: Gerard Houllier

SPONSORS

Carlsberg

FANZINES

All Day and All of the Night
Red All Over the Land
Another Vintage Liverpool Performance

COLOURS

Home: Red shirts, shorts and stockings
Away: Green shirts with white and navy trim, navy shorts, green stockings

NICKNAME

The Reds

HONOURS

League Champions: 1900–01, 1905–06, 1921–22, 1922–23, 1946–47, 1963–64, 1965–66, 1972–73, 1975–76, 1976–77, 1978–79, 1979–80, 1981–82, 1982–83, 1983–84, 1985–86, 1987–88, 1989–90
Division Two Champions: 1893–94, 1895–96, 1904–05, 1961–62
FA Cup: 1965, 1974, 1986, 1989, 1992
League Cup: 1981, 1982, 1983, 1984, 1995
European Cup: 1976–77, 1977–78, 1980–81, 1983–84
UEFA Cup: 1972–73, 1975–76
European Super Cup: 1977

RECORD GOALSCORER

Roger Hunt – 245 league goals, 1959–69

BIGGEST WIN

10–1 v Rotherham Town – Division Two, 18 February 1896

BIGGEST DEFEAT

1–9 v Birmingham City – Division Two, 11 December 1954

SEASON REVIEW

Liverpool made big strides in 1999–2000, and it is a measure of their progress that qualification for the UEFA Cup ultimately represented a big disappointment to the team from Anfield. No doubt they would have been happier with such an outcome three games into the season when, after beating Sheffield Wednesday 2–1 on the opening day, they slumped to two successive 1–0 defeats by Watford and Middlesbrough.

Paul Ince, who had been offloaded to Middlesbrough in the summer, went as far as to claim that Gerard Houllier and his assistant Phil Thompson should be sacked. Losing the services of Steve McManaman to Real Madrid had been beyond the club's control, but as well as selling the likes of Ince and David James, Houllier had added plenty of new faces to his squad, so it was bound to take the team some time to gel. Injuries to Stephane Henchoz and Dietmar Hamann did not help matters, while the absence of Michael Owen had deprived the side of a key player up front.

"Of course we would prefer to play in the Champions League, but my job is to view the season from an overall perspective and we have made sound progress."
Gerard Houllier

Titi Camara filled in well, scoring in his first game and quickly becoming a real favourite with the Kop, but with Robbie Fowler departing the scene with a bad long-term injury after just eight games and Owen struggling to regain full fitness, Liverpool found it difficult to field an effective strikeforce until they signed Emile Heskey from Leicester.

For all their problems up front, there was a new steel about Liverpool's defence. Not since the days of Alan Hansen and Mark Lawrenson had Anfield seen as effective a central defensive pairing as Sami Hyypia and Stephane Henchoz. With Dutch goalkeeper Sander Westerveld in good form, Dominic Matteo the club's most improved player and Jamie Carragher also playing well, Liverpool finished the 1999–2000 season with the best defensive record in the Premiership.

The familiar weakness in the air was in evidence when arch-rivals Manchester United ran out 3–2 winners at Anfield courtesy of two Jamie Carragher own-goals. Liverpool found it impossible to defend against David Beckham's crosses that day, but the Champions were the only side to score more than two goals against them all season.

Defeat by Everton in a chaotic Merseyside derby, on the back of the Manchester United result and a 2–2 draw against Leicester, left Liverpool in 12th place. They then went unbeaten in their next seven games, though, climbing to fifth place in the process.

Injuries to key players were worrying, but there was a plus point in the shape of the young players who stepped up to replace them. Steven Gerrard, in particular, proved to be one of the finds of the season, not only for Liverpool but for England, too.

The 19-year-old looked comfortable at right-back, but really came into his own when he moved into midfield where, along with David Thompson and Danny Murphy, he impressed whenever he played, eventually earning an England call-up.

In fact, the introduction of Gerrard and Thompson seemed to provide the team with new impetus, and although they fell to defeats in London at both West Ham and Tottenham, they were steadily climbing the Premiership table, eventually hitting second place in March.

The defeat at Tottenham proved to be their last in the league for 13 games, a period in which the team conceded just seven goals and kept seven clean sheets. This new mean streak was particularly

0 Liverpool were the only side not to lose

SEASON REVIEW

pleasing for Houllier who, unlike his recent predecessors, had successfully tackled the defensive weaknesses that had blighted Liverpool for a decade.

The cups proved less fruitful. Third Division Hull City were beaten in the second round of the Worthington Cup, but when third-round opponents Southampton knocked the Reds out in October, the FA Cup represented their only realistic hope of a trophy. Huddersfield were beaten 2–0 in the third round but Blackburn Rovers momentarily put their troubles behind them to pull off a shock 1–0 win at Anfield.

At least that left Liverpool free to concentrate on their quest for Champions League football. With Leeds and Arsenal both stuttering, it meant the Merseyside club could take the opportunity to consolidate their second-placed position.

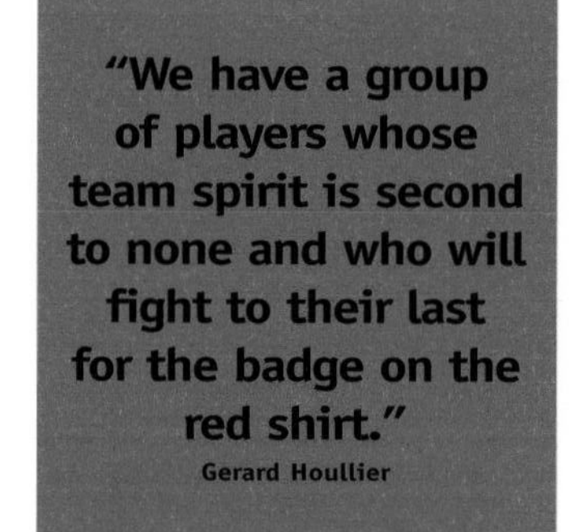

"We have a group of players whose team spirit is second to none and who will fight to their last for the badge on the red shirt."
Gerard Houllier

With five games to go Liverpool were five points clear of their two nearest rivals and also appeared to be certainties for the Champions League. Emile Heskey had taken a bit of time to settle but was forging a useful-looking partnership with Owen.

When Heskey grabbed both goals in a comfortable 2–1 victory against Wimbledon, few would have believed that Liverpool would fail to find the net again in the five remaining games of the season. Robbie Fowler was on the comeback trail, as was Jamie Redknapp, so the team's haul of just two points out of a possible 15 was hard to explain.

They were still expected to beat Bradford on the last day of the season. With Leeds only managing a draw at Upton Park against West Ham, a victory would have taken them into third place, but they were unable to match Bradford's desire and went down 1–0.

Houllier professed that he was satisfied with the season. His side still need to score more goals – their final tally of 51 was beaten by 10 other Premiership sides. There is no doubt that the absence of Fowler and Owen for large chunks of the 1999–2000 season was a significant factor in Liverpool's failure to qualify for the Champions League.

As well as their defence played, the Reds found it particularly hard to break down the massed defences of visiting teams to Anfield, dropping points against the likes of Leicester City, Watford, Middlesbrough and Southampton at home.

But Houllier's team have finally shed the "Spice Boys" tag with which they were saddled, replacing it with a new sense of resolve typified by the likes of Hyypia and Henchoz. With the addition of more proven winners like Markus Babbel, the club's future looks in fine shape. If they can keep their opponents to the average of 0.79 goals a game that they managed in 1999–2000 and improve in attack, the current Liverpool side could well be the one to bring glory back to Anfield.

They will start the 2000–01 season among the favourites to win the Premiership and, while Houllier may publicly play down his side's Championship chances, privately he must feel that he is close to finding the winning formula.

Money is available to improve a squad that is already looking strong. And even if the title proves beyond them, Liverpool look well placed for another tilt at the Champions League places.

If they can achieve that aim and combine it with a successful run in either the UEFA or FA Cup then they will have taken another significant step in the right direction.

a Premiership match after taking a lead

LIVERPOOL

DATE	OPPONENT	SCORE	ATT.	BERGER	CAMARA	CARRAGHER	FOWLER	FRIEDEL	GERRARD	HAMANN	HEGGEM	HENC
7.8.99	Sheff Wed A	2–1	34,853	90	89^{1}	90	90^{1}	–	–	25	90	–
14.8.99	Watford H	0–1	44,174	90	90	90	90	–	57	–	81	–
21.8.99	Middlesbro A	0–1	34,783	65	90□	90	90□	–	90□	–	90	–
23.8.99	Leeds Utd A	2–1*	39,703	90	90^{1}□	90	90	–	90	–	–	–
28.8.99	Arsenal H	2–0	44,886	90^{1}□	87	90	90^{1}	–	90	–	s20	–
11.9.99	Man Utd H	2–3	44,929	90^{1}	64□	90	90	–	64	–	s26	–
18.9.99	Leicester A	2–2	21,623	90	56	90	–	–	90□	–	90	–
27.9.99	Everton H	0–1	44,802	90	s20	90	65	–	s24■	65	90	–
2.10.99	Aston Villa A	0–0	39,217	90	s9□	s14	–	–	s58	76□	–	90□
16.10.99	Chelsea H	1–0	44,826	–	–	90	–	90	–	–	s10	90
23.10.99	Southampton A	1–1	15,241	–	90^{1}	90	–	90	–	–	s17	90□
27.10.99	West Ham H	1–0	44,012	90	78^{1}	90□	–	–	–	–	s17	90
1.11.99	Bradford H	3–1	40,483	90	90^{1}	s18□	–	–	–	90	$s13^{1}$	90
6.11.99	Derby Co H	2–0	44,467	–	57	90	–	–	s10	90	90	90
20.11.99	Sunderland A	2–0	42,015	90^{1}	–	–	–	–	81□	90	s1	90□
27.11.99	West Ham A	0–1	26,043	19	–	–	–	–	90	90	90	90
5.12.99	Sheff Wed H	4–1	42,517	–	90	s17	s9	–	90^{1}	90	–	90□
18.12.99	Coventry H	2–0	44,024	90	86^{1}	90	–	–	90	90	s4	90
26.12.99	Newcastle A	2–2	36,445	90	70	90	s8	–	90	90	s20	–
28.12.99	Wimbledon H	3–1	44,107	90^{1}	89	90	$s30^{1}$	–	90	–	90	90
03.1.00	Tottenham A	0–1	36,044	73	90□	58□	–	–	90	90	90	90
15.1.00	Watford A	3–2	21,367	90^{1}	85	90	–	–	90	63□	–	90□
22.1.00	Middlesbro H	0–0	44,324	90	–	90	–	–	90	90	–	90
5.2.00	Leeds Utd H	3–1	44,793	90^{1}	71	90	–	–	90□	90^{1}□	–	90
13.2.00	Arsenal A	1–0	38,098	90	90^{1}□	90	–	–	33	90	s57	90
4.3.00	Man Utd A	1–1	61,592	90^{1}	77	90	–	–	–	90	19	90
11.3.00	Sunderland H	1–1	44,693	90^{1}	s7	90□	–	–	45□	90	–	90
15.3.00	Aston Villa H	0–0	43,615	90	s24	90	–	–	78	90	–	90
18.3.00	Derby Co A	2–0	33,378	90	$s18^{1}$	90	–	–	90	90	–	90
25.3.00	Newcastle H	2–1	44,743	88	90^{1}	90	–	–	79	90	–	90
1.4.00	Coventry A	3–0	23,098	90	s10	90	–	–	70	90□	–	84
9.4.00	Tottenham H	2–0	44,536	90^{1}	s3	90	–	–	–	90	s8	90
16.4.00	Wimbledon A	2–1	26,102	90	s11	90	–	–	90	90	–	90
21.4.00	Everton A	0–0	40,052	90	–	90	s45	–	90	90□	s34	90□
29.4.00	Chelsea A	0–2	34,957	90	s24	90	s15	–	51	66	–	90
3.5.00	Leicester H	0–2	43,456	90□	s24□	90	s38	–	–	52	–	90□
7.5.00	Southampton H	0–0	44,015	90	80	90	59	–	–	s14	–	90
14.5.00	Bradford A	0–1	18,276	61	s29	90	–	–	61	90□	–	90□

□ Yellow card, ■ Red card, s Substitute, 90^{2} Goals scored

*including one own goal

1999–2000 PREMIERSHIP APPEARANCES

HESKEY	HYYPIA	MATTEO	MEIJER	MURPHY	NEWBY	OWEN	REDKNAPP	RIEDLE	SMICER	SONG	STAUNTON	THOMPSON	WESTERVELD	TOTAL
–	90	90	s1	–	–	–	90	–	90	–	s5	s60□	90	990
–	90	90	–	–	–	–	90	s18	72	s9	–	s33□	90	990
–	90	90	s19	–	–	–	90	–	–	–	71	s25	90	990
–	90	90	–	–	–	–	90	–	–	90□	–	90	90	990
–	90	90	–	–	–	s3	90	–	–	90	–	70	90	990
–	90[1]	90	–	–	–	s26	90□	–	s45	90□	–	45	90	990
–	90	90	s34	s11	–	90[2]	79	–	–	–	–	89■	90	989
–	90	–	s25	–	–	90□	90□	–	70	–	90□	–	75■	974
–	90□	–	90□	–	–	81	90□	–	32	90	31■	–	90	931
–	90	–	s4	80□	–	86	90□	–	90	90	90□	90[1]□	–	990
–	90	–	58	58	–	s21	90	–	73	90	90	s32	–	979
–	90	90	90	–	–	–	90	–	s12	90	–	73	90	990
–	90	–	s9	–	–	–	72[1]	–	81	90	90	77	90	990
–	90	–	s33	s76[1]	–	80	90[1]	–	14	–	90	–	90	990
–	90	90	s16	74	–	89[1]	90	–	–	90	–	s9□	90	990
–	90	90	s21	90	–	74□	–	–	–	69	s16	s71□	90	990
–	90[1]	90	–	76[1]	–	81	–	–	–	73	s14	90[1]□	90	990
–	90	90	–	s2	–	90[1]	–	–	s52	–	–	36	90	990
–	90	90	–	82	–	90[2]	–	–	–	90	–	–	90	990
–	90	90	–	60	–	65[1]	–	–	s25	s1	–	–	90	990
–	90	90□	–	s17	–	–	–	–	81□	–	s9	s32	90	990
–	90□	90□	–	s16	–	74	–	–	s27[1]	–	s5	90[1]	90	990
–	90	90	s62	s33	s14	28	–	–	76	–	–	57	90	990
–	90	90	90	s19[1]	–	–	–	–	90	–	–	–	90	990
–	90	90	54	s36	–	–	–	–	90	–	–	–	90	990
–	45	90	90□	s45	–	s13	–	–	90	s71	–	–	90	990
90	90	90	77	s45	–	s13	–	–	–	83	–	–	90	990
90	90	90	s8	–	–	66	s12	–	–	–	–	82	90	990
88	90	90	–	–	–	72[1]	s2	–	–	–	–	90	90	990
90	90	90	s14	s2	–	–	s11[1]	–	–	–	–	76	90	990
90[1]	90	90	–	s20	–	80[2]	–	–	–	s6	–	90	90	990
90	90	90	–	82□	–	87[1]	–	–	s17	–	–	73	90	990
79[2]	90	90	–	s7	–	83	–	–	s28	–	–	62	90	990
45	90	90	–	–	–	90	–	–	–	–	–	56□	90	990
90	90	90	–	75	–	90	s39	–	–	–	–	–	90	990
90	90	90	–	s16□	–	66	90	–	–	–	–	74	90	990
90	90	90	s10	–	–	–	90	–	–	76	–	s31	90	990
90	90	82	s8	–	–	90	90	–	s29	–	–	–	90	990

THE MANAGER

GERARD HOULLIER

Former French national manager Gerard Houllier has been at Liverpool for two seasons but 1999–2000 was his first in sole charge of the club, and he can look back with pride on a job well done so far.

Houllier will recognise the beginning and end of the season as costing Liverpool at least a top three finish; they won just three of their opening nine games of the season and failed to score in their last five matches, picking up just two points.

The Frenchman won the title with Le Touquet during his spell as a player there between 1973–76, but it is as a manager that he has made his name, guiding Lens to UEFA Cup qualification and Paris St Germain to the French Championship.

His spell as French national coach ended disappointingly with failure to qualify for the 1994 World Cup, but he has also been boss of the French under-18 and under-20 sides.

Houllier's experience in coaching promising young players has been evident at Liverpool, with the likes of Steven Gerrard and David Thompson emerging during his reign.

Houllier is already in the process of strengthening his squad, and the expectant Anfield fans will be looking for their side to challenge for the Premiership title in 2000–01.

LEAGUE POSITION

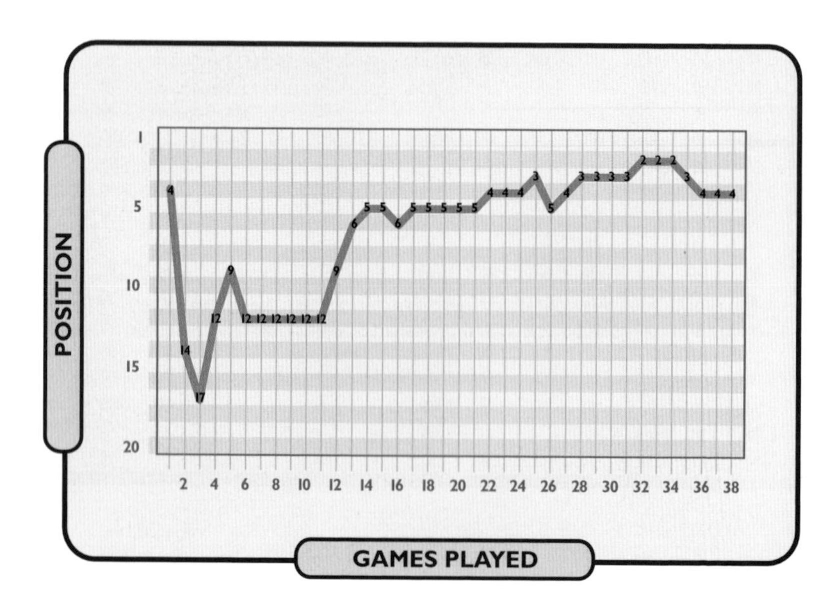

THE GOALS

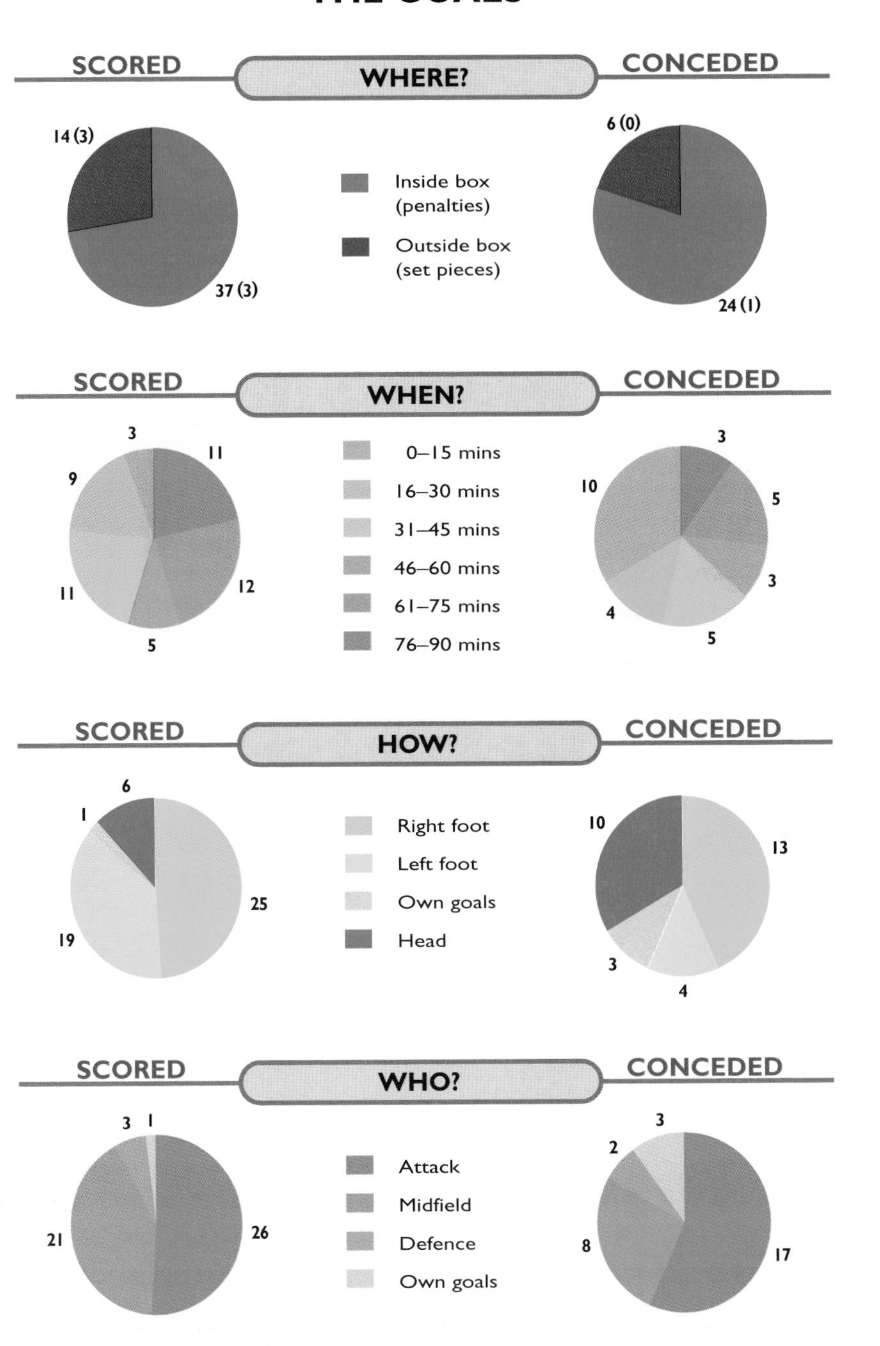

goals from headers in the Premiership

LIVERPOOL

	BERGER	CAMARA	CARRAGHER	FOWLER	GERRARD	HAMANN	HEGGEM	HENCHOZ	HESKEY	HYY
APPEARANCES										
Start	34	22	33	8	26	27	10	29	12	38
Sub	0	11	3	6	3	1	12	0	0	0
Minutes on pitch	2916	1978	2987	809	2151	2251	1047	2604	1022	3375
GOAL ATTEMPTS										
Goals	9	9	0	3	1	1	1	0	3	2
Shots on target	35	31	2	18	10	14	4	1	12	5
Shots off target	35	33	7	10	20	27	3	1	5	14
Shooting accuracy	50%	48%	22%	64%	33%	34%	57%	50%	71%	26%
PASSING										
Goal assists	3	1	0	0	3	2	0	0	1	2
Long passes	221	119	348	20	311	321	58	357	39	499
Short passes	1005	643	1036	282	865	946	394	574	455	956
PASS COMPLETION										
Own half %	80%	67%	86%	84%	83%	86%	74%	87%	79%	83%
Opposition half %	69%	60%	70%	58%	65%	74%	65%	57%	62%	61%
CROSSING										
Total crosses	191	42	22	5	38	23	26	7	23	18
Cross completion %	21%	19%	32%	40%	32%	35%	0%	43%	13%	28%
DRIBBLING										
Dribbles & runs	110	190	25	26	70	76	73	37	51	67
Dribble completion %	80%	72%	96%	62%	70%	79%	75%	100%	82%	99%
DEFENDING										
Tackles made	83	18	120	18	114	88	39	93	13	112
Tackles won %	49%	33%	51%	67%	53%	51%	49%	42%	62%	54%
Blocks	12	3	46	1	20	15	10	80	2	85
Clearances	28	3	225	6	54	22	62	249	16	538
Interceptions	19	5	32	1	35	21	3	18	0	38
DISCIPLINE										
Fouls	44	36	36	15	38	45	13	37	29	34
Offside	20	18	0	7	1	1	0	0	4	0
Yellow cards	2	7	4	1	5	6	0	8	0	2
Red cards	0	0	0	0	1	0	0	0	0	0

GOALKEEPER NAME	START/ (SUB)	TIME ON PITCH	GOALS CONCEDED	MINS/GOALS CONCEDED	SAVES MADE	SAVES/ SHOTS
FRIEDEL	2	180	1	180	5	83%
WESTERVELD	36	3225	29	111	94	76%

PLAYERS' STATISTICS

MATTEO	MEIJER	MURPHY	NEWBY	OWEN	REDKNAPP	RIEDLE	SMICER	SONG	STAUNTON	THOMPSON	TOTAL	RANK
32	7	9	0	22	18	0	12	14	7	19		
0	14	14	1	5	4	1	9	4	5	8		
2872	813	1022	14	1818	1655	18	1184	1288	601	1703		
0	0	3	0	11	3	0	1	0	0	3	51*	11th
1	8	9	0	30	23	0	6	0	0	21	230	3rd
3	7	5	0	19	18	0	14	0	2	27	250	3rd
25%	53%	64%	0%	61%	56%	0%	30%	0%	0%	44%	48%	7th
5	1	2	0	3	1	0	4	1	1	3	33	14th
342	24	99	1	37	230	0	85	99	97	165	3472	4th
1127	311	373	2	419	786	8	446	287	236	699	11850	5th
80%	78%	88%	100%	79%	87%	0%	83%	78%	84%	83%	83%	5th
68%	61%	67%	50%	65%	75%	80%	68%	58%	70%	65%	67%	6th
58	12	26	0	21	53	0	46	25	31	70	737	12th
28%	25%	46%	0%	29%	28%	0%	41%	12%	29%	17%	25%	20th
105	20	54	0	89	70	1	78	34	25	87	1289	5th
90%	80%	72%	0%	61%	83%	100%	78%	88%	88%	76%	79%	5th
88	33	27	0	24	64	0	28	43	13	63	1085	3rd
49%	48%	44%	0%	58%	55%	0%	54%	44%	54%	46%	50%	17th
33	1	6	0	2	5	0	6	26	6	9	368	14th
165	5	11	0	4	26	0	12	182	49	31	1701	5th
16	7	7	0	6	10	0	11	27	13	15	284	5th
33	34	14	0	21	21	1	21	26	6	39	544	11th
1	8	2	0	26	0	0	4	0	0	5	97	20th
2	2	3	0	2	4	0	1	2	2	7	60	11th
0	0	0	0	0	0	0	0	0	1	1	4	=5th

*Including one own goal

ROSSES AUGHT	CROSSES PUNCHED	CROSSES NOT CLAIMED	CATCH SUCCESS	THROWS/ SHORT KICKS	% COMPLETION	LONG KICKS	% COMPLETION
2	1	0	100%	7	86%	65	35%
65	26	9	88%	203	92%	886	41%

PLAYER OF THE SEASON

PLAYER	INDEX SCORE
SAMI HYYPIA	**1,039**
Patrik Berger	954
Steven Gerrard	891
Jamie Redknapp	860*
Dominic Matteo	859
Dietmar Hamann	852
Jamie Carragher	844
Titi Camara	784*
Stephane Henchoz	707
Sander Westerveld	655

All players played 75 minutes in at least 19 matches except those marked * who featured in just 17 games.

In recent seasons Liverpool fans have pointed the finger at their shaky defence as the reason why silverware has been conspicuous by its absence at Anfield. But manager Gerard Houllier pledged to put this right, and with his signings in the summer of 1999 he appeared to do this.

One of his most important captures was Finnish international Sami Hyypia from Dutch side Willem II Tilburg. Hyypia dominated the Reds' back-line helping them to become the league's tightest defensive unit, conceding only 30 goals.

Hyypia's total of 538 clearances was the second highest in the league and he also made 112 tackles to help preserve the Premiership's best defensive record. The Finn also managed two goals as he achieved an average of 1,039 Opta Season Index points.

Liverpool will now be hoping to build on their strong defence as they look to return to the trophy-winning ways of the 70s and 80s. Czech midfielder Patrik Berger also had a good season, following on from being Opta's player of the season for Liverpool in 1998–99.

Berger averaged 954 points thanks to his nine goals from midfield – which helped make him the Merseysiders' joint-second highest scorer. His potency from free-kicks led to three goals coming from set-pieces, with no Premiership player scoring more from dead-ball situations.

Young midfielder Steven Gerrard made a big impression, earning himself recognition at international level as well as in the Premiership. The product of Liverpool's youth set-up had three goal assists from his 1,176 passes and also attempted 114 tackles as he earned himself an average of 891 points.

A further four of Houllier's new signings finished in the top 10 – Titi Camara Dietmar Hamann, Stephane Henchoz and Sander Westerveld. Hamann in particular, followed up an impressive campaign at Newcastle United with some consistent performances in the Liverpool midfield.

25% Liverpool's crossing accuracy was

FIVE OF THE BEST

Sandwiched between two bad spells, Liverpool's season was a clear indication of the progress the club are making under Gerard Houllier. After crashing to defeats at home to Watford and away to Middlesbrough, the Reds climbed the table. A Champions League berth looked to be in the club's grasp before a goal drought saw them finish fourth.

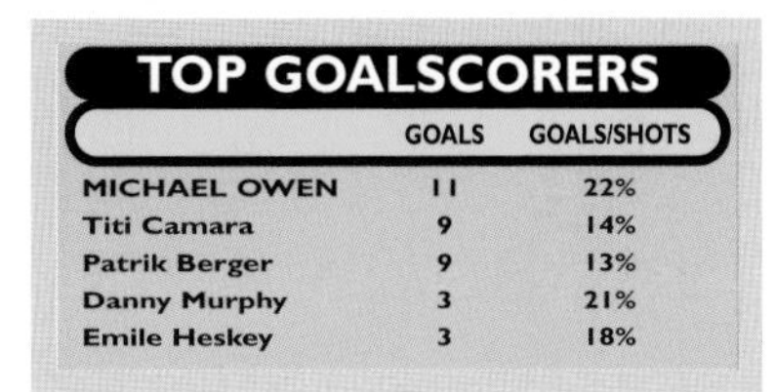

TOP GOALSCORERS

	GOALS	GOALS/SHOTS
MICHAEL OWEN	11	22%
Titi Camara	9	14%
Patrik Berger	9	13%
Danny Murphy	3	21%
Emile Heskey	3	18%

1999–2000 proved to be Michael Owen's trickiest yet as a professional footballer. He finished as Liverpool's top scorer again but missed 11 games because of his troublesome hamstring. His goals-to-shots ratio of 22% showed that he had not lost his predatory instincts, though. Summer '99 signing Titi Camara scored nine times and became a favourite with the Kop, while midfielder Patrik Berger also scored nine, five of them from outside the penalty area.

In the season that saw Steven Gerrard touted as a future England international it was another youngster, Jamie Carragher, who ended the campaign with the most successful passes at the club. Defenders Sami Hyypia and Dominic Matteo were not far behind, their ball skills part of the reason why 'Pool had the tightest defence in the Premiership. German international Dietmar Hamann was the most accurate, with 79% of his passes finding a red shirt.

TOP PASSERS

	SUCC PASSES	COMPLETION
JAMIE CARRAGHER	1,073	78%
Sami Hyypia	1,066	73%
Dominic Matteo	1,063	72%
Dietmar Hamann	998	79%
Patrik Berger	880	72%

TOP TACKLERS

	WON	SUCCESS
SAMI HYYPIA	61	54%
Jamie Carragher	61	51%
Steven Gerrard	60	53%
Dietmar Hamann	45	51%
Dominic Matteo	43	49%

Sami Hyypia and Jamie Carragher both made 61 successful tackles for Liverpool, the Finn easily making the Opta Team of the Season thanks to his commanding presence in the heart of the side. The emerging Steven Gerrard made just one challenge fewer, and it looks likely that he will be one of the best England players of his generation. Dominic Matteo is in another of the top fives, suggesting that the club's search for a new left-back is not as desperate as is made out.

Liverpool rarely have disciplinary problems and the 1999–2000 season was no different. The bad boy of the team was midfielder David Thompson, who only conceded 39 fouls but was booked seven times and sent off once. The red card came in the game at Leicester when Matt Elliott infamously elbowed Michael Owen. Interestingly, all of Liverpool's red cards came in a five-game spell in late September and October 1999.

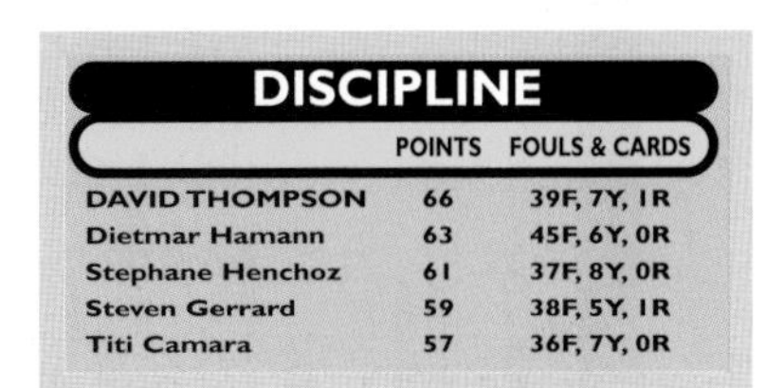

DISCIPLINE

	POINTS	FOULS & CARDS
DAVID THOMPSON	66	39F, 7Y, 1R
Dietmar Hamann	63	45F, 6Y, 0R
Stephane Henchoz	61	37F, 8Y, 0R
Steven Gerrard	59	38F, 5Y, 1R
Titi Camara	57	36F, 7Y, 0R

ACTION	CAMARA	CARRAGHER	FOWLER	GERRARD	HAMANN	HENCHOZ	HYYPIA	MATTEO	MURPHY	OWEN	SONG	STAUNTON	THOMPSON	WESTERVELD	TOTAL	SHEFF WED
Time on pitch	90	17	9	90	90	90	90	90	76	81	73	14	90	90	990	990
GOALS																
Goal	–	–	–	1	–	–	1	–	1	–	–	–	1	–	4	1
Shot on target	1	–	1	–	1	–	–	–	1	–	–	–	2	–	6	2
Shot off target	–	–	–	–	1	–	1	–	2	–	–	–	2	–	6	2
Blocked shot	–	–	–	–	2	–	–	–	–	2	–	–	4	–	8	3
Own goal	–	–	–	–	–	–	–	–	–	–	–	–	–	–	–	–
PASSES																
Pass to own player	25	4	4	54	41	27	32	50	27	22	32	7	33	–	358	244
Pass to opposition	12	4	–	13	9	6	9	8	11	4	9	2	24	–	111	114
Cross to own player	–	–	–	–	2	–	–	1	1	–	–	1	2	–	7	3
Cross to opposition player	2	–	–	1	–	–	1	4	1	2	–	1	10	–	22	11
Goal assist	–	–	–	–	1	–	–	–	–	–	1	–	1	–	3	1
Pass completion %	64%	50%	100%	79%	83%	82%	76%	81%	70%	79%	79%	73%	51%	0%	73%	66%
TACKLES & CLEARANCES																
Tackle	1	1	–	2	3	2	5	4	1	1	2	2	4	–	28	34
Clearances, blocks and interceptions	–	5	–	1	2	8	8	4	2	–	7	–	2	1	40	73
DRIBBLES & RUNS																
Dribble ball retained	4	–	1	2	1	–	–	2	1	4	3	–	5	–	23	12
Dribble ball lost	1	–	–	–	–	–	–	–	1	2	–	–	1	–	5	2
Dribble success %	80%	0%	100%	100%	100%	0%	0%	100%	50%	67%	100%	0%	83%	0%	82%	86%
DISCIPLINE																
Fouls	1	–	–	1	–	2	1	1	1	1	2	–	2	–	12	10
Penalty conceded	–	–	–	–	–	–	–	–	–	–	–	–	–	–	–	–
Free kick – offside	2	–	–	–	–	–	–	–	–	–	–	–	–	–	2	2
Yellow cards	–	–	–	–	–	1	–	–	–	–	–	–	1	–	2	2
Red cards	–	–	–	–	–	–	–	–	–	–	–	–	–	–	–	–
GOALKEEPERS																
Distribution to own player	–	–	–	–	–	–	–	–	–	–	–	–	–	14	14	24
Distribution to opposition player	–	–	–	–	–	–	–	–	–	–	–	–	–	14	14	8
Goalkeeper distribution %	0%	0%	0%	0%	0%	0%	0%	0%	0%	0%	0%	0%	0%	50%	50%	75%
Save	–	–	–	–	–	–	–	–	–	–	–	–	–	2	2	6
Ball caught	–	–	–	–	–	–	–	–	–	–	–	–	–	1	1	1
Ball dropped	–	–	–	–	–	–	–	–	–	–	–	–	–	1	1	1
Goal conceded	–	–	–	–	–	–	–	–	–	–	–	–	–	1	1	4

97 Liverpool were caught offside fewer

Amid criticism levelled at Gerard Houllier that he was importing too many foreign players, Liverpool put on a televised performance that showed they are more than prepared to rely on home-grown talent, with Michael Owen, David Thompson, Steven Gerrard, Dominic Matteo, Jamie Carragher and Robbie Fowler all playing in this game.

In fact, the Liverpool team cost just £6.95m more than the Wednesday side that played at Anfield and was relegated by the end of the season, and it is worth noting that Sander Westerveld and Dietmar Hamann accounted for nearly half the cost of the 14 players that the home side used.

In the opening 15 minutes, Thompson, Owen, Gerrard and Danny Murphy all linked up well and created the first clear-cut chance, with Kevin Pressman saving well at the feet of Owen. Titi Camara then started to show some of his repertoire of tricks and was repeatedly turning the Owls' defence inside-out.

But it was the visitors that took a shock lead after 19 minutes. A Wednesday free-kick on the left touchline was squared across the area and Niclas Alexandersson rifled the ball past Westerveld.

But Liverpool soon reimposed themselves. Houllier's side made more than a hundred more passes than the Owls, who were constantly put under pressure, with their back four being forced into making 60 clearances, blocks and interceptions throughout the game.

In fact, it only took the Reds two minutes to level the score. Heavy Liverpool dominance led to a corner and, from Thompson's outswinging cross, Sami Hyypia scored with a strong downward header. The stand-in captain was leading the Anfield charge with the Shankly-era "attack from the back" philosophy.

It was through Thompson's endeavour, though, that Liverpool took the lead after a neat Camara dummy let the youngster in. His angled shot just before the break was parried up and outwards, where Murphy was on hand to volley in his fifth goal of the season. Houllier and Phil Thompson celebrated as enthusiastically as the fans on the Kop itself.

The second half saw no respite from the Reds – and after 69 minutes Liverpool increased their lead.

Gerrard scored his first goal for Liverpool and showed composure beyond his years. After picking up a pass from Rigobert Song, the 19-year-old skipped past Emerson Thome, then dropped his shoulder to dummy the experienced Walker before steering the ball past Pressman.

While Anfield sides of the late 90s might have settled for that scoreline, this team sensed blood. Hamann headed the ball out to Thompson on the right and the little dynamo ran at the tired Wednesday defence, cut inside and curled the ball over Pressman and into the far corner to make it 4–1.

Half of the team that beat Wednesday grew up as Liverpool fans and that passion and pride in the shirt was evident on the pitch. Houllier – who stood on the Kop himself in the '60s – showed that his vision of Liverpool's future entailed a mix of imported and not just English, but local, talent.

MANCHESTER UNITED

ADDRESS

Sir Matt Busby Way, Old Trafford,
Manchester M16 0RA

CONTACT NUMBERS

Telephone: 0161 868 8000
Fax: 0161 868 8668
Ticket and Match Information:
0161 868 8020
Megastore: 0161 868 8567
Museum and Tour Centre:
0161 868 8631
Website: www.manutd.com

KEY PERSONNEL

Chairman: C M Edwards
Directors: Professor R Smith, E M Watkins
A Al Midani, P F Kenyon, D A Gill
Club Secretary: K R Merrett
Manager: Sir Alex Ferguson CBE

SPONSORS

1999–2000 Sharp
2000–2001 Vodafone

FANZINES

Red News
United We Stand
Red Attitude
Red Army

COLOURS

Home: Red shirts, White shorts,
black stockings
Away: Navy blue shirts, black shorts,
white stockings

NICKNAME

The Red Devils

HONOURS

League Champions: 1907–08, 1910–11,
1951–52, 1955–56, 1956–57, 1964–65,
1966–67, 1992–93, 1993–94, 1995–96,
1996–97, 1998–99, 1999–00
Division Two Champions:
1935–36, 1974–75
FA Cup: 1909, 1948, 1963,
1977, 1983, 1985, 1990, 1994,
1996, 1999
League Cup: 1992
European Cup: 1968, 1999
European Cup Winners' Cup: 1991
World Club Championship: 1999
European Super Cup: 1991

RECORD GOALSCORER

Bobby Charlton –
199 league goals, 1956–73

BIGGEST WIN

(as Manchester United) 9–0 v Ipswich
Town – FA Premier League, 4 March 1995

BIGGEST DEFEAT

0–7 v Blackburn Rovers – Division One,
10 April 1926
0–7 v Aston Villa – Division One,
27 December 1930
0–7 v Wolverhampton Wanderers –
Division Two, 26 December 1931

SEASON REVIEW

Manchester United played below their best for much of the 1999–2000 season, yet they won the Premiership by a record margin of 18 points, scored a record number of Premiership goals (97) and broke Arsenal's record of 10 consecutive Premiership wins when they made it 11 out of 11 on the last day of the campaign. Unbeaten at home (no side has even managed to stop them scoring at Old Trafford in the Premiership since Newcastle in November 1998) they also had four separate hat-trick scorers and drew the usual capacity crowds wherever they went.

Their season started controversially with withdrawal from the FA Cup so that they could participate in the inaugural World Club Championship in Brazil. National newspapers campaigned for the club to reverse its decision and at least field a reserve team in the Cup – but United refused.

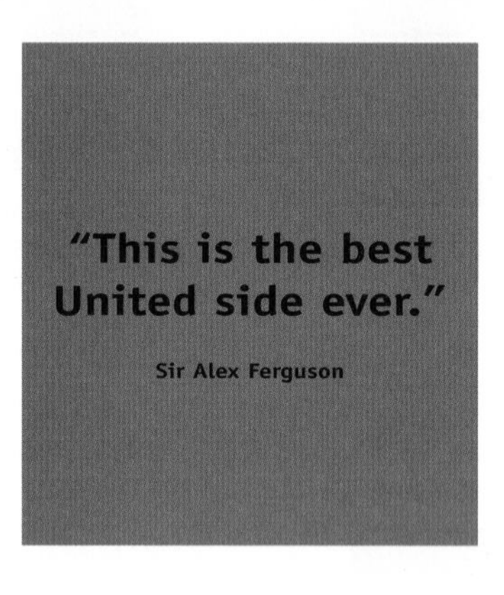

"This is the best United side ever."
Sir Alex Ferguson

On the pitch, most of the attention was focused on Mark Bosnich. A summer signing from Aston Villa, the former United trainee was under the spotlight as the man with the unenviable task of following Peter Schmeichel. He had some shaky moments in the opening-day draw with Everton and then a relatively uneventful time in a 4–0 demolition of Sheffield Wednesday. In the next match, though, a 2–0 victory over Leeds United, his hamstring gave way and he was replaced by Raimond van der Gouw.

Better news came on the same day with the announcement by Roy Keane that he would at least see out the remaining year of his contract. The skipper was eventually to commit his long-term future to the club, taking home a cool £50,000 a week in the process, but for a while there was a real possibility that his services might be lost to the club. Not that his performances on the pitch suffered, as he drove his team on to six straight wins including a 2–1 victory at title rivals Arsenal, where he scored both of United's goals.

After losing the European Super Cup to Lazio in Monaco, United returned to the Premiership to beat Newcastle United 5–1 and Liverpool 3–2. New signing Massimo Taibi – at £4.5 million the most expensive goalkeeper in English football history – recovered from a nervous start to play a major part in the win at Anfield, but some of the Italian's other performances for the club were to be disastrous. In just four Premiership games he conceded 11 goals at the rate of one every 32 minutes, an appalling record that saw him farmed out to Italian club Reggina on loan, probably never to return.

Progress to the second group stage of the Champions League was assured, with only Marseille in a group containing Croatia Zagreb and Austrian minnows Sturm Graz managing to beat United. The opening game of the second group stage against Fiorentina was lost 2–0. But some consolation was to be had with victory in the Intercontinental Cup, when a Roy Keane goal proved enough to earn a 1–0 victory over Palmeiras of Brazil.

The Worthington Cup was treated with United's usual disdain, a reserve side losing 3–0 to Aston Villa in the third round of the competition.

With the World Club Championships and a month-long absence from the Premiership looming, United moved up a gear, scoring 15 times in the space of four games in December to depart for Brazil one point behind Leeds. By the time they returned they were four points behind Leeds and level with Arsenal, but with three games in hand on both.

42 Manchester United earned the fewest

SEASON REVIEW

The World Club Championships had not gone smoothly, with United drawing 1–1 with Necaxa – a game in which David Beckham was sensationally sent off – and then a 3–1 defeat to Vasco Da Gama due to some bad defending by Gary Neville.

The break in the sun seemed to do them no harm in the Premiership, though. Arsenal were held to a 1–1 draw at Old Trafford in their first game back and, with their main rivals stuttering after that, United merely accelerated away, losing just one Premiership game in the year 2000.

While they looked shaky at the back, no other team could live with United's attack. They scored goals from all over the pitch, notching an overall goals-to-shots rate of 19%, comfortably higher than any of their rivals.

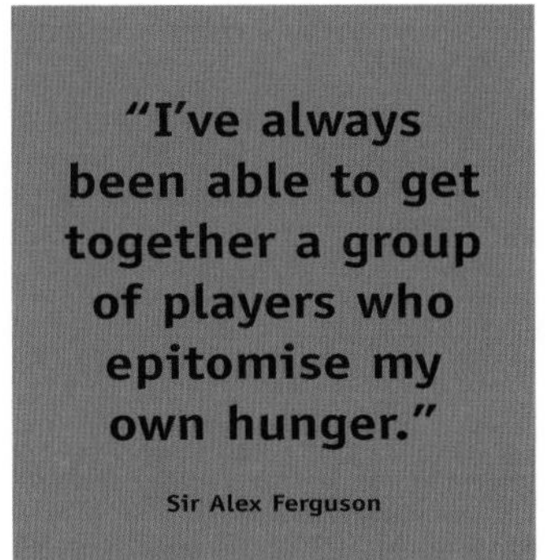

"I've always been able to get together a group of players who epitomise my own hunger."
Sir Alex Ferguson

Negotiating the second group phase of the Champions League proved an easy enough task. Despite the loss to Fiorentina in their opening game, Bordeaux and Valencia were both beaten, and when the Italians were hammered 3–1 in the return, the stage was set for an epic quarter-final clash with the legendary Real Madrid.

United's defeat came as a great shock to many of their fans who had come to expect victory as a matter of course, whoever the opponents might be. They, like the team, were able to content themselves with the fact that the league was wrapped up three days after the Madrid defeat with a 3–1 victory at Southampton.

While few denied that their league success was well-deserved, there were those who disagreed with the award of both the PFA and Sportswriters' Player of the Year awards to United's talismanic captain Roy Keane.

The Irishman had an inspirational season, but in the year that Stanley Matthews died, many questioned the appropriateness of giving the awards to a player who, along with his team-mates, had harassed referee Andy D'Urso for daring to award a penalty at Old Trafford and been sent off at Newcastle for two bookable offences, one of which was for questioning an official's eyesight.

In his defence, Keane could argue that his team's disciplinary record was the best in the Premiership. No team picked up fewer bookings or committed fewer fouls, a record of which Sir Alex Ferguson was rightly proud.

Whatever the critics think of Keane and his Manchester United team-mates, there is no doubt they are the yardstick against which all other sides must measure their progress. Before the season had even ended Sir Alex Ferguson was looking to add Ruud Van Nistelrooy to his squad. That deal fell through due to a failed medical, but United added more world-class talent to their squad when they signed French number one Fabien Barthez for £7.8 million from Monaco in a move that could well spell the end for Bosnich as first-choice goalkeeper.

In Barthez, Ferguson may have finally found the dominant figure needed to organise a defence that suffered in comparison to United's multi-talented attack during the 1999–2000 season.

Seeing that the club has already proved itself to be some way ahead of its main domestic rivals, the fact that international stars are queuing up to join Old Trafford's already star-studded squad list merely underlines the fact that United will once again be the team to beat.

It is difficult to see any of their rivals overhauling them at the moment, and the Red Devils will start as clear favourites to retain their title.

MANCHESTER UNITED

DATE	OPPONENT	SCORE	ATT.	BECKHAM	BERG	BOSNICH	BUTT	CLEGG	COLE	CRUYFF	CULKIN	CURTIS	FORTUNE	GIG
8.8.99	Everton A	1–1	39,141	90	90	90	s15	–	90	–	–	–	–	–
11.8.99	Sheff Wed H	4–0	54,941	56	90	90	s34	–	90^{1}	–	–	–	–	56
14.8.99	Leeds Utd H	2–0	55,187	90	90	22	s21	–	90□	–	–	–	–	90□
22.8.99	Arsenal A	2–1	38,147	90□	90□	–	s29	–	77	–	s1	–	–	90
25.8.99	Coventry A	2–1	22,024	90□	90	–	61	–	–	–	–	s12	–	90
30.8.99	Newcastle H	5–1	55,190	75	90	–	90	s9	90^{4}	–	–	–	s20	90^{1}
11.9.99	Liverpool A	3–2**	44,929	90□	90	–	39	s6	72^{1}■	–	–	–	–	90
18.9.99	Wimbledon H	1–1	55,189	–	90	–	–	–	s23	$s60^{1}$	–	–	–	30
25.9.99	Southampton H	3–3	55,249	90	90□	–	90	–	–	–	–	–	–	–
3.10.99	Chelsea A	0–5	34,909	65	90	–	22■	–	65	–	–	–	–	–
16.10.99	Watford H	4–1	55,188	90	–	90	90	–	66^{2}	–	–	–	–	70
23.10.99	Tottenham A	1–3	36,072	68□	–	90	–	–	90	–	–	–	–	90^{1}
30.10.99	Aston Villa H	3–0	55,211	90	–	90	–	–	79^{1}	s11	–	–	–	79
6.11.99	Leicester H	2–0	55,191	–	s8	90	–	–	90^{2}	–	–	–	–	90
20.11.99	Derby Co A	2–1	33,370	86	s13	–	90^{1}□	–	90^{1}	–	–	–	–	90
4.12.99	Everton H	5–1	55,133	–	–	8	90□	–	s26	–	–	–	–	64
18.12.99	West Ham A	4–2	26,037	77	–	–	s13	–	–	–	–	–	–	90^{2}
26.12.99	Bradford H	4–0	55,188	–	–	90	90	–	$s24^{1}$	–	–	–	90^{1}	–
28.12.99	Sunderland A	2–2	42,026	84	–	90	90^{1}	–	89	–	–	–	–	90□
24.1.00	Arsenal H	1–1	58,293	90	–	90	90	–	66	–	–	–	–	90
29.1.00	Middlesbro H	1–0	61,267	90^{1}	–	90	90	–	s10	–	–	–	–	90
2.2.00	Sheff Weds A	1–0	39,640	90	–	90	45	–	–	–	–	–	–	90
5.2.00	Coventry H	3–2	61,380	90	–	90	s20	–	90^{2}	s10	–	–	–	–
12.2.00	Newcastle A	0–3	36,470	90	–	90	s21	–	90□	–	–	–	–	90
20.2.00	Leeds Utd A	1–0	40,160	–	–	90	90	–	90^{1}	–	–	–	–	90
26.2.00	Wimbledon A	2–2	26,129	90	s20	90	90	–	90^{1}	70^{1}	–	–	–	90
4.3.00	Liverpool H	1–1	61,592	90	–	–	90	–	s10	–	–	–	–	90
11.3.00	Derby Co H	3–1	61,619	90	90	90	s19	–	–	–	–	–	71	–
18.3.00	Leicester A	2–0	22,170	90^{1}	90	90	s5	–	84	–	–	–	–	85
25.3.00	Bradford A	4–0	18,276	90^{1}□	90	90	–	–	90	–	–	–	–	83
1.4.00	West Ham H	7–1	61,611	90^{1}	–	90	s33	–	68^{1}	–	–	–	90	–
10.4.00	Middlesbro A	4–3	34,775	90	90	90	s9	–	90^{1}	–	–	–	$s9^{1}$	81^{1}
15.4.00	Sunderland H	4–0	61,612	s25	$s34^{1}$	45	90^{1}	–	–	–	–	–	90	–
22.4.00	Southampton A	3–1*	15,245	90^{1}	–	–	90	–	71	–	–	–	–	58
24.4.00	Chelsea H	3–2	61,593	90□	s58	–	90	–	–	s27	–	–	–	90
29.4.00	Watford A	3–2	20,250	–	90	–	64■	–	–	$s18^{1}$	–	–	–	90^{1}
6.5.00	Tottenham H	3–1	61,629	90^{1}	s63	–	62	–	–	s11	–	–	–	90
14.5.00	Aston Villa A	1–0	39,217	–	90	–	–	–	–	s57□	–	–	–	90

□ Yellow card, ■ Red card, s Substitute, 90^{2} Goals scored

*including one own goal **including two own goals

1999–2000 PREMIERSHIP APPEARANCES

GREENING	HIGGINBOTHAM	IRWIN	JOHNSEN	KEANE	MAY	G NEVILLE	P NEVILLE	SCHOLES	SHERINGHAM	SILVESTRE	SOLSKJAER	STAM	TAIBI	VAN DER GOUW	WALLWORK	WILSON	YORKE	TOTAL
–	–	90	–	90□	–	–	90	90	–	–	75	90	–	–	–	–	90[1]	990
–	–	90	–	90	–	–	90	90[1]□	s45	–	s34[1]	90□	–	–	–	–	45[1]	990
–	–	90	–	90	–	–	90	69	s9	–	–	90	–	s68	–	–	81[2]	990
–	–	90	–	90[2]	–	–	90□	61□	s13	–	–	90	–	89	–	–	90	990
–	–	90	–	90	–	–	78	s29[1]	73	–	s17	90	–	90	–	–	90[1]	990
–	–	–	–	–	–	81	90	70	s15	–	–	90	–	90	–	–	90	990
–	–	–	–	–	–	–	84□	90	–	90	–	90	90	–	s51	–	90	972
–	–	90	–	–	–	–	90	90	90	90	67	90	90	–	–	–	90	990
–	–	90	–	–	–	–	–	90□	90[1]	90	90	90	90	–	–	–	90[2]	990
–	–	90	–	–	–	–	90	65□	s25	90	s25	90	90	–	–	s25	90	922
s20	–	90[1]	–	s36	–	–	90□	90	–	90	s24	54	–	–	–	–	90[1]	990
s8	–	82	–	90□	–	–	90	90	–	90	s22	90	–	–	–	–	90	990
–	–	90	–	90[1]	–	–	90	90[1]	–	90	s24	90	–	–	–	s11	66	990
–	78	–	–	90	s12	–	82	90	–	90	90	90	–	–	–	–	90	990
–	–	–	–	90	–	90	90	–	–	77	s4	90	–	90	–	–	90	990
–	–	90[1]	–	90	–	90	s26	90	90	64	90[4]	90	–	s82	–	–	–	990
–	–	45	–	90	–	90	s45	90	90	90	–	90	–	90	–	–	90[2]	990
–	–	–	–	90[1]	–	90	90	66	66	90	90	81	–	–	s9	–	s24[1]	990
–	–	77	–	90[1]	–	90	s1	–	s13	90	s6	90□	–	–	–	–	90	990
–	–	87	–	90	–	90	s3	–	s24[1]	90	–	90	–	–	–	–	90	990
–	–	80	–	90□	–	68	–	s22	80	90	s10	90	–	–	–	–	90	990
–	–	90	–	90	–	90	–	s45	90[1]	90	–	90	–	–	–	–	90	990
–	–	–	–	90	–	90	90	90[1]	80	90	70□	90	–	–	–	–	–	990
–	–	69	–	64■	–	90	–	90□	75	90	s15	90□	–	–	–	–	–	964
–	–	90□	–	90	–	90	–	90	s60	90	–	90□	–	–	–	–	30	990
–	–	–	–	–	–	90	71	–	90	90	s19	90	–	–	–	–	–	990
–	–	90	–	90□	–	90	–	–	s5	90	80[1]	90	–	90	–	–	85□	990
–	–	–	–	75	–	90	90	90	–	90	90	–	–	–	s15	–	90[3]	990
–	–	90	–	90	–	90	–	90	s6	–	–	90	–	–	–	–	90[1]	990
–	–	–	–	75	–	90	90	90[1]	–	90	s7	–	–	–	s15	–	90[2]	990
–	–	90[1]	–	57	–	90	–	69[3]	s22	90	s21[1]	90	–	–	–	–	90	990
–	–	32	–	81□	–	90	–	90[1]	–	s58	–	90	–	–	–	–	90	990
–	–	–	–	90□	–	90	90	65	90	90	90[2]	56□	–	s45	–	–	–	990
–	–	–	s32	90□	–	90	90	–	s19	90	71[1]	90	–	90	–	–	s19	990
–	–	–	90	49	–	32	90	s41	–	90	63[1]□	–	–	90	–	–	90[2]	990
72	s27	–	63	–	–	–	90□	–	90	90	90	–	–	90	–	45	s45[1]	964
s28	–	90	–	–	–	–	90	90□	90[1]	90	79[1]	27	–	90	–	–	–	990
–	45	90	–	–	–	–	90	90□	90[1]	90	33	–	–	90	s45	–	90	990

THE MANAGER

SIR ALEX FERGUSON

The 2000–01 season will be Sir Alex Ferguson's 15th in charge at Old Trafford, and arguably the finest domestic manager of his generation will be keen to regain the European crown that his side relinquished before he steps down.

Ferguson started his managerial career with East Stirling, but just three months into his reign he joined St Mirren, with whom he won the First Division Championship.

From there he went to Aberdeen in 1978, and while guiding the Dons to three Scottish Premier League titles, his highlight came in 1983 when his Aberdeen side won the European Cup Winners' Cup.

He turned down many big offers after that, including the Scotland job, but the chance to manage Manchester United was too tempting to resist.

That was in November 1986, and since then he has won six Premiership titles, four FA Cups, a European Cup Winners' Cup and the Champions League in 1999, the third leg of United's historic "Treble" that season.

Despite their controversial absence from the 1999–2000 FA Cup United still played for a total of seven trophies, and whatever 2000–01 brings them, you can be sure that Ferguson's will and desire will be as strong as ever.

LEAGUE POSITION

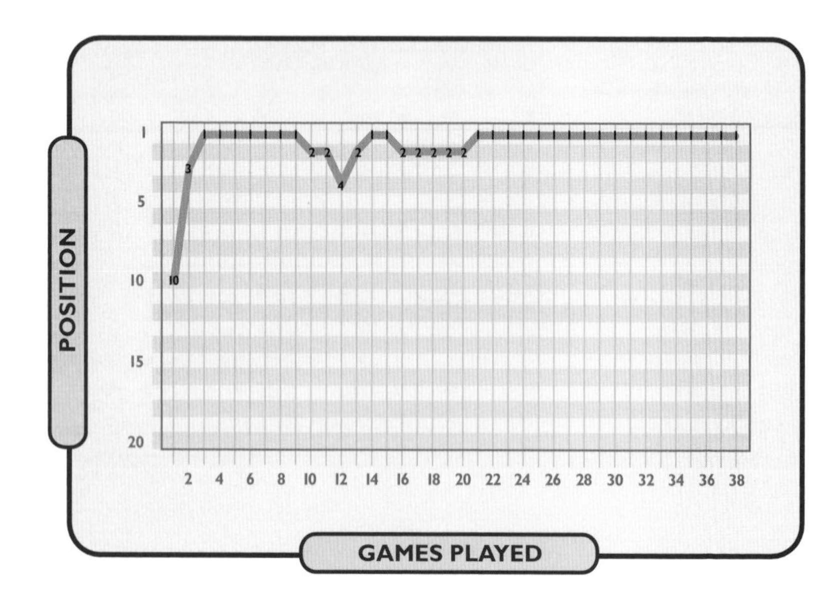

8 Dwight Yorke scored more headed goals

THE GOALS

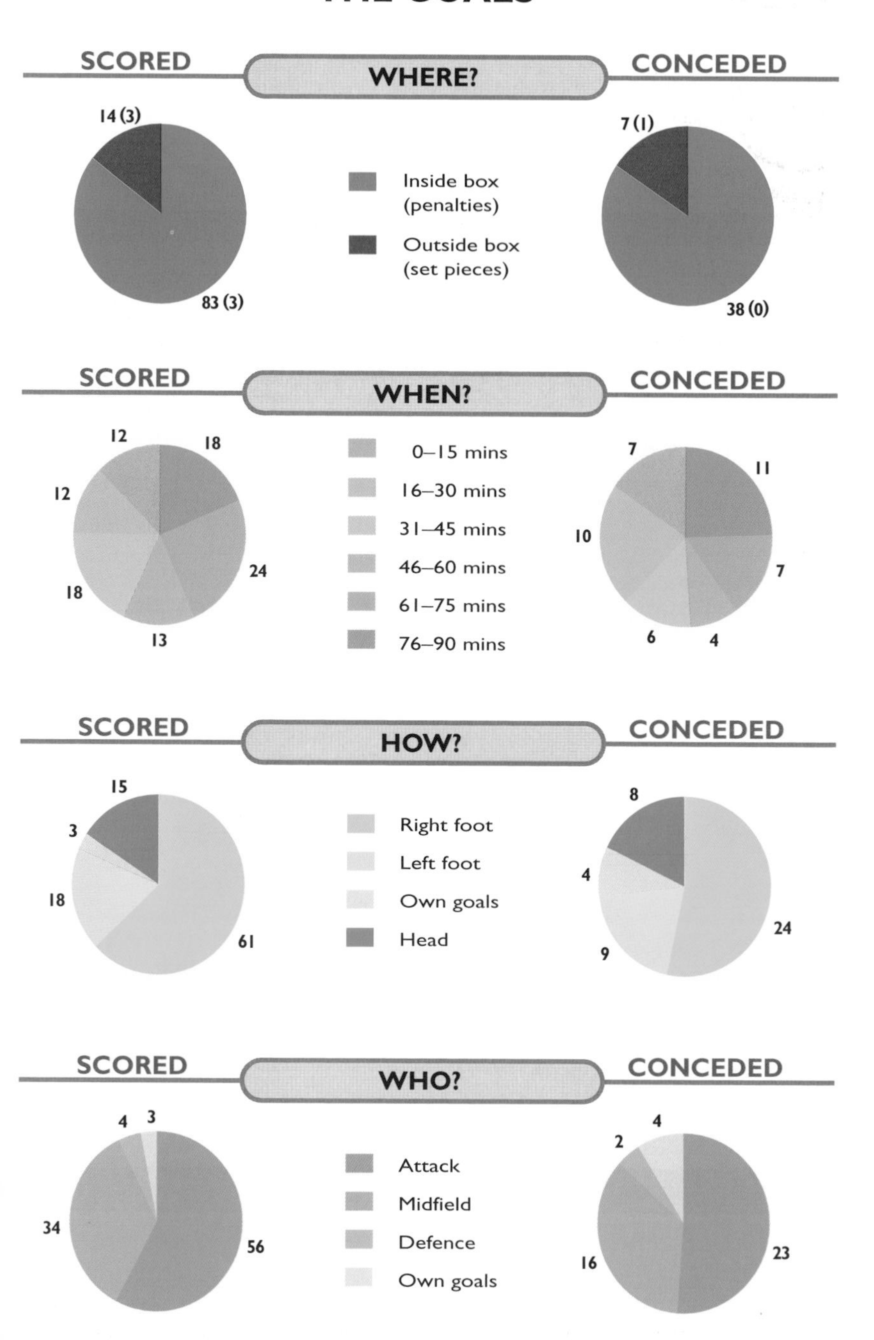

than any other Premiership player

MANCHESTER UNITED

	BECKHAM	BERG	BUTT	CLEGG	COLE	CRUYFF	CURTIS	FORTUNE	GIGGS	GREENING	HIGGINB
Start	30	16	21	0	23	1	0	4	30	1	2
Sub	1	6	10	2	5	7	1	2	0	3	1
Minutes on pitch	2606	1636	1862	15	2000	264	12	370	2496	128	150
GOAL ATTEMPTS											
Goals	6	1	3	0	19	3	0	2	6	0	0
Shots on target	20	6	12	0	39	7	0	4	20	2	0
Shots off target	22	5	16	0	23	4	0	2	28	4	0
Shooting accuracy	48%	55%	43%	0%	63%	64%	0%	67%	42%	33%	0%
PASSING											
Goal assists	15	0	3	0	5	0	0	1	12	0	0
Long passes	538	195	151	0	69	27	1	14	204	7	28
Short passes	1234	549	895	6	579	84	1	154	948	54	73
PASS COMPLETION											
Own half %	85%	89%	89%	100%	84%	83%	100%	89%	72%	89%	82%
Opposition half %	67%	64%	76%	100%	71%	77%	0%	79%	63%	84%	65%
CROSSING											
Total crosses	372	5	12	1	13	5	1	23	150	16	7
Cross completion %	27%	20%	33%	0%	38%	40%	0%	22%	28%	25%	29%
DRIBBLING											
Dribbles & runs	104	10	64	0	67	27	1	16	222	8	9
Dribble completion %	89%	90%	73%	0%	63%	74%	0%	69%	68%	75%	78%
DEFENDING											
Tackles made	54	41	121	0	19	5	0	9	55	4	4
Tackles won %	50%	59%	55%	0%	42%	40%	0%	44%	44%	75%	25%
Blocks	9	37	9	0	1	1	0	2	7	2	3
Clearances	31	156	24	2	1	2	2	1	12	1	12
Interceptions	18	15	16	0	2	2	0	0	20	0	0
DISCIPLINE											
Fouls	45	20	31	0	58	5	0	7	24	2	3
Offside	9	0	2	0	26	2	0	0	12	0	0
Yellow cards	6	2	2	0	2	1	0	0	2	0	0
Red cards	0	0	2	0	1	0	0	0	0	0	0

GOALKEEPER NAME	START/ (SUB)	TIME ON PITCH	GOALS CONCEDED	MINS/GOALS CONCEDED	SAVES MADE	SAVES/ SHOTS
BOSNICH	23	1875	21	89	45	68%
CULKIN	0(1)	1	0	0	0	0%
TAIBI	4	360	11	33	15	58%
VAN DER GOUW	11(3)	1184	13	91	49	79%

PLAYERS' STATISTICS

JOHNSEN	KEANE	MAY	NEVILLE G	NEVILLE P	SCHOLES	SHERINGHAM	SILVESTRE	SOLSKJAER	STAM	WALLWORK	WILSON	YORKE	TOTAL	RANK
2	28	0	22	25	27	15	30	15	33	0	1	29		
1	1	1	0	4	4	12	1	13	0	5	2	3		
185	2417	12	1891	2280	2402	1530	2719	1396	2828	135	81	2555		
0	5	0	0	0	9	5	0	12	0	0	0	20	97*	1st
0	15	0	2	0	31	14	0	31	3	0	0	42	255	2nd
0	22	0	3	5	31	14	6	21	9	1	1	21	241	6th
0%	41%	0%	40%	0%	50%	50%	0%	60%	25%	0%	0%	67%	51%	3rd
0	1	0	2	2	5	6	0	7	1	0	0	3	64	1st
19	373	4	364	343	288	87	462	61	312	20	9	117	4013	1st
51	1546	1	694	1100	1242	742	930	531	1091	53	29	1289	14797	1st
84%	92%	100%	83%	84%	91%	88%	86%	88%	89%	74%	81%	92%	87%	1st
48%	80%	67%	71%	74%	78%	75%	58%	68%	78%	77%	68%	84%	73%	1st
0	19	0	90	70	32	14	25	19	11	3	1	22	959	1st
0%	32%	0%	24%	34%	28%	21%	52%	11%	55%	0%	100%	27%	28%	14th
1	89	0	48	80	84	31	78	48	57	3	1	117	1218	6th
100%	91%	0%	92%	84%	82%	74%	92%	81%	95%	67%	0%	72%	79%	3rd
8	111	0	45	63	90	19	128	21	99	6	5	31	1013	11th
0%	56%	0%	53%	54%	53%	47%	52%	62%	54%	33%	80%	55%	52%	10th
3	34	0	34	41	14	3	56	1	69	7	1	7	359	15th
10	55	0	74	127	19	9	247	3	268	5	3	20	1209	19th
2	15	0	14	17	15	1	28	1	35	1	0	6	228	15th
1	36	1	12	28	34	26	26	37	45	2	2	78	414	20th
0	0	0	2	1	4	12	0	18	0	0	0	36	125	12th
0	7	0	0	4	7	0	0	2	5	0	0	1	42	20th
0	1	0	0	0	0	0	0	0	0	0	0	0	4	=5th

*Including three own goals

ROSSES AUGHT	CROSSES PUNCHED	CROSSES NOT CLAIMED	CATCH SUCCESS	THROWS/ SHORT KICKS	% COMPLETION	LONG KICKS	% COMPLETION
32	11	3	91%	155	94%	584	42%
0	0	0	0%	0	0%	1	100%
5	3	1	83%	58	98%	89	26%
26	9	1	96%	122	90%	405	41%

PLAYER OF THE SEASON

PLAYER	INDEX SCORE
DWIGHT YORKE	1283
Roy Keane	1252
Paul Scholes	1219
David Beckham	1137
Denis Irwin	1030
Jaap Stam	967
Phil Neville	955
Mickael Silvestre	925
Ryan Giggs	913
Gary Neville	872

Another season of success for Manchester United saw their players perform at their peak throughout the campaign, allowing them to romp home to Premiership success in record-breaking fashion.

It was one of Alex Ferguson's expensive signings who repaid him by clinching the player of the season spot in the Opta Season Index. Dwight Yorke arrived for £12.75 million early in the 1998–99 season and, after winning the Treble that year, he contributed greatly to his second Premiership title – and United's sixth – this time around.

The Trinidad and Tobago star scored an average of 1,283 points after being United's top scorer in the league with 20 goals. Yorke is more than just an out-and-out goalscorer, though, making more passes than any other Premiership striker and creating three goals.

United skipper Roy Keane was close behind Yorke in the ratings, justifying the club's decision to break their pay structure in order to keep the influential midfielder. The Irishman made 1,634 successful passes – the highest total in the Premiership – and scored five goals on his way to ending the season in style by lifting the Premiership trophy.

England midfield pair David Beckham and Paul Scholes both enjoyed another good season, with Beckham claiming the joint highest number of assists in the league with 15. He also attempted 372 crosses and corners – more than any other Premiership player.

Scholes found the back of the net nine times from midfield as United clocked up a record Premiership goals total, but it will be his stunning strikes against Bradford and Middlesbrough which people will remember the most.

One omission from the United top 10 is striker Andy Cole, who had an outstanding season. Unfortunately for the former Newcastle striker, he failed to qualify for the Index as he started fewer than half of United's matches.

11 Manchester United won 11 consecutive

FIVE OF THE BEST

Manchester United smashed a host of records as they galloped to the Premiership title, scoring more goals, collecting more points and winning more games in a row than ever before. Alex Ferguson's claim that the team are the finest yet at Old Trafford does not seem like an exaggeration. What next for the all-conquering Champions?

TOP GOALSCORERS

	GOALS	GOALS/SHOTS
DWIGHT YORKE	20	32%
Andy Cole	19	31%
Ole Gunnar Solskjaer	12	23%
Paul Scholes	9	15%
David Beckham	6	14%

Some accused Dwight Yorke of having a poor season, but he was the first Manchester United player since Brian McClair in 1988 to score 20 league goals in a season, finishing with a superb goals-to-shots ratio of 32%. Just one goal behind him was Andy Cole, who also had a clinical rate of more than 30%. Perennial substitute Ole Gunnar Solskjaer chipped in with 12 and David Beckham's haircut seemed to help the midfielder; he scored five of his six goals after his well-documented trip to the barbers.

It was a season of triumph in the league for Roy Keane. The United skipper made more successful passes than any other player in the country and won the PFA and Football Writers' Player of the Year awards. Jaap Stam finished the campaign with a marginally better completion rate than his captain, and Dwight Yorke and Paul Scholes also had completion rates of more than 80%. Beckham was on just 71% but he is frequently looking for the "killer" pass rather than the easy option.

TOP PASSERS

	SUCC PASSES	COMPLETION
ROY KEANE	1,634	85%
David Beckham	1,260	71%
Paul Scholes	1,259	82%
Jaap Stam	1,197	85%
Dwight Yorke	1,179	84%

TOP TACKLERS

	WON	SUCCESS
NICKY BUTT	67	55%
Mickael Silvestre	66	52%
Roy Keane	62	56%
Jaap Stam	53	54%
Paul Scholes	48	53%

Nicky Butt featured in 32 of Manchester United's league games and he finished as the most prolific tackler at the club, winning just one more than his team-mate Mickael Silvestre. Roy Keane and Jaap Stam were never far away from a challenge, either, and like the great sides of yesteryear United have a biting edge that gives their players the chance to create when they have the ball.

One of the most enduring images of Manchester United's 1999–2000 season was half the team, led by Roy Keane, berating referee Andy D'Urso after he gave Middlesbrough a penalty at Old Trafford. It was the Irish international who topped the Red Devils' disciplinary table with seven yellow cards and one red, but the team were the cleanest in the Premier League, conceding fewer fouls and collecting fewer yellow cards than any other side.

DISCIPLINE

	POINTS	FOULS & CARDS
ROY KEANE	63	36F, 7Y, 1R
Jaap Stam	60	45F, 5Y, 0R
David Beckham	54	36F, 6Y, 0R
Paul Scholes	51	30F, 7Y, 0R
Nicky Butt	47	29F, 2Y, 2R

ACTION	BECKHAM	BOSNICH	BUTT	COLE	FORTUNE	IRWIN	KEANE	G NEVILLE	SCHOLES	SHERINGHAM	SILVESTRE	SOLSKJAER	STAM	YORKE	TOTAL	WEST HAM
Time on pitch	90	90	33	68	90	90	57	90	69	22	90	21	90	90	990	990
GOALS																
Goal	1	–	–	1	–	1	–	–	3	–	–	1	–	–	7	1
Shot on target	1	–	–	1	1	1	–	–	1	–	–	–	–	–	5	1
Shot off target	1	–	–	1	–	–	–	–	–	–	–	1	–	–	3	7
Blocked shot	–	–	–	1	–	–	–	–	–	–	–	–	–	–	1	1
Own goal	–	–	–	–	–	–	–	–	–	–	–	–	–	–	–	–
PASSES																
Pass to own player	78	–	13	16	33	56	45	60	42	14	26	16	26	49	474	237
Pass to opposition	20	–	6	14	9	15	9	5	9	1	6	3	3	9	109	102
Cross to own player	2	–	–	–	–	–	–	2	–	–	–	–	–	–	4	1
Cross to opposition player	3	1	–	1	4	–	–	5	1	–	–	–	–	–	15	3
Goal assist	2	–	–	–	–	–	–	–	–	1	–	–	–	–	3	1
Pass completion %	78%	0%	68%	52%	72%	79%	83%	86%	81%	94%	81%	84%	90%	84%	80%	69%
TACKLES & CLEARANCES																
Tackle	–	–	3	–	2	3	2	5	1	1	3	–	5	–	25	26
Clearances, blocks and interceptions	–	–	1	–	–	1	2	3	–	–	3	–	4	–	14	35
DRIBBLES & RUNS																
Dribble ball retained	6	–	1	2	3	3	3	4	4	–	1	–	1	2	30	28
Dribble ball lost	–	–	–	1	–	–	1	–	–	–	–	1	–	–	3	3
Dribble success %	100%	0%	100%	67%	100%	100%	75%	100%	100%	0%	100%	0%	100%	100%	91%	90%
DISCIPLINE																
Fouls	2	–	1	–	3	1	2	–	1	–	1	–	2	2	15	7
Penalty conceded	–	–	–	–	–	–	–	–	–	–	–	–	–	–	–	2
Free kick – offside	–	–	1	–	–	–	–	–	–	–	–	–	–	1	2	5
Yellow cards	–	–	–	–	–	–	–	–	–	–	–	–	–	–	–	1
Red cards	–	–	–	–	–	–	–	–	–	–	–	–	–	–	–	–
GOALKEEPERS																
Distribution to own player	–	16	–	–	–	–	–	–	–	–	–	–	–	–	16	20
Distribution to opposition player	–	10	–	–	–	–	–	–	–	–	–	–	–	–	10	12
Goalkeeper distribution %	0%	62%	0%	0%	0%	0%	0%	0%	0%	0%	0%	0%	0%	0%	62%	63%
Save	–	1	–	–	–	–	–	–	–	–	–	–	–	–	1	5
Ball caught	–	1	–	–	–	–	–	–	–	–	–	–	–	–	1	–
Ball dropped	–	–	–	–	–	–	–	–	–	–	–	–	–	–	–	–
Goal conceded	–	1	–	–	–	–	–	–	–	–	–	–	–	–	1	7

19 Manchester United scored three or more

On the back of three straight victories, Sir Alex Ferguson's Champions-elect entertained West Ham at Old Trafford. Little did the watching hordes realise that it would transpire to be one of United's most commanding performances of the 1999–2000 season and one of the Hammers' worst.

West Ham were immediately into their stride as Harry Redknapp's skilful outfit began the brighter, closing United down all over the pitch and disrupting the league leaders' natural passing game with some biting challenges.

United pushed up in an attempt to pressurise the Hammers' back-line but were dealt a sucker-punch after just 10 minutes. Frederic Kanouté flicked on for his languid and oft-maligned striking partner Paulo Wanchope, who duly slotted the ball past Mark Bosnich.

But West Ham's lead lasted just 13 minutes, as United swept them away. For Hammers 'keeper Craig Forrest, who was in goal for Ipswich when United inflicted a Premiership record 9–0 defeat on Town in March 1995, it was a case of déjà vu.

First, on 23 minutes, England midfielder Paul Scholes drilled in from 20 yards via a Frank Lampard deflection. Then Roy Keane fell to the ground following a Steve Potts challenge and referee Mike Riley awarded a hotly-disputed penalty.

The decision seemed harsh on Potts, but full-back Denis Irwin was not complaining and, although Forrest parried the spot-kick, the Irishman netted the rebound.

Two became three on the stroke of half-time, as David Beckham's curling cross found Andy Cole unmarked at the near post, and he nodded home his 21st goal of the campaign.

United carried their momentum into the second half, and it took them only five minutes to open up a three-goal advantage as Beckham crossed for Scholes's second of the game – this time, a cheeky flick past the hapless Forrest.

The England midfielder's hat-trick followed soon after. Substitute Nicky Butt was clumsily brought down by youngster Rio Ferdinand and the ginger demon smashed United's second penalty into the roof of the net on 61 minutes.

Beckham curled a sweet 25-yard free-kick past Forrest to make it 6–1 and then the rout was completed by super-sub Ole Gunnar Solskjaer, who struck in the 73rd minute after being put through by fellow-substitute Teddy Sherringham.

United completed nearly 500 passes in total – a commendable 80% of all attempts – with the prolific David Beckham making more than a hundred passes and crosses combined and registering two goal assists. Hat-trick hero Scholes was comfortably Opta's man of the match. In addition to his goals, the England international linked well with his team-mates, completing 42 out of 51 passes, while also embarking on four successful dribbles.

The Hammers could not compete with red-hot United as they fired in only two shots on target during the 90 minutes, one of which was Wanchope's goal. It was a performance by Ferguson's men that epitomised their attacking ethos.

errea
ZIEGE

MIDDLESBROUGH

ADDRESS

BT Cellnet Riverside Stadium,
Middlesbrough TS3 6RS

CONTACT NUMBERS

Telephone: 01642 877700
Fax: 01642 877840
Ticket Office: 01642 877745
Ticket Office Fax: 01642 877843
Ticket Information Line: 01642 877809
Club Call: 09068 121181
Stadium Store: 01642 877720
e-mail: user@mfc.bdx.co.uk
Website: www.mfc.co.uk

KEY PERSONNEL

Chairman: Steve Gibson
Chief Executive: Keith Lamb
Club Secretary: Karen Nelson
Manager: Bryan Robson

SPONSORS

BT Cellnet

FANZINES

Fly Me To The Moon

COLOURS

Home: Red shirts, red and white shorts and red stockings, all with white trim
Away: White and purple shirts, purple shorts with white and purple stockings

NICKNAME

Boro

HONOURS

Division One Champions: 1994–95
Division Two Champions:
1926–27, 1928–29, 1973–74
Anglo-Scottish Cup: 1976

RECORD GOALSCORER

George Camsell –
326 league goals, 1925–39

BIGGEST WIN

9–0 v Brighton & Hove Albion –
Division Two, 28 August 1958

BIGGEST DEFEAT

0–9 v Blackburn Rovers – Division Two,
6 November 1954

SEASON REVIEW

Middlesbrough finished 12th in the 1999–2000 Premiership, failing to achieve Bryan Robson's pre-season target of at least eighth place. Ultimately, though, many of the club's fans were happy to see the club finish where they did, aware that at one stage the spectre of relegation had threatened to cast its shadow over the Riverside Stadium.

The atmosphere in Middlesbrough before the opening game against Bradford was one of optimism. The arrival of German international Christian Ziege and England's Paul Ince proved that the club were still ambitious enough to invest in the best players.

Ince, in particular, had a point to prove, feeling that the management team at Anfield had been wrong to let him go and calling for the sacking of Gerard Houllier and Phil Thompson in a national newspaper article.

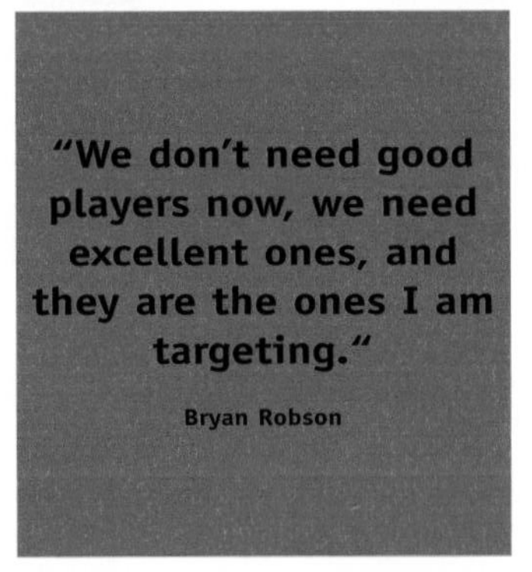

"We don't need good players now, we need excellent ones, and they are the ones I am targeting."
Bryan Robson

The former Liverpool man was absent for the Bradford game, which provided the Premiership with its first shock of the season, as Dean Saunders struck to earn the visitors an unexpected 1–0 victory in their first league game in the top flight for 77 years.

Three successive wins followed – away at Wimbledon and Derby, and then (much to Paul Ince's satisfaction) at home to Liverpool – which lifted the team up to third place and even prompted talk of a title challenge. With news filtering through to the press that Boro were in talks with Atletico Madrid over a deal to bring Juninho back to Teesside, spirits were as high as they had been in a long time at The Riverside.

Back-to-back defeats by Leicester and Aston Villa provided a wake-up call. Rumours that AC Milan's Ibrahim Ba was also about to make the move to Teesside turned out to be unfounded, but Juninho's return – albeit on loan – papered over the cracks. The little Brazilian failed to provide the immediate spark that his team needed as Boro stumbled to two defeats in his first two appearances.

His return did start another debate, though. There were those who saw his arrival as the end for Paul Gascoigne. Even though Robson insisted there was room in his team for two entertainers, the rumours grew more heated after Gascoigne was sent off in the 1–0 home defeat by Chelsea for swearing. The team improved in his absence, winning three games in a row and advancing to the fourth round of the Worthington Cup with victory over Watford.

Chesterfield provided stubborn opposition in the second round of the competition but were eventually beaten 2–1 on aggregate. Arsenal, who had trounced Boro 5–1 in the league, were their next opponents in the competition. Arsene Wenger fielded a shadow side and, although the Gunners' second string put up a good fight, the home side eventually came through after a penalty shoot-out.

The crowd were less than impressed with the team's Premiership form, though. The first murmurs of discontent were heard in the 0–0 draw with Wimbledon when some fans chanted "You don't know what you're doing" at Robson after he had substituted Juninho. Robson was clearly hurt by the criticism but he was determined not to let it get to him, saying that Juninho had been taken off for the good of the team.

Calls for Robson's head grew even louder in December as Middlesbrough fell to an unwanted double in the cups. Their misery began in the third round of the FA Cup with defeat at the hands of Second Division Wrexham and continued in the

79% Mark Schwarzer's saves-to-shots ratio

SEASON REVIEW

quarter-finals of the Worthington Cup as eventual runners-up Tranmere bundled them out of the competition with a 2–1 victory at Prenton Park.

After a 4–1 home defeat by Derby County, Robson promised to review his position at the end of the season. With his team nine points clear of relegation and just three points outside the top 10, he was entitled to some breathing-space.

The fans were also entitled to be worried, though. Their team was allowing the opposition too many goal attempts and they were paying the price with some bad results. No goalkeeper made as many saves as Mark Schwarzer in the 1999–2000 season and only one other team, Bradford, were forced into as many last-ditch blocks. When Aston Villa thrashed Boro 4–0 at The Riverside in a game during which Gascoigne broke his own arm while elbowing Villa player George Boateng in the face, the calls for Robson's resignation grew deafening.

"If you look, we've notoriously gone up one season and then back down the next. But we've broken that cycle in the last two seasons and now we have to start to improve our position in the league."
Bryan Robson

With just one point since Christmas, the club were now only four points off the relegation zone. Amazingly, they took this as the cue for a seven-game unbeaten run that saved their season.

The form of Paul Ince, in a run that included wins against Coventry, Arsenal and Tottenham, was particularly good. But there were also fine performances from the likes of Hamilton Ricard and England under-21 international Andy Campbell, who staked his place for a regular starting role with a series of intelligent displays up front for the team.

The cries for Robson's resignation had long since died away by the time Manchester United arrived at The Riverside in April. The crowd were still given plenty to shout about when some controversial decisions during a 4–3 defeat led to the Middlesbrough team surrounding the officials, just as Manchester United had done in the first game of the season between the two clubs at Old Trafford. Unlike United, Middlesbrough were charged, leading Robson to accuse the FA of hypocrisy over their failure to apply the same rules to his former club.

One man who would have been disgusted by the scenes at The Riverside was Wilf Mannion. The former Middlesbrough great died just four days after the game with United at the age of 81. He would have been happier with his beloved club's continued membership of the Premiership.

Boro eventually finished 19 points clear of the relegation zone, but there were times when they looked anything but certainties for survival.

While the calls for Bryan Robson's dismissal have subsided, he will once again come under pressure if the club makes a poor start to the 2000–01 season.

At least Robson has a sympathetic chairman behind him. Steve Gibson is likely to be asked to put his hand in his pocket again before 2000–01 kicks off.

He has already backed Robson's judgement with several expensive forays into the transfer market and can be expected to do so again.

Christian Karembeu's expected arrival from Real Madrid shows that Robson's name still has pulling power. However, he still needs to integrate youth into his experienced side.

While more world-class players would be welcome at The Riverside it remains to be seen whether they can be moulded into a consistent enough team to turn Middlesbrough into a significant force in Premiership football.

was the best in the division

MIDDLESBROUGH

DATE	OPPONENT	SCORE	ATT.	ARMSTRONG	BERESFORD	CAMPBELL	COOPER	CUMMINS	DEANE	FESTA	FLEMING	GASCOIGNE	GAVIN	GORDON
7.8.99	Bradford H	0–1	33,762	–	–	70	–	–	90	90	–	90	–	90
10.8.99	Wimbledon A	3–2	11,036	–	–	s1	–	–	90	90	–	90	–	90□
14.8.99	Derby Co A	3–1	24,045	s7	–	–	–	–	90^{1}	90	–	–	–	59
21.8.99	Liverpool H	1–0	34,783	–	–	s2	–	–	90^{1}	90	–	19	–	–
24.8.99	Leicester H	0–3	33,126	–	–	s46	–	–	90	90	–	–	–	–
28.8.99	Aston Villa A	0–1	28,728	–	–	s20	–	–	90	–	–	–	90	–
11.9.99	Southampton H	3–2	32,165	s26	–	–	90□	–	90^{1}□	–	–	90^{1}	s26	–
19.9.99	Leeds Utd A	0–2	34,122	72	–	–	90	–	90	90□	–	–	–	–
25.9.99	Chelsea H	0–1	34,183	s1	–	–	90□	–	70	90	90	s19■	–	–
3.10.99	Newcastle A	1–2	36,421	–	–	s45	90□	–	90^{1}	90□	90□	–	–	–
17.10.99	West Ham H	2–0	31,862	$s30^{1}$	–	–	90	–	90^{1}	–	90	–	–	–
24.10.99	Watford A	3–1*	16,081	s45	–	–	90	–	90	–	90	–	–	–
30.10.99	Everton H	2–1	33,916	–	–	–	–	–	90^{1}	–	90	–	–	–
6.11.99	Sunderland H	1–1	34,793	–	–	–	90	–	90□	–	–	–	–	–
20.11.99	Arsenal A	1–5	38,082	–	–	s15	90	–	90□	90□	90	90□	90	–
27.11.99	Wimbledon H	0–0	31,400	s29	–	–	90	–	90	90	–	–	–	–
4.12.99	Bradford A	1–1	17,708	–	–	–	–	–	90□	90	50	74	–	–
18.12.99	Tottenham H	2–1	33,129	s5	–	–	–	–	90^{1}	90	–	–	–	–
26.12.99	Sheff Wed A	0–1	28,531	45	–	–	–	–	90□	45□	90	–	s45	–
15.1.00	Derby Co H	1–4	32,745	45	–	$s45^{1}$	–	–	–	90	90□	–	–	–
22.1.00	Liverpool A	0–0	44,324	–	–	82	90	–	–	90	90	–	s22	–
29.1.00	Man Utd A	0–1	61,267	–	–	80	90	–	–	90	90	–	s69	–
5.2.00	Leicester A	1–2	17,550	–	–	90^{1}	90	–	–	90	90	–	–	–
14.2.00	Aston Villa H	0–4	31,571	s17	90	73	90□	–	–	90□	77	44	–	–
19.2.00	Coventry H	2–0	32,798	–	–	90	90	–	–	90^{1}	90	–	–	–
26.2.00	Leeds Utd H	0–0	34,800	s16	–	74	90	s16	–	86■	90	–	–	–
4.3.00	Southampton A	1–1	15,223	–	–	–	90□	–	90□	–	90	–	–	s73
12.3.00	Arsenal H	2–1	34,244	–	–	85	90	–	90	–	90	–	–	–
18.3.00	Sunderland A	1–1	42,013	–	–	s22	90	–	90	s5	90	–	–	–
25.3.00	Sheff Wed H	1–0	32,748	–	–	90^{1}	90	–	90	90	90	–	–	–
3.4.00	Tottenham A	3–2*	31,796	–	–	90	90	–	90	–	90□	–	–	–
10.4.00	Man Utd H	3–4	34,775	–	–	90^{1}	12	–	90	s78	90	–	–	–
15.4.00	Coventry A	1–2	19,345	–	–	89	–	–	90	90	61	–	–	–
22.4.00	Chelsea A	1–1	34,467	–	–	s12	90	–	90	90	90□	–	–	–
29.4.00	West Ham A	1–0	25,472	–	–	73	90	–	90^{1}	90	90□	–	–	–
2.5.00	Newcastle H	2–2	34,744	–	–	87	90	–	–	90^{1}	90	–	–	–
6.5.00	Watford H	1–1	32,930	–	–	45	90	–	–	90	90	–	–	–
14.5.00	Everton A	2–0	34,663	–	–	82	90	–	90^{1}	90□	90□	–	–	–

□ Yellow card, ■ Red card, s Substitute, 90^{2} Goals scored

*including one own goal

1999–2000 PREMIERSHIP APPEARANCES

JUNINHO	KILGANNON	MADDISON	MARINELLI	MUSTOE	O'NEILL	ORMEROD	PALLISTER	RICARD	SCHWARZER	STAMP	STOCKDALE	SUMMERBELL	TOWNSEND	VICKERS	ZIEGE	
–	–	–	–	90□	90	–	–	s20	90	90	–	–	s12	78	90	990
–	–	–	–	s13	s45	–	–	89[2]	90	90□	–	–	90	90	45[1]	990
–	–	–	–	90	90□	–	–	83[1]	90	90	–	–	s31	90	90[1]□	990
–	–	–	–	s6	s71□	–	90	88	90	84□	–	–	90□	90	90	990
–	–	s41□	–	90□	3	–	90□	90	90	–	90	–	–	90	90□	990
–	–	–	–	90	–	–	90	70	90	90	90	s14□	76	90	–	990
–	–	–	–	90	–	–	90[1]	64□	90	64	s26	–	–	64	90	990
–	–	–	–	90	90	–	90□	s18	90	–	–	–	–	90	90□	990
89	–	–	–	s55	90□	–	90	90□	90	–	–	–	–	–	90□	989
45	–	–	–	90	90	–	10	–	90	–	–	–	–	s80	90	990
90	–	–	–	–	90	–	90	60	90	–	–	–	–	90	90	990
77[1]	–	–	–	–	90	–	90	45	90	s13	–	–	–	90	90□	990
90	–	–	–	–	90	–	90□	90	90	90	–	–	–	90	90[1]	990
90	–	–	–	–	90□	–	90	90[1]	90	90	–	–	–	90□	90	990
75	–	–	–	s45	–	–	–	90[1]	90	–	s32	–	–	13	–	990
62	–	–	–	s28□	90	–	–	61	90	90	–	–	–	90	90	990
90	–	s40	–	90	–	–	–	90[1]	90	90□	–	s16	–	90	90	990
90	–	90	–	90	90□	–	–	85	90	–	90	s1	–	90□	89[1]	990
90	–	90	s45	90	–	–	–	s15	90	75□	90	–	–	90	–	990
90	–	s45	–	90	–	–	90	90	90	–	45	–	–	90	–	990
90□	–	–	–	90	–	–	90	s8□	90	–	–	90	–	68	–	990
90	–	s10	–	–	–	s45	21	45	90□	–	–	90	–	–	60■	960
90	–	–	–	–	80	–	90	s10	90	–	–	90□	–	–	90	990
90	–	s13	–	–	90	–	90	–	–	s46	–	90	–	–	–	990
89	–	s1	–	–	–	–	90	90[1]	90	–	–	90	–	–	90	990
90	–	74	–	–	–	–	90□	87	90	–	–	90	–	s3	90□	986
85	–	90	–	s5	–	–	90	90[1]	90	–	–	90□	–	90	17□	990
s5	–	79	–	s11	–	–	–	90[1]	90	–	–	90	–	90	90	990
s14	–	68	–	–	–	–	90	76□	90	–	–	90	–	90□	85[1]	990
75	–	–	–	s15	–	–	90□	–	90	–	–	90	–	–	90	990
–	–	–	–	90	–	–	–	90[2]□	90	–	–	90	–	90	90	990
s20[1]	–	–	–	70	–	–	–	90□	90	–	–	90□	–	90	90□	990
s29	–	–	–	90	–	–	–	90	90	s29	s1	61	–	90□	90[1]	990
–	–	–	–	90	–	–	–	78[1]	90	–	–	90	–	90	90	990
82	–	–	–	s17	–	–	–	s8	90	90□	–	90	–	90	–	990
90[1]	s3	–	–	76	–	–	–	90	90	–	s16	s14	–	90□	74□	990
90	–	–	s45	90	–	–	–	90□	90	–	90[1]	–	–	90	–	990
90[1]	–	s8	–	90□	–	–	–	–	90	69□	s21	–	–	90	–	990

THE MANAGER

BRYAN ROBSON

Middlesbrough boss and former Manchester United legend Bryan Robson came through a testing 1999–2000 – arguably his toughest season to date as a manager.

After a 4–0 hammering at home to Aston Villa on Valentine's night, Boro fans were left almost heartbroken as their side lay just four points off the bottom three.

Middlesbrough were booed off the pitch – but Robson vowed to "instil some confidence in the players". And how it worked, with his side losing just two of their remaining 14 Premiership matches and finishing the season in a respectable 12th place.

Boro has been Robson's only managerial port of call, although he gained further experience when joining the England coaching staff under the reign of Terry Venables.

But he is best known for his 345 appearances for Manchester United and 90 England caps, gaining the well-earned nickname "Captain Marvel".

Believed by many to possibly be the successor to Sir Alex Ferguson at Old Trafford, Robson will be hoping that his seventh season in charge on Teesside will be his most successful yet at the club.

LEAGUE POSITION

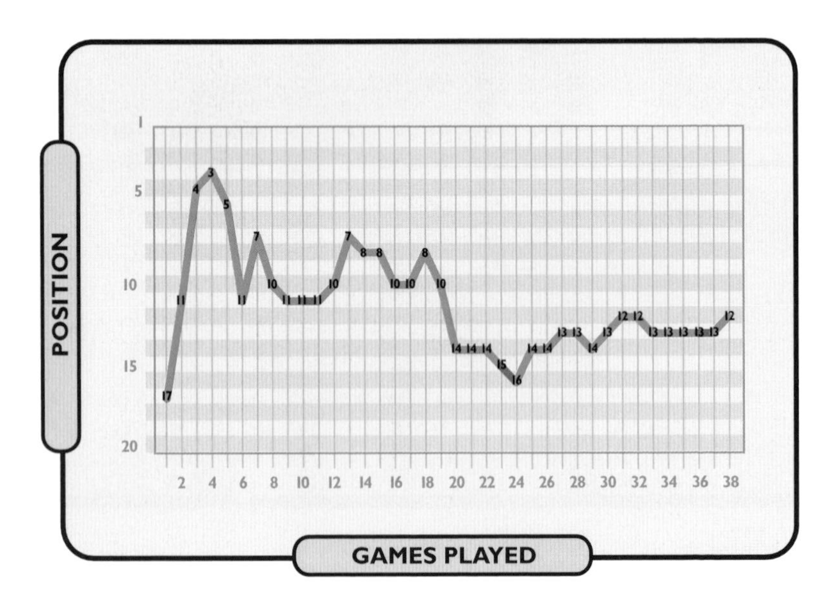

0 Boro did not concede a single goa

THE GOALS

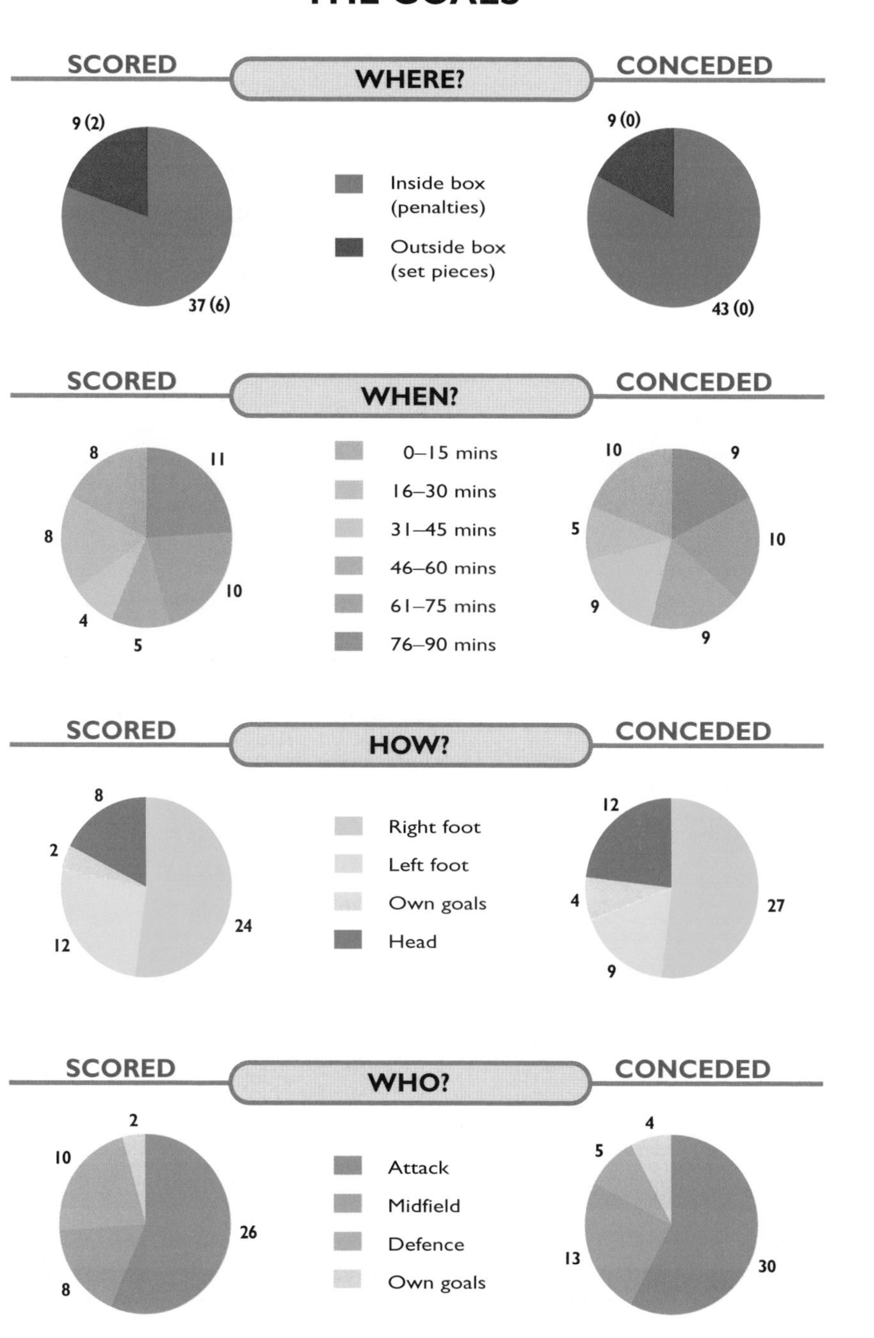

from either a penalty or direct free-kick

MIDDLESBROUGH

	ARMSTRONG	CAMPBELL	COOPER	CUMMINS	DEANE	FESTA	FLEMING	GASCOIGNE	GAVIN	GORDON	INCE	JUNIN
APPEARANCES												
Start	3	16	26	0	29	27	27	7	2	3	32	24
Sub	9	9	0	1	0	2	0	1	4	1	0	4
Minutes on pitch	338	1498	2262	16	2590	2464	2348	516	342	312	2812	2097
GOAL ATTEMPTS												
Goals	1	4	0	0	9	2	0	1	0	0	3	4
Shots on target	3	13	1	0	29	6	2	1	0	0	19	25
Shots off target	5	6	8	0	29	9	6	3	0	3	28	30
Shooting accuracy	38%	68%	11%	0%	50%	40%	25%	25%	0%	0%	40%	45%
PASSING												
Goal assists	0	2	1	0	4	1	1	1	0	0	1	2
Long passes	16	42	333	0	58	233	203	56	23	29	249	161
Short passes	110	316	507	3	969	642	583	198	55	87	942	808
PASS COMPLETION												
Own half %	85%	83%	75%	100%	81%	75%	69%	92%	85%	77%	84%	80%
Opposition half %	67%	65%	54%	100%	61%	55%	63%	73%	72%	69%	70%	65%
CROSSING												
Total crosses	2	10	16	1	23	23	34	25	3	6	13	89
Cross completion %	100%	10%	69%	0%	22%	17%	41%	36%	67%	17%	46%	31%
DRIBBLING												
Dribbles & runs	6	62	32	0	55	61	47	21	3	11	71	220
Dribble completion %	83%	69%	94%	0%	69%	84%	87%	71%	100%	91%	85%	62%
DEFENDING												
Tackles made	2	7	74	0	29	60	113	27	15	11	125	47
Tackles won %	0%	14%	46%	0%	66%	62%	40%	44%	47%	55%	62%	40%
Blocks	0	3	69	1	20	59	45	3	16	5	44	8
Clearances	2	2	220	1	57	238	90	7	56	39	93	10
Interceptions	2	5	18	0	9	28	16	7	1	6	22	11
DISCIPLINE												
Fouls	12	34	22	0	97	50	27	8	2	4	42	31
Offside	8	23	0	0	24	0	0	1	0	0	1	8
Yellow cards	0	0	5	0	6	6	6	1	0	1	8	1
Red cards	0	0	0	0	0	1	0	1	0	0	0	0

GOALKEEPER NAME	START/ (SUB)	TIME ON PITCH	GOALS CONCEDED	MINS/GOALS CONCEDED	SAVES MADE	SAVES/ SHOTS
BERESFORD	1	90	4	23	1	20%
SCHWARZER	37	3330	48	69	184	79%

PLAYERS' STATISTICS

KILGANNON	MADDISON	MARINELLI	MUSTOE	O'NEILL	ORMEROD	PALLISTER	RICARD	STAMP	STOCKDALE	SUMMERBELL	TOWNSEND	VICKERS	ZIEGE	TOTAL	RANK
0	6	0	19	14	0	21	28	13	6	15	3	30	29		
1	7	2	9	2	1	0	6	3	5	4	2	2	0		
3	649	90	1871	1279	45	1741	2360	1190	591	1366	299	2646	2440		
0	0	0	0	0	0	1	12	0	1	0	0	0	6	46*	=13th
0	1	2	2	4	0	1	33	1	3	2	0	2	22	172	13th
0	4	1	7	7	0	6	25	8	4	3	1	2	27	222	7th
0%	20%	67%	22%	36%	0%	14%	57%	11%	43%	40%	0%	50%	45%	44%	16th
0	0	0	0	1	0	0	3	1	1	0	0	1	6	26	18th
0	62	5	118	97	3	182	99	89	32	54	12	257	249	2662	20th
1	190	25	565	334	12	453	694	236	122	326	106	478	696	9458	17th
0%	81%	80%	76%	75%	100%	80%	77%	76%	67%	79%	84%	80%	77%	78%	14th
0%	61%	75%	67%	65%	60%	61%	58%	51%	62%	62%	71%	53%	60%	62%	15th
0	15	4	8	40	1	8	35	41	18	8	4	9	184	620	20th
0%	20%	50%	25%	25%	0%	63%	31%	34%	17%	13%	25%	56%	24%	30%	11th
0	8	6	19	76	0	30	99	70	7	17	3	15	78	1017	13th
0%	75%	83%	68%	70%	0%	83%	63%	64%	100%	71%	67%	93%	83%	73%	19th
0	9	2	84	44	2	69	33	24	14	71	6	62	85	1017	9th
0%	56%	100%	57%	43%	50%	57%	52%	46%	50%	41%	17%	53%	55%	51%	14th
0	9	0	13	18	0	60	6	10	4	20	1	79	23	516	2nd
0	16	0	41	75	5	268	6	66	23	23	8	297	77	1737	4th
0	3	0	15	13	0	24	4	8	5	12	0	20	35	264	8th
0	14	2	45	27	0	19	138	25	6	26	3	36	34	570	4th
0	1	1	0	1	0	0	54	5	1	1	0	0	5	134	=8th
0	1	0	4	5	0	5	7	6	0	4	1	5	9	82	3rd
0	0	0	0	0	0	0	0	0	0	0	0	0	1	3	=12th

*Including two own goals

ROSSES AUGHT	CROSSES PUNCHED	CROSSES NOT CLAIMED	CATCH SUCCESS	THROWS/ SHORT KICKS	% COMPLETION	LONG KICKS	% COMPLETION
2	0	0	100%	2	0%	36	28%
75	34	5	94%	169	85%	1220	42%

PLAYER OF THE SEASON

PLAYER	INDEX SCORE
MARK SCHWARZER	**1,047**
Gary Pallister	**1,012**
Christian Ziege	**971**
Paul Ince	**937**
Juninho	**918**
Gianluca Festa	**741**
Colin Cooper	**734**
Brian Deane	**718**
Steve Vickers	**682**
Hamilton Ricard	**681**

Middlesbrough were the only club to have a goalkeeper as their highest-ranking player of the 1999–2000 in the Opta Season Index.

Mark Schwarzer earned this accolade after a fine season of shot-stopping which saw him make 184 saves – more than any other Premiership 'keeper. The big Australian twice saved penalties and kept nine clean sheets for the Teessiders as they finished the season in mid-table.

The 1998–99 Boro Opta player of the season Gary Pallister once again produced consistently good performances throughout the campaign to achieve an average score of 1,012 points.

Boro veteran "Pally" used his head to make 220 clearances – more than any other Middlesbrough player – and he won a better-than-average 57% of his attempted tackles.

German import Christian Ziege settled into English football well and enjoyed a good first season at The Riverside. He received the supporters' vote as Player of the Year, scoring six goals and making another six from his wide role during the course of the campaign. His versatility was also a great advantage to Bryan Robson as he excelled in a variety of positions.

Paul Ince once again proved he was the "Guv'nor" as he earned an average of 937 points in the middle of the park for Boro. He won an impressive 62% of the tackles he made and, despite not being renowned for his goalscoring ability, he was on target on three occasions for the Teessiders.

The returning Juninho managed to gain an average of 918 points while other foreign imports such as Gianluca Festa and Hamilton Ricard also found themselves ranked in the Boro top 10. The experienced homegrown trio of Colin Cooper, Brian Deane and Steve Vickers also scored highly.

Bryan Robson's faith in the more mature players has been rewarded with six of the top 10 being aged over 30.

184 Mark Schwarzer made more saves

FIVE OF THE BEST

Middlesbrough finished the season in 12th place, well clear of relegation, but there was a tangible air of disappointment around The Riverside Stadium as the campaign ended. The team had flattered to deceive in the Premiership and crashed out of both cup competitions to sides from the lower leagues. Bryan Robson knows he will have to produce a better team in 2000–01.

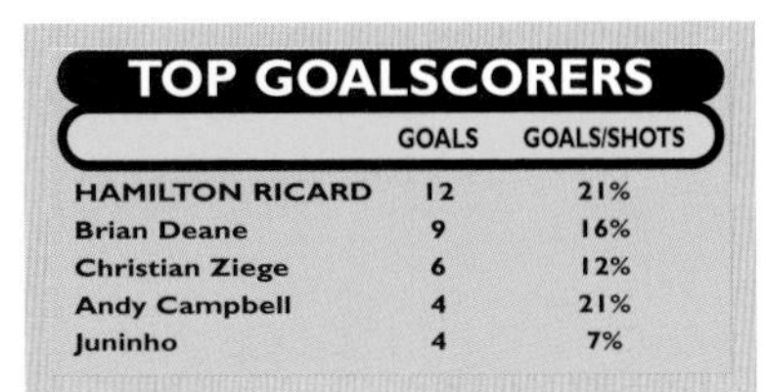

TOP GOALSCORERS

	GOALS	GOALS/SHOTS
HAMILTON RICARD	12	21%
Brian Deane	9	16%
Christian Ziege	6	12%
Andy Campbell	4	21%
Juninho	4	7%

Hamilton Ricard ended as Boro's top scorer for the second successive season, and while he may have scored three goals fewer, his goals-to-shots ratio had improved. The only man who could match him for deadliness was the young forward Andy Campbell. His four goals promise much for the future, while a man from the past, Brian Deane, proved that he could still play at the highest level. The returning Juninho managed to score with only 7% of his efforts.

Paul Ince had a lot to prove when he left Liverpool for Middlesbrough, and he played well enough on Teesside to regain his place in the England team. Only Bradford, Watford and Wimbledon made fewer successful passes than Middlesbrough, but Ince was always looking for the telling delivery and was comfortably superior to his colleagues. Juninho was behind him in second place, but often looked out-of-sorts, finding a team-mate with just 68% of his passes during the campaign.

TOP PASSERS

	SUCC PASSES	COMPLETION
PAUL INCE	886	74%
Juninho	657	68%
Christian Ziege	624	66%
Gianluca Festa	577	66%
Brian Deane	562	55%

TOP TACKLERS

	WON	SUCCESS
PAUL INCE	77	62%
Robbie Mustoe	48	57%
Christian Ziege	47	55%
Curtis Fleming	45	40%
Gary Pallister	39	57%

Paul Ince was the best tackler at The Riverside Stadium, proving to his critics that he still has the desire and heart to play in the Premiership. His nearest challengers were Robbie Mustoe and German import Christian Ziege, the latter being one of the few bright spots in Boro's season. Veteran defender Gary Pallister missed 17 league games but still made 39 successful tackles, winning 57% of his challenges.

Hamilton Ricard topped 100 Opta disciplinary points mainly due to his 84 fouls. He also picked up seven yellow cards during the campaign as he battled hard for the Teessiders. Christian Ziege may not have committed many indiscretions, but is in the top five due to his nine yellow cards and his sending-off at Old Trafford. It was certainly an explosive introduction to English football for the international wing-back.

DISCIPLINE

	POINTS	FOULS & CARDS
HAMILTON RICARD	105	84F, 7Y, 0R
Brian Deane	91	73F, 6Y, 0R
Gianluca Festa	74	50F, 6Y, 1R
Paul Ince	65	41F, 8Y, 0R
Christian Ziege	62	29F, 9Y, 1R

than any other top flight goalkeeper

ACTION	CAMPBELL	COOPER	DEANE	FLEMING	INCE	JUNINHO	MADDISON	MUSTOE	RICARD	SCHWARZER	SUMMERBELL	VICKERS	ZIEGE	TOTAL	ARSENAL
Time on pitch	85	90	90	90	90	5	79	11	90	90	90	90	90	990	990
GOALS															
Goal	–	–	–	–	1	–	–	–	1	–	–	–	–	2	1
Shot on target	–	–	1	–	–	–	–	–	3	–	–	–	1	5	5
Shot off target	–	–	1	–	1	–	–	–	–	–	–	–	2	4	5
Blocked shot	–	–	–	–	–	–	–	–	–	–	–	–	–	–	5
Own goal	–	–	–	–	–	–	–	–	–	–	–	–	–	–	–
PASSES															
Pass to own player	13	12	17	23	24	1	17	2	10	–	10	17	17	163	344
Pass to opposition	3	11	16	17	12	2	8	1	22	–	12	10	6	120	117
Cross to own player	–	–	–	–	–	–	1	–	2	–	–	–	–	3	9
Cross to opposition player	–	–	3	–	–	–	5	–	1	–	–	–	5	14	26
Goal assist	–	–	–	1	–	–	–	–	–	–	–	–	–	1	1
Pass completion %	81%	52%	47%	59%	67%	33%	58%	67%	34%	0%	45%	63%	61%	55%	71%
TACKLES & CLEARANCES															
Tackle	1	–	2	5	9	–	3	1	1	–	4	2	1	29	20
Clearances, blocks and interceptions	–	13	10	5	7	1	2	–	1	–	4	17	8	68	35
DRIBBLES & RUNS															
Dribble ball retained	2	1	–	2	1	1	1	–	5	–	–	–	–	13	14
Dribble ball lost	2	–	–	–	–	–	–	–	1	–	–	–	–	3	5
Dribble success %	50%	100%	0%	100%	100%	100%	100%	0%	83%	0%	0%	0%	0%	81%	74%
DISCIPLINE															
Fouls	–	2	2	–	1	–	2	2	7	–	4	1	–	21	16
Penalty conceded	–	–	–	–	–	–	–	–	–	–	–	–	–	–	–
Free kick – offside	–	–	–	–	–	–	–	–	4	–	–	–	–	4	7
Yellow cards	–	–	–	–	–	–	–	–	–	–	–	–	–	–	1
Red cards	–	–	–	–	–	–	–	–	–	–	–	–	–	–	–
GOALKEEPERS															
Distribution to own player	–	–	–	–	–	–	–	–	–	17	–	–	–	17	15
Distribution to opposition player	–	–	–	–	–	–	–	–	–	19	–	–	–	19	15
Goalkeeper distribution %	0%	0%	0%	0%	0%	0%	0%	0%	0%	47%	0%	0%	0%	47%	50%
Save	–	–	–	–	–	–	–	–	–	5	–	–	–	5	5
Ball caught	–	–	–	–	–	–	–	–	–	3	–	–	–	3	1
Ball dropped	–	–	–	–	–	–	–	–	–	–	–	–	–	–	–
Goal conceded	–	–	–	–	–	–	–	–	–	1	–	–	–	1	2

24 No team won more points against

Prior to this game, Arsenal were losing ground at the top of the table and needed a win from their trip to The Riverside to stay in with a chance of the title. Middlesbrough, on the other hand, were fighting to secure their place in the Premiership and Arsenal were one of the last teams they would have wanted to face.

The Gunners had fired in 11 goals against Bryan Robson's team in the previous two league meetings, while Middlesbrough had the worst scoring record at home – few would have predicted anything other than a win for the Londoners.

The opening exchanges were fairly even, with both sides opting to attack, and Boro came close to scoring after 15 minutes. Neil Maddison put a high cross into the box and Brian Deane beat Silvinho, only to see David Seaman stop the ball right on the line. Throughout the game, Silvinho at 5'8" struggled to cope with the dominating presence of Deane who towered above him at 6'3" and caused problems for the makeshift Arsenal defence.

Stand-in centre-back Emmanuel Petit was also struggling to come to terms with his responsibilities, and was being given a torrid time by the skilful Hamilton Ricard.

At the other end, Mark Schwarzer was called into action early on, making a good save from Thierry Henry, before relying on his post to help him out when he was beaten by a Ray Parlour effort.

Paul Ince was in magnificent form throughout the afternoon, winning six out of nine tackles as well as getting back to help out the defence. Ince set an example that his team-mates followed, by putting in a gutsy performance. Throughout the game, Boro went in for 29 tackles and completed 68 clearances, blocks and interceptions to keep the Gunners at bay.

The injured David Seaman was replaced at half-time by Alex Manninger and the home side were delighted to beat the Austrian soon after the restart.

Deane forced a corner down the right during a period of home pressure. Christian Ziege swung in the set-piece and when the Arsenal defenders only half-cleared it, Curtis Fleming played the ball back in. As Arsenal tried to push up for offside, Ince was on hand to back-head the ball over Manninger and into the net.

The second Boro goal was a gift from Patrick Vieira. Under pressure from Andy Campbell, the Frenchman played the ball back without looking and it fell to Ricard. The South American ran at the visiting defence, nutmegged Petit and passed the ball into the corner of the net. It was no more than Boro deserved. Ricard was on target with all four of his shots, scoring once and completing five out of six dribbles and runs that he attempted.

However, Arsenal did pull a goal back with 20 minutes to go. Kanu laid a pass through to substitute Dennis Bergkamp and the Dutchman played a one-two with Henry before lobbing the ball over Schwarzer and into the net. The home side could have scored again in the final 10 minutes, but Manninger pulled off a superb double save from Ricard. Boro bravely held out and claimed the win that moved them nearer to safety and ended Arsenal's bid for the title.

NEWCASTLE UNITED

ADDRESS

St James's Park,
Newcastle-upon-Tyne NE1 4ST

CONTACT NUMBERS

Telephone: 0191 201 8400
Fax: 0191 201 8600
Ticket Office: 0191 261 1571
Club Call: 09068 121190
Superstore: 0191 201 8426
Website: www.nufc.co.uk

KEY PERSONNEL

President: Sir John Hall
Patron: Trevor Bennett
Chairman: W F Shepherd
Deputy Chairman: D S Hall
Directors: A O Fletcher, R Jones, L Wheatley
Honorary President: Bob Young
Director of Football Administration: R Cushing
Manager: Bobby Robson CBE

SPONSORS

1999– 2000 Scottish and Newcastle Breweries
2000–2001 NTL

FANZINES

The Mag
Talk Of The Tyne
True Faith

COLOURS

Home: Black and white striped shirts with black shorts and stockings
Away: White shirts with teal half-sleeve, white shorts and white stockings

NICKNAME

The Magpies

HONOURS

League Champions: 1904–05, 1906–07, 1908–09, 1926–27
Division One Champions: 1992–93
Division Two Champions: 1964–65
FA Cup: 1910, 1924, 1932, 1951, 1952, 1955
Fairs Cup: 1969

RECORD GOALSCORER

Jackie Milburn – 177 league goals, 1946–57

BIGGEST WIN

13–0 v Newport County – Division Two, 5 October 1946

BIGGEST DEFEAT

0–9 v Burton Wanderers – Division Two, 15 April 1895

SEASON REVIEW

Newcastle United started the 1999–2000 season as they had finished the 1998–99 campaign: by losing. Defeat in the previous season's cup final came on the back of seven league games without a win, form that did not bode well for the new campaign.

Ruud Gullit had brought in plenty of new blood, paying almost £10 million for the services of Marcelino and Alain Goma and a further £6.75 million for Ipswich's Kieron Dyer. Franck Dumas also arrived for £500,000 and some of this outlay was recouped with the sale of Dietmar Hamann to Liverpool.

For all the injection of talent, though, Gullit was having real problems with his existing playing staff. He had consigned Alessandro Pistone and Rob Lee to the reserves and, more importantly, his relationship with club captain Alan Shearer had deteriorated to the point where the two barely spoke.

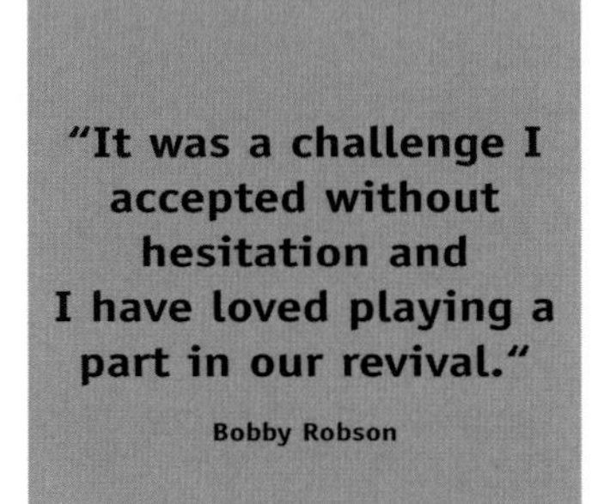

"It was a challenge I accepted without hesitation and I have loved playing a part in our revival."
Bobby Robson

It was against this background of internal division that the team went into their first game of the season against Aston Villa. The match was memorable for referee Uriah Rennie's controversial dismissal of Shearer and a Julian Joachim goal that consigned the Magpies to a depressing defeat.

Things went downhill rapidly as the team slipped to heavy defeats at Tottenham and Southampton. By the time they faced deadly rivals Sunderland on a rainy night at the end of August, Newcastle were 18th in the Premiership with one point, separated from the foot of the table by goal difference alone.

Gullit's decision to leave both Shearer and Duncan Ferguson on the bench for the game was a huge gamble, designed to underline his authority. It failed miserably, as Sunderland ran out 2–1 winners.

Gullit defended his selection policy by saying that the team had only lost after he had brought the duo on, but his time at St James's Park was clearly at an end. He resigned three days later.

Newcastle were in turmoil, crashing to their fifth defeat of the season at Old Trafford, former Gallowgate idol Andy Cole rubbing salt into his old club's wounds with four goals in a 5–1 drubbing.

Speculation about the identity of Gullit's successor was rife, with everyone from Johan Cruyff to Alan Shearer linked with the job. A poll in a local newspaper revealed the people's choice, though, as 87% of those asked expressed a preference for Bobby Robson. They were to get their wish.

Robson arrived in time for the visit to Chelsea and, although the team lost, they played with more spirit than they had managed all season. The new manager's first task was to pick up Alan Shearer. The England skipper had had a dreadful start to the campaign, scoring just one goal for his club and playing so badly for his country that the press had begun to question his right to pull on an England shirt. The criticism undoubtedly had an influence on his decision to announce his retirement from international football after the Euro 2000 tournament.

It did not take long for Shearer to respond to his new boss. After the team had chalked up their first victory of the season with a 2–0 win against CSKA Sofia in Bulgaria, they returned to St James's Park for a crucial game against fellow-strugglers Sheffield Wednesday.

The game proved to be the turning-point of the season, as Newcastle destroyed their hapless visitors with a breathtaking display of attacking football that saw Shearer notch five goals in an 8–0 victory.

59 Nolberto Solano delivered the highest

SEASON REVIEW

By the time October had come an end, Shearer had taken his tally to 11 and Newcastle were on the way up. The one downside to a fantastic month came with elimination from the Worthington Cup after a 2–0 defeat by Trevor Francis's Birmingham City at St Andrews.

With Rob Lee restored to the side and Kieron Dyer playing some great football, Newcastle moved out of the bottom three after a 2–0 win against Derby County and never looked back. UEFA Cup elimination at the hands of Roma was disappointing, but progress in the FA Cup was smoother.

"There were a few careers going backwards here and they didn't have any character. It was a leaking ship. But I have put a smile back on their faces on the training ground."

Bobby Robson

After escaping White Hart Lane with a 1–1 draw, Newcastle took Spurs back to St James's Park for a third-round replay where they won 6–1. Their fourth-round opponents Sheffield United were beaten 4–1. And in the fifth round Shearer rammed the taunts of his former fans down their throats with both goals in a 2–1 victory against Blackburn Rovers – a game in which the England skipper amazed everyone by abandoning his famous one-handed salute to unveil two "trendy" new goal celebrations.

The club went into their game against Manchester United on a high. Even they could not have predicted a 3–0 win, though – a result that confirmed their resurrection under Robson.

The team was playing with plenty of style, but they had added new grit to their game evident in the United game. Shearer admitted that his team had gone in hard on the Champions on purpose, saying: "We got among them and they didn't like it".

That spirit was in evidence again in the sixth round of the FA Cup when Newcastle held off a brave Tranmere side to win 3–2 and book a semi-final date with Chelsea. Further good news came with the revelation that Robson had signed a new 12-month rolling contract, a fact that provided the board at the club with some much-needed positive publicity after a bitter dispute with season ticket-holders over the relocation of seats.

A Gustavo Poyet header in the 1–0 home defeat by Chelsea provided a taste of things to come at the beginning of March but the team continued their revival, reaching the 40-point mark by the end of the month to secure their Premiership status.

The FA Cup semi-final at Wembley turned out to be a desperately disappointing affair, as Newcastle put in one of their best performances of the season only to lose 2–1 courtesy of two more Poyet goals. With three Wembley defeats in as many years, it was easy to understand Shearer's sentiments when he said he could not wait for the place to be knocked down, although he did make a happier return at the end of the season as he captained England to a 2–0 international friendly victory over Ukraine in his last game for his country at the famous old stadium.

Wembley disappointment was tinged with satisfaction over achievements in the league. Newcastle eventually finished 11th but, had the season started after Robson's first game in charge, they would have ended the campaign in sixth place, a position that is well within their reach in 2000–01.

After the disappointment of the Kenny Dalglish and Ruud Gullit eras on Tyneside, the Robson revival has provided the Toon Army with real hope of a trophy-winning season. While silverware is by no means guaranteed, Newcastle are at least in a position to challenge for the major trophies. More signings are expected to bolster the squad, and with Robson at the helm, Newcastle could well surprise a few people in 2000–01.

NEWCASTLE UNITED

DATE	OPPONENT	SCORE	ATT.	BARTON	BEHARALL	CHARVET	DABIZAS	DOMI	DUMAS	DYER	FERGUSON	FUMACA	GALLACHER	GAVILAN	GIVEN	GLASS	GO
7.8.99	Aston Villa H	0–1	36,600	90□	–	–	–	90	90	s45	–	–	–	–	–	–	90
9.8.99	Tottenham A	1–3	28,701	90□	–	–	–	90	73	90	–	–	–	–	–	–	90
15.8.99	Southampton A	2–4	15,030	90	–	–	–	90	–	90	–	–	–	–	–	–	90
21.8.99	Wimbledon H	3–3	35,809	90	s31	–	–	90^{1}	–	90	s28	–	–	–	–	–	59
25.8.99	Sunderland H	1–2	36,600	90	–	–	90	90□	–	90^{1}	s32	–	–	–	–	–	90
30.8.99	Man Utd A	1–5*	55,190	90□	s15	–	47■	–	–	90	79	–	–	–	–	–	90
11.9.99	Chelsea A	0–1	35,092	90□	–	–	90□	90	–	90□	73	–	–	–	–	–	90
19.9.99	Sheff Wed H	8–0	36,619	90	–	–	–	81	–	63^{1}	–	–	–	–	–	s9	90
25.9.99	Leeds Utd A	2–3	40,192	90	–	s17	–	90□	–	90	–	–	–	–	–	–	90
3.10.99	Middlesbro H	2–1	36,421	90	–	–	90□	90	–	90	–	–	83	–	–	s2	90
16.10.99	Coventry A	1–4	23,031	30■	–	–	90□	90^{1}	–	90	–	–	90	–	90	–	–
25.10.99	Derby Co H	2–0*	35,614	56	–	–	90	–	–	37	s10	–	80	–	90	–	–
30.10.99	Arsenal A	0–0	38,106	–	–	–	90□	90	90	–	s1	–	90	–	–	–	–
7.11.99	Everton H	1–1	36,164	–	–	–	90	90	90□	–	84	–	90	–	–	–	–
20.11.99	Watford A	1–1	19,539	–	–	–	90^{1}	–	90	–	–	–	s8	–	–	s9	–
28.11.99	Tottenham H	2–1	36,460	–	–	90	90^{1}	–	–	–	s14	81	–	–	–	90^{1}	–
4.12.99	Aston Villa A	1–0	34,531	s4	–	–	90□	–	90	–	$s32^{1}$	–	–	–	–	–	–
18.12.99	Bradford A	0–2	18,286	90	–	–	–	–	–	s20	90	s6	73	–	–	s17	–
26.12.99	Liverpool H	2–2	36,445	90	–	–	90	–	–	52	89^{1}	–	s16	–	–	s38	–
28.12.99	Leicester A	2–1	21,225	90	–	–	90	–	–	–	90^{1}	–	90	–	–	–	–
3.1.00	West Ham H	2–2	36,314	90	–	–	90^{1}	–	–	–	78	s38	76	–	–	s14	–
16.1.00	Southampton H	5–0**	35,623	84	–	–	90	s14	–	90	90^{2}	–	76	–	–	–	–
22.1.00	Wimbledon A	0–2	22,118	90	–	–	90	s16	–	90	90	–	74	–	–	–	–
5.2.00	Sunderland A	2–2	42,192	90	–	–	90□	89^{1}	–	90	90	–	s1	s1	–	–	–
12.2.00	Man Utd H	3–0	36,470	90	–	–	90	s7	–	83	62^{1}	–	83	s7	–	–	–
26.2.00	Sheff Wed A	2–0	29,212	90□	–	–	90	s15	–	90	45	–	75^{1}	–	90	–	–
4.3.00	Chelsea H	0–1	36,448	90	–	–	90	45	–	90	90	–	–	–	90	–	–
11.3.00	Watford H	1–0	36,433	90	–	–	90	s45	–	–	90	–	90^{1}	–	90	–	–
19.3.00	Everton A	2–0	32,512	90	–	–	90	s22	–	$s13^{1}$	90□	–	68	–	90	–	–
25.3.00	Liverpool A	1–2	44,743	90	–	–	90	s32	–	90	90	–	s25	–	90	–	58
1.4.00	Bradford H	2–0	36,572	90	–	–	–	90	–	73	90	–	–	–	–	–	90
12.4.00	West Ham A	1–2	25,817	90	–	–	50	90	–	86	–	–	–	–	90	–	90
15.4.00	Leicester H	0–2	36,246	90	–	–	–	90	–	80	–	s10	–	s22	90	–	90
23.4.00	Leeds Utd H	2–2	36,460	90	–	–	90	90	–	80	–	s4	–	86	90	–	–
29.4.00	Coventry H	2–0	36,408	90	–	–	90	39	–	90	–	–	–	89^{1}	90	–	–
2.5.00	Middlesbro A	2–2	34,744	90	–	–	90	–	–	82	–	–	–	–	90	–	–
6.5.00	Derby Co A	0–0	32,724	90	–	–	90	s78	–	90	–	–	s25	s6	90	–	–
14.5.00	Arsenal H	4–2	36,450	90	–	–	90	–	–	90	–	–	s19	–	90	–	–

□ Yellow card, ■ Red card, s Substitute, 90^{2} Goals scored

*including one own goal **including two own goals

1999–2000 PREMIERSHIP APPEARANCES

GRIFFIN	HARPER	HELDER	HOWEY	HUGHES	KARELSE	KETSBAIA	LEE	MARCELINO	MARIC	MCCLEN	PISTONE	ROBINSON	SERRANT	SHEARER	SOLANO	SPEED	WRIGHT	TOTAL
–	90	–	–	–	–	90	–	45	s15	–	–	s5	75	70■	85	90□	–	970
–	90	–	–	68	–	90□	–	–	s22	–	–	s17	–	90	90^{1}□	90□	–	990
–	–	–	–	90	90	90	–	–	s59	–	–	s18	13	90^{1}	90	90^{1}	–	990
–	–	–	–	–	90	62	–	90	–	90□	–	90	–	–	90^{1}	90^{1}	–	990
–	–	–	–	–	–	–	–	–	72	90□	–	58	–	s18	90	90	90	990
–	–	–	–	90	–	–	70	–	–	s20	–	s11	–	90	75□	90	90	947
–	–	–	–	s3	–	–	77	–	s13	–	–	s17	–	90	87□	90	90	990
–	90	–	–	90^{1}	–	78	90	–	–	s12	–	s27	–	90^{5}	90	90^{1}	–	990
–	90	–	–	–	–	43	–	90□	–	73	–	s47	–	90^{2}	90	90□	–	990
–	90	–	–	–	–	–	90	–	–	–	–	s7	–	90^{2}	88	90	–	990
–	–	–	–	90	–	–	90	–	–	–	–	–	–	90	90□	90	–	930
–	–	–	–	s34	–	–	90	90	s53	–	90	–	–	90^{1}	90	90	–	990
–	–	–	–	–	90	–	90□	90	–	–	90	–	–	90	89	90	–	990
–	90	–	–	–	–	–	90	–	s6	–	90	–	–	90^{1}	90	90□	–	990
–	90	–	–	90	–	82	90□	90□	81	–	90	–	–	90	–	90	–	990
–	90	90	–	90	–	76	90	–	s4	s9	–	–	–	90	86□	–	–	990
–	90	90	–	s6	–	84	90	–	58	–	90□	–	–	90	86	90□	–	990
–	90	90□	–	90	–	–	84	–	–	–	90	–	–	90	70	90	–	990
–	90	–	–	90	–	s1	90	–	–	–	90	–	–	90^{1}	74	90	–	990
–	90	–	–	–	–	–	90	90	–	–	90	–	–	90^{1}	90	90	–	990
–	90	–	–	–	–	s12	52	90	–	–	90	–	–	90	90	90^{1}	–	990
–	90	–	–	s6	–	s9	–	90	–	–	90	–	–	90	81^{1}	90	–	990
–	90	–	–	–	–	–	–	90	–	–	90	–	–	90	90	90	–	990
–	90	90^{1}	–	s53	–	–	89□	–	–	–	37	–	–	90	–	90	–	990
–	90	90	–	90	–	s28	90	–	–	–	–	–	–	90^{2}□	–	90	–	990
–	–	69	s21	90	–	s45	90	–	–	–	–	–	–	90^{1}	–	90	–	990
–	–	–	90	90	–	s15	75	–	–	–	–	–	–	90	s45	90	–	990
–	–	–	90	45	–	–	90	–	–	–	–	–	–	90	90	90	–	990
–	–	–	90□	90^{1}	–	–	90	–	–	–	–	–	–	90	77	90□	–	990
–	–	–	90	90	–	–	65	–	–	–	–	–	–	90^{1}	–	90	–	990
–	90	90	–	90	–	s17	90	–	–	–	–	–	–	90^{1}	–	90^{1}	–	990
–	–	–	s40	90	–	s4	90□	–	–	–	–	–	–	90	90□	90^{1}	–	990
–	–	–	90	68	–	–	90	–	–	–	–	s22	–	90	68	90	–	990
–	–	65	90	90	–	–	90	s25	s10	–	–	–	–	90^{2}□	–	–	–	990
s1	–	–	–	90	–	s51	89	–	–	s1	90	–	–	90^{1}	–	90	–	990
s4	–	–	–	90	–	87	90	–	s3	s8	90^{1}	–	–	90	86	90^{1}	–	990
–	–	–	–	90	–	84	90□	–	–	–	12	–	–	90	65	90	–	990
90^{1}	–	–	90	–	–	71	89	–	s4	s1	–	–	–	90^{1}	86	90^{2}	–	990

THE MANAGER

BOBBY ROBSON

After collecting just one point from their opening five games, and losing at home to north-east rivals Sunderland, Ruud Gullit left Newcastle United.

Bobby Robson was installed as the new boss, charged with the responsibility of saving Newcastle from the drop and he did that and more, guiding his side to 11th place – a remarkable achievement considering Newcastle's plight at the time.

As a player, Robson won 20 England caps, but it is in management where he has excelled. He won the FA Cup and UEFA Cup with Ipswich Town, before managing England from 1982–90. He took the national side to the World Cup quarter-finals in 1986, and the semi-finals in 1990, before returning to club management.

He won the Dutch League title twice with PSV Eindhoven, nurturing Ronaldo along the way, then enjoyed success in Portugal, where he won the league twice with FC Porto and the Cup with Sporting Lisbon.

Robson was then appointed Barcelona coach and guided the Catalan side to the Spanish Cup and European Cup Winners' Cup in 1997, before becoming Technical Director.

Rewarded with a rolling one-year contract, Robson will want to take Newcastle into the top six and beyond.

LEAGUE POSITION

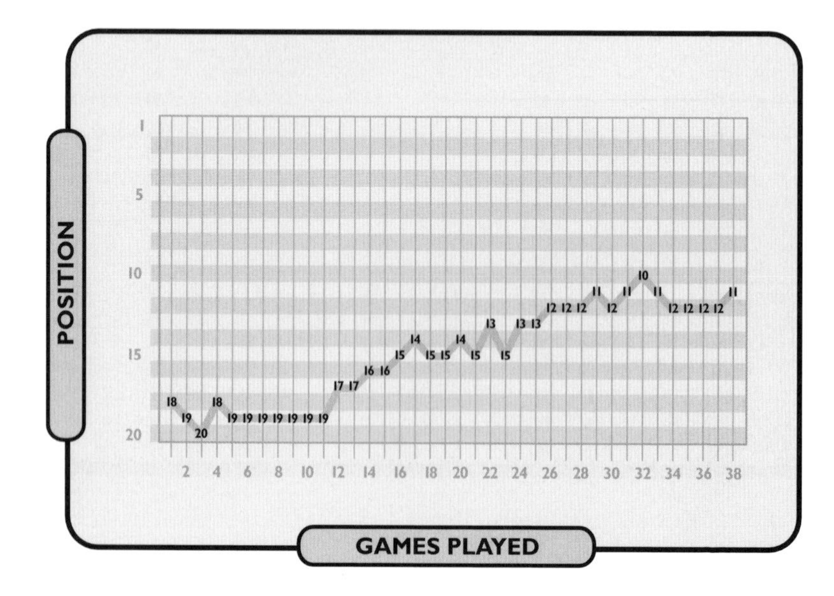

19 Newcastle scored more headed goals than

THE GOALS

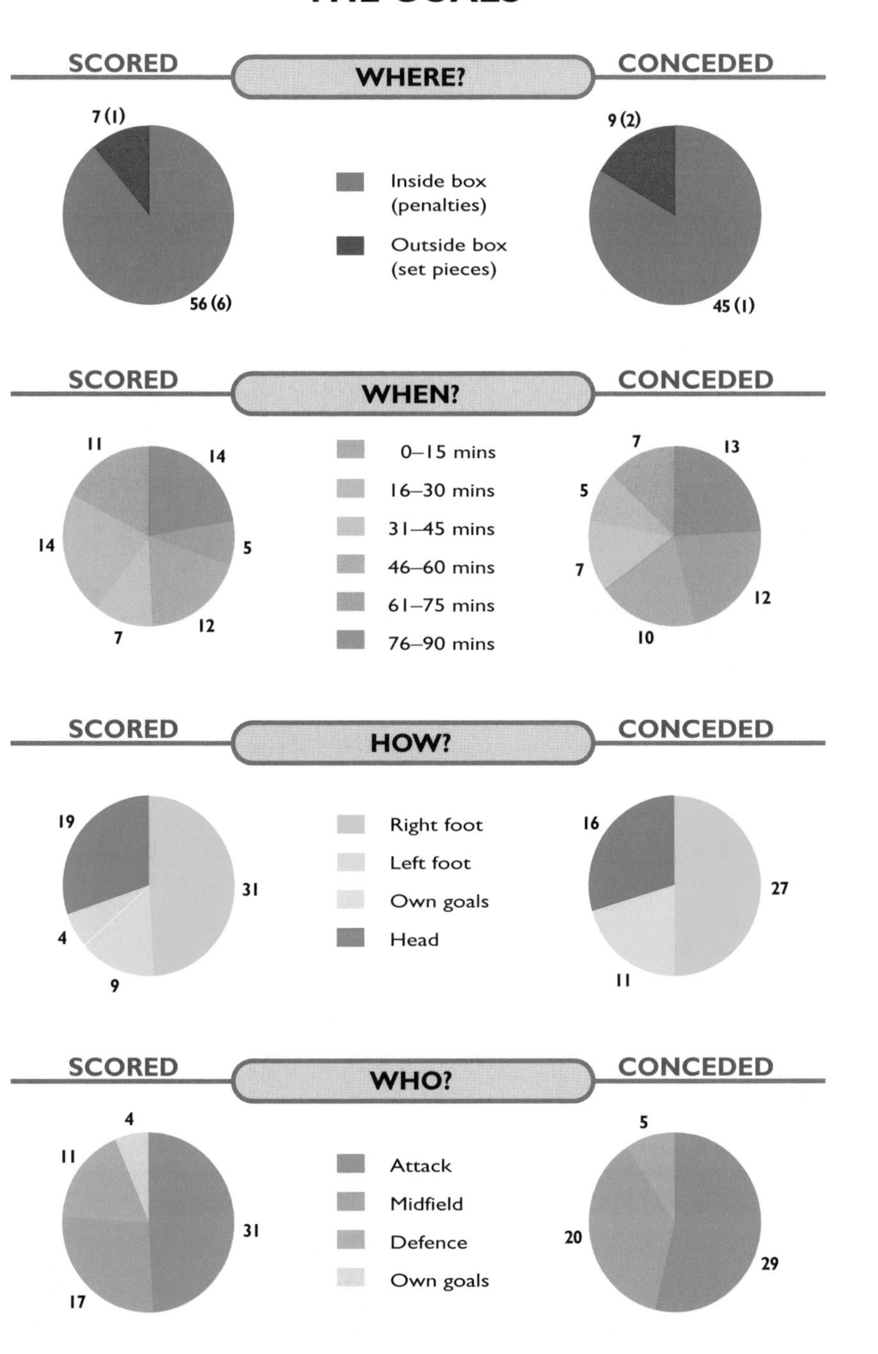

any of their Premiership counterparts

NEWCASTLE UNITED

	BARTON	BEHERALL	CHARVET	DABIZAS	DOMI	DUMAS	DYER	FERGUSON	FUMACA	GALLACHER	GAVILAN	GLASS
APPEARANCES												
Start	33	0	1	29	19	6	27	17	1	14	2	1
Sub	1	2	1	0	8	0	3	6	4	6	4	6
Minutes on pitch	2874	46	107	2527	1833	523	2334	1527	139	1232	211	179
GOAL ATTEMPTS												
Goals	0	0	0	3	3	0	3	6	0	2	1	1
Shots on target	1	0	0	7	9	2	17	20	1	16	2	2
Shots off target	10	0	0	3	11	1	20	25	1	19	0	2
Shooting accuracy	9%	0%	0%	70%	45%	67%	46%	44%	50%	46%	100%	50%
PASSING												
Goal assists	3	0	0	0	3	0	6	1	0	0	0	0
Long passes	608	3	9	343	174	83	108	68	10	86	16	5
Short passes	1103	6	37	776	525	167	906	717	52	459	69	43
PASS COMPLETION												
Own half %	84%	86%	76%	80%	80%	83%	86%	84%	77%	78%	75%	71%
Opposition half %	62%	50%	56%	62%	64%	73%	83%	69%	71%	70%	62%	53%
CROSSING												
Total crosses	80	0	1	15	86	6	55	12	1	46	18	8
Cross completion %	36%	0%	0%	60%	31%	67%	36%	8%	100%	22%	33%	13%
DRIBBLING												
Dribbles & runs	105	1	7	54	103	13	157	30	4	38	9	12
Dribble completion %	91%	100%	86%	94%	79%	92%	73%	67%	75%	66%	67%	67%
DEFENDING												
Tackles made	88	0	3	87	57	16	61	8	5	25	2	3
Tackles won %	50%	0%	33%	49%	51%	50%	57%	50%	60%	24%	0%	67%
Blocks	50	2	5	61	16	15	2	4	0	13	0	0
Clearances	144	5	12	300	90	41	7	23	3	5	0	1
Interceptions	25	0	6	18	9	7	8	0	5	3	1	1
DISCIPLINE												
Fouls	37	1	0	43	33	7	32	64	7	19	3	0
Offside	4	0	0	3	4	0	13	13	0	6	1	0
Yellow cards	5	0	0	6	2	1	1	1	0	0	0	0
Red cards	1	0	0	1	0	0	0	0	0	0	0	0

GOALKEEPER NAME	START/ (SUB)	TIME ON PITCH	GOALS CONCEDED	MINS/GOALS CONCEDED	SAVES MADE	SAVES/ SHOTS
GIVEN	14	1260	17	74	34	67%
HARPER	18	1620	22	74	45	67%
KARELSE	3	270	7	39	8	53%
WRIGHT	3	270	8	34	11	58%

For more information visit our website:

PLAYERS' STATISTICS

…IFFIN	HELDER	HOWEY	HUGHES	KETSBAIA	LEE	MARCELINO	MARIC	McCLENE	PISTONE	ROBINSON	SERRANT	SHEARER	SOLANO	SPEED	TOTAL	RANK
	8	7	22	12	30	10	3	3	15	2	2	36	29	36		
	0	2	5	9	0	1	10	6	0	9	0	1	1	0		
	674	691	1993	1119	2580	880	400	304	1219	319	88	3238	2508	3240		
	1	0	2	0	0	0	0	0	1	0	0	23	3	9	63*	3rd
	4	0	2	10	7	0	0	0	2	4	0	43	14	24	190	8th
	0	1	1	17	14	1	0	1	2	5	0	37	8	26	207	10th
%	100%	0%	67%	37%	33%	0%	0%	0%	50%	44%	0%	54%	64%	48%	48%	8th
	0	0	2	3	1	0	0	0	0	1	0	7	15	3	45	3rd
	91	86	238	57	412	143	16	11	173	8	2	165	220	373	3589	3rd
	196	158	535	439	1167	244	153	113	440	89	20	1107	1058	1405	12324	4th
%	85%	85%	77%	83%	87%	78%	77%	96%	84%	85%	78%	82%	82%	86%	83%	4th
%	66%	68%	64%	68%	76%	55%	70%	86%	65%	64%	77%	66%	70%	73%	69%	2nd
	5	3	39	16	50	9	9	1	44	5	6	44	312	25	901	3rd
%	40%	33%	23%	44%	40%	44%	33%	0%	36%	20%	0%	30%	37%	28%	34%	1st
	12	6	43	47	60	17	14	8	35	29	1	80	98	85	1079	9th
	92%	100%	81%	83%	85%	88%	86%	75%	80%	59%	100%	68%	80%	80%	79%	4th
	28	17	57	30	98	34	8	8	30	7	2	26	76	124	940	19th
%	46%	29%	53%	43%	53%	44%	38%	25%	43%	14%	50%	42%	63%	52%	50%	16th
	11	19	28	2	16	31	1	1	14	1	0	10	19	20	356	17th
	43	43	138	1	45	101	1	5	64	0	1	40	40	95	1392	17th
	3	0	13	3	23	7	1	3	2	0	1	2	14	17	183	18th
	14	12	11	19	59	13	14	5	6	11	1	121	45	59	547	9th
	1	1	0	7	1	0	1	0	3	2	1	42	11	4	118	=16th
	1	1	0	1	5	2	0	2	1	0	0	2	6	6	48	17th
	0	0	0	0	0	0	0	0	0	0	0	1	0	0	3	=12th

*Including four own goals

…ROSSES …AUGHT	CROSSES PUNCHED	CROSSES NOT CLAIMED	CATCH SUCCESS	THROWS/ SHORT KICKS	% COMPLETION	LONG KICKS	% COMPLETION
22	10	0	100%	92	88%	493	56%
23	9	4	85%	136	96%	508	50%
6	4	0	100%	19	100%	84	29%
5	1	0	100%	39	100%	78	46%

PLAYER OF THE SEASON

PLAYER	INDEX SCORE
NOLBERTO SOLANO	1,093
Gary Speed	958
Kieron Dyer	941
Didier Domi	897*
Alan Shearer	851
Nikos Dabizas	850
Warren Barton	849
Robert Lee	804
Aaron Hughes	794*
Steve Harper	555*

All players played 75 minutes in at least 19 matches except those marked * who played in just 18 games.

A depressing start to the season for the Geordies picked up after the appointment of Bobby Robson and, under him, Newcastle's attacking players have flourished, none more so than Peruvian winger Nolberto Solano.

A signing by Kenny Dalglish in the summer of 1998, Solano struggled to adapt to the pace of the Premiership in his first season on Tyneside. But he progressed in 1999–2000 and became a valuable supply-line for the likes of Alan Shearer and Duncan Ferguson.

The Peruvian made more successful crosses than any other Premiership player and had the joint highest number of assists in the league, as his creativity became a key factor behind Newcastle's spirited revival.

Welsh midfielder Gary Speed also featured highly in the Index with an average of 958 points. He scored nine times and was always a threat with his aerial ability. As well as his goalscoring, Speed was able to provide a good all-round contribution to the side, making 1,778 passes and 124 tackles during the course of the season.

The Tyneside club spent big on Kieron Dyer in the summer but promising displays from him at both club and international level made him look worth every penny.

The youngster's season was hampered by several niggling injuries, but he still managed to score three goals and create another six in his first Premiership campaign.

Captain Alan Shearer's season got off to a bad start, but as Newcastle's fortunes changed so did his, and he ended the campaign as the Premiership's second-highest scorer with 23 goals from 80 attempts. This also took his career goals tally to 300.

Former England stars Warren Barton and Robert Lee also featured in the top 10, while Aaron Hughes proved there is still room for youth at Newcastle among the expensive imported players.

FIVE OF THE BEST

Newcastle started the season appallingly, and after defeat at home to arch-rivals Sunderland, Ruud Gullit left the club. Local lad Bobby Robson steadied the ship and guided the Toon to an 11th-placed finish. He managed to rejuvenate Alan Shearer and steady the once-rocky United defence. Hopes are high that 2000–01 will bring better times to St James's Park.

TOP GOALSCORERS

	GOALS	GOALS/SHOTS
ALAN SHEARER	23	29%
Gary Speed	9	18%
Duncan Ferguson	6	13%
Nikos Dabizas	3	30%
Didier Domi	3	15%

Alan Shearer was struggling under the management of Ruud Gullit, but Bobby Robson helped him recapture his golden days and he smashed home 23 goals, finishing with a superb goals-to-shots ratio of 29%. Goals were harder to find among the rest of the team, although Gary Speed scored nine times from midfield. Duncan Ferguson was once again hampered by injury, managing to score just six times. His fitness will be vital if Newcastle are to succeed in 2000–01.

Three players who had suffered during the Gullit regime ended as United's top passers in 1999–2000. Gary Speed, Robert Lee and Warren Barton all prospered under the genial Robson, Lee finishing with a pass completion of 80%. New boy Kieron Dyer went even better, his incisive distribution adding a new dimension to Newcastle's play. The former Ipswich man looks to have a gigantic future in the game.

TOP PASSERS

	SUCC PASSES	COMPLETION
GARY SPEED	1,359	76%
Robert Lee	1,264	80%
Warren Barton	1,218	71%
Nolberto Solano	939	73%
Kieron Dyer	844	83%

TOP TACKLERS

	WON	SUCCESS
GARY SPEED	64	52%
Robert Lee	52	53%
Nolberto Solano	48	63%
Warren Barton	44	50%
Nikos Dabizas	43	49%

Gary Speed heads another top five after making 64 successful tackles during the season. But Peruvian winger Nolberto Solano was the most consistent tackler, having won 63% of his challenges. He became a vital player to the team during 1999–2000 and his defensive work was something that often went unnoticed. Nikos Dabizas, another player revitalised by the manager, is in fifth place, something that may have helped him clinch a new four-year contract.

Alan Shearer was in all the headlines on the opening weekend of the campaign after receiving the first red card of his career. His season improved dramatically after that but it was a low point for the England captain. He committed more fouls than any other United player, but it was the midfield pairing of Gary Speed and Robert Lee that racked up the most yellow cards. Duncan Ferguson also deserves mention, conceding 51 fouls in just 1,527 minutes of football.

DISCIPLINE

	POINTS	FOULS & CARDS
ALAN SHEARER	91	79F, 2Y, 1R
Robert Lee	73	58F, 5Y, 0R
Gary Speed	73	55F, 6Y, 0R
Nikos Dabizas	64	40F, 6Y, 1R
Duncan Ferguson	54	51F, 1Y 0R

Sheffield Wednesday was the quickest of the season

ACTION	BARTON	DABIZAS	DOMI	DYER	FERGUSON	GALLACHER	GAVILAN	HARPER	HELDER	HUGHES	KETSBAIA	LEE	SHEARER	SPEED	TOTAL	MAN UTD
Time on pitch	90	90	7	83	62	83	7	90	90	90	28	90	90	90	990	964
GOALS																
Goal	–	–	–	–	1	–	–	–	–	–	–	–	2	–	3	–
Shot on target	–	–	–	–	–	–	–	–	–	–	–	–	1	1	2	1
Shot off target	–	–	–	–	2	4	–	–	–	–	1	1	1	2	11	4
Blocked shot	–	–	–	1	1	1	–	–	–	–	–	–	2	–	5	–
Own goal	–	–	–	–	–	–	–	–	–	–	–	–	–	–	–	–
PASSES																
Pass to own player	36	28	2	39	34	28	7	–	34	19	11	51	32	41	362	302
Pass to opposition	23	8	1	6	7	9	3	–	10	20	1	24	15	17	144	140
Cross to own player	2	1	–	2	–	–	–	–	–	–	1	–	1	–	7	8
Cross to opposition player	1	1	–	3	1	3	–	–	–	2	–	1	2	–	14	11
Goal assist	–	–	1	–	–	–	–	–	–	–	–	–	1	1	3	–
Pass completion %	61%	76%	75%	82%	81%	70%	70%	0%	77%	46%	92%	67%	67%	71%	70%	67%
TACKLES & CLEARANCES																
Tackle	5	4	1	2	–	4	–	–	4	3	–	2	–	4	29	18
Clearances, blocks and interceptions	9	12	–	1	–	–	–	–	2	–	–	4	2	2	32	33
DRIBBLES & RUNS																
Dribble ball retained	3	1	2	6	1	2	1	–	2	2	1	2	1	4	28	26
Dribble ball lost	–	–	1	2	–	–	–	–	–	–	1	1	1	–	6	5
Dribble success %	100%	100%	67%	75%	100%	100%	100%	0%	100%	100%	50%	67%	50%	100%	82%	84%
DISCIPLINE																
Fouls	–	–	–	1	2	1	–	–	–	–	3	1	1	1	10	12
Penalty conceded	–	–	–	–	–	–	–	–	–	–	–	–	–	–	–	–
Free kick – offside	–	–	–	–	–	–	–	–	–	–	–	1	2	–	3	4
Yellow cards	–	–	–	–	–	–	–	–	–	–	–	–	1	–	1	3
Red cards	–	–	–	–	–	–	–	–	–	–	–	–	–	–	–	1
GOALKEEPERS																
Distribution to own player	–	–	–	–	–	–	–	29	–	–	–	–	–	–	29	17
Distribution to opposition player	–	–	–	–	–	–	–	13	–	–	–	–	–	–	13	21
Goalkeeper distribution %	0%	0%	0%	0%	0%	0%	0%	69%	0%	0%	0%	0%	0%	0%	69%	45%
Save	–	–	–	–	–	–	–	1	–	–	–	–	–	–	1	2
Ball caught	–	–	–	–	–	–	–	3	–	–	–	–	–	–	3	1
Ball dropped	–	–	–	–	–	–	–	–	–	–	–	–	–	–	–	–
Goal conceded	–	–	–	–	–	–	–	–	–	–	–	–	–	–	–	3

34% Newcastle's crossing accuracy

Recent history did not favour Newcastle with the visit of Manchester United. The Magpies had only won once in their last 13 attempts against the league leaders who came to the north–east unbeaten in their last 11 games. The home side would also be looking for revenge after a 5–1 drubbing at Old Trafford earlier in the season.

12 February 2000
3–0
NEWCASTLE UNITED
VS.
MANCHESTER UNITED

Alex Ferguson's men had cruised to victory in their previous three games against Coventry, Middlesbrough and Sheffield Wednesday without ever really getting into top gear. When they came to Tyneside, though, they took the game straight to Newcastle and Teddy Sheringham and David Beckham both put early chances over the bar.

The home side quickly hit back, and a spectacular strike from Duncan Ferguson quickly had the Champions rocking. Warren Barton played a long ball towards Alan Shearer who flicked the ball on to Ferguson. From 20 yards, the big Scotsman gave Mark Bosnich no chance by crashing a left-foot volley into the top corner.

The striker, whose Newcastle career has been blighted by injury, was then inspired and could have helped himself to more goals. A second chance was hammered inches over and there were other chances that almost saw the Magpies extending their lead as they dominated the opening period. The busy Kevin Gallacher and Gary Speed also came close as Newcastle tore into their opponents.

After the break the visitors fought back and nine minutes into the second half they were sure they had equalised. A lob from former Newcastle striker Andy Cole appeared to be heading in but 'keeper Steve Harper scrambled back to make a desperate save on the line. Cole was convinced he had scored but neither the referee nor his assistant believed the whole of the ball had crossed the line.

Within minutes United skipper Roy Keane was dismissed for a second bookable offence after cutting down Speed. The visitors' tempers frayed with Cole, Paul Scholes and Jaap Stam also cautioned.

As the game entered the final 15 minutes, Shearer sent the Toon Army wild when his low drive beat the despairing dive of Bosnich. The game was then put out of sight when Shearer grabbed his second and Newcastle's third with a simple finish from Didier Domi's cross.

The Magpies dominated United in all areas of the pitch, Shearer, Speed and Barton each scoring more than 1,000 Opta points. Shearer ended up as man of the match after scoring twice and setting up Ferguson for his opener.

Newcastle attempted more than three times as many shots as United, with Cole's controversial effort being the visitors' only attempt on target. The Champions proved to be the best passers in the league over the season but they were put in their place on the day by Newcastle, who attempted more than 500 passes with a completion rate of 70%.

The performance of Newcastle was a far cry from some of their early-season showings and by inflicting United's third defeat of the season, demonstrated the progress that the north-east giants had made under Bobby Robson.

was the highest in the Premiership

SANDERSON

SHEFFIELD WEDNESDAY

ADDRESS

Hillsborough, Sheffield S6 1SW

CONTACT NUMBERS

Telephone: 0114 221 2121
Fax: 0114 221 2122
Ticket Office: 0114 221 2400
Ticket Office Fax: 0114 221 2401
Club Call: 09068 121186
Owls Superstore: 0114 221 2345
e-mail: enquiries@swfc.co.uk
Website: www.swfc.co.uk

KEY PERSONNEL

Chairman: H E Culley
Vice Chairman/President: K T Addy
Directors: G K Hulley, R M Grierson, G A H Thorpe
Company Secretary: Alan D Sykes
Manager: Peter Shreeves

SPONSORS

Sanderson

FANZINES

Boddle
Spitting Feathers
The Blue And White Wizard
Out Of The Blue

COLOURS

Home: Blue and white striped shirts with black shorts and stockings
Away: Yellow shirts with black and white trim, with navy shorts and yellow stockings

NICKNAME

The Owls

HONOURS

League Champions: 1902–03, 1903–04 1928–29, 1929–30
Division Two Champions: 1899–00, 1925–26, 1951–52, 1955–56, 1958–59
FA Cup: 1896, 1907, 1935
League Cup: 1991

RECORD GOALSCORER

Andy Wilson – 199 league goals, 1900–20

BIGGEST WIN

9–1 v Birmingham – Division One, 13 December 1930

BIGGEST DEFEAT

0–10 v Aston Villa – Division One, 5 October 1912

SEASON REVIEW

Sheffield Wednesday's disastrous 1999–2000 campaign saw them relegated from the Premiership. Never out of the bottom three after their first game of the season, they occasionally looked capable of pulling off a remarkable escape, but their eventual demise came as no surprise to anyone.

The pre-season signings of Gilles De Bilde and Gerald Sibon from Dutch rivals PSV Eindhoven and Ajax respectively, for a combined cost of £5 million, and the capture of exciting Celtic youngsters Phil O'Donnell and Simon Donnelly on free transfers promised much, but in truth none of them (with the possible exception of De Bilde) made a significant impact.

The pattern for a depressing campaign was set early on with defeat by Liverpool on the opening day and a meek performance in the 4–0 thrashing at Manchester United. Benito Carbone's reluctance to sit on the bench against Southampton saw the want-away striker storm out of the Dell before the kick-off. Wednesday lost the game, leaving them with just one point from their opening five games.

Wednesday chairman Dave Richards blasted Carbone and former Wednesday player Paolo Di Canio for the team's troubles, claiming that they had created unrest at the club, but it was difficult to see how either of the Italians – particularly Di Canio, who was no longer even at the club - were in any way at fault for a run of results that reached a new low with a disastrous 8–0 thrashing by Newcastle at St James's Park.

After nine games of the season, Wednesday found themselves firmly rooted to the bottom of the table. The team was averaging a pitiful 0.33 goals a game while conceding at the rate of 2.7 per match – a surefire recipe for relegation.

"It looked like it was going to be difficult from the start of the season. It was difficult in the middle and it's going to be difficult in the end."

Danny Wilson

With Carbone departing for Aston Villa and the team registering their first win of the season with a 5–1 victory over Wimbledon at Hillsborough, things momentarily looked up in October, particularly when the team followed up the Wimbledon game with a 4–1 victory over Nottingham Forest in the Worthington Cup.

But results soon resumed a depressingly familiar pattern with defeats at Leeds and Leicester sandwiching a draw with Coventry. Wednesday finished the month four points adrift at the foot of the table.

The situation got worse in November as the club were dumped out of the Worthington Cup by plucky Bolton Wanderers, and, despite putting in a spirited performance, lost 4–3 against West Ham in a game that left them with just six points.

With Wilson's team haemmorhaging goals at an alarming rate, it came as a bitter blow to Owls fans when their best defender Emerson Thome was sold to Chelsea in December. Although the move freed up money for the manager to spend in the transfer market, it did little to boost Richards' popularity.

A silent protest against the chairman before the 1–1 draw with Arsenal proved that his approval ratings had reached an all-time low. Sheffield MPs Joe Ashton, David Blunkett, Bill Michie and Clive Betts did little to help when they called for Wilson to be sacked on the eve of a crucial game against relegation rivals Bradford.

Wednesday won that game, and for a while the criticism directed at Wilson seemed to have a positive effect on the team as they went on a run of five unbeaten games in all competitions,

4 Gilles De Bilde hit the woodwork more times

SEASON REVIEW

lifting themselves off the bottom of the table for the first time in five months with a 1–0 win at Tottenham Hotspur.

There was bad news in the FA Cup, though, as after safely negotiating a path that took them past Bristol City and Wolverhampton Wanderers – albeit on a penalty shoot-out – Wednesday were the victims of a giant-killing by Gillingham, the Kent side beating them 3–1 in a fifth-round tie. This shock result made Wilson's Manager of the Month award a little embarrassing.

The beleaguered manager had earned plenty of sympathy from his fellow-bosses and, in general, the supporters had stayed behind him as well, preferring to vent their frustrations on the board. But after a 1–0 home defeat by Southampton the crowd turned on Wilson for the first time.

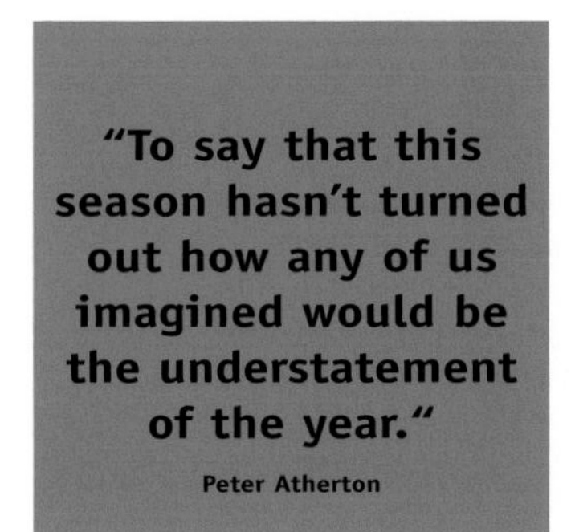

"To say that this season hasn't turned out how any of us imagined would be the understatement of the year."
Peter Atherton

Richards quit soon afterwards and Wilson lasted just four more games, finally getting the sack after a 1–0 defeat at Watford that left Wednesday seven points off the safety zone with just nine games of the season left to play.

Peter Shreeves was appointed in Wilson's place, but could not stop his team from slipping to 1–0 defeats against Middlesbrough and Aston Villa. Publicly he was bullish about the team's chances of survival, but it took back-to-back wins against Wimbledon and Chelsea before anyone seriously believed Wednesday might have a chance of survival.

The win against Chelsea moved Shreeves' team above Bradford in the table and put them five points behind 17th-placed Derby, with five games to play.

Any real hopes of survival disappeared in Wednesday's next few games as they slumped to defeats against Sunderland, Leeds and Coventry. In their penultimate game of the season, hopes of a great escape were briefly reignited when the team surged into a shock 3–1 lead against Arsenal at Highbury, but the Gunners came back well to level the scores at 3–3 and relegate Wednesday in the process.

Even the most die-hard of Wednesday fans had to admit that their side were not good enough for the Premiership. Only rarely did they show the stomach for a relegation fight, finishing the season with the joint second worst goalscoring record and the third most goals conceded.

The team secured entry into the lucky dip for a UEFA Cup place courtesy of an exemplary disciplinary record, but there is no doubt that the club's fans would gladly have suffered a few more yellow and red cards in exchange for the continuation of Premiership football at Hillsborough in the 2000–01 season. As it is, they will have to content themselves with the resumption of hostilities in the Sheffield derby.

As soon as the 1999–2000 season ended, Wednesday attempted to bring Joe Kinnear to Hillsborough – a move which failed, so the club looked to Yorkshire rivals Bradford, appointing Paul Jewell on a three-year contract just weeks after he had saved the Bantams from relegation

Jewell will have little money to spend and even less chance of attracting top quality players to Sheffield.

Certainly the experiment of importing mid-range foreign players at bargain prices has failed and the club will be reluctant to go down that route again. Instead the Owls will have to rely on the exciting young talents of the likes of Steven Haslam, Mark McKeever and Alan Quinn as they bid to make a quick return to the top flight in 2000–01.

from shots outside the area than any other Premiership player

SHEFFIELD WEDNESDAY

DATE	OPPONENT	SCORE	ATT.	ALEXANDERSSON	ATHERTON	BOOTH	BRISCOE	CARBONE	CRESSWELL	DE BILDE	DONNELLY	HASLAM	HINC
7.8.99	Liverpool H	1–2	34,853	90	–	–	s13	s23^{1}	s31	67	77□	–	90
11.8.99	Man Utd A	0–4	54,941	90	90	–	s27	s32	s14	76	–	–	90
14.8.99	Bradford A	1–1*	18,276	90	90	s13	s40	90	–	77□	s13	–	50
21.8.99	Tottenham H	1–2	24,027	90	90□	s33	–	90^{1}	–	90	–	90	–
25.8.99	Derby Co H	0–2	20,943	90	90	–	–	90	s45	45	–	59	–
28.8.99	Southampton A	0–2	14,815	90	90□	–	90	–	90	62	s28	74	–
11.9.99	Everton H	0–2	23,539	63	90	90	90□	s27	–	63	s27□	–	–
19.9.99	Newcastle A	0–8	36,619	90□	–	s28	–	62	–	90	83	s45	–
25.9.99	Sunderland A	0–1	41,132	90	–	90	90	–	s27	63□	83	–	–
2.10.99	Wimbledon H	5–1	18,077	90	90	88	–	–	–	90^{2}	s5	–	–
16.10.99	Leeds Utd A	0–2	39,437	90	90□	90	–	–	–	90	–	–	90
23.10.99	Coventry H	0–0	23,296	90	90□	80	s29	–	–	90	–	–	61
30.10.99	Leicester A	0–3	19,046	90	90	–	–	–	s28	90	–	–	90
6.11.99	Watford H	2–2	21,658	45	75	90	–	–	s45□	90^{2}□	–	–	90
21.11.99	West Ham A	3–4	23,015	90	90	90^{1}□	–	–	s10	90	–	–	90
5.12.99	Liverpool A	1–4	42,517	90^{1}	90	90	81	–	s9	81	–	–	–
18.12.99	Aston Villa A	1–2	23,885	90	90	90	–	–	–	90^{1}	–	s34	–
26.12.99	Middlesbro H	1–0	28,531	90	90^{1}	90□	–	–	s3□	90	–	s25	90
29.12.99	Chelsea A	0–3	32,938	90□	90	71□	62	–	s19	90	–	s28	90
3.1.00	Arsenal H	1–1	26,155	90	90	–	45	–	s12	90	–	–	90
15.1.00	Bradford H	2–0*	24,682	70^{1}	90	–	–	–	–	90	s20	90	90
22.1.00	Tottenham A	1–0	35,897	90^{1}	90	–	–	–	–	88	s2	90	90
2.2.00	Man Utd H	0–1	39,640	90	90	–	–	–	s7	70	s20	90	90
5.2.00	Derby Co A	3–3	30,100	57	90	–	–	–	–	82^{1}	s8^{1}	90	90
12.2.00	Southampton H	0–1	23,470	90	90	s22	–	–	–	60	s30	68	90
26.2.00	Newcastle H	0–2	29,212	90	90	–	–	–	s34	56	–	90	90
4.3.00	Everton A	1–1	32,020	90	90	–	s45	–	–	90	–	90	90
11.3.00	West Ham H	3–1	21,147	90^{1}	90	–	–	–	s45^{1}	90	–	90	90^{1}
18.3.00	Watford A	0–1	15,840	90	90	–	–	–	90	90	–	90	90
25.3.00	Middlesbro A	0–1	32,748	90	90	–	–	–	s8	82	–	80	90
5.4.00	Aston Villa H	0–1	18,136	90	90	80	61	–	s10	90	–	–	90
12.04.00	Wimbledon A	2–0	8,248	90	90	90	s6	–	–	84^{1}	–	s1	90
15.4.00	Chelsea H	1–0	21,743	90	90	90	s25	–	–	73	–	90	90
22.4.00	Sunderland H	0–2	28,072	86	90	80	–	–	s10□	90	–	90	90
30.4.00	Leeds Utd H	0–3	23,416	77	90	90	s13	–	–	77	–	–	90
6.5.00	Coventry A	1–4	19,921	61	90□	90	–	–	–	90^{1}	–	s37	90
9.5.00	Arsenal A	3–3	37,271	–	90	90	s7	–	–	s35^{1}	–	55	90
14.5.00	Leicester H	4–0	21,656	69^{1}	90	90^{1}	–	–	s3	90^{1}	–	s13	90

□ Yellow card, ■ Red card, s Substitute, 90^{2} Goals scored

*including one own goal

1999–2000 PREMIERSHIP APPEARANCES

HORNE	JONK	McKEEVER	NEWSOME	NOLAN	O'DONNELL	PRESSMAN	QUINN	RUDI	SCOTT	SIBON	SONNER	SRNICEK	THOME	WALKER	TOTAL
–	–	–	90	–	–	–	–	90	–	59	90	90	90	90	990
–	–	–	90	–	–	–	–	90	–	58	63□	90	90	90	990
–	77	–	90□	–	–	90	–	90	–	–	–	–	90□	90	990
–	81	–	–	90	–	90	–	57	s9	–	–	–	90	90	990
–	90	–	s76	90□	–	90	–	90	–	s31	–	–	90	14	990
–	–	–	90	–	–	90	–	90	90□	s16□	–	–	90	–	990
–	–	–	–	90	s45□	90	–	45	–	–	90	–	90	90	990
–	–	–	90	90	–	90	–	45	–	s7	90	–	90	90	990
–	s27	–	–	90	–	–	–	63	–	s7	90	90	90	90	990
–	90[1]	–	–	90	–	–	–	90[1]	–	s2[1]	85	90	90	90	990
–	90	–	–	–	–	–	–	90□	–	–	90□	90	90	90	990
–	90	–	–	–	–	–	–	90	–	s10	90	90	90	90	990
–	90	–	–	–	–	–	–	62	–	90	90	90	90□	90	990
–	90	–	–	s15	–	90	–	90	–	–	90	–	90	90	990
–	90[1]□	–	–	84□	–	90	–	80[1]	–	–	68■	–	s6	90	968
–	90	–	–	90	–	90	s1	89□	–	s9	–	–	90□	90	990
–	82	–	–	90	–	–	56□	–	–	s8	90□	90	90	90	990
–	90□	87	–	90	–	–	–	–	–	–	65□	90	–	90	990
–	90	–	–	90	–	–	–	–	–	s28	62	90	–	90	990
–	90	s45	–	90□	–	–	–	–	–	78[1]	90	90	–	90	990
–	90	–	–	90	–	–	90	–	–	90	–	90	–	90	990
–	90	–	–	90	–	–	73	–	s17	90	–	90	–	90	990
–	90	–	–	90□	–	–	–	s30	60	83	–	90	–	90	990
–	76	–	–	90	–	–	90	–	s33	90[1]	s14	90	–	90	990
–	–	–	–	90	–	–	90	48	–	90	s42	90	–	90	990
–	–	–	–	90	–	–	90	s6	–	90	84	90	–	90	990
–	–	–	–	45	–	–	90[1]	–	–	90□	90	90	–	90	990
–	80□	–	–	90	–	–	90	–	–	45	s10	90	–	90	990
–	90	–	–	90	–	s59	89□	–	–	s1	–	31	–	90	990
–	90	–	–	90	–	90□	90	90	–	–	s10	–	–	90	990
–	90	–	–	90	–	90	90□	–	–	–	s29	–	–	90	990
90	89	–	–	90	–	90	84	–	–	s6[1]	–	–	–	90	990
65	90[1]	–	–	–	–	90	90	–	–	s17	–	–	–	90	990
86	90	–	–	–	–	90	90	–	–	s4	s4	–	–	90	990
63	90	–	–	90	–	90	90	–	–	s27	s13	–	–	90	990
67	90□	–	–	90	–	90	90	–	–	s29	s23	–	–	53	990
83	90	–	–	90	–	90	90[1]	–	–	s35[1]	55	–	–	90	990
87	90	–	–	90	–	90	90[1]	–	–	–	s21	–	–	77	990

THE MANAGER

PETER SHREEVES

Sheffield Wednesday collected just one point from the opening 27 on offer and never climbed out of the bottom three after this disasterous start , and consequently Danny Wilson was sacked in March after a 1–0 defeat to bottom club Watford.

Peter Shreeves was installed as caretaker manager, but despite seeing the team win two of his first four games in charge it was not enough to preserve Wednesday's Premiership status.

The new caretaker-manager had already spent two-and-a-half years at the club working with David Pleat and Ron Atkinson, and has been involved at seven senior clubs in coaching and management roles, most notably at Tottenham.

Shreeves had two spells in charge of Spurs, managing them for two years between 1984–86 and again between July 1991–May 1992, and has made it clear that he would relish the Wednesday position full-time.

It remains to be seen whether or not he is given the opportunity, but whoever takes charge will have the fans' expectations to live up to, and that means a return to the Premiership as quick as possible.

LEAGUE POSITION

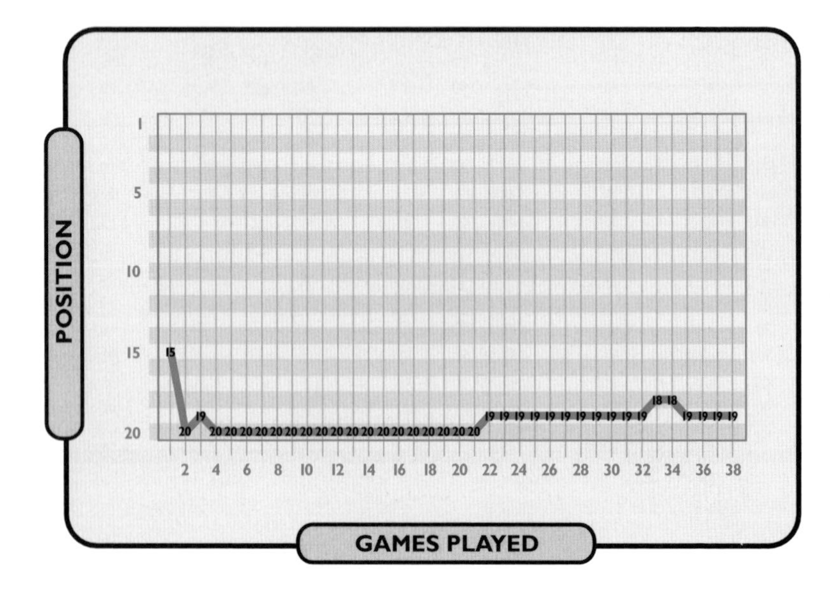

THE GOALS

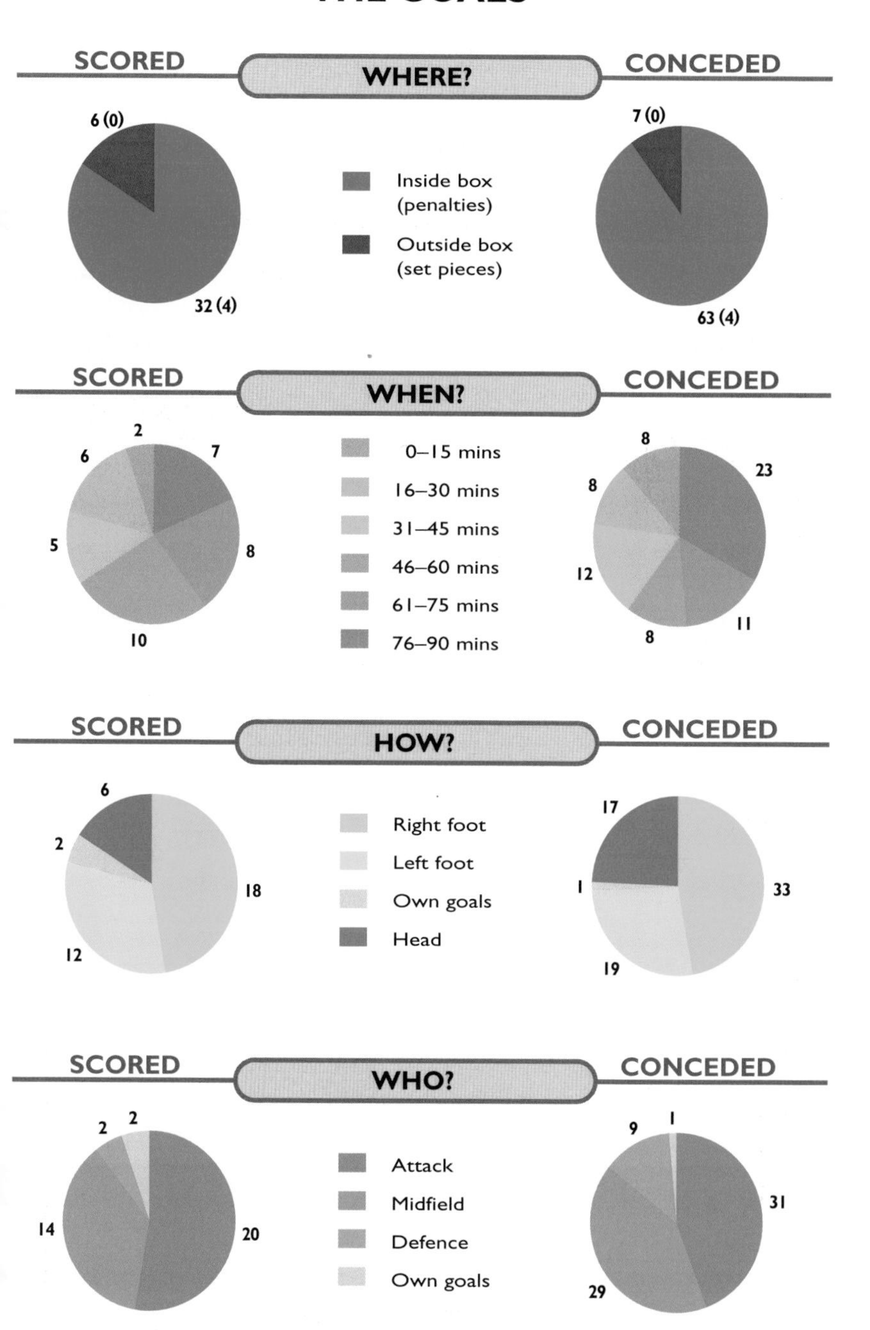

of Premiership goals in the first 15 minutes of matches

SHEFFIELD WEDNESDAY

	ALEXANDERSSON	ATHERTON	BOOTH	BRISCOE	CARBONE	CRESSWELL	DE BILDE	DONNELLY	HASLAM	HIN
APPEARANCES										
Start	37	35	19	7	4	2	37	3	16	29
Sub	0	0	4	9	3	18	1	9	7	0
Minutes on pitch	3138	3135	1755	724	414	540	3041	396	1509	2541
GOAL ATTEMPTS										
Goals	5	1	2	0	2	1	10	1	0	1
Shots on target	25	2	15	1	6	3	42	1	0	7
Shots off target	24	12	20	3	9	4	30	2	3	2
Shooting accuracy	51%	14%	43%	25%	40%	43%	58%	33%	0%	78%
PASSING										
Goal assists	4	0	3	1	0	0	3	1	0	2
Long passes	179	339	49	67	23	8	99	7	136	581
Short passes	932	780	776	195	190	182	1058	187	495	775
PASS COMPLETION										
Own half %	72%	79%	81%	76%	84%	82%	82%	80%	81%	76%
Opposition half %	64%	57%	61%	56%	62%	53%	63%	75%	64%	59%
CROSSING										
Total crosses	89	23	14	31	11	6	63	7	5	150
Cross completion %	27%	43%	43%	35%	18%	0%	21%	29%	20%	33%
DRIBBLING										
Dribbles & runs	122	25	40	17	36	21	181	17	12	40
Dribble completion %	78%	96%	60%	88%	47%	43%	60%	76%	92%	100%
DEFENDING										
Tackles made	126	124	33	29	12	12	55	15	78	48
Tackles won %	51%	45%	30%	38%	58%	67%	53%	53%	51%	54%
Blocks	20	76	11	11	0	2	2	1	11	53
Clearances	54	306	25	62	0	7	3	3	51	172
Interceptions	35	32	8	7	3	0	9	1	17	16
DISCIPLINE										
Fouls	30	35	70	8	17	24	117	5	25	14
Offside	8	0	14	1	11	6	56	0	0	0
Yellow cards	2	5	3	1	0	3	3	2	0	0
Red cards	0	0	0	0	0	0	0	0	0	0

GOALKEEPER NAME	START/ (SUB)	TIME ON PITCH	GOALS CONCEDED	MINS/GOALS CONCEDED	SAVES MADE	SAVES/ SHOTS
PRESSMAN	18(1)	1679	42	40	76	64%
SRNICEK	20	1741	28	62	84	75%

PLAYERS' STATISTICS

HORNE	JONK	MCKEEVER	NEWSOME	NOLAN	O'DONNELL	QUINN	RUDI	SCOTT	SIBON	SONNER	THOME	WALKER	TOTAL	RANK
7	29	1	5	28	0	18	18	2	12	18	16	37		
0	1	1	1	1	1	1	2	3	16	9	1	0		
541	2582	132	526	2484	45	1563	1425	209	1190	1638	1446	3204		
0	3	0	0	0	0	3	2	0	5	0	0	0	38*	=18th
0	16	0	0	1	0	17	4	0	16	4	2	1	163	15th
1	10	1	1	3	0	18	4	0	18	15	6	0	186	19th
0%	62%	0%	0%	25%	0%	49%	50%	0%	47%	21%	25%	100%	47%	10th
0	8	0	0	1	0	2	0	0	1	1	0	0	27	=16th
80	433	10	35	355	3	78	112	6	63	175	132	273	3243	9th
196	1084	29	116	714	15	446	582	65	565	673	309	643	11007	7th
87%	87%	82%	78%	79%	83%	74%	87%	87%	80%	83%	83%	79%	80%	7th
66%	69%	73%	60%	60%	73%	66%	66%	71%	66%	66%	52%	51%	63%	12th
2	131	9	6	45	0	23	26	6	8	23	1	5	684	18th
100%	31%	22%	17%	33%	0%	13%	15%	17%	38%	17%	0%	40%	29%	13th
4	53	7	1	67	2	103	52	8	35	30	17	34	924	16th
100%	85%	57%	0%	87%	0%	65%	83%	75%	66%	77%	100%	94%	73%	17th
33	77	1	15	68	1	56	50	9	56	46	56	65	1067	6th
67%	53%	100%	47%	38%	100%	34%	60%	44%	52%	67%	73%	60%	52%	11th
4	6	1	7	39	0	4	8	1	4	15	32	94	402	9th
5	28	1	76	125	1	9	36	11	15	41	259	507	1813	2nd
2	23	0	7	19	0	12	17	3	5	6	23	49	296	2nd
9	23	1	6	15	4	58	25	3	31	30	32	16	481	17th
0	2	0	0	0	0	13	3	0	1	3	0	0	118	=16th
0	4	0	1	4	1	3	2	1	2	5	3	0	46	18th
0	0	0	0	0	0	0	0	0	0	1	0	0	1	=17th

*Including two own goals

OSSES UGHT	CROSSES PUNCHED	CROSSES NOT CLAIMED	CATCH SUCCESS	THROWS/ SHORT KICKS	% COMPLETION	LONG KICKS	% COMPLETION
31	16	3	91%	91	87%	601	40%
25	22	4	86%	100	81%	617	42%

PLAYER OF THE SEASON

PLAYER	INDEX SCORE
ANDY HINCHCLIFFE	892
Des Walker	875
Wim Jonk	865
Niclas Alexandersson	849
Pavel Srnicek	836
Gilles De Bilde	807
Peter Atherton	797
Ian Nolan	695
Andy Booth	692*
Kevin Pressman	536*

All players played 75 minutes in at least 19 matches except those marked * who played in just 18 games

It was not a happy time for Wednesday during 1999–2000, but former England international Andy Hinchcliffe will have been pleased with his form after his return from injury.

The former Everton player topped Wednesday's Opta Season Index with an average of 892 points. His crossing ability with his left foot has long been admired and, in a dismal season for the Owls, he still managed to attempt 150 crosses and corners, with a better-than-average completion rate.

Hinchcliffe was also on the scoresheet once for the South Yorkshire side in a rare victory over West Ham and created two more, thanks to his high-quality centres.

Former Forest favourite Des Walker also featured highly for Wednesday. The veteran defender won 60% of his tackles and made 507 clearances – the third-highest total in the Premiership – as he tried in vain to maintain the Owls' status in the top flight. He also had one of the best disciplinary records in the league, committing just 16 fouls all season was never cautioned.

Overseas signings Wim Jonk, Niclas Alexandersson, Pavel Srnicek and Gilles De Bilde all managed to make an impact in the struggling Wednesday side.

Belgian international De Bilde, a summer signing from PSV Eindhoven, finished as the club's top scorer with 10 goals – although many of these came late in the campaign with the club already in deep trouble. Fellow striker Andy Booth also made it into the top 10 after a season in which he was the subject of much transfer speculation.

Skipper Peter Atherton recorded an average of 797 points with 124 tackles and 306 clearances in a disappointing season for Wednesday, but it was not enough to save them from the drop into the Nationwide League. Both 'keepers at Hillsborough fiercely contested the number one spot but it was Pavel Srnicek who came out on top with an average Index score of 836 points.

48% Sheffield Wednesday were the most accurat

FIVE OF THE BEST

Having taken just one point from a possible 27 at the start of the Premiership campaign, it was pretty clear from the outset that 1999–2000 was to be a season of struggle for Sheffield Wednesday. Despite changing managers and enjoying one or two good results, the Owls never clawed their way out of the bottom three and face Division One football in 2000–01.

TOP GOALSCORERS

	GOALS	GOALS/SHOTS
GILLES DE BILDE	10	14%
Gerald Sibon	5	15%
Niclas Alexandersson	5	10%
Wim Jonk	3	12%
Alan Quinn	3	9%

Belgian striker Gilles De Bilde failed to live up to his pre-season billing for Sheffield Wednesday, despite notching 10 Premiership goals in 1999–2000. His strikes came only in sporadic bursts and were not enough to keep the Owls afloat in the top flight. In the absence of the injured Andy Booth, De Bilde's support in attack came mainly from Gerald Sibon, but he managed only five goals, despite having the best goals-to-shots ratio among the strikers.

Despite being criticised in some quarters for a seemingly relaxed attitude in 1999–2000, Holland international Wim Jonk's passing always had a touch of class about it. The former Inter star completed 75% of his passes as he tried in vain to fashion some chances. Jonk's greatest passing allies were full-back Andy Hinchcliffe, who made 876 successful passes, and skipper Peter Atherton, who completed 70% of his distribution around the park. Gilles De Bilde and Niclas Alexandersson completed the top five Owls.

TOP PASSERS

	SUCC PASSES	COMPLETION
WIM JONK	1,145	75%
Andy Hinchcliffe	876	65%
Peter Atherton	779	70%
Gilles De Bilde	772	67%
Niclas Alexandersson	734	66%

TOP TACKLERS

	WON	SUCCESS
N ALEXANDERSSON	64	51%
Peter Atherton	56	45%
Emerson Thome	41	73%
Wim Jonk	41	53%
Steven Haslam	40	51%

Workaholic midfielder Niclas Alexandersson had no shortage of admirers come the end of 1999–2000, despite Wednesday's relegation from the Premiership. The right-sided Swede made 64 successful challenges for the Hillsborough side. In terms of success ratio, though, top man for the Owls was Brazilian stopper Emerson Thome, who won 73% of his challenges before moving on to Chelsea in December. Thome's departure allowed Peter Atherton to move into the heart of the defence and in all he won 56 tackles.

The Premiership's cleanest team in 1998–99, Sheffield Wednesday made few enemies in 1999–2000, ending up with the third best Opta disciplinary record in the Premiership. The only blip on the Owls' record was the dismissal of midfielder Danny Sonner against West Ham in November. Sonner earned the fifth-highest total of Opta disciplinary points in the chart headed by striker Gilles De Bilde. He committed 61 fouls and was booked three times to beat Andy Booth into second place.

DISCIPLINE

	POINTS	FOULS & CARDS
GILLES DE BILDE	70	61F, 3Y, 0R
Andy Booth	65	56F, 3Y, 0R
Alan Quinn	54	45F, 3Y, 0R
Peter Atherton	50	35F, 5Y, 0R
Danny Sonner	48	27F, 5Y, 1R

marksmen from outside the penalty area

ACTION	ALEXANDERSSON	ATHERTON	BOOTH	DE BILDE	DONNELLY	JONK	NOLAN	RUDI	SIBON	SONNER	SRNICEK	THOME	WALKER	TOTAL	WIMBLEDON
Time on pitch	90	90	88	90	5	90	90	90	2	85	90	90	90	990	990
GOALS															
Goal	–	–	–	2	–	1	–	1	1	–	–	–	–	5	1
Shot on target	1	–	–	2	–	–	–	–	–	–	–	–	–	3	3
Shot off target	–	1	2	3	–	–	–	1	–	1	–	–	–	8	5
Blocked shot	–	–	–	–	–	–	–	–	–	–	–	–	–	–	2
Own goal	–	–	–	–	–	–	–	–	–	–	–	–	–	–	–
PASSES															
Pass to own player	19	24	28	28	5	36	40	46	4	29	–	23	29	311	205
Pass to opposition	14	8	9	10	1	14	12	15	–	9	–	7	–	99	127
Cross to own player	2	–	–	1	–	4	–	–	–	–	–	–	–	7	3
Cross to opposition player	2	–	1	2	–	5	1	3	–	2	–	–	1	17	15
Goal assist	–	–	–	1	1	2	–	–	–	1	–	–	–	5	1
Pass completion %	57%	75%	74%	71%	86%	69%	75%	72%	100%	73%	0%	77%	97%	74%	60%
TACKLES & CLEARANCES															
Tackle	5	6	3	3	–	4	–	5	–	2	–	1	1	30	33
Clearances, blocks and interceptions	8	7	4	3	–	3	11	11	–	5	–	20	31	103	64
DRIBBLES & RUNS															
Dribble ball retained	2	–	–	7	–	3	3	3	–	1	–	1	1	21	9
Dribble ball lost	2	–	1	4	–	–	–	–	–	–	–	–	1	8	8
Dribble success %	50%	0%	0%	64%	0%	100%	100%	100%	0%	100%	0%	100%	50%	72%	53%
DISCIPLINE															
Fouls	–	2	1	1	–	–	–	3	–	1	–	2	–	10	11
Penalty conceded	–	–	–	–	–	–	–	–	–	–	–	–	–	–	–
Free kick – offside	–	–	–	2	–	–	–	–	–	–	–	–	–	2	4
Yellow cards	–	–	–	–	–	–	–	–	–	–	–	–	–	–	–
Red cards	–	–	–	–	–	–	–	–	–	–	–	–	–	–	–
GOALKEEPERS															
Distribution to own player	–	–	–	–	–	–	–	–	–	–	17	–	–	17	18
Distribution to opposition player	–	–	–	–	–	–	–	–	–	–	18	–	–	18	23
Goalkeeper distribution %	0%	0%	0%	0%	0%	0%	0%	0%	0%	0%	49%	0%	0%	49%	44%
Save	–	–	–	–	–	–	–	–	–	–	3	–	–	3	3
Ball caught	–	–	–	–	–	–	–	–	–	–	4	–	–	4	4
Ball dropped	–	–	–	–	–	–	–	–	–	–	–	–	–	–	–
Goal conceded	–	–	–	–	–	–	–	–	–	–	1	–	–	1	5

14 Kevin Pressman made the highest numbe

Wednesday could never have imagined a worse start to the season. Just one point from their opening nine matches had left them rooted to the bottom of the table from the start. Five consecutive league games without a goal – including an 8–0 drubbing at Newcastle – had already left them fighting for survival early on in the season.

However, the visit of Wimbledon gave Owls fans signs of hope and for the first time Wednesday played to their full potential, breaking their goal drought in emphatic style.

At times during the season, Danny Wilson's men were unfortunate not to get the result that their performance deserved but on this occasion they were well worth the three points. From the kick-off to the final whistle Wednesday showed their total commitment, fighting and battling for every ball.

For the first time, summer signing Gilles De Bilde looked every bit the £3 million player that Wednesday bought, with an emphatic performance that boosted Sheffield spirits and crushed the Dons.

Wednesday had gone eight hours 37 minutes without scoring but it took them just nine minutes to get off the mark against Egil Olsen's men. De Bilde picked up on Petter Rudi's pass and surged down the left-hand side. His low cross was missed by everyone except Wim Jonk, who coolly slipped the ball past Neil Sullivan.

Within six minutes the visitors were back on level terms, though, when a Marcus Gayle shot took a fortunate deflection off John Hartson and Pavel Srnicek was beaten in the Wednesday goal. The Owls' momentum remained unaffected, and with De Bilde in control it was only a matter of time before Wednesday threatened again.

On 23 minutes, De Bilde controlled a Jonk pass and, with Dean Blackwell losing his footing, the Belgian found the space to surge into the area and fire past Sullivan for his first league goal as he restored the advantage.

It was not until the 71st minute that they added to their tally, though. A long ball over the top from Jonk found Rudi in space and he shot across Sullivan into the bottom right-hand corner.

More was to come when De Bilde tricked his way past three Dons defenders to claim his second. Then with just two minutes remaining another summer signing, Gerald Sibon, made it five.

In one afternoon Wednesday had more than doubled their goals tally for the season and put in a performance that belied their lowly league position.

Belgian De Bilde was a class act and was, not surprisingly, man of the match with 2,623 Opta points. Not only did he score his first two league goals in English football, but he also created the opener for Jonk and attempted a further five shots on goal.

Wimbledon did not really stand a chance against a rampant Wednesday, who blew away the memories of their dismal start to the season with an emphatic showing. They managed 16 attempts at goal and made a total of 410 passes during the afternoon.

Sadly for Owls followers, this performance proved to be a one-off as they remained in the bottom three for the remainder of the campaign.

of saves in a single match (v West Ham away)

SOUTHAMPTON

ADDRESS

The Dell, Milton Road,
Southampton SO15 2XH

CONTACT NUMBERS

Telephone: 023 8022 0505
Fax: 023 8033 0360
Ticket Office: 023 8022 8575
Ticket Office Fax: 023 8023 0882
Merchandise Shop: 023 8033 6450
Club Call: 09068 121178
e-mail: sfc@saintsfc.co.uk
Website: www.saintsfc.co.uk

KEY PERSONNEL

President: E T Bates
Chairman: R J G Lowe
Vice Chairman: B H D Hunt
Directors: A E Cowen, I L Gordon
M R Richards, K St J Wiseman
R M Withers
Company Secretary: Brian Truscott
Manager: Glenn Hoddle

SPONSORS

Friends Provident

FANZINES

The Ugly Inside

COLOURS

Home: Red and white shirts, black shorts and stockings
Away: Dark navy shirts and shorts with yellow stockings

NICKNAME

The Saints

HONOURS

FA Cup 1976
Division Three (South) Champions: 1921–22
Division Three Champions: 1959–60

RECORD GOALSCORER

Mike Channon – 185 league goals, 1966–77, 1979–82

BIGGEST WIN

9–3 v Wolverhampton Wanderers – Division Two, 18 September 1965

BIGGEST DEFEAT

0–8 v Tottenham Hotspur – Division Two, March 28, 1936
0–8 v Everton – Division One, 20 November 1971

SEASON REVIEW

After the scrapes they have had in recent years, Southampton enjoyed a relatively comfortable end to the 1999–2000 season. That is not to say that the club experienced a completely trouble-free season. For a long time they looked to be heading for their usual nail-biting brush with relegation.

The only significant pre-season signing was defender Dean Richards, a player who had never quite fulfilled his potential at Wolves. After a 1–0 win at Coventry on the opening day, though, manager Dave Jones moved into the transfer market. Egil Ostenstad, who had scored the winner at Coventry, moved to Blackburn, with Kevin Davies returning to the south coast in exchange. Trond-Egil Soltvedt also joined from Coventry.

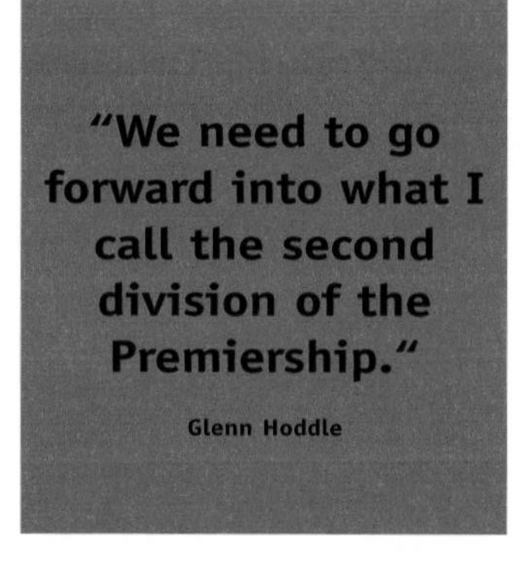

"We need to go forward into what I call the second division of the Premiership."
Glenn Hoddle

The opening month proved to be an up-and-down affair. While the team lost heavily to Leeds and Everton, they managed good wins against Coventry, Newcastle and Sheffield Wednesday to end the month a creditable 10th in the Premiership.

September proved less happy, as the club was left reeling from the bombshell that manager Dave Jones would have to defend himself against serious allegations dating back to his time as a social worker. The club pledged to stick by him and, to their credit, the team produced several hard-working performances on the pitch. They fell to unfortunate defeats against Middlesbrough and Arsenal and, thanks to some comical goalkeeping by Massimo Taibi, secured a thrilling 3–3 draw against Manchester United at Old Trafford.

Less satisfaction could be drawn from the next game, another 3–3 draw, this time with Derby, for whom Mikkel Beck equalised with the latest goal of the 1999–2000 season to deny Saints all three points.

At least progress in the Worthington Cup was ensured, a 0–0 draw at Maine Road providing no clue of the drama to come in the second leg of the second-round clash with Manchester City. Leading 3–1 with just 15 minutes to go, Southampton were pegged back to 3–3 and reduced to 10 men when Mark Hughes was red-carded. Despite this they came through, a Dean Richard goal winning the tie in extra-time.

When Liverpool were beaten 2–1 in the following round, there were hopes of a run. Unfortunately, the team surrendered meekly to Aston Villa, going down to a 4–0 defeat in the fourth round.

Results in the league suggested that the club were in for a familia season of struggle. Afte the three wins in August, Saints managed just one more victory in their next 14 games. Many fans questioned the judgment of Dave Jones, their chief gripe being the continued absence of Matt Le Tissier from the side.

With the team struggling to score, it wa certainly hard to understand why Le Tissie was on the bench. The mercurial midfielde expressed his dissatisfaction with the situation by giving Jones an ultimatum to play him before Christmas or lose his services to another club.

Jones eventually gave way to Le Tisser albeit one day late, naming the talented Channel Islander in his starting line-up fo the Boxing Day clash with Chelsea Southampton lost the game, but no before Le Tissier had set up Kevin Davies' goal and come close to securing a poin with a free-kick which he slammed agains the bar.

At the turn of the year, Southampton found themselves in 16th place, just one point outside the relegation zone. The

10 Saints had more shots cleared off the line

SEASON REVIEW

pressure was mounting on Jones – and not merely on the football front. The club that had stood by him since the beginning decided that the pressure of his impending court case was having an adverse effect on his day-to-day running of the team. In January it was announced that he had been given "a year's leave of absence" to concentrate solely on his court case. His replacement was Glenn Hoddle.

Hoddle enjoyed considerable success in what remained of the season, making it doubtful whether Jones will ever return.

When Hoddle arrived at Southampton, the team were floundering in 16th place, just two points clear of the relegation zone. By the time the season ended they were up to 15th place, 11 points ahead of relegated Wimbledon.

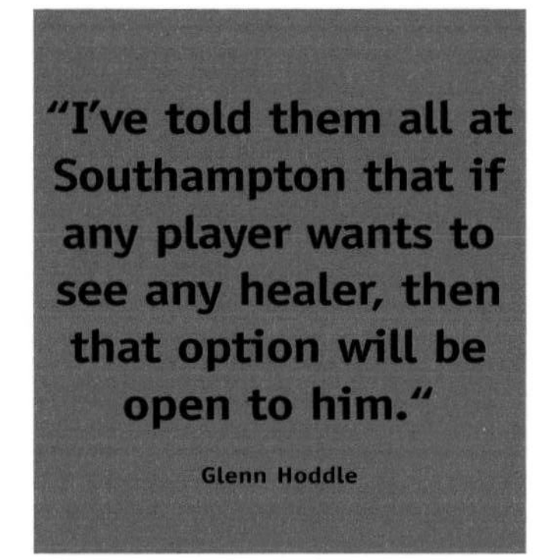

"I've told them all at Southampton that if any player wants to see any healer, then that option will be open to him."
Glenn Hoddle

The recovery began almost immediately. Free of FA Cup commitments after a fourth-round exit at Aston Villa, the team turned their full attention to the league.

February has traditionally been a bad month for Southampton, but back-to-back wins against West Ham and Sheffield Wednesday in Hoddle's first two games took them five points clear of the relegation zone with a game in hand.

With building work started on a new stadium and results picking up in the league, there was a new mood of optimism around The Dell. But bad results against Arsenal and Tottenham, (who thrashed Saints 7–2), reminded everyone at the club that there was still plenty of hard work to be done in what remained of the season.

A 2–1 win at Bradford courtesy of a Dean Windass own goal in an early April six-pointer left the team 11 points ahead of the Bantams and virtually guaranteed survival. Mathematically speaking, the club secured their Premiership status on 22 April when, despite losing 3–1 to Manchester United, Sheffield Wednesday's 2–0 loss to Sunderland made them safe.

Understandably, the media chose to focus on United's title win but, for all the praise showered on Alex Ferguson's men, Saints fans could still afford a smile at the news that their last four games of the season would be trouble-free.

Hoddle will clearly have to bring in some new faces if he is to implement his preferred style of play successfully at The Dell. But in Marian Pahars, Jo Tessem and Player of the Season Dean Richards, to name just three, he clearly has some star performers at his disposal.

In his final programme notes of the season, he declared that his aim for the 2000–01 campaign was to take the club into what he called "the second division of the Premiership" and compete with the likes of Leicester City, Middlesbrough and West Ham. To do that he must improve on certain key areas: Saints finished as the third-least accurate short passers and second-worst tacklers.

If Hoddle can address these problems, there is no reason why Southampton should not achieve a higher finish in season 2000–01.

Having said that everyone at the club must guard against any complacency. Southampton are by no means guaranteed survival. The 2000–01 Premiership is likely to be every bit as strong as it was in 1999-2000 and Saints will have to maintain their improved form if they are to avoid trouble.

While their fans have grown used to avoiding the drop – in some seasons more comfortably than others – if they are not able to make progress, then like Wimbledon and Sheffield Wednesday found in 1999–2000, one day Saints may not be so fortunate.

than any other top-flight side

SOUTHAMPTON

DATE	OPPONENT	SCORE	ATT.	ALMEIDA	BEATTIE	BENALI	BERESFORD	BOA MORTE	BRADLEY	BRIDGE	COLLETER	DAVIES	DODD	DR
7.8.99	Coventry A	1–0	19,915	–	–	90	s1	–	–	–	–	–	90□	–
11.8.99	Leeds Utd H	0–3	15,206	–	–	90□	–	–	–	–	–	–	90	–
15.8.99	Newcastle H	4–2	15,030	–	–	90□	–	–	–	s1	–	–	–	–
21.8.99	Everton A	1–4	31,755	–	–	90	–	–	s13□	s33	–	90□	–	–
28.8.99	Sheff Wed H	2–0	14,815	–	–	90	–	s11	–	–	–	–	90	–
11.9.99	Middlesbro A	2–3	32,165	–	s18	90	–	67■	–	s18	–	–	90	–
18.9.99	Arsenal H	0–1	15,242	s19	90□	90	–	–	–	82	–	–	90□	–
25.9.99	Man Utd A	3–3	55,249	–	s1	90	–	–	–	–	–	–	90	–
4.10.99	Derby Co H	3–3	14,208	–	s12	90	–	s1	–	–	–	–	90	–
16.10.99	Leicester A	1–2	19,556	–	–	88	–	s2	–	–	–	s9■	90	–
23.10.99	Liverpool H	1–1	15,241	–	s4	90	–	–	–	–	–	–	90□	–
30.10.99	Wimbledon A	1–1	15,754	–	s20	90	–	–	–	–	–	–	90	–
6.11.99	Aston Villa A	1–0	26,474	–	s4	–	–	s15	–	–	90□	–	90	–
20.11.99	Tottenham H	0–1	15,248	–	78	–	–	s5	–	–	90□	–	–	–
28.11.99	Leeds Utd A	0–1	39,288	–	s14	–	–	–	–	–	87■	–	s3	–
4.12.99	Coventry H	0–0	15,168	–	90	90	–	–	–	–	90	s26	90	–
18.12.99	Sunderland A	0–2	40,860	–	s41□	90□	–	–	–	–	–	–	90	–
26.12.99	Chelsea H	1–2	15,232	–	53	90	–	s37	–	–	–	$s37^{1}$	90	–
28.12.99	Watford A	2–3	18,459	–	s14	90	–	90^{1}	–	–	–	90^{1}□	90	–
3.1.00	Bradford H	1–0	15,027	–	–	–	–	90	–	90	–	90^{1}	90	–
16.1.00	Newcastle A	0–5	35,623	–	90	s45	s18	23	–	–	45	90	–	72
22.1.00	Everton H	2–0	15,232	–	s2	90	s9	81□	–	–	–	88	–	–
5.2.00	West Ham H	2–1*	15,257	–	–	90	–	66	–	68	s22	90	90	–
12.2.00	Sheff Wed A	1–0	23,470	–	–	90	–	–	–	–	69	90	90	–
26.2.00	Arsenal A	1–3	38,044	–	18	90	–	s45	–	–	45	90□	90□	–
4.3.00	Middlesbro H	1–1	15,223	–	–	90	–	s14	–	90	–	90	90	–
8.3.00	West Ham A	0–2	23,484	–	–	90	–	–	–	90	–	90□	90	–
11.3.00	Tottenham A	2–7	36,024	–	–	90□	–	–	–	90	–	–	–	–
18.3.00	Aston Villa H	2–0	15,218	–	–	–	–	–	–	90	–	90^{2}□	90	–
25.3.00	Chelsea A	1–1	34,956	–	–	–	–	–	–	90	–	90	90	–
1.4.00	Sunderland H	1–2	15,245	–	–	–	–	–	–	90	–	90	90	–
8.4.00	Bradford A	2–1*	17,439	–	–	90	–	–	–	90	–	90	90	–
15.4.00	Watford H	2–0	15,252	–	56	–	–	–	–	90	–	90^{1}	–	–
22.4.00	Man Utd H	1–3	15,245	–	–	45	–	–	–	90	–	71□	90	–
24.4.00	Derby Co A	0–2	29,403	–	70	–	–	–	–	90	–	s45	90	–
29.4.00	Leicester H	1–2	15,178	–	–	–	–	–	–	90	–	90□	90	–
7.5.00	Liverpool A	0–0	44,015	–	–	–	–	–	–	90	–	90	90□	–
14.5.00	Wimbledon H	2–0	15,249	–	–	–	–	–	–	90^{1}	–	90	90	–

□ Yellow card, ■ Red card, s Substitute, 90^{2} Goals scored

*including one own goal

For more information visit our website:

1999–2000 PREMIERSHIP APPEARANCES

EL-KHALEJ	HILEY	HUGHES	JONES	KACHLOUL	LE TISSIER	LUNDEKVAM	MARSDEN	MONK	MOSS	OAKLEY	OSTENSTAD	PAHARS	RICHARDS	RIPLEY	RODRIGUES	SOLTVEDT	TESSEM	TOTAL
–	–	90	90	89	85	90	90	–	–	–	90[1]□	90	90	s5	–	–	–	990
–	–	90□	90	66	90□	90	45	–	–	s45	90□	90	90	s24	–	–	–	990
–	90	90[1]□	90	89[2]	45	90	–	–	–	45	90	90[1]	90	s45	–	s45	–	990
–	90	90□	90	57	–	90	–	–	–	–	–	77[1]	90	90	–	90	–	990
–	–	90	90	79[1]	–	90	–	–	–	90[1]	–	90	90	90	–	90	–	990
–	–	90	90	72[1]	–	90	–	–	–	s63	–	72[1]	90	27	–	90	–	967
–	–	90	90	90	s8	71	–	–	–	90□	–	–	90	–	–	90	–	990
–	–	90	90	90	s45[2]	68	s22	–	–	90	–	89[1]	90	90	–	45	–	990
–	90	90□	90	89	78	–	–	–	–	90[1]	–	90[1]	90	90[1]	–	–	–	990
–	–	67	90	90□	s45	90□	90	–	–	–	–	90[1]	90	45	–	90	–	976
–	–	90	90	90	53	90	–	–	–	90□	–	90	90	s37	–	86[1]	–	990
–	–	90	90	90	–	90	–	–	–	90	–	70[1]	90	90	–	90	–	990
–	–	90	90	90□	–	90	–	–	–	90	–	90	90[1]□	75	–	86	–	990
–	–	85□	90	85	s5	89■	–	–	–	90	–	90□	90□	90	–	s12	90	989
–	–	76□	90	90□	–	90	–	–	–	90	–	87□	90	90	–	90	90	987
–	–	–	90	90	–	–	–	–	–	90	–	64	90	90	–	–	90	990
–	–	–	33	90□	s24□	90□	–	–	s57	90	–	90	90	66	–	90	49	990
–	–	–	90	53	90□	90	–	–	–	75□	–	90	90	–	–	90	s15	990
–	–	76□	90	s8	41	90	–	–	–	–	–	–	90□	s41	–	90	90	990
–	–	–	90	–	–	90	90	–	–	–	–	90	90	90	–	–	90	990
–	–	90□	90	–	–	–	–	s67	–	–	–	–	90	90	–	90	90	990
–	–	–	90	–	–	90□	90□	90	–	72[1]	–	90□	90	–	–	s18	90[1]	990
–	–	s24	90	–	–	–	90	–	–	90	–	89[1]	90	–	–	s1	90	990
–	–	–	90	90	–	s21	90□	–	–	90	–	90	90	–	–	–	90[1]	990
–	–	s72	90	90□	–	s45	90□	–	–	90	–	–	90[1]	–	–	–	45	990
–	–	–	90	76	–	90	90	–	–	90	–	90[1]	–	–	–	–	90	990
–	–	–	90	66	–	90	90	–	–	90	–	90	–	–	–	s24	90	990
90[1]	–	90	90	68□	s22	–	90	–	–	90	–	90	90	–	–	–	90[1]	990
90□	–	–	90	90□	–	–	90□	–	–	90	–	89	90	–	–	s1	90	990
90	–	–	90	90	–	–	90	–	–	90	–	90	90	–	–	–	90[1]	990
90	–	–	45	s9	s45[1]	90	90	–	s45	45	–	90	90□	–	–	–	81	990
90□	–	–	–	–	75	–	90	–	90	–	–	s15[1]	90	78□	–	s12	90	990
90	–	–	–	–	90	90	90	–	90	s6	–	s34[1]	90	90	–	–	84	990
82	–	–	–	s45	s8	90	90	–	90	s19	–	90[1]□	90	–	–	–	90	990
90	–	–	–	82□	s20	–	45□	–	90	90	–	–	90	90	–	90	s8	990
90□	–	–	–	90[1]□	–	–	72□	–	90	s18	–	90	89■	58	s32	–	90	989
90	–	–	–	90	–	–	–	–	90	90	–	90	90	–	–	90	90	990
90	–	–	–	85	–	90	s13	–	90	90	–	90[1]	–	–	s5	77	90	990

THE MANAGER

GLENN HODDLE

After a 2–0 home win against Everton, the then-Southampton manager Dave Jones was temporarily relieved of his managerial duties to allow him to concentrate on his personal legal battle.

Glenn Hoddle took over and guided the Saints to safety, losing just seven of his 16 matches in charge to preserve Southampton's Premiership status.

As a player, Hoddle was arguably the most gifted footballer of his generation, scoring eight goals in 53 England appearances, as well as winning two FA Cups and the UEFA Cup at Tottenham, for whom he made nearly 500 appearances.

Hoddle started his managerial career at Swindon Town, and guided them into the Premiership in 1992–93 after victory in the play-off final at Wembley.

He then joined Chelsea as player-manager in June 1993, and took them to an FA Cup final.

He stayed at Stamford Bridge for three seasons before taking over from Terry Venables in 1996 as England manager.

Hoddle guided England to the 1998 World Cup Finals, but after losing the England job in 1999 he gleefully accepted the offer from Southampton to return to club management, and he will be looking towards the top half of the Premiership for the Saints in 2000–01.

LEAGUE POSITION

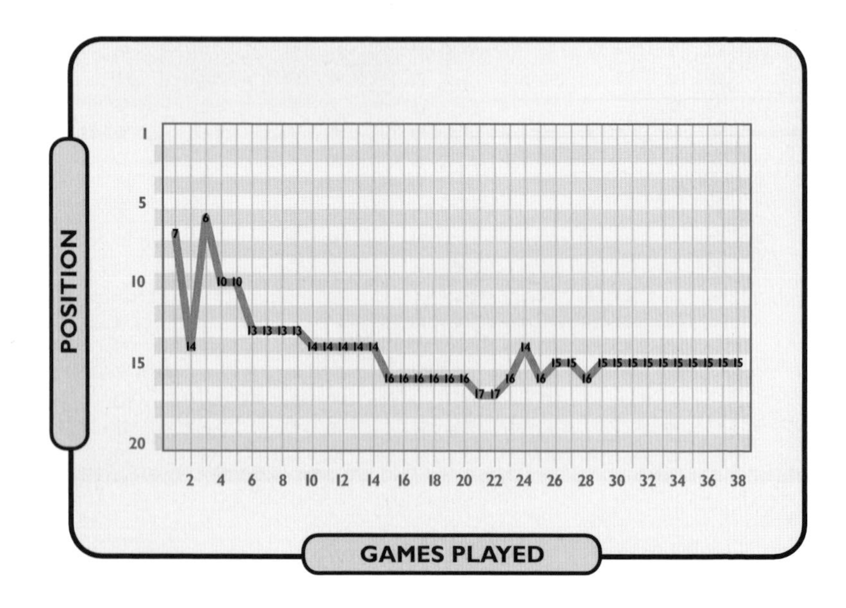

73% of Saints' goals came

THE GOALS

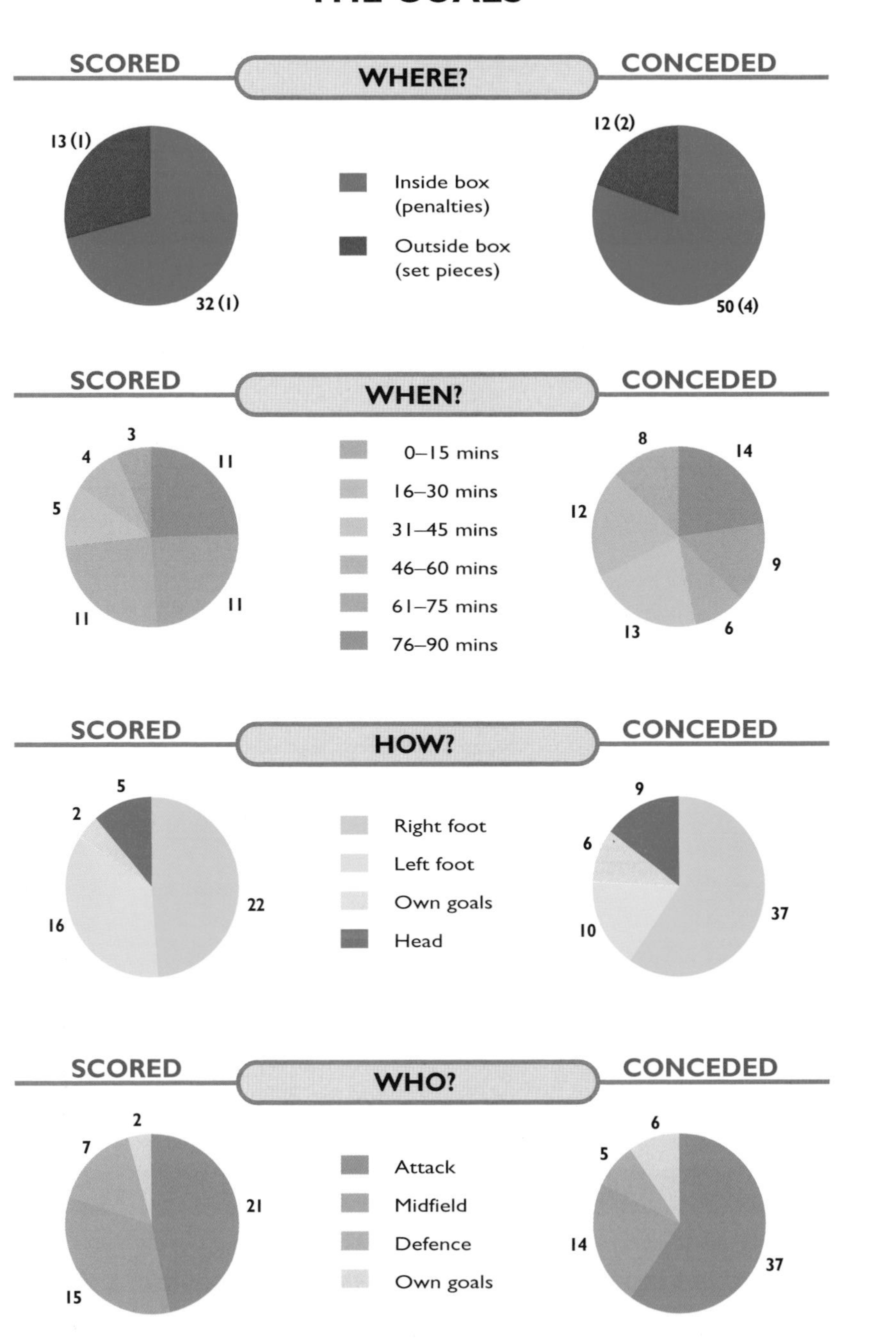

after the break – the highest ratio in the Premiership

SOUTHAMPTON

	ALMEIDA	BEATTIE	BENALI	BERESFORD	BOA MORTE	BRADLEY	BRIDGE	COLLETER	DAVIES	DODD	DRYDEN	EL-
APPEARANCES												
Start	0	8	25	0	6	0	16	7	19	30	1	11
Sub	1	10	1	3	8	1	3	1	4	1	0	0
Minutes on pitch	19	675	2248	28	547	13	1462	538	1806	2703	72	982
GOAL ATTEMPTS												
Goals	0	0	0	0	1	0	1	0	6	0	0	1
Shots on target	0	7	2	0	3	0	3	2	22	2	1	7
Shots off target	0	7	1	0	3	0	0	0	13	2	1	2
Shooting accuracy	0%	50%	67%	0%	50%	0%	100%	100%	63%	50%	50%	78%
PASSING												
Goal assists	0	0	0	0	1	0	2	0	3	2	0	0
Long passes	1	20	335	5	25	0	167	62	91	412	10	76
Short passes	1	210	659	11	96	3	379	140	612	813	14	208
PASS COMPLETION												
Own half %	100%	74%	76%	100%	58%	100%	71%	64%	66%	78%	22%	59%
Opposition half %	0%	53%	51%	67%	56%	0%	61%	57%	53%	63%	47%	47%
CROSSING												
Total crosses	0	11	28	0	30	0	37	6	22	42	3	3
Cross completion %	0%	27%	32%	0%	27%	0%	38%	17%	32%	17%	67%	67%
DRIBBLING												
Dribbles & runs	0	22	30	0	47	0	48	14	55	50	2	22
Dribble completion %	0%	32%	87%	0%	57%	0%	90%	86%	75%	90%	100%	95%
DEFENDING												
Tackles made	1	13	53	1	30	0	36	26	47	81	1	37
Tackles won %	100%	31%	53%	0%	47%	0%	39%	42%	38%	48%	0%	41%
Blocks	0	2	43	0	5	0	30	10	6	58	5	29
Clearances	3	1	187	3	3	0	45	30	26	161	4	75
Interceptions	0	0	13	0	4	0	10	7	3	17	1	3
DISCIPLINE												
Fouls	0	31	26	0	15	1	6	5	57	29	2	32
Offside	0	14	0	0	3	0	0	0	11	0	0	3
Yellow cards	0	2	4	0	1	1	0	2	7	5	0	3
Red cards	0	0	0	0	1	0	0	1	1	0	0	0

GOALKEEPER NAME	START/ (SUB)	TIME ON PITCH	GOALS CONCEDED	MINS/GOALS CONCEDED	SAVES MADE	SAVES/ SHOTS
JONES	31	2688	52	52	121	70%
MOSS	7(2)	732	10	73	30	75%

PLAYERS' STATISTICS

HILEY	HUGHES	KACHLOUL	LETISSIER	LUNDEKVAM	MARSDEN	MONK	OAKLEY	OSTENSTAD	PAHARS	RICHARDS	RIPLEY	RODRIGUES	SOLTVEDT	TESSEM	TOTAL	RANK
3	18	29	9	25	19	1	26	3	31	35	18	0	17	23		
0	2	3	9	2	2	1	5	0	2	0	5	2	7	2		
270	1660	2468	869	2274	1637	157	2368	270	2756	3149	1581	37	1577	1992		
0	1	5	3	0	0	0	3	1	13	2	1	0	1	4	45*	16th
0	4	21	16	1	2	0	12	1	36	13	7	1	9	15	187	9th
0	14	30	6	1	6	0	19	2	19	10	8	0	6	15	165	20th
0%	22%	41%	73%	50%	25%	0%	39%	33%	65%	57%	47%	100%	60%	50%	53%	1st
0	3	1	5	2	1	0	3	0	2	0	6	0	3	0	34	=12th
44	122	147	91	227	211	14	246	0	108	282	97	2	109	159	3063	15th
77	603	865	262	448	573	36	760	86	759	597	421	10	376	544	9563	16th
84%	85%	77%	83%	79%	86%	75%	79%	88%	80%	72%	68%	100%	77%	73%	76%	18th
56%	73%	56%	55%	49%	69%	59%	65%	72%	65%	52%	55%	67%	63%	57%	59%	18th
8	7	74	75	11	20	4	50	2	65	18	165	2	9	43	736	13th
25%	43%	26%	35%	36%	25%	25%	24%	0%	15%	44%	25%	0%	22%	40%	28%	15th
5	41	137	27	28	27	2	66	12	164	40	92	3	36	71	1041	11th
80%	85%	64%	56%	93%	85%	100%	83%	58%	68%	98%	77%	100%	81%	75%	75%	13th
2	47	92	13	52	85	2	77	6	30	89	43	1	42	66	973	16th
0%	49%	60%	31%	56%	52%	50%	56%	33%	63%	54%	37%	100%	55%	41%	49%	19th
3	2	9	5	58	17	2	15	2	3	91	6	0	11	8	420	8th
25	11	32	5	329	39	14	38	2	4	410	14	1	39	37	1558	13th
2	5	16	2	15	3	0	8	0	6	20	4	0	9	3	151	19th
1	55	61	23	35	37	2	31	8	82	47	33	1	20	45	563	5th
0	7	9	6	0	0	0	3	2	46	1	2	1	2	13	123	13th
0	8	9	3	3	6	0	3	2	4	4	1	0	0	0	68	8th
0	0	0	0	1	0	0	0	0	0	1	0	0	0	0	5	=3rd

*Including two own goals

OSSES UGHT	CROSSES PUNCHED	CROSSES NOT CLAIMED	CATCH SUCCESS	THROWS/ SHORT KICKS	% COMPLETION	LONG KICKS	% COMPLETION
56	28	10	85%	126	90%	1001	39%
4	6	0	100%	32	75%	248	41%

PLAYER OF THE SEASON

PLAYER	INDEX SCORE
DEAN RICHARDS	**811**
Hassan Kachloul	774
Jason Dodd	771
Marian Pahars	749
Claus Lundekvam	724
Matthew Oakley	706
Paul Jones	698
Kevin Davies	656*
Jo Tessem	652
Francis Benali	645

All players played 75 minutes in at least 19 matches except those marked * who played in just 18 games.

Southampton can look back on their capture of Dean Richards from Wolves as one of the bargains of last summer, after the former Bradford man came to The Dell free of charge under the Bosman ruling.

The centre-back picked up the supporters' Player of the Year award and it is easy to see why as he also tops the Opta Season Index for the Saints.

"Deano" formed a good relationship with Claus Lundekvam in the heart of the Saints' defence and made 410 clearances at the back.

The former England under-21 international also made 89 tackles, 879 passes and even scored twice as he helped the Saints end the season clear of the drop zone.

After an impressive campaign in 1998–99, Moroccan Hassan Kachloul once again figured high up in the end-of-season Index for Southampton.

He scored five times from midfield and made 1,012 passes, making him one of the Saints' most consistent performers in recent seasons.

Reliable skipper Jason Dodd is another who repeated his high performance rating from the previous season for the Saints. The defender made 81 tackles and 161 clearances from right-back as he once again led by example.

Top scorer Marian Pahars also rated highly after bagging 13 Premiership goals. The Latvian enhanced his growing reputation in English football by combining pace and clinical finishing ability to steer the Saints clear of their usual flirtation with the drop zone. He may not like the comparison with Michael Owen which is often made, but should his form continue then players will soon start being compared to Marian Pahars.

Richards's defensive partner Lundekvam also featured among the top five players on the Index, and the returning striker Kevin Davies made it into the top 10 after scoring six times since ending his frustrating time at Blackburn.

6 Southampton scored more owr

FIVE OF THE BEST

Comfortable survival in the Premiership, achieved by a team containing several excellent young players, meant that 1999–2000 was a season to be proud of for Southampton. Despite the upheaval of changing managers midway through the campaign, the Saints never looked in danger of dropping into the bottom three – an achievement in itself.

TOP GOALSCORERS

	GOALS	GOALS/SHOTS
MARIAN PAHARS	13	24%
Kevin Davies	6	17%
Hassan Kachloul	5	10%
Jo Tessem	4	13%
Matt Le Tissier	3	14%

Once described by ex-Southampton boss Dave Jones as "the Baltic Michael Owen", striker Marian Pahars enjoyed a fantastic first full season at The Dell, even outscoring the Liverpool man he was compared to. Pahars's total of 13 Premiership goals puts him way out in front as Southampton's top marksman in 1999–2000, while he also had the best goals-to-shots ratio at the club – 24%. Kevin Davies netted six goals, one more than Moroccan midfielder Hassan Kachloul.

Ever-reliable skipper Jason Dodd was the player involved in the most successful passing moves for Southampton in 1999–2000. But the Bath-born defender only completed 69% of his passes, whereas Dodd had found a team-mate with 74% of his distribution in 1998–99. In terms of accuracy, grafter Chris Marsden was top man, completing 76% of his passes, while he was also the third most prolific user of the ball at The Dell, despite missing the first half of the season because of injury.

TOP PASSERS

	SUCC PASSES	COMPLETION
JASON DODD	840	69%
Matthew Oakley	699	69%
Francis Benali	615	62%
Hassan Kachloul	611	60%
Chris Marsden	594	76%

TOP TACKLERS

	WON	SUCCESS
HASSAN KACHLOUL	55	60%
Dean Richards	48	54%
Chris Marsden	44	52%
Matthew Oakley	43	56%
Jason Dodd	39	48%

Like his compatriots Youssef Chippo and Moustapha Hadji at Coventry, Moroccan midfielder Hassan Kachloul was never far away from the action in 1999–2000, his first full season of football in England. The Saints man, adept enough to play anywhere in midfield or attack, won 55 tackles, more than any other player for the south coast side. Centre-back Dean Richards was his closest contender, having won 48 challenges, with a success rate of 54%.

Despite earning his reputation for being a skilful and attacking midfielder, Southampton star Hassan Kachloul certainly looked after himself in 1999–2000. In fact, the Opta disciplinary points mark him out as the Saints' dirtiest player during the campaign after he committed 52 fouls and received nine bookings in the Premiership. Striker Kevin Davies and defender Dean Richards were both shown one red card in 1999–2000, explaining their presence in the top five.

DISCIPLINE

	POINTS	FOULS & CARDS
HASSAN KACHLOUL	79	52F, 9Y, 0R
Kevin Davies	73	46F, 7Y, 1R
Mark Hughes	72	48F, 8Y, 0R
Dean Richards	64	46F, 4Y, 1R
Chris Marsden	55	37F, 6Y, 0R

goals than any other team

ACTION	BENALI	BRIDGE	HILEY	HUGHES	JONES	KACHLOUL	LE TISSIER	LUNDEKVAM	OAKLEY	OSTENSTAD	PAHARS	RICHARDS	RIPLEY	SOLTVEDT	TOTAL	NEWCASTLE
Time On Pitch	90	1	90	90	90	89	45	90	45	90	90	90	45	45	990	990
GOALS																
Goal	–	–	–	1	–	2	–	–	–	–	1	–	–	–	4	2
Shot on Target	–	–	–	–	–	–	–	–	–	–	–	1	–	1	2	2
Shot off Target	–	–	–	2	–	–	–	–	–	1	–	–	–	2	5	6
Blocked Shot	–	–	–	1	–	–	–	–	1	–	–	–	–	1	3	6
Own Goal	–	–	–	–	–	–	–	–	–	–	–	–	–	–	–	–
PASSES																
Pass to Own Player	33	1	34	34	–	21	23	29	11	22	19	17	17	7	268	314
Pass to Opposition	16	–	11	14	–	24	9	11	4	8	11	5	8	3	124	124
Pass to Scoring Zone – Own Player	1	–	2	–	–	1	2	–	–	–	–	1	4	–	11	12
Pass to Scoring Zone – Opposition Player	1	–	4	–	–	1	3	–	–	1	2	1	5	–	18	13
Goal Assist	–	–	–	–	–	–	–	–	–	–	–	–	2	2	4	1
Pass Completion %	67%	100%	71%	71%	0%	47%	68%	73%	73%	71%	59%	75%	64%	75%	67%	70%
TACKLES & CLEARANCES																
Tackle	2	–	–	6	–	6	–	2	–	3	4	8	–	2	33	35
Clearances, Blocks and Interceptions	3	–	2	–	–	2	–	13	2	2	–	18	–	–	42	52
DRIBBLES & RUNS																
Dribble ball retained	–	–	2	–	–	–	–	–	–	3	2	2	5	3	17	17
Dribble ball lost	–	–	–	1	–	5	1	–	–	4	2	–	1	–	14	6
Dribble Success %	0%	0%	100%	0%	0%	0%	0%	0%	0%	43%	50%	100%	83%	100%	55%	74%
DISCIPLINE																
Free kick – foul	–	–	–	3	–	2	–	1	–	1	–	–	–	1	8	13
Penalty Conceded	–	–	–	–	–	–	–	1	–	–	–	–	–	–	1	–
Free kick – offside	–	–	–	–	–	–	–	–	–	2	2	–	–	–	4	3
Yellow Cards	1	–	–	1	–	–	–	–	–	–	–	–	–	–	2	–
Red Cards	–	–	–	–	–	–	–	–	–	–	–	–	–	–	–	–
GOALKEEPERS																
Distribution to Own Player	–	–	–	–	19	–	–	–	–	–	–	–	–	–	19	11
Distribution to Opposition Player	–	–	–	–	22	–	–	–	–	–	–	–	–	–	22	18
Goalkeeper Distribution %	0%	0%	0%	0%	46%	0%	0%	0%	0%	0%	0%	0%	0%	0%	46%	38%
Save	–	–	–	–	2	–	–	–	–	–	–	–	–	–	2	2
Ball Caught	–	–	–	–	4	–	–	–	–	–	–	–	–	–	4	3
Ball Dropped	–	–	–	–	–	–	–	–	–	–	–	–	–	–	–	–
Goal Conceded	–	–	–	–	2	–	–	–	–	–	–	–	–	–	2	4

53% Southampton's shooting accuracy

It had been a mixed start to the season for the Saints. Next up were Newcastle, whose manager Ruud Gullit was coming under increasing pressure to get results after defeats in their two opening games. In front of the TV cameras, Southampton came from behind to destroy the Magpies with a devastating second-half performance.

15 August 1999
4–2
SOUTHAMPTON
vs.
NEWCASTLE UNITED

Former Saints star Alan Shearer gave the visitors the lead from the penalty spot in the 22nd minute, after Claus Lundekvam had brought down the lively Kieron Dyer. Following the goal, Newcastle began to apply more pressure on the Southampton defence, with Dyer going close to increasing the lead.

Manager David Jones replaced the ineffective Matt Le Tissier and Matthew Oakley with Stuart Ripley and Trond-Egil Soltvedt at the start of the second half and this had an immediate effect. Ripley was a constant threat to Newcastle down the right-hand side and he was instrumental in bringing the Saints back into contention.

In the 59th minute he collected a flick from Egil Ostenstad, wrong-footed Didier Domi and drove the ball low across the face of the goal to Hassan Kachloul, who converted the simplest of chances.

Southampton could now see that Newcastle were struggling, and with confidence growing after the equaliser they stepped up a gear. Ripley was again involved in the second goal with a raking pass beyond the Newcastle back line. 'Keeper John Karelse hesitated in the visitors' goal and that was enough incentive for Latvian Marian Pahars to collect the ball and smash it into the bottom corner to put the Saints ahead.

Newcastle had not recovered before Southampton went further in front. This time it was set up by the other half-time substitute, Soltvedt. Scott Hiley's high ball was won in the air by the £300,000 capture from Coventry and it dropped perfectly for Kachloul to drive home his second.

The Magpies were now well and truly on the rack, but the best was still yet to come for Southampton. More good work from Soltvedt saw the ball fall to Mark Hughes on the edge of the area. Not for the first time in his career, Hughes attempted a spectacular volley, smashing the ball beyond Karelse and into the top corner for the second goal of his Southampton career.

Dave Jones's men had scored four times in a dramatic 20-minute spell and could have had more, as they increased the agony for suffering Newcastle. Gary Speed pulled a goal back for the visitors, but it was a mere consolation after they had been swept aside by the rampant Saints.

Summer signing Dean Richards was Opta's man of the match for the south coast side with 1,613 points, after thwarting Newcastle's attacking efforts with eight tackles and an impressive 18 clearances, blocks, and interceptions. His contribution was vital in the first half when the Magpies had the upper hand but were unable to capitalise on their possession and only had the penalty goal to show for their efforts.

Southampton's four goals came from 11 efforts and, despite making fewer passes than Newcastle, their electrifying 20-minute spell in the second half was more than enough to crush the visitors.

was the best in the Premiership

REG VARDY

SUNDERLAND

ADDRESS

The Stadium of Light, Stadium Park,
Sunderland SR5 1SU

CONTACT NUMBERS

Telephone: 0191 551 5000
Fax: 0191 551 5123
Ticket Office: 0191 551 5151
Ticket Office Fax: 0191 551 5150
Club Call: 0891 121140
Club Shop: 0191 551 5050
Club Shop Fax: 0191 551 5123
e-mail: communications@
sunderland-afc.com
Website: www.sunderland-afc.com

KEY PERSONNEL

Chairman: R S Murray
Chief Executive: J M Fickling
Directors: R S Murray, J M Fickling
G M McDonnell, D C Stonehouse
Club Secretary: M Blackbourne
Manager: Peter Reid

SPONSORS

Reg Vardy

FANZINES

Love Supreme
Sex and Chocolate
The Wearside Roar

COLOURS

Home: Red shirts with white stripes,
black shorts, black stockings
with red turnover
Away: Navy blue shirts with red and
white hoops, navy blue shorts and
stockings with red and white trim

NICKNAMES

The Black Cats
The Mackems

HONOURS

League Champions: 1891–92, 1892–93
1894–95, 1901–02, 1912–13, 1935–36
Division One Champions: 1995–96,
1998–99
Division Two Champions: 1975–76
Division Three Champions: 1987–88
FA Cup: 1937, 1973

RECORD GOALSCORER

Charlie Buchan –
209 league goals, 1911–25

BIGGEST WIN

9–1 v Newcastle United – Division One,
5 December 1908

BIGGEST DEFEAT

0–8 v West Ham United – Division One,
19 October 1968
0–8 v Watford – Division One,
25 September 1982

SEASON REVIEW

If Sunderland were in any doubt about the size of the task facing them in 1999–2000, they were given an early wake-up call on a sunny afternoon at Stamford Bridge. Runaway winners of Division One in the 1998–99 season, Peter Reid's men were soundly thrashed 4–0 by Chelsea in their first game back in the Premiership.

In retrospect, the result was the best thing that could have happened to Sunderland. As Reid himself was to admit later in the season: "I honestly believe the Chelsea result was a brilliant one for us...it woke us up."

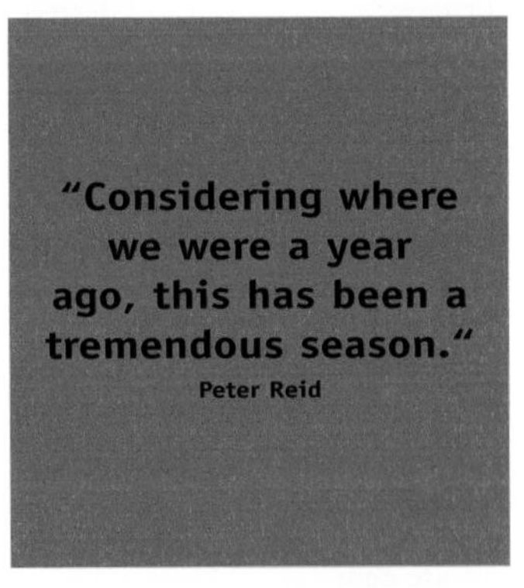

"Considering where we were a year ago, this has been a tremendous season."
Peter Reid

By the end of August, Sunderland had chalked up a win over Watford, held Arsenal to a 0–0 draw and, in a game that provided their fervent supporters with the highlight of the season, had beaten bitter rivals Newcastle at St James's Park. That game left the Magpies in turmoil at the foot of the table and proved to be the last game of Ruud Gullit's stormy reign in the St James's Park hotseat. Their style took on a more physical look, a deliberate tactic that proved costly in disciplinary terms but rattled plenty of opposition sides and brought the club success on the field.

Even with their desire to win, though, it is doubtful whether Sunderland would have managed to do so well had it not been for Kevin Phillips. At the start of the season the former Watford man was a 40-to-one shot to finish the season as the Premiership's top scorer; six games and five goals later he was second favourite and by the end of the year it was almost impossible to bet against him.

Phillips's strike partner Niall Quinn received less credit but was, in many ways, just as important to the Sunderland cause. The Irishman scored 14 goals and set up a further eight – most of them for Phillips – to ensure that Peter Reid rarely regretted his decision to sell Michael Bridges to Leeds before the season had started.

Surprisingly, established German international Thomas Helmer found it much harder to adjust to the Premiership, departing on loan for Hertha Berlin soon after the start of the season, but Reid's other close-season signings, Steve Bould and Stefan Schwarz, were finding life on Wearside much more to their liking.

September was the month Sunderland's season really took off. Three successive wins in the Premiership, which included a 5–0 romp at Derby (where Phillips scored a hat-trick), and an 8–2 aggregate victory over Walsall in the Worthington Cup left players and fans alike confident that survival would be no problem.

A 4–0 victory at Bradford in early October propelled them to third place in the Premiership and, although few people seriously spoke about the Championship, Europe was the word on everyone's lips. Even a third-round Worthington Cup exit at the hands of Wimbledon did little to dampen spirits, the team picking itself up to record a fifth successive league win with a controversial 2–1 victory over Aston Villa courtesy of two more goals from Phillips at the Stadium of Light.

Chris Makin was dismissed against Middlesbrough two games later and, with the club's tough-tackling style leading to a host of bookings, suspensions began to bite. By the time Liverpool arrived on 20 November Sunderland were missing five players through suspension, a fact that undoubtedly contributed to the end of their 10-game unbeaten run as Gerard Houllier's resurgent Reds ran out comfortable 2–0 winners.

SEASON REVIEW

Normal service was resumed with a 3–2 victory at Watford the following week and, when Kevin Phillips and Niall Quinn grabbed two goals each in the 4–1 win over Chelsea, the progress the club had made since their opening-day defeat by the same club was there for everyone to see.

Peter Reid continued to strengthen his squad with the signing of Kevin Kilbane from West Bromwich Albion, a move that spelled the end of Allan Johnston's Sunderland career, and progress to the fourth round of the FA Cup was ensured with a 1–0 win against Portsmouth at the Stadium of Light.

Two more goals for Phillips in his next game – his 18th and 19th of the season – against Southampton nicely maintained Sunderland's superb start and left them just two points behind first-placed Manchester United.

No one could have predicted that they would fail to win any of their next 12 games. Ironically Everton, the team that started Sunderland's slide with a 5–0 win on Boxing Day, were the ones who would provide Peter Reid's men with their first win of the Millennium three months later.

The slump was hard to take. From looking certainties for a European place, Sunderland dropped to a final position of seventh and were beaten 1–0 in the FA Cup by Tranmere in a game that caused plenty of controversy, thanks to the failure of referee Rob Harris to notice that Tranmere had brought on an illegal substitute in the dying seconds.

Harris was suspended for one month but there was to be no second chance for Sunderland, who resumed their Premiership campaign with a 4–1 defeat at Arsenal.

Rumours of training-ground bust-ups between players contributed to the feeling that all was not well but, on the pitch at least, the team stuck together and played their way through the bad patch, eventually getting back to winning ways with a 2–1 victory against Everton.

With a new nickname – The Black Cats – Sunderland improved rapidly, picking up a further 13 points out of a possible 24. Phillips reached the 30-goal mark with the only goal in a 1–0 win against West Ham to win the Golden Boot, and although the club missed out on Europe, seventh place still represented a satisfactory finish to the season.

"The Stadium of Light is a great place to be. The atmosphere and the spirit about the place is superb. It's something that we can all be proud of and now we can build on it."

Peter Reid

While a similar finish in the 2000–01 campaign would represent healthy consolidation, the target for Sunderland must now be Europe and a good run in at least one of the two domestic cup competitions.

Reid will undoubtedly move into the transfer market to strengthen his squad further, but he has also acted quickly to tie the club's most prized asset, Phillips, to a long-term deal that should keep the prolific frontman on Wearside for another six years.

This may not deter bigger clubs from making advances, but potential suitors will have to fork out a hefty transfer fee if the Black Cats are to part with their prolific goalscorer.

Expectations among the supporters are higher than ever and little wonder. The 1999–2000 season saw Sunderland take Newcastle's title as the north-east's premier club and Phillips beat Alan Shearer to the Golden Boot.

To move on a step, the team will have to tighten up defensively, particularly away from home against the league's best sides (Arsenal, Chelsea and Manchester United all put four goals past the Black Cats on their travels in 1999–2000), but there is no doubt that Sunderland on the up.

SUNDERLAND

DATE	OPPONENT	SCORE	ATT.	BALL	BOULD	P BUTLER	T BUTLER	CRADDOCK	DICHIO	FREDGAARD	GRAY	HELMER	HOLLO
7.8.99	Chelsea A	0–4	34,831	60	90	90	–	–	–	s30	90	–	–
10.8.99	Watford H	2–0	40,630	–	90□	90	–	–	s14□	–	90	–	–
14.8.99	Arsenal H	0–0	41,680	90□	53	90	–	–	–	–	90	s37	–
21.8.99	Leeds Utd A	1–2	39,064	89□	–	73□	–	–	s1	–	63	90□	s27
25.8.99	Newcastle A	2–1	36,600	s21	90	90□	–	–	–	–	90	–	–
29.8.99	Coventry H	1–1	39,427	–	90□	90	–	–	–	–	90	–	–
11.9.99	Leicester H	2–0	40,105	90	90□	90^{1}	–	–	s11	–	90	–	–
18.9.99	Derby Co A	5–0	28,264	59□	90	90□	–	–	s31□	–	90	–	–
25.9.99	Sheff Wed H	1–0	41,132	45	90	90	–	–	s5	–	90	–	–
2.10.99	Bradford A	4–0	18,204	–	90	90	–	–	s4	–	90	–	–
18.10.99	Aston Villa H	2–1	41,045	s6	90	90	–	–	–	–	90	–	–
24.10.99	West Ham A	1–1	26,022	–	20■	90	–	–	s17	–	24	–	–
31.10.99	Tottenham H	2–1	41,904	s18	90	90	–	–	s30	–	90	–	–
6.11.99	Middlesbro A	1–1	34,793	s20□	90	90□	–	–	–	–	76	–	–
20.11.99	Liverpool H	0–2	42,015	–	–	90□	–	90	–	–	90	–	–
27.11.99	Watford A	3–2	21,590	s14	–	90□	–	90	–	–	90	–	–
4.12.99	Chelsea H	4–1	41,377	–	–	–	–	90	–	–	90	–	s6
18.12.99	Southampton H	2–0	40,860	–	90	90	–	–	–	–	90	–	–
26.12.99	Everton A	0–5	40,017	–	90	90	–	–	–	–	45	–	–
28.12.99	Man Utd H	2–2	42,026	–	90	90	–	–	–	–	90	–	–
3.1.00	Wimbledon A	0–1	17,621	–	90	90	–	–	–	–	90	–	–
15.1.00	Arsenal A	1–4	38,039	–	90	90	–	–	–	–	90	–	–
23.1.00	Leeds Utd H	1–2	41,947	–	77	90	–	s13	–	–	45	–	s45
5.2.00	Newcastle H	2–2	42,192	–	–	90	–	90	–	–	90	–	–
12.2.00	Coventry A	2–3	22,101	–	–	90	–	90	–	–	–	–	s27
26.2.00	Derby Co H	1–1	41,960	–	–	90	–	90	–	–	90	–	s30
5.3.00	Leicester A	2–5	20,432	–	–	90	–	90	–	–	–	–	45
11.3.00	Liverpool A	1–1	44,693	–	–	–	–	90	–	–	–	–	90
18.3.00	Middlesbro H	1–1	42,013	–	–	–	–	90	–	–	–	–	90□
25.3.00	Everton H	2–1	41,934	–	s16	–	–	90	–	–	–	–	90
1.4.00	Southampton A	2–1	15,245	–	–	–	–	90	s1	–	s45	–	90
8.4.00	Wimbledon H	2–1	41,592	–	–	–	–	90	–	–	76	–	90
15.4.00	Man Utd A	0–4	61,612	–	–	s15	–	90	–	–	54	–	90
22.4.00	Sheff Wed A	2–0	28,072	–	–	90	–	90	s15	–	90	–	55
24.4.00	Bradford H	0–1	40,628	–	–	90	–	83	s7	–	90	–	–
29.4.00	Aston Villa A	1–1	33,949	–	–	90	–	90□	–	–	90	–	–
6.5.00	West Ham H	1–0	41,684	–	–	90	s6	90	s46	–	90	–	s1
14.5.00	Tottenham A	1–3	36,070	–	–	90	–	90	–	–	90	–	s17

□ Yellow card, ■ Red card, s Substitute, 90^{2} Goals scored

*including one own goal

1999–2000 PREMIERSHIP APPEARANCES

KILBANE	LUMSDON	MAKIN	MARRIOTT	McCANN	NUNEZ	OSTER	PHILLIPS	QUINN	RAE	REDDY	ROY	SCHWARZ	SORENSEN	SUMMERBEE	THIRWELL	WILLIAMS	TOTAL
–	45	90□	–	s45	–	–	90	90□	90□	–	–	–	90	90	–	–	990
–	–	90□	–	s22	–	68	90[2]	76	90	–	–	90	90	90	–	–	990
–	–	90□	–	s45	–	45	78	s12	90	–	–	90□	90	90	–	–	990
–	–	90	–	90	–	–	90[1]	s17□	43■	–	–	90□	90	90	–	–	943
–	–	90	–	90□	–	–	90[1]□	90[1]	90	–	–	69	90	90	–	–	990
–	–	90	–	72	–	s18	90[1]□	90	90□	–	–	90	90	90	–	–	990
–	–	90	–	86[1]□	–	–	90	79□	–	–	s4	74	90□	90	–	s16	990
–	–	90	–	71[1]	–	–	90[3]	59[1]	s19	–	–	90	90	90□	–	s31	990
–	–	90	–	90	–	–	90	85	s45	–	–	90[1]	90	90	–	–	990
–	–	90□	–	61□	–	–	90[2]	86[1]	73[1]□	–	s29	90	90	90□	–	s17	990
–	–	90	–	84	–	–	90[2]	90	75	s9	s15	90□	90	81	–	–	990
–	–	90□	–	90□	–	–	90[1]	73	68	–	s22	90□	90	90	–	s66	920
–	–	90	–	90	–	–	60	90[2]	–	–	72	90	90	87	–	s3	990
–	–	32■	–	70	–	–	90□	90□	–	s14[1]	35	90□	90	90	–	s55□	932
–	–	–	–	90□	–	–	90	90	84□	s6	90	–	90	90	–	90	990
–	–	–	–	90[1]	–	–	89[2]	90	–	s1	76	90□	90	90□	–	90	990
–	–	90	–	–	–	–	90[2]	90[2]	–	–	90	90	90	84	90	90	990
s3	–	90□	–	90	–	–	90[2]□	90	–	–	65	87	90	90	–	s25	990
90□	–	90	–	90□	–	–	–	90	–	s45	32	90	90	90	–	s58	990
89	–	90□	–	90[1]	–	–	–	90[1]	61□	s1	–	90□	90	90	–	s29	990
90	–	71□	90	90□	–	s19	90	90□	–	–	–	90	–	35	–	s55	990
s20	–	61□	–	90	–	–	90	90[1]	–	–	90□	90	90	70	–	s29	990
90	–	–	–	90	–	–	90[1]	–	90	s26	64	90	90	–	–	90	990
90	–	90	–	90	–	–	90[2]	90	–	s14	–	90□	90	76	–	–	990
90	–	90□	–	66□	–	–	90[1]	90	s12[1]	–	s24	90□	90	78	–	63	990
90	–	–	–	–	–	–	90	90	90[1]□	–	60	–	90	–	90	90□	990
90□	–	90	–	–	–	s18	90[1]	90[1]□	90	–	72	90	90	s45	–	–	990
90	–	90□	–	–	–	–	90[1]	90	90	–	–	90	90	–	90□	90	990
90	–	90	–	–	–	–	90	90[1]	90□	–	–	90□	90	s35	55	90	990
90	–	90	–	–	–	–	90[1]	90	90	–	–	74□	90	90[1]	–	90	990
90	–	90	–	–	–	–	90[1]	89[1]	90	–	90□	–	90	45	–	90	990
90[1]	–	90	–	–	s14	–	90	90[1]	90	–	86	–	90	–	s4	90	990
90	–	90	–	–	–	–	90	90	90□	–	90	–	90	s36	–	75	990
66	–	90	–	–	–	s24	90[2]	75	90	–	90	–	90	–	–	s35	990
90	–	90	–	–	–	s48	90	90	90	–	90	–	90	–	–	42	990
45	–	90	–	–	–	s45	90□	90[1]	–	–	90	–	90	90	90	–	990
–	–	90	–	–	–	89□	90[1]□	44	–	–	84	–	90	90	90□	–	990
s28	–	73[1]	–	–	–	62	90	90	s24■	–	90	–	90	90	65	–	989

THE MANAGER

PETER REID

Peter Reid has been in charge of Sunderland for five full seasons now, but 1999–2000 was by far his most successful.

Having already experienced one relegation from the Premiership, Reid's main priority was not to allow history to repeat itself, but what he and the players achieved surpassed mere survival.

Sunderland's seventh-placed finish was more than most fans could have hoped for, with Kevin Phillips, a Reid signing, finishing the season as the division's top scorer with 30 goals.

From September onwards Sunderland were never out of the top seven, and it is a credit to Reid that relegation was never an issue, while European qualification was always possible.

Famed for his terrier-like performances in midfield with Everton and England, for whom he won 13 caps, the former Manchester City boss took charge of Sunderland in March 1995, and is already being suggested as a future England coach.

Sunderland certainly have the potential at least to repeat their successful 1999–2000 campaign, and the fans' expectations will now be much higher than 12 months ago.

But with Reid at the helm, their future would appear to be in safe hands.

LEAGUE POSITION

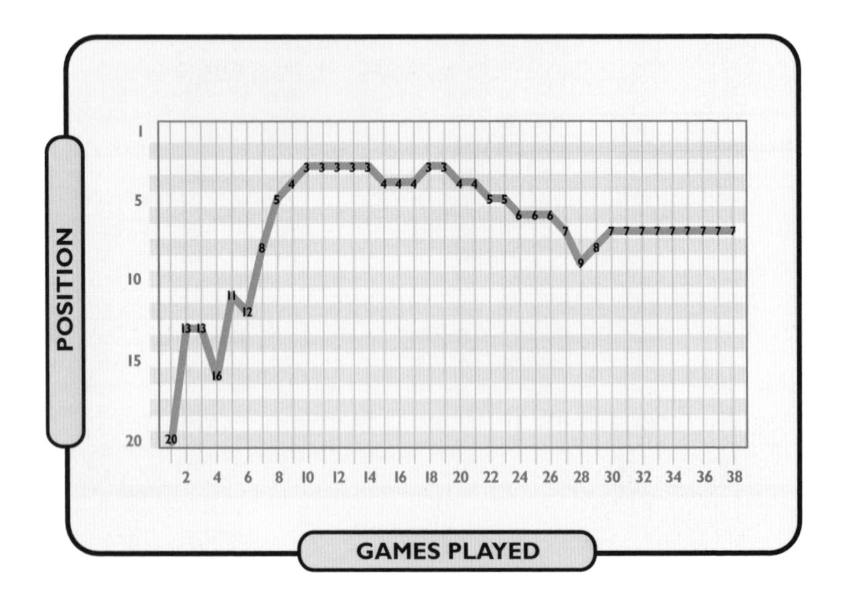

79% of Sunderland's goals were scored by strikers

THE GOALS

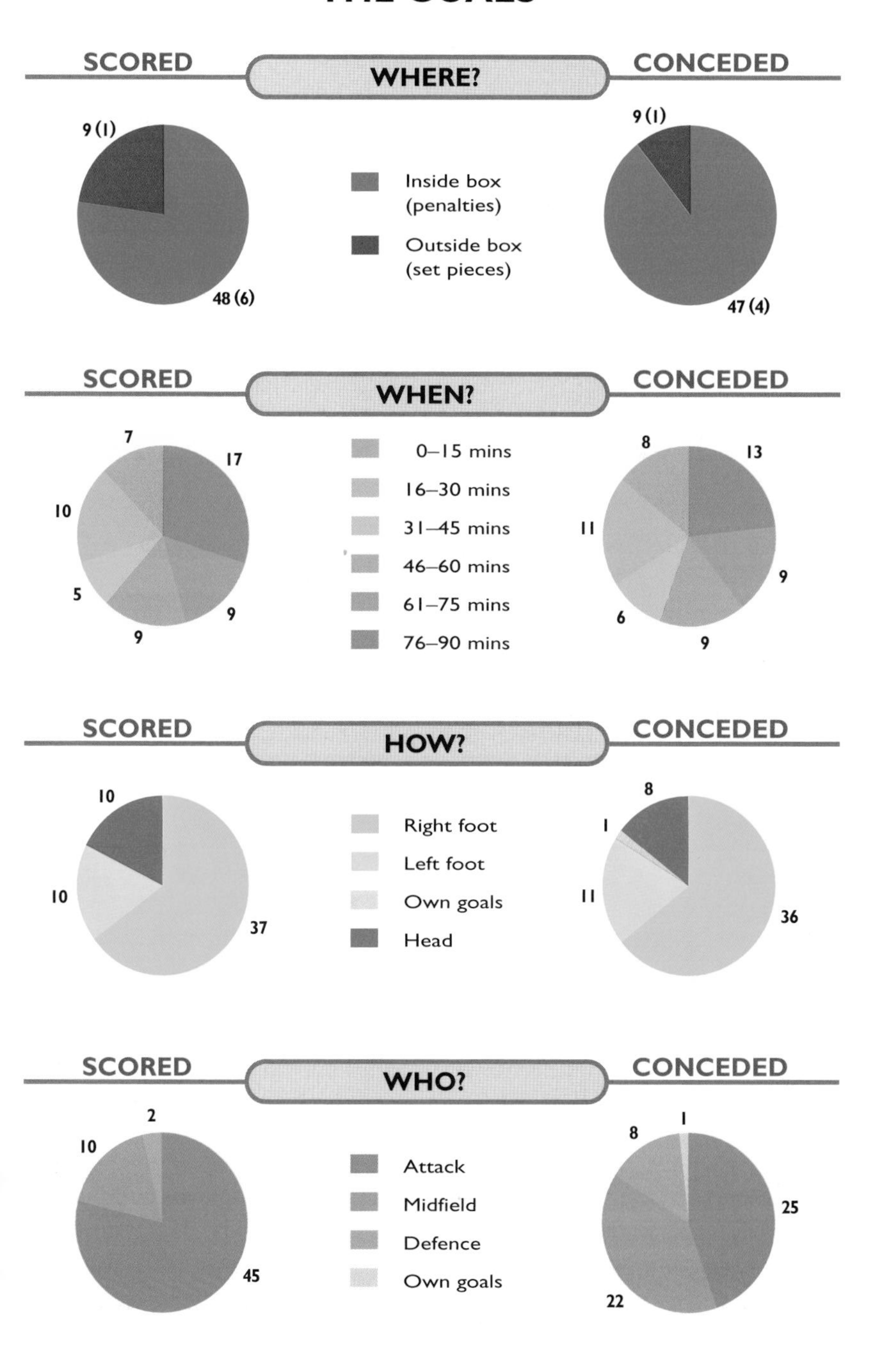

– the highest ratio in the top flight

SUNDERLAND

	BALL	BOULD	BUTLER	BUTLER	CRADDOCK	DICHIO	FREDGAARD	GRAY	HELMER	HOLLOWAY	KILBA
APPEARANCES											
Start	6	19	31	0	18	0	0	32	1	8	17
Sub	5	1	1	1	1	12	1	1	1	7	3
Minutes on pitch	512	1606	2788	6	1626	182	30	2678	127	793	1511
GOAL ATTEMPTS											
Goals	0	0	1	0	0	0	0	0	0	0	1
Shots on target	0	1	2	0	2	2	1	3	0	0	12
Shots off target	2	6	4	0	1	1	0	4	0	1	12
Shooting accuracy	0%	14%	33%	0%	67%	67%	100%	43%	0%	0%	50%
PASSING											
Goal assists	0	0	1	0	0	1	0	4	0	1	1
Long passes	16	110	342	1	263	8	0	510	1	144	99
Short passes	145	390	599	0	340	77	10	906	29	229	463
PASS COMPLETION											
Own half %	79%	87%	84%	0%	73%	80%	100%	81%	81%	74%	67%
Opposition half %	73%	51%	49%	0%	52%	63%	67%	64%	33%	62%	62%
CROSSING											
Total crosses	0	1	11	0	6	2	0	122	0	18	92
Cross completion %	0%	0%	45%	0%	17%	0%	0%	30%	0%	33%	30%
DRIBBLING											
Dribbles & runs	2	17	22	0	21	2	4	139	0	27	76
Dribble completion %	50%	88%	95%	0%	95%	100%	25%	81%	0%	85%	67%
DEFENDING											
Tackles made	33	42	69	0	62	5	0	77	2	42	30
Tackles won %	61%	62%	52%	0%	50%	40%	0%	34%	50%	62%	37%
Blocks	4	30	66	0	47	0	0	24	3	7	12
Clearances	24	211	433	0	181	3	1	121	17	24	16
Interceptions	2	27	31	0	9	1	0	19	2	4	8
DISCIPLINE											
Fouls	16	28	39	0	32	19	0	24	2	21	15
Offside	1	1	0	0	1	1	0	2	0	0	0
Yellow cards	4	3	6	0	1	2	0	0	1	1	2
Red cards	0	1	0	0	0	0	0	0	0	0	0

GOALKEEPER NAME	START/ (SUB)	TIME ON PITCH	GOALS CONCEDED	MINS/GOALS CONCEDED	SAVES MADE	SAVES/ SHOTS
MARRIOTT	1	90	1	90	4	80%
SORENSEN	37	3330	55	61	132	71%

PLAYERS' STATISTICS

LUMSDON	MAKIN	McCANN	NUNEZ	OSTER	PHILLIPS	QUINN	RAE	REDDY	ROY	SCHWARZ	SUMMERBEE	THIRLWELL	WILLIAMS	TOTAL	RANK
1	34	21	0	4	36	35	22	0	19	27	29	7	13		
0	0	3	1	6	0	2	4	8	5	0	3	1	12		
45	2937	1882	14	436	3197	3035	1944	116	1550	2374	2562	574	1499		
0	1	4	0	0	30	14	3	1	0	1	1	0	0	57	=6th
0	5	8	0	0	65	38	16	2	5	8	8	3	0	181	10th
0	8	17	0	5	57	35	13	2	9	9	7	1	0	194	16th
0%	38%	32%	0%	0%	53%	52%	55%	50%	36%	47%	53%	75%	0%	48%	5th
0	0	3	0	1	4	8	5	0	2	2	5	0	1	40	7th
2	359	148	0	43	136	95	234	3	155	152	211	50	201	3283	8th
13	1025	654	3	168	842	1393	680	27	555	658	621	193	351	10371	11th
100%	81%	85%	100%	89%	89%	74%	86%	25%	81%	85%	83%	86%	69%	81%	6th
86%	72%	67%	50%	68%	67%	57%	65%	42%	73%	65%	61%	66%	55%	63%	11th
3	43	83	0	26	34	42	59	3	9	35	233	2	15	839	7th
0%	37%	33%	0%	50%	24%	24%	31%	0%	33%	26%	36%	0%	27%	32%	6th
0	81	49	0	18	91	47	55	4	26	44	193	7	32	957	15th
0%	90%	69%	0%	83%	69%	81%	78%	50%	69%	75%	60%	71%	88%	75%	14th
1	114	100	0	8	13	24	82	3	69	112	50	15	62	1016	10th
0%	48%	53%	0%	13%	62%	38%	50%	33%	65%	60%	50%	40%	48%	51%	12th
0	30	9	0	1	1	15	12	0	10	14	12	5	26	328	19th
0	126	30	0	1	4	49	32	1	27	37	27	5	103	1488	16th
1	15	25	0	1	7	8	22	1	7	20	6	3	12	232	13th
0	50	60	1	4	81	154	40	2	23	38	36	7	29	621	2nd
0	0	2	1	0	34	52	0	1	0	0	2	1	1	100	19th
0	11	8	0	1	6	6	8	0	2	11	3	2	2	81	4th
0	1	0	0	0	0	0	2	0	0	0	0	0	0	4	=5th

OSSES UGHT	CROSSES PUNCHED	CROSSES NOT CLAIMED	CATCH SUCCESS	THROWS/ SHORT KICKS	% COMPLETION	LONG KICKS	% COMPLETION
1	0	0	100%	8	100%	42	43%
61	18	5	92%	210	88%	1097	53%

PLAYER OF THE SEASON

PLAYER	INDEX SCORE
KEVIN PHILLIPS	**1,034**
Alex Rae	**849***
Paul Butler	**826**
Niall Quinn	**795**
Michael Gray	**787**
Chris Makin	**764**
Jody Craddock	**733***
Thomas Sorensen	**719**
Stefan Schwarz	**653**
Nicky Summerbee	**624**

All players played 75 minutes in at least 19 matches except those marked * who featured in just 18 games.

Premiership passions returned to Wearside with a bang as Sunderland's players revelled in their return to the top flight, none more so than Kevin Phillips.

The striker had made his England debut at the tail end of the 1998–99 season during the Mackems' successful promotion campaign, but many doubted whether he could be as effective in the top flight. The former Watford player proved those doubters wrong by finishing the season as the Premiership's top scorer and helping Sunderland to a seventh-placed finish.

Phillips scored 30 times from 122 attempted shots, giving him an average of 1,034 Index points as Premiership defences struggled to cope with his formidable strike partnership alongside Niall Quinn.

Midfielder Alex Rae appears second in the Index with three goals and five assists in a solid Premiership season, while big centre-back Paul Butler coped with the step up admirably, making 433 clearances and 66 blocks in the heart of the Sunderland defence.

Quinn had to play second fiddle to Phillips upfront, but the big Irishman still managed to grab 14 goals and eight assists, as his awkward presence proved to be more than a nuisance for opposing defences.

The experienced forward's double-act with Phillips proved to be the most prolific strike pairing in the league and was the main reason why Sunderland performed as well as they did in their first season back in the top flight.

Many of Peter Reid's men who made up the promotion-winning side continued to perform well in the Premiership, with the likes of Michael Gray, Chris Makin and Jody Craddock all achieving good Index scores.

New signing Stefan Schwarz performed well on his return to English football, while 'keeper Thomas Sorensen put some indifferent mid-season form behind him to achieve a respectable average Index score of 719 points.

6 Kevin Phillips scored more penaltie

FIVE OF THE BEST

Before the 1999–2000 season, teams promoted from Division One to the Premiership had struggled badly to maintain top-flight status. But Sunderland bucked the trend in style after bouncing back to the big time, with their strike partnership smashing in 44 goals between them and the future looks bright at the Stadium of Light.

TOP GOALSCORERS

	GOALS	GOALS/SHOTS
KEVIN PHILLIPS	30	25%
Niall Quinn	14	19%
Gavin McCann	4	16%
Alex Rae	3	10%
Nicky Summerbee	1	7%

Although Kevin Phillips confidently set himself a target of 20 Premiership goals in the summer of 1999, few could have foreseen the huge impact the former Watford striker was to make in his first season in top-flight football. The England international finished up with 30 goals, while his strike partner Niall Quinn netted 14. The fact that the next top scorer was Gavin McCann with just four strikes illustrates how important the striking duo are to the Black Cats.

A mid-season fall-out with boss Peter Reid threatened to jeopardise the future of gritty Chris Makin at the Stadium of Light. However, the former Marseille man proved himself to be a crucial player to the Mackems, completing 1,048 successful passes. He recorded a passing accuracy of 76%, prompting moves from either full-back slot. Michael Gray was Makin's nearest challenger in terms of successful passes – he made 981 of them and had a 69% completion ratio.

TOP PASSERS

	SUCC PASSES	COMPLETION
CHRIS MAKIN	1,048	76%
Michael Gray	981	69%
Niall Quinn	818	55%
Kevin Phillips	679	69%
Alex Rae	657	72%

TOP TACKLERS

	WON	SUCCESS
STEFAN SCHWARZ	67	60%
Chris Makin	55	48%
Gavin McCann	53	53%
Eric Roy	45	65%
Alex Rae	41	50%

Tough-tackling Swede Stefan Schwarz returned to the Premiership for 1999–2000 and showed that none of his competitive spirit had deserted him in four years away from England. The former Arsenal man won 67 tackles for Sunderland, more than any other Black Cat, although his success rate of 60% was bettered by another European midfielder. That man was Frenchman Eric Roy, who won 65% of his challenges and impressed the north-east hordes despite a relatively low-key season on the whole.

Despite his "one of football's gentlemen" tag, Niall Quinn illustrated the tougher side of his character on a regular basis throughout 1999–2000. Admittedly, Sunderland's big Irishman was booked just six times and never dismissed, but he committed 102 fouls, a total second only to West Ham's Paulo Wanchope in the Premiership. It could be argued that Alex Rae was the club's real bad boy. He was dismissed twice and hauled up before the FA for a misconduct charge after an elbow on Derby's Darryl Powell.

DISCIPLINE

	POINTS	FOULS & CARDS
NIALL QUINN	120	102F, 6Y, 0R
Chris Makin	89	50F, 11Y, 1R
Gavin McCann	82	58F, 8Y, 0R
Alex Rae	76	40F, 8Y, 2R
Stefan Schwarz	71	38F, 11Y, 0R

han any other player

ACTION	CRADDOCK	GRAY	HOLLOWAY	MAKIN	PHILLIPS	QUINN	ROY	SCHWARZ	SORENSEN	SUMMERBEE	THIRLWELL	WILLIAMS	TOTAL	CHELSEA
Time on pitch	90	90	6	90	90	90	90	90	90	84	90	90	990	990
GOALS														
Goal	–	–	–	–	2	2	–	–	–	–	–	–	4	1
Shot on target	–	–	–	–	4	1	–	–	–	–	1	–	6	3
Shot off target	–	–	–	–	1	–	–	–	–	–	–	–	1	6
Blocked shot	–	–	–	–	2	–	–	–	–	–	–	–	2	1
Own goal	–	–	–	–	–	–	–	–	–	–	–	–	–	–
PASSES														
Pass to own player	16	34	2	35	15	34	39	25	–	25	29	17	271	242
Pass to opposition	11	20	–	13	13	25	10	10	–	14	10	10	136	134
Cross to own player	1	1	–	1	–	2	–	–	–	1	–	–	6	3
Cross to opposition player	–	1	–	–	1	1	–	3	–	2	1	–	9	13
Goal assist	–	–	–	–	–	–	1	–	–	–	–	1	2	1
Pass completion %	61%	63%	100%	73%	52%	58%	80%	66%	0%	62%	73%	64%	66%	63%
TACKLES & CLEARANCES														
Tackle	5	3	–	4	–	–	3	1	–	2	4	1	23	32
Clearances, blocks and interceptions	9	6	–	5	–	4	–	–	–	–	1	7	32	29
DRIBBLES & RUNS														
Dribble ball retained	–	3	–	5	2	–	2	2	–	5	1	–	20	19
Dribble ball lost	–	2	–	–	–	–	–	–	–	1	2	–	5	1
Dribble success %	0%	60%	0%	100%	100%	0%	100%	100%	0%	83%	33%	0%	80%	95%
DISCIPLINE														
Fouls	4	1	–	1	4	3	1	–	–	2	1	4	21	14
Penalty conceded	–	–	–	–	–	–	–	–	–	–	–	–	–	–
Free kick – offside	–	–	–	–	–	–	–	–	–	–	1	–	1	3
Yellow cards	–	–	–	–	–	–	–	–	–	–	–	–	–	2
Red cards	–	–	–	–	–	–	–	–	–	–	–	–	–	–
GOALKEEPERS														
Distribution to own player	–	–	–	–	–	–	–	–	20	–	–	–	20	10
Distribution to opposition player	–	–	–	–	–	–	–	–	11	–	–	–	11	18
Goalkeeper distribution %	0%	0%	0%	0%	0%	0%	0%	0%	65%	0%	0%	0%	65%	36%
Save	–	–	–	–	–	–	–	–	3	–	–	–	3	6
Ball caught	–	–	–	–	–	–	–	–	4	–	–	–	4	1
Ball dropped	–	–	–	–	–	–	–	–	–	–	–	–	–	–
Goal conceded	–	–	–	–	–	–	–	–	1	–	–	–	1	4

124 Niall Quinn made more successful flick-on

The Wearsiders still held bitter memories of their opening-day mauling at Stamford Bridge as they entered this fixture. Despite performing well on their return to the Premiership, the 4–0 drubbing back in August was a black mark in Sunderland's copybook.

Peter Reid was forced to make changes to his line-up with four players out through suspension, but Sunderland looked anything but understrength as they went for Chelsea straight from the kick-off.

Gianluca Vialli's men were rocked as the Mackems set about them right from the first whistle. Vialli had said that Chelsea would be waving goodbye to their title hopes if they failed to win at the Stadium of Light, and it took just 44 seconds for him to begin his farewells.

The red and white shirts swarmed all over the Chelsea defence and Eric Roy's jinking run wrong-footed the Blues' defence. He cut the ball back to Niall Quinn who had the simplest of tasks to tap the ball home from close range.

Chelsea were shell-shocked as the Stadium of Light erupted. Boosted by their early lead, Sunderland were rampant and tore into their stunned opponents.

With the Londoners reeling after 23 minutes, Sunderland broke quickly, and as the ball fell to Kevin Phillips 30 yards from goal he unleashed a searing volley that dipped over Ed De Goey into the top corner for one of the goals of the season.

World Cup winner Marcel Desailly and Jes Hogh in the Chelsea defence were being overwhelmed by Quinn and Phillips as the home side continued to drive forward. Phillips and debutant Paul Thirlwell both had efforts blocked in a goalmouth scramble as there was little respite for Vialli's men.

In the 36th minute, Michael Gray's cross from the left found Niall Quinn, who controlled on his chest before firing in a shot which De Goey could only parry. The ball fell kindly for the unmarked Phillips, though, and he smashed the rebound home.

Before the fans had stopped celebrating, along came goal number four. A Nicky Summerbee corner was not cleared and Quinn was able to fire home his second to leave Chelsea three down even before the end of the first period.

The second half could not possibly live up to the excitement of the first and so it proved, with Sunderland happy to sit on their lead and soak up the pressure from the visitors. Chelsea managed to pull one back 10 minutes from time through Uruguayan international Gustavo Poyet from Gianfranco Zola's corner.

There were impressive displays all through the Sunderland side, but England striker Phillips was the Opta man of the match with 2,030 points for his two goals and four other shots on target.

Chelsea simply had no answer to the Wearsiders, who made a total of 407 passes and enjoyed 10 shots on target compared to the visitors' four. Sunderland also pressed the Blues all over the park, making more clearances, blocks and interceptions as the memories of their opening-day humiliation were wiped away in the best possible style.

han any other player in the Premiership

adidas
HOLSTEN

TOTTENHAM HOTSPUR

ADDRESS

Bill Nicholson Way, 748 High Road,
Tottenham, London N17 0AP

CONTACT NUMBERS

Telephone: 020 8365 5000
Fax: 020 8365 5005
Ticket Office: 020 8365 5050
Club Call: 09068 100 500
Club Superstore: 020 8365 5041
Website: www.spurs.co.uk

KEY PERSONNEL

Chairman: A M Sugar
Vice-Chairman: N Soloman
Directors: J Sedgwick, A G Berry
D A Alexiou, I Yawetz, C T Sandy
Club Secretary: Peter Barnes
Director of Football: David Pleat
Manager: George Graham

SPONSORS

Holsten

FANZINES

Cock A Doodle Doo
My Eyes Have Seen the Glory

COLOURS

Home: White shirts, navy shorts,
navy stockings
Away: Yellow and navy shirts,
white shorts and stockings

NICKNAME

Spurs
The Lilywhites

HONOURS

League Champions: 1950–51, 1960–61
Division Two Champions: 1919–20,
1949–50
FA Cup: 1901, 1921, 1961, 1962,
1967, 1981, 1982, 1991
League Cup: 1971, 1973, 1999
European Cup Winners' Cup: 1963
UEFA Cup: 1972, 1984

RECORD GOALSCORER

Jimmy Greaves –
220 league goals, 1961–70

BIGGEST WIN

9–0 v Bristol Rovers – Division Two,
22 October 1977

BIGGEST DEFEAT

0–8 v Cologne – UEFA Inter Toto Cup,
22 July 1995

SEASON REVIEW

Tottenham finished six points and one position higher in the 1999–2000 season than they had the previous campaign, but there was still a feeling of disappointment around White Hart Lane at the club's inability to add another trophy to the Worthington Cup that they claimed in 1998–99.

Despite George Graham's failure to secure the services of a top-quality striker in the summer, the former Arsenal man had added £8.5 million-worth of new talent in the form of Chris Perry, Oyvind Leonhardsen and Willem Korsten to his growing squad.

Spurs certainly looked on course for success at the start of the season, rubbing shoulders with Manchester United at the top of the table after taking nine points from their opening four games, with new signings Leonhardsen and Perry particularly impressive.

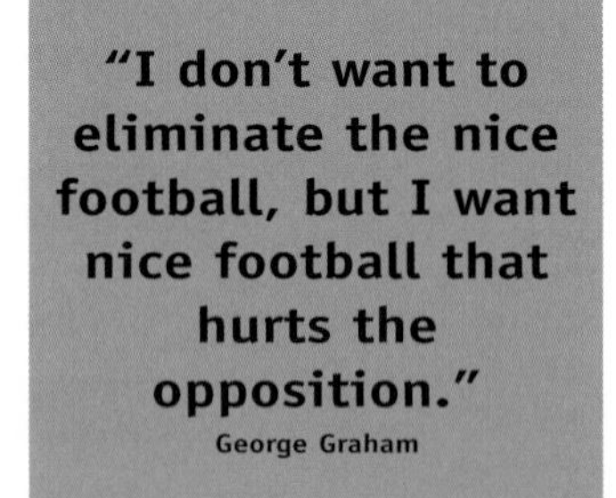

"I don't want to eliminate the nice football, but I want nice football that hurts the opposition."
George Graham

September saw the manager celebrate a year at White Hart Lane with an unbeaten run, although many supporters were less than impressed with draws against Bradford and Wimbledon that saw the club drop to ninth place by the end of the month.

Of even more concern was the future of England internationals Darren Anderton and Sol Campbell. Both players were stalling on new deals, Campbell in particular refusing to discuss a contract until the end of the season. With press reports linking the pair to Manchester United, there was an understandable desire on the part of the fans to see both players signed up to long-term deals with Spurs as quickly as possible.

Anderton eventually signed a one-year extension, but even though Campbell gave the club verbal assurances that he would stay until the end of the 2000–01 season, he is yet to commit his long-term future to Tottenham Hotspur.

For that to happen, Spurs will have t sustain more of an assault on maj honours than they did in 1999–200 Progress in the UEFA Cup was halted i early November with a last-minute Stephe Carr own-goal giving Kaiserslauten a 2- victory on aggregate. And although th team recorded some good results in th league before the New Year – notab against Manchester United and Arsenal – serious challenge for a European spot i 2000–01 never real materialised.

Graham certainly g his players battlin Only three teams Liverpool, Manchest United and Aston Villa beat them by more tha one clear goal in th Premiership and n other side attempte more tackles or made a many interceptions characteristics th occasionally got the into trouble, as in th game against Leeds a Elland Road where a ful scale brawl resulted in a heavy fine.

But at Tottenham – a club where th supporters demand that the team pla with style – effort is never enoug especially when it is accompanied by po results. A double cup exit in Decemb proved too much for some supporter After watching their team relinquish the hold on the Worthington Cup with a 3- defeat at Fulham and crash out of the F Cup with a humiliating 6–1 defeat b Newcastle, many turned their wrath c Alan Sugar for not providing the money t make the high-profile signings needed t match the ambitions of the likes c Anderton and Campbell.

Graham, who did not escape criticisn described the moaners as "profession whingers", ignoring the boos of his ow supporters in the home game again Watford when he substituted th

622 Tottenham were the most foule

SEASON REVIEW

inspirational David Ginola shortly after the Frenchman had scored the Goal of the Month. Graham lambasted the critical fans claiming that with the game virtually won he was resting Ginola for the next match.

Promising Peterborough youngsters Matthew Etherington and Simon Davies were added to the squad in December, but neither provided the immediate answer to Tottenham's most pressing need: a top-quality striker.

Graham, as always, would not be pushed into any rash moves in the transfer market. He reacted to Chelsea's signing of George Weah by calling the move a "quick fix"; words that came back to haunt him after the Liberian scored the winner against Spurs on his debut.

No one could accuse Tottenham's next signing, Dave McEwen, of being a quick fix. The former Dulwich Hamlet man was definitely bought with the future in mind, but with just five goals in their opening eight games of the New Year, Spurs fans were more concerned with the here and now.

A £7 million move for former Arsenal man John Hartson fell through when the burly target man failed a medical – a fact that obviously spurred Chris Armstrong and Steffen Iversen into action. The duo lashed a combined total of five goals past Southampton in a fantastic 7–2 victory that left the fans surprised and delighted.

Armstrong emerged from the second half of the season with plenty of credit, ignoring the catcalls of the fans to score 11 goals in the New Year and boost his tally for the season to 14, a figure that his fellow-frontman Iversen matched.

Armstrong and Iversen's form merely papered over the cracks, though. Spurs won just six of their last 19 games, dropping out of European contention and into mid-table in the process.

A sequence of five games without a win after the victory over Southampton saw them reach a low point when, after going 2–0 up against Aston Villa at White Hart Lane, they collapsed to a 4–2 defeat after which Alan Sugar was once again the target of supporters' discontent.

George Graham, facing a personal battle of his own against rheumatoid arthritis, was not at the game, but he would have been upset to see his team concede four for the first time in the Premiership since he had assumed control of the club.

"The last game of the season presents the ideal time to reflect on the campaign as a whole. And, unfortunately my illness just about sums it all up!"
George Graham

Happier news came at the end of the season with the £11 million signing of Sergei Rebrov. The arrival of the highly-rated Ukrainian finally ended the search for a big-name striker which had occupied directors, manager and supporters alike for much of the season.

With more high-profile signings on the way and promising youngsters like Gary Doherty and Anthony Gardner added to the squad, Graham clearly has a long-term plan for Tottenham. Supporters will probably have to wait a little longer before those plans come to fruition, but Spurs will at least be expected to challenge for a European place in the 2000–01 season.

Failure to reach that target for a second successive season would see the once proud club fall even further behind bitter London rivals Arsenal and Chelsea. Graham has proved that the club can attract top quality players with the signings of Rebrov and Neil Sullivan, but it is now time for Spurs to start producing the goods on a regular basis.

Only then will Tottenham be able to convince their more established players that they can achieve their ambitions at White Hart Lane.

TOTTENHAM HOTSPUR

DATE	OPPONENT	SCORE	ATT.	ANDERTON	ARMSTRONG	CAMPBELL	CARR	CLEMENCE	DAVIES	DOHERTY	DOMINGUEZ	EDINBURGH	ETHERINGTON	FE
7.8.99	West Ham A	0–1	26,010	90	–	27□	90	–	–	–	45	90	–	s45□
9.8.99	Newcastle H	3–1	28,701	90	–	–	90	–	–	–	s35	–	–	45^{1}
14.8.99	Everton H	3–2	34,539	85	–	–	90	–	–	–	–	–	–	90
21.8.99	Sheff Wed A	2–1	24,027	90	–	–	90	–	–	–	–	–	–	90^{1}□
28.8.99	Leeds Utd H	1–2	36,012	–	–	–	90	–	–	–	s39	–	–	45
12.9.99	Bradford A	1–1	18,143	–	s18	–	90	–	–	–	–	–	–	72
19.9.99	Coventry H	3–2	35,224	–	85^{1}□	–	90	–	–	–	s30	–	–	–
26.9.99	Wimbledon A	1–1	17,368	–	76	–	90^{1}	–	–	–	s14	–	–	–
3.10.99	Leicester H	2–3	35,591	–	90	–	90	–	–	–	–	–	–	–
16.10.99	Derby Co A	1–0	29,815	–	77^{1}	90	90□	–	–	–	–	–	–	–
23.10.99	Man Utd H	3–1*	36,072	–	–	90	90^{1}	–	–	–	–	–	–	–
31.10.99	Sunderland A	1–2	41,904	–	–	90□	90	90	–	–	s45	–	–	–
7.11.99	Arsenal H	2–1	36,085	–	90	90	90□	90□	–	–	s1	90□	–	–
20.11.99	Southampton A	1–0	15,248	–	90	90□	–	–	–	–	s26	90	–	–
28.11.99	Newcastle A	1–2	36,460	–	68^{1}□	90	–	s5	–	–	s22	90□	–	–
6.12.99	West Ham H	0–0	36,233	–	s10	90	–	–	–	–	80	–	–	–
18.12.99	Middlesbro A	1–2	33,129	–	82	90	–	–	–	–	–	s45	–	–
26.12.99	Watford H	4–0	36,089	–	90	90	90	90	–	–	s15	–	–	–
29.12.99	Aston Villa A	1–1	39,217	–	90	90	90	90	–	–	–	–	–	–
3.1.00	Liverpool H	1–0	36,044	–	90^{1}	90□	90	90□	–	–	–	–	–	–
12.1.00	Chelsea A	0–1	34,969	90	90□	90	90	90	–	–	–	90	–	–
15.1.00	Everton A	2–2*	36,144	90	90^{1}	90	90	90□	–	–	–	81□	–	–
22.1.00	Sheff Wed H	0–1	35,897	90	62	90	90	62	–	–	–	62	–	–
5.2.00	Chelsea H	0–1	36,041	86	90	90	90	90	–	–	–	–	–	–
12.2.00	Leeds Utd A	0–1	40,127	90□	90□	90	90	74□	–	–	s12	–	–	–
26.2.00	Coventry A	1–0	23,077	90	90^{1}	90	90	s46	–	–	–	–	–	–
4.3.00	Bradford H	1–1	35,472	90	90	90	90	–	–	–	–	–	–	s17
11.3.00	Southampton H	7–2*	36,024	90^{1}	90^{2}	90	90□	–	–	–	–	–	–	–
19.3.00	Arsenal A	1–2	38,131	90□	90^{1}	73	90□	–	–	–	–	–	–	s30□
25.3.00	Watford A	1–1	20,050	90	90^{1}	–	90	64	–	–	–	–	–	s14
3.4.00	Middlesbro H	2–3	31,796	90	90^{1}	90	90□	s22	–	–	–	–	–	–
9.4.00	Liverpool A	0–2	44,536	90	90	90	90	78□	s12	–	–	–	s12	–
15.4.00	Aston Villa H	2–4	35,304	90□	90^{1}	90□	90	90	–	–	–	–	–	–
19.4.00	Leicester A	1–0	19,764	90□	74	90	90	90	–	–	–	–	s16	–
22.4.00	Wimbledon H	2–0	33,086	90^{1}	90^{1}	90	90	90	–	–	–	–	s17	–
29.4.00	Derby Co H	1–1	33,044	90□	90	90□	90	90^{1}	s45	–	–	–	s20	–
6.5.00	Man Utd A	1–3	61,629	90	71^{1}	90	90	90	90	s19	–	–	84	–
14.5.00	Sunderland H	3–1	36,070	90^{1}	90	90	90^{1}	–	–	s45	–	–	–	–

□ Yellow card, ■ Red card, s Substitute, 90^{2} Goals scored

*including one own goal

For more information visit our website:

1999–2000 PREMIERSHIP APPEARANCES

FOX	FREUND	GINOLA	IVERSEN	KING	KORSTEN	LEONHARDSEN	McEWAN	NIELSEN	PERRY	PIERCY	SCALES	SHERWOOD	TARICCO	VEGA	WALKER	YOUNG	TOTAL
–	90□	45	90	–	–	s45	–	–	90	–	s63	90	–	–	90	–	990
–	s10	90	90[1]	–	–	90	–	–	90	–	90	90[1]	89	–	90	s1	990
–	s5	90	90[1]	–	–	90[1]	–	–	90	–	90	90[1]	90	–	90□	–	990
–	s45□	45	90□	–	–	90[1]	–	–	90	–	–	90	90	–	90	90	990
–	90□	90	90	–	–	90	–	s6	90	–	–	90[1]	90□	–	90	90	990
–	90□	89	90□	–	–	90	–	s1	90[1]	–	–	90□	90	–	90	90□	990
–	90	60	90[1]	–	–	90[1]	–	s5	90	–	–	90	90	–	90	90	990
–	90	–	90	–	–	90	–	90	90	–	–	90□	90□	–	90	90	990
–	90	72	90[2]	–	–	90□	–	s18□	90	–	–	90□	90	s17	90	73	990
–	–	89	90	90	–	90	–	77	90	s13	–	s1	90□	s13	90	–	990
87□	90□	90	90[1]	–	–	90	–	–	–	s3	–	90□	90	s15	90	75	990
–	90	45	90[1]□	–	–	78	–	–	s45	45	–	s12	90□	90	90	–	990
s3	–	89	90[1]	–	–	87□	–	–	90	–	–	90[1]	–	–	90	–	990
–	90	64	90	–	–	90[1]□	–	–	90	–	–	90	90	–	90	–	990
–	85	90□	90	–	–	90	–	–	90□	–	–	90□	90□	–	90	–	990
–	90□	90	90	–	–	90	–	s14	90□	–	–	76	90	–	90	90	990
s8	33	45□	90	–	–	–	–	89■	90	–	–	s57□	90□	90[1]	90	90□	989
–	–	75[1]	90[1]	–	–	–	–	90	90	–	–	90[2]	90□	–	90	–	990
–	–	90	90□	–	–	–	–	85	90	–	–	90[1]	90	–	90	s5	990
–	–	90	90	–	–	–	–	–	90□	–	–	90	90	–	90	90	990
–	–	90	90□	–	–	–	–	–	90	–	–	90□	–	–	90	–	990
–	–	68	90	–	–	–	–	s22□	90	–	–	90□	–	–	90	s9	990
–	–	90	90	–	s28	–	–	s28	90	–	–	90	–	–	90	s28	990
–	–	90	79	–	s11	–	–	s4	90	–	–	90	90	–	90	–	990
–	–	78	–	–	90	–	–	s16	90	–	–	90□	90□	–	90	–	990
–	90	90	–	–	–	90	–	–	90	–	–	44	62	–	90	s28	990
–	90	90	90[1]	–	–	73	–	–	90	–	–	–	77	–	90	s13	990
–	90□	90	90[3]	–	–	90	–	–	29	–	–	–	90	–	90	s61	990
–	90	85	60	–	s5	90	–	–	90	–	–	–	90	–	90	s17	990
–	90	90	76	–	–	s26	–	–	90	–	90	–	90	–	90	–	990
–	90	90[1]□	90	–	68	–	–	–	90□	–	–	–	90	–	90	–	990
–	90□	78	90	–	–	–	–	–	90□	–	–	–	90□	–	90	–	990
–	90	90	90[1]	–	–	–	–	–	90□	–	–	–	90□	–	90	–	990
–	90	90[1]	74	–	s16	–	–	–	90□	–	–	–	37	–	90	s53	990
–	90	73	90	–	90	–	–	–	90	–	–	–	–	–	90	–	990
–	–	70	70	–	45□	–	s20	–	90□	–	–	–	–	–	90	90	990
–	90□	–	71	s6	s19	–	–	–	90	–	–	–	–	–	90	–	990
–	90	90	45	90	–	42	–	–	90	–	–	s48[1]	–	–	90	–	990

THE MANAGER

GEORGE GRAHAM

At the start of 1999–2000, most Spurs fans were not hoping for a top six finish – they were expecting it.

Much of this optimism was due to George Graham's appointment. After all, while it was hard for the fans to take, the fact remained that the Scot had been very successful at Arsenal and had won Spurs' first trophy for eight years in his first season.

As a player, Graham was part of the 1971 Arsenal Double-winning side, and won 12 Scotland caps during what was a successful career.

His first managerial post was at Millwall but Arsenal appointed him boss in May 1986 to inaugurate a golden era for the Gunners.

Graham guided Arsenal to two Championships, an FA Cup, two League Cups, and, in 1994, the European Cup Winners' Cup.

Spurs supporters will be hoping that he can bring similar success to the White Hart Lane outfit.

Hanging on to Sol Campbell and signing the likes of Sergei Rebrov will certainly raise hopes that with a few more signings, combined with the Scot's experience and ability, 2000–01 could be the season Spurs fans have been waiting for.

LEAGUE POSITION

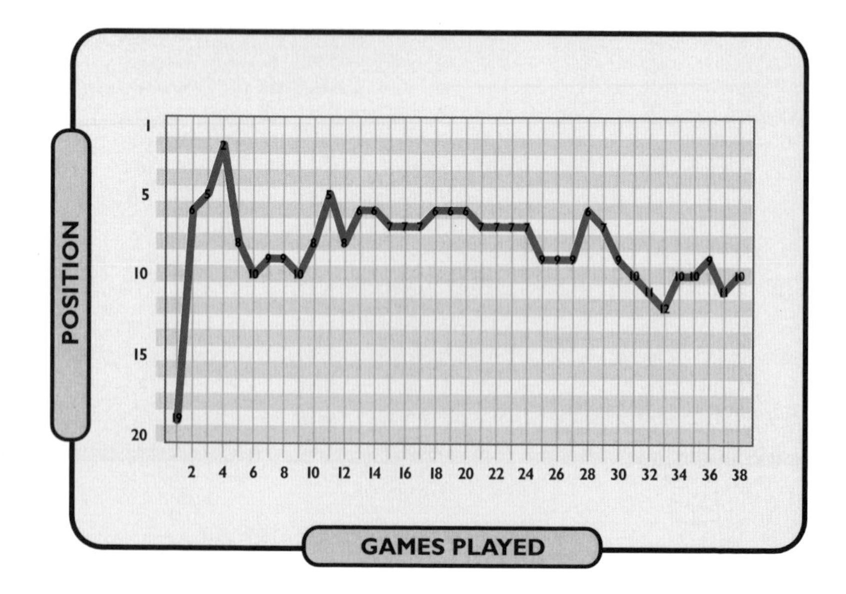

60% Spurs scored the highest ratio of

THE GOALS

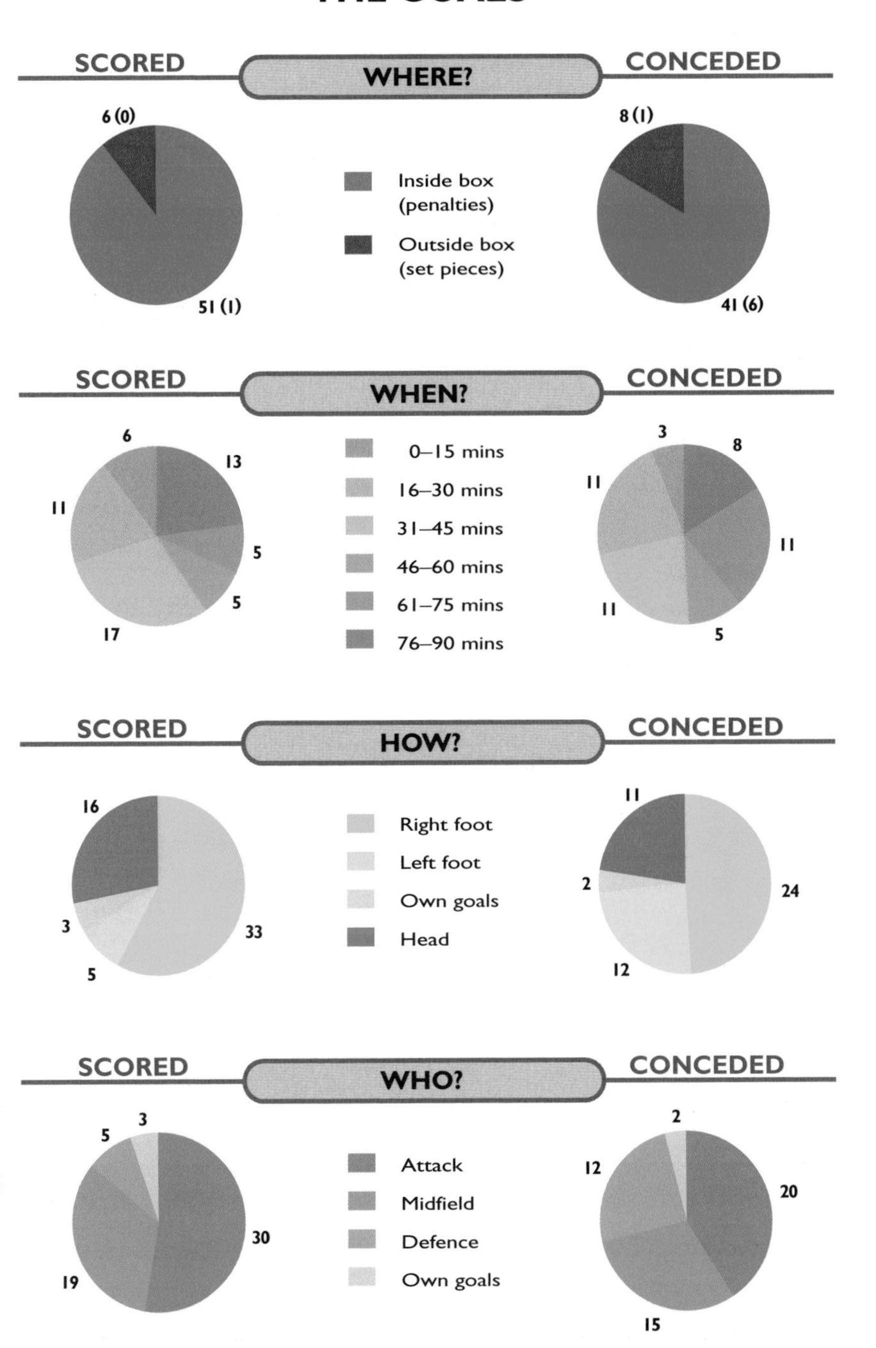

first-half goals in the 1999–2000 Premiership

TOTTENHAM HOTSPUR

	ANDERTON	ARMSTRONG	CAMPBELL	CARR	CLEMENCE	DAVIES	DOHERTY	DOMINGUEZ	EDINBURGH	ETHERINGTON	FERDINAND	FO
APPEARANCES												
Start	22	29	29	34	17	1	0	2	7	1	5	1
Sub	0	2	0	0	3	2	2	10	1	4	4	2
Minutes on pitch	1971	2513	2530	3060	1521	147	64	364	638	149	448	98
GOAL ATTEMPTS												
Goals	3	14	0	3	1	0	0	0	0	0	2	0
Shots on target	18	30	5	7	4	1	1	1	2	0	6	1
Shots off target	25	40	8	13	3	1	1	0	2	1	7	1
Shooting accuracy	42%	43%	38%	35%	57%	50%	50%	100%	50%	0%	46%	50%
PASSING												
Goal assists	6	1	3	3	1	0	0	0	0	1	0	0
Long passes	287	54	222	436	153	15	1	10	50	8	4	5
Short passes	855	639	550	1032	571	34	16	86	142	48	194	29
PASS COMPLETION												
Own half %	78%	79%	76%	75%	78%	93%	67%	80%	75%	65%	89%	82%
Opposition half %	67%	54%	55%	66%	69%	77%	45%	68%	66%	69%	71%	55%
CROSSING												
Total crosses	139	38	7	84	53	3	1	23	12	8	1	6
Cross completion %	36%	29%	57%	24%	25%	33%	0%	17%	25%	13%	0%	50%
DRIBBLING												
Dribbles & runs	60	82	43	161	42	5	0	65	12	12	12	5
Dribble completion %	80%	65%	91%	82%	88%	100%	0%	57%	92%	67%	42%	100%
DEFENDING												
Tackles made	75	28	123	90	57	2	1	11	28	5	13	1
Tackles won %	44%	39%	60%	49%	47%	50%	0%	27%	39%	20%	31%	100%
Blocks	7	4	83	52	15	2	0	0	7	0	0	0
Clearances	18	10	328	213	31	4	1	1	46	0	6	2
Interceptions	16	6	61	61	19	0	0	4	10	0	5	0
DISCIPLINE												
Fouls	40	138	54	36	37	1	5	9	15	1	15	1
Offside	3	66	2	4	0	0	0	4	0	0	3	0
Yellow cards	5	4	6	5	5	0	0	0	3	0	3	1
Red cards	0	0	0	0	0	0	0	0	0	0	0	0

GOALKEEPER NAME	START/ (SUB)	TIME ON PITCH	GOALS CONCEDED	MINS/GOALS CONCEDED	SAVES MADE	SAVES/ SHOTS
WALKER	38	3420	49	70	113	70%

PLAYERS' STATISTICS

FREUND	GINOLA	IVERSEN	KING	KORSTEN	LEONHARDSEN	MCEWAN	NIELSEN	PERRY	PIERCY	SCALES	SHERWOOD	TARICCO	VEGA	YOUNG	TOTAL	RANK
24	36	36	2	4	20	0	5	36	1	3	23	29	2	11		
3	0	0	1	5	2	1	9	1	2	1	4	0	3	9		
2158	2880	3085	186	372	1791	20	545	3224	61	333	2128	2515	225	1173		
0	3	14	0	0	4	0	0	1	0	0	8	0	1	0	57*	=6th
6	28	48	1	3	15	0	1	4	0	0	17	4	2	0	205	6th
7	43	46	2	3	9	3	3	10	1	1	11	3	0	4	248	4th
46%	39%	51%	33%	50%	63%	0%	25%	29%	0%	0%	61%	57%	100%	0%	45%	13th
1	8	7	0	0	1	0	1	0	0	0	0	5	1	0	39	=8th
118	276	84	11	27	79	1	41	215	2	13	213	276	11	80	2692	19th
702	1016	1016	51	118	653	5	180	530	18	76	848	789	42	277	10517	10th
80%	82%	74%	58%	69%	77%	100%	71%	80%	80%	75%	84%	74%	77%	78%	78%	15th
72%	64%	61%	73%	53%	69%	100%	61%	60%	62%	71%	70%	70%	41%	63%	65%	7th
22	229	14	1	11	46	0	10	9	0	0	19	42	5	11	794	9th
36%	31%	21%	0%	18%	30%	0%	50%	33%	0%	0%	37%	24%	40%	18%	30%	10th
32	415	87	4	10	86	0	24	38	4	1	37	71	7	47	1368	3rd
81%	70%	76%	75%	90%	83%	0%	83%	100%	25%	100%	92%	92%	86%	72%	77%	11th
78	45	38	5	9	86	0	32	145	1	6	86	92	10	41	1109	1st
55%	42%	45%	40%	67%	55%	0%	53%	52%	0%	50%	51%	41%	70%	51%	50%	18th
25	3	16	2	1	5	0	2	85	0	10	19	36	6	14	394	10th
43	4	41	8	1	17	0	12	387	0	59	64	163	37	106	1625	9th
25	13	18	6	0	26	0	12	68	0	7	33	38	2	19	452	1st
29	38	50	0	6	45	0	8	37	3	6	40	43	6	11	546	10th
2	6	22	0	0	7	0	1	0	2	0	4	1	3	0	130	10th
9	3	5	0	1	3	0	2	8	0	0	9	10	0	2	85	2nd
0	0	0	0	0	0	0	1	0	0	0	0	0	0	0	1	=17th

*Including three own goals

ROSSES AUGHT	CROSSES PUNCHED	CROSSES NOT CLAIMED	CATCH SUCCESS	THROWS/ SHORT KICKS	% COMPLETION	LONG KICKS	% COMPLETION
70	9	7	91%	152	91%	1363	42%

PLAYER OF THE SEASON

PLAYER	INDEX SCORE
SOL CAMPBELL	1,034
Stephen Carr	1,004
Tim Sherwood	977
Darren Anderton	946
David Ginola	911
Steffen Iversen	906
Chris Perry	904
Mauricio Taricco	861
Steffen Freund	671
Ian Walker	629

George Graham's sides have a reputation for being built around a strong defence, so the Spurs boss will be happy to see England centre-back Sol Campbell leading the way in the 1999–2000 Opta Season Index for Tottenham Hotspur.

Despite an average campaign for the White Hart Lane outfit, the big centre-back proved himself to be one of the country's best defenders with an Index score of 1,034. He won an above-average 60% of his tackles and made the second-highest number of interceptions in the whole Premiership in 1999–2000.

The defender, who was a product of the Tottenham youth team, also made three goals in the league last season, although he failed to hit the back of the net himself from his 13 attempts at goal.

Another defender, Stephen Carr, closely followed Campbell in the Index with 1,004 points. The Republic of Ireland full-back ended the season with a spectacular strike against Sunderland for his third goal of the campaign. He also made 90 tackles and 230 clearances as he enhanced his reputation as one of the best right-backs in the division.

The presence of Tim Sherwood in the centre of midfield was sorely missed in the latter part of the season, as the former Blackburn man had been enjoying a promising campaign. He notched up eight goals and weighed in with 86 challenges before succumbing to injury.

Wingers Darren Anderton and David Ginola also scored highly and, along with Norwegian Steffen Iversen, posed the greatest attacking threat for Spurs. Ginola made more successful dribbles and runs than any other player in the Premiership while Iversen attempted the third-highest number of shots in the league with 94 attempts at goal.

But it was the defensive-minded players, on the whole, who dominated for Spurs, with Chris Perry, Mauricio Taricco, Steffen Freund and 'keeper Ian Walker all featuring in the top 10.

75 Chris Perry won more tackles than

FIVE OF THE BEST

After their Worthington Cup triumph in 1998–99, Tottenham failed to build on the early success George Graham had brought to White Hart Lane. Spurs' European adventure ended prematurely and excellent wins, like the 3–1 victory over Manchester United, were all too often followed up with disappointing defeats.

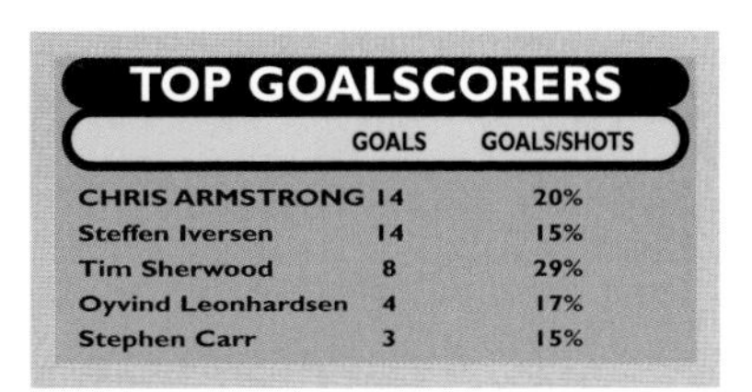

TOP GOALSCORERS

	GOALS	GOALS/SHOTS
CHRIS ARMSTRONG	14	20%
Steffen Iversen	14	15%
Tim Sherwood	8	29%
Oyvind Leonhardsen	4	17%
Stephen Carr	3	15%

Tottenham's lambasted attacking partnership of Chris Armstrong and Steffen Iversen silenced one or two critics in 1999–2000 by accruing 14 goals apiece come the end of the campaign. In Iversen's case it could have been a few more, with only Harry Kewell and Kevin Phillips having more shots than the Norwegian during the Premiership season. Tim Sherwood was Spurs' third highest scorer, netting eight goals from his midfield berth, while defender Stephen Carr scored three times, including a pair of real scorchers.

Stephen Carr looks like being the latest in a long line of top-quality Irish full-backs. Despite his tender years, Carr was always looking to get involved in the action and made more successful passes (1,012) than any other Tottenham player. But England international Tim Sherwood was the most accurate passer for the north London side. He found a team-mate with 74% of his distribution, while David Ginola's pass completion rate was a disappointingly low 67% – a drop of two percentage points from 1998–99.

TOP PASSERS

	SUCC PASSES	COMPLETION
STEPHEN CARR	1,012	69%
David Ginola	871	67%
Darren Anderton	794	70%
Tim Sherwood	790	74%
Mauricio Taricco	758	71%

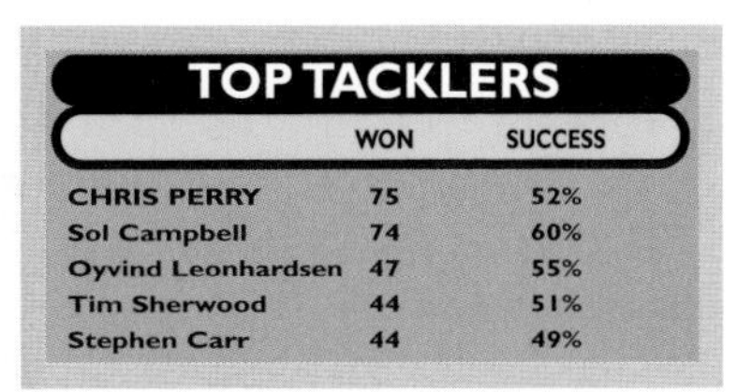

TOP TACKLERS

	WON	SUCCESS
CHRIS PERRY	75	52%
Sol Campbell	74	60%
Oyvind Leonhardsen	47	55%
Tim Sherwood	44	51%
Stephen Carr	44	49%

Former Wimbledon man Chris Perry was not put off his game by the brighter lights of Tottenham and enjoyed an excellent first season for the Lilywhites. He was top tackler at the Lane, winning 75 challenges in the Premiership, one more than his defensive partner Sol Campbell. But Spurs' big skipper could boast the best tackling success ratio of any regular defender at the club, winning 60% of his meaty challenges. Midfielder Oyvind Leonhardsen won 47 tackles – not bad considering the number of games he missed.

Under the management of George Graham, Tottenham were never going to be anything but competitive, but their disciplinary record was very impressive all the same. The Opta points system marks out striker Chris Armstrong as Spurs' dirtiest player, but he was booked just four times and the 72 fouls he conceded were the result of the Premiership's hurly-burly nature as opposed to anything malicious. Argentinean full-back Mauricio Taricco was the only Spurs man to reach double figures in bookings.

DISCIPLINE

	POINTS	FOULS & CARDS
CHRIS ARMSTRONG	84	72F, 4Y, 0R
Mauricio Taricco	72	42F, 10Y, 0R
Sol Campbell	70	52F, 6Y, 0R
Tim Sherwood	63	36F, 9Y, 0R
Chris Perry	61	37F, 8Y, 0R

any other Premiership defender

ACTION	CAMPBELL	CARR	FOX	FREUND	GINOLA	IVERSEN	LEONHARDSEN	PIERCY	SHERWOOD	TARICCO	VEGA	WALKER	YOUNG	TOTAL	MAN UTD
Time on pitch	90	90	87	90	90	90	90	3	90	90	15	90	75	990	990
GOALS															
Goal	–	1	–	–	–	1	–	–	–	–	–	–	–	2	1
Shot on target	–	–	1	–	1	–	1	–	–	–	–	–	–	3	6
Shot off target	–	–	1	–	1	2	2	–	–	–	–	–	–	6	4
Blocked shot	–	–	–	1	1	1	–	–	1	–	–	–	–	4	7
Own goal	–	–	–	–	–	–	–	–	–	–	–	–	–	–	1
PASSES															
Pass to own player	11	19	17	23	16	16	28	1	39	25	3	–	10	208	493
Pass to opposition	9	12	12	11	21	13	10	–	7	12	1	–	3	111	130
Cross to own player	1	–	2	–	–	–	1	–	–	–	–	–	–	4	6
Cross to opposition player	–	–	3	–	5	–	2	–	–	–	–	–	–	10	15
Goal assist	–	–	–	–	–	–	–	–	–	–	–	–	–	–	1
Pass completion %	57%	61%	56%	68%	38%	55%	71%	100%	85%	68%	75%	0%	77%	64%	78%
TACKLES & CLEARANCES															
Tackle	4	2	–	6	1	–	4	–	1	3	1	–	2	24	27
Clearances, blocks and interceptions	21	7	1	3	–	3	2	–	3	6	8	2	13	69	41
DRIBBLES & RUNS															
Dribble ball retained	1	2	4	2	19	2	5	1	5	3	1	–	1	46	45
Dribble ball lost	–	–	–	–	1	–	–	–	–	–	–	–	–	1	2
Dribble success %	100%	100%	100%	100%	95%	100%	100%	100%	100%	100%	100%	0%	100%	98%	96%
DISCIPLINE															
Fouls	2	–	1	2	1	–	1	–	3	1	–	–	–	11	12
Penalty conceded	–	–	–	–	–	–	–	–	–	–	–	–	–	–	–
Free kick – offside	–	–	–	–	–	1	–	–	1	–	–	–	–	2	1
Yellow cards	–	–	1	1	–	–	–	–	1	–	–	–	–	3	2
Red cards	–	–	–	–	–	–	–	–	–	–	–	–	–	–	–
GOALKEEPERS															
Distribution to own player	–	–	–	–	–	–	–	–	–	–	–	17	–	17	34
Distribution to opposition player	–	–	–	–	–	–	–	–	–	–	–	23	–	23	6
Goalkeeper distribution %	0%	0%	0%	0%	0%	0%	0%	0%	0%	0%	0%	43%	0%	43%	85%
Save	–	–	–	–	–	–	–	–	–	–	–	6	–	6	3
Ball caught	–	–	–	–	–	–	–	–	–	–	–	2	–	2	2
Ball dropped	–	–	–	–	–	–	–	–	–	–	–	–	–	–	–
Goal conceded	–	–	–	–	–	–	–	–	–	–	–	1	–	1	3

1,109 Tottenham attempted more tackles

Manchester United travelled to north London as champions of Europe and the Premiership and on the back of their best-ever start to a league campaign under Alex Ferguson. But Tottenham fought the Red Devils from start to finish and snatched all three points with a 3–1 win at a waterlogged White Hart Lane.

23 October 1999
3–1
TOTTENHAM HOTSPUR
vs.
MANCHESTER UNITED

However, during the opening exchanges, it was United who looked the more likely winners. They were rewarded for their pressure in the 23rd minute when Cole threaded an incisive through-ball to Ryan Giggs. The Welsh international eluded both Sol Campbell and Luke Young before deftly chipping the onrushing Ian Walker to open the scoring.

Spurs did not allow their heads to drop, though, and started to create some scoring opportunities with their skilful approach play. David Ginola did not disappoint in the 1999–2000 clash, being successful with 19 of the 20 dribbles and runs that he embarked upon.

But it was through good fortune rather than Gallic genius that George Graham's team eventually found their way back into the game on 37 minutes. A Mickael Silvestre error led to a corner, and Oyvind Leonhardsen's swerving centre found Tim Sherwood, whose flick landed in the path of Steffen Iversen. There was a suspicion of handball as the Norwegian international struck the post with his first shot, before he bundled the ball into the back of the net with his second attempt.

And if Spurs were somewhat lucky on that occasion, they could count themselves doubly fortunate two minutes later. Ginola threaded an intricate pass into the path of Iversen, but saw Silvestre cut it out to concede another corner. This time former Newcastle winger whipped in a powerful cross that Paul Scholes headed into his own net, under pressure from Young, to give Spurs a 2–1 half-time lead that had seemed highly unlikely just minutes before.

Over the 90 minutes, Ferguson's side completed a staggering 493 passes – 285 more than Spurs – but were simply unable to make their possession count. Tottenham, of course, must take great credit for halting the attacking might of the Red Devils. The Lilywhites won 46% of their challenges and took advantage of the wet conditions to turn the game into a midfield melee.

And as the pitch became increasingly unplayable, tempers began to fray. Referee Jeff Winter gave second-half bookings to Tim Sherwood, Roy Keane, Steffen Freund and David Beckham.

Spurs wrapped up their win in the 71st minute with a blockbusting shot from Stephen Carr. The Republic of Ireland international latched on to the ball on the half-way line and proceeded to speed up the right wing. And, as Phil Neville back-pedalled away from him, the Tottenham defender fired an unstoppable shot that flew past Mark Bosnich to send the White Hart Lane crowd wild with delight and seal a famous victory. Carr was Tottenham's man of the match, scoring from his one attempt on goal, completing 61% of his passes and winning both his challenges to end up with an Opta Index score of 1,175.

than any other team in the Premiership

phones
4u

WATFORD

ADDRESS

Vicarage Road Stadium,
Watford WD1 8ER

CONTACT NUMBERS

Telephone: 01923 496000
Fax: 01923 496001
Ticket Office: 01923 496010
Ticket Office Fax: 01923 351145
Club Call: 09068 104104
Hornet Shop: 01923 496005
Hornet Shop Fax: 01923 496238
Website: www.watfordfc.com

KEY PERSONNEL

Chairman: Sir E John CBE
Vice-Chairman: H Oundjian
Directors: B Anderson, D Lester
C Lissack, D Meller, C Norton, T Shaw
M Sherwood, G Simpson, N Wray
Club Secretary: J Alexander
Manager: Graham Taylor

SPONSORS

Phones 4 U

FANZINES

Clap Your Hands, Stamp Your Feet
The Horn

COLOURS

Home: Yellow shirt with red sleeves and black collar and cuffs, red shorts with yellow tops and two black hoops
Away: Blue and silver striped shirts with red pinstripes, blue shorts and blue stockings with red tops and two black hoops

NICKNAME

The Hornets

HONOURS

Division Two Champions: 1997–98
Division Three Champions: 1968–69
Division Four Champions: 1977–78

RECORD GOALSCORER

Luther Blissett – 148 league goals
1976–83, 1984–88, 1991–92

BIGGEST WIN

8–0 v Sunderland – Division One,
25 September 1982

BIGGEST DEFEAT

0–10 v Wolverhampton Wanderers –
FA Cup 1st Round Replay,
24 January 1912

SEASON REVIEW

Watford started the 1999–2000 season as favourites for the Premiership "wooden spoon" and, despite some spirited displays, they rarely looked like proving the bookmakers wrong.

Graham Taylor was realistic about the task facing his team from the start, but the former England boss was also determined not to ruin Watford's long-term future by bankrupting the club in a vain attempt to secure top-flight football.

Unfortunately the gulf in class between Watford and the rest of the Premiership was immediately apparent. Wimbledon did not achieve their 3–2 victory at Vicarage Road on the opening day without a fight, but they still had too much in their locker for the Hornets, who became the first and last team to lose at home to the Dons all season.

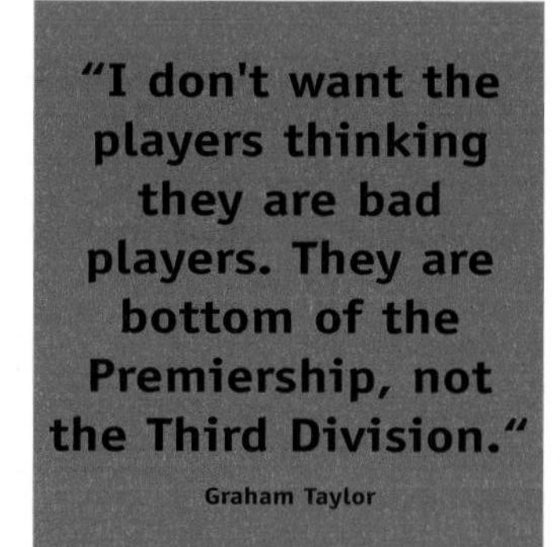

"I don't want the players thinking they are bad players. They are bottom of the Premiership, not the Third Division."
Graham Taylor

Defeat at Sunderland's Stadium of Light three days later, courtesy of two goals by Watford old boy Kevin Phillips, confirmed the suspicion that Watford were in for a long, hard season.

The players, though, were determined to prove their critics wrong and pulled off one of the shocks of the season in their next game, as Tommy Mooney scored an unlikely winner to give the Hornets a fantastic 1–0 win against Liverpool. That result gave Graham Taylor his first victory at Anfield in 22 years of management.

When Mooney struck again a week later to earn another 1–0 win, this time against Bradford, Watford moved up to ninth place in the Premiership. That game was followed by three 1–0 defeats, though, and Watford began to slide.

Taylor reacted by moving into the transfer market. His first signing, Nordin Wooter, cost £950,000 – a fee that broke the club's long-standing transfer record, but was still cheap by Premiership standards – while his second, Charlie Miller cost just £450,000 from Rangers.

Wooter made an immediate impact, playing a major part in the build-up to Allan Smart's goal in the 1–0 victory over Chelsea, but despite some bright displays was rarely as effective again.

After beating Wigan on away goals in the second round of the Worthington Cup, Watford's interest in the competition came to an end with a 1–0 defeat at Middlesbrough. Events also took a turn for the worse in the Premiership.

After two months in which Watford had lost plenty of games but never been hammered, the floodgates began to creak open. Predictably, the visit to free-scoring Premiership favourites Manchester United proved to be the catalyst.

Even without playing well, United put four past the Hornets, with Mark Williams's dismissal for a rash foul merely compounding the visitors' misery.

Things got worse, though. A week later Middlesbrough romped to a 3–1 win at Vicarage Road, teenage striker Tommy Smith providing Watford fans with their only bright moment, scoring with a fantastic strike.

Taylor remained calm, reassuring fans that signings would be made, but stressing once again that he was not prepared to bankrupt the club or break its carefully-weighted wage structure.

It was clear to everyone connected with the club, however, that drastic action would be needed for the club to escape relegation. Watford's first-choice XI was already the weakest in the Premiership, but the lack of quality in reserve was even more worrying.

Nowhere was this better illustrated than in Watford's game against Coventry at the

SEASON REVIEW

end of October. With injuries to five key players, including Mooney and Smart, Taylor was forced to promote untried youngsters to the first team. They proved too raw to contain the Sky Blues, who romped to an easy 4–0 victory. That result left Watford in 19th place – and from there the only way was down.

Taylor moved to sign two more players before the end of the year, Neil Cox and Xavier Gravelaine, but neither man was able to arrest the Hornets' slide. The team did pick up points against Sheffield Wednesday and versus Newcastle, but those results were offset by an FA Cup exit at the hands of Birmingham City and heavy defeats by the likes of Wimbledon, Everton and Tottenham.

The team finally picked up another win on 28 December when Southampton were defeated 3–2 at Vicarage Road. That result left them just three points off the safety zone, but hopes of a great escape were quickly dashed when Branko Strupar swooped to score the first Premiership goal of the Millennium after just two minutes in a 2–0 defeat by Derby that left Watford five points behind the Rams.

"This club has never just been about winning, winning, winning."
Graham Taylor

Taylor blamed injuries for his team's poor start to the year 2000 which saw them lose their first four games and slump to the foot of the Premiership table, but even the return of several first-teamers made little difference.

Watford reacted by breaking their transfer record for the second time in the campaign to bring Lillestrom's promising striker Heidar Helguson to Vicarage Road. Helguson proved an instant success, scoring twice in his first two games for the club, although both strikes were consolations in 3–2 defeats.

In an attempt to bring some solidity to the team's defence, efforts were made to sign the experienced German international Lothar Matthaeus. Unfortunately the former World Cup winner chose New York over Hertfordshire, opting for the Metro Stars rather than Watford.

After a 2–0 defeat at Southampton which left his team 12 points from safety with just five games left to play, Taylor admitted publicly that his team were as good as relegated; a fact that was confirmed a week later when Bradford grabbed a shock 1–0 win at Sunderland to put themselves out of the Hornets' reach in 17th place.

The club accepted relegation with the good grace that had marked their entire season. No team scored fewer or conceded more goals than Watford, but few sides put in as much hard work as the Hornets.

The team were clearly not good enough to compete at the highest level, collectively registering the lowest tackle success rate, the worst goals-to-shots ratio and fewer passes than any other team bar Wimbledon and Bradford.

But the club returns to Division One with its finances still intact, a sensible wage structure and some promising young players. With a prudent manager in Graham Taylor at the helm, Watford are well-placed for another tilt at promotion in 2000–01.

If they do return to the Premiership, Watford can expect to struggle again. Taylor has publicly stated that he would be happy for them to become a "yo-yo club", and it is difficult to disagree with him.

Watford's fans certainly seem content with the progress their team have made under Taylor in his second spell in charge at the club and, like their optimistic manager, they will start life back in Division One in a positive frame of mind.

for the fewest points earned in a season

WATFORD

DATE	OPPONENT	SCORE	ATT.	BAKALLI	BONNOT	BROOKER	CHAMBERLAIN	COX	DAY	EASTON	FOLEY	GIBBS	GRAVELAINE	GUDMUN	H
7.8.99	Wimbledon H	2–3	15,511	–	90	s5	–	–	90	90	–	–	–	–	–
10.8.99	Sunderland A	0–2	40,630	–	76	–	–	–	90	90□	–	–	–	s14	–
14.8.99	Liverpool A	1–0	44,174	–	–	–	–	–	90	s38	s21	–	–	–	–
21.8.99	Bradford H	1–0	15,564	–	–	–	–	–	90	90	s12	–	–	–	–
24.8.99	Aston Villa H	0–1	19,161	–	s13	–	–	–	90	77	s13	–	–	s13	–
30.8.99	Leicester A	0–1	17,920	s19	–	–	–	–	90	71□	–	–	–	s19	–
11.9.99	West Ham A	0–1	25,310	–	–	–	90	–	–	–	–	–	–	s22□	–
18.9.99	Chelsea H	1–0	21,244	–	–	–	90	–	–	90	–	90	–	–	–
25.9.99	Arsenal A	0–1	38,127	–	–	–	90	–	–	s2	88	90	–	–	–
3.10.99	Leeds Utd H	1–2	19,677	–	–	–	90	–	–	s10	70	s45	–	–	–
16.10.99	Man Utd A	1–4	55,188	–	–	–	90	–	–	–	–	90	–	–	–
24.10.99	Middlesbro H	1–3	16,081	–	–	–	90	–	–	s15	–	90	–	–	–
31.10.99	Coventry A	0–4	21,700	–	–	–	90	–	–	90	–	90	–	s18	–
6.11.99	Sheff Wed A	2–2	21,658	–	–	–	90	90	–	90	–	s26	–	–	–
20.11.99	Newcastle H	1–1	19,539	s46	–	–	90	90	–	44	–	–	90	–	–
27.11.99	Sunderland H	2–3	21,590	–	–	–	90	90	–	–	–	s45	89■	–	–
4.12.99	Wimbledon A	0–5	14,021	–	–	–	90	90□	–	–	–	–	90	–	–
18.12.99	Everton H	1–3	17,346	–	–	–	90	90■	–	–	s2	–	–	–	–
26.12.99	Tottenham A	0–4	36,089	–	–	–	90	90	–	–	s45	–	–	s45	–
28.12.99	Southampton H	3–2	18,459	–	–	–	90	90	–	–	s23	s6	78[2]□	84	–
3.1.00	Derby Co A	0–2	28,072	–	–	–	90	–	–	–	s17	90	90	–	–
15.1.00	Liverpool H	2–3	21,367	–	s1	–	90	–	–	–	–	90	90	–	80
22.1.00	Bradford A	2–3	16,864	–	s22	–	90	90	–	–	–	–	90	–	90
5.2.00	Aston Villa A	0–4	27,647	–	90	–	–	64	90	45	–	90	–	–	9
12.2.00	Leicester H	1–1	16,814	–	90□	–	–	–	90	–	–	90	–	–	84
26.2.00	Chelsea A	1–2	34,928	–	87	–	90	–	–	–	–	90	–	–	90
4.3.00	West Ham H	1–2	18,619	–	45	–	90	s45	–	–	–	45	–	–	90[1]
11.3.00	Newcastle A	0–1	36,433	–	s3	–	90	90	–	–	–	–	–	–	9
18.3.00	Sheff Wed H	1–0	15,840	–	–	–	90	90	–	–	–	–	–	–	6
25.3.00	Tottenham H	1–1	20,050	–	–	–	90	90	–	–	–	–	–	–	66
1.4.00	Everton A	2–4	31,960	–	–	–	90	90	–	90	–	–	–	–	–
8.4.00	Derby Co H	0–0	16,579	–	s17	–	90	90	–	73	–	–	–	–	s25
15.4.00	Southampton A	0–2	15,252	–	–	–	90	73	–	90	–	–	–	s17	s4
23.4.00	Arsenal H	2–3	19,670	–	–	–	90	90	–	–	–	–	–	s18	90[1]
29.4.00	Man Utd H	2–3	20,250	–	–	–	90	84	–	–	45	s6	–	–	87
3.5.00	Leeds Utd A	1–3	36,324	–	–	–	–	90	90	–	66[1]	–	–	–	66
6.5.00	Middlesbro A	1–1	32,930	–	–	–	–	90	90	–	45	–	–	–	9
14.5.00	Coventry H	1–0	18,977	–	90	–	–	51	90	–	–	s39	–	–	90

□ Yellow card, ■ Red card, s Substitute, 90[1] Goals scored

*including one own goal

1999–2000 PREMIERSHIP APPEARANCES

HYDE	JOHNSON	KENNEDY	LYTTLE	MILLER	MOONEY	NGONGE	NOEL-WILLIAMS	PAGE	PALMER	PANAYI	PERPETUINI	ROBINSON	SMART	SMITH	WARD	WILLIAMS	WOOTER	WRIGHT	TOTAL
–	90	90[1]	90	–	90	90[1]	–	45	90	–	–	–	–	s40	–	90	–	–	990
–	90□	90	90	–	90	90□	–	90	90	–	–	–	–	–	–	90	–	–	990
90	52	90	90	–	90[1]□	69	–	90□	90	–	–	90	–	–	–	90□	–	–	990
90	–	90	90	–	90[1]	78	–	90	90	–	–	90□	–	–	–	90□	–	–	990
77	–	90	90	–	90	77	–	90	90	–	–	90	–	–	–	90□	–	–	990
90□	–	90□	90	–	90	71	–	90	90	–	–	90	–	–	–	90	–	–	990
90	–	90	90	–	90□	s22	–	90	90	–	–	90	68	–	–	90	–	68	990
90□	–	90	–	–	s6	s4	–	90□	90	–	–	90	80[1]	–	–	90	65	s25	990
90	–	90□	–	–	–	s36	–	90□	90	–	–	90□	54	–	–	90□	85	s5	990
90	–	80	45	s20	–	90	–	90□	90	–	–	90□	–	–	–	90[1]	90	–	990
45	90[1]	90□	–	s30□	–	60	–	90□	83	–	–	90□	–	s7	–	88■	90	s45	988
90	90	–	–	90	–	–	–	90	90	–	–	90	–	75[1]	–	90□	90	–	990
90	90	–	90	45	–	s45	–	–	90	45	–	–	–	72	s45	–	90	–	990
90	90	–	–	90	–	82[1]	s49	90[1]	90	64	–	–	–	s8	–	–	41	–	990
90	–	–	–	90	–	63[1]	90□	90□	90	–	–	90	–	–	–	–	s27	–	990
s11	90[1]	–	–	45□	–	79[1]	s11	90	90	–	–	90	–	–	–	90□	79	–	989
90	79	–	–	–	–	90	–	90	90	–	–	90	–	–	–	90□	90	–	990
88	90□	–	–	90□	–	90[1]	–	90	90	–	–	90□	–	90	–	90	–	–	990
90□	90	–	–	s45	–	45	–	90	90	–	45□	90	–	90	–	45	–	–	990
90□	90	–	–	–	–	67	–	90	90	–	90[1]□	90□	–	s12□	–	–	–	–	990
90	90	–	–	73	–	73	–	90□	90	–	90	90	–	s17	–	–	–	–	990
–	89[1]□	–	84	90	–	s10	–	90	90	–	90	90	–	s6	–	–	–	–	990
90[1]	–	–	90□	68	–	–	–	90	90	–	68	90	–	s22	–	–	–	–	990
90	–	s45	–	–	–	–	–	90□	90	–	–	90□	s45	45	–	–	s26	–	990
90	–	84	–	–	–	s6	–	90	90	–	–	s6	90	–	–	90	90[1]	–	990
90□	–	90	–	s3	–	s10	–	90	90	–	–	–	90[1]	–	–	90	80	–	990
90	s45	90□	–	–	–	–	–	90□	90	–	–	s45	90	–	–	45	90	–	990
90	87	90	–	–	–	–	–	90	90	–	–	90	90	–	–	s12	78	–	990
90	90	90	–	–	–	–	–	90□	90	–	–	90	90[1]	s21	–	–	90	–	990
90	90□	66	–	–	–	–	–	74	90	–	s24	90□	90[1]	s24	–	s16□	90	–	990
90[1]□	90	–	–	s45	–	–	–	–	90	–	–	90	90[1]	90	s45	45	45	–	990
90	90	–	–	–	–	–	–	90□	90	–	90	–	65	90	90	–	–	–	990
90	90	–	–	–	–	–	–	90	90	–	73	s17	45□	90	90	–	–	–	990
90[1]	s3	–	–	–	–	–	–	90□	90	–	87	90	72	90	90	–	–	–	990
64■	s3	–	–	–	s45	–	–	90	90	–	90□	90	–	90[1]	90	–	–	–	964
90□	–	–	–	–	s24	–	–	90	90	–	90	90	–	90	90	–	s24	–	990
90	–	–	–	–	s45	–	–	90	90	–	45	90□	–	90	90[1]	–	s45	–	990
–	–	–	–	–	90	–	–	90	90	–	90□	90	–	90	90	–	–	–	990

THE MANAGER

GRAHAM TAYLOR

When Watford won promotion to the Premiership with a 2–0 win over Bolton at Wembley in May 1999, manager Graham Taylor knew it would be difficult to keep his team there for more than a season.

The Hornets may have been buzzing in Division One, but the Premiership proved too much for them, and despite wins against Chelsea at home and a fantastic 1–0 victory at Anfield against Liverpool, Watford finished bottom.

After beginning his playing career at Grimsby Town, Taylor moved on to Lincoln City where he remained as manager. He guided the Imps to the Fourth Division title in 1975–76 before moving to Vicarage Road for his first spell at Watford.

Taylor then moved to Aston Villa, and was appointed England manager in 1990. But after failing to qualify for the 1994 World Cup, he returned to club management with Wolves, before coming back to Watford in 1997.

Despite the disappointment of relegation, Taylor has been quick to point out that the club is in better shape now than ever before, and with money behind them and some promising young players coming through, a return to the top flight cannot be ruled out.

LEAGUE POSITION

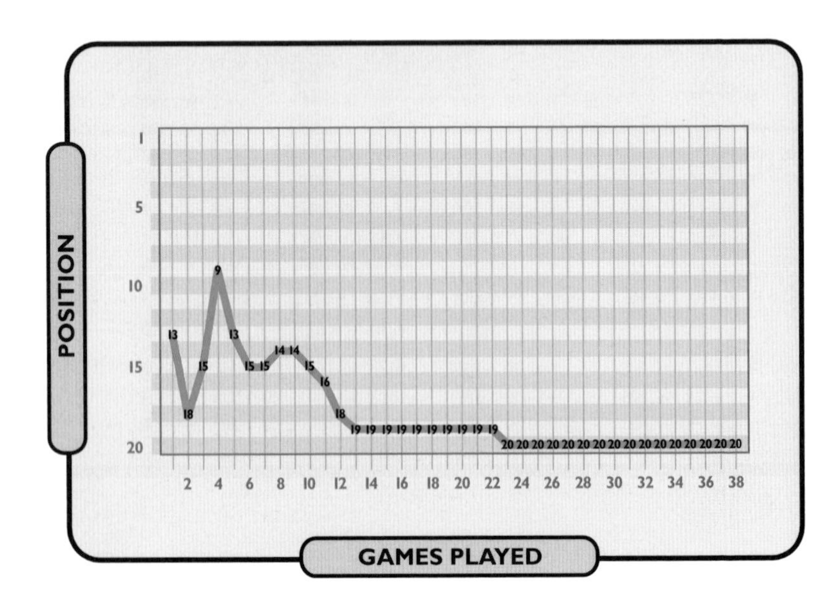

13 Watford conceded more goals from shots outside

THE GOALS

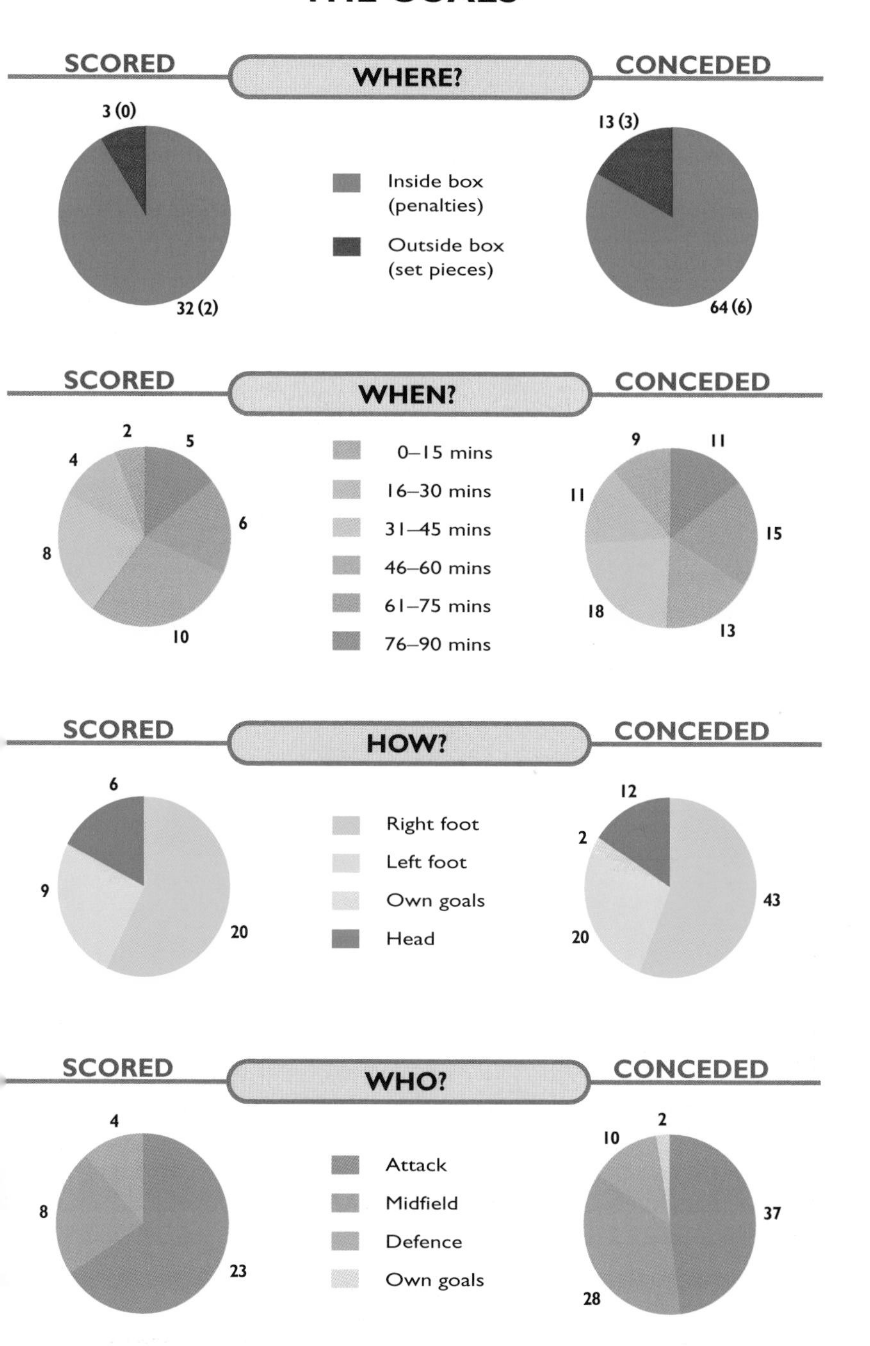

the area than any other Premiership side

WATFORD

	BAKALLI	BONNOT	BROOKER	COX	EASTON	FOLEY	GIBBS	GRAVELAINE	GUDMUNDSSON	HELGUSON	HYDE	JOHNSON	KEN
APPEARANCES													
Start	0	7	0	20	13	5	11	7	1	14	33	20	17
Sub	2	5	1	1	4	7	6	0	8	2	1	3	1
Minutes on pitch	65	624	5	1757	1095	447	1112	617	250	1242	2895	1798	1535
GOAL ATTEMPTS													
Goals	0	0	0	0	0	1	0	2	0	6	3	3	1
Shots on target	0	2	0	0	4	9	1	6	1	18	16	11	5
Shots off target	0	4	0	9	4	6	0	3	3	20	12	22	12
Shooting accuracy	0%	33%	0%	0%	50%	60%	100%	67%	25%	47%	57%	33%	29%
PASSING													
Goal assists	0	0	0	1	0	0	1	2	0	2	5	1	2
Long passes	5	62	0	272	89	17	134	32	14	40	299	248	151
Short passes	21	211	1	381	374	104	228	153	52	395	1007	616	393
PASS COMPLETION													
Own half %	80%	74%	0%	61%	77%	84%	67%	81%	73%	70%	79%	79%	69%
Opposition half %	50%	60%	100%	49%	59%	68%	57%	52%	57%	56%	65%	61%	53%
CROSSING													
Total crosses	1	10	0	72	46	2	33	16	2	8	79	23	98
Cross completion %	0%	20%	0%	28%	24%	50%	21%	19%	50%	38%	27%	43%	26%
DRIBBLING													
Dribbles & runs	1	15	1	25	24	7	10	21	10	21	94	37	41
Dribble completion %	100%	60%	100%	92%	92%	71%	90%	67%	60%	71%	80%	92%	85%
DEFENDING													
Tackles made	1	26	0	52	44	3	36	12	7	22	133	59	41
Tackles won %	100%	54%	0%	35%	43%	33%	61%	58%	43%	50%	44%	39%	39%
Blocks	1	3	0	57	10	1	21	1	0	2	24	21	14
Clearances	0	15	0	96	49	1	60	0	3	4	52	42	49
Interceptions	1	6	0	10	16	2	6	1	2	0	14	14	10
DISCIPLINE													
Fouls	2	11	0	18	15	16	7	25	4	38	44	24	17
Offside	0	0	0	0	1	3	0	15	2	16	1	0	2
Yellow cards	0	1	0	1	2	0	0	1	1	6	7	4	4
Red cards	0	0	0	1	0	0	0	1	0	0	1	0	0

GOALKEEPER NAME	START/ (SUB)	TIME ON PITCH	GOALS CONCEDED	MINS/GOALS CONCEDED	SAVES MADE	SAVES/ SHOTS
CHAMBERLAIN	27	2430	61	40	107	64%
DAY	11	990	16	62	33	67%

For more information visit our website:

PLAYERS' STATISTICS

LYTTLE	MILLER	MOONEY	NGONGE	NOEL-WILLIAMS	PAGE	PALMER	PANAYI	PERPETUINI	ROBINSON	SMART	SMITH	WARD	WILLIAMS	WOOTER	WRIGHT	TOTAL	RANK
11	9	8	16	1	36	38	2	12	29	13	13	7	20	16	1		
0	5	4	7	2	0	0	0	1	3	1	8	2	2	4	3		
939	824	840	1347	150	3179	3413	109	972	2678	1059	1249	720	1691	1405	143		
0	0	2	5	0	1	0	0	1	0	5	2	1	1	1	0	35	20th
2	4	12	18	2	4	4	0	4	3	17	14	1	3	11	1	173	12th
2	7	8	17	0	0	13	0	3	5	12	1	3	2	18	1	187	18th
50%	36%	60%	51%	100%	100%	24%	0%	57%	38%	59%	93%	25%	60%	38%	50%	48%	6th
0	1	1	0	1	2	0	0	1	1	1	3	1	0	1	0	27	=16th
87	79	17	25	5	447	300	9	66	393	30	30	56	126	43	2	3078	14th
204	230	204	373	56	586	608	12	223	626	305	373	127	241	424	41	8569	20th
79%	81%	81%	81%	33%	73%	70%	70%	68%	67%	84%	78%	61%	76%	75%	54%	73%	19th
48%	55%	56%	56%	63%	39%	54%	45%	57%	49%	52%	66%	45%	45%	62%	54%	55%	20th
27	12	9	22	1	19	24	0	48	54	16	25	1	6	47	1	702	=16th
41%	17%	0%	32%	0%	37%	33%	0%	10%	19%	25%	24%	0%	33%	28%	0%	25%	19th
16	34	12	64	11	22	23	1	16	54	16	71	2	6	116	8	779	20th
88%	74%	42%	75%	55%	91%	91%	100%	81%	91%	69%	72%	50%	83%	69%	25%	77%	10th
15	22	13	16	0	88	88	1	35	122	12	18	15	64	43	2	991	14th
67%	50%	54%	69%	0%	56%	53%	100%	37%	45%	58%	44%	27%	48%	44%	50%	47%	20th
10	5	2	5	0	94	65	3	15	67	3	0	24	45	4	0	497	3rd
82	11	2	13	0	421	213	16	21	157	5	4	71	251	10	0	1677	6th
12	4	1	5	0	19	13	3	5	21	1	6	2	12	4	0	191	17th
7	17	16	76	6	72	32	2	16	45	46	27	11	46	45	5	549	8th
3	3	6	28	0	1	0	0	1	1	20	20	0	0	18	0	141	7th
1	3	2	1	1	12	0	0	4	9	1	1	0	8	0	0	70	=6th
0	0	0	0	0	0	0	0	0	0	0	0	0	1	0	0	4	=5th

OSSES UGHT	CROSSES PUNCHED	CROSSES NOT CLAIMED	CATCH SUCCESS	THROWS/ SHORT KICKS	% COMPLETION	LONG KICKS	% COMPLETION
41	18	1	98%	59	78%	1091	37%
27	10	1	96%	25	84%	344	33%

PLAYER OF THE SEASON

PLAYER	INDEX SCORE
MICAH HYDE	**762**
Mark Williams	**718*****
Nordin Wooter	**692***
Richard Johnson	**670**
Robert Page	**667**
Paul Robinson	**659**
Neil Cox	**574*****
Peter Kennedy	**560****
Steve Palmer	**529**
Alec Chamberlain	**439**

All players played 75 minutes in at least 19 matches except those marked *who featured in just 13 games, ** who featured in 16 games and *** who featured in 17 games.

It was always going to be a tough season for Graham Taylor's Watford after their second successive promotion brought them back into the top flight. He had stuck with many of the players that had helped them get out of the Second Division and it was vital that they could raise themselves to be able to compete in the Premiership.

One player who did just this was Micah Hyde, who came top of the Opta Season Index for Watford with 762 points.

The midfielder, who joined the Hornets from Cambridge United, scored three and created five from midfield in his first season in the Premiership.

He was more than prepared to get stuck in, making 133 tackles, and attempting 1,306 passes as the Watford side often looked to him to provide a creative spark.

Northern Ireland international Mark Williams had the unenviable task of trying to plug the gaps in the Premiership's leakiest defence. He managed to make 251 clearances and 14 blocks, whic helped gain him an average of 718 points

Record signing Nordin Woote struggled to repay Watford's investmen in him, but recorded an average of 69 Opta points. The Dutch under-2 international scored one, made one an managed 29 shots for the Hornets.

Supporters' Player of the Seaso Robert Page picked up an average of 66 points thanks to the 421 clearances an 1,033 passes attempted as he tried i vain to keep Watford's heads above wate in the Premiership.

Fellow-defenders Paul Robinson, Nei Cox and Peter Kennedy all foun themselves in the firing line at the bac for the Hornets but were ranked in the to 10 Watford players of the season, whil 'keeper Alec Chamberlain just made it i with an average of 439 points.

He beat off competition from fello shot-stopper Chris Day to be the to 'keeper at Vicarage Road in a difficul season for the Hornets.

55% Watford's pass completion rat

FIVE OF THE BEST

After the whirlwind of consecutive promotions to the Premiership, the 1999–2000 season was always likely to be a struggle for Graham Taylor's Watford. One or two good early results gave cause for some optimism, but the Hornets dropped into the bottom three in October and failed to reappear in the safety zone.

TOP GOALSCORERS

	GOALS	GOALS/SHOTS
HEIDAR HELGUSON	6	16%
Allan Smart	5	17%
Michel Ngonge	5	14%
Micah Hyde	3	11%
Richard Johnson	3	9%

Icelandic striker Heidar Helguson started just 14 league games for Watford in 1999–2000, but still ended up as their top scorer in the Premiership with six goals. While that is a record to be proud of for Helguson, it is a pretty sad indictment of the Hornets' attacking prowess before the striker arrived from Lillestrom. Scotsman Allan Smart and Michel Ngonge were joint-second in the scoring chart with five apiece, despite the fact neither man was a regular starter for the Vicarage Road outfit.

Former Cambridge midfielder Micah Hyde's all-action style was certainly not out of place in the Premiership and 897 successful passes indicated his ability to stamp his mark on top-flight games. Of the players usually dictating Watford's play, Hyde had the highest pass completion ratio at 69%, his usual midfield partner Richard Johnson mustering 66%. Robert Page was the second most prolific player in terms of successful passes – he found a team-mate with 578.

TOP PASSERS

	SUCC PASSES	COMPLETION
MICAH HYDE	897	69%
Robert Page	578	56%
Paul Robinson	576	57%
Richard Johnson	568	66%
Steve Palmer	545	60%

TOP TACKLERS

	WON	SUCCESS
MICAH HYDE	59	44%
Paul Robinson	55	45%
Robert Page	49	56%
Steve Palmer	47	53%
Mark Williams	31	48%

As well as being Watford's best passer in 1999–2000, Micah Hyde also earned the accolade of top tackler and never gave up fighting for the cause, no matter how desperate the Hornets' situation became. The gritty midfield man won 59 challenges, retaining possession for his side in some vital positions. But centre-back Robert Page had the highest success ratio, winning 56% of the tackles he slid into, three percentage points ahead of veteran Steve Palmer.

Welsh international defender Robert Page may have been voted Watford's Player of the Year but he was never in contention for any fair play awards. The Watford skipper racked up 107 Opta disciplinary points, mainly the product of 12 yellow cards. Only Lee Bowyer and Derby's Seth Johnson picked up more bookings in the 1999–2000 Premiership season. Micah Hyde also made the top five, although he fell foul of one red card – dished out for his part in a late-season skirmish with Manchester United's Nicky Butt.

DISCIPLINE

	POINTS	FOULS & CARDS
ROBERT PAGE	107	71F, 12Y, 0R
Mark Williams	76	46F, 8Y, 1R
Paul Robinson	71	44F, 9Y, 0R
Micah Hyde	70	43F, 7Y, 1R
Michel Ngonge	51	48F, 1Y, 0R

was lower than any other side

ACTION	DAY	EASTON	FOLEY	HYDE	JOHNSON	KENNEDY	LYTTLE	MOONEY	NGONGE	PAGE	PALMER	ROBINSON	WILLIAMS	TOTAL	LIVERPOOL
Time on pitch	90	38	21	90	52	90	90	90	69	90	90	90	90	990	990
GOALS															
Goal	–	–	–	–	–	–	–	1	–	–	–	–	–	1	–
Shot on target	–	1	–	–	1	1	1	1	–	–	1	–	–	6	5
Shot off target	–	–	–	–	–	1	–	–	–	–	–	–	–	1	11
Blocked shot	–	–	–	1	–	–	–	–	1	–	–	–	–	2	6
Own goal	–	–	–	–	–	–	–	–	–	–	–	–	–	–	–
PASSES															
Pass to own player	–	6	4	9	17	16	5	10	5	6	8	10	10	106	331
Pass to opposition	–	2	2	13	10	15	11	15	17	3	10	5	2	105	131
Cross to own player	–	–	–	1	–	1	–	–	–	–	–	–	–	2	6
Cross to opposition player	–	–	–	–	1	2	–	–	2	–	–	–	–	5	17
Goal assist	–	–	–	–	–	–	–	–	–	1	–	–	–	1	–
Pass completion %	0%	75%	67%	43%	61%	50%	31%	40%	21%	70%	44%	67%	83%	50%	69%
TACKLES & CLEARANCES															
Tackle	–	1	2	4	3	3	1	2	1	3	1	7	5	33	25
Clearances, blocks and interceptions	3	4	1	4	5	4	19	1	–	29	12	15	17	114	75
DRIBBLES & RUNS															
Dribble ball retained	–	1	–	1	–	1	–	–	1	–	1	–	–	5	22
Dribble ball lost	–	–	–	–	–	–	–	–	1	–	–	–	–	1	2
Dribble success %	0%	100%	0%	100%	0%	100%	0%	0%	50%	0%	100%	0%	0%	83%	92%
DISCIPLINE															
Fouls	–	–	1	1	–	–	–	1	3	1	2	1	4	14	7
Penalty conceded	–	–	–	–	–	–	–	–	–	–	–	–	–	–	–
Free kick – offside	–	–	–	–	–	–	–	2	–	–	–	–	–	2	1
Yellow Cards	–	–	–	–	–	–	–	1	–	1	–	–	1	3	1
Red cards	–	–	–	–	–	–	–	–	–	–	–	–	–	–	–
GOALKEEPERS															
Distribution to own player	12	–	–	–	–	–	–	–	–	–	–	–	–	12	17
Distribution to opposition player	29	–	–	–	–	–	–	–	–	–	–	–	–	29	12
Goalkeeper distribution %	29%	0%	0%	0%	0%	0%	0%	0%	0%	0%	0%	0%	0%	29%	59%
Save	5	–	–	–	–	–	–	–	–	–	–	–	–	5	6
Ball caught	4	–	–	–	–	–	–	–	–	–	–	–	–	4	2
Ball dropped	–	–	–	–	–	–	–	–	–	–	–	–	–	–	–
Goal conceded	–	–	–	–	–	–	–	–	–	–	–	–	–	–	1

4 Robert Page made the joint-highest

In the first month of the season, most pundits were already predicting a swift return to the First Division for Watford, but Graham Taylor has never been a man to give up without a fight. And after the defeat against Sunderland the previous Saturday, Taylor had predicted that his side were going to win at Liverpool.

The assembled members of the press scoffed and the bookies were just as doubtful, after quoting Watford at odds of 8–1 to win, but Taylor was deadly serious. A week later, Watford duly won their first-ever game at Anfield.

When the match kicked off, it seemed that Taylor's players shared his optimism and got stuck into the home side with a confidence and self-belief that those outside the club had not shared. After 11 minutes the Hornets fired a warning blast across the Anfield bows. Tommy Mooney drove a low shot that Sander Westerveld spilled and the Reds escaped punishment thanks to Steven Gerrard's swift clearance.

The Watford fans were encouraged by the early exchanges and struck up chants of "We're staying up". In the 16th minute, there was even more for them to sing and dance about.

Des Lyttle swung in a free-kick from the right wing that was not dealt with by the home side. The Liverpool centre-backs reverted to their pre-Gerard Houllier defensive "after you" hesitancy, and it fell to former Koppite Tommy Mooney, who fired home from six yards.

The Hornets were constantly closing down, not letting the Liverpool players settle on the ball and breaking up the home side's passing game. The visiting team won an incredible 74% of the 33 tackles that they attempted, putting a spanner in the cogs of the Red Machine.

Visiting 'keeper Chris Day tipped away drives from Jamie Redknapp and then a Patrik Berger free-kick before denying the Czech again with a good block.

Liverpool were often reduced to long-range shooting and hit the target with only five of their 22 efforts throughout the match, as they were frustrated time and time again.

As the game moved into the final 10 minutes, the home side started to become more desperate and pushed forward, leaving inevitable gaps at the back, and Watford almost sealed the win in spectacular style.

Westerveld rushed out to block a Mooney shot and Micah Hyde chipped the ball goalward from 30 yards, just being denied by a Rigobert Song header right on the line.

The heroic Hertfordshire side completed a huge total of 114 clearances, blocks and interceptions that afternoon, with their player of the season Robert Page making 29 of those himself.

Only three other teams in the Premiership came away from Anfield with maximum points, and afterwards Taylor praised the Liverpool fans who applauded them off and said: "I will remember this for a long time."

It might not have been too pretty, but it was three vital points. It was to be the only away league win for the Hornets and gave the travelling fans a fantastic memory of their sojourn in the Premiership.

umber of last man saving tackles

Martens

WEST HAM UNITED

ADDRESS

Boleyn Ground, Green Street,
Upton Park, London E13 9AZ

CONTACT NUMBERS

Contact Numbers
Telephone: 020 8548 2748
Fax: 020 8548 2758
Ticket Office: 020 88 548 2700
Club Call: 09068 121165
Club Merchandise: 020 8548 2722
Website: www.westhamunited.co.uk

KEY PERSONNEL

Chairman: Terence Brown
Vice-Chairman: Martin Cearns
Directors: Terence Brown, Martin Cearns, Paul Aldridge (Managing) Charles Warner, Nick Igoe
Football Secretary: Peter Barnes
Manager: Harry Redknapp

SPONSORS

Dr Martens

FANZINES

On The Terraces
On A Mission
Over Land And Sea

COLOURS

Home: Claret shirts with blue sleeves, white shorts, light blue stockings with claret hoops
Away: White shirts with dark blue and claret trim, dark blue shorts, white stockings with dark blue tops

NICKNAME

The Hammers
The Irons

HONOURS

Division Two Champions: 1957–58, 1980–81
FA Cup: 1964, 1975, 1980
European Cup Winners' Cup: 1964–65

RECORD GOALSCORER

Vic Watson – 298 league goals, 1920–35

BIGGEST WIN

8–0 v Rotherham United – Division Two, 8 March 1958

BIGGEST DEFEAT

2–8 v Blackburn Rovers – Division One, 26 December 1963

SEASON REVIEW

West Ham promised much in 1999–2000 but, as has so often been the case with the Hammers, they were unable to win any silverware.

As England's representatives in the much-maligned Intertoto Cup, West Ham's season started while their Premiership rivals were still enjoying their summer holidays. FC Jokerit were the club's first opponents in July. The Hammers beat them 2–1 on aggregate, but were clearly not match-fit.

They looked better against Dutch outfit Heerenveen in the next round, winning both legs 1–0 to book a showdown with Metz. When the French side left Upton Park with a 1–0 win the Intertoto cup campaign looked to be ending in disaster, but West Ham played one of their best games of the season in the return leg to win 3–1 and progress to the UEFA Cup proper.

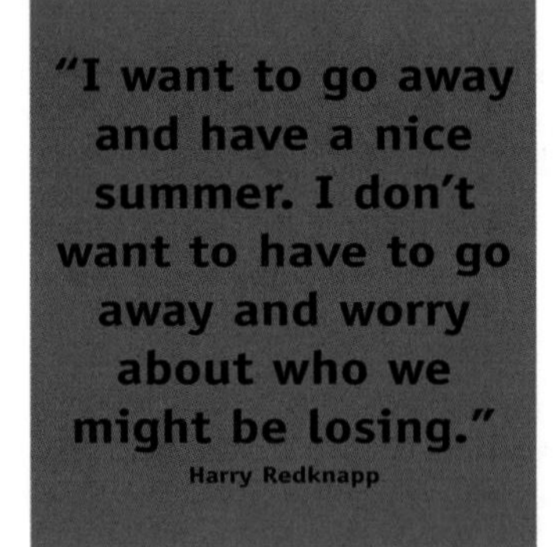

"I want to go away and have a nice summer. I don't want to have to go away and worry about who we might be losing."
Harry Redknapp

Fears that the Intertoto Cup might work against the Hammers seemed to be misplaced, as they got their Premiership season underway with a 1–0 victory against Tottenham. That was the first of five unbeaten games that took the team to fifth place in the table with games in hand over most of their rivals.

However, injuries began to bite with Rio Ferdinand, Scott Minto, Neil Ruddock and Javier Margas joining long-term casualties Ian and Stuart Pearce on the Upton Park treatment table.

But despite their problems at the back the Hammers continued to make progress in Europe, beating first-round UEFA Cup opponents Osijek 6–1 on aggregate.

Back in the Premiership, the team recorded a morale-boosting victory over Arsenal courtesy of two goals from the inspirational Paolo Di Canio. The match was soured by the sendings-off of Marc Vivien Foe and Patrick Vieira and th Frenchman's subsequent spat with Ne Ruddock, but Hammers fans still left Upto Park that day feeling that they were well placed to make an assault on the uppe echelons of the Premiership.

All the optimistic predictions wer shelved in the club's next league game though, as they fell to a 2–0 defea against Middlesbrough. Shaka Hislop di not help his team after seeing red fc handling the ba outside his area.

His dismissal was th third in as many leagu games and helped se the pattern for a seaso in which West Ham sa red more often than an other team, a total c eight times.

Surprisingly for player with hi reputation, Paolo Canio was not amon West Ham's list c miscreants. In fact, th fiery Italian was a example to all his team mates, starting the season in blisterin fashion and playing at a consistentl excellent level for the rest of th campaign, eventually winning Opta' Player of the Season award.

Even Di Canio was unable to prevent hi team slipping to their fifth away defeat c the season at Leeds, however, a result tha saw West Ham drop into the bottom half c the table by the end of October.

Di Canio's strike partner Paulo Wanchop became the scapegoat for many of th team's indifferent performances aroun this time. The gangly Costa Rican suffere in comparison to his brilliant team-mat and was the latest in a long line of playe to become the target of the Upton Pa boo-boys. It took until January before hi tormentors showed any signs of easing u on him.

Of more immediate concern to Redknap

71% Paolo Di Canio's shooting accuracy was highe

SEASON REVIEW

vas the team's exit from the UEFA Cup at he hands of Steaua Bucharest. West Ham ad played a total of 10 European natches, yet only reached the second ound of the UEFA Cup – a disappointing tatistic.

Better news came in a fourth-round Vorthington Cup clash with Birmingham ity. Joe Cole had made his debut in the 998–99 campaign, but Redknapp chose he 1999–2000 season to give his highly-ated young player an extended run in the eam. Cole had already nade a number of 'remiership appearances efore the Birmingham natch, but his last-ninute winner at St ndrews was his first oal for the club and roved that he had the bility to be a match-vinner on his day.

> **"They (West Ham's young players) want to stay here but they want to see us go out and buy new players and I can understand that."**
> Harry Redknapp

The next round of the Vorthington Cup was to rovide less happy nemories, though, as an dministrative error cost he Hammers their place n the semi-final. After eating Aston Villa on penalties at Upton ark, it was revealed that West Ham's late ubstitute Manny Omonyimni had already layed in the competition while on loan at illingham and was thus ineligible for West am in that particular tournament.

The tie was replayed, West Ham lost and pton Park was plunged into depression. lready out of the FA Cup after losing 2–1 o Tranmere Rovers, the club's quest for ome long overdue silverware was over efore the turn of the year.

Europe was still a target, but a run of six ames without a win between 6 December nd 22 January left West Ham in eighth lace, six points behind fifth-placed underland. The introduction of another utstanding young prospect, Michael arrick, to the first team provided upporters with some cheer, but a broken eg sustained by Shaka Hislop in the opening minutes of the home game against Bradford soon sent spirits crashing once more.

West Ham struggled to find a replacement for Hislop. Reserve 'keeper Stephen Bywater immediately conceded four in the Bradford game (although West Ham won 5–4!) and his replacement, on-loan Charlton 'keeper Sasa Ilic, shipped another four the following week.

Preferred back-up goalkeeper Craig Forrest eventually returned to the side, but even he was unable to stop the odd avalanche of goals, conceding seven as West Ham collapsed against Manchester United at Old Trafford.

Considering the problems that they were experiencing at the back, it came as a surprise to many that West Ham chose to sign a striker on their run-in. Frederic Kanouté proved a great success but was unable to inspire the Hammers to a European place, the club eventually finishing in ninth position.

Supporters and playing staff will be expecting a more tangible reward in the 2000–01 season. West Ham have some outstanding players but, despite repeated denials from the management, the club may find it hard to hang on to the likes of Cole, Ferdinand and Lampard if a challenge for honours fails to materialise.

To start competing with the Premiership heavyweights, the club will have to have more luck with injuries and add more players to a squad that, at times, looked far too thin in key areas. Redknapp has little in the way of hard cash to work with and may have to sell again before he can buy. This scenario will make it hard for the club to make a significant improvement on the achievements of the 1998–99 and 1999–2000 seasons.

WEST HAM UNITED

DATE	OPPONENT	SCORE	ATT.	BYRNE	BYWATER	CARRICK	CHARLES	COLE	DI CANIO	FERDINAND	FEUER	FOE	FORREST	HIS
7.8.99	Tottenham H	1–0	26,010	–	–	–	–	s1	89□	90	–	90□	–	90
16.8.99	Aston Villa A	2–2*	26,250	–	–	–	–	–	90	90	–	90	–	90
21.8.99	Leicester H	2–1	23,631	–	–	–	–	–	90^1	90	–	90	–	90
28.8.99	Bradford A	3–0	17,926	–	–	s11	–	–	90^1□	79	–	–	–	90
11.9.99	Watford H	1–0	25,310	–	–	s9	–	–	90^1	–	–	–	–	90
19.9.99	Everton A	0–1	35,154	–	–	–	–	–	90□	–	–	–	–	90
25.9.99	Coventry A	0–1	19,993	–	–	–	–	–	90	–	–	90	–	90
3.10.99	Arsenal H	2–1	26,009	–	–	–	–	–	90^2	–	–	89■	–	90
17.10.99	Middlesbro A	0–2	31,862	–	–	–	–	s15	90□	90	–	–	s62	28□
24.10.99	Sunderland H	1–1	26,022	–	–	–	–	90	90	90□	–	–	–	90
27.10.99	Liverpool A	0–1	44,012	–	–	–	–	90	–	90	–	–	–	90
30.10.99	Leeds Utd A	0–1	40,190	–	–	–	–	s20	–	90	–	70□	–	90
7.11.99	Chelsea A	0–0	34,935	–	–	–	–	87□	–	90	–	90	90	–
21.11.99	Sheff Wed H	4–3	23,015	–	–	–	–	90	90^1	90	–	90^1□	–	90
27.11.99	Liverpool H	1–0	26,043	–	–	–	–	90	90	90	–	–	–	90
6.12.99	Tottenham A	0–0	36,233	–	–	–	–	90	85	90	–	90	–	90
18.12.99	Man Utd H	2–4	26,037	–	–	–	–	–	90^2□	90	–	90	–	90
26.12.99	Wimbledon A	2–2	21,180	–	–	–	–	90	90	90	–	90□	–	90
28.12.99	Derby Co H	1–1	24,998	–	–	–	–	90	90^1	90□	–	90	–	90
3.1.00	Newcastle A	2–2	36,314	s10	–	90	–	90	–	90	–	90	–	90
15.1.00	Aston Villa H	1–1	24,237	–	–	–	–	90	90^1	90	–	–	–	90
22.1.00	Leicester A	3–1	19,019	–	–	s52	–	90	90^1	90	–	–	s64	26
5.2.00	Southampton A	1–2	15,257	–	–	–	90□	90	–	90	–	–	90	–
12.2.00	Bradford H	5–4	25,417	–	s88	–	57	90^1	90^1	90	–	–	–	2
26.2.00	Everton H	0–4	26,025	–	–	–	–	90	–	90	–	–	–	–
4.3.00	Watford A	2–1	18,619	–	–	–	–	–	–	90	–	90	90	–
8.3.00	Southampton H	2–0	23,484	–	–	–	–	73	s17	90	–	90	90	–
11.3.00	Sheff Wed A	1–3	21,147	–	–	–	–	s22	90	90	–	90	90	–
18.3.00	Chelsea H	0–0	26,041	–	–	–	–	s5	90	90	–	90□	90	–
26.3.00	Wimbledon H	2–1	22,438	–	–	–	–	–	90^1	90	–	90	90	–
1.4.00	Man Utd A	1–7	61,611	–	–	–	–	–	–	90	–	90	90	–
12.4.00	Newcastle H	2–1	25,817	–	–	–	s37	90	90	90	–	90	90	–
15.4.00	Derby Co A	2–1	31,202	–	–	s43	s8	47	90	90	90	90	–	–
22.4.00	Coventry H	5–0	24,719	–	–	90^1	–	–	90^2	90	90	–	–	–
29.4.00	Middlesbro H	0–1	25,472	–	–	–	–	–	90	90	90□	90	–	–
2.5.00	Arsenal A	1–2	38,092	–	90	90	–	–	90^1□	–	–	90□	–	–
6.5.00	Sunderland A	0–1	41,684	–	90	90	–	–	90	90	–	90	–	–
14.5.00	Leeds Utd H	0–0	26,044	–	90	–	–	–	90	90	–	89■	–	–

□ Yellow card, ■ Red card, s Substitute, 90^2 Goals scored

*including one own goal

1999–2000 PREMIERSHIP APPEARANCES

…LIC	KANOUTE	KELLER	KITSON	LAMPARD	LOMAS	MARGAS	MINTO	MONCUR	NEWTON	I PEARCE	S PEARCE	POTTS	RUDDOCK	SINCLAIR	STIMAC	WANCHOPE	TOTAL
–	–	s53	–	90[1]	–	–	90	–	–	37	90	90	–	90	–	90	990
–	–	s45	s8	90□	–	–	45	82□	–	–	90□	90	–	90[1]	–	90	990
–	–	–	–	90	90	–	–	90	–	–	90□	90	–	90	–	90[1]	990
–	–	90□	–	90	90□	–	–	90	–	–	90□	90	–	90[1]	–	90[1]	990
–	–	90	–	90	90	s44	–	81	–	–	46	90	–	90	90	90	990
–	–	90	–	90□	90	90	–	90	–	–	–	90	–	90	90□	90	990
–	–	77	–	90	90	–	–	71■	s13	–	–	90	–	90	90□	90□	971
–	–	–	s10	90	90□	s2	–	88□	–	–	–	90	90	90	90□	80□	989
–	–	75	–	90	90	–	–	28	–	–	–	–	90□	90	90	90□	928
–	–	90	s27	90	73□	90	–	s17	–	–	–	–	s38□	90[1]□	52	63	990
–	–	90□	90	90	90	–	–	–	–	–	–	90	90	90	–	90	990
–	–	90	90	90	90□	90	–	90□	–	–	–	–	90	–	–	90	990
–	–	90	–	90	90□	86■	–	–	–	–	–	–	s3	90	90□	90	986
–	–	90	–	90[1]	–	–	–	–	–	–	–	90	90	90	–	90[1]	990
–	–	90□	s8	90	90	90	–	–	–	–	–	–	90	90[1]	–	82	990
–	–	–	45	90	44■	67	s45	–	–	–	–	s23	90□	90	–	s5	944
–	–	90	–	90	90	–	90	–	–	–	–	–	90	90	–	90	990
–	–	–	–	90[1]□	–	90	90	–	–	–	–	–	90	90[1]	–	90□	990
–	–	s31	–	90	–	90	59	–	–	–	–	90	–	90□	–	90□	990
–	–	80	–	90[1]	–	–	90	–	–	–	–	90□	–	90	90[1]	–	990
–	–	90	–	90	90	90	–	–	–	–	–	–	–	90	90□	90	990
–	–	72	–	90	38	90	s18□	–	–	–	–	–	90	90	–	90[2]	990
–	–	–	–	90[1]	90	45	90	s45	–	–	–	–	–	90	90□	90	990
–	–	–	s33	90[1]□	90	–	90	90[1]	–	–	–	–	–	90[1]	90	–	990
0	–	90	90	–	90	–	–	90	–	–	90	–	–	90	90	90	990
–	–	–	–	90	90[1]	–	90	90□	–	–	90	–	–	90	90	90[1]	990
–	–	–	–	90	90	–	s81	90	–	–	9	–	–	90[1]	90	90[1]	990
–	–	–	–	90[1]	90	–	–	68	–	–	–	–	90□	90□	90	90	990
–	–	–	s17	90	90	–	90	85□	–	–	–	–	s13	90	71■	60	971
–	90[1]	s1	–	90	90	–	90	89	–	–	–	–	–	90	90	–	990
–	90	–	–	90	90	–	90	90	–	–	–	90	–	90□	–	90[1]	990
–	90	53	–	90	–	s11	90□	–	–	–	–	–	53	–	79□	s37[2]	990
–	–	–	–	90	–	90□	90	–	–	–	–	–	–	90	82	90[2]□	990
–	90[1]	–	–	90	–	90[1]	86	–	s4	–	–	–	–	90	90□	90	990
–	90	90	–	90	–	90	–	–	–	–	–	–	–	90□	90	90	990
–	90	90□	–	–	–	–	–	90□	–	–	–	90	–	89■	90□	90□	989
–	90	–	–	–	–	–	–	90	–	–	–	90	–	90	90	90	990
–	90□	–	–	–	–	90	–	90□	–	–	–	90	–	90	90	90	989

THE MANAGER

HARRY REDKNAPP

After finishing fifth in 1998–99, West Ham were always going to have their work cut out to repeat such a feat the following season. But Harry Redknapp can nonetheless be proud of his players and himself after the Hammers finished in the top 10 for the third successive season.

The Hammers boss started his managerial career with Bournemouth in 1983, guiding them to the Associate Members' Cup final in his first season and the Division Three (South) Championship in 1986–87, and has now been at West Ham for six seasons, with the east London club looking in safe hands.

West Ham were only denied a place in the Worthington Cup semi-finals in 1999–2000 by an administrative error, and enjoyed 10 European games in all after getting through the Intertoto Cup and reaching the second round of the UEFA Cup.

The future also looks promising, with Redknapp giving Joe Cole, Michael Carrick, Adam Newton and Stephen Bywater first-team opportunities to add to the likes of Frank Lampard and Rio Ferdinand, already established at Upton Park.

Redknapp still has to sell in order to buy, and it is another string to his bow that he has strengthened the squad considerably over the last few seasons without having to sell his top stars.

LEAGUE POSITION

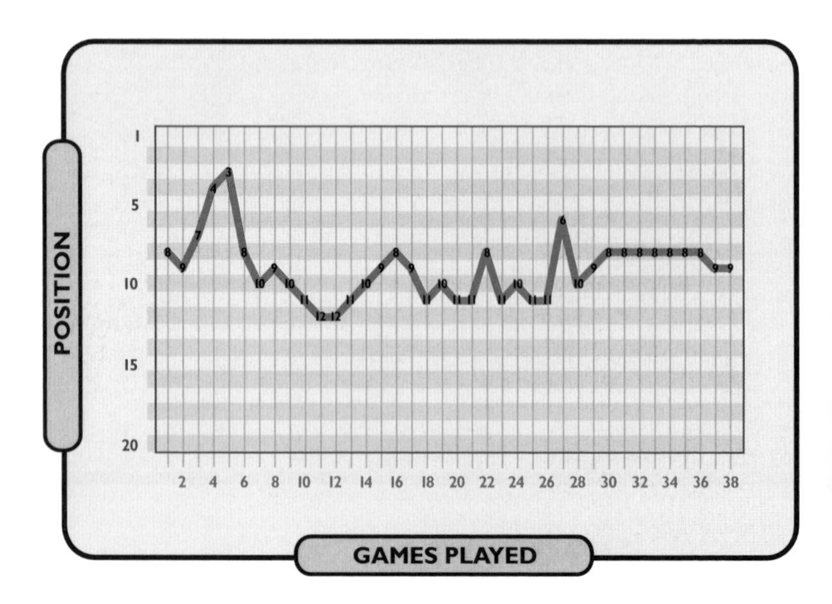

THE GOALS

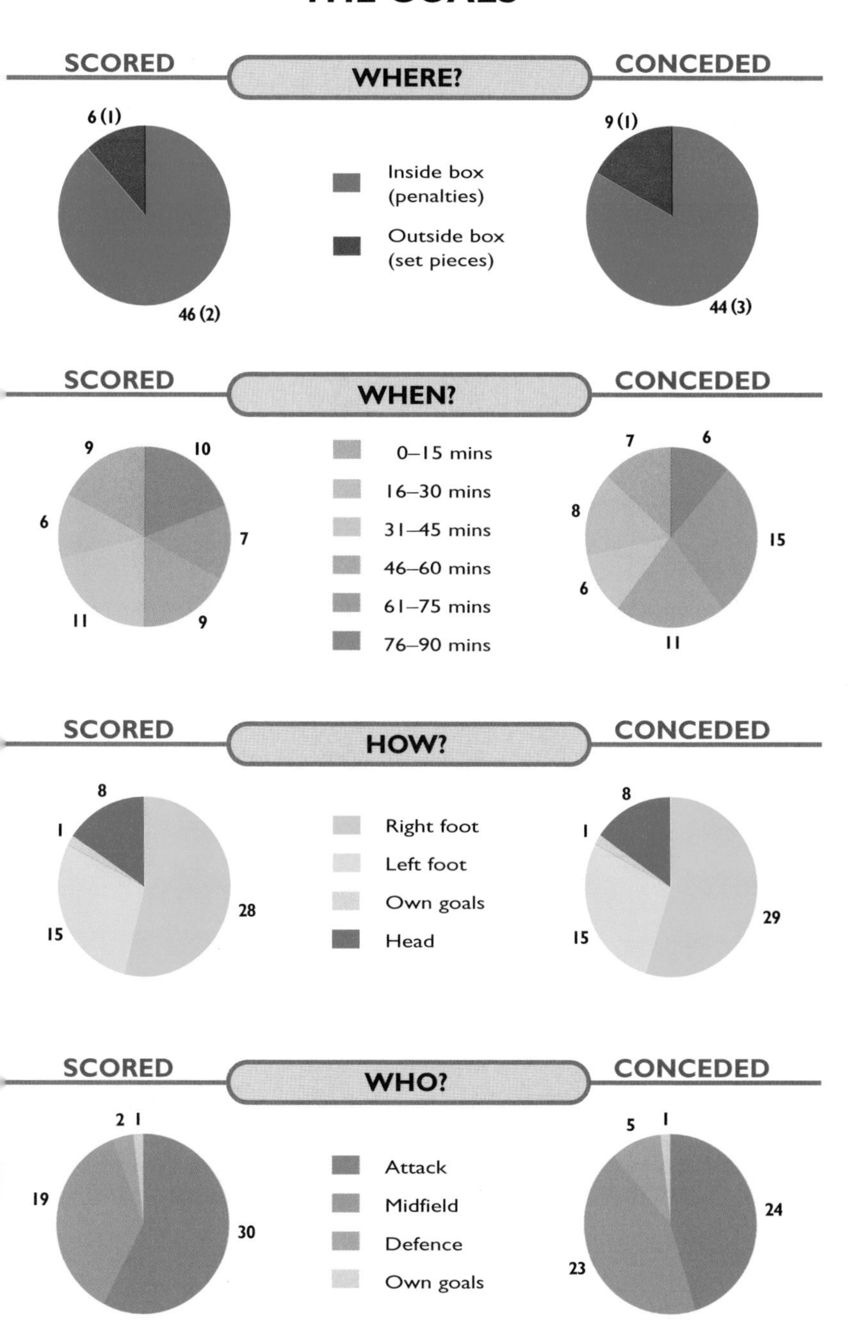

between 61–75 minutes in Premiership matches

WEST HAM UNITED

	BYRNE	CARRICK	CHARLES	COLE	DI CANIO	FERDINAND	FOE	KANOUTE	KELLER	KITS
APPEARANCES										
Start	0	4	2	17	29	33	25	8	19	4
Sub	1	4	2	5	1	0	0	0	4	6
Minutes on pitch	10	475	192	1530	2621	2959	2228	720	1747	418
GOAL ATTEMPTS										
Goals	0	1	0	1	16	0	1	2	0	0
Shots on target	0	3	0	8	45	2	7	16	7	1
Shots off target	0	4	0	13	18	5	19	14	9	5
Shooting accuracy	0%	43%	0%	38%	71%	29%	27%	53%	44%	17%
PASSING										
Goal assists	0	2	0	1	13	0	2	1	1	0
Long passes	2	46	26	137	158	488	209	21	129	12
Short passes	3	161	52	634	1102	702	603	211	462	132
PASS COMPLETION										
Own half %	67%	79%	77%	87%	78%	80%	77%	73%	82%	87%
Opposition half %	0%	63%	70%	76%	70%	53%	64%	65%	68%	66%
CROSSING										
Total crosses	1	3	9	26	238	22	7	7	115	6
Cross completion %	0%	67%	11%	38%	35%	50%	29%	29%	21%	0%
DRIBBLING										
Dribbles & runs	0	15	2	134	204	83	63	47	103	11
Dribble completion %	0%	60%	100%	66%	66%	84%	84%	66%	75%	100%
DEFENDING										
Tackles made	0	26	2	41	42	83	92	7	41	8
Tackles won %	0%	50%	0%	41%	57%	48%	62%	57%	54%	63%
Blocks	0	7	4	2	7	98	25	2	12	0
Clearances	0	9	7	7	3	326	120	9	77	4
Interceptions	0	1	0	9	12	44	20	0	20	0
DISCIPLINE										
Fouls	0	4	3	17	75	15	61	29	28	15
Offside	0	0	0	1	40	0	0	20	4	7
Yellow cards	0	0	1	1	6	2	6	1	4	0
Red cards	0	0	0	0	0	0	2	0	0	0

GOALKEEPER NAME	START/ (SUB)	TIME ON PITCH	GOALS CONCEDED	MINS/GOALS CONCEDED	SAVES MADE	SAVES/ SHOTS
BYWATER	3(1)	358	7	51	14	67%
FEUER	3	270	2	135	12	86%
FORREST	9(2)	936	17	55	32	65%
HISLOP	22	1766	23	77	78	77%
ILIC	1	90	4	23	3	43%

PLAYERS' STATISTICS

LAMPARD	LOMAS	MARGAS	MINTO	MONCUR	NEWTON	I PEARCE	S PEARCE	POTTS	RUDDOCK	SINCLAIR	STIMAC	WANCHOPE	TOTAL	RANK
34	25	15	15	20	0	1	8	16	12	36	24	33		
0	0	3	3	2	2	0	0	1	3	0	0	2		
3060	2135	1335	1414	1734	17	37	595	1463	1097	3239	2084	2937		
7	1	1	0	1	0	0	0	0	0	7	1	12	38*	10th
50	7	3	0	3	0	0	2	0	1	21	1	41	163	5th
35	6	4	4	9	0	0	3	0	3	17	2	34	186	=11th
59%	54%	43%	0%	25%	0%	0%	40%	0%	25%	55%	33%	55%	47%	2nd
3	4	1	2	0	0	0	0	0	1	8	0	5	27	4th
265	297	157	129	244	1	4	84	83	109	221	333	69	3243	11th
1080	743	237	384	770	5	15	201	314	173	1194	494	1011	11007	9th
83%	82%	77%	70%	85%	33%	86%	84%	85%	74%	78%	78%	80%	80%	8th
69%	69%	51%	68%	76%	67%	0%	60%	67%	56%	67%	58%	65%	63%	5th
47	50	5	27	16	2	0	3	4	2	122	14	33	684	11th
23%	28%	40%	41%	38%	50%	0%	0%	50%	50%	30%	71%	12%	29%	8th
82	71	15	40	57	2	0	6	15	7	226	28	158	924	2nd
83%	83%	80%	85%	79%	100%	0%	100%	93%	100%	70%	100%	62%	73%	16th
97	70	47	50	60	1	1	13	37	22	92	69	55	1067	17th
61%	56%	49%	36%	63%	100%	0%	54%	43%	59%	54%	84%	55%	52%	2nd
22	28	39	31	9	0	1	8	20	54	32	66	15	402	4th
47	113	154	46	34	0	6	76	93	145	102	197	31	1813	8th
20	22	25	6	8	0	0	7	23	19	11	22	11	296	6th
40	23	17	24	42	0	0	13	14	20	62	46	185	481	6th
10	0	0	0	0	0	0	0	0	0	24	1	66	118	2nd
4	5	1	2	7	0	0	3	1	4	5	9	7	46	=6th
0	1	1	0	1	0	0	0	0	0	1	1	0	1	1st

*Including one own goal

ROSSES AUGHT	CROSSES PUNCHED	CROSSES NOT CLAIMED	CATCH SUCCESS	THROWS/ SHORT KICKS	% COMPLETION	LONG KICKS	% COMPLETION
3	2	1	75%	11	73%	99	36%
4	0	0	100%	17	94%	57	37%
13	3	0	100%	35	89%	255	52%
39	4	3	93%	106	97%	497	38%
0	1	0	0%	4	100%	14	36%

PLAYER OF THE SEASON

PLAYER	INDEX SCORE
PAOLO DI CANIO	1,290
Frank Lampard	1,040
Trevor Sinclair	967
Steve Lomas	923
Rio Ferdinand	855
Paulo Wanchope	811
Shaka Hislop	777
Igor Stimac	757
John Moncur	722*
Marc-Vivien Foe	697

All players played 75 minutes in at least 19 matches except those marked * who played in just 17 games

Harry Redknapp's sanity was questioned when he paid £1.75 million to Sheffield Wednesday for the maverick Paolo Di Canio.

But Harry must be laughing now, as the Italian has fully recaptured his form and lit up the East End with his sublime skills.

He averaged 1,290 points in the Opta Season Index, not only putting him at the top of the West Ham rankings but at the top of the Premiership overall.

He was the Hammers' top scorer with 16 goals and also made 13 for his team-mates, making him directly responsible for 29 of West Ham's 52 goals in the 1999–2000 season.

His contribution was such that Redknapp even named him as captain in order that he should lead by example.

Young midfielder Frank Lampard was the closest challenger to Di Canio with an average of 1,040 points. The England under-21 star, who made his full international debut earlier in 1999–2000, scored seven goals from midfield and made another three. He clearly enjoyed getting forward, having more attempts at goal than any other Premiership midfielder.

Another young England star, Rio Ferdinand, also featured among the top players along with England "B" international Trevor Sinclair, who recorded eight assists – the second-highest number in the Hammers' side after Di Canio, and finished just above club captain Steve Lomas in the Index.

Manager Redknapp will also be pleased to see that, even despite his previous difficulties with overseas players, his current foreign legion did not let him down, with Paulo Wanchope, Igor Stimac and Marc-Vivien Foe all averaging respectable Index scores.

Goalkeeper Shaka Hislop also produced some consistent performances before his season was sadly cut short by injury.

8 West Ham had more players sent

FIVE OF THE BEST

West Ham had won silverware in 1999–2000 before the summer suntans of most Premiership footballers had faded. But the Intertoto Cup triumph proved a false dawn, as the Hammers crashed out of the UEFA Cup and struggled to maintain their form of 1998–99. The fantastic individual performances from Paolo Di Canio merely glossed over the gaps.

TOP GOALSCORERS

	GOALS	GOALS/SHOTS
PAOLO DI CANIO	16	25%
Paulo Wanchope	12	16%
Trevor Sinclair	7	18%
Frank Lampard	7	8%
Frederic Kanouté	2	7%

Opta's Player of the Year Paolo Di Canio rattled 16 Premiership goals into the back of the net in 1999–2000 and proved wrong all those who doubted Harry Redknapp's decision to snap up the controversial Italian. Not only was Di Canio the Hammers' top scorer, but he also had the best goals-to-shots ratio at the club and was a threat to all opposing defences. His support up front came from Paulo Wanchope who scored 12 goals, although he recorded a less impressive goals-to-shots record of just 16%.

Young midfielder Frank Lampard had much to cheer in 1999–2000. He made his England debut, scored seven Premiership goals and came out on top of the Opta passing table for his constructive displays. A total of 998 successful passes illustrates how much involvement Lampard had in the Hammers' best moves, while only John Moncur bettered his passing accuracy among the midfielders at the Boleyn Ground. England hopefuls Trevor Sinclair and Rio Ferdinand also made the top five list of United's best passers.

TOP PASSERS

	SUCC PASSES	COMPLETION
FRANK LAMPARD	998	74%
Trevor Sinclair	976	69%
Paolo Di Canio	898	71%
John Moncur	803	79%
Rio Ferdinand	798	67%

TOP TACKLERS

	WON	SUCCESS
FRANK LAMPARD	59	61%
Igor Stimac	58	84%
Marc-Vivien Foe	57	62%
Trevor Sinclair	50	54%
Rio Ferdinand	40	48%

He may have earned a reputation for being a classy playmaker, but home-grown West Ham star Frank Lampard does not shy away from the nitty-gritty when the situation arises. In 1999–2000 Lampard won 59 tackles, more than any other Hammer – even those recognised for their defensive skills like Marc-Vivien Foe and Rio Ferdinand. However, Igor Stimac's tackle success rate of 84% was not only the best at the club, but also the best in the Premiership of any player to make more than 50 challenges.

Costa Rican striker Paulo Wanchope bore the brunt of West Ham's dreadful disciplinary record in 1999–2000. He often fell foul of the referee's whistle, committing 119 fouls – more than any other Premiership player. The team as a whole received eight red cards, the most shown to one top-flight side in 1999–2000. Midfielder Marc-Vivien Foe was one of seven Premiership players to be sent off twice during the season, the latter of his red cards coming in a farewell appearance against Leeds for a kick on the grounded Matthew Jones.

DISCIPLINE

	POINTS	FOULS & CARDS
PAULO WANCHOPE	140	119F, 7Y, 0R
Marc-Vivien Foe	91	61F, 6Y, 2R
Igor Stimac	78	45F, 9Y, 1R
John Moncur	69	42F, 7Y, 1R
Trevor Sinclair	59	38F, 5Y 1R

off than any other team

ACTION	CARRICK	DI CANIO	FERDINAND	FEUER	KANOUTE	LAMPARD	MARGAS	MINTO	NEWTON	SINCLAIR	STIMAC	WANCHOPE	TOTAL	COVENTRY
Time On Pitch	90	90	90	90	90	90	90	86	4	90	90	90	990	990
GOALS														
Goal	1	2	–	–	1	–	1	–	–	–	–	–	5	–
Shot on Target	2	2	–	–	3	–	–	–	–	–	–	2	9	2
Shot off Target	–	–	1	–	3	1	–	–	–	–	–	2	7	4
Blocked Shot	–	–	–	–	1	–	–	–	–	–	–	2	3	1
Own Goal	–	–	–	–	–	–	–	–	–	–	–	–	–	–
PASSES														
Pass to Own Player	28	31	24	–	19	32	18	24	2	28	32	17	255	359
Pass to Opposition	13	18	13	–	5	8	16	12	2	13	14	13	127	125
Pass to Scoring Zone – Own Player	–	5	–	–	–	–	–	1	1	–	–	–	7	2
Pass to Scoring Zone – Opposition Player	–	7	–	–	1	1	–	1	–	2	–	–	12	11
Goal Assist	1	3	–	–	–	–	–	1	–	–	–	–	5	–
Pass Completion %	69%	61%	65%	0%	76%	78%	53%	67%	60%	65%	70%	57%	66%	73%
TACKLES & CLEARANCES														
Tackle	1	2	3	–	–	4	1	3	–	1	2	2	19	26
Clearances, Blocks and Interceptions	2	–	3	–	–	2	8	2	–	3	6	–	26	25
DRIBBLES & RUNS														
Dribble ball retained	1	10	4	–	6	3	1	4	1	6	2	6	44	41
Dribble ball lost	–	3	1	–	2	–	–	1	–	1	–	5	13	8
Dribble Success %	100%	77%	80%	0%	75%	100%	100%	80%	100%	86%	100%	55%	77%	84%
DISCIPLINE														
Free kick – foul	–	–	–	–	1	3	–	3	–	–	2	2	11	13
Penalty Conceded	–	–	–	–	–	–	–	–	–	–	–	–	–	–
Free kick – offside	–	–	–	–	1	–	–	–	–	–	1	1	3	2
Yellow Cards	–	–	–	–	–	–	–	–	–	–	1	–	1	–
Red Cards	–	–	–	–	–	–	–	–	–	–	–	–	–	–
GOALKEEPERS														
Distribution to Own Player	–	–	–	3	–	–	–	–	–	–	–	–	3	11
Distribution to Opposition Player	–	–	–	10	–	–	–	–	–	–	–	–	10	20
Goalkeeper Distribution %	0%	0%	0%	23%	0%	0%	0%	0%	0%	0%	0%	0%	23%	35%
Save	–	–	–	2	–	–	–	–	–	–	–	–	2	9
Ball Caught	–	–	–	1	–	–	–	–	–	–	–	–	1	2
Ball Dropped	–	–	–	–	–	–	–	–	–	–	–	–	–	–
Goal Conceded	–	–	–	–	–	–	–	–	–	–	–	–	–	5

56% Paolo Di Canio either scored or directly set-up

Coventry's form away from Highfield Road during the 1999–2000 season was dire, but they can rarely have been so convincingly beaten as when they took on West Ham at Upton Park. Harry Redknapp went into this clash with an embarrassment of attacking riches at his disposal but even he could not have predicted the goal-feast that was to follow.

22 April 2000
5–0
WEST HAM UNITED
vs.
COVENTRY CITY

Frederic Kanouté had made an excellent start to his Upton Park career since joining on loan from Lyon, Paolo Di Canio was in sparkling form and even Paulo Wanchope was banging the goals in, firing nine in the previous 11 games. Redknapp selected all three for this game.

In the absence of England prospect Joe Cole, fellow-FA Youth Cup winner Michael Carrick stepped into the Hammers' midfield and got the match off to a flier. Di Canio burst down the right wing and eluded a couple of challenges before releasing the youngster just inside the Sky Blues' half. And Carrick netted with the first goal of his career, a 25-yard shot that wrong-footed Magnus Hedman in the Coventry goal.

Redknapp's team rained in shots on the Coventry goal. They fired in 24 efforts over the 90 minutes – 17 more than Gordon Strachan's side – in what was one of the most breathtaking displays of attacking football seen at Upton Park in years.

Javier Margas scored his first goal in claret and blue five minutes later. The Chilean international converted a corner from his Italian captain, despite close attention from Gary Breen.

Coventry rallied and almost pulled a goal back through Noel Whelan on 19 minutes. But the Hammers rarely allowed Strachan's players any room in midfield, the home side winning 68% of their challenges during the match.

Three minutes into the second half, Di Canio scored arguably the best goal of the game. The former AC Milan forward received the ball from Carrick before eluding the challenge of David Burrows to fire a thumping drive from the edge of the box into the bottom right corner of Hedman's net.

And the Italian made the score 4–0 after 67 minutes following another well-worked West Ham move. Di Canio exchanged passes with Scott Minto on the edge of the box, brilliantly wrong-footed Richard Shaw and Breen before beating Coventry's Swedish 'keeper with a low shot.

Coventry's torment did not end there, as more calamitous defending allowed West Ham to further increase their tally. Hedman fumbled a corner and Kanouté finished with a simple header. It was no more than the French under-21 international deserved after a tireless performance. He fired in eight shots, more than any other player on the pitch.

There was, however, no doubting the real star of the show. Di Canio had terrorised the Coventry back-line from the opening whistle, embarking on 10 successful dribbles and runs and making 31 accurate passes. He also scored from two of his four attempts on goal and set up the Hammers' other three strikes to amass an Opta Index score of 2,975 – the highest total by any player during the 1999–2000 campaign.

56% of all West Ham's Premiership goals

lotto
tiny
ULTIMAX

WIMBLEDON

ADDRESS

Selhurst Park Stadium,
South Norwood, London SE25 6PY

CONTACT NUMBERS

Telephone: 020 8771 2233
Fax: 020 8768 0640/1
Ticket Office: 020 8771 8841
Ticket Office Fax: 020 8653 4708
Club Call: 09068 121175
Club shop: 020 8768 6100
Ticket e-mail: Crazy.box@virgin.net
Website: www.wimbledon-fc.co.uk

KEY PERSONNEL

Chairman: B Gjelsten
Deputy Chairman: C Koppel
Directors: K Rokke, S Reed, J Lelliott
P Cork, P Lloyd-Cooper, P Miller
M Hauger, C Stromberg
Chief Executive: D Barnard
Club Secretary: S Rooke
Manager: Terry Burton

SPONSORS

Tiny Computers

FANZINES

Yidaho!
Sour Grapes
Hoof The Ball Up
Route One

COLOURS

Home: All navy with yellow trim
Away: All white with black trim

NICKNAME

The Dons

HONOURS

Division Four Champions: 1982–83
FA Cup: 1988

RECORD GOALSCORER

Alan Cork – 145 league goals, 1977–92

BIGGEST WIN

6–0 v Newport County – Division Three,
3 September 1983

BIGGEST DEFEAT

0–8 v Everton – League Cup 2nd
Round, 29 August 1978

SEASON REVIEW

Egil Olsen and Wimbledon were supposed to be a perfect match. The wellie-wearing Norwegian with a taste for geography and a love of the long ball was in many ways even more eccentric than the club he was about to take over. Yet for various reasons the marriage never worked, and although Olsen was not at the helm as Wimbledon finally sank at Southampton there is no doubt that he, more than anyone else, must take responsibility for the Dons' demise.

Olsen arrived in south London determined to impose his own style of play on the club. With no in-depth knowledge of the English transfer market he turned to Norway for his first signings, recruiting Tore Pedersen and Kjetil Waehler on free transfers and splashing out a total of £4.3 million on Trond Andersen and Martin Andresen. Israeli Arab Walid Badir also arrived for £800,000.

> **"I didn't think I'd ever watch a Wimbledon side where the spirit evaporated. They were treading water and raised the white flag."**
> **Bobby Gould**

The players already at the club clearly found it difficult to adjust to his system of zonal defending, a task made even harder by the departure of defensive lynchpin Chris Perry to Tottenham in the summer. In their first game of the season at Watford, they won – but not without some decidedly shaky moments along the way.

Olsen realised that his players were finding his style of play difficult to come to terms with, conceding that it would take until Christmas for them to get used to his methods. He was right. After their opening-day victory the Dons won just once more in their next 12 games, slipping further into the bottom half of the table as they went.

With the exception of Trond Andersen, none of Olsen's signings seemed to settle in and murmurs of discontent from those players who had been at the club under Joe Kinnear were beginning to find thei way out of the dressing room and into th public domain.

Fans found it hard to agree with Olse that Michael Hughes did not deserve place in the side because he lacke defensive capabilities. And, even thoug he retained his place until later on in th season, there were rumours that clu captain Robbie Earle did not see eye-to eye with his manager either.

Further Scandinavian blood was adde to the team in Octobe when hulking Herman Hreidarsson arrived fror Brentford for £2. million, but though th Icelandic internationa slotted in quite well Wimbledon continued t slip up in the league.

The team were farin slightly better in th Worthington Cup, bu after beating Cardif City, Sunderland an Huddersfield they wer beaten by Bolton in th fifth round.

A 5–0 victory ove Watford in December brought some hop that the players were finally adjusting t Olsen's tactics, but by the time they slumpe to a spiritless 3–1 defeat at Anfield in thei last match of the century, Wimbledon stoo just six points above the relegation zone.

Out of the FA Cup after a 3–0 defeat b Fulham in the fouth round, the team the lost John Hartson to injury, an urgen operation on his knee ruling him out o action for four months. With Olse determined to play Carl Cort and Marcu Gayle as midfielders in a complicate 4–5–1 formation, the Dons were strippe of their spearhead. As hard as Carl Leabur laboured, he did not carry the same threa as the Welshman. Andreas Lund wa brought in to replace Hartson but he, too proved largely ineffective, despite one o two good performances.

More depressing news for Dons fan

8 Neil Sullivan conceded more goal

SEASON REVIEW

ame with the announcement that Sam
lammam would be selling his remaining
:0% in Wimbledon to the club's Norwegian
wners. He had fallen out over the
roposed sale of top players, which the
lorwegians felt was essential to clear a
lebt of £3 million and maintain the club's
inancial security.

Hammam's departure was seen by many
s the final curtain call for the old Crazy
ang. When a £6 million fee was agreed
vith Tottenham for Hartson, the clearout
eemed about to begin.

lartson's transfer
ollapsed, however, after
failed medical, and on
he pitch the team were
n even poorer health.

Their home record had
een all that had kept
hem out of the
elegation zone in the
irst half of the season,
ut once that collapsed
Vimbledon, who had
ailed to pick up an away
vin since the opening
lay, went into free-fall.

Between 19 March and
0 April they lost eight
ames in a row, the worst run in the club's
istory and one that took them into the
ottom four. This appalling sequence of
esults coincided with a period in which
radford were starting to pick up vital
oints, and by the time the two teams met
n a crunch game at Valley Parade,
Vimbledon were just two points above
heir relegation rivals.

While Bradford went to ground to
repare for the match, Wimbledon were
aught up in a demoralising round of
abloid speculation, as various players
vent on record as saying they had lost
aith in Olsen and wanted to leave the
truggling club.

The game itself proved to be the final
ne of Egil Olsen's short reign as
Vimbledon manager. Beaten 3–0, albeit
vith the help of some controversial
efereeing by Jeff Winter, the Dons
dropped into the bottom three for the first
time in 1999-2000.

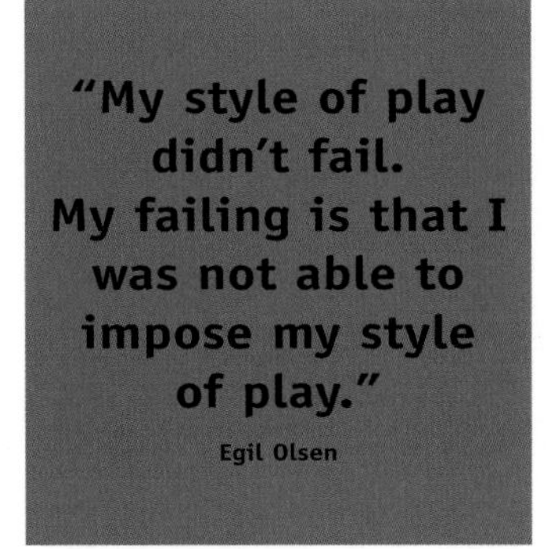

"My style of play didn't fail.
My failing is that I was not able to impose my style of play."
Egil Olsen

Ironically, they had lost the game at
Bradford because they were outfought by a
side that embodied all the qualities
Wimbledon themselves had once stood for.
The Bantams, like Wimbledon, were a
limited side, but they had pulled together
at the right time, flying into tackles and
contesting every inch of the pitch. By
contrast, Egil Olsen's side had attempted
fewer tackles and interceptions than any
other Premiership side
over the course of the
season.

Olsen's immediate
replacement was Terry
Burton, a former
assistant to Joe Kinnear,
who had already been
promoted to the
position of Olsen's
assistant in an attempt
to quell the increasing
mood of despair among
the players.

While he managed to
pull the club out of the
bottom three with a
draw against Aston Villa
on the same day as Bradford lost 3–0 to
Leicester, Burton could do nothing to stop
his side sliding to a 2–0 defeat by
Southampton on the final day. That result,
coupled with Bradford's victory over
Liverpool, condemned the Dons to Division
One after 14 years in the top flight.

The fear for Wimbledon fans is that
their team may never make a return to
the Premiership. Burton will certainly
find it hard to hang onto his best
players. Influential goalkeeper Neil
Sullivan departed for Tottenham shortly
after the 1999-2000 season ended, and
other key men were also linked with
moves. Whoever Burton has at his
disposal, his first objective must be to
restore some of the club's famous
fighting spirit. Without that, Wimbledon
could well find themselves with another
struggle on their hands.

rom the penalty spot than any other 'keeper

WIMBLEDON

DATE	OPPONENT	SCORE	ATT.	AINSWORTH	ANDERSEN	ANDRESEN	ARDLEY	BADIR	BLACKWELL	CORT	CUNNINGHAM	EARLE	EUEL
7.8.99	Watford A	3–2*	15,511	–	–	–	s24	–	16■	90^1	90	90	s14
10.8.99	Middlesbro H	2–3	11,036	–	–	–	–	–	90	90^1	90□	83	s21
14.8.99	Coventry H	1–1	10,635	–	90□	–	s11	–	90	90^1	90	59	s31
21.8.99	Newcastle A	3–3	35,809	$s31^2$□	59	–	–	–	–	90□	90	59	s31
25.8.99	Everton A	0–4	32,818	s32	s45	–	–	–	90	90	90	58	90
28.8.99	Chelsea H	0–1	22,167	–	90	–	–	65	–	90	90	74	s25□
11.9.99	Derby Co H	2–2	12,282	–	90	–	–	76	–	90	90	s14	90^1
18.9.99	Man Utd A	1–1	55,189	–	90	–	–	90^1	90	79	90	–	90
26.9.99	Tottenham H	1–1	17,368	–	85	–	–	90	90	90	90	–	90
2.10.99	Sheff Wed A	1–5	18,077	–	36	–	–	57	90	90	90	s33	90
16.10.99	Bradford H	3–2	10,029	–	90	–	–	–	80	90^1	90	90	90
23.10.99	Aston Villa A	1–1	27,160	–	90	s28	–	–	–	90	90	90^1	90
30.10.99	Southampton H	1–1	15,754	–	77	–	–	s25	–	90□	90	65	90
7.11.99	Leeds Utd H	2–0	18,747	–	90	s1	–	s10	–	89	90	90	90
20.11.99	Leicester A	1–2	18,255	–	90	–	–	s2	88□	90	90	90	90
27.11.99	Middlesbro A	0–0	31,400	–	90	–	–	–	–	90	90	90	90□
4.12.99	Watford H	5–0	14,021	–	90	s23	–	–	–	78^1	90	90^1□	90^1
18.12.99	Arsenal A	1–1	38,052	–	90	s23	–	–	–	67^1	90	90	90
26.12.99	West Ham H	2–2	21,180	–	90	–	90^1	90	–	–	90	90	90□
28.12.99	Liverpool A	1–3	44,107	–	90	s25	–	76□	–	57	90	90	90□
3.1.00	Sunderland H	1–0	17,621	–	90	86□	s25	65□	–	90^1	90	–	90
15.1.00	Coventry A	0–2	19,012	–	90	90	80	s10	–	90	90	90	90
22.1.00	Newcastle H	2–0	22,118	–	90	–	s30	90	–	90	90	90^1	90
6.2.00	Everton H	0–3	13,172	–	90	s25	s25	75	–	90	90	65	90
12.2.00	Chelsea A	1–3	34,826	–	90□	68	s22	–	–	90	90	85	90
26.2.00	Man Utd H	2–2	26,129	–	90	s15	75	s2	–	90^1	90	–	90^1
4.3.00	Derby Co A	0–4	28,384	–	90	–	71	s19	–	90	90	–	90□
11.3.00	Leicester H	2–1	14,319	–	90	s10	82^1	–	–	90^1	90	90	90
19.3.00	Leeds Utd A	1–4	39,256	–	90	–	90	s45	–	45	90	90□	90^1
26.3.00	West Ham A	1–2	22,438	–	90	–	75	–	s18	–	90	65	90□
1.4.00	Arsenal H	1–3	25,858	–	90	66	s24	s14	90	–	90	–	88■
8.4.00	Sunderland A	1–2*	41,592	–	90	–	–	83	90	–	90	–	90□
12.4.00	Sheff Wed H	0–2	8,248	–	90	–	–	56	90	s34	90	–	90
16.4.00	Liverpool H	1–2	26,102	–	90□	$s32^1$	–	–	87□	90	90	–	–
22.4.00	Tottenham A	0–2	33,086	–	90	s20	–	–	–	90	90	–	90
30.4.00	Bradford A	0–3	18,276	–	90□	–	90	–	62	90	90	–	90
6.5.00	Aston Villa H	2–2*	19,188	–	90	–	90	–	90	75	29	–	90
14.5.00	Southampton A	0–2	15,249	–	90	–	90	s15	83□	90	–	–	90□

□ Yellow card, ■ Red card, s Substitute, 90^2 Goals scored

*including one own goal

For more information visit our website:

1999–2000 PREMIERSHIP APPEARANCES

FRANCIS	GAYLE	GRAY	HARTSON	HEALD	HREIDARSSON	C HUGHES	M HUGHES	JUPP	KIMBLE	LEABURN	LUND	PEDERSEN	ROBERTS	SULLIVAN	THATCHER	WILLMOTT	TOTAL
–	76[1] □	–	66 □	–	–	–	21	s69	90	–	–	90	90	90	–	–	916
–	90	–	90[1]	–	–	–	69	–	61 □	s7	–	90	90	90	s29	–	990
–	79	–	90 □	–	–	s20	–	–	–	–	–	90 □	70	90	90	–	990
–	90	–	–	–	–	–	76[1]	–	90	s14	–	90	90	90	90	–	990
–	90	–	–	–	–	–	80	–	90	s10	–	–	45	90	90 □	–	990
–	90	–	–	–	–	–	90 □	–	s45	s16	–	45	90	90	90 □	–	990
–	90	–	90[1]	–	–	–	–	–	–	–	–	90 □	90	90	90 □	–	990
–	90	–	90	–	–	–	–	s11	–	–	–	–	90	90	90	–	990
–	90	–	78[1] ■	–	–	–	–	–	s5	–	–	–	90 □	90	90	–	978
–	90	–	90[1]	–	–	–	–	–	s54	s15	–	–	75	90	90	–	990
–	86	–	90[2]	–	90	–	–	–	s25	s4	–	–	s10	90	65	–	990
–	82	–	62	–	90	–	–	–	90	s8	–	–	–	90	90	–	990
–	90[1]	–	90	–	90 □	–	–	–	90	s13	–	–	–	90	90	–	990
–	80[1]	–	88[1]	–	90 □	–	–	–	90 □	s2	–	–	–	90	90	–	990
–	90[1]	–	90	–	90	–	–	–	90	–	–	–	–	90	–	–	990
–	90	–	–	–	90	–	s10	–	90	80	–	–	–	90	90	–	990
–	90[1]	–	90[1]	–	90	–	s12	–	67	–	–	–	s45	90	45 □	–	990
–	27	–	90 □	–	90	–	s63	–	90	–	–	–	90	90	–	–	990
–	90	–	–	–	90[1]	–	s18	–	90	72	–	–	–	90	–	–	990
s14	90[1]	–	–	–	90	–	–	–	s33	65	–	–	–	90	90	–	990
s4	90 □	–	–	–	90 □	–	–	–	–	–	–	–	–	90	90	90	990
80	–	s10	–	–	90	–	–	–	90	–	–	–	–	90	–	–	990
–	90[1]	–	–	–	90	–	–	–	90	60	–	–	–	90	–	–	990
s15	90	–	–	–	90	–	–	–	90	65	–	–	–	90	–	–	990
s5	–	–	–	–	90	–	–	–	90	–	90[1] □	–	–	90	–	90	990
–	90	–	–	–	90	–	–	–	90	–	88	–	–	90	–	90	990
–	90	–	–	–	90	–	–	–	90	–	90	–	–	90	–	90	990
–	90	–	–	90	–	–	s8	–	90	–	80	–	–	–	–	90	990
–	90	–	–	–	–	–	s25	–	90	–	65	–	–	90	–	90	990
s25 □	90	–	–	–	–	–	90[1]	–	90	s15	90	–	–	90	–	72	990
–	90	–	–	–	–	–	90	90	–	–	90[1]	–	76	90	–	–	988
–	90	–	–	–	90	–	90	90 □	–	s7	90	–	–	90	–	–	990
–	90	–	–	–	90	–	90	90	–	s20	70	–	–	90	–	–	990
–	90	–	–	–	90	–	90	90	–	s3	58	–	90	90	–	–	990
s11	82	–	–	–	90	–	90	90	90 □	–	s8	–	59	90	–	–	990
–	s28	–	51 ■	–	90	–	90 □	–	–	–	–	–	–	90 □	90	–	951
s47	90	–	s15[1]	–	90	–	43	s61	–	–	–	–	–	90	90	–	990
s7	75	–	–	–	90	–	–	90	60 □	–	s30	–	–	90	90	–	990

THE MANAGER

TERRY BURTON

May 14th has been a glorious date for Wimbledon in the past, but on that date in 2000, Dons fans were in tears as their side were relegated to the Nationwide League after failing to beat Southampton on the final day of the season.

Former Norway boss Egil Olsen took charge of Wimbledon in the summer of 1999 but was sacked at the end of April 2000 after a 3–0 defeat by relegation rivals Bradford.

Assistant manager Terry Burton was then asked by Chairman Bjorn Gjelsten if he wanted the job, to which his answer was a resounding "Yes".

Burton was number two to Joe Kinnear as well as Olsen, but had a spell as Academy Director in between.

Reportedly confirmed as manager for next season, Burton has vowed to "bring back Wimbledon as quickly as possible", but he has a tough task ahead.

He will have the assistance of coaches Stewart Robson and Mick Harford, who have also spent many years with the Dons, and between them they will be hoping to get Wimbledon back into the Premiership at the end of 2000–01.

LEAGUE POSITION

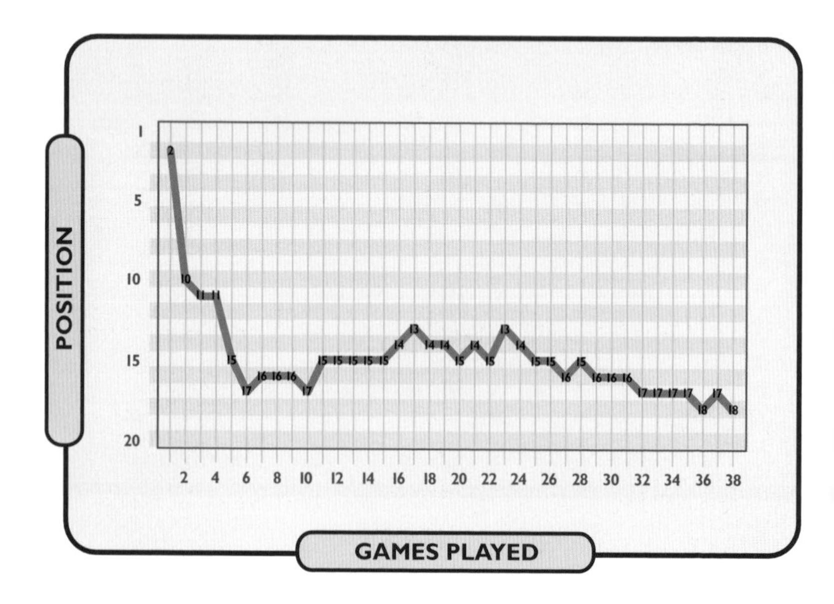

92% Wimbledon conceded the highest ratio o

THE GOALS

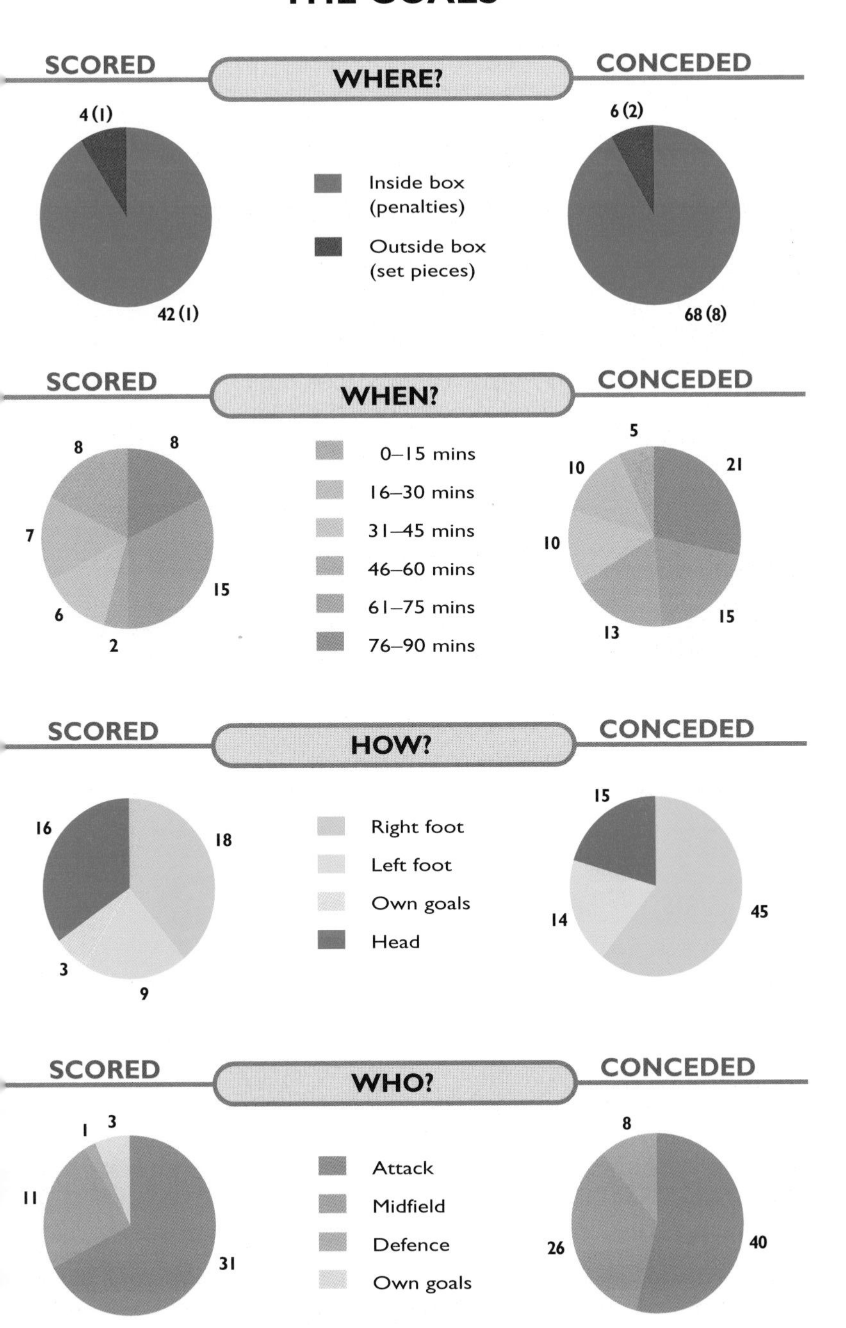

goals from shots inside the area in the Premiership

WIMBLEDON

	AINSWORTH	ANDERSEN	ANDRESEN	ARDLEY	BADIR	BLACKWELL	CORT	CUNNINGHAM	EARLE	EUELL	FRA
APPEARANCES											
Start	0	35	4	10	12	16	33	37	23	32	1
Sub	2	1	10	7	9	1	1	0	2	5	8
Minutes on pitch	63	3092	512	994	1055	1334	2864	3269	1920	3000	208
GOAL ATTEMPTS											
Goals	2	0	1	2	1	0	9	0	3	4	0
Shots on target	3	1	1	6	11	0	23	1	10	14	0
Shots off target	0	9	6	3	12	1	39	4	17	28	1
Shooting accuracy	100%	10%	14%	67%	48%	0%	37%	20%	37%	33%	0%
PASSING											
Goal assists	0	2	1	1	0	0	6	3	0	5	0
Long passes	2	344	43	86	67	88	100	435	113	233	15
Short passes	2	782	177	294	328	166	1134	877	490	837	88
PASS COMPLETION											
Own half %	100%	70%	70%	81%	73%	74%	77%	72%	76%	72%	73%
Opposition half %	0%	58%	48%	56%	63%	39%	64%	58%	56%	62%	58%
CROSSING											
Total crosses	1	49	25	59	14	2	60	170	11	44	4
Cross completion %	0%	39%	40%	24%	14%	0%	23%	36%	18%	30%	25%
DRIBBLING											
Dribbles & runs	7	53	24	33	29	9	121	76	19	97	8
Dribble completion %	29%	89%	67%	61%	69%	100%	75%	87%	84%	75%	75%
DEFENDING											
Tackles made	0	81	12	21	37	46	60	101	64	117	6
Tackles won %	0%	60%	50%	48%	57%	43%	57%	40%	52%	56%	83%
Blocks	0	52	2	5	10	19	11	72	25	17	5
Clearances	1	207	2	7	17	145	42	272	56	43	2
Interceptions	1	14	0	1	5	8	7	23	5	11	0
DISCIPLINE											
Fouls	2	33	12	15	25	18	98	21	21	60	1
Offside	0	0	3	4	5	0	35	0	3	10	0
Yellow cards	1	4	1	0	2	3	2	1	2	8	1
Red cards	0	0	0	0	0	1	0	0	0	1	0

GOALKEEPER NAME	START/ (SUB)	TIME ON PITCH	GOALS CONCEDED	MINS/GOALS CONCEDED	SAVES MADE	SAVES/ SHOTS
HEALD	1	90	1	90	4	80%
SULLIVAN	37	3330	73	46	176	71%

PLAYERS' STATISTICS

GAYLE	GRAY	HARTSON	HREIDARSSON	C HUGHES	M HUGHES	JUPP	KIMBLE	LEABURN	LUND	PEDERSEN	ROBERTS	THATCHER	WILLMOTT	TOTAL	RANK
35	0	15	24	0	13	6	23	5	10	6	14	19	7		
1	1	1	0	1	6	3	5	13	2	0	2	1	0		
3045	10	1260	2160	20	1145	681	2150	476	849	495	1190	1669	612		
7	0	9	1	0	2	0	0	0	2	0	0	0	0	46*	=13th
25	0	21	4	0	11	0	0	2	10	0	3	0	0	146	20th
37	0	14	3	0	17	2	2	4	12	0	4	1	1	217	8th
40%	0%	60%	57%	0%	39%	0%	0%	33%	45%	0%	43%	0%	0%	40%	20th
4	0	4	0	0	1	0	3	0	1	0	1	2	0	34	=13th
132	0	23	219	1	115	101	413	15	28	24	104	189	63	2953	17th
850	2	424	343	5	302	144	350	182	235	44	339	196	80	8671	19th
73%	0%	75%	54%	0%	71%	68%	56%	78%	82%	91%	82%	65%	61%	70%	20th
54%	0%	63%	49%	67%	65%	52%	48%	64%	53%	58%	55%	50%	56%	57%	19th
74	0	9	16	1	82	20	181	1	4	0	11	28	1	867	6th
24%	0%	44%	63%	0%	27%	25%	36%	0%	0%	0%	36%	25%	100%	31%	7th
101	0	14	63	1	32	17	28	7	8	2	7	26	3	785	19th
67%	0%	86%	90%	100%	81%	94%	96%	71%	63%	50%	86%	88%	100%	78%	7th
26	0	9	64	2	24	24	64	2	9	16	40	52	8	886	20th
50%	0%	44%	50%	100%	42%	63%	42%	100%	44%	56%	68%	37%	75%	51%	13th
10	0	2	83	0	7	10	36	0	1	3	8	26	28	432	7th
47	0	8	220	2	9	26	125	4	4	71	68	185	60	1637	7th
6	0	1	11	0	2	2	12	0	0	5	12	11	3	141	20th
54	2	73	43	0	12	13	22	12	29	8	17	20	7	514	16th
20	0	15	0	0	0	0	0	1	8	0	0	0	0	104	18th
2	0	3	3	0	2	1	4	0	1	2	1	4	0	49	16th
0	0	2	0	0	0	0	0	0	0	0	0	0	0	4	=5th

*Including three own goals

ROSSES AUGHT	CROSSES PUNCHED	CROSSES NOT CLAIMED	CATCH SUCCESS	THROWS/ SHORT KICKS	% COMPLETION	LONG KICKS	% COMPLETION
2	2	0	100%	0	0%	27	41%
79	19	9	90%	63	76%	1389	49%

PLAYER OF THE SEASON

PLAYER	INDEX SCORE
KENNY CUNNINGHAM	**875**
Neil Sullivan	**862**
Carl Cort	**747**
Hermann Hreidarsson	**633**
Ben Thatcher	**615***
Jason Euell	**612**
Robbie Earle	**606***
Trond Andersen	**597**
Alan Kimble	**588**
Marcus Gayle	**566**

All players played 75 minutes in at least 19 matches except those marked * who played in just 17 games.

In a depressing season for the Dons, culminating in relegation, it was left to some of the more experienced members of their side to try and stop the slide into Division One.

Full-back Kenny Cunningham put in several consistent performances on the right-hand side, even taking on the responsibility of captaincy in the absence of Robbie Earle.

Cunningham was also voted the supporters' Player of the Year for the 1999–2000 season as he fought harder than most in the relegation battle.

The Republic of Ireland international made the second-highest number of successful crosses in the Premiership and claimed three goal assists, although he had to spend a great deal of his time with defensive duties. He made 101 tackles and 272 clearances in his attempts to lead his team to safety.

'Keeper Neil Sullivan also pulled out all the stops to try and preserve the Dons' place in the Premiership. The Scottish international made 176 saves – the second-highest number in the Premiership – and kept five clean sheets, despite his goal coming under great pressure during the season. Despite the Dons' relegation, Sullivan will continue to play Premiership football in 2000–01 following a summer move to Tottenham.

The Dons' talented youngsters also made an impact during the campaign with Carl Cort, Ben Thatcher and Jason Euell all making an impression in the top 10 of the Opta Season Index, catching the eye of several other Premiership clubs in the process.

The versatile Trond Andersen was the only one of the Dons' Norwegian imports to make his mark during the season, making 1,126 passes and 207 clearances, after performing in both defence and midfield.

Other established Crazy Gang members such as Robbie Earle and Marcus Gayle also appeared in the top 10 but could not do enough to stop the Dons' last-day heartache.

40% Wimbledon's shooting accuracy was

FIVE OF THE BEST

The rot had set in at Wimbledon before Egil Olsen took control but the eccentric Norwegian could not stamp his authority on the team. After a spell of just one defeat in nine games between October and December it seemed as if the Dons were as solid as ever. But a spring collapse saw them finish 18th and slide out of the top flight 14 years after arriving.

TOP GOALSCORERS

	GOALS	GOALS/SHOTS
JOHN HARTSON	9	26%
Carl Cort	9	15%
Marcus Gayle	7	11%
Jason Euell	4	10%
Robbie Earle	3	11%

Nine goals from a £7.5 million man is a poor return, caused by John Hartson's regular absences through suspension and injury. He ended the campaign with a goals-to-shots ratio of 26% – a much greater rate than any of his team-mates. Carl Cort also scored nine times, but received a lot of praise from the critics. Cort may need to improve on a success rate of 15% if he is to secure a move away from Selhurst Park.

Wimbledon made fewer successful passes than any other team in the Premiership, and less than half as many as Manchester United. Kenny Cunningham made the most with 825, with an accuracy of 63%. Jason Euell finished with the same completion rate, while Cort and Trond Anderson were both on 62%. The Dons have never been famed for their passing, but it fell in standard considerably this year and will need to improve if they are to challenge for promotion.

TOP PASSERS

	SUCC PASSES	COMPLETION
KENNY CUNNINGHAM	825	63%
Carl Cort	760	62%
Trond Andersen	699	62%
Jason Euell	677	63%
Marcus Gayle	526	54%

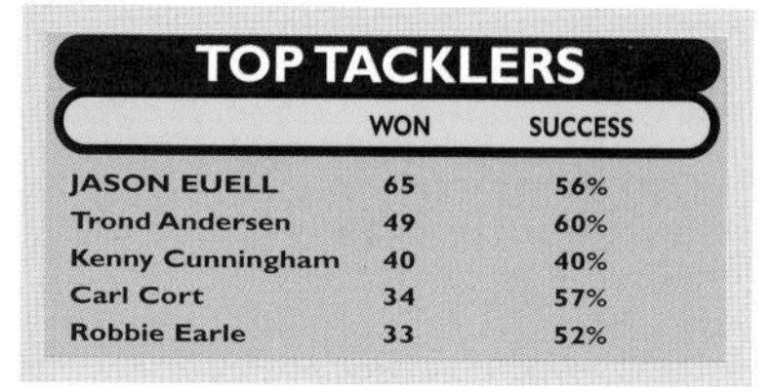

TOP TACKLERS

	WON	SUCCESS
JASON EUELL	65	56%
Trond Andersen	49	60%
Kenny Cunningham	40	40%
Carl Cort	34	57%
Robbie Earle	33	52%

Jason Euell was one of Wimbledon's most consistent players in 1999–2000, and he ended the season with 65 successful tackles. Trond Andersen was statistically most likely to win the ball, but he slid into fewer challenges. Kenny Cunningham, Carl Cort and Robbie Earle make up the top five, although the latter's biggest challenge was recovering from a stomach injury that threatened his life.

Fiery Jason Euell racked up the most disciplinary points at Wimbledon, but the worst-behaved player was surely John Hartson. He featured in just 16 league games but committed 58 fouls and picked up three yellow cards. He was also sent off twice, the second red card meaning he missed the final game of the season at Southampton, where his presence could have been more than useful.

DISCIPLINE

	POINTS	FOULS & CARDS
JASON EUELL	80	50F, 8Y, 1R
John Hartson	79	58F, 3Y, 2R
Carl Cort	69	63F, 2Y, 0R
Hermann Hreidarsson	52	43F, 3Y, 0R
Trond Andersen	45	33F, 4Y, 0R

ACTION	ANDERSEN	ANDRESEN	BADIR	CORT	CUNNINGHAM	EARLE	EUELL	GAYLE	HARTSON	HREIDARSSON	KIMBLE	LEABURN	SULLIVAN	THATCHER	TOTAL	LEEDS UNITED
Time on pitch	90	1	10	89	90	90	90	80	88	90	90	2	90	90	990	990
GOALS																
Goal	–	–	–	–	–	–	–	1	1	–	–	–	–	–	2	–
Shot on target	–	–	–	–	–	–	1	–	4	–	–	–	–	–	5	5
Shot off target	1	–	–	1	–	–	1	1	1	–	–	–	–	–	5	4
Blocked shot	–	–	1	–	–	–	–	1	1	–	–	–	–	–	3	6
Own goal	–	–	–	–	–	–	–	–	–	–	–	–	–	–	–	–
PASSES																
Pass to own player	28	–	2	29	18	11	26	12	15	10	20	1	–	11	183	343
Pass to opposition	19	1	2	11	14	14	15	9	16	9	8	–	–	8	126	120
Cross to own player	1	–	–	–	3	–	–	–	–	–	3	–	–	–	7	5
Cross to opposition player	–	–	–	3	2	2	1	3	1	–	3	–	–	–	15	23
Goal assist	–	–	–	–	–	–	–	–	–	–	1	–	–	–	1	–
Pass completion %	60%	0%	50%	67%	57%	41%	62%	50%	47%	53%	69%	100%	0%	58%	58%	71%
TACKLES & CLEARANCES																
Tackle	5	–	1	5	7	3	2	–	–	4	2	–	–	3	32	18
Clearances, blocks and interceptions	12	–	–	2	15	2	2	1	–	22	9	–	–	24	89	69
DRIBBLES & RUNS																
Dribble ball retained	2	–	1	4	2	–	2	4	–	4	2	–	–	3	24	39
Dribble ball lost	–	–	–	1	–	–	–	1	–	–	–	–	–	–	2	3
Dribble success %	100%	0%	100%	80%	100%	0%	100%	80%	0%	100%	100%	0%	0%	100%	92%	93%
DISCIPLINE																
Fouls	4	–	–	1	1	–	2	–	4	4	1	–	–	–	17	11
Penalty conceded	–	–	–	–	–	–	–	–	–	–	–	–	–	–	–	–
Free kick – offside	–	–	–	–	–	–	–	–	2	–	–	–	–	–	2	4
Yellow cards	–	–	–	–	–	–	–	–	–	1	1	–	–	–	2	–
Red cards	–	–	–	–	–	–	–	–	–	–	–	–	–	–	–	–
GOALKEEPERS																
Distribution to own player	–	–	–	–	–	–	–	–	–	–	–	–	25	–	25	16
Distribution to opposition player	–	–	–	–	–	–	–	–	–	–	–	–	9	–	9	17
Goalkeeper distribution %	0%	0%	0%	0%	0%	0%	0%	0%	0%	0%	0%	0%	74%	0%	74%	48%
Save	–	–	–	–	–	–	–	–	–	–	–	–	5	–	5	5
Ball caught	–	–	–	–	–	–	–	–	–	–	–	–	5	–	5	–
Ball dropped	–	–	–	–	–	–	–	–	–	–	–	–	–	–	–	–
Goal conceded	–	–	–	–	–	–	–	–	–	–	–	–	–	–	–	2

5 Wimbledon kept fewer clean sheets

Only the most optimistic of Wimbledon supporters would have predicted a win over Leeds when the sides met at a drizzly Selhurst Park in November. Leeds had gone on a 13-game unbeaten run before their trip to SE25, while the Dons had won just once in their previous 12 Premiership fixtures.

Wimbledon's record signing, John Hartson, was clearly keyed up for the game and held his head in his hands after his 20-yard drive flew wide of the target with just 30 seconds gone. Two minutes later the bustling Welshman was presented with another chance, but Lucas Radebe bravely threw himself in the way of Hartson's goalbound effort.

Michael Bridges was missing from the Leeds line-up with a back injury and the visitors were clearly missing their £5 million striker, who had scored nine goals in the previous 11 away games. Manager David O'Leary was forced to play a makeshift partnership of Alan Smith and Darren Huckerby.

With 12 minutes on the clock, England international goalkeeper Nigel Martyn produced the save of the match, diving low to his right to superbly turn away Hartson's header. But 18 minutes later, the Dons opened the scoring.

The goal came on the break, immediately after Lee Bowyer had seen a weak header saved by Neil Sullivan in Wimbledon's goal. Instead of retreating to their positions, the Leeds midfielder and his team-mate Harry Kewell stopped to debate whether Bowyer should have gone for goal or passed.

The gap left by Kewell allowed Wimbledon's Kenny Cunningham to dash down the flank and whip over a cross that found its way to Hartson who, from an unmarked position, slotted coolly under the advancing Martyn.

Leeds fared little better in the second half, with Hartson again finding himself in space, only to scuff his shot at Martyn just after the restart. Another outlet for the Dons was skipper Cunningham, who was being given the freedom of the right wing to deliver his crosses.

Wimbledon got an inevitable second goal after 65 minutes when Alan Kimble's corner from the right was headed home by Marcus Gayle. The absence of a Leeds defender guarding the near post was to prove costly, as Martyn was too far from the ball to attempt a save.

Leeds struggled to make an impact going forward as hard-working Wimbledon suffocated all their slick passing moves. The Yorkshire side's best chance did not come until three minutes from time when substitute Eirik Bakke's header was cleared off the line by the Dons' tireless Trond Andersen.

The Opta stats reveal that Wimbledon's clean sheet-keeping Neil Sullivan was man of the match, although Hartson was the choice of the fans, scooping 48% of the votes in Sky's post-match poll.

However, Sullivan's five saves and immaculate catch success rate earned him 1,964 Index points, nearly 500 more than Hartson. Leeds' top man was David Batty, who won three tackles and completed 82% of his passes.

Nationwide
Nationwide
Nationwide
MESH
MESH

CHARLTON ATHLETIC

ADDRESS

The Valley, Floyd Road,
Charlton, London SE7 8BL

CONTACT NUMBERS

Telephone: 020 8333 4000
Fax: 020 8333 4001
Box Office: 020 8333 4010
Club Call: 09068 121146
Club Shop: 020 8333 4010
E-Mail: info@cafc.co.uk
Website: www.cafc.co.uk

KEY PERSONNEL

Chairman: M Simons
Deputy Chairman: R Murray
Chief Executive: P Varney
Directors: R Alwen, D G Bone
R Collins, G Franklin, D Hughes
W Perfect, M Stevens, D Sumners
D Ufton, R Whitehand
Club Secretary: C Parkes
Manager: Alan Curbishley

SPONSORS

1999–2000 Mesh
2000–2001 Redbus

FANZINES

The Voice of the Valley
Goodbye Horse

COLOURS

Home: Red shirt, white
shorts with red stockings
Away: White shirt, red shorts,
white stockings (2000–01)

NICKNAME

The Addicks

HONOURS

Division One Champions: 1999–2000
Division Three (South) Champions:
1928–29, 1934–35
FA Cup Winners: 1947

RECORD GOALSCORER

Stuart Leary – 153 league goals,
1953–62

BIGGEST WIN

8–1 v Middlesbrough – Division One,
12 September 1953

BIGGEST DEFEAT

1–11 v Aston Villa – Division Two,
14 November 1959

SEASON REVIEW

Charlton Athletic may have won the hearts of fans everywhere for their gutsy displays in the 1998–99 Premiership season, but that did not save them from relegation from the top flight. Their opening fixture in the 1999–2000 season was at The Valley on 7 August against Barnsley, who had approached life in the top flight with similar zest during the 1997–98 campaign.

Charlton saw off the Tykes 3–1 thanks to a Clive Mendonca hat-trick – a throwback to their first home match in the Premiership when Mendonca's finishing skills helped annihilate Southampton 5–0.

The team that lined up to face the Tykes included new signing Dean Kiely, who joined the club for £1 million from Bury during the summer. His arrival solved the goalkeeping conundrum that had surfaced during 1998–99 when Sasa Ilic, Andy Petterson and Simon Royce all failed to hold their places once given their opportunity between the sticks for the Addicks.

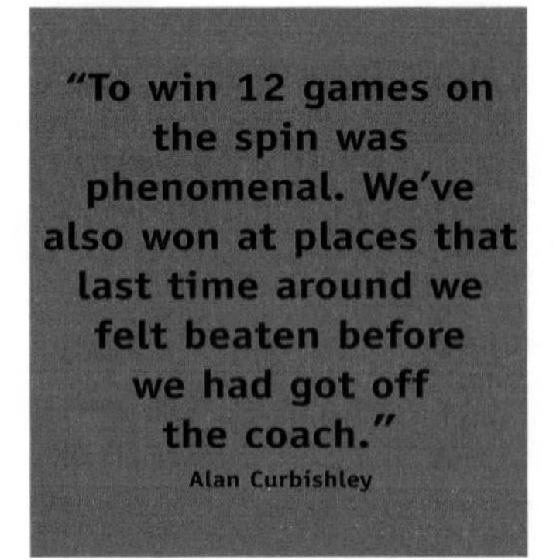

"To win 12 games on the spin was phenomenal. We've also won at places that last time around we felt beaten before we had got off the coach."
Alan Curbishley

Alan Curbishley used more of the money from the £4 million sale of Danny Mills to Leeds to sign highly-rated right-back Greg Shields from Dunfermline for £580,000, and also secured the services of former England international John Salako. After an initial loan spell from Fulham, the former Crystal Palace star agreed a permanent move across London for a fee of £150,000.

Kiely's form in goal and Andy Hunt's shooting boots helped the Addicks reach October with just one defeat – a 2–1 loss at moneybags Fulham in August. They also scored in all their matches until a goalless encounter at The Valley against West Bromwich Albion on 23 October.

November saw Charlton's most impressive result to date, a 5–2 win at Grimsby, but they were soon brought back down to earth by a 1–0 defeat at home to Manchester City, courtesy of a 48th-minute Shaun Goater effort. This result was the catalyst for a poor run of form in which only six points were picked up out of a possible 15, but this slump was more than made up for, as the next 12 league matches were all won.

One of the more impressive results in this sequence was the 3–2 win at Molineux, which will probably be best remembered for Martin Pringle's two goals. Unfortunately, the second effort beat his own 'keeper Dean Kiely, bringing Wolves back into the game for the final quarter of the match. But Charlton managed to hold on to the victory, which placed them at the top of the table, where they remained for the rest of the season.

A more impressive goalscoring feat was Andy Hunt's two hat-tricks in successive weeks against Norwich City and Stockport County. Other goals in this period came from all quarters, not just the forwards, as John Robinson, Graham Stuart and Richard Rufus all found the target to build the lead at the top of the table to eight points after 32 matches.

Mark Kinsella was an absentee from the scoresheet during much of this period, until the trip to Walsall. The Irishman netted his first of the campaign against Tranmere at the end of September, but had to wait for the visit to the Bescot Stadium for his next goal, which came on the stroke of half-time. Having gone 27 games without scoring, he then doubled his tally on 66 minutes, captaining his side to an emphatic 4–2 victory against the struggling Saddlers.

During this period, Alan Curbishley

SEASON REVIEW

ecured the services of Bolton centre-back ndy Todd for £1 million. He found himself laying alongside Richard Rufus at the eginning of the unbeaten run as Eddie ouds injured knee ligaments in the 2–1 win at Huddersfield at the end of ecember.

It was not long before Crystal Palace triker Matt Svensson was added to the anks to boost Charlton's attacking ptions, as his height and ability to hold a all up were seen as ideal skills to omplement Andy Hunt's inishing prowess.

The Addicks' one isappointment at this tage was the FA Cup uarter-final defeat by a ingle Eidur Gudjohnsen oal at the hands of olton Wanderers. Their up run will be best emembered for the win t Coventry City in a ive-goal thriller in ound five, with John obinson, Shaun Newton nd Andy Hunt leading he fightback after the ddicks had been two oals down.

The club record for straight league wins ame to an end in bizarre fashion – a 1–0 ome defeat to bottom-of-the-table windon, with the goal coming from a rare ean Kiely fumble. The giant stopper let lip a cross from Steve Cowe and appeared lmost to throw it into the goal, having ived on the ball in his six-yard box. But his defeat was then followed by three vins out of the next four matches.

The Sky cameras descended for the home atches against both Huddersfield and ortsmouth in the hope that promotion ould be captured for the live television udience. Unfortunately, big-game nerves inally got to the players. Defeat against uddersfield was followed by a Good Friday oint against a Pompey outfit much nproved from the one outplayed 2–0 at ratton Park six months earlier. Thankfully, rivals Ipswich were defeated by QPR 3–1 the next day to secure promotion, so the race was now on to be crowned Champions.

Three days after the Portsmouth game Charlton travelled north to Blackburn, knowing that if Manchester City failed to beat Tony Pulis's Pompey side at Fratton Park, the Division One Championship would be secure. Blackburn were held in a 1–1 draw, but this result was academic, as on the south coast Lee Bradbury, whose goal 72 hours earlier muted the Charlton faithful at The Valley, netted a late equaliser to ensure that City were held to just a single point, with the match ending in a 2–2 draw.

> **"We're going back to the Premiership stronger as a club, with a stronger squad and with a little bit of money to spend."**
> Alan Curbishley

This combination of results was enough to secure the Championship and finally allowed the fans and the players to celebrate, but it was a slight disappointment for the supporters that they did not see a win in the last seven games of the season.

Peter Middleton, chairman of the Football League, and Peter Gandolfi, the sponsorship manager of Nationwide Building Society, presented the trophy to Mark Kinsella after the final home match of the season against Ipswich Town.

The efforts of the players were rewarded by their fellow-professionals at the annual PFA dinner. Five Addicks were included in the final XI: Rufus, Kinsella, Hunt, Robinson and Chris Powell.

Previous Division One winners Sunderland pushed for a UEFA Cup spot during 1999–2000, but most Charlton fans will probably not mind how the 2000–01 season goes, provided they are still in the Premiership come May.

Alan Curbishley may have a tough task ahead, but as one of the most promising coaches in the game, he will be much better prepared for the top flight second time around.

han any other Nationwide league side

CHARLTON ATHLETIC

DATE	OPPONENT	SCORE	ATT.	BARNESS	BROWN	HUNT	ILIC	K JONES	S JONES	KIELY	KINSELLA	KITSON	KON
7.8.99	Barnsley H	3–1	19,268	–	90□	70	–	s20	–	90	90□	–	–
21.8.99	Norwich H	1–0	19,623	–	90	60	–	–	s30	90	90	–	–
28.8.99	Fulham A	1–2*	15,154	–	75	s45	–	–	45	90	90	–	–
11.9.99	Bolton W H	2–1	19,028	–	s1	–	–	–	–	90	90	–	–
18.9.99	Sheff Utd A	2–1	13,216	–	s7	90^{2}	–	–	–	90	90	–	90
25.9.99	Tranmere A	2–2	5,846	s2	–	–	–	–	–	90	90^{1}□	–	90□
28.9.99	Stockport H	4–0	19,842	–	s14	90^{3}	–	–	–	90	90	–	–
2.10.99	Birmingham H	1–0	19,753	–	s40	90	–	–	–	90	90□	–	–
16.10.99	Portsmouth A	2–0	14,812	–	–	74	–	90	–	90	90	–	–
19.10.99	Ipswich A	2–4	17,940	s67	s20	90^{2}	–	70	–	90	90	–	–
23.10.99	West Brom H	0–0	19,346	–	–	90	–	80	–	90	90	–	90□
26.10.99	Tranmere H	3–2	19,491	–	$s45^{1}$	90□	–	90	–	90	–	–	66
30.10.99	Birmingham A	0–1	19,172	–	s25	90	–	86	–	90	–	–	–
2.11.99	Crewe A A	2–0	4,741	–	90	90	–	90	–	90	90	–	–
6.11.99	Walsall H	2–1	18,663	–	s7	83^{1}□	–	75□	–	90	90□	–	–
12.11.99	Grimsby A	5–2*	6,849	–	s4	90^{1}	90	90	–	–	83	–	–
20.11.99	Man City H	0–1	20,043	–	90	90	–	90	–	90	90	–	–
23.11.99	Swindon A	2–1	6,515	–	s18	90	–	90	–	90	90	–	–
27.11.99	Port Vale H	2–2	19,256	–	90□	73	–	80	–	90	90	–	–
30.11.99	Blackburn H	1–2	18,939	–	90□	90	–	73	–	90	90	–	–
4.12.99	Barnsley A	1–1	14,553	–	90	90	–	90^{1}	–	90	90□	–	–
18.12.99	QPR A	0–0	14,708	–	–	90□	–	90	–	90	–	–	–
26.12.99	C Palace H	2–1	20,043	–	90□	90	–	88	–	90	90	–	–
28.12.99	Huddersfield A	2–1	17,415	–	s45	90^{1}	–	90	–	90	45	–	–
3.1.00	Nottm Forest H	3–0	19,787	–	90	87^{1}	–	–	–	90	–	–	–
11.1.00	Wolves A	3–2	18,464	–	90	90	–	–	–	90	90	–	–
15.1.00	Crewe A H	1–0	19,125	–	90	90	–	–	–	90	90	–	90
22.1.00	Norwich A	3–0	15,642	–	90	90^{3}	–	–	–	90	–	–	–
5.2.00	Stockport A	3–1	8,185	90	90	90^{3}	–	–	–	90	–	–	–
12.2.00	Wolves H	2–0	20,043	90	90^{1}	90	–	–	–	90	–	–	–
15.2.00	Fulham H	1–0	19,940	55	90	90	–	–	–	90	–	–	–
26.2.00	Sheff Utd H	1–0	19,249	79	90	67	–	–	–	90	90□	–	–
4.3.00	Bolton W A	2–0	15,000	90	90	90^{1}	–	–	–	90	90	–	s42
7.3.00	Walsall A	4–2	6,227	90	90	90^{2}	–	–	–	90	90^{2}	–	–
11.3.00	Swindon H	0–1	19,569	90	90	72	–	–	–	90	90	–	–
19.3.00	Man City A	1–1	32,139	90	90	90	–	–	–	90□	90□	–	–
22.3.00	Grimsby H	4–0	19,364	90	45	62^{1}	–	–	–	90	90	s28	–
25.3.00	C Palace A	1–0	22,577	90	–	76	–	–	–	90	90	$s14^{1}$	s6
31.3.00	QPR H	2–1	19,617	83	90□	90	–	–	–	90	90	s19	–
4.4.00	Port Vale A	2–2	4,513	62□	90□	90^{1}	–	–	–	90	90	82	–
8.4.00	Nottm Forest A	1–1	20,922	90	90	90^{1}	–	–	–	90	90	–	–
14.4.00	Huddersfield H	0–1	19,739	90	90	90	–	–	–	90	90	–	–
21.4.00	Portsmouth H	1–1	20,043	90	90	90	–	–	–	90	90	–	–
24.4.00	Blackburn A	1–1	18,587	90	90□	76	–	–	–	90	90	s14	–
29.4.00	Ipswich H	1–3	20,043	–	90	90^{1}	–	–	–	90	90	45	–
7.5.00	West Brom A	0–2	22,101	90	–	90	–	–	–	90	90	–	90□

□ Yellow card, ■ Red card, s Substitute, 90^{2} Goals scored *including one own goal

1999–2000 DIVISION ONE APPEARANCES

MACDONALD	McCAMMON	MENDONCA	NEWTON	PARKER	POWELL	PRINGLE	ROBINSON	RUFUS	SALAKO	SHIELDS	STUART	SVENSSON	TILER	TODD	YOUDS	TOTAL
–	–	90[3]	70	–	90	s20	90	90	–	–	90	–	–	–	90□	990
–	–	86	90	–	90	s4	90	90[1]	–	–	90	–	–	–	90	990
–	–	90	45	s45	90	s15	90□	90□	–	–	90	–	–	–	90	990
–	s17	89[1]	90	–	90	73	62	90	s28	90	44[1]■	–	–	–	90□	944
–	–	90	90	–	–	–	88	90	s2	90	83	–	–	–	90	990
–	68	90[1]	90	88	–	s22	68	90□	s22	90	–	–	–	–	90□	990
–	–	86[1]	90	76	90	s4	86□	90□	s4	90	–	–	–	–	90	990
–	–	85	90	50	90	s5	89	90	s1	90[1]	–	–	–	–	90□	990
–	–	90	88	–	90	s16	90[1]□	90	s2[1]	90	–	–	–	–	90	990
–	–	–	90	–	23	–	90	90□	s20	90	70	–	–	–	90	990
–	s10	75	69□	–	–	–	90	90	s21	90□	s15	–	–	–	90	990
–	–	90	45	–	–	–	90[1]	90[1]	s24	90	90	–	–	–	90	990
–	–	90□	–	s4	79	s11	90	90□	65	90	90	–	–	–	90□	990
–	–	–	s16	–	90	81[1]	74	–	s9	90	90[1]	–	–	–	90	990
–	s15	–	–	–	90	68	90	90	s22	90	90[1]	–	–	–	90	990
–	–	90[1]	–	–	90	–	90□	90[2]	s7	90	90	–	–	–	86□	990
–	–	90	–	–	90	s14	90□	90	s45	76	45	–	–	–	–	990
–	–	72	89[1]	–	90	s18	90[1]	90	–	72	–	–	–	s1	90□	990
–	–	90[2]	73	–	90	s17	90	90	s17	–	s10	–	–	–	90	990
–	–	90	90[1]	–	79	s11	63	90	s27	–	s17	–	–	–	90	990
–	–	60	90	–	90	s30□	–	90□	76	–	–	–	–	s14	90□	990
–	–	90	83□	90	90	s7	s25	90□	65	90	–	–	–	–	90	990
–	–	–	90	–	90	90[1]	s13	90□	77[1]	–	–	–	–	s2	90	990
–	–	–	77	–	90	90	90[1]	90	s13□	90	–	–	–	s45	45	990
s11	–	–	90	s9	90	79	90	90	s3	90[1]	81[1]	–	–	90	–	990
s7	–	–	90	–	90	83[1]□	83[1]	90[1]	s7	90	67	–	–	s23	–	990
–	–	–	73	–	–	90	88	90	s17	90	90[1]	–	–	s2	–	990
–	–	–	90	–	90	90	90	90	–	90	90	–	–	90	–	990
–	–	–	90	–	90	68	82	90	s8	–	90□	s22	–	90□	–	990
–	–	–	90	–	90	78	90	90	–	–	90[1]□	s12	–	90	–	990
–	–	–	90	–	90	52	90[1]□	90	–	–	90	s38	s35	90	–	990
–	–	–	90	–	90	s23	88[1]□	90	–	–	90	90	s11	s2	–	990
–	–	–	90	–	86	s21[1]	48	90□	–	–	90	69	s4	–	–	990
–	–	–	90	–	90	s15	90	90	–	–	68	75	s22	–	–	990
–	–	–	90	–	66	s18	90	90	s24	–	90	90	–	–	–	990
–	–	–	90[1]	–	90	s24	90	–	–	–	90	66	90	–	–	990
–	–	–	90[1]	s21	90	–	69	90	–	–	90	90[1]	s45[1]	–	–	990
–	–	–	76	–	90	–	84	90	s14	–	90	90	90	–	–	990
–	–	–	78[1]	s7[1]	90□	–	90	90	–	–	90	71	s12	–	–	990
–	–	–	90	s28	90	–	62	90[1]	–	–	90	s8	s28	–	–	990
–	–	–	87	s3	90	s21	90	90	–	–	90□	69□	–	–	–	990
s14	–	–	64	s26	76	–	90	90	–	–	90	90	–	–	–	990
–	–	–	90	–	90	–	90□	90	–	–	90[1]	90	–	–	–	990
–	–	–	90	s9	90	–	81	90	–	–	90	90[1]	–	–	–	990
–	–	–	90	s26	90	–	90□	90	–	–	64	s45	90	–	–	990
–	–	–	67	90□	–	–	90□	90	s9	–	s23	81	90	–	–	990

THE MANAGER

ALAN CURBISHLEY

Alan Curbishley began his management career at Charlton Athletic in tandem with Steve Gritt in 1991. Once the club returned to The Valley in 1992, the foundations were laid to bring top-flight football back to SE7, a task which fell to Curbishley alone after Gritt's departure in 1995.

Charlton first reached the Premiership under Curbishley following their play-off victory on penalties against Sunderland in 1998. But they were relegated on the last day of the 1998–99 campaign, despite the efforts of players such as Mark Kinsella, who had little trouble adjusting to Premiership life.

A great deal of credit for Charlton's amazing 1999–2000 campaign should go to Curbishley, who stuck with the majority of his Premiership side, while adding solid performers such as Dean Kiely from Bury and Matt Svensson from Crystal Palace.

Curbishley's next task is to decide if he should continue his trend of signing up-and-coming youngsters and experienced pros, or start buying more expensive players of proven quality at the highest level, in order to deliver a side worthy of long-term survival in the Premiership.

LEAGUE POSITION

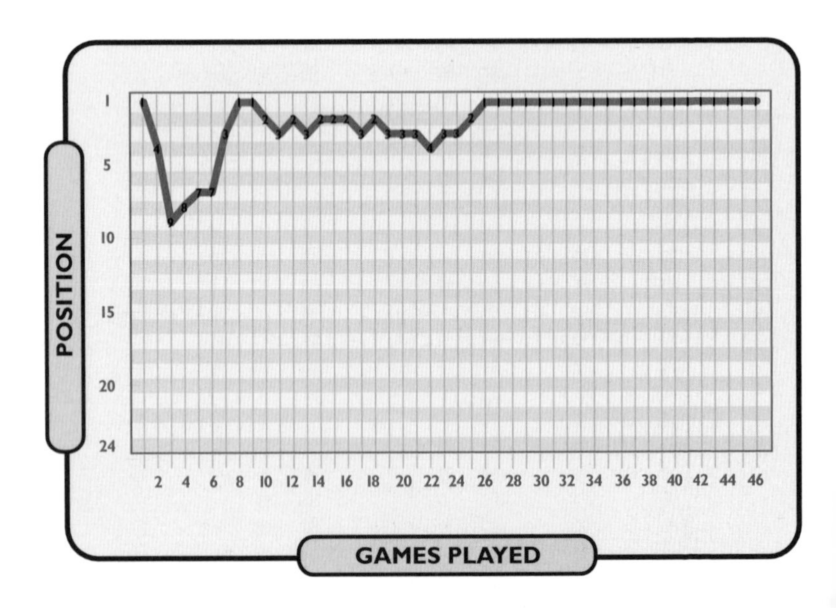

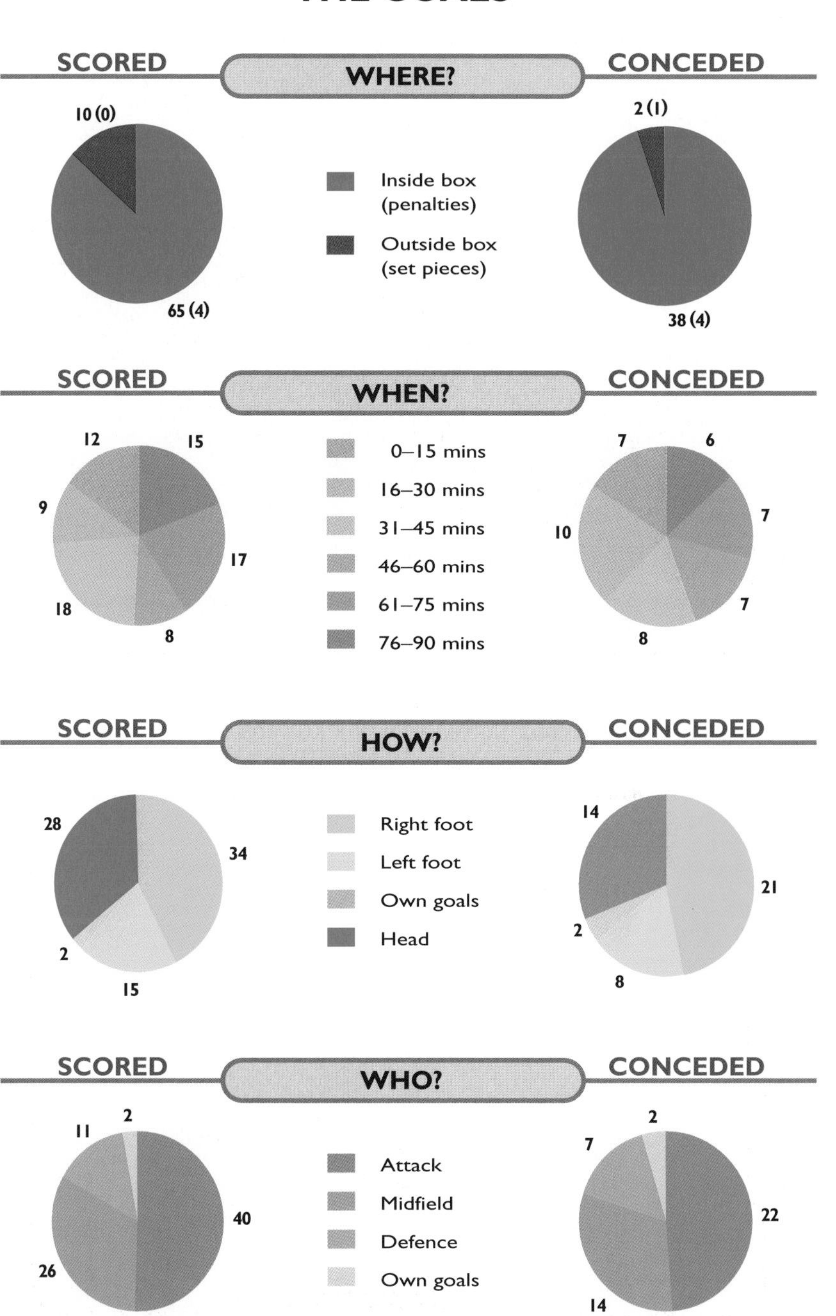
THE GOALS
SCORED
WHERE?
CONCEDED
10 (0)
65 (4)
Inside box (penalties)
Outside box (set pieces)
2 (1)
38 (4)
SCORED
WHEN?
CONCEDED
12
15
9
17
18
8
0–15 mins
16–30 mins
31–45 mins
46–60 mins
61–75 mins
76–90 mins
7
6
7
10
7
8
SCORED
HOW?
CONCEDED
28
34
2
15
Right foot
Left foot
Own goals
Head
14
21
2
8
SCORED
WHO?
CONCEDED
11
2
40
26
Attack
Midfield
Defence
Own goals
7
2
22
14

won in a row – a club record

CLAPHAM
3
8
PUNCH

IPSWICH TOWN

ADDRESS

Portman Road, Ipswich,
Suffolk, IP1 2DA

CONTACT NUMBERS

Telephone: 01473 400 500
Fax: 01473 400 040
Ticket Office:
0845 605 0129 (local rate)
Club Call: 09068 121068
Superstore: 01473 400 563
E-Mail: enquiries@itfc.co.uk
Website: www.itfc.co.uk

KEY PERSONNEL

Chairman: D Sheepshanks
Chief Executive: H Wells
Directors: R Finbow, P Hope-Cobbold
J Kerr MBE, R Moore
Rt. Hon Lord Ryder OBE
Club Secretary: D Rose
Manager: George Burley

SPONSORS

Greene King

FANZINES

Dribble
Those Were The Days
Without A Care In The World
A Load Of Cobbolds
Score!

COLOURS

Home: Blue shirts, white
shorts and blue stockings
Away: White shirts, black shorts
and white stockings (2000–01)

NICKNAME

The Blues
Town

HONOURS

Division One Champions: 1961–62
Division Two Champions: 1960–61,
1967–68, 1991–92
Division Three (South) Champions:
1953–54, 1956–57
FA Cup Winners: 1978
UEFA Cup Winners: 1981
Texaco Cup Winners: 1973

RECORD GOALSCORER

Ray Crawford – 203 league goals
1958–63, 1966–69

BIGGEST WIN

7–0 v Portsmouth – Division Two,
7 November 1964
7–0 v Southampton – Division One,
2 February 1974
7–0 v WBA – Division One,
6 November 1976

BIGGEST DEFEAT

1–10 v Fulham – Division One,
26 December 1963

SEASON REVIEW

Following heartbreak in the play-off semi-finals once again, Ipswich Town began the 1999–2000 season in defiant mood, winning their first three matches and avoiding defeat until the 1–0 reverse at home to Trevor Francis's Birmingham City on 18 September.

This good start to the campaign dispelled fears that the club would struggle to come to terms with the loss of Kieron Dyer, who completed a £6.5 million move to Newcastle United over the summer of 1999.

Rather than spend all the money in one go, George Burley sensibly added promising Crewe midfielder Jermaine Wright to his squad and also signed Jonas Axeldal, a Swedish striker who had been plying his trade at Foggia in Italy.

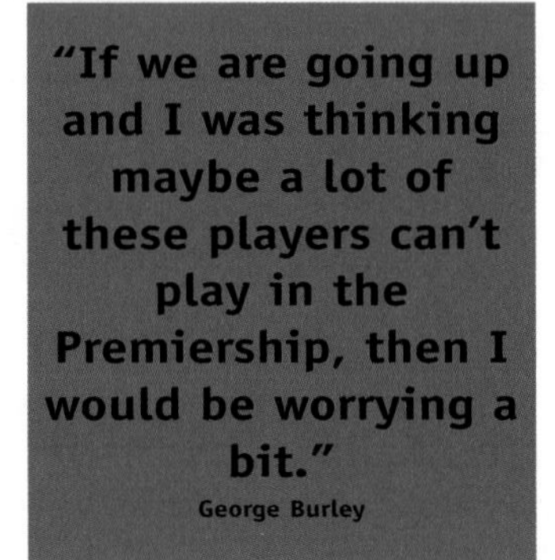

"If we are going up and I was thinking maybe a lot of these players can't play in the Premiership, then I would be worrying a bit."
George Burley

Axeldal had to be content with cameo appearances from the bench as the scoring form of David Johnson helped keep Town in top spot after their first six matches. The most emphatic win in this period was the 6–1 drubbing of Barnsley on August Bank Holiday Monday. Johnson scored two in this fixture, but, impressively, goals came from all over the field as Dave Bassett's side were sent back to South Yorkshire in total disarray.

Burley's next move was to sign Blackburn right-back Gary Croft, but after he joined the club for a fee of £540,000 it became apparent that the police wanted to talk to the former Grimsby man. Croft's subsequent conviction for a motoring offence gave him the dubious honour of becoming the first professional to play in a match wearing an electronic tag on his ankle, coming on as a substitute against Swindon on 15 January.

Another impressive result occurred at Portman Road on 19 October. Charlton Athletic were beaten 4–2 thanks to goa from Jamie Scowcroft, Mark Venu Johnson and Mick Stockwell. This matc also marked Tony Mowbray's first start the season. "Mogga" was supposed to hav taken a back seat to concentrate o coaching duties but, once selected, h missed just one game during the rest the season.

Although Town had no trouble in findir the back of the net in the league, defe by a single goal to Southampton in the F Cup forced Burley to us the remaining millior from the Dyer sale. I perhaps the mos amazing deal of th season in Division On Huddersfield Town, wh were chasing promotio themselves, parte company with st striker Marcus Stewar who had scored 1 league goals for th Terriers already.

Stewart did lac Premiership experienc but was seen as th ideal man to partn Johnson now that Scowcroft was showin promise in midfield.

It took Stewart just 60 minutes to ope his Town account, doubling the lead Oakwell against Barnsley a minute aft Scowcroft's opener. The duo scored agai in the next match to secure a wi ironically against Stewart's form Huddersfield team-mates.

Stewart's scoring form then deserte him, but this did not hamper Town progress until a shock 1–0 home defeat the hands of Portsmouth. This loss marke the end of Manchester United youngst Michael Clegg's loan spell with the clu Clegg had been brought in to cover for spate of defensive injuries, but returned t the Red Devils having played just thre times for the Blues.

The Pompey defeat did not he confidence and Town had to wait until th

18 Number of clean sheets kept by Richard Wrigh

SEASON REVIEW

visit to Prenton Park, four games later, to earn their next three points. This victory was then followed by a win against Fulham, which elevated Town to the second automatic promotion spot.

Unfortunately for Burley's side, this was the last time they were in second place. But, thanks to a 3–1 win over Champions Charlton Athletic at The Valley, they went into the final game of the season at home to Walsall knowing that second spot could still be obtained if Manchester City lost at Blackburn Rovers.

When news filtered through that Blackburn had taken the lead shortly before half-time, Ipswich started their second half knowing that a win would take them up. Johnson duly bagged the opener, but up at Ewood Park Manchester City's nerves had settled and by the time Johnson had netted his second strike of the game, City were well on the way to victory.

> **"You can imagine the heartbreak of the last few seasons, but the support has got stronger, the club has got stronger and the players have got better."**
> **George Burley**

As if déjà-vu was not apparent enough, with this being Ipswich's fourth attempt at play-off success, the side they faced in the semi-final was the team which had beaten them at that stage a year previously – Bolton Wanderers.

The first leg at the Reebok Stadium began in disastrous fashion. After 32 minutes Bolton had scored twice and both Johnson and Mowbray had gone off injured. But Town fought back and two superb Stewart strikes set things up nicely for the second leg.

The 21,543 crowd at Portman Road witnessed one of the most incident-packed matches in play-off history. Ipswich came from behind three times, courtesy of a Jim Magilton hat-trick, to take the game into extra-time. Magilton could have had a fourth but, having scored his first goal from the penalty spot, a second spot-kick was saved by Jussi Jaaskelainen.

In extra-time a third penalty was awarded, but this time Jamie Clapham took the responsibility and made no mistake. Bolton's cause was not helped when Robbie Elliott was dismissed, reducing their side to nine men, following Mike Whitlow's red card in the 90th minute. Martijn Reuser got Town's fifth to secure the victory and ensure Ipswich's first trip to Wembley for 22 years.

Their opponents in the final were Barnsley, who had conceded eight goals in the league meetings between the two sides. This was another enthralling encounter in which Ipswich came from behind again after Craig Hignett's strike had hit the bar and rebounded in off 'keeper Richard Wright.

A Mowbray header levelled matters, but on the stroke of half-time Wright conceded a penalty. However, the England squad member made amends by saving Darren Barnard's resulting spot-kick.

Come the second half, Ipswich took control with goals from Richard Naylor and Marcus Stewart, whose performances in the play-offs justified his transfer fee.

Barnsley were later awarded another penalty which was converted by Hignett, but Martijn Reuser, as he had done in the second leg against Bolton, secured the victory in the final minute.

Inevitably, before they had left Wembley questions were being asked concerning Ipswich's chances of staying up. Burley's squad contains some highly-rated youngsters in Scowcroft, Clapham and Wright, as well as current internationals Matt Holland and Magilton.

There could be a bright future for the club – if they survive their first season back in the Premiership.

earning him a place in England's Euro 2000 squad

IPSWICH TOWN

DATE	OPPONENT	SCORE	ATT.	AXELDAL	BROWN	CLAPHAM	CLEGG	CROFT	FRIARS	HOLLAND	JOHNSON	LOGAN
7.8.99	Nottm Forest H	3–1	20,830	s5	–	90	–	–	–	90	85^{1}	–
15.8.99	Swindon A	4–1	6,195	s6	s2	90	–	–	–	90	84^{2} □	–
21.8.99	Bolton W H	1–0	17,696	s1	–	90	–	–	–	90	84^{1}	–
28.8.99	Sheff Utd A	2–2	12,445	–	–	90	–	–	–	90	90^{1}	–
30.8.99	Barnsley H	6–1	18,037	–	s45	90	–	–	–	90	90^{2}	–
11.9.99	Portsmouth A	1–1	16,034	s1	90	90 □	–	–	–	90	89 □	–
18.9.99	Birmingham H	0–1	19,758	–	s44	90	–	–	–	90	90	–
26.9.99	Man City H	2–1	19,406	–	s13	s45	–	90^{1}	–	90	90^{1} □	–
2.10.99	Grimsby A	1–2	6,531	–	–	90	–	–	–	90	90	–
16.10.99	QPR H	1–4	17,544	–	–	90	–	45	–	90^{1}	79	–
19.10.99	Charlton H	4–2	17,940	–	–	90 □	–	–	–	90	90^{1} □	–
23.10.99	Walsall A	1–0	6,526	s17 □	–	90	–	–	–	90	73	–
27.10.99	Man City A	0–1	32,799	s21	–	90	–	s14	–	90	45	–
30.10.99	Grimsby H	2–0	16,617	s8	–	90^{1}	–	s8	–	90	82	–
2.11.99	Huddersfield A	1–3	12,093	s13	–	90	–	s15	–	90^{1}	77	s4
6.11.99	Blackburn A	2–2	18,512	90	–	90	–	–	–	90^{1}	–	–
12.11.99	Tranmere H	0–0	14,514	s13	–	90	–	–	–	90	90	–
21.11.99	Norwich A	0–0	19,948	–	90	90	–	–	–	90	90	–
24.11.99	Wolves H	1–0	15,731	–	90	90	–	–	–	90	87	–
27.11.99	Crewe A H	2–1	15,211	–	70	90	–	90 □	s20	90	90^{2}	–
5.12.99	Nottm Forest A	1–0	15,724	–	90	90	–	90	–	90^{1}	90	–
7.12.99	C Palace A	2–2	13,176	s38	90 □	90	–	90	–	90^{1}	52^{1}	–
18.12.99	West Brom H	3–1	14,712	s7	90	90	–	–	–	90	32^{1} □	–
26.12.99	Fulham A	0–0	17,255	–	90	90	–	–	–	90	80	–
28.12.99	Stockport H	1–0	20,671	–	–	90	–	–	–	90	81	–
3.1.00	Port Vale A	2–1	6,908	s13	–	90	–	–	–	90^{1}	–	–
15.1.00	Swindon H	3–0	17,326	s8	–	90	–	s20	–	85	82	–
22.1.00	Bolton W A	1–1	11,924	s30	–	90	–	s25	–	90^{1}	90	–
29.1.00	Sheff Utd H	1–1	17,350	s9	–	90	–	90	–	90	90^{1}	–
5.2.00	Barnsley A	2–0	17,601	–	90	81	–	90	–	90	88	–
12.2.00	Huddersfield H	2–1	21,233	–	90	87	–	s2	–	90	88	–
19.2.00	Crewe A A	2–1	6,393	–	–	90^{1}	90	–	–	90	90	–
27.2.00	Birmingham A	1–1	20,493	–	90	90	90	–	–	90	90^{1}	–
4.3.00	Portsmouth H	0–1	20,305	–	90	90	90 □	–	–	90	90	–
7.3.00	Blackburn H	0–0	18,871	–	90	90	–	–	–	90	90	–
11.3.00	Wolves A	1–2	22,652	–	90	90	–	–	–	90	90	–
19.3.00	Norwich H	0–2	21,760	–	–	90	–	–	–	90	90	–
22.3.00	Tranmere A	2–0	6,933	–	s20	90	–	90	–	90^{1}	89^{1}	–
25.3.00	Fulham H	1–0	20,168	–	–	90	–	90	–	90	90	–
4.4.00	West Brom A	1–1	12,536	–	–	90	–	90	–	90^{1}	60	–
8.4.00	Port Vale H	3–0	19,663	–	90	90	–	90	–	90^{1}	84^{1}	–
15.4.00	Stockport A	1–0	8,501	–	90	90	–	90 □	–	90	90^{1}	–
22.4.00	QPR A	1–3	14,920	–	90	90	–	45	–	90	90	–
25.4.00	C Palace H	1–0	18,798	–	90	90	–	–	–	90	90^{1} □	–
29.4.00	Charlton A	3–1	20,043	–	90	s18	–	90	–	90	90^{1}	–
7.5.00	Walsall H	2–0	21,908	–	90	90	–	s9	–	90	90^{2}	–

□ Yellow card, ■ Red card, s Substitute, 90^{2} Goals scored, *including one own goal

1999–2000 DIVISION ONE APPEARANCES

McGREAL	MAGILTON	MIDGLEY	MOWBRAY	NAYLOR	REUSER	SCOWCROFT	STEWART	STOCKWELL	THETIS	VENUS	WILNIS	J WRIGHT	R WRIGHT	TOTAL
90□	–	–	–	90[1]	–	90[1]	–	81	90	90	s9	90	90	990
90	–	–	–	90[2]	–	–	–	90	90	88□	90	90	90	990
90	s6	–	–	89	–	90	–	61	81■	90	s29	90	90	981
90□	90	–	s25	90□	–	90[1]	–	s25	65	90	65	–	90	990
90	s10[1]	–	–	90[1]	–	90[1]	–	s10	90	45[1]	80	80	90	990
43■	s45□	–	–	45	–	90[1]	–	s45	–	90□	45□	90	90	943
90	s16	–	–	90	–	90	–	s4	46□	90□	86	74	90	990
–	90	–	–	s7	–	90	–	83	90	90□	77□	45	90	990
90□	90[1]□	–	–	90	–	90	–	90	73	90	s17□	–	90	990
90	45■	–	–	s11	–	90	–	s45	90□	90	–	90	90	945
90	90	–	90	–	–	90[1]	–	90[1]	–	90[1]	90	–	90	990
90	89	–	90	s45[1]	–	90	–	45	–	90	90	s1	90	990
90	90	–	90	s45	–	90	–	69	–	90	76	–	90	990
90	–	–	90	90[1]	–	–	–	90	–	90	82	90	90	990
90	–	–	–	90	–	–	–	86	90	90	75	90□	90	990
90	–	–	90[1]	90□	–	–	–	90	–	90□	90□	90□	90	990
90	s25	–	90	77	–	s45	–	90	–	90	45	65	90	990
–	90	–	90	s4□	–	90	–	86	90	–	90	–	90	990
90	90	–	90	s3	–	90[1]	–	76	–	–	90	s14	90	990
90□	90	–	90	–	–	90	–	70	–	–	–	s20	90	990
90	90	–	90	–	–	90	–	68	–	–	–	s22	90	990
90	90	–	90	–	–	90	–	71	–	–	–	s19	90	990
90	90	s58[1]	90	83	–	90[1]	–	59	–	–	–	s31	90	990
90	90	s10	90□	90	–	90	–	–	–	–	90□	–	90	990
90	45	s19	90	71	–	90[1]	–	s9	–	90	90	s45	90	990
90	–	77	90	66	–	90[1]	–	s24	–	90□	90	90	90	990
90	90	–	90□	90[2]	–	90	–	70[1]	–	90	–	s5	90	990
90	–	–	90	–	–	90	–	60	–	90	65	90	90	990
90	–	–	90	81	–	90□	–	s9	–	81	–	90	90	990
90	90	–	90	s2	–	90[1]	90[1]	–	–	–	s9	–	90	990
90	90	–	90	s2	–	90[1]	90[1]	s1	–	–	90	–	90	990
90	90	–	90□	45	–	90	–	–	–	–	90□	s45[1]	90	990
90	90	–	90	–	–	90	90	–	–	–	–	–	90	990
–	90	–	90□	–	–	45	90	–	–	–	90	s45	90	990
–	90	–	90	s5	–	–	85	s14	90	–	90	76	90	990
90	90	–	90	s19	–	90[1]	–	–	–	–	90	71	90	990
–	90	–	90□	s44	–	90□	46	s17	73	90	90□	–	90	990
–	90	–	90	s1	–	90	–	s63	–	70	27	90	90	990
90	90	–	90	s14	s14[1]	76	–	s9	–	81□	–	76	90	990
–	90	–	90	–	s40	90	s30	50	–	90	–	90	90	990
–	90	–	90	s6	s20	90[1]	68	–	–	70□	–	s22	90	990
14	90	–	90	–	45	90	–	s37	–	–	s39	s45	90	990
–	90[1]	–	90	s21	s45	90	–	–	–	–	90	69	90	990
–	90	–	90	s2	90	88	–	–	74	–	90	s16	90	990
–	90[1]	–	90	–	s34[1]	90	56	–	s9□	81	72	–	90	990
–	90	–	90	s19	s24	71	66	–	90□	–	81□	–	90	990

THE MANAGER

GEORGE BURLEY

After a brief spell in charge of Colchester United, George Burley moved to Portman Road in December 1994, returning to the club where he made more than 390 league appearances, as well as playing in both the 1978 FA Cup final win over Arsenal and the 1981 UEFA Cup final victory against Dutch side AZ Alkmaar. On the international stage with Scotland, he won 11 full caps.

His appointment as Ipswich boss at the mid-way stage of the 1994–95 Premiership season did not give him enough time to save the club from relegation. He was, however, taken on to do a long-term job with the goal of reaching the top flight with the new breed of youngsters coming through the ranks.

Burley deployed reliable campaigners such as Mick Stockwell and Tony Mowbray alongside young stars Richard Wright, James Scowcroft and Kieron Dyer to produce a series of teams that reached the Division One play-off semi-finals from 1996–97 to 1998–99.

Now that he has finally overcome Town's play-off hoodoo, Burley will need to keep Ipswich in the top flight, as relegation will result in established Premiership sides making offers which his most promising players may find too tempting to turn down.

LEAGUE POSITION

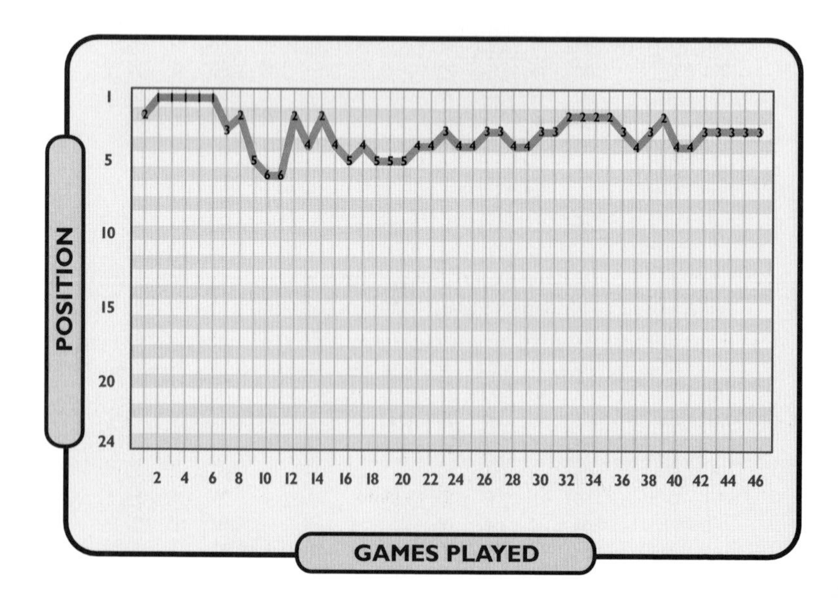

4,135 Minutes played in the league by Matt Holland

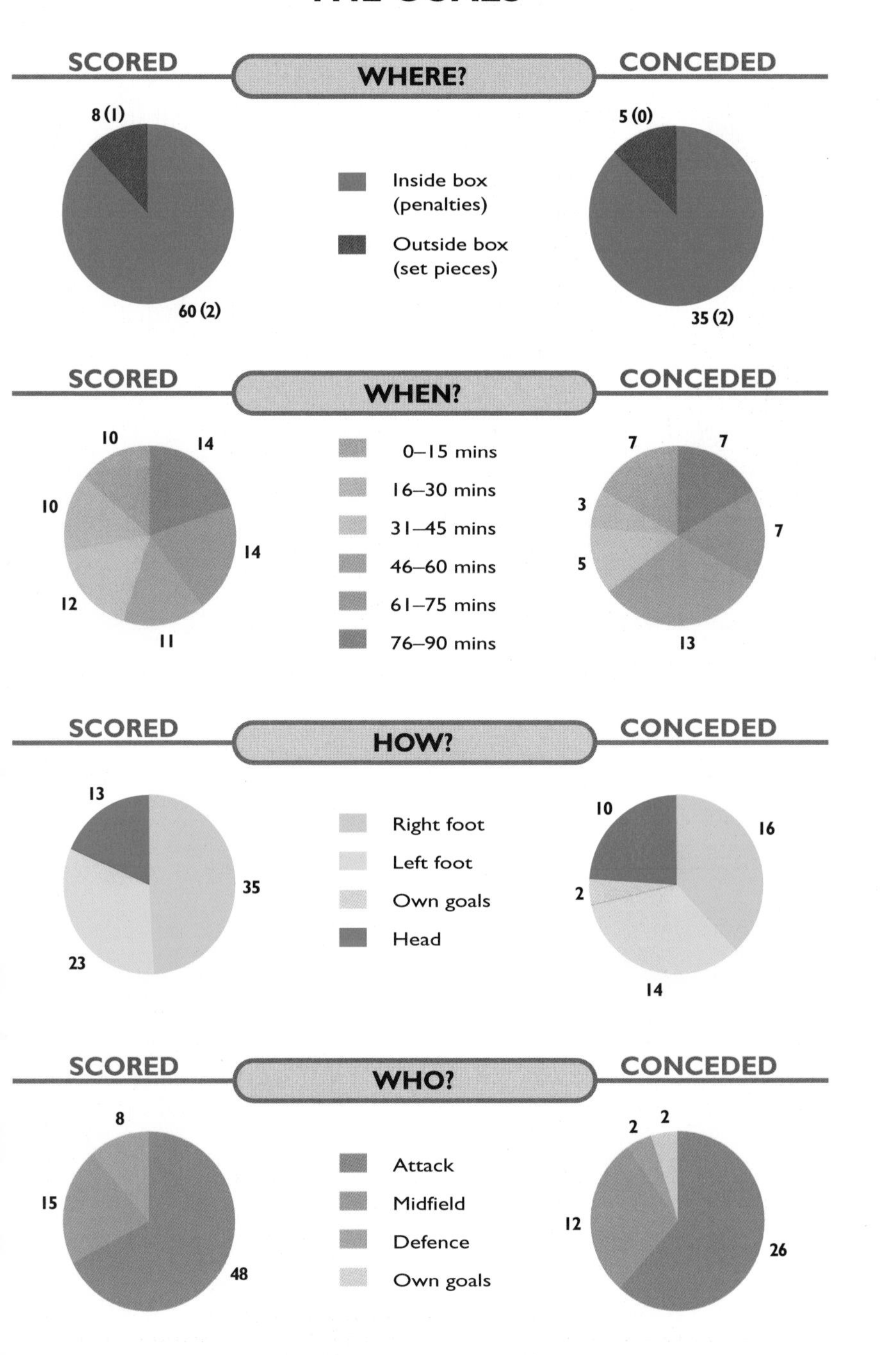
THE GOALS
SCORED
WHERE?
CONCEDED
8 (1)
60 (2)
Inside box
(penalties)
Outside box
(set pieces)
5 (0)
35 (2)
SCORED
WHEN?
CONCEDED
10
14
10
14
12
11
0–15 mins
16–30 mins
31–45 mins
46–60 mins
61–75 mins
76–90 mins
7
7
3
7
5
13
SCORED
HOW?
CONCEDED
13
35
23
Right foot
Left foot
Own goals
Head
10
16
2
14
SCORED
WHO?
CONCEDED
8
15
48
Attack
Midfield
Defence
Own goals
2
2
12
26

He was not booked all season

MANCHESTER CITY

ADDRESS

Maine Road, Moss Side,
Manchester, M14 7WN

CONTACT NUMBERS

Telephone: 0161 232 3000
Fax: 0161 232 8999
Ticket Office: 0161 226 2224
24 hour Booking: 0161 227 9229
Clubcall: 0891 121191
Superstore: 0161 232 1111
E-Mail: mcfc@mcfc.co.uk
Website: www.mcfc.co.uk

KEY PERSONNEL

Chairman: D Bernstein
Deputy Chairman: J Wardle
Directors: C Bird, B Bodek
A Lewis, A Mackintosh
A Thomas, D Tueart
Club Secretary: B Halford
Manager: Joe Royle

SPONSORS

Eidos

FANZINES

Bert Trautmann's Helmet
King of the Kippax
This Charming Fan
Chips 'n' Gravy
City Til I Cry

COLOURS

Home: Sky blue shirts, white shorts and navy stockings
Away: White shirts, navy shorts, white stockings

NICKNAME

The Blues
The Citizens

HONOURS

Division One Champions:
1936–37, 1967–68
Division Two Champions:
1898–99, 1902–03, 1909–10,
1927–28, 1946–47, 1965–66
FA Cup Winners:
1904, 1934, 1956, 1969
League Cup Winners: 1970, 1976
European Cup Winners' Cup Winners:
1970

RECORD GOALSCORER

Tommy Johnson – 158 league goals, 1919–30

BIGGEST WIN

10–1 v Huddersfield Town – Division Two, 7 November 1987

BIGGEST DEFEAT

1–9 v Everton – Division One, 3 September 1906

SEASON REVIEW

Following their dramatic victory on penalties against Gillingham in the play-off final at Wembley, Manchester City returned to Division One with renewed optimism following one of the most difficult periods in the club's history.

The 1999–2000 season began in typically rollercoaster fashion. Joe Royle's side took four points from their first three matches – a 1–0 defeat at home to Wolves, a goalless draw at Fulham and then, just as pundits began to predict more dismal times on Moss Side, an emphatic 6–0 mauling of Sheffield United at Maine Road.

The form of £1 million signing Mark Kennedy was having a profound effect on the team, as he not only weighed in with a goal in that Blades demolition and the winner at Bolton, but also created numerous chances for other members of the Manchester side.

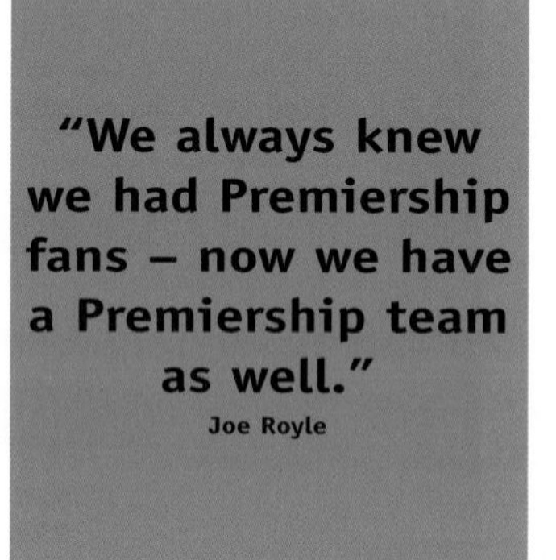

"We always knew we had Premiership fans – now we have a Premiership team as well."
Joe Royle

The 1–0 win at Walsall on 18 September put City on the top of the First Division, but they failed to hold this spot for more than a week as their next two matches, both in East Anglia, ended in defeat at Ipswich Town and Norwich City.

These losses acted as the catalyst for some excellent results in October and November. In these months, 26 points were won out of a possible 33, meaning an unbroken run of 10 weeks at the top of the Division One table.

During this period Joe Royle decided to increase the size of his squad by signing Lee Peacock from Mansfield for £500,000. He failed to hit the back of the net in a City shirt and his cause was not helped by Royle's next addition – Robert Taylor.

Back in May it had been Taylor's effort that had left City looking dead and buried as he netted Gillingham's second goal in the play-off final, but now he was moving up a division to Maine Road in a deal worth £1.5 million. He, too, was the subject of some criticism, having been handed his debut in arguably City's worst performance of the season, a 4–1 defeat at Molineux.

In the long term, however, his signing was justified. Once he had scored his first goal in the 3–0 win against basement boys Swindon, he struck up a formidable partnership with Shaun Goater that would ultimately fire the team all the way to the Premiership.

Another player to join City just before the Millennium festivities was Everton midfielder Tony Grant, who had experienced Division One life earlier in the campaign with a loan spell at Tranmere Rovers.

The FA Cup trail started with an emphatic 4–1 third round win at the Deva Stadium against Chester City. The fourth-round draw proved to be the toughest tie possible – at home to the then-Premiership leaders Leeds United. Many considered the match would give a good indication of City's prospects for survival in the top flight.

Leeds, in perhaps their best spell of form of the season, emerged victorious by five goals to two, but City had taken the lead twice in the match to suggest that if promotion followed, their forwards were capable of netting at the highest level.

City's next league game against Fulham looked tough on paper, but they dispelled any fears that the cup defeat would have an adverse effect on their league form by winning 4–0. Shaun Goater netted a brilliant hat-trick which boosted his confidence as he went on to score seven goals in the next nine games.

Come deadline day, Joe Royle decided to add a final piece to his jigsaw. Experienced centre-back Spencer Prior joined from

38 Manchester City recorded the best goal

SEASON REVIEW

Derby County for a £750,000 fee. This allowed the manager to move Gerard Wiekens into midfield, but meant Prior had to quickly forge a partnership with Richard Jobson.

Jobson took over from Andy Morrison in the heart of the defence following the latter's suspension back in August. Morrison did return to the side following his ban, but his season was ended in November because of injury. Thankfully the reliable Jobson, a mainstay of Royle's giant-killing Oldham sides, was in truly outstanding form for much of the campaign and adapted well to playing alongside Prior. In their nine matches together City conceded only five goals, a record that proved crucial in the battle for the second automatic promotion place.

> **"It's amazing – the first call from an agent came within an hour of us winning promotion at Blackburn."**
> Joe Royle

Prior's attributes at the other end of the field were also vital. He scored the opener against Crewe, which settled nerves and opened the flood gates as Dario Gradi's side crashed to a 4–0 defeat. Joe Royle revealed that the City players were so thrilled with their performance that they were "bouncing off the walls" in jubilation.

In the next game Prior's sixth-minute effort secured a win away at Grimsby Town, while his header at Portsmouth got the ball rolling for what was to be a dramatic south coast encounter.

A second goal followed in the 40th minute with a smart finish by Robert Taylor from a Mark Kennedy cross. City were cruising, but gave away a spot-kick on the stroke of half-time after the ball struck Taylor on the arm from close range. The decision infuriated City; and to make matters worse, former Citizen Lee Bradbury made no mistake from the spot. He also got the Pompey equaliser in the game's dying moments.

This result meant that City could no longer win the title, but instead had to focus their attention on retaining second place ahead of George Burley's Ipswich.

Another important Taylor goal against Birmingham City meant that only a point was needed from the final match of the season against Blackburn, but Ipswich could pip them to the post if City lost and Town won their last two matches.

Despite the club's reputation for cracking under similar pressures at the other end of the table in recent years, the defeat of Birmingham heralded jubilant celebrations, culminating in a pitch invasion when the final whistle was blown.

Some observers suggested the premature celebration might be regretted if City failed to beat Rovers but, despite conceding an early goal at Ewood Park, they overcame the jitters to come through 4–1 victors. Had City lost, Ipswich would have replaced them in second place as they beat Walsall 2–0 at Portman Road, but instead Town had to settle for a fourth successive stint in the play-offs.

Nicky Weaver, Shaun Goater and Mark Kennedy were all selected in the Division One PFA Team of the Year, but great credit must go to unsung heroes such as Richard Edghill, Jeff Whitley and Richard Jobson, who all played such a big part in taking the club back to the big time.

The rise in fortunes of Manchester City in the last two seasons has been as dramatic as their decline in the previous few. Successive promotions would not normally augur well for a successful Premiership campaign, but City's size and Joe Royle's wily management should see them fare better than Watford – the last team to achieve the Citizens' feat.

difference in Division One

MANCHESTER CITY

DATE	OPPONENT	SCORE	ATT.	ALLSOPP	BISHOP	COOKE	CROOKS	DICKOV	EDGHILL	GOATER	GRANT	GRANVILLE	HORL
8-8-99	Wolves H	0–1	31,755	–	–	90	s54	90	90	90	–	15	90
14.8.99	Fulham A	0–0	16,754	–	90	–	90 □	90 □	–	90	–	–	–
21.8.99	Sheff Utd H	6–0	30,110	–	s56	90	–	90^{1}	90	70^{1}	–	–	90^{2}
28.8.99	Bolton W A	1–0	21,671	–	s55	35	s4	90 □	90 □	75	–	–	90 □
30.8.99	Nottm Forest H	1–0	31,857	–	s17	73	s17	90	90	83^{1}	–	–	90
11.9.99	C Palace H	2–1	31,541	–	s35	75	s15	47	90	90	–	–	90
18.9.99	Walsall A	1–0	7,260	–	90	–	s25	90	90	90^{1}	–	–	90
26.9.99	Ipswich A	1–2	19,406	–	73	s17	90	90	–	90^{1}	–	s12	90
28.9.99	Norwich A	0–1	15,130	s22	90 □	s29	90 □	59	–	90	–	90	90 □
2.10.99	Port Vale H	2–1	31,608	s56	90^{2}	s9	90	81	–	34	–	90	90
16.10.99	Tranmere A	1–1	13,208	–	90	–	90 □	90 □	s1	–	–	90 □	82^{1} ■
19.10.99	Birmingham A	1–0	22,126	s1	90	–	s7	89	90	–	–	90	90 □
23.10.99	Blackburn H	2–0	33,027	–	81	–	s9	90	90^{1} □	81	–	90	90
27.10.99	Ipswich H	1–0	32,799	–	72	–	s18	67	90	90	–	90	90^{1}
30.10.99	Port Vale A	2–1*	10,250	–	s45	45	45	–	90	–	–	90^{1}	–
3.11.99	Portsmouth H	4–2	31,660	–	58	s42	–	–	90	–	–	90	90
6.11.99	QPR A	1–1	19,002	–	90	s45	45	–	90	–	–	90 □	90^{1}
20.11.99	Charlton A	1–0	20,043	–	–	s20	–	–	90	90^{1}	–	90	90 □
24.11.99	Barnsley H	3–1	32,692	–	–	–	s10	–	90	80^{1}	–	90	90^{1}
27.11.99	Huddersfield H	0–1	32,936	–	–	s45	–	–	90	90	–	90	90
3.12.99	Wolves A	1–4	21,635	–	90	–	–	–	90	90^{1}	–	55	90
7.12.99	Stockport H	1–2	32,686	–	90	–	–	–	90	90	–	90 □	90
18.12.99	Swindon H	3–0	31,751	–	90	–	–	–	90	64^{1}	–	90	90
26.12.99	West Brom A	2–0	19,589	–	90	–	–	s17	90 □	90^{1}	s12	90^{1}	–
28.12.99	Grimsby H	2–1	32,607	–	89	–	s1	s34	90	90	s11	90	90^{2}
3.1.00	Crewe A A	1–1	10,066	–	90	–	90^{1}	s44	–	90	73	49	90
16.1.00	Fulham H	4–0	30,057	–	90	–	–	–	90	90^{3}	90	90	90^{1}
22.1.00	Sheff Utd A	0–1	23,862	–	90	–	90	s26	90	90	90	–	90
5.2.00	Nottm Forest A	3–1	25,846	–	69	–	–	s13	90	90^{2}	–	s24	90
12.2.00	Norwich H	3–1	32,681	s29	90	–	–	61 □	79	90^{1}	–	90	90
18.2.00	Huddersfield A	1–1	18,173	–	89	–	–	90	90 □	90^{1}	–	90	78
26.2.00	Walsall H	1–1	32,438	–	90	–	s10 □	45	90	90^{1}	s45	80	45 □
4.3.00	C Palace A	1–1	21,052	–	–	–	–	–	90 □	–	–	72	–
8.3.00	QPR H	1–3	31,353	–	s45	–	–	s30	90	90	–	45	s21
11.3.00	Barnsley A	1–2	22,650	–	s45	–	–	s11	90 □	90^{1}	–	45	–
19.3.00	Charlton H	1–1	32,139	–	63	–	–	–	90	90^{1}	–	s27	–
21.3.00	Stockport A	2–2	11,212	–	61	–	–	s29	90	90	–	90	–
25.3.00	West Brom H	2–1	32,072	–	–	–	–	s45	90	90^{1}	s26	64	–
1.4.00	Swindon A	2–0	12,397	–	s42	–	–	90	90	85^{1}	48	–	–
5.4.00	Bolton W H	2–0	32,927	–	–	–	–	90^{1}	90	51	–	s17	90^{1}
8.4.00	Crewe A H	4–0	32,433	–	s9	–	–	90^{2}	90	90	–	–	90
15.4.00	Grimsby A	1–1	8,166	–	s35	–	–	63	90	90	–	–	55
22.4.00	Tranmere H	2–0	32,842	–	s16	–	–	69	90	90^{1}	–	–	90
24.4.00	Portsmouth A	2–2	19,015	–	–	–	–	s29	90	90	–	s4	s23
28.4.00	Birmingham H	1–0	32,062	–	–	–	–	s6	90	90	–	s6	88
7.5.00	Blackburn A	4–1*	29,913	–	s43	–	–	$s37^{1}$	90	90^{1}	–	s11	90

□ Yellow card, ■ Red card, s Substitute, 90^{2} Goals scored, *including one own goal

1999–2000 DIVISION ONE APPEARANCES

JOBSON	KENNEDY	MILLS	MORRISON	PEACOCK	POLLOCK	PRIOR	G TAYLOR	R TAYLOR	TIATTO	VAUGHAN	WEAVER	JEFF WHITLEY	JIM WHITLEY	WIEKENS	WRIGHT	WRIGHT-PHILLIPS	TOTAL
–	90	–	90	–	–	–	s21	–	–	–	90	90	–	90	–	–	990
–	70	–	70■	–	90	–	–	–	90	s20	90	90□	–	90	–	–	970
s25	90[1]	–	65□	–	–	–	s20[1]	–	34	–	90	90	–	90	–	–	990
90	90[1]	–	–	–	–	–	s15	–	86	–	90	90	–	90	–	–	990
90	90	–	90	–	–	–	s7	–	73	–	90	90	–	–	–	–	990
90[1]	90	–	90	–	–	–	s43[1]	–	55	–	90	90	–	–	–	–	990
90	90	–	–	–	–	–	–	–	90	–	90	90	–	65□	–	–	990
90	90	–	–	–	–	–	–	–	78□	–	90	90	–	90□	–	–	990
61	90□	–	90	–	–	–	s9	–	–	–	90	90	–	–	–	–	990
90	90	–	90□	–	–	–	–	–	–	–	90	90	–	–	–	–	990
90	89	–	90	–	–	–	90	–	–	–	90	90	–	–	–	–	982
90[1]	90	–	90	–	–	–	83	–	–	–	90□	90	–	–	–	–	990
90	90	–	90	–	–	–	s9	–	–	–	90	90[1]	–	–	–	–	990
90	80	–	90	–	–	–	s23	–	s10	–	90	90	–	–	–	–	990
90	90	–	57	–	90	–	90	–	–	–	90	90	–	s33	–	s45	990
90	90	–	–	–	s32[1]	–	90[2]	–	s13	–	90	90[1]	–	48	–	77	990
90	81	–	–	s45	–	–	90	–	s9	–	90	90	–	–	–	45	990
90	–	–	–	–	90	–	90	–	70	–	90	90	–	90	–	–	990
90	–	–	–	s10	90	–	90[1]	–	80	–	90	90	–	90	–	–	990
90	–	–	–	s30	90	–	60	–	45	–	90	90	–	90	–	–	990
90	90	–	–	–	s35□	–	–	90	s35	–	90	55	–	90	–	–	990
90	90	–	–	–	s15	–	s7□	83	–	–	90	75	–	90[1]	–	–	990
90	49	–	–	s26	90[1]	–	–	90[1]	s41	–	–	–	–	90	90	–	990
90	25	–	–	73	78	–	–	–	s65	–	90	90	–	90□	–	–	990
90	–	–	–	79	90	–	–	–	56	–	90	–	–	90	–	–	990
90	–	–	–	–	90	–	–	46	s41□	–	90	s17	–	90□	–	–	990
90	76□	–	–	–	–	–	–	90	s14	–	90	–	–	90	–	–	990
90	90	–	–	–	–	–	–	64□	90□	–	90	–	–	–	–	–	990
90	90	–	–	–	s21	–	–	77[1]	66□	–	90	90	–	90□	–	–	990
90	90[2]	–	–	–	s11	–	–	–	–	–	90	90	–	90	–	–	990
90	90	–	–	–	–	–	–	–	s12	–	90	90	s1	90	–	–	990
90	90	–	–	–	–	–	–	s45	–	–	90	90	–	90	–	–	990
90□	90	–	–	90	90	–	–	90[1]	90	–	90	90	–	90	–	s18	990
90	90	–	–	90	60	–	–	–	69	–	90	90[1]	–	90	–	–	990
90□	90	90	–	–	79	–	–	–	90	–	90	90□	–	90	–	–	990
90	90	–	–	–	90	–	–	90	90	–	90	90	–	90	–	–	990
90[1]□	90	–	–	–	90[1]□	–	–	90	–	–	90	90	–	90	–	–	990
90	90[1]	–	–	–	90	90	–	45□	90	–	90	90	–	–	–	–	990
90	90[1]□	–	–	–	90	90	–	–	90□	–	90	90□	–	s5	–	–	990
90	90	s39	–	–	–	90	–	–	73	–	90	90	–	90	–	–	990
90□	90[1]	–	–	–	–	90[1]	–	–	90	–	90	90	–	81	–	–	990
90	90	s27	–	–	–	90[1]	–	–	90	–	90	90	–	90	–	–	990
90	74	–	–	–	s13	90	–	s21	90□	–	90	77[1]	–	90	–	–	990
90	86	–	–	–	90	90[1]	–	61[1]□	90	–	90	90	–	67	–	–	990
90	84	–	–	–	s2	90	–	84[1]	90	–	90	90	–	90	–	–	990
90	79[1]	–	–	–	47	90	–	53	90	–	90	90	–	–	–	–	990

THE MANAGER

JOE ROYLE

As manager of Oldham Athletic, Joe Royle reached a League Cup final, two FA Cup semi-finals and helped the Latics cheat relegation on a regular basis once they were in the top flight.

He moved to Everton in 1994, where he had scored 119 goals in his playing career. As manager he won the 1995 FA Cup and achieved a sixth-placed finish in the Premiership in 1995–96, before leaving the club in 1997.

Royle joined Manchester City, another club where he had experience as a player, in February 1998 with the threat of relegation to the Second Division a distinct possiblility. Royle could not save City from the drop, but his appointment heralded a turnaround in the club's fortunes, starting with promotion via the Division Two play-offs in May 1999.

Goals from signings Robert Taylor and latterly Spencer Prior, helped secure second spot in Division One – and City's second successive promotion.

Royle has said that he wants to stick to the players who got the club up. Considering City's reputation for signing expensive flops during the close season under previous regimes, this tactic may be of benefit.

LEAGUE POSITION

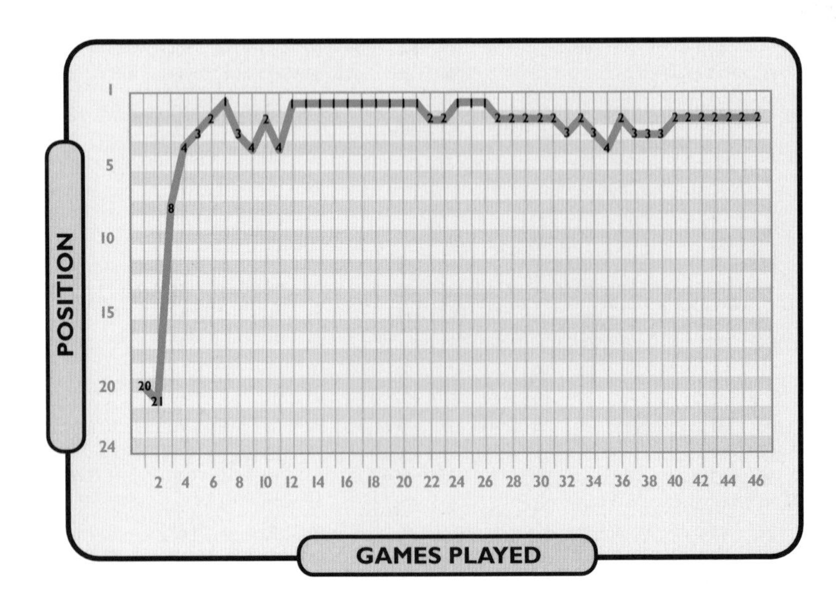

13 At 13 of their 23 away games Manchester City attracted

THE GOALS

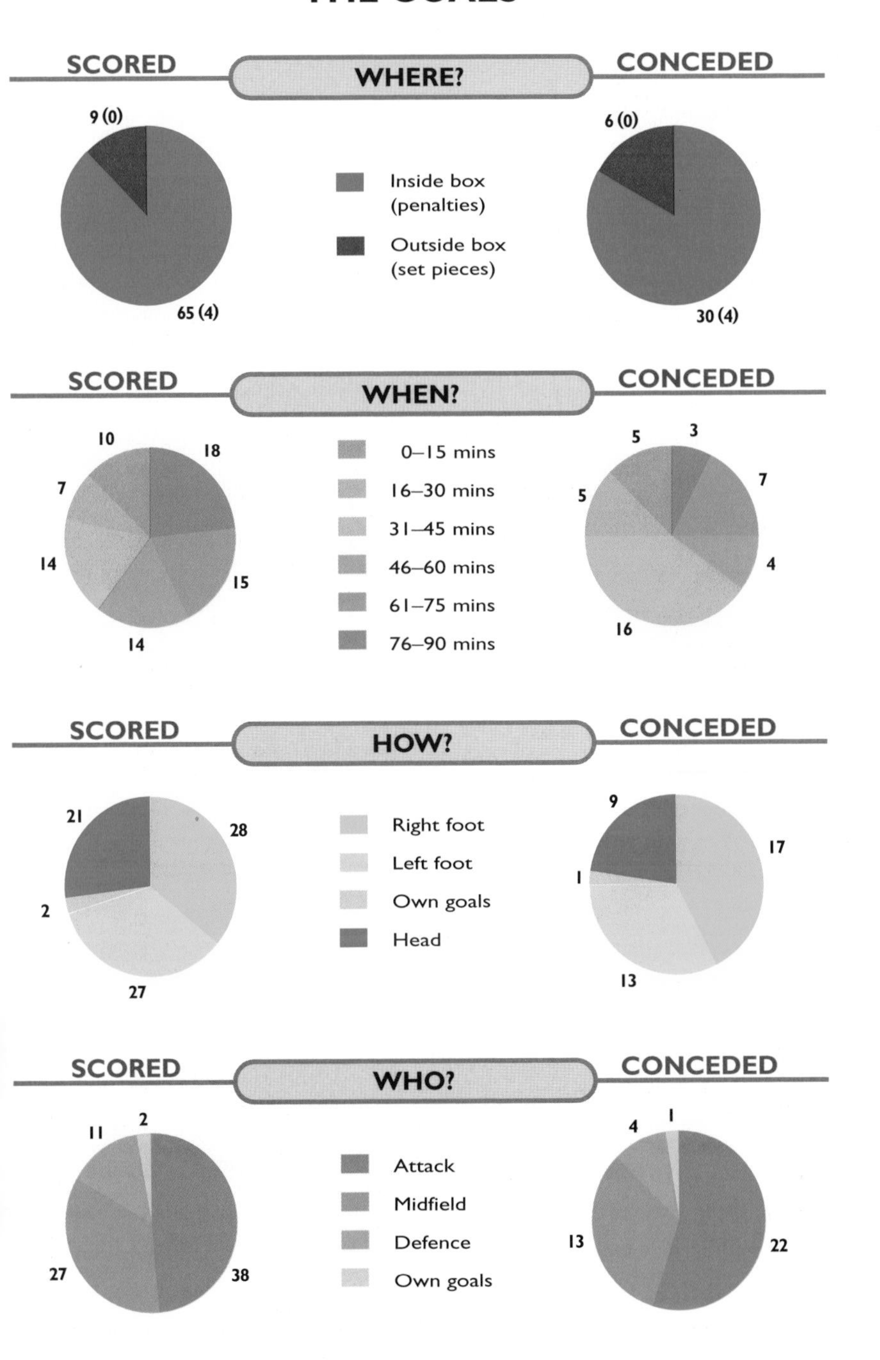

their opponents' highest gate of the season

HARP

THE PLAYERS

During the 1999–2000 season, 542 players made an appearance on the pitch – just three more than in 1998–99. Each player is featured in the following section, whether he was ever-present or played just one match as a substitute.

The players are featured in alphabetical order and the statistics that are shown are an individual's total contribution in 1999–2000, even if he played for more than one club. If you would like to see a player's contribution to a particular club, all you have to do is turn to the relevant page in the Team Section showing all players' performances for that particular team. The page references for these more detailed statistics are highlighted at the bottom of each player profile.

The club colours shown are for the team with which the player finished the season or for whom he made his last appearance in the 1999–2000 Premiership.

The small lozenge alongside each player's name indicates his usual position.

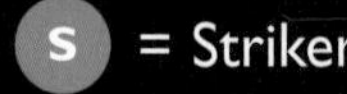

You will find that the categories of statistics vary according to the players' positions. Clearly more emphasis has been placed on goal attempts for strikers, whereas defenders will have tackling and defensive clearances featured. All players feature discipline figures for the season too and you should note that the statistics are for Premiership matches only.

PLAYERS' AVERAGES

CATEGORY	STRIKER	ATTACKING MIDFIELDER	MIDFIELDER	DEFENDER
Goals/Shots	16%	11%	9%	10%
Shooting Accuracy	52%	45%	42%	40%
Passing Accuracy	64%	70%	74%	68%
Short Pass Accuracy	64%	73%	77%	76%
Long Pass Accuracy	58%	56%	60%	51%
Crossing Accuracy	26%	30%	29%	32%
Dribble Success	68%	72%	80%	87%
Tackle Success	51%	50%	56%	51%

GOALKEEPER
Saves/Shots 72%   Catch Success rate 93%

CB Tony ADAMS • 6

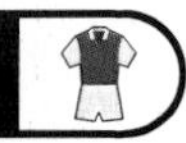

ARSENAL • BORN: 10.10.66

In a 1999–2000 season troubled by injury, Arsenal captain Tony Adams once again came close to landing a major honour. But for the second season in a row, Arsenal fell short on two fronts – finishing second in the Premiership and losing the UEFA Cup final to Galatasaray on penalties.

The Romford-born star is still considered one of the best defenders in the country and continued to prove his importance to the north London club, which undoubtedly missed his commanding presence when the 33-year-old was sidelined. Arsene Wenger's men conceded more than half their league goals in 1999–2000 when Adams was missing.

Arsenal's inspirational figurehead may not have appeared on the Gunners' scoresheet, but Wenger's intelligent approach to management has clearly augmented Adams's already impressive all-round game. Arsenal's skipper passed the ball out of defence with precision – finding a team-mate with 77% of his distribution – while completing more than 170 defensive clearances.

APPEARANCES	
Start (sub)	21(0)
Minutes on pitch	1890
GOAL ATTEMPTS	
Goals	0
DEFENDING	
Blocks	31
Shots cleared off line	0
Headed clearances	138
Other clearances	34
Interceptions	33
Last man saving tackles	0
Tackles won	44
Tackles won %	60%
PASSING	
Passing accuracy own half	84%
Passing accuracy opp half	65%
DISCIPLINE	
Fouls	25
Fouls in danger area	10
Yellow cards	2
Red cards	0

SEE PAGE 38 FOR FULL STATS

AM Gareth AINSWORTH • 18

WIMBLEDON • BORN: 10.5.73

Former Port Vale winger Gareth Ainsworth may only have made two substitute appearances for the Dons during the 1999–2000 season, but still managed to score a brace against Newcastle on August 21, before a niggling injury kept him out for the rest of the Wombles' unsuccessful Premiership campaign.

Ainsworth must be confident that he can play a more prominent role in Wimbledon's attempt to bounce straight back to the top flight and the fact that the diminutive player is still only 27 years of age should imbue the £2 million signing with the confidence to break into the first team when fit.

In his brief time in a Dons shirt, Ainsworth displayed his clinical instinct in front of goal by thumping in three shots on target, two of which found the back of the net, in just an hour of game-play. The Lancastrian clearly has a lot to offer the Selhurst Park faithful in the future, and will be hoping to help the Dons bounce straight back up.

SEE PAGE 304 FOR FULL STATS

Commanding: Tony Adams

A

Niclas ALEXANDERSSON • 16

SHEFFIELD WEDNESDAY • BORN: 29.12.71

Niclas Alexandersson was one of Wednesday's more consistent performers during their disastrous Premiership campaign, missing just one match in 1999–2000. Ironically, the skilful midfielder was absent for the Owls' penultimate fixture against Arsenal at Highbury, where a 3–3 draw saw Peter Shreeves's men relegated.

Alexandersson managed to rack up five goals, including what may prove to be his last strike in a Wednesday shirt on the final day of the season. The former Gothenburg star lashed in a left-footed shot, as the Owls mystified their ardent supporters by thrashing Leicester 4–0 to end a season that had seen so much disappointing football from the Yorkshiremen.

The tall Swede created 16 goalscoring opportunities for his team-mates from his wide position and whipped more than 80 crosses into the box. The fact that Alexandersson also tracked back to complete 109 defensive clearances, blocks and interceptions demonstrates the total commitment displayed by the talented player.

APPEARANCES	
Start (sub)	37(0)
Minutes on pitch	3138
GOAL ATTEMPTS	
Goals	5
Shots on target	25
Shooting accuracy	51%
Goals/shots ratio	10%
PASSING	
Goal assists	4
Passes in opp half	724
Passing accuracy in opp half	64%
Successful crosses	24
Crossing accuracy	27%
DRIBBLING	
Dribbles & runs	122
Dribble completion	78%
Corners forced	27
DISCIPLINE	
Fouls	22
Yellow cards	2
Red cards	0

SEE PAGE 220 FOR FULL STATS

Marco ALMEIDA • 29

SOUTHAMPTON • BORN: 4.4.77

Young Saints defender Marco Almeida had little opportunity to impress in the Premiership, playing for just 19 minutes against Arsenal on September 18.

Almeida was loaned from Portuguese giants Sporting Lisbon to Southampton at the start of the 1999–2000 season, but failed to break into the Saints' first team and was subsequently released back to his home country in December.

The Barreiro-born player did make the substitutes' bench five times, but then-manager Dave Jones only felt the need to bring Almeida on to the pitch on one occasion, after an injury to central defender Claus Lundekvam in the Saints' 1–0 defeat against the Gunners.

Unfortunately for the youngster, his rather ignominious introduction and, as it also transpired, final appearance at The Dell ended with Thierry Henry turning Almeida inside-out before despatching the ball past Paul Jones.

SEE PAGE 234 FOR FULL STATS

John ALOISI • 9

COVENTRY CITY • BORN: 5.2.76

A nasty hamstring injury sustained in Coventry's exciting 4–3 defeat at the hands of Leeds back in early September resulted in a premature end to John Aloisi's first full season with the Sky Blues.

Picked up for what many believed was a bargain fee of £650,000 from cash-strapped Portsmouth, the likeable Australian banged in two strikes before his unfortunate injury, just as he looked to be forging an impressive partnership with Irish international Robbie Keane up front for Coventry.

Aloisi's two goals, including one against the title-holders Manchester United, both came from inside the penalty area. This demonstrated the Aussie's natural finishing instinct, while he also managed to fire in a further three efforts on target.

The 6'0" striker displayed a real willingness to run at defenders, completing 60% of his attempted dribbles – and this can only be an asset to Gordon Strachan's team in 2000–01.

SEE PAGE 94 FOR FULL STATS

was the highest in the Premiership

Gabriele AMBROSETTI • 18

CHELSEA • BORN: 7.8.73

Gabriele Ambrosetti was brought in by Gianluca Vialli from Vicenza, although the pacy star struggled to hold down a regular starting place in the Chelsea line-up.

With just nine starts to his name, the 27-year-old hardly helped his cause by failing to score in the Premiership. But he proved to be extremely adept at passing and will have impressed the south-west London masses by winning all but one of his attempted challenges in a Blues shirt.

The striker-cum-midfielder was favourably compared with Manchester United's star Ryan Giggs by Vialli, but the Chelsea fans are still waiting to see the best from the Italian. Ambrosetti did embark on nearly 50 runs and dribbles, but a crossing accuracy from open play of just 13% does not exactly measure up to the Welshman's lofty standards.

Nonetheless, Ambrosetti looks to be a hot prospect and given the number of over-30s at Stamford Bridge, this 20-something should have sufficient time to make a name for himself in the Premiership.

APPEARANCES	
Start (sub)	9(7)
Minutes on pitch	739
GOAL ATTEMPTS	
Goals	0
Shots on target	4
Shooting accuracy	33%
Goals/shots ratio	0%
PASSING	
Goal assists	0
Passes in opp half	183
Passing accuracy in opp half	67%
Successful crosses	17
Crossing accuracy	22%
DRIBBLING	
Dribbles & runs	49
Dribble completion	80%
Corners forced	12
DISCIPLINE	
Fouls	10
Yellow cards	0
Red cards	0

SEE PAGE 80 FOR FULL STATS

CB

Trond ANDERSEN • 29

WIMBLEDON • BORN: 6.1.75

APPEARANCES	
Start (sub)	35(1)
Minutes on pitch	3092
GOAL ATTEMPTS	
Goals	0
DEFENDING	
Blocks	52
Shots cleared off line	2
Headed clearances	147
Other clearances	60
Interceptions	14
Last man saving tackles	0
Tackles won	49
Tackles won %	60%
PASSING	
Passing accuracy own half	70%
Passing accuracy opp half	58%
DISCIPLINE	
Fouls	33
Fouls in danger area	8
Yellow cards	4
Red cards	0

SEE PAGE 304 FOR FULL STATS

Norwegian Trond Andersen was brought in by erstwhile Wimbledon boss Egil Olsen from Molde back at the start of 1999–2000.

Equally comfortable at the back as in midfield, Andersen was ever-present for the Dons following his introduction against Coventry on August 14. But the Kristiansund-born player could not stop his side experiencing the agonising slide into Nationwide Division One.

The Norwegian international showed that he is far more comfortable completing his defensive duties rather than supporting the front men, after firing all but one of his 10 efforts on goal off target. Unsurprisingly then, Andersen failed to score for the Dons in the Premiership, but did show an admirable rearguard ability. The 25-year-old made more than 200 vital defensive clearances, along with 66 blocks and interceptions.

After experiencing three runners-up finishes in his five years at Molde, Andersen's athleticism will be put to the test in the unrelenting world of Division One football.

A

Darren ANDERTON • 7

TOTTENHAM HOTSPUR • BORN: 3.3.72

In yet another season stunted by injury, it is some consolation that Darren Anderton's Achilles tendon problem did not stop him completing more than 1,800 minutes of first team action for Spurs during 1999–2000.

The former Pompey star came back into the team to good effect by helping himself to three goals, including Tottenham's second in their 7–2 drubbing of Southampton – arguably Spurs' best performance of what was an ultimately disappointing season.

Anderton's natural skill on the ball continues to outfox defenders and this was epitomised through the lanky winger retaining possession in 80% of his dribbles. The experienced top-flight player proved that he still has the ability to create chances for his grateful team-mates, providing six assists and 23 key passes, while whipping in almost 140 centres.

Undoubtedly, a fit Anderton is one of the country's top midfielders. If he can replicate the 1998–99 season when he was virtually injury-free, Tottenham's next campaign could prove more fruitful.

APPEARANCES	
Start (sub)	22(0)
Minutes on pitch	1971
GOAL ATTEMPTS	
Goals	3
Shots on target	18
Shooting accuracy	42%
Goals/shots ratio	7%
PASSING	
Goal assists	6
Passes in opp half	832
Passing accuracy in opp half	67%
Successful crosses	50
Crossing accuracy	36%
DRIBBLING	
Dribbles & runs	60
Dribble completion	80%
Corners forced	21
DISCIPLINE	
Fouls	37
Yellow cards	5
Red cards	0

SEE PAGE 262 FOR FULL STATS

Martin ANDRESEN • 20

WIMBLEDON • BORN: 2.2.77

APPEARANCES	
Start (sub)	4(10)
Minutes on pitch	512
GOAL ATTEMPTS	
Goals	1
Shots on target	1
Shooting accuracy	14%
Goals/shots ratio	14%
PASSING	
Goal assists	1
Passes in opp half	164
Passing accuracy in opp half	48%
Successful crosses	10
Crossing accuracy	40%
DRIBBLING	
Dribbles & runs	24
Dribble completion	67%
Corners forced	7
DISCIPLINE	
Fouls	9
Yellow cards	1
Red cards	0

SEE PAGE 304 FOR FULL STATS

Another of former Dons boss Egil Olsen's Norwegian signings, Martin Andresen came to Selhurst Park during the 1999–2000 season for £2 million from Stabæk.

Unfortunately for the talented midfielder, Andresen's first team starts were extremely limited and the tag of being voted "the sexiest man in Norway" by a glamour magazine was perhaps the most prominent feature of his first season in England.

Andresen represented his country at under-21 level, but the fact that he only scored one league goal did not impress many Dons fans. Certainly, there was a distinct lack of sexy football in south London considering that strike was the Scandinavian's only shot on target for the Dons.

The 23-year-old former Ski player held on to the ball with 67% of his attempted dribbles and won back possession with exactly half of his challenges. But if Andresen is to play an integral part in Wimbledon bouncing straight back to the Premiership, then he will have to improve on 1999–2000's tame debut.

Neal ARDLEY • 12

WIMBLEDON • BORN: 1.9.72

Versatile midfielder Neal Ardley is Wimbledon through and through after having graduated through the club's youth system, but suffered from former boss Egil Olsen's preference for his Scandinavian imports.

The Epsom-born player only completed 90 minutes on five occasions during the 1999–2000 season and two of those were under new manager Terry Burton. But, despite his limited time on the pitch, Ardley still managed to net a couple of strikes and created six goalscoring chances for his fellow Dons.

The former England under-21 international's experience, tenacious tackling and hard work will be needed by Burton's men for next season's slog in the Football League. The Dons star completed more than 20 challenges for the ball, although he will want to improve on his 48% tackling success ratio.

Ardley is usually involved in Wimbledon's dead-ball situations and, although the 27-year-old did not score from a free-kick during 1999–2000, he did net the Dons' only spot-kick against Leicester back in November.

APPEARANCES	
Start (sub)	10(7)
Minutes on pitch	994
GOAL ATTEMPTS	
Goals	2
Shots on target	6
Shooting accuracy	67%
Goals/shots ratio	22%
PASSING	
Goal assists	1
Passes in opp half	294
Passing accuracy in opp half	56%
Successful crosses	14
Crossing accuracy	24%
DRIBBLING	
Dribbles & runs	33
Dribble completion	61%
Corners forced	18
DISCIPLINE	
Fouls	11
Yellow cards	0
Red cards	0

SEE PAGE 304 FOR FULL STATS

Alun ARMSTRONG • 20

MIDDLESBROUGH • BORN: 22.2.75

APPEARANCES	
Start (sub)	3(9)
Minutes on pitch	338
GOAL ATTEMPTS	
Goals inside box	1
Goals outside box	0
Minutes per goal scored	338.0
Goals/shots ratio	13%
SHOOTING	
Shots on target inside box	2
Shots on target outside box	1
Shooting accuracy	38%
PASSING	
Goal assists	0
Key passes	4
Passing accuracy in opp half	67%
DISCIPLINE	
Fouls committed	4
Fouls won	5
Offside	8
Yellow cards	0
Red cards	0

SEE PAGE 192 FOR FULL STATS

Ever since joining Boro from Stockport County during the 1997–1998 season, Alun Armstrong has struggled to break into the first team at The Riverside, and the 1999–2000 campaign was no exception.

The Gateshead-born forward made only 1 appearances for Bryan Robson's men before joining First Division side Huddersfield Town on loan until the end of the season. Armstrong did manage to score in the Premiership before his temporary move, knocking in a rebound against West Ham in October.

In his brief time on the pitch, Armstrong displayed a willingness to run at defences and successfully retained possession 83% of the time. The 6'1" striker also created fou goalscoring opportunities for his team-mate and found a fellow-Boro player with a impressive 71% of his passes.

At the age of just 25, the Middlesbroug attacker would fancy his chances of featurin more regularly in Robson's plans for next season Certainly Armstrong has shown in glimpses the potential to be a permanent fixture.

I Chris Armstrong was the only Premiership player to

A

Chris ARMSTRONG • 16

TOTTENHAM HOTSPUR • BORN: 19.6.70

Although Chris Armstrong has attracted plenty of critics, he was Tottenham's joint-top scorer along with Steffen Iversen during 1999–2000, with 14 Premiership goals to his name.

The man Spurs paid £4.5 million for back in 1995 certainly hit back at the cynics and looked to be building a healthy striking partnership with Iversen in George Graham's new-look side.

Armstrong bore the brunt of a torrent of abuse from the White Hart Lane crowd, most of which appeared unnecessary considering the 6'0" forward scored with 20% of his efforts on goal. This percentage was higher than north London rival Thierry Henry and experienced Sunderland attacker Niall Quinn, who both finished along with the Tottenham attacker in the top 10 scorers chart.

The Newcastle-born player also reaffirmed his talent in the air, with only seven top-flight players surpassing Armstrong's tally of four headed goals during the campaign. Certainly, very few efforts will top the 30-year-old's diving header at Old Trafford.

APPEARANCES	
Start (sub)	29(2)
Minutes on pitch	2513
GOAL ATTEMPTS	
Goals inside box	13
Goals outside box	1
Minutes per goal scored	179.5
Goals/shots ratio	20%
SHOOTING	
Shots on target inside box	27
Shots on target outside box	3
Shooting accuracy	43%
PASSING	
Goal assists	1
Key passes	5
Passing accuracy in opp half	54%
DISCIPLINE	
Fouls committed	72
Fouls won	52
Offside	66
Yellow cards	4
Red cards	0

SEE PAGE 262 FOR FULL STATS

Pegguy ARPHEXAD • 22

LEICESTER CITY • BORN: 18.5.73

APPEARANCES	
Start (sub)	9(2)
Minutes on pitch	973
SHOT STOPPING	
Goals conceded (inside box)	15
Goals conceded (outside box)	2
Minutes per goal conceded	57.2
Clean sheets	3
Saves (shots inside box)	24
Saves (shots outside box)	24
Saves/shots	74%
DISTRIBUTION	
Long kick %	44%
Throws/short passes %	87%
CATCHING	
Crosses caught	18
Crosses punched	1
Crosses dropped	0
Catch success %	100%
DISCIPLINE	
Yellow cards	0
Red cards	0

SEE PAGE 150 FOR FULL STATS

Leicester's number two goalkeeper Pegguy Arphexad did manage to feature in more than 900 minutes of Premiership football during the 1999–2000 season after a number of injuries to first-choice 'keeper Tim Flowers. He also most memorably replaced the England stopper in the FA Cup game with Arsenal and saved Gilles Grimandi's spot-kick to win the game for the elated Foxes.

Arphexad kept three clean sheets in nine starts for Martin O'Neill's men, although he did concede 17 goals in that time. Heavy defeats against Derby (3–0) and Sheffield Wednesday (4–0) rather offset the fact that the French 'keeper had a decent record for the Foxes, with excellent handling skills and good reactions.

The former Lens number one eased the pressure on his defence by successfully dealing with all crosses into the box, while saving 74% of shots on the Leicester goal. For a 'keeper who played out most of the season in the reserves, this represents a pretty healthy set of statistics. More of Arphexad's reliability may well be needed wherever he plies his trade.

score for both teams in the same match (v Arsenal – 19 March)

FB Peter ATHERTON • 2

SHEFFIELD WEDNESDAY • BORN: 6.4.70

It was an unfortunate 1999–2000 campaign for Wednesday captain Peter Atherton, culminating in personal relegation from the top flight for the first time, despite playing in a poor Coventry defence in the early 1990s.

The Owls' back-line did not perform much better than his former employers, shipping 70 goals as they plummeted from the top flight. But the versatile player did still manage to surpass the 300 mark for defensive clearances and put in 124 tackles, plying his trade in midfield for some of the season.

The experienced Atherton notched up a single strike – scoring the winner against Middlesbrough at Hillsborough – and thumped in 14 efforts on goal. The Owls' fans were also quick to point out that, despite his hard-tackling reputation, the former Wigan stalwart did not see red and received just five yellow cards in the league over the course of the 1999–2000 season.

Atherton ended the campaign out of contract, and was rumoured to be a target for Wigan Athletic and Manchester City.

APPEARANCES	
Start (sub)	35(0)
Minutes on pitch	3135
GOAL ATTEMPTS	
Goals	1
Goal assists	0
Passing	1119
Passing accuracy	70%
PASSING & CROSSING	
Crosses	23
Crossing accuracy	43%
DEFENDING	
Tackles	124
Tackles won %	45%
Blocks	76
Interceptions	32
Clearances	306
Shots cleared off line	2
DISCIPLINE	
Fouls	35
Yellow cards	5
Red cards	0

SEE PAGE 220 FOR FULL STATS

FB Celestine BABAYARO • 3

CHELSEA • BORN: 29.8.78

APPEARANCES	
Start (sub)	23(2)
Minutes on pitch	2055
GOAL ATTEMPTS	
Goals	0
PASSING & CROSSING	
Goal assists	0
Passing	1054
Passing accuracy	79%
Successful crosses	53
Crossing accuracy	28%
DEFENDING	
Tackles	53
Tackles won %	47%
Blocks	29
Interceptions	17
Clearances	119
Shots cleared off line	0
DISCIPLINE	
Fouls	32
Yellow cards	3
Red cards	0

SEE PAGE 80 FOR FULL STATS

Nigerian international Celestine Babayaro wa at the centre of several club-versus-countr rows during the 1999–2000 season. Only th postponement of a friendly with Qatar allowe "Baba" to participate in the FA Cup final.

And, following the African Nations Cup i January, he went AWOL for two weeks befor finally returning to Stamford Bridge.

Despite this, a long-term injury to left-bac Graeme Le Saux saw Babayaro establis himself on the left-hand side. His stamina an determination enabled him to get forward a every opportunity, although his passin accuracy of 79% was a decline on 1998–99.

Nevertheless, his cross completion rat improved, as his solid running down the flan was a useful attacking outlet.

He had an eventful Champions Leagu scoring against Skonto Riga in the preliminar round and at home to Feyenoord.

But it all turned sour for Babayaro when h was dismissed at the Nou Camp for professional foul as the Blues crashed out a the quarter-final stage to Barcelona.

Walid BADIR • 19

WIMBLEDON • BORN: 12.3.74

)espite being known as "the hardest man in sraeli football", Walid Badir was unable to ave the Dons from the dreaded drop after heir 14-year stay in the top flight.

He joined the club in July 1999 for £1.6 nillion, snubbing moves to Sheffield Vednesday and Spanish side Rayo Vallecano to ›ly his trade at Selhurst Park.

Badir made a dream start in his first full jame, putting the Dons one-up at Old Trafford. 3ut, like the story of Wimbledon's season, they vere unable to hold on to a lead and Jordi Cruyff soon levelled for the Champions.

Used as a winger later in the season, it may)e argued that Badir was better employed hrough the centre, as his poor crossing ccuracy demonstrated.

He attempted a lot of shots from outside the)ox, but they usually failed to trouble most keepers in the Premiership.

It remains to be seen if Wimbledon's new nanager will keep Badir at the club when they eek an instant return to the Premiership in eason 2000–01.

APPEARANCES	
Start (sub)	12(9)
Minutes on pitch	1055
GOAL ATTEMPTS	
Goals	1
Shots on target	11
Shooting accuracy	48%
Goals/shots ratio	4%
PASSING	
Goal assists	0
Passes in opp half	256
Passing accuracy in opp half	63%
Successful crosses	2
Crossing accuracy	14%
DRIBBLING	
Dribbles & runs	29
Dribble completion	69%
Corners forced	9
DISCIPLINE	
Fouls	20
Yellow cards	2
Red cards	0

SEE PAGE 304 FOR FULL STATS

Francesco BAIANO • 27

DERBY COUNTY • BORN: 24.2.68

Francesco Baiano's two-year spell with the Rams ended when he joined Italian side Ternana in November 1999.

The immensely-skilful striker found himself surplus to requirements at Pride Park with the arrival of Belgian international Branko Strupar and the emergence of exciting youngster Malcolm Christie.

A fine provider to his team-mates, he set up two goals and had an above-average passing accuracy for a centre-forward, picking out a fellow-Ram with 71% of his distribution.

But the former Italian international struggled to cope with the frenetic pace of the Premiership and, at 32 years of age, his slow build-up play was better suited to the continental game.

His last match for the club was in the televised 2–0 defeat at Newcastle in late October and his number 27 shirt was later worn by new crowd favourite at Pride Park Georgi Kinkladze.

SEE PAGE 108 FOR FULL STATS

Adrian BAKALLI • 25

WATFORD • BORN: 22.11.76

Former Belgian under-21 international Adrian Bakalli played a minor role in the Hornets' doomed bid to avoid relegation.

Originally he joined the club for a trial period, making his Watford debut as a second-half substitute in the 1–0 defeat at Leicester.

Manager Graham Taylor was suitably impressed and shelled out £100,000 for his services in January. But Bakalli found it hard to make the breakthrough because of the disciplined performances of Steve Palmer in the centre of the park.

Watford's version of the "muscles from Brussels" is versatile enough to play at right-back or in the midfield. He is excellent in the air and, for such a tall player, possesses a good touch.

Although his completion rate of 62% from 26 passes could have been better, he was a valuable squad player and could be given more of a chance in the Football League Division One in 2000–01.

SEE PAGE 276 FOR FULL STATS

Eirik BAKKE • 19

LEEDS UNITED • BORN: 13.9.77

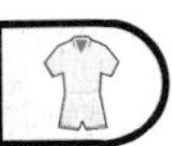

Elegant Eirik Bakke boosted Leeds' squad when he joined United for £1.75 million in the summer of 1999.

The Norwegian Euro 2000 star was subsequently voted Young Player of the Year at Elland Road after a series of fine performances. A stylish and creative midfielder, he showed an eye for goal, netting twice in the league and another six times in cup competitions.

Both his Premiership goals came in a terrific team performance when United demolished Wimbledon 4–1 in March.

Bakke is not afraid to shoot from distance, although his long-rangers rarely troubled opposition 'keepers. He also showed strength in the tackle, winning 60% of his challenges, although poor timing on occasions saw him booked seven times.

With Leeds finishing third and qualifying for the Champions League, season 2000–01 will see Bakke parade his talents on an even bigger stage, where football connoisseurs across the continent will witness his talents.

APPEARANCES	
Start (sub)	24(5)
Minutes on pitch	2232
GOAL ATTEMPTS	
Goals	2
Shots on target	11
Shooting accuracy	28%
PASSING	
Goal assists	1
Passes in opp half	744
Passing accuracy in opp half	63%
Successful crosses	8
Cross completion	19%
DEFENDING	
Interceptions	15
Clearances	37
Tackles	81
Tackles won %	60%
DISCIPLINE	
Fouls	52
Yellow cards	7
Red cards	0

SEE PAGE 136 FOR FULL STATS

M

Kevin BALL • 4

SUNDERLAND • BORN: 12.11.64

APPEARANCES	
Start (sub)	6(5)
Minutes on pitch	512
GOAL ATTEMPTS	
Goals	0
Shots on target	0
Shooting accuracy	0%
PASSING	
Goal assists	0
Passes in opp half	85
Passing accuracy in opp half	73%
Successful crosses	0
Cross completion	0%
DEFENDING	
Interceptions	2
Clearances	24
Tackles	33
Tackles won %	61%
DISCIPLINE	
Fouls	15
Yellow cards	4
Red cards	0

SEE PAGE 248 FOR FULL STATS

Inspirational skipper Kevin Ball ended his nine-year association with the Black Cats when he moved to Fulham for £200,000 in December 1999.

Ball found himself surplus to requirements at the Stadium of Light because of the arriva[l] of Swedish international Stefan Schwarz and the form of youngster Gavin McCann.

Tough-tackling Ball is a whole-hearted player, whose unerring commitment and desire to win endeared him to the fans. Indeed, they turned out in force for his benefit match against Sampdoria in the summer of 1999.

The 35-year-old captained the Mackems to the Division One Championship in 1996 and 1999, and his holding role saw him make a creditable 24 clearances in the 1999–2000 Premiership campaign.

His last goal for the club was a consolation effort in Sunderland's 3–2 defeat at Wimbledon in the Worthington Cup in October before he moved south to play alongside former Black Cat team-mate Lee Clark at Craven Cottage.

FB Michael BALL • 3

EVERTON • BORN: 2.10.79

APPEARANCES	
Start (sub)	14(11)
Minutes on pitch	1420
GOAL ATTEMPTS	
Goals	1
PASSING	
Goal assists	0
Passing	560
Passing accuracy	61%
Crosses	23
Crossing accuracy	4%
DEFENDING	
Tackles	56
Tackles won %	54%
Blocks	25
Interceptions	9
Clearances	72
Shots cleared off line	0
DISCIPLINE	
Fouls	13
Yellow cards	3
Red cards	0

SEE PAGE 122 FOR FULL STATS

. reported £5 million bid from Manchester nited seemed to affect the form of Everton's ichael Ball during the 1999–2000 season.

The 20-year-old left-back failed to claim a egular spot in the Toffees' rearguard, as alter Smith preferred to utilise the xperience of David Unsworth rather than call pon the raw talent of Ball.

Statistically, he endured a disappointing eason, with a notable decline in his passing nd crossing accuracy from 1998–99.

Many observers believe that he will be a ermanent fixture in the England set-up efore too long.

A sharp tackler, winning 54% of his hallenges, he displayed great composure by oolly slotting home a penalty in the 2–1 win ver Derby in February.

Ball is one of the club's most prized assets nd season 2000–01 should see him in more irst-team action as Walter Smith aims to uild on well-laid foundations and help boost verton's chances of finishing higher than 3th place in the league.

AM Nick BARMBY • 8

EVERTON • BORN: 11.2.74

APPEARANCES	
Start (sub)	37(0)
Minutes on pitch	3098
GOAL ATTEMPTS	
Goals	9
Shots on target	25
Shooting accuracy	54%
Goals/shots ratio	20%
PASSING	
Goal assists	8
Passes in opp half	1019
Passing accuracy in opp half	65%
Successful crosses	38
Crossing accuracy	26%
DRIBBLING	
Dribbles & runs	108
Dribble completion	80%
Corners forced	34
DISCIPLINE	
Fouls	25
Yellow cards	7
Red cards	0

SEE PAGE 122 FOR FULL STATS

After nearly four years in the international wilderness, Nick Barmby made a shock return when he was called into Kevin Keegan's squad for Euro 2000 after a series of fine displays for Everton during 1999–2000.

Barmby has excellent technical ability and a real footballing brain; witness his ability to deliver telling through-balls. His total of 1,437 attempted passes throughout the season was the most by an Everton player with the exception of midfielder John Collins – and Don Hutchison.

He also made the highest number of crosses and dribbles of any Everton star.

One of his best performances came in a 4–0 thumping of West Ham in February when he smashed a hat-trick past the hapless Sasa Ilic.

He also scored the Toffees' last goal of the 1999–2000 campaign, when he pounced on a mistake by Nigel Martyn to equalise in a stormy encounter at Elland Road.

Similar displays from Barmby in the future could see him become a more regular fixture in Kevin Keegan's England squads.

he area was the highest in the Premiership

S Graham BARRETT • 35

ARSENAL • BORN: 6.10.81

Arsenal's Irish starlet Graham Barrett is a fantastic prospect for the north London giants. Captaining the Gunners to a 5–1 aggregate success in the FA Youth Cup, Barrett is a prolific striker at reserve and youth levels.

Manager Arsene Wenger rates him very highly and gave him a brief taste of the Premiership when he brought him on as sub in the comfortable victories at Leicester and at home to Sunderland, when he replaced leading scorer Thierry Henry.

Barrett has represented the Republic of Ireland at under-15, 16 and 17 levels – and, under the watchful eye of Arsenal youth supremo Liam Brady, could well blossom into a full international.

The 18-year-old Dubliner scored seven goals in 12 reserve appearances and another five strikes on the road to Youth Cup glory.

Barrett would now appear to have a very promising future in the game.

SEE PAGE 38 FOR FULL STATS

CB Gareth BARRY • 15

ASTON VILLA • BORN: 23.2.81

Cultured defender Gareth Barry continued his football education with a series of fine performances in the Villa Park classroom.

Playing alongside the more experienced duo of Ugo Ehiogu and Gareth Southgate, Barry earned himself an England debut in February during the friendly international with Argentina at Wembley.

Making more clearances than he did in the 1998–99 season, Barry also utilised his fine positional sense to make 13 vital interceptions during the course of the season.

His solitary goal was a header in front of the Holte End, from an Alan Thompson corner, during the 1–1 draw with Sunderland.

One of the best passers at the club, only Villa's Player of the Year Paul Merson and wing-back Alan Wright made more successful passes during the course of 1999–2000.

He also boasted the best tackle success rate at the club and achieved a 94% dribble completion rate.

Barry ended the season with a call-up to England's Euro 2000 squad.

Call-up: Gareth Barry

APPEARANCES	
Start (sub)	30(0)
Minutes on pitch	2700
GOAL ATTEMPTS	
Goals	1
DEFENDING	
Blocks	53
Shots cleared off line	0
Headed clearances	152
Other clearances	74
Interceptions	13
Last man saving tackles	3
Tackles won	43
Tackles won %	58%
PASSING	
Passing accuracy own half	68%
Passing accuracy opp half	57%
DISCIPLINE	
Fouls	37
Fouls in danger area	9
Yellow cards	6
Red cards	0

SEE PAGE 52 FOR FULL STATS

B

Warren BARTON • 2

NEWCASTLE UNITED • BORN: 19.3.69

Flaxen-haired full-back Warren Barton made up for an early-season indiscretion at Coventry by enjoying a consistent 1999–2000 campaign for the Magpies.

The former Wimbledon man was sent off in Newcastle's 4–1 defeat at Highfield Road in October for an alleged punch on Moroccan international Youssef Chippo.

The well-dressed ex-England defender loves to get forward and his excellent stamina levels enabled him to make a number of surging runs down the flank.

In fact, he had the best dribble completion rate at St James's Park in 1999–2000, ahead of pacy team-mates Kieron Dyer and wing wizard Nolberto Solano.

Barton's crossing accuracy of 36% was a nine-point improvement on his 1998–99 total and his versatility is an asset to the squad.

The former England international received special praise from Newcastle boss Bobby Robson for his professionalism throughout the season, suggesting that he has a big part to play in the Magpies' future.

APPEARANCES	
Start (sub)	33(1)
Minutes on pitch	2874
GOAL ATTEMPTS	
Goals	0
PASSING & CROSSING	
Goal assists	3
Passing	1711
Passing accuracy	71%
Crosses	80
Crossing accuracy	36%
DEFENDING	
Tackles	88
Tackles won %	50%
Blocks	50
Interceptions	25
Clearances	144
Shots cleared off line	2
DISCIPLINE	
Fouls	33
Yellow cards	5
Red cards	1

SEE PAGE 206 FOR FULL STATS

M

David BATTY • 23

LEEDS UNITED • BORN: 2.12.68

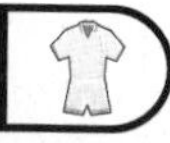

APPEARANCES	
Start (sub)	16(0)
Minutes on pitch	1380
GOAL ATTEMPTS	
Goals	0
Shots on target	2
Shooting accuracy	25%
PASSING	
Goal assists	3
Passes in opp half	654
Passing accuracy in opp half	80%
Successful crosses	2
Cross completion	33%
DEFENDING	
Interceptions	28
Clearances	31
Tackles	67
Tackles won %	52%
DISCIPLINE	
Fouls	21
Yellow cards	4
Red cards	0

SEE PAGE 136 FOR FULL STATS

The 1999–2000 season was one of huge disappointment for Leeds' midfield hardman David Batty.

After a calf injury ruled him out from December onwards, he had to sit and watch from the sidelines as David O'Leary's youngsters produced a series of fearless performances both at home and in abroad in the UEFA Cup.

Before his injury, Batty's incisive through-balls laid on three goals and he had an above-average passing accuracy of 84%. On the other hand, his tackle success rate was in decline from last season, perhaps as he feared aggravating his long-standing injury.

Missing out on Euro 2000 will have hurt Batty's pride after his last outing for Kevin Keegan's side ended in dismissal in the qualifying match against Poland in 1999.

Batty aimed to train throughout the summer in a bid to get fully fit, so expect the tough-tackling Yorkshireman to form a fearsome partnership with Olivier Dacourt in the centre of the park in 2000–01.

Peter BEAGRIE • 11

BRADFORD CITY • BORN: 28.11.65

Flying winger Peter Beagrie played through the pain barrier in the last few weeks of the 1999–2000 season as the Bantams successfully avoided relegation.

The somersaulting former Everton wideman had to undergo a double Achilles operation in the summer of 1999 in a bid to patch him up for the season.

He was the club's regular penalty-taker and weighed in with seven goals, including a brace in the relegation six-pointer with Wimbledon.

His total of 284 crosses was comfortably the most by any Bradford man and only three Premiership players (David Beckham, Steve Guppy and David Ginola) put in more deliveries throughout the whole season.

Beagrie was also one of the top dribblers in the Premiership, embarking on 212 forays with the ball during the campaign.

His commitment was also evident in his defensive work, as illustrated by his 135 attempted tackles. Only another member of City's "Dad's Army", the feisty Stuart McCall, made more challenges.

APPEARANCES	
Start (sub)	30(5)
Minutes on pitch	2764
GOAL ATTEMPTS	
Goals	7
Shots on target	19
Shooting accuracy	41%
Goals/shots ratio	15%
PASSING	
Goal assists	5
Passes in opp half	745
Passing accuracy in opp half	53%
Successful crosses	91
Crossing accuracy	32%
DEFENDING	
Dribbles & runs	212
Dribble completion	67%
Corners forced	45
DISCIPLINE	
Fouls	55
Yellow cards	5
Red cards	0

SEE PAGE 66 FOR FULL STATS

Geriatric acrobatics: Peter Beagrie

82 Peter Beagrie lost mor

S James BEATTIE • 16

SOUTHAMPTON • BORN: 27.2.78

B

fter being voted Southampton's Player of the ear in his first term at The Dell, the 1999–2000 eason must have been one of personal isappointment for striker James Beattie.

Failing to find the back of the net hurt his onfidence and, with the arrival of Glenn oddle, he saw his first-team opportunities mited as the former England boss preferred he combination of Marian Pahars and Kevin avies up top.

Excellent in the air with a fine physical resence, Beattie also had an above-average rossing accuracy for a striker, with a 27% ompletion rate.

The former Blackburn youngster is a fine rospect, and has the possibility of an nternational career ahead of him after naking appearances for Howard Wilkinson's ngland under-21s.

Don't bet against Beattie making a omeback in 2000–01, as he aims to prove his orth. With calf and ankle problems clearing p, he should be able to justify his place in oddle's saintly strikeforce.

APPEARANCES	
Start (sub)	8(10)
Minutes on pitch	675
GOAL ATTEMPTS	
Goals inside box	0
Goals outside box	0
Minutes per goal scored	n/a
Goals/shots ratio	0%
SHOOTING	
Shots on target inside box	7
Shots on target outside box	0
Shooting accuracy	50%
PASSING	
Goal assists	0
Key passes	3
Passing accuracy in opp half	53%
DISCIPLINE	
Fouls committed	17
Fouls won	15
Offside	14
Yellow cards	2
Red cards	0

SEE PAGE 234 FOR FULL STATS

S Mikkel BECK • 25

DERBY COUNTY • BORN: 12.5.73

APPEARANCES	
Start (sub)	5(6)
Minutes on pitch	541
GOAL ATTEMPTS	
Goals inside box	1
Goals outside box	0
Minutes per goal scored	541.0
Goals/shots ratio	7%
SHOOTING	
Shots on target inside box	5
Shots on target outside box	2
Shooting accuracy	47%
PASSING	
Goal assists	0
Key passes	3
Passing accuracy in opp half	62%
DISCIPLINE	
Fouls committed	8
Fouls won	13
Offside	6
Yellow cards	0
Red cards	0

SEE PAGE 108 FOR FULL STATS

Mikkel Beck failed to make an impression on the pitch at Pride Park following his move from Middlesbrough in March 1999. But off the park, he cut a fine figure as he turned up for training in a leather trousers and fur coat combination. Nice!

He made just 11 appearances for the Rams in 1999–2000, and only lasted the full 90 minutes twice.

His only goal was the last-gasp equaliser in the dramatic 3–3 draw with Southampton at The Dell in October – it proved to be the latest strike over the whole campaign, timed at 94 minutes and 31 seconds – and he soon found himself travelling up the A52 to join rivals Nottingham Forest on loan.

The hard-working striker failed to settle at the City Ground, the Forest fans so unimpressed with his performances that they presented the club with his bus fare back to Derby.

After controversially declining a move to poverty-stricken Crystal Palace in February, he joined their London rivals QPR, where he netted four times in 11 appearances.

ackles than any other player

David BECKHAM • 7

AM

MANCHESTER UNITED • BORN: 2.5.75

David Beckham's hairstyles and tattoos were the subject of close scrutiny in 1999–2000 – but Premiership performance analysts Opta studied more than just his fashion sense.

Beckham picked up the pieces of his season after a terrible start to the new Millennium, when he was dismissed in Brazil during the FIFA World Club Championships.

Selected by his fellow-professionals in the PFA award-winning Premiership team of the season for the second successive year, Beckham attempted 372 crosses, substantially more than any other player in the league.

One of the most technically gifted midfielders in the world, Beckham weighed in with six goals – five of them post-crop – as United retained their Championship at a canter. He scored several stunning free-kicks, including a textbook effort in the 7–1 demolition of West Ham in April.

He was credited with the highest number of assists (15) alongside Newcastle's Nolberto Solano, while only Frank Leboeuf completed more successful long passes.

APPEARANCES	
Start (sub)	30(1)
Minutes on pitch	2606
GOAL ATTEMPTS	
Goals	6
Shots on target	20
Shooting accuracy	48%
Goals/shots ratio	14%
PASSING	
Goal assists	15
Passes in opp half	1366
Passing accuracy in opp half	67%
Successful crosses	99
Crossing accuracy	27%
DRIBBLING	
Dribbles & runs	104
Dribble completion	89%
Corners forced	63
DISCIPLINE	
Fouls	36
Yellow cards	6
Red cards	0

SEE PAGE 178 FOR FULL STATS

Top of the crops: David Beckham

CB

David BEHERALL • 27

NEWCASTLE UNITED • BORN: 8.3.79

romising Newcastle centre-back David eherall made just two substitute appearances uring the 1999–2000 season.

After making his Magpies debut at the tail nd of the 1998–99 campaign, Beherall was nable to win regular first-team football ecause of the defensive form of Greek ternational Nikos Dabizas, among others.

The lithe defender came on in the sappointing 3–3 draw with Wimbledon and e 5–1 thumping courtesy of Manchester nited at Old Trafford.

He made five clearances and two blocks uring his brief appearances and had an bove-average passing accuracy for a defender ith a 78% success rate.

The 21-year-old Geordie will hope 2000–01 ill herald more first-team appearances under opular manager Bobby Robson, although a ove to the Nationwide Football League could e on the cards on a loan deal or even a ermanent basis.

SEE PAGE 206 FOR FULL STATS

FB

Francis BENALI • 15

SOUTHAMPTON • BORN: 30.12.68

ints' longest-serving player Francis Benali ded the 1999–2000 season as second-oice left-back due to the form of young left-ded defender Wayne Bridge, who impressed ter establishing himself under new boss enn Hoddle.

Unfortunately, Benali's suspect discipline eteriorated from the 1998–99 season, as he rned four cautions in his 2,248 minutes on e pitch. Other areas of decline in Benali's ats included his passing and crossing curacy, but he did attempt more tackles, ith a 53% success rate.

A loyal and dedicated servant to the club, e defender has played all his football with e Saints and will probably come back in 00–01, hoping to reclaim his place in oddle's back line.

Benali has always been a solid if nspectacular player who concentrates on his fensive duties. He made a significant umber of clearances, blocks and terceptions, just trailing behind the club's ayer of the Year, Dean Richards.

Loyal: Francis Benali

APPEARANCES	
Start (sub)	25(1)
Minutes on pitch	2248
GOAL ATTEMPTS	
Goals	0
PASSING & CROSSING	
Goal assists	0
Passing	994
Passing accuracy	62%
Crosses	28
Crossing accuracy	32%
DEFENDING	
Tackles	53
Tackles won %	53%
Blocks	43
Interceptions	13
Clearances	187
Shots cleared off line	0
DISCIPLINE	
Fouls	26
Yellow cards	4
Red cards	0

SEE PAGE 234 FOR FULL STATS

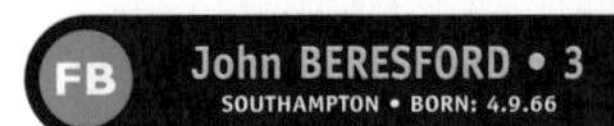

FB John BERESFORD • 3

SOUTHAMPTON • BORN: 4.9.66

Yet again, injuries ruined the season for John Beresford, who hardly featured in Southampton's Premiership campaign during season 1999–2000.

After appearing as a last-minute substitute in the opening-day victory against Coventry at Highfield Road, his next appearance was on loan in Division One for Birmingham City. But injuries even managed to curtail his time at St Andrews.

In his 28 minutes of action for the Saints, the former Newcastle defender completed three-quarters of his passes, but the usually pacy left-back, who loves to get forward, rather surprisingly failed to make a single forward foray with the ball.

It remains to be seen if Beresford can recover from his long-term injuries and regain the sort of form that saw him earn international caps for England at "B" level during his successful spell at St James's Park with Newcastle United.

SEE PAGE 234 FOR FULL STATS

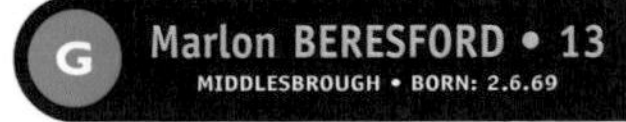

G Marlon BERESFORD • 13

MIDDLESBROUGH • BORN: 2.6.69

Middlesbrough's deputy 'keeper Marl… Beresford found first-team opportuniti… limited at The Riverside during 1999–2000.

His only Premiership appearance was in t… St Valentine's Day massacre, when Aston Vi… blitzed Bryan Robson's men 4–0, a destructi… witnessed by millions on live television.

The defeat was the first Beresford h… suffered as a Premiership player wi… Middlesbrough. Signed from Burnley in Mar… 1998, he had gained a reputation as one … the best 'keepers in the lower divisions.

But despite this promise, the tall a… commanding former Owl has played seco… fiddle to Mark Schwarzer.

His only contribution in the humiliati… defeat to Villa was one save and two catch… – as well as picking the ball out of the back … the net four times.

It was a disappointing night for Beresfo… and Boro as a whole, as they slumped … defeat against the eventual FA Cup finalists…

SEE PAGE 192 FOR FULL STATS

CB Henning BERG • 21

MANCHESTER UNITED • BORN: 1.9.69

APPEARANCES	
Start (sub)	16(6)
Minutes on pitch	1636
GOAL ATTEMPTS	
Goals	1
DEFENDING	
Blocks	37
Shots cleared off line	2
Headed clearances	113
Other clearances	43
Interceptions	15
Last man saving tackles	0
Tackles won	24
Tackles won %	59%
PASSING	
Passing accuracy own half	89%
Passing accuracy opp half	64%
DISCIPLINE	
Fouls	20
Fouls in danger area	5
Yellow cards	2
Red cards	0

SEE PAGE 178 FOR FULL STATS

Norwegian international Henning Berg was… regular fixture in the Manchester United lir… up during their 1999–2000 Championshi… winning campaign.

With compatriot Ronny Johnsen missing t… majority of the season due to injury, it w… left to Berg to contest the second centre-ba… slot with Frenchman Mickael Silvestre for t… right to partner Dutch mainstay Jaap Stam.

Composed Berg is an exquisite tackler w… has a very good disciplinary record. He w… shown only two cards during the ent… Premiership season.

He also made more clearances, blocks a… interceptions in 1999–2000 than he did … United's Treble-winning campaign, althou… his overall passing accuracy of 81% was a 1… point decrease on the previous campaign.

Despite his impeccable timing a… judgement, Berg actually won more tackles … the 1998–99 season.

He scored his first Premiership goal in almo… two-and-a-half years in the 4–0 drubbing … Sunderland at Old Trafford in April.

3 Patrik Berger scored the joint-highest number of goa…

B

AM

Patrik BERGER • 15

LIVERPOOL • BORN: 10.11.73

iverpool's Czech mate Patrik Berger had one of his most productive seasons in a red shirt ince his arrival at the club shortly after the uro 96 tournament.

He was ranked seventh in the Opta Attacking 1idfielders Index for the season, behind such layers as David Beckham and Gustavo Poyet. innish defender Sami Hyypia was the only layer with a higher average score at Anfield han the straggly-haired left-winger.

He scored some fantastic long-range efforts, ncluding a free-kick at Old Trafford in the 1–1 draw with United and some dipping left-ooted pile-drivers from outside the box that aw off the likes of Leeds, Spurs and Arsenal.

His penetrating runs at pace saw an mproved dribble completion rate of 80% and e had a better disciplinary record, picking up nly two cautions, in contrast to the four ellow cards he received in 1998–99.

Berger attempted more crosses and corners han anyone else at the club, a fact which elped him pick up three goal assists during he course of the season.

APPEARANCES	
Start (sub)	34(0)
Minutes on pitch	2916
GOAL ATTEMPTS	
Goals	9
Shots on target	35
Shooting accuracy	50%
Goals/shots ratio	13%
PASSING	
Goal assists	3
Passes in opp half	878
Passing accuracy in opp half	69%
Successful crosses	41
Crossing accuracy	21%
DRIBBLING	
Dribbles & runs	110
Dribble completion	80%
Corners forced	28
DISCIPLINE	
Fouls	44
Yellow cards	2
Red cards	0

SEE PAGE 164 FOR FULL STATS

One heck of a Czech: Patrik Berger

direct from set-pieces, along with David Beckham

Dennis BERGKAMP • 10

ARSENAL • BORN: 18.5.69

Despite a fine start to the season, when he netted two goals in the opening two matches, Dennis Bergkamp suffered a disappointing 1999–2000 campaign, epitomised by his performance in the UEFA Cup final against Galatasaray, in which he was substituted.

The Opta stats for the Premiership reveal that he had an inferior goals-to-shots ratio to his 15% average during the 1998–99 season.

Overshadowed by the explosive goalscoring talents of Thierry Henry, Bergkamp was forced to take a back seat as the speedy Frenchman took all the plaudits.

Bergkamp netted only six Premiership goals, making him joint-fifth leading scorer along with Freddie Ljungberg, but did improve his shooting accuracy from 58% in 1998–99.

Bergkamp's precision passing meant he was the top provider at Highbury, laying on nine goals for his grateful team-mates, one more than Henry. His total of 39 shots on target was only bettered by Henry's 51.

The non-flying Dutchman will hope season 2000–01 is more successful.

APPEARANCES	
Start (sub)	23(5)
Minutes on pitch	1881
GOAL ATTEMPTS	
Goals inside box	5
Goals outside box	1
Minutes per goal scored	313.5
Goals/shots ratio	9%
SHOOTING	
Shots on target inside box	20
Shots on target outside box	19
Shooting accuracy	61%
PASSING	
Goal assists	9
Key passes	17
Passing accuracy in opp half	61%
DISCIPLINE	
Fouls committed	35
Fouls won	52
Offside	14
Yellow cards	6
Red cards	0

SEE PAGE 38 FOR FULL STATS

Robert BETTS • 38

COVENTRY CITY • BORN: 21.12.81

Teenage midfielder Robert Betts made his senior debut for the Sky Blues at the tail end of the 1999–2000 season.

Playing just 18 minutes of Premiership football was hardly enough time to test his true credentials, but his stats made impressive reading nonetheless.

He managed an above-average 86% accuracy from his 22 attempted passes and both of his dribbles and runs were successfully completed.

Betts was a member of the Coventry team that lost the FA Youth Cup final to Arsenal and made a significant number of reserve appearances under the watchful eye of Coventry legend Trevor Peake, before earning his call-up to the senior squad.

The youngster actually made his professional debut for Doncaster Rovers at the tender age of 16 in April 1998 before Gordon Strachan snapped him up as the South Yorkshire side were relegated to the Conference.

SEE PAGE 94 FOR FULL STATS

Non-flying Dutchman: Dennis Bergkamp

FB Jonathan BEWERS • 30

ASTON VILLA • BORN: 10.9.82

Jonathan Bewers made his Premiership debut for the Villans when he came on as a last-minute substitute for Mark Delaney in the remarkable 4–2 win at Tottenham in April.

Versatile enough to play in defence or midfield, the highly-rated youngster has impressed Villa's coaching staff of Gordon Cowans and Kevin MacDonald in FA Premier under-17 and under-19 fixtures.

Bewers has been with the FA Cup finalists since signing schoolboy forms in 1997. And his development is a testament to the hard work done behind the scenes by the youth development officers at Villa Park.

Kettering-born Bewers was not fazed at being thrown in at the deep end in front of 35,000 fans at White Hart Lane, and John Gregory will doubtless be looking to give the youngster more first-team chances in the claret and blue shirt. Along with the likes of Jlloyd Samuel and Darius Vassell, Bewers could feature more during the 2000–01 Premiership season.

SEE PAGE 52 FOR FULL STATS

AM Tommy BLACK • 33

ARSENAL • BORN: 26.11.79

Arsene Wenger gave tricky winger Tommy Black his Premiership debut in the Gunners' 1–0 win at Goodison Park in April.

Replacing goalscorer Marc Overmars in the 86th minute, Black suggested he is capable of playing at the highest level.

He made 16 appearances in the reserve team, but was also farmed out on loan to gain first-team experience.

He was sent off on his Carlisle debut in the 1–1 draw at Mansfield, but overcame that disappointment to score in the 4–2 win over Plymouth two days later.

Black actually made his Arsenal debut in the fourth round Worthington Cup defeat to Middlesbrough in November, before heading along the M4 to Bristol City on a month's loan.

Black was the subject of a £500,000 bid from Second Division Brentford towards the end of 1999–2000. The fact that Arsenal swiftly rejected it indicates how highly the club rate the promising forward.

SEE PAGE 38 FOR FULL STATS

B

CB Dean BLACKWELL • 5

WIMBLEDON • BORN: 5.12.69

APPEARANCES	
Start (sub)	16(1)
Minutes on pitch	1334
GOAL ATTEMPTS	
Goals	0
DEFENDING	
Blocks	19
Shots cleared off line	0
Headed clearances	101
Other clearances	44
Interceptions	8
Last man saving tackles	0
Tackles won	20
Tackles won %	43%
PASSING	
Passing accuracy own half	74%
Passing accuracy opp half	39%
DISCIPLINE	
Fouls	18
Fouls in danger area	7
Yellow cards	3
Red cards	1

SEE PAGE 304 FOR FULL STATS

Wimbledon centre-back Dean Blackwell endured a nightmare season as the club were relegated back to the First Division after a 14-year stay in the top flight.

Following the departure of defensive partner Chris Perry to Spurs in the summer of 1999, it was always going to be an uncomfortable term for the club's longest-serving player.

The cleanest player in the previous Premiership campaign, Blackwell was dismissed in the opening day win at Vicarage Road against Watford. It was the first red card of his career, shown for a mis-timed challenge that resulted in a penalty kick. It was indicative of what was to come, as he recorded a below-average tackle success rate of 43% over the campaign.

Missing a large proportion of the season through injury, Blackwell returned to the side for the run-in but was unable to prevent the Dons' heartbreaking slide into the Nationwide League, despite his 145 clearances. He will be hoping to contribute significantly to a swift return to top-flight football for the south Londoners in 2000–01.

Robbie BLAKE • 8

BRADFORD CITY • BORN: 4.3.76

After starring in Bradford's promotion campaign of 1998–99, Robbie Blake was only a squad player during the club's successful fight against relegation.

Versatile enough to play on either flank or up front, his close control and ability to ghost past defenders made him a fans' favourite.

Only Peter Beagrie attempted more dribbles for the Bantams, but then the ex-Everton winger was on the field for a considerably longer period during the 1999–2000 season.

Despite bagging 16 goals in Bradford's promotion-winning season, he only managed two in the top flight, against Leicester City and Southampton, both at Valley Parade. But his goal against the Foxes was a blinding strike into the top corner and he did complete two-thirds of his passes – an above-average ratio for a frontman.

As the West Yorkshire side attempt to consolidate again during the 2000–01 campaign, expect the silky skills and deft touches of Robbie Blake to play a more prominent part in the Bantams' season.

APPEARANCES	
Start (sub)	15(13)
Minutes on pitch	1651
GOAL ATTEMPTS	
Goals inside box	2
Goals outside box	0
Minutes per goal scored	825.5
Goals/shots ratio	8%
SHOOTING	
Shots on target inside box	8
Shots on target outside box	5
Shooting accuracy	54%
PASSING	
Goal assists	1
Key passes	4
Passing accuracy in opp half	62%
DISCIPLINE	
Fouls committed	12
Fouls won	36
Offside	14
Yellow cards	0
Red cards	0

SEE PAGE 66 FOR FULL STATS

Luis BOA MORTE • 35

SOUTHAMPTON • BORN: 4.8.77

APPEARANCES	
Start (sub)	6(10)
Minutes on pitch	597
GOAL ATTEMPTS	
Goals	1
Shots on target	4
Shooting accuracy	50%
Goals/shots ratio	13%
PASSING	
Goal assists	1
Passes in opp half	105
Passing accuracy in opp half	55%
Successful crosses	31
Crossing accuracy	29%
DRIBBLING	
Dribbles & runs	50
Dribble completion	54%
Corners forced	13
DISCIPLINE	
Fouls	17
Yellow cards	1
Red cards	1

SEE PAGES 38 & 234 FOR FULL STATS

Luis Boa Morte suffered a disappointin campaign after his £500,000 switch fron Arsenal in August 1999.

The Portuguese under-21 international wa unable to claim a regular first-team spot a Highbury due to the plethora of attackin options available to Arsene Wenger.

Moving on to The Dell to gain first-tean football, he marked his full debut for th Saints by getting sent off in the 3–2 defeat a Middlesbrough in September.

Capable of playing on either flank o through the middle, Boa Morte used hi blistering pace to give defenders a hard time

But his progress was halted due to succession of injuries, including a hamstrin problem that saw him fail to make anothe first-team appearance after March.

He did manage one goal, at home t Watford, but clearly has much to do to impres the Saints faithful. With his first child bein born on the south coast early in the new year the 2000–01 campaign may herald the start o a more productive season.

9 George Boateng earned more yellow cards

B

M George BOATENG • 6

ASTON VILLA • BORN: 5.9.75

George Boateng endured a miserable end to the 1999–2000 season as Aston Villa were beaten by Chelsea in the last FA Cup final beneath the Twin Towers, despite his efforts on the Wembley turf.

John Gregory snapped up the Dutch midfielder for £4.5 million in the 1999 close season from Midlands rivals Coventry City.

He possesses a good engine which enables him to travel from box to box consistently throughout a game, but nevertheless found it hard to settle into Villa's system after being used to a more conventional 4–4–2 formation at Highfield Road.

His two Premiership goals both came against lowly Derby; a header at Pride Park on Boxing Day and an emphatic finish past Mart Poom in the 2–0 success at Villa Park in March.

Boateng attempted more tackles than any other player at the club and his success rate was average for a Premiership midfielder.

But he will hope to improve his disciplinary record after picking up nine bookings for his misdemeanours in a claret and blue shirt.

APPEARANCES	
Start (sub)	30(3)
Minutes on pitch	2489
GOAL ATTEMPTS	
Goals	2
Shots on target	11
Shooting accuracy	44%
PASSING	
Goal assists	0
Passes in opp half	714
Passing accuracy in opp half	68%
Successful crosses	7
Cross completion	19%
DEFENDING	
Interceptions	20
Clearances	53
Tackles	126
Tackles won %	56%
DISCIPLINE	
Fouls	58
Yellow cards	9
Red cards	0

SEE PAGE 52 FOR FULL STATS

Paul BOERTIEN • 23

DERBY COUNTY • BORN: 20.1.79

Twenty-one-year-old Paul Boertien made his first appearance of the season in the vital 2–0 win over Southampton in April, replacing Tony Dorigo at half-time in a match that virtually sealed the Rams' Premiership status.

Like team-mate Rory Delap, Boertien was signed from Carlisle United for £250,000 in March 1999 but, unlike Delap, he failed to establish himself in the first team after making his debut against Chelsea in 1998–99.

The composed defender was sent out on loan to Crewe in February and got two games under his belt as he built up some useful first-team experience.

Opta's stats reveal that Boertien needs to work on the accuracy of his passing, as he completed just 58% of his distribution when venturing over the halfway line.

Along with Malcolm Christie, Richard Jackson and Seth Johnson, Boertien is a player that manager Jim Smith regards as one for the future at Pride Park.

SEE PAGE 108 FOR FULL STATS

Good engine: George Boateng

than any other Villa player

Lars BOHINEN • 14

DERBY COUNTY • BORN: 8.9.69

Derby's Norwegian midfielder Lars Bohinen started off the 1999–2000 campaign with a knee injury, ended it with hamstring problems and in between times was fined for criticising County's training policies on his own website.

Not the smoothest of seasons, then, for the classy playmaker, who struggled to make an impact at Pride Park with problems of one sort or another never far away.

Bohinen failed to start more than two Premiership matches in a row, did not manage to score for the Rams and was credited with just one goal assist. In October, Bohinen came very close to joining the Scandinavian revolution at Wimbledon but, after overcoming his differences with boss Jim Smith, decided to stick it out in the east Midlands.

In the 13 league games he was involved in, the ex-Blackburn man won an impressive 63% of 40 tackles and also completed 76% of his dribbles. Having played the last two games of the season, Bohinen is clearly still in the thoughts of Smith and may feature more regularly in 2000–01.

APPEARANCES	
Start (sub)	8(5)
Minutes on pitch	673
GOAL ATTEMPTS	
Goals	0
Shots on target	3
Shooting accuracy	43%
PASSING	
Goal assists	1
Passes in opp half	225
Passing accuracy in opp half	67%
Successful crosses	2
Cross completion	14%
DEFENDING	
Interceptions	4
Clearances	7
Tackles	40
Tackles won %	63%
DISCIPLINE	
Fouls	10
Yellow cards	1
Red cards	0

SEE PAGE 108 FOR FULL STATS

Alexandre BONNOT • 24

WATFORD • BORN: 31.7.73

APPEARANCES	
Start (sub)	7(5)
Minutes on pitch	624
GOAL ATTEMPTS	
Goals	0
Shots on target	2
Shooting accuracy	33%
PASSING	
Goal assists	0
Passes in opp half	167
Passing accuracy in opp half	60%
Successful crosses	2
Cross completion	20%
DEFENDING	
Interceptions	6
Clearances	15
Tackles	26
Tackles won %	54%
DISCIPLINE	
Fouls	11
Yellow cards	1
Red cards	0

SEE PAGE 276 FOR FULL STATS

Former France under-20 midfielder Alexandre Bonnot earned his chance in Watford's starting line-up at the start of 1999–2000 after injuries had sidelined regular starters such as Nick Wright and Micah Hyde.

But the return of the first-teamers from the treatment room saw Bonnot drop out of the side after two games, and boss Graham Taylor used him sparingly thereafter.

Bonnot, who started his career at Paris St Germain in the same squad as David Ginola and George Weah, is a neat, compact midfielder whose total of 26 tackles illustrates his willingness to get stuck in.

He also ventured forward from midfield to strike six shots at goal, two of which tested opposing goalkeepers. The one blot on Bonnot's season was a booking against Leicester in February for a foul.

With a year still to run on his contract, Bonnot is likely to remain at Watford, but he will be aiming for a longer stretch of football in the Hornets' first team as he tries to make a name for himself in England.

S

Andy BOOTH • 10

SHEFFIELD WEDNESDAY • BORN: 6.12.73

B

If every Sheffield Wednesday player had matched striker Andy Booth for effort in 1999–2000, then the Owls could well be looking forward to another season of Premiership football in 2000–01.

The former Huddersfield target man could never claim to be the most skilful player in the top flight, but he gave his all for the team and there were several clubs willing to take Booth off Wednesday's hands.

In fact, Nottingham Forest and Bradford both showed an interest in Booth, while Leicester had agreed a £2.7 million fee to take the Yorkshireman to Filbert Street, but the deal fell through after a medical.

A nagging groin strain also helped to disrupt Booth's season and he ended up with just two goals to his name in the Premiership. He did, however, rattle a further 13 accurate shots at goal, contributed three assists and helped out his defence with 25 clearances.

If the Owls are to regain Premiership status by winning promotion in 2000–01, then Booth's form and fitness will be a key factor.

APPEARANCES	
Start (sub)	19(4)
Minutes on pitch	1755
GOAL ATTEMPTS	
Goals inside box	2
Goals outside box	0
Minutes per goal scored	877.5
Goals/shots ratio	6%
SHOOTING	
Shots on target inside box	11
Shots on target outside box	4
Shooting accuracy	43%
PASSING	
Goal assists	3
Key passes	8
Passing accuracy in opp half	61%
DISCIPLINE	
Fouls committed	56
Fouls won	70
Offside	14
Yellow cards	3
Red cards	0

SEE PAGE 220 FOR FULL STATS

FB

Vassilis BORBOKIS • 22

DERBY COUNTY • BORN: 10.2.69

APPEARANCES	
Start (sub)	6(6)
Minutes on pitch	655
GOAL ATTEMPTS	
Goals	0
PASSING & CROSSING	
Goal assists	0
Passing	269
Passing accuracy	69%
Crosses	58
Crossing accuracy	36%
DEFENDING	
Tackles	22
Tackles won %	77%
Blocks	0
Interceptions	4
Clearances	32
Shots cleared off line	0
DISCIPLINE	
Fouls	10
Yellow cards	2
Red cards	0

SEE PAGE 108 FOR FULL STATS

After ending the 1998–99 season with some impressive performances down Derby's right flank, Greek wing-back Vassilis Borbokis started the Millennium campaign as an integral member of Jim Smith's squad.

The former Sheffield United man was involved in 12 of the Rams' first 15 Premiership fixtures and impressed with his mazy runs and teasing crosses from the flank. But the arrival of strikers Esteban Fuertes and Branko Strupar at Pride Park freed up Rory Delap to play in the wing-back role and Borbokis was squeezed out of the picture.

The 31-year-old international was allowed to move on in December and signed for PAOK Salonika in his homeland for a nominal fee.

In his appearances for Derby in 1999–2000, Borbokis excelled at tackling, winning 77% of his 22 challenges – way above the 51% average for a Premiership defender.

He failed to score in the league, but found the net with a stunning strike in a 3–1 Worthington Cup win over Swansea, his first and final goal for Derby.

Mark BOSNICH • 1

MANCHESTER UNITED • BORN: 13.1.72

Manchester United's only major summer signing of 1999, goalkeeper Mark Bosnich was the man faced with the thankless task of replacing Peter Schmeichel.

Despite one or two blips on his record, the Australian 'keeper could be fairly content at the end of 1999–2000, considering the immense pressure any player is under when arriving at Old Trafford.

Despite a niggling hamstring injury, Bosnich turned out 23 times in the Premiership, keeping nine clean sheets and making a total of 45 saves.

Although he did not immediately endear himself to United's fans, the brief and disastrous spell of Massimo Taibi in goal convinced the watching faithful and boss Sir Alex Ferguson that Bosnich was the best man to guard the net for the Champions.

However, the signing of French international Fabien Barthez in June places a huge question mark over the future of the former Aston Villa 'keeper and he may well find himself surplus to requirements.

APPEARANCES	
Start (sub)	23(0)
Minutes on pitch	1875
SHOT STOPPING	
Goals conceded (inside box)	16
Goals conceded (outside box)	5
Minutes per goal conceded	89.3
Clean sheets	9
Saves (shots inside box)	21
Saves (shots outside box)	24
Saves/shots	68%
DISTRIBUTION	
Long kick %	42%
Throws/short passes %	94%
CATCHING	
Crosses caught	32
Crosses punched	11
Crosses dropped	3
Catch success %	91%
DISCIPLINE	
Yellow cards	0
Red cards	0

SEE PAGE 178 FOR FULL STATS

CB

Steve BOULD • 5

SUNDERLAND • BORN: 16.11.62

APPEARANCES	
Start (sub)	19(1)
Minutes on pitch	1606
GOAL ATTEMPTS	
Goals	0
DEFENDING	
Blocks	30
Shots cleared off line	0
Headed clearances	161
Other clearances	50
Interceptions	27
Last man saving tackles	0
Tackles won	26
Tackles won %	62%
PASSING	
Passing accuracy own half	87%
Passing accuracy opp half	51%
DISCIPLINE	
Fouls	27
Fouls in danger area	5
Yellow cards	3
Red cards	1

SEE PAGE 248 FOR FULL STATS

Phased out of the first team picture at Arsenal in 1998–99, promoted Sunderland held enough belief in veteran Steve Bould to give him their number five squad number and install him as first-choice centre-back.

The first day debacle at Chelsea apart, Bould repaid that faith in the early stages of 1999–2000, fully justifying his £500,000 fee and steadying the relatively inexperienced Sunderland back-line.

Bould featured in 13 of the Black Cats' first 14 Premiership matches but was dismissed for an alleged headbutt on Paulo Wanchope in the game against West Ham on 24 October. Bould's season took a further blow in January when a torn hamstring kept him out for all but one of the last 15 games.

In the football he did manage, Bould was always quietly assured, winning 62% of his tackles, making 211 clearances and finding a team-mate with 78% of his passes. But injury and age may combine to take their toll on Bould, who is unlikely to be more than a squad player in 2000–01.

M

Lee BOWYER • 11

LEEDS UNITED • BORN: 3.1.77

ne of the top flight's ultimate Jekyll and yde footballers, Lee Bowyer showed flashes f his vast talent in 1999–2000, but all too ften spoiled things by letting his aggressive emperament get the better of him.

The England under-21 midfielder was the irst player to pick up 13 bookings in the 999–2000 Premiership season and, with a oul on Stephen Clemence, sparked off the gly scenes against Spurs that landed both eams with an FA misconduct charge.

On the positive side, Bowyer was one of the ıost effective midfielders around, bagging ive Premiership goals and six more in the ups. He also created three goals, completed 4% of his dribbles and runs and won more ıan half of his tackles. His form was so good t one stage, that it seemed only a matter of ime before Bowyer was handed a full England ebut under Kevin Keegan.

Still aged only 23, Bowyer still has a great hance of making the national team – if he an curb his disciplinary problems and show reater maturity both on and off the pitch.

APPEARANCES	
Start (sub)	31(2)
Minutes on pitch	2768
GOAL ATTEMPTS	
Goals	5
Shots on target	30
Shooting accuracy	42%
PASSING	
Goal assists	3
Passes in opp half	735
Passing accuracy in opp half	64%
Successful crosses	8
Cross completion	17%
DEFENDING	
Interceptions	25
Clearances	23
Tackles	105
Tackles won %	55%
DISCIPLINE	
Fouls	55
Yellow cards	13
Red cards	0

SEE PAGE 136 FOR FULL STATS

Shayne BRADLEY • 31

SOUTHAMPTON • BORN: 8.12.79

diligent worker in the youth and reserve eams, Gloucester-born striker Shayne Bradley vas given his one and only Premiership outing or Southampton early on in the 1999–2000 eason in a heavy defeat at Everton.

Sent on for Marian Pahars with the Saints ılready 4–1 down, Bradley strove to get into he action, but only managed to get himself n the book, for a foul on Everton defender)avid Weir.

With several more experienced strikers ıhead of him in the queue for first-team ootball, Bradley moved on loan to Division Three side Exeter City in September, but his pell there was tarnished by a red card in the A Cup first round tie against non-league astwood Town.

With just one goal to his name in 19 league ıppearances for three clubs, it seems unlikely hat Bradley will get any kind of run in the aints team in 2000–01 and may have to nove on to further his career.

SEE PAGE 234 FOR FULL STATS

Aggressive: Lee Bowyer

Gary BREEN • 17

COVENTRY CITY • BORN: 12.12.73

Irish defender Gary Breen was one of several Coventry City players dogged by injury in 1999–2000, in his case with an annoyingly persistent groin problem.

In the 20 Premiership starts he did manage, Breen was often shifted from right-back to centre-back as boss Gordon Strachan shuffled his pack to deal with the Sky Blues' injury crisis. The unsettled nature of Breen's campaign did not help him, although he remained an important squad member for both his club and country.

In 1,816 minutes of top-flight action, Breen still managed to clear the ball 158 times and won almost half of the tackles he slid into during the campaign. But, like his defensive partners, his distribution was quite poor when venturing out from the back and for the second season running he failed to score a league goal.

City's dreadful away record in the Premiership will undoubtedly improve in 2000–01 if the club can keep fit its key defenders – of which Breen is most certainly one.

APPEARANCES	
Start (sub)	20(1)
Minutes on pitch	1816
GOAL ATTEMPTS	
Goals	0
DEFENDING	
Blocks	42
Shots cleared off line	0
Headed clearances	117
Other clearances	41
Interceptions	8
Last man saving tackles	0
Tackles won	17
Tackles won %	49%
PASSING	
Passing accuracy own half	77%
Passing accuracy opp half	55%
DISCIPLINE	
Fouls	28
Fouls in danger area	7
Yellow cards	2
Red cards	0

SEE PAGE 94 FOR FULL STATS

FB

Wayne BRIDGE • 18

SOUTHAMPTON • BORN: 5.8.80

APPEARANCES	
Start (sub)	16(3)
Minutes on pitch	1462
GOAL ATTEMPTS	
Goals	1
Shots on target	3
Shooting accuracy	100%
Goals/shots ratio	33%
PASSING	
Goal assists	2
Passes in opp half	300
Passing accuracy in opp half	61%
Successful crosses	14
Crossing accuracy	38%
DRIBBLING	
Dribbles & runs	48
Dribble completion	90%
Corners forced	11
DISCIPLINE	
Fouls	6
Yellow cards	0
Red cards	0

SEE PAGE 234 FOR FULL STATS

Southampton's Wayne Bridge fulfilled eve schoolboy's dream in 1999–2000 by playin and scoring, for his hometown club.

A debutant in 1998–99, Bridge was careful nurtured by former Saints boss Dave Jones ar was given just two Premiership starts up unt January in the 1999–2000 campaign.

But Glenn Hoddle's arrival as manager at Th Dell was the catalyst for Bridge's season t really take off. Playing either at left-back c wide in midfield, the England under-21 starle did not miss a minute of football i Southampton's final 13 Premiership matche and during that run netted his first-ever goa

That strike came from a spectacular free-kic against Wimbledon on the final day of th season, sending the Dons on their way t Division One. Bridge also made two goals i 1999–2000 and completed an impressive 90 of his dribbles down the flank.

With a sweet left foot and an abundance c pace, Bridge is likely to be a regular starter fo the Saints again in 2000–01 and caps fo England in the future are not beyond him.

B

S Michael BRIDGES • 8

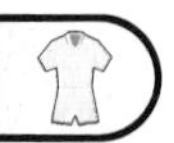

LEEDS UNITED • BORN: 5.8.78

ngland under-21 striker Michael Bridges urpassed the expectations of even the most ptimistic of Leeds supporters by netting 19 oals in his first full Premiership season.

Having been mainly used as a substitute in underland's Division One Championship-inning team of 1998–99, more than a few yebrows were raised when Leeds forked out 5 million for the confident striker.

He repaid the faith of his new boss David 'Leary, netting a hat-trick against outhampton in just his second match for the lland Road side, before playing a key role as eeds rose to the top of the Premiership table.

Despite United's season tailing off a little in he league, Bridges carried on finding the net, ever going more than five consecutive games ithout a Premiership goal. He proved himself o be more than just a goalscorer, though, reating four strikes for team-mates and inning 70% of 20 attempted tackles.

With a more experienced strike partner and greater supply of scoring chances, don't bet gainst Bridges improving further in 2000–01.

APPEARANCES	
Start (sub)	32(2)
Minutes on pitch	2356
GOAL ATTEMPTS	
Goals inside box	16
Goals outside box	3
Minutes per goal scored	124.0
Goals/shots ratio	24%
SHOOTING	
Shots on target inside box	27
Shots on target outside box	15
Shooting accuracy	54%
PASSING	
Goal assists	4
Key passes	17
Passing accuracy in opp half	60%
DISCIPLINE	
Fouls committed	65
Fouls won	49
Offside	56
Yellow cards	6
Red cards	0

SEE PAGE 136 FOR FULL STATS

Lee BRISCOE • 21

SHEFFIELD WEDNESDAY • BORN: 30.9.75

ttacking left-back Lee Briscoe was once gain little more than a squad player for heffield Wednesday in 1999–2000.

With £3 million signing Andy Hinchcliffe learly ahead of him in the pecking order at illsborough, Briscoe's only opportunities to mpress came as a substitute or when his xpensive team-mate was injured.

The highlight of Briscoe's season probably ame on the opening day when, at 2–0 down, e fed Benito Carbone to chip past Liverpool's ander Westerveld.

Briscoe's other notable contributions of the ampaign were 11 accurate crosses (one every 6 minutes on average), an 88% dribble ompletion rate and an impressive amount of learances – 62 in 724 minutes.

With his contract running out in the summer f 2000, Briscoe has been linked with a move to ortsmouth, but Wednesday could do worse han retain the signature of the enthusiastic ull-back as they prepare for life in Division One.

SEE PAGE 220 FOR FULL STATS

Stephen BROOKER • 31

WATFORD • BORN: 21.5.81

A regular goalscorer in Watford's under-19 academy team, striker Stephen Brooker was given his initial taste of first-team football on the opening day of the 1999–2000 Premiership season when he came off the bench against Wimbledon at Vicarage Road.

A late replacement for another young striker, Tommy Smith, Brooker made just two contributions, but completed his one pass and solitary dribble. But his presence was not nearly enough to help prevent Watford losing the game 3–2, something of an anti-climax for the expectant Hornets faithful.

Surprisingly, Graham Taylor never gave the Newport Pagnall-born hitman another chance to prove his worth in the Premiership, although Brooker was an unused sub on a couple of other occasions.

Strong and quick with an eye for goal, Brooker may get the chance to add to his limited first-team experience when Watford bid for a Premiership return in 2000–01.

SEE PAGE 276 FOR FULL STATS

Craig BURLEY • 33

DERBY COUNTY • BORN: 24.9.71

Having endured a dreadful run of just one win in nine Premiership matches, Derby boss Jim Smith moved swiftly into the transfer market in November 1999 to try to rectify the situation. Along with Georgi Kinkladze, who joined on loan from Ajax, Craig Burley returned to English football after two-and-a-half seasons north of the border with Celtic.

And the midfield duo made all the difference to the Rams as they gradually pulled away from the threat of relegation. But while Kinkladze took most of the plaudits for some improved County performances, Scotland international Burley was equally as important following his £3 million move.

He netted five times in his 1,595 minutes of Premiership football and would probably have got a couple more had he not missed four games in a row with a hamstring injury. He also made one goal and got wide to deliver 49 crosses and corners.

In defensive terms, Burley won 54% of 54 tackles and helped out his defence with 17 clearances and 10 blocks.

APPEARANCES	
Start (sub)	18(0)
Minutes on pitch	1595
GOAL ATTEMPTS	
Goals	5
Shots on target	11
Shooting accuracy	46%
PASSING	
Goal assists	1
Passes in opp half	458
Passing accuracy in opp half	60%
Successful crosses	11
Cross completion	22%
DEFENDING	
Interceptions	8
Clearances	17
Tackles	54
Tackles won %	54%
DISCIPLINE	
Fouls	24
Yellow cards	7
Red cards	0

SEE PAGE 108 FOR FULL STATS

FB

David BURROWS • 3

COVENTRY CITY • BORN: 25.10.68

APPEARANCES	
Start (sub)	12(3)
Minutes on pitch	989
GOAL ATTEMPTS	
Goals	0
PASSING & CROSSING	
Goal assists	0
Passing	465
Passing accuracy	71%
Crosses	36
Crossing accuracy	36%
DEFENDING	
Tackles	27
Tackles won %	56%
Blocks	10
Interceptions	4
Clearances	55
Shots cleared off line	0
DISCIPLINE	
Fouls	13
Yellow cards	0
Red cards	1

SEE PAGE 94 FOR FULL STATS

A disappointing 1999–2000 season fo Coventry full-back David Burrows, ravaged b suspension and injury, threatened to spoil hi chances of earning a new contract a Highfield Road for 2000–01.

Things started off well enough for th experienced defender. He was selected b Gordon Strachan for the first four games c the season and displayed his usual thrust an persistence going down the left.

But after 70 minutes of the game agains Leicester in August, Burrows was dismissed fo catching Robbie Savage with a flailing elbov And just a few weeks later he was sent of again for elbowing Tranmere's Alan Morgan i the Worthington Cup defeat.

The subsequent lengthy suspension coincided with a knee injury that kep Burrows sidelined for the best part of 2 Premiership matches. In the 989 minutes c football Burrows did manage, he showed som glimpses of his quality – delivering 1 accurate crosses and completing 80% of hi forward runs.

Deon BURTON • 9

DERBY COUNTY • BORN: 25.10.76

S

espite scoring eight goals from 14 remiership starts in 1998–99, Jamaican nternational striker Deon Burton was used poradically by the Rams for the second season n a row in 1999–2000.

Burton started just 15 times in the league nd was withdrawn by boss Jim Smith on eight ccasions. However, the livewire hitman still agged four goals from just nine shots on arget – his most important strike being the ne that set the Rams on the way to a 3–1 ictory over Chelsea on 30 October.

Always a willing worker, Burton won an mpressive 68% of the 22 tackles he attempted nd drifted wide to whip in 17 crosses, while e was also credited with one goal assist.

Having started and finished the final two natches of the season, the 1999–2000 term inished on a high note for Burton. Yet with Malcolm Christie, Branko Strupar, Dean turridge and Marvin Robinson all competing or first-team places in attack, little looks like hanging for Burton in 2000–01 as Smith erseveres with a squad rotation system.

APPEARANCES	
Start (sub)	15(4)
Minutes on pitch	1262
GOAL ATTEMPTS	
Goals inside box	3
Goals outside box	1
Minutes per goal scored	315.5
Goals/shots ratio	18%
SHOOTING	
Shots on target inside box	7
Shots on target outside box	2
Shooting accuracy	41%
PASSING	
Goal assists	1
Key passes	6
Passing accuracy in opp half	58%
DISCIPLINE	
Fouls committed	44
Fouls won	21
Offside	26
Yellow cards	6
Red cards	0

SEE PAGE 108 FOR FULL STATS

Paul BUTLER • 6

SUNDERLAND • BORN: 2.11.72

CB

APPEARANCES	
Start (sub)	31(1)
Minutes on pitch	2788
GOAL ATTEMPTS	
Goals	1
DEFENDING	
Blocks	66
Shots cleared off line	1
Headed clearances	335
Other clearances	98
Interceptions	31
Last man saving tackles	0
Tackles won	36
Tackles won %	52%
PASSING	
Passing accuracy own half	84%
Passing accuracy opp half	49%
DISCIPLINE	
Fouls	39
Fouls in danger area	12
Yellow cards	6
Red cards	0

SEE PAGE 248 FOR FULL STATS

After winning international honours and a place in the Division One PFA Team of the Year in 1999, Sunderland defender Paul Butler made sure he completed the perfect year by making the step up into the Premiership with a good deal of solid and competent performances.

Butler, who was a team-mate of boss Peter Reid at Bury, was an unsung hero for most of 1999–2000, missing just one match in the first 27 Premiership fixtures and keeping some of the country's most prolific strikers under wraps. However, a loss of form culminating in a 5–2 defeat at Leicester, prompted Reid to leave Butler out of the side for six consecutive matches starting in March.

The Eire international returned for the final five games of the campaign and proved once again that he can be a crucial player for club and country when he is on top form.

The Opta stats show that Butler made 433 clearances (the fourth highest total in the top flight after David Wetherall, Sami Hyypia and Des Walker) and won more than half of his 69 attempted tackles.

bookings than those from any other side

Thomas BUTLER • 27

SUNDERLAND • BORN: 25.4.81

Young Irish midfielder Thomas Butler was given his first taste of Premiership football in the penultimate game of Sunderland's 1999–2000 season.

Butler came off the substitutes' bench to replace Frenchman Eric Roy with six minutes remaining of the Black Cats' 1–0 win over West Ham on 6 May. He touched the ball just once, conceding possession with an inaccurate pass, but has proved himself to be a busy and tidy midfielder in youth team football.

In 1997, Butler scooped the Ireland under-15 Player of the Year award and represented his country in the Youth World Cup in 1999. Sunderland competed with West Ham and Aston Villa for the signature of Butler, whose older brother John came through the Leeds youth system alongside Jonathon Woodgate, Stephen McPhail and Matthew Jones.

With Peter Reid always willing to give homegrown talent a chance in his first team, Butler could feature more in 2000–01.

SEE PAGE 248 FOR FULL STATS

Shaun BYRNE • 37

WEST HAM UNITED • BORN: 21.1.81

A popular and integral member of Tony Carr's all-conquering West Ham youth team, Ireland under-21 international Shaun Byrne was entrusted to make his Premiership debut as a substitute in the Hammers' trip to Newcastle in January 2000.

Coming on for Marc Keller in the left wing-back role, Byrne was understandably nervous in his top-flight bow and gave the ball away on three of the five occasions he gained possession in 10 minutes on the pitch.

He did venture forward to deliver one cross with his trusty left foot and, with Scott Minto spending as much time in the treatment room as he did on the pitch in 1999–2000, Byrne could feature more regularly in the 2000–01 Premiership campaign.

Like Joe Cole, Michael Carrick and Stephen Bywater, Byrne is definitely one to watch for the future at Upton Park, and his progress over coming months will be monitored closely by the Hammers' faithful.

SEE PAGE 290 FOR FULL STATS

Nicky BUTT • 8

MANCHESTER UNITED • BORN: 21.1.75

Midfield enforcer Nicky Butt featured in a but six games of Manchester United' 1999–2000 Premiership-winning campaign.

But, frustratingly for the Englan international, he missed many of th important games, domestically and in Europ as Sir Alex Ferguson made it pretty clear tha the combination of Roy Keane and Pau Scholes was his first choice partnership i central midfield.

Despite that, the Opta stats still make ver impressive reading for a player who was by n means an automatic starter in 1999–200 From his preferred deep-lying midfield rol Butt got forward to net three times in th Premiership, the most important of which wa a late equaliser in the 2–2 draw at Sunderlan just after Christmas.

Butt's season was tarnished, though, by tw red cards in the Premiership – the first for petulant reaction to some goading b Chelsea's Dennis Wise and the second for skirmish with Watford's Micah Hyde Unfortunately for Butt, his suspec temperament seems to have diminished hi chances of a regular place in the Englan team, which is a shame for an undoubtedl talented midfielder.

APPEARANCES	
Start (sub)	21(11)
Minutes on pitch	1862
GOAL ATTEMPTS	
Goals	3
Shots on target	12
Shooting accuracy	43%
PASSING	
Goal assists	3
Passes in opp half	639
Passing accuracy in opp half	76%
Successful crosses	4
Cross completion	33%
DEFENDING	
Interceptions	16
Clearances	24
Tackles	121
Tackles won %	55%
DISCIPLINE	
Fouls	29
Yellow cards	2
Red cards	2

SEE PAGE 178 FOR FULL STATS

G Stephen BYWATER • 32

WEST HAM UNITED • BORN: 7.6.81

laving replaced broken leg victim Shaka lislop after just two minutes of West Ham's 'remiership match against Bradford in ebruary, teenage goalkeeper Stephen Bywater ndured the worst of inductions into top-light football.

Left pretty exposed by his defence, Bywater onceded four goals, two of which resulted rom his slip-ups. Thankfully for Bywater, the lammers scored five times at the other end to ake all three points.

To his credit Bywater, whose father was a oalkeeper at Halifax Town, bounced back rom his debut despair to produce some very ood performances in the final three 'remiership matches of 1999–2000, when Vest Ham's injury crisis deepened.

Starting the games at Arsenal and underland, Bywater earned glowing eferences from his boss Harry Redknapp and vent on to keep his first Premiership clean heet against Leeds on the final day. In all, he former Rochdale youngster made 14 saves nd conceded seven goals.

APPEARANCES	
Start (sub)	3(1)
Minutes on pitch	358
SHOT STOPPING	
Goals conceded (inside box)	5
Goals conceded (outside box)	2
Minutes per goal conceded	51.1
Clean sheets	1
Saves (shots inside box)	7
Saves (shots outside box)	7
Saves/shots	67%
DISTRIBUTION	
Long kick %	36%
Throws/short passes %	73%
CATCHING	
Crosses caught	3
Crosses punched	2
Crosses dropped	1
Catch success %	75%
DISCIPLINE	
Yellow cards	0
Red cards	0

SEE PAGE 290 FOR FULL STATS

Danny CADAMARTERI • 16

EVERTON • BORN: 12.10.79

APPEARANCES	
Start (sub)	3(14)
Minutes on pitch	524
GOAL ATTEMPTS	
Goals inside box	1
Goals outside box	0
Minutes per goal scored	524.0
Goals/shots ratio	9%
SHOOTING	
Shots on target inside box	7
Shots on target outside box	1
Shooting accuracy	73%
PASSING	
Goal assists	2
Key passes	0
Passing accuracy in opp half	72%
DISCIPLINE	
Fouls committed	10
Fouls won	9
Offside	6
Yellow cards	2
Red cards	0

SEE PAGE 122 FOR FULL STATS

Despite starting just two games for the Toffeemen during the 1999–2000 season, Danny Cadamarteri did not lose any of his enthusiasm or determination to succeed in the top flight. The pacy striker had to compete with more experienced attackers in the shapes of Kevin Campbell and Mark Hughes for a place in the Everton forward line.

Following a loan spell at First Division Fulham, Cadamarteri forced his way into Walter Smith's side for the televised game at Wimbledon. It was in this fixture that the Bradford-born 20-year-old advertised his strongest assets, providing two pinpoint crosses which in turn produced two Campbell headed goals in a 3–0 win.

When he did play, 73% of his efforts found the target, but with a return of just one goal, Cadamarteri was not able to demonstrate the sort of consistency needed in a free-flowing Everton team that scored 59 league goals.

With young hopeful Francis Jeffers coming to the fore, Cadamarteri may find his opportunities becoming even more limited in 2000–01.

Jorge CADETE • 33

BRADFORD CITY • BORN: 27.7.68

Proven goalscorer Jorge Cadete was drafted in by Bradford boss Paul Jewell in February to add some much-needed firepower to the Bantams' attack in a bid to stave off the threat of relegation.

The former Portuguese international failed to find the back of the net during his brief stay at Valley Parade and featured in only seven games during his loan period. He did not have much of an opportunity to make an impact, managing to fire just two efforts on target in less than five hours of Premier League football.

In the matches Cadete was involved in, the team lost five times and drew twice. He looked out of sorts and registered a poor 49% overall pass completion rate.

Unable to demonstrate the clinical finishing that he displayed at Celtic during the 1996–1997 season – when he scored 32 league goals – Cadete headed back to Benfica. He was not the saviour that the Bantams' faithful had hoped to see – but that credit was gleefully received by Dean Windass and co.

APPEARANCES	
Start (sub)	2(5)
Minutes on pitch	272
GOAL ATTEMPTS	
Goals inside box	0
Goals outside box	0
Minutes per goal scored	n/a
Goals/shots ratio	0%
SHOOTING	
Shots on target inside box	2
Shots on target outside box	0
Shooting accuracy	100%
PASSING	
Goal assists	0
Key passes	1
Passing accuracy in opp half	43%
DISCIPLINE	
Fouls committed	3
Fouls won	4
Offside	3
Yellow cards	0
Red cards	0

SEE PAGE 66 FOR FULL STATS

CB

Colin CALDERWOOD • 34

ASTON VILLA • BORN: 20.1.65

APPEARANCES	
Start (sub)	15(3)
Minutes on pitch	1372
GOAL ATTEMPTS	
Goals	0
DEFENDING	
Blocks	15
Shots cleared off line	0
Headed clearances	108
Other clearances	50
Interceptions	14
Last man saving tackles	0
Tackles won	15
Tackles won %	58%
PASSING	
Passing accuracy own half	86%
Passing accuracy opp half	56%
DISCIPLINE	
Fouls	14
Fouls in danger area	1
Yellow cards	1
Red cards	0

SEE PAGE 52 FOR FULL STATS

Experienced Scottish defender Coli Calderwood was a regular in the Aston Vill rearguard during the first half of th 1999–2000 league campaign. But th continued emergence of promising youngste Gareth Barry left the 35-year-old on the fring of a team building for the future.

In 18 appearances, the 6'0" centre-bac displayed his strength and consistency b completing 108 headed clearances an winning 58% of his tackles. Calderwood foun a Villa man with 73% of his passes, showin plenty of composure on the ball.

The former Tottenham player was at th centre of transfer speculation at the turn c the year as he was linked with a move to Firs Division Portsmouth. Instead he plumped fo a move to Nottingham Forest for a cut-pric £70,000. Forest manager David Platt bough Calderwood as cover for an injury crisis, whic saw seven defenders sidelined.

But both Forest's and Calderwood's problem were heightened when the defender broke hi leg against Birmingham on 15 April.

4 Andy Campbell won the joint-highest number of

Titi CAMARA • 22

LIVERPOOL • BORN: 7.11.72

C

Liverpool manager Gerard Houllier used his French connections to snap up Titi Camara from Marseille for £2.6 million in the summer of 1999. The 6'0" striker forged an instant partnership with Robbie Fowler at the start of the campaign, resulting in both marksmen scoring twice in the opening six matches.

Proving a livewire in attack, Camara fired in 31 shots on target, nine of which found the back of the net. Liverpool did not lose a league game when Camara got on the scoresheet, including a 1–0 victory at Highbury where the Guinean fired home with precision from the edge of the area.

Houllier attempted to tailor Camara's playing style to suit the traditional Anfield method of "pass and move". His 60% pass completion rate was below par, but he did contribute a goal assist and 11 key passes which led to scoring opportunities.

His man-of-the-match performances are best appreciated by his mother, who, not sharing Camara's Muslim faith, gratefully receives the celebratory champagne.

APPEARANCES	
Start (sub)	22(11)
Minutes on pitch	1978
GOAL ATTEMPTS	
Goals inside box	4
Goals outside box	5
Minutes per goal scored	219.8
Goals/shots ratio	14%
SHOOTING	
Shots on target inside box	13
Shots on target outside box	18
Shooting accuracy	48%
PASSING	
Goal assists	1
Key passes	11
Passing accuracy in opp half	60%
DISCIPLINE	
Fouls committed	36
Fouls won	43
Offside	18
Yellow cards	7
Red cards	0

SEE PAGE 164 FOR FULL STATS

S

Andy CAMPBELL • 18

MIDDLESBROUGH • BORN: 18.4.79

APPEARANCES	
Start (sub)	16(9)
Minutes on pitch	1498
GOAL ATTEMPTS	
Goals inside box	2
Goals outside box	2
Minutes per goal scored	374.5
Goals/shots ratio	21%
SHOOTING	
Shots on target inside box	7
Shots on target outside box	6
Shooting accuracy	68%
PASSING	
Goal assists	2
Key passes	8
Passing accuracy in opp half	65%
DISCIPLINE	
Fouls committed	11
Fouls won	42
Offside	23
Yellow cards	0
Red cards	0

SEE PAGE 192 FOR FULL STATS

A great young prospect at The Riverside, 21-year-old Andy Campbell edged his way into the Middlesbrough first team, becoming a regular towards the climax of 1999–2000.

He is a successful product of Boro's youth policy and was rewarded for his persistent rise up the ranks with a new four-year contract earlier in the year.

The nippy youngster demonstrated his potential with both consolation goals in the defeats by Derby and Leicester, before scoring a classy winning lob against Sheffield Wednesday. That feat was followed up with a volleyed opening goal against Champions Manchester United.

Goals and measured shots rained in from both inside and outside the box illustrate Campbell's versatility as a forward. Four goals from 19 shots gave him a 21% goals-to-shots ratio that offers further evidence of his potency in the danger area.

If he continues to perform with such a deadly eye for goal, England under-21 caps may soon become senior caps.

penalties in the Premiership, along with Kevin Phillips

Kevin CAMPBELL • 9

EVERTON • BORN: 4.2.70

Sidelined through injury from early March 2000, big Kevin Campbell still ended the season as Everton's top marksman with 12 goals. This was a continuation of his goalscoring form during a loan period that almost single-handedly saved the club from relegation at the climax of the 1998–99 season.

Everton manager Walter Smith shelled out £3 million for Campbell's services back in July 1999 and the striker has gone a long way to paying back that fee. The former England under-21 international has achieved cult status on Merseyside like so many former Everton number nines down the years.

The former Gunner sent 37 rockets goal-bound, with only 11 fizzing past the woodwork. A 70% shooting accuracy is evidence enough that at 6'1" Campbell is as deadly with his feet as he is with his effective heading ability.

The 30-year-old offered experience to youngster Francis Jeffers in a partnership that yielded 18 goals. Campbell also weighed in with an invaluable seven goal assists.

APPEARANCES	
Start (sub)	26(0)
Minutes on pitch	2340
GOAL ATTEMPTS	
Goals inside box	12
Goals outside box	0
Minutes per goal scored	195.0
Goals/shots ratio	32%
SHOOTING	
Shots on target inside box	24
Shots on target outside box	2
Shooting accuracy	70%
PASSING	
Goal assists	7
Key passes	14
Passing accuracy in opp half	72%
DISCIPLINE	
Fouls committed	58
Fouls won	37
Offside	64
Yellow cards	2
Red cards	0

SEE PAGE 122 FOR FULL STATS

CB

Sol CAMPBELL • 5

TOTTENHAM HOTSPUR • BORN: 18.9.74

APPEARANCES	
Start (sub)	29(0)
Minutes on pitch	2530
GOAL ATTEMPTS	
Goals	0
DEFENDING	
Blocks	83
Shots cleared off line	1
Headed clearances	240
Other clearances	88
Interceptions	61
Last man saving tackles	0
Tackles won	74
Tackles won %	60%
PASSING	
Passing accuracy own half	76%
Passing accuracy opp half	55%
DISCIPLINE	
Fouls	52
Fouls in danger area	18
Yellow cards	6
Red cards	0

SEE PAGE 262 FOR FULL STATS

For the second successive season, Sol Campbell earned himself a place in the Opta Team of the Season. The adept centre-back had a solid 1999–2000 campaign and his Herculean performances led to a rash of transfer speculation.

But manager George Graham convinced Campbell to see out the remaining two years of his contract, which is testament to how highly he rates his skipper. The imposing 6'2" defender was commanding on the ground and dominant in the air, completing a total of 328 clearances. His leggy stride enabled him to block 83 shots and crosses.

The 25-year-old demonstrated his ability in carrying the ball out of defence, embarking upon 43 marauding dribbles and runs with a 91% success rate, evidence that Campbell's sophisticated game involves more than pumping the ball upfield.

Campbell's consistency has made him an integral component in Kevin Keegan's England team and he has all the right leadership qualities to become a future captain.

Stuart CAMPBELL • 16

LEICESTER CITY • BORN: 9.12.77

C

Midfielder Stuart Campbell found first-team opportunities hard to come by at Filbert Street, featuring in just four matches during the 1999–2000 season. The form of Leicester midfielders Neil Lennon, Muzzy Izzet and Robbie Savage severely restricted right-sided Campbell's progress at the club.

The 22-year-old did make a telling contribution in the home game against Newcastle – providing a goal assist for Theo Zagorakis – and was rewarded three weeks later with a full 90 minutes in the defeat at West Ham.

The young Fox was successful with three-quarters of his dribbles and runs but his crossing was disappointing with only nine crosses or corners finding their target. Having proved his ability, Campbell snapped up the chance of a loan move to the First Division to further advertise his capabilities.

Trevor Francis took the Scottish under-21 player to St Andrews in March in a bid to strengthen Birmingham's drive to make the play-offs.

APPEARANCES	
Start (sub)	1(3)
Minutes on pitch	182
GOAL ATTEMPTS	
Goals	0
Shots on target	0
Shooting accuracy	0%
PASSING & CROSSING	
Goal assists	1
Passes in opp half	27
Passing accuracy in opp half	63%
Successful crosses	1
Cross completion	11%
DEFENDING	
Interceptions	4
Clearances	1
Tackles	3
Tackles won %	67%
DISCIPLINE	
Fouls	2
Yellow cards	0
Red cards	0

SEE PAGE 150 FOR FULL STATS

Horacio CARBONARI • 2

DERBY COUNTY • BORN: 2.5.74

APPEARANCES	
Start (sub)	29(0)
Minutes on pitch	2509
GOAL ATTEMPTS	
Goals	2
DEFENDING	
Blocks	78
Shots cleared off line	1
Headed clearances	178
Other clearances	119
Interceptions	28
Last man saving tackles	2
Tackles won	47
Tackles won %	49%
PASSING	
Passing accuracy own half	76%
Passing accuracy opp half	49%
DISCIPLINE	
Fouls	34
Fouls in danger area	18
Yellow cards	10
Red cards	0

SEE PAGE 108 FOR FULL STATS

Signed in 1998 for a sum of £2.7 million, Horacio Carbonari was again an integral part of the Derby County defence. The Argentinean appeared 29 times for the Rams despite carrying an injury, which is a tribute to his commitment.

Affectionately named "Boom-Boom" by the Derby faithful on account of his power-stacked thunder boots, Carbonari lived up to the hype, thumping home an unstoppable shot against Tottenham in a 1–1 draw. It is surprising that he only found the back of the net twice, having fired in 37 shots, with 10 testing the goalkeeper and 12 blocked by defenders.

The big Ram was not shy of a physical encounter, collecting 10 yellow cards throughout the course of the season. Tackling was not at the forefront of his game, though, as he won fewer than 50% of his challenges.

Clearly Carbonari's ability lies in his strength, as he managed to put his frame in the way of 78 shots and crosses and completed almost 300 clearances. A summer hernia operation should see him back to full strength and power.

Benito CARBONE • 18

ASTON VILLA • BORN: 14.8.71

John Gregory made an astute signing when he swooped for unsettled Sheffield Wednesday striker Benito Carbone in October 1999. The Italian provided a much-needed spark that ignited Villa's ailing start to the campaign.

The diminutive striker made an immediate impact, forcing four saves out of Wimbledon 'keeper Neil Sullivan on his debut before orchestrating a goal for Dion Dublin in a sparkling display.

Carbone was a constant threat throughout 1999–2000, but only managed five league goals in return. Perseverance was there in abundance as he rifled in 66 shots, under half of which called the 'keeper into action.

Running with the ball as if it were tied to his foot, "Beni" tormented defenders 145 times with his mazy dribbles that proved successful missions 54% of the time.

Carbone enjoys the big occasion and was instrumental in guiding Villa to the FA Cup final, with his never-say-die attitude prominent as he scored a stunning hat-trick against Leeds in the fifth round.

APPEARANCES	
Start (sub)	26(5)
Minutes on pitch	2284
GOAL ATTEMPTS	
Goals inside box	1
Goals outside box	4
Minutes per goal scored	456.8
Goals/shots ratio	6%
SHOOTING	
Shots on target inside box	9
Shots on target outside box	20
Shooting accuracy	44%
PASSING	
Goal assists	5
Key passes	8
Passing accuracy in opp half	60%
DISCIPLINE	
Fouls committed	42
Fouls won	48
Offside	76
Yellow cards	1
Red cards	0

SEE PAGES 52 & 220 FOR FULL STATS

Stephen CARR • 2

TOTTENHAM HOTSPUR • BORN: 29.8.76

APPEARANCES	
Start (sub)	34(0)
Minutes on pitch	3060
GOAL ATTEMPTS	
Goals	3
PASSING & CROSSING	
Goal assists	3
Passing	1468
Passing accuracy	69%
Crosses	84
Crossing accuracy	24%
DEFENDING	
Tackles	90
Tackles won %	49%
Blocks	52
Interceptions	61
Clearances	213
Shots cleared off line	2
DISCIPLINE	
Fouls	32
Yellow cards	5
Red cards	0

SEE PAGE 262 FOR FULL STATS

Stephen Carr has now missed just five league matches in the last three seasons, which is a testament to how accomplished he has become in the right-back slot. His performances were so consistent during the 1999–2000 campaign that Carr made the Opta Team of the Season.

The Eire international has flourished under the management of George Graham and plays in a style that is synonymous with the Scotsman. Carr is a solid defender, tough in the tackle but also confident in bringing the ball out of defence, storming up the wing on the overlap and delivering balls into the box.

The youngster displayed composure on the ball and attempted more passes than any of his team-mates, with 69% of his deliveries finding a white shirt. He ventured into the opponents' half on surging runs and scored superb goals at White Hart Lane against Manchester United and Sunderland.

Fitness and stamina are an intrinsic part of his game, which should ensure that Carr is an automatic choice in 2000–01.

76 Benito Carbone strayed offside more

Jamie CARRAGHER • 23

LIVERPOOL • BORN: 28.1.78

C

Despite his tender years, Jamie Carragher made 36 league appearances in 1999–2000, becoming a regular fixture in the Liverpool rearguard. The 22-year-old defender displayed his versatility, appearing in midfield on occasions before being utilised in the right-back berth.

While limited in attacking prowess, Carragher is solid and reliable in his defensive duties, having launched the ball clear on 225 occasions. He is not afraid to put himself in the face of potential danger, blocking 46 threatening balls with his 6'1" frame.

The Liverpudlian managed to channel his aggression into positive energy, receiving just four yellow cards – an improvement over his disciplinary record during the 1998–99 season. But, he did not shy away from confrontation, winning 51% of his tackles.

The Bootle-born player made it into the record books by becoming the most capped England under-21 player, after making his 23rd appearance in the national side against Argentina in February 2000.

APPEARANCES	
Start (sub)	33(3)
Minutes on pitch	2987
GOAL ATTEMPTS	
Goals	0
DEFENDING	
Blocks	46
Shots cleared off line	1
Headed clearances	165
Other clearances	60
Interceptions	32
Last man saving tackles	0
Tackles won	61
Tackles won %	51%
PASSING	
Passing accuracy own half	86%
Passing accuracy opp half	70%
DISCIPLINE	
Fouls	36
Fouls in danger area	6
Yellow cards	4
Red cards	0

SEE PAGE 164 FOR FULL STATS

Michael CARRICK • 21

WEST HAM UNITED • BORN: 28.7.81

APPEARANCES	
Start (sub)	4(4)
Minutes on pitch	475
GOAL ATTEMPTS	
Goals	1
Shots on target	3
Shooting accuracy	43%
PASSING & CROSSING	
Goal assists	2
Passes in opp half	120
Passing accuracy in opp half	63%
Successful crosses	2
Cross completion	67%
DEFENDING	
Interceptions	1
Clearances	9
Tackles	26
Tackles won %	50%
DISCIPLINE	
Fouls	4
Yellow cards	0
Red cards	0

SEE PAGE 290 FOR FULL STATS

One young man's downfall proved to be another young man's gain at Upton Park, as Michael Carrick stepped in to replace the injured Joe Cole. Carrick is a product of the West Ham youth team and, though less hyped than his contemporary, he is no less talented.

The 19-year-old played just 475 minutes of Premiership football, but has been touted by Harry Redknapp as a future England international. He made his debut against Bradford in August, then enjoyed loan spells with Swindon and Birmingham before returning to Upton Park.

His first telling contribution was a goal assist against Leicester, followed swiftly by an impressive display against Coventry. Carrick opened the scoring in the 5–0 romp by rifling home from 20 yards and then created a goal for Paolo Di Canio. His precision was emphasised by a 67% cross completion rate and a 70% pass completion rate.

The Geordie's impact was rewarded with the Young Hammer of the Year award and a call-up to the England under-21 squad.

Alec CHAMBERLAIN • 1

WATFORD • BORN: 20.6.64

Signed from Sunderland in 1996, Alec Chamberlain has been a worthy last line of defence for the Hornets for four seasons.

He was Player of the Year when Watford won the Division Two Championship in 1997–1998 and runner-up the following season as the team won promotion to the dizzy heights of the Premiership. Unfortunately, relegation from the top flight after the 1999–2000 campaign is likely to coincide with Chamberlain's last stint between the posts for his eighth league club.

The 6'2" stopper conceded 61 goals in 27 appearances, maintaining a meagre three clean sheets in the process. He can take solace in the fact that he was the club's cleanest player, receiving no cards and not committing a single foul.

In a very pressured season, Chamberlain was often left exposed and made more than 100 saves from shots from all angles. He confidently marshalled his penalty box when called upon, dropping just a solitary ball from 42 attempted catches and punching clear 18 times.

APPEARANCES	
Start (sub)	27(0)
Minutes on pitch	2430
SHOT STOPPING	
Goals conceded (inside box)	53
Goals conceded (outside box)	8
Minutes per goal conceded	39.8
Clean sheets	3
Saves (shots inside box)	70
Saves (shots outside box)	37
Saves/shots	64%
DISTRIBUTION	
Long kick %	37%
Throws/short passes %	78%
CATCHING	
Crosses caught	41
Crosses punched	18
Crosses dropped	1
Catch success %	98%
DISCIPLINE	
Yellow cards	0
Red cards	0

SEE PAGE 276 FOR FULL STATS

Gary CHARLES • 2

WEST HAM UNITED • BORN: 13.4.70

APPEARANCES	
Start (sub)	2(2)
Minutes on pitch	192
GOAL ATTEMPTS	
Goals	0
PASSING & CROSSING	
Goal assists	0
Passing	78
Passing accuracy	72%
Crosses	9
Crossing accuracy	11%
DEFENDING	
Tackles	2
Tackles won %	0%
Blocks	4
Interceptions	0
Clearances	7
Shots cleared off line	0
DISCIPLINE	
Fouls	3
Yellow cards	1
Red cards	0

SEE PAGE 290 FOR FULL STATS

Harry Redknapp rescued Gary Charles from his turbulent spell in Portuguese football when he signed him from Benfica in October 1999. Charles was returning to his roots, having been brought up in Canning Town and being a lifelong Hammers fan.

Having played just five games in Portugal due to a stomach problem, Charles has continued to be dogged by injury since his return to England. He suffered a thigh strain shortly after signing and was badly injured at Birmingham in the Worthington Cup.

The right-back's comeback proved to be a nightmare, as the Hammers went down 2–1 at Southampton with Charles scoring his first ever own-goal to decide the game. Coupled with a booking, it was 90 minutes that he would probably rather forget.

Charles started just one more game and made two substitute appearances. Despite playing only 192 minutes, a 72% pass completion rate and nine attempted crosses indicate that he Charles offers a mixture of purposeful possession and attacking flair.

Laurent CHARVET • 16

NEWCASTLE UNITED • BORN: 8.5.73

Since arriving on English soil in January 1998, Laurent Charvet has experienced mixed fortunes under three different managers.

Originally on loan at Chelsea courtesy of Ruud Gullit, Charvet was brought from the south of France to the north-east of England by Kenny Dalglish in July 1998. A month and one twist of fate later and the Frenchman was reunited with Gullit, who took over the reins at St James's Park.

But, when Bobby Robson took over, Charvet largely fell out of favour and played a paltry 107 minutes of football in a disappointing 1999–2000 season. He was also dogged by injury, which meant spells on the treatment table led only to infrequent appearances on the bench.

Charvet's first league appearance came at Elland Road, where his lack of match fitness was exposed by a youthful Leeds attack that scored three times. Renowned as a tough but skilful full-back, he did not commit a single foul but only won a third of his tackles during his two games.

APPEARANCES	
Start (sub)	1(1)
Minutes on pitch	107
GOAL ATTEMPTS	
Goals	0
PASSING & CROSSING	
Goal assists	0
Passing	46
Passing accuracy	65%
Crosses	1
Crossing accuracy	0%
DEFENDING	
Tackles	3
Tackles won	33%
Blocks	5
Interceptions	6
Clearances	12
Shots cleared off line	0
DISCIPLINE	
Fouls	0
Yellow cards	0
Red cards	0

SEE PAGE 206 FOR FULL STATS

AM

Youssef CHIPPO • 18

COVENTRY CITY • BORN: 10.5.73

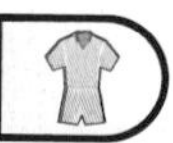

APPEARANCES	
Start (sub)	32(1)
Minutes on pitch	2781
GOAL ATTEMPTS	
Goals	2
Shots on target	17
Shooting accuracy	55%
Goals/shots ratio	6%
PASSING	
Goal assists	3
Passes in opp half	710
Passing accuracy in opp half	69%
Successful crosses	9
Crossing accuracy	23%
DRIBBLING	
Dribbles & runs	162
Dribble completion	77%
Corners forced	7
DISCIPLINE	
Fouls	68
Yellow cards	9
Red cards	1

SEE PAGE 94 FOR FULL STATS

African export Youssef Chippo arrived on English soil in May 1999 as the first half of Coventry's Moroccan dream team. The pony-tailed midfielder made a spectacular impact for his national team during the 1998 World Cup in France and was snapped up by Gordon Strachan for £1 million.

The former FC Porto player is an integral part of the Coventry squad, combining an ambitious attacking flair with a gritty determination to win the ball. He attempted and won more tackles than any of his team-mates during the 1999–2000 season, but also paraded a fiery side to his temperament. Chippo amassed a total of nine yellow cards and one red during a turbulent season.

The Moroccan is a threat in the opponents' half and, despite finding the back of the net just twice, had 15 shots saved and nine blocked en route to goal. A 77% dribble success rate is indicative of his confidence on the ball and undoubtedly makes him a fans' favourite. At 27, he will have a definite say in any future success at Highfield Road.

Malcolm CHRISTIE • 12

DERBY COUNTY • BORN: 11.4.79

Jim Smith proved that homegrown talent still exists in the lower leagues by poaching Malcolm Christie from the Dr Martens League. The former Nuneaton Borough striker played a vital role in ensuring Derby maintained their Premier League status.

Cast into the limelight for his first-ever Premiership start at The Riverside, the 21-year-old refused to be overawed by the occasion and looked very comfortable in a Derby side short on confidence. Cool Christie bagged two goals in a 4–1 victory that was swiftly followed up with an opportunist goal at Sunderland to earn a precious point.

The livewire youngster oozes enthusiasm the moment he dons the white shirt and is a fine example of determination breeding success. A consistent threat around the penalty area, Christie fired in 20 shots on target and contributed two goal assists.

It is a far cry from his days as a supermarket shelf-stacker in Stamford. He has certainly shown in the Premiership that he has packets of talent.

APPEARANCES	
Start (sub)	10(11)
Minutes on pitch	1179
GOAL ATTEMPTS	
Goals inside box	5
Goals outside box	0
Minutes per goal scored	235.80
Goals/shots ratio	19%
SHOOTING	
Shots on target inside box	17
Shots on target outside box	3
Shooting accuracy	77%
PASSING	
Goal assists	2
Key passes	5
Passing accuracy in opp half	58%
DISCIPLINE	
Fouls committed	22
Fouls won	23
Offside	19
Yellow cards	2
Red cards	0

SEE PAGE 108 FOR FULL STATS

G

Matt CLARKE • 13

BRADFORD CITY • BORN: 3.11.73

APPEARANCES	
Start (sub)	21(0)
Minutes on pitch	1875
SHOT STOPPING	
Goals conceded (inside box)	29
Goals conceded (outside box)	7
Minutes per goal conceded	52.1
Clean sheets	5
Saves (shots inside box)	52
Saves (shots outside box)	39
Saves/shots	72%
DISTRIBUTION	
Long kick %	42%
Throws/short passes %	77%
CATCHING	
Crosses caught	40
Crosses punched	23
Crosses dropped	1
Catch success %	98%
DISCIPLINE	
Yellow cards	0
Red cards	0

SEE PAGE 66 FOR FULL STATS

Matt Clarke was highly instrumental in Bradford's great escape from the clutches of Division One football during the 1999–2000 campaign. The Bantams utilised four goalkeepers throughout the season, but Clarke proved that he was the pick of the bunch.

The former Sheffield Wednesday man maintained five of the team's seven clean sheets during his 21 appearances. Having ousted injured Gary Walsh from between the sticks, Clarke took up the position against Liverpool where he performed heroics despite Bradford going down 3–1. A consistent vein of form ensued before he suffered a knee injury in the win over Watford. Clarke returned to the side in time for the run-in, which saw Bradford win three of their last four games.

The 26-year-old 'keeper saved 72% of the shots aimed towards his goal – the average percentage for a top-flight goalie – and commanded his penalty area, plucking an impressive 98% of balls from the air.

Clarke will be seeking to make the number one jersey his own in 2000–01.

77% Malcolm Christie's shooting accuracy was higher than an

Michael CLEGG • 23

MANCHESTER UNITED • BORN: 3.7.77

;ompeting against the likes of the Neville ›rothers and Denis Irwin for a slot in the Jnited back four proved a mountainous task or Michael Clegg.

The 23-year-old full-back played just 15 ninutes for the Premier League champions, ›ut rose to the challenge of playing on loan in he lower leagues.

Clegg played three times for Ipswich Town s cover for Gary Croft before heading back to he north west to end the 1999–2000 season vith promotion-chasing Wigan. Although ›rimarily a right-back, Clegg showed his ersatility by playing at right midfield on ›ccasion at the JJB stadium.

At Wigan, the former Manchester United rainee combined composure on the ball with lecent crossing ability. With more talent eading into Old Trafford, Clegg may be urplus to requirements and would be an asset o any ambitious team looking for a sound nvestment to better their cause.

SEE PAGE 178 FOR FULL STATS

Alex CLELAND • 2

EVERTON • BORN: 10.12.70

Since arriving at Goodison Park in July 1998, Alex Cleland has been plagued by injury and spent much of his time on the periphery of the first team. He made 16 starts as an emergency centre-back at the start of the 1998–99 season before suffering a torn calf muscle at Ipswich, which put him out of action for the remainder of the season.

The Glaswegian was reunited with former boss Walter Smith at Everton, for whom he had played more than 100 games at Rangers. He is adept at attacking down the flanks and has a no-nonsense approach to defending, making 20 blocks and clearances in less than four hours of football.

The addition of Scottish international defender David Weir to the Everton squad left Cleland fighting for a starting position. He made just three starts for the club in 1999 before suffering another calf injury at Bradford in December, which brought his season to a premature end.

SEE PAGE 122 FOR FULL STATS

Stephen CLEMENCE • 25

TOTTENHAM HOTSPUR • BORN: 31.3.78

APPEARANCES	
Start (sub)	17(3)
Minutes on pitch	1521
GOAL ATTEMPTS	
Goals	1
Shots on target	4
Shooting accuracy	57%
PASSING & CROSSING	
Goal assists	1
Passes in opp half	424
Passing accuracy in opp half	69%
Successful crosses	13
Cross completion	25%
DEFENDING	
Interceptions	19
Clearances	31
Tackles	57
Tackles won %	47%
DISCIPLINE	
Fouls	37
Yellow cards	5
Red cards	0

SEE PAGE 262 FOR FULL STATS

Ensuring that the name Clemence remains synonymous with Tottenham into the new Millennium, young Stephen enjoyed a positive season at White Hart Lane, playing a part in 20 Premiership games.

Having undergone surgery for an ankle injury during the 1998–99 season, he did not make an appearance until the October defeat at Sunderland but enjoyed a further 16 starts as the season progressed.

Clemence, a former England youth international, made notable strides to improve his game, showing that he can be a threat in attacking positions by making 42 dribbles and runs and setting up one goal.

He found the back of the net in front of the Spurs faithful with a contender for "cheekiest goal of the season". Executed in the last minute against Derby, Clemence deftly back-heeled the ball between the posts to earn Spurs a draw.

His tackling ability may have to improve if he is to meet George Graham's ideals, and he did pick up five bookings – but this may indicate a competitive edge and a growth in confidence.

Andy COLE • 9

MANCHESTER UNITED • BORN: 15.10.71

S

Andy Cole reached a personal milestone and equalled a club record, in a season when he received his fourth league winners' medal. The former Newcastle hitman scored his 100th goal for the Champions against Wimbledon and netted his 14th European Cup goal to match Denis Law's long-standing record.

Cole played a pivotal role in United's quest for the Championship, bagging 19 league goals and contributing five goal assists. He continued his quasi-telepathic relationship with strike partner Dwight Yorke as they yielded a combined total of 39 goals.

The persistent striker started 23 games for the Reds and his consistent movement around the box led to 39 shots on target and a further 23 flying wide of the mark. A 72% pass completion rate was indicative of his increased awareness of his team-mates.

Cole remains one of the Premiership's top marksmen and, despite a number of verbal assaults on the England set-up, he figured in Kevin Keegan's preliminary squad before injury ended his Euro 2000 dream.

APPEARANCES	
Start (sub)	23(5)
Minutes on pitch	2000
GOAL ATTEMPTS	
Goals inside box	18
Goals outside box	1
Minutes per goal scored	105.3
Goals/shots ratio	31%
SHOOTING	
Shots on target inside box	36
Shots on target outside box	3
Shooting accuracy	63%
PASSING	
Goal assists	5
Key passes	9
Passing accuracy in opp half	71%
DISCIPLINE	
Fouls committed	32
Fouls won	23
Offside	26
Yellow cards	2
Red cards	1

SEE PAGE 178 FOR FULL STATS

Ashley COLE • 34

ARSENAL • BORN: 20.12.80

Andy Cole is no relation, but Arsenal's teenage full-back Ashley Cole seems to enjoy scoring goals just as much as his illustrious namesake.

Cole joined Crystal Palace on loan for the final three months of 1999–2000 and became a massive hit with the Eagles' faithful with his pacy, direct running, crunching tackles and penchant for long-range shooting.

He promised the fans he would not return to Highbury without scoring – and he duly netted with a superb rising drive at home to Blackburn, a goal which helped Palace avoid relegation from Division One.

Cole then bade farewell to Selhurst Park and started Arsenal's final game of the season at Middlesbrough, pushing left-back Nigel Winterburn into midfield.

He fired in two shots at goal in his 90 minutes for the Gunners, made six trademark tackles and completed 71% of his passes. It will now be interesting to see how many chances he gets in the Gunners' first team in 2000–01.

SEE PAGE 38 FOR FULL STATS

Ton-up: Andy Cole

Joe COLE • 26

WEST HAM UNITED • BORN: 8.11.81

C

here are very few sports stars who have had ıeir name trademarked, but the youngest ust be Joe Cole.

Not that this decision should be questioned, ; Cole is the protégé whose name was ıentioned by many of football's elite even efore he had made a first-team appearance.

After making the breakthrough in the 998–99 season, the young midfielder managed ɔ establish himself as a regular in 1999–2000. e soon scored his debut senior goal in the 'orthington Cup trip to Birmingham City.

The twinkle-toed youngster has justified his eam place, particularly as he supplied many <iller" passes to his team-mates. He boasted ı above-average pass completion rate of 8%, higher even than skilful stars Paolo Di anio and Trevor Sinclair.

But as Euro 2000 approached and, with it, ıe prospects of an England squad place, Cole xperienced his first footballing heartbreak 'hen he broke his leg at Derby. Kevin Keegan ɔnsoled him by urging him to look forward to ıe 2002 World Cup.

APPEARANCES	
Start (sub)	17(5)
Minutes on pitch	1530
GOAL ATTEMPTS	
Goals	1
Shots on target	8
Shooting accuracy	38%
Goals/shots ratio	5%
PASSING	
Goal assists	1
Passes in opp half	554
Passing accuracy in opp half	76%
Successful crosses	10
Crossing accuracy	38%
DRIBBLING	
Dribbles & runs	134
Dribble completion	66%
Corners forced	8
DISCIPLINE	
Fouls	16
Yellow cards	1
Red cards	0

SEE PAGE 290 FOR FULL STATS

FB

Patrick COLLETER • 24

SOUTHAMPTON • BORN: 6.11.65

APPEARANCES	
Start (sub)	7(1)
Minutes on pitch	538
GOAL ATTEMPTS	
Goals	0
PASSING & CROSSING	
Goal assists	0
Passing	202
Passing accuracy	60%
Crosses	6
Crossing accuracy	17%
DEFENDING	
Tackles	26
Tackles won %	42%
Blocks	10
Interceptions	7
Clearances	30
Shots cleared off line	0
DISCIPLINE	
Fouls	5
Yellow cards	2
Red cards	1

SEE PAGE 234 FOR FULL STATS

An experienced left-back, Patrick Colleter is probably best remembered in English football for his debut performance, when the Frenchman produced a crunching challenge on Gustavo Poyet, which could have ended the Chelsea player's career.

But despite his "B" international status in France, Colleter had little opportunity to leave his mark at Southampton in the 1999–2000 campaign. During his performances, the Frenchman showed his combative side by making 26 challenges. But he came out on top in only 42%, a big drop on his efforts during his first season in the Premiership.

He also seemed to lose his attacking instincts, with only 17% of his crosses finding their intended target and 40% of his passes going astray.

After playing a part in each of Glenn Hoddle's first three games in charge at The Dell, he did not make the starting line-up again. And at 34, Colleter will need to make a bright start to the 2000–01 campaign if he is to resurrect his Saints career.

John COLLINS • 7

EVERTON • BORN: 31.1.68

A virtual ever-present for the Toffees during 1999–2000, John Collins showed himself to be one of the most complete midfielders in the Premiership with his combination of silky skills and hard tackling.

The former Scotland international was successful with 107 challenges – more than any other top-flight player. But Collins was equally instrumental in his team's attacking play, with the majority of their best moves going through him. He made 1,724 passes – the sixth-highest total in the division – and contributed massively to Everton becoming the fourth-highest scorers in the Premiership.

The former Monaco midfielder also fired a couple of goals himself, but will now be hoping his efforts can result in some silverware for the Goodison Park trophy cabinet. Collins, now 32, has stated that he wants to make his final years of top-class football as memorable as possible. And if he can retain his form and fitness, he will stand a good chance of achieving the success he craves with the Toffees during 2000–01.

APPEARANCES	
Start (sub)	33(2)
Minutes on pitch	2931
GOAL ATTEMPTS	
Goals	2
Shots on target	14
Shooting accuracy	33%
PASSING & CROSSING	
Goal assists	1
Passes in opp half	979
Passing accuracy in opp half	77%
Successful crosses	15
Cross completion	33%
DEFENDING	
Interceptions	44
Clearances	38
Tackles	176
Tackles won %	61%
DISCIPLINE	
Fouls	52
Yellow cards	4
Red cards	1

SEE PAGE 122 FOR FULL STATS

Stan COLLYMORE • 8

LEICESTER CITY • BORN: 22.1.71

APPEARANCES	
Start (sub)	6(0)
Minutes on pitch	473
GOAL ATTEMPTS	
Goals inside box	3
Goals outside box	1
Minutes per goal scored	118.3
Goals/shots ratio	22%
SHOOTING	
Shots on target inside box	5
Shots on target outside box	6
Shooting accuracy	61%
PASSING	
Goal assists	1
Key passes	1
Passing accuracy in opp half	63%
DISCIPLINE	
Fouls committed	8
Fouls won	11
Offside	9
Yellow cards	1
Red cards	0

SEE PAGE 150 FOR FULL STATS

After his disastrous spell at Aston Villa, St Collymore moved on to Filbert Street to t and rediscover the talent that had once ma him Britain's most expensive player. Aft costing Villa a staggering £1 million for ea league goal that he scored, many pundi wrote off his chances of making a comebac

However, despite the infamous fi extinguisher incident in Spain just days in his Leicester career, Collymore defied h critics and won over the Leicester fa instantly: "Stan The Man" grabbed a hat-tri on his home debut against Sunderland.

But, unfortunately, he managed just o more strike before his season was end cruelly when he broke his leg against Derby

Collymore's performances left Foxes fa drooling at what he might achieve in t 2000–01 campaign. He fired 61% of his sho on target and linked well with his tea mates, completing 59% of his passes. The are clear signs that if he can recov sufficiently from his injury, Collymore mig well return to set the Premiership on fire.

8 Carl Cort missed the target with more shots from insid

Colin COOPER • 28

MIDDLESBROUGH • BORN: 28.2.67

Colin Cooper had a steady second season at The Riverside in 1999–2000. The £2.5 million signing had returned to his first club from Nottingham Forest to renew his "old boys" centre-back partnership with Gary Pallister.

But, despite him providing the side with the defensive solidity needed for Premiership survival, Boro have yet to make the leap to the upper echelons of the top flight, the promise of which prompted grizzled Cooper's return to Teesside.

During the 1999–2000 campaign, the 33-year-old used his experience to make 18 interceptions as well as 69 blocks – the second highest total at the club. But despite challenging for the ball on 74 occasions, the former Millwall defender came out on top in only 46% of his tackles – five percentage points worse than the season average.

Cooper will be slightly disappointed with his lack of success in the tackle. But the former England international's contribution in other areas should see him marshalling the Boro back-line once again in 2000–01.

APPEARANCES	
Start (sub)	26(0)
Minutes on pitch	2262
GOAL ATTEMPTS	
Goals	0
DEFENDING	
Blocks	69
Shots cleared off line	0
Headed clearances	146
Other clearances	74
Interceptions	18
Last man saving tackles	1
Tackles won	34
Tackles won %	46%
PASSING	
Passing accuracy own half	75%
Passing accuracy opp half	54%
DISCIPLINE	
Fouls	22
Fouls in danger area	8
Yellow cards	5
Red cards	0

SEE PAGE 192 FOR FULL STATS

S

Carl CORT • 7

WIMBLEDON • BORN: 1.11.77

APPEARANCES	
Start (sub)	33(1)
Minutes on pitch	2864
GOAL ATTEMPTS	
Goals inside box	9
Goals outside box	0
Minutes per goal scored	318.2
Goals/shots ratio	15%
SHOOTING	
Shots on target inside box	18
Shots on target outside box	5
Shooting accuracy	37%
PASSING	
Goal assists	6
Key passes	9
Passing accuracy in opp half	64%
DISCIPLINE	
Fouls committed	63
Fouls won	38
Offside	35
Yellow cards	2
Red cards	0

SEE PAGE 304 FOR FULL STATS

Big Carl Cort showed immense versatility in 1999–2000, switching between the right-wing and centre-forward positions for the Dons.

Egil Olsen's tactics meant that Cort got fewer goalscoring opportunities than he would have liked, but still ended up as Wimbledon's joint-top scorer with nine league goals – and a brilliant hat-trick against Sunderland in the Worthington Cup.

It was not enough to steer the Dons clear of relegation, however, and with Olsen now gone, Cort will probably move back permanently to his more favoured role as a striker, either with Wimbledon or elsewhere.

Cort has often stated that his skills are best employed up front – and the Opta statistics for the 1999–2000 season certainly back up his point of view. He completed a disappointing 23% of his crosses, showing his deficiencies as a winger, but excelled when in front of goal. The Southwark-born player fired in 62 shots – the joint-highest total at the club – and will be relishing the prospect of improving on his shooting skills in 2000–01.

he six-yard box than any other Premiership player

Tony COTTEE • 27

LEICESTER CITY • BORN: 11.7.65

After a career spanning 18 seasons, Tony Cottee finally picked up the winner's medal he so desperately wanted when his Leicester side triumphed in the Worthington Cup. It was no more than the veteran striker deserved after his superb performances for Leicester over the 1999–2000 campaign.

Cottee finished as the club's top scorer with 13 league goals and, if he retains his form and fitness, he could easily go on for another season in the Premiership. He certainly appears to have retained all the finishing skills that prompted Everton to splash out a British record fee of £2.3 million for him in 1988.

An incredible 33% of the former West Ham forward's shots found their way into the back of the net – the highest rating of any regular top-flight striker – highlighting his vast importance to the Leicester cause.

The pint-sized frontman will hope to play a starring role once again in 2000–01, just as he did at the City Christmas party, when he turned up to the fancy-dress gig dressed as a garden gnome.

APPEARANCES	
Start (sub)	30(3)
Minutes on pitch	2491
GOAL ATTEMPTS	
Goals inside box	12
Goals outside box	1
Minutes per goal scored	191.6
Goals/shots ratio	33%
SHOOTING	
Shots on target inside box	21
Shots on target outside box	3
Shooting accuracy	60%
PASSING	
Goal assists	1
Key passes	5
Passing accuracy in opp half	74%
DISCIPLINE	
Fouls committed	28
Fouls won	48
Offside	31
Yellow cards	1
Red cards	0

SEE PAGE 150 FOR FULL STATS

Neil COX • 36

WATFORD • BORN: 8.10.71

APPEARANCES	
Start (sub)	20(1)
Minutes on pitch	1757
GOAL ATTEMPTS	
Goals	0
PASSING & CROSSING	
Goal assists	1
Passing	653
Passing accuracy	52%
Crosses	72
Crossing accuracy	28%
DEFENDING	
Tackles	52
Tackles won %	35%
Blocks	57
Interceptions	10
Clearances	96
Shots cleared off line	0
DISCIPLINE	
Fouls	18
Yellow cards	1
Red cards	1

SEE PAGE 276 FOR FULL STATS

Neil Cox now suffers the unfortuna distinction of having experienced relegati from the Premiership with three different clul His spells with Middlesbrough, Bolton and nc Watford all ended with the dreaded drop.

However, the former England under- defender showed enough skill a determination after his transfer to Vicara Road to indicate that he and his club cou be back in the top flight in the near future

Despite not playing a full Premiersh campaign in 1999–2000, Cox still made clearances and 52 challenges in the Horne troubled defence. But the Scunthorpe-bc player will certainly want to improve upon h below-par 35% tackle success rate next ter

Although plying his trade in one of t Premiership's most overworked defences, C still found the time to get forward to suppc the Watford attack on a regular basis. whipped in 56 crosses – the highest total the club – and will surely be one of his sid key players as the Hornets attempt to boun straight back to the Premiership.

Jody CRADDOCK • 17

SUNDERLAND • BORN: 25.7.75

ody Craddock moved to Sunderland from ambridge United in July 1997 on the same ay as the Stadium of Light opened. But after eturning from a month's loan at Sheffield nited at the beginning of the 1999–2000 eason, he eventually started to see the light imself and fought his way into Peter Reid's igh-flying side.

The 25-year-old played 1,626 minutes at the eart of the defence, where he completed 181 learances, as well as winning exactly half of he 62 tackles that he attempted.

During his spell in the side, he rarely shirked is responsibilities and stood tall to protect is goal, blocking 47 shots and crosses and aking nine interceptions. In his days at the bbey Stadium, he was voted into the Third ivision's PFA team of the season and is earning all the time.

With plenty of experience under his belt, raddock's best years are still ahead of him nd, under the stern leadership of Reid, he hould develop into a commanding addition o the improving Sunderland squad.

APPEARANCES	
Start (sub)	18(1)
Minutes on pitch	1626
GOAL ATTEMPTS	
Goals	0
DEFENDING	
Blocks	47
Shots cleared off line	1
Headed clearances	114
Other clearances	67
Interceptions	9
Last man saving tackles	2
Tackles won	31
Tackles won %	50%
PASSING	
Passing accuracy own half	73%
Passing accuracy opp half	52%
DISCIPLINE	
Fouls	31
Fouls in danger area	6
Yellow cards	1
Red cards	0

SEE PAGE 248 FOR FULL STATS

Richard CRESSWELL • 12

SHEFFIELD WEDNESDAY • BORN: 20.9.77

APPEARANCES	
Start (sub)	2(18)
Minutes on pitch	540
GOAL ATTEMPTS	
Goals inside box	1
Goals outside box	0
Minutes per goal scored	540.0
Goals/shots ratio	14%
SHOOTING	
Shots on target inside box	2
Shots on target outside box	1
Shooting accuracy	43%
PASSING	
Goal assists	0
Key passes	0
Passing accuracy in opp half	53%
DISCIPLINE	
Fouls committed	18
Fouls won	19
Offside	6
Yellow cards	3
Red cards	0

SEE PAGE 220 FOR FULL STATS

Lissom Richard Cresswell joined Wednesday from York City in a £1 million deal minutes before the transfer deadline in March 1999. It followed a season at Bootham Crescent in which he scored 19 goals and earned England recognition with the under-21s.

Cresswell is seen as potentially one of the best young strikers in the country, but had limited appearances during the 1999–2000 season. In the 540 minutes he played for the Owls he fired off seven shots, scoring just once in a rare Premiership win against West Ham.

His below-average pass completion rate of 57% shows he struggled to make the transition to the Premiership, but he did manage to force five corners for the beleaguered Owls.

The 6'0" striker was linked with a move to Division Two Champions Preston North End, but this was blocked, indicating that the club have future plans for him. There is still time for this player to make his mark and he should find more opportunities against the Division One defences in the 2000–01 season.

Jordi CRUYFF • 14

MANCHESTER UNITED • BORN: 9.2.74

There was talk at the turn of the year that Jordi Cruyff might be on his way back to his father's former club, Barcelona.

Cruyff junior is proud to be a Catalonian: indeed Jordi is the name of the patron saint of the city, and he even plays for their national side in exhibition matches – despite being an international for Holland.

The indications are that he would do a good job wherever he went. Despite only playing 264 minutes for Manchester United in the 1999–2000 season, Cruyff managed to score three goals from just 11 shots.

The blond 26-year-old has also recorded an excellent 77% pass completion rate while in the opposition's half.

But despite this, the versatile attacking midfielder has not been able to command a regular place in Alex Ferguson's team and his loan spell at Celta Vigo implies it may be time for Cruyff to turn elsewhere if he is to resurrect his career.

SEE PAGE 178 FOR FULL STATS

Carlo CUDICINI • 23

CHELSEA • BORN: 6.9.73

Carlo Cudicini joined Chelsea in the summer c
1997 from Italian side Atalanta Juniors an
has been tipped to succeed Ed De Goey if an
when the Dutchman moves on.

Cudicini's only appearance in the 1999–200
season was in the final game against Derb
when he kept a clean sheet.

The 26-year-old Italian pulled off four save
claimed the one cross that he came for an
also recorded an excellent distributio
accuracy of 76%.

At 6'3" he has a commanding presence an
reports say he has been outstanding i
training, impressing everyone at the club.

Manager Gianluca Vialli was one of thos
admirers and rewarded him with a new twc
year contract.

In the next few seasons, Cudicini could well b
following in the footsteps of his father, wh
was an international in the 1960s, but for no
the former Lazio stopper will keep pushing f
the number one jersey at Stamford Bridge.

SEE PAGE 80 FOR FULL STATS

Nick CULKIN • 31

MANCHESTER UNITED • BORN: 6.7.78

Despite being the fourth-choice goalkeeper at Old Trafford, Nick Culkin made his Manchester United debut at Highbury against Arsenal in United's 2–1 win at the beginning of the 1999–2000 season.

The 22-year-old came on for the injured Raimond van der Gouw in the 90th minute and his only touch of the ball during that appearance was to take a goal kick.

Alex Ferguson loaned him out to Hull in December to gain some valuable first-team experience. He made four appearances and was beaten just once while in goal for the Tigers at Boothferry Park.

Rumours that United were in the market for another 'keeper, after the calamitous Massimo Taibi was sent back to Italy and Van der Gouw turned 37, came true as United swooped for French international 'keeper Fabien Barthez. But as a goalkeeper, Culikin's prime is still a long way ahead of him, and his progress so far has been highly commendable.

SEE PAGE 178 FOR FULL STATS

Michael CUMMINS • 30

MIDDLESBROUGH • BORN: 1.6.78

The only appearance that Michael Cummir
made for Middlesbrough in the 1999–20C
season was as a substitute against Leec
United. In that brief 16-minute appearanc
the Republic of Ireland under-21 play
completed all three of his passes and mac
one clearance.

The strong-tackling midfielder will no dou
have learned from training with players lik
Paul Ince, a man whose style of play Cummir
clearly admires.

Cummins is a hard-working player who lik
to cover every blade of grass on the pitch ar
impose himself on the opposition.

Unfortunately for Cummins, he will not b
covering any more turf at The Riverside. Aft
being unable to gain a regular place in th
first team he moved to Port Vale on a fre
transfer in March, making his debut in the 1-
draw at Crystal Palace. He appeared 12 tim
for Vale and scored once for the club but cou
not save them from the drop.

SEE PAGE 192 FOR FULL STATS

5 Wimbledon kept fewer clean sheets

Kenny CUNNINGHAM • 2

WIMBLEDON • BORN: 28.6.71

e versatile Kenny Cunningham's sixth
ason for the Dons was certainly not his most
ccessful, but it was again one in which he
d by example. The Dons' skipper recorded an
'mirable disciplinary record involving only
 fouls and one booking in some 3,269
inutes of Premiership football.

Cunningham's consistently good form was
e of the bright spots in an otherwise
sperate Dons campaign. Appearing in every
inute of the first 36 games of the season, he
issed only the final match defeat at The
ell, having been substituted in the 29th
inute during the penultimate fixture against
ton Villa because of injury.

Defensively, Cunningham was Wimbledon's
ost effective performer, making a total of
'2 clearances and winning 40% of his 101
ckles. Still searching for his first senior goal
r the club, his performances in the attacking
alf of the field were also impressive. He made
 successful crosses with a 36% accuracy,
aking him the 10th most prolific crosser in
e Premiership.

APPEARANCES	
Start (sub)	37(0)
Minutes on pitch	3269
GOAL ATTEMPTS	
Goals	0
PASSING & CROSSING	
Goal assists	3
Passing	1312
Passing accuracy	63%
Crosses	170
Crossing accuracy	36%
DEFENDING	
Tackles	101
Tackles won %	40%
Blocks	72
Interceptions	23
Clearances	272
Shots cleared off line	0
DISCIPLINE	
Fouls	21
Yellow cards	1
Red cards	0

SEE PAGE 304 FOR FULL STATS

John CURTIS • 13

MANCHESTER UNITED • BORN: 3.9.78

e 1999–2000 Premiership campaign was a
ustrating one for England under-21 defender
hn Curtis. But this is not to say that the
ason itself was not a successful one, as
pressive form for Barnsley in the Nationwide
eague while on loan from Old Trafford led to
terest from a host of clubs.

Competition for defensive places at United
as fierce, with the Neville brothers, Jaap
tam, Henning Berg, Ronny Johnsen, Denis
win and Wes Brown all seemingly above
urtis in the pecking order.

In all, Curtis made only one substitute
ppearance for United in the 1999–2000
ason – against Coventry – accumulating a
ere 12 minutes of Premiership action.

Barnsley were keen to sign Curtis on a
ermanent basis, but Graeme Souness
vooped to snare the youngster for Blackburn
overs in a £1.5 million deal. He will no doubt
ay an important role in the Scot's rebuilding
ogramme at Ewood Park.

SEE PAGE 178 FOR FULL STATS

Neil CUTLER • 13

ASTON VILLA • BORN: 3.9.76

After the sale of Michael Oakes to Wolves, goalkeeper Neil Cutler moved up the pecking order at Villa Park and made his debut for John Gregory's team as a substitute on Valentine's Day 2000.

On for the injured David James, Cutler only played seven minutes and his contribution to his team's 4–0 victory was four goal kicks – three of which were accurate.

The Birmingham-born stopper cost Villa nothing when he joined from Chester City in late 1999, and has bags of potential.

This former England Youth and schoolboy international is still under 25 and time is most certainly on his side, so he will not be too worried about the lack of first-team action during the 1999–2000 season. Although the near future might find him occupying the bench more than the goalmouth, Villa could well look back on him as a bargain acquisition in years to come if, as hoped, he goes on to make the first-team.

SEE PAGE 52 FOR FULL STATS

an any other Premiership team

Nikolaos DABIZAS • 34

NEWCASTLE UNITED • BORN: 3.8.73

Like Robert Lee, Greek defender Nikos Dabizas started the 1999–2000 season at Newcastle seemingly left out in the cold by enigmatic coach Ruud Gullit.

Having missed the first four games of the campaign, Dabizas was recalled for the derby against Sunderland at St James's Park, but United crashed to a 2–1 defeat, a result which signalled Gullit's departure.

Dabizas went on to play a key role under the tutelage of Bobby Robson, holding the defence together at times, despite having seven different partners at the back. He also chipped in with three goals in the Premiership, including two in two games against Watford and Tottenham in November.

His passing and tackling completion rates were not as impressive as they were in 1998–99, although for the second season running he made more than 1,000 passes from defence. With a new four-year contract under his belt, it is a safe bet to say that Dabizas will not start the 2000–01 season as an outcast in the north east.

APPEARANCES	
Start (sub)	29(0)
Minutes on pitch	2527
GOAL ATTEMPTS	
Goals	3
DEFENDING	
Blocks	61
Shots cleared off line	0
Headed clearances	223
Other clearances	77
Interceptions	18
Last man saving tackles	0
Tackles won	43
Tackles won %	49%
PASSING	
Passing accuracy own half	80%
Passing accuracy opp half	62%
DISCIPLINE	
Fouls	40
Fouls in danger area	19
Yellow cards	6
Red cards	1

SEE PAGE 206 FOR FULL STATS

Sam DALLA BONA • 24

CHELSEA • BORN: 6.2.81

Having captained the Italy under-18 team and scored 16 goals from midfield for Chelsea reserves in 1998–99, it was only a matter of time before Sam Dalla Bonna made his debut for Gianluca Vialli's first team.

It came in the 2–1 win over Coventry in April when he replaced Roberto Di Matteo after 55 minutes, three minutes before Gianfranco Zola netted the winner.

Three days later, Dalla Bonna made his second appearance in a Chelsea shirt, replacing Frenchman Didier Deschamps at half-time at Sheffield Wednesday – but to no avail, as the Blues went down 1–0.

In his two brief run-outs for Chelsea, Dalla Bonna was never far from the action, making 48 passes in just 80 minutes and even getting forward to strike a shot on target.

With the Stamford Bridge squad not getting any younger, teenager Dalla Bonna could well be used more often in 2000–01 as Vialli re-jigs his ageing team.

SEE PAGE 80 FOR FULL STATS

Greek chic: Nikos Dabizas

Kevin DAVIES • 10

S

SOUTHAMPTON • BORN: 26.3.77

As forecast in the 1999–2000 Opta Yearbook, Kevin Davies completed his return from Blackburn to Southampton in August, with Norwegian striker Egil Ostenstad moving the other way in a swap deal.

Davies's reintroduction into the Saints' team was far from smooth, though, and he was injured and sent off before he found his feet again on the south coast. When he did, Southampton fans were reminded of the form that saw Davies earn a £7 million price tag and linked with an England call-up.

He scored in three consecutive Premiership games over the turn of the Millennium, including the winner against Bradford City in what was then a crucial relegation clash for both sides.

Three more goals and a trio of assists before the season's end were a big factor in Southampton's unexpectedly comfortable Premiership survival. With strikers like Davies and Marian Pahars about, seasons of struggle could be a thing of the past at The Dell from now on.

APPEARANCES	
Start (sub)	19(4)
Minutes on pitch	1806
GOAL ATTEMPTS	
Goals inside box	5
Goals outside box	1
Minutes per goal scored	301.0
Goals/shots ratio	17%
SHOOTING	
Shots on target inside box	17
Shots on target outside box	5
Shooting accuracy	63%
PASSING	
Goal assists	3
Key passes	6
Passing accuracy in opp half	53%
DISCIPLINE	
Fouls committed	46
Fouls won	43
Offside	11
Yellow cards	7
Red cards	1

SEE PAGE 234 FOR FULL STATS

D

Simon DAVIES • 29

AM

TOTTENHAM HOTSPUR • BORN: 23.10.79

APPEARANCES	
Start (sub)	1(2)
Minutes on pitch	147
GOAL ATTEMPTS	
Goals	0
Shots on target	1
Shooting accuracy	50%
Goals/shots ratio	0%
PASSING	
Goal assists	0
Passes in opp half	35
Passing accuracy in opp half	77%
Successful crosses	1
Crossing accuracy	33%
DRIBBLING	
Dribbles & runs	5
Dribble completion	100%
Corners forced	1
DISCIPLINE	
Fouls	1
Yellow cards	0
Red cards	0

SEE PAGE 262 FOR FULL STATS

Having spent the summer of 1999 training with Manchester United, it was fitting that Welsh midfielder Simon Davies should make his first Premiership start at Old Trafford – albeit against the Champions in the colours of Tottenham Hotspur.

After his transfer from Spurs to Peterborough last December, Davies quickly made the step from Division Three to top-flight football, coming on as a substitute at Liverpool for his debut and quickly impressing with his determination and skill.

Another sub appearance against Derby followed before the United match, in which Davies performed well in front of a live television audience. He made 49 passes in his first-team outings, with an excellent success rate of 82%. He also completed all five of the dribbles he attempted.

At his current rate of progress, Davies is sure to be a regular in the Welsh national team before long, following in the footsteps of his uncle Ian Walsh, who played for Crystal Palace and Wales in the early 1980s.

Aidan DAVISON • 31

BRADFORD CITY • BORN: 11.5.68

Unable to break into Sheffield United's team after his arrival from Grimsby, Northern Ireland international goalkeeper Aidan Davison joined Bradford in January to fill in for the injured Gary Walsh and Matt Clarke.

Initially signed on loan, Davison struggled to come to terms with the quality of the Premiership, conceding 13 goals in just six games for the Bantams after making his debut as a substitute against Watford.

His spell in the first team was interrupted when his loan deal expired and he could not agree terms on a permanent move, forcing City to field veteran Neville Southall in goal against Leeds.

The situation was soon rectified and Davison moved full-time immediately before making his last appearance of the season in the 4–0 defeat at Coventry in March.

Despite having a saves-to-shots ratio of just 63% (one of the worst records in the Premiership), Davison impressed many at Valley Parade and is likely to push Walsh and Clarke hard for a starting place in 2000–01.

APPEARANCES	
Start (sub)	5(1)
Minutes on pitch	465
SHOT STOPPING	
Goals conceded (inside box)	10
Goals conceded (outside box)	3
Minutes per goal conceded	35.8
Clean sheets	0
Saves (shots inside box)	10
Saves (shots outside box)	12
Saves/shots	63%
DISTRUBUTION	
Long kick %	34%
Throws/short passes %	78%
CATCHING	
Crosses caught	14
Crosses punched	5
Crosses dropped	0
Catch success %	100%
DISCIPLINE	
Yellow cards	1
Red cards	0

SEE PAGE 66 FOR FULL STATS

Chris DAY • 13

WATFORD • BORN: 28.7.75

APPEARANCES	
Start (sub)	11(0)
Minutes on pitch	990
SHOT STOPPING	
Goals conceded (inside box)	11
Goals conceded (outside box)	5
Minutes per goal conceded	61.9
Clean sheets	3
Saves (shots inside box)	20
Saves (shots outside box)	13
Saves/shots	67%
DISTRIBUTION	
Long kick %	33%
Throws/short passes %	84%
CATCHING	
Crosses caught	27
Crosses punched	10
Crosses dropped	1
Catch success %	96%
DISCIPLINE	
Yellow cards	0
Red cards	0

SEE PAGE 276 FOR FULL STATS

After two years sitting on the sidelines a Watford, former England under-21 goalkeepe Chris Day was thrust into first-team action o the opening day of the 1999–2000 season i the absence of injured Alec Chamberlain.

The 3–2 home defeat against Wimbledo that day was a taste of things to come for th Hornets, although they went on to enjoy som good results with Day between the sticks including consecutive 1–0 wins over Liverpoo and Bradford in August.

But Chamberlain's return from the treatmen room saw Day drop back to the bench for 2 of the next 32 games, as Watford's relegatio to Division One was confirmed.

Interestingly, the former Crystal Palace ma conceded 1.45 goals a game on average whereas Chamberlain let through 61 goals i his 27 games – an average of 2.26. Day als kept three clean sheets, which was as many a Chamberlain managed.

Those facts suggest that Day may play a bigger part in 2000–01, as Watford aim t make an immediate return to the Premiership.

16 Ed De Goey kept more clean sheets

Gilles DE BILDE • 23

SHEFFIELD WEDNESDAY • BORN: 9.6.71

D

en goals in his first Premiership season may ot look like a bad return for Sheffield Vednesday's Gilles De Bilde, but in truth the elgian striker flattered to deceive for much f the 1999–2000 campaign, following his £3 nillion move from PSV Eindhoven.

Apart from braces against eventually-elegated sides Watford and Wimbledon, De Bilde managed just three goals in 33 remiership appearances as Wednesday lipped out of the top flight for the first time ince 1991.

A further three goals in the last three games f the term took De Bilde into double figures, ut it was not enough to stave off the readed drop.

Goals aside, De Bilde acquitted himself easonably well in England, setting up three trikes and whipping over 63 crosses.

But Hillsborough supporters rarely saw the iery, committed image with which De Bilde rrived in England and few eyebrows will be aised if the Belgian international is back on he continent come the start of 2000–01.

APPEARANCES	
Start (sub)	37(1)
Minutes on pitch	3041
GOAL ATTEMPTS	
Goals inside box	10
Goals outside box	0
Minutes per goal scored	304.1
Goals/shots ratio	14%
SHOOTING	
Shots on target inside box	35
Shots on target outside box	7
Shooting accuracy	58%
PASSING	
Goal assists	3
Key passes	12
Passing accuracy in opp half	63%
DISCIPLINE	
Fouls committed	61
Fouls won	46
Offside	56
Yellow cards	3
Red cards	0

SEE PAGE 220 FOR FULL STATS

Ed DE GOEY • 1

CHELSEA • BORN: 20.12.66

APPEARANCES	
Start (sub)	37(0)
Minutes on pitch	3330
SHOT STOPPING	
Goals conceded (inside box)	28
Goals conceded (outside box)	6
Minutes per goal conceded	97.9
Clean sheets	16
Saves (shots inside box)	57
Saves (shots outside box)	39
Saves/shots	74%
DISTRIBUTION	
Long kick %	47%
Throws/short passes %	88%
CATCHING	
Crosses caught	53
Crosses punched	41
Crosses dropped	4
Catch success %	93%
DISCIPLINE	
Yellow cards	1
Red cards	0

SEE PAGE 80 FOR FULL STATS

Ed De Goey capped another term of consistency between the sticks for Chelsea by breaking Peter Bonetti's club record of clean sheets kept in a season.

A shut-out against Newcastle in March was De Goey's record-breaking 22nd of the 1999–2000 campaign in all competitions, as Chelsea progressed to the latter stages of the Champions League and FA Cup, while maintaining a top five Premiership position.

The 6'5" Dutchman, Chelsea's tallest-ever player, ended up with 16 Premiership clean sheets to his name (three more than in the 1998–99 season) and was an ever-present in the league right up until the final game, when he was rested before the FA Cup final.

Just like in 1998–99, De Goey made more punches (41) than any other Premiership goalkeeper and was a crucial figure as Chelsea came runners-up in the top-flight defensive stakes for the second successive season. De Goey looks to have assured his status as number one 'keeper at the Bridge for a few more years at least.

han any other Premiership 'keeper

Brian DEANE • 10

MIDDLESBROUGH • BORN: 7.2.68

Brian Deane's relatively quiet season in the Middlesbrough attack erupted in November when he was charged with misconduct by the FA following an incident in the north-east derby against Sunderland.

The former Leeds striker was caught by TV cameras elbowing Sunderland's Paul Butler in the face as the players jostled for position at a corner. Deane consequently picked up a one-match ban after his "trial by television".

His suspension coincided with a knee injury that kept him out for seven Premiership games, during which Boro picked up just five points and raised fears of a late slump towards the relegation places.

On his return, Deane made a big difference to Boro as they beat Tottenham and Arsenal and he scored the only goal from the penalty spot to defeat West Ham. During this run, Deane was moved wider to the right to accommodate Hamilton Ricard and Andy Campbell up front.

In all, Deane netted nine Premiership goals and created four others.

APPEARANCES	
Start (sub)	29(0)
Minutes on pitch	2590
GOAL ATTEMPTS	
Goals inside box	9
Goals outside box	0
Minutes per goal scored	287.8
Goals/shots ratio	16%
SHOOTING	
Shots on target inside box	25
Shots on target outside box	4
Shooting accuracy	50%
PASSING	
Goal assists	4
Key passes	7
Passing accuracy in opp half	61%
DISCIPLINE	
Fouls committed	73
Fouls won	30
Offside	24
Yellow cards	6
Red cards	0

SEE PAGE 192 FOR FULL STATS

Mark DELANEY • 24

ASTON VILLA • BORN: 13.5.76

APPEARANCES	
Start (sub)	25(3)
Minutes on pitch	2290
GOAL ATTEMPTS	
Goals	1
PASSING & CROSSING	
Goal assists	2
Passing	885
Passing accuracy	64%
Crosses	73
Crossing accuracy	30%
DEFENDING	
Tackles	125
Tackles won %	39%
Blocks	35
Interceptions	19
Clearances	107
Shots cleared off line	0
DISCIPLINE	
Fouls	21
Yellow cards	6
Red cards	0

SEE PAGE 52 FOR FULL STATS

Mark Delaney's meteoric rise from non-leag Carmarthen Town to the Premiersh continued at pace during the 1999–2000 he notched his first top-flight goal, earn international honours for Wales and help Aston Villa reach the FA Cup final.

Delaney started the campaign as first-choi right wing-back for Villa, despite havi appeared just twice as a substitute 1998–99. He played in every minute of t first seven Premiership fixtures, during whi he scored his only goal of the season – superb strike as Villa beat Watford 1–0.

In October, Delaney made his eagerl awaited debut for the Welsh national si against Switzerland, but he was back in t press for the wrong reasons after bei dismissed in the FA Cup semi-final again Bolton Wanderers at Wembley in April.

Apart from that, Delaney can consider t 1999–2000 term a success, with two assists show for his efforts. In addition, he deliver 73 crosses, embarked on 99 dribbles and sl into 125 tackles to impress the Villa faithfu

Rory DELAP • 10

DERBY COUNTY • BORN: 6.7.76

D

Despite Derby's struggle to retain Premiership status in 1999–2000, Ireland international Rory Delap blossomed into one of County's finest players and earned national accolades for being the top-scoring wing-back in the top flight.

A total of eight goals was a fine return for a player who also made 110 tackles and 124 clearances from an essentially defensive position. Delap did spend an early part of the season playing in attack, though, before the arrivals of Esteban Fuertes and Branko Strupar from the continent.

A tally of four goal assists means that Delap either scored or created 12 goals during the campaign, more than a quarter of the 44 strikes Derby managed in the Premiership. He also attempted more than 1,000 passes, whipped in 66 crosses and went on 116 dribbles and runs with the ball.

But his passing and tackling success rates are both poorer than they were in 1998–99, which illustrates the fact that there are still plenty of things to work on for this vastly promising Derby wing-back.

APPEARANCES	
Start (sub)	34(0)
Minutes on pitch	2925
GOAL ATTEMPTS	
Goals	8
Shots on target	18
Shooting accuracy	39%
Goals/shots ratio	17%
PASSING	
Goal assists	4
Passes in opp half	708
Passing accuracy in opp half	57%
Successful crosses	21
Crossing accuracy	32%
DRIBBLING	
Dribbles & runs	116
Dribble completion	77%
Corners forced	18
DISCIPLINE	
Fouls	35
Yellow cards	6
Red cards	1

SEE PAGE 108 FOR FULL STATS

Marcel DESAILLY • 6

CHELSEA • BORN: 17.9.68

APPEARANCES	
Start (sub)	23(0)
Minutes on pitch	1930
GOAL ATTEMPTS	
Goals	1
DEFENDING	
Blocks	44
Shots cleared off line	0
Headed clearances	130
Other clearances	63
Interceptions	22
Last man saving tackles	0
Tackles won	30
Tackles won %	48%
PASSING	
Passing accuracy own half	88%
Passing accuracy opp half	77%
DISCIPLINE	
Fouls	20
Fouls in danger area	8
Yellow cards	2
Red cards	1

SEE PAGE 80 FOR FULL STATS

A star of Chelsea's 1998–99 season, Marcel Desailly was expected to be the rock upon which the Blues built their Championship challenge in the 1999–2000 campaign.

The fact that the Frenchman missed 15 league matches and failed to live up to the reputation he earned during his first season in England was possibly a big factor in Chelsea's domestic failings, as they ended up 26 points behind Manchester United.

Desailly did notch up two personal Premiership firsts in 1999–2000. He netted his first league goal for Chelsea against Watford on 26 February when he accurately headed Gianfranco Zola's free-kick past Alec Chamberlain; but before that he had been dismissed for the first time, when Mike Reed produced the second of two yellow cards for a foul on Liverpool's Danny Murphy at Anfield.

It is fair to say that Desailly's best form was saved for the Champions League, against opposing strikers like Andriy Shevchenko, Marcelo Salas and Patrick Kluivert, as Chelsea progressed to the quarter-finals.

Didier DESCHAMPS • 7

CHELSEA • BORN: 15.10.68

Of all the foreign players to have joined Chelsea over the last few years, Didier Deschamps arrived with the most impressive CV of all, having won all manner of honours in France and Italy before captaining his country to their first-ever World Cup win in 1998.

As such, Deschamps's first season in England must go down as a disappointment and he barely justified his big wages and the £3 million transfer fee paid to Juventus.

While he was always quietly effective playing the holding role in Chelsea's midfield, Deschamps set few pulses racing at Stamford Bridge, failing to score in the Premiership and creating only one goal.

An overall passing accuracy of 79% and dribble success rate of 93% illustrates the Frenchman's talent and comfort on the ball, yet he spent as much time complaining about the physical side of the English game as he did trying to make his mark on it.

And Chelsea's failure to secure a Champions League place for 2000–01 could well signal the end of Deschamps's brief spell in London.

APPEARANCES	
Start (sub)	24(3)
Minutes on pitch	2052
GOAL ATTEMPTS	
Goals	0
Shots on target	5
Shooting accuracy	25%
PASSING & CROSSING	
Goal assists	1
Passes in opp half	813
Passing accuracy in opp half	73%
Successful crosses	10
Cross completion	25%
DEFENDING	
Interceptions	25
Clearances	67
Tackles	96
Tackles won %	61%
DISCIPLINE	
Fouls	52
Yellow cards	5
Red cards	0

SEE PAGE 80 FOR FULL STATS

Impressive CV: Didier Deshamps (left)

56% Paolo Di Canio scored or

S

Paolo DI CANIO • 10

WEST HAM UNITED • BORN: 9.7.68

D

›era and soap opera: Paolo Di Canio (right)

APPEARANCES	
Start (sub)	29(1)
Minutes on pitch	2621
GOAL ATTEMPTS	
Goals inside box	14
Goals outside box	2
Minutes per goal scored	163.8
Goals/shots ratio	25%
SHOOTING	
Shots on target inside box	33
Shots on target outside box	12
Shooting accuracy	71%
PASSING	
Goal assists	13
Key passes	34
Passing accuracy in opp half	70%
DISCIPLINE	
Fouls committed	35
Fouls won	53
Offside	40
Yellow cards	6
Red cards	0

SEE PAGE 290 FOR FULL STATS

The omission of Paolo Di Canio from the PFA Player of the Season shortlist caused amazement within football, not least of all to manager Harry Redknapp.

But the enigmatic forward can take pleasure from the statistics, which made him the Opta player of the season for 1999–2000.

Di Canio bagged 16 goals and created 13 others, meaning he had a direct hand in 56% of all his team's league goals.

Di Canio's 71% passing accuracy was slightly poorer than in 1998–99, although his crossing improved, with more than a third of his 238 deliveries finding a team-mate.

The Hammers' Player of the Year even introduced the Upton Park faithful to operatic tunes, a far cry from the moment of madness when he pushed over referee Paul Alcock in his Sheffield Wednesday swansong.

Repaying the faith shown in him by Redknapp, Di Canio calmed his firebrand temperament, being booked only six times and even being honoured with the captain's armband in the absence of Steve Lomas.

›et up 56% of West Ham's goals

Roberto DI MATTEO • 16

CHELSEA • BORN: 29.5.70

One of the Premiership's longest-serving foreign players, Roberto Di Matteo was regularly absent from Gianluca Vialli's early-season plans following ankle surgery.

The Swiss-born Italian international started just one of the Blues' first 15 Premiership matches and made only sporadic substitute appearances in between. It was midway through the 1999–2000 season before the midfielder appeared regularly and reminded Chelsea fans of his smooth passing style and ability to create chances for others.

Two assists and a 76% passing accuracy exemplify Di Matteo's distribution qualities, while his comfort on the right or in the centre of midfield was an obvious plus.

His two league goals came in the last three games of the season: the first in the 2–0 win over Liverpool and the other against Derby on the final day. And, of course, he netted the only goal of the game in the FA Cup final.

Di Matteo's goalscoring form came at the right time of the season to re-establish himself firmly in Vialli's plans for 2000–01.

APPEARANCES	
Start (sub)	14(4)
Minutes on pitch	1311
GOAL ATTEMPTS	
Goals	2
Shots on target	11
Shooting accuracy	50%
PASSING & CROSSING	
Goal assists	2
Passes in opp half	400
Passing accuracy in opp half	74%
Successful crosses	12
Cross completion	30%
DEFENDING	
Interceptions	8
Clearances	11
Tackles	40
Tackles won %	63%
DISCIPLINE	
Fouls	19
Yellow cards	3
Red cards	0

SEE PAGE 80 FOR FULL STATS

Daniele DICHIO • 12

SUNDERLAND • BORN: 19.10.74

APPEARANCES	
Start (sub)	0(12)
Minutes on pitch	182
GOAL ATTEMPTS	
Goals inside box	0
Goals outside box	0
Minutes per goal scored	n/a
Goals/shots ratio	0%
SHOOTING	
Shots on target inside box	1
Shots on target outside box	1
Shooting accuracy	67%
PASSING	
Goal assists	1
Key passes	0
Passing accuracy in opp half	63%
DISCIPLINE	
Fouls committed	18
Fouls won	1
Offside	1
Yellow cards	2
Red cards	0

SEE PAGE 248 FOR FULL STATS

With Kevin Phillips and Niall Quinn missi just three Premiership matches between the in 1999–2000, it proved a fruitless season f Sunderland's back-up striker Danny Dichio.

The former QPR and Sampdoria man was n helped by a freak injury to his back, inflam by his penchant for spinning the vinyl as part-time DJ at his local nightclub.

In all, Dichio played just 182 minutes Premiership football in 12 substitu appearances and missed 17 games in t middle of the campaign because of his inju

He made his comeback in March, scoring f Sunderland's reserves in a friendly against Brann, before having brief substitute run-ou against Southampton, Sheffield Wednesd and Bradford. Against West Ham in t penultimate game of the season, Dichio ma his longest appearance of 1999–2000, comi on at half-time for Quinn.

Dichio's one assist came early when he p Phillips in for a stunning goal again Watford. One of his two bookings also came that match at the Stadium of Light.

FB

Lee DIXON • 2

ARSENAL • BORN: 17.3.64

D

Arsenal's signing of Dynamo Kiev right-back Oleg Luzhny in the summer of 1999 cast doubt over the future of long-serving Lee Dixon at Highbury. Come the end of 1999–2000, Dixon had proved wrong all his doubters, playing more Premiership football than any other Gunner apart from Patrick Vieira.

And he played it effectively, too, scoring three goals and creating one other, while completing 76% of his passes and 88% of his dribbles and runs.

Dixon's defensive duties never suffered from the foraging runs he frequently made down the right flank, with 60 tackles attempted and 57 clearances completed.

And he did not succumb to serious fatigue in 1999–2000 (two games in a row being his longest absence), despite celebrating his 36th birthday midway through the season.

With Arsenal back in the Champions League, new signings will be expected at Highbury before the start of 2000–01, but Dixon has seen off challenges for his position in the past and there is no reason why he cannot do it again.

APPEARANCES	
Start (sub)	28(0)
Minutes on pitch	2467
GOAL ATTEMPTS	
Goals	3
PASSING & CROSSING	
Goal assists	1
Passing	1172
Passing accuracy	76%
Crosses	86
Crossing accuracy	30%
DEFENDING	
Tackles	60
Tackles won %	47%
Blocks	28
Interceptions	11
Clearances	57
Shots cleared off line	1
DISCIPLINE	
Fouls	18
Yellow cards	3
Red cards	0

SEE PAGE 38 FOR FULL STATS

FB

Jason DODD • 2

SOUTHAMPTON • BORN: 2.11.70

APPEARANCES	
Start (sub)	30(1)
Minutes on pitch	2703
GOAL ATTEMPTS	
Goals	0
PASSING & CROSSING	
Goal assists	2
Passing	1225
Passing accuracy	69%
Crosses	42
Crossing accuracy	17%
DEFENDING	
Tackles	81
Tackles won %	48%
Blocks	58
Interceptions	17
Clearances	161
Shots cleared off line	2
DISCIPLINE	
Fouls	29
Yellow cards	5
Red cards	0

SEE PAGE 234 FOR FULL STATS

Southampton skipper Jason Dodd enjoyed another consistent season on the south coast, no doubt basking in one of the Saints' more relaxed flirtations with relegation.

Dodd, who has scored just nine times in more than 300 games for the club, failed to find the net in 1999–2000 and had just two shots on target in the Premiership. But he did make two goals and was a willing worker down the right flank.

Bath-born Dodd was at his best when travelling with the ball, completing 90% of his dribbles and runs but won fewer than half of his tackles and only found a team-mate with 17% of his crosses.

Yet he remains a crucial player for boss Glenn Hoddle, who sometimes used his captain in the sweeper role towards the end of 2000–01 after Dodd had spent most of the campaign in his more recognised full-back position. The former England coach may deploy Dodd in the centre more often in 1999–2000 to utilise fully the calming influence of one of the Premiership's most respected pros.

Gary DOHERTY • 12

TOTTENHAM HOTSPUR • BORN: 31.1.80

Having joined Tottenham from Luton Town after the transfer deadline day in 1999–2000, Irishman Gary Doherty probably thought he would have to wait until 2000–01 for his Premiership debut.

Not so; because, with permission from the Premiership authorities and opponents Manchester United, Doherty turned out at Old Trafford in Spurs' penultimate game as a late sub for Chris Armstrong.

And he appeared again on the final day of 1999–2000, coming on at half-time for Steffen Iversen to play in attack against Sunderland. Doherty had a great chance to make an immediate impact on the top flight, but had a weak shot saved from a good position – his only effort on target in the Premiership.

During his time at Luton, Doherty filled both defensive and attacking roles with accomplishment and is likely to prove a useful addition to the Tottenham Hotspur squad in future seasons.

SEE PAGE 262 FOR FULL STATS

Didier DOMI • 4

NEWCASTLE UNITED • BORN: 2.5.78

Newcastle's young Frenchman Didier Domi was one of the main beneficiaries of Bobby Robson's arrival at St James's Park in September 1999.

Under Ruud Gullit's management, Domi was always used as the left full-back but Robson made the most of his attacking abilities by moving him further up the flank to supply balance and crosses for Alan Shearer and Duncan Ferguson.

Domi thrived on having licence to get forward and began causing problems for opposition defences, rather than vice-versa. In 1,833 minutes of Premiership football, he created three goals and delivered 86 crosses with a success rate of 31% – an improvement on his 1998–99 record.

The ex-Paris St Germain star found the net himself on a trio of occasions, the first in a 3–3 draw with Wimbledon, followed by a consolation strike in the 4–1 defeat at Coventry in October. His third and final goal was a deflected effort to open the scoring in the Tyne and Wear derby draw against Sunderland in the Stadium of Light.

Three goals: Didier Domi

APPEARANCES	
Start (sub)	19(8)
Minutes on pitch	1833
GOAL ATTEMPTS	
Goals	3
PASSING & CROSSING	
Goal assists	3
Passing	699
Passing accuracy	70%
Crosses	86
Crossing accuracy	31%
DEFENDING	
Tackles	57
Tackles won %	51%
Blocks	16
Interceptions	9
Clearances	90
Shots cleared off line	0
DISCIPLINE	
Fouls	29
Yellow cards	2
Red cards	0

SEE PAGE 206 FOR FULL STATS

AM

Jose DOMINGUEZ • 20

TOTTENHAM HOTSPUR • BORN: 16.2.74

 tireless worker and one never afraid to run
: opponents, Portuguese winger Jose
ominguez was used at surprisingly
frequent intervals by Tottenham Hotspur in
999–2000.

Dominguez started the first game of the
eason for Spurs, but was withdrawn at half-
me and appeared just once more from the
art in 1999–2000 – the 0–0 draw with West
am at White Hart Lane. A loan deal to his old
ub Birmingham fell through midway into the
rm and Dominguez had just the occasional
imeo run-out before disappearing completely
om the scene in February.

When he did play, the international winger
iowed that none of his skill had deserted
im, dribbling 65 times in 364 minutes and
elivering 23 crosses in total.

For such a hard-working and popular player,
 seems unlikely that Dominguez will struggle
 find a club for 2000–01 if, as seems likely,
ottenham decide to let him go.

SEE PAGE 262 FOR FULL STATS

Simon DONNELLY • 18

SHEFFIELD WEDNESDAY • BORN: 1.12.74

Simon Donnelly burst on to the scene in Scotland in the mid-1990s, playing up front for Celtic and even earning generous comparisons to a young Kenny Dalglish.

So it was no mean feat for Sheffield Wednesday when, in the summer of 1999, they brought Donnelly and his Celtic team-mate Phil O'Donnell to Hillsborough under freedom of contract. But both players suffered dreadfully from injury in 1999–2000, just one of the many factors contributing to Wednesday's eventual relegation from the Premiership.

When not being troubled by the painful back problem sciatica in 1999–2000, Donnelly managed 396 minutes of Premiership football, mostly as a substitute and to excellent effect. He set up one goal and came off the bench at Derby in February to score a goal in a 3–3 draw at Pride Park.

If he can steer clear of more injury in 2000–01, Donnelly is likely to be a key man in Wednesday's challenge for promotion.

SEE PAGE 220 FOR FULL STATS

D

FB

Tony DORIGO • 5

DERBY COUNTY • BORN: 31.12.65

APPEARANCES	
Start (sub)	20(3)
Minutes on pitch	1673
GOAL ATTEMPTS	
Goals	0
PASSING & CROSSING	
Goal assists	0
Passing	624
Passing accuracy	69%
Crosses	54
Crossing accuracy	33%
DEFENDING	
Tackles	56
Tackles won %	63%
Blocks	30
Interceptions	17
Clearances	85
Shots cleared off line	0
DISCIPLINE	
Fouls	22
Yellow cards	4
Red cards	0

SEE PAGE 108 FOR FULL STATS

Impressive in 1998–99, his first season with Derby, Tony Dorigo started the Millennium campaign back in the County line-up and performed well in a 0–0 draw with his old club Leeds on the opening day.

But the former England left-back missed the next seven matches and when he returned to the side, directly after a 5–0 home defeat against Sunderland, it was clear that 1999–2000 was going to be a season of struggle for the Rams.

Despite that, Dorigo was a calming influence in the 20 games he started, helping young team-mates like Steve Elliott and Seth Johnson overcome the nerves they were bound to feel in their first full season of top-flight football.

Dorigo's passing accuracy of 69% was not as good as his 1998–99 record, but he got forward to strike three shots on target.

Derby's 4–0 defeat by Chelsea on the last day of the season turned out to be Dorigo's final game for the club, as he was released in the summer having helped the Rams to secure top-flight status.

Mark DRAPER • 8

ASTON VILLA • BORN: 11.11.70

Despite having almost a decade of Premiership experience behind him, Aston Villa midfielder Mark Draper was banished to the reserves for the vast majority of 1999–2000; so much so that he played just one minute of top-flight football throughout the campaign.

His one cameo appearance for Villa was way back in August 1999, when he replaced Steve Stone in the dying minutes of a 1–0 defeat against Chelsea. He touched the ball just four times in that match.

Villa boss John Gregory usually favoured George Boateng, Ian Taylor and Lee Hendrie in central midfield and made it clear to Draper that he could move on.

Much interest was shown in the classy playmaker, although reports of transfers to Blackburn, Wolves, Nottingham Forest and Derby never came to fruition. Draper eventually moved to Spain's Rayo Vallecano on loan, but is likely to return to England to rebuild his career in 2000–01.

SEE PAGE 52 FOR FULL STATS

Richard DRYDEN • 12

SOUTHAMPTON • BORN: 14.6.69

Having made just four Premiersh appearances in 1998–99, Southampt defender Richard Dryden was an even mo peripheral figure in 1999–2000, starting ju one game before trying to further his stalli career elsewhere.

The burly stopper was farmed out on loan Division Two side Stoke in November, but w drafted back into the Saints' first-team squ for the fixture at Newcastle in January. In t absence of Claus Lundekvam and Jason Dod Dryden started the game, but was given t runaround by Alan Shearer and co Newcastle won 5–0. He was withdrawn aft 72 minutes, having completed just 38% of h intended passes and losing the solitary tack he attempted.

The former Bristol City man then rejoin Stoke on a permanent basis in March a featured at Wembley in the Auto Windscree Shield final, as well as helping the Potters a play-off place in Division Two.

SEE PAGE 234 FOR FULL STATS

John DREYER • 20

BRADFORD CITY • BORN: 11.6.63

APPEARANCES	
Start (sub)	11(3)
Minutes on pitch	978
GOAL ATTEMPTS	
Goals	1
DEFENDING	
Blocks	18
Shots cleared off line	1
Headed clearances	82
Other clearances	33
Interceptions	6
Last man saving tackles	2
Tackles won	21
Tackles won %	55%
PASSING	
Passing accuracy own half	75%
Passing accuracy opp half	52%
DISCIPLINE	
Fouls	19
Fouls in danger area	6
Yellow cards	4
Red cards	0

SEE PAGE 66 FOR FULL STATS

The highlight of John Dreyer's 1999–20 season undoubtedly came at Sunderland April, when he popped up to head Bradford's first winning goal for 10 games.

Not only was it a crucial goal in re-igniti the Bantams' bid for Premiership survival b it was also a pretty significant one for Drey who had not found the net since Novem 1996 – that is if you discount his own-go against Sheffield Wednesday in August.

Alnwick-born Dreyer, the sixth-olde outfield player in the Premiership, played vital role in the last few matches 1999–2000, freeing up Dean Windass to p in Bradford's attack by filling in the gap l in the midfield.

While he rarely got forward to support t frontmen, Dreyer anchored midfield qu effectively, winning more than half of the tackles he attempted and completing a to of 115 clearances throughout the campaign

While he is unlikely to be a regular starter 2000–01, he is a reliable player who can fil hole in defence or midfield.

Michael DUBERRY • 22

LEEDS UNITED • BORN: 14.10.75

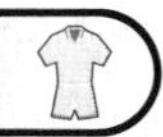

With the likes of Frank Leboeuf and Marcel Desailly blocking his path into the Chelsea first team, young English centre-back Michael Duberry moved on in the summer of 1999, joining Leeds in a £4.5 million deal.

But Duberry fared little better at Elland Road, with Jonathon Woodgate and Lucas Radebe both enjoying excellent campaigns at the heart of the Leeds defence.

Duberry made just 12 starts in the Premiership and indiscipline often got the better of him as he picked up four league bookings. He also received his marching orders for two bookable offences against Everton at the tail-end of 1999–2000 – just one game after he had opened his scoring account for Leeds with a fine strike against Watford.

Of the 34 tackles Duberry attempted, he won an above-average 56% and was a formidable barrier in the back line, making 133 clearances and 22 blocks. But 1999–2000 was not his best season, so he will hope 2000–01 will see him rediscover the form that once saw him targeted by Manchester United.

APPEARANCES	
Start (sub)	12(1)
Minutes on pitch	1054
GOAL ATTEMPTS	
Goals	1
DEFENDING	
Blocks	22
Shots cleared off line	1
Headed clearances	100
Other clearances	33
Interceptions	9
Last man saving tackles	1
Tackles won	19
Tackles won %	56%
PASSING	
Passing accuracy own half	67%
Passing accuracy opp half	45%
DISCIPLINE	
Fouls	42
Fouls in danger area	10
Yellow cards	4
Red cards	1

SEE PAGE 136 FOR FULL STATS

S

Dion DUBLIN • 9

ASTON VILLA • BORN: 22.4.69

APPEARANCES	
Start (sub)	23(3)
Minutes on pitch	2030
GOAL ATTEMPTS	
Goals inside box	12
Goals outside box	0
Minutes per goal scored	169.2
Goals/shots ratio	19%
SHOOTING	
Shots on target inside box	18
Shots on target outside box	4
Shooting accuracy	35%
PASSING	
Goal assists	4
Key passes	2
Passing accuracy in opp half	62%
DISCIPLINE	
Fouls committed	48
Fouls won	44
Offside	12
Yellow cards	1
Red cards	0

SEE PAGE 52 FOR FULL STATS

The recipient of 1999–2000's most-publicised injury, Dion Dublin bounced back superbly from a broken neck sustained just before Christmas to play a key role in Aston Villa's final few Premiership games and their run to the FA Cup final.

At one point the specialists feared Dublin might lose the ability to walk, let alone play football again, so the speed of his recovery from the injury he picked up in a freak clash with Sheffield Wednesday's Gerald Sibon was all the more remarkable.

Despite spending a dozen Premiership games on the sidelines, Dublin still managed to break the double-figure mark for league goals, netting 12 times in 2,030 minutes. He could have had a few more, too, but saw 41 efforts go wide of the target.

In just his second full game back from the treatment room Dublin notched a brace at Tottenham, including a superb overhead kick. That came just a fortnight after he had scored the deciding penalty in the FA Cup semi-final shoot-out against Bolton.

Lawrie DUDFIELD • 28

LEICESTER CITY • BORN: 7.5.80

Ex-Leicester boss Martin O'Neill threw London-born youngster Lawrie Dudfield into the Premiership fray in April 2000 after senior strikers Darren Eadie and Stan Collymore sustained injuries in the game at Derby.

Impressive all season in City's reserve team, YTS product Dudfield came on as a substitute for his debut against Everton at Filbert Street, replacing Tony Cottee with 25 minutes left. Although he failed to get in a shot at goal, Dudfield quickly impressed with his assured touch, a surprisingly good one for a powerful six-footer.

He made his second substitute appearance two weeks later, replacing midfielder Stefan Oakes in the Foxes' 2–2 draw at Villa Park. With Leicester City seemingly willing to give youth its chance in the absence of senior pros, Dudfield could add to the 56 minutes he has played with a few more run-outs in the 2000–01 Premiership campaign under new boss Peter Taylor.

SEE PAGE 150 FOR FULL STATS

Franck DUMAS • 8

NEWCASTLE UNITED • BORN: 9.1.68

Signed from Monaco for £500,000 in the summer of 1999, French defender Franck Dumas spent only a short and unsettled spell in England playing for Newcastle.

One of Ruud Gullit's five pre-season signings for United, Dumas went to the north-east with a reputation for being a classy continental-style sweeper, but was surprisingly used in midfield for the opening two games of the Premiership season.

From that position Dumas impressed, but a broken shoulder sidelined the former international for 10 games, during which time Bobby Robson took over the managerial reins from Gullit at St James's Park.

Robson used Dumas in his favoured sweeper position for four matches out of five towards the end of 1999, but a £1 million-plus offer from Marseille was too good to turn down for a 32-year-old and Newcastle doubled their money on the player just five months after signing him.

SEE PAGE 206 FOR FULL STATS

Richard DUNNE • 15

EVERTON • BORN: 21.9.79

APPEARANCES	
Start (sub)	27(4)
Minutes on pitch	2327
GOAL ATTEMPTS	
Goals	0
DEFENDING	
Blocks	53
Shots cleared off line	0
Headed clearances	115
Other clearances	90
Interceptions	28
Last man saving tackles	1
Tackles won	49
Tackles won %	48%
PASSING	
Passing accuracy own half	68%
Passing accuracy opp half	54%
DISCIPLINE	
Fouls	32
Fouls in danger area	12
Yellow cards	4
Red cards	2

SEE PAGE 122 FOR FULL STATS

Richard Dunne firmly established himself in Everton's defence in 1999–2000, filling in comfortably at right or centre-back and earning himself international honours in the process.

A powerful Irishman, Dunne won his first full cap in April against Greece in a 1–0 defeat and ended up with 27 Premiership starts to his name as he confirmed his standing as one of the top flight's best young stoppers.

Benefiting from playing alongside the cool-headed Richard Gough, Dunne particularly excelled in the heart of the Toffees' defence making 205 clearances and more than 100 tackles. His distribution was not great though, with just 60% of his passes reaching their intended target.

Dunne's discipline was sometimes a bit of a problem, too. He was harshly dismissed against Derby in August, but towards the end of 1999–2000 was rightly shown the red card for a second time, following a bad foul on Leeds striker Michael Bridges. He is clearly part of Walter Smith's plans, though, and will no doubt feature regularly in 2000–01.

83% Kieron Dyer's passing accuracy in the opposition half was higher

AM Kieron DYER • 7

NEWCASTLE UNITED • BORN: 29.12.78

ollowing Ipswich's third consecutive play-off 'efeat in 1998–99, Kieron Dyer decided the ime was right to take his considerable skills on to the Premiership stage and joined Newcastle for £6.5 million in July 1999.

From day one he impressed the Toon Army with his inimitable combination of hard graft, pace and skill. He further endeared himself to he fans by scoring in the Tyne and Wear derby against Sunderland in August, before going on o make an impressive England debut against Luxembourg at Wembley later that month playing at right wing-back.

Despite doing everything at considerable pace, Dyer's passing accuracy of 83% was excellent, while he managed to find a team-mate with 36% of his 55 crosses and weighed n with six goal assists.

Dyer chipped in with three goals in his first Premiership season, the most spectacular of which came against Everton in March. That classy run and chip confirmed beyond doubt that Dyer is one of the best midfield prospects England has produced in years.

APPEARANCES	
Start (sub)	27(3)
Minutes on pitch	2334
GOAL ATTEMPTS	
Goals	3
Shots on target	17
Shooting accuracy	46%
Goals/shots ratio	8%
PASSING	
Goal assists	6
Passes in opp half	738
Passing accuracy in opp half	83%
Successful crosses	20
Crossing accuracy	36%
DRIBBLING	
Dribbles & runs	157
Dribble completion	73%
Corners forced	24
DISCIPLINE	
Fouls	19
Yellow cards	1
Red cards	0

SEE PAGE 206 FOR FULL STATS

S Darren EADIE • 10

LEICESTER CITY • BORN: 10.6.75

APPEARANCES	
Start (sub)	15(1)
Minutes on pitch	1277
GOAL ATTEMPTS	
Goals inside box	0
Goals outside box	0
Minutes per goal scored	n/a
Goals/shots ratio	0%
SHOOTING	
Shots on target inside box	3
Shots on target outside box	6
Shooting accuracy	56%
PASSING	
Goal assists	0
Key passes	3
Passing accuracy in opp half	64%
DISCIPLINE	
Fouls committed	15
Fouls won	33
Offside	4
Yellow cards	0
Red cards	0

SEE PAGE 150 FOR FULL STATS

Martin O'Neill's main Christmas extravagance was spending a club record £3 million on Norwich City's talented but injury-prone forward Darren Eadie. The former England under-21 international had been repeatedly linked with a move to the Premiership and Leicester fans were justifiably excited about the prospect of Eadie linking up with Emile Heskey.

But his impact was less than dramatic, his campaign once again hampered by injury. He made his debut in the home defeat by bitter rivals Derby County, and the Rams proved to be a bogey team. The return match at Pride Park, largely remembered for Stan Collymore's broken leg, also saw Eadie hobble off. And he made headlines when he was red-carded in controversial circumstances at Arsenal in the FA Cup.

Eadie managed just nine shots on target, failing to score in 16 games and creating precious little. His earlier spell at Carrow Road had produced just one goal, and for a man mooted as an answer to England's problems down the left side, 1999–2000 will be a season he will probably want to forget.

than any other midfielder who attempted more than 700 passes

Robbie EARLE • 8

WIMBLEDON • BORN: 27.1.65

As one of the more articulate members of the Crazy Gang, Robbie Earle occupies a senior position at the club, but his role under managerial incumbent Egil Olsen certainly put a strain on the Jamaican international. Olsen's ill-fated new system meant that Earle was no longer an automatic choice at Selhurst Park, and a series of injuries made matters worse.

He scored three times for the Dons in 1999–2000, including a comic effort in the 2–0 win over Newcastle in January.

The attacking flair of old was curtailed, though, as his Norwegian manager played him in front of the defence. And while Earle might have been disappointed with this new role, he did not shirk the task, sliding into 64 tackles and winning 52%.

Earle committed only 18 fouls, picking up two yellow cards, before a serious stomach disorder saw the 35-year-old confined to hospital. And so it came to pass that he watched Wimbledon's proud stay in the top flight end from his sickbed, a fitting image for the ailing Dons.

APPEARANCES	
Start (sub)	23(2)
Minutes on pitch	1920
GOAL ATTEMPTS	
Goals	3
Shots on target	10
Shooting accuracy	37%
Goals/shots ratio	11%
PASSING	
Goal assists	0
Passes in opp half	396
Passing accuracy in opp half	56%
Successful crosses	2
Crossing accuracy	18%
DRIBBLING	
Dribbles & runs	19
Dribble completion	84%
Corners forced	10
DISCIPLINE	
Fouls	18
Yellow cards	2
Red cards	0

SEE PAGE 304 FOR FULL STATS

Clint EASTON • 19

WATFORD • BORN: 1.10.77

APPEARANCES	
Start (sub)	13(4)
Minutes on pitch	1095
GOAL ATTEMPTS	
Goals	0
Shots on target	4
Shooting accuracy	50%
PASSING & CROSSING	
Goal assists	0
Passes in opp half	291
Passing accuracy in opp half	59%
Successful crosses	11
Cross completion	24%
DEFENDING	
Interceptions	16
Clearances	49
Tackles	44
Tackles won %	43%
DISCIPLINE	
Fouls	14
Yellow cards	2
Red cards	0

SEE PAGE 276 FOR FULL STATS

It is doubtful that Ennio Morricone wou have envisaged one of his Spaghetti Wester movie scores being used as a football chan but "Uh-ah-ah-ah-aaah! Clint Easton" to th soundtrack of *The Good, The Bad and The Ug* was a popular refrain around Vicarage Road i 1999–2000.

Well-groomed left midfielder Easton looke overwhelmed by the rigours of the Premiersh in 1999–2000, but occasionally showed tha he can play at this level.

He played for just over 1,000 minutes, wit the majority of his appearances at the start c the season, when the Hornets were still i their honeymoon period, and he played 9 minutes in each of Watford's famous wins ove Liverpool and Chelsea.

As the team became firmly rooted to the foc of the table Graham Taylor eased Easton out c the team, and after being substituted at hal time in the game against Newcastle i November he featured in just four more games But his enthusiastic style will surely come t the fore again in Division One in 2000–01.

FB Justin EDINBURGH • 12

TOTTENHAM HOTSPUR • BORN: 18.12.69

eorge Graham finally froze Justin Edinburgh ut of the first XI at Spurs in 1999–2000, elling him to Portsmouth in March. The left-ack had done little to persuade his manager o keep him at the club.

Now 30, Edinburgh made just 192 passes in he famous white shirt, ending his spell with less-than-impressive pass completion rate of 8%. His marauding runs of old became less equent and just 12 crosses left his boot.

The high point of his campaign came in ovember when he was recalled for the north ondon derby. His experience shored up a purs defence that had kept only one clean heet in their first 12 games and Tottenham ıanaged to beat their old foes 2–1. The ooking Edinburgh picked up in this game was he first of three he would earn in just eight ppearances, frustration perhaps getting the etter of the former Southend man.

His final appearance for the Lilywhites was n the 1–0 home defeat to Sheffield /ednesday, a decidedly inauspicious way to nd a lengthy Premiership career.

APPEARANCES	
Start (sub)	7(1)
Minutes on pitch	638
GOAL ATTEMPTS	
Goals	0
PASSING & CROSSING	
Goal assists	0
Passing	192
Passing accuracy	68%
Crosses	12
Crossing accuracy	25%
DEFENDING	
Tackles	28
Tackles won %	39%
Blocks	7
Interceptions	10
Clearances	46
Shots cleared off line	1
DISCIPLINE	
Fouls	15
Yellow cards	3
Red cards	0

SEE PAGE 262 FOR FULL STATS

E

FB Marc EDWORTHY • 2

COVENTRY CITY • BORN: 24.12.72

APPEARANCES	
Start (sub)	10(0)
Minutes on pitch	882
GOAL ATTEMPTS	
Goals	0
PASSING & CROSSING	
Goal assists	1
Passing	349
Passing accuracy	76%
Crosses	16
Crossing accuracy	25%
DEFENDING	
Tackles	30
Tackles won %	60%
Blocks	13
Interceptions	10
Clearances	90
Shots cleared off line	1
DISCIPLINE	
Fouls	10
Yellow cards	3
Red cards	0

SEE PAGE 94 FOR FULL STATS

The departure of Roland Nilsson from Highfield Road must have filled former Crystal Palace full-back Marc Edworthy with joy. He had been unable to displace the Swedish international from the right-back slot but started 1999–2000 in fine form, making some swashbuckling runs down the flank and supporting Moustapha Hadji and Youssef Chippo well.

Unfortunately, the Devon-born defender suffered a knee injury in City's 4–1 romp against Newcastle in October and he did not play for the first team again all season. His stats illustrate why Coventry missed him so much, as they show a good combination of defending and attacking.

He completed 76% of his passes and also had an assist to his name. A tackle success rate of 60% in the late summer meant that Edworthy ranked eighth in the Opta Defender's Index on August 31. He seemed to have been a victim of the early-season refereeing strictness, though, picking up three yellow cards from just 10 fouls.

Ugo EHIOGU • 5

ASTON VILLA • BORN: 3.11.72

Yet another international tournament passes by without Aston Villa's consistent defender Ugo Ehiogu in the England squad. Many in the game wonder what the powerful player has to do to add to his solitary senior cap, especially after another solid season at Villa Park.

He missed just seven league games for the club in 1999–2000 and it was duly noted that Villa did not manage to win a single match in that period. Ten goals were conceded, too, and under-pressure manager John Gregory was delighted to be able to slot the big man back into the defence, alongside the two Gareths (Southgate and Barry).

Ehiogu made 332 clearances and 81 tackles for the team, succeeding in 44% of his challenges. His reading of the game and partnership with Southgate meant that Villa's defence became the third-meanest in the Premiership. At the other end, Ehiogu was an occasional threat, scoring his only goal in the 1–0 win over bitter rivals Coventry City in March, a result that meant so much to the Holte End faithful.

APPEARANCES	
Start (sub)	31(0)
Minutes on pitch	2767
GOAL ATTEMPTS	
Goals	1
DEFENDING	
Blocks	58
Shots cleared off line	1
Headed clearances	231
Other clearances	101
Interceptions	15
Last man saving tackles	2
Tackles won	36
Tackles won %	44%
PASSING	
Passing accuracy own half	74%
Passing accuracy opp half	51%
DISCIPLINE	
Fouls	53
Fouls in danger area	20
Yellow cards	5
Red cards	0

SEE PAGE 52 FOR FULL STATS

CB

Tahar EL-KHALEJ • 27

SOUTHAMPTON • BORN: 16.6.68

APPEARANCES	
Start (sub)	11(0)
Minutes on pitch	982
GOAL ATTEMPTS	
Goals	1
PASSING & CROSSING	
Goal assists	0
Passing	284
Passing accuracy	54%
Crosses	3
Crossing accuracy	67%
DEFENDING	
Tackles	37
Tackles won %	41%
Blocks	29
Interceptions	3
Clearances	75
Shots cleared off line	0
DISCIPLINE	
Fouls	29
Yellow cards	3
Red cards	0

SEE PAGE 234 FOR FULL STATS

Glenn Hoddle looked to the Algarve when h snapped up powerful defender Tahar El-Khale in March. Benfica were willing to let th Moroccan move to The Dell and it proved to b a successful venture.

He started his south coast career in dramati fashion as Hoddle took his new charges t White Hart Lane, only to see his defence lea seven goals. The new signing demonstrate his ability, though, powerfully heading hom Southampton's second goal in the first hal He also slid into three tackles in a kee attempt to impress the former England an Chelsea manager.

El-Khalej finished the campaign with a pas completion rate of just 54%, something tha he will want to improve on in 2000–01. Hi powerful style of play certainly endeared hi to the regulars at The Dell, and he complete 95% of his dribbles and runs. If he can ad some more composure to his strength, then i is more than likely that El-Khalej will becom an integral part of the Glenn Hoddl revolution.

6 The joint-highest scoring defenders from open pla

Matt ELLIOTT • 18

LEICESTER CITY • BORN: 1.11.68

'He's quite mobile for his size." So said Matt
lliott in August about Benson, his 13-stone
t Bernard dog. But the same characteristics
pply to the inspirational Leicester skipper,
nd he led the team to another successful
eason in 1999–2000, culminating in the
Vorthington Cup triumph over Tranmere
Rovers at Wembley.

Elliott scored twice beneath the Twin
owers, but also notched six times in the
eague as Martin O'Neill guided his underdog
eroes to a highest-ever eighth-placed finish
n the Premiership. The former Oxford United
ruiser was often utilised as a makeshift
triker, a role in which he excelled. His
resence created three goals for the Foxes and
97% dribble completion rate was the result
f some battering runs.

Defensively he was as strong as ever, clearing
he ball on 360 occasions and putting his
onsiderable bulk behind the ball whenever
ossible. He missed just one game all season,
nd even the most fair-weather of Leicester
ans will know how important Elliott is.

APPEARANCES	
Start (sub)	37(0)
Minutes on pitch	3330
GOAL ATTEMPTS	
Goals	6
DEFENDING	
Blocks	90
Shots cleared off line	1
Headed clearances	250
Other clearances	110
Interceptions	21
Last man saving tackles	0
Tackles won	35
Tackles won %	48%
PASSING	
Passing accuracy own half	79%
Passing accuracy opp half	63%
DISCIPLINE	
Fouls	54
Fouls in danger area	7
Yellow cards	2
Red cards	0

SEE PAGE 150 FOR FULL STATS

Bald bruiser: Matt Elliott

were both Leicester players – Gerry Taggart and Matt Elliott

Steve ELLIOTT • 19

DERBY COUNTY • BORN: 29.10.78

Up-and-coming central defender Steve Elliott was pitched into Derby County's bitter relegation struggle in November as Jim Smith attempted to shuffle his squad and produce a winning formula. It was no reflection on the former Pride Park Young Player of the Year that he did not stem the decline, as he was often one of the more consistent players in the Rams' defence.

A tackle success rate just shy of 50% was only just below the Premiership average – and the accuracy of his tackling is illustrated by the fact that he conceded just 18 fouls in 1,566 minutes of football. Elliott featured in five of Derby's nine wins and just half of their 18 defeats.

While young players can suffer from being pitched into tough situations, many can prosper, and the signs are that Elliott will continue to play an important role in the County defence for the next few years. But his last appearance of the season, in the 4–0 thrashing at Chelsea, should remind him of the excessive rigours of life in the Premiership.

APPEARANCES	
Start (sub)	18(2)
Minutes on pitch	1566
GOAL ATTEMPTS	
Goals	0
DEFENDING	
Blocks	44
Shots cleared off line	0
Headed clearances	88
Other clearances	44
Interceptions	16
Last man saving tackles	1
Tackles won	35
Tackles won %	49%
PASSING	
Passing accuracy own half	69%
Passing accuracy opp half	49%
DISCIPLINE	
Fouls	18
Fouls in danger area	7
Yellow cards	1
Red cards	0

SEE PAGE 108 FOR FULL STATS

G

Peter ENCKELMAN • 39

ASTON VILLA • BORN: 10.3.77

APPEARANCES	
Start (sub)	9(1)
Minutes on pitch	849
SHOT STOPPING	
Goals conceded (inside box)	8
Goals conceded (outside box)	1
Minutes per goal conceded	94.3
Clean sheets	4
Saves (shots inside box)	20
Saves (shots outside box)	12
Saves/shots	78%
DISTRIBUTION	
Long kick %	31%
Throws/short passes %	88%
CATCHING	
Crosses caught	18
Crosses punched	4
Crosses dropped	1
Catch success %	95%
DISCIPLINE	
Yellow cards	0
Red cards	0

SEE PAGE 52 FOR FULL STATS

Aston Villa paid Finnish club Jalkapallo TP £200,000 in January 1999 for highly-rate goalkeeper Peter Enckelman, and the under-2 international finally made his debut for th club at Highbury after David James suffered recurrence of his knee injury. The Fin proceeded to let in just one goal on wha must have been an anxious first appearance.

Enckelman played 849 minutes of football i 1999–2000, conceding just nine goals an keeping four clean sheets. His saves-to-shot ratio of 78% compares well with virtuall every goalkeeper in the Premiership, while h dropped only one cross in the campaign.

His finest moment was when Villa travelle to Anfield to face Liverpool and a fit-agai Michael Owen. Enckelman, like so man goalkeepers before him, was inspired by th Kop and produced a superb display. He wa somewhat fortunate when Owen crashed penalty against the bar, but his confiden display in one of the cauldrons of Englis football suggests that he has an excitin career ahead of him.

Stefano ERANIO • 29

DERBY COUNTY • BORN: 29.12.66

With Derby County's squad in a state of flux, the fact that Stefano Eranio has expressed his desire to finish his career at Pride Park will come as a great comfort to the Rams' supporters. Like the team as a whole, Eranio had a mixed campaign in 1999–2000, culminating in him breaking a bone in his leg as Derby lost 2–0 at Anfield in November.

And after two seasons of creativity and skill, Eranio ended the campaign without a single goal or assist to his name, something that will worry both the player and his army of supporters. His passing was slightly less accurate than in 1998–99, but on the plus side his deliveries from the flanks were better.

His lowest point was probably Derby's 5–0 home defeat to Sunderland, when his passing was woeful and he was substituted after 54 minutes. It was a sad moment for all concerned, a modern County legend in poor form. He did recover, though, and in games such as the 4–0 drubbing of Wimbledon he was back to his best, whipping the ball in from the right flank with deadly accuracy.

APPEARANCES	
Start (sub)	17(2)
Minutes on pitch	1388
GOAL ATTEMPTS	
Goals	0
Shots on target	3
Shooting accuracy	43%
Goals/shots ratio	0%
PASSING	
Goal assists	0
Passes in opp half	460
Passing accuracy in opp half	72%
Successful crosses	15
Crossing accuracy	33%
DRIBBLING	
Dribbles & runs	52
Dribble completion	83%
Corners forced	9
DISCIPLINE	
Fouls	20
Yellow cards	4
Red cards	0

SEE PAGE 108 FOR FULL STATS

Matthew ETHERINGTON • 28

TOTTENHAM HOTSPUR • BORN: 14.8.81

APPEARANCES	
Start (sub)	1(4)
Minutes on pitch	149
GOAL ATTEMPTS	
Goals	0
Shots on target	0
Shooting accuracy	0%
Goals/shots ratio	0%
PASSING	
Goal assists	1
Passes in opp half	36
Passing accuracy in opp half	69%
Successful crosses	1
Crossing accuracy	13%
DRIBBLING	
Dribbles & runs	12
Dribble completion	67%
Corners forced	0
DISCIPLINE	
Fouls	1
Yellow cards	0
Red cards	0

SEE PAGE 262 FOR FULL STATS

Much is expected of youthful left-winger Matthew Etherington, signed from Division Three side Peterborough United in January in a deal which could eventually net the minnows £4 million. He was the youngest player to feature in the 1998–99 Division Three PFA team and he carried his form into 1999–2000, scoring three times for Posh.

Spurs had been tracking Etherington for some time and, despite considerable interest from Manchester United and Newcastle, he chose to move to White Hart Lane. Ironically, after just four substitute appearances for the Lilywhites, he made his full debut at Old Trafford, and belied his lack of experience with an assured display.

He finished the season with one assist for Tottenham, his cross having set up David Ginola for the last-minute equaliser against Leicester at Filbert Street. His dribble completion rate of 67% was relatively low, but as he gains in strength he will become a more powerful force. His biggest challenge may be replacing the aforementioned Frenchman.

S

Jason EUELL • 10

WIMBLEDON • BORN: 6.2.77

When the Wimbledon players look back on the disastrous 1999–2000 season, the men who led the bitter revolt against beleaguered boss Egil Olsen may regret their actions. One of those revolutionaries was highly-rated powerhouse Jason Euell, a player who performed in a way that encouraged clubs such as Tottenham and Arsenal to enquire about his services.

Operating in a role similar to that of David Platt in his heyday, Euell was unfortunate to be playing in a team that struggled so much, particularly after Christmas.

He scored on just four occasions, six fewer than in 1998–99, but his surging runs saw him create five goals for the Dons.

His defensive play improved dramatically, though, and only 24 players in the Premiership made more than his 117 tackles. But such effort came at a cost. He received eight yellow cards, and was ordered from the field of play in the home defeat to Arsenal, the third loss in a run of eight that was to prove so costly to the Crazy Gang.

APPEARANCES	
Start (sub)	32(5)
Minutes on pitch	3000
GOAL ATTEMPTS	
Goals inside box	4
Goals outside box	0
Minutes per goal scored	750.0
Goals/shots ratio	10%
SHOOTING	
Shots on target inside box	14
Shots on target outside box	0
Shooting accuracy	33%
PASSING	
Goal assists	5
Key passes	10
Passing accuracy in opp half	62%
DISCIPLINE	
Fouls committed	50
Fouls won	28
Offside	10
Yellow cards	8
Red cards	1

SEE PAGE 304 FOR FULL STATS

M

John EUSTACE • 24

COVENTRY CITY • BORN: 3.11.79

APPEARANCES	
Start (sub)	13(3)
Minutes on pitch	1152
GOAL ATTEMPTS	
Goals	1
Shots on target	8
Shooting accuracy	57%
PASSING & CROSSING	
Goal assists	0
Passes in opp half	285
Passing accuracy in opp half	65%
Successful crosses	4
Cross completion	27%
DEFENDING	
Interceptions	8
Clearances	18
Tackles	41
Tackles won %	63%
DISCIPLINE	
Fouls	30
Yellow cards	2
Red cards	0

SEE PAGE 94 FOR FULL STATS

After playing well during a loan spell at Dundee United in 1998–99, John Eustace was elevated to the Coventry City first team by Gordon Strachan in the club's Worthington Cup second round humiliation at Tranmere. The young midfielder must have wondered if he had blown his chance at the top level, but he was called into the first XI for the game against Wimbledon on 15 January, and missed only two more games for the Sky Blues.

His first goal in English football came as he knocked home a penalty in the 4–0 romp against Bradford at Highfield Road, and his growing confidence in each game was a joy to the Coventry fans. A pass completion rate of 71% was respectable enough, while his tackling gave Moustapha Hadji and Youssef Chippo room to weave their magic.

Coventry have to improve their atrocious away form if they want to progress in the 2000–01 campaign, and the impressive Eustace could well become a vital source of strength in the middle of the park for an entertaining Sky Blues side.

65 Jason Euell won more tackles than

S Graham FENTON • 21

LEICESTER CITY • BORN: 22.5.74

Martin O'Neill is one of the most astute managers in the modern game, able to resurrect the careers of players such as Tony Cottee, but Graham Fenton has not been one of his better buys. Any thoughts that Fenton might make more of an impact in 1999–2000 were soon dashed as he was restricted to just two appearances in January.

He did manage to create Emile Heskey's penultimate goal for the Foxes in the 3–1 home defeat to West Ham. But with a total of just three shots, and all of them off target, it was no surprise that the former Aston Villa and Blackburn man did not feature in the first team again.

He was shipped off on loan to Walsall in March and briefly showed promise, scoring in the basement battle with Port Vale in his second game. But the goal drought that has blighted his recent career kicked in and he struggled once more.

It is hard to see a future for him at Filbert Street but with O'Neill's departure, Fenton has a new chance to impress.

APPEARANCES	
Start (sub)	1(1)
Minutes on pitch	142
GOAL ATTEMPTS	
Goals inside box	0
Goals outside box	0
Minutes per goal scored	n/a
Goals/shots ratio	0%
SHOOTING	
Shots on target inside box	0
Shots on target outside box	0
Shooting accuracy	0%
PASSING	
Goal assists	1
Key passes	0
Passing accuracy in opp half	55%
DISCIPLINE	
Fouls committed	4
Fouls won	2
Offside	1
Yellow cards	1
Red cards	0

SEE PAGE 150 FOR FULL STATS

E
F

S Les FERDINAND • 9

TOTTENHAM HOTSPUR • BORN: 18.12.66

APPEARANCES	
Start (sub)	5(4)
Minutes on pitch	448
GOAL ATTEMPTS	
Goals inside box	2
Goals outside box	0
Minutes per goal scored	224.0
Goals/shots ratio	15%
SHOOTING	
Shots on target inside box	4
Shots on target outside box	2
Shooting accuracy	46%
PASSING	
Goal assists	0
Key passes	1
Passing accuracy in opp half	71%
DISCIPLINE	
Fouls committed	12
Fouls won	11
Offside	3
Yellow cards	3
Red cards	0

SEE PAGE 262 FOR FULL STATS

If the 1998–99 season was a disappointment for Les Ferdinand, then 1999–2000 was an unmitigated disaster for the former England international. He started just five games, with four brief substitute appearances. His persistent injury problems have wreaked havoc with his career at Spurs, and finishing the season with a total of just two goals will upset him.

His strikes came in the home win over Newcastle and the away triumph at Sheffield Wednesday, a period when the season ahead looked promising for the Spurs fans. But a loss of form and the loss of Ferdinand, among others, meant that the progress made by George Graham in 1998–99 was not built upon.

Ferdinand's pace is gradually receding, but he remains a great threat with his aerial prowess and he is something of a talismanic figure in the game.

Whether he has a future in the Tottenham team with the arrival of Sergei Rebrov remains to be seen. His popularity has never waned, and that could certainly help him in his quest to return to regular football.

any other Premiership striker

CB Rio FERDINAND • 15

WEST HAM UNITED • BORN: 7.11.78

Despite not progressing as quickly as some may have wanted in 1999–2000, Rio Ferdinand is still one of the most highly-rated defensive talents in the English game and is on the shopping list of a host of clubs. He missed just five Premiership games for West Ham, and Harry Redknapp's men lost three of those matches.

His passing and tackling were less successful than in 1998–99, but he added a lot of experience to his CV. Ferdinand featured in two England games and was a guiding force in the Hammers' Intertoto and UEFA Cup campaigns, Harry Redknapp's team beating Metz in the final of the former competition.

He made 326 clearances overall, and only 19 players in the Premiership logged a higher tally. More impressive was the fact that he only conceded 15 fouls all season, a testament to his calm and assured play. The 21-year-old is still in a strong position career-wise, and, despite missing out on Euro 2000, he should be a fixture in the England squad for years to come.

APPEARANCES	
Start (sub)	33(0)
Minutes on pitch	2959
GOAL ATTEMPTS	
Goals	0
DEFENDING	
Blocks	98
Shots cleared off line	0
Headed clearances	211
Other clearances	115
Interceptions	44
Last man saving tackles	1
Tackles won	40
Tackles won %	48%
PASSING	
Passing accuracy own half	80%
Passing accuracy opp half	53%
DISCIPLINE	
Fouls	15
Fouls in danger area	7
Yellow cards	2
Red cards	0

SEE PAGE 290 FOR FULL STATS

Steady season: Rio Ferdinand

Duncan FERGUSON • 20

S

NEWCASTLE UNITED • BORN: 27.12.71

F

Injury-prone: Duncan Ferguson

APPEARANCES	
Start (sub)	17(6)
Minutes on pitch	1527
GOAL ATTEMPTS	
Goals inside box	4
Goals outside box	2
Minutes per goal scored	254.5
Goals/shots ratio	13%
SHOOTING	
Shots on target inside box	17
Shots on target outside box	3
Shooting accuracy	44%
PASSING	
Goal assists	1
Key passes	5
Passing accuracy in opp half	69%
DISCIPLINE	
Fouls committed	51
Fouls won	20
Offside	13
Yellow cards	1
Red cards	0

SEE PAGE 206 FOR FULL STATS

When compared to his first season as a Newcastle player, Duncan Ferguson's 1999–2000 campaign was more impressive. He finished with six goals and one assist, but was again dogged by a series of injuries.

He was used sparingly until November when he had recovered sufficiently well enough to play the last half-hour at Aston Villa. Within seven minutes of coming on he had scored to give Newcastle their first away win of the season and made Bobby Robson a very happy man.

Ferguson then started 14 matches in a row, an unprecedented spell for the big man, and he started to show the Newcastle fans why Ruud Gullit had spent £7 million bringing him to St James's Park. He scored four goals in four games over Christmas and the New Year, but saved his best for the visit of Manchester United on 12 February.

Sadly, though, this was to be his last league goal of the campaign. Everybody knows what Ferguson is capable of, but he needs to stay clear of the treatment room if he is to provide value for money.

FB Albert FERRER • 17

CHELSEA • BORN: 6.6.70

Albert Ferrer was again superbly consistent for Chelsea in 1999–2000. He missed out on the FA Cup final through injury, but was a solid outlet on the right flank during the season and always popular with the Stamford Bridge faithful. His form in the Blues' European Cup adventure was a key reason why Gianluca Vialli's side progressed to the quarter-finals.

After the inaugural Opta Yearbook highlighted the Spaniard's wayward crossing, it was pleasing to see that "Chapi" had vastly improved. He delivered 62 centres and 35% of them reached a team-mate. He also finished the campaign with three assists, his teasing balls proving tempting for the misfiring Chelsea frontmen.

Ferrer's defending was as fiery as usual, and he slid into 85 tackles. Importantly, he won more than half of them and committed just 25 fouls in the process. There are strong rumours that the Spaniard may be leaving Chelsea soon and there is no doubt that if he does go, he will be greatly missed by everybody associated with the west London club.

APPEARANCES	
Start (sub)	24(1)
Minutes on pitch	2100
GOAL ATTEMPTS	
Goals	0
PASSING & CROSSING	
Goal assists	3
Passing	1049
Passing accuracy	74%
Crosses	62
Crossing accuracy	35%
DEFENDING	
Tackles	85
Tackles won %	55%
Blocks	31
Interceptions	31
Clearances	139
Shots cleared off line	0
DISCIPLINE	
Fouls	25
Yellow cards	4
Red cards	0

SEE PAGE 80 FOR FULL STATS

CB Gianluca FESTA • 5

MIDDLESBROUGH • BORN: 15.3.69

APPEARANCES	
Start (sub)	27(2)
Minutes on pitch	2464
GOAL ATTEMPTS	
Goals	2
DEFENDING	
Blocks	59
Shots cleared off line	1
Headed clearances	153
Other clearances	85
Interceptions	28
Last man saving tackles	0
Tackles won	37
Tackles won %	62%
PASSING	
Passing accuracy own half	75%
Passing accuracy opp half	55%
DISCIPLINE	
Fouls	50
Fouls in danger area	14
Yellow cards	6
Red cards	1

SEE PAGE 192 FOR FULL STATS

Popular Italian defender Gianluca Festa was again involved in much of whatever action Middlesbrough found themselves in during 1999–2000. It was a season that promised much for Bryan Robson's team, but cup exits to clubs from the lower leagues cast a dark shadow over The Riverside.

Festa scored twice, first in the home win over Coventry and, more memorably, in the 2–2 draw with local rivals Newcastle in April. Such goals have endeared the Sicilian to the Boro fans and his exuberant celebrations illustrate the fondness he has for the club.

His tackling was as keen as ever, and a 62% success rate made Festa one of the sternest defenders in the Premiership. Sometimes, though, his eagerness went too far, and while committing 50 fouls he managed to pick up six yellow cards. The game against Leeds in February saw Festa red-carded for hauling down Darren Huckerby when the pacy forward was through on goal. But at a club where certain foreign imports have been less than dedicated, the Italian's commitment cannot be faulted.

17 Chelsea kept more clean

G Ian FEUER • 29

WEST HAM UNITED • BORN: 20.5.71

Vhen players decide to return to a club, they ›ften find the second outing less prosperous. ›ut after spells with Luton, Cardiff, Rushden ›nd Diamonds and in America, Ian Feuer eturned to West Ham with his allegiance all he stronger.

In his previous spell with the Hammers, the iant American lived in the shadow of Ludek Aiklosko and Shaka Hislop. But in the 999–2000 campaign, when injuries struck ›oth Hislop and Craig Forrest, Feuer felt there /ere "voodoo dolls" working at Upton Park as ›e pulled on the number one jersey.

The 'keeper conceded two goals in three ›ames, but successfully managed to keep a lean sheet in the 5–0 rout of Coventry while ›laying with a thigh injury.

That knock forced him out of action near the nd of the 1999–2000 season. But as Feuer is /ithout a permanent contract, he will hope he ›erformed well enough to figure in Harry ›edknapp's plans for 2000–01 or to have ›mpressed another club sufficiently to take a hance on him.

APPEARANCES	
Start (sub)	3(0)
Minutes on pitch	270
SHOT STOPPING	
Goals conceded (inside box)	2
Goals conceded (outside box)	0
Minutes per goal conceded	135.0
Clean sheets	1
Saves (shots inside box)	9
Saves (shots outside box)	3
Saves/shots	86%
DISTRIBUTION	
Long kick %	37%
Throws/short passes %	94%
CATCHING	
Crosses caught	4
Crosses punched	0
Crosses dropped	0
Catch success %	100%
DISCIPLINE	
Yellow cards	1
Red cards	0

SEE PAGE 290 FOR FULL STATS

F

FB Curtis FLEMING • 2

MIDDLESBROUGH • BORN: 8.10.68

APPEARANCES	
Start (sub)	27(0)
Minutes on pitch	2348
GOAL ATTEMPTS	
Goals	0
PASSING & CROSSING	
Goal assists	1
Passing	786
Passing accuracy	65%
Crosses	34
Crossing accuracy	41%
DEFENDING	
Tackles	113
Tackles won %	40%
Blocks	45
Interceptions	16
Clearances	90
Shots cleared off line	0
DISCIPLINE	
Fouls	27
Yellow cards	6
Red cards	0

SEE PAGE 192 FOR FULL STATS

The 1999–2000 campaign was Curtis Fleming's ninth season at Middlesbrough, and the Irish international was his usual consistent self. Due to a long-term knee injury he did not play until late September, when Boro lost at home to Chelsea, but missed only three league games from that point. His running on the flank was as powerful as ever and he recorded a cross completion rate of 41%. Given this above-average accuracy, it is somewhat surprising that Fleming finished the season with just one assist.

He careered into 113 tackles, although he enjoyed less success than team-mates such as Gianluca Festa. But after facing competition for his place from young Robbie Stockdale in 1998–99, it must have pleased him to play so much football.

His competitive temperament saw him receive six yellow cards, three of them coming in the last five games of the season. Fleming showed admirable tenacity in winning his first XI place back, and he will need to display a similar attitude in 2000–01 if Middlesbrough are to progress.

›heets than any other team

Tore Andre FLO • 19

CHELSEA • BORN: 15.6.73

Tore Andre Flo climbed off the bench in 1999–2000 and played a much fuller role in the Chelsea campaign than in previous years. He featured in all but four of the Blues' league games, scoring 10 goals in the process. His image as a super-sub was proven to be a fallacy, as nine of his league goals came during matches he had started. He was also superb in the Champions League, bagging eight goals, including three in two games against Barcelona.

He finished the Premiership season with just one assist, though, and a below-par pass completion rate of 64%. But his crossing was perceptive, with 41% of his deliveries finding a blue shirt.

Flo was caught offside 35 times, and only 16 players in the whole division were flagged more often, but his tireless work-rate meant that the Chelsea midfield could release the ball in confidence. His partnership with Gianfranco Zola was the most consistent of Vialli's pairings and, after seeing off the £10 million man Chris Sutton, Flo's standing continues to rise.

APPEARANCES	
Start (sub)	20(14)
Minutes on pitch	1906
GOAL ATTEMPTS	
Goals inside box	10
Goals outside box	0
Minutes per goal scored	190.6
Goals/shots ratio	16%
SHOOTING	
Shots on target inside box	30
Shots on target outside box	4
Shooting accuracy	55%
PASSING	
Goal assists	1
Key passes	2
Passing accuracy in opp half	65%
DISCIPLINE	
Fouls committed	38
Fouls won	30
Offside	35
Yellow cards	1
Red cards	0

SEE PAGE 80 FOR FULL STATS

Tim FLOWERS • 1

LEICESTER CITY • BORN: 3.2.67

APPEARANCES	
Start (sub)	29(0)
Minutes on pitch	2447
SHOT STOPPING	
Goals conceded (inside box)	33
Goals conceded (outside box)	5
Minutes per goal conceded	64.4
Clean sheets	4
Saves (shots inside box)	45
Saves (shots outside box)	33
Saves/shots	67%
DISTRIBUTION	
Long kick %	47%
Throws/short passes %	90%
CATCHING	
Crosses caught	31
Crosses punched	19
Crosses dropped	1
Catch success %	97%
DISCIPLINE	
Yellow cards	1
Red cards	0

SEE PAGE 150 FOR FULL STATS

If 1998–99 was an unmitigated disaster for Ti Flowers, 1999–2000 was a triumph for th amiable goalkeeper. Despite an unpromisir start, when he misplaced his lucky glove within 48 hours of first joining the club, Flowe will consider his first Foxes season a success.

The only misfortunes he endured we several brief injuries, one of which forced hi to wear an all-in-one rubber flak jacket to a his recovery. Apparently they are regular used by jockeys, but there were plenty quips about him looking like "a model out one of those shady fetish magazines."

The former Blackburn 'keeper turned in som superb displays, producing a series of amazir stops, although he kept just four clean shee in the league.

Leicester's march to Worthington Cup glo was heavily influenced by Flowers. He kept go when the Foxes beat Leeds at Filbert Stree and certainly enjoyed his day out at Wemble

Flowers made the majority of his stops fro shots struck inside the box, and dropped ju one cross in the whole campaign.

Marc-Vivien FOE • 13

WEST HAM UNITED • BORN: 1.5.75

An up-and-down season and the ability to rake in a reasonable fee were mitigating factors in Harry Redknapp's decision to sell Marc-Vivien Foe at the end of 1999–2000.

In the early season, the Cameroon star displayed little of the talent that had previously caused Liverpool's and then West Ham's interest in him.

But, as the campaign progressed, he became a reliable force in the Hammers' midfield, particularly defensively; witness the fact that he won 62% of his tackles.

Redknapp is renowned for his honest remarks, yet his declaration that Foe was a mild-mannered player was completely contradicted on the pitch. He made 61 fouls, received six yellow cards and two reds, the more infamous being his unsavoury exit for a wild kick at Matthew Jones of Leeds on the last day of the season.

The manner of that sending-off probably eased fans' disappointment as Foe moved for £6 million to Lyon, funding striker Frederic Kanouté's permanent move.

APPEARANCES	
Start (sub)	25(0)
Minutes on pitch	2228
GOAL ATTEMPTS	
Goals	1
Shots on target	7
Shooting accuracy	27%
PASSING & CROSSING	
Goal assists	2
Passes in opp half	449
Passing accuracy in opp half	64%
Successful crosses	2
Cross completion	29%
DEFENDING	
Interceptions	20
Clearances	120
Tackles	92
Tackles won %	62%
DISCIPLINE	
Fouls	61
Yellow cards	6
Red cards	2

SEE PAGE 290 FOR FULL STATS

S

Dominic FOLEY • 33

WATFORD • BORN: 7.7.76

APPEARANCES	
Start (sub)	5(7)
Minutes on pitch	447
GOAL ATTEMPTS	
Goals inside box	1
Goals outside box	0
Minutes per goal scored	447.0
Goals/shots ratio	7%
SHOOTING	
Shots on target inside box	7
Shots on target outside box	2
Shooting accuracy	60%
PASSING	
Goal assists	0
Key passes	0
Passing accuracy in opp half	68%
DISCIPLINE	
Fouls committed	13
Fouls won	8
Offside	3
Yellow cards	0
Red cards	0

SEE PAGE 276 FOR FULL STATS

After a disappointing season with Wolves in 1998–99, free agent Dominic Foley was surprisingly snapped up by Graham Taylor in the summer. The Irishman had been on loan at Vicarage Road in 1997–98 but scored just once. He was now asked to play at the highest level and coped with it relatively well.

He made his second debut for the Hornets in the high-pressure atmosphere at Anfield, coming on for Michel Ngonge with 21 minutes to play. In what was Watford's finest hour of their brief sojourn in the Premiership he touched the ball just nine times, but could at least say that he was part of the team that embarrassed Liverpool.

Foley scored his only goal of the season in April when he bagged a shock equaliser at Elland Road. Leeds eventually triumphed, but Foley showed in spells that he could cope with the level of football.

With Watford enriched by top-level experience, the amiable 24-year-old could very well enjoy a successful season back in the Nationwide Football League.

Craig FORREST • 22

WEST HAM UNITED • BORN: 20.9.67

Living in the shadow of the ever-improving Shaka Hislop had, until the tail end of 1999–2000, proved to be Craig Forrest's main role at West Ham.

The big Canadian made his club debut in October 1997, but only injury to Hislop in 1999–2000 allowed the former Ipswich man to have a decent run in the team.

Forrest's excellent shot-stopping skills ensured he kept three clean sheets, but he might well have wished he had remained in his former career of ice hockey after facing Manchester United in March.

Before that clash, the 'keeper had only conceded five goals in five games. But nightmares dating back to March 1995, when he conceded nine times while in goal for Ipswich at the Theatre of Dreams, came back to haunt him. The same team, just a different scoreline – 7–1.

He showed good composure in coming back in the Hammers' 2–1 win at home to Newcastle, and would have continued in the first team had he not aggravated his hernia.

APPEARANCES	
Start (sub)	9(2)
Minutes on pitch	936
SHOT STOPPING	
Goals conceded (inside box)	13
Goals conceded (outside box)	4
Minutes per goal conceded	55.1
Clean sheets	3
Saves (shots inside box)	17
Saves (shots outside box)	15
Saves/shots	65%
DISTRIBUTION	
Long kick %	52%
Throws/short passes %	89%
CATCHING	
Crosses caught	13
Crosses punched	3
Crosses dropped	0
Catch success %	100%
DISCIPLINE	
Yellow cards	0
Red cards	0

SEE PAGE 290 FOR FULL STATS

Quinton FORTUNE • 25

MANCHESTER UNITED • BORN: 21.5.77

APPEARANCES	
Start (sub)	4(2)
Minutes on pitch	370
GOAL ATTEMPTS	
Goals	2
Shots on target	4
Shooting accuracy	67%
PASSING & CROSSING	
Goal assists	1
Passes in opp half	108
Passing accuracy in opp half	79%
Successful crosses	5
Cross completion	22%
DEFENDING	
Interceptions	0
Clearances	1
Tackles	9
Tackles won %	44%
DISCIPLINE	
Fouls	7
Yellow cards	0
Red cards	0

SEE PAGE 178 FOR FULL STATS

Quinton Fortune left the sunny climes soon-to-be-relegated Atletico Madrid for rai Manchester and looked to be a valuab addition to the squad at Old Trafford. He ma his league debut for the Red Devils in a 2 minute substitute appearance again Newcastle United, but made only four sta toward the end of the campaign.

The athletic midfielder will have a hard ta displacing Ryan Giggs down United's le flank, but looked an able deputy in t absence of Jesper Blomqvist. He completed a excellent 81% of all his passes, but h crossing was somewhat wayward, with ju 22% finding a team-mate in the box.

The South African international certain seemed to be a catalyst for goals. He featur in only six Premiership games, but Manchest United managed 27 goals in those fixtures.

Fortune scored two of these, one again Bradford and one versus Middlesbrough. I also excelled in the jaunt to Brazil, scori twice in the tropical heat, as the rest of t team looked somewhat shaky.

8 Liverpool won more matches against Londo

S

Robbie FOWLER • 9

LIVERPOOL • BORN: 9.4.75

obbie Fowler endured his most difficult eason in 1998–99, and he must have hoped hat the good times were returning when he cored Liverpool's first goal of 1999–2000 at heffield Wednesday.

His second strike of the campaign came three eeks later when he scored his obligatory racker against Arsenal to give the Reds a vital in. But his performance in that game was the enith of another disappointing term for rguably England's most natural finisher.

Sadly for Fowler, niggling injuries ruined his eason and, apart from a few appearances over hristmas, he did not feature in another game ntil the Merseyside derby in April. nsurprisingly he was not match-fit, and failed o score during the rest of the campaign.

The season ended in more controversy for the triker when 'Pool boss Gerard Houllier dropped im prior to the vital game with Bradford. The vent further fuelled speculation that Fowler ould be leaving the club. Such a transfer ould command a huge fee, though – an ndication of Fowler's undoubted ability.

APPEARANCES	
Start (sub)	8(6)
Minutes on pitch	809
GOAL ATTEMPTS	
Goals inside box	2
Goals outside box	1
Minutes per goal scored	269.7
Goals/shots ratio	11%
SHOOTING	
Shots on target inside box	11
Shots on target outside box	7
Shooting accuracy	64%
PASSING	
Goal assists	0
Key passes	3
Passing accuracy in opp half	58%
DISCIPLINE	
Fouls committed	15
Fouls won	8
Offside	7
Yellow cards	1
Red cards	0

SEE PAGE 164 FOR FULL STATS

F

Ruel FOX • 18

TOTTENHAM HOTSPUR • BORN: 14.1.68

ormer Newcastle United wingman Ruel Fox igned for Spurs in 1995, but it looks as if his areer at White Hart Lane is now drawing to a lose. He featured in just three games all eason, but did manage to play 87 minutes of purs' 3–1 triumph over Champions lanchester United in October.

Apart from that, he did little else during a isappointing campaign for most at the club. le fired just one shot on target, and another hat flew wide, while the 34 passes that he ttempted found a team-mate on just 21 ccasions.

Fox was shown a yellow card in the lanchester United game – a colour he may be ore familiar with very soon, as it is rumoured hat Norwich City are interested in bringing im back to Carrow Road. Conventional isdom says you should never go back, but he former Canary will just be happy to be laying first-team football after a couple of easons on the sidelines.

SEE PAGE 262 FOR FULL STATS

'Pool prowler: Robbie Fowler

ides than any other team in the Premiership

Damien FRANCIS • 24

WIMBLEDON • BORN: 27.2.79

In a season of woe for the Dons, young Damien Francis continued to emerge as a genuine prospect at Selhurst Park. He did not play until December, when Egil Olsen introduced him to Anfield in Wimbledon's 3–1 defeat. All in all he appeared in nine matches, and eight of them were as a substitute.

His one start was in the 2–0 loss at Coventry, when he was relatively ineffective, although the City defenders had to block two of his shots. It was his tackling that impressed most. He won 83% of his challenges and, with the team dropping into the Nationwide League, he could prove a crucial player in the efforts to return to the Premiership at the first attempt.

Certainly with many Wimbledon fans complaining of a lack of effort from some of their foreign imports, they will hope budding stars such as Francis will be able to reassert the Crazy Gang spirit in a new era for the south London club.

SEE PAGE 304 FOR FULL STATS

Carsten FREDGAARD • 15

SUNDERLAND • BORN: 20.5.76

Twenty-four-year-old Carsten Fredgaard faile to make as much of an impact as he woul have liked at Sunderland, playing just 3 minutes in the 1999–2000 campaign, and th in the 4–0 opening day drubbing by Chelsea a Stamford Bridge.

He did manage a shot on target during th half-hour, but Ed De Goey dealt with it easil His passing was also sharp, but with Nia Quinn and Kevin Phillips performing brilliant and Danny Dichio ahead of him in the peckir order, Peter Reid did not call on the form Lyngby player again for action in th 1999–2000 Premiership.

He scored a brace of goals for the Black Ca in the Worthington Cup win over Walsall, b was loaned out to struggling Division One sic West Brom in February. That stay was cut sho after the Danish striker picked up an inju that forced him to return to the Stadium Light, where he will be hoping to enjoy mo luck in 2000–01.

SEE PAGE 248 FOR FULL STATS

Steffen FREUND • 4

TOTTENHAM HOTSPUR • BORN: 19.1.70

APPEARANCES	
Start (sub)	24(3)
Minutes on pitch	2158
GOAL ATTEMPTS	
Goals	0
Shots on target	6
Shooting accuracy	46%
PASSING & CROSSING	
Goal assists	1
Passes in opp half	489
Passing accuracy in opp half	72%
Successful crosses	8
Cross completion	36%
DEFENDING	
Interceptions	25
Clearances	43
Tackles	78
Tackles won %	55%
DISCIPLINE	
Fouls	27
Yellow cards	9
Red cards	0

SEE PAGE 263 FOR FULL STATS

German midfield powerhouse Steffen Freu has more than his fair share of critics, but does exactly what his manager demands. T Euro 96 winner crashed into 78 tackles 1999–2000, winning more than half of the while his distribution was solid, with 75% his passes finding a Tottenham team-mate.

His shooting is widely regarded as bei wayward, and once again he failed to sco The majority of his shots were blocke though seven of them went well wide.

Perhaps the most memorable incident Freund's season was during Tottenham's fine hour, the 3–1 win over Manchester Unite The German was yellow-carded, but he al managed to aggravate Roy Keane so mu that the Irishman chased his counterpa around the pitch. That booking was one nine for Freund, an aspect of his game that needs to curtail.

Spurs fans will be looking for the form Borussia Dortmund star to step up a gear 2000–01, and drive the Lilywhites to sor much-needed glory.

Brad FRIEDEL • 19

LIVERPOOL • BORN: 18.5.71

After a 1998–99 season in which Brad Friedel was alternated with David James, 1999–2000 saw the American restricted to just two league games as new boy Sander Westerveld made the goalkeeping position his own. With work permit regulations, Friedel's Liverpool career looks like ending very soon.

He did well enough in his three hours of Premiership football, keeping a clean sheet at home against Chelsea and then conceding just one goal at Southampton. In those two games he had to make five saves, four of which were shots from close range.

Friedel's other two games came in the Worthington Cup. Unfortunately for the American, he conceded two goals at The Dell as Liverpool crashed out of the competition in the third round.

There is no doubting Friedel's ability, but it seems that he has hit a brick wall at Anfield. Any club wanting a solid shot-stopper could do a lot worse than the affable 'keeper, who may have to return to America if a new club is not found.

APPEARANCES	
Start (sub)	2(0)
Minutes on pitch	180
SHOT STOPPING	
Goals conceded (inside box)	1
Goals conceded (outside box)	0
Minutes per goal conceded	180.0
Clean sheets	1
Saves (shots inside box)	4
Saves (shots outside box)	1
Saves/shots	83%
DISTRIBUTION	
Long kick %	35%
Throws/short passes %	86%
CATCHING	
Crosses caught	2
Crosses punched	1
Crosses dropped	0
Catch success %	100%
DISCIPLINE	
Yellow cards	0
Red cards	0

SEE PAGE 164 FOR FULL STATS

F

AM

Stephen FROGGATT • 16

COVENTRY CITY • BORN: 9.3.73

APPEARANCES	
Start (sub)	21(5)
Minutes on pitch	1872
GOAL ATTEMPTS	
Goals	1
Shots on target	4
Shooting accuracy	44%
Goals/shots ratio	11%
PASSING	
Goal assists	2
Passes in opp half	434
Passing accuracy in opp half	62%
Successful crosses	18
Crossing accuracy	22%
DRIBBLING	
Dribbles & runs	121
Dribble completion	74%
Corners forced	14
DISCIPLINE	
Fouls	21
Yellow cards	5
Red cards	0

SEE PAGE 94 FOR FULL STATS

Steve Froggatt is a pacy and direct player, from whom Gordon Strachan has coaxed some excellent performances. The former Wolves man was even drafted into Kevin Keegan's Euro 2000 play-off squad although, in truth, this was more to do with England's lack of options wide on the left than Froggatt's form.

Switching between left-back and the winger's role in the City team, he scored just once but created two others. His tackling was not altogether successful, but he was never reluctant to challenge the opposition.

His lone goal came as the Sky Blues routed Watford 4–0 at Highfield Road, and this was a game when his powerful running came to the fore. During the season Froggatt embarked on 121 dribbles and runs and, considering that he only played for 1,872 minutes, that is an impressive total.

After suffering an injury against Sunderland in February he only played five more times, and he will hope that he can continue his gradual rise in 2000–01 and perhaps make a return to the England squad.

Esteban FUERTES • 20

DERBY COUNTY • BORN: 26.12.72

As Derby slipped towards the foot of the table, Jim Smith decided that another foreign striker might arrest the slump, so he plumped for Argentinean Esteban Fuertes. The bustling forward enjoyed only a short but incident-packed career at Pride Park.

In his first home appearance he slammed home a goal to give the Rams a vital win over Everton. His arrival brought some life into the Derby team, but there were constant rumours about his work permit – and, indeed, whether he had one.

He hit the headlines again in the home defeat to Bradford when he was sent off after a scuffle with David Wetherall. Worse followed in November when the Rams returned from a training trip to Portugal. Passport irregularities resulted in Fuertes being refused entry to the country and his Derby career was over.

His stats indicate that he could have been an effective force for Jim Smith's team but, with little chance of a return to England, Fuertes will go down as a bizarre footnote in the Derby history books.

APPEARANCES	
Start (sub)	8(0)
Minutes on pitch	538
GOAL ATTEMPTS	
Goals inside box	1
Goals outside box	0
Minutes per goal scored	538.0
Goals/shots ratio	20%
SHOOTING	
Shots on target inside box	3
Shots on target outside box	0
Shooting accuracy	60%
PASSING	
Goal assists	0
Key passes	2
Passing accuracy in opp half	45%
DISCIPLINE	
Fouls committed	13
Fouls won	13
Offside	11
Yellow cards	2
Red cards	1

SEE PAGE 109 FOR FULL STATS

Jose Antunes FUMACA • 38

NEWCASTLE UNITED • BORN: 15.7.76

APPEARANCES	
Start (sub)	1(4)
Minutes on pitch	139
GOAL ATTEMPTS	
Goals	0
Shots on target	1
Shooting accuracy	50%
PASSING & CROSSING	
Goal assists	0
Passes in opp half	35
Passing accuracy in opp half	71%
Successful crosses	1
Cross completion	100%
DEFENDING	
Interceptions	5
Clearances	3
Tackles	5
Tackles won %	60%
DISCIPLINE	
Fouls	7
Yellow cards	0
Red cards	0

SEE PAGE 206 FOR FULL STATS

When Bobby Robson decided to take the reir at St James's Park, he brought in forme Colchester United manager and Crystal Palac coach Mick Wadsworth.

Wadsworth is a far cry from Ruud Gullit bu he did persuade Robson to sign a Brazilia midfielder he had worked with at Layer Roa and Selhurst Park on loan. José Antune Fumaca was his name, and he ended u making five appearances for the Magpies i the 1999–2000 campaign.

His only start came in United's 2–1 wi against Tottenham, and he played relativel well, making four tackles and forcing a sav from Ian Walker in the Spurs goal. Hi subsequent four games were all as substitute, and the only game of note was th 2–2 draw with West Ham when he played fc most of the second half.

With Newcastle's burgeoning squad, it i more than likely Fumaca will not be makin his move to the north-east permanent, and hi ability and experience do seem more suited t a club outside the Premiership.

Kevin GALLACHER • 32

NEWCASTLE UNITED • BORN: 23.11.66

cottish international striker Kevin Gallacher enewed his acquaintance with England and lewcastle captain Alan Shearer when he oined the Toon Army from Blackburn in ctober for £700,000.

Goals have hardly been flowing, with just wo strikes to the Clydebank-born forward's ame in 14 starts for Newcastle, but this is nainly because Gallacher was asked to adopt midfield role behind United's front two, hearer and Duncan Ferguson.

The former Coventry attacker did display rief glimpses of his predatory instinct in ront of goal during the 1999–2000 campaign. 'he 5'8" player netted both of his strikes from nside the box and fired in a further eight fforts on target within the penalty area.

And Gallacher did prove his worth in nidfield, creating six goalscoring pportunities and finding a team-mate with n impressive 70% of his passes. The Scot was articularly adroit at banging in crosses, hipping in more than 40 centres, usually rom the left flank.

APPEARANCES	
Start (sub)	14(6)
Minutes on pitch	1232
GOAL ATTEMPTS	
Goals inside box	2
Goals outside box	0
Minutes per goal scored	616.0
Goals/shots ratio	6%
SHOOTING	
Shots on target inside box	10
Shots on target outside box	6
Shooting accuracy	46%
PASSING	
Goal assists	0
Key passes	6
Passing accuracy in opp half	70%
DISCIPLINE	
Fouls committed	13
Fouls won	17
Offside	6
Yellow cards	0
Red cards	0

SEE PAGE 206 FOR FULL STATS

M

Paul GASCOIGNE • 8

MIDDLESBROUGH • BORN: 27.5.67

APPEARANCES	
Start (sub)	7(1)
Minutes on pitch	516
GOAL ATTEMPTS	
Goals	1
Shots on target	1
Shooting accuracy	25%
PASSING & CROSSING	
Goal assists	1
Passes in opp half	152
Passing accuracy in opp half	73%
Successful crosses	9
Cross completion	36%
DEFENDING	
Interceptions	7
Clearances	7
Tackles	27
Tackles won %	44%
DISCIPLINE	
Fouls	7
Yellow cards	1
Red cards	1

SEE PAGE 192 FOR FULL STATS

It was a poor season for Paul Gascoigne, with just seven starts to his name during 1999–2000. Gazza's lack of first-team action was exacerbated by a dismissal against Chelsea for swearing at the referee's assistant and a self-inflicted injury sustained in Boro's 4–0 loss against Villa in February.

The creative genius's elbow on the Villans' George Boateng resulted in a broken bone for the former Spurs star along with a shattered season. Gazza's proneness to injury – especially when caused by his often overly-zealous approach to the game he so loves – has undoubtedly stunted what could have been a world-beating career.

Now at the age of 33, Gascoigne is reaching the end of his playing days. In his brief time in a Middlesbrough shirt in 1999–2000, the Newcastle-born maestro scored just one goal – against Southampton – which was his only shot on target all season. Gazza did show small glimpses of his talent, finding a team-mate in the opposition's half with a solid 73% of his distribution.

nidfield than any other side in the Premiership

Diego GAVILAN • 8

NEWCASTLE UNITED • BORN: 1.3.80

Young South American Diego Gavilan was bought by Bobby Robson in January for £2 million and he has impressed in his limited time in a Newcastle shirt.

Employed on the right wing, Gavilan scored his first-ever goal for the Toon Army in their 2–0 win over Coventry on 29 April. Overlapping the front two on a breakaway, the Portuguese player displayed a cool head to slot the ball past Magnus Hedman in the Sky Blues' goal.

Although that strike was one of only two efforts on goal from Gavilan, the talented youngster did show a willingness to take on defenders and displayed a good touch, not uncommon with South American footballers. United's attacking midfielder successfully found his team-mates with 72% of his short passes.

Opportunities in Bobby Robson's side were limited, but this starlet definitely looks one for the future. If the Magpies are to have a more successful Premiership campaign in 2000–01, then young players such as Gavilan could be key to the former England boss's plans.

APPEARANCES	
Start (sub)	2(4)
Minutes on pitch	211
GOAL ATTEMPTS	
Goals	1
Shots on target	2
Shooting accuracy	100%
Goals/shots ratio	50%
PASSING	
Goal assists	0
Passes in opp half	61
Passing accuracy in opp half	62%
Successful crosses	6
Crossing accuracy	33%
DRIBBLING	
Dribbles & runs	9
Dribble completion	67%
Corners forced	2
DISCIPLINE	
Fouls	2
Yellow cards	0
Red cards	0

SEE PAGE 206 FOR FULL STATS

Jason GAVIN • 29

MIDDLESBROUGH • BORN: 14.3.80

APPEARANCES	
Start (sub)	2(4)
Minutes on pitch	342
GOAL ATTEMPTS	
Goals	0
DEFENDING	
Blocks	16
Shots cleared off line	0
Headed clearances	29
Other clearances	27
Interceptions	1
Last man saving tackles	1
Tackles won	7
Tackles won %	47%
PASSING	
Passing accuracy own half	85%
Passing accuracy opp half	72%
DISCIPLINE	
Fouls	2
Fouls in danger area	1
Yellow cards	0
Red cards	0

SEE PAGE 192 FOR FULL STATS

Youngster Jason Gavin is being touted as prodigious talent and already has bags experience at under-21 level with his nativ Republic of Ireland. But first-team chances f the Dubliner were limited during th 1999–2000 campaign and it looks as if Gavi will have to be patient.

Graduating from the Boro trainee system i 1997, the central defender turned in som impressive performances when Bryan Robso called upon his services. Unfortunately f Gavin, he was involved in Middlesbrough' biggest defeat of the season, a 5–1 reverse a Highbury against Arsenal, and looked a littl out of his depth trying to halt the world-clas pairing of Kanu and Dennis Bergkamp.

That match aside, the precocious defende looked reasonably solid at the back, winnin nearly 50% of his attempted tackles an making more than 70 important defensiv clearances, blocks and interceptions. The fac that Gavin was called into making one last man challenge demonstrates the young man' awareness in so little playing time.

Marcus GAYLE • 11

WIMBLEDON • BORN: 27.9.70

amaican international Marcus Gayle's enchant for grabbing vital goals could not top Wimbledon dropping out of the remiership at the end of a disastrous 999–2000 campaign.

The experienced striker-cum-midfielder vice doubled Wimbledon leads to see off eeds United and Newcastle at Selhurst Park, ut his lack of scoring in the final quarter of ne campaign was indicative of the Dons' ltimate demise as they plunged into the ationwide Football League.

All in all, Gayle's tally of seven strikes esulted in the Hammersmith-born star being ew boss Terry Burton's third-highest scorer ehind forward pair John Hartson and Carl Cort.

The former Brentford attacker also displayed ne many facets to his game in what was a oubled season for the Dons. Gayle created ine goalscoring chances for his team-mates hile the 29-year old also tracked back to ood effect, winning 50% of his challenges nd completing more than 50 clearances and terceptions for his beleagured defenders.

APPEARANCES	
Start (sub)	35(1)
Minutes on pitch	3045
GOAL ATTEMPTS	
Goals inside box	5
Goals outside box	2
Minutes per goal scored	435.0
Goals/shots ratio	11%
SHOOTING	
Shots on target inside box	17
Shots on target outside box	8
Shooting accuracy	40%
PASSING	
Goal assists	4
Key passes	5
Passing accuracy in opp half	54%
DISCIPLINE	
Fouls committed	34
Fouls won	18
Offside	20
Yellow cards	2
Red cards	0

SEE PAGE 305 FOR FULL STATS

Scott GEMMILL • 11

EVERTON • BORN: 2.1.71

APPEARANCES	
Start (sub)	6(8)
Minutes on pitch	626
GOAL ATTEMPTS	
Goals	1
Shots on target	1
Shooting accuracy	50%
PASSING & CROSSING	
Goal assists	0
Passes in opp half	175
Passing accuracy in opp half	71%
Successful crosses	4
Cross completion	80%
DEFENDING	
Interceptions	8
Clearances	11
Tackles	20
Tackles won %	40%
DISCIPLINE	
Fouls	8
Yellow cards	1
Red cards	0

SEE PAGE 122 FOR FULL STATS

Everton bought Scottish international Scott Gemmill from Nottingham Forest back in March 1999 for a cut-price £250,000 and, although the midfield maestro only played just over 600 minutes of Premiership football during the 1999–2000 season, he did show glimpses of the talent that interested the Toffees' boss Walter Smith in the first place.

He is certainly not known for his tenacity – Forest fans used to nickname him "Mavis" – but he has proved to be a real box-to-box runner throughout his career and this, combined with his natural talent on the ball, resulted in the Scot starting for Everton at the beginning of the 1999–2000 campaign. But an injury sustained in Everton's 4–4 draw with Leeds essentially ended his season prematurely, to the disappointment of the Goodison Park faithful.

The Paisley-born midfielder scored his one and only goal of the season against strugglers Sheffield Wednesday back in September but had little opportunity to build on his modest scoring record for Forest.

Paul GERRARD • 13

EVERTON • BORN: 22.1.73

One man's misfortune is often another's opportunity and so it proved when 1998–99 ever-present Thomas Myrhe broke his leg. It proved to be a lucky break for Paul Gerrard, who had previously struggled to make an impression at first-team level at Goodison Park.

The former Oldham shot-stopper made 138 saves in the Premiership, 90 of which were from shots inside his own penalty area, displaying the erstwhile England under-21 'keeper's excellent reactions.

But despite notching up a total of nine clean sheets through Everton's mediocre season, Gerrard did experience a few nightmare matches. Most notably, the 27-year-old could not stop Leeds and Arsenal both scoring four goals in successive clashes with the Toffees or, indeed, Champions Manchester United thumping five past them at Old Trafford.

Gerrard did show worrying signs of susceptibility in the air by dropping eight crosses, but it is a testament to his promise that he established himself as the Everton number one.

APPEARANCES	
Start (sub)	34(0)
Minutes on pitch	2977
SHOT STOPPING	
Goals conceded (inside box)	37
Goals conceded (outside box)	8
Minutes per goal conceded	66.2
Clean sheets	9
Saves (shots inside box)	90
Saves (shots outside box)	48
Saves/shots	75%
DISTRIBUTION	
Long kick %	38%
Throws/short passes %	82%
CATCHING	
Crosses caught	54
Crosses punched	11
Crosses dropped	8
Catch success %	87%
DISCIPLINE	
Yellow cards	3
Red cards	0

SEE PAGE 122 FOR FULL STATS

Steven GERRARD • 28

LIVERPOOL • BORN: 30.5.80

APPEARANCES	
Start (sub)	26(3)
Minutes on pitch	2151
GOAL ATTEMPTS	
Goals	1
Shots on target	10
Shooting accuracy	33%
PASSING & CROSSING	
Goal assists	3
Passes in opp half	735
Passing accuracy in opp half	65%
Successful crosses	12
Cross completion	32%
DEFENDING	
Interceptions	35
Clearances	54
Tackles	114
Tackles won %	53%
DISCIPLINE	
Fouls	38
Yellow cards	5
Red cards	1

SEE PAGE 164 FOR FULL STATS

As another exponent of Liverpool's successf youth system, Steven Gerrard broke into t Reds' starting line-up during the 1999–20 season to join fellow youngsters Jam Carragher and David Thompson.

In a season with more highs than lows f the Reds, Gerrard featured prominently in t Liverpool midfield, linking up efficiently wi the frontmen and tackling tenaciously in t middle of the park. The 20-year-old al netted his first and only goal for the club wi a sublime effort against Sheffield Wednesda

In keeping with the Liverpool ethos, t Huyton-born star displayed great composu on the ball, retaining possession with decent 70% of his 70 dribbles and runs a creating 11 goalscoring chances. Certain Gerrard's hard work impressed the Reds' bo Gerard Houllier, earning the former Engla youth international 26 league starts duri the 1999–2000 campaign.

Gerrard ended 1999–2000 by earning a ca up to Kevin Keegan's Euro 2000 squad a should prove a fixture for years to come.

71% Paul Gerrard's saves-to-shots ratio from efforts struc

Najwan GHRAYIB • 20

ASTON VILLA • BORN: 30.1.74

he Israeli international found first-team hances limited during Villa's 1999–2000 ampaign, but Najwan Ghrayib did make his full ebut three games before the conclusion of the remiership season, playing 87 minutes in the 'illans' 1–1 draw with Sunderland at Villa Park.

Ghrayib cost John Gregory £1.5 million to empt him away from Hapoel Haifa, but ecause of the fine form of left-back Alan Vright the diminutive defender has spent a arge amount of time studying the woodgrain n a variety of substitutes' benches.

However, he did impress in his brief ppearances, coming out with the ball in half f his challenges and completing 11 defensive learances, blocks and interceptions.

Ghrayib nearly signed for Spurs before the tart of the season, but perhaps the fact that 'illa reached the FA Cup final suggests the sraeli made the right decision to move to the Vest Midlands.

Certainly, Gregory has demonstrated an astute urchasing ability in the past and the Nazareth-orn player should prove no exception.

APPEARANCES	
Start (sub)	1(4)
Minutes on pitch	173
GOAL ATTEMPTS	
Goals	0
PASSING & CROSSING	
Goal assists	0
Passing	59
Passing accuracy	61%
Crosses	8
Crossing accuracy	25%
DEFENDING	
Tackles	4
Tackles won %	50%
Blocks	6
Interceptions	1
Clearances	4
Shots cleared off line	0
DISCIPLINE	
Fouls	5
Yellow cards	0
Red cards	0

SEE PAGE 52 FOR FULL STATS

G

FB

Nigel GIBBS • 16

WATFORD • BORN: 20.11.65

APPEARANCES	
Start (sub)	11(6)
Minutes on pitch	1112
GOAL ATTEMPTS	
Goals	0
PASSING & CROSSING	
Goal assists	1
Passing	362
Passing accuracy	60%
Crosses	33
Crossing accuracy	21%
DEFENDING	
Tackles	36
Tackles won%	61%
Blocks	21
Interceptions	6
Clearances	60
Shots cleared off line	0
DISCIPLINE	
Fouls	7
Yellow cards	0
Red cards	0

SEE PAGE 276 FOR FULL STATS

Veteran Watford stalwart Nigel Gibbs could not have expected to play much of a part in the Hornets' return to the top flight, but a combination of the 34-year-old's reliability and the poor form of fellow right-back Des Lyttle resulted in Gibbs playing more than 1,000 minutes of football during 1999–2000.

It was the St Albans-born defender's 15th season of senior appearances for the Hornets and his first venture back into the fray ended in arguably Watford's most impressive performance of the campaign, a 1–0 win over Chelsea at Vicarage Road. But it did not help Graham Taylor's men avoid the drop.

The erstwhile England manager's mid-season purchase of Neil Cox from Bolton may not augur well for Gibbs's first-team opportunities in 2000–01, but the experienced player certainly turned in solid displays in his 11 starts. Strong in the tackle, the former England under-21 international won an impressive 61% of his attempted challenges and only lost the ball on one occasion when embarking on a dribble or run from the back.

inside the box was the highest of all first-choice 'keepers

Ryan GIGGS • 11

MANCHESTER UNITED • BORN: 29.11.73

Welsh international Ryan Giggs once again had a stunning campaign in a Manchester United shirt as they strolled to their second successive Premiership title and the sixth in eight seasons.

Haring down the left flank, Giggs has tortured top-flight defenders for many seasons now and the Cardiff-born winger whipped in more than 130 during 1999–2000. His crossing accuracy also vastly improved, from 1998–99's wayward 14% to a more respectable 28% completion rate.

The 26-year-old's natural skill on the ball and pace were a constant threat to oppositions' defences and the fact that only three other Premiership players made more successful runs and dribbles epitomises Giggs's value to the Champions of England.

He scored six times, set up double that number and shocked the world of football by turning out in a friendly for Wales against Finland in March 2000 – his first non-competitive fixture, despite having made 24 previous international appearances.

APPEARANCES	
Start (sub)	30(0)
Minutes on pitch	2496
GOAL ATTEMPTS	
Goals	6
Shots on target	20
Shooting accuracy	42%
Goals/shots ratio	13%
PASSING	
Goal assists	12
Passes in opp half	854
Passing accuracy in opp half	63%
Successful crosses	42
Crossing accuracy	28%
DRIBBLING	
Dribbles & runs	222
Dribble completion	68%
Corners forced	37
DISCIPLINE	
Fouls	12
Yellow cards	2
Red cards	0

SEE PAGE 178 FOR FULL STATS

CB

Phil GILCHRIST • 15

LEICESTER CITY • BORN: 25.8.73

APPEARANCES	
Start (sub)	17(10)
Minutes on pitch	1658
GOAL ATTEMPTS	
Goals	1
DEFENDING	
Blocks	44
Shots cleared off line	1
Headed clearances	109
Other clearances	59
Interceptions	12
Last man saving tackles	0
Tackles won	19
Tackles won %	34%
PASSING	
Passing accuracy own half	65%
Passing accuracy opp half	59%
DISCIPLINE	
Fouls	13
Fouls in danger area	4
Yellow cards	0
Red cards	0

SEE PAGE 150 FOR FULL STATS

Ex-Nottingham Forest junior Phil Gilchrist spe many an afternoon at the City Ground cleanin ex-Leicester legend Garry Parker's boots.

But considering Emile Heskey and Le Hendrie also buffed Parker's footwear to radiant shine in their formative year Gilchrist is in good company.

The ex-Oxford man started most of th 1999–2000 campaign in central defence fo Leicester after only being used sporadicall the previous season. He epitomised the hard working ethos of Martin O'Neill's side and th 5'11" player has already been rewarded with League Cup winner's medal and the chance play in the UEFA Cup.

The City centre-back earned his place with combination of pace and stoicism that wer down well at Filbert Street. In addition to th fact that Gilchrist completed more than 20 defensive clearances and blocks, he only los possession on one occasion when bringing th ball out from defence.

He also popped up in attack to head home the Foxes' excellent 2–0 win over Liverpool.

AM David GINOLA • 14

TOTTENHAM HOTSPUR • BORN: 25.1.67

purs' French superstar David Ginola once gain mesmerised Premiership defenders with is unique brand of skill and precision.

The Frenchman signed a lucrative new ontract with Spurs, presumably because George raham agreed with Ginola's reasons for hoosing his shampoo – "Because I'm worth it!"

But critics point out that the former ewcastle master-improviser was substituted y George Graham on no fewer than 17 ccasions during the 1999–2000 season, ieaning that all is not well at White Hart Lane.

Either way, Ginola started nearly every game or Tottenham and the sight of the 1998–1999 ootball Writers and PFA Player of the Year linking past defenders is still a joy to behold.

Ginola embarked on more dribbles and runs han any other top-flight player in 999–2000, successfully retaining possession n an amazing 70% of his 415 jaunts.

His attack-minded play also resulted in 28 hots on target, although the 33-year-old will e disappointed that his seasonal tally did not mount to more than three strikes.

APPEARANCES	
Start (sub)	36(0)
Minutes on pitch	2880
GOAL ATTEMPTS	
Goals	3
Shots on target	28
Shooting accuracy	39%
Goals/shots ratio	4%
PASSING	
Goal assists	8
Passes in opp half	951
Passing accuracy in opp half	64%
Successful crosses	70
Crossing accuracy	31%
DRIBBLING	
Dribbles & runs	415
Dribble completion	70%
Corners forced	46
DISCIPLINE	
Fouls	32
Yellow cards	3
Red cards	0

SEE PAGE 263 FOR FULL STATS

G Shay GIVEN • 1

NEWCASTLE UNITED • BORN: 24.4.76

APPEARANCES	
Start (sub)	14(0)
Minutes on pitch	1260
SHOT STOPPING	
Goals conceded (inside box)	12
Goals conceded (outside box)	5
Minutes per goal conceded	74.1
Clean sheets	6
Saves (shots inside box)	23
Saves (shots outside box)	11
Saves/shots	67%
DISTRIBUTION	
Long kick %	56%
Throws/short passes %	88%
CATCHING	
Crosses caught	22
Crosses punched	10
Crosses dropped	0
Catch success %	100%
DISCIPLINE	
Yellow cards	0
Red cards	0

SEE PAGE 206 FOR FULL STATS

Sharing the goalkeeping duties with Steve Harper, Newcastle's Shay Given started fewer than half of the Magpies' matches in the 1999–2000 season, but he did finish the campaign as Bobby Robson's first choice for the Toon Army's number one spot.

The Republic of Ireland international shot-stopper has experienced mixed fortunes since joining United from Blackburn back in 1997, but coped well with the divided 'keeping duties. The likeable Irishman racked up six clean sheets in his limited starts, making more than 30 saves, and did not spill one of the 32 crosses he attempted to claim.

Newcastle did concede at a rate of just over a strike per game when Given was between the sticks and the 24-year-old would want to improve the fact that he was beaten by 33% of shots on the Magpies' goal.

But a run in the team at the start of the 2000–01 season could be enough to prove to Robson that Given is the undisputed number one in the Magpies' goalkeeping pecking order at St James's Park.

Stephen GLASS • 17

NEWCASTLE UNITED • 23.5.76

In a 1999–2000 season hit by injury, young Stephen Glass only made one start for the Magpies, and the Toon Army will be keen to see this prodigious talent running around in a black and white shirt more often in the 2000–01 campaign.

Glass's forward thinking resulted in the former Aberdeen star arriving in the penalty area just five minutes into his only start of the season, when Spurs visited St James's Park back in November last year. The youngster's glancing header beat Ian Walker in the Tottenham goal to register Glass's one and only striking contribution in the 1999–2000 campaign.

Aside from several substitute appearances, Glass remained frustrated in the Newcastle wings and eventually racked up just under 180 minutes of game-play time. But when on the pitch the Scottish international displayed a real enthusiasm, although he will need to brush up on his passing.

Glass is certainly a player for the future and the fee of £650,000 should still turn out to be a real bargain.

APPEARANCES	
Start (sub)	1(6)
Minutes on pitch	179
GOAL ATTEMPTS	
Goals	1
Shots on target	2
Shooting accuracy	50%
Goals/shots ratio	25%
PASSING	
Goal assists	0
Passes in opp half	30
Passing accuracy in opp half	53%
Successful crosses	1
Crossing accuracy	13%
DRIBBLING	
Dribbles & runs	12
Dribble completion	67%
Corners forced	2
DISCIPLINE	
Fouls	0
Yellow cards	0
Red cards	0

SEE PAGE 206 FOR FULL STATS

Bjarne GOLDBAEK • 12

CHELSEA • BORN: 6.10.68

APPEARANCES	
Start (sub)	2(4)
Minutes on pitch	293
GOAL ATTEMPTS	
Goals	0
Shots on target	4
Shooting accuracy	44%
Goals/shots ratio	0%
PASSING	
Goal assists	0
Passes in opp half	88
Passing accuracy in opp half	78%
Successful crosses	1
Crossing accuracy	9%
DRIBBLING	
Dribbles & runs	14
Dribble completion	93%
Corners forced	5
DISCIPLINE	
Fouls	3
Yellow cards	0
Red cards	0

SEE PAGE 80 FOR FULL STATS

Denmark international Bjarne Goldbaek' 1999–2000 season in the Premiership laste just 293 minutes.

He was all set to sign for Nottingham Fores in August, but Goldbaek's wife was keen t stay in London and the midfielder signed fo Chelsea's neighbours Fulham.

Goldbaek only started two Premiership game for Chelsea, losing 1–0 to Watford in Septembe in one of them. The Dane was substituted o 61 minutes.

The much-travelled player did once agai look promising in a Blues shirt at the start o the 1999–2000 season with his exceller control and willingness to run at defenders o the right wing. Indeed, Goldbaek retaine possession in an impressive 93% of hi attempted runs and dribbles and was willin to take a pot-shot at goal by striking seve efforts from outside the box.

The lack of first-team football proved to frustrating for Goldbaek at Chelsea and h rewarded his new club, Fulham, by notchin three goals in Nationwide Division One.

32 Newcastle fielded more

Alain GOMA • 5

NEWCASTLE UNITED • BORN: 5.10.72

ought by erstwhile Newcastle manager Ruud ullit, Alain Goma found life tough at St ames's Park and made just 14 starts during ne 1999–2000 season.

Goma started the first 10 games of ewcastle's 1999–2000 campaign. nfortunately for the former PSG star, the lagpies' Premiership season got off to a errible start as the Toon Army conceded 23 oals. The Sault-born defender only took the eld on four more occasions under Bobby obson and it was injury that stopped the rench international showing more of his ndoubted natural ability.

Playing in the shadow of Marcel Desailly, aurent Blanc and Frank Leboeuf, Goma would urely have given his international career a oost if he had more time on the pitch, but he brief glimpses of the defender suggested he price-tag of £4.75 million was not as verblown as many critics claimed.

Goma proved to be tough in the tackle, vinning an excellent 68% of his challenges, nd completed 128 clearances.

APPEARANCES	
Start (sub)	14(0)
Minutes on pitch	1197
GOAL ATTEMPTS	
Goals	0
DEFENDING	
Blocks	14
Shots cleared off line	1
Headed clearances	85
Other clearances	43
Interceptions	11
Last man saving tackles	0
Tackles won	26
Tackles won %	68%
PASSING	
Passing accuracy own half	85%
Passing accuracy opp half	66%
DISCIPLINE	
Fouls	28
Fouls in danger area	10
Yellow cards	5
Red cards	0

SEE PAGE 206 FOR FULL STATS

G

Tommy GOODWIN • 38

LEICESTER CITY • BORN: 8.11.79

ocal lad Tommy Goodwin discovered that ife in the Premiership can be extremely rustrating, but also that patience pays off vhen he was finally given his senior debut n Leicester's 3–1 home defeat against West lam United.

The young defender played the entire 90 ninutes against the Hammers at Filbert Street fter making his first appearance on the ubstitutes' bench three days previously. lthough the Foxes lost the game, Goodwin lisplayed some of the talent that saw him raduate through the youth system.

Goodwin came out with the ball in two of is three challenges, while showing enough omposure to find a fellow-Fox with 83% of is short passes.

Unfortunately for Goodwin he did not get ny more opportunities to impress Martin 'Neill but, with time on his side, he could ecome a more regular fixture in the Foxes' ine-up under a new regime.

SEE PAGE 150 FOR FULL STATS

Tough tackler: Alain Goma

layers than any other side

Dean GORDON • 3

MIDDLESBROUGH • BORN: 10.2.73

Signed by Bryan Robson for £900,000, Gordon was one of only eight Premiership players to feature in every single minute of the 1998-1999 season and the value of the player to Boro was underlined when the former Eagle was named the supporters' Player of the Year. Unfortunately for the England left-back contender, injury ruined 1999–2000.

A cruciate ligament injury against Derby County in August put paid to Dean Gordon's season and Middlesbrough have certainly missed the wholehearted effort consistently put in by their full-back.

Gordon displayed his tenacious tackling ability and made 11 challenges, coming out on top in 55% of them. The Croydon-born defender also demonstrated his forward-thinking nature by tearing up the wing to whip in six crosses, while also firing in a couple of shots from distance to boot.

Despite an outing as a substitute in March at The Dell, further minor surgery on some debris in Gordon's cartilage meant that he finished with just a handful of appearances.

APPEARANCES	
Start (sub)	3(1)
Minutes on pitch	312
GOAL ATTEMPTS	
Goals	0
PASSING & CROSSING	
Goal assists	0
Passing	116
Passing accuracy	70%
Crosses	6
Crossing accuracy	17%
DEFENDING	
Tackles	11
Tackles won %	55%
Blocks	5
Interceptions	6
Clearances	39
Shots cleared off line	0
DISCIPLINE	
Fouls	4
Yellow cards	1
Red cards	0

SEE PAGE 192 FOR FULL STATS

CB

Richard GOUGH • 4

EVERTON • BORN: 5.4.62

APPEARANCES	
Start (sub)	29(0)
Minutes on pitch	2582
GOAL ATTEMPTS	
Goals	1
DEFENDING	
Blocks	60
Shots cleared off line	1
Headed clearances	284
Other clearances	68
Interceptions	30
Last man saving tackles	2
Tackles won	48
Tackles won %	68%
PASSING	
Passing accuracy own half	83%
Passing accuracy opp half	61%
DISCIPLINE	
Fouls	41
Fouls in danger area	16
Yellow cards	3
Red cards	0

SEE PAGE 122 FOR FULL STATS

Everton's purchase of Richard Gough naturall raised a few eyebrows. Nonetheless, the 38 year-old defender has impressed considerabl at Goodison Park and appears to have los none of the stalwart qualities that earned hi more than 60 international caps in a illustrious career.

Gough picked up a record nine Scottis Premier League Championship medals wit Glasgow Rangers and his stoic performances a the back for the Toffees were rewarded wit several Man of the Match awards during th 1999–2000 season. Ironically, the Sweden born centre-back missed out on the accolac of being the Premiership's oldest outfiel player because his team-mate Dave Watso was born five months earlier than him.

Gough performed with aplomb, completin 284 headed clearances – the eighth-highes number in the Premiership. In addition, th Scot won an impressive 68% of his challenge and only picked up three bookings, provin that experience is a valuable commodity i the top flight.

S Gareth GRANT • 24

BRADFORD CITY • BORN: 6.9.80

'oungster Gareth Grant did feature in Paul
'ewell's plans in Nationwide Division One at
he start of the 1998–1999 season, but only
nade one appearance as a substitute in the
'remiership, which came as a surprise to many
ıt Valley Parade.

This precocious striker entered the field with
.8 minutes left against Watford back in
August 1999, but failed to make an impact
ınd could not muster a shot on goal.
Jnfortunately, that was the end of Grant's
irst-team opportunities.

He was loaned out to both Halifax Town and
3olton Wanderers during 1999, but failed to
ick up any first-team experience at either.
3ut Bradford's Premiership survival was good
ıews to everyone at the club, and given that
he pacy forward was a prodigious scorer at
oth youth and reserve level at Valley Parade,
he 2000–01 season promises to hold a
righter future for him if he can impress the
ıew boss sufficiently.

SEE PAGE 66 FOR FULL STATS

M Tony GRANT • 24

EVERTON • BORN: 14.11.74

Manchester City boss Joe Royle made the purchase of Tony Grant an early Christmas present for supporters of the Citizens when he signed him on Christmas Eve 1999.

Grant, who had played only 23 minutes for Everton, had just experienced playing in the glamour surroundings of Old Trafford but, along with his team-mates, returned to Merseyside red-faced after Manchester United had dished out a 5–1 hiding.

Royle splashed out £450,000 on the midfielder, who he claimed was a "rare commodity in modern football, who could give the team more direction." However, things did not turn out quite as Grant would have wished as he struggled to hold down a first team place at Maine Road.

More often than not, the former England under-21 international was used as a substitute, but he will be glad to have played a small part in getting the Manchester club back into the Premiership.

SEE PAGE 122 FOR FULL STATS

G

S Xavier GRAVELAINE • 21

WATFORD • BORN: 5.10.68

APPEARANCES	
Start (sub)	7(0)
Minutes on pitch	617
GOAL ATTEMPTS	
Goals inside box	1
Goals outside box	1
Minutes per goal scored	308.5
Goals/shots ratio	22%
SHOOTING	
Shots on target inside box	3
Shots on target outside box	3
Shooting accuracy	67%
PASSING	
Goal assists	2
Key passes	1
Passing accuracy in opp half	52%
DISCIPLINE	
Fouls committed	10
Fouls won	7
Offside	15
Yellow cards	1
Red cards	1

SEE PAGE 276 FOR FULL STATS

Watford will consider the sale of Xavier Gravelaine as good business after his brief two-month spell in Hertfordshire. He joined the Hornets on a free transfer in November 1999 from Paris St Germain where he helped the French giants win the title, but in January 2000 he left to join Le Havre in a £300,000 deal.

His brief sojourn at Vicarage Road was certainly eventful, with him being sent off in only his second game with the club. His late challenge on Darren Williams saw him shown the red card against Sunderland.

While this was probably the lowest point of his brief career at Watford, he made up for it with a two-goal salvo, which disposed of Southampton at Vicarage Road.

Soon after, though, a homesick and unhappy Gravelaine returned to his native France. His two goals came from only nine shots in England, but the Frenchman contributed to Watford's cause with two further assists.

Watford invested some of the money they received for Gravelaine in the purchase of record signing Heidar Helguson.

Julian GRAY • 38

ARSENAL • BORN: 21.9.79

Julian Gray tasted Premiership action for the first time in the final league game of the season against Newcastle United. The promising midfielder was a substitute for Nwankwo Kanu, as Arsene Wenger rested his key players only days before the UEFA Cup final against Galatasaray.

Gray was given a 19-minute run-out by the Gunners boss, but his form for the reserve side in 1999–2000 would suggest he could follow in the footsteps of David Rocastle, Michael Thomas and Ray Parlour as a midfield graduate of the Arsenal youth academy.

In 1998, Gray scored both goals as the junior Gunners beat QPR in the final of the Southern Junior Floodlit Cup. Since then, he has gone on to break into the reserve team, but with the likes of Patrick Vieira, Emmanuel Petit, Ray Parlour and Marc Overmars in front of him, he still has some way to go to break into the first team.

SEE PAGE 38 FOR FULL STATS

Wayne GRAY • 32

WIMBLEDON • BORN: 7.11.80

Many at Selhurst Park have high hopes of Wayne Gray as this pacy young striker is another promising prospect to roll off the Wimbledon production line.

Gray only managed 10 minutes of first-team action for the Dons as a substitute in the 2–0 defeat to Coventry City at Highfield Road, but he made his full Dons debut in their embarrassing 3–0 FA Cup defeat against Fulham at Craven Cottage.

With Wimbledon embroiled in a desperate relegation battle, the timing was never really right to give Gray a run out in the first XI, but in an attempt to increase his first-team experience, he spent some time on loan at Swindon Town.

In eight starts for the Wiltshire club, Gray notched two goals, and the former schoolboy sprint champion will be hoping for more of a chance in 2000–01 as the Dons attempt to bounce straight back into the Premiership at the first attempt.

SEE PAGE 305 FOR FULL STATS

Michael GRAY • 3

SUNDERLAND • BORN: 3.8.74

Michael Gray enjoyed a good 1999–20(campaign, and may feel slightly aggrieved n to have been included in Kevin Keegan's squa for Euro 2000.

The national team's lack of left-sided playe is well-documented, and after becoming th first Sunderland player for 23 years t represent England, the attacking full-ba may be disappointed at missing out.

Gray supplied a string of dangerous crosses f Sunderland's dynamic duo of Kevin Phillips ar Niall Quinn, and assisted in four of Sunderland goals that saw the Mackems end the season a respectable seventh place.

Thirty per cent of the Sunderland-born ful back's crosses found a team-mate, but h forward forays occasionally left him vulnerab defensively and he will be looking to impro his tackle success rate of just 34%. Despite th lamentable statistic, he achieved a supe disciplinary record, committing just 22 fou and not being booked once.

Gray is the only current Sunderland play who featured in Peter Reid's first game charge of the Mackems more than four yea ago, and following Kevin Ball's departure t Fulham, the 26-year-old is now the longes serving player at the Stadium of Light.

APPEARANCES	
Start (sub)	32(1)
Minutes on pitch	2678
GOAL ATTEMPTS	
Goals	0
PASSING & CROSSING	
Goal assists	4
Passing	1416
Passing accuracy	69%
Crosses	122
Crossing accuracy	30%
DEFENDING	
Tackles	77
Tackles won %	34%
Blocks	24
Interceptions	19
Clearances	121
Shots cleared off line	1
DISCIPLINE	
Fouls	22
Yellow cards	0
Red cards	0

SEE PAGE 248 FOR FULL STATS

34% Michael Gray's tackle success rate was the lowest o

AM Jonathan GREENING • 34

MANCHESTER UNITED • BORN: 2.1.79

›espite a string of impressive displays for the Jnited reserve side, including a four-goal salvo ıgainst Marine, Jonathan Greening is still vaiting to be given a fair crack in the first team.

Comfortable either as a striker or on the ight wing, it is easy to see why his chances ıt Old Trafford are limited with the likes of 'orke, Cole, Solskjaer, Sheringham and 3eckham in front of him.

As a result, the former York City player nitially turned down United's offer of a new ontract and was placed on the transfer list. 3ut following a rare start at Watford, Greening lecided to put pen to paper on a new deal.

Greening, whose appearance and style of ılay is reminiscent of Real Madrid's Champions .eague-winning winger Steve McManaman, nade a strong impression on United legend Eric Cantona when he returned for a estimonial and, after solving his contractual lifferences, Greening may feature more often 'or the Red Devils.

SEE PAGE 178 FOR FULL STATS

FB Andy GRIFFIN • 12

NEWCASTLE UNITED • BORN: 17.3.79

After a promising first season at Newcastle United that saw him start the 1999 FA Cup Final and pushing for a regular full-back slot, for the most part 1999–2000 was a frustrating campaign for the former Stoke City man Andy Griffin.

Injury followed injury for the England under-21 international, but he rounded off his disappointing season by scoring the fourth in the Geordies' 4–2 win over Arsenal on the final day of the season. When fit, he has shown his capabilities, and even in his brief outings in 1999–2000 he completed an excellent 86% of the 58 passes he attempted.

Not only has he been plagued by injury since joining Newcastle, but the supremely talented youngster also suffered the embarrassment of driving his Porsche Boxster through a railway crossing barrier and into the side of a passing Metro train. "I couldn't see the lights flashing," claimed Griffin. "The sun was too bright!"

SEE PAGE 207 FOR FULL STATS

G

CB Gilles GRIMANDI • 18

ARSENAL • BORN: 11.11.70

APPEARANCES	
Start (sub)	27(1)
Minutes on pitch	2328
GOAL ATTEMPTS	
Goals	2
DEFENDING	
Blocks	32
Shots cleared off line	1
Headed clearances	108
Other clearances	10
Interceptions	18
Last man saving tackles	0
Tackles won	54
Tackles won %	61%
PASSING	
Passing accuracy own half	84%
Passing accuracy opp half	68%
DISCIPLINE	
Fouls	46
Fouls in danger area	13
Yellow cards	8
Red cards	1

SEE PAGE 38 FOR FULL STATS

Gilles Grimandi is another of the French contingent at Highbury, having joined the Gunners from Monaco in June 1997 at the same time as colleague Emmanuel Petit.

He had just won the French Championship with Monaco, and followed that up by winning the Premiership in his first season.

Grimandi, who allegedly learned English by watching cult cartoon *The Simpsons*, is widely regarded as the most improved player at Highbury. He boasted a 76% pass completion rate, while his competitive nature is underlined by the fact that he won 61% of his tackles. The versatile utility player looked equally at home standing in for Petit or Patrick Vieira in midfield or Martin Keown or Tony Adams in central defence.

However, Grimandi faced heartbreak when the Gunners crashed out of the 1999–2000 FA Cup campaign, as Pegguy Arphexad saved his crucial penalty. The hot-headed Frenchman also saw red on two occasions during 1999–2000 – in the north London derby with Spurs, and in a Champions League clash with Barcelona.

all Premiership defenders who played at least 1,500 minutes

Johann GUDMUNDSSON • 20

WATFORD • BORN: 7.12.77

After catching the eye of Hornets boss Graham Taylor during a trial period, Johann Gudmundsson signed for Watford on transfer deadline day in 1998 in an £85,000 deal. The skilful midfielder failed to recapture the form he showed during his trial spell, though, and spent the majority of the season on the bench for the Hornets.

Gudmundsson has been capped at under-21 and full international level for Iceland, but made only one start during the Hornets' spell in the Premiership.

However, following the arrival of Nordin Wooter and a lack of first-team opportunities, the Icelander's days at Vicarage Road would appear to be numbered.

In his first game for Watford, Gudmundsson made a sensational start, scoring both goals in a 2–2 draw against Port Vale at Vicarage Road. His attacking instinct seemed to desert him, though, as these were the only goals he scored in a Watford shirt, and a move away from Hertfordshire may be the only option to get his career back on track.

APPEARANCES	
Start (sub)	1(8)
Minutes on pitch	250
GOAL ATTEMPTS	
Goals	0
Shots on target	1
Shooting accuracy	25%
Goals/shots ratio	0%
PASSING	
Goal assists	0
Passes in opp half	47
Passing accuracy in opp half	57%
Successful crosses	1
Crossing accuracy	50%
DRIBBLING	
Dribbles & runs	10
Dribble completion	60%
Corners forced	2
DISCIPLINE	
Fouls	2
Yellow cards	1
Red cards	0

SEE PAGE 276 FOR FULL STATS

Arnar GUNNLAUGSSON • 13

LEICESTER CITY • BORN: 6.3.73

APPEARANCES	
Start (sub)	2(0)
Minutes on pitch	110
GOAL ATTEMPTS	
Goals inside box	0
Goals outside box	0
Minutes per goal scored	n/a
Goals/shots ratio	0%
SHOOTING	
Shots on target inside box	0
Shots on target outside box	0
Shooting accuracy	0%
PASSING	
Goal assists	0
Key passes	1
Passing accuracy in opp half	72%
DISCIPLINE	
Fouls committed	4
Fouls won	0
Offside	1
Yellow cards	0
Red cards	0

SEE PAGE 150 FOR FULL STATS

Icelandic international Arnar Gunnlaugsso failed to live up to expectations following club-record £2.1 million move from Bolto Wanderers. While with the Trotters, "Arnie earned himself a reputation for scorin spectacular, long-range goals, but he ha failed to recreate that form at Filbert Street.

After making only two starts for the Foxes Gunnlaugsson jumped at the opportunity of loan move, and his spell at Stoke City resulte in the Potters reaching the 1999–2000 play offs. He netted three goals as City won eigh of their last nine league games to claim th final play-off place.

But any aspirations the Icelander had o Wembley were quickly dispelled when th Potters crashed in the semi-finals t Gillingham. He had also earlier missed out o the euphoria of the Foxes' Worthington Cu success over Tranmere Rovers.

Gunnlaugsson's meagre contribution t Leicester's Premiership season contained jus 31 attempted passes at a reasonabl completion rate of 68%.

AM Steve GUPPY • 11

LEICESTER CITY • BORN: 29.3.69

Steve Guppy has proved a bargain since his £950,000 move from Port Vale, and some impressive performances saw him called up to the full England squad.

But despite playing the full 90 minutes in a friendly with Belgium, the former Wycombe Wanderers player failed to make Kevin Keegan's squad for Euro 2000.

Widely regarded as being one of the best crossers in the Premiership, his ability has been compared to that of David Beckham, and as a result many pundits have called for his inclusion at international level to give England some much-needed balance. In season 1998–99 Guppy supplied 255 crosses, with an accuracy of 35%.

His seven assists were the most by any Leicester player over the course of 1999–2000, and the one-time bailiff made just short of 1,000 passes during the course of the campaign. He missed the middle part of the season with a knee injury, but returned in time to supply the goals for Matt Elliott to head the Foxes to Worthington Cup glory at Wembley.

APPEARANCES	
Start (sub)	29(1)
Minutes on pitch	2580
GOAL ATTEMPTS	
Goals	2
Shots on target	5
Shooting accuracy	31%
Goals/shots ratio	13%
PASSING	
Goal assists	7
Passes in opp half	675
Passing accuracy in opp half	58%
Successful crosses	89
Crossing accuracy	35%
DRIBBLING	
Dribbles & runs	114
Dribble completion	72%
Corners forced	25
DISCIPLINE	
Fouls	21
Yellow cards	2
Red cards	0

SEE PAGE 150 FOR FULL STATS

G

Left out: Steve Guppy

Tomas GUSTAFSSON • 32

COVENTRY CITY • BORN: 7.5.73

With City facing an injury crisis, Gordon Strachan signed Swedish international Tomas Gustafsson for £250,000 in December 1999. Thankfully, he had no trouble in understanding broad Scot Strachan, as the City boss is the third Scottish manager with whom the Swede has worked.

Recommended to the Sky Blues boss by Coventry stars Magnus Hedman and Roland Nilsson, Strachan wasted no time in bringing Gustafsson to England from AIK Solna.

After making brief substitute appearances against Arsenal and Derby, the Swede was given his full debut against Manchester United at Old Trafford.

During his short time at Highfield Road Gustafsson made just under 300 passes, and he supplied 13 crosses into opposition penalty boxes, with 38% of them successful.

Equally good in a defensive capacity, he won more than 50% of his challenges.

Coventry is not Gustafsson's first foreign club; indeed, he spent a brief spell in Canada playing for Winnipeg Fury.

APPEARANCES	
Start (sub)	7(3)
Minutes on pitch	636
GOAL ATTEMPTS	
Goals	0
PASSING & CROSSING	
Goal assists	0
Passing	299
Passing accuracy	65%
Crosses	13
Crossing accuracy	38%
DEFENDING	
Tackles	32
Tackles won %	53%
Blocks	5
Interceptions	3
Clearances	15
Shots cleared off line	0
DISCIPLINE	
Fouls	7
Yellow cards	1
Red cards	0

SEE PAGE 94 FOR FULL STATS

Alf-Inge HAALAND • 4

LEEDS UNITED • BORN: 23.11.72

APPEARANCES	
Start (sub)	7(6)
Minutes on pitch	749
GOAL ATTEMPTS	
Goals	0
PASSING & CROSSING	
Goal assists	0
Passing	259
Passing accuracy	64%
Crosses	8
Crossing accuracy	38%
DEFENDING	
Tackles	19
Tackles won %	63%
Blocks	9
Interceptions	2
Clearances	39
Shots cleared off line	0
DISCIPLINE	
Fouls	24
Yellow cards	4
Red cards	0

SEE PAGE 136 FOR FULL STATS

A versatile player who is equally comfortable in defence or midfield, Alfie Haaland was unable to hold down a regular first-team place during the 1999–2000 season. Injury and the emergence of Leeds' young defenders restricted the Norwegian's appearances, but Haaland began to appear more regularly towards the end of the campaign, helping his side to Champions League qualification.

The former Nottingham Forest star will be hoping his tough-tackling skills earn him a more settled place in Joe Royle's side during the 2000–01 season. He was successful with 63% of his challenges during 1999–2000 – 12 percentage points above the seasonal average for a defender – indicating that his physical presence could be a key asset.

The one area of Haaland's game that appeared to let him down was his distribution. He completed only 64% of his passes during 1999–2000 and, if he can improve upon this, he should see himself on the team sheet more often in the future at his new club Manchester City.

47% of Coventry's goals were scored by midfielders,

Moustapha HADJI • 11

COVENTRY CITY • BORN: 16.11.71

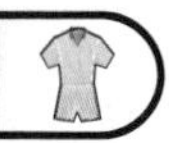

After his outstanding performances during the 1998 World Cup, Moustapha Hadji became one of the hottest African footballers on the market. But he was still unable to hold down a place at Deportivo La Coruna and agreed a move to Highfield Road in the summer of 1999.

And it was certainly an eventful first season in the Premiership, with Hadji's sublime skills terrorising opposing defences. Even a foot injury, which Hadji treated by wearing a steak inside his boot, did not impinge upon his contribution. The lean Moroccan tucked into 52 meaty challenges and only 11 Premiership players embarked upon more dribbles and runs in 1999–2000.

Hadji also beefed up the Sky Blues' attack, setting up seven goals over the campaign – more than any other Coventry player – and scoring six himself. Gordon Strachan certainly has to be commended on his judgement in bringing the two Moroccans to Highfield Road and Sky Blues fans will be delighted that Steak and Chippo will continue to be on the menu in 2000–01.

APPEARANCES	
Start (sub)	33(0)
Minutes on pitch	2871
GOAL ATTEMPTS	
Goals	6
Shots on target	34
Shooting accuracy	44%
Goals/shots ratio	8%
PASSING	
Goal assists	7
Passes in opp half	849
Passing accuracy in opp half	62%
Successful crosses	13
Crossing accuracy	20%
DRIBBLING	
Dribbles & runs	177
Dribble completion	70%
Corners forced	26
DISCIPLINE	
Fouls	41
Yellow cards	5
Red cards	0

SEE PAGE 94 FOR FULL STATS

G H

Paul HALL • 29

COVENTRY CITY • BORN: 3.7.72

Paul Hall's performances in the 1998 World Cup earned him a £300,000 transfer from Portsmouth to Coventry.

But his failure to adapt to the rigours of Premiership football meant that his first-team opportunities at Highfield Road have been limited, and after playing only seven minutes of Premiership football during the 1999–2000 season, the Jamaican international decided to look elsewhere in order to further his career.

After loan spells at Sheffield United and West Brom, Hall switched to Walsall, a move that was made permanent on transfer deadline day. But despite firing four goals in 10 appearances for the Saddlers, he was unable to halt their slide towards the Nationwide Second Division.

But, with his confidence back, the Manchester-born winger can now set his sights on using his pace and dribbling skills to help his new club to bounce right back to Division One.

SEE PAGE 94 FOR FULL STATS

Marcus HALL • 19

COVENTRY CITY • BORN: 24.3.76

A former England under-21 defender, Marcus Hall saw his first-team opportunities blighted by injury in the 1999–2000 season for Coventry City.

But, in the matches he did play, Hall was able to show that he has what it takes to compete at the highest level.

He played 90 minutes for the first time in the 1–0 win over West Ham and remained in the starting line-up for the following six matches, during which time the Sky Blues went on their longest unbeaten run of the 1999–2000 campaign.

Also able to play in midfield, Hall's attacking instincts came to the fore during his brief stint in the first team.

He was successful with 94% of his dribbles and runs, but will need to improve upon his tackle success rate of 44% if he is to displace fellow-England hopeful Steve Froggatt in the Coventry side and fulfil his potential for the Sky Blues in the top flight.

SEE PAGE 94 FOR FULL STATS

the highest ratio in the Premiership

Gunnar HALLE • 18

BRADFORD CITY • BORN: 11.8.65

After signing from Leeds for £200,000 before the 1999–2000 season, Gunnar Halle became one of the key performers in the Bradford side which surprised most people by avoiding relegation in their first Premiership season.

While his most memorable contribution was probably his goal-line clearance from Michael Owen on the last day of the season, Halle was equally dependable throughout the 1999–2000 campaign. A virtual ever-present in the Bantams' starting line-up, he made 106 challenges, 63 blocks and 193 clearances in his team's overworked defence.

Capped 62 times for Norway, Halle has also operated in midfield for both club and country and displayed his versatility for Paul Jewell's side by getting forward whenever the opportunity arose. He whipped in 56 crosses – the joint-third highest total at the club – and set up four vital goals in the Bantams' battle against the drop.

Although Halle is now 35, he will relish the prospect of another season of top-flight football as his career nears its twilight.

APPEARANCES	
Start (sub)	37(1)
Minutes on pitch	3163
GOAL ATTEMPTS	
Goals	0
PASSING & CROSSING	
Goal assists	4
Passing	950
Passing accuracy	62%
Crosses	56
Crossing accuracy	20%
DEFENDING	
Tackles	106
Tackles won %	50%
Blocks	63
Interceptions	26
Clearances	193
Shots cleared off line	3
DISCIPLINE	
Fouls	55
Yellow cards	8
Red cards	0

SEE PAGE 66 FOR FULL STATS

Dietmar HAMANN • 16

LIVERPOOL • BORN: 27.8.73

APPEARANCES	
Start (sub)	27(1)
Minutes on pitch	2251
GOAL ATTEMPTS	
Goals	1
Shots on target	14
Shooting accuracy	34%
PASSING & CROSSING	
Goal assists	2
Passes in opp half	764
Passing accuracy in opp half	74%
Successful crosses	8
Cross completion	35%
DEFENDING	
Interceptions	21
Clearances	22
Tackles	88
Tackles won %	51%
DISCIPLINE	
Fouls	45
Yellow cards	6
Red cards	0

SEE PAGE 164 FOR FULL STATS

After an excellent first campaign in Englan prompted Gerard Houllier to pay £8 million fc him, much was expected of Dietmar Haman at Anfield. He had been the highest-rate player in the Opta Index during the 1998–9 season, with his vision and work-rate shinin through in an average Newcastle side.

Unfortunately, an ankle injury sustained o the opening day of the 1999–2000 seaso meant that the German international did nc complete a full 90 minutes for Liverpool unt November. But upon his return to full fitnes Hamann's accomplished performances i midfield had an instant impact. He attempte 88 challenges, winning more than half, an his protection of Liverpool's back four wa instantly felt. The Reds conceded only 1 goals in the 21 games immediately after hi return and finished with the Premiership tightest defence.

Hamann has yet to score with the regularit that he did at Newcastle. But he will still be key performer for the Reds during 2000–01 a they attempt to mount a title challenge.

Jon HARLEY • 34

CHELSEA • BORN: 26.9.79

After signing for Chelsea in 1997, Jon Harley finally made his mark on the Premiership during the 1999–2000 campaign.

Taking advantage of injuries to Graeme Le Saux and Celestine Babayaro, the former England youth international put in some excellent performances down the left side of Gianluca Vialli's team to establish himself in the first team squad.

Equally comfortable in midfield or defence, the Maidstone-born player clearly benefited from his opportunity to rub shoulders with the Blues' more established players. And as Harley's confidence in himself grew with every game, so his performances became increasingly accomplished.

He embarked upon 77 dribbles and runs and whipped in 52 crosses. But undoubtedly the highlights of his season were the goals he scored against Watford and Leeds, which both clinched wins for Chelsea.

Clearly excited by Harley's performances, Vialli rewarded his protégé with a new long-term contract during the campaign.

APPEARANCES	
Start (sub)	13(4)
Minutes on pitch	1209
GOAL ATTEMPTS	
Goals	2
PASSING & CROSSING	
Goal assists	0
Passing	516
Passing accuracy	59%
Crosses	52
Crossing accuracy	25%
DEFENDING	
Tackles	43
Tackles won %	53%
Blocks	17
Interceptions	14
Clearances	23
Shots cleared off line	0
DISCIPLINE	
Fouls	13
Yellow cards	1
Red cards	0

SEE PAGE 80 FOR FULL STATS

Kevin HARPER • 11

DERBY COUNTY • BORN: 15.1.76

APPEARANCES	
Start (sub)	0(5)
Minutes on pitch	130
GOAL ATTEMPTS	
Goals	0
Shots on target	2
Shooting accuracy	100%
Goals/shots ratio	0%
PASSING	
Goal assists	0
Passes in opp half	41
Passing accuracy in opp half	66%
Successful crosses	3
Crossing accuracy	60%
DRIBBLING	
Dribbles & runs	8
Dribble completion	50%
Corners forced	1
DISCIPLINE	
Fouls	0
Yellow cards	1
Red cards	0

SEE PAGE 109 FOR FULL STATS

After signing from Hibernian in 1998, great things were expected of Kevin Harper at Derby County. But, despite scoring on his debut against Liverpool, the inconsistency of his performances for the Rams led to him being placed on the transfer list at the start of the 1999–2000 campaign.

A loan spell at Walsall followed during which Harper impressed sufficiently to secure a permanent move to Portsmouth before transfer deadline day. And the former Scotland under-21 international appeared to settle in well at Fratton Park, scoring twice in the final 11 games of the campaign as Pompey steered clear of the relegation zone.

A versatile performer, Harper is equally adept on the wing, in midfield or up front, but is clearly at his most dangerous when using his pace to run at the opposition. The Oldham-born player will be hoping he can establish himself as a first team regular at Portsmouth in the 2000–01 campaign but he will need to improve on the modest pass completion rate he recorded for Derby.

Steve HARPER • 13

G

NEWCASTLE UNITED • BORN: 14.3.75

A qualified referee, Steve Harper had spent the majority of his Newcastle career on loan at Nationwide League clubs. But despite interest from several teams, he refused to blow the whistle on his time at St James's Park and was subsequently rewarded with an extended run in the first team.

Although he was in the starting line-up for both of the Magpies' opening two fixtures of 1999–2000, the Easington-born 'keeper paid the price for Newcastle's poor start to the season and was axed by Ruud Gullit.

He returned under Bobby Robson for the morale-boosting 8–0 win over Sheffield Wednesday, and managed to keep a further four clean sheets during his 18 starts. But Harper seemed vulnerable on crosses, catching only 85% of those he went for – eight percentage points worse than the seasonal average for a Premiership 'keeper. He lost his place to Shay Given towards the end of the season, but is highly-rated by Robson and will surely get another chance to establish himself in the 2000–01 campaign.

APPEARANCES	
Start (sub)	18(0)
Minutes on pitch	1620
SHOT STOPPING	
Goals conceded (inside box)	19
Goals conceded (outside box)	3
Minutes per goal conceded	73.6
Clean sheets	5
Saves (shots inside box)	30
Saves (shots outside box)	15
Saves/shots	67%
DISTRIBUTION	
Long kick %	50%
Throws/short passes %	96%
CATCHING	
Crosses caught	23
Crosses punched	9
Crosses dropped	4
Catch success %	85%
DISCIPLINE	
Yellow cards	0
Red cards	0

SEE PAGE 206 FOR FULL STATS

Ian HARTE • 3

FB

LEEDS UNITED • BORN: 31.8.77

APPEARANCES	
Start (sub)	33(0)
Minutes on pitch	2868
GOAL ATTEMPTS	
Goals	6
PASSING & CROSSING	
Goal assists	5
Passing	1517
Passing accuracy	66%
Crosses	181
Crossing accuracy	33%
DEFENDING	
Tackles	67
Tackles won %	36%
Blocks	47
Interceptions	13
Clearances	154
Shots cleared off line	1
DISCIPLINE	
Fouls	33
Yellow cards	7
Red cards	1

SEE PAGE 136 FOR FULL STATS

The 1999–2000 campaign saw Ian Harte enjo his best season in the Premiership yet. Th full-back combined his tough-tackling skill with marauding runs down the left flank which were an integral part of Leeds attacking play as the Whites challenged fo the Championship.

The Republic of Ireland internationa whipped in 181 crosses – the 12th highes total in the top flight – and created five goal for David O'Leary's young guns. But the mai reason that Harte rose to national prominenc was his undeniable talent from set-pieces.

Having established himself as Leeds principal free-kick and penalty taker, th Drogheda-born defender quickly set abou gaining a reputation for his lethal left boot He scored six goals, helping to earn him place in the PFA team of the year, and Hart stands every chance of experiencing succes in O'Leary's exciting young side. But he mus temper his youthful enthusiasm with bette discipline after earning seven yellow card and one red.

7 John Hartson was one of seven player

S John HARTSON • 9

WIMBLEDON • BORN: 5.4.75

Wimbledon's record signing John Hartson looked set for a mid-season move to Spurs in March. But the burly centre-forward failed his medical at White Hart Lane and returned for the remainder of his side's disappointing campaign.

In fact, Hartson's fitness was a major concern during the 1999–2000 season, with injury restricting his time on pitch. But he still managed to finish as the Dons' joint-top scorer with nine league goals, showing that his eye for goal had not deserted him.

When not missing through injury, Hartson's disciplinary problems also produced costly absences. He was dismissed against Bradford in a crucial relegation clash in April – his second red card of the campaign.

Hartson did grab an injury-time equaliser against Aston Villa in the penultimate game of the season to move the Dons out of the relegation zone. But he could only watch from the sidelines as suspension kept him out of his team's last game of the season, when, short on firepower, the Dons slipped unceremoniously out of the Premiership.

APPEARANCES	
Start (sub)	15(1)
Minutes on pitch	1260
GOAL ATTEMPTS	
Goals inside box	9
Goals outside box	0
Minutes per goal scored	140.0
Goals/shots ratio	26%
SHOOTING	
Shots on target inside box	18
Shots on target outside box	3
Shooting accuracy	60%
PASSING	
Goal assists	4
Key passes	11
Passing accuracy in opp half	63%
DISCIPLINE	
Fouls committed	58
Fouls won	18
Offside	15
Yellow cards	3
Red cards	2

SEE PAGE 305 FOR FULL STATS

H

CB Steven HASLAM • 22

SHEFFIELD WEDNESDAY • BORN: 6.9.79

APPEARANCES	
Start (sub)	16(7)
Minutes on pitch	1509
GOAL ATTEMPTS	
Goals	0
Shots on target	0
Shooting accuracy	0%
PASSING & CROSSING	
Goal assists	0
Passes in opp half	362
Passing accuracy in opp half	64%
Successful crosses	1
Cross completion	20%
DEFENDING	
Interceptions	17
Clearances	51
Tackles	78
Tackles won %	51%
DISCIPLINE	
Fouls	25
Yellow cards	0
Red cards	0

SEE PAGE 220 FOR FULL STATS

Much is expected of stylish young defender Steven Haslam at Sheffield Wednesday. But although the 1999–2000 season saw him establish himself firmly in the Owls' first-team squad, he will struggle to look back fondly on a season of toil that resulted in relegation to Division One.

Still, Haslam showed immense composure in a struggling side. He successfully completed 71% of his passes and showed his versatility by playing in midfield when called upon.

But his aim is to make the grade as a centre-back, and Haslam certainly showed that he has the spirit and determination needed to succeed as a defender at the highest level. He attempted 78 challenges, the third-highest total at the club – an impressive tally considering that he started fewer than half of Wednesday's games.

With a mass exodus expected at Hillsborough in the wake of the Owls' relegation, Haslam should have even more opportunities to improve his game, as his side bid to return to the top flight at the first attempt.

sent off twice in the 1999–2000 Premiership

Paul HEALD • 13

WIMBLEDON • BORN: 20.9.68

Now entering his sixth season at Wimbledon, Paul Heald has rarely emerged from the shadow of first-choice 'keeper Neil Sullivan. But with the Scotland international moving to pastures new, it seems likely that Heald will be locked in a head-to-head battle with youth team goalie Kelvin Davies for the number one jersey at Selhurst Park.

Although Heald played only one Premiership fixture in the 1999–2000 campaign, he was certainly impressive as the Dons won 2–1 against Leicester.

He was especially dominant in the air, claiming all the crosses that he went for. And by saving 80% of the shots fired at his goal, he helped the Dons to their last Premiership win of the season.

An extremely popular player among Wimbledon players and fans alike, Heald will be desperate to prove himself in the First Division and help the club he loves gain promotion back to the Premiership.

SEE PAGE 304 FOR FULL STATS

Swede dreams: Magnus Hedman

Magnus HEDMAN • 1

COVENTRY CITY • BORN: 19.3.73

During the 1999–2000 season, Magnus Hedman again showed what a bargain he has been since Gordon Strachan signed him for £500,000. The Swedish international kept nine clean sheets – the fifth-highest total in the division – adding assurance to Coventry's normally overworked defence.

Hedman is renowned for his shot-stopping skills, and he enhanced this reputation saving an impressive 74% of the efforts fired at his goal. And he was certainly missed when injury forced him out of the team, Strachan's side falling to heavy defeats in each of the three Premiership games where Hedman was absent.

But the former AIK Solna 'keeper's command of the penalty area was brought into question on several occasions.

He claimed a below-average 91% of crosses that he went for and had his aerial vulnerability exposed at West Ham, when the Swede's errors resulted in a 5–0 defeat. If he can improve this aspect of his game, however, Hedman has the talent to be a fixture at Highfield Road for many years to come.

APPEARANCES	
Start (sub)	35(0)
Minutes on pitch	3150
SHOT STOPPING	
Goals conceded (inside box)	40
Goals conceded (outside box)	7
Minutes per goal conceded	67.02
Clean sheets	9
Saves (shots inside box)	82
Saves (shots outside box)	54
Saves/shots	74%
DISTRIBUTION	
Long kick %	36%
Throws/short passes %	94%
CATCHING	
Crosses caught	62
Crosses punched	13
Crosses dropped	6
Catch success %	91%
DISCIPLINE	
Yellow cards	0
Red cards	0

SEE PAGE 94 FOR FULL STATS

Vegard HEGGEM • 14

LIVERPOOL • BORN: 13.7.75

After a promising first season in the Premiership, the 1999–2000 campaign must have felt like a step backwards for Vegard Heggem. He struggled with injuries throughout the season and, when fit, was rarely given the opportunities he needed to force his way back into the first team.

Originally a forward, the Norwegian international has been used at full-back and in midfield by the Reds, but his performances in both positions were disappointing. Heggem won only 49% of his challenges and was not his usual self when going forward, either. He whipped in 26 crosses, but was unable to find a Liverpool player with any of them, indicating why he found himself on the bench so often.

Although a wonderful individual goal against Bradford signalled his intention to fight for a place, Heggem was largely ignored and did not start a single game after January. And with the arrival from Bayern Munich of right-back Markus Babbel, the former Rosenborg player may find his Anfield opportunities further restricted in future.

APPEARANCES	
Start (sub)	10(12)
Minutes on pitch	1047
GOAL ATTEMPTS	
Goals	1
PASSING & CROSSING	
Goal assists	0
Passing	452
Passing accuracy	69%
Crosses	26
Crossing accuracy	0%
DEFENDING	
Tackles	39
Tackles won %	49%
Blocks	10
Interceptions	3
Clearances	62
Shots cleared off line	1
DISCIPLINE	
Fouls	13
Yellow cards	0
Red cards	0

SEE PAGE 164 FOR FULL STATS

H

HELDER Rodrigues • 39

NEWCASTLE UNITED • BORN: 21.3.71

APPEARANCES	
Start (sub)	8(0)
Minutes on pitch	674
GOAL ATTEMPTS	
Goals	1
DEFENDING	
Blocks	11
Shots cleared off line	0
Headed clearances	26
Other clearances	17
Interceptions	3
Last man saving tackles	0
Tackles won	13
Tackles won %	46%
PASSING	
Passing accuracy own half	85%
Passing accuracy opp half	66%
DISCIPLINE	
Fouls	13
Fouls in danger area	6
Yellow cards	1
Red cards	0

SEE PAGE 207 FOR FULL STATS

Well-known to Bobby Robson after the Newcastle manager's four-year spell in Portugal, Helder Rodrigues sacrificed Championship glory with Deportivo La Coruna in Spain to move to St James's Park on loan in November 1999.

The Portuguese defender added class to the Magpies' previously beleaguered defence. He rarely wasted possession, successfully completing an impressive 77% of his passes. And Helder's assurance at the back clearly had an impact, as he was on the losing side only once in his eight league starts.

Helder endeared himself to the Newcastle fans by scoring his side's second goal in the derby game against Sunderland. But doubts remained about his ability to cope with the physical aspect of the English game. He won just 46% of his challenges – five percentage points worse than the seasonal average for a Premiership defender. And after sustaining an injury in the game against Sheffield Wednesday in February, he was unable to hold down a regular first-team place for the remainder of the 1999–2000 campaign.

Heidar HELGUSON • 37

WATFORD • BORN: 22.8.77

After paying £1.5 million for Heidar Helguson in January 2000, Graham Taylor bemoaned the current cost of a player with "potential".

But the Icelandic striker quickly lived up to his billing as the most expensive player in Watford's history. On his debut against Liverpool, he terrorised the best defence in the Premiership for the full 90 minutes, scoring with a powerful header and forcing a series of fouls. In fact, Helguson proved to be a handful for most defences during the 1999–2000 campaign, forcing 47 fouls – the joint-highest total at the club.

And the former Lillestrom forward also showed himself to be composed in front of goal. Sixteen per cent of his shots ended up in the back of the net and, despite playing less than half of the campaign, he consequently finished the season as the Hornets' top goalscorer with six goals.

Helguson rounded off 1999–2000 with a spectacular bicycle-kick goal, which clinched a victory over Coventry and left Watford fans hoping for more in Division One.

APPEARANCES	
Start (sub)	14(2)
Minutes on pitch	1242
GOAL ATTEMPTS	
Goals inside box	6
Goals outside box	0
Minutes per goal scored	207.0
Goals/shots ratio	16%
SHOOTING	
Shots on target inside box	13
Shots on target outside box	5
Shooting accuracy	47%
PASSING	
Goal assists	2
Key passes	2
Passing accuracy in opp half	56%
DISCIPLINE	
Fouls committed	22
Fouls won	47
Offside	16
Yellow cards	6
Red cards	0

SEE PAGE 276 FOR FULL STATS

Thomas HELMER • 8

SUNDERLAND • BORN: 21.4.65

After starring for Germany in their successful Euro 96 campaign, Thomas Helmer jumped at the chance to return to England.

Peter Reid brought the veteran to the Stadium of Light to add some experience to the Sunderland back-line. But from the opening game of the season, it seemed clear that the Black Cats' manager preferred fellow-veteran Steve Bould and, after just two appearances, Helmer was on his way back to Germany on loan with Hertha Berlin.

Helmer was in the Bayern Munich squad which lost the 1999 Champions League final to Manchester United. And he suffered more bad luck in the competition during 1999–2000, suffering an injury against Chelsea in November, which resulted in his return to the north-east. Despite some committed performances in the reserves, Helmer was unable to force his way back into the first team and will struggle to re-establish himself at Sunderland in the future.

SEE PAGE 248 FOR FULL STATS

Handful: Heidar Helguson

10% Watford's goals-to-shots ratic

CB Stephane HENCHOZ • 2

LIVERPOOL • BORN: 9.9.74

espite helping Liverpool to form the remiership's tightest defence during the 999–2000 season, Stephane Henchoz anaged to keep a relatively low profile. 'hile his partner at the heart of the Reds' ack-line Sami Hyypia grabbed the headlines, ıe Swiss international simply got on with his ɔb in a typically efficient manner.

Henchoz showed his defensive solidity by ıaking 249 clearances – the second-highest ɔtal at the club – and blocking 80 shots and rosses. He also demonstrated genuine ɔmposure with his distribution, integrating imself effortlessly into Liverpool's playing tyle. The former Blackburn player was uccessful with 77% of his passes and was the tarting point for many of the Reds' attacks uring the campaign.

But Henchoz rarely dominated games in the 'ay that he did at Ewood Park. He won only 2% of his challenges – 21 percentage points 'orse than the 1998–99 campaign – and will eed to be more successful in the tackle if he ; to step out of Hyypia's shadow at Anfield.

APPEARANCES	
Start (sub)	29(0)
Minutes on pitch	2604
GOAL ATTEMPTS	
Goals	0
DEFENDING	
Blocks	80
Shots cleared off line	0
Headed clearances	159
Other clearances	90
Interceptions	18
Last man saving tackles	2
Tackles won	39
Tackles won %	42%
PASSING	
Passing accuracy own half	87%
Passing accuracy opp half	57%
DISCIPLINE	
Fouls	37
Fouls in danger area	15
Yellow cards	8
Red cards	0

SEE PAGE 164 FOR FULL STATS

H

AM Lee HENDRIE • 17

ASTON VILLA • BORN: 18.5.77

APPEARANCES	
Start (sub)	18(11)
Minutes on pitch	1676
GOAL ATTEMPTS	
Goals	1
Shots on target	8
Shooting accuracy	42%
Goals/shots ratio	5%
PASSING	
Goal assists	0
Passes in opp half	618
Passing accuracy in opp half	70%
Successful crosses	16
Crossing accuracy	33%
DRIBBLING	
Dribbles & runs	103
Dribble completion	81%
Corners forced	9
DISCIPLINE	
Fouls	25
Yellow cards	6
Red cards	0

SEE PAGE 53 FOR FULL STATS

An exceptional start to the 1998–99 season saw Lee Hendrie earn an England debut against the Czech Republic. But he began the 1999–2000 campaign inconsistently and Hendrie's loss of form for Villa saw him dropped in favour of the rejuvenated Paul Merson and demoted to the under-21s at international level.

Although Hendrie possesses an abundance of natural talent, questions have been raised about his effectiveness at the highest level. He successfully completed an above-average 73% of his passes. But despite his passing abilities he failed to set up a single goal, and consequently struggled to gain regular first-team action.

The youngster came back strongly, however, and finished the 1999–2000 campaign somewhere near his best form. He was successful with an impressive 81% of his dribbles and runs over the season and scored in the draw with Wimbledon.

John Gregory now anticipates that Hendrie will command a more regular place in his side in the future and, should he impress, may get the chance to add to his solitary England cap.

vas the lowest in the Premiership

Colin HENDRY • 35

COVENTRY CITY • BORN: 7.12.65

After sitting on the Rangers bench for the better part of two seasons, Colin Hendry decided it was time to put an end to his Ibrox career in March.

During the opening months of the 1999–2000 campaign, the former Blackburn star had played more minutes on the pitch for Scotland than he had for Rangers. But his lack of match fitness did not stop Hendry stepping straight into the Sky Blues' first team.

Disappointingly for a player who prides himself on the physical side of his game, Hendry won only 47% of the challenges he attempted while at Highfield Road. But after suffering consecutive defeats in his first two games for the Sky Blues, the Scotland international's influence began to tell.

His organisational skills steered Coventry to wins over Everton, Bradford and Boro before his campaign was ended prematurely by an eye-socket injury. But Hendry is confident he will have plenty to offer the Sky Blues when he returns to full fitness at the start of the 2000–01 season.

APPEARANCES	
Start (sub)	9(0)
Minutes on pitch	777
GOAL ATTEMPTS	
Goals	0
DEFENDING	
Blocks	24
Shots cleared off line	0
Headed clearances	43
Other clearances	16
Interceptions	4
Last man saving tackles	0
Tackles won	17
Tackles won %	47%
PASSING	
Passing accuracy own half	72%
Passing accuracy opp half	43%
DISCIPLINE	
Fouls	9
Fouls in danger area	4
Yellow cards	0
Red cards	0

SEE PAGE 94 FOR FULL STATS

Thierry HENRY • 14

ARSENAL • BORN: 17.8.77

APPEARANCES	
Start (sub)	26(5)
Minutes on pitch	2251
GOAL ATTEMPTS	
Goals inside box	14
Goals outside box	3
Minutes per goal scored	132.4
Goals/shots ratio	18%
SHOOTING	
Shots on target inside box	35
Shots on target outside box	16
Shooting accuracy	55%
PASSING	
Goal assists	8
Key passes	9
Passing accuracy in opp half	62%
DISCIPLINE	
Fouls committed	54
Fouls won	32
Offside	42
Yellow cards	6
Red cards	0

SEE PAGE 38 FOR FULL STATS

Arsene Wenger knew what he was getting f his money when he signed pacy striker Thier Henry from Juventus in August 1999. Th young Frenchman began his career und Wenger at Monaco and was keen to link u with his former mentor at Highbury after a unhappy time in Turin.

After a slow start, Henry became revelation, bursting into life with a raspin drive to secure three points at Southampto The young marksman went on to score 1 times in the Premiership – hitting the targ with 51 shots – making him the third bes performing striker in the top flight.

Standing an imposing 6'1", the young Wor Cup winner operated as a centre-forward f Arsenal, showing pace and strength in attac He finished 1999–2000 scoring in seve consecutive games to equal the Premiersh record and will set a new mark if he nets in h first fixture of 2000–01.

An asset to both club and country, Henry tender years ensure that he has a long-ter future terrorising defences at the highest leve

Emile HESKEY • 8

LIVERPOOL • BORN: 11.1.78

iverpool's record signing Emile Heskey rrived at Anfield in March for £11 million nortly after winning the Worthington Cup ith Leicester.

Forming a good partnership with Michael wen, "Bruno" soon endeared himself to the ans by winning a penalty at the Kop end just wo minutes into his debut against underland. It was no real surprise that eskey was awarded the spot-kick, as he was ne most-fouled player during the Premiership uring the 1999–2000 season.

Despite the comments of John Gregory, who issed: "I see Emile's brought his skates with im from Leicester," the centre-forward was legally challenged 100 times.

Heskey is extremely powerful, and when unning at defenders he can be impossible to andle, as the Wimbledon back four found out when he grabbed a brace in the April ncounter at Selhurst Park.

Despite grabbing four goal assists, Heskey as pledged to be more selfish in 2000–01 in bid to improve his goal tally.

APPEARANCES	
Start (sub)	35(0)
Minutes on pitch	3045
GOAL ATTEMPTS	
Goals inside box	8
Goals outside box	2
Minutes per goal scored	304.5
Goals/shots ratio	14%
SHOOTING	
Shots on target inside box	30
Shots on target outside box	7
Shooting accuracy	43%
PASSING	
Goal assists	4
Key passes	20
Passing accuracy in opp half	64%
DISCIPLINE	
Fouls committed	75
Fouls won	100
Offside	29
Yellow cards	5
Red cards	0

SEE PAGE 151 & 164 FOR FULL STATS

ed alert: Emile Heskey

Martin HIDEN • 21

LEEDS UNITED • BORN: 11.3.73

Austrian defender Martin Hiden had another wretched season spoiled by injury, and his only senior appearance was a 15-minute spell as substitute for Ian Harte in the 2–0 defeat at Manchester United in August.

It was a strange coincidence that he played at Old Trafford, as the previous season Hiden had suffered a serious cruciate ligament injury there on a poor surface.

After this brief appearance he suffered a setback in a reserve game, injuring his ribs, and the former Rapid Vienna player was not expected to return until pre-season training for the 2000–01 campaign.

When fit, the £1.3 million George Graham signing is a tremendous reader of the game and is capable of some perfectly-timed challenges. Versatile enough to play as full-back, centre-back or sweeper, at the time of going to press he was about to return to Austria after Leeds accepted a £500,000 bid from SV Salzburg.

SEE PAGE 136 FOR FULL STATS

Danny HIGGINBOTHAM • 28

MANCHESTER UNITED • BORN: 29.12.78

Reserve left-back Danny Higginbotham spe just 105 minutes on the pitch as th Champions easily retained their title. An ab deputy for Denis Irwin, he made his fir Premiership appearance of the campaign the 2–0 win over Leicester City in Novembe

Opta's stats reveal that Higginbotham had a above-average passing ratio of 72% from th 101 passes he made in the 1999–2000 seaso

After his start against the Foxes, he did n return to the first team until the Championsh was won, replacing Ronny Johnsen at Watfo and playing the first half of the final match Aston Villa.

Higginbotham may return to Belgian sic Royal Antwerp after he spent a successf period on loan with United's nursery outf during season 1998–1999. If he stays at O Trafford, Higginbotham will hope to featu more regularly, as veteran defender Irw reaches the twilight of his highly successf club career.

SEE PAGE 178 FOR FULL STATS

Scott HILEY • 23

SOUTHAMPTON • BORN: 27.9.68

APPEARANCES	
Start (sub)	3(0)
Minutes on pitch	270
GOAL ATTEMPTS	
Goals	0
PASSING & CROSSING	
Goal assists	0
Passing	121
Passing accuracy	64%
Crosses	8
Crossing accuracy	25%
DEFENDING	
Tackles	2
Tackles won %	0%
Blocks	3
Interceptions	2
Clearances	25
Shots cleared off line	1
DISCIPLINE	
Fouls	1
Yellow cards	0
Red cards	0

SEE PAGE 235 FOR FULL STATS

Full-back Scott Hiley made three appearanc for the Saints before a £200,000 switch south coast rivals Portsmouth in December.

In those three games, Hiley was made work hard for a beleaguered Saints defen that conceded a total of nine goals while was on the pitch.

Hiley's passing was well below par with ju 64% of his distribution finding a team-mat a factor that meant the 30-somethi defender was not in the forefront of the manager Dave Jones's plans.

The former Birmingham defender made h last appearance in a red and white shirt in t 3–3 draw with Derby, when the Saints let two-goal lead slip. He contributed tw interceptions, three blocks and 25 clearanc to Southampton's campaign before movi along the coast to Fratton Park seekir regular first-team football.

But it proved to be a bad move for Hiley, he found himself out of favour with Pompey new manager Tony Pulis and was placed c the transfer list at the end of the season.

37 Andy Hinchcliffe made more successfu

Andy HINCHCLIFFE • 3

SHEFFIELD WEDNESDAY • BORN: 5.2.69

ıgland international Andy Hinchcliffe ıffered the cruel fate of relegation as ıeffield Wednesday finished in 19th place.

His wholehearted approach makes him a firm vourite with Wednesday fans, who hope the ub will be able to keep hold of him, as mours of a switch back to his native ıncashire with Blackburn Rovers circulated ıring the close season.

A dead-ball expert, Hinchcliffe attempted ore crosses than anyone at the club and only ıree players in the Premiership played more ng-range passes than Hinchcliffe's total of 31. He picked up an injury in the Yorkshire erby with Bradford City that saw him miss ine games, but on his return he was a regular the Owls' defence. His only Premiership oal was a 25-yard piledriver past Craig orrest in the 3–1 defeat of West Ham and he armed the fingers of several top-flight eepers with seven more shots on target.

Hinchcliffe, though, will have been isappointed to be part of a porous back-line ıat conceded 70 goals.

APPEARANCES	
Start (sub)	29(0)
Minutes on pitch	2541
GOAL ATTEMPTS	
Goals	1
PASSING & CROSSING	
Goal assists	2
Passing	1356
Passing accuracy	65%
Crosses	150
Crossing accuracy	33%
DEFENDING	
Tackles	48
Tackles won %	54%
Blocks	53
Interceptions	16
Clearances	172
Shots cleared off line	2
DISCIPLINE	
Fouls	14
Yellow cards	0
Red cards	0

SEE PAGE 220 FOR FULL STATS

H

ead-ball expert: Andy Hinchcliffe

rosses than any other Wednesday player

Shaka HISLOP • 1

WEST HAM UNITED • BORN: 22.2.69

In 1999–2000 Shaka Hislop displayed the goalkeeping stature he had shown in becoming Opta Goalkeeper of the Season during the previous campaign, until the first curse of the West Ham 'keepers struck in the Bradford game in February.

He suffered a broken leg after just two minutes, forcing 18-year-old Stephen Bywater to experience a daunting Premiership debut.

In 22 games Hislop conceded only 23 goals, keeping five clean sheets. And while the other Hammers goalkeepers deputised to varying degrees, it was acknowledged all around Upton Park that Hislop was sorely missed when absent.

He put his time studying mechanical engineering at a Washington university to good use in terms of getting his angles right, keeping out 77% of shots faced. And he came seventh in the Opta Goalkeepers Index.

Fans were pleased to see Hislop walking after the final game of 1999–2000 and, after his speedy recovery, he should reclaim his number one shirt.

APPEARANCES	
Start (sub)	22(0)
Minutes on pitch	1766
SHOT STOPPING	
Goals conceded (inside box)	20
Goals conceded (outside box)	3
Minutes per goal conceded	76.8
Clean sheets	5
Saves (shots inside box)	41
Saves (shots outside box)	37
Saves/shots	77%
DISTRIBUTION	
Long kick %	38%
Throws/short passes %	97%
CATCHING	
Crosses caught	39
Crosses punched	4
Crosses dropped	3
Catch success %	93%
DISCIPLINE	
Yellow cards	0
Red cards	1

SEE PAGE 290 FOR FULL STATS

CB

Jes HOGH • 4

CHELSEA • BORN: 7.5.66

APPEARANCES	
Start (sub)	6(3)
Minutes on pitch	548
GOAL ATTEMPTS	
Goals	0
DEFENDING	
Blocks	9
Shots cleared off line	0
Headed clearances	41
Other clearances	23
Interceptions	1
Last man saving tackles	0
Tackles won	12
Tackles won %	63%
PASSING	
Passing accuracy own half	91%
Passing accuracy opp half	71%
DISCIPLINE	
Fouls	7
Fouls in danger area	3
Yellow cards	0
Red cards	0

SEE PAGE 80 FOR FULL STATS

Chelsea boss Gianluca Vialli used veter defender Jes Hogh sparingly during seas 1999–2000. But the Italian boss held t Dane up as "an example for everybody" for h professional approach.

The £330,000 signing from Turkish out Fenerbahce was mainly used as defensi cover for the likes of Marcel Desailly and Fra Leboeuf. With the arrival of Emerson Thon from Sheffield Wednesday, his first-tea opportunities became even more limited.

Good in the air, as his 41 headed clearanc suggest, Hogh is powerfully built and an 84 passing accuracy is highly admirable for a b man. Hogh was also solid in the tackl winning 12 out of his 19 challenges – a above-average rate for a Premiership defende

His last start in the Premiership was in t Blues' 4–1 thrashing at the hands of Sunderla at the Stadium of Light in December. Hogh w unable to cope with the partnership of Ni Quinn and Kevin Phillips, who both help themselves to a brace in Chelsea's blackest d of their Premiership campaign.

Darren HOLLOWAY • 14

SUNDERLAND • BORN: 3.10.77

ull-back Darren Holloway was just a squad layer in the Black Cats' terrific first season ack in the Premiership. The England under-1 international has made more than 60 ppearances for the Mackems, but struggled to reak into the first team on a regular basis.

The Bishop Auckland-born lad spent a month n loan with First Division Bolton Wanderers in ecember, as he was unable to get in Peter eid's side ahead of Chris Makin or Michael Gray.

Nevertheless, when called into action he ave a reasonable account of himself, making 4 clearances and accurately distributing two-hirds of his passes. Holloway's tackle success ate of 62% was an excellent return from his 2 challenges in the Premiership.

The youngster received just one booking, eeing yellow in the Tees-Wear derby with iddlesbrough in March. But he did concede a enalty in the April Fool's Day 2–1 success at outhampton.

Holloway will hope to play a bigger part in underland's second season back in the top ight of English football.

APPEARANCES	
Start (sub)	8(7)
Minutes on pitch	793
GOAL ATTEMPTS	
Goals	0
PASSING & CROSSING	
Goal assists	1
Passing	373
Passing accuracy	67%
Crosses	18
Crossing accuracy	33%
DEFENDING	
Tackles	42
Tackles won %	62%
Blocks	7
Interceptions	4
Clearances	24
Shots cleared off line	0
DISCIPLINE	
Fouls	21
Yellow cards	1
Red cards	0

SEE PAGE 248 FOR FULL STATS

H

David HOPKIN • 7

LEEDS UNITED • BORN: 21.8.70

APPEARANCES	
Start (sub)	10(4)
Minutes on pitch	971
GOAL ATTEMPTS	
Goals	1
Shots on target	9
Shooting accuracy	56%
PASSING & CROSSING	
Goal assists	1
Passes in opp half	253
Passing accuracy in opp half	66%
Successful crosses	8
Cross completion	30%
DEFENDING	
Interceptions	5
Clearances	21
Tackles	30
Tackles won %	60%
DISCIPLINE	
Fouls	12
Yellow cards	1
Red cards	0

SEE PAGE 136 FOR FULL STATS

Scottish midfielder David Hopkin had a stop-start campaign as Leeds United booked their place in the Champions League by finishing third in the Premiership.

Hopkin was unable to gain a regular place due to the emergence of talented youngsters such as Matthew Jones, Stephen McPhail and Norwegian import Eirik Bakke.

Nevertheless, the flame-haired schemer still has a lot to offer the Elland Road outfit. He scored one goal in the 3–0 win at Hillsborough in April and set up another goal during the course of the 1999–2000 season.

Other contributions included an above-average crossing accuracy from his 27 centres and the former Crystal Palace stalwart's tenacious tackling saw him emerge with the ball 18 times from his 30 challenges.

Hopkin was forced to undergo surgery for a hernia problem in November, which saw him miss a large proportion of the season, although he returned to the Leeds first team after Christmas, chalking up four appearances, and helping the side to three wins.

Barry HORNE • 26

SHEFFIELD WEDNESDAY • BORN: 18.5.62

Veteran midfielder Barry Horne surprisingly arrived at Hillsborough on transfer deadline day after failing to break into the team at First Division Huddersfield.

The Welsh international produced a string of steady displays at the tender age of 38, as Sheffield Wednesday bravely fought to avoid relegation in 1999–2000.

He was brought to the club by acting manager Peter Shreeves to add his wealth of experience alongside youngsters such as Danny Sonner and Alan Quinn. He set an example to them by completing three-quarters of his passes and winning two-thirds of his challenges with his tenacious tackling ability.

Although he may have lacked the stamina and a certain level of fitness for the pace of the Premiership, in his seven appearances for the club Horne did inspire the Owls to three wins – over Chelsea, Leicester and Wimbledon – and a draw at Highbury.

Currently PFA Chairman, Horne is expected to be playing for Football League newboys Kidderminster Harriers in 2000–01.

APPEARANCES	
Start (sub)	7(0)
Minutes on pitch	541
GOAL ATTEMPTS	
Goals	0
Shots on target	0
Shooting accuracy	0%
PASSING & CROSSING	
Goal assists	0
Passes in opp half	158
Passing accuracy in opp half	66%
Successful crosses	2
Cross completion	100%
DEFENDING	
Interceptions	2
Clearances	5
Tackles	33
Tackles won %	67%
DISCIPLINE	
Fouls	9
Yellow cards	0
Red cards	0

SEE PAGE 221 FOR FULL STATS

Russell HOULT • 1

DERBY COUNTY • BORN: 22.11.72

APPEARANCES	
Start (sub)	10(0)
Minutes on pitch	900
SHOT STOPPING	
Goals conceded (inside box)	16
Goals conceded (outside box)	1
Minutes per goal conceded	52.9
Clean sheets	2
Saves (shots inside box)	16
Saves (shots outside box)	16
Saves/shots	65%
DISTRIBUTION	
Long kick %	37%
Throws/short passes %	85%
CATCHING	
Crosses caught	24
Crosses punched	7
Crosses dropped	1
Catch success %	96%
DISCIPLINE	
Yellow cards	1
Red cards	0

SEE PAGE 108 FOR FULL STATS

Derby County shot-stopper Russell Hoult ma just 10 Premiership appearances for the Rar during the opening three months of the seaso

Unable to see off the challenge of dedicat Estonian international Mart Poom, wh outperformed him in every key area, Hou moved to First Division Portsmouth in Janua seeking first-team football and eventua helped the south coast side cruise clear of t relegation zone.

While at Pride Park he kept two clean sheet but conceded a goal on average every minutes in the Premiership. One game he w want to forget was the 5–0 home defeat Sunderland, when Kevin Phillips blasted stunning hat-trick.

The 27-year-old custodian has a safe pair hands, a fact demonstrated by the fact that claimed 96% of crosses, but Jim Smith will keen that Hoult curbs his tendency to co for crosses that he cannot get.

Hoult also recorded a poor saves-to-sho ratio, beating off just 65% of all efforts on h goal, a poor return for a Premiership 'keepe

Steve HOWEY • 6

CB

NEWCASTLE UNITED • BORN: 26.10.71

ıltured centre-back Steve Howey missed the ajority of the 1999–2000 campaign after ıpturing his Achilles tendon during the 1999 A Cup semi-final victory over Spurs. In fact, ıjury has seen the talented centre-back make ewer than 200 league appearances in 10 easons at the club.

The Magpies' longest-serving player returned ı February, replacing Helder in the 2–0 win at ıeffield Wednesday, and went on to make ıother eight appearances.

Converted from a striker, Howey possesses eat pace and is very composed when the ball at his feet. Preferring to pick out a olleague with an accurate ball rather than a ng punt, his 77% passing accuracy for 999–2000 makes impressive reading.

Determined in the air, having made 30 eaded clearances, Howey was quick to spot anger by anticipating opponents' attacks.

Now in his late 20s, Howey suffered isappointment at Wembley when Newcastle st 2–1 to eventual winners Chelsea in the FA ıp semi-final.

APPEARANCES	
Start (sub)	7(2)
Minutes on pitch	691
GOAL ATTEMPTS	
Goals	0
DEFENDING	
Blocks	19
Shots cleared off line	0
Headed clearances	30
Other clearances	13
Interceptions	0
Last man saving tackles	0
Tackles won	5
Tackles won %	29%
PASSING	
Passing accuracy own half	85%
Passing accuracy opp half	68%
DISCIPLINE	
Fouls	11
Fouls in danger area	3
Yellow cards	1
Red cards	0

SEE PAGE 207 FOR FULL STATS

H

Hermann HREIDARSSON • 30

CB

WIMBLEDON • BORN: 11.7.74

APPEARANCES	
Start (sub)	24(0)
Minutes on pitch	2160
GOAL ATTEMPTS	
Goals	1
DEFENDING	
Blocks	83
Shots cleared off line	0
Headed clearances	172
Other clearances	48
Interceptions	11
Last man saving tackles	0
Tackles won	32
Tackles won %	50%
PASSING	
Passing accuracy own half	54%
Passing accuracy opp half	49%
DISCIPLINE	
Fouls	43
Fouls in danger area	14
Yellow cards	3
Red cards	0

SEE PAGE 305 FOR FULL STATS

Wily stopper Hermann Hreidarsson thwarted his Crazy Gang team-mates when he arrived at Selhurst Park from Brentford midway through the 1999–2000 season.

Well aware of the traditional Wimbledon "welcome" afforded to new players, Hreidarsson deliberately donned a cheap tracksuit for training to avoid his expensive togs being burnt.

The former Crystal Palace man was equally thrifty in defence, although his best efforts could not prevent the Dons from suffering an ignominious slump into the Nationwide League.

He made 24 starts for the Dons in his third season in English football, missing just four games due to a knee cartilage complaint that required minor surgery.

The 6'0" defender was a consistent performer, completing 220 clearances and winning 50% of his tackles. The Wimbledon faithful held their breath every week in anticipation of his famed surging runs out of defence and Hreidarsson opened his account for the Dons with a headed goal against West Ham.

ıhan any other Premiership side

S Darren HUCKERBY • 12

LEEDS UNITED • BORN: 23.4.76

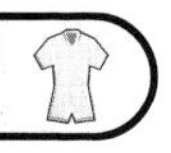

Lightning-quick Darren Huckerby experienced a frustrating first season at Elland Road after arriving from Coventry in August 1999. The former darling of Highfield Road failed to command a regular place in David O'Leary's side, making just nine league starts.

The rampaging striker possessed the prerequisites that were demanded by a Leeds team striding into Europe and contending the Championship: youth and a British passport. Unfortunately for Huckerby, Michael Bridges also fitted the bill and the former Sunderland striker's electrifying form at the start of the 1999–2000 campaign, alongside Harry Kewell, left Huckerby on the bench.

Renowned for haring down the wing and terrifying defenders, the former England "B" international only showed glimpses of his capabilities, embarking upon 122 raids but retaining possession just 57% of the time. Huckerby did score twice and set up three further Leeds goals, but will have to make the most of his few chances if he is to convince O'Leary that he is worthy of retaining.

APPEARANCES	
Start (sub)	10(24)
Minutes on pitch	1296
GOAL ATTEMPTS	
Goals inside box	2
Goals outside box	0
Minutes per goal scored	648.0
Goals/shots ratio	7%
SHOOTING	
Shots on target inside box	7
Shots on target outside box	8
Shooting accuracy	54%
PASSING	
Goal assists	3
Key passes	11
Passing accuracy in opp half	53%
DISCIPLINE	
Fouls committed	25
Fouls won	24
Offside	31
Yellow cards	0
Red cards	0

SEE PAGE 95 & 137 FOR FULL STATS

CB Aaron HUGHES • 18

NEWCASTLE UNITED • BORN: 8.11.79

APPEARANCES	
Start (sub)	22(5)
Minutes on pitch	1993
GOAL ATTEMPTS	
Goals	2
DEFENDING	
Blocks	28
Shots cleared off line	0
Headed clearances	76
Other clearances	62
Interceptions	13
Last man saving tackles	0
Tackles won	30
Tackles won %	53%
PASSING	
Passing accuracy own half	77%
Passing accuracy opp half	64%
DISCIPLINE	
Fouls	11
Fouls in danger area	5
Yellow cards	0
Red cards	0

SEE PAGE 207 FOR FULL STATS

Under the guidance of Bobby Robso versatile defender Aaron Hughes establish himself in the Newcastle rearguard. The you defender made 22 league starts in t 1999–2000 season, achieving a run of 13 succession after proving his potential.

Hughes has not been overawed playing front of 36,000 fanatical Geordies at James's Park – after all, he made his debut the imposing Nou Camp in 1999. The Irishm is a valuable asset to Robson who utilised h at full-back, centre-back and in midfield.

Hughes won 53% of his tackles in t Premiership and distributed the ball w comfort, completing 70% of his passes. successfully combined these traits in Europ receiving good reviews for his man-to-m marking job on Roma star Francesco Totti.

The Cookstown-born talent can inclu being one of the cleanest players in t Premier League in his growing list accolades. With 10 full Northern Ireland ca to his name, Hughes is maturing into a play with an exciting future ahead of him.

M Ceri HUGHES • 26

WIMBLEDON • BORN: 26.2.71

A bizarre set of circumstances led to Welsh international Ceri Hughes playing just 20 minutes of Premier League football for Wimbledon during the 1999–2000 campaign. Nearing his 40th appearance, the club refused to play him as they would have to pay his former club Luton Town £250,000 in appearance fees.

The aggressive midfielder was rescued by new Portsmouth boss Tony Pulis who made Hughes his first signing for the south coast club. He played an instrumental role in maintaining Pompey's First Division status, scoring on his debut at Stockport to earn a precious point. He repeated this feat at Blackburn, firing home from the edge of the box to ease the team away from the relegation melée.

The tough-tackler made 15 starts at Fratton Park, adding bite to a revitalised midfield. His notorious temperament was transferred with him as Hughes received four yellow cards in his first 12 games at his new club.

SEE PAGE 305 FOR FULL STATS

S Mark HUGHES • 26

EVERTON • BORN: 1.11.63

Mark Hughes had a hectic 1999–2000 campaign. He played a significant part in Southampton's season, was recruited to bolster Walter Smith's strikeforce at Everton and was appointed coach of the Welsh national side.

Sparky, as he is fondly known, clearly had plenty to ponder and probably spent his few quiet moments in his downstairs cloakroom. The exotic water closet contains a custom-made lavatory bowl in the shape of a Welsh dragon, complete with wings, and provides the perfect place to reflect on his packed schedule.

But far from being bogged down by his dual role as player and coach, Hughes would have been flushed with his success.

The veteran striker scored one goal apiece for his two Premiership clubs, recorded an above-average pass completion rate and improved his disciplinary record. Hughes, who was once described by author Jim White as a "centre-forward with the on-pitch disposition of something let loose on the streets of Pamplona", picked up just 10 yellow cards – an improvement on 1998–99's tally of 14.

Bullish: Mark Hughes

APPEARANCES	
Start (sub)	27(2)
Minutes on pitch	2425
GOAL ATTEMPTS	
Goals inside box	1
Goals outside box	1
Minutes per goal scored	1212.5
Goals/shots ratio	6%
SHOOTING	
Shots on target inside box	5
Shots on target outside box	4
Shooting accuracy	27%
PASSING	
Goal assists	4
Key passes	10
Passing accuracy in opp half	73%
DISCIPLINE	
Fouls committed	87
Fouls won	69
Offside	22
Yellow cards	10
Red cards	0

SEE PAGE 122 & 235 FOR FULL STATS

H

Michael HUGHES • 16

WIMBLEDON • BORN: 2.8.71

Tricky winger Michael Hughes suffered a disenchanting season at Wimbledon, plagued by injury and consigned to long spells on the subs' bench. Having undergone pre-season groin surgery, he fell out of favour with controversial Dons manager Egil Olsen, who questioned his defensive capabilities.

Hughes played the full 90 minutes at Upton Park where he scored a cracking consolation goal. Despite making a vital contribution, Olsen pointed the finger at Hughes for not clearing the danger that led to Paolo Di Canio's scintillating volley.

Hughes possessed quality on the ball, arrowing in 82 centres, with 27% finding a Dons player. He demonstrated his prowess around the box by launching 28 goal-bound efforts, with 11 testing the 'keeper.

Making just 13 starts in a Wimbledon shirt, Hughes enjoyed his best run in the side towards the end of the campaign. But in the penultimate league fixture against Aston Villa, an awkward challenge by Mark Delaney left Hughes with a broken leg.

APPEARANCES	
Start (sub)	13(6)
Minutes on pitch	1145
GOAL ATTEMPTS	
Goals	2
Shots on target	11
Shooting accuracy	39%
Goals/shots ratio	7%
PASSING	
Goal assists	1
Passes in opp half	334
Passing accuracy in opp half	65%
Successful crosses	22
Crossing accuracy	27%
DRIBBLING	
Dribbles & runs	32
Dribble completion	81%
Corners forced	17
DISCIPLINE	
Fouls	12
Yellow cards	2
Red cards	0

SEE PAGE 305 FOR FULL STATS

Stephen HUGHES • 18

EVERTON • BORN: 18.9.76

APPEARANCES	
Start (sub)	12(1)
Minutes on pitch	1002
GOAL ATTEMPTS	
Goals	1
Shots on target	2
Shooting accuracy	25%
PASSING & CROSSING	
Goal assists	3
Passes in opp half	290
Passing accuracy in opp half	66%
Successful crosses	7
Cross completion	19%
DEFENDING	
Interceptions	1
Clearances	4
Tackles	30
Tackles won %	63%
DISCIPLINE	
Fouls	13
Yellow cards	1
Red cards	0

SEE PAGE 38 & 123 FOR FULL STATS

Stephen Hughes began the 1999–2000 season on loan at Fulham. After a bust-up at the end of the previous campaign Arsenal had resigned themselves to losing the talented youngster, but Hughes failed to agree moves to several interested parties and then returned early to Highbury from west London after an unhappy time at Craven Cottage.

After a couple of fleeting performances for the Gunners, Walter Smith swooped for Hughes as an effective acquisition for the Everton midfield, paying Arsenal £3 million.

The left-footed player returned to the capital to make his Everton debut in the 1–1 draw with Chelsea and started every game up to the end of the season. Hughes is meticulous on the ball and found his man with 71% of his passes overall, as well as setting up three goals. He proved that he is committed in the challenge and won 63% of his 30 attempted tackles.

Capped at under-21 level, Hughes could eventually prove a valuable asset to England in filling the problem left-sided role.

Don HUTCHISON • 10

EVERTON • BORN: 9.5.71

Industrious midfielder Don Hutchison enjoyed a continued resurgence of his career at Everton, captaining the side with passion and commitment. His consistency and leadership qualities led to Hutchison becoming a regular in the Scotland team, and it was with the Tartan Army that he achieved a highlight of his career – leading the Scots to victory over England at Wembley.

He doubled his tally of three league goals from the 1998–1999 season, carving out opportunities with his lively running and hitting 15 shots on target. A highlight for the Gateshead-born player was firing home the first two goals in the 5–0 Boxing Day rout over Sunderland.

He can mix it up in the middle of the park with a combination of creativity and aggression. The tough tackler won 59% of his challenges and distributed the ball with vision, providing 20 defence-splitting passes and four goal assists. Transfer-listed in March due to ongoing contract talks, Hutchison would prove difficult to replace.

APPEARANCES	
Start (sub)	28(3)
Minutes on pitch	2482
GOAL ATTEMPTS	
Goals	6
Shots on target	15
Shooting accuracy	41%
PASSING & CROSSING	
Goal assists	4
Passes in opp half	1005
Passing accuracy in opp half	65%
Successful crosses	18
Cross completion	35%
DEFENDING	
Interceptions	20
Clearances	54
Tackles	81
Tackles won %	59%
DISCIPLINE	
Fouls	69
Yellow cards	7
Red cards	1

SEE PAGE 123 FOR FULL STATS

Micah HYDE • 8

WATFORD • BORN: 10.11.74

APPEARANCES	
Start (sub)	33(1)
Minutes on pitch	2895
GOAL ATTEMPTS	
Goals	3
Shots on target	16
Shooting accuracy	57%
PASSING & CROSSING	
Goal assists	5
Passes in opp half	907
Passing accuracy in opp half	65%
Successful crosses	21
Cross completion	27%
DEFENDING	
Interceptions	14
Clearances	52
Tackles	133
Tackles won %	44%
DISCIPLINE	
Fouls	43
Yellow cards	7
Red cards	1

SEE PAGE 276 FOR FULL STATS

Graham Taylor swooped for Micah Hyde after he impressed while on tour in Finland with the Hornets in the summer of 1997. The former Cambridge United skipper played an essential role in Watford's two successive promotion seasons and carried his form into the Premiership.

His stamina and fitness levels were in evidence as he made 33 starts and one substitute appearance – making him the third most-utilised player at the club during 1999–2000. He was also prominent in linking the team together, making more successful passes than any of his team-mates.

Hyde was an essential part of the midfield, scoring three times – against Bradford, Everton and Arsenal – and weighing in with five goal assists. His vision was a valued resource helping him thread 11 key passes through opposing defences to create attacking opportunities.

One area Hyde needs to improve is his tackling ability, as he won just 44% of his challenges, well below average.

than any other Everton player

Sami HYYPIA • 12

LIVERPOOL • BORN: 7.10.73

Gerard Houllier made a shrewd investment when he splashed out £2.6 million for the services of Sami Hyypia in May 1999. The determined defender was a revelation in his first season at Anfield.

The centre-back played all but 45 minutes throughout the 1999–2000 campaign. His 100% appearance record was ruined because of an injury received courtesy of an Ole Gunnar Solskjaer challenge in the 1–1 draw at Manchester United. To rub salt into the wound, the Norwegian netted while Hyypia was getting stitches.

The Finnish international amassed 538 clearances – the second-highest number for a Premiership player – and provided the Liverpool rearguard with much-needed aerial power. He won 54% of his tackles and his defensive contribution helped the Merseysiders achieve the status of the tightest rearguard in all four divisions.

The former Willem II player also proved to be a confident captain in Jamie Redknapp's frequent absence.

APPEARANCES	
Start (sub)	38(0)
Minutes on pitch	3375
GOAL ATTEMPTS	
Goals	2
DEFENDING	
Blocks	85
Shots cleared off line	0
Headed clearances	416
Other clearances	122
Interceptions	38
Last man saving tackles	0
Tackles won	61
Tackles won %	54%
PASSING	
Passing accuracy own half	83%
Passing accuracy opp half	61%
DISCIPLINE	
Fouls	34
Fouls in danger area	13
Yellow cards	2
Red cards	0

SEE PAGE 164 FOR FULL STATS

Revelation: Sami Hyypia

G Sasa ILIC • 28

WEST HAM UNITED • BORN: 18.7.72

A bar graph charting the highs and lows of Sasa Ilic's career would certainly have an interesting pattern on it. Signed from non-league football by Charlton Athletic, he was heralded a hero as he helped propel the Addicks to the Premiership.

But a dip in form led to a long spell on the bench after the big goalie had paper aeroplanes thrown at him by disenchanted Charlton fans. So it was a big surprise for Hammers supporters when Harry Redknapp, desperate to replace broken leg victim Shaka Hislop, brought Ilic on loan to Upton Park.

Surprise undoubtedly turned to despair when the 'keeper, on his debut, was blamed for the four goals he conceded in the 4–0 defeat against Everton.

This was the only game that Ilic endured between the posts for West Ham. Craig Forrest established himself as an adequate replacement, and Ilic quickly made the short trip back to The Valley.

SEE PAGE 290 FOR FULL STATS

FB Andy IMPEY • 24

LEICESTER CITY • BORN: 13.9.71

The Foxes' flying wing-back Andy Impey enjoyed a productive 1999–2000 campaign as he helped Leicester win the Worthington Cup final against Tranmere Rovers. That victory also secured the Foxes a coveted place in the 2000–01 UEFA Cup.

Keener to attack than defend, the former England under-21 international made a total of 101 crosses throughout the season, and set up two of City's goals.

Impey also got on the scoresheet himself, his only goal coming in a 3–1 defeat at Bradford. That was his first strike since a £1.6 million switch from West Ham in November 1998.

Impey made a total of 132 dribbles and runs throughout the 1999–2000 season, with 72% of them successful. He has also proved more than adequate in the tackle, winning over half of his 67 challenges, and the Hammersmith-born ace can also be proud of an immaculate disciplinary record, having not been booked nor sent off all season. He committed just 13 fouls and earned himself a spot in Opta's Clean Team of the Season.

Clean: Andy Impey

APPEARANCES	
Start (sub)	28(1)
Minutes on pitch	2399
GOAL ATTEMPTS	
Goals	1
PASSING & CROSSING	
Goal assists	2
Passing	787
Passing accuracy	68%
Crosses	101
Crossing accuracy	35%
DEFENDING	
Tackles	67
Tackles won %	58%
Blocks	17
Interceptions	20
Clearances	76
Shots cleared off line	1
DISCIPLINE	
Fouls	13
Yellow cards	0
Red cards	0

SEE PAGE 151 FOR FULL STATS

Paul INCE • 9

MIDDLESBROUGH • BORN: 21.10.67

Boro's self-styled "Guv'nor" settled in well on Teesside and quickly established himself as the lynchpin of Bryan Robson's ageing team.

Ince chipped in with three goals as Boro ended the season comfortably in mid-table, dispelling any fears of relegation that haunted the terraces of The Riverside.

Ince's form throughout the 1999–2000 campaign caught the eye of England boss Kevin Keegan, who selected the superstitious star for his Euro 2000 squad, with the former Manchester United ace back to his best after an unhappy spell at Liverpool. A £1 million move to join up with Bryan Robson, his one-time midfield partner at United, ended his misery on Merseyside after a two-year stint.

Ince was as reliable as ever during the 1999–2000 season, with 74% of his 1,191 passes finding a colleague, and the one-time West Ham hardman proved he had lost none of his bottle, going in for 125 tackles and winning 62% of them. He also made 71 dribbles and runs throughout the campaign with an 85% completion rate.

APPEARANCES	
Start (sub)	32(0)
Minutes on pitch	2812
GOAL ATTEMPTS	
Goals	3
Shots on target	19
Shooting accuracy	40%
PASSING & CROSSING	
Goal assists	1
Passes in opp half	741
Passing accuracy in opp half	70%
Successful crosses	6
Cross completion	46%
DEFENDING	
Interceptions	22
Clearances	93
Tackles	125
Tackles won %	62%
DISCIPLINE	
Fouls	41
Yellow cards	8
Red cards	0

SEE PAGE 192 FOR FULL STATS

Denis IRWIN • 3

MANCHESTER UNITED • BORN: 31.10.65

APPEARANCES	
Start (sub)	25(0)
Minutes on pitch	2092
GOAL ATTEMPTS	
Goals	3
PASSING & CROSSING	
Goal assists	1
Passing	1241
Passing accuracy	77%
Crosses	47
Crossing accuracy	23%
DEFENDING	
Tackles	74
Tackles won %	45%
Blocks	18
Interceptions	19
Clearances	104
Shots cleared off line	1
DISCIPLINE	
Fouls	15
Yellow cards	1
Red cards	0

SEE PAGE 178 FOR FULL STATS

Denis Irwin picked up another winner's medal as the Red Devils romped to their sixth title in eight years. United's longest-serving player even retired from international football in 1999–2000 in an attempt to prolong his career at Old Trafford, and at just £625,000 the Irishman must rank as one of Sir Alex Ferguson's best-ever buys.

After 10 years at the Theatre of Dreams, his statistics would suggest there is plenty of life left in him yet. He recorded an impressive 77% pass completion, and the Cork-born ace whipped in 47 crosses for United's goal-hungry strikers.

Irwin also made 53 dribbles and runs with a completion rate of 85%, and as well as making one goal he chipped in with three himself, two of which were penalties.

The Irishman also broke the club record for appearances in the European Cup in 1999–2000. The defeat by Real Madrid was his 47th match in the competition and, after his sixth title medal, he will hope to add to his tally in 1999–2000.

S Steffen IVERSEN • 10

TOTTENHAM HOTSPUR • BORN: 10.11.76

ter an injury-plagued start to his White Hart ne career, 1999–2000 proved to be a ccessful season for Spurs' Steffen Iversen. ended the term with 14 league goals, aring the honour of top scorer at the Lane th strike partner Chris Armstrong.

Prior to the 1999–2000 campaign, Iversen ıjoyed a prolific pre-season, but as the mpaign wore on and Spurs' lack of strikers came apparent, Iversen began to tire. But s total of 94 efforts on goal was only bettered Kevin Phillips and Harry Kewell in the emiership and the blond-haired striker ensured ro status with Spurs fans by scoring against ch-rivals Arsenal in a 2–1 win in November.

As well as scoring 14 goals in a sappointing season for Spurs, he managed ven assists, with only David Ginola anaging more for the Lilywhites. Iversen will hoping the arrival of Ukrainian ace arksman Sergei Rebrov will take some of the orkload off his shoulders and that he can fire e goals to take Spurs back into European mpetition.

APPEARANCES	
Start (sub)	36(0)
Minutes on pitch	3085
GOAL ATTEMPTS	
Goals inside box	13
Goals outside box	1
Minutes per goal scored	220.4
Goals/shots ratio	15%
SHOOTING	
Shots on target inside box	38
Shots on target outside box	10
Shooting accuracy	51%
PASSING	
Goal assists	7
Key passes	14
Passing accuracy in opp half	61%
DISCIPLINE	
Fouls committed	28
Fouls won	53
Offside	22
Yellow cards	5
Red cards	0

SEE PAGE 263 FOR FULL STATS

I

M Muzzy IZZET • 6

LEICESTER CITY • BORN: 31.10.74

APPEARANCES	
Start (sub)	32(0)
Minutes on pitch	2796
GOAL ATTEMPTS	
Goals	8
Shots on target	24
Shooting accuracy	53%
PASSING & CROSSING	
Goal assists	3
Passes in opp half	814
Passing accuracy in opp half	71%
Successful crosses	34
Cross completion	32%
DEFENDING	
Interceptions	31
Clearances	62
Tackles	114
Tackles won %	68%
DISCIPLINE	
Fouls	29
Yellow cards	3
Red cards	0

SEE PAGE 151 FOR FULL STATS

Muzzy Izzet may have been a driving force in the Leicester midfield in 1999–2000, but when it came to driving his red Ford Fiesta, he proved significantly less effective.

The Mile End-born son of a Turk failed his second driving test in December without even leaving the test centre, because his car did not have a second, interior driving mirror.

Fortunately Izzet had no problem getting out of first gear on the pitch, his partnership with Neil Lennon proving once again to be one of the most effective in the Premiership.

Izzet's form was excellent but his failure to earn international recognition from Kevin Keegan prompted him to turn his back on England and pledge his allegiance to Turkey.

As well as scoring eight league goals for the Foxes, he proved himself once again to be a fine passer and tackler, winning 68% of his challenges and underlining his natural all-round ability – and Kevin Keegan's decision to omit him from the England squad could prove to be a wrong one. England's loss could well be Turkey's gain.

Vorthington Cup, European club competitions and Euro 2000 qualifiers

FB Richard JACKSON • 18

DERBY COUNTY • BORN: 18.4.80

Richard Jackson signed from Scarborough for a fee of £30,000 – which may rise to £250,000 depending on appearances – on transfer deadline day in March 1999.

His exciting performances for the coastal side had caught the attention of Derby manager Jim Smith, who offered him a trial at Pride Park and was impressed enough to sign him. The 20-year-old right-back made a one-minute debut against Newcastle and enjoyed a further 26 minutes against Chelsea on the last day of the season.

During that outing against Gianluca Vialli's star-studded London side he blocked a shot, made a clearance and completed nine passes. Hardly spectacular; but while his team were lambs to the slaughter and lost 4–0 that afternoon, the highly-rated Jackson is fast developing into a sturdy Ram.

The 2000–01 season should see Jackson making more appearances and he appears to have the confidence to step into the Derby side.

SEE PAGE 109 FOR FULL STATS

FB Wayne JACOBS • 22

BRADFORD CITY • BORN: 3.2.69

Wayne Jacobs was grateful to a faith healer who laid her hands on and cured his troublesome knee while he was at Hull. That gave the 31-year-old the opportunity to play later at the highest level and to help keep Bradford in the Premiership, against all the odds.

Paul Jewell's men battled to save their Premiership lives and Jacobs chipped in with 123 clearances, 63 tackles (winning 51% of them) and cleared the ball off the line twice to aid the overworked defence.

While Valley Parade was beset on all sides by those who doubted, the gutsy left-back played an integral part in helping Jewell's side perform miracles to stay in the Premiership.

The Sheffield-born defender is a firm favourite with the Bradford faithful and loves to get forward. Jacobs made 815 passes and embarked on 23 dribbles during the 1999–2000 season, successfully completing 83% of his runs.

His contribution has been rewarded by the offer of a new contract that would keep him at Bradford for the rest of his career.

Keeping the faith: Wayne Jacobs

APPEARANCES	
Start (sub)	22(2)
Minutes on pitch	1861
GOAL ATTEMPTS	
Goals	0
PASSING & CROSSING	
Goal assists	0
Passing	815
Passing accuracy	67%
Crosses	31
Crossing accuracy	16%
DEFENDING	
Tackles	63
Tackles won %	51%
Blocks	21
Interceptions	11
Clearances	123
Shots cleared off line	2
DISCIPLINE	
Fouls	10
Yellow cards	3
Red cards	0

SEE PAGE 66 FOR FULL STATS

G

David JAMES • 1

ASTON VILLA • BORN: 1.8.70

ccording to Villa boss John Gregory, only eter Schmeichel is superior to David James in urope. But after some inauspicious errors – ot least the three fumbles in the FA Cup final few would agree that he has totally shaken ff his "Calamity" tag.

James made the £1.7 million move to Villa in ne summer of 1999 and, despite only onceding a goal every 99 minutes, no other eeper dropped the ball more than the 10 mes that James did, underlining his ropensity for lapses in concentration.

The former Armani model has always been egarded as a good shot-stopper and saved 5% of the efforts that he faced during the 999–2000 season – above-average for the remiership. But even at 6'5" his catch success ate was just 85%, which is eight percentage oints lower than average for the top flight.

Clearly his manager feels that his occasional angers are overshadowed by his ability in ther areas – and with Villa recording the third ghtest defence in the Premiership, it is hard argue with Gregory's opinion.

APPEARANCES	
Start (sub)	29(0)
Minutes on pitch	2564
SHOT STOPPING	
Goals conceded (inside box)	23
Goals conceded (outside box)	3
Minutes per goal conceded	98.6
Clean sheets	11
Saves (shots inside box)	40
Saves (shots outside box)	36
Saves/shots	75%
DISTRIBUTION	
Long kick %	38%
Throws/short passes %	81%
CATCHING	
Crosses caught	58
Crosses punched	20
Crosses dropped	10
Catch success %	85%
DISCIPLINE	
Yellow cards	0
Red cards	0

SEE PAGE 52 FOR FULL STATS

S

Francis JEFFERS • 17

EVERTON • BORN: 25.1.81

APPEARANCES	
Start (sub)	16(5)
Minutes on pitch	1443
GOAL ATTEMPTS	
Goals inside box	6
Goals outside box	0
Minutes per goal scored	240.5
Goals/shots ratio	14%
SHOOTING	
Shots on target inside box	16
Shots on target outside box	7
Shooting accuracy	53%
PASSING	
Goal assists	6
Key passes	3
Passing accuracy in opp half	65%
DISCIPLINE	
Fouls committed	7
Fouls won	17
Offside	37
Yellow cards	0
Red cards	1

SEE PAGE 123 FOR FULL STATS

Francis Jeffers began the season in inauspicious circumstances, putting in a transfer request and finding himself dropped by Walter Smith. But after sorting out his contract wrangle with Everton, the 19-year-old striker put in a good season for the Toffeemen.

Jeffers scored six times for Everton and set up another six goals for team-mates. Although not blessed with blistering pace, he has a quick footballing brain and good movement.

Jeffers's eye for goal is sharp and his finishing is excellent, as his goals-to-shots ratio of 14% illustrates.

But despite appearing in 21 league games for Walter Smith's side, Jeffers completed the full 90 minutes on only six occasions. An ankle injury picked up playing for the England under-21 team meant he missed most of the second half of the 1999–2000 season, making just four substitute appearances towards the end of the campaign.

After forging a fine partnership with Kevin Campbell, Jeffers has shown he has a great future for Everton – and possibly England.

S Phil JEVONS • 20

EVERTON • BORN: 1.8.79

First-team opportunities were again very limited for Phil Jevons, with the 21-year-old spending only 149 minutes on the pitch in the 1999–2000 Premiership.

In that brief time Jevons recorded a passing accuracy of 69%, which was above average for a striker, but only managed to fire one shot on target from the three he attempted.

The local lad won the FA Youth Cup with Everton in 1998 and the following season was the club's reserve team top scorer. But with Joe-Max Moore and Mark Hughes joining the club, his outings were extremely limited during the campaign.

Jevons will also have been disappointed to see the younger Francis Jeffers move ahead of him in the pecking order. But he is a talented prospect, and with more and more clubs employing a rotation system to cope with the number of games, it is likely he will feature more often in 2000–01 as long as he continues his current progress.

SEE PAGE 123 FOR FULL STATS

Second fiddle: Julian Joachim

Julian JOACHIM • 12

ASTON VILLA • BORN: 20.9.74

Julian Joachim showed glimpses of his talent in front of goal during the 1999–2000 season. He managed to hit the target with 59% of his efforts at goal, but scored only six times. His shooting gave him an above-average 15% goals-to-shots ratio, indicating that it was probably a lack of chances that saw him net so irregularly.

But his contribution outside the box could have been better. Despite setting up five goals, Joachim completed just 63% of his passes.

The pint-sized forward went on 81 dribbles and runs but successfully completed just 69% of them, highlighting one of the reasons he often played second fiddle to Benito Carbone, Paul Merson and Dion Dublin.

Ignored by Kevin Keegan when in good form early in the campaign, Joachim hoped to play for the island of St Vincent, but his international dreams were dashed after he had already flown out for a fixture. Unfortunately, he had played three games for England in the World Youth Championships of 1993 and was ineligible to play for any other team.

APPEARANCES	
Start (sub)	27(6)
Minutes on pitch	2382
GOAL ATTEMPTS	
Goals inside box	6
Goals outside box	0
Minutes per goal scored	397.0
Goals/shots ratio	15%
SHOOTING	
Shots on target inside box	20
Shots on target outside box	3
Shooting accuracy	59%
PASSING	
Goal assists	5
Key passes	5
Passing accuracy in opp half	65%
DISCIPLINE	
Fouls committed	35
Fouls won	38
Offside	34
Yellow cards	0
Red cards	0

SEE PAGE 53 FOR FULL STATS

4 Ronny Johnsen has won four trophies in fou

Ronny JOHNSEN • 5

MANCHESTER UNITED • BORN: 10.6.69

ɔnny Johnsen holds the incredible record of ıaving won four trophies in four consecutive ımes for Manchester United.

He played in the Championship title-clincher 1999 against Tottenham, then the FA Cup ıal and the Champions League final against ayern Munich. The Norwegian was injured for e vast majority of the 1999–2000 season, ıt made his comeback in the game at The ell where United won the title again – ırning himself a personal quadruple, though he did not play enough to gain a edal in 1999–2000.

The 31-year-old only played 185 minutes in e 1999–2000 season and took time to re-ljust to the frenetic pace of the Premiership. e lost all eight of the tackles that he went in r, and although his overall pass completion te of 73% was above average for a defender, fell to 48% in the opposition half.

Johnsen still has two years left to run on his ıntract and, if he can put his injury troubles ehind him, he is sure to be a key figure for ıited in 2000–01.

APPEARANCES	
Start (sub)	2(1)
Minutes on pitch	185
GOAL ATTEMPTS	
Goals	0
DEFENDING	
Blocks	3
Shots cleared off line	0
Headed clearances	9
Other clearances	1
Interceptions	2
Last man saving tackles	0
Tackles won	0
Tackles won %	0%
PASSING	
Passing accuracy own half	84%
Passing accuracy opp half	48%
DISCIPLINE	
Fouls	1
Fouls in danger area	1
Yellow cards	0
Red cards	0

SEE PAGE 179 FOR FULL STATS

J

Richard JOHNSON • 10

WATFORD • BORN: 27.4.74

APPEARANCES	
Start (sub)	20(3)
Minutes on pitch	1798
GOAL ATTEMPTS	
Goals	3
Shots on target	11
Shooting accuracy	33%
PASSING & CROSSING	
Goal assists	1
Passes in opp half	583
Passing accuracy in opp half	61%
Successful crosses	10
Cross completion	43%
DEFENDING	
Interceptions	14
Clearances	42
Tackles	59
Tackles won%	39%
DISCIPLINE	
Fouls	24
Yellow cards	4
Red cards	0

SEE PAGE 276 FOR FULL STATS

Despite Watford finishing bottom of the table and making a swift return to Division One, Richard Johnson can be proud of some of his performances.

The Australian, who has been at the club since he was 16, was one of the Hornets' best players throughout 1999–2000 as they battled to make their mark in the top flight.

He scored goals against Liverpool, Sunderland and Manchester United and, although his shooting accuracy was a disappointing 33%, he was not afraid to shoot from distance, hitting 30 shots from outside the area.

The versatile midfielder is composed in possession and likes to get forward, recording an excellent 43% crossing accuracy. He picked up an injury in the win at Liverpool, causing him to miss seven games, but Johnson recovered well and his confident performances were rewarded when he made his international debut for Australia against Brazil.

His experience and commitment to Watford will be valuable to Graham Taylor as they fight for promotion in 2000–01.

onsecutive appearances for Manchester United

Seth JOHNSON • 7

DERBY COUNTY • BORN: 12.3.79

Seth Johnson became Derby County's record signing when he made the £3 million move from Crewe Alexandra.

The tenacious midfielder added bite to Jim Smith's side by going in for 121 tackles in just over 3,000 minutes on pitch. But his tackle success rate of 46% was 11 percentage points below the average for a midfielder and he picked up 13 yellow cards over the campaign – no other player was booked more times.

Defensively he made a significant contribution with 35 interceptions and 19 blocks, but Johnson also made an impact when going forward for the Rams, putting in 46 accurate crosses.

Despite his hardman image, Johnson likes to collect toy fire engines and, according to room-mate Rory Delap, he keeps quite a collection in display cabinets at home.

Joining Derby rather than Liverpool has undoubtedly given him more first-team opportunities and in the 2000–01 season he should continue to develop into an excellent combative midfielder.

APPEARANCES	
Start (sub)	36(0)
Minutes on pitch	3156
GOAL ATTEMPTS	
Goals	1
Shots on target	5
Shooting accuracy	26%
PASSING & CROSSING	
Goal assists	4
Passes in opp half	823
Passing accuracy in opp half	65%
Successful crosses	46
Cross completion	34%
DEFENDING	
Interceptions	35
Clearances	74
Tackles	121
Tackles won %	46%
DISCIPLINE	
Fouls	47
Yellow cards	13
Red cards	0

SEE PAGE 109 FOR FULL STATS

Tommy JOHNSON • 26

EVERTON • BORN: 15.1.71

Tommy Johnson was struggling to get in the Celtic side under John Barnes at the start of the season and was looking for a way out.

He was rescued by Walter Smith, who snapped up the pacy striker on a loan move to Everton. But it proved just as tough to get a game on Merseyside as it did in Glasgow. Johnson only played 66 minutes for the Toffees, making brief substitute appearances against Leeds United, Newcastle United and Middlesbrough.

Johnson did not even manage a shot during those outings and recorded a poor pass completion rate of 52% – figures that hardly inspired the Everton faithful.

Once Barnes departed, Johnson returned north of the border and scored nine goals in seven starts for the Glasgow club. The 2000–01 season might see more action for him, but with another change in management, there could be tough and uncertain times ahead for the 29-year-old.

SEE PAGE 123 FOR FULL STATS

Matthew JONES • 20

LEEDS UNITED • BORN: 1.9.80

By the time Matthew Jones made his fir team debut for Leeds he already had We youth and under-21 caps to his name, a rounded off the 1999–2000 season by playi for the full Wales team against Brazil.

Although Jones only played for 380 minut he made a solid contribution to Lee excellent season. His tackle success rate 71% was superb and although he did not on the score sheet himself, he managed to up two goals for other players. But t Welshman's pass completion rate of 65% l room for improvement.

Jones has been tipped as one of the m exciting talents to emerge from the you team which won the FA Youth Cup in 19 With Leeds in the Champions League duri the 2000–01 season, squad rotation will vital and there will be more opportunities this prodigious talent to show what he can and perhaps even the chance to establ himself in the side.

SEE PAGE 137 FOR FULL STATS

Paul JONES • 1

G

SOUTHAMPTON • BORN: 18.4.67

Former Southampton manager Dave Jones brought goalkeeper Paul Jones to The Dell with him from Stockport in the summer of 1997. After a nervy start, Jones the 'keeper put in some excellent performances and was voted Player of the Season in 1997–98.

Now a full Welsh international, Jones is Southampton's undisputed number one but had a less-than-outstanding 1999–2000 season. Despite being regarded as a very good shot-stopper and keeping eight clean sheets, he only saved 70% of the efforts he faced, which was below the Premiership average. In fact, Jones conceded 11 goals from shots outside the area – more than any other 'keeper.

His handling ability has also been called into question, as no 'keeper dropped the ball more times than Jones, who fumbled crosses on 10 occasions.

The Welsh stopper picked up a serious back injury against Sunderland which ruled him out for the remaining seven games. Although the injury was feared to be career-threatening, he then targeted a return for Saints in August.

APPEARANCES	
Start (sub)	31(0)
Minutes on pitch	2688
SHOT STOPPING	
Goals conceded (inside box)	41
Goals conceded (outside box)	11
Minutes per goal conceded	51.7
Clean sheets	8
Saves (shots inside box)	61
Saves (shots outside box)	60
Saves/shots	70%
DISTRIBUTION	
Long kick %	39%
Throws/short passes %	90%
CATCHING	
Crosses caught	56
Crosses punched	28
Crosses dropped	10
Catch success %	85%
DISCIPLINE	
Yellow cards	0
Red cards	0

SEE PAGE 234 FOR FULL STATS

Wim JONK • 4

M

SHEFFIELD WEDNESDAY • BORN: 12.10.66

APPEARANCES	
Start (sub)	29(1)
Minutes on pitch	2582
GOAL ATTEMPTS	
Goals	3
Shots on target	16
Shooting accuracy	62%
PASSING & CROSSING	
Goal assists	8
Passes in opp half	962
Passing accuracy in opp half	69%
Successful crosses	41
Cross completion	31%
DEFENDING	
Interceptions	23
Clearances	28
Tackles	77
Tackles won %	53%
DISCIPLINE	
Fouls	21
Yellow cards	4
Red cards	0

SEE PAGE 221 FOR FULL STATS

Wim Jonk was Danny Wilson's first buy as manager of Sheffield Wednesday. The Dutchman's laid-back style was supposed to act as a calming influence on the rest of the team, especially the younger players, but at times he has looked lost in the hurly-burly of the Premiership.

The experienced playmaker has nearly 50 international appearances behind him, as well as having played for Holland in the World Cup, and his pedigree is clear. But the former Inter Milan, Ajax and PSV Eindhoven midfielder completed only 75% of his passes in 1999–2000, which was eight percentage points inferior to his distribution in 1998–99.

He did create eight goals and scored three himself, but the apocalyptic mix of lack of firepower and defensive frailty of his team meant that he was unable to help prevent the inexorable slide into Division One.

If Jonk remains at Hillsborough, his ability and experience will be invaluable as Wednesday fight to get back into the Premiership at the first time of asking.

JUNINHO • 23

MIDDLESBROUGH • BORN: 22.2.73

Prime Minister and Newcastle fan Tony Blair intervened to help get Juninho a work permit so that the Brazilian could return to The Riverside. But the initial excitement of Juninho's return wore off and the Boro public were ultimately left frustrated and disillusioned by his lack of form.

The little Brazilian scored four times in the 2,097 minutes he played, but those four strikes came from a substantial 55 efforts. Only 45% of those shots hit the target and he finished with a very poor goals-to-shots ratio of 7%.

His pass completion rate of 68% was also below average, although he did set up two goals for Boro.

There are no doubts that the twinkle toes are still there – and only five players in the Premiership completed more successful dribbles and runs than the 136 that Juninho did.

The 27-year-old is still only on loan at Middlesbrough from his club Atletico Madrid, but if he is to stay in the north-east permanently an all-round improvement will be required in the 2000–01 season.

APPEARANCES	
Start (sub)	24(4)
Minutes on pitch	2097
GOAL ATTEMPTS	
Goals	4
Shots on target	25
Shooting accuracy	45%
Goals/shots ratio	7%
PASSING	
Goal assists	2
Passes in opp half	743
Passing accuracy in opp half	65%
Successful crosses	28
Crossing accuracy	31%
DRIBBLING	
Dribbles & runs	220
Dribble completion	62%
Corners forced	23
DISCIPLINE	
Fouls	23
Yellow cards	1
Red cards	0

SEE PAGE 192 FOR FULL STATS

FB

Duncan JUPP • 21

WIMBLEDON • BORN: 25.1.75

APPEARANCES	
Start (sub)	6(3)
Minutes on pitch	681
GOAL ATTEMPTS	
Goals	0
PASSING & CROSSING	
Goal assists	0
Passing	245
Passing accuracy	58%
Crosses	20
Crossing accuracy	25%
DEFENDING	
Tackles	24
Tackles won %	63%
Blocks	10
Interceptions	2
Clearances	26
Shots cleared off line	0
DISCIPLINE	
Fouls	13
Yellow cards	1
Red cards	0

SEE PAGE 305 FOR FULL STATS

Duncan Jupp experienced another season of frustration, having been on the fringe of the Wimbledon first team since his move from Fulham in 1996.

He was utilised on the opening day of the season as a strategic measure when Dean Blackwell was sent off at Watford, but had to wait six weeks for his next opportunity, which was an 11-minute substitute appearance at Old Trafford.

The Scottish under-21 international enjoyed a run of five starts in April as injuries forced a reshuffle at the back. Jupp's main competitor for the right-back slot was Kenny Cunningham, who was the captain in Robbie Earle's absence and only missed one game.

Jupp enjoyed running down the flanks and managed to hit 20 centres into the box during his brief outings, five of which found their target. His tackling was sound but he was let down by poor distribution, with only 58% of his passes finding a Wimbledon colleague. A move to another club may refresh his touch and rebuild his confidence.

4,111 In more than 4,000 minutes for Southampton

AM Hassan KACHLOUL • 30

SOUTHAMPTON • BORN: 19.2.73

After becoming a cult figure at The Dell in 1998–99, Hassan Kachloul made further progress in 1999–2000, playing a key role in a Southampton side comfortably anchored in mid-table for much of the campaign.

He scored five times for the Saints, four of them coming in a late summer burst. Glenn Hoddle was happy to keep the Moroccan in the first XI when he arrived at the club – a clear indication of Kachloul's importance.

His passing was disappointing, but his 137 dribbles made him one of the top 25 runners in the Premiership. Kachloul racked up nine yellow cards during the season, the most publicised being when he dived at Villa Park after anticipating a challenge from Alan Wright that never came.

His temperament can produce moments of madness, but moments of genius too. And though St Etienne, the band with the same name as Kachloul's former club, once sang *Only Love Can Break Your Heart*, Saints fans will disagree. If their tricky midfielder left the south coast, they would be heartbroken.

APPEARANCES	
Start (sub)	29(3)
Minutes on pitch	2468
GOAL ATTEMPTS	
Goals	5
Shots on target	21
Shooting accuracy	41%
Goals/shots ratio	10%
PASSING	
Goal assists	1
Passes in opp half	600
Passing accuracy in opp half	56%
Successful crosses	19
Crossing accuracy	26%
DRIBBLING	
Dribbles & runs	137
Dribble completion	64%
Corners forced	19
DISCIPLINE	
Fouls	52
Yellow cards	9
Red cards	0

SEE PAGE 235 FOR FULL STATS

S Frederic KANOUTE • 14

WEST HAM UNITED • BORN: 2.9.77

APPEARANCES	
Start (sub)	8(0)
Minutes on pitch	720
GOAL ATTEMPTS	
Goals inside box	2
Goals outside box	0
Minutes per goal scored	360.0
Goals/shots ratio	7%
SHOOTING	
Shots on target inside box	13
Shots on target outside box	3
Shooting accuracy	53%
PASSING	
Goal assists	1
Key passes	7
Passing accuracy in opp half	65%
DISCIPLINE	
Fouls committed	9
Fouls won	20
Offside	20
Yellow cards	1
Red cards	0

SEE PAGE 290 FOR FULL STATS

With two Frenchmen already established at Upton Park, the arrival of lesser-known striker Frederic Kanouté on loan from Lyon did not seem as much of a gamble as some of Harry Redknapp's previous ventures in the foreign transfer market.

This was quickly confirmed when the pacy forward exploded into the English game with a superb performance against Wimbledon. That culminated in a debut goal, endearing him to the East End crowd immediately.

In seven games, Kanouté demonstrated his enjoyment of picking the ball up deep and running at opposition defenders.

He constantly looked a danger in front of goal and, by netting two strikes in seven games, hinted to Redknapp that he could have a great strikeforce if he could sign the Frenchman permanently.

This was made possible at the end of 1999–2000, as midfielder Marc-Vivien Foe moved in the opposite direction and Kanouté should prove to be yet another example of Redknapp's shrewdness.

Hassan Kachloul has set up just one goal

Nwankwo KANU • 25

ARSENAL • BORN: 1.8.76

After Nwankwo Kanu experienced difficulties bringing his family to England for a visit he expressed his dismay, qualifying it with the statement: "But I will not kill myself or anything like that."

Arsenal fans were delighted to hear that, after the Nigerian starred once again for the north London side.

After scoring six times in 1998–99, he doubled his contribution in 1999–2000, and was an imperious sight with the ball. His finest moment came against Chelsea at Stamford Bridge when the Gunners trailed 2–0 to their west London rivals. Kanu scored three times in the final 15 minutes to send the fans wild. His third goal was something to behold, a curling effort from an almost impossible angle for an injury-time winner.

Of the Arsenal squad, only Marc Overmars made more dribbles than Kanu, and the majestic Super Eagle looks likely to play a considerable role at Arsenal in the future, particularly with the club keen to make more of an impact in the Champions League.

APPEARANCES	
Start (sub)	24(7)
Minutes on pitch	2160
GOAL ATTEMPTS	
Goals inside box	11
Goals outside box	1
Minutes per goal scored	180.0
Goals/shots ratio	15%
SHOOTING	
Shots on target inside box	20
Shots on target outside box	14
Shooting accuracy	43%
PASSING	
Goal assists	4
Key passes	21
Passing accuracy in opp half	66%
DISCIPLINE	
Fouls committed	35
Fouls won	48
Offside	14
Yellow cards	2
Red cards	0

SEE PAGE 38 FOR FULL STATS

John KARELSE • 29

NEWCASTLE UNITED • BORN: 17.5.70

APPEARANCES	
Start (sub)	3(0)
Minutes on pitch	270
SHOT STOPPING	
Goals conceded (inside box)	6
Goals conceded (outside box)	1
Minutes per goal conceded	38.6
Clean sheets	1
Saves (shots inside box)	7
Saves (shots outside box)	1
Saves/shots	53%
DISTRIBUTION	
Long kick %	29%
Throws/short passes %	100%
CATCHING	
Crosses caught	6
Crosses punched	4
Crosses dropped	0
Catch success %	100%
DISCIPLINE	
Yellow cards	0
Red cards	0

SEE PAGE 206 FOR FULL STATS

The signs were not good for Newcastle when Ruud Gullit spent £750,000 on hulking Dutch goalkeeper John Karelse.

He had never played outside of Holland and this quickly seemed to weigh heavily on the player's shoulders.

He conceded seven goals in his first two games for the club, although much of this can be attributed to the calamitous defence he was playing behind.

He was quickly dropped from the team and it looked as if he would never grace the famous shirt again. But a 'keeper crisis before the visit to Arsenal meant that Bobby Robson had to plunge Karelse into the fray, and he shocked the supporters by keeping a clean sheet, the team's first shut-out away from home in eight months.

It was to be his finest and last hour, as he played no further part in Newcastle United's season. After demanding a transfer in January, Robson waited until the end of the season before buying out his contract and bidding him farewell.

Robbie KEANE • 7

COVENTRY CITY • BORN: 8.7.80

Coventry City ignored Sir Alex Ferguson's claim that "the lad would struggle to get in our reserves" when they made Robbie Keane the most expensive teenager in English football.

The £6 million was money well spent, though, and by the end of the season Keane's performances would surely have graced the Manchester United first XI.

He scored 12 times for his new club and finished with four assists as well. Two strikes on his debut against Derby and his athletic celebration was already burned into the minds of the Highfield Road faithful.

Aston Villa's John Gregory must have wondered if he had blundered in not buying the Irish youngster, and Keane gave him further food for thought when he scored the winner for the Sky Blues when they played their local rivals in November.

He embarked on 194 dribbles, and only seven men in the Premiership were more eager than that. Keane only scored once in his last 10 appearances of the season, but he is sure to come again.

APPEARANCES	
Start (sub)	31(0)
Minutes on pitch	2692
GOAL ATTEMPTS	
Goals inside box	12
Goals outside box	0
Minutes per goal scored	224.3
Goals/shots ratio	21%
SHOOTING	
Shots on target inside box	29
Shots on target outside box	5
Shooting accuracy	61%
PASSING	
Goal assists	4
Key passes	7
Passing accuracy in opp half	69%
DISCIPLINE	
Fouls committed	34
Fouls won	54
Offside	26
Yellow cards	3
Red cards	0

SEE PAGE 95 FOR FULL STATS

K

Eager teen: Robbie Keane

Roy KEANE • 16

MANCHESTER UNITED • BORN: 10.8.71

"Most of the time I don't like to get involved in the silly things that happen on the field and I think I've changed in that respect." Many people would disagree with that assertion by the United captain, but few would deny that undisputed Footballer of the Year Roy Keane is the most inspirational footballer in England, and probably worth the reported £52,000 a week he is paid.

After bagging just two goals in 1998–99, Keane stepped up a gear and scored five times, most memorably with a brace at Highbury that saw off Arsenal in August. His presence in the side cannot be underestimated and United's lowest point of the season, a 5–0 defeat at Chelsea, came without their skipper.

Keane was the most prolific distributor in the Premiership, making almost 1,634 successful passes, and weighed in with 111 tackles too.

But, the lasting memory of Roy Keane in 1999–2000 will be his hounding of referee Andy D'Urso in January. It gave plenty of ammunition to his critics, but Keane's packed trophy cabinet is ample consolation.

APPEARANCES	
Start (sub)	28(1)
Minutes on pitch	2417
GOAL ATTEMPTS	
Goals	5
Shots on target	15
Shooting accuracy	41%
PASSING & CROSSING	
Goal assists	1
Passes in opp half	1047
Passing accuracy in opp half	80%
Successful crosses	6
Cross completion	32%
DEFENDING	
Interceptions	15
Clearances	55
Tackles	111
Tackles won %	56%
DISCIPLINE	
Fouls	36
Yellow cards	7
Red cards	1

SEE PAGE 179 FOR FULL STATS

Inspirational: Roy Keane

1,634 Roy Keane made more successful passes

Marc KELLER • 7

WEST HAM UNITED • BORN: 14.1.68

arry Redknapp demonstrated his shrewdness the transfer market once again when he anaged to sign French international Marc eller on a free transfer at the end of 1997–98.

Because Keller can play on either flank, in idfield or as wing-back, he was mainly used s a utility player during 1999–2000. edknapp has sometimes been criticised for is 5–3–2 formation – and Keller may mpathise with the critics, because this ystem meant he was not always a first-choice eam member, with Scott Minto preferred at ft-back and Trevor Sinclair on the right.

This lack of stability invariably had an npact on his statistics. He made a ubstantial 115 crosses, but achieved a isappointing completion rate of 21%. And, hile his passing accuracy was adequate, he ade fewer than 600 passes over the course f the season.

The former Karlsruhe star is likely to stay ith West Ham but he will need to work hard o prove to Redknapp that, at 32, there is life till left in him.

APPEARANCES	
Start (sub)	19(4)
Minutes on pitch	1747
GOAL ATTEMPTS	
Goals	0
Shots on target	7
Shooting accuracy	44%
Goals/shots ratio	0%
PASSING	
Goal assists	1
Passes in opp half	364
Passing accuracy in opp half	68%
Successful crosses	24
Crossing accuracy	21%
DRIBBLING	
Dribbles & runs	103
Dribble completion	75%
Corners forced	23
DISCIPLINE	
Fouls	24
Yellow cards	4
Red cards	0

SEE PAGE 290 FOR FULL STATS

K

FB

Gary KELLY • 2

LEEDS UNITED • BORN: 9.7.74

APPEARANCES	
Start (sub)	28(3)
Minutes on pitch	2618
GOAL ATTEMPTS	
Goals	0
PASSING & CROSSING	
Goal assists	0
Passing	1102
Passing accuracy	64%
Crosses	62
Crossing accuracy	23%
DEFENDING	
Tackles	59
Tackles won %	56%
Blocks	28
Interceptions	34
Clearances	170
Shots cleared off line	0
DISCIPLINE	
Fouls	25
Yellow cards	6
Red cards	0

SEE PAGE 137 FOR FULL STATS

While his nephew and team-mate Ian Harte received more attention from the media in Leeds' exciting 1999–2000 campaign, stand-in captain and consistent right-back Gary Kelly was a model professional for the Whites and was rewarded with a new five-year contract.

In a team persistently termed "my babies" by manager David O'Leary, Kelly – alongside Nigel Martyn, Lucas Radebe, David Batty, Jason Wilcox and David Hopkin – provided enough experience to steady the ship.

Kelly's passing was not overly impressive but he was always willing to overlap on the flank and whip in dangerous crosses for the Leeds United frontmen.

Handed the captain's armband when Radebe went to play in the African Nations Cup, Kelly performed well. He did not play at all in the 1998–99 campaign due to a knee injury, and the manner in which he came back was admirable. If he could add a goalscoring string to his bow in 2000–01, Leeds will be able to boast one of the most complete full-backs in the Premiership.

han any other Premiership player

Peter KENNEDY • 3

WATFORD • BORN: 10.9.73

Peter Kennedy proved himself to be one of the most consistent Watford players in the club's rise from Division Two to the Premiership.

The Irishman must have hoped that he could make a considerable impact in the top flight, but a combination of injury and playing for the league's whipping-boys meant that he struggled to fulfil his ambition.

Kennedy scored the Hornets' first goal of the season, a penalty against Wimbledon, but that was to be his only strike. He played in the 4–1 defeat against Manchester United at Old Trafford but then missed 12 games with a knee injury. He returned in the New Year but again succumbed to a fitness problem and missed the run-in.

His passing was wayward but he did manage to whip in 98 crosses in just 1,535 minutes of football. Vicarage Road regulars were disappointed that the Premiership did not see the best of their Irish wing-back, and he himself will be eager to play a full role in Watford's first season back in the Nationwide Football League.

APPEARANCES	
Start (sub)	17(1)
Minutes on pitch	1535
GOAL ATTEMPTS	
Goals	1
PASSING & CROSSING	
Goal assists	2
Passing	544
Passing accuracy	57%
Crosses	98
Crossing accuracy	26%
DEFENDING	
Tackles	41
Tackles won %	39%
Blocks	14
Interceptions	10
Clearances	49
Shots cleared off line	0
DISCIPLINE	
Fouls	15
Yellow cards	4
Red cards	0

SEE PAGE 276 FOR FULL STATS

Martin KEOWN • 5

ARSENAL • BORN: 24.7.66

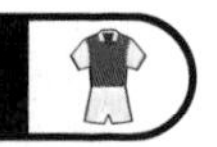

APPEARANCES	
Start (sub)	27(0)
Minutes on pitch	2404
GOAL ATTEMPTS	
Goals	1
DEFENDING	
Blocks	51
Shots cleared off line	0
Headed clearances	271
Other clearances	61
Interceptions	31
Last man saving tackles	0
Tackles won	33
Tackles won %	70%
PASSING	
Passing accuracy own half	87%
Passing accuracy opp half	65%
DISCIPLINE	
Fouls	38
Fouls in danger area	12
Yellow cards	5
Red cards	1

SEE PAGE 38 FOR FULL STATS

Martin Keown had an average season by h high standards, but was still a vital cog in team that finished second in the Premiersh and reached the final of the UEFA Cup. As 1998–99, Keown scored just once in th league, the strike coming in the Gunners' 4- romp at Leeds.

The stopper made 999 passes as he police the defence in his usual dogged manner ar played his way out of trouble. A tackle succe rate of 70% compared favourably wit virtually every defender in the Premiershi and it was no surprise when Kevin Keega named him in the squad for Euro 2000.

Despite a red card in the north London derb at White Hart Lane, Keown's disciplina record improved on 1998–99. Arsenal were f calmer as a team, although five leagu dismissals were still accrued.

Arsene Wenger will be hungry for his side t regain the Premiership title in 2000–01, an while Keown is not the youngest play around, he still has the requisite ability t help the Gunners achieve that aim.

Temuri KETSBAIA • 14

NEWCASTLE UNITED • BORN: 18.3.68

·muri Ketsbaia, the wild chicken of the ·emiership, did not have his best season in ·999–2000, playing for just 1,119 minutes of ·ewcastle's campaign.

His cult appeal to the fans had been ·egated by his constant attempts to dribble ·ast the entire opposition, but the arrival of ·obby Robson seemed to make Ketsbaia more · a team player.

He embarked on just 47 runs in 1999–2000, ·hile his passing declined in accuracy when ·mpared to 1998–99. He did manage to ·eate three goals for the Toon, one of them ·r Nikos Dabizas in United's 1–1 draw at ·atford, and another for Duncan Ferguson in ·ewcastle's first away win of the campaign at ·ston Villa.

But the return of Ferguson from injury ·eant that Ketsbaia was a frequent spectator · mid-season, and although the Scotsman fell ·ul of his fitness problems again, the result ·eing a return to action for the Georgian, it is ·kely that the bald forward will not enjoy ·uch of a future at St James's Park.

APPEARANCES	
Start (sub)	12(9)
Minutes on pitch	1119
GOAL ATTEMPTS	
Goals inside box	0
Goals outside box	0
Minutes per goal scored	n/a
Goals/shots ratio	0%
SHOOTING	
Shots on target inside box	3
Shots on target outside box	7
Shooting accuracy	37%
PASSING	
Goal assists	3
Key passes	3
Passing accuracy in opp half	68%
DISCIPLINE	
Fouls committed	12
Fouls won	12
Offside	7
Yellow cards	1
Red cards	0

SEE PAGE 207 FOR FULL STATS

K

AM

Harry KEWELL • 10

LEEDS UNITED • BORN: 22.9.78

APPEARANCES	
Start (sub)	36(0)
Minutes on pitch	3199
GOAL ATTEMPTS	
Goals	10
Shots on target	43
Shooting accuracy	40%
Goals/shots ratio	9%
PASSING	
Goal assists	4
Passes in opp half	917
Passing accuracy in opp half	65%
Successful crosses	22
Crossing accuracy	23%
DRIBBLING	
Dribbles & runs	336
Dribble completion	57%
Corners forced	65
DISCIPLINE	
Fouls	65
Yellow cards	6
Red cards	0

SEE PAGE 137 FOR FULL STATS

David O'Leary once said: "Harry Kewell will one day be a truly great player and it's my duty to help him along that path." And the Irishman certainly did so in 1999–2000. Kewell blossomed from a highly-rated player to a fully-fledged Premiership lynchpin, and Leeds' prized asset.

After scoring six times in 1998–99, he blasted 10 goals for the Yorkshire side in 1999–2000, finishing with four assists as well. He was always prepared to shoot, and only Kevin Phillips was more trigger-happy. Unfortunately, the majority of Kewell's efforts were off target, but his silky skills and accurate deliveries caused opponents great problems.

His crossing declined, but with a team playing with strikers as weak in the air as Michael Bridges and Alan Smith rather than the departed Jimmy Floyd Hasselbaink, this is unsurprising. A host of European clubs have been linked with Kewell, and though Leeds have qualified for the 2000–01 Champions League, they will face a battle to keep one of the best left-sided players in the world.

Kevin KILBANE • 4

SUNDERLAND • BORN: 1.2.77

Many Sunderland fans unfairly claimed that Kevin Kilbane was a curse on the Black Cats when he joined, as his arrival coincided with Sunderland's 11-game winless run after Christmas.

But the £2.5 million left-winger was a good acquisition by manager Peter Reid, filling the gap left by contract rebel Allan Johnston.

His cross completion rate of 30% was solid, with the ex-Preston star providing a series of dangerous balls for Kevin Phillips and Niall Quinn to feed on.

His skill also saw him earn more caps for the Republic of Ireland, something that has helped him develop into a fine player.

He scored his first league goal for Sunderland against Wimbledon, a late winner that gave the club their ninth home win of the season. Kilbane is a capable defender, too, and could be utilised as a wing-back in future. Peter Reid will be desperate to build on a solid first season back in the top flight, and Kilbane certainly has enough ability to play a big part in any progress made.

APPEARANCES	
Start (sub)	17(3)
Minutes on pitch	1511
GOAL ATTEMPTS	
Goals	1
Shots on target	12
Shooting accuracy	50%
Goals/shots ratio	4%
PASSING	
Goal assists	1
Passes in opp half	368
Passing accuracy in opp half	62%
Successful crosses	28
Crossing accuracy	30%
DRIBBLING	
Dribbles & runs	76
Dribble completion	67%
Corners forced	21
DISCIPLINE	
Fouls	15
Yellow cards	2
Red cards	0

SEE PAGE 248 FOR FULL STATS

Sean KILGANNON • 35

MIDDLESBROUGH • BORN: 8.3.81

Young Middlesbrough forward Sean Kilgannon played just three minutes of Middlesbrough's 1999–2000 season, coming on as a substitute in the 2–2 draw with Newcastle in May.

As he stepped on to the park, Newcastle brought Silvio Maric into the game. The £3.6 million man looked no more impressive than the Boro youngster. Kilgannon managed to touch the ball just once in that game, a flick-on that was cleared by the United defence.

The Dundee-born player first made the Boro squad when the team played Liverpool in January, but he did not feature. Although he could play for either the Republic of Ireland or Scotland, the tousle-haired player has elected to play for the latter.

The Middlesbrough youth team has produced such players as Andy Campbell and Robbie Stockdale in recent seasons. There is no reason why Kilgannon cannot follow in their footsteps and make a considerable impression in the north-east club's future.

SEE PAGE 193 FOR FULL STATS

Wide man: Kevin Kilbane

1,109 Tottenham attempted more tackle

Alan KIMBLE • 3

WIMBLEDON • BORN: 6.8.66

ɪw 34, Alan Kimble has been a loyal servant r Wimbledon since joining the club in 1993. is strength on the left flank has helped the ɔns' cause considerably, and while 1999–2000 as not one of his better seasons, he still had ɪme good moments in the blue shirt.

The former Cambridge United man finished ɪe season with three assists, but his pass ɪmpletion of 50% was woeful. His running ɔwn the wing and accurate delivery helped m fire in 181 crosses, and with an impressive ɪccess rate too.

He did not cause opposition goalkeepers too any problems, though, and the two shots he t went wide. But Kimble did manage to get ı the scoresheet in the Dons' Worthington ɪp victory at Huddersfield, with a thumping ee-kick that gave Terriers' goalkeeper Nico ıesen no chance.

Kimble played a lot of football in the lower agues in the early 1990s, and fate has etermined that he will have to do so again in)00–01. He, more than most, will be suited ı the task.

APPEARANCES	
Start (sub)	23(5)
Minutes on pitch	2150
GOAL ATTEMPTS	
Goals	0
PASSING & CROSSING	
Goal assists	3
Passing	763
Passing accuracy	50%
Crosses	181
Crossing accuracy	36%
DEFENDING	
Tackles	64
Tackles won %	42%
Blocks	36
Interceptions	12
Clearances	125
Shots cleared off line	0
DISCIPLINE	
Fouls	22
Yellow cards	4
Red cards	0

SEE PAGE 305 FOR FULL STATS

K

Ledley KING • 26

TOTTENHAM HOTSPUR • BORN: 16.12.80

edley King has been lazily tagged as the ıew Sol Campbell", but he does seem to have ıough ability to emulate the Spurs and ıgland defensive colossus. After making his ebut at Liverpool in 1998–99, King made ıree appearances for Tottenham in 1999–2000.

The first came in the 1–0 win at Derby, when e played 90 minutes and managed to get ɔrward enough to have two attempts at goal. nfortunately, they both went wide. He also efended stoutly, making nine defensive earances, blocks and interceptions.

His second appearance was a six-minute ameo in the defeat at Old Trafford, while he layed his second full game of the season as purs defeated Sunderland. In those three ıatches he looked a strong defender and ıanaged to avoid giving away a single free-ick. George Graham is sure to utilise King ıore and more in the future as the youngster ains in strength and confidence through ıore experience.

SEE PAGE 263 FOR FULL STATS

Determined: Alan Kimble

Georgi KINKLADZE • 27

DERBY COUNTY • BORN: 6.11.73

Jim Smith's move to buy Georgi Kinkladze seemed to smack of desperation, but it turned out to be one of the main reasons why the Rams avoided relegation. The former Manchester City wizard was not in the best shape when he arrived at Pride Park but he gradually rediscovered his undoubted genius.

He finished the campaign with six goal assists and a pass completion of 81% as he guided the team away from danger and gave the fans hope for 2000–01.

Despite starting just 12 matches, Kinkladze embarked on 110 dribbles, a total which put him in the top 50 for the whole division. His only goal for County came when he opened the scoring in Derby's 4–0 rout of Wimbledon, a result that was to prove crucial in the relegation scrap.

For a man with such talent, Kinkladze seems to be constantly involved in basement battles, but hopes are high that the Georgian can form an impressive midfield with Craig Burley and Seth Johnson. That trio could propel Derby up the Premiership in 2000–01.

APPEARANCES	
Start (sub)	12(5)
Minutes on pitch	1090
GOAL ATTEMPTS	
Goals	1
Shots on target	2
Shooting accuracy	17%
Goals/shots ratio	8%
PASSING	
Goal assists	6
Passes in opp half	376
Passing accuracy in opp half	79%
Successful crosses	13
Crossing accuracy	32%
DRIBBLING	
Dribbles & runs	110
Dribble completion	75%
Corners forced	10
DISCIPLINE	
Fouls	14
Yellow cards	2
Red cards	0

SEE PAGE 109 FOR FULL STATS

Paul KITSON • 9

WEST HAM UNITED • BORN: 9.1.71

APPEARANCES	
Start (sub)	4(6)
Minutes on pitch	418
GOAL ATTEMPTS	
Goals inside box	0
Goals outside box	0
Minutes per goal scored	n/a
Goals/shots ratio	0%
SHOOTING	
Shots on target inside box	0
Shots on target outside box	1
Shooting accuracy	17%
PASSING	
Goal assists	0
Key passes	0
Passing accuracy in opp half	66%
DISCIPLINE	
Fouls committed	8
Fouls won	4
Offside	7
Yellow cards	0
Red cards	0

SEE PAGE 290 FOR FULL STATS

When Paul Kitson and John Hartson we bought in a last-ditch attempt to save We Ham from relegation in 1997–1998, few wou have believed that their partnership would b so explosive.

But this harmony did not last long an while Hartson is no longer at the club, Kitsc probably wishes he was elsewhere too.

During 1999–2000, the ex-Newcast player's quest to gain a first-team spot w hampered by various injuries and Kitson on took part in 10 games in total.

His nightmare time was epitomised in th home game to Chelsea, when he came on as substitute and played for just 17 minute before the manager took him off again to r shuffle the team.

This was obviously the last straw and withi a week Kitson was on loan at Charlton. H only played two games for them, but hit ba at the critics by scoring the winner in the tr to Crystal Palace.

He remains a West Ham player, at least c paper, for the present.

Muhamed KONJIC • 6

COVENTRY CITY • BORN: 14.5.70

Bosnian international Muhamed Konjic has experienced some difficult periods in his life, and the 1999–2000 season at Highfield Road was no different.

After spending much of 1998–99 on the bench, he must have been looking forward to first-team action. Unfortunately he made just four appearances before going off injured in City's 1–1 draw at Everton.

His form in that brief spell was indicative of a man on top of his game, and it must have disheartened Gordon Strachan, the man who paid £2 million for the former Monaco stopper as the fiery Scot assembles a cosmopolitan squad in Warwickshire.

Konjic's passing was crisp, and of the 12 tackles he slid into he won nine – an impressive ratio.

He is a remarkably strong man and if he had stayed clear of injury then Coventry's disastrous away record might not have evolved. If he can recover in time for the new campaign, then the Sky Blues will surely reap the benefits of their Balkan purchase.

APPEARANCES	
Start (sub)	3(1)
Minutes on pitch	243
GOAL ATTEMPTS	
Goals	0
DEFENDING	
Blocks	6
Shots cleared off line	0
Headed clearances	40
Other clearances	18
Interceptions	8
Last man saving tackles	0
Tackles won	9
Tackles won %	75%
PASSING	
Passing accuracy own half	100%
Passing accuracy opp half	50%
DISCIPLINE	
Fouls	5
Fouls in danger area	4
Yellow cards	1
Red cards	0

SEE PAGE 95 FOR FULL STATS

K

Willem KORSTEN • 11

TOTTENHAM HOTSPUR • BORN: 21.1.75

APPEARANCES	
Start (sub)	4(5)
Minutes on pitch	372
GOAL ATTEMPTS	
Goals	0
Shots on target	3
Shooting accuracy	50%
Goals/shots ratio	0%
PASSING	
Goal assists	0
Passes in opp half	92
Passing accuracy in opp half	53%
Successful crosses	2
Crossing accuracy	18%
DRIBBLING	
Dribbles & runs	10
Dribble completion	90%
Corners forced	4
DISCIPLINE	
Fouls	6
Yellow cards	1
Red cards	0

SEE PAGE 263 FOR FULL STATS

After snubbing Leeds United and David O'Leary to join George Graham at Spurs, Willem Korsten finally made his full Tottenham debut at Elland Road against his former team!

The Dutch under-21 international was a victim of the White Hart Lane injury jinx and only featured for the Lilywhites in nine games. He looked reasonably lively but failed to score, with only three of his shots hitting the target.

Spurs fans will have been disappointed with his passing, as only 58% of his distribution reached a team-mate, and this is something that he will have to improve. Too often he was peripheral during games and did not offer the side much of an option.

He also had the problem of playing in the same position as David Ginola, although time has shown that Graham is willing to drop the flamboyant Frenchman.

Korsten is clearly a talented player, but at present, Premiership football seems slightly too much for him. George Graham will have to utilise all of his powers to turn the Dutchman into an effective force.

Bernard LAMBOURDE • 21

CHELSEA • BORN: 11.5.71

Like so many Chelsea players, Bernard Lambourde failed to play a full part in Gianluca Vialli's plans, instead filling in when required as a result of the squad rotation system employed at Stamford Bridge.

His first selection in the league during the 1999–2000 season was for the visit to The Riverside to play Middlesbrough and he endeared himself to the travelling fans by scoring the only goal of the game.

When given the opportunity, Lambourde looked comfortable on the ball, completing 93% of his dribbles and finding a Chelsea player with a respectable 70% of his passes.

It was against Tottenham that he scored his second goal of the season, which again proved to be the match-winner, following on from his exploits on Teesside a matter of five months earlier.

He may well prosper if given an extended run in the side. If not, there is always his promising modelling career to fall back on. Given his versatility, however, the likelihood is Vialli will hold on to the former Bordeaux utility man.

APPEARANCES	
Start (sub)	12(3)
Minutes on pitch	1123
GOAL ATTEMPTS	
Goals	2
DEFENDING	
Blocks	20
Shots cleared off line	0
Headed clearances	45
Other clearances	22
Interceptions	8
Last man saving tackles	0
Tackles won	32
Tackles won %	57%
PASSING	
Passing accuracy own half	77%
Passing accuracy opp half	63%
DISCIPLINE	
Fouls	37
Fouls in danger area	11
Yellow cards	3
Red cards	0

SEE PAGE 81 FOR FULL STATS

Frank LAMPARD • 18

WEST HAM UNITED • BORN: 20.6.78

APPEARANCES	
Start (sub)	34(0)
Minutes on pitch	3060
GOAL ATTEMPTS	
Goals	7
Shots on target	50
Shooting accuracy	59%
PASSING & CROSSING	
Goal assists	3
Passes in opp half	829
Passing accuracy in opp half	69%
Successful crosses	11
Cross completion	23%
DEFENDING	
Interceptions	20
Clearances	47
Tackles	97
Tackles won %	61%
DISCIPLINE	
Fouls	30
Yellow cards	4
Red cards	0

SEE PAGE 291 FOR FULL STATS

At the age of 22, Frank Lampard is now seen as one of the "old hands" at West Ham, but despite the high standards set in 1998–99 critics still question the youngster's place in the team.

He failed to win over some of the Upton Park faithful, as he sometimes seemed rather anonymous, and cynics at the Boleyn Ground blamed Lampard's family connections for the fact he was never dropped.

But his statistics demonstrate that during 1999–2000 he honed his class act. He must question his exclusion from the Euro 2000 squad, particularly as his performances have made him an Opta England team member.

His dribble completion rate of 83% was above the Premiership average, and he won an impressive 61% of the tackles he made. Despite this tenacity, he is still a bit of a homeboy, preferring to drive on his mother's car insurance!

The England under-21 captain must now set his sights on being part of Kevin Keegan's 2002 World Cup squad.

50 Frank Lampard fired more shots on target

Jacob LAURSEN • 16

DERBY COUNTY • BORN: 6.10.71

Reliable defender Jacob Laursen had a busy season at the heart of the Derby defence in 1999–2000, thanks to his side's rather patchy league form.

Not surprisingly, given Derby's lowly position in the league table, Laursen spent most of his time defending and managed just a single goal from eight attempts.

The goal was an important one, though, as it helped Derby to a 3–3 draw with Southampton at The Dell.

Defensively Laursen won 62% of his tackles – 11 points above the divisional average for a defender – and cleared 261 balls from danger.

Laursen showed great composure too, completing 94% of his dribbles and runs, and had a knack for spotting the loose ball. His total of 34 interceptions was only one behind Seth Johnson, who attempted the most for the Rams.

Darryl Powell may now have replaced him as captain, but minus the armband Laursen's influence was still there for all to see and will be of vital importance if Derby's performances are to improve in the 2000–01 season.

APPEARANCES	
Start (sub)	36(0)
Minutes on pitch	3167
GOAL ATTEMPTS	
Goals	1
DEFENDING	
Blocks	94
Shots cleared off line	0
Headed clearances	131
Other clearances	130
Interceptions	34
Last man saving tackles	1
Tackles won	50
Tackles won %	62%
PASSING	
Passing accuracy own half	81%
Passing accuracy opp half	50%
DISCIPLINE	
Fouls	30
Fouls in danger area	14
Yellow cards	5
Red cards	0

SEE PAGE 109 FOR FULL STATS

Jamie LAWRENCE • 7

BRADFORD CITY • BORN: 8.3.70

APPEARANCES	
Start (sub)	19(4)
Minutes on pitch	1657
GOAL ATTEMPTS	
Goals	3
Shots on target	7
Shooting accuracy	58%
Goals/shots ratio	25%
PASSING	
Goal assists	0
Passes in opp half	264
Passing accuracy in opp half	47%
Successful crosses	4
Crossing accuracy	21%
DRIBBLING	
Dribbles & runs	73
Dribble completion	75%
Corners forced	5
DISCIPLINE	
Fouls	24
Yellow cards	3
Red cards	0

SEE PAGE 66 FOR FULL STATS

Jamie Lawrence hit the headlines on numerous occasions during the 1999-2000 season – but not always for his skills on the football field.

The colourfully-coiffured winger sported a host of dyes in his hair which made him the darling of the media. The results of his regular trips to the salon were rarely out of the national newspapers.

On the field of play, however, only 50% of his passes and 21% of his centres found a Bradford player, a return which would have been higher had a recognised target man been used by Paul Jewell to challenge more effectively in the goalmouth.

His most productive spell in the side occurred between mid-January and the end of March. During this period he scored three times, although two of these could not save the Bantams from an agonizing 5–4 defeat at West Ham.

Lawrence's aim should now be to see if he can earn himself a permanent place at the start of 2000–01 in the Bradford line-up.

Graeme LE SAUX • 14

CHELSEA • BORN: 17.10.68

The 1999–2000 season will not be remembered with any great fondness by Graeme Le Saux. The cultured left-back failed to play a single match for the Blues from November onwards due to injury and this lack of fitness robbed him of a chance of making the England squad for the European Championships in Holland and Belgium.

In what little Premiership football he did play, Le Saux passed the ball with 71% accuracy, while his crosses found a team-mate an impressive 41% of the time.

Le Saux's injury could not have happened at a worse time from his point of view, as Chelsea went on to enjoy a memorable Champions League campaign and, of course, victory in the last FA Cup final to be played at Wembley before the bulldozers move in.

The good news for both Chelsea and England is that in May, Le Saux returned to light training. He will be keen to make up for lost time at both club and international level during 2000–01 by winning back his place from a host of pretenders.

APPEARANCES	
Start (sub)	6(2)
Minutes on pitch	441
GOAL ATTEMPTS	
Goals	0
PASSING & CROSSING	
Goal assists	2
Passing	180
Passing accuracy	71%
Crosses	22
Crossing accuracy	41%
DEFENDING	
Tackles	23
Tackles won %	52%
Blocks	2
Interceptions	1
Clearances	20
Shots cleared off line	0
DISCIPLINE	
Fouls	9
Yellow cards	3
Red cards	0

SEE PAGE 81 FOR FULL STATS

Matthew LE TISSIER • 7

SOUTHAMPTON • BORN: 14.10.68

APPEARANCES	
Start (sub)	9(9)
Minutes on pitch	869
GOAL ATTEMPTS	
Goals	3
Shots on target	16
Shooting accuracy	73%
Goals/shots ratio	14%
PASSING	
Goal assists	5
Passes in opp half	240
Passing accuracy in opp half	55%
Successful crosses	26
Crossing accuracy	35%
DRIBBLING	
Dribbles & runs	27
Dribble completion	56%
Corners forced	11
DISCIPLINE	
Fouls	17
Yellow cards	3
Red cards	0

SEE PAGE 235 FOR FULL STATS

Glenn Hoddle's appointment as manager at The Dell was widely predicted to bring out the best in south coast messiah Matt Le Tissier. Unfortunately for Southampton fans, the Channel Islander failed to hold down a place, managing to complete 90 minutes on just three occasions in the league.

Despite his perennial struggle to retain match fitness, "Le God" was still able to contribute in a positive fashion to Southampton's 1999–2000 Premiership campaign.

Ever the man for the big occasion, Le Tissier's most impressive display came at Old Trafford where he scored two goals, having come off the bench for the second half.

His 56% dribble completion rate suggests that he still sees gaps to run into, but his slowing legs do not allow him to escape defenders as he did in his prime in the early 1990s.

The five goals he created during the season prove that he is still capable of influencing games, but a tough decision will soon have to be made about the future of Southampton's favourite son.

Carl LEABURN • 15

WIMBLEDON • BORN: 30.3.69

Carl Leaburn had little to cheer about in 1999–2000. Egil Olsen restricted him to substitute appearances for much of the season, even though John Hartson's injuries meant that there was often a place in the first team up for grabs.

When given the opportunity to play from the off, the former Charlton man was always withdrawn from the action prematurely and thus failed to play the full 90 minutes in all five Dons matches he started. He also failed to make an impact from the bench.

Leaburn's statistics do not make good reading, but it has to be remembered that he was always on the fringes of the first team without ever being given any great opportunity to prove his worth.

Leaburn may find himself released by the club at the end of the season as the Dons look to cut costs to help cope with their drop into Division One. At the age of 31, Leaburn will be keen to resume his career with a new club in order to score his first league goal for more than two years.

APPEARANCES	
Start (sub)	5(13)
Minutes on pitch	476
GOAL ATTEMPTS	
Goals inside box	0
Goals outside box	0
Minutes per goal scored	n/a
Goals/shots ratio	0%
SHOOTING	
Shots on target inside box	2
Shots on target outside box	0
Shooting accuracy	33%
PASSING	
Goal assists	0
Key passes	1
Passing accuracy in opp half	64%
DISCIPLINE	
Fouls committed	11
Fouls won	8
Offside	1
Yellow cards	0
Red cards	0

SEE PAGE 305 FOR FULL STATS

Frank LEBOEUF • 5

CHELSEA • BORN: 22.1.68

APPEARANCES	
Start (sub)	28(0)
Minutes on pitch	2315
GOAL ATTEMPTS	
Goals	2
DEFENDING	
Blocks	57
Shots cleared off line	0
Headed clearances	141
Other clearances	68
Interceptions	29
Last man saving tackles	0
Tackles won	53
Tackles won %	58%
PASSING	
Passing accuracy own half	82%
Passing accuracy opp half	56%
DISCIPLINE	
Fouls	30
Fouls in danger area	15
Yellow cards	7
Red cards	2

SEE PAGE 81 FOR FULL STATS

Classy centre-back Frank Leboeuf had another incident-packed season at Stamford Bridge that ended on the high note of FA Cup victory against Aston Villa.

Leboeuf courted controversy in November when he was dismissed in the 1–1 draw with Everton, having collected two yellow cards.

He next played a month later in a fiery encounter with Leeds United in which he was again on the receiving end of a red card, brandished by Jeff Winter for halting Harry Kewell's progress with a late challenge. He appeared to react by stamping on the Aussie, and bedlam ensued.

His more positive contributions to Chelsea's exploits included a 70% pass completion rate and an above-average tackle success.

Following FA Cup victory at Wembley, his future at the club was uncertain as a host of French clubs enquired about the availability of his services.

A move back to France could unsettle one member of his family, though. Will pet pooch Chelsea have to undergo a change of name?

Robert LEE • 37

NEWCASTLE UNITED • BORN: 1.2.66

Ruud Gullit's refusal to give Robert Lee a squad number at the start of 1999–2000 was an obvious indication that the former England man was not going to feature in the Dutchman's plans.

But once Gullit had departed following Newcastle's disastrous start to the campaign, caretaker Steve Clarke wasted no time in handing Lee the number 37 shirt, although his return to the side was not enough to stop the Magpies crashing to a 5–1 defeat against Manchester United at Old Trafford.

Things did improve, though, after Bobby Robson took over – a man who was a big admirer of the former Charlton midfielder. Over the course of the season, Lee was well worth his place in the side, successfully completing 80% of his passes and crossing the ball with a high degree of accuracy.

His international days may well be over, but if he can continue to contribute to such great effect at club level, it is likely he will remain at Newcastle United for the remainder of his current contract.

APPEARANCES	
Start (sub)	30(0)
Minutes on pitch	2580
GOAL ATTEMPTS	
Goals	0
Shots on target	7
Shooting accuracy	33%
Goals/shots ratio	0%
PASSING	
Goal assists	1
Passes in opp half	957
Passing accuracy in opp half	76%
Successful crosses	20
Crossing accuracy	40%
DRIBBLING	
Dribbles & runs	60
Dribble completion	85%
Corners forced	13
DISCIPLINE	
Fouls	58
Yellow cards	5
Red cards	0

SEE PAGE 207 FOR FULL STATS

Neil LENNON • 7

LEICESTER CITY • BORN: 25.6.71

APPEARANCES	
Start (sub)	31(0)
Minutes on pitch	2767
GOAL ATTEMPTS	
Goals	1
Shots on target	8
Shooting accuracy	47%
PASSING & CROSSING	
Goal assists	6
Passes in opp half	1085
Passing accuracy in opp half	79%
Successful crosses	21
Cross completion	39%
DEFENDING	
Interceptions	25
Clearances	45
Tackles	149
Tackles won %	70%
DISCIPLINE	
Fouls	32
Yellow cards	7
Red cards	1

SEE PAGE 151 FOR FULL STATS

Best friends Neil Lennon and Muzzy Izzet have spent three seasons dominating the centre of the park with their dynamic displays, part of their success attributed to their excellent relationship off the field.

Sadly, the charismatic pair are room-mates no longer after the ginger midfielder's snoring proved too much for his weary friend. But their displays on the field continued to dazzle, Lennon enhancing his reputation as one of the most effective midfielders in the Premiership.

The Northern Ireland international had exceptional passing statistics, but an equally impressive attribute was his tackling. His total of 149 challenges was second in the Premiership only to John Collins.

Lennon decided to take up tango lessons in 1999–2000, and the crop-haired schemer displayed plenty of twinkle-toed trickery in dancing through the Filbert Street midfield.

He only managed a single league goal during the campaign, but it was an important one: the equaliser in Leicester's 2–2 draw at Aston Villa in April.

Oyvind LEONHARDSEN • 17

TOTTENHAM HOTSPUR • BORN: 17.8.70

eorge Graham's £3 million signing Oyvind eonhardsen was an instant hit at White Hart ane following his move from Liverpool in the uild-up to the 1999–2000 campaign.

By Christmas, Leonhardsen was really njoying his football again following his rustrating period on Merseyside. He had cored four goals, including the winner against outhampton at The Dell in November.

Unfortunately a recurring hamstring injury truck, and the skilful Norwegian was not the ame for the rest of the season.

He returned in February, but again his fitness et him down. In a final effort to be fit for Euro 000 he made a comeback in the final league atch of the season, but unfortunately had to e withdrawn from the action after 42 minutes s the hamstring gave way again.

Statistically, "Leo" contributed well in all reas of the pitch, particularly when it came to ollecting the loose ball, as his perceptive ature ensured an impressive 26 interceptions.

Should he remain fit, he has a big part to lay for Spurs in 2000–01.

APPEARANCES	
Start (sub)	20(2)
Minutes on pitch	1791
GOAL ATTEMPTS	
Goals	4
Shots on target	15
Shooting accuracy	63%
Goals/shots ratio	17%
PASSING	
Goal assists	1
Passes in opp half	500
Passing accuracy in opp half	69%
Successful crosses	14
Crossing accuracy	30%
DRIBBLING	
Dribbles & runs	86
Dribble completion	83%
Corners forced	16
DISCIPLINE	
Fouls	38
Yellow cards	3
Red cards	0

SEE PAGE 263 FOR FULL STATS

Fredrik LJUNGBERG • 8

ARSENAL • BORN: 16.4.77

APPEARANCES	
Start (sub)	22(4)
Minutes on pitch	1815
GOAL ATTEMPTS	
Goals	6
Shots on target	24
Shooting accuracy	63%
Goals/shots ratio	16%
PASSING	
Goal assists	2
Passes in opp half	513
Passing accuracy in opp half	67%
Successful crosses	11
Crossing accuracy	28%
DRIBBLING	
Dribbles & runs	128
Dribble completion	67%
Corners forced	17
DISCIPLINE	
Fouls	25
Yellow cards	2
Red cards	1

SEE PAGE 39 FOR FULL STATS

Fredrik Ljungberg scored the first of his six goals of the 1999–2000 season against Manchester United in the 2–1 defeat at Highbury in August.

It was a real case of déjà vu for the Swede, as he had scored his only previous Arsenal goal the season before against the Red Devils on his Gunners debut.

Ljungberg had a very impressive campaign, with more than half of his efforts at goal being on target, and he was very tidy in possession too.

But the Swede blotted his copybook with a dismissal. His red card was incurred against Spurs at White Hart Lane for pushing Justin Edinburgh, a moment of madness that earned him a three-match ban. On leaving the field he gestured at the referee, David Elleray, for which he received a stern warning from the Football Association.

A rib injury affected the latter part of his campaign, but he will be back in 2000–01 to play as big a part as possible in any future Arsenal success.

Steve LOMAS • 11

WEST HAM UNITED • BORN: 18.1.74

Steve Lomas was a consistent team member until injury struck, even prepared to play in an uncustomary right-back role when team injuries forced him there.

While his vocal chords are famously used for karaoke off the pitch, they are better utilised on the field for keeping his team motivated, and his leadership skills led to Harry Redknapp making him captain.

Better equipped in his terrier-like role in midfield, it was there that his performances were most effective particularly in his passing and dribbling. However, he often looked susceptible at right-back and he did not figure in the top five tacklers at the club, emphasising this weakness.

The Northern Ireland international is never one to shy away from confrontation, and it is for this reason he received his one red card.

He suffered a broken toe in early April, but at only 26 he will no doubt return fit for the new battles of 2000–01. But his biggest struggle may be wresting the captain's armband from equally fiery Paolo Di Canio!

APPEARANCES	
Start (sub)	25(0)
Minutes on pitch	2135
GOAL ATTEMPTS	
Goals	1
Shots on target	7
Shooting accuracy	54%
PASSING & CROSSING	
Goal assists	4
Passes in opp half	601
Passing accuracy in opp half	69%
Successful crosses	14
Cross completion	28%
DEFENDING	
Interceptions	22
Clearances	113
Tackles	70
Tackles won %	56%
DISCIPLINE	
Fouls	23
Yellow cards	5
Red cards	1

SEE PAGE 291 FOR FULL STATS

Chris LUMSDON • 23

SUNDERLAND • BORN: 15.12.79

Sunderland youngster Chris Lumsdon was given the opportunity to impress in the opening fixture of the 1999–2000 season against Chelsea at Stamford Bridge. He played on the left side of midfield in preference to Allan Johnston, who was in dispute with Peter Reid regarding his new contract.

In Lumsdon's only half of Premiership football, he was able to complete 93% of his 15 passes and have an effort at goal blocked by the star-studded Chelsea defence.

Unfortunately he failed to represent the Black Cats again following the Chelsea match, but had a successful loan spell at Second Division Blackpool, in which he scored one goal in five games.

Lumsdon's future at the Stadium of Light will now depend on how confident Peter Reid is in giving the youngster a chance to prove himself following his side's impressive displays with more experienced players during the 1999–2000 season.

SEE PAGE 249 FOR FULL STATS

Consistent crooner: Steve Lomas

Andreas LUND • 34

WIMBLEDON • BORN: 7.5.75

ndreas Lund was signed by Egil Olsen for a ee of £2.8 million from Molde, making his ebut for Wimbledon in the Dons' visit to helsea in February.

He made an immediate impact by scoring at tamford Bridge, but despite adding to his ally with a stunning strike in the 3–1 defeat t home to Arsenal, he could not save the /ombles from their relegation to Nationwide ivision One.

Lund was impressive in the air, but his pass ompletion rate of 53% in the opposition half /as extremely disappointing.

In the final weeks of the season he lost his lace in the side to John Hartson, who eturned following injury. Lund's final ppearance was as a substitute in the ill-fated ncounter at Southampton on the last day of he season.

He will have to wait to find out who takes ver at Selhurst Park to discover if he, like so nany of Egil Olsen's signings, still has a part o play in the future plans of Wimbledon ootball Club.

APPEARANCES	
Start (sub)	10(2)
Minutes on pitch	849
GOAL ATTEMPTS	
Goals inside box	2
Goals outside box	0
Minutes per goal scored	424.5
Goals/shots ratio	9%
SHOOTING	
Shots on target inside box	10
Shots on target outside box	0
Shooting accuracy	45%
PASSING	
Goal assists	1
Key passes	3
Passing accuracy in opp half	53%
DISCIPLINE	
Fouls committed	21
Fouls won	16
Offside	8
Yellow cards	1
Red cards	0

SEE PAGE 305 FOR FULL STATS

Claus LUNDEKVAM • 5

SOUTHAMPTON • BORN: 22.3.73

APPEARANCES	
Start (sub)	25(2)
Minutes on pitch	2274
GOAL ATTEMPTS	
Goals	0
DEFENDING	
Blocks	58
Shots cleared off line	0
Headed clearances	231
Other clearances	98
Interceptions	15
Last man saving tackles	2
Tackles won	29
Tackles won %	56%
PASSING	
Passing accuracy own half	79%
Passing accuracy opp half	49%
DISCIPLINE	
Fouls	35
Fouls in danger area	17
Yellow cards	3
Red cards	1

SEE PAGE 235 FOR FULL STATS

Norwegian Claus Lundekvam had a solid first half of the season in the Saints' defence, but occasionally looked out of his depth against some of the Premiership's cosmopolitan array of star strikers.

The signing of Dean Richards took some of the pressure off Lundekvam, as in previous seasons the Norwegian did not benefit from having a strong centre-back partner. The pair swept away 739 balls from defence between them, which shows how effective their partnership was at clearing the danger.

Lundekvam's lowest point of the season came in the 1–0 defeat at home to Tottenham when he was sent off. Referee Steve Bennett brandished the red card in stoppage-time at the end of 90 minutes for the Norwegian's second bookable offence, a foul on Steffen Iversen, who was also his victim for the first caution.

Now that Richards is installed as Glenn Hoddle's first choice centre-back, it remains to be seen if Lundekvam will be a regular in the team at the start of 2000–01 if Hoddle gets the opportunity to strengthen his squad.

Oleg LUZHNY • 22

ARSENAL • BORN: 5.8.68

Much was expected of Arsene Wenger's £1.8 million man Oleg Luzhny when he signed from Dynamo Kiev for the Gunners during the summer of 1999. It was believed that he was nicknamed "The Horse" – for his rampaging runs up the flank – but it transpired that his Ukrainian moniker meant "The Moose".

The Ukraine captain had impressed during the two sides' Champions League meetings in 1998–99, but struggled to break into the Arsenal first team because of the form of the evergreen Lee Dixon. Luzhny had more opportunities to impress in the second half of the season, but mostly at centre-back. His longest stint in the starting line-up ended abruptly thanks to referee Uriah Rennie, who sent him off in the win at Wimbledon.

At the end of the 1999–2000 season, Luzhny had at least understood the rivalry between Arsenal and Tottenham. He endeared himself to Gunners fans by advising fellow-countryman Sergei Rebrov not to join Spurs, but instead to choose a club that had a chance of winning something.

APPEARANCES	
Start (sub)	16(5)
Minutes on pitch	1462
GOAL ATTEMPTS	
Goals	0
PASSING & CROSSING	
Goal assists	1
Passing	715
Passing accuracy	75%
Crosses	44
Crossing accuracy	27%
DEFENDING	
Tackles	56
Tackles won %	50%
Blocks	23
Interceptions	12
Clearances	83
Shots cleared off line	0
DISCIPLINE	
Fouls	10
Yellow cards	2
Red cards	1

SEE PAGE 39 FOR FULL STATS

FB

Des LYTTLE • 2

WATFORD • BORN: 26.9.71

APPEARANCES	
Start (sub)	11(0)
Minutes on pitch	939
GOAL ATTEMPTS	
Goals	0
PASSING & CROSSING	
Goal assists	0
Passing	291
Passing accuracy	55%
Crosses	27
Crossing accuracy	41%
DEFENDING	
Tackles	15
Tackles won %	67%
Blocks	10
Interceptions	12
Clearances	82
Shots cleared off line	0
DISCIPLINE	
Fouls	4
Yellow cards	1
Red cards	0

SEE PAGE 277 FOR FULL STATS

Following his move from Nottingham Forest on a free transfer before the start of the 1999–2000 season, Des Lyttle started Watford's Premiership campaign in the right-back slot. He proved to be something of a disappointment, though, and failed to hold down a place from mid-September onwards.

This was partly due to Nigel Gibbs's presence in the squad and Graham Taylor's signing of Neil Cox from Bolton Wanderers.

In his time at Vicarage Road, Lyttle won a solid 67% of his tackles but was guilty of too many basic errors at the back.

Such competition for the Hornets at right-back forced Lyttle to take a loan spell at West Brom, where he was thrown into another relegation dogfight.

He appeared in all of the Baggies' last nine matches and helped them remain in Division One. It would seem that he is more comfortable at this level, and he may well try to secure a permanent deal at The Hawthorns, having been told by Taylor that his services were no longer required at Vicarage Road.

Neil MADDISON • 15

MIDDLESBROUGH • BORN: 2.10.69

he archetypal squad player, 1999–2000 was nother season of frustration for ⁄iddlesbrough's Neil Maddison, who was only sed by boss Bryan Robson in times of injury risis on Teesside.

After just one appearance as a substitute in he opening 16 Premiership games of 999–2000, Maddison finally got a fair crack f the whip when Boro's luck was out on the itness front. Starting with the game against radford in December, Maddison appeared in 1 of the next 13 Premiership fixtures, once gain proving his versatility by filling the aps in defence or midfield.

Maddison was on the pitch for 649 minutes n 1999–2000 and, while he failed to score or reate a goal, was quietly effective in nanipulating games. The former Southampton nan completed 67% of the 252 passes he ttempted and was never shy on the ball.

But with Middlesbrough constantly being inked with various foreign players on a egular basis, it is difficult to see Maddison orcing his way into Robson's first-team plans.

APPEARANCES	
Start (sub)	6(7)
Minutes on pitch	649
GOAL ATTEMPTS	
Goals	0
Shots on target	1
Shooting accuracy	20%
PASSING & CROSSING	
Goal assists	0
Passes in opp half	155
Passing accuracy in opp half	61%
Successful crosses	3
Cross completion	20%
DEFENDING	
Interceptions	3
Clearances	16
Tackles	9
Tackles won %	56%
DISCIPLINE	
Fouls	13
Yellow cards	1
Red cards	0

SEE PAGE 193 FOR FULL STATS

Chris MAKIN • 2

SUNDERLAND • BORN: 8.5.73

APPEARANCES	
Start (sub)	34(0)
Minutes on pitch	2937
GOAL ATTEMPTS	
Goals	1
PASSING & CROSSING	
Goal assists	0
Passing	1384
Passing accuracy	76%
Crosses	43
Crossing accuracy	37%
DEFENDING	
Tackles	114
Tackles won %	48%
Blocks	30
Interceptions	15
Clearances	126
Shots cleared off line	1
DISCIPLINE	
Fouls	50
Yellow cards	11
Red cards	1

SEE PAGE 249 FOR FULL STATS

Consistent full-back Chris Makin was one of Sunderland's unsung heroes in their romp through Division One in 1998–99 and transferred his form into the Premiership.

Be it on the right or left of defence, the former Marseille man was a dependable figure in 1999–2000 who few opposing wingers got the better of – as 114 attempted tackles and 126 clearances illustrates. And going forward, his completion rates in terms of passing, crossing and dribbling were all superior to the Premiership's average for defenders.

However, Makin's season threatened to collapse in January when, after a 4–1 defeat against Arsenal, he was spotted on a highly-publicised night-time sortie and incurred the subsequent wrath of boss Peter Reid.

Along with team-mate Nicky Summerbee, Makin was dropped for the next match against Leeds, but soon returned to the starting line-up for all but one of the Black Cats' last 15 games of 1999–2000. There is little doubt that Makin will play just as big a part at the Stadium of Light in 2000–01.

vas the lowest in the Premiership

Stefan MALZ • 19

ARSENAL • BORN: 15.6.72

Completing one of the least glamorous signings in Arsenal's history, Arsene Wenger surprised the Highbury faithful in the summer of 1999 by snapping up midfielder Stefan Malz from German side 1860 Munich.

With Marc Overmars ahead of him in the pecking order, Malz was unable to force his way into the Gunners' first team and did not make his Premiership debut until November, when he came off the bench for the last nine minutes of the game against Derby County.

The sale of Stephen Hughes to Everton in February opened the door a little further for Malz in the first-team reckoning, but led to Arsenal fans questioning the decision to let a promising English player who had come through the ranks go, while persevering with a foreigner who seemed merely a reserve.

However, Malz was to justify his place in the Arsenal squad on the final day of the Premiership campaign by scoring one goal and creating another in his first full Premiership run-out for the north London side – a 4–2 defeat against Newcastle.

APPEARANCES	
Start (sub)	2(3)
Minutes on pitch	246
GOAL ATTEMPTS	
Goals	1
Shots on target	2
Shooting accuracy	29%
PASSING & CROSSING	
Goal assists	1
Passes in opp half	67
Passing accuracy in opp half	72%
Successful crosses	4
Cross completion	57%
DEFENDING	
Interceptions	1
Clearances	4
Tackles	2
Tackles won %	50%
DISCIPLINE	
Fouls	6
Yellow cards	0
Red cards	0

SEE PAGE 39 FOR FULL STATS

Alex MANNINGER • 13

ARSENAL • BORN: 4.6.77

APPEARANCES	
Start (sub)	14(1)
Minutes on pitch	1305
SHOT STOPPING	
Goals conceded (inside box)	12
Goals conceded (outside box)	4
Minutes per goal conceded	81.6
Clean sheets	5
Saves (shots inside box)	17
Saves (shots outside box)	12
Saves/shots	64%
DISTRIBUTION	
Long kick %	42%
Throws/short passes %	93%
CATCHING	
Crosses caught	20
Crosses punched	9
Crosses dropped	0
Catch success %	100%
DISCIPLINE	
Yellow cards	0
Red cards	0

SEE PAGE 38 FOR FULL STATS

The calf injury Arsenal goalkeeper Davi Seaman picked up in a pre-season friendl with Monaco allowed his understudy Ale Manninger to start the Gunners' first nin Premiership fixtures of 1999–2000.

However, Seaman's return to fitness and th first team in October renewed speculatio about the future of Manninger.

Gossip increased further when Manninger national team coach, Otto Baric, stated that move and regular first-team action woul increase the young 'keeper's chances c becoming Austria's number one choice.

But Manninger stuck out 1999–2000 wit Arsenal, appearing in the league and cup when Seaman was either rested or injured. H ended up with five clean sheets from 14 start and had an immaculate 100% catc completion rate.

Although the vast majority of Premiershi sides would love to have Manninger in the first team, chances are that 2000–01 wi herald more disappointment for a 'keeper wh deserves more than sporadic appearances.

CB Elena MARCELINO • 3

NEWCASTLE UNITED • BORN: 26.9.71

A big, confident centre-back who had excelled in Mallorca's run to the Cup Winners' Cup final in 1998–99, Spaniard Marcelino was expected to solve Newcastle's defensive problems.

The £5 million fee splashed out on Marcelino looked like money well spent by coach Ruud Gullit, but the 6'2" stopper appeared in just six games in the first half of 1999–2000.

And, by refusing to play against Roma in a UEFA Cup tie in November, the Spanish international did not do himself many favours in the popularity stakes. Claiming he would have to miss the game because of a groin strain, Marcelino upset boss Bobby Robson, who commented: "There are bottlers at this club and we don't want them."

Marcelino bounced back to appear in four consecutive Premiership games over the turn of the new year, forming a decent-looking partnership with Nikos Dabizas and making 101 clearances. However, the arrival of Helder on loan from Deportivo La Coruña forced Marcelino back on to the sidelines, where he stayed for the remainder of 1999–2000.

APPEARANCES	
Start (sub)	10(1)
Minutes on pitch	880
GOAL ATTEMPTS	
Goals	0
DEFENDING	
Blocks	31
Shots cleared off line	0
Headed clearances	77
Other clearances	24
Interceptions	7
Last man saving tackles	0
Tackles won	15
Tackles won %	44%
PASSING	
Passing accuracy own half	78%
Passing accuracy opp half	55%
DISCIPLINE	
Fouls	13
Fouls in danger area	7
Yellow cards	2
Red cards	0

SEE PAGE 207 FOR FULL STATS

M

CB Javier MARGAS • 30

WEST HAM UNITED • BORN: 10.5.69

APPEARANCES	
Start (sub)	15(3)
Minutes on pitch	1335
GOAL ATTEMPTS	
Goals	1
DEFENDING	
Blocks	39
Shots cleared off line	0
Headed clearances	104
Other clearances	50
Interceptions	25
Last man saving tackles	0
Tackles won	23
Tackles won %	49%
PASSING	
Passing accuracy own half	77%
Passing accuracy opp half	51%
DISCIPLINE	
Fouls	17
Fouls in danger area	3
Yellow cards	1
Red cards	1

SEE PAGE 291 FOR FULL STATS

After going AWOL over the summer, Javier Margas, with the aid of a good English teacher, returned from Chile to Chadwell Heath to surprise his manager and West Ham fans.

Chile's most-capped player was welcomed back, and in some of his performances rekindled the impressive displays he made in World Cup 1998. Surprisingly, Harry Redknapp was keener to play Neil Ruddock in the centre of the defence, and Margas spent some of the season only on the bench.

When he did play he was a capable force, making an impressive 154 clearances in only 1,335 minutes on the pitch. Equally as good as his defensive clearances were his passes to team-mates, and he successfully completed two-thirds of his distribution.

Painting his hair claret and blue, the former Colo Colo player has demonstrated his commitment to the Irons and, if he remains free from his recurring knee injury, his defensive competence and experience should help to sustain West Ham's tentative back line in the 2000–01 Premiership campaign.

Silvio MARIC • 10

NEWCASTLE UNITED • BORN: 20.3.75

Another of Ruud Gullit's signings for Newcastle not to deliver on his reputation, Silvio Maric ended a season of frustration at St James's Park by going AWOL in May 2000.

The £3.65 million signing was scarcely used in 1999–2000 and a move to his old club Croatia Zagreb fell through shortly before Christmas when a transfer fee could not be agreed.

Things reached boiling-point shortly after the season finished when Maric failed to show for the club's trip to Trinidad, sparking fresh rumours that his spell in the north-east was all but over.

On his day, Maric is one of Europe's most skilful midfielders and attracted interest from AC Milan and Juventus before joining Newcastle in February 1999.

In the 400 minutes of football he managed in 1999–2000, Maric had five blocked shots and found a team-mate with 72% of the 169 passes he attempted. His dribble completion rate of 86% was six points above the average for a Premiership midfielder, but in truth, he has been a costly mistake for the Magpies.

APPEARANCES	
Start (sub)	3(10)
Minutes on pitch	400
GOAL ATTEMPTS	
Goals	0
Shots on target	0
Shooting accuracy	0%
Goals/shots ratio	0%
PASSING	
Goal assists	0
Passes in opp half	115
Passing accuracy in opp half	70%
Successful crosses	3
Crossing accuracy	33%
DRIBBLING	
Dribbles & runs	14
Dribble completion	86%
Corners forced	2
DISCIPLINE	
Fouls	13
Yellow cards	0
Red cards	0

SEE PAGE 207 FOR FULL STATS

Carlos Arturo MARINELLI • 34

MIDDLESBROUGH • BORN: 28.8.80

With the arrival of young Argentinean midfielder Carlos Marinelli at Middlesbrough in September 1999 came the inevitable comparisons to Diego Maradona, both players having started their careers at Boca Juniors.

The early indications suggest that Marinelli will not disappoint the Teesside faithful, 7,000 of whom turned up to see the teenager's debut for Boro's reserves against Barnsley. He let nobody down, scoring the only goal of the game with a 25-yard free-kick.

Boss Bryan Robson, who had signed the skilful starlet for £1.5 million after he had played against Middlesbrough's youth team in the annual Irish Milk Cup, handed Marinelli his Premiership debut on Boxing Day against Sheffield Wednesday.

Replacing striker Alun Armstrong at half-time, Marinelli quickly found his way into the action, successfully dribbling with the ball twice, whipping over three crosses and linking up impressively with Juninho.

SEE PAGE 193 FOR FULL STATS

Andy MARRIOTT • 13

SUNDERLAND • BORN: 11.10.70

Sunderland's Welsh international goalkeeper Andy Marriott had to be content with playing second fiddle to Thomas Sorensen in the 1999–2000 season.

Having started his career at Arsenal, Marriott made his name at Wrexham, proving himself to be one of the best 'keepers in the lower divisions. Mackems boss Peter Reid snapped him up in the summer of 1998 but played Marriott just once in 1998–99.

And he was given just one more chance in 1999–2000, stepping in for the flu-stricken Sorensen in the game against Wimbledon in January. Despite lacking match practice, Marriott performed impressively, making four saves. He denied Carl Cort and Jason Euell, as well as stopping two efforts from Walid Badir.

Unfortunately, a headed goal by Cort denied Marriott a clean sheet and sent Sunderland home without a point. Unlikely to displace Sorensen, Marriott is sure to prove a reliable deputy again in 2000–01.

SEE PAGE 248 FOR FULL STATS

Chris MARSDEN • 4

SOUTHAMPTON • BORN: 3.1.69

Chris Marsden was a useful member of Southampton's squad in 1999–2000 which, despite him now being 31 years old, was his first full season of Premiership football.

An intelligent and sensible midfielder, Marsden was always looking to get the ball down and start new moves, having broken up opposition attacks with his tackling. On 85 occasions Marsden made challenges, and he completed 76% of his passes.

The departure of Dave Jones, the manager who had brought Marsden to the club after they had been together at Stockport, did not affect the balding schemer who went on to play a key role under Glenn Hoddle's tutelage.

Marsden's return from injury in January coincided with a three-game winning run for the Saints, which more or less secured another season of top-flight football.

Having scored twice at the tail end of the 1998–99 campaign, Marsden will have been disappointed not to find the net in 1999–2000, but his midfield holding role restricted him to just eight shots at goal.

APPEARANCES	
Start (sub)	19(2)
Minutes on pitch	1637
GOAL ATTEMPTS	
Goals	0
Shots on target	2
Shooting accuracy	25%
PASSING & CROSSING	
Goal assists	1
Passes in opp half	467
Passing accuracy in opp half	69%
Successful crosses	5
Cross completion	25%
DEFENDING	
Interceptions	3
Clearances	39
Tackles	85
Tackles won %	52%
DISCIPLINE	
Fouls	37
Yellow cards	6
Red cards	0

SEE PAGE 235 FOR FULL STATS

M

S

Ian MARSHALL • 20

LEICESTER CITY • BORN: 20.3.66

APPEARANCES	
Start (sub)	2(19)
Minutes on pitch	535
GOAL ATTEMPTS	
Goals inside box	0
Goals outside box	0
Minutes per goal scored	n/a
Goals/shots ratio	0%
SHOOTING	
Shots on target inside box	6
Shots on target outside box	1
Shooting accuracy	47%
PASSING	
Goal assists	0
Key passes	1
Passing accuracy in opp half	63%
DISCIPLINE	
Fouls committed	12
Fouls won	14
Offside	9
Yellow cards	1
Red cards	0

SEE PAGE 151 FOR FULL STATS

Following three eventful years at Filbert Street, Leicester striker Ian Marshall was released in the summer of 2000, taking with him a Worthington Cup winner's medal and the memories of some vital goals in his time at the club.

A left-footed frontrunner with the incredible knack of scoring when it matters, Marshall could not shake off a persistent hamstring injury in 1999–2000 and, according to O'Neill, spent the majority of time "smoking cigarettes in the treatment room", while managing just 535 minutes of Premiership football.

The highlight of Marshall's season came in the Worthington Cup quarter-final against Fulham in January when he scored two crucial goals in a 3–3 draw, before the Foxes won on penalties.

With Emile Heskey, Tony Cottee and latterly Darren Eadie and Stan Collymore ahead of him in the pecking order Marshall only started two Premiership matches, neither of which he finished. He failed to score or create a goal but caused defenders problems with his robust style after he had entered the fray as a sub.

1999–2000 than any other Premiership team

Nigel MARTYN • 1

LEEDS UNITED • BORN: 11.8.66

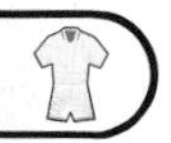

One of the older heads in Leeds' team of young upstarts, Nigel Martyn enjoyed another excellent season in 1999–2000.

But the former Crystal Palace 'keeper struggled to force his way into Kevin Keegan's England team ahead of David Seaman, despite earning a place in the PFA Premiership select XI for the second season running.

The Opta stats illustrate, if further proof were needed, how consistently Martyn performed in the Premiership. He did not miss a single minute of football in 1999–2000 and made 144 saves – only Middlesbrough's Mark Schwarzer and Neil Sullivan of Wimbledon made more.

But, having let in only 28 goals in 1998–99, Martyn will have been disappointed to concede 43 strikes in 1999–2000 and his catch success rate of 95% was inferior to his record of the previous campaign.

That said, Martyn is still rated highly by his manager, fellow-professionals and supporters alike. But at 34, time is running out for Martyn to fulfill his real ambition of becoming England's first-choice goalkeeper.

APPEARANCES	
Start (sub)	38(0)
Minutes on pitch	3420
SHOT STOPPING	
Goals conceded (inside box)	38
Goals conceded (outside box)	5
Minutes per goal conceded	79.6
Clean sheets	13
Saves (shots inside box)	71
Saves (shots outside box)	73
Saves/shots	77%
DISTRIBUTION	
Long kick %	41%
Throws/short passes %	87%
CATCHING	
Crosses caught	37
Crosses punched	13
Crosses dropped	2
Catch success %	95%
DISCIPLINE	
Yellow cards	2
Red cards	0

SEE PAGE 136 FOR FULL STATS

Consistent performer: Nigel Martyn

Dominic MATTEO • 21

LIVERPOOL • BORN: 24.4.74

Best defence: Dominic Matteo

APPEARANCES	
Start (sub)	32(0)
Minutes on pitch	2872
GOAL ATTEMPTS	
Goals	0
DEFENDING	
Blocks	33
Shots cleared off line	0
Headed clearances	104
Other clearances	61
Interceptions	16
Last man saving tackles	1
Tackles won	43
Tackles won %	49%
PASSING	
Passing accuracy own half	80%
Passing accuracy opp half	68%
DISCIPLINE	
Fouls	33
Fouls in danger area	12
Yellow cards	2
Red cards	0

SEE PAGE 165 FOR FULL STATS

Dominic Matteo finally established himself in the Liverpool line-up in 1999–2000, having flitted in and out of the team after making his debut in 1993.

Although he was used mainly in central defence in the early stages of his career, Reds boss Gerard Houllier utilised Matteo in the troublesome left-back position for the majority of the 1999–2000 campaign. In that role Matteo had a fine season, despite being criticised by some Liverpool fans for his attacking play.

The 26-year-old started all but six Premiership games and was an integral part of the best defence in the top flight. He made 165 clearances and attempted 88 tackles – 38 more than he went in for in 1998–99.

Belying his critics, Matteo created five goals when venturing forward and his dribble success rate of 90% was three points above the Premiership's average for a defender. Although he failed to score in the league, Matteo did find the net with a vital strike against Huddersfield in the third round of the FA Cup.

CB David MAY • 4

MANCHESTER UNITED • BORN: 24.6.70

Instrumental in Manchester United's FA Cup win and Champions League celebrations in 1998–99, David May endured a nightmare campaign in 1999–2000, managing to play just two games in the league.

Only one of those was for the Champions – a 12-minute substitute appearance in the 2–0 win over Leicester in November. He touched the ball just five times.

His other game in 1999–2000 came during a loan spell with Huddersfield, but he was forced off the pitch after 77 minutes of his debut against Crewe on Boxing Day.

A hamstring injury sidelined him that day but a worse stroke of luck was to follow. On his first training session back with United, May ruptured his Achilles tendon, an injury serious enough to raise question marks over May's future in football.

Even if he can recover sufficiently, the former Blackburn man may have to leave Old Trafford if he is to get first-team football.

SEE PAGE 179 FOR FULL STATS

M Gary McALLISTER • 10

COVENTRY CITY • BORN: 25.12.64

Even the more confident of Coventry's supporters could not have predicted what a fantastic season lay in store for veteran midfielder Gary McAllister.

The former Scotland international ended the campaign as Coventry's Player of the Year and the Premiership's top-scoring midfielder with 11 league goals. A surprise move to Liverpool in July resulted for McAllister, who has re-established himself as one of the top-flight's most effective midfield men.

Even without his goals, it was a pretty amazing season for the Coventry skipper. Manchester United's Roy Keane aside, McAllister made more passes (1,820) than any other top-flight player and drifted wide to deliver 207 crosses and corners.

McAllister also contributed an exceptional amount of defensive work, including 92 tackles and 31 interceptions.

Although he will be 35 years old at the beginning of 2000–01, McAllister looks like being an excellent addition to Liverpool's squad as they seek trophies on four fronts.

Mersey-bound: Gary McAllister

APPEARANCES	
Start (sub)	38(0)
Minutes on pitch	3364
GOAL ATTEMPTS	
Goals	11
Shots on target	27
Shooting accuracy	51%
PASSING & CROSSING	
Goal assists	4
Passes in opp half	1184
Passing accuracy in opp half	67%
Successful crosses	53
Cross completion	26%
DEFENDING	
Interceptions	31
Clearances	76
Tackles	92
Tackles won %	51%
DISCIPLINE	
Fouls	24
Yellow cards	2
Red cards	0

SEE PAGE 95 FOR FULL STATS

11 Gary McAllister was the top-scorin

Stuart McCALL • 4

M — BRADFORD CITY • BORN: 10.6.64

A legend at Valley Parade, Stuart McCall would have been the most disappointed man in Bradford had the Bantams been relegated from the Premiership in 1999–2000.

As it was, his influence and enthusiasm in midfield were among the main factors in Bradford's last-day survival, which prompted celebrations equivalent to those seen on the day when City were promoted a year earlier.

McCall, who started his career in West Yorkshire before moving on to Everton and Rangers, skippered Bradford admirably through 1999–2000, anchoring the midfield to great effect and never letting his head drop, even when those around him might have.

In the 33 starts and one substitute appearance McCall made, he attempted more passes (1,459) than any other City player with a success rate of 71%, while his total of 45 interceptions was the most made by a Premiership midfielder.

The 36-year-old scored just one goal in the league but it was a vital one – a last minute equaliser in the 1–1 draw with Spurs.

APPEARANCES	
Start (sub)	33(1)
Minutes on pitch	2997
GOAL ATTEMPTS	
Goals	1
Shots on target	4
Shooting accuracy	50%
PASSING & CROSSING	
Goal assists	2
Passes in opp half	942
Passing accuracy in opp half	68%
Successful crosses	9
Cross completion	39%
DEFENDING	
Interceptions	45
Clearances	111
Tackles	137
Tackles won %	53%
DISCIPLINE	
Fouls	51
Yellow cards	6
Red cards	0

SEE PAGE 66 FOR FULL STATS

Gavin McCANN • 21

SUNDERLAND • BORN: 10.1.78

APPEARANCES	
Start (sub)	21(3)
Minutes on pitch	1882
GOAL ATTEMPTS	
Goals	4
Shots on target	8
Shooting accuracy	32%
PASSING & CROSSING	
Goal assists	3
Passes in opp half	500
Passing accuracy in opp half	67%
Successful crosses	27
Cross completion	33%
DEFENDING	
Interceptions	25
Clearances	30
Tackles	100
Tackles won %	53%
DISCIPLINE	
Fouls	58
Yellow cards	8
Red cards	0

SEE PAGE 249 FOR FULL STATS

Signed midway through Sunderland's Division One Championship-winning campaign of 1998–99, midfielder Gavin McCann was an unexpected fixture in the Black Cats' team.

On signing McCann for £500,000 from Everton in November 1998, Sunderland boss Peter Reid said: "He's just an outstanding player and I can't believe I got him at the price I did."

He proved his pedigree in 1999–2000, scoring four times, including the winner against Watford in November and a goal against Manchester United in a 2–2 draw just after Christmas. McCann could have scored more, but on 17 occasions wayward finishing let him down. His hard work in midfield resulted in exactly 100 tackles and 802 passes with a success rate of 72%.

However, McCann's season ended on a sour note when he badly damaged knee ligaments in a game against Coventry in February. That injury sidelined McCann for the rest of the season, but 2000–01 should see a return for a player Reid has tipped for England honours.

Jamie McCLEN • 19

NEWCASTLE UNITED • BORN: 13.5.79

By ostracising half his Newcastle squad in the summer of 1999, Dutch coach Ruud Gullit was forced to call upon inexperienced youngsters like Jamie McClen at the start of the 1999–2000 season.

Having played just once in 1998–99, local lad McClen was selected to play two consecutive games in August, starting the fixtures against Wimbledon and Sunderland at St James's Park.

The latter match signalled the end of Gullit's reign in the north-east and McClen was to start just one more Premiership game in 1999–2000.

In the 304 minutes he did play, McClen had just one shot at goal but enjoyed an amazingly good pass completion rate of 91% from 124 passes. However, he was booked in two of the three games he started.

He was recalled to the Newcastle squad for the last four games of the season, showing that he may well be in the plans of Bobby Robson for the 2000–01 campaign.

SEE PAGE 207 FOR FULL STATS

Dave McEWEN • 23

TOTTENHAM HOTSPUR • BORN: 2.11.77

Of the five players Tottenham signed from th lower leagues in 1999–2000, striker Dav McEwen arrived at White Hart Lane with th lowest level of publicity.

The young striker had been close to signin for Brentford after trials in summer 1999, bu was playing his football in the Ryman Leagu for Dulwich Hamlet. Eleven goals in 25 game attracted the attention of Spurs' director c football, David Pleat.

A small transfer fee took McEwen to Whit Hart Lane and he was handed his debut in th game against Derby in April. Coming off th substitutes' bench for Steffen Iversen with 2 minutes remaining, McEwen quickly gc involved in the action and came close t scoring with three good chances.

A University of London undergraduate i Business Studies, McEwen only trained part time with Spurs in 1999–2000 but goes on t the full-time payroll for the beginning of th 2000–01 campaign.

SEE PAGE 263 FOR FULL STATS

Brian McGOVERN • 36

ARSENAL • BORN: 28.4.80

Unable to break into Arsene Wenger's first-team squad on a regular basis, Arsenal's young defender Brian McGovern ended the 1999–2000 season thinking about a move away from Highbury to further his career.

A 20-year-old Irishman, McGovern aimed to use the annual Toulon under-21 international tournament to put himself in the shop window, saying: "My agent has told me that a lot of clubs will have representatives watching and I aim to impress."

Having shone in a month's loan at QPR at the turn of the year, McGovern was given his Premiership debut by the Gunners on the final day of 1999–2000 against Newcastle, when Wenger had rested several senior players in preparation for the UEFA Cup final.

Coming on for the final 23 minutes of the match, McGovern impressed the travelling Arsenal fans by making one clearance, one block and finding a red and white shirt with nine passes.

SEE PAGE 39 FOR FULL STATS

Mark McKEEVER • 24

SHEFFIELD WEDNESDAY • BORN: 16.11.78

After impressing for three different clubs i 1998–99, Sheffield Wednesday winger Mar McKeever was expected to be a regula member of the Owls' first-team set-up i 1999–2000.

But the poor start the Hillsborough side mad to the campaign was not conducive to bloodin inexperienced players and that, coupled with serious foot injury, kept McKeever out of th reckoning for the majority of 1999–2000.

In the two games he featured in, the forme Eire under–21 man showed flashes of hi talent, completing 77% of his passes an whipping over nine crosses. The one game h started was a 1–0 win over Middlesbrough which gave the Owls only their second taste o victory in 18 Premiership games.

Loaned to Reading and Bristol Rovers i 1998–99, McKeever has some decen experience of Nationwide League football something that could stand him in good stea in 2000–01 if he steers clear of injury.

SEE PAGE 221 FOR FULL STATS

AM Stephen McPHAIL • 14

LEEDS UNITED • BORN: 9.12.79

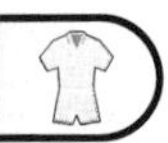

Stephen McPhail started the 1999–2000 season as one of the lesser-known faces in Leeds' exciting squad, but ended it with 23 Premiership starts under his belt, international recognition for Ireland and the reputation of being one of the Premiership's best up-and-coming midfielders.

Injuries to senior midfielders David Batty and David Hopkin gave McPhail his chance to become a first-team regular; one he took with both hands, starting 10 Premiership games in a row from October onwards.

During that period McPhail scored the first, and only, league goals of his season, netting both of the strikes that beat Chelsea 2–0 just before Christmas. Compared by many to a young Liam Brady, McPhail displayed fine distribution skills by creating four goals for team-mates and completing 77% of his 1,057 passes.

In 2,068 minutes of league football, McPhail escaped a single caution or red card and has the kind of temperament that Lee Bowyer, his midfield ally at Elland Road, could do worse than try to emulate.

APPEARANCES	
tart (sub)	23(1)
Minutes on pitch	2068
GOAL ATTEMPTS	
Goals	2
Shots on target	6
Shooting accuracy	33%
Goals/shots ratio	11%
PASSING	
Goal assists	4
Passes in opp half	753
Passing accuracy in opp half	74%
Successful crosses	22
Crossing accuracy	31%
DRIBBLING	
Dribbles & runs	42
Dribble completion	81%
Corners forced	13
DISCIPLINE	
Fouls	24
Yellow cards	0
Red cards	0

SEE PAGE 137 FOR FULL STATS

M

S Gary McSHEFFREY • 28

COVENTRY CITY • BORN: 13.8.82

Record-breaking Coventry youngster Gary McSheffrey achieved a personal goal in 1999–2000 by making his first-team debut at Highfield Road.

McSheffrey, who grew up just a goal-kick away from City's ground, said: "It was my ambition to play for the club, which I am now doing, but my dream is to run out with the first team at home."

Having become the youngest-ever Premiership player when he made his debut as a sub at Aston Villa in 1998–99, he fulfilled his dream of playing in front of the Highfield Road fans in September when he replaced Steve Froggatt for the final 15 minutes of a 4–3 defeat to Leeds.

McSheffrey's home bow was sandwiched between two other brief outings as substitute in 1999–2000, giving him a combined total of 28 Premiership minutes. If he continues to progress, then the teenage striker can expect a larger slice of the action in 2000–01.

SEE PAGE 95 FOR FULL STATS

Lean, keen and clean: Stephen McPhail

Erik MEIJER • 18

LIVERPOOL • BORN: 2.8.69

Bosman signing Erik Meijer joined Liverpool in summer 1999, happy to play second fiddle to Robbie Fowler and Michael Owen. But injuries to the England duo gave Meijer more chances than he might have bargained for, while leaving him plenty of time to indulge in his favourite hobby – cooking.

Meijer's own website pages detail his passion for cooking, be it Spaghetti Bolognese or Cantonese stir-fry chicken – Uncle Ben's-style.

In the 813 minutes he played, Meijer did not serve up too many treats for the Liverpool faithful, failing to score in the Premiership, although he netted twice in a 5–1 Worthington Cup victory over Hull.

More often than not, the powerfully-built 6'2" striker would be feeding team-mates chances with through-balls and flick-ons, a skill that resulted in one goal assist.

After starting four Premiership games in a row in February and March, Meijer was forced out of the line-up by the introduction of Emile Heskey and it seems likely that he will struggle to gain a regular place in 2000–01.

APPEARANCES	
Start (sub)	7(14)
Minutes on pitch	813
GOAL ATTEMPTS	
Goals inside box	0
Goals outside box	0
Minutes per goal scored	n/a
Goals/shots ratio	0%
SHOOTING	
Shots on target inside box	7
Shots on target outside box	1
Shooting accuracy	53%
PASSING	
Goal assists	1
Key passes	1
Passing accuracy in opp half	61%
DISCIPLINE	
Fouls committed	34
Fouls won	13
Offside	8
Yellow cards	2
Red cards	0

SEE PAGE 165 FOR FULL STATS

Mario MELCHIOT • 15

CB

CHELSEA • BORN: 4.11.76

APPEARANCES	
Start (sub)	4(1)
Minutes on pitch	400
GOAL ATTEMPTS	
Goals	0
DEFENDING	
Blocks	8
Shots cleared off line	0
Headed clearances	5
Other clearances	2
Interceptions	1
Last man saving tackles	0
Tackles won	5
Tackles won %	50%
PASSING	
Passing accuracy own half	83%
Passing accuracy opp half	79%
DISCIPLINE	
Fouls	6
Fouls in danger area	2
Yellow cards	0
Red cards	0

SEE PAGE 81 FOR FULL STATS

A product of the world-famous Ajax yout academy, Mario Melchiot shows all th versatility one would associate with a playe from the Dutch side. Comfortable i midfield, at right-back or in central defenc Melchiot is a versatile addition to th Chelsea squad.

A foot injury restricted his opportunities a the beginning of the 1999–2000 campaigr But he came back to feature strongly in th Blues' closing Premiership fixtures, startin four of their last five matches. And h certainly impressed the Chelsea faithful wit his calm, assured performances, completin 81% of his passes – much better than th average for a Premiership defender.

Melchiot was rewarded for his fine form wit a place in the starting line-up for the FA Cu final. And he did not disappoint, with hi surging runs down the right flank a starrin feature in Chelsea's win. If he can reproduc his end-of-season form in 1999–200 Melchiot should find himself a regular fixtur in the Blues team.

48% Paul Merson was the most accurate corner taker of al

Paul MERSON • 10

ASTON VILLA • BORN: 20.3.68

player who has certainly endured ups and owns during his career, Paul Merson's 999–2000 season was again something of a ollercoaster ride.

He was dropped for the start of the season n favour of Lee Hendrie, but returned with ome outstanding performances to win the arling Player of the Month award in February.

Over the 1999–2000 season, Merson made 47 passes in the opposition half – more than ny other Villa player – and revelled in his ole behind the main strikers.

Merson rewarded his team by creating eight oals during the campaign – the joint-seventh ighest total in the Premiership – with the ormer Gunner's form prompting calls for his nclusion in the England squad for Euro 2000. lowever, after announcing his retirement from nternational football he was unable to inspire 'illa to a European place. And after their FA up final defeat, manager John Gregory nformed Merson that his opportunities at Villa vould be limited in the future. Merson may herefore be playing elsewhere in 2000–01.

APPEARANCES	
Start (sub)	24(8)
Minutes on pitch	2225
GOAL ATTEMPTS	
Goals	5
Shots on target	16
Shooting accuracy	38%
Goals/shots ratio	12%
PASSING	
Goal assists	8
Passes in opp half	847
Passing accuracy in opp half	68%
Crosses	74
Crossing accuracy	38%
DRIBBLING	
Dribbles & runs	114
Dribble completion	75%
Corners forced	32
DISCIPLINE	
Fouls	22
Yellow cards	2
Red cards	0

SEE PAGE 53 FOR FULL STATS

Charlie MILLER • 35

WATFORD • BORN: 18.3.76

APPEARANCES	
Start (sub)	9(5)
Minutes on pitch	824
GOAL ATTEMPTS	
Goals	0
Shots on target	4
Shooting accuracy	36%
PASSING & CROSSING	
Goal assists	1
Passes in opp half	219
Passing accuracy in opp half	55%
Successful crosses	2
Cross completion	17%
DEFENDING	
Interceptions	4
Clearances	11
Tackles	22
Tackles won %	50%
DISCIPLINE	
Fouls	14
Yellow cards	3
Red cards	0

SEE PAGE 277 FOR FULL STATS

A product of the Rangers youth system, Charlie Miller won trophies galore during his spell with the Scottish giants. But, when pushed on to the fringes of Dick Advocaat's squad, the Scotland under-21 international moved south to join Watford.

And it was not an easy 1999–2000 season for the Glasgow-born midfielder. Early on in his Hornets career, Miller had his appearances restricted through lack of fitness. But he returned to feature in the game against Leeds in October and remained a regular in the first team until January, when injury again forced him out of contention for a long spell.

During his stint in the Watford first team, Miller was unable to recreate the form that saw him star in the Rangers midfield. He successfully completed just 62% of his passes – 12 percentage points worse than the Premiership average for a midfielder. And he was consequently unable to reclaim his place in the team when he returned from injury, prompting speculation linking him with a summer move away from Vicarage Road.

Premiership players who attempted at least 75 corners

Jamie MILLIGAN • 36

EVERTON • BORN: 3.1.80

Jamie Milligan played alongside Francis Jeffers and Phil Jevons in the Everton side which won the FA Youth Cup in 1998. But, unlike his team-mates, Milligan has been unable to make the breakthrough to the first team that he would have wanted.

However, great things are expected of Milligan at Goodison Park. And despite playing only 45 minutes of Premiership football in the 1999–2000 campaign, manager Walter Smith rates him very highly. So much so, in fact, that the Everton boss berated his young protégé for choosing England under-18s instead of pledging his future to Scotland – the manager's homeland.

During his time on pitch, Milligan showed his attacking instincts by whipping in seven crosses, finding his intended target with 29% of them. And if the left-sided midfielder can impress his manager in 2000–01, he should get more opportunities to establish himself at Everton in the near future.

SEE PAGE 123 FOR FULL STATS

Danny MILLS • 18

LEEDS UNITED • BORN: 18.5.77

After bursting on to the Premiership scene during Charlton's relegation battle, Danny Mills moved to Leeds in a £4 million deal in order to further his career.

The England under-21 international started promisingly, scoring the winner in the Whites' clash with Sunderland in August. And as David O'Leary's young side climbed up the Premiership table, so Mills began to look worth every penny that Leeds had spent on him.

He made 150 clearances and blocked 20 shots and crosses, with Mills's form prompting calls for his inclusion in the full England team. But the return to fitness of Gary Kelly saw the Norwich-born defender's opportunities at right-back restricted and he subsequently failed to feature in the first team for long periods of the 1999–2000 campaign.

However, Mills returned to start the last five Premiership games of the season, during which time Leeds sealed qualification for the Champions League. And if he can start the new campaign in the same vein of form, he should see more chances in the 2000–01 season.

Determined: Danny Mills

APPEARANCES	
Start (sub)	16(1)
Minutes on pitch	1463
GOAL ATTEMPTS	
Goals	1
PASSING & CROSSING	
Goal assists	1
Passing	554
Passing accuracy	60%
Crosses	27
Crossing accuracy	30%
DEFENDING	
Tackles	64
Tackles won %	48%
Blocks	20
Interceptions	9
Clearances	150
Shots cleared off line	0
DISCIPLINE	
Fouls	31
Yellow cards	5
Red cards	0

SEE PAGE 137 FOR FULL STATS

S Lee MILLS • 9

BRADFORD CITY • BORN: 10.7.70

One of the stars of Bradford's promotion campaign, Lee Mills struggled to find his goalscoring touch in the Premiership at the start of the 1999–2000 season.

With the Bantams struggling at the foot of the table, Mills spent much of his time tracking back to cover his side's overworked defence. But he seemed to excel under the pressure. The former Port Vale player won 63% of his challenges – 12 percentage points greater than the seasonal average for a Premiership striker.

And after finding the back of the net against Wimbledon in October he seemed to regain his confidence, and by January was Bradford's top scorer with five league goals.

Unfortunately, Mills was ruled out through injury just as his form was improving. And after his return to fitness, he found himself unable to force his way back into the first team and was loaned to Manchester City. In 2000–01, Mills will be back at Valley Parade for Bradford's second season in the Premiership and will be desperate to make his mark.

APPEARANCES	
Start (sub)	19(2)
Minutes on pitch	1719
GOAL ATTEMPTS	
Goals inside box	5
Goals outside box	0
Minutes per goal scored	343.8
Goals/shots ratio	13%
SHOOTING	
Shots on target inside box	14
Shots on target outside box	4
Shooting accuracy	45%
PASSING	
Goal assists	3
Key passes	6
Passing accuracy in opp half	60%
DISCIPLINE	
Fouls committed	21
Fouls won	32
Offside	20
Yellow cards	1
Red cards	0

SEE PAGE 66 FOR FULL STATS

M

FB Scott MINTO • 20

WEST HAM UNITED • BORN: 6.8.71

APPEARANCES	
Start (sub)	15(3)
Minutes on pitch	1414
GOAL ATTEMPTS	
Goals	0
PASSING & CROSSING	
Goal assists	2
Passing	513
Passing accuracy	69%
Crosses	27
Crossing accuracy	41%
DEFENDING	
Tackles	50
Tackles won %	36%
Blocks	31
Interceptions	6
Clearances	46
Shots cleared off line	0
DISCIPLINE	
Fouls	24
Yellow cards	2
Red cards	0

SEE PAGE 291 FOR FULL STATS

Former Chelsea man Scott Minto struggled to make an impact at West Ham due to a run of injuries following his signing from Benfica in January 1999.

The Achilles heel really was Minto's weakness in 1999–2000. The heel injury he sustained at Aston Villa in August kept him out until 21 November, when he was on the bench in the 4–3 win at Sheffield Wednesday. He waited a further two weeks for any on-field action, appearing at White Hart Lane on 6 December.

Minto's initial performances at left-back looked slightly vulnerable, highlighted in his tackle success rate of only 36%. But when Harry Redknapp favoured a 3–5–2 formation and played him as left wing-back, the plucky defender's confidence surged.

Minto looked happier on the ball and enjoyed making forward runs down the left flank, his 85% dribble completion rate demonstrating that his positive action was usually beneficial.

As Redknapp has shown interest in Minto since his Charlton days, the manager will no doubt maintain faith in him in 2000-01.

John MONCUR • 16

WEST HAM UNITED • BORN: 22.9.66

As well-known for his tricks off the pitch as his on-field talent, John Moncur is definitely the practical joker of West Ham – and it is rumoured that he may know something about the disappearance of Paolo Di Canio's famous white boots!

Moncur is often the unsung hero in the midfield and, even in his mid-30s, his eagerness to give everything over 90 minutes is much-respected by fans. He will never run away from winning the ball, and his 63% tackle success rate was the third best at the club during the campaign.

But his passion came at a price: the tenacious ball-winner picked up seven yellow cards and one red over 1999–2000, making him a member of Opta's "Dirty Dozen".

His pass completion rate of 79% was second only to Joe Cole but, by being a less tricky midfielder, his talent often goes unrecognised.

Moncur, who always wears his shirt outside his shorts, is likely to stay with the Hammers, until following former colleague Julian Dicks on to the golfing circuit.

APPEARANCES	
Start (sub)	20(2)
Minutes on pitch	1734
GOAL ATTEMPTS	
Goals	1
Shots on target	3
Shooting accuracy	25%
PASSING & CROSSING	
Goal assists	0
Passes in opp half	608
Passing accuracy in opp half	76%
Successful crosses	6
Cross completion	38%
DEFENDING	
Interceptions	8
Clearances	34
Tackles	60
Tackles won %	63%
DISCIPLINE	
Fouls	42
Yellow cards	7
Red cards	1

SEE PAGE 291 FOR FULL STATS

Gary MONK • 25

SOUTHAMPTON • BORN: 6.3.79

A classy young defender, Gary Monk signed for Southampton from Torquay in 1997. But in the future he will be praying he has more opportunities to impress with the Saints than he was offered during 1999–2000.

As a good passer of the ball, Monk's style should certainly appeal to manager Glenn Hoddle. He showed excellent vision by successfully completing 50% of his long range passes – a better rating than all but one of the Saints' other central defenders.

However, Monk's inexperience cost Southampton dear during his first Premiership start of the season. Newcastle's in-form strikeforce tormented him, and the Saints crashed to a 5–0 defeat.

But Dave Jones showed his faith in the youngster by retaining him for the next game, a 2–0 win over Everton, when Monk looked extremely composed. And if he can reproduce that form, he should play a more prominent role for the Saints in the future.

SEE PAGE 235 FOR FULL STATS

Practical joker: John Moncur

Tommy MOONEY • 9

WATFORD • BORN: 11.8.71

Famously rejected by Graham Taylor at Aston Villa, Tommy Mooney became something of a talisman for the former England boss during Watford's promotion campaign. And he continued to confound his manager's judgment in the opening games of the 1999–2000 season, securing 1–0 wins for Watford with goals in consecutive games against Liverpool and Bradford in August.

Over the season, Mooney fired 60% of his shots on target – eight percentage points greater than the seasonal average.

Unfortunately, a September injury curtailed his campaign and he failed to start another league match until the final game of the season. Without their inspirational striker, Watford won only two league matches in eight months. So by the time he had helped them to a last-day win over Coventry City, the Hornets were already consigned to relegation.

The former Southend player certainly showed enough quality to indicate he could be a powerful weapon as the Hornets attempt to bounce back to the Premiership.

APPEARANCES	
Start (sub)	8(4)
Minutes on pitch	840
GOAL ATTEMPTS	
Goals inside box	2
Goals outside box	0
Minutes per goal scored	420.0
Goals/shots ratio	10%
SHOOTING	
Shots on target inside box	8
Shots on target outside box	4
Shooting accuracy	60%
PASSING	
Goal assists	1
Key passes	1
Passing accuracy in opp half	56%
DISCIPLINE	
Fouls committed	10
Fouls won	18
Offside	6
Yellow cards	2
Red cards	0

SEE PAGE 277 FOR FULL STATS

Joe-Max MOORE • 23

EVERTON • BORN: 23.2.71

APPEARANCES	
Start (sub)	11(4)
Minutes on pitch	927
GOAL ATTEMPTS	
Goals inside box	6
Goals outside box	0
Minutes per goal scored	154.5
Goals/shots ratio	32%
SHOOTING	
Shots on target inside box	8
Shots on target outside box	3
Shooting accuracy	58%
PASSING	
Goal assists	1
Key passes	2
Passing accuracy in opp half	66%
DISCIPLINE	
Fouls committed	11
Fouls won	19
Offside	7
Yellow cards	1
Red cards	0

SEE PAGE 123 FOR FULL STATS

A vastly-experienced striker in the USA national team, Joe-Max Moore was given his chance in the Premiership by Everton boss Walter Smith in December after joining from MLS side New England Revolution on a free transfer.

Recommended to the Toffees' management team by veteran defender Richard Gough – who spent some of 1998–99 in the US – Moore took his time to settle on Merseyside, starting just one game in his first month with the club.

But an injury-time equaliser against Tottenham in January sparked off one of the best runs of form any player enjoyed in the 1999–2000 Premiership campaign. Including that goal against Spurs, Moore scored in six out of seven games, forcing highly-rated striker Francis Jeffers on to the Goodison Park subs' bench. Moore ended the campaign with six league goals and also created one.

A knee ligament injury ruled him out of Everton's final five Premiership games of the season but, with the summer to get fit, the 29-year-old will be ready and raring to go for the 2000–01 season.

Lee MORRIS • 6

DERBY COUNTY • BORN: 30.4.80

Lee Morris is perhaps the most exciting player to come out of Sheffield United's youth team in many seasons. Operating as a forward or on the left of midfield, he scored eight goals in 16 starts and was rewarded with a call-up to the England under-21 side.

But the youngster caused outrage among Blades fans by signing for Derby at the start of the 1999–2000 campaign.

Since his transfer, Morris has struggled to live up to his £3 million price tag, as a series of niggling injuries have restricted his appearances in the Premiership.

The youngster will be keen to impress in 2000–01 after a disappointing start. He attempted just 36 passes and one shot, as Derby struggled at the foot of the table. Despite looking somewhat lightweight in the Premiership, Morris certainly has potential and will surely have more opportunities to show the Derby faithful what he can do when he returns to fitness.

SEE PAGE 109 FOR FULL STATS

Jody MORRIS • 20

CHELSEA • BORN: 22.12.78

During the 1999–2000 season, Jody Morris featured strongly in Chelsea's assault on the Premiership, FA Cup and Champions League. Despite the battle for places in central midfield at Stamford Bridge, he starred in all but eight of the Blues' league fixtures – and the club's annual paintballing competition.

Allying a fierce work-rate to undeniable skill, Morris looked extremely comfortable as one of the few Englishmen among Chelsea's cosmopolitan squad. He completed 76% of his passes and won 57% of his challenges – both above average for a Premiership midfielder – and scored his first goal of the campaign during the 5–0 rout of Manchester United.

He scored two more goals and created two others over the season, as his performances for the Blues became increasingly influential. Morris was rewarded for his excellent performances by being named as Chelsea's skipper during their 2–1 triumph over Coventry. Boss Gianluca Vialli indicated that the midfielder will eventually take this on permanently if he keeps progressing.

Paintball king: Jody Morris

APPEARANCES	
Start (sub)	19(11)
Minutes on pitch	1762
GOAL ATTEMPTS	
Goals	3
Shots on target	10
Shooting accuracy	53%
PASSING & CROSSING	
Goal assists	2
Passes in opp half	533
Passing accuracy in opp half	70%
Successful crosses	6
Cross completion	35%
DEFENDING	
Interceptions	3
Clearances	21
Tackles	46
Tackles won %	57%
DISCIPLINE	
Fouls	41
Yellow cards	4
Red cards	0

SEE PAGE 81 FOR FULL STATS

Neil MOSS • 13

SOUTHAMPTON • BORN: 10.5.75

After making just two substitute appearances before April, Neil Moss took advantage of an injury to Paul Jones to start the last seven Premiership fixtures of the 1999–2000 season.

The young 'keeper deputised ably for Southampton, looking solid in the air and keeping three clean sheets.

He was successful with each of the 10 crosses he dealt with, whether he chose to catch or punch, and saved 75% of the efforts that were fired at his goal.

But although he helped the Saints record wins over Bradford and Watford in his first two starts, Moss's inexperience told in later games. He was at fault as Manchester United won at The Dell to clinch the Premiership and, with Jones returning to full fitness in time for the start of 2000–01, Moss's Southampton future must remain in doubt.

During his five-year career at The Dell, Moss has started just 17 league fixtures, indicating that he will perhaps need to move elsewhere in the future if he wants to further his career with first-team football.

APPEARANCES	
Start (sub)	7(2)
Minutes on pitch	732
SHOT STOPPING	
Goals conceded (inside box)	9
Goals conceded (outside box)	1
Minutes per goal conceded	73.2
Clean sheets	3
Saves (shots inside box)	17
Saves (shots outside box)	13
Saves/shots	75%
DISTRIBUTION	
Long kick %	41%
Throws/short passes %	75%
CATCHING	
Crosses caught	4
Crosses punched	6
Crosses dropped	0
Catch success %	100%
DISCIPLINE	
Yellow cards	0
Red cards	0

SEE PAGE 234 FOR FULL STATS

M

Danny MURPHY • 24

LIVERPOOL • BORN: 18.3.77

APPEARANCES	
Start (sub)	9(14)
Minutes on pitch	1022
GOAL ATTEMPTS	
Goals	3
Shots on target	9
Shooting accuracy	64%
PASSING & CROSSING	
Goal assists	2
Passes in opp half	323
Passing accuracy in opp half	67%
Successful crosses	12
Cross completion	46%
DEFENDING	
Interceptions	7
Clearances	11
Tackles	27
Tackles won %	44%
DISCIPLINE	
Fouls	14
Yellow cards	3
Red cards	0

SEE PAGE 165 FOR FULL STATS

After impressing in the World Youth Championships in Malaysia, Danny Murphy was brought to Liverpool to recreate his England under-18s partnership with Michael Owen. But a disappointing start to his Anfield career saw him loaned out to Crewe during the 1998–1999 campaign. And by the time he returned, even Murphy himself felt that his Anfield career was over.

However, after some excellent performances for the reserves, Murphy was offered a well-deserved chance in the first team, starting the 1–0 win over Chelsea in October. He remained a fringe player for much of 1999–2000, but impressed Gerard Houllier enough during his appearances to earn a new contract.

Linking well with the attack, Murphy found his target with 46% of his crosses – the best rating at the club – and was equally potent when getting into scoring positions. He scored with 21% of his shots, including a fantastic 25-yard strike against Leeds, to indicate that Murphy could well go on to fulfil his enormous potential.

Adam MURRAY • 28

DERBY COUNTY • BORN: 30.9.81

The Derby management team have very high hopes for young midfield player Adam Murray, who continued to impress everyone at Pride Park in 1999–2000.

Having made his first-team debut and won Derby's Young Player of the Year award in 1998–99, Murray progressed by earning a four-year contract, playing for England's under-18s and making his first Premiership start in 1999–2000. He capped it off by starring in the Rams' Championship-winning reserve team.

Murray was given eight league outings, although he started just the one match – a 0–0 draw with Newcastle. In his 139 minutes on the pitch, the tenacious grafter struck two shots on target, completed 73% of his passes and was booked in the game against Tottenham in October for a foul on David Ginola.

Able to combine skill with determination, Murray could well be a star player at Derby in years to come though 2000–01 will likely see him continue with cameo roles.

SEE PAGE 109 FOR FULL STATS

Tackling with gusto: Robbie Mustoe

Robbie MUSTOE • 7

MIDDLESBROUGH • BORN: 28.8.68

Despite the talk, and in some cases arrivals, of big-name signings at The Riverside Stadium in the summer of 1999, wily veteran Robbie Mustoe once again managed to hold down a place in the Middlesbrough team for the Millennium campaign.

Utilised in a holding midfield role, Mustoe rarely broke forward to support the attack: in fact he failed to score or create a goal during 1999–2000. But his disciplined performances allowed the likes of Paul Ince and Christian Ziege to get forward and grab the headlines.

In 1,871 minutes of Premiership action, Mustoe won an above-average 57% of his tackles and distributed the ball with a 71% success rate. However, he did concede 45 fouls and was booked on four occasions.

A testimonial against German giants Borussia Dortmund in the summer of 2000 is unlikely to prove Mustoe's swansong in the north-east.

He should still have a part to play in 2000–01, even if Bryan Robson manages to attract more big names to Teesside.

APPEARANCES	
Start (sub)	19(9)
Minutes on pitch	1871
GOAL ATTEMPTS	
Goals	0
Shots on target	2
Shooting accuracy	22%
PASSING & CROSSING	
Goal assists	0
Passes in opp half	395
Passing accuracy in opp half	67%
Successful crosses	2
Cross completion	25%
DEFENDING	
Interceptions	15
Clearances	41
Tackles	84
Tackles won %	57%
DISCIPLINE	
Fouls	45
Yellow cards	4
Red cards	0

SEE PAGE 193 FOR FULL STATS

4 Middlesbrough scored fewer goals from central midfield

FB

Andy MYERS • 3

BRADFORD CITY • BORN: 3.11.73

n £800,000 signing from Chelsea, Andy Iyers failed to make an impact at his new lub, Bradford, and was shipped out on loan o Portsmouth as the 1999–2000 season drew o a close.

A former England under-21 international, Iyers was frustrated at the lack of first-team pportunities for him at Chelsea and made the nove north in the summer of 1999.

A fresh challenge looked just what Myers eeded, but in only his second start for the antams he was sent off for two bookable ffences in a stormy match at Pride Park gainst Derby in September.

He returned from suspension to start seven ames out of eight over the turn of the New ear, but failed to impress boss Paul Jewell espite making an impressive 75 clearances and ompleting a respectable 77% of his dribbles.

A pacy operator, Myers filled in at left or entre-back during his three-month spell with ortsmouth and played a quietly-efficient role n the south coast side's eventual survival in ivision One.

APPEARANCES	
Start (sub)	10(3)
Minutes on pitch	888
GOAL ATTEMPTS	
Goals	0
PASSING & CROSSING	
Goal assists	0
Passing	335
Passing accuracy	61%
Crosses	16
Crossing accuracy	25%
DEFENDING	
Tackles	29
Tackles won %	52%
Blocks	19
Interceptions	15
Clearances	75
Shots cleared off line	0
DISCIPLINE	
Fouls	13
Yellow cards	0
Red cards	1

SEE PAGE 67 FOR FULL STATS

M

G

Thomas MYHRE • 1

EVERTON • BORN: 16.10.73

APPEARANCES	
Start (sub)	4(0)
Minutes on pitch	360
SHOT STOPPING	
Goals conceded (inside box)	2
Goals conceded (outside box)	0
Minutes per goal conceded	180.0
Clean sheets	2
Saves (shots inside box)	10
Saves (shots outside box)	2
Saves/shots	86%
DISTRIBUTION	
Long kick %	33%
Throws/short passes %	91%
CATCHING	
Crosses caught	6
Crosses punched	4
Crosses dropped	0
Catch success %	100%
DISCIPLINE	
Yellow cards	0
Red cards	0

SEE PAGE 122 FOR FULL STATS

During the close season of 1999, Everton goalkeeper Thomas Myhre broke an ankle in training with Norway and then a few weeks later cracked a bone in his foot as he got out of the bath, moving him to say: "It wasn't the best summer I have ever had, that's for sure."

Effectively, the injuries ruined Myhre's 1999–2000 campaign, as he could not regain his first-team place on his return from the treatment room because of Paul Gerrard's form.

The Norwegian international played only four Premiership games and would not have appeared at all had it not been for an injury to Gerrard. The quartet of matches Myhre appeared in yielded two clean sheets and 10 points out of 12 for Everton.

Despite that, Myhre was loaned to Birmingham in April, his second temporary transfer of 1999–2000 after a brief spell at Glasgow Rangers.

In the Midlands, Myhre performed very impressively, keeping five shut-outs in seven matches as the Blues reached the Division One play-offs, where they lost to Barnsley.

han any other side in the Premiership

FB Gary NEVILLE • 2

MANCHESTER UNITED • BORN: 18.2.75

By his high standards, England full-back Gary Neville will look back on the 1999–2000 campaign as a disappointing one, but will still be content with another title medal.

In January, his two howlers in the inaugural FIFA World Club Championship tournament in Brazil ended any lingering hopes the Red Devils had of winning the trophy, but Neville bounced back well to help United retain their Premiership crown.

Neville made more than 1,000 passes throughout the 1999–2000 season, with 75% of them finding a colleague, and he showed his attacking prowess by successfully completing 92% of his dribbles and runs.

Although his tackle success rate was far less than the 76% he achieved during United's historic 1998–99 campaign, Neville still won more than half of his challenges.

Equally effective in the centre of defence or at right-back, David Beckham's best man missed much of the start of the 1999–2000 campaign after injuring himself while on international duty.

APPEARANCES	
Start (sub)	22(0)
Minutes on pitch	1891
GOAL ATTEMPTS	
Goals	0
PASSING & CROSSING	
Goal assists	2
Passing	1058
Passing accuracy	75%
Crosses	90
Crossing accuracy	24%
DEFENDING	
Tackles	45
Tackles won %	53%
Blocks	34
Interceptions	14
Clearances	74
Shots cleared off line	0
DISCIPLINE	
Fouls	10
Yellow cards	0
Red cards	0

SEE PAGE 179 FOR FULL STATS

FB Philip NEVILLE • 12

MANCHESTER UNITED • BORN: 21.1.77

APPEARANCES	
Start (sub)	25(4)
Minutes on pitch	2280
GOAL ATTEMPTS	
Goals	0
PASSING & CROSSING	
Goal assists	2
Passing	1443
Passing accuracy	78%
Crosses	70
Crossing accuracy	34%
DEFENDING	
Tackles	63
Tackles won %	54%
Blocks	41
Interceptions	17
Clearances	127
Shots cleared off line	2
DISCIPLINE	
Fouls	27
Yellow cards	4
Red cards	0

SEE PAGE 179 FOR FULL STATS

Despite being only 23, Phil Neville has alrea clocked up more than 150 appearances for t Red Devils. In that time, the attack-minded fu back has picked up four Championship meda two FA Cup winner's medals and a Champio League medal, but it could have been qui different for the England international.

At a young age, Neville was regarded as outstanding cricketer and could well ha reached county level, but chose instead career in football, following in the footsteps his brother Gary.

Phil made his United debut less than months after signing junior forms, in Manchester derby at Maine Road in 1995.

In fact, he enjoyed more first-team footb than his brother in 1999–2000, and contributed towards United's latest tit success with two assists. Neville provided total of 70 crosses, with 34% of them findi a red shirt, and with Denis Irwin approachi the end of his career at Old Trafford, Nevi may soon find himself a regular in Sir Al Ferguson's all-conquering team.

S

John NEWBY • 32

LIVERPOOL • BORN: 28.11.78

fter coming through the Anfield youth ranks, ot-shot John Newby made his debut for iverpool when he appeared as a second-half ıbstitute in the 0–0 stalemate with iddlesbrough at Anfield.

Newby joined Liverpool in 1988 when he was ıst nine years old, and fronted the Liverpool outh side that won the FA Youth Cup in 1996 ith Michael Owen. In fact it was Newby who et the Reds on their way, scoring the first oal in the first leg against West Ham United t Upton Park.

Although he failed to get a start for the iverpool first team, he ended the 1999–2000 ampaign as the reserve team's top goalscorer.

In March, Newby was shipped out on a onth's loan to Liverpool's feeder club Crewe, ut the pacy, two-footed striker failed to find ne scoresheet in five starts for the ailwaymen. However, the experience will ave done him good, and he will be hoping for first-team opportunity in 2000–01.

SEE PAGE 165 FOR FULL STATS

FB

Adam NEWTON • 38

WEST HAM UNITED • BORN: 4.12.80

Upton Park outsiders, the name of Adam ewton may not be as well known as his Youth cademy counterparts Joe Cole and Michael arrick, but scouts for the club were interested ı him when he was just seven years old.

Newton's progress has been steady, and his erformances in the latter stages of West am's Youth Cup-winning side of 1998–1999 ignified there were better things to come for ne young defender.

Newton was loaned to Portsmouth in early 999–2000 and he received his first call-up r the England under-21s against Denmark.

Comfortable in the right-back position, he is ost effective when playing at wing-back. His wo substitute performances against Coventry uggest Harry Redknapp will use him more in eason 2000–01.

With a lack of defensive cover and some ammers in their twilight years, the right-back osition is there for the taking, so the future ooks bright for another starlet.

SEE PAGE 291 FOR FULL STATS

CB

Jon NEWSOME • 19

SHEFFIELD WEDNESDAY • BORN: 6.9.70

Devastated defender Jon Newsome ended a bitterly disappointing 1999–2000 season by announcing his enforced retirement.

The dependable centre-back never recovered from a string of injuries and, after starting the season alongside Des Walker, failed to appear again for the Owls after their 8–0 mauling at the hands of Newcastle. It was revealed in May that a crippling knee injury had put paid to his career. It seems a far cry from the heady days of 1991–92 when the giant defender scored some crucial goals for Leeds United, helping them to the old First Division Championship.

Newsome made five starts for the Owls in 1999–2000, and in that short space of time made 76 clearances for the Hillsborough club. But the Owls lost five of the six games in which Newsome appeared, and drew the other.

He joined Wednesday in a £1.6 million move from Norwich in 1996, where he captained the East Anglian club. He ended a bitterly-disappointing season watching from the sidelines as his team-mates plunged into the Nationwide League. Newsome was probably hit particularly hard as he had a strong affiliation with the club – he is a Sheffield lad and had come up through Wednesday's youth system.

N

APPEARANCES	
Start (sub)	5(1)
Minutes on pitch	526
GOAL ATTEMPTS	
Goals	0
DEFENDING	
Blocks	7
Shots cleared off line	1
Headed clearances	55
Other clearances	21
Interceptions	7
Last man saving tackles	0
Tackles won	7
Tackles won %	47%
PASSING	
Passing accuracy own half	78%
Passing accuracy opp half	60%
DISCIPLINE	
Fouls	6
Fouls in danger area	0
Yellow cards	1
Red cards	0

SEE PAGE 221 FOR FULL STATS

Michel NGONGE • 7

WATFORD • BORN: 10.1.67

After starting the 1999–2000 season as first choice for the Hornets, Michel Ngonge found himself out of favour at Vicarage Road following the arrival of Heidar Helguson.

Frustrated by his lack of first-team action, Ngonge joined Huddersfield Town on loan, but the Democratic Republic of Congo international made only four substitute appearances for the Terriers.

Before then, Ngonge had scored five goals for the Hornets, including a spell of three in three games in November, when Sheffield Wednesday, Newcastle and then Sunderland were the victims of his predatory instincts.

His five goals were the result of 18 shots on target, but Ngonge's statistics reveal the all-round ability he possesses. He is comfortable on the ball, with 75% of his dribbles and runs completed, and the free transfer capture from Samsunspor also won 69% of his challenges.

At the age of 33, his Premiership days would appear to be over, but he will be hoping Graham Taylor gives him the opportunity to fire Watford back into the big time.

APPEARANCES	
Start (sub)	16(7)
Minutes on pitch	1347
GOAL ATTEMPTS	
Goals inside box	5
Goals outside box	0
Minutes per goal scored	269.4
Goals/shots ratio	14%
SHOOTING	
Shots on target inside box	13
Shots on target outside box	5
Shooting accuracy	51%
PASSING	
Goal assists	0
Key passes	0
Passing accuracy in opp half	56%
DISCIPLINE	
Fouls committed	48
Fouls won	30
Offside	28
Yellow cards	1
Red cards	0

SEE PAGE 277 FOR FULL STATS

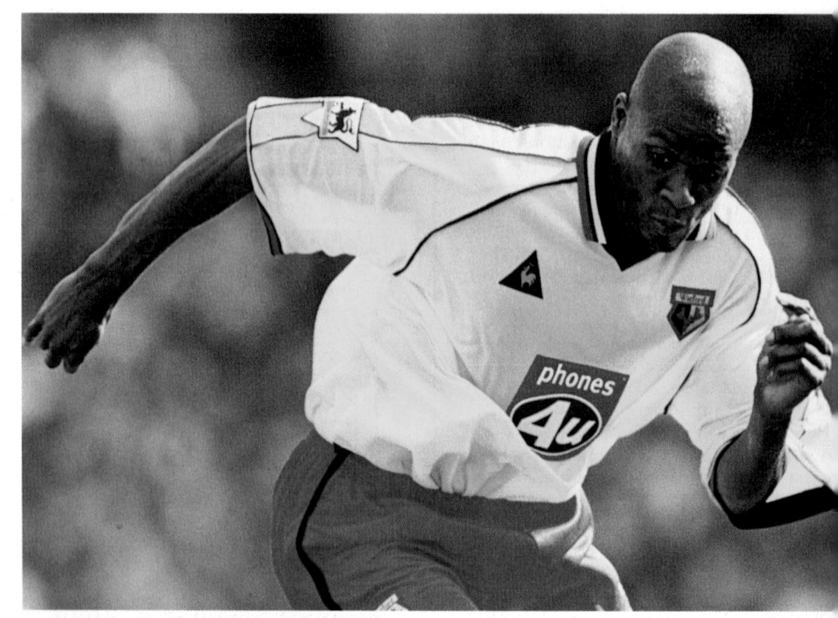

It's all gone wronge: Michel Ngonge

10% Watford's goal-to-shots rati

Allan NIELSEN • 22

TOTTENHAM HOTSPUR • BORN: 13.3.71

.fter scoring the goal that won the 1999 Vorthington Cup final against Leicester City – strike that took Tottenham back into Europe or the first time since the 1991–92 season – llan Nielsen endured a torrid 1999–2000 ampaign. The Dane was largely ignored by eorge Graham, and was loaned to Wolves at he tail end of the season.

Nielsen started only five games for Spurs ith his only notable incident being a red ard in the 2–1 defeat at Middlesbrough. But he former Danish Footballer of the Year njoyed his loan spell with the Midlanders and is performances earned him a recall from the nternational wilderness.

The hard-working midfielder is generally onsidered to be more tenacious and ependable than particularly skilful and he won 3% of his 32 tackles. While his pass ompletion could have been better, an 83% ribbles and runs completion rate underlined is confidence on the ball, and many might rgue he supplied the steel often lacking from he Spurs midfield.

APPEARANCES	
Start (sub)	5(9)
Minutes on pitch	545
GOAL ATTEMPTS	
Goals	0
Shots on target	1
Shooting accuracy	25%
PASSING & CROSSING	
Goal assists	1
Passes in opp half	155
Passing accuracy in opp half	61%
Successful crosses	5
Cross completion	50%
DEFENDING	
Interceptions	12
Clearances	12
Tackles	32
Tackles won %	53%
DISCIPLINE	
Fouls	7
Yellow cards	2
Red cards	1

SEE PAGE 263 FOR FULL STATS

Avi NIMNI • 13

DERBY COUNTY • BORN: 26.4.72

sraeli midfielder Avi Nimni joined the Rams n a three-month loan spell from fallen panish giants Atletico Madrid, and was lunged straight into Premiership action gainst Arsenal at Highbury.

Nimni, a left-sided midfielder, scored one oal during his sojourn in Derbyshire, in a 2–1 efeat away to Everton, but the Israeli nternational was borrowed for his creativity ather than his goalscoring.

Unfortunately, a bout of flu restricted the umber of first-team appearances he made, nd his only real contribution to Derby's eason was his goal at Goodison Park.

A 75% pass completion rate underlined the bility he possesses, and given more time in ne Premiership, he could have made a similar npact at Derby as his Israeli team-mate Eyal erkovic did at West Ham. But after two starts nd two substitute appearances for the Rams, would appear we have seen the last of Avi imni playing on English soil.

SEE PAGE 109 FOR FULL STATS

Gifton NOEL-WILLIAMS • 15

WATFORD • BORN: 21.1.80

The 1999–2000 campaign was a frustrating season for Watford's highly-rated striker Gifton Noel-Williams, who is Watford's youngest-ever goalscorer. He made only one start in the Premiership, which was a huge disappointment to the former England youth striker, as he had ended 1998–99 as the Hornets' top scorer, despite missing the second half of the campaign with a hip injury.

However, a knee injury did not respond to intensive treatment from a range of specialists in England. This left the popular frontrunner with no option but to see another specialist in America in an attempt to resolve the problem.

With such complications, many questions are being asked as to whether the prodigious talent will ever play again.

He still has time on his side, but Watford fans will be desperately hoping he can return fully fit and ready to lead the Hornets' campaign to regain their Premiership status.

SEE PAGE 277 FOR FULL STATS

vas the lowest in the Premiership

Ian NOLAN • 17

SHEFFIELD WEDNESDAY • BORN: 9.7.70

Ian Nolan was a virtual ever-present during 1999–2000 for the Owls, but was powerless to stop the Hillsborough club from falling out of the Premiership. Signed by Trevor Francis in 1994, the Northern Ireland international could slot in well at left-back despite being a predominantly right-footed player.

Former Tranmere manager Johnny King brought Nolan into the professional game, after taking his car for a service at the garage where Nolan was working. The chirpy Scouser, playing for non-league Marine at the time, persuaded King to take a look at him, and he was obviously impressed, offering Nolan a professional contract.

Nolan often attracts criticism because of his desire to get forward, and this is reflected in his statistics. He had only a 38% tackle success rate, while making 67 dribbles during 1999–2000. He supplied a total of 45 crosses with 33% of them finding a team-mate, but not enough of them were converted and, hence, Wednesday found themselves tumbling from the Premiership stage.

APPEARANCES	
Start (sub)	28(1)
Minutes on pitch	2484
GOAL ATTEMPTS	
Goals	0
PASSING & CROSSING	
Goal assists	1
Passing	1069
Passing accuracy	68%
Crosses	45
Crossing accuracy	33%
DEFENDING	
Tackles	68
Tackles won %	38%
Blocks	39
Interceptions	19
Clearances	125
Shots cleared off line	2
DISCIPLINE	
Fouls	15
Yellow cards	4
Red cards	0

SEE PAGE 221 FOR FULL STATS

Runar NORMANN • 20

COVENTRY CITY • BORN: 1.3.78

Norwegian under-21 international Runar Normann endured a frustrating 1999–2000 campaign, following a £1 million move from Lillestrom. He suffered a number of niggling injuries that kept him sidelined for the best part of the season.

However, he made his first start of the campaign as a second-half substitute in a 2–0 defeat by Liverpool at Anfield and ended the season making a number of substitute appearances, before getting his first start in a 5–0 thrashing at West Ham United.

Normann, whose name translates as "man from the north" in Norwegian, will be hoping his injury nightmare is behind him and he can help the Sky Blues to end their horrific away record which has not seen them win on their travels since a 2–1 victory at Sheffield Wednesday on 3 April 1999.

The Sky Blues' away form is obviously something Gordon Strachan will be looking to improve on.

SEE PAGE 95 FOR FULL STATS

Milton NUNEZ • 33

SUNDERLAND • BORN: 30.10.72

Despite being only 5'5", Milton Nunez powerful, stocky build earned him th nickname of "Tyson".

But Black Cat supporters have seen little s far of their Honduran international, signed fro Nacional Montevideo in Uruguay.

More than 25,000 fans turned up at th Stadium of Light to witness his debut, a 2- win in a reserve clash with Manchester Unite but Nunez had to wait until April before makin his Premiership bow.

He came on for the final 14 minutes of th Wearsiders' 2–1 win over Wimbledon, but on managed three touches during his brief foray With a full, intensive pre-season behind hir though, Nunez should be a prominent feature f the Mackems in 2000–01.

However, he will certainly have his work c out in gaining a first-team spot, with Nia Quinn and 1999–2000 Premiership top scor Kevin Phillips forging a dangerous, and at time unstoppable, partnership for Peter Reid's side

SEE PAGE 249 FOR FULL STATS

Stefan OAKES • 29

LEICESTER CITY • BORN: 6.9.78

Ex-Leicester City manager Martin O'Neill was forced to blood Stefan Oakes in 1998–99 due to a rash of injuries in the midfield, and the youngster took his chance with aplomb. As predicted in the inaugural Opta Yearbook, he played a much greater role in Leicester's 1999–2000 campaign, playing 1,345 minutes for the Foxes.

He also bagged his first goal, a 25-yard free-kick to complete the scoring in the 5–2 rout of Sunderland at Filbert Street.

It was fully deserved, too, as the younger brother of Scott Oakes had impressed everyone at the club.

He created three of Leicester's goals and his crossing was consistent. He also won 58% of his challenges. In terms of discipline, he only committed 10 fouls all season and was not booked at all.

With a midfield as strong as Leicester's, he will find it hard to maintain a regular first-team spot, but it must be heartening for everybody at Filbert Street to know that players such as Oakes are waiting in the wings.

APPEARANCES	
Start (sub)	15(7)
Minutes on pitch	1345
GOAL ATTEMPTS	
Goals	1
Shots on target	2
Shooting accuracy	18%
PASSING & CROSSING	
Goal assists	3
Passes in opp half	445
Passing accuracy in opp half	59%
Successful crosses	28
Cross completion	35%
DEFENDING	
Interceptions	5
Clearances	20
Tackles	50
Tackles won %	58%
DISCIPLINE	
Fouls	10
Yellow cards	0
Red cards	0

SEE PAGE 151 FOR FULL STATS

M

Matthew OAKLEY • 8

SOUTHAMPTON • BORN: 17.8.77

APPEARANCES	
Start (sub)	26(5)
Minutes on pitch	2368
GOAL ATTEMPTS	
Goals	3
Shots on target	12
Shooting accuracy	39%
PASSING & CROSSING	
Goal assists	3
Passes in opp half	639
Passing accuracy in opp half	65%
Successful crosses	12
Cross completion	24%
DEFENDING	
Interceptions	8
Clearances	38
Tackles	77
Tackles won %	56%
DISCIPLINE	
Fouls	28
Yellow cards	3
Red cards	0

SEE PAGE 235 FOR FULL STATS

Glenn Hoddle was delighted to inherit players such as Matthew Oakley when he took over at Southampton.

The England under-21 international is a genuinely talented midfielder who certainly saw his form improve after the former England manager started coaching him.

But the three goals he scored all came when Dave Jones was manager, and all of them at The Dell. He ended the season with three assists, an indication of his value to the team. His defensive work was also impressive, as he won more than half of his 77 tackles and made 61 blocks, clearances and interceptions during 1999–2000.

But his distribution declined and he registered a pass completion rate of 69%, a fact that must disappoint the youngster.

Oakley clearly has a lot of ability, but has yet to make the Premiership sit up and take notice. But with Hoddle coaching him, he should be able to make progress in 2000–01 and establish himself as a key performer for Southampton.

Andrew O'BRIEN • 14

BRADFORD CITY • BORN: 29.6.79

Bradford City's 1999–2000 season will go down in the club's history books as being one of the finest the Yorkshire side have ever experienced. A dramatic last-day escape from the relegation zone means that players such as Andy O'Brien will be playing in the Premiership for a second season.

O'Brien was an unqualified success for the Bantams, playing in all but two of the club's league fixtures.

He managed to make 128 tackles, and only nine men in the entire division could boast more than that. He also made 395 clearances, a total bettered by just six players.

Even more importantly, O'Brien managed to score what turned out to be the winner in the crucial basement clash with Watford in January. Although this goal was deemed important at the time, its real value was only seen at the end of the season.

Bradford know they have to reduce the average age of their team in the future, but thankfully they can call on the 21-year-old in the heart of their defence for many seasons to come.

APPEARANCES	
Start (sub)	36(0)
Minutes on pitch	3195
GOAL ATTEMPTS	
Goals	1
DEFENDING	
Blocks	126
Shots cleared off line	0
Headed clearances	289
Other clearances	106
Interceptions	52
Last man saving tackles	0
Tackles won	73
Tackles won %	57%
PASSING	
Passing accuracy own half	71%
Passing accuracy opp half	49%
DISCIPLINE	
Fouls	30
Fouls in danger area	10
Yellow cards	2
Red cards	0

SEE PAGE 67 FOR FULL STATS

Phil O'DONNELL • 11

SHEFFIELD WEDNESDAY • BORN: 25.3.72

Ex-Owls boss Danny Wilson must have thought that he had picked up a real bargain when Simon Donnelly and Phil O'Donnell left Celtic for Hillsborough in summer 1999. They were both out of contract and keen to play in England, but both struggled with injury, particularly the latter.

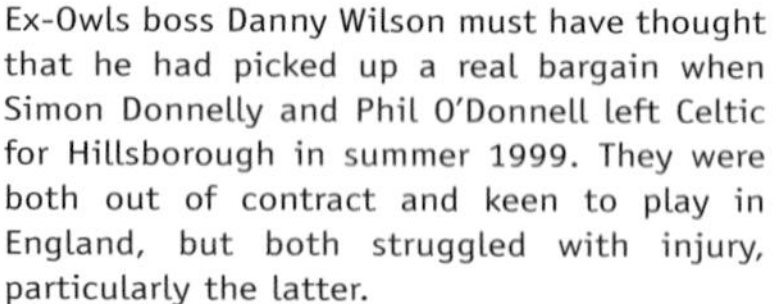

O'Donnell managed just 45 minutes of football for the Owls in their doomed season, coming on as a half-time substitute in the 0–2 home defeat against Everton. The main impact he had was to get booked for fouling Kevin Campbell, though 72% of his passes found a blue-and-white shirt.

He attempted two dribbles on that September afternoon but neither were completed, a sad indication of the lack of fulfilment O'Donnell was to experience in his campaign. He played no further part as Wednesday plunged into the Nationwide Football League, and there must be serious questions about his long-term future with the Owls.

SEE PAGE 221 FOR FULL STATS

Steve OGRIZOVIC • 26

COVENTRY CITY • BORN: 12.9.57

Arsene Wenger described Steve Ogrizovic's performance in goal for Coventry against the Gunners as "unbelievable" and it did seem incredible that a man with the honour of being the second-oldest Premiership player in history made save after save at Highbury. Unfortunately for the veteran, the north London team managed to score three times past him.

But 1999–2000 proved to be the gnarled 'keeper's final season, and he bade an emotional farewell to Highfield Road in the club's 4–1 win over Sheffield Wednesday. His career has had such highs as scoring a goal against Wednesday in 1986 and winning the FA Cup a year later.

He also played in 241 consecutive games between 1984 and 1989, a remarkable record. He can look back on his final spell in goal with pride, as he made 18 stops in just 270 minutes of action, finishing the campaign with a saves-to-shots ratio of 72%.

SEE PAGE 95 FOR FULL STATS

Keith O'NEILL • 11

MIDDLESBROUGH • BORN: 16.2.76

AM

Middlesbrough have still not seen the best from Keith O'Neill since paying Norwich City 700,000 for the Irish winger. He played for just 1,279 minutes in 1999–2000, failing to score a single goal for the Teessiders.

The Irish international has suffered with a series of calamitous injuries in his career, and he struggled to break into the Boro team due to the form of Christian Ziege. The German played much of the season in midfield and Bryan Robson then played O'Neill in the unfamiliar position of left-back.

O'Neill did create one goal during the season but his passing was less than impressive. He only managed to deliver 40 crosses, while of his 76 dribbles, he completed just 70%.

The Irishman played in just two games in the new Millennium, and he must know that he will have to overcome his fitness difficulties if he is to make his Premiership career work. He certainly has enough ability to play at the highest level but, like his injury-prone former Norwich team-mate, Darren Eadie, he must steer clear of the treatment table.

APPEARANCES	
Start (sub)	14(2)
Minutes on pitch	1279
GOAL ATTEMPTS	
Goals	0
Shots on target	4
Shooting accuracy	36%
Goals/shots ratio	0%
PASSING	
Goal assists	1
Passes in opp half	271
Passing accuracy in opp half	65%
Successful crosses	10
Crossing accuracy	25%
DRIBBLING	
Dribbles & runs	76
Dribble completion	70%
Corners forced	14
DISCIPLINE	
Fouls	26
Yellow cards	5
Red cards	0

SEE PAGE 193 FOR FULL STATS

Anthony ORMEROD • 26

MIDDLESBROUGH • BORN: 31.3.79

AM

Famous at the club for his acrobatic goal celebrations, Middlesbrough midfield player Anthony Ormerod featured for just 45 minutes in the Premiership during 1999–2000, but luckily for him it was during the Teessiders' match at Old Trafford.

And while the pacy forward did not manage a shot in his second-half appearance, he showed enough composure to suggest that he could be another classy graduate from the Middlesbrough youth academy.

Ormerod made 15 passes on the Old Trafford turf, with 73% of them reaching a team-mate. He also made five clearances and two tackles as his side fought hard to contain the Champions, eventually losing 1–0.

He spent a spell on loan at York where he played 12 times for the struggling Division Three team. His performances there had lower-division pundits drooling, and he should feature in the Boro first XI much more in 2000–01.

SEE PAGE 193 FOR FULL STATS

Egil OSTENSTAD • 10

SOUTHAMPTON • BORN: 2.1.72

S

Popular at Southampton due to his powerful running and impressive goalscoring rate, it came as a revelation to Saints fans when, just three games into the season, then-Blackburn manager Brian Kidd negotiated a deal whereby the Norwegian forward left the south coast for Ewood Park. Southampton also paid Rovers a fee, but received Kevin Davies back after his disastrous spell in Lancashire.

Ostenstad only played three games in the Premiership in 1999–2000, but he certainly looked as explosive as ever. A goal on the opening day to give the Saints an away win at Coventry showed his hunger had not abated, and the two bookings he accrued in that two-week period were an indication of his somewhat abrasive playing style.

It was surprising, therefore, that he did not settle too well at Blackburn. Despite scoring twice in his second game, he finished the season with just eight goals for the Lancastrian side.

SEE PAGE 235 FOR FULL STATS

O

John OSTER • 28

SUNDERLAND • BORN: 8.12.78

Sunderland snapped up Everton's out-of-sorts winger John Oster before the 1999–2000 season, with Black Cats manager Peter Reid feeling that he could coax some of the Welshman's undoubted talent out of him.

But Oster's campaign never really got going, and despite featuring in Sunderland's last five games he will have to work hard to become a fixture in the team.

The stats show that although he did not score, he did finish the season with an assist. His crossing, which let him down at Goodison Park, improved too. Although he only whipped in 26 deliveries, exactly half of them reached a team-mate. Oster's passing was also crisp, and he certainly gave Sunderland an option down their left flank, helping the club to forget about the departure of contract rebel Allan Johnston.

The former Grimsby man is still only 21, and has time on his side. But after failing to make the grade at Everton, he will not get many better opportunities than the one he currently has at the Stadium of Light.

APPEARANCES	
Start (sub)	4(6)
Minutes on pitch	436
GOAL ATTEMPTS	
Goals	0
Shots on target	0
Shooting accuracy	0%
Goals/shots ratio	0%
PASSING	
Goal assists	1
Passes in opp half	136
Passing accuracy in opp half	68%
Successful crosses	13
Crossing accuracy	50%
DRIBBLING	
Dribbles & runs	18
Dribble completion	83%
Corners forced	2
DISCIPLINE	
Fouls	4
Yellow cards	1
Red cards	0

SEE PAGE 249 FOR FULL STATS

Marc OVERMARS • 11

ARSENAL • BORN: 29.3.73

APPEARANCES	
Start (sub)	22(9)
Minutes on pitch	1927
GOAL ATTEMPTS	
Goals	7
Shots on target	29
Shooting accuracy	48%
Goals/shots ratio	11%
PASSING	
Goal assists	8
Passes in opp half	578
Passing accuracy in opp half	71%
Successful crosses	28
Crossing accuracy	29%
DRIBBLING	
Dribbles & runs	169
Dribble completion	72%
Corners forced	29
DISCIPLINE	
Fouls	8
Yellow cards	1
Red cards	0

SEE PAGE 39 FOR FULL STATS

Marc Overmars, Holland's fastest export, had a inconsistent season at Arsenal in 1999–200 but still helped the club to second place in th Premiership and to the UEFA Cup final.

After scoring six goals in 1998–99, he we one better in 1999–2000, his final effort well-taken goal against West Ham.

The Dutchman created eight goals, too, ar only six men in the Premiership could boa more assists than that. His 169 dribbles ar runs put him 13th in that category, and eve right-back in the Premiership will testify t the danger that Overmars poses.

As a boy, Overmars sometimes used to pu his family's farm-cart along by himself and h still has all that strength in abundance. H ability is admired throughout Europe ar there are a host of clubs who would lik nothing more than to sign the winger.

Overmars courted publicity by suggestin that his career might be better served b moving abroad, but whatever happens, he w still be recognised as one of the mos impressive Gunners in recent history.

S Michael OWEN • 10

LIVERPOOL • BORN: 14.12.79

ome Liverpool fans felt that the hamstring ŋjury Michael Owen suffered at Leeds towards he end of the 1998–99 season was a blessing ı disguise, in that it would give the "Boy Vonder" a deserved rest. Unfortunately, the njury plagued Owen throughout the 999–2000 campaign, and it was only in April nd May that he looked properly fit.

Nevertheless, the England striker still ıanaged to score 11 goals in a progressive eason for the Merseyside club, creating three thers as well. The pacy forward managed to et the majority of his shots on target, inishing the season with a good accuracy ating of 61%.

He continued his exceptional scoring record gainst Newcastle at St James's Park with a race on Boxing Day, while another two-goal alvo was recorded at Highfield Road.

Owen is still vitally important, both for his lub and his country. The 2000–01 season hould represent the start of his peak, if he an put his injury troubles behind him, and he goals will surely continue to flow.

APPEARANCES	
Start (sub)	22(5)
Minutes on pitch	1818
GOAL ATTEMPTS	
Goals inside box	11
Goals outside box	0
Minutes per goal scored	165.3
Goals/shots ratio	22%
SHOOTING	
Shots on target inside box	26
Shots on target outside box	4
Shooting accuracy	61%
PASSING	
Goal assists	3
Key passes	6
Passing accuracy in opp half	65%
DISCIPLINE	
Fouls committed	21
Fouls won	33
Offside	26
Yellow cards	2
Red cards	0

SEE PAGE 165 FOR FULL STATS

CB Robert PAGE • 4

WATFORD • BORN: 3.9.74

APPEARANCES	
Start (sub)	36(0)
Minutes on pitch	3179
GOAL ATTEMPTS	
Goals	1
DEFENDING	
Blocks	94
Shots cleared off line	0
Headed clearances	271
Other clearances	150
Interceptions	19
Last man saving tackles	4
Tackles won	49
Tackles won %	56%
PASSING	
Passing accuracy own half	73%
Passing accuracy opp half	39%
DISCIPLINE	
Fouls	71
Fouls in danger area	21
Yellow cards	12
Red cards	0

SEE PAGE 277 FOR FULL STATS

Touted as the hardman of the Hornets team, skipper Robert Page featured in all but two of Watford's games in the Premiership. His previous claim to fame was that he had played in matches against Brazil and Barnet in the same week, but his debut season at the highest level showed him to be a surprisingly steady head.

Page made 421 clearances during the season, and only four men could boast a busier campaign than that.

He also clattered into 88 tackles, winning a healthy 56%. He managed to score once, too, the second goal in the team's 2–2 draw at Sheffield Wednesday.

Page was the first Watford player to hold a trophy aloft at Wembley, after the Hornets' triumphant victory over Bolton in the 1999 play-off final.

He saw further silverware in 2000, in the form of the club's Player of the Year award. It provided some consolation to the Welsh international, proving that he is one of the most valuable assets at Vicarage Road.

S Marian PAHARS • 17

SOUTHAMPTON • BORN: 5.8.76

After saving the Saints from relegation on the last day of the 1998–99 season, Marian Pahars continued to show that Latvia can produce something other than timber. His searing pace gave almost every defender problems and he finished the season with 13 goals.

Glenn Hoddle's arrival at Southampton saw an upsurge in Pahars's form and he was occasionally employed on the wing. While his pace caught the eye once again, the stats show that his crossing was less impressive.

The vast majority of his shots were on target, and as Pahars has said that the comparisons between him and Michael Owen are "boring", perhaps the Liverpool striker should be called the "English Marian Pahars". There is little doubt that the Southampton man had a better 1999–2000 league season.

Wimbledon supporters will not have good memories of the little hitman, as it was he who danced through the Dons' defence to condemn the south London club to relegation. There seems little chance that he will have to play at that level himself.

APPEARANCES	
Start (sub)	31(2)
Minutes on pitch	2756
GOAL ATTEMPTS	
Goals inside box	10
Goals outside box	3
Minutes per goal scored	212.0
Goals/shots ratio	24%
SHOOTING	
Shots on target inside box	25
Shots on target outside box	11
Shooting accuracy	65%
PASSING	
Goal assists	2
Key passes	14
Passing accuracy in opp half	65%
DISCIPLINE	
Fouls committed	36
Fouls won	42
Offside	46
Yellow cards	4
Red cards	0

SEE PAGE 235 FOR FULL STATS

CB Gary PALLISTER • 6

MIDDLESBROUGH • BORN: 30.6.65

APPEARANCES	
Start (sub)	21(0)
Minutes on pitch	1741
GOAL ATTEMPTS	
Goals	1
DEFENDING	
Blocks	60
Shots cleared off line	0
Headed clearances	220
Other clearances	48
Interceptions	24
Last man saving tackles	0
Tackles won	39
Tackles won %	57%
PASSING	
Passing accuracy own half	80%
Passing accuracy opp half	61%
DISCIPLINE	
Fouls	19
Fouls in danger area	5
Yellow cards	5
Red cards	0

SEE PAGE 193 FOR FULL STATS

Like Des Walker, Gary Pallister is a vastl experienced defender who seems to hav drifted out of the public consciousness but still very much alive and playing well.

The former "most expensive defender" wa as steady as usual for Middlesbrough 1999–2000, and while his pace is not quit as it was, his experience gives him a hea start. He made 69 tackles for Boro during h 1,741 minutes of play and won more tha half of them. Only five teams conceded fewe goals than Middlesbrough away from hom and Pallister can take some of the credit f that.

He missed large chunks of the season b managed to get on the scoresheet in Boro 3–2 win over Southampton, his fist-wavin celebrations indicating to anyone watchin how much the club still means to him.

Time is against Pallister now, and h troublesome back caused him to miss the la eight games of the season. But his love the game and Middlesbrough Football Cl should see him feature in 2000–01.

Carlton PALMER • 14

COVENTRY CITY • BORN: 5.12.65

t quickly became clear in autumn 1999 that ew Nottingham Forest manager David Platt vas not too keen on keeping the lanky Carlton almer at the City Ground.

The signs were there when Palmer vented his ury after being named as a substitute in a re-season friendly at Bradford.

Gordon Strachan was quick to snap up the ormer Sheffield Wednesday and Leeds United nan and take him to Coventry.

And though injury restricted him to just 15 ames for the Sky Blues, he inspired the team o an eight-match unbeaten run when he rrived and a spell of bad form began after his amstring injury in February.

He made 70 tackles during his 1,350 ninutes, winning 60% of them. He also nanaged to get on the scoresheet once, in the –1 rout of Newcastle.

With Gary McAllister moving to Liverpool, almer's role in the Coventry team is even nore important. If he can stay fit, he will add n effective edge to the team.

APPEARANCES	
Start (sub)	15(0)
Minutes on pitch	1350
GOAL ATTEMPTS	
Goals	1
Shots on target	3
Shooting accuracy	33%
PASSING & CROSSING	
Goal assists	0
Passes in opp half	341
Passing accuracy in opp half	63%
Successful crosses	4
Cross completion	67%
DEFENDING	
Interceptions	20
Clearances	55
Tackles	70
Tackles won %	60%
DISCIPLINE	
Fouls	27
Yellow cards	4
Red cards	0

SEE PAGE 95 FOR FULL STATS

Steve PALMER • 5

WATFORD • BORN: 31.3.68

P

APPEARANCES	
Start (sub)	38(0)
Minutes on pitch	3413
GOAL ATTEMPTS	
Goals	0
Shots on target	4
Shooting accuracy	24%
PASSING & CROSSING	
Goal assists	0
Passes in opp half	522
Passing accuracy in opp half	54%
Successful crosses	8
Cross completion	33%
DEFENDING	
Interceptions	13
Clearances	213
Tackles	88
Tackles won %	53%
DISCIPLINE	
Fouls	32
Yellow cards	0
Red cards	0

SEE PAGE 277 FOR FULL STATS

Many footballers are nicknamed "Prof", usually when they have amassed two or three GCSEs, but Watford's Steve Palmer is far more deserving of such a moniker. He can boast a first-class degree from Cambridge University, and a cricket career that saw him play alongside Mike Atherton.

Whether Palmer attended all of his lectures is unknown, but he was certainly a fixture in the Watford team, playing all but seven minutes of the Hornets' campaign. Many supporters believe that it was his partnership with Robert Page that helped the team into the Premiership but Palmer featured mostly in midfield in season 1999–2000.

Despite making 88 challenges, Palmer committed only 32 fouls all season, and did not accrue a single booking. He could certainly give a tutorial in behaviour to some of the Premiership's more badly-behaved participants.

But Palmer failed to score during the campaign, something that will disappoint him greatly. He, especially, knows the difference between a 2–1 and a 2–2.

than those from any other side

James PANAYI • 27

WATFORD • BORN: 24.1.80

Hammersmith-born James Panayi had not made an appearance in the Watford first XI before the start of the 1999–2000 season, but Graham Taylor deemed that the youngster was ready for action on Halloween and plunged him into the scary world of the Premiership.

Unfortunately for Panayi, he was given a fright as a rampant Coventry team tore the Hornets apart, leaving the fans ghostly-white. He made 20 clearances, blocks and interceptions in his 45 minutes on the field and as Taylor decided to substitute him he must have been disappionted.

Panayi's other appearance came seven days later, just after Guy Fawkes Day, and there were more fireworks from the team as they managed to draw 2–2 with fellow-strugglers Sheffield Wednesday. Panayi managed 64 minutes of play this time, and again looked no worse than his colleagues.

With Watford back in the Nationwide Football League, the 20-year-old will surely get more opportunities to impress the Hertfordshire masses.

APPEARANCES	
Start (sub)	2(0)
Minutes on pitch	109
GOAL ATTEMPTS	
Goals	0
DEFENDING	
Blocks	3
Shots cleared off line	0
Headed clearances	6
Other clearances	10
Interceptions	3
Last man saving tackles	0
Tackles won	1
Tackles won %	100%
PASSING	
Passing accuracy own half	70%
Passing accuracy opp half	45%
DISCIPLINE	
Fouls	2
Fouls in danger area	1
Yellow cards	0
Red cards	0

SEE PAGE 277 FOR FULL STATS

Ray PARLOUR • 15

ARSENAL • BORN: 7.3.73

APPEARANCES	
Start (sub)	29(1)
Minutes on pitch	2430
GOAL ATTEMPTS	
Goals	1
Shots on target	12
Shooting accuracy	35%
Goals/shots ratio	3%
PASSING	
Goal assists	2
Passes in opp half	777
Passing accuracy in opp half	69%
Successful crosses	17
Crossing accuracy	22%
DRIBBLING	
Dribbles & runs	123
Dribble completion	67%
Corners forced	31
DISCIPLINE	
Fouls	45
Yellow cards	3
Red cards	0

SEE PAGE 39 FOR FULL STATS

Ray Parlour is one of the most energeti midfielders in English football and hi performances for the Gunners in 1999–200 were almost, but not quite, up to his recen high standards.

He embarked on 123 dribbles and runs, figure which put him in the Premiership to 30, and no one will need a reminder of th energy that Parlour possesses.

One aspect of his game that declined wa his goalscoring. While he had smashed si goals into the net during the 1998–99 season he managed just one in 1999–2000, and tha one was at Watford – a disappointing retur for an England international.

His passing was also slightly mor inaccurate, and with Arsene Wenger more tha keen to add to the squad at Highbury befor the commencement of the 2000–01 term Parlour will know that he will face a fight t keep his spot in the first team.

But Wenger will struggle to find someon with Parlour's level of passion and enthusiasm for the game.

Stuart PEARCE • 3

WEST HAM UNITED • BORN: 24.4.62

Taking on a defender who is 38 for the Premiership would usually seem foolish, but not when that player is Stuart Pearce, a man with experience and the desire to win.

His free transfer arrival at the beginning of 1999–2000 was designed to ease Harry Redknapp's defensive worries, and Pearce soon aided the back line, particularly with his clearances: he made 76 in only 595 minutes.

But Hammers fans did not have time to see "Psycho" peak, because he broke his leg playing against Watford in September.

Remarkably, the defender made a quick comeback, only to suffer the heartbreak of breaking the same leg playing Southampton five months later. If he held any dreams of reaching Euro 2000, they were now dashed.

Speculation suggests that Redknapp will offer Pearce a rolling monthly contract, so Hammers fans may still see more of him yet. Forest fans certainly love him – a successful campaign by Forest fanzine *Everywhere We Go* resulted in Pearce receiving the MBE in the 1999 New Year's Honours List.

APPEARANCES	
Start (sub)	8(0)
Minutes on pitch	595
GOAL ATTEMPTS	
Goals	0
DEFENDING	
Blocks	8
Shots cleared off line	0
Headed clearances	47
Other clearances	29
Interceptions	7
Last man saving tackles	0
Tackles won	7
Tackles won %	54%
PASSING	
Passing accuracy own half	84%
Passing accuracy opp half	60%
DISCIPLINE	
Fouls	13
Fouls in danger area	3
Yellow cards	3
Red cards	0

SEE PAGE 291 FOR FULL STATS

Ian PEARCE • 19

WEST HAM UNITED • BORN: 7.5.74

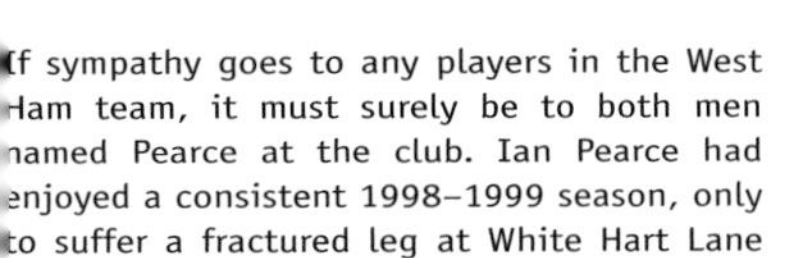

If sympathy goes to any players in the West Ham team, it must surely be to both men named Pearce at the club. Ian Pearce had enjoyed a consistent 1998–1999 season, only to suffer a fractured leg at White Hart Lane near the end of the campaign.

Pearce will want to forget the visit of Tottenham on the opening day of the 1999–2000 season, because it was in that game that he damaged knee ligaments after playing only 36 minutes. At the time, Harry Redknapp stated the defender would only be out for seven months, yet the injury ruled him out for the whole season, raising question marks about his future.

Recent speculation has suggested Pearce will not be back in first-team action until Christmas 2000.

He can take comfort from recoveries made by Alan Shearer and Paul Gascoigne from similar injuries to believe his career can yet be restarted.

SEE PAGE 291 FOR FULL STATS

Tore PEDERSEN • 14

WIMBLEDON • BORN: 29.9.69

The summer of 1999 was an optimistic time to be a Wimbledon fan. New manager Egil Olsen had arrived and had attracted players from clubs such as Eintracht Frankfurt, in the form of Tore Pedersen.

The Norwegian international defender had had spells at Oldham and Blackburn in the past but had failed to excite.

He settled in well at Selhurst Park, playing in six of the Dons' first seven games. In 650 minutes, he recorded a tidy pass completion rate of 74% in 1999–2000 and a tackle success rate of 56% made it look like he would be a good addition to the squad. But he soon succumbed to "jumper's knee", a problem that kept him out of the team for the rest of the 1999–2000 season.

It remains to be seen whether he can regain a spot in the Wimbledon team, but seeing as he comes from the same town as the deposed Olsen, it seems likely that he will depart the club in similar fashion.

SEE PAGE 305 FOR FULL STATS

P

Mark PEMBRIDGE • 12

EVERTON • BORN: 29.11.70

When Frank Dobson attacked Chris Evans's support for Ken Livingstone in the London Mayoral elections by lambasting his ginger hair, it was just the latest brickbat in a long history of abusing red-headed people.

Everton's resident redhead Mark Pembridge had suffered a certain amount of maltreatment from Toffees fans who were less than impressed by his play, but his form in the latter stages of 1999–2000 did a lot to quieten them.

By the end of the season he had secured a regular place in the team, and finished the campaign with two goals and five assists. Forced to play at left-back for a spell, he showed skill and vision, making more than 1,200 passes for the Merseyside club.

He also slid into 84 tackles, as he proved to the Goodison Park faithful that he may have been taken to Portugal by Graeme Souness, but he was more than capable of holding his own in the Premiership. If he can continue to improve in 2000–01, the remaining sceptics at the club might finally accept him.

APPEARANCES	
Start (sub)	29(2)
Minutes on pitch	2566
GOAL ATTEMPTS	
Goals	2
Shots on target	9
Shooting accuracy	38%
PASSING & CROSSING	
Goal assists	5
Passes in opp half	778
Passing accuracy in opp half	69%
Successful crosses	23
Cross completion	19%
DEFENDING	
Interceptions	13
Clearances	37
Tackles	84
Tackles won %	48%
DISCIPLINE	
Fouls	43
Yellow cards	4
Red cards	0

SEE PAGE 123 FOR FULL STATS

David PERPETUINI • 26

WATFORD • BORN: 29.9.79

APPEARANCES	
Start (sub)	12(1)
Minutes on pitch	972
GOAL ATTEMPTS	
Goals	1
Shots on target	4
Shooting accuracy	57%
PASSING & CROSSING	
Goal assists	1
Passes in opp half	195
Passing accuracy in opp half	57%
Successful crosses	5
Cross completion	10%
DEFENDING	
Interceptions	5
Clearances	21
Tackles	35
Tackles won %	37%
DISCIPLINE	
Fouls	15
Yellow cards	4
Red cards	0

SEE PAGE 277 FOR FULL STATS

Promising left-sided youngster Davi Perpetuini could be the most exciting thing t come out of Watford since the Metropolita Line. The exotic-sounding player actually hai from Hitchin and, after thumbing a lift into th Hornets' team at the tail end of 1998–99, h went on to make 13 appearances in Watford Premiership campaign.

Graham Taylor looked fully justified in playin him when, in his second top-flight start, h scored in Watford's 3–2 win over Southampto at Vicarage Road. It was to be the youngster only goal of the season, although he did finis 1999–2000 with an assist as well.

His crossing will need to improve after onl 10% of his deliveries found a team-mate. Hi tackling also occasionally looked weak but h was certainly thrown into the maelstrom at tender age.

Watford are proud of their system fo producing young players and Perpetuini is sur to get a chance to shine in the Nationwid Football League, where he will be given th opportunity to dazzle plenty of defences.

9 Tottenham's opponents receive

Chris PERRY • 6

TOTTENHAM HOTSPUR • BORN: 26.4.73

ieorge Graham was more than happy to spend :4 million of Spurs' money on Wimbledon lefender Chris Perry in summer 1999, in the iope that he would form an effective central lefensive partnership with Sol Campbell. That lid not turn out to be the case, although Perry y no means disgraced himself in his first eason at White Hart Lane.

Nicknamed "The Rash" by Wimbledon upporters, Perry did not seem his usual teady self, especially when playing alongside :ampbell, and after a few well-publicised jaffes, his confidence looked shaken.

But he still ended the season with 387 learances, more than any other Spurs player, ind the seventh-highest total in the Premiership. His first league goal for the ilywhites came as the team drew 1–1 with Bradford in September, the diminutive stopper scoring after 76 minutes.

Many fans thought that the move to Tottenham could finally see Perry called up to the England squad – but that is something that has still not happened.

APPEARANCES	
Start (sub)	36(1)
Minutes on pitch	3224
GOAL ATTEMPTS	
Goals	1
DEFENDING	
Blocks	85
Shots cleared off line	0
Headed clearances	260
Other clearances	127
Interceptions	68
Last man saving tackles	1
Tackles won	75
Tackles won %	52%
PASSING	
Passing accuracy own half	80%
Passing accuracy opp half	60%
DISCIPLINE	
Fouls	37
Fouls in danger area	17
Yellow cards	8
Red cards	0

SEE PAGE 263 FOR FULL STATS

Emmanuel PETIT • 17

ARSENAL • BORN: 22.9.70

P

APPEARANCES	
Start (sub)	24(2)
Minutes on pitch	2056
GOAL ATTEMPTS	
Goals	3
Shots on target	12
Shooting accuracy	39%
PASSING & CROSSING	
Goal assists	7
Passes in opp half	806
Passing accuracy in opp half	67%
Successful crosses	41
Cross completion	31%
DEFENDING	
Interceptions	15
Clearances	54
Tackles	94
Tackles won %	61%
DISCIPLINE	
Fouls	29
Yellow cards	5
Red cards	0

SEE PAGE 39 FOR FULL STATS

Known affectionately by Gunners fans as "Porno Flick", Emmanuel Petit continued to show the public that he was one of the world's most eminent midfielders, helping to inspire Arsenal to second places in both the Premiership and the UEFA Cup.

Petit has said that he wants to go into the fashion industry after his footballing career has ended, and if he can cut cloth as well as he can cut open defences then he should be a great success. Three goals and seven assists are a clear indication of his value to the Arsenal side. He also made almost 100 tackles for the Gunners, winning more than 60% of them. More importantly, Petit avoided a red card in the league, after being dismissed twice in 1998–99.

His season was not without problems, though. A persistent knee injury and constant rumours that he wanted to leave Highbury for European pastures meant that the previously excellent relationship he had with the fans deteriorated slightly, and his future at Arsenal is no clearer.

a league-high nine red cards

Dan PETRESCU • 2

CHELSEA • BORN: 22.12.67

Although Dan Petrescu is a foreigner playing at Chelsea, he is the second longest-serving player in the team and is universally loved by the fans at Stamford Bridge. He even named his daughter after the club, and there will be great disappointment when he does quit west London for pastures new.

That day might be nearer after an alleged disagreement between the outspoken Romanian and Chelsea manager Gianluca Vialli. It meant that Petrescu was not even on the bench for the FA Cup victory against Aston Villa in May.

But there is no doubt that Petrescu is still an excellent player. Four goals and five assists in the league illustrate his creativity. Even more impressively, he found a colleague with 49% of his 63 crosses, making him one of the best wide men in the Premiership.

No-one is likely to get rid of the Romanian easily. He saw off the competition from Brian Laudrup at Stamford Bridge and he will be as keen as ever to start the 2000–01 season in the blue of Chelsea.

APPEARANCES	
Start (sub)	24(5)
Minutes on pitch	1995
GOAL ATTEMPTS	
Goals	4
Shots on target	14
Shooting accuracy	50%
Goals/shots ratio	14%
PASSING	
Goal assists	5
Passes in opp half	579
Passing accuracy in opp half	74%
Successful crosses	31
Crossing accuracy	49%
DRIBBLING	
Dribbles & runs	87
Dribble completion	80%
Corners forced	21
DISCIPLINE	
Fouls	9
Yellow cards	2
Red cards	0

SEE PAGE 81 FOR FULL STATS

Terry PHELAN • 18

EVERTON • BORN: 16.3.67

In danger of becoming one of the forgotten men of football, Terry Phelan made just one appearance for Everton in 1999–2000 before drifting out of the Premiership. He came on for the last five minutes of the Toffees' game with Manchester United on the opening day, his only actions being two passes, one dribble and one clearance.

It was to be the last time the former Manchester City and Wimbledon man played a league game for the club. Walter Smith doled him out on loan to Crystal Palace but, although Phelan played well, the cash-starved Eagles could barely afford to give him a shirt and were not able to make him a full-time squad member.

He finally left Everton permanently for Fulham in February, where he excelled for the Cottagers and scored his first senior goal in six years. Everton are unlikely to miss Phelan, but he will be be a real asset to his new club.

SEE PAGE 123 FOR FULL STATS

Long-serving: Dan Petrescu

Kevin PHILLIPS • 10

SUNDERLAND • BORN: 25.7.73

After cleaning Alan Shearer's boots at Southampton, Kevin Phillips metaphorically shoved them down the England captain's throat after smashing home 30 league goals in his first season in the Premiership. Shearer had claimed that no player would again reach that magical figure in one season, but the hero of the Stadium of Light did it with one game to spare.

What was more remarkable was that the two previous players to bag 30 goals, Shearer and Andy Cole, both did so in a 42-game season.

Phillips attempted 15 more shots than any other player in the Premiership and got a massive 65 of them on target. He also created four other goals for the Black Cats in their largely successful return to the top tier of English football.

Bizarrely, some critics claimed that Phillips has still not proved himself, although 90 goals in three seasons on Wearside suggest otherwise. The next challenge for the former Watford man is to establish himself as a regular England international.

APPEARANCES	
Start (sub)	36(0)
Minutes on pitch	3197
GOAL ATTEMPTS	
Goals inside box	24
Goals outside box	6
Minutes per goal scored	106.6
Goals/shots ratio	25%
SHOOTING	
Shots on target inside box	45
Shots on target outside box	20
Shooting accuracy	53%
PASSING	
Goal assists	4
Key passes	8
Passing accuracy in opp half	67%
DISCIPLINE	
Fouls committed	47
Fouls won	69
Offside	34
Yellow cards	5
Red cards	0

SEE PAGE 249 FOR FULL STATS

John PIERCY • 32

TOTTENHAM HOTSPUR • BORN: 18.9.79

Young striker John Piercy became the 500th player to appear in league football for Spurs when he came on for Chris Armstrong with 13 minutes of the game at Derby County in October remaining.

He went on to make two further appearances for Tottenham, one as a sub in the 3–1 triumph against Manchester United, while his first start came at Sunderland's Stadium of Light, the latter match being the first time he tasted Premiership defeat.

In total he played for 61 minutes, managing just one shot off target in that time. He showed willingness to run, but only completed 25% of his dribbles for the north London side. A local lad, he is a keen fan of the club and will be hoping that George Graham gives him more time to taste first-team football in what could be a make-or-break 2000–01 season.

With Sergei Rebrov arriving, though, he may well find himself sent out on loan.

SEE PAGE 263 FOR FULL STATS

Remarkable: Kevin Phillips

P

Alessandro PISTONE • 36

NEWCASTLE UNITED • BORN: 27.7.75

All the signs at the end of the 1998–99 season pointed to the fact that Alessandro Pistone's Newcastle United career was over. Ruud Gullit was obviously less than impressed by the Italian and shipped him off to Venezia. But once the dreadlocked supremo had been overthrown, Pistone saw a revival in his career on Tyneside.

By the end of the season he had played in 15 games for United, with the club losing only two of them. A broken leg during the derby with Sunderland in February interrupted his return to favour but, to the delight of many Newcastle fans, he now seems to be firmly in the first-team picture.

He even managed a goal, scoring the Toon's second strike in their 2–2 draw with Middlesbrough in May. Even more impressive was that in 1,219 minutes of football he only conceded three fouls, a clear illustration of his firm but fair tackling technique. And with Paolo Maldini nearing the end of his career, Pistone could yet establish himself in the Italian senior squad.

APPEARANCES	
Start (sub)	15(0)
Minutes on pitch	1219
GOAL ATTEMPTS	
Goals	1
PASSING & CROSSING	
Goal assists	0
Passing	613
Passing accuracy	73%
Crosses	44
Crossing accuracy	36%
DEFENDING	
Tackles	30
Tackles won %	43%
Blocks	14
Interceptions	2
Clearances	64
Shots cleared off line	0
DISCIPLINE	
Fouls	3
Yellow cards	1
Red cards	0

SEE PAGE 207 FOR FULL STATS

Mart POOM • 21

DERBY COUNTY • BORN: 3.2.72

APPEARANCES	
Start (sub)	28(0)
Minutes on pitch	2520
SHOT STOPPING	
Goals conceded (inside box)	35
Goals conceded (outside box)	5
Minutes per goal conceded	63.0
Clean sheets	9
Saves (shots inside box)	60
Saves (shots outside box)	44
Saves/shots	72%
DISTRIBUTION	
Long kick %	41%
Throws/short passes %	90%
CATCHING	
Crosses caught	89
Crosses punched	20
Crosses dropped	2
Catch success %	98%
DISCIPLINE	
Yellow cards	2
Red cards	0

SEE PAGE 108 FOR FULL STATS

One of Mart Poom's heroes is the lat comedian Benny Hill, one of the few "artists" shown on Estonian television when it was communist state.

Unfortunately for the Derby Count goalkeeper, it must have seemed for lon periods as if the defence he was behin consisted of some old men and some scantily clad nurses running at double-speed aroun Pride Park, such was their lack of effectivenes at repelling attacks.

After playing the first four games of th season, none of them victories, Poom wa dropped, and the future must have looke bleak for the international 'keeper. But h recovered in inimitable style and ended th campaign by being overwhelmingly voted a the Rams' Player of the Season.

In a poor season for the east Midlands club he still kept nine clean sheets and was one o only 10 goalkeepers in the Premiership t make more than 100 saves.

He battled with Russell Hoult to be Derby' first-choice but saw off the challenge.

89 Mart Poom caught more crosse

CB Steve POTTS • 4

WEST HAM UNITED • BORN: 7.5.67

n an era where footballers' wages are piralling and big-money deals are the norm, t is now extremely rare for a player to remain t one club throughout his career.

But 1999–2000 was the 17th year at West Ham for Steve Potts, and yet again he proved his worth to the club.

The tidy defender filled in at centre-back nd right-back when required and never howed a lack of fitness when Harry Redknapp alled on his services.

Being one of the shortest players at the lub, he only made 59 headed clearances; he lso won only 43% of his challenges, but he naintained his professionalism by receiving nly one yellow card over the course of the 999–2000 campaign.

And his services to the club were rewarded vhen he enjoyed a testimonial match near the nd of the season.

Born in America, the East End crowd have dopted him as one of their own. And the opular Potts is unlikely to be hanging up his laying boots just yet.

APPEARANCES	
Start (sub)	16(1)
Minutes on pitch	1463
GOAL ATTEMPTS	
Goals	0
DEFENDING	
Blocks	20
Shots cleared off line	1
Headed clearances	59
Other clearances	34
Interceptions	23
Last man saving tackles	0
Tackles won	16
Tackles won %	43%
PASSING	
Passing accuracy own half	85%
Passing accuracy opp half	67%
DISCIPLINE	
Fouls	14
Fouls in danger area	7
Yellow cards	1
Red cards	0

SEE PAGE 291 FOR FULL STATS

M Darryl POWELL • 4

DERBY COUNTY • BORN: 15.11.71

APPEARANCES	
Start (sub)	31(0)
Minutes on pitch	2785
GOAL ATTEMPTS	
Goals	2
Shots on target	12
Shooting accuracy	41%
PASSING & CROSSING	
Goal assists	1
Passes in opp half	673
Passing accuracy in opp half	71%
Successful crosses	5
Cross completion	31%
DEFENDING	
Interceptions	21
Clearances	62
Tackles	95
Tackles won %	58%
DISCIPLINE	
Fouls	44
Yellow cards	6
Red cards	0

SEE PAGE 109 FOR FULL STATS

Derby County skipper Darryl Powell was stuck in a Chicago lift with Dean Sturridge and Deon Burton in the Rams' pre-season tour of the USA, and became extremely disturbed by their hysterical wailing.

But perhaps the two strikers had just had a premonition of how bad the club's 1999–2000 campaign was going to be.

Powell was one of the few players to emerge with any credit after the Rams finished 16th. His midfield partnership with Craig Burley was one of the main reasons the team pulled clear of danger with a few weeks to go.

After failing to score in 1998–99, Powell responded with two goals, including the important first strike in the side's 2–0 win over Southampton in April. His passing was relatively crisp and he made almost 100 tackles for the Rams.

A year ago, Powell's future in the Premiership looked less than secure, but he can look forward to the 2000–01 campaign with optimism. He has developed into a reliable and effective midfielder.

than any other goalkeeper

Gustavo POYET • 8

CHELSEA • BORN: 15.11.67

Gustavo Poyet captured many of the back-page headlines on the opening day of the season with a spectacular volley against Sunderland. He had added nine more goals to his total by the end of the season as he proved once again that he is one of the most dangerous and effective midfielders in the Premiership.

Poyet claimed in September that he would "rather have a Championship medal at the end of this season than winning the European Cup", but unfortunately he finished with neither. Nevertheless, he can look back on some exceptional performances in both competitions, creating five league goals with his power in the air and his strength.

Like Gianfranco Zola and Dan Petrescu, Poyet has adapted to life in England well and seems more than happy to play for the Blues. But with his 33rd birthday looming, it remains to be seen how much longer he will remain an integral part of the side, particularly with Gianluca Vialli seeking to reduce the average age of the squad.

APPEARANCES	
Start (sub)	25(8)
Minutes on pitch	2350
GOAL ATTEMPTS	
Goals	10
Shots on target	31
Shooting accuracy	41%
Goals/shots ratio	13%
PASSING	
Goal assists	5
Passes in opp half	752
Passing accuracy in opp half	70%
Successful crosses	9
Crossing accuracy	38%
DRIBBLING	
Dribbles & runs	55
Dribble completion	87%
Corners forced	12
DISCIPLINE	
Fouls	42
Yellow cards	5
Red cards	0

SEE PAGE 81 FOR FULL STATS

Kevin PRESSMAN • 1

SHEFFIELD WEDNESDAY • BORN: 6.11.67

APPEARANCES	
Start (sub)	18(1)
Minutes on pitch	1679
SHOT STOPPING	
Goals conceded (inside box)	36
Goals conceded (outside box)	6
Minutes per goal conceded	39.98
Clean sheets	3
Saves (shots inside box)	36
Saves (shots outside box)	40
Saves/shots	64%
DISTRIBUTION	
Long kick %	40%
Throws/short passes %	87%
CATCHING	
Crosses caught	31
Crosses punched	16
Crosses dropped	3
Catch success %	91%
DISCIPLINE	
Yellow cards	1
Red cards	0

SEE PAGE 220 FOR FULL STATS

Kevin Pressman spent 1999–2000 battling wit Pavel Srnicek for the goalkeeping jersey a Sheffield Wednesday, but neither man coul stop the Owls from dropping into Division One

Pressman kept only three clean sheets in hi 18 starts. He finished with a saves-to-shot ratio of 64% and the only regular goalkeeper t have a worse record was David Seaman c Arsenal and England.

Nevertheless, when Peter Shreeves took ove as caretaker-manager at Hillsborough, h preferred the bulky Pressman to the maveric Czech. Pressman has made the headlines i recent seasons for his penalty taking in cu shoot-outs, but unfortunately Wednesday season was so poor he did not have a chance t add to his record.

With the once-proud club now languishing i the Nationwide Football League, Pressman' career in Sheffield remains uncertain. He ha been at the club for his entire career, and woul be loathe to leave, but if he cannot command first-team place in the First Division th situation would surely be untenable.

Spencer PRIOR • 17

CB

DERBY COUNTY • BORN: 22.4.71

Having started the season as a first-choice player at Pride Park, Spencer Prior was gradually edged out of the first-team picture at Derby County. Originally signed to replace Christian Dailly, Prior's fall from grace was somewhat surprising, considering his excellent first season at the club.

His passing might not have been the crispest, but he won nearly 60% of his challenges and made numerous vital clearances. Derby manager Jim Smith preferred the emerging Steve Elliott, though, and after being dropped for the visit of Tottenham in October, Prior made only five more starts for the Rams.

His season was rescued by Manchester City manager Joe Royle who decided that Prior was just the man to bolster the Citizens' defence. He duly made a £500,000 switch and helped spur the Maine Road side to second place in Division One.

There is no doubt that Prior will be fired-up for the 2000–01 season, trying to prove, to Smith in particular, that he can be an effective defensive force in the top flight.

APPEARANCES	
Start (sub)	15(5)
Minutes on pitch	1479
GOAL ATTEMPTS	
Goals	0
DEFENDING	
Blocks	30
Shots cleared off line	0
Headed clearances	149
Other clearances	56
Interceptions	24
Last man saving tackles	1
Tackles won	23
Tackles won %	58%
PASSING	
Passing accuracy own half	84%
Passing accuracy opp half	55%
DISCIPLINE	
Fouls	22
Fouls in danger area	9
Yellow cards	6
Red cards	0

SEE PAGE 109 FOR FULL STATS

Alan QUINN • 33

S

SHEFFIELD WEDNESDAY • BORN: 13.6.79

APPEARANCES	
Start (sub)	18(1)
Minutes on pitch	1563
GOAL ATTEMPTS	
Goals inside box	3
Goals outside box	0
Minutes per goal scored	521.0
Goals/shots ratio	9%
SHOOTING	
Shots on target inside box	8
Shots on target outside box	9
Shooting accuracy	49%
PASSING	
Goal assists	2
Key passes	2
Passing accuracy in opp half	66%
DISCIPLINE	
Fouls committed	45
Fouls won	39
Offside	13
Yellow cards	3
Red cards	0

SEE PAGE 221 FOR FULL STATS

One of the few bright spots in a terribly disappointing season for Sheffield Wednesday fans was talented youngster Alan Quinn.

The 21-year-old Dubliner established himself in the first team despite getting sent off just two minutes into his home debut against Bristol City in the FA Cup.

After serving his suspension, Quinn was deployed by Danny Wilson to play just behind the strikers and impressed everyone with his strong running and great awareness.

There were question marks over his ability to cope with the physical demands of the Premiership, but he answered the sceptics, showing plenty of stamina.

Quinn scored three goals during the 1999–2000 Premiership campaign, including superb solo efforts against both Arsenal, when he rounded England goalkeeper David Seaman, and Leicester City in the Owls' 4–0 success on the last day of the season.

He was rumoured to be a target for Spurs but, if he does not move south, expect Quinn to be an impressive figure in Division One.

Barry QUINN • 22

COVENTRY CITY • BORN: 9.5.79

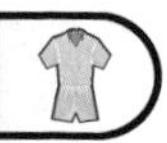

Coventry's Barry Quinn was used primarily as a squad player in the Sky Blues' 1999–2000 Premiership campaign. His only appearance before Christmas saw him booked and substituted in the 4–3 defeat by Leeds.

Nevertheless, after the New Year, he became a more regular fixture in Gordon Strachan's first-team line-ups.

The skipper of the Republic of Ireland under-21s, Quinn enjoys the responsibility that the role brings and that was reflected in his performances for Coventry. He had a better tackle success rate than in 1998–99, his first season of top-flight football.

Despite Quinn's disappointing passing accuracy of 69%, a decrease on his previous rate, he showed occasional glimpses of his ability to open the tightest of Premiership defences with a precision through-ball.

Quinn is a product of the Sky Blues' youth system and, following the departure of veteran Gary McAllister to Liverpool, season 2000–2001 could see him finally establish himself as a first-choice midfielder for Coventry.

APPEARANCES	
Start (sub)	5(6)
Minutes on pitch	560
GOAL ATTEMPTS	
Goals	0
Shots on target	0
Shooting accuracy	0%
PASSING & CROSSING	
Goal assists	0
Passes in opp half	190
Passing accuracy in opp half	62%
Successful crosses	1
Cross completion	13%
DEFENDING	
Interceptions	7
Clearances	24
Tackles	27
Tackles won %	63%
DISCIPLINE	
Fouls	5
Yellow cards	2
Red cards	0

SEE PAGE 95 FOR FULL STATS

Niall QUINN • 9

SUNDERLAND • BORN: 15.8.66

APPEARANCES	
Start (sub)	35(2)
Minutes on pitch	3035
GOAL ATTEMPTS	
Goals inside box	13
Goals outside box	1
Minutes per goal scored	216.8
Goals/shots ratio	19%
SHOOTING	
Shots on target inside box	30
Shots on target outside box	8
Shooting accuracy	52%
PASSING	
Goal assists	8
Key passes	25
Passing accuracy in opp half	57%
DISCIPLINE	
Fouls committed	102
Fouls won	94
Offside	52
Yellow cards	6
Red cards	0

SEE PAGE 249 FOR FULL STATS

Rangy striker Niall Quinn proved he could still cut it at the highest level, finishing 15th in the Opta strikers Index for the 1999–2000 season.

Quinn demonstrated his goalscoring prowess by chalking up 14 goals, including excellent braces against Chelsea and Tottenham.

A model professional off the pitch, Quinn also led by example on it, and his total of eight goal assists was the highest number recorded by a Sunderland player during the course of the 1999–2000 season.

His partnership with 30-goal hot-shot Kevin Phillips made the pair one of the most potent attacking strikeforces in the Premiership. And, although Quinn did not always receive the same attention as his partner, he was equally important to the Black Cats.

Quinn possesses not just aerial strength, but deftness on the ground. As Crystal Palace boss Steve Coppell once said of him: "He's the most difficult player to defend against," a statement supported by the fact that only Emile Heskey and David Ginola were fouled more often during the course of the season.

124 Niall Quinn made more successful flick-ons

CB Lucas RADEBE • 5

LEEDS UNITED • BORN: 12.4.69

Leeds skipper Lucas Radebe was rated sixth-best defender in the Opta Index for his performances during 1999–2000.

Many Leeds fans believe him to be the best defender at the club since the Don Revie era, and the South African international was once again incredibly consistent in a rearguard that conceded just 43 goals all season.

Radebe made more blocks and headed clearances than he did during the previous campaign of 1998–99, although he made fewer interceptions. It could be argued that his rearguard was under less pressure than in previous years.

The 31-year-old is an excellent man-marker, and a great reader of the game; his tackle success rate of 60% and 77% passing accuracy marked him out as a class act.

Little surprise, then, that the Leeds manager David O'Leary quashed speculation about the possibility of Radebe leaving the club, when he said simply: "Over my dead body". A strong statement from the Irishman – but a clear indication of how highly Radebe is regarded.

APPEARANCES	
Start (sub)	31(0)
Minutes on pitch	2697
GOAL ATTEMPTS	
Goals	0
DEFENDING	
Blocks	74
Shots cleared off line	0
Headed clearances	266
Other clearances	108
Interceptions	49
Last man saving tackles	4
Tackles won	64
Tackles won %	60%
PASSING	
Passing accuracy own half	84%
Passing accuracy opp half	60%
DISCIPLINE	
Fouls	32
Fouls in danger area	13
Yellow cards	2
Red cards	0

SEE PAGE 137 FOR FULL STATS

M Alex RAE • 16

SUNDERLAND • BORN: 13.6.69

APPEARANCES	
Start (sub)	22(4)
Minutes on pitch	1944
GOAL ATTEMPTS	
Goals	3
Shots on target	16
Shooting accuracy	55%
PASSING & CROSSING	
Goal assists	5
Passes in opp half	575
Passing accuracy in opp half	65%
Successful crosses	18
Cross completion	31%
DEFENDING	
Interceptions	22
Clearances	32
Tackles	82
Tackles won %	50%
DISCIPLINE	
Fouls	40
Yellow cards	8
Red cards	2

SEE PAGE 249 FOR FULL STATS

Alex Rae's season ended on a sour note when he was dismissed for an elbow on David Ginola in the Black Cats' 3–1 defeat at Spurs in the last minute of the final day of the 1999–2000 Premiership campaign.

It was all the more disappointing for the hard-working Scottish midfielder, who had just returned to the side after serving a two-match suspension and a £2,000 fine for a similar elbow on Derby County's Darryl Powell in February.

When not in trouble with the men in black, Rae had a good term for Peter Reid's side, grafting away in the centre of the park, winning half of his attempted challenges and setting up five of Sunderland's 57 Premiership goals scored during the course of the Wearsiders' solid campaign.

The possibility of a call-up to Craig Brown's Scotland squad was mooted after Rae's good form during the early part of the 1999–2000 season. A former Scottish under-21 and "B" international, a full cap would be a tremendous boost to Rae's confidence.

than any other Premiership player

Isaiah RANKIN • 19

BRADFORD CITY • BORN: 22.5.78

Pacy marksman Isaiah Rankin made just nine substitute appearances during Bradford's heroic survival campaign of 1999–2000.

The club's record signing when Paul Jewell paid £1.3 million for his services in August 1998, Rankin was instrumental in the side that won promotion to the Premiership.

But Rankin found his first-team opportunities limited during the Bantams' first season in the top flight, as Jewell preferred the more experienced partnership of Dean Windass and Dean Saunders.

He was farmed out on loan to Birmingham City, impressing the St Andrews faithful by scoring four goals in 11 starts for Trevor Francis's team.

Rankin was unfortunate not to seal Bradford's dramatic last-day win over Liverpool, when he saw a late effort just skim wide of Sander Westerveld's left-hand post.

Nevertheless, he displayed good passing skills and a perfect tackle success rate.

SEE PAGE 67 FOR FULL STATS

Michael REDDY • 31

SUNDERLAND • BORN: 24.3.80

Centre-forward Michael Reddy became a firn favourite with the Sunderland fans after h scored the equaliser just two minutes afte coming off the bench in the Tees-Wear derby a The Riverside Stadium last November.

After Kevin Phillips had seen his penalty brilliantly saved by Mark Schwarzer in the 78t minute, 20-year-old Irishman Reddy was o hand to earn the Black Cats a share of th spoils in a hotly-contested affair between th two bitter rivals.

Reddy made eight substitute appearances fo Sunderland during their 1999–2000 Premiershi campaign and, alongside midfielder Pau Thirwell, is a graduate of the Black Cats' yout team. He also put in a fine performance agains Wimbledon in the Worthington Cup.

He initially arrived at the club from Kilkenn City in July 1999 after being chased by number of Premiership clubs includin Newcastle United, but opted for a move to th Stadium of Light after a successful trial period

SEE PAGE 249 FOR FULL STATS

Neil REDFEARN • 26

BRADFORD CITY • BORN: 20.6.65

APPEARANCES	
Start (sub)	14(3)
Minutes on pitch	1254
GOAL ATTEMPTS	
Goals	1
Shots on target	6
Shooting accuracy	26%
PASSING & CROSSING	
Goal assists	0
Passes in opp half	303
Passing accuracy in opp half	63%
Successful crosses	4
Cross completion	22%
DEFENDING	
Interceptions	20
Clearances	32
Tackles	45
Tackles won %	56%
DISCIPLINE	
Fouls	43
Yellow cards	6
Red cards	0

SEE PAGE 67 FOR FULL STATS

When midfielder Neil Redfearn left Bradford t join Wigan Athletic in March, it was a grea relief for supporters of the Bantams.

After Redfearn suffered two successiv Premiership relegations with Barnsley an Charlton, his transfer to the JJB Stadium wa like the removing of a giant albatross fron around the necks of the club's supporters.

Not that there was anything bad abou Redfearn's performances in the claret an amber shirt. He scored one goal, a flick in th 3–1 defeat of Leicester in October, following great cross from Robbie Blake.

Redfearn was a strong and determine performer, who made more interception during 1999–2000 than he did during hi season with the Addicks.

Although his tackle success rate declined he always applied himself in City's bid t avoid relegation.

The midfielder originally arrived at the clu in July 1999, after his spell at Charlton ende when his family failed to settle and requeste a return to their native Yorkshire.

Jamie REDKNAPP • 11

LIVERPOOL • BORN: 25.6.73

It was a mixed campaign for Liverpool midfielder Jamie Redknapp.

He had the honour of being made club captain by Gerard Houllier in July after the sale of Paul Ince to Middlesbrough. But his luck took a downward spiral when he was forced to undergo surgery on his knee in November and was unable to start another first-team match for the Reds until May.

Up until then the husband of pop star Louise was playing quite well, scoring two goals in successive wins over Bradford and Derby. Redknapp also fulfilled a boyhood dream when he scored his first goal for England, a 25-yard screamer to earn a 2–1 victory over Belgium.

The former "Spice Boy" is renowned for his passing ability and his accuracy improved during 1999–2000, despite distributing fewer balls than his total during 1998–1999.

Redknapp will spend the 2000–2001 season competing with Germany's Dietmar Hamann, England's Steven Gerrard and new boy Gary McAllister in the midfield engine room at Anfield.

APPEARANCES	
Start (sub)	18(4)
Minutes on pitch	1655
GOAL ATTEMPTS	
Goals	3
Shots on target	23
Shooting accuracy	56%
PASSING & CROSSING	
Goal assists	1
Passes in opp half	659
Passing accuracy in opp half	75%
Successful crosses	15
Cross completion	28%
DEFENDING	
Interceptions	10
Clearances	26
Tackles	64
Tackles won %	55%
DISCIPLINE	
Fouls	21
Yellow cards	4
Red cards	0

SEE PAGE 165 FOR FULL STATS

Hamilton RICARD • 19

MIDDLESBROUGH • BORN: 12.1.74

APPEARANCES	
Start (sub)	28(6)
Minutes on pitch	2360
GOAL ATTEMPTS	
Goals inside box	10
Goals outside box	2
Minutes per goal scored	196.7
Goals/shots ratio	21%
SHOOTING	
Shots on target inside box	23
Shots on target outside box	10
Shooting accuracy	57%
PASSING	
Goal assists	3
Key passes	9
Passing accuracy in opp half	58%
DISCIPLINE	
Fouls committed	84
Fouls won	72
Offside	54
Yellow cards	7
Red cards	0

SEE PAGE 193 FOR FULL STATS

For the only time during his Middlesbrough career, Hamilton Ricard scored and actually ended up on the losing side when he grabbed a 68th-minute consolation in Boro's 5–1 thrashing at Arsenal last November.

Nevertheless it was another great season for the "lucky charm" as he ended up as the club's top scorer for the second consecutive campaign. Rated 20th in the Opta strikers Index for 1999–2000, the big, strong talisman forged a good partnership with Brian Deane.

Although Ricard scored fewer goals during 1999–2000 than the previous term he did improve on his goals-to-shots ratio, and his 33 shots on target meant an improved shooting accuracy for the Colombian hitman.

He improved his all-round game by setting up more goals than he did in 1998–1999, but did concede more fouls and was also flagged offside more frequently.

Ricard was expected to be in peak condition for the start of 2000–2001 after undergoing an operation on a hernia, caused by three years of non-stop football.

CB Dean RICHARDS • 6

SOUTHAMPTON • BORN: 9.6.74

Dean Richards will miss the first two games of the 2000–2001 campaign after earning a red card for fouling Leicester's Robbie Savage in the Saints' penultimate home game of the season in April.

But overall, the commanding defender had a fantastic debut season in the top flight following his arrival at The Dell on a free transfer in July 1999 from First Division Wolverhampton Wanderers.

He formed a good partnership with Claus Lundekvam in the middle of the Saints' back-line, and his ability to challenge well was reflected in his 54% tackle success rate.

Only a handful of players actually made more clearances and blocks than Richards during the course of the 1999–2000 season.

On the other hand, he was part of the team that conceded the most own-goals in the Premiership, with six.

Richards contributed by inflicting capital punishment on his team-mates when he put through his own net twice in the successive outings to Spurs and Chelsea in March.

APPEARANCES	
Start (sub)	35(0)
Minutes on pitch	3149
GOAL ATTEMPTS	
Goals	2
DEFENDING	
Blocks	91
Shots cleared off line	2
Headed clearances	312
Other clearances	98
Interceptions	20
Last man saving tackles	3
Tackles won	48
Tackles won %	54%
PASSING	
Passing accuracy own half	72%
Passing accuracy opp half	52%
DISCIPLINE	
Fouls	46
Fouls in danger area	16
Yellow cards	4
Red cards	1

SEE PAGE 235 FOR FULL STATS

S Karl-Heinz RIEDLE • 13

LIVERPOOL • BORN: 16.9.65

Karl-Heinz Riedle was once described by ex-Liverpool manager Roy Evans as "the best professional I have ever worked with" – but as he drifted into his twilight years, his German efficiency waned.

The former European Cup winner only played 18 Premiership minutes in a Liverpool shirt during the 1999–2000 season, as a substitute in the shocking home defeat to Watford. Word around Liverpool said the club were keen to keep him on as a staff member for his outstanding technical expertise and to maintain links with the Riedle Soccer Academy back in Germany.

But the lure of first-team football at Fulham tempted Riedle him to Craven Cottage for £200,000 in September.

He even had a short spell as caretaker manager following the sacking of Paul Bracewell. And Riedle brought in Roy Evans to help out, the pair successfully reverting the Cottagers to a 4–4–2 formation.

SEE PAGE 165 FOR FULL STATS

CB Chris RIGGOTT • 31

DERBY COUNTY • BORN: 1.9.80

Teenage defender Chris Riggott only made one 33-minute substitute appearance for Derby, in the final game of the season against Chelsea.

There are few things that fill the heart of a footballer with pride like playing for his local team and, far from looking sheepish, the 19-year-old appeared mature beyond his years and never looked in awe of the superstars he was up against.

Derby were beaten 4–0 at Stamford Bridge that afternoon, but in his brief cameo appearance the young centre-back made five clearances, two blocks and won two tackles. After the final whistle, Riggott left the field surely feeling it would not be too long before he returned.

After assuring Premiership safety, Jim Smith was clearly using the final game as an opportunity to blood some of the up-and-coming players, and the Bald Eagle will have seen that there is nothing woolly about this particular young Ram.

SEE PAGE 109 FOR FULL STATS

6 Southampton scored more own goals

AM Stuart RIPLEY • 14

SOUTHAMPTON • BORN: 20.11.67

The talented Mr Ripley was so disappointed with his first season in a Southampton shirt, he wrote a letter to the local paper apologising for his poor performances.

The apology was firmly accepted by the Southampton faithful at the beginning of the 1999–2000 season, when he certainly improved his form.

"Rips", as he is known on the south coast, embarked on 92 dribbles and runs and successfully completed 77% of them. His crossing at Blackburn was a key feature, but for Saints during 1999–2000 his crossing accuracy of 25% was below average and his passing accuracy of 56% was poor.

Nevertheless, the Middlesbrough-born winger set up six goals and got on the scoresheet himself with a rare strike. But when Glenn Hoddle took over as manager, he preferred to use five at the back and Ripley fell out of favour, then picked up a groin injury.

The veteran might find it progressively harder to get into the team but his drive and dribbling skills could still be an asset.

APPEARANCES	
Start (sub)	18(5)
Minutes on pitch	1581
GOAL ATTEMPTS	
Goals	1
Shots on target	7
Shooting accuracy	47%
Goals/shots ratio	7%
PASSING	
Goal assists	6
Passes in opp half	349
Passing accuracy in opp half	55%
Successful crosses	41
Crossing accuracy	25%
DRIBBLING	
Dribbles & runs	92
Dribble completion	77%
Corners forced	33
DISCIPLINE	
Fouls	31
Yellow cards	1
Red cards	0

SEE PAGE 235 FOR FULL STATS

M Andy ROBERTS • 4

WIMBLEDON • BORN: 20.3.74

APPEARANCES	
Start (sub)	14(2)
Minutes on pitch	1190
GOAL ATTEMPTS	
Goals	0
Shots on target	3
Shooting accuracy	43%
PASSING & CROSSING	
Goal assists	1
Passes in opp half	270
Passing accuracy in opp half	55%
Successful crosses	4
Cross completion	36%
DEFENDING	
Interceptions	12
Clearances	68
Tackles	40
Tackles won %	68%
DISCIPLINE	
Fouls	17
Yellow cards	1
Red cards	0

SEE PAGE 305 FOR FULL STATS

Andy Roberts played just over 1,000 minutes for Wimbledon, but could yet prove to be the player that fills the void left by cult hero Vinnie Jones.

His ability to sit in midfield and break up opposition attacks took some of the pressure off the overworked Wimbledon defence in 1999–2000. He made 40 tackles and won a respectable 68% of them, as well as getting back to help out the defence and make 68 important clearances.

Bearing in mind Wimbledon's penchant for direct football, his 65% pass completion rate was reasonable, while his 86% dribble success rate illustrated how he should possibly have pushed forward a bit more.

With the departure of Egil Olsen, perhaps there will be more opportunities for Roberts to play in the first team.

The 26-year-old's ability to play in midfield and as a sweeper could be invaluable to the Dons during 2000–01, when they will have a fight on their hands to get back into the top flight at the first time of asking.

Marvin ROBINSON • 26

DERBY COUNTY • BORN: 4.11.80

Young Marvin Robinson started 1999–2000 in good form, but, playing for a total of just 393 minutes throughout the season, he did little to secure a first-team place for the Rams.

He failed to get a single shot on target and was only able to find a team-mate with 54% of his passes.

Things took a downward turn when he was charged by the FA for abusive language in a game against Sheffield Wednesday, but the worst was still to come for the promising prospect.

In April, just after signing a three-year deal at Pride Park, the 20-year-old striker was sentenced to eight months' detention in a young offenders' institution after an incident outside a Wolverhampton nightclub. Derby said they would be standing by the player and would welcome the Ram back to the flock after his release.

Gaffer Jim Smith will be hoping that the 2000–01 season sees this young talent put his many troubles behind him and re-integrate himself into the game.

APPEARANCES	
Start (sub)	3(5)
Minutes on pitch	393
GOAL ATTEMPTS	
Goals inside box	0
Goals outside box	0
Minutes per goal scored	n/a
Goals/shots ratio	0%
SHOOTING	
Shots on target inside box	0
Shots on target outside box	0
Shooting accuracy	0%
PASSING	
Goal assists	0
Key passes	1
Passing accuracy in opp half	48%
DISCIPLINE	
Fouls committed	12
Fouls won	16
Offside	10
Yellow cards	1
Red cards	0

SEE PAGE 109 FOR FULL STATS

Paul ROBINSON • 28

NEWCASTLE UNITED • BORN: 15.10.79

APPEARANCES	
Start (sub)	2(9)
Minutes on pitch	319
GOAL ATTEMPTS	
Goals inside box	0
Goals outside box	0
Minutes per goal scored	n/a
Goals/shots ratio	0%
SHOOTING	
Shots on target inside box	2
Shots on target outside box	2
Shooting accuracy	44%
PASSING	
Goal assists	1
Key passes	2
Passing accuracy in opp half	64%
DISCIPLINE	
Fouls committed	9
Fouls won	8
Offside	2
Yellow cards	0
Red cards	0

SEE PAGE 207 FOR FULL STATS

Paul Robinson signed from Darlington in March 1998 for an initial fee of £250,000 but is yet to integrate himself fully into the Newcastle side, having played just 319 minutes throughout the 1999–2000 season.

Robinson was retained at the club after manager Bobby Robson's spring clearout and could turn out to be a valuable asset to the Magpies' squad.

Like his late-80s Australian namesake from TV's *Neighbours*, he is confident, tricky and should not be underestimated. However, his shooting was even less accurate than the hunter who mistook Kerry Mangle for a duck, with only 44% of his shots hitting the target.

His distribution was better, though, with two-thirds of his passes finding a fellow-Magpie. And in the short time he played he won a penalty and set up a goal.

Several lower-league clubs have had bids for the forward turned down, a fact that suggests he is highly-rated. But it looks unlikely that he will be displacing the Alan Shearer-Duncan Ferguson partnership any time soon.

Paul ROBINSON • 6

WATFORD • BORN: 14.12.78

One of three Paul Robinsons on the books of Premiership clubs, Watford's was more involved than his Leeds and Newcastle namesakes in 1999–2000, playing more than 2,500 minutes for the Hornets.

The local left-back was an all-action figure in Graham Taylor's team during the season, although the statistics suggest that there is still room for improvement.

The 21-year-old went in for 122 tackles, highlighting his commitment to the cause at Vicarage Road, but unfortunately only emerged victorious 45% of the time. He also made more than 1,000 passes, but only 57% of them reached their target.

Robinson made three saving tackles as the last man and two goal-line clearances to help endear him to the Watford faithful, but his enthusiasm sometimes got the better of him, and that led to nine bookings.

Robinson will be a vital player in Watford's promotion bid during 2000–01, and as a local lad there will be few players more passionate about getting the Hornets back up than him.

APPEARANCES	
Start (sub)	29(3)
Minutes on pitch	2678
GOAL ATTEMPTS	
Goals	0
PASSING & CROSSING	
Goal assists	1
Passing	1019
Passing accuracy	57%
Crosses	54
Crossing accuracy	19%
DEFENDING	
Tackles	122
Tackles won %	45%
Blocks	67
Interceptions	21
Clearances	157
Shots cleared off line	2
DISCIPLINE	
Fouls	44
Yellow cards	9
Red cards	0

SEE PAGE 277 FOR FULL STATS

Dani RODRIGUES • 19

SOUTHAMPTON • BORN: 3.3.80

Portuguese striker Dani Rodrigues made only two appearances for Southampton: one in the defeat against Leicester City and the other in a brief run-out in the final game at home to Wimbledon.

In the 37 minutes he did play, his one shot was on target and nine of his 12 passes found a fellow Saint.

The little Mediterranean hitman moved down the south coast from Bournemouth where he was on loan. Southampton paid his club Farense £170,000 for his services in February 1999, but he is yet to really show what he can do for Glenn Hoddle's team.

He has been in good form for the reserve side, for whom he finished the season as top scorer with eight goals from 20 starts, and has shown what a handful he can be.

Hopefully the 2000–01 season should see more first-team action for the little dynamo down at The Dell as Hoddle remoulds the Saints' style of play.

SEE PAGE 235 FOR FULL STATS

Bruno RODRIGUEZ • 29

BRADFORD CITY • BORN: 25.11.72

Much was expected of French loan star Bruno Rodriguez at Valley Parade, but the French forward played only 58 Premiership minutes for the Bantams, failing to muster a single shot during brief outings against Tottenham Hotspur and Aston Villa.

To call his loan period at Valley Parade from early September to late October a failure would be an understatement, though he might argue that he was not given the opportunity to prove himself to the Bradford fans.

After his return to French outfit RC Lens, he was given the chance to show his ability when he made a 15-minute appearance against Arsenal in the UEFA Cup semi-final, but was again rather anonymous when faced with Premiership opposition.

In years to come, when Bradford fans sit back and reminisce about their dramatic first season in the Premiership, it is unlikely that the name of Bruno Rodriguez will crop up too often in their thoughts.

SEE PAGE 67 FOR FULL STATS

S Cedric ROUSSEL • 31

COVENTRY CITY • BORN: 6.1.78

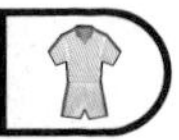

When Coventry boss Gordon Strachan sold Dion Dublin and Darren Huckerby, eyebrows were raised in the Midlands, but the partnership that Cedric Roussel forged with fellow-new signing Robbie Keane allayed the fears at homely Highfield Road.

The tall, powerful striker proved more than a handful for world-class defenders such as Tony Adams and Marcel Desailly and his loan move from Belgian club Ghent became permanent thanks to a £1.2 million deal.

He scored six times and set up another six goals for team-mates, and although his goals-to-shots ratio of 14% and his shooting accuracy of 40% were below average, he proved to be a worthy addition to the Coventry side.

Despite his height, Roussel demonstrated ability on the ground, completing 31 out of the 35 dribbles he attempted, which highlighted his keenness to run at defences.

The Belgian under-21 international said: "I love this club and the city. The atmosphere at the stadium and the supporters are fantastic." The feeling is fast becoming mutual.

APPEARANCES	
Start (sub)	18(4)
Minutes on pitch	1614
GOAL ATTEMPTS	
Goals inside box	6
Goals outside box	0
Minutes per goal scored	269.0
Goals/shots ratio	14%
SHOOTING	
Shots on target inside box	16
Shots on target outside box	1
Shooting accuracy	40%
PASSING	
Goal assists	6
Key passes	6
Passing accuracy in opp half	59%
DISCIPLINE	
Fouls committed	29
Fouls won	26
Offside	29
Yellow cards	1
Red cards	0

SEE PAGE 95 FOR FULL STATS

Givin' 'em hell: Cedric Roussel

Eric ROY • 29

SUNDERLAND • BORN: 26.9.67

ric Roy joined Sunderland from Marseille in ugust 1999 for £200,000 after first mpressing Peter Reid when playing in Kevin all's testimonial match against Sampdoria – nd added steel to an already strong midfield.

The former French international accurately ompleted three-quarters of his passes and von a splendid 65% of the 69 tackles that he vent in for. Such strength and precision was a eature of the Black Cats' play.

Despite Sunderland having the worst isciplinary record in the Premiership, Roy onceded only 23 free-kicks and received just wo bookings in more than 1,500 minutes of remiership football.

It appears that he can keep his head while ll those around him are losing theirs, and ome of his performances have been like intage Peter Reid of the 1980s.

Now in his 30s, it is unclear how many more easons he will be playing for Sunderland, but s Reid tries to build on the successes of 999–2000, Roy will no doubt play some part n his plans.

APPEARANCES	
Start (sub)	19(5)
Minutes on pitch	1550
GOAL ATTEMPTS	
Goals	0
Shots on target	5
Shooting accuracy	36%
PASSING & CROSSING	
Goal assists	2
Passes in opp half	444
Passing accuracy in opp half	73%
Successful crosses	3
Cross completion	33%
DEFENDING	
Interceptions	7
Clearances	27
Tackles	69
Tackles won %	65%
DISCIPLINE	
Fouls	23
Yellow cards	2
Red cards	0

SEE PAGE 249 FOR FULL STATS

Neil RUDDOCK • 6

WEST HAM UNITED • BORN: 9.5.68

APPEARANCES	
Start (sub)	12(3)
Minutes on pitch	1097
GOAL ATTEMPTS	
Goals	0
DEFENDING	
Blocks	54
Shots cleared off line	0
Headed clearances	100
Other clearances	45
Interceptions	19
Last man saving tackles	0
Tackles won	13
Tackles won %	59%
PASSING	
Passing accuracy own half	74%
Passing accuracy opp half	56%
DISCIPLINE	
Fouls	20
Fouls in danger area	5
Yellow cards	4
Red cards	0

SEE PAGE 291 FOR FULL STATS

Neil Ruddock's long-standing allegiance to Tottenham Hotspur did little to help him win over West Ham fans. And in his two seasons with the club he has done little to improve the relationship.

"Razor" has received plenty of taunts for his lack of pace, and for looking rather clumsy when trying to defend in his own area.

He made just 22 tackles in 1999–2000, but at least proved his aerial ability; of the 145 clearances he made, 100 were with his head. Equally, he made 54 blocks, the third-highest total in the Hammers' squad.

By his own admission, Ruddock had a "black book" of players he wished revenge on. But his temper was subdued in 1999–2000, apart from his behaviour in the game against Arsenal at Upton Park, which resulted in Patrick Vieira being sent off.

Links to Portsmouth and Millwall suggest that Harry Redknapp is ready to offload the 32-year-old, a move that would probably upset few supporters at Upton Park who are used to more cultured defenders.

han any other team

Petter RUDI • 14

SHEFFIELD WEDNESDAY • BORN: 17.9.73

Injury problems ruled Petter Rudi out for large chunks of Sheffield Wednesday's dismal 1999–2000 Premiership campaign and he will be hoping for an extended injury-free run in 2000–01, albeit in Division One.

Despite his height, which can often make him appear ungainly, Rudi is an exciting wide player with bags of skill and plenty of potential. The 1999–2000 season saw him embark on 52 dribbles and runs, successfully completing 83% of them.

For all his ball skills and good approach work, though, he failed to set up a single goal for a team-mate and out of 26 attempted crosses, only four found a Wednesday player – a highly disappointing return for a man with such obvious talent.

Brondby coach Age Hareide, who managed him at Molde and sold him to Wednesday in 1997, believed at the time that his star man was rated as "the best player in Norway." Unfortunately, 2000–01 will see him fighting to earn the tag of the best Norwegian player in the Nationwide League.

APPEARANCES	
Start (sub)	18(2)
Minutes on pitch	1425
GOAL ATTEMPTS	
Goals	2
Shots on target	4
Shooting accuracy	50%
Goals/shots ratio	25%
PASSING	
Goal assists	0
Passes in opp half	439
Passing accuracy in opp half	66%
Successful crosses	4
Crossing accuracy	15%
DRIBBLING	
Dribbles & runs	52
Dribble completion	83%
Corners forced	5
DISCIPLINE	
Fouls	22
Yellow cards	2
Red cards	0

SEE PAGE 221 FOR FULL STATS

CB

Jlloyd SAMUEL • 31

ASTON VILLA • BORN: 24.5.79

APPEARANCES	
Start (sub)	5(4)
Minutes on pitch	518
GOAL ATTEMPTS	
Goals	0
Shots on target	0
Shooting accuracy	0%
PASSING & CROSSING	
Goal assists	0
Passes in opp half	59
Passing accuracy in opp half	61%
Successful crosses	2
Cross completion	100%
DEFENDING	
Interceptions	2
Clearances	27
Tackles	11
Tackles won %	73%
DISCIPLINE	
Fouls	8
Yellow cards	2
Red cards	0

SEE PAGE 53 FOR FULL STATS

A product of the Villa youth academy ar tipped by many to reach the top level of th game, Jlloyd Samuel experienced th Premiership at the tail end of 1999–2000.

He came in for Gareth Southgate after th Villa captain was given time off and made h full debut in a 2–0 win over Derby County a Villa Park.

Although Samuel did not venture as far a the opposition's penalty box, his statisti would suggest he is definitely one for th future. From Samuel's 11 tackles, he emerge with a creditable 73% success rate and h showed his confidence and ability on the ba by successfully keeping possession after a his dribbles and runs.

His strong defensive play is underlined i Villa's defensive record in games he played i with the Villans conceding just four goals i the five starts Samuel made. His impressiv performances warranted him a place on th bench for the 2000 FA Cup final, and a call-u to the England under-21 squad would appe to be within the talented youngster's grasp.

S Dean SAUNDERS • 28

BRADFORD CITY • BORN: 21.6.64

eteran striker Dean Saunders played a crucial ɔle as Bradford defied the odds and secured ɿeir place in the Premiership but, at 36, his remiership days would appear to be umbered. The Yorkshire outfit are the 12th lub Saunders has joined since he made his ebut for Swansea City in 1982.

Only 24 hours after joining the Bantams on free transfer from Benfica, Saunders wrote imself into the City record books by notching heir first-ever goal in the Premiership – an 9th-minute winner at Middlesbrough. In ıct, it seemed a season of records for the /elshman, who also equalled the highest umber of Welsh international caps for an utfield player, when he made his 73rd ppearance in a friendly with Brazil.

Age would appear to be creeping up on the wansea-born hitman, who only managed hree goals all season. But they all proved ıvaluable to Paul Jewell's side, as each goal roved to be a winning strike. Saunders also hipped in with two assists, as Bradford tayed up at Wimbledon's expense.

APPEARANCES	
Start (sub)	28(6)
Minutes on pitch	2451
GOAL ATTEMPTS	
Goals inside box	3
Goals outside box	0
Minutes per goal scored	817.0
Goals/shots ratio	5%
SHOOTING	
Shots on target inside box	12
Shots on target outside box	9
Shooting accuracy	38%
PASSING	
Goal assists	2
Key passes	8
Passing accuracy in opp half	66%
DISCIPLINE	
Fouls committed	41
Fouls won	48
Offside	44
Yellow cards	1
Red cards	0

SEE PAGE 67 FOR FULL STATS

AM Robbie SAVAGE • 14

LEICESTER CITY • BORN: 18.10.74

APPEARANCES	
Start (sub)	35(0)
Minutes on pitch	3002
GOAL ATTEMPTS	
Goals	1
Shots on target	5
Shooting accuracy	42%
Goals/shots ratio	8%
PASSING	
Goal assists	1
Passes in opp half	544
Passing accuracy in opp half	60%
Successful crosses	12
Crossing accuracy	24%
DRIBBLING	
Dribbles & runs	71
Dribble completion	72%
Corners forced	14
DISCIPLINE	
Fouls	44
Yellow cards	4
Red cards	0

SEE PAGE 151 FOR FULL STATS

Much loved around Filbert Street, Welsh international Robbie Savage nonetheless has a reputation for dizziness. Steve Guppy, for example, was left somewhat bemused when, having told the tenacious midfielder that his parents had bought a new house with a sea view, Savage replied: "Whereabouts in Leicester is that, then?"

Fortunately for the Foxes, Savage knows the geography of the Filbert Street pitch rather better and missed only three games all season.

Full of energy, and never lacking in self-confidence, Savage was regularly used as a wing-back, but was equally at home in the centre of midfield. He possesses a midfield engine somewhat more reliable than that of his new Porsche, which failed to start just a day after it was delivered to his home.

His one goal came in the 2–0 win at Newcastle, when he unleashed an unstoppable shot which flew into the top corner of Shay Given's goal. And despite his reputation for being a tough tackler, the one-time Manchester United trainee received only four yellow cards all season.

John SCALES • 19

TOTTENHAM HOTSPUR • BORN: 4.7.66

Three years after joining Spurs in a £2.6 million deal, George Graham decided to hand injury-prone centre-back John Scales a free transfer. The Harrogate-born defender made only 29 starts in a Spurs shirt, including just three during the 1999–2000 campaign.

His bubbly character will be sorely missed around the dressing room, though, and he was once the source of great amusement when a friendly bet somewhat backfired. Scales had placed a wager on himself eating three Mexican chillies at once, but 30 seconds after finishing, he came out in a serious sweat and blotchy rash.

The 34-year-old stalwart will attract the interest of a number of clubs, as he showed he has certainly lost none of his ability, managing a 73% pass completion during the course of 1999–2000 in his brief outings.

After featuring in the first three games of the season, Scales had to wait until a trip to Vicarage Road, Watford in March before playing for the first team again, as a result of yet another injury.

APPEARANCES	
Start (sub)	3(1)
Minutes on pitch	333
GOAL ATTEMPTS	
Goals	0
DEFENDING	
Blocks	10
Shots cleared off line	0
Headed clearances	49
Other clearances	10
Interceptions	7
Last man saving tackles	0
Tackles won	3
Tackles won %	50%
PASSING	
Passing accuracy own half	75%
Passing accuracy opp half	71%
DISCIPLINE	
Fouls	6
Fouls in danger area	0
Yellow cards	0
Red cards	0

SEE PAGE 263 FOR FULL STATS

FB

Stefan SCHNOOR • 3

DERBY COUNTY • BORN: 24.4.71

APPEARANCES	
Start (sub)	22(7)
Minutes on pitch	1867
GOAL ATTEMPTS	
Goals	0
PASSING & CROSSING	
Goal assists	1
Passing	615
Passing accuracy	67%
Crosses	42
Crossing accuracy	38%
DEFENDING	
Tackles	78
Tackles won %	40%
Blocks	42
Interceptions	13
Clearances	168
Shots cleared off line	1
DISCIPLINE	
Fouls	31
Yellow cards	4
Red cards	2

SEE PAGE 109 FOR FULL STATS

Since his arrival at Pride Park, Stefan Schno has had a stop-start couple of seasons Derby. A strange injury in the Rams' seco match of the season against Arsenal appear to be incurred with no contact with opposition player.

German Schnoor was then sent off twice – home to Manchester United and away Tottenham – though he was perha unfortunate on at least one of those occasio

He won under 50% of his challenges duri the 1999–2000 campaign and would appear be more comfortable when going forward wi the ball, as he recorded a 93% dribb completion rate, while 38% of his 42 cross fell to a Rams shirt.

Schnoor was faced with a difficult task aft his free transfer move. Following in t footsteps of the hugely popular Chris Pow was never going to be easy, and after n really impressing, and Jim Smith allowi Tony Dorigo to leave on a free transfer, Der may look to strengthen at left-back in t close season.

Paul SCHOLES • 18

MANCHESTER UNITED • BORN: 16.11.74

he 1999–2000 season was one of personal riumph for United's Paul Scholes after being 'oted the England Supporters' Club Player of he Year for 1999.

This followed his two-goal heroics that shot lown Scotland in the European Championship lay-offs, and Scholes went on to help the Red Devils to their sixth Championship in eight easons with some exquisite strikes.

Scholes once scored eight goals in a school ame, all with his head, and despite growing ıp in the shadow of Old Trafford he was a ervent Oldham Athletic supporter as a boy. le then became one of "Fergie's Fledglings" aving played in the same youth team as the ikes of Gary Neville, Nicky Butt, David Beckham and Ryan Giggs.

In 1999–2000, Scholes maintained the form hat contributed towards United's historic reble, with an impressive 82% of his passes inding their intended target. But the one lownside in Scholes's game must be his liscipline, with the tenacious midfielder being ooked in seven of United's league games.

APPEARANCES	
Start (sub)	27(4)
Minutes on pitch	2402
GOAL ATTEMPTS	
Goals	9
Shots on target	31
Shooting accuracy	50%
Goals/shots ratio	15%
PASSING	
Goal assists	5
Passes in opp half	964
Passing accuracy in opp half	78%
Successful crosses	9
Crossing accuracy	28%
DRIBBLING	
Dribbles & runs	84
Dribble completion	82%
Corners forced	13
DISCIPLINE	
Fouls	30
Yellow cards	7
Red cards	0

SEE PAGE 179 FOR FULL STATS

Stefan SCHWARZ • 20

SUNDERLAND • BORN: 18.4.69

APPEARANCES	
Start (sub)	27(0)
Minutes on pitch	2374
GOAL ATTEMPTS	
Goals	1
Shots on target	8
Shooting accuracy	47%
PASSING & CROSSING	
Goal assists	2
Passes in opp half	515
Passing accuracy in opp half	65%
Successful crosses	9
Cross completion	26%
DEFENDING	
Interceptions	20
Clearances	37
Tackles	112
Tackles won %	60%
DISCIPLINE	
Fouls	38
Yellow cards	11
Red cards	0

SEE PAGE 249 FOR FULL STATS

Sunderland's record £4 million signing has become a cult hero on Wearside following his move from Valencia. The blond-haired playmaker has been capped on 60 occasions by Sweden, and was voted the Swedish Player of the Year for 1999. But after rupturing his Achilles tendon in a friendly with Austria, the tough-tackling midfielder was forced to miss the tail end of the 1999–2000 campaign, as well as Euro 2000.

Schwarz is already looking forward to the World Cup in 2002, but will be doing his utmost to bring European football to the Stadium of Light in 2000–01. Many people questioned whether he would settle on Wearside after an unhappy spell at Arsenal, but Schwarz quickly allayed those fears by helping the Mackems make a blistering start to the season.

Schwarz's Premiership statistics – notably a 72% passing accuracy and 60% tackle success rate – underlined the all-round ability he possesses. Black Cat supporters will be hoping he can reproduce that form following his injury.

Mark SCHWARZER • 1

G

MIDDLESBROUGH • BORN: 6.10.72

Since signing for Middlesbrough, Mark Schwarzer has quickly established himself as one of the best 'keepers currently plying their trade in the Premiership. The Australian shot-stopper has five international caps for the Socceroos, and joined Boro in a £1.5 million deal from Bradford City.

He joined the Bantams from German side Kaiserslautern in a £350,000 deal in November 1996, and played only 13 games for the West Yorkshire club before his big money move to The Riverside.

Such is his importance to Bryan Robson's side that the club offered him a seven-year contract, the biggest in the club's history.

Schwarzer kept nine clean sheets for Boro during the 1999–2000 campaign, making 184 saves, the most by a 'keeper in the Premiership. He also took 94% of crosses coming into the Boro box.

Born in Sydney, the 6'4" stopper has become a huge favourite at The Riverside and his demanding presence gives the Boro defence some much-needed stability.

APPEARANCES	
Start (sub)	37(0)
Minutes on pitch	3330
SHOT STOPPING	
Goals conceded (inside box)	40
Goals conceded (outside box)	8
Minutes per goal conceded	69.4
Clean sheets	9
Saves (shots inside box)	96
Saves (shots outside box)	88
Saves/shots	79%
DISTRIBUTION	
Long kick %	42%
Throws/short passes %	85%
CATCHING	
Crosses caught	75
Crosses punched	34
Crosses dropped	5
Catch success %	94%
DISCIPLINE	
Yellow cards	1
Red cards	0

SEE PAGE 192 FOR FULL STATS

Philip SCOTT • 15

M

SHEFFIELD WEDNESDAY • BORN: 14.11.74

APPEARANCES	
Start (sub)	2(3)
Minutes on pitch	209
GOAL ATTEMPTS	
Goals	0
Shots on target	0
Shooting accuracy	0%
PASSING & CROSSING	
Goal assists	0
Passes in opp half	48
Passing accuracy in opp half	71%
Successful crosses	1
Cross completion	17%
DEFENDING	
Interceptions	3
Clearances	11
Tackles	9
Tackles won %	44%
DISCIPLINE	
Fouls	3
Yellow cards	1
Red cards	0

SEE PAGE 221 FOR FULL STATS

Former Scottish under-21 international Phili Scott joined the Owls from Scottish Premie League side St Johnstone in a bargai £75,000 deal. The fee could have been a lo more for the Scottish side, but they had t cash in on him before his contract expired. H signed for Wednesday shortly before th transfer deadline in March 1998.

A number of clubs were said to be looking a "Phizzy" before he put pen to paper on a dea at the Yorkshire club. But an Achilles hee injury ruled him out of the remainder of th 1998–99 campaign, and the following seaso was one of frustration as injury continued t dog the highly-rated Scot.

He made only two starts in the Owls disastrous campaign; but, if he can steer clea of injury, he could play a key role i Wednesday's attempts to regain the Premiership spot.

Scott showed glimpses of his ability whe he was called upon for the Owls and a 76% pass completion underlined his composure o the ball.

G David SEAMAN • 1

ARSENAL • BORN: 19.9.63

Since arriving in a £1.3 million deal from Queens Park Rangers in what was then a British transfer record for a goalkeeper, David Seaman has gone on to establish himself as Arsenal and England's first choice.

Whether he is still an automatic choice for the Gunners in 2000–01 remains to be seen, with Arsenal boss Arsene Wenger rumoured to be seeking a new number one. Seaman has been an outstanding servant for Arsenal and holds the club record number of appearances for a goalkeeper.

Injuring himself prior to the start of the 1999–2000 campaign, Seaman did not seem his usual assured self when he finally recovered his fitness and his saves-to-shots ratio of 61% was the lowest among the Premiership's first-choice 'keepers.

But he could boast an impeccable catch success rate, with every cross he came for being claimed by "Safe Hands".

Despite his heroics in the Euro 96 campaign, Seaman is now very much under pressure for his England place.

APPEARANCES	
Start (sub)	24(0)
Minutes on pitch	2115
SHOT STOPPING	
Goals conceded (inside box)	21
Goals conceded (outside box)	6
Minutes per goal conceded	78.3
Clean sheets	5
Saves (shots inside box)	26
Saves (shots outside box)	17
Saves/shots	61%
DISTRIBUTION	
Long kick %	40%
Throws/short passes %	94%
CATCHING	
Crosses caught	28
Crosses punched	11
Crosses dropped	0
Catch success %	100%
DISCIPLINE	
Yellow cards	0
Red cards	0

SEE PAGE 38 FOR FULL STATS

FB Carl SERRANT • 21

NEWCASTLE UNITED • BORN: 12.9.75

After arriving at St James's Park with the tag "England's next left-back", the career of Carl Serrant has stalled somewhat. He joined Newcastle in a £500,000 deal from Oldham Athletic with Latics supporters claiming they had been ripped off, but the Lancashire club risked losing him for free had he stayed at Boundary Park.

Serrant's spell on Tyneside got off to the worst possible start when former manager Ruud Gullit hauled him off on his debut at half-time. It was the Dutchman's first game in charge and Newcastle were 4–1 down at the time against a rampant Liverpool.

The 1999–2000 season was no better for Serrant, as he managed just 88 minutes of action for the first team.

In that time he completed an above-average 77% of his passes and worked himself into six crossing positions. Under Bobby Robson's management, Serrant could feature more in the 2000–01 season.

SEE PAGE 207 FOR FULL STATS

Under pressure: David Seaman

Lee SHARPE • 16

AM

BRADFORD CITY • BORN: 27.5.71

After bursting on to the scene, swapping his school uniform for a football kit, the career of Lee Sharpe has been disrupted by a combination of injury and loss of form. He left the humble surroundings of Torquay United for Manchester United at 16 and quickly broke into the first team at Old Trafford. He made a name for himself with a hat-trick as the Red Devils thrashed Arsenal 6–2 in a League Cup tie at Highbury.

After winning medals for three Championships, an FA Cup and a Cup Winners' Cup, not to mention several England caps, the popular Brummie moved to Leeds United as one of Howard Wilkinson's last signings at the Elland Road club.

Largely ignored by George Graham and not wanted by David O'Leary, Sharpe had a brief spell in Italy with Sampdoria before joining Bradford in a £200,000 deal. The versatile left-footer was part of the squad that defied the odds to preserve their Premiership status, starting 13 league games in the Bantams' historic season.

APPEARANCES	
Start (sub)	13(5)
Minutes on pitch	1189
GOAL ATTEMPTS	
Goals	0
Shots on target	3
Shooting accuracy	75%
Goals/shots ratio	0%
PASSING	
Goal assists	1
Passes in opp half	336
Passing accuracy in opp half	52%
Successful crosses	13
Crossing accuracy	22%
DRIBBLING	
Dribbles & runs	30
Dribble completion	73%
Corners forced	15
DISCIPLINE	
Fouls	13
Yellow cards	1
Red cards	0

SEE PAGE 67 FOR FULL STATS

Richard SHAW • 5

CB

COVENTRY CITY • BORN: 11.9.68

APPEARANCES	
Start (sub)	27(2)
Minutes on pitch	2508
GOAL ATTEMPTS	
Goals	0
DEFENDING	
Blocks	64
Shots cleared off line	0
Headed clearances	177
Other clearances	93
Interceptions	18
Last man saving tackles	0
Tackles won	32
Tackles won %	59%
PASSING	
Passing accuracy own half	83%
Passing accuracy opp half	64%
DISCIPLINE	
Fouls	28
Fouls in danger area	8
Yellow cards	3
Red cards	0

SEE PAGE 95 FOR FULL STATS

Five years after joining the Sky Blues in a £1 million deal from Crystal Palace, Richard Shaw was voted Coventry City's Player of the Year for 1998–99.

Rated by Michael Owen as one of the toughest defenders to play against in the Premiership, Shaw was successful with nearly 60% of his challenges. His distribution of the ball was equally impressive, with 76% of his passes finding a colleague.

Widely regarded as one of the best man-markers in the game, Shaw also posted an excellent disciplinary record, picking up only three yellow cards all season.

Shaw spent nine years at Selhurst Park after joining the Eagles from school, and was part of the Crystal Palace team which played Manchester United in the 1990 FA Cup final, drawing 3–3.

He has now clocked up more than 150 games for Coventry, but is yet to find the scoresheet in that time. In fact, throughout the whole of the 1999–2000 campaign, Shaw failed even to register an effort on goal.

6 Alan Shearer hit the woodwork more times

Alan SHEARER • 9

NEWCASTLE UNITED • BORN: 13.8.70

Alan Shearer began the season in conflict with Ruud Gullit, enduring scathing criticism for his poor performances by the media and contemplating a move away from his beloved Newcastle. But the appointment of Bobby Robson as manager saw the skipper enjoy a productive season for the Magpies, as the former England boss changed the tactics to play to Shearer's strengths.

Shearer netted 23 league goals – bringing his overall tally to 300 – but he will be disappointed that Newcastle lost to Chelsea in the FA Cup semi-final, with the heartache of defeat at Wembley for the third year running.

Shearer, dubbed "Mary Poppins" by disgraced Newcastle directors, also set up seven goals, as he led from the front in steering the club away from the relegation zone to mid-table security.

He announced he would retire from the international scene after Euro 2000, insisting he needs to pace himself if he wants to continue playing in the Premiership. It is widely believed that he may eventually move into a coaching role at St James's Park.

APPEARANCES	
Start (sub)	36(1)
Minutes on pitch	3238
GOAL ATTEMPTS	
Goals inside box	20
Goals outside box	3
Minutes per goal scored	140.8
Goals/shots ratio	29%
SHOOTING	
Shots on target inside box	33
Shots on target outside box	10
Shooting accuracy	54%
PASSING	
Goal assists	7
Key passes	14
Passing accuracy in opp half	66%
DISCIPLINE	
Fouls committed	79
Fouls won	79
Offside	42
Yellow cards	2
Red cards	1

SEE PAGE 207 FOR FULL STATS

Talk of the Toon: Alan Shearer

S

than any other player in the Premiership

S Teddy SHERINGHAM • 10

MANCHESTER UNITED • BORN: 2.4.66

After the euphoria of scoring his side's vital first goal in the 1999 European Cup final, Teddy Sheringham will be disappointed with a lack of first-team football at Old Trafford.

Despite that, he still ended up with another winner's medal in his pocket, which was the rationale behind his move to Old Trafford. Before picking up three medals in United's historic 1998–99 campaign, Sheringham's trophy cabinet was fairly bare, consisting of a Second Division Championship medal from his Millwall days and a Zenith Data Systems Cup medal he won at Nottingham Forest.

He scored five goals as United won the first title of the new Millennium and Sheringham, more a goal provider than a goalscorer, underlined that reputation by setting up six other strikes. Always cool with the ball at his feet, Sheringham achieved a decent 75% pass completion rate.

Sheringham seemed to be on his way out of Old Trafford, but the collapse of the Ruud van Nistelrooy deal saw him sign a one-year contract to stay at United.

APPEARANCES	
Start (sub)	15(12)
Minutes on pitch	1530
GOAL ATTEMPTS	
Goals inside box	5
Goals outside box	0
Minutes per goal scored	306.0
Goals/shots ratio	18%
SHOOTING	
Shots on target inside box	11
Shots on target outside box	3
Shooting accuracy	50%
PASSING	
Goal assists	6
Key passes	13
Passing accuracy in opp half	75%
DISCIPLINE	
Fouls committed	14
Fouls won	18
Offside	12
Yellow cards	0
Red cards	0

SEE PAGE 179 FOR FULL STATS

M Tim SHERWOOD • 8

TOTTENHAM HOTSPUR • BORN: 2.2.69

APPEARANCES	
Start (sub)	23(4)
Minutes on pitch	2128
GOAL ATTEMPTS	
Goals	8
Shots on target	17
Shooting accuracy	61%
PASSING & CROSSING	
Goal assists	0
Passes in opp half	686
Passing accuracy in opp half	70%
Successful crosses	7
Cross completion	37%
DEFENDING	
Interceptions	33
Clearances	64
Tackles	86
Tackles won %	51%
DISCIPLINE	
Fouls	36
Yellow cards	9
Red cards	0

SEE PAGE 263 FOR FULL STATS

After a spell at Blackburn Rovers in which he won a League Championship medal, Tim Sherwood moved south to White Hart Lane for £4 million in February 1999.

He made an impressive start to his career with Spurs, but suffered with a hernia problem during the 1999–2000 campaign which saw him miss the last two months of the season. On making his comeback, he scored the second goal in a 3–1 win against Sunderland on the final day of the season.

This was the eighth goal of the campaign for the former Watford and Norwich midfielder, who could well have featured in Euro 2000 had it not been for his injury. Sherwood made his international debut shortly after signing for Spurs in the 3–1 win over Poland.

A good passer of the ball, Sherwood successfully completed 74% of his passes, and his leadership qualities were sorely missed in the latter stages of the campaign. In his absence, Spurs won just three of their 11 games and disappointed their fans by finishing in mid-table.

S Gerald SIBON • 9

SHEFFIELD WEDNESDAY • BORN: 19.4.74

Gerald Sibon arrived at Hillsborough in a £2 million deal from Ajax Amsterdam, and hopes were high that he could build a lethal partnership with another new recruit, Belgian striker Gilles De Bilde.

Sadly for Owls fans, it was not the case. While De Bilde went on to earn himself some credibility in Wednesday's disastrous season, Sibon was left to face the flak of the Wednesday faithful and regularly received a torrent of abuse whenever he entered the field of play.

His one outstanding moment came when he cracked an unstoppable volley into the top corner of the Derby goal to put Wednesday 2–0 up. But after also leading 3–1, Wednesday conceded two goals in stoppage-time to let the Rams snatch a point.

At 6'3", and unheard of on these shores, Sibon arrived having scored 51 goals in just over 100 games in the Dutch League. But even the man responsible for his signing, Danny Wilson, must have been worried about his new boy when the giant front-runner claimed he was "not really that good with headers".

APPEARANCES	
Start (sub)	12(16)
Minutes on pitch	1190
GOAL ATTEMPTS	
Goals inside box	4
Goals outside box	1
Minutes per goal scored	238.0
Goals/shots ratio	15%
SHOOTING	
Shots on target inside box	10
Shots on target outside box	6
Shooting accuracy	47%
PASSING	
Goal assists	1
Key passes	5
Passing accuracy in opp half	66%
DISCIPLINE	
Fouls committed	30
Fouls won	13
Offside	1
Yellow cards	2
Red cards	0

SEE PAGE 221 FOR FULL STATS

FB Mickael SILVESTRE • 27

MANCHESTER UNITED • BORN: 9.8.77

APPEARANCES	
Start (sub)	30(1)
Minutes on pitch	2719
GOAL ATTEMPTS	
Goals	0
PASSING & CROSSING	
Goal assists	0
Passing	1392
Passing accuracy	74%
Crosses	25
Crossing accuracy	52%
DEFENDING	
Tackles	128
Tackles won %	52%
Blocks	56
Interceptions	28
Clearances	247
Shots cleared off line	1
DISCIPLINE	
Fouls	26
Yellow cards	0
Red cards	0

SEE PAGE 179 FOR FULL STATS

United splashed out £4 million to bring Mickael Silvestre to Old Trafford, pinching him from under the noses of Liverpool.

Sir Alex Ferguson had been impressed with the French under-21 international's performance in a European Cup tie against United en route to their historic Treble, and wasted no time in handing Silvestre his debut.

That came, ironically, in a thrilling 3–2 win at Anfield over Liverpool, and despite taking his time in coming to terms with the English game, he showed glimpses of the pace and ability that prompted Ferguson to buy him.

He soon established himself in the heart of the United defence alongside Jaap Stam, winning 52% of his 128 tackles. Silvestre also showed he is comfortable on the ball by completing 92% of his dribbles and runs, while the speedy Frenchman also saw an excellent 52% of his crosses pick out a red shirt.

Nonetheless, with Ronny Johnsen and Wes Brown regaining full fitness after missing almost all of the 1999–2000 campaign, Silvestre has a battle to hold his place in the United first team.

SILVINHO • 16

ARSENAL • BORN: 12.4.74

Arsenal have ostensibly had three left-backs for the past 30 years – Sammy Nelson, Kenny Sansom and Nigel Winterburn – and Brazilian Silvinho has begun the unenviable task of following in the footsteps of the Gunners legends as first-choice left-back.

Silvinho signed in a £4 million deal from Corinthians and impressed with his committed attitude, close control and dangerous crossing ability. Like many Brazilians, he also packs a mean shot, but surprisingly had to wait until the penultimate game of the season against Sheffield Wednesday to open his account, with a stunning long-range thunderbolt.

Despite his Brazilian nationality, he claims to have no interest in samba, but his dancing dribbling skills were much in evidence against Leeds United when he set up a goal for Kanu with a mesmerising run.

Silvinho loves to get forward, but this means he sometimes gets caught out of position. Tony Adams can often be seen reminding the full-back of his defensive responsibilities, but Silvinho did win more than half of his tackles.

APPEARANCES	
Start (sub)	23(8)
Minutes on pitch	2177
GOAL ATTEMPTS	
Goals	1
PASSING & CROSSING	
Goal assists	3
Passing	1076
Passing accuracy	73%
Crosses	90
Crossing accuracy	26%
DEFENDING	
Tackles	103
Tackles won %	52%
Blocks	19
Interceptions	17
Clearances	67
Shots cleared off line	1
DISCIPLINE	
Fouls	32
Yellow cards	3
Red cards	0

SEE PAGE 39 FOR FULL STATS

Steve SIMONSEN • 35

EVERTON • BORN: 3.4.79

After moving to Goodison Park from Tranmere Rovers in a £3.3 million deal, Steve Simonsen has found first-team opportunities hard to come by. The fee for the England under-21 shot-stopper was a British record for a goalkeeper, but Simonsen has found himself third in the pecking order behind Paul Gerrard and then Thomas Myhre.

The former Nottingham Forest junior had played only 35 games for Tranmere and made an immediate impact, keeping seven successive clean sheets.

But he caused quite a stir when he missed a training session at Tranmere, thinking – quite wrongly – that his move to Everton had been completed. He was soon made aware that it was not in a heated conversation with Rovers chief John Aldridge, who told him in no uncertain terms to "get back here at once".

The youngster made one appearance as a substitute against Southampton, making four saves and conceding two goals.

SEE PAGE 122 FOR FULL STATS

Thunderbolt: Silvinho

27% of Leicester's goals were scored by defenders,

Frank SINCLAIR • 3

LEICESTER CITY • BORN: 3.12.71

Frank Sinclair endured the worst possible start to the 1999–2000 campaign when he scored own-goals in the Foxes' first two games of the season against Arsenal and Chelsea. What made it worse for Martin O'Neill's side was that they were both scored in injury-time!

This earned him the nickname "Frank Spencer", but Leicester's one-time record £2-million signing from Chelsea bounced back well from his "whoopsies"!

He was an integral member of the team that defeated Tranmere Rovers in the Worthington Cup at Wembley, something that made up for him missing out in the League Cup final of 1998. His "serious breach of discipline" shortly before the game with Tottenham saw him promptly dropped by O'Neill.

The 1999–2000 season saw no such problems, with the pacy defender a virtual ever-present in O'Neill's side. His total of 79 blocks was bettered only by Matt Elliott in the Foxes team, and he can be pleased with his 55% tackle success rate – four percentage points above the average for a Premiership defender.

APPEARANCES	
Start (sub)	34(0)
Minutes on pitch	2926
GOAL ATTEMPTS	
Goals	0
DEFENDING	
Blocks	79
Shots cleared off line	1
Headed clearances	204
Other clearances	111
Interceptions	25
Last man saving tackles	0
Tackles won	66
Tackles won %	55%
PASSING	
Passing accuracy own half	78%
Passing accuracy opp half	56%
DISCIPLINE	
Fouls	43
Fouls in danger area	15
Yellow cards	7
Red cards	1

SEE PAGE 151 FOR FULL STATS

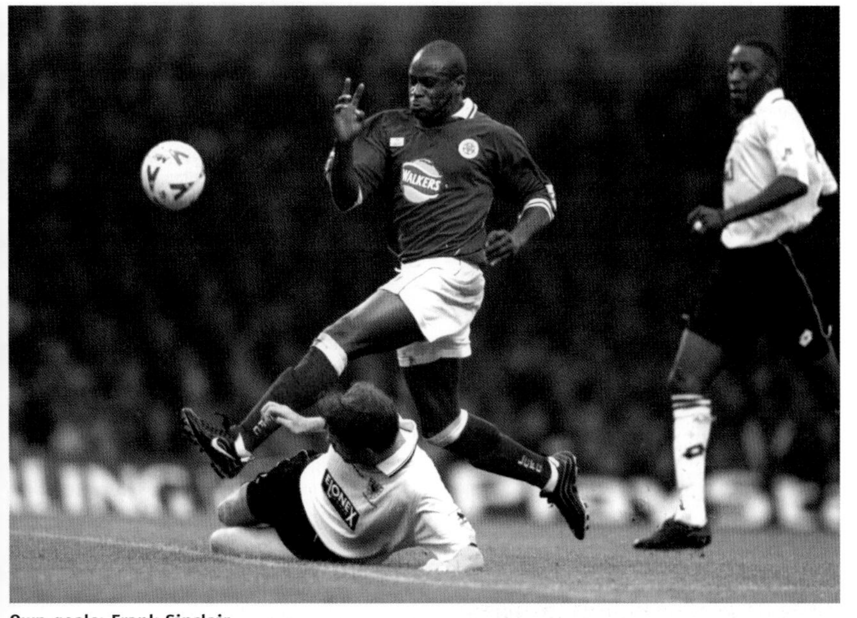

Own-goals: Frank Sinclair

Trevor SINCLAIR • 8

WEST HAM UNITED • BORN: 2.3.73

Any manager would be delighted to have a player who can skilfully perform in virtually any position – and Harry Redknapp has just that in Trevor Sinclair.

The pacy midfielder more than thanked Redknapp for reviving his flagging career with consistent performances throughout 1999–2000. Only the presence of a certain Italian pushed Sinclair into the runner-up spot in the Hammers' Player of the Year poll.

Sinclair played on the left and right flanks for West Ham, as a wing-back and in midfield. These constant changes in position did not seem to affect him and he was a regular supplier of passes to his team-mates, making 1,415 in total. He also scored seven goals, revelling in the opportunity to get into the box.

Many Hammers supporters were surprised to see his name omitted from England's Euro 2000 squad, especially since his league stats earned him a place in the Opta England team.

But press reports linking him with a move to Chelsea showed his worth and he must now set his sights on World Cup 2002.

APPEARANCES	
Start (sub)	36(0)
Minutes on pitch	3239
GOAL ATTEMPTS	
Goals	7
Shots on target	21
Shooting accuracy	55%
Goals/shots ratio	18%
PASSING	
Goal assists	8
Passes in opp half	934
Passing accuracy in opp half	67%
Successful crosses	36
Crossing accuracy	30%
DRIBBLING	
Dribbles & runs	226
Dribble completion	70%
Corners forced	42
DISCIPLINE	
Fouls	38
Yellow cards	5
Red cards	1

SEE PAGE 291 FOR FULL STATS

Allan SMART • 12

WATFORD • BORN: 8.7.74

APPEARANCES	
Start (sub)	13(1)
Minutes on pitch	1059
GOAL ATTEMPTS	
Goals inside box	5
Goals outside box	0
Minutes per goal scored	211.8
Goals/shots ratio	17%
SHOOTING	
Shots on target inside box	12
Shots on target outside box	5
Shooting accuracy	59%
PASSING	
Goal assists	1
Key passes	1
Passing accuracy in opp half	52%
DISCIPLINE	
Fouls committed	26
Fouls won	17
Offside	20
Yellow cards	1
Red cards	0

SEE PAGE 277 FOR FULL STATS

Allan Smart moved to the Hornets at the beginning of 1998–99 and immediately impressed with his ability to shield the ball and bring others into play. Smart went on to score eight goals that season, including a crisp drive at Wembley that secured Watford's place in the Premiership.

He then bagged five goals during the 1999–2000 season, the most notable being the winner in the 1–0 triumph over Chelsea. In fact, Smart also scored at Stamford Bridge against the Blues, but could not prevent Watford slipping to a 2–1 defeat.

Injury robbed him of the chance to make a major impact on the Premiership, but he wasted no time in breaking his goalscoring duck. His winning strike against Gianluca Vialli's side came in only his second start. His five strikes resulted from 17 efforts on target, but he managed just one assist.

Smart will be looking for an injury-free start to the 2000–2001 season to help Watford back into the Premiership after their brief flirtation with the top flight.

Vladimir SMICER • 7

LIVERPOOL • BORN: 24.5.73

After arriving at Anfield in a £4.2 million move from RC Lens, Vladimir Smicer endured a torrid 1999–2000 as injury followed injury for the Czech international.

Steve McManaman's departure to Real Madrid paved the way for Smicer to move to Liverpool and join up with close friend and international team-mate Patrik Berger. After an impressive pre-season, hopes were high that he would be the natural successor to "Macca".

But in only his second game, Smicer sustained an ankle injury that kept him out for the best part of a month.

He made his comeback as a second-half substitute against Manchester United, as Liverpool went down 3–2.

When he has played, Smicer has shown the Liverpool fans glimpses of his class. A total of 72% of his passes found a red shirt and he set up four of Liverpool's goals. But, as he concedes, whenever he felt his football, form and confidence returning, he sustained another injury, and Liverpool are yet to see the best of the Czech star.

APPEARANCES	
Start (sub)	12(9)
Minutes on pitch	1184
GOAL ATTEMPTS	
Goals	1
Shots on target	6
Shooting accuracy	30%
Goals/shots ratio	5%
PASSING	
Goal assists	4
Passes in opp half	351
Passing accuracy in opp half	68%
Successful crosses	19
Crossing accuracy	41%
DRIBBLING	
Dribbles & runs	78
Dribble completion	78%
Corners forced	13
DISCIPLINE	
Fouls	21
Yellow cards	1
Red cards	0

SEE PAGE 165 FOR FULL STATS

Alan SMITH • 17

LEEDS UNITED • BORN: 28.10.80

APPEARANCES	
Start (sub)	20(6)
Minutes on pitch	1733
GOAL ATTEMPTS	
Goals inside box	4
Goals outside box	0
Minutes per goal scored	433.3
Goals/shots ratio	13%
SHOOTING	
Shots on target inside box	10
Shots on target outside box	4
Shooting accuracy	47%
PASSING	
Goal assists	3
Key passes	12
Passing accuracy in opp half	66%
DISCIPLINE	
Fouls committed	57
Fouls won	38
Offside	26
Yellow cards	5
Red cards	1

SEE PAGE 137 FOR FULL STATS

After making a sensational impact in his first season at Leeds, hot-shot Alan Smith endured a disappointing 1999–2000 campaign.

He made a memorable debut as a sub at Anfield in 1998, scoring with his first touch in professional football. His natural goalscoring instinct and aggressive nature have earned comparisons to Leeds legend Allan Clarke.

Smith has represented England at under-16 and under-18 level, and capped his under-21 debut with a goal and two assists.

But after netting against Spurs and twice against Sheffield Wednesday during 1999–2000, Smith failed to register another goal after his strike in the 2–1 victory over Bradford.

His biggest problem seems to be his temperament. Smith often appears to concentrate too much on the physical aspect of the game rather than his football. He committed 57 fouls, earned five yellow cards and one dismissal in 1999–2000, earning a place in Opta's "Dirty Dozen".

Tommy SMITH • 17

WATFORD • BORN: 22.5.80

Hemel Hempstead-born Tommy Smith was spotted playing park football when Hornets boss Graham Taylor decided to offer him a full-time contract. Still only 20, Smith is highly thought-of at Watford and in his debut season in the Premiership he netted two goals – a brilliant solo effort against Middlesbrough and a neatly-taken strike against Manchester United in a narrow 3–2 defeat.

He started the 1999–2000 season making fleeting appearances as a substitute, but as Watford's fate was sealed, he was first choice in every game from April onwards.

The Hornets hitman scored twice from 15 attempts at goal, but he can be delighted with his accuracy, as 14 of his efforts were on target. He also chipped in with three assists as Watford's season ended in disappointment.

The experience Smith has gained from a season in the top flight will hold him in good stead and he clearly has a bright future. He will now be hoping he gets the opportunity to launch Watford's assault on a Premiership return in 2000–01.

APPEARANCES	
Start (sub)	13(8)
Minutes on pitch	1249
GOAL ATTEMPTS	
Goals inside box	2
Goals outside box	0
Minutes per goal scored	624.5
Goals/shots ratio	13%
SHOOTING	
Shots on target inside box	12
Shots on target outside box	2
Shooting accuracy	93%
PASSING	
Goal assists	3
Key passes	2
Passing accuracy in opp half	66%
DISCIPLINE	
Fouls committed	7
Fouls won	19
Offside	20
Yellow cards	1
Red cards	0

SEE PAGE 277 FOR FULL STATS

Nolberto SOLANO • 15

NEWCASTLE UNITED • BORN: 12.12.74

APPEARANCES	
Start (sub)	29(1)
Minutes on pitch	2508
GOAL ATTEMPTS	
Goals	3
Shots on target	14
Shooting accuracy	64%
Goals/shots ratio	14%
PASSING	
Goal assists	15
Passes in opp half	919
Passing accuracy in opp half	70%
Successful crosses	116
Crossing accuracy	37%
DRIBBLING	
Dribbles & runs	98
Dribble completion	80%
Corners forced	38
DISCIPLINE	
Fouls	34
Yellow cards	6
Red cards	0

SEE PAGE 207 FOR FULL STATS

The Premiership's first Peruvian footballer has settled in well on Tyneside following a £2.5 million move from Boca Juniors of Argentina, and Nolberto Solano has become a firm favourite with the Geordie faithful.

Despite being a right-back at international level (he is also captain of the national side), Solano has revelled in a right-wing role under Bobby Robson, and his total of 312 crosses throughout the 1999–2000 campaign was bettered only by David Beckham.

Many doubted whether "Nobby" would settle in the north-east, and he has admitted that learning the language has been difficult – especially in Newcastle. But despite the communication problems, Solano played an integral part in the Magpies' run to the semi-final of the FA Cup.

He is seen as the ideal man to provide the ammunition for Alan Shearer, and Solano's total of 15 assists was the best in the Premiership along with Beckham. Newcastle will now be keen to resist rumoured interest from Real Madrid.

Ole Gunnar SOLSKJAER • 20

MANCHESTER UNITED • BORN: 26.2.73

ʼle Gunnar Solskjaer earned legendary status at ʼld Trafford for his injury-time heroics in the ʼ999 Champions League final against Bayern ɬunich, and the popular striker enjoyed another ɹccessful season in 1999–2000.

Again, the United hitman spent plenty of time ɒondering life on the substitutes' bench, which ɘd to many clubs, including Spurs and Leeds, ɲquiring about his availability. But, when ɑlled upon, he again delivered the goods for ɦe Red Devils.

Solskjaer, who amazingly suffers from an ɭlergy to grass, blasted 12 league goals for ʼnited, including four in the 5–1 win over ɿverton at Old Trafford, and contributed seven ssists for Sir Alex Ferguson's side. His all-round ɔility is underlined with his 62% tackle success ɑte, but it is his incredible scoring touch for ɿhich he is idolised by the Stretford End.

Solskjaer became an instant hit with the ʼnited fans after netting on his first team ɘbut. He became the 87th United player to do ɔ when he fired home in a 2–2 draw with lackburn in 1996.

APPEARANCES	
Start (sub)	15(13)
Minutes on pitch	1396
GOAL ATTEMPTS	
Goals inside box	12
Goals outside box	0
Minutes per goal scored	116.3
Goals/shots ratio	23%
SHOOTING	
Shots on target inside box	24
Shots on target outside box	7
Shooting accuracy	60%
PASSING	
Goal assists	7
Key passes	4
Passing accuracy in opp half	68%
DISCIPLINE	
Fouls committed	19
Fouls won	14
Offside	18
Yellow cards	2
Red cards	0

SEE PAGE 179 FOR FULL STATS

Trond-Egil SOLTVEDT • 32

SOUTHAMPTON • BORN: 15.2.67

APPEARANCES	
Start (sub)	17(7)
Minutes on pitch	1577
GOAL ATTEMPTS	
Goals	1
Shots on target	9
Shooting accuracy	60%
PASSING & CROSSING	
Goal assists	3
Passes in opp half	305
Passing accuracy in opp half	63%
Successful crosses	2
Cross completion	22%
DEFENDING	
Interceptions	9
Clearances	39
Tackles	42
Tackles won %	55%
DISCIPLINE	
Fouls	18
Yellow cards	0
Red cards	0

SEE PAGE 235 FOR FULL STATS

After spending two years with Coventry City, Trond-Egil Soltvedt moved to The Dell in a £350,000 deal after two games of the 1999–2000 campaign. His debut came as a second-half substitute in the superb 4–2 win over Newcastle United.

But after Glenn Hoddle took over the reins for the Saints, Soltvedt found himself out of favour at The Dell, possibly not helped by a lowly 67% pass completion rate.

He started only three games under Hoddle's regime, but made a number of appearances from the subs' bench. The Norwegian midfielder managed only one goal in a disappointing campaign; that came in a 1–1 draw with Liverpool. He also netted against Liverpool in a League Cup tie at The Dell, which the Saints won 2–1.

Despite reports that he may leave the south coast, assistant manager John Gorman has stated he does not want Soltvedt to leave. But if he continues to play only a bit-part role for the Saints, his future may well lie away from the Hampshire club.

S

:orners than any other player in the Premiership

Rigobert SONG • 4

LIVERPOOL • BORN: 1.7.76

CB

Cameroon international Rigobert Song arrived on British shores with a reputation for aggression. He was sent off in two successive World Cup campaigns for the Africans, and regularly found himself in trouble with referees. A poor start to his Liverpool career hardly enhanced his credentials as a Premiership star.

But Song claims he is a more mature player these days and points to only one yellow card during the African Nations Cup as proof. His decisive penalty secured the Cup for the Cameroonians in February.

His efficient defensive style has earned him the nickname of "German" from his international team-mates, but he has become a firm favourite among Koppites despite his lack of first-team action. The impressive form of Sami Hyypia and Stephan Henchoz has seen his chances limited, and Song has mainly played at full-back.

Song failed to register an attempt at goal during the 1999–2000 campaign, but was credited with one assist. He attempted 43 tackles but will be looking to improve on his modest success rate of 44%.

APPEARANCES	
Start (sub)	14(4)
Minutes on pitch	1288
GOAL ATTEMPTS	
Goals	0
DEFENDING	
Blocks	26
Shots cleared off line	3
Headed clearances	127
Other clearances	55
Interceptions	27
Last man saving tackles	0
Tackles won	19
Tackles won %	44%
PASSING	
Passing accuracy own half	78%
Passing accuracy opp half	58%
DISCIPLINE	
Fouls	26
Fouls in danger area	7
Yellow cards	2
Red cards	0

SEE PAGE 165 FOR FULL STATS

Danny SONNER • 7

SHEFFIELD WEDNESDAY • BORN: 9.1.72

M

APPEARANCES	
Start (sub)	18(9)
Minutes on pitch	1638
GOAL ATTEMPTS	
Goals	0
Shots on target	4
Shooting accuracy	21%
PASSING & CROSSING	
Goal assists	1
Passes in opp half	498
Passing accuracy in opp half	66%
Successful crosses	4
Cross completion	17%
DEFENDING	
Interceptions	6
Clearances	41
Tackles	46
Tackles won %	67%
DISCIPLINE	
Fouls	27
Yellow cards	5
Red cards	1

SEE PAGE 221 FOR FULL STATS

Former Owls chief Danny Wilson made Dan Sonner his third signing for Wednesday whe he paid only £75,000 for his services fro Ipswich Town. The fee should have been a l more for the diminutive midfielder, but Wilsc took advantage of a clause in Sonner's contra to take him to Hillsborough for a minimal fe

Skilful and creative, Sonner's statistics for t 1999–2000 campaign underline his abilit with 73% of his passes successfully finding team-mate. But a lack of goals and only o assist saw him relegated to the bench aft starting the season in the first team.

One aspect of his game that does nee improving is his shooting, with only four Sonner's 19 shots troubling the keeper. But has shown there is more to his game than ju his passing by making 46 challenges – ar winning two-thirds of them.

After falling out of favour at Hillsboroug Northern Irish international Sonner will l looking to regain his first-team place ar help Wednesday back into the Premiership 2000–01.

Thomas SORENSEN • 1

SUNDERLAND • BORN: 12.6.76

Thomas Sorensen has proved a bargain buy for Peter Reid's side following a £500,000 move from Danish club OB Odense. He received offers from Ajax and Udinese but decided his future was on Wearside and signed for the Mackems in the summer of 1998.

In his first season for Sunderland, he broke the club record for the highest number of clean sheets in a season, and was prominent in their promotion back to the Premiership, winning the club's Player of the Year award to boot.

He has already made more than 20 appearances for the Danish under-21 side and is widely tipped to be the successor to Danish legend Peter Schmeichel as the country's number one.

Ever reliable, the Danish shot-stopper missed only one game for the Black Cats during 1999–2000, keeping nine clean sheets in his first season of Premiership action. He also achieved a 71% saves-to-shots ratio, and he will be looking to help Sunderland in their quest for Europe during 2000–01 after signing a new deal to stay on Wearside.

APPEARANCES	
Start (sub)	37(0)
Minutes on pitch	3330
SHOT STOPPING	
Goals conceded (inside box)	46
Goals conceded (outside box)	9
Minutes per goal conceded	60.5
Clean sheets	9
Saves (shots inside box)	72
Saves (shots outside box)	60
Saves/shots	71%
DISTRIBUTION	
Long kick %	53%
Throws/short passes %	88%
CATCHING	
Crosses caught	61
Crosses punched	18
Crosses dropped	5
Catch success %	92%
DISCIPLINE	
Yellow cards	1
Red cards	0

SEE PAGE 248 FOR FULL STATS

Neville SOUTHALL • 32

BRADFORD CITY • BORN: 16.9.58

Welsh legend Neville Southall made a shock Premiership comeback in 1999–2000 at the age of 41.

He appeared for Bradford City in their derby clash with Leeds United because of City's goalkeeping crisis, with Gary Walsh and Matt Clarke both injured. Clarke had fallen down some stairs at home after only recently returning from injury, and the larger-than-life Southall was given the nod to play.

He had signed on a match-to-match basis after beginning the season at Torquay, but was powerless to stop Leeds from winning 2–1 in front of the Sky TV cameras. Southall was even selected for a 15-minute cameo role on Sky's Digital TV PlayerCam.

Despite conceding two goals, Southall kept the score down by making three saves. But after a career that has seen him win many of the game's top honours, it would appear the Premiership has finally seen the last of the eccentric Welshman.

SEE PAGE 66 FOR FULL STATS

Shock comeback: Neville Southall

Gareth SOUTHGATE • 4

ASTON VILLA • BORN: 3.9.70

When ex-Villa boss Brian Little paid Crystal Palace a club record £2.5 million for Gareth Southgate, many expected the ex-Eagle to continue to play in midfield.

But Little decided to switch him to centre-back, where Southgate excelled and went on to establish himself as an England international in that position.

Southgate, whose nickname is "The Model" after Villa boss John Gregory stated he had the highest standards of conduct, will always be remembered as the player whose penalty miss saw England bow out of Euro 96.

And against West Ham in a League Cup clash at Upton Park, the ghost of that fateful night seemed to return as he missed again in a shoot-out. Luckily for him, the Manny Omoyimni fiasco meant a replay was ordered – and Villa went on to win.

The 1999–2000 season again saw Southgate as consistent as ever, but it all ended miserably when a lacklustre Villa side lost 1–0 in the FA Cup final to Chelsea. And in June, Southgate slapped in a transfer request at Villa Park.

APPEARANCES	
Start (sub)	31(0)
Minutes on pitch	2727
GOAL ATTEMPTS	
Goals	2
DEFENDING	
Blocks	68
Shots cleared off line	0
Headed clearances	217
Other clearances	129
Interceptions	35
Last man saving tackles	0
Tackles won	50
Tackles won %	57%
PASSING	
Passing accuracy own half	78%
Passing accuracy opp half	51%
DISCIPLINE	
Fouls	33
Fouls in danger area	8
Yellow cards	0
Red cards	1

SEE PAGE 53 FOR FULL STATS

Gary SPEED • 11

NEWCASTLE UNITED • BORN: 8.9.69

APPEARANCES	
Start (sub)	36(0)
Minutes on pitch	3240
GOAL ATTEMPTS	
Goals	9
Shots on target	24
Shooting accuracy	48%
Goals/shots ratio	18%
PASSING	
Goal assists	3
Passes in opp half	1160
Passing accuracy in opp half	73%
Successful crosses	7
Crossing accuracy	28%
DRIBBLING	
Dribbles & runs	85
Dribble completion	80%
Corners forced	13
DISCIPLINE	
Fouls	55
Yellow cards	6
Red cards	0

SEE PAGE 207 FOR FULL STATS

Welsh international Gary Speed has only bee suspended twice during his decade at the to level, the second of which was in 1999–2000

"You can't afford to mistime a tackle," sai Speed who, after serving his suspension, wa booked just once in his last 1,710 minutes c Premiership football, maintaining hi reputation as a hard-working midfielder.

While everyone connected with Newcastl would prefer to forget the first month of th 1999–2000 campaign, Speed's form, alon with the rest of his team-mates', improve dramatically with the arrival of Bobby Robson

Speed's nine league goals made hin Newcastle's second-highest scorer, and hi five headed strikes not only proved h prowess in the air, but also highlighted hi team's ability to get quality balls in from wid areas. The Welshman's passing in th opposition half was highly accurate, provin that he is a well-rounded player.

With much optimism around St James's Par for the 2000–01 season, Newcastle could b moving up the table with Speed.

2 Pavel Srnicek was the only 'keepe

G Pavel SRNICEK • 28

SHEFFIELD WEDNESDAY • BORN: 10.3.68

Pavel Srnicek certainly had a busy time in the Sheffield Wednesday goal, but showed some good form in the 1999–2000 season.

The Czech saved three-quarters of the shots on target he faced, a far superior saves-to-shots ratio than his rival for the number one spot, Kevin Pressman.

Even so, Danny Wilson seemed unable to decide which man he preferred between the sticks, with Srnicek twice losing his place to Pressman but each time forcing his way back into the side. His second "comeback" game was at Villa Park, where he saved two penalties but still saw the Owls lose 2–1 to John Gregory's team.

Srnicek's season was cut short in March when he had to be taken off against Watford with a shoulder injury and, frustratingly for him, could only sit and watch as his team-mates were unable to haul themselves out of the relegation zone.

But if he can keep up his good form in the Nationwide League, Srnicek could bounce straight back to the Premiership with the Owls.

APPEARANCES	
Start (sub)	20(0)
Minutes on pitch	1741
SHOT STOPPING	
Goals conceded (inside box)	27
Goals conceded (outside box)	1
Minutes per goal conceded	62.2
Clean sheets	4
Saves (shots inside box)	45
Saves (shots outside box)	39
Saves/shots	75%
DISTRIBUTION	
Long kick %	42%
Throws/short passes %	81%
CATCHING	
Crosses caught	25
Crosses punched	22
Crosses dropped	4
Catch success %	86%
DISCIPLINE	
Yellow cards	0
Red cards	0

SEE PAGE 220 FOR FULL STATS

CB Jaap STAM • 6

MANCHESTER UNITED • BORN: 17.7.72

APPEARANCES	
Start (sub)	33(0)
Minutes on pitch	2828
GOAL ATTEMPTS	
Goals	0
DEFENDING	
Blocks	69
Shots cleared off line	0
Headed clearances	203
Other clearances	65
Interceptions	35
Last man saving tackles	1
Tackles won	53
Tackles won %	54%
PASSING	
Passing accuracy own half	89%
Passing accuracy opp half	78%
DISCIPLINE	
Fouls	45
Fouls in danger area	13
Yellow cards	5
Red cards	0

SEE PAGE 179 FOR FULL STATS

Only two Premiership teams finished 1999–2000 without a player who could boast that they made more clearances than Jaap Stam, but while the giant Dutchman may not have been the busiest defender in the top flight he was certainly one of the most efficient.

His task was made all the harder by the lack of a regular partner in central defence, with Mickael Silvestre and Henning Berg both playing alongside Stam, and Ronny Johnsen only returning from injury towards the end of the campaign.

Stam would also have been bemused by the constant change of goalkeeping personnel, as the former PSV man appeared to be the only regular feature in United's rearguard.

Stam's pass completion rate in his own half of 89% was higher than any other regular Premiership centre-back, and confirmed not only his coolness in possession but also his reputation as one of the best defenders in the world. But he also recorded a good rate in the opposition half, as he strode forward with comfort on the ball.

to save two penalties in one match

Phil STAMP • 14

MIDDLESBROUGH • BORN: 12.12.75

The 1999–2000 campaign was a frustrating one for Phil Stamp, whose hamstring injury restricted the midfielder's appearances for Middlesbrough.

Stamp's entire Boro career has been anything but consistent; he has been with the club since signing forms from the junior ranks in February 1993, yet has only made 91 league appearances for the club.

But while the Premiership is yet to see a first-class Stamp, Bryan Robson clearly believes that the 24-year-old can cut it at the highest level and has kept faith in him.

Stamp recorded a poor pass completion rate of just 59% and won fewer than half his attempted tackles, so it is unlikely that he will become a first-team regular unless he can improve. But his versatility helps make him a valuable member of the Boro squad.

Of his injury problems, Stamp said: "The new season can't come soon enough for me", and if he can endure an injury-free 2000–01 and get a consistent run in the first team, we may yet see the best of him.

APPEARANCES	
Start (sub)	13(3)
Minutes on pitch	1190
GOAL ATTEMPTS	
Goals	0
Shots on target	1
Shooting accuracy	11%
PASSING & CROSSING	
Goal assists	1
Passes in opp half	211
Passing accuracy in opp half	51%
Successful crosses	14
Cross completion	34%
DEFENDING	
Interceptions	8
Clearances	66
Tackles	24
Tackles won %	46%
DISCIPLINE	
Fouls	20
Yellow cards	6
Red cards	0

SEE PAGE 193 FOR FULL STATS

CB

Steve STAUNTON • 5

LIVERPOOL • BORN: 19.1.69

APPEARANCES	
Start (sub)	7(5)
Minutes on pitch	601
GOAL ATTEMPTS	
Goals	0
DEFENDING	
Blocks	6
Shots cleared off line	0
Headed clearances	35
Other clearances	14
Interceptions	13
Last man saving tackles	0
Tackles won	7
Tackles won %	54%
PASSING	
Passing accuracy own half	84%
Passing accuracy opp half	70%
DISCIPLINE	
Fouls	6
Fouls in danger area	2
Yellow cards	2
Red cards	1*

SEE PAGE 165 FOR FULL STATS

Equally adept as a left-back or in the centre of defence, one position where Steve Staunton would not claim to be proficient is in goal.

Yet in the Merseyside derby at Anfield in September, Staunton was forced to don the goalkeeping gloves after Sander Westerveld was sent off. The Irishman made two saves without conceding a goal.

It was not the first strange incident for Staunton in 1999–2000, though. The Irishman was sent off for encroaching at a free-kick although TV replays clearly showed the ball being touched twice before Staunton moved. The red card was later rescinded*.

In his more orthodox outfield role Staunton's appearances were limited, thanks to the good form of Sami Hyypia and Stephane Henchoz in central defence, and the emergence of Dominic Matteo as first-choice left-back.

Staunton failed to start a Premiership match from mid-November and spent the majority of the campaign watching Liverpool's season from the bench.

Jordan STEWART • 46

LEICESTER CITY • BORN: 3.3.82

Jordan Stewart made his City debut when coming on as a substitute for Theo Zagorakis in the Foxes' 3–1 defeat at home to West Ham, at a time when Leicester were facing a serious injury crisis.

The highly-rated midfielder joined from Aston Villa when he impressed in a couple of trial games for Leicester. He is quick and enthusiastic and has the ability to play in either midfield or defence. The Birmingham-born ace has progressed well at Leicester and his impressive form for the juniors and reserve team earned him a first-team call-up.

The Leicester backroom staff predict a bright future for their prodigious talent, who also started one game in a loan spell with Bristol Rovers in 1999–2000. Now he must impress new boss Peter Taylor.

Stewart, whose nickname is "Shark Head", is in the second year of his apprenticeship at Filbert Street and is also said to be the ladies' favourite at the training ground.

SEE PAGE 151 FOR FULL STATS

Igor STIMAC • 5

WEST HAM UNITED • BORN: 6.9.67

Having helped Croatia to third place in World Cup 1998, and turned in a series of sturdy performances for Derby County, Stimac seemed the perfect defensive signing for West Ham.

With the club's well-documented injury problems in defence, his overall consistency was vital to the Hammers' back line.

But Stimac will have empathised more than anyone with Manny Omoyimni, having experienced a similar memory lapse to the young winger when playing in the Intertoto Cup game against Osijek. His European two-match suspension from four years earlier was still outstanding, and West Ham were lucky to escape punishment for their oversight.

His main attribute is his strength, and Stimac's superb tackle success rate of 84% was the best at the club. His vigour can also be his downfall, and the defender received nine yellow cards and one red in 1999–2000.

Being top of the charts at the Boleyn will come as no surprise – his Christmas number one hit in Croatia has proved he can be a success at whatever he puts his hands to.

Number one hit: Igor Stimac

APPEARANCES	
Start (sub)	24(0)
Minutes on pitch	2084
GOAL ATTEMPTS	
Goals	1
DEFENDING	
Blocks	66
Shots cleared off line	0
Headed clearances	148
Other clearances	49
Interceptions	22
Last man saving tackles	0
Tackles won	58
Tackles won %	84%
PASSING	
Passing accuracy own half	78%
Passing accuracy opp half	58%
DISCIPLINE	
Fouls	45
Fouls in danger area	19
Yellow cards	9
Red cards	1

SEE PAGE 291 FOR FULL STATS

S

Robbie STOCKDALE • 27

MIDDLESBROUGH • BORN: 30.11.79

The fine form of Curtis Fleming meant that young Robbie Stockdale started only six matches for Middlesbrough in 1999–2000.

However, the England under-21 international did score the first goal of his Boro career in the 1–1 draw with Watford, proving his ability to get forward and have a shot when given the opportunity to do so from right-back.

As he plays more games he will look to improving his pass completion rate and the accuracy of his crosses: important facets of a player who wants to carve out a career as a buccaneering wing-back.

Stockdale may find that if he cannot force his way into the starting line-up, there will be no shortage of clubs outside the top flight who would like to give him a chance away from The Riverside Stadium.

His lack of experience contributed to his failure to be included for the European under-21 Championships squad. To avoid future disappointments, Stockdale will have to decide if he can afford to be a bit-part player and still hope to realise his potential.

APPEARANCES	
Start (sub)	6(5)
Minutes on pitch	591
GOAL ATTEMPTS	
Goals	1
PASSING & CROSSING	
Goal assists	1
Passing	154
Passing accuracy	63%
Crosses	18
Crossing accuracy	17%
DEFENDING	
Tackles	14
Tackles won %	50%
Blocks	4
Interceptions	5
Clearances	23
Shots cleared off line	0
DISCIPLINE	
Fouls	5
Yellow cards	0
Red cards	0

SEE PAGE 193 FOR FULL STATS

Steve STONE • 26

ASTON VILLA • BORN: 20.8.71

APPEARANCES	
Start (sub)	10(14)
Minutes on pitch	1046
GOAL ATTEMPTS	
Goals	1
Shots on target	5
Shooting accuracy	50%
Goals/shots ratio	10%
PASSING	
Goal assists	2
Passes in opp half	333
Passing accuracy in opp half	71%
Successful crosses	17
Crossing accuracy	36%
DRIBBLING	
Dribbles & runs	44
Dribble completion	84%
Corners forced	6
DISCIPLINE	
Fouls	28
Yellow cards	1
Red cards	0

SEE PAGE 53 FOR FULL STATS

Steve Stone once famously crashed his ca into a set of closed iron gates outside the Cit Ground in front of a crowd of Forest fan queuing for tickets. But despite his dubiou driving skills in Nottingham, at least he ha no problems keeping his place in their team.

Sadly, in 1999–2000 at Aston Villa, h struggled to be a regular part of Joh Gregory's rigid 5–3–2 formation, so he had t be content with the majority of hi appearances from the substitutes' bench.

Stone scored just once during th 1999–2000 season, but still showed touche of class, harking back to his England days. H boasted a 36% cross completion rate and 73% passing accuracy, illustrating why some Vill fans felt he should be in the side.

The emergence of Mark Delaney was anothe contributing factor in Stone's lack of footba as the young Welshman proved himself to b an accomplished right wing-back.

Unless John Gregory switches to a 4–4–2 system, Stone's opportunities are unlikely t increase at Villa Park.

1 Derby County were the only club where

M

Gavin STRACHAN • 21

COVENTRY CITY • BORN: 23.12.78

\ tireless midfielder who draws inevitable :omparisons with his father Gordon, Gavin 5trachan returned to the first-team picture at :oventry in 1999–2000 after missing out :ompletely the previous season because of njuries.

A Scottish under-21 international, Strachan ıdded to the experience he gained with City in 1997–98 and during a loan spell with Dundee n 1998–99 by appearing in three Premiership james in the Millennium season.

Strachan appeared twice as a substitute in james against Derby and Leeds in the early part of 1999–2000 before starting his only game of :he term in a 0–0 draw with the Rams in January.

In the 98 minutes he spent on the pitch, 5trachan proved he has the makings of a quality player by getting forward to hit two shots at joal and completing 76% of his passes. The 2000–01 season is likely to be a make-or-break campaign for young Strachan's Coventry career.

SEE PAGE 95 FOR FULL STATS

Cutting edge: Branko Strupar

S

Branko STRUPAR • 35

DERBY COUNTY • BORN: 9.2.70

Belgian international Branko Strupar joined the Rams for a fee of £3 million in December and made his first appearance as a substitute in the 1–0 win at Leicester on 18 December.

His first two goals for the club were vitally important, helping Jim Smith's side beat Watford 2–0 and also putting him into Derby County history as the first player to score for the club in the new Millennium.

His selfish style of play meant that he did not create a goal, but come the end of the campaign Strupar had scored five times, giving Derby a much-needed cutting edge.

Should Strupar continue his impressive ability to finish off the chances his Derby team-mates create in the 2000–01 campaign, Rams supporters will hope that a nail-biting end to the season can this time be avoided.

Smith will need Strupar to justify his price tag following the doomed signing of the Belgian's predecessor Esteban Fuertes, who was denied entry back into the UK following a training trip.

APPEARANCES	
Start (sub)	13(2)
Minutes on pitch	1111
GOAL ATTEMPTS	
Goals inside box	3
Goals outside box	2
Minutes per goal scored	222.2
Goals/shots ratio	15%
SHOOTING	
Shots on target inside box	8
Shots on target outside box	7
Shooting accuracy	44%
PASSING	
Goal assists	0
Key passes	9
Passing accuracy in opp half	65%
DISCIPLINE	
Fouls committed	19
Fouls won	24
Offside	19
Yellow cards	1
Red cards	0

SEE PAGE 109 FOR FULL STATS

Dean STURRIDGE • 8

DERBY COUNTY • BORN: 27.7.73

Following a successful loan spell with Torquay United during the 1994–95 season, Dean Sturridge returned to Derby where his career exploded into life. He scored 20 goals as the Rams won promotion in 1995–96, and he maintained that form, frightening many Premiership defences with his electric pace.

But Sturridge's career has been plagued by niggling injuries ever since and the 1999–2000 campaign saw him start only 14 games.

In that time he scored six goals as Derby battled to avoid relegation, and the fact they came from only 29 efforts on goal is testament to his clinical finishing.

After bursting on to the Premiership scene, Sturridge was dubbed "the new Ian Wright" and his impressive form caught the eye of a number of top clubs, including Arsenal.

Sturridge signed a lucrative new deal at Pride Park in 1997, though, but the following campaign was one of frustration for the former trainee. Jim Smith then placed him on the transfer list, but a lack of interest saw Sturridge removed and further interest has been minimal.

APPEARANCES	
Start (sub)	14(11)
Minutes on pitch	1219
GOAL ATTEMPTS	
Goals inside box	6
Goals outside box	0
Minutes per goal scored	203.2
Goals/shots ratio	21%
SHOOTING	
Shots on target inside box	15
Shots on target outside box	2
Shooting accuracy	59%
PASSING	
Goal assists	0
Key passes	3
Passing accuracy in opp half	65%
DISCIPLINE	
Fouls committed	36
Fouls won	17
Offside	12
Yellow cards	3
Red cards	0

SEE PAGE 109 FOR FULL STATS

Davor SUKER • 9

ARSENAL • BORN: 1.1.68

APPEARANCES	
Start (sub)	8(14)
Minutes on pitch	969
GOAL ATTEMPTS	
Goals inside box	7
Goals outside box	1
Minutes per goal scored	121.1
Goals/shots ratio	17%
SHOOTING	
Shots on target inside box	26
Shots on target outside box	5
Shooting accuracy	66%
PASSING	
Goal assists	1
Key passes	12
Passing accuracy in opp half	65%
DISCIPLINE	
Fouls committed	13
Fouls won	13
Offside	17
Yellow cards	4
Red cards	0

SEE PAGE 39 FOR FULL STATS

Hopes were high that Davor Suker, the ma with shares in Manchester United, would b the man to score the goals to bring th Premiership title back to Highbury.

But, despite bagging a brilliant brace o his full debut against Aston Villa, things di not work out as well as Suker would hav hoped, and the 1999–2000 season will se him best remembered as one of the player who missed a spot-kick in the penalt shoot-out defeat to Turkish side Galatasara in the UEFA Cup final.

The top scorer in the 1998 World Cup wit six goals started only eight games fo Arsenal, and made 14 substitut appearances. But he scored eigh Premiership goals.

With the successful transformation o Thierry Henry from a winger to a strike Suker was released by Arsene Wenger. H opted to stay in London and completed free transfer switch to West Ham in June. H and Paolo Di Canio could forge a very usefu partnership in 2000–01.

G Neil SULLIVAN • 1

WIMBLEDON • BORN: 24.2.70

fter 180 league appearances for Wimbledon, eil Sullivan decided it was time to move on nd joined Tottenham Hotspur soon after the ons' relegation from the Premiership.

Sullivan had come through the youth ranks ith the Dons and, following the retirements f Jim Leighton and Andy Goram from nternational football, the Sutton-born hot-stopper became Scotland's number one, hanks to his grandmother's roots.

He was part of the squad that travelled to he 1998 World Cup but he failed to start a ame for the Scots, who fell at the first urdle. Sullivan responded by taking the Dons' layer of the Year award for 1999. He was owerless, though, as the Dons 14-year stint n the top flight came to an end.

Only Middlesbrough's Mark Schwarzer ettered Sullivan's total of 176 saves during 999-2000, but the Scottish number one will e disappointed to have kept only five clean heets. With a better defence in front of him, e will be hoping things will improve ollowing his move to White Hart Lane.

APPEARANCES	
Start (sub)	37(0)
Minutes on pitch	3330
SHOT STOPPING	
Goals conceded (inside box)	67
Goals conceded (outside box)	6
Minutes per goal conceded	45.6
Clean sheets	5
Saves (shots inside box)	109
Saves (shots outside box)	67
Saves/shots	71%
DISTRIBUTION	
Long kick %	49%
Throws/short passes %	76%
CATCHING	
Crosses caught	79
Crosses punched	19
Crosses dropped	9
Catch success %	90%
DISCIPLINE	
Yellow cards	1
Red cards	0

SEE PAGE 304 FOR FULL STATS

Best foot forward: Neil Sullivan

S

Nicky SUMMERBEE • 7

SUNDERLAND • BORN: 26.8.71

Peter Reid pulled off a shrewd bit of business by capturing right-winger Nicky Summerbee from Manchester City in a straight swap involving Craig Russell, valued at £1 million.

Since his arrival, he has gone on to provide the ammunition for Niall Quinn and Kevin Phillips to bag a hatful of goals, and he was a key figure as the Black Cats narrowly missed out on Europe during the 1999–2000 campaign.

The son of former England international Mike Summerbee, the young starlet still holds a place in the Guiness Book of Records for having the fastest shot in football, though he could only manage one goal throughout the 1999–2000 Premiership season.

But it is not his goalscoring for which he is renowned, as Summerbee supplied a constant torrent of crosses throughout the campaign. He attempted 233 in total, with an impressive 36% of them successful, and he also chipped in with five assists.

If he can carry on supplying that kind of service, a European place may well be within reach in 2000–01.

APPEARANCES	
Start (sub)	29(3)
Minutes on pitch	2562
GOAL ATTEMPTS	
Goals	1
Shots on target	8
Shooting accuracy	53%
Goals/shots ratio	7%
PASSING	
Goal assists	5
Passes in opp half	542
Passing accuracy in opp half	61%
Successful crosses	83
Crossing accuracy	36%
DRIBBLING	
Dribbles & runs	193
Dribble completion	60%
Corners forced	40
DISCIPLINE	
Fouls	34
Yellow cards	3
Red cards	0

SEE PAGE 249 FOR FULL STATS

Mark SUMMERBELL • 22

MIDDLESBROUGH • BORN: 30.10.76

APPEARANCES	
Start (sub)	15(4)
Minutes on pitch	1366
GOAL ATTEMPTS	
Goals	0
Shots on target	2
Shooting accuracy	40%
Goals/shots ratio	0%
PASSING	
Goal assists	0
Passes in opp half	201
Passing accuracy in opp half	62%
Successful crosses	1
Crossing accuracy	13%
DRIBBLING	
Dribbles & runs	17
Dribble completion	71%
Corners forced	3
DISCIPLINE	
Fouls	25
Yellow cards	4
Red cards	0

SEE PAGE 193 FOR FULL STATS

After captaining the Boro reserve team for th past two years, Mark Summerbell failed t establish himself in the first team, makin just 15 starts during the 1999–2000 season.

Combative and hard-working, Summerbe came through the youth ranks at Th Riverside, and his 71 challenges underline his willingness to tackle, although he wi surely be disappointed with a below-par 41% success rate.

He is also regarded as a good passer of th ball on Teesside, but a 69% pass completio would suggest he is yet to come to terms wit the demands of the Premiership. Nonetheles his form towards the end of the season wa enough for Boro chief Bryan Robson to offe him a new contract.

A similar type of player to team-mat Robbie Mustoe, Summerbell has had to b patient for an opportunity at The Riverside but he has proved his worth when calle upon. He will be hoping he can impres Robson and get an extended run of first-tear action during the 2000–01 campaign.

Chris SUTTON • 9

CHELSEA • BORN: 10.3.73

helsea's record signing Chris Sutton revealed arlier in the season that he would probably ave been an undertaker had he not made the rade in football – and there were times during he campaign when he must have wanted the round to open up and swallow him.

Sutton buried just one of his 32 goal efforts Chelsea's second strike against Manchester nited – and judging by his grave demeanour t times, "The Funeral March" would have been ppropriate accompanying music as he trudged ff at the end of games.

The ex-England international recorded an bysmal shooting accuracy of 29% from inside he area, with some observers reading the last ites on his Chelsea career.

Despite his problems in front of goal, the ormer Blackburn striker retained the respect f his manager and fellow players. He even amed a pig he bought during the season after eorge Weah, but after making a pig's ear of a ilt-edged chance against Sunderland on the pening day, Sutton's form entered a trough rom which it rarely ascended.

APPEARANCES	
Start (sub)	21(7)
Minutes on pitch	1850
GOAL ATTEMPTS	
Goals inside box	1
Goals outside box	0
Minutes per goal scored	1850.0
Goals/shots ratio	3%
SHOOTING	
Shots on target inside box	6
Shots on target outside box	4
Shooting accuracy	31%
PASSING	
Goal assists	2
Key passes	5
Passing accuracy in opp half	59%
DISCIPLINE	
Fouls committed	78
Fouls won	40
Offside	16
Yellow cards	7
Red cards	0

SEE PAGE 81 FOR FULL STATS

Gerry TAGGART • 4

LEICESTER CITY • BORN: 18.10.70

APPEARANCES	
Start (sub)	30(1)
Minutes on pitch	2620
GOAL ATTEMPTS	
Goals	6
DEFENDING	
Blocks	65
Shots cleared off line	0
Headed clearances	251
Other clearances	108
Interceptions	29
Last man saving tackles	1
Tackles won	51
Tackles won %	52%
PASSING	
Passing accuracy own half	73%
Passing accuracy opp half	52%
DISCIPLINE	
Fouls	46
Fouls in danger area	16
Yellow cards	5
Red cards	1

SEE PAGE 151 FOR FULL STATS

Leicester City fans saw Gerry spring a surprise during 1999–2000, as his six league goals made him the joint highest-scoring central defender from open play, along with team-mate Matt Elliott. The Northern Ireland international scored twice in the 3–0 win over Sheffield Wednesday, but still performed admirably in his orthodox defensive role.

Taggart made more headed clearances than any other City player, as he formed an impressive central back-line with Elliott and Frank Sinclair.

He was sent off in the away fixture against Sunderland for two bookable fouls on Kevin Phillips, but throughout the season he committed just 16 fouls in the danger area.

His tackle success rate of 52% was higher than the 1999–2000 average for a defender, and he was a key member of Martin O'Neill's squad, missing just seven matches.

The fact that he only started six games in 1998–99 proves how much he has adjusted to the top flight; and, with European football for the Foxes in 2000–01, Taggart has much to look forward to.

10 shots on target in the Premiership

Massimo TAIBI • 26

MANCHESTER UNITED • BORN: 18.2.70

Despite picking up Mark Bosnich on a free transfer from Aston Villa, Sir Alex Ferguson splashed out £4.5 million on Italian 'keeper Massimo Taibi.

Taibi made his debut away to Liverpool and, although he was at fault for one of the goals, made some impressive saves to indicate that he had what it takes to become the regular number one.

But it all went horribly wrong after that, most noticeably against Southampton, when a weakly-struck Matt Le Tissier shot squirmed under his body and gave the Saints a point.

After letting in five goals at Stamford Bridge he never played for United again, and was sent on loan to Reggina where he stayed for the remainder of the campaign.

Nicknamed "The Blind Venetian" by the popular press, Taibi's days at Old Trafford seemed numbered, with the Champions being linked with many of the world's best 'keepers.

With the arrival of Fabien Barthez at the Theatre of Dreams it seems certain that Taibi will continue his career back in his homeland.

APPEARANCES	
Start (sub)	4(0)
Minutes on pitch	360
SHOT STOPPING	
Goals conceded (inside box)	10
Goals conceded (outside box)	1
Minutes per goal conceded	32.7
Clean sheets	0
Saves (shots inside box)	8
Saves (shots outside box)	7
Saves/shots	58%
DISTRIBUTION	
Long kick %	26%
Throws/short passes %	98%
CATCHING	
Crosses caught	5
Crosses punched	3
Crosses dropped	1
Catch success %	83%
DISCIPLINE	
Yellow cards	0
Red cards	0

SEE PAGE 178 FOR FULL STATS

FB

Mauricio TARICCO • 3

TOTTENHAM HOTSPUR • BORN: 10.3.73

APPEARANCES	
Start (sub)	29(0)
Minutes on pitch	2515
GOAL ATTEMPTS	
Goals	0
PASSING & CROSSING	
Goal assists	5
Passing	1065
Passing accuracy	71%
Crosses	42
Crossing accuracy	24%
DEFENDING	
Tackles	92
Tackles won %	41%
Blocks	36
Interceptions	38
Clearances	163
Shots cleared off line	0
DISCIPLINE	
Fouls	42
Yellow cards	10
Red cards	0

SEE PAGE 263 FOR FULL STATS

Argentine full-back Mauricio Taricco starte all but nine of Tottenham's 1999-200 Premiership matches, settling well into th left-back position.

The former Ipswich Town defender wa effective going forward, setting up five Spur goals and giving George Graham's defence more balanced look, with Stephen Carr on th opposite flank.

While Taricco's tackling was below averag for a Premiership defender, his passing wa crisp, and he firmly established himself a Tottenham's first choice left-back.

His crossing accuracy was a disappointin 24%, but with the likes of Sergei Rebrov t aim for in 2000-01, he is more than capabl of improving on that.

With David Ginola supporting him furthe upfield Taricco has helped to form formidable threat, and will be hoping to d more of the same in 2000-01.

His 10 cautions during the campaign ma cause some concern, but hopefully Taricco ca adjust further to the Premiership.

Ian TAYLOR • 7

ASTON VILLA • BORN: 4.6.68

Midfield stalwart and lifelong Villa fan Ian Taylor continued to be a vital member of John Gregory's squad, and was instrumental in his side's excellent 1999–2000 campaign.

The central midfielder scored five goals in the league, one of which was the 32nd-minute winner at home to Sheffield Wednesday that started a Villa run of just two defeats in their last 21 Premiership matches.

His shooting accuracy was above average for a central midfielder, and his 26% goals-to-shots ratio was 17 percentage points higher than average.

His 70% pass completion rate in the opposition half was bettered only by Steve Stone at the club, and the 32-year-old former Wednesday player clearly still has much to offer in the top flight.

Competition for places in the Villa midfield was hot, with George Boateng, Lee Hendrie, Paul Merson, Alan Thompson and Stone all vying for a place in the starting line-up.

Of these players, though, only Boateng started more matches than Taylor.

APPEARANCES	
Start (sub)	25(4)
Minutes on pitch	2369
GOAL ATTEMPTS	
Goals	5
Shots on target	9
Shooting accuracy	47%
PASSING & CROSSING	
Goal assists	0
Passes in opp half	528
Passing accuracy in opp half	70%
Successful crosses	2
Cross completion	22%
DEFENDING	
Interceptions	37
Clearances	74
Tackles	109
Tackles won %	55%
DISCIPLINE	
Fouls	44
Yellow cards	8
Red cards	0

SEE PAGE 53 FOR FULL STATS

Paul TELFER • 12

COVENTRY CITY • BORN: 21.10.71

APPEARANCES	
Start (sub)	25(5)
Minutes on pitch	2371
GOAL ATTEMPTS	
Goals	0
Shots on target	3
Shooting accuracy	30%
Goals/shots ratio	0%
PASSING	
Goal assists	0
Passes in opp half	756
Passing accuracy in opp half	60%
Successful crosses	30
Crossing accuracy	34%
DRIBBLING	
Dribbles & runs	61
Dribble completion	82%
Corners forced	8
DISCIPLINE	
Fouls	14
Yellow cards	2
Red cards	0

SEE PAGE 95 FOR FULL STATS

Coventry City midfielder Paul Telfer had a solid 1999–2000, the highlight of which was a call-up to the Scotland squad for a friendly against World Champions France.

Telfer was called up for the next two squads after that, which is indicative of his consistently good form for the Sky Blues.

Such were the injury problems facing Gordon Strachan during the campaign that Telfer was often required to play as a full-back rather than in his more orthodox right-midfield role, but he took to the task well.

His tackle success rate of 55% was above average for a Premiership defender and only one percentage point below the average for a midfielder, as Telfer proved equally adept in both positions.

The Scot dramatically improved his disciplinary record; 11 yellow cards in 1998–99 was followed by just two cautions throughout the 1999–2000 campaign, and his tally of 14 fouls was lower than any other City player who spent at least 1,000 minutes on the pitch.

John TERRY • 26

CHELSEA • BORN: 7.12.80

Young centre-back John Terry made twice as many appearances for Chelsea in 1999–2000 than he managed the season before, but still found his opportunities limited and ended up on loan at Nottingham Forest.

The 19-year-old played 90 minutes in Chelsea's 1-1 draw at Bradford, and also appeared in the following match at home to Tottenham Hotspur.

For both of his substitute appearances, Terry replaced Marcel Desailly in the heart of the Blues' defence, although he will have been a little disappointed when Chelsea signed Emerson Thome in December, as this limited his chances even further.

Terry won half the challenges he attempted and, in more than four hours on the pitch, Blues fans saw enough to convince them that he can become a regular for the club in the future.

Reports emanating from Nottingham suggest that the youngster is indeed a special talent. Although Forest are keen to hang on to his services it is doubtful whether he will spend too much longer outside of the Premiership.

APPEARANCES	
Start (sub)	2(2)
Minutes on pitch	259
GOAL ATTEMPTS	
Goals	0
DEFENDING	
Blocks	5
Shots cleared off line	0
Headed clearances	16
Other clearances	4
Interceptions	5
Last man saving tackles	0
Tackles won	3
Tackles won %	50%
PASSING	
Passing accuracy own half	86%
Passing accuracy opp half	60%
DISCIPLINE	
Fouls	1
Fouls in danger area	0
Yellow cards	0
Red cards	0

SEE PAGE 81 FOR FULL STATS

Jo TESSEM • 21

SOUTHAMPTON • BORN: 28.2.72

APPEARANCES	
Start (sub)	23(2)
Minutes on pitch	1992
GOAL ATTEMPTS	
Goals	4
Shots on target	15
Shooting accuracy	50%
Goals/shots ratio	13%
PASSING	
Goal assists	0
Passes in opp half	452
Passing accuracy in opp half	57%
Successful crosses	17
Crossing accuracy	40%
DRIBBLING	
Dribbles & runs	71
Dribble completion	75%
Corners forced	12
DISCIPLINE	
Fouls	32
Yellow cards	0
Red cards	0

SEE PAGE 235 FOR FULL STATS

Bought for £600,000 from Norwegian outfi Molde in November, Jo Tessem proceeded t appear in every Premiership match from the until the end of the season.

He immediately settled, and scored four goal in total, the best of which was agains Tottenham at White Hart Lane, although Saint lost the match 7-2.

Half the Norwegian's shots tested th goalkeeper, and his 13% goals-to-shots rati was above the 1999–2000 Premiership averag for a midfielder.

Tessem was also impressive from wide areas with two out of five crosses on averag reaching a team-mate, and he proved to be a excellent addition to the Southampton squad.

Under the guidance of Glenn Hoddle, Tessen may yet develop further, and could prove to b even more of a bargain as the 2000–01 seasor unfolds, as he and his colleagues look t consolidate on their strong finish t 1999–2000 and finish in the middle of th table, rather than fall into another season-lon struggle against the dreaded drop.

Ben THATCHER • 6

WIMBLEDON • BORN: 30.11.75

Ben Thatcher played consistently well for Wimbledon in 1999–2000, yet he will not enjoy reflecting on the club's Premiership campaign one little bit.

He and his Wimbledon team-mates suffered relegation on the final day of the season, while an elbow to the face of Nicky Summerbee in Wimbledon's 1–0 win against Sunderland cost Thatcher a place in the England squad.

To add further insult to injury, Thatcher injured his ankle in the dying moments of that match, and did not feature again until the away match against Bradford City, for which he was made captain.

Unfortunately that match also ended in heartbreak, as Thatcher was controversially penalised for handball allowing Bradford to score the first goal in a 3–0 rout.

While the accuracy of his passing was below average for a defender, Thatcher was playing in the second-leakiest defence in the league, and his battling performances attracted the attention of a host of top managers.

APPEARANCES	
Start (sub)	19(1)
Minutes on pitch	1669
GOAL ATTEMPTS	
Goals	0
PASSING & CROSSING	
Goal assists	2
Passing	385
Passing accuracy	54%
Crosses	28
Crossing accuracy	25%
DEFENDING	
Tackles	52
Tackles won %	37%
Blocks	26
Interceptions	11
Clearances	185
Shots cleared off line	0
DISCIPLINE	
Fouls	20
Yellow cards	4
Red cards	0

SEE PAGE 305 FOR FULL STATS

M

Paul THIRLWELL • 19

SUNDERLAND • BORN: 13.2.79

APPEARANCES	
Start (sub)	7(1)
Minutes on pitch	574
GOAL ATTEMPTS	
Goals	0
Shots on target	3
Shooting accuracy	75%
PASSING & CROSSING	
Goal assists	0
Passes in opp half	145
Passing accuracy in opp half	66%
Successful crosses	0
Cross completion	0%
DEFENDING	
Interceptions	3
Clearances	5
Tackles	15
Tackles won %	40%
DISCIPLINE	
Fouls	6
Yellow cards	2
Red cards	0

SEE PAGE 249 FOR FULL STATS

Promising Sunderland midfielder Paul Thirlwell was recalled from a loan spell at Swindon Town when Peter Reid's side were decimated by suspensions in November.

The 21-year-old played 12 games for the Robins without missing a single minute. He looked impressive, and Reid threw him in at the deep end for the Premiership home game against Chelsea, in which Thirlwell and his team-mates enjoyed a 4–1 win.

He then had to wait nine games for his next appearance, but did start the last three league games of the season.

The youngster won just 40% of his challenges, but when coming forward his passing was better, with two-thirds of his passes in the opposition half reaching a Sunderland player.

It would be bad luck on Thirlwell if he were not to make more first-team appearances in 2000–01, as he definitely seems to be one for the future on Wearside.

Should that fail to materialise, there is bound to be interest in him from other clubs in the top two divisions.

than any other Premiership team

Danny THOMAS • 34

LEICESTER CITY • BORN: 1.5.81

Young attacking midfielder Danny Thomas made his Premiership debut on December 28 at home to Newcastle United.

He then appeared as a substitute in two of Leicester's next three league games, but failed to play a single minute after that.

While not being given much of a chance to show how well he could do in the Premiership, Thomas did find time to deliver a successful cross from out wide, while two-thirds of his passes in the opposition half also found one of his team-mates.

More than half of Thomas's dribbles and runs were successful, as the youngster certainly did not seem fazed by the top flight and its collection of cosmopolitan stars.

With Leicester City quite short of creative midfielders, Thomas may find himself given more opportunities during 2000-01, and he certainly moved in the right direction in his short amount of time on the pitch during the 1999-2000 campaign.

SEE PAGE 151 FOR FULL STATS

Emerson THOME • 30

CHELSEA • BORN: 30.3.72

Brazilian centre-back Emerson Thome started the season with Sheffield Wednesday but in December Gianluca Vialli splashed out £2.5 million to acquire his services – and it proved to be very fortunate for Thome.

His former club were relegated, while Chelsea went on to qualify for the 2000-01 UEFA Cup.

Thome made 20 appearances for the Blues, as opposed to 17 for the Owls, but, perhaps surprisingly, it was his form for the Yorkshire side that was the more impressive.

His tackle success rate at Wednesday was 73%, but with Chelsea he won just 45% of his challenges, despite being under far less pressure with Vialli's team.

In the 1999-2000 Premiership, only David Wetherall, Sami Hyypia and Thome's former team-mate Des Walker made more clearances than the Brazilian.

Thome's disciplinary record was admirable. Despite his huge physical presence, he committed just 65 fouls and earned only four yellow cards.

Brawny: Emerson Thome

APPEARANCES	
Start (sub)	34(3)
Minutes on pitch	3136
GOAL ATTEMPTS	
Goals	0
DEFENDING	
Blocks	89
Shots cleared off line	2
Headed clearances	335
Other clearances	111
Interceptions	35
Last man saving tackles	2
Tackles won	68
Tackles won %	59%
PASSING	
Passing accuracy own half	80%
Passing accuracy opp half	54%
DISCIPLINE	
Fouls	65
Fouls in danger area	24
Yellow cards	4
Red cards	0

SEE PAGE 81 & 221 FOR FULL STATS

Alan THOMPSON • 11

ASTON VILLA • BORN: 22.11.73

t was another season of frustration at Aston 'illa for midfielder Alan Thompson. The ieordie was John Gregory's first signing for he Villans in the summer of 1998, and, after disappointing first season which was lighted by injuries, he would have hoped for etter in 1999–2000.

Thompson began the campaign in the first eam, but struggled to find the form which aw Villa shell out £4.5 million for him and onsequently was only able to start 16 games or the West Midlanders.

A last-minute winner at Sheffield Vednesday was the highlight of "Thommo"'s 'remiership season but he will be hoping for nuch more in 2000–01.

The midfielder has a cultured left foot but vill be disappointed at only completing 25% of his attempted crosses. His pass completion ate of 70% was also below average for a 'remiership midfielder and, with strong ompetition for the central positions at Villa, ie will have to improve if he is going to truly ulfil his potential.

APPEARANCES	
Start (sub)	16(5)
Minutes on pitch	1412
GOAL ATTEMPTS	
Goals	2
Shots on target	8
Shooting accuracy	42%
Goals/shots ratio	11%
PASSING	
Goal assists	2
Passes in opp half	464
Passing accuracy in opp half	64%
Successful crosses	23
Crossing accuracy	25%
DRIBBLING	
Dribbles & runs	53
Dribble completion	79%
Corners forced	16
DISCIPLINE	
Fouls	23
Yellow cards	7
Red cards	0

SEE PAGE 53 FOR FULL STATS

Frustration: Alan Thompson

T

David THOMPSON • 25

LIVERPOOL • BORN: 12.9.77

Youngster David Thompson enjoyed his best season to date at Liverpool, as some fine performances saw him make his mark in Gérard Houllier's side.

A product of Liverpool's school of excellence and part of their FA Youth Cup-winning side of 1996, the England under-21 international's enthusiasm and work-rate have seen him become a crowd favourite at Anfield, as he has tried to nail down a first-team place despite some intense competition.

The boy from Birkenhead came off the bench to produce consistently impressive displays early on in the season, although his progress was marred by a sending-off at Leicester.

He scored three times during the 1999–2000 campaign including the winner against Chelsea and a spectacular solo effort in front of the television cameras against Sheffield Wednesday, to enhance his reputation.

His strikes came from 48 attempts at goal, and after several man-of-the-match performances he will be hoping to continue his progress during 2000–01.

APPEARANCES	
Start (sub)	19(8)
Minutes on pitch	1703
GOAL ATTEMPTS	
Goals	3
Shots on target	21
Shooting accuracy	44%
PASSING & CROSSING	
Goal assists	3
Passes in opp half	570
Passing accuracy in opp half	65%
Successful crosses	12
Cross completion	17%
DEFENDING	
Interceptions	15
Clearances	31
Tackles	63
Tackles won %	46%
DISCIPLINE	
Fouls	39
Yellow cards	7
Red cards	1

SEE PAGE 165 FOR FULL STATS

Andy TOWNSEND • 16

MIDDLESBROUGH • BORN: 27.7.63

APPEARANCES	
Start (sub)	3(2)
Minutes on pitch	299
GOAL ATTEMPTS	
Goals	0
Shots on target	0
Shooting accuracy	0%
PASSING & CROSSING	
Goal assists	0
Passes in opp half	73
Passing accuracy in opp half	71%
Successful crosses	1
Cross completion	25%
DEFENDING	
Interceptions	0
Clearances	8
Tackles	6
Tackles won %	17%
DISCIPLINE	
Fouls	3
Yellow cards	1
Red cards	0

SEE PAGE 193 FOR FULL STATS

The Premiership has surely seen the last of Andy Townsend after he left Middlesbrough to link up with former manager Brian Little at West Brom in September.

Former Republic of Ireland skipper Townsend made just three starts and two substitute appearances for Boro in the 1999–2000 campaign before joining the Baggies. His final game was against former side Aston Villa on August 28 before moving on to The Hawthorns for £50,000.

The veteran was skipper at The Riverside during the 1998–99 season, but with 37-year-old Townsend recognising that his career in the top flight was coming to an end, he decided to move on and look towards a future career in coaching or management.

He showed that he still has ability by making 118 passes in his limited appearances for the Teessiders during the campaign, with a creditable completion rate of 75%, and Boro fans will miss the effort and enthusiasm he put into the game, which inspired his team-mates and often belied his years.

6 David Unsworth scored the joint

David UNSWORTH • 6

EVERTON • BORN: 16.10.73

David Unsworth was an automatic choice at Goodison Park, as manager Walter Smith opted for the chunky defender's strength and experience in central defence or at left-back.

Affectionately known by the Everton faithful as "Rhino" because of his build and stomping runs down the left flank, Unsworth's bullish determination helped him win nearly 50 challenges for the Blues during the season.

While Smith converted Everton in 1999–2000 into a more controlled passing side than in recent seasons, the team still relied on Unsworth to pump direct balls towards the box. The stocky defender attempted more long passes than any of his colleagues, and subsequently recorded a below-average 57% completion rate overall.

He won his only England cap in the Umbro tournament in 1995 but has since faded from the international scene. If his all-round game was of a higher quality, England would surely benefit from his trusty left peg, which saw him score six league goals – five as a result of his lethal penalty-taking.

APPEARANCES	
Start (sub)	32(1)
Minutes on pitch	2762
GOAL ATTEMPTS	
Goals	6
DEFENDING	
Blocks	44
Shots cleared off line	0
Headed clearances	146
Other clearances	88
Interceptions	24
Last man saving tackles	3
Tackles won	47
Tackles won %	51%
PASSING	
Passing accuracy own half	74%
Passing accuracy opp half	46%
DISCIPLINE	
Fouls	47
Fouls in danger area	22
Yellow cards	4
Red cards	0

SEE PAGE 123 FOR FULL STATS

Matthew UPSON • 20

ARSENAL • BORN: 18.4.79

APPEARANCES	
Start (sub)	5(3)
Minutes on pitch	449
GOAL ATTEMPTS	
Goals	0
DEFENDING	
Blocks	5
Shots cleared off line	0
Headed clearances	44
Other clearances	7
Interceptions	1
Last man saving tackles	0
Tackles won	5
Tackles won %	63%
PASSING	
Passing accuracy own half	84%
Passing accuracy opp half	65%
DISCIPLINE	
Fouls	7
Fouls in danger area	3
Yellow cards	1
Red cards	0

SEE PAGE 39 FOR FULL STATS

Arsene Wenger has a quality centre-back waiting in the wings in the form of young Matthew Upson. The former Luton Town trainee was snapped up by the Gunners in 1997 as an 18-year-old and is patiently learning his trade at Highbury, having made just a handful of first-team appearances to date.

Upson deputised for the injured Tony Adams at the start of the 1999–2000 season, starting three games including the heated confrontation against Manchester United. The youngster was involved in the thick of the action, hitting the woodwork with a volley and almost grabbing a share of the spoils with an injury-time header.

The England under-21 international is a solid tackler and won an impressive 63% of his challenges. He also used the ball intelligently and with vision, finding a team-mate with a commendable 80% of his passes.

Unfortunately his season came to a premature end after he suffered knee ligament damage at Leicester in December, but he should be pushing hard for a place in the starting line-up when he recovers from the setback.

highest number of goals by a defender

Raimond VAN DER GOUW • 17

MANCHESTER UNITED • BORN: 24.3.63

Raimond Van Der Gouw played more first-team football for Manchester United during the 1999–2000 campaign than he did in the previous three seasons combined. He was utilised sporadically over the season but proved resilient whenever called upon.

Primarily acting as cover for new 'keeper Mark Bosnich, the Dutchman made 11 league starts and was never on the losing side. He was flung into the action as early as the 68th minute of the third game of the season, when Bosnich aggravated a hamstring injury.

Van Der Gouw performed consistently between the posts, saving 79% of goal-bound efforts – well above the average ratio for a Premiership goalie. The towering 6'3" stopper used his height to maximum potential, leaping to claim 96% of the balls launched into his vicinity.

Having won previous FA Cup and Champions League silverware just for being there, Van Der Gouw can now feel satisfied in the knowledge that he has earned his Championship winner's medal on merit.

APPEARANCES	
Start (sub)	11(3)
Minutes on pitch	1184
SHOT STOPPING	
Goals conceded (inside box)	12
Goals conceded (outside box)	1
Minutes per goal conceded	91.08
Clean sheets	1
Saves (shots inside box)	22
Saves (shots outside box)	27
Saves/shots	79%
DISTRIBUTION	
Long kick %	41%
Throws/short passes %	90%
CATCHING	
Crosses caught	26
Crosses punched	9
Crosses dropped	1
Catch success %	96%
DISCIPLINE	
Yellow cards	0
Red cards	0

SEE PAGE 178 FOR FULL STATS

Darius VASSELL • 22

ASTON VILLA • BORN: 13.6.80

APPEARANCES	
Start (sub)	1(10)
Minutes on pitch	233
GOAL ATTEMPTS	
Goals inside box	0
Goals outside box	0
Minutes per goal scored	n/a
Goals/shots ratio	0%
SHOOTING	
Shots on target inside box	1
Shots on target outside box	0
Shooting accuracy	25%
PASSING	
Goal assists	2
Key passes	0
Passing accuracy in opp half	65%
DISCIPLINE	
Fouls committed	7
Fouls won	4
Offside	6
Yellow cards	1
Red cards	0

SEE PAGE 53 FOR FULL STATS

John Gregory labelled prospect Darius Vassell "an important member of the squad" and he must have been as disappointed as the youngster when injury cut his season short.

A product of the Aston Villa youth academy, Vassell had made just one start and a handful of substitute appearances before his imposing performance against Derby in December. The game was locked at 0–0 when the speedy striker was introduced to the fray with 34 minutes remaining. Villa ran out 2–0 winners, with Vassell creating both goals for George Boateng and Ian Taylor.

His successful contribution led to four consecutive appearances from the bench before he damaged an ankle against Chelsea, which was later diagnosed as broken.

The skilful striker's hunger for the ball was illustrated by 26 dribbles and runs in less than four hours of football. He fired in four shots on goal – one on target – showing a glimpse of the deadly touch that helped him achieve the youth team scoring record of 39 goals during the 1996–1997 season.

Ramon VEGA • 15

TOTTENHAM HOTSPUR • BORN: 14.6.71

After two and a half seasons at Spurs, Ramon Vega finally managed to strut his stuff in north London. However, it was not his footballing skills that caught the eye during the 1999–2000 season – it was his fashion sense. The former Cagliari defender showed incredible bravery when making his catwalk debut, donning a sexy little black dress that can hardly have enhanced his reputation as a tough-tackling defender.

After the fashion show, Vega found his appearances at White Hart Lane during the 1999–2000 campaign restricted by Chris Perry's emerging partnership with Sol Campbell.

However, when he was on the pitch Vega showed some of the class that prompted Gerry Francis to pay £3.75 million for his services in 1997. The Swiss international won an impressive 70% of his challenges, but failed to force his way back into the first team and was consequently placed on the transfer list late in the season.

SEE PAGE 263 FOR FULL STATS

Paolo VERNAZZA • 30

ARSENAL • BORN: 1.11.79

Finding his appearances at Highbury restricted by Emmanuel Petit and Patrick Vieira, Paolo Vernazza moved on loan to Portsmouth in January 2000 in search of first-team opportunities. And the midfielder made an instant impact, winning the Man of the Match award on his debut against Wolves.

However, Vernazza failed to reach that level of performance in later games, and after a defeat at home to Tranmere he was sent back to Arsenal two months ahead of schedule.

The only full first-team game of Vernazza's Arsenal career was away to Panathinaikos in the Champions League in 1998, where the youngster showed great skill and composure.

The former England under-18 international will be hoping to make use of his undeniable talent in the 2000–2001 campaign. But with so many established players standing in Vernazza's way, he may have to remain patient as he bids for a place in Arsene Wenger's multi-national team.

SEE PAGE 39 FOR FULL STATS

Steve VICKERS • 4

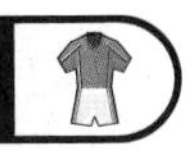

MIDDLESBROUGH • BORN: 13.10.67

APPEARANCES	
Start (sub)	30(2)
Minutes on pitch	2646
GOAL ATTEMPTS	
Goals	0
DEFENDING	
Blocks	79
Shots cleared off line	0
Headed clearances	193
Other clearances	104
Interceptions	20
Last man saving tackles	0
Tackles won	33
Tackles won %	53%
PASSING	
Passing accuracy own half	80%
Passing accuracy opp half	53%
DISCIPLINE	
Fouls	36
Fouls in danger area	13
Yellow cards	5
Red cards	0

SEE PAGE 193 FOR FULL STATS

In what was ultimately a disappointing season for Middlesbrough, central defender Steve Vickers can hold his head up and be proud of his performances for the Teesside team.

The veteran defender has employed a no-nonsense approach throughout his career that has seemingly served him well. Never one to dilly-dally in defence, Vickers completed 297 clearances for Boro during the 1999–2000 Premiership, yet recorded a fair passing accuracy of 68% – indicating that he can pick out a pass when he needs to.

Thoroughly committed to Bryan Robson's side, the often-unsung Vickers converted a few more followers to the Boro cause with his determined displays at the back. He made 79 blocks throughout the campaign and came away with the ball from 53% of challenges.

Now in his 30s, some players would be thinking of opening a nice little pub or doing some commentary for a local radio station, but this centre-back is made of sterner stuff and will hope to be a key player for Robson's team in 2000–01 and beyond.

Patrick VIEIRA • 4

ARSENAL • BORN: 23.6.76

On his day, he is one of the best midfielders in the Premiership, but Patrick Vieira showed the other side of his game too often in 1999–2000.

The Frenchman was banned for six games after being sent off at West Ham and then spitting at Neil Ruddock after his dismissal, and was then involved in an ugly fracas with Watford's Heidar Helguson. But despite his sending-off, and nine yellow cards, there were some excellent displays by the marauding midfielder.

Only two other Premiership players won more challenges than Vieira in 1999–2000, with the World Cup star claiming the ball 88 times when tackling opponents – a very sturdy 68% of all challenges. Once in possession, Vieira regularly passed with aplomb, attempting more than 1,500 passes, with 78% of these finding their intended target.

His partnership with Emmanuel Petit has been a formidable one for the Gunners in recent campaigns, and it is no coincidence that Arsenal faltered earlier in 1999–2000, considering that Vieira and Petit started only four matches together in the first half of the season.

APPEARANCES	
Start (sub)	29(1)
Minutes on pitch	2627
GOAL ATTEMPTS	
Goals	2
Shots on target	7
Shooting accuracy	24%
PASSING & CROSSING	
Goal assists	3
Passes in opp half	963
Passing accuracy in opp half	74%
Successful crosses	8
Cross completion	62%
DEFENDING	
Interceptions	19
Clearances	81
Tackles	130
Tackles won %	68%
DISCIPLINE	
Fouls	63
Yellow cards	9
Red cards	1

SEE PAGE 39 FOR FULL STATS

Nelson VIVAS • 7

ARSENAL • BORN: 18.10.69

APPEARANCES	
Start (sub)	1(4)
Minutes on pitch	213
GOAL ATTEMPTS	
Goals	0
PASSING & CROSSING	
Goal assists	2
Passing	94
Passing accuracy	74%
Crosses	14
Crossing accuracy	50%
DEFENDING	
Tackles	8
Tackles won %	88%
Blocks	4
Interceptions	3
Clearances	12
Shots cleared off line	0
DISCIPLINE	
Fouls	8
Yellow cards	1
Red cards	0

SEE PAGE 39 FOR FULL STATS

Argentinean international Nelson Vivas began his career playing for the steelworks teams of Somisa. The little right-back moved on from the rough and tough world of molten metal and hot sparks and found his way to the Premiership, but has found it hard graft to make himself a permanent fixture within the Arsenal framework.

Excellent in the air for his size, he is able to play in the midfield as well as defence, but he struggled to hold down a regular place in Arsene Wenger's team.

He only played 213 minutes for Arsenal during the 1999–2000 campaign and was loaned out to Celta Vigo for the remainder of the season in January 2000. In the time he had played for Arsenal, he won 88% of his tackles and found a red and white shirt with 74% of his passes.

Unfortunately for Vivas, it won't be any easier in 2000–01 to break into the Arsenal side, but if Wenger needs to bring someone in on the right, then Vivas is a more than capable deputy.

Des WALKER • 6

SHEFFIELD WEDNESDAY • BORN: 26.11.65

Sheffield Wednesday suffered the ignominy of relegation from the Premiership despite the stoic efforts of the ex-England international Des Walker in the centre of their defence. The former Nottingham Forest and Sampdoria stalwart defender may have reached the age of 34, but the Londoner showed that his pace and positioning sense have not diminished.

After a disappointing spell in Italy, Wednesday's faith in their £2.7-million signing has been paid off fully by Walker with season upon season of good service. The 1999–2000 campaign has been no exception, with the 5'11" defender absent for just one match.

Walker made 507 defensive clearances and only David Wetherall and Sami Hyypia completed more in the Premiership.

In addition, Walker once again proved to be robust in the tackle, winning 60% of his challenges and making 49 interceptions.

The Hillsborough crowd still await their hero's first goal in a Wednesday shirt, but he at least went one better than 1998–99 by registering a shot on target.

APPEARANCES	
Start (sub)	37(0)
Minutes on pitch	3204
GOAL ATTEMPTS	
Goals	0
DEFENDING	
Blocks	94
Shots cleared off line	0
Headed clearances	335
Other clearances	172
Interceptions	49
Last man saving tackles	0
Tackles won	39
Tackles won %	60%
PASSING	
Passing accuracy own half	79%
Passing accuracy opp half	51%
DISCIPLINE	
Fouls	16
Fouls in danger area	4
Yellow cards	0
Red cards	0

SEE PAGE 221 FOR FULL STATS

G

Ian WALKER • 1

TOTTENHAM HOTSPUR • BORN: 31.10.71

APPEARANCES	
Start (sub)	38(0)
Minutes on pitch	3420
SHOT STOPPING	
Goals conceded (inside box)	41
Goals conceded (outside box)	8
Minutes per goal conceded	69.79
Clean sheets	8
Saves (shots inside box)	47
Saves (shots outside box)	66
Saves/shots	70%
DISTRIBUTION	
Long kick %	42%
Throws/short passes %	91%
CATCHING	
Crosses caught	70
Crosses punched	9
Crosses dropped	7
Catch success %	91%
DISCIPLINE	
Yellow cards	1
Red cards	0

SEE PAGE 262 FOR FULL STATS

Spurs stopper Ian Walker is one of three Premiership players to have played every single minute of the 1999–2000 season and appears to have become far more disciplined since George Graham took over as the Tottenham manager back in October 1998.

Walker put in some mature performances between the sticks for Spurs during the season. The defensive qualities of Graham as a manager seem to have come just at the right time for the Watford-born 'keeper, and Walker has repaid the Scot by racking up eight clean sheets during the 1999–2000 season.

However, the old questions surrounding his reliability in the air returned to the fore, highlighted by the fact that Walker dropped seven crosses whipped into the Tottenham penalty area and registered a saves-to-shots ratio of 70% – below the Premiership average for a 'keeper.

The son of the former Norwich boss Mike Walker is undoubtedly a talented goalie, but may find his position usurped by new signing Neil Sullivan.

was the highest in the Premiership

Richard WALKER • 19

ASTON VILLA • BORN: 8.11.77

Having never been able to hold down a first-team place since graduating from the Villa youth ranks in 1995, striker Richard Walker experienced a frustrating 1999–2000 season, starting just two games towards the conclusion of the Villans' relatively successful campaign.

Despite the fact that Walker's family were Birmingham city fans, the youngster went against his father's wishes and supported Villa as a boy. His dreams were fulfilled when he signed as a professional in 1996, but like the much-maligned striker Stan Collymore, Walker has been disappointed to find he did not figure predominantly in John Gregory's plans.

However, the 6'0" forward did net his debut goal for Villa in their 4–0 demolition of Watford and quickly followed that up with his second coming against Arsenal at Villa Park. Certainly, the fans are keen on their homegrown talent and a Darius Vassell-Walker partnership is not out of the question in the future.

SEE PAGE 53 FOR FULL STATS

Ronnie WALLWORK • 30

MANCHESTER UNITED • BORN: 10.9.77

A young defender with much promise, United's Ronnie Wallwork may be one of the future generation of Alex Ferguson's babes, but just don't ask him to go to Belgium.

Local lad Wallwork was involved in a fracas with a referee while on loan for Royal Antwerp, which resulted in a lifetime ban from playing again. Luckily for the gifted youngster, the sentence was reduced to three years and limited to Belgium so Wallwork could return to Manchester United and turn out for the Red Devils.

If this incident demonstrates nothing else, it is Wallwork's no-nonsense attitude when plying his trade at Old Trafford. The young talent may have only come off the substitutes' bench on five occasions during the 1999–2000 season but impressed in his limited time on the pitch, including a solid performance in a highly-charged clash with Liverpool.

However, first-team football may only be achieved elsewhere.

SEE PAGE 179 FOR FULL STATS

Gary WALSH • 1

BRADFORD CITY • BORN: 21.3.68

APPEARANCES	
Start (sub)	11(0)
Minutes on pitch	990
SHOT STOPPING	
Goals conceded (inside box)	15
Goals conceded (outside box)	2
Minutes per goal conceded	58.2
Clean sheets	2
Saves (shots inside box)	32
Saves (shots outside box)	26
Saves/shots	77%
DISTRIBUTION	
Long kick %	34%
Throws/short passes %	90%
CATCHING	
Crosses caught	31
Crosses punched	7
Crosses dropped	1
Catch success %	97%
DISCIPLINE	
Yellow cards	0
Red cards	0

SEE PAGE 66 FOR FULL STATS

Although goalkeeper Gary Walsh lost his place to fellow-Bantam Matt Clarke through injury and failed to regain it when fit, the experienced goalie is still highly regarded and will be hopeful of featuring in Bradford's 2000–2001 campaign.

Walsh is possibly most famous for being the back-up 'keeper at Manchester United for 10 years and being in goal when the Red Devils were thumped 4–0 by Barcelona at the Nou Camp in the Champions League. However, he has made a more positive name for himself in Yorkshire, epitomised by the fact that the agile stopper won the Player of the Year award in his first season at the club.

Walsh played in the first 11 matches of the 1999–2000 campaign, but unfortunately for the 32-year-old the Bantams picked up just three victories in that time and conceded an unhealthy 17 goals.

This was despite the heroic efforts of the 'keeper, though, who made 58 saves and stopped an impressive 77% of the shots levelled at his goal.

Steve WALSH • 5

LEICESTER CITY • BORN: 3.11.64

Usually Mr Reliable, veteran centre-back Steve Walsh unfortunately suffered a knee injury in Leicester's opening game of the 1999–2000 season against Arsenal at Highbury which hampered the experienced campaigner's contribution to the Foxes's cause.

It was a particularly bad blow for Leicester that the centre-back could not play more of a part in the Foxes's back line, given the fact that injury problems forced defender Matt Elliott to play up front for much of 1999–2000.

During Walsh's limited exposure in 1999–2000, the former Wigan player did manage to thump away 88 clearances, and the fact that 74 of these were with his head demonstrates the stalwart defender's aerial prowess.

Although the central defender failed to find the net in the Premiership, Walsh did belt in a scorcher against Fulham in the Worthington Cup that helped the Foxes on their way to winning the competition and earning a place in Europe for the 2000–2001 season. His experience could prove vital for the forthcoming campaign.

APPEARANCES	
Start (sub)	5(6)
Minutes on pitch	532
GOAL ATTEMPTS	
Goals	0
DEFENDING	
Blocks	17
Shots cleared off line	0
Headed clearances	74
Other clearances	14
Interceptions	4
Last man saving tackles	0
Tackles won	9
Tackles won %	50%
PASSING	
Passing accuracy own half	67%
Passing accuracy opp half	45%
DISCIPLINE	
Fouls	12
Fouls in danger area	8
Yellow cards	2
Red cards	0

SEE PAGE 151 FOR FULL STATS

Paulo WANCHOPE • 12

WEST HAM UNITED • BORN: 31.7.76

APPEARANCES	
Start (sub)	33(2)
Minutes on pitch	2937
GOAL ATTEMPTS	
Goals inside box	12
Goals outside box	0
Minutes per goal scored	244.8
Goals/shots ratio	16%
SHOOTING	
Shots on target inside box	36
Shots on target outside box	5
Shooting accuracy	55%
PASSING	
Goal assists	5
Key passes	11
Passing accuracy in opp half	65%
DISCIPLINE	
Fouls committed	119
Fouls won	69
Offside	66
Yellow cards	7
Red cards	0

SEE PAGE 291 FOR FULL STATS

The relationship between leggy striker Paulo Wanchope and the Upton Park faithful could hardly be described as a love affair.

An unfortunate knack of missing clear goalscoring opportunities and being caught offside a staggering 66 times – the second highest total of any Premiership player – did not help the ex-Ram gain any positive allegiance with the Hammers fans.

Unfortunately for Wanchope, his lack of rapport with the crowd was magnified by the fans' adoration of partner Paolo Di Canio.

And he may not have made too many friends outside the Boleyn Ground thanks to his 119 fouls – a Premiership high – that saw him head Opta's "Dirty Dozen" table.

But the arrival of Frederic Kanouté meant a change of formation to 4–3–3, and this brought out the best in the Costa Rican. He scored five goals in three games in April.

These impressive performances helped silence the "boo-boys" and talk of a close-season move to Leicester soon subsided thanks to his improved form.

Darren WARD • 23

WATFORD • BORN: 13.9.78

Graham Taylor has always been committed to developing talent within the ranks of Watford Football Club, and centre-back Darren Ward was one of several Hornets' youngsters to get their chance in the 1999–2000 Premiership.

Ward made his debut in Watford's 4–0 capitulation away to Coventry – with regular centre-backs Robert Page and Mark Williams both absent – and did not feature again until April when Watford's season was all but over.

But in his limited time on the pitch, Ward made good use of his height and strength in the air.

He completed more than 50 headed clearances in just 720 minutes of football, and in only his second-ever Premiership match – away to Everton – he came on as a substitute and dealt impressively with the aerial threat of Mark Hughes.

The powerful defender also had an impact at the other end of the pitch, scoring the Hornets' equaliser at Middlesbrough and setting up Heidar Helguson's last-day winner against Coventry with a well-directed header.

APPEARANCES	
Start (sub)	7(2)
Minutes on pitch	720
GOAL ATTEMPTS	
Goals	1
DEFENDING	
Blocks	24
Shots cleared off line	0
Headed clearances	51
Other clearances	20
Interceptions	2
Last man saving tackles	0
Tackles won	4
Tackles won %	27%
PASSING	
Passing accuracy own half	61%
Passing accuracy opp half	45%
DISCIPLINE	
Fouls	11
Fouls in danger area	4
Yellow cards	0
Red cards	0

SEE PAGE 277 FOR FULL STATS

FB Mitch WARD • 21

EVERTON • BORN: 19.6.71

APPEARANCES	
Start (sub)	6(4)
Minutes on pitch	476
GOAL ATTEMPTS	
Goals	0
PASSING & CROSSING	
Goal assists	0
Passing	181
Passing accuracy	67%
Crosses	25
Crossing accuracy	24%
DEFENDING	
Tackles	18
Tackles won %	50%
Blocks	3
Interceptions	4
Clearances	12
Shots cleared off line	0
DISCIPLINE	
Fouls	10
Yellow cards	1
Red cards	0

SEE PAGE 123 FOR FULL STATS

Everton's versatile defender Mitch Ward has rarely been given a chance to impress under Walter Smith since the Scot took charge of the Toffees in July 1998. 1999–2000 saw little change in the former Sheffield United player's fortunes, with just six starts to his name.

Although Ward can play on either side, the Sheffield-born full-back failed to oust either Richard Dunne, Michael Ball or David Unsworth from the starting line-up after beginning five of the first seven games of the 1999–2000 campaign.

Howard Kendall's purchase has coped admirably with playing reserve-team football and seems to be hanging on patiently for a chance to figure in Smith's plans for the Toffees. It is ironic that, during Ward's brief appearances in an Everton shirt, the Merseysiders kept four clean sheets, with the 29-year-old winning half of his challenges.

Ward proved quite effective when going forward, connecting with roughly a quarter of the 25 crosses he attempted in his brief 1999–2000 season.

38 Dave Watson was the oldest

Dave WATSON • 5

EVERTON • BORN: 20.11.61

As the oldest outfield player in the Premiership in the 1999–2000 season, Everton's central defender Dave Watson seems to have discovered the secret of longevity. But when quizzed on the subject, the former Norwich star answered: "I don't know, really. Look after yourself, determination, and really that's it – just dedication."

The Everton stalwart defender is now 38 years old and many predict that the Liverpudlian will one day manage the Toffees after already having a spell in charge as caretaker boss following Howard Kendall's departure from the club during the 1997–1998 season.

Never one to shirk a challenge, Watson's robust defending was evident in his limited time on the pitch, as he won 58% of his attempted tackles and completed more than 70 vital clearances, blocks and interceptions. But it is perhaps his experience that is most useful to Everton, with the veteran campaigner turning his hand to coaching more and more.

APPEARANCES	
Start (sub)	5(1)
Minutes on pitch	471
GOAL ATTEMPTS	
Goals	0
DEFENDING	
Blocks	7
Shots cleared off line	0
Headed clearances	44
Other clearances	26
Interceptions	7
Last man saving tackles	0
Tackles won	7
Tackles won %	58%
PASSING	
Passing accuracy own half	86%
Passing accuracy opp half	60%
DISCIPLINE	
Fouls	9
Fouls in danger area	5
Yellow cards	3
Red cards	0

SEE PAGE 123 FOR FULL STATS

FB

Steve WATSON • 2

ASTON VILLA • BORN: 1.4.74

APPEARANCES	
Start (sub)	13(1)
Minutes on pitch	1084
GOAL ATTEMPTS	
Goals	0
PASSING & CROSSING	
Goal assists	2
Passing	469
Passing accuracy	52%
Crosses	36
Crossing accuracy	28%
DEFENDING	
Tackles	34
Tackles won %	59%
Blocks	9
Interceptions	5
Clearances	37
Shots cleared off line	0
DISCIPLINE	
Fouls	12
Yellow cards	4
Red cards	0

SEE PAGE 53 FOR FULL STATS

England "B" international Steve Watson experienced a disappointing season in 1999–2000 making just 13 starts for the Villans and missing out on the FA Cup final.

The excellent form of Mark Delaney kept the Geordie out of the right wing-back position which he had made his own in 1998–99, and there was much transfer speculation throughout the season linking Watson with a return to his native north east.

Watson – who made his league debut aged just 16 for Newcastle – will be disappointed with his distribution from the right flank with both his passing accuracy of 52% and crossing accuracy of 28% falling below average for a Premiership defender.

The £4 million man impressed with his tough tackling though, putting in a total of 34 challenges and coming out on top in 59% of these. This sometimes led him into trouble, though, as despite limited appearances he still managed to pick up four cautions. He will be hoping that 2000–01 brings about a better change in fortune all round.

outfield player to appear

George WEAH • 31

CHELSEA • BORN: 1.10.66

Chelsea's Liberian striker George Weah has received many accolades and awards including being named World Footballer of the Year in 1995 and twice winning Serie A with AC Milan, but the superstar has not quite grasped the concept of the English public transport system in his short spell at Chelsea.

Clearly, Weah's years in the game have paid off financially, as was shown when Africa's demi-god was asked the last time he took public transport and the Chelsea forward responded: "Two weeks ago I took a taxi".

Luckily for the former Monaco attacker, Weah has let his feet do the talking on the pitch by racking up three Premiership strikes – two more than team-mate and friend Chris Sutton managed throughout all the 1999–2000 season – and created three goal assists in just nine starts for the west London outfit.

Weah certainly made an impact at Stamford Bridge, and topped it all by appearing alongside Gianfranco Zola in the Blues' 1–0 FA Cup final win against Aston Villa in possibly his final game for Chelsea.

APPEARANCES	
Start (sub)	9(2)
Minutes on pitch	876
GOAL ATTEMPTS	
Goals inside box	3
Goals outside box	0
Minutes per goal scored	292.0
Goals/shots ratio	15%
SHOOTING	
Shots on target inside box	8
Shots on target outside box	2
Shooting accuracy	50%
PASSING	
Goal assists	3
Key passes	6
Passing accuracy in opp half	57%
DISCIPLINE	
Fouls committed	14
Fouls won	9
Offside	31
Yellow cards	0
Red cards	0

SEE PAGE 81 FOR FULL STATS

David WEIR • 14

EVERTON • BORN: 10.5.70

APPEARANCES	
Start (sub)	35(0)
Minutes on pitch	3092
GOAL ATTEMPTS	
Goals	2
DEFENDING	
Blocks	80
Shots cleared off line	0
Headed clearances	242
Other clearances	114
Interceptions	44
Last man saving tackles	2
Tackles won	62
Tackles won %	63%
PASSING	
Passing accuracy own half	76%
Passing accuracy opp half	57%
DISCIPLINE	
Fouls	27
Fouls in danger area	11
Yellow cards	3
Red cards	1

SEE PAGE 123 FOR FULL STATS

David Weir missed only three games during the 1999–2000 season and would have a case for getting a new nickname after being dubbed "peas and gravy" from his days at Hearts.

The reason that Weir received this handle from his Scottish team-mates was apparently because "Davey" rhymes with "gravy", but the Toffees' defender's play in 1999–2000 was far tastier than his epitaph suggests.

The Scottish international was arguably one of Walter Smith's shrewdest purchases at just £250,000 in February 1999 and has repaid the former Rangers supremo with some extremely consistent performances for Everton.

Weir displayed strength in the tackle, winning a very impressive 63% of his 99 challenges, and only four regular top-flight centre-backs can boast a superior record.

In addition, the Scot was a danger up-front, slamming six efforts on target and netting twice. The Falkirk-born player demonstrated his dogged determination when grabbing Everton's injury-time equaliser in their 4–4 draw with Leeds.

G Sander WESTERVELD • 1

LIVERPOOL • BORN: 23.10.74

Wearing the number one jersey at Anfield has proved a difficult task in recent seasons, but after a successful debut campaign with Liverpool £4 million signing Sander Westerveld will not have regretted joining the Reds from Vitesse Arnheim.

Aided by some classy performances from several of their key defenders, Westerveld helped Liverpool become the stingiest defence in the Premiership, conceding a miserly 29 goals in 36 games.

Westerveld used his size and agility to good effect between the sticks, making 94 stops in total – an impressive 76% of efforts on his goal. The Dutchman showed magnificent reactions when facing close-range shots, beating away 68% of efforts struck from inside the area – seven percentage points higher than the Premiership average.

While there is no doubting his shot-stopping abilities, the Dutch international was occasionally suspect when coming for the high ball, dropping nine crosses and registering a poor catch success rate of 88%.

APPEARANCES	
Start (sub)	36(0)
Minutes on pitch	3225
SHOT STOPPING	
Goals conceded (inside box)	23
Goals conceded (outside box)	6
Minutes per goal conceded	111.2
Clean sheets	14
Saves (shots inside box)	50
Saves (shots outside box)	44
Saves/shots	76%
DISTRIBUTION	
Long kick %	41%
Throws/short passes %	92%
CATCHING	
Crosses caught	65
Crosses punched	26
Crosses dropped	9
Catch success %	88%
DISCIPLINE	
Yellow cards	0
Red cards	1

SEE PAGE 164 FOR FULL STATS

CB Rhys WESTON • 32

ARSENAL • BORN: 27.10.80

Another member of the Gunners' youth system on the verge of breaking into the first team, defender Rhys Weston made his senior debut in Arsenal's final game of the 1999–2000 season. Unfortunately, the youngster's first taste of Premiership football was somewhat soured by the result of the match, as the Gunners succumbed to a 4–2 defeat at Newcastle.

Weston graduated through the FA School of Excellence at Lilleshall and has already been capped for England at under-16 level, and the 19-year-old possesses terrific potential for the future. Arsene Wenger was confident enough to bring on Weston for the injured Gilles Grimandi in the Worthington Cup clash with Middlesbrough at the Riverside.

The Kingston-born defender should feature in the Gunners' plans more and more through the coming seasons, and if Arsenal are to follow the successful youth policies of Manchester United and Leeds, then players such as Weston will be vital to that cause.

SEE PAGE 39 FOR FULL STATS

CB Ashley WESTWOOD • 6

BRADFORD CITY • BORN: 31.8.76

Former Manchester United trainee Ashley Westwood joined Bradford at the start of the 1998–1999 season and played a significant part in winning the Bantams promotion from Division One in the centre of their defence.

Despite the stopper's evident talent, which persuaded Paul Jewell to sign Westwood from Crewe, his opportunities in the Bradford team were severely limited during the 1999–2000 campaign. The Bridgnorth-born defender can play anywhere across the back and midfield, but such versatility failed to attract the attention of the Bantams' management team and the former England under-21 international made only one start and four substitute appearances. A niggling injury did not help matters for the young player.

The 24-year-old was, however, something of a talisman for City. He never played on the losing side in his brief excursions on to the pitch in 1999–2000 – and he was the only Bantams player to achieve this distinction.

SEE PAGE 67 FOR FULL STATS

W

David WETHERALL • 5

BRADFORD CITY • BORN: 14.3.71

Central defender David Wetherall is part of folklore in Yorkshire and will be for ever more – the former Leeds centre back scored the goal that kept Bradford in the Premiership on the final day of the 1999–2000 season.

Wetherall's bullet header in the 13th minute against Liverpool proved enough to secure victory and earn Bradford's second successive season in the Premiership. If that was not enough to earn the key to the city, then add to the mix the fact that Wetherall was the only outfield player in the Premiership not to miss a single minute of action in 1999–2000, and you get an idea of how crucial to the City cause the likeable 29-year-old was.

The Bantams' centre-back had an outstanding time in Bradford's rearguard in 1999–2000 and it was little surprise that Wetherall completed more defensive clearances than any other Premiership player. The Sheffield-born defender also won an outstanding 64% of his challenges and was arguably the shrewdest of all the signings Paul Jewell made for the 1999–2000 campaign, driving the Bantams to safety.

APPEARANCES	
Start (sub)	38(0)
Minutes on pitch	3420
GOAL ATTEMPTS	
Goals	2
DEFENDING	
Blocks	124
Shots cleared off line	4
Headed clearances	429
Other clearances	132
Interceptions	42
Last man saving tackles	2
Tackles won	57
Tackles won %	64%
PASSING	
Passing accuracy own half	73%
Passing accuracy opp half	47%
DISCIPLINE	
Fouls	56
Fouls in danger area	10
Yellow cards	7
Red cards	0

SEE PAGE 67 FOR FULL STATS

Gareth WHALLEY • 10

BRADFORD CITY • BORN: 19.12.73

APPEARANCES	
Start (sub)	16(0)
Minutes on pitch	1283
GOAL ATTEMPTS	
Goals	1
Shots on target	3
Shooting accuracy	43%
PASSING & CROSSING	
Goal assists	1
Passes in opp half	341
Passing accuracy in opp half	67%
Successful crosses	9
Cross completion	47%
DEFENDING	
Interceptions	11
Clearances	25
Tackles	49
Tackles won %	45%
DISCIPLINE	
Fouls	4
Yellow cards	0
Red cards	0

SEE PAGE 67 FOR FULL STATS

Another of the ex-Crewe contingent now plying their trade at Valley Parade, midfielder Gareth Whalley was named the Players' Player of the Year during Bradford's promotion campaign in 1998–1999.

Whalley began the 1999–2000 season in the Bantams' midfield and put in some impressive performances in the early stages of Bradford's inaugural Premiership campaign. The Manchester-born player made good use of possession and was City's most accurate passer, picking out a team-mate with 74% of attempts – in line with the Premiership average for midfielders.

Employed chiefly as a ball-winner and supplier in the midfield, the defence-minded Whalley rarely broke forward to join the attack. But the former Liverpool and Spurs trialist did find the back of the net on one occasion – netting a crucial first-half strike in the Bantams' 3–2 win against Watford in January 2000 – and also supplied one direct assist for a colleague. He will hope to figure more prominently in 2000–01.

Noel WHELAN • 8

COVENTRY CITY • BORN: 30.12.74

Injured for much of 1999, Noel Whelan came back to the fore toward the end of Coventry's 1999–2000 season and is generally known to be one of Gordon Strachan's favourite players at Highfield Road.

Whelan was hampered by his injuries and struggled to maintain a consistent standard on the pitch, only sporadically displaying the kind of form that brought him to the Midlands in the first place. Rumours abound that the former England youth and under-21 international was unhappy at Coventry and hoping for a move back to his native Leeds.

Strachan's £2-million signing netted just once during 1999–2000 in 19 starts for the club, and with the partnership of Robbie Keane and Cedric Roussel taking precedence when both were fit, Whelan may feel his days at Highfield Road are numbered.

The striker recorded an abysmal goals-to-shots ratio of just 3% – the lowest of any regular Premiership striker – and was relieved when he finally broke his 1999–2000 duck against Bradford City.

APPEARANCES	
Start (sub)	19(7)
Minutes on pitch	1785
GOAL ATTEMPTS	
Goals inside box	0
Goals outside box	1
Minutes per goal scored	1785.0
Goals/shots ratio	3%
SHOOTING	
Shots on target inside box	12
Shots on target outside box	4
Shooting accuracy	40%
PASSING	
Goal assists	2
Key passes	8
Passing accuracy in opp half	63%
DISCIPLINE	
Fouls committed	34
Fouls won	28
Offside	34
Yellow cards	3
Red cards	0

SEE PAGE 95 FOR FULL STATS

Jason WILCOX • 16

LEEDS UNITED • BORN: 15.7.71

APPEARANCES	
Start (sub)	15(5)
Minutes on pitch	1423
GOAL ATTEMPTS	
Goals	3
Shots on target	11
Shooting accuracy	58%
Goals/shots ratio	16%
PASSING	
Goal assists	2
Passes in opp half	436
Passing accuracy in opp half	62%
Successful crosses	41
Crossing accuracy	34%
DRIBBLING	
Dribbles & runs	74
Dribble completion	78%
Corners forced	21
DISCIPLINE	
Fouls	15
Yellow cards	1
Red cards	0

SEE PAGE 137 FOR FULL STATS

Pacy winger Jason Wilcox has been a revelation at Elland Road since joining Leeds in December last year and clearly looks to have augmented his international credibility after a number of top-class performances for David O'Leary's skilful young side.

It was a surprise to many that Blackburn allowed Wilcox to fly the nest and hook up with O'Leary, but less of a shock was how the England international quickly demonstrated his worth with a succession of powerful runs down the left flank and a plethora of top-quality crosses into the box.

Wilcox played out the majority of the 1999–2000 season on the United left and notched up three Premiership goals in the process. However, it was in his crossing where the 29-year-old excelled, and Wilcox whipped in nearly 80 centres from his wide position – more than any other Leeds player bar Aussie Harry Kewell.

Wilcox appeared to really enjoy his football at Elland Road and the transfer fee of £3 million now looks like an absolute bargain.

on average, the most infrequent in the Premiership

Darren WILLIAMS • 18

SUNDERLAND • BORN: 28.4.77

Sunderland's versatile defender Darren Williams must be glad he ended up in his first choice profession after being given a run in the side at the turn of the year. If the youngster hadn,t succeeded as a footballer, then the Middlesbrough-born starlet wanted to join the army.

Despite limited opportunities for a regular place in the starting line up, the England under-21 player certainly did not receive many barrackings from his manager after some steady performances in Sunderland's defence towards the end of 1999-2000.

The former York star can perform in most defensive and midfield positions, but Reid employed Williams mainly as a centre back when Steve Bould and Paul Butler were missing.

Williams made more than 100 clearances and won 30 tackles at the back, while also getting forward to provide ammunition for his forward line, where he supplied one goal assist for Reid,s men. He also managed to get himself on the scoresheet in the 3-2 Worthington Cup victory over Walsall.

APPEARANCES	
Start (sub)	13(12)
Minutes on pitch	1499
GOAL ATTEMPTS	
Goals	0
DEFENDING	
Blocks	26
Shots cleared off line	0
Headed clearances	69
Other clearances	34
Interceptions	12
Last man saving tackles	0
Tackles won	30
Tackles won %	48%
PASSING	
Passing accuracy own half	69%
Passing accuracy opp half	55%
DISCIPLINE	
Fouls	28
Fouls in danger area	11
Yellow cards	2
Red cards	0

SEE PAGE 249 FOR FULL STATS

CB

Mark WILLIAMS • 32

WATFORD • BORN: 28.9.70

APPEARANCES	
Start (sub)	20(2)
Minutes on pitch	1691
GOAL ATTEMPTS	
Goals	1
DEFENDING	
Blocks	45
Shots cleared off line	0
Headed clearances	152
Other clearances	99
Interceptions	12
Last man saving tackles	1
Tackles won	31
Tackles won %	48%
PASSING	
Passing accuracy own half	76%
Passing accuracy opp half	45%
DISCIPLINE	
Fouls	46
Fouls in danger area	10
Yellow cards	7
Red cards	1

SEE PAGE 277 FOR FULL STATS

Watford's centre-back Mark Williams displayec his prophetic capabilities by finishing seconc in the Watford players' result predictior competition, but he couldn't have foreseer that the Hornets would disappear so meekly from the top flight.

Finishing with the lowest points total in the Premiership's history, Williams couldn't stop his team leaking goals at an alarming rate.

The Northern Ireland international came to Vicarage Road before the start of the 1990–2000 season straight from the seconc division, and despite an impressive start to his top-flight career he often looked out of his depth in the Premiership. He also fell foul of officials on occasion, picking up a hefty total of seven yellow cards during the season and was also sent off in a heavy defeat at Old Trafford.

Watford's defender did manage to find the back of the net against Leeds in Octobe 1999, but a below-average tackling success rate pretty much sums up Williams' difficulty in acclimatising to Premiership life.

Paul WILLIAMS • 4

COVENTRY CITY • BORN: 26.3.71

There was speculation that erstwhile Coventry central defender Paul Williams would be leaving Highfield Road after the 1999–2000 season, but the former England under-21 international pledged his future to the club when he signed a new contract at the end of the campaign.

Williams chipped in with some impressive play in the Sky Blues' back line. The 29-year-old came out with the ball in an excellent 59% of his challenges and completed more than 300 defensive clearances.

Aside from his much-appreciated exertions, the solid centre-back managed to make his mark in spectacular style at the other end of the pitch, thumping in a screamer in the Sky Blues' 4–1 demolition of Newcastle.

That strike certainly earned Williams the plaudits from his boss Gordon Strachan, although the fiery Scot found fault with others' appreciation of the goal, moaning: "If anyone else had scored that goal it would have been talked about for weeks, but because it was a Coventry defender it was just seen as a fluke."

APPEARANCES	
Start (sub)	26(2)
Minutes on pitch	2312
GOAL ATTEMPTS	
Goals	1
DEFENDING	
Blocks	48
Shots cleared off line	0
Headed clearances	210
Other clearances	108
Interceptions	41
Last man saving tackles	3
Tackles won	57
Tackles won %	59%
PASSING	
Passing accuracy own half	82%
Passing accuracy opp half	47%
DISCIPLINE	
Fouls	31
Fouls in danger area	12
Yellow cards	4
Red cards	0

SEE PAGE 95 FOR FULL STATS

CB

Chris WILLMOTT • 22

WIMBLEDON • BORN: 30.9.77

APPEARANCES	
Start (sub)	7(0)
Minutes on pitch	612
GOAL ATTEMPTS	
Goals	0
DEFENDING	
Blocks	28
Shots cleared off line	0
Headed clearances	46
Other clearances	14
Interceptions	3
Last man saving tackles	0
Tackles won	6
Tackles won %	75%
PASSING	
Passing accuracy own half	61%
Passing accuracy opp half	56%
DISCIPLINE	
Fouls	7
Fouls in danger area	5
Yellow cards	0
Red cards	0

SEE PAGE 305 FOR FULL STATS

Promising defender Chris Willmott played a minor role in the Dons' campaign of 1999–2000 that ended in the cruel disappointment of relegation to the First Division.

He was signed from Luton Town in July 1999 in a deal that also saw Hatters' goalie Kelvin Davies' move to Selhurst. With the Bedfordshire club in administration they were forced to sell their most prize assets at a bargain price.

A tall commanding centre-back who is equally at home in the full-back position, Willmott was brought to the club as cover for Tore Pedersen and Dean Blackwell.

In his seven Premiership appearances, Wilmott was a reliable and steady performer, winning three-quarters of his challenges.

The young defender pitched in with 28 blocks and nearly 50 headed clearances for the Dons, and featured in Wimbledon's final victory of the campaign, against Leicester.

Wimbledon have high hopes for the 22-year-old, and Wilmott's displays suggest that he will acquit himself reasonably well in the First Division.

Mark WILSON • 33

MANCHESTER UNITED • BORN: 9.2.79

Mark Wilson is the latest in a long line of Manchester United's youngsters on the fringes of first-team action.

United's ever expanding fixture list means that Wilson has already seen action in the Champions League and World Club Championships as well as the Premiership in his short career.

The midfielder made his debut for the Red Devils against Brondby in 1998–99. He then had the unenviable task of trying to replace Roy Keane during United's pre-season tour of Australia before making his Premiership bow as a substitute against Chelsea in October.

Another substitute appearance against Aston Villa followed and he made his first start for United against Watford at the end of April – although only played 45 minutes.

With the likes of Keane, Paul Scholes and Nicky Butt providing competition for central midfield places, Wilson will always struggle to find a regular place in the United side.

SEE PAGE 179 FOR FULL STATS

Dean WINDASS • 15

BRADFORD CITY • BORN: 1.4.69

Dean Windass will be looking forward to the challenge of another season in the top flight after his goals helped Bradford preserve their Premiership status by the narrowest of margins.

The Bantams paid Oxford United £1 million for Windass to help with their promotion push of 1998–99. He scored three times in the season's run-in, and after helping them achieve their place in the Premiership, Windass went on to become their top scorer with 10 top flight goals – including a first-half hat-trick against Derby County.

The former Aberdeen hitman played a part in every single one of Bradford's league games and his goals came from 72 shots.

Despite an ungainly appearance Windass is surprisingly adept with the ball with his passing accuracy far higher than average for a Premiership striker. He made 1,155 passes, creating two goals in the process.

He was a shining example of Bradford's collective spirit which helped them survive, also helping out defensively with 73 tackles and 58 clearances.

Ungainly: Dean Windass

APPEARANCES	
Start (sub)	36(2)
Minutes on pitch	3083
GOAL ATTEMPTS	
Goals inside box	7
Goals outside box	3
Minutes per goal scored	308.3
Goals/shots ratio	14%
SHOOTING	
Shots on target inside box	18
Shots on target outside box	16
Shooting accuracy	47%
PASSING	
Goal assists	2
Key passes	6
Passing accuracy in opp half	66%
DISCIPLINE	
Fouls committed	72
Fouls won	47
Offside	20
Yellow cards	6
Red cards	0

SEE PAGE 67 FOR FULL STATS

Nigel WINTERBURN • 3

ARSENAL • BORN: 11.12.63

Nigel Winterburn completed his 12th season at Highbury in May 2000, but will be disappointed that he finally lost his place in the famous "back five" as manager Arsene Wenger introduced fresher faces to his defence.

The form of Brazilian Silvinho forced Winterburn out of his customary left-back role and saw him spend much of the latter part of the season on the bench, but he returned before the end of the campaign playing in an unfamiliar midfield position.

Whether he was playing from the start or coming off the bench, Winterburn remained the reliable professional throughout. He had an impressive pass completion rate for a defender of 77% from the 1,059 passes he made while he was on the pitch.

He attempted 99 tackles – the third-highest total by an Arsenal player during the season – and he won just over half of them.

In June, Winterburn followed team-mate Davor Suker to West Ham seeking first-team football, for a fee of £250,000.

APPEARANCES	
Start (sub)	19(9)
Minutes on pitch	1907
GOAL ATTEMPTS	
Goals	0
PASSING & CROSSING	
Goal assists	0
Passing	1059
Passing accuracy	77%
Crosses	57
Crossing accuracy	30%
DEFENDING	
Tackles	99
Tackles won %	52%
Blocks	21
Interceptions	15
Clearances	53
Shots cleared off line	0
DISCIPLINE	
Fouls	21
Yellow cards	3
Red cards	0

SEE PAGE 39 FOR FULL STATS

M

Dennis WISE • 11

CHELSEA • BORN: 16.12.66

APPEARANCES	
Start (sub)	29(1)
Minutes on pitch	2603
GOAL ATTEMPTS	
Goals	4
Shots on target	15
Shooting accuracy	52%
PASSING & CROSSING	
Goal assists	5
Passes in opp half	1042
Passing accuracy in opp half	75%
Successful crosses	52
Cross completion	31%
DEFENDING	
Interceptions	22
Clearances	37
Tackles	95
Tackles won %	57%
DISCIPLINE	
Fouls	62
Yellow cards	7
Red cards	1

SEE PAGE 81 FOR FULL STATS

The 1999–2000 season ended in now-familiar style for Chelsea captain Dennis Wise – with him lifting another piece of silverware. Wise is the most successful captain in Chelsea's history and it is a record he's keen to keep extending.

It was a fitting end to the season for "Dennis the Menace" whose outstanding performances earned him an England recall. Surrounded by expensive overseas talent at Stamford Bridge, Wise led by example, proving to be the heart and soul of the Chelsea side.

He scored crucial goals in Europe, as well as four in the Premiership, as he drove the Blues through another successful season.

Famed for his ferocious tackling, Wise won 57% of the challenges he attempted. The Londoner's passing ability goes unnoticed by some, but he made 1,595 passes with a higher-than-average completion rate of 79% and created five Premiership goals for Gianluca Vialli's men.

Although generally composed, Wise still showed he had not lost his fiery edge with seven yellow cards and one red during the campaign.

Robert WOLLEASTEN • 28

CHELSEA • BORN: 21.12.79

Robert Wolleaston is one of several exciting prospects from the Chelsea youth side and he made his debut for the Blues in 1999–2000.

The 20-year-old's first appearance came as a substitute against Huddersfield in the Worthington Cup, but he had to wait until December to make his Premiership bow, replacing Dennis Wise for the last 13 minutes in Chelsea's 4–1 defeat at Sunderland.

Wolleaston had little chance to make an impression that day, making four passes and getting one cross in, but with other Chelsea youngsters being give a chance in the first team he will be hoping his time will come sooner rather than later.

He spent the last two months of the season out on loan at Second Division Bristol Rovers, where he featured in four matches. Wolleaston will be hoping to make the most of this experience as he pushes for a place in Chelsea's star-studded starting line-up at some point during 2000–01.

SEE PAGE 81 FOR FULL STATS

Formidable: Jonathon Woodgate

CB Jonathon WOODGATE • 6

LEEDS UNITED • BORN: 22.1.80

The 1998–99 season proved sensational for centre-back Jonathon Woodgate. After he broke into the first team early on in the season, he went on to win an England cap against Bulgaria in June.

It was always going to be hard for Woodgate to follow this up in 1999–2000, but consistent displays at the heart of the Leeds defence have seen him attract many plaudits from all corners, with Watford's Tommy Smith rating Woodgate as the best defender he had faced.

"Woody" was part of the Leeds side which won the 1997 FA Youth Cup, and while George Graham was at Elland Road, he marked the young defender out as having a big future.

Since then Graham has been proved right, with Woodgate forming a formidable partnership alongside Lucas Radebe at the back for the Whites.

Woodgate won a better-than-average 56% of the tackles he attempted during the 1999–2000 campaign, made a total of 369 clearances and was comfortable spreading the ball, completing 72% of all passes.

APPEARANCES	
Start (sub)	32(2)
Minutes on pitch	2826
GOAL ATTEMPTS	
Goals	1
DEFENDING	
Blocks	80
Shots cleared off line	1
Headed clearances	290
Other clearances	79
Interceptions	33
Last man saving tackles	1
Tackles won	65
Tackles won %	56%
PASSING	
Passing accuracy own half	80%
Passing accuracy opp half	58%
DISCIPLINE	
Fouls	32
Fouls in danger area	10
Yellow cards	0
Red cards	0

SEE PAGE 137 FOR FULL STATS

AM

Nordin WOOTER • 14

WATFORD • BORN: 24.8.76

Graham Taylor smashed the Hornets' 15-year transfer record when he paid Real Zaragoza £950,000 for Nordin Wooter in September 1999, but the dreadlocked Dutch star failed to deliver on his promises at Vicarage Road.

When signing for Watford, Wooter said: "I want to score goals but I am as much a maker of goals as I am a scorer of goals." He will be disappointed, then, that he managed just one goal and one assist during the season for Taylor's battlers.

The under-21 international enjoyed a promising debut in Watford's 1–0 win over Chelsea in September, but his progress with the Hornets was restricted after he received an ankle injury in the FA Cup tie with Birmingham City.

The former Ajax player has plenty of pace and tried to use it to good effect by making 116 dribbles. However, with a passing accuracy of 65%, he still has a fair way to go to live up to Taylor's billing as an "exciting creative midfield player", although he may excel in Nationwide Division One.

APPEARANCES	
Start (sub)	16(4)
Minutes on pitch	1405
GOAL ATTEMPTS	
Goals	1
Shots on target	11
Shooting accuracy	38%
Goals/shots ratio	3%
PASSING	
Goal assists	1
Passes in opp half	322
Passing accuracy in opp half	62%
Successful crosses	13
Crossing accuracy	28%
DRIBBLING	
Dribbles & runs	116
Dribble completion	69%
Corners forced	18
DISCIPLINE	
Fouls	27
Yellow cards	0
Red cards	0

SEE PAGE 277 FOR FULL STATS

FB

Alan WRIGHT • 3

ASTON VILLA • BORN: 28.9.71

APPEARANCES	
Start (sub)	31(1)
Minutes on pitch	2642
GOAL ATTEMPTS	
Goals	1
PASSING & CROSSING	
Goal assists	5
Passing	1192
Passing accuracy	66%
Crosses	95
Crossing accuracy	34%
DEFENDING	
Tackles	57
Tackles won %	37%
Blocks	28
Interceptions	19
Clearances	109
Shots cleared off line	1
DISCIPLINE	
Fouls	15
Yellow cards	5
Red cards	0

SEE PAGE 53 FOR FULL STATS

Alan Wright saw his run of playing in 97 consecutive Premiership matches for Aston Villa come to an end early in the season when injury forced him to sit out five games.

The 5'4" defender – more commonly known as "Titch" in the West Midlands – has been one of Villa's most consistent and reliable performers since Brian Little brought him to the club in 1995, and has made the left wing-back spot his own.

He not only provides Villa with strong defensive qualities, but he also has good crossing ability and enjoys getting forward down the left flank.

Wright was Villa's chief supplier down the left side, and the diminutive defender supplied a total of 95 crosses during the 1999–2000 campaign, completing an impressive 34% of these. His deadly delivery directly resulted in five goals for colleagues.

Wright rarely gets his name on the scoresheet, but when he does it is usually spectacular, as was the case with his stunning strike into the top corner against Tottenham.

Nick WRIGHT • 11

WATFORD • BORN: 15.10.75

Watford's Wembley hero Nick Wright suffered a disappointing season with his chances of playing Premiership football being severely restricted through injury.

Wright etched his name into Watford folklore by scoring a stunning overhead kick against Bolton beneath the Twin Towers in the 1999 play-off final. But since then things have gone downhill for the former Carlisle man.

The unlucky midfielder has been hit hard by knee and hernia problems which sidelined him for most of the season. Reports suggested that his career hung in the balance, but the Derbyshire-born player is battling back and hoping to be fit for the start of the 2000–01 campaign.

He started just one game in the Premiership – at West Ham in September – and made three appearances as a substitute before injury cruelly struck again and meant he was unable to play any part in the Hornets' battle at the foot of the table.

SEE PAGE 277 FOR FULL STATS

Tommy WRIGHT • 32

NEWCASTLE UNITED • BORN: 29.8.63

A goalkeeper crisis at Newcastle at the start of the season saw a shock return to Tyneside for Tommy Wright, and he was straight in at the deep end against local rivals Sunderland.

Wright had been part of Kevin Keegan's promotion-winning side at Newcastle in 1992–93, before Frank Clark took him to Nottingham Forest and then on to Manchester City. However, a series of early-season injuries to 'keepers at St James's Park saw Ruud Gullit take the veteran Wright back to his former stomping ground on loan.

It was not the happiest of returns for Wright, though, as he conceded eight goals as Newcastle fast approached crisis point. He could do little to stop Sunderland on his return and this was followed by a 5–1 drubbing at Old Trafford. In total Wright managed to save 58% of the shots he faced in three games, before he returned to Maine Road where he made one appearance in the drive to promotion.

SEE PAGE 206 FOR FULL STATS

Abel XAVIER • 19

EVERTON • BORN: 30.11.72

APPEARANCES	
Start (sub)	18(2)
Minutes on pitch	1655
GOAL ATTEMPTS	
Goals	0
Shots on target	3
Shooting accuracy	25%
Goals/shots ratio	0%
PASSING	
Goal assists	0
Passes in opp half	358
Passing accuracy in opp half	69%
Successful crosses	2
Crossing accuracy	22%
DRIBBLING	
Dribbles & runs	12
Dribble completion	83%
Corners forced	6
DISCIPLINE	
Fouls	33
Yellow cards	0
Red cards	0

SEE PAGE 123 FOR FULL STATS

When Everton signed Abel Xavier, fans on Merseyside were quick to ask "Abel who?" but Walter Smith's recruit from PSV Eindhoven was a big hit at Goodison Park following his £1.5 million move.

He made his debut as a substitute in a 2–0 win at Sheffield Wednesday in September 1999, but had his longest run in the side in early 2000, retaining his place for 11 matches in a row from 26 February.

Mozambique-born Xavier had been known to play anywhere in the back four or midfield, making him a shining example of the type of versatile player that managers want to have in their squads.

His crisp, clean passing resulted in a 73% completion rate, although his tackles were not quite as successful, with just 40% of his challenges retaining possession of the ball.

His performances have been as noteworthy as his hair, and if he continues to play with such versatility and skill he is likely to add to his growing tally of Portuguese caps during the 2000–01 season.

8 Dwight Yorke scored more headed goals

Dwight YORKE • 19

MANCHESTER UNITED • BORN: 3.11.71

Red Devils striker Dwight Yorke was given the keys to the capital of his native Tobago in March 1999 – the country's highest honour – and after yet another free-scoring 1999–2000 season with United, the keys to the Old Trafford domain must surely follow soon.

Although critics argue that Yorke failed to repeat his stunning form of the 1998–1999 campaign, the Trinidad and Tobagan international still racked up 20 Premiership goals to leave him as the club's top scorer in the league. Add to that his second successive Premiership winner's medal and the diminutive star looks to have had the last laugh.

Yorke, who surprisingly scored with more headers than any other player, netted with an excellent 32% of his total efforts – one of the best records in the Premiership – and thumped in 67% of his shots on target. Yorke was also the most accurate passer of the ball in the opposition half, finding a team-mate with 84% of all his distribution, illustrating why Opta ranked him as the second most effective Premiership striker.

APPEARANCES	
Start (sub)	29(3)
Minutes on pitch	2555
GOAL ATTEMPTS	
Goals inside box	19
Goals outside box	1
Minutes per goal scored	128.8
Goals/shots ratio	32%
SHOOTING	
Shots on target inside box	36
Shots on target outside box	6
Shooting accuracy	67%
PASSING	
Goal assists	3
Key passes	26
Passing accuracy in opp half	84%
DISCIPLINE	
Fouls committed	42
Fouls won	62
Offside	36
Yellow cards	1
Red cards	0

SEE PAGE 179 FOR FULL STATS

Luke YOUNG • 21

TOTTENHAM HOTSPUR • BORN: 19.7.79

APPEARANCES	
Start (sub)	11(9)
Minutes on pitch	1173
GOAL ATTEMPTS	
Goals	0
DEFENDING	
Blocks	14
Shots cleared off line	0
Headed clearances	61
Other clearances	45
Interceptions	19
Last man saving tackles	0
Tackles won	21
Tackles won %	51%
PASSING	
Passing accuracy own half	78%
Passing accuracy opp half	63%
DISCIPLINE	
Fouls	11
Fouls in danger area	5
Yellow cards	2
Red cards	0

SEE PAGE 263 FOR FULL STATS

Luke Young's mature performances for Tottenham during 1998–99 meant that great things were expected of him the following season. Unfortunately, Young failed to get a permanent place because of the signing of Chris Perry in the summer of 1999.

Young remained a valuable squad player and had some opportunities to appear in the middle of defence, as well as at left-back when Mauricio Taricco was unavailable.

Should the Essex youngster get more opportunities during 2000–01, he will look to improve his 69% pass completion rate and get forward more often so that he can get his first goal in Tottenham colours.

Despite his limited opportunities, he was still able to impress Howard Wilkinson enough to be part of the England squad for the European under-21 Championships which took place during the summer of 2000.

It may be a while before Young can claim a regular place in the Tottenham line-up, but experience gained in the under-21s will be of benefit as he waits for his chance.

Theo ZAGORAKIS • 37

LEICESTER CITY • BORN: 27.10.71

Theo Zagorakis found himself on the substitutes bench for most of the 1999–2000 season, unable to force his way past the consistent midfield trio of Neil Lennon, Muzzy Izzet and Robbie Savage.

His name was in the headlines after City's Worthington Cup win at Wembley following a touchline altercation with Tranmere manager John Aldridge.

When he did get a chance to play, Zagorakis made important contributions in all areas and scored his only goal of the season in the 2–1 home defeat against Newcastle United. He even played in goal in the Worthington Cup match at Crystal Palace!

Understandably, though, the Greek international was frustrated with his lack of first-team opportunities at Leicester and, after Martin O'Neill allowed him to leave the club, Zagorakis will start the 2000–01 season back in his homeland. His deal with AEK Athens will give him the opportunity to play in the UEFA Cup and could see him return to Filbert Street if the two cup-winning sides are drawn together.

APPEARANCES	
Start (sub)	6(11)
Minutes on pitch	690
GOAL ATTEMPTS	
Goals	1
Shots on target	3
Shooting accuracy	33%
Goals/shots ratio	11%
PASSING	
Goal assists	1
Passes in opp half	169
Passing accuracy in opp half	60%
Successful crosses	10
Crossing accuracy	36%
DRIBBLING	
Dribbles & runs	22
Dribble completion	82%
Corners forced	4
DISCIPLINE	
Fouls	7
Yellow cards	2
Red cards	0

SEE PAGE 151 FOR FULL STATS

FB

Christian ZIEGE • 17

MIDDLESBROUGH • BORN: 1.2.72

APPEARANCES	
Start (sub)	29(0)
Minutes on pitch	2440
GOAL ATTEMPTS	
Goals	6
PASSING & CROSSING	
Goal assists	6
Passing	945
Passing accuracy	66%
Crosses	184
Crossing accuracy	24%
DEFENDING	
Tackles	85
Tackles won %	55%
Blocks	23
Interceptions	35
Clearances	77
Shots cleared off line	0
DISCIPLINE	
Fouls	29
Yellow cards	9
Red cards	1

SEE PAGE 193 FOR FULL STATS

Inspirational German international midfielder Christian Ziege had a solid start to his Premiership career in the north-east, although he may have been left questioning his choice of club following his debut, in which Boro crashed to a disappointing 1–0 home defeat to Bradford City on the opening day of the season.

Finishing the season as the club's third-highest scorer with six goals, including three from outside the penalty area, Ziege became a vital part of the Boro first team, also contributing six assists.

His passing was often wayward, with only 66% of all passes reaching the intended target and a crossing accuracy of just 24%. But he was sorely missed when he was absent from the team – of the nine games in which he did not feature, Boro were beaten in five.

One of Germany's few consistent performers in the build-up to Euro 2000, Ziege has proved a real hit in the Premiership. His experience will be vital as the club looks to challenge for a UEFA Cup place in 2000–01.

Gianfranco ZOLA • 25

CHELSEA • BORN: 5.7.66

Gianfranco Zola played in all but five of Chelsea's Premiership matches and continued to provide the crucial link between midfield and attack that has made him so vital to the Blues' pattern of play.

He may have scored only four times, but Zola's nine goal assists and 73% pass completion rate proved that he is still a handful in the opposition half. He was able to distribute the ball from the centre of the field and the flanks, looking equally dangerous from both areas of the pitch.

His popularity with Chelsea fans was never higher than in 1999–2000, so rumours linking him with a move to Fenerbahce upset supporters, who hope he will finish his career at Stamford Bridge.

Zola had reportedly been seen shaking hands with the Fenerbahce president. And with Napoli also claiming to be keen on him, it remains to be seen if he will see out the remaining years on his contract in London, although, he himself has said that he is very happy at Chelsea.

APPEARANCES	
Start (sub)	25(8)
Minutes on pitch	2226
GOAL ATTEMPTS	
Goals inside box	4
Goals outside box	0
Minutes per goal scored	556.5
Goals/shots ratio	7%
SHOOTING	
Shots on target inside box	17
Shots on target outside box	13
Shooting accuracy	51%
PASSING	
Goal assists	9
Key passes	22
Passing accuracy in opp half	72%
DISCIPLINE	
Fouls committed	11
Fouls won	28
Offside	30
Yellow cards	0
Red cards	0

SEE PAGE 81 FOR FULL STATS

Ysrael ZUNIGA • 34

COVENTRY CITY • BORN: 27.8.76

APPEARANCES	
Start (sub)	3(4)
Minutes on pitch	224
GOAL ATTEMPTS	
Goals inside box	2
Goals outside box	0
Minutes per goal scored	112.0
Goals/shots ratio	50%
SHOOTING	
Shots on target inside box	3
Shots on target outside box	1
Shooting accuracy	100%
PASSING	
Goal assists	0
Key passes	0
Passing accuracy in opp half	56%
DISCIPLINE	
Fouls committed	1
Fouls won	3
Offside	7
Yellow cards	0
Red cards	0

SEE PAGE 95 FOR FULL STATS

Gordon Strachan initially admitted that the signing of Ysrael Zuniga was a gamble, as he had never seen him play live. So he was relieved when the Peruvian striker showed a great deal of promise in his first three months in the Premiership, following his £750,000 move from FCB Melgar in February.

Zuniga, also known as "Cachete", may turn out to be one of the best gambles of Strachan's short managerial career, as the player is a previous winner of the South American Golden Boot and proved more than a handful for Premiership defences.

He made seven appearances and, although he only played for 224 minutes, he managed to notch a goal in each of the home victories against Bradford and Sheffield Wednesday. His only four shots were all on target.

If Zuniga can sustain his impressive start in English football he may not only prove to be one of the bargains of recent years, he may even manage to bring a smile to the face of Scotsman Strachan, widely regarded as one of the hardest tasks in football.

OPTA PLAYERS TO WATCH

Youth is often the driving force behind the top leagues across the world and the English Premiership is no exception. But which players are destined to be the top-flight stars of the future?

Opta have used their expert knowledge of football to uncover those players who are expected to make the grade in the coming seasons. Here they present a team of 11 young players who are either set for their Premiership debuts or are likely to be snapped up by a big-name club in the near future.

Liverpool starlet Steven Gerrard and Chelsea ace John Harley are just two examples of such meteoric rises to fame during the 1999–2000 season, and these young hopefuls will be looking to follow in their lofty footsteps.

Converted from an out-and-out winger in his days at Aylesbury United, Rangers' Jermaine Darlington fitted into his defensive role at Loftus Road with aplomb during the 1999–2000 season and, despite being 26, promises to have a long career in front of him.

Darlington dropped to non-league football after being released by Charlton in 1993 and supplemented his part-time soccer wages by working as a glazier.

Ironically West Ham, the team reputedly after the signature of the skilful wing-back, used to be sponsored by BAC Windows!

The Londoner's pace and excellent ball control aided his forward play on the wing for the Rs, and the fact that Darlington loves to attack defenders was illustrated in the pint-sized player's tally of two league goals in the 1999–2000 campaign.

Although the Hackney-born star's season ended prematurely with an injury at the start of April, Darlington should stand a good chance of gracing the Premiership in the near future if he can maintain his form.

FB
David WRIGHT
BORN: 1.5.80 GOALS 1999–2000: 0
APPEARANCES 1999–2000: 45

Young players at Crewe are usually hyped as "the next big thing" or linked with moves to the Premiership. And in the case of right-back David Wright, the talk of future stardom looks well justified.

Likened to former Liverpool, Crewe and England player Rob Jones, Wright progressed from captaining the youth side at Gresty Road to being a first-team regular in 1999–2000.

He managed to force Marcus Bignot, another highly-promising player, out of the first-team picture and Wright's marauding, attacking runs down the right flank earned him plenty of rave reviews.

Wright, an England under-18 international, has attracted the attention of Middlesbrough and Blackburn in 1999–2000. And Derby, who signed Seth Johnson from Crewe in the summer of 1999, are the latest top-flight team to have been linked with a swoop for Wright, who looks sure to grace the Premiership at some point in his career.

G Nicky WEAVER

BORN: 2.3.79 GOALS 1999–2000: 0
APPEARANCES 1999–2000: 45

England under-21 goalkeeper Nicky Weaver has experienced two successive promotions under Joe Royle at Manchester City and the youngster is about to savour his first taste of the top flight during the 2000–2001 season.

The 21-year-old shot to fame by saving two penalties in the 1998–99 Division Two play-off final to break Gillingham's hearts, and has been an instrumental figure in 1999–2000, helping the Blues hold the best defensive record in the Nationwide's top league with just 40 goals conceded in 46 games.

Expect fireworks from the Sheffield-born starlet if he can augment his reputation for possessing astute judgement alongside a penchant for the spectacular.

Newcastle have already shown an interest in the youngster, allegedly preparing a £5 million bid. Nevertheless, Weaver will be plying his trade in the Premiership, whatever the speculation following the Citizens' promotion to the big time.

Fireworks: Nicky Weaver

CB
Darren POWELL
BORN: 10.3.76 GOALS 1999–2000: 2
APPEARANCES 1999–2000: 36

Brentford's central defender Darren Powell was plucked from non-league obscurity at the start of the 1998–1999 season and immediately won over the Bees' supporters with his excellent timing in the tackle and solid performances.

Powell was rewarded by being named the club's Player of the Year and picked up a Division Three winner's medal to boot. The 24-year-old augmented his reputation during the 1999–2000 campaign, coping admirably with the loss of defensive partner Hermann Hreidarsson to Wimbledon in October.

The Londoner also netted for the Bees in their 2–0 defeat of Oxford which, coincidently, was Powell's first game without Hreidarsson by his side. It cannot be too long a wait until the talented player receives the chance to follow his former Icelandic team-mate into the Premiership – although Powell would hope to last longer in the top flight than his erstwhile colleague, who was part of the Wimbledon side relegated in 1999–2000.

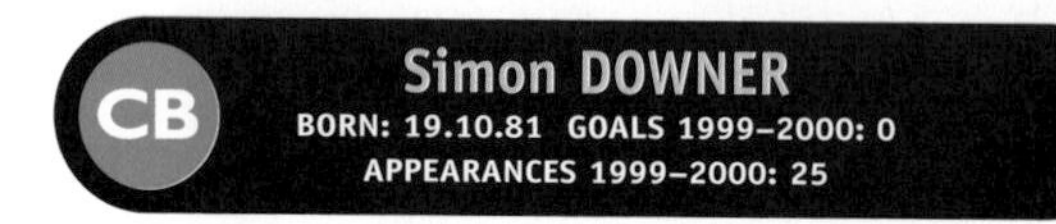

As a product of Leyton Orient's successful youth system, Simon Downer broke into the first team in December and, after solid performances at the back, finished the 1999–2000 season linked with a proposed £1 million move to Spurs.

The heavily-touted 18-year-old slotted into the centre-back position at Brisbane Road following injuries to key players and established himself as a prodigious talent, combining his natural skill and pace with a mature attitude to the game.

In the Londoner's opening 17-game spell for the club, Tommy Taylor's men kept seven clean sheets and dragged themselves from the foot of the table with nine victories. Certainly, Downer was integral to this turnaround with his strong tackling and presence on the pitch.

One part of his game that Downer will be keen to improve is his goalscoring potential, since he failed to find the back of the net during the 1999–2000 campaign, but there is no doubting the teenager's innate talent.

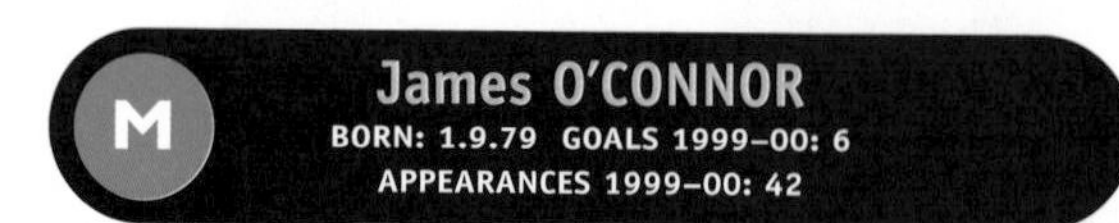

In the summer of 1999, 20-year-old midfielder James O'Connor had played just four games for Stoke's first team and was very much on the fringes of former boss Gary Megson's squad.

A year on, and the Irish-born schemer enters the 2000–01 campaign with a reputation for being one of the best young midfield players outside the Premiership. He also has a Wembley winner's medal to show off and a Player of the Year award to put on his mantelpiece.

O'Connor forms a highly-effective central midfield partnership with his fellow-Irishman Graham Kavanagh for Stoke, and the pair were key players as City reached the Division Two play-offs and won the Auto Windscreens Shield.

A tenacious and tough-tackling player, O'Connor also possesses a fair amount of skill and is likely to be plying his trade at a higher level in the not-too-distant future, should he continue to progress at a similar rate.

Alan MAHON

BORN: 4.4.78 GOALS 1999–2000: 4
APPEARANCES 1999–2000: 36

Republic of Ireland under-21 international midfielder Alan Mahon is widely believed to be one of the most skilful players outside the Premiership and Leeds, Spurs and Celtic are among some of the clubs rumoured to be keen to get the Irishman's signature.

Currently out of contract at Tranmere, the Dublin-born star quickly matured after graduating from the Rovers youth system in 1995 and impressed greatly during the 1999–2000 season following the Merseysiders' respectable league finish and success in both cup competitions.

Mahon has proved to be extremely reliable in the middle for John Aldridge's team and displayed his natural composure by slotting home all three penalties he elected to take in 1999–2000.

The 22-year-old also bagged a strike from open play against QPR and consistently combined his forward-thinking with dogged defensive work in the Rovers' midfield.

The Dubliner certainly controls his own destiny and could well be settling in to the top flight by the start of 2000–01.

Composure: Alan Mahon

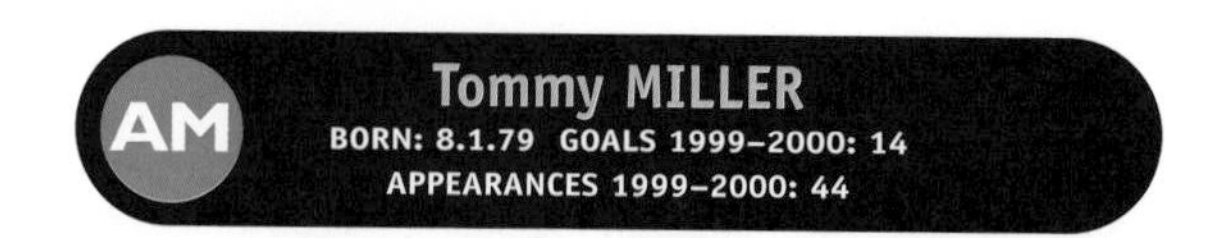

AM
Tommy MILLER
BORN: 8.1.79 GOALS 1999–2000: 14
APPEARANCES 1999–2000: 44

A powerful 21-year-old who loves to get forward, Hartlepool's Tommy Miller was the top-scoring midfielder in Division Three in 1999–2000 with 14 goals.

Those strikes also made Miller 'Pool's top scorer and helped them achieve a play-off placing in the Third Division table.

Miller, a local lad who progressed through the club's youth system, made his first-team debut in 1997–98, and has been a regular ever since. When former England striker Peter Beardsley signed for Hartlepool towards the end of the 1998–99, he and Miller linked up superbly, helping to secure the club's highly prized Division Three status.

Miller's form in 1999–2000 has attracted representatives from clubs like Spurs, Arsenal, Chelsea and Celtic to Victoria Park and he has certainly given them food for thought. But Hartlepool boss Chris Turner sees Miller as a big part of his plans, as the North-East side aim for promotion in 2000–01.

After breaking into the first team in Millwall's 3–1 victory at Oxford in October, winger Paul Ifill was never dropped by the Lions as he tormented Division Two defenders from his wide right position.

Brighton boy Ifill signed professional from the Lions' youth academy in 1998 and, despite graduating as a striker, the 6'0" player adapted impressively on to the wing while retaining his eye for goal, bagging 11 strikes during the 1999–2000 campaign.

The youngster's enthusiasm and willingness to take players on made him a crowd favourite at the Lions' Den – as did his ability to pop up in the box to net vital strikes.

In addition, the 20-year-old whipped in a multitude of dangerous centres from the right and fast became the kind of attacking midfielder that would stand a good chance of excelling against a better quality of defender. No doubt Ifill's time will soon come to grace a bigger stage.

S
Lomano TRESOR LUA LUA
BORN: 28.12.80 GOALS 1999–2000: 12
APPEARANCES 1999–2000: 41

Zairian forward Lomano Tresor Lua Lua greatly impressed in his first full season in the Football League and his unusual name should become far wider known come the end of the 2000–01 league season.

French national Lua Lua was spotted playing for Leyton College in September 1998 and Colchester United snapped up the highly-skilled forward, instantly recognising the teenager's quality. Their faith was repaid when the agile attacker netted within minutes of his debut as a second-half substitute, and the 1999–2000 campaign has seen the youngster continue that very promising trend.

Lua Lua arrived off the bench and scored on no less than six occasions for Colchester during the 1999–2000 season, racking up 12 strikes in total. The Us starlet also showed he enjoys shooting from distance, with four of his tally being fired in from outside the penalty area.

Certainly, the future looks bright for the man from Zaire and it should not be long before this prodigious talent is picked up by a bigger club, from a higher division.

S Eidur GUDJOHNSEN

BORN: 15.9.78 GOALS 1999–2000: 13
APPEARANCES 1999–2000: 41

Eidur Gudjohnsen drew favourable comparisons with his striking partner Ronaldo when playing at PSV Eindhoven near the start of his career and the Icelandic international has not failed to continued to impress in his first full season in England.

The 21-year-old knocked in 13 goals during the Trotters' ultimately disappointing 1999–2000 season, although he missed out on the chance to help his team-mates in the play-off semi-final second leg at Ipswich after limping off injured in the first clash.

The skilful forward did score a cracker in the first leg, however, cutting in to deliciously curl a 20-yard effort with unnerving precision beyond the dive of Richard Wight.

The Icelandic star proved he was capable of featuring regularly on the scoresheet and, following Sam Allardyce's confirmation that he was resigned to losing the services of Gudjohnsen for the 2000–01 season, Chelsea boss Gianluca Vialli snapped him up for a fee of £4 million in June.

Cracker: Eidur Gudjohnsen

SUTTON
9

COMPARATIVE TABLES

Debates will inevitably rage about which team is the best, which players are better than others and which referee is the strictest in the league. Now you can settle all those arguments with the definitive guide to the 1999–2000 Premiership season. Our comparative tables show how teams fared relative to each other, how the top 20 players ranked in certain categories and who were the top players of the season.

This section is divided up to analyse key aspects of the game.

THE TEAMS

All the Premiership teams are compared and contrasted over a number of categories. Find out which team were the best and worst passers, tacklers and defenders, plus which sides had the best and worst disciplinary records.

THE PLAYERS

The top 20 players in each category are compared and contrasted to highlight the best goalscorers, passers, tacklers and goalkeepers, as well as the players with the poorest disciplinary records.

THE INDEX

Who was the best player in each position and who was the most influential player of the season? The Opta Index reveals all.

TEAMS OF THE SEASON

Everybody's favourite pastime with a twist. Opta select their teams of the season based on actual performance in key areas.

REFEREES

An in-depth look at the disciplinary record of the 1999–2000 season in terms of the fouls and penalties awarded and yellow and red cards issued by referees.

THE TEAMS

How did your team rate against the other Premiership sides in key categories? You will find the answer in this section. All 20 teams are featured in each table and are ranked according to a key category which will be explained below each chart.

The tables will show you the main areas of strength and weakness within each team and will go some way to explaining why certain teams were successful and why others struggled over the course of the 1999–2000 season.

For example on page 610 you will see that Watford managed a goals-to-shots ratio of just 9.7% compared with Manchester United's 19.0%. This shows how the Hornets had to attempt nearly twice as many shots to score a goal as the Premiership Champions, which is clearly a key factor in the relative success of each team.

You can discover which team scored the most headed goals, which won the most tackles, which earned the most disciplinary points and which side suffered most at the hands of their opponents.

There is an explanation beneath each of the charts showing how the ranking is calculated and how to access the information.

The most important table of all, of course, is the Premiership league table. Opposite you will see how all 20 teams finished in the 1999–2000 Premiership season, their home and away records and what they achieved.

Manchester United won the title by a record 18 points from Arsenal, who finished second and qualified for the Champions League. Third-placed Leeds United also qualified for the 2000–01 Champions League, but they will enter the competition only if they progress past a qualifying round. If they are eliminated at that stage, they will enter the UEFA Cup.

Liverpool's fourth position secured them a spot in the UEFA Cup alongside Worthington Cup winners Leicester City and FA Cup winners Chelsea, while Aston Villa will enter the Intertoto Cup in a bid to reach the UEFA Cup.

Watford were the first side to be relegated when Bradford City beat Sunderland on Easter Monday. The Hornets were joined by Sheffield Wednesday after the Owls' 37th match – the 3–3 draw away at Arsenal – and Wimbledon, who were leapfrogged by Bradford on the last day of the season and were relegated after 14 seasons in the top flight.

FA CARLING PREMIERSHIP
SEASON 1999–2000

		HOME					AWAY						
	PLD	W	D	L	F	A	W	D	L	F	A	PTS	GD
Man Utd	38	15	4	0	59	16	13	3	3	38	29	91	52
Arsenal	38	14	3	2	42	17	8	4	7	31	26	73	30
Leeds Utd	38	12	2	5	29	18	9	4	6	29	25	69	15
Liverpool	38	11	4	4	28	13	8	6	5	23	17	67	21
Chelsea	38	12	5	2	35	12	6	6	7	18	22	65	19
Aston Villa	38	8	8	3	23	12	7	5	7	23	23	58	11
Sunderland	38	10	6	3	28	17	6	4	9	29	39	58	1
Leicester	38	10	3	6	31	24	6	4	9	24	31	55	0
West Ham	38	11	5	3	32	23	4	5	10	20	30	55	-1
Tottenham	38	10	3	6	40	26	5	5	9	17	23	53	8
Newcastle	38	10	5	4	42	20	4	5	10	21	34	52	9
Middlesbro	38	8	5	6	23	26	6	5	8	23	26	52	-6
Everton	38	7	9	3	36	21	5	5	9	23	28	50	10
Coventry	38	12	1	6	38	22	0	7	12	9	32	44	-7
Southampton	38	8	4	7	26	22	4	4	11	19	40	44	-17
Derby Co	38	6	3	10	22	25	3	8	8	22	32	38	-13
Bradford	38	6	8	5	26	29	3	1	15	12	39	36	-30
Wimbledon	38	6	7	6	30	28	1	5	13	16	46	33	-28
Sheff Wed	38	6	3	10	21	23	2	4	13	17	47	31	-32
Watford	38	5	4	10	24	31	1	2	16	11	46	24	-42

GOALSCORING

	GOALS/SHOTS RATIO	GOALS SCORED (GOALS PER MATCH)
Man Utd	19.0%	97 (2.55)
Everton	15.5%	59 (1.55)
Sunderland	15.2%	57 (1.50)
Leicester	14.9%	55 (1.45)
Newcastle	14.9%	63 (1.66)
Arsenal	12.5%	73 (1.92)
Aston Villa	12.4%	46 (1.21)
Southampton	12.2%	45 (1.18)
West Ham	12.1%	52 (1.37)
Coventry	12.0%	47 (1.24)
Tottenham	11.9%	57 (1.50)
Derby Co	11.9%	44 (1.16)
Wimbledon	11.8%	46 (1.21)
Middlesbro	11.2%	46 (1.21)
Leeds Utd	11.1%	58 (1.53)
Chelsea	10.7%	53 (1.39)
Bradford	10.6%	38 (1.00)
Liverpool	10.4%	51 (1.34)
Sheff Wed	10.3%	38 (1.00)
Watford	9.7%	35 (0.92)

There were two new goalscoring records set in the 1999–2000 Premiership. Manchester United netted 97 times in the league, more than any side has ever managed in the Premiership, while the combined total of 1,060 strikes registered by all clubs throughout the 1999–2000 campaign is the highest tally reached since the Premiership was reduced to 20 clubs.

For the second successive season Manchester United were the deadliest team in front of goal, with an outstanding 19% of all efforts finding the net.

As in the 1998–99 season, the Champions averaged more than two goals per game and were the only side in the top flight to achieve this feat. Indeed, no fewer than eight United players chipped in with at least five goals in the league – more than at any other club.

Thanks largely to the predatory skills of Kevin Phillips, Premiership newcomers Sunderland were the third-deadliest side, while Everton, Newcastle and Leicester saw their goals-to-shots ratios increase by more than four percentage points in 1999–2000 on the previous term.

Leicester's Tony Cottee had a league-high goals-to-shots ratio of 32.5%, Kevin Campbell of Everton was a close second and Newcastle registered the 1999–2000's Premiership's biggest win – 8–0 at home to Sheffield Wednesday.

Crucially, three of Manchester United's biggest rivals – Leeds, Chelsea and Liverpool – all scored less frequently during 1999–2000 than they did in 1998–99. The trio occupied 15th, 16th and 18th spots respectively in the goals-to-shots table.

United's closest challengers Arsenal had more shots at goal than any other top-flight side, but with only 12.5% of strikes finding the net, they were no match for United either.

SHOOTING

	SHOOTING ACCURACY	SHOTS ON TARGET	SHOTS OFF TARGET
Southampton	53.1%	187	165
West Ham	51.7%	218	204
Man Utd	51.4%	255	241
Arsenal	49.8%	280	282
Sunderland	48.3%	181	194
Watford	48.1%	173	187
Liverpool	47.9%	230	250
Newcastle	47.9%	190	207
Coventry	46.7%	179	204
Sheff Wed	46.7%	163	186
Everton	46.5%	171	197
Leicester	45.7%	159	189
Tottenham	45.3%	205	248
Chelsea	45.2%	202	245
Derby Co	44.0%	159	202
Middlesbro	43.7%	172	222
Bradford	43.1%	151	199
Leeds Utd	42.9%	220	293
Aston Villa	42.3%	153	209
Wimbledon	40.2%	146	217

Opta statistics prove that teams in the 1999–2000 Premiership were more accurate in front of goal than they were during the 1998–99 campaign.

The average shooting accuracy for a top-flight side increased from 45.3% in 1998–99 to 46.6% in 1999–2000 – not surprising, considering that there were 101 more goals scored.

Southampton scored a mediocre 45 goals, but were surprisingly the most accurate of all sides in 1999–2000. The shot-shy Saints attempted just 352 goal efforts, but managed to strike 53.1% of these on target and they would surely have benefited from creating more shooting chances with such accuracy.

Perhaps a bigger surprise was the fact that the 1998–99 Premiership's most accurate side, Leeds United, were the third most profligate team in the 1999–2000 campaign, and this cost them dearly as their title challenge faltered.

The Yorkshire outfit finished with a shooting accuracy of 42.9%, a decline of more than six percentage points on 1998–99, and fired nearly 300 shots off target – more than any other side.

The only other top-flight teams who could boast a shooting accuracy greater than 50% were West Ham – who increased their ratio of shots on target from a below-par 44.5% in 1998–99 to 51.7% in 1999–2000 – and Manchester United.

United registered 255 shots on target during the season – second only to league rivals Arsenal who mustered 280 – to boost their accuracy to 51.4%, with the Gunners just below them.

Chelsea registered a below-average shooting accuracy for the second season running, Watford's 48.1% accuracy suggests that they were unfortunate not to net more than 35 goals, while Wimbledon tested 'keepers fewer times than any other Premiership side.

than any other team

PASSING OVERALL

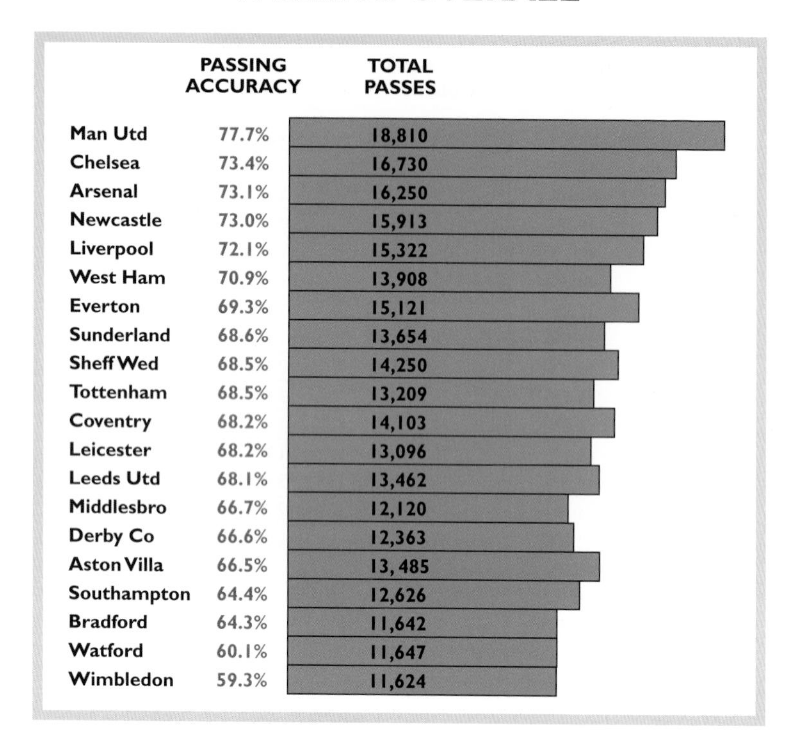

	PASSING ACCURACY	TOTAL PASSES
Man Utd	77.7%	18,810
Chelsea	73.4%	16,730
Arsenal	73.1%	16,250
Newcastle	73.0%	15,913
Liverpool	72.1%	15,322
West Ham	70.9%	13,908
Everton	69.3%	15,121
Sunderland	68.6%	13,654
Sheff Wed	68.5%	14,250
Tottenham	68.5%	13,209
Coventry	68.2%	14,103
Leicester	68.2%	13,096
Leeds Utd	68.1%	13,462
Middlesbro	66.7%	12,120
Derby Co	66.6%	12,363
Aston Villa	66.5%	13, 485
Southampton	64.4%	12,626
Bradford	64.3%	11,642
Watford	60.1%	11,647
Wimbledon	59.3%	11,624

The gulf between the top and the bottom of the Premiership is illustrated in Opta's overall passing table.

Manchester United completed 14,615 passes more than 2,000 clear of their closest rivals Chelsea and double the number of successful passes played by relegated clubs Wimbledon and Watford. United dominated the majority of matches they played in and made excellent use of the ball. In fact six of their stars were among the Premiership's top 15 for passes completed during the season.

As per the 1998–99 campaign, teams generally associated with a patient playing style are near the top of the passing table, although overall passing accuracy dropped in 1999–2000 compared to 1998–99 with more teams adopting a direct approach.

Arsenal looked to find Thierry Henry with long balls over the back line, Chelsea searched for the height of Chris Sutton or Tore Andre Flo, as did Newcastle with Alan Shearer and Duncan Ferguson, while Liverpool employed Titi Camara and latterly Emile Heskey as target men.

Newcomers Watford, Bradford and Sunderland replaced the more renowned passing sides Blackburn, Nottingham Forest and Charlton, and none of the sides promoted after the 1998–99 season came close to matching the three relegated teams in terms of passing accuracy.

Aston Villa saw the biggest decline of all 1999–2000 Premiership sides in their overall pass success rate compared to 1998–99. Villa adopted a more direct style of play to exploit Dion Dublin's height and Julian Joachim's speed with long balls into the opposition half; hence their passing accuracy slumped 9.8%.

Wimbledon struggled to come to terms with Egil Olsen's zonal system of play and were the worst passers in the top-flight for the second successive season.

59.3% Wimbledon were the only team not

PASSING IN OPPOSITION HALF

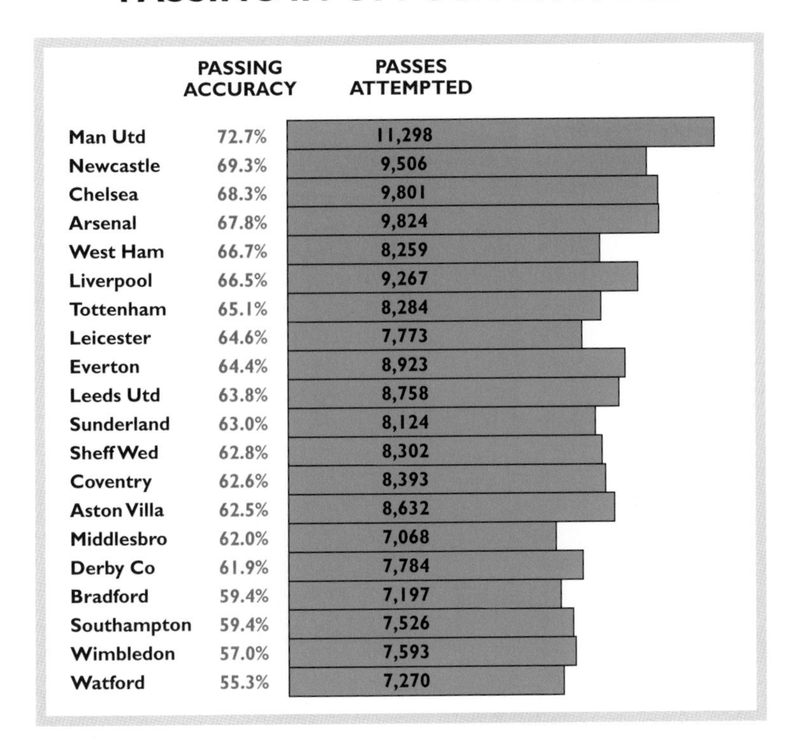

	PASSING ACCURACY	PASSES ATTEMPTED
Man Utd	72.7%	11,298
Newcastle	69.3%	9,506
Chelsea	68.3%	9,801
Arsenal	67.8%	9,824
West Ham	66.7%	8,259
Liverpool	66.5%	9,267
Tottenham	65.1%	8,284
Leicester	64.6%	7,773
Everton	64.4%	8,923
Leeds Utd	63.8%	8,758
Sunderland	63.0%	8,124
Sheff Wed	62.8%	8,302
Coventry	62.6%	8,393
Aston Villa	62.5%	8,632
Middlesbro	62.0%	7,068
Derby Co	61.9%	7,784
Bradford	59.4%	7,197
Southampton	59.4%	7,526
Wimbledon	57.0%	7,593
Watford	55.3%	7,270

Most teams are comfortable enough on the ball in their own territory, but the real test of a side's ability is what they do with possession in their opponent's half. Not surprisingly it is Manchester United who feature at the top of Opta's table for passes attempted in the opposition half in 1999–2000.

No other team nailed more than 70% of all passes in their opponents' territory and United were also the only top-flight side to attempt at least 10,000 outside of their own half.

Newcastle were top of this table during 1998–99 and improved from fourth in terms of overall passing to second when seeking to pick out a colleague in the opposition half for 1999–2000.

Sheffield Wednesday struggled to make an impression in the final third and were not helped by a passing accuracy that fell nearly six percentage points in their opponents' half – dropping them from ninth in the overall passing table to 12th in this table.

While distribution success rates in opposition territory in 1999–2000 were down across the board on 1998–99, Tottenham and Everton suffered the smallest decline. Spurs were 14th in 1998–99 but improved to seventh in 1999–2000, while Everton went from 19th to ninth, thanks in part to Kevin Campbell's ability to hold on to possession in the attacking domain.

Seventy per cent of all passes made by Wimbledon were played in the opposition half – the highest ratio of any top-flight side – and as a result there is little difference between the Dons' overall pass completion rate and the success they enjoyed further up field.

Meanwhile, Premiership defenders dealt very effectively with Watford's offensive threat, and the Hornets replace the Dons at the foot of this table.

to complete more than 60% of their passes

SHORT PASSING

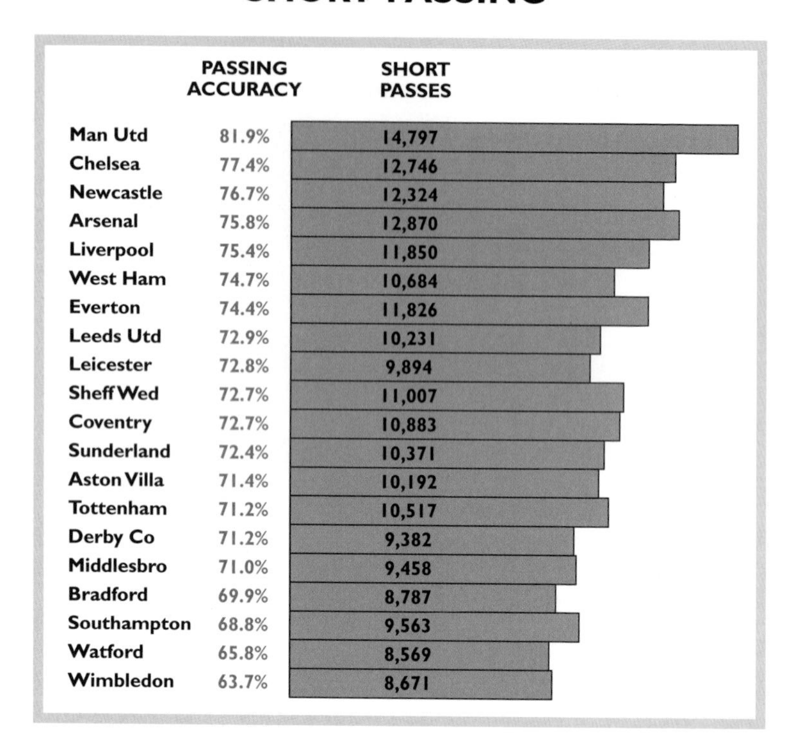

PASSING ACCURACY
SHORT PASSES
Man Utd 81.9% 14,797
Chelsea 77.4% 12,746
Newcastle 76.7% 12,324
Arsenal 75.8% 12,870
Liverpool 75.4% 11,850
West Ham 74.7% 10,684
Everton 74.4% 11,826
Leeds Utd 72.9% 10,231
Leicester 72.8% 9,894
Sheff Wed 72.7% 11,007
Coventry 72.7% 10,883
Sunderland 72.4% 10,371
Aston Villa 71.4% 10,192
Tottenham 71.2% 10,517
Derby Co 71.2% 9,382
Middlesbro 71.0% 9,458
Bradford 69.9% 8,787
Southampton 68.8% 9,563
Watford 65.8% 8,569
Wimbledon 63.7% 8,671

One of the secrets of Manchester United's success is their ability to keep hold of the ball for long periods and dictate the game, frustrating the opposition and making it difficult for them to settle.

Opta's stats illustrate just how competent they were at doing so during the 1999–2000 Premiership. United were the only team to complete more than 80% of short passes – defined as those struck under a distance of 25 yards – and none of their rivals came close to the 14,797 passes they played in total.

It was the second consecutive season that United have been the most accurate short-range distributors, and in fact the top three in terms of accuracy remained unchanged from 1998–99 to 1999–2000, with Chelsea and then Newcastle below the Champions.

Sheffield Wednesday were the fifth-most accurate side in 1998–99 in terms of short distribution, but one of their downfalls in 1999–2000 was that they gave far too many simple passes away to the opposition. Their accuracy subsequently dropped more than 10 percentage points in the latter season – the biggest decline of any top-flight side.

Surprisingly, Tottenham played a higher ratio of short passes than any of their rivals. While they connected with a below-average 71.2% of these, Spurs still improved to 14th in the 1999–2000 table compared to 19th the season before.

Leeds and Everton both moved up eight places in the 1999–2000 standings from their respective positions in the 1998–99 table. Nick Barmby, John Collins and Don Hutchison linked well for Walter Smith's side, while David O'Leary's youngsters made excellent progress in the 1999–2000 Premiership and showed greater composure and control on the ball than in the previous campaign.

4,013 Manchester United made more

LONG PASSING

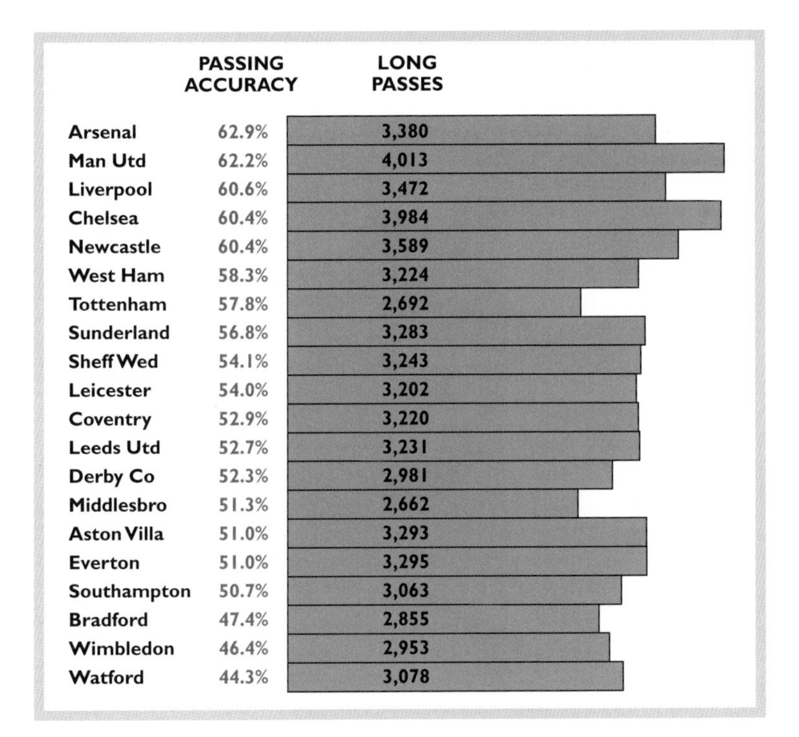

	PASSING ACCURACY	LONG PASSES
Arsenal	62.9%	3,380
Man Utd	62.2%	4,013
Liverpool	60.6%	3,472
Chelsea	60.4%	3,984
Newcastle	60.4%	3,589
West Ham	58.3%	3,224
Tottenham	57.8%	2,692
Sunderland	56.8%	3,283
Sheff Wed	54.1%	3,243
Leicester	54.0%	3,202
Coventry	52.9%	3,220
Leeds Utd	52.7%	3,231
Derby Co	52.3%	2,981
Middlesbro	51.3%	2,662
Aston Villa	51.0%	3,293
Everton	51.0%	3,295
Southampton	50.7%	3,063
Bradford	47.4%	2,855
Wimbledon	46.4%	2,953
Watford	44.3%	3,078

It will not surprise too many people to learn that of all the sides in the 1999–2000 Premiership, Watford, Wimbledon and Bradford City relied most heavily on the long ball.

More than a quarter of all passes played by the Hornets covered a distance of more than 25 yards – the highest ratio in the league – with Wimbledon and then Bradford not far behind.

Throughout the season, all three teams were often under intense pressure in their own half and forced to hurry the ball upfield, with precious few opportunities to take their time and pick out their intended target. As a result, they were the only top-flight sides not to connect with at least 50% of long passes, and thus occupy the bottom three spots.

As was the case in 1998–99, Arsenal were the most accurate long passers in the 1999–2000 Premiership. Nwankwo Kanu and Patrick Vieira completed an impressive ratio of long passes, while in Thierry Henry the Gunners had a willing and competent target to aim for.

Manchester United's hugely-successful, direct style of attacking was founded mainly on their ability to pass accurately over distance, from all areas of the pitch. The Champions completed more long balls than any of their rivals and Dwight Yorke had the best completion rate of any Premiership player attempting at least a hundred such passes.

Chelsea and Liverpool also fared well when striking long balls, thanks largely to the accuracy of their midfield men, while Newcastle's strike duo Alan Shearer and Duncan Ferguson were excellent foils for the likes of Kieron Dyer to pick out.

Everton were less comfortable when hitting long passes compared to short, while Middlesbrough went one worse than in 1998–99, attempting fewer long passes than any other side.

ong passes than any other side

CROSSING

	CROSSING ACCURACY	CROSSES COMPLETED	CROSSES AWAY
Newcastle	34.4%	310	591
Derby Co	33.0%	232	470
Leicester	33.0%	290	589
Chelsea	32.8%	285	584
Aston Villa	31.9%	255	545
Sunderland	31.8%	267	572
Wimbledon	31.4%	272	595
West Ham	30.8%	234	525
Arsenal	30.4%	280	642
Tottenham	29.7%	236	558
Middlesbro	29.7%	184	436
Leeds Utd	29.2%	228	552
Sheff Wed	28.7%	196	488
Man Utd	27.8%	267	692
Southampton	27.6%	203	533
Bradford	27.4%	194	514
Everton	27.2%	182	487
Coventry	25.6%	181	527
Watford	25.5%	179	523
Liverpool	25.0%	184	553

With the aerial strength of Alan Shearer and Duncan Ferguson in attack and the precision delivery of Nolberto Solano on the wing, no Premiership team could match Newcastle in terms of cross completion. They were the only team to nail more than a third of all centres and moved from 12th in the 1998–99 crossing table to first in the 1999–2000 standings.

Derby County were again among the best crossers in the Premiership, finishing second behind Newcastle. The Rams used Branko Strupar's height effectively when centring the ball, with the alert Malcolm Christie another good target.

Leicester shot up from 19th in the 1998–99 standings to third in the following campaign, with Steve Guppy supplying some quality service to Emile Heskey and then highly effective stand-in striker Matt Elliott.

Chelsea picked out their tall strikers frequently and completed a fourth-best 32.8% of crosses, while Arsenal were helped by Thierry Henry's aerial ability and went from last in 1998–99 to ninth in the 1999–2000 crossing table.

Sheffield Wednesday were the 1998–99 Premiership's most accurate crossers, but they struggled to make an impact in 1999–2000 up front, with the diminutive Gilles De Bilde replacing target man Andy Booth, and slumped to 13th in the crossing table.

Southampton were largely deprived of the services of Matt Le Tissier and fell from second-best crossers in 1998–99 to 15th in the following campaign, scoring just five times with headers all season.

Despite David Beckham and Ryan Giggs's reputation, Manchester United had a below-par crossing accuracy, while without a recognised target man, Liverpool recorded the worst completion rate of all.

620 Middlesbrough attempted fewer crosse

TACKLING

	TACKLES WON %	TACKLES WON	TACKLES LOST
Arsenal	59.3%	619	425
West Ham	55.9%	534	422
Leicester	55.6%	600	479
Chelsea	54.6%	545	453
Leeds Utd	54.5%	515	430
Everton	54.2%	590	499
Derby Co	52.6%	543	490
Coventry	52.5%	516	466
Bradford	52.3%	562	512
Man Utd	51.9%	526	487
Sheff Wed	51.7%	552	515
Sunderland	51.3%	521	495
Wimbledon	51.1%	453	433
Middlesbro	50.8%	517	500
Aston Villa	50.6%	509	496
Newcastle	50.4%	474	466
Liverpool	50.3%	546	539
Tottenham	49.6%	550	559
Southampton	49.2%	479	494
Watford	47.3%	469	522

Arsenal possess some of the most gifted individuals in the Premiership, but they showed in 1999–2000 there is ample graft to go with their craft.

With the likes of Patrick Vieira, Emmanuel Petit and Tony Adams in the side, the north Londoners made more successful tackles than any of their top-flight rivals and won the highest percentage of challenges in the league.

West Ham were near the bottom of the 1998–99 tackling table but they improved massively during 1999–2000 and were Arsenal's closest rivals in terms of tackle success. The Hammers had to battle hard in the face of an extended injury list, with Marc-Vivien Foe, Frank Lampard and Igor Stimac in particular proving highly-effective ball winners.

But the most significant changes from 1998–99 to 1999–2000 involved Wimbledon and Leicester. The Foxes were the second-least effective tacklers in 1998–99 but leapt to third best in 1999–2000. Martin O'Neill's side won a second-highest 600 tackles while committing the second-fewest fouls, with the tough-but-fair approach of Neil Lennon, Robbie Savage and Muzzy Izzet reaping its reward – eighth place in the Premiership and Worthington Cup success.

Egil Olsen's zonal system of play had huge repercussions on Wimbledon's season. In 1998–99 the Dons were second in terms of tackle success rate, but slumped to 13th in the 1999–2000 campaign and won fewer challenges than any Premiership side. The "Crazy Gang" spirit that had made the Dons successful in the past seemed to be lacking, and Opta's stats back this up.

While there was no doubting Watford's commitment, they lacked strength in the tackle and had trouble winning back possession, recording the lowest tackle success rate in the division.

and corners than any other side

DISCIPLINE – FOULS CONCEDED

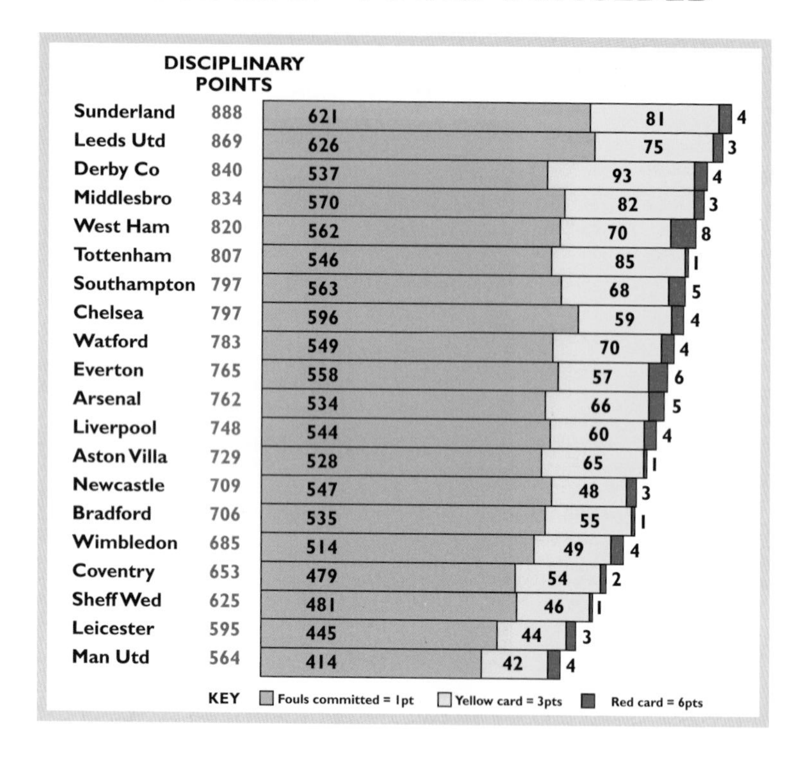

From Dean Blackwell's 16th-minute dismissal on the opening day against Watford, to Alex Rae's sending-off for his elbow on David Ginola in the last minute of the final weekend, the issue of discipline was never far from the spotlight in the 1999–2000 Premiership.

A letter from the FA to all Premier League officials in January, urging greater leniency towards players, resulted in a 46% reduction in the number of red cards and a 31% drop in yellow cards shown in the second half of the season compared to the first. Consequently 1999–2000 saw 135 fewer yellow cards and one less red than 1998–99.

Despite this, Sunderland accumulated 888 disciplinary points to head Opta's sinners table – just two fewer than 1998–99's worst offenders Everton. The Black Cats had four players dismissed, while Chris Makin and Stefan Schwarz both reached double figures for cautions.

David O'Leary's Leeds sit second in the 1999–2000 discipline table, having committed more fouls than any other side for the second season running.

Derby County accrued the most yellow cards in the league and were third in Opta's table. West Ham, two places below them, suffered the most dismissals.

Everton and Chelsea were first and second respectively in the 1998–99 sinners rankings, but cleaned up their acts noticeably in 1999–2000 – Everton, with 48% fewer cautions falling to 10th and Chelsea, having reduced their yellow card count by 26, dropping to eighth.

Despite two high-profile spats with officials involving skipper Roy Keane, Manchester United were the best-disciplined side, committing the fewest fouls and earning the fewest yellow cards. Leicester finished 19th in this table for the second season running, just below 1998–99's saintly Sheffield Wednesday.

DISCIPLINE – FOULS WON

Team	Disciplinary Points	Fouls committed	Yellow cards	Red cards
Tottenham	913	622	79	9
Leeds Utd	887	560	95	7
Arsenal	880	619	79	4
Leicester	847	601	72	5
Sunderland	810	579	71	3
Middlesbro	808	565	71	5
Everton	790	541	73	5
West Ham	782	578	62	3
Liverpool	760	520	70	5
Newcastle	753	534	71	1
Derby Co	746	545	61	3
Chelsea	737	524	63	4
Bradford	723	543	54	3
Aston Villa	719	509	64	3
Watford	709	541	52	2
Southampton	700	493	69	
Coventry	685	520	51	2
Man Utd	671	482	53	5
Sheff Wed	586	490	32	
Wimbledon	470	383	27	1

KEY: Fouls committed = 1pt; Yellow card = 3pts; Red card = 6pts

Martin O'Neill learned his trade under the iron fist of Brian Clough, and Opta's stats suggest he instilled that kind of discipline in his Leicester side.

The Foxes were the third most fouled team in the league in 1999–2000, while Emile Heskey drew 66 fouls at Filbert Street and 100 in all during the season – more than any other top-flight player. Yet Leicester responded with the second-fewest illegal challenges in the top flight and finished 19th in the sinners table.

Tottenham's opponents were shown a league-high nine red cards against the north Londoners and accrued 913 disciplinary points in total, with David Ginola just behind Heskey in terms of fouls won – all of which left Spurs at the top of Opta's sinned against table.

David O'Leary encouraged Leeds United's fully committed approach to their football, and matches involving Leeds tended to be highly competitive. Teams playing against them were shown an average of 2.5 yellow cards per match and a total of seven red cards, as they finished just below Spurs in this table.

While incidents such as the dismissals for Patrick Vieira at Upton Park and Martin Keown and Freddie Ljungberg at Tottenham portrayed them in a bad light, Arsenal in fact drew more fouls from opponents than any other side barring Spurs and finished high up in the sinned against rankings.

Given the fact that they finished below halfway in the sinned against table, Derby's record of collecting the most cautions in the league seems to suggest that the Rams were generally the aggressors in their matches.

Manchester United finished 18th in the sinned against table and although they were the second-least fouled side during the season, only two teams had more players sent off against them.

than any other side in the top flight

GOALS CONCEDED

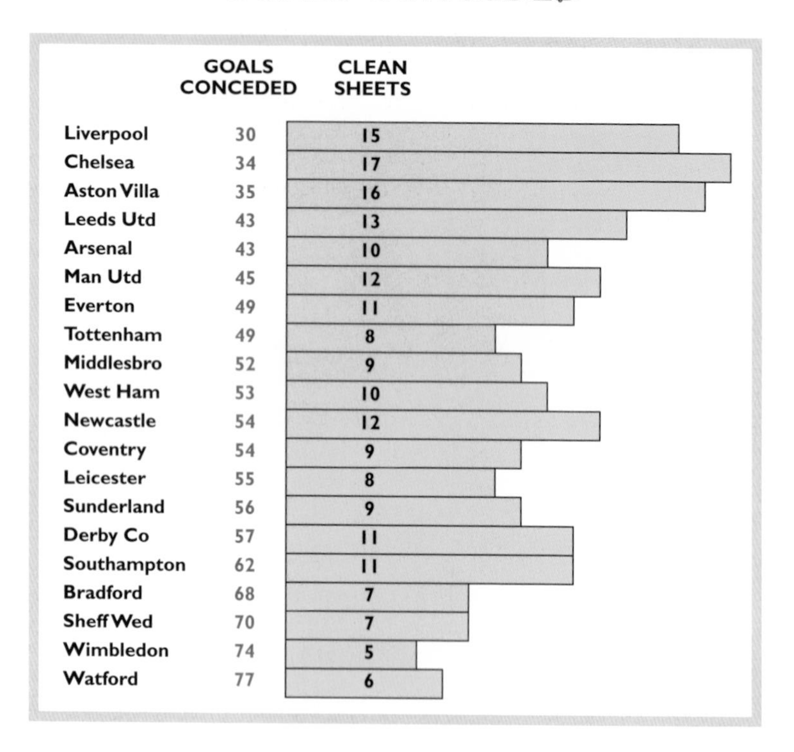

GOALS CONCEDED
CLEAN SHEETS
Liverpool 30 15
Chelsea 34 17
Aston Villa 35 16
Leeds Utd 43 13
Arsenal 43 10
Man Utd 45 12
Everton 49 11
Tottenham 49 8
Middlesbro 52 9
West Ham 53 10
Newcastle 54 12
Coventry 54 9
Leicester 55 8
Sunderland 56 9
Derby Co 57 11
Southampton 62 11
Bradford 68 7
Sheff Wed 70 7
Wimbledon 74 5
Watford 77 6

Gerard Houllier shored up the Liverpool defence during the summer of 1999 with the captures of Sander Westerveld, Stephane Henchoz and Sami Hyypia, and in doing so created the Premiership's meanest back-line.

Westerveld stopped 76% of all shots faced and kept 14 clean sheets and Hyypia made 538 clearances as the Reds conceded just 30 goals – 19 fewer than they did in 1998–99 when they finished 10th in the goals against table.

Chelsea's Ed De Goey kept 16 clean sheets in the Premiership, more than any other 'keeper, but the Blues could not take advantage of a strong defence and won just four times when their opponents scored – a major factor in their failure to qualify for the Champions League.

Aston Villa were the only other side to concede less than a goal per game, but were also hindered by a relatively poor goalscoring record. Twelve top-flight sides registered more strikes than Villa, who only qualified for the Intertoto Cup thanks to their superior goal difference over Sunderland.

Arsenal's new-look defence failed to live up to 1998–99 standards when they set a Premiership record for the fewest goals conceded. They shipped 43 goals as David Seaman recorded the lowest saves-to-shots ratio of any regular 'keeper.

Manchester United's attacking style meant opponents often caught them out at the back, but this was of little concern to the Champions thanks to their phenomenal scoring record.

Meanwhile Derby County went from having the sixth best defence in 1998–99 to the sixth worse a year later, and consequently they struggled in the 1999–2000 Premiership.

It is no coincidence that the three teams who conceded the most goals were relegated from the Premiership.

16 Ed De Goey kept more clean sheets

TEAM RECORDS – SHOTS, PASSES, OFFSIDES, FOULS

There is nothing more frustrating for the fans than to see their team dominate a game, yet fail to take their chances, or to be constantly brought to book by those in charge. Here, Opta show the matches in which one team were keeping either the officials or the opposing defence extremely busy.

MOST SHOTS IN ONE GAME

MATCH	SHOTS	(ON TARGET)	RESULT
Bradford v CHELSEA	29	(11)	1–1
ARSENAL v Watford	28	(10)	1–0
LEEDS v Middlesbro	25	(13)	0–0
ARSENAL v Everton	24	(13)	4–1
ARSENAL v Coventry	24	(11)	3–0

Arsene Wenger's Gunners lived up to their moniker in 1999–2000 firing in 562 shots in total – nearly 50 more than nearest challengers Leeds United.

Not surprisingly, Arsenal featured three times in the top five for most shots attempted in a single match by a team.

But no side could match Chelsea's efforts away to Bradford, when the Blues attempted 29 shots – roughly one every three minutes. Incredibly, the Bantams held on for a point.

MOST PASSES IN ONE GAME

The 1999–2000 Premiership's most prolific passers – Manchester United – occupy four of the top five spots for the highest number of successful passes made in a match by a team.

Ironically, though, it was against the champions that the record for distribution completed was set for the 1999–2000 campaign, when Chelsea connected with 524 attempted passes at Stamford Bridge. The dismissal of Nicky Butt allowed Gianluca Vialli's side to dominate the game and run out 5–0 victors.

TEAM		OPPONENTS	PASSES COMPLETED
CHELSEA	v	Man Utd (h)	524
MAN UTD	v	Everton (a)	518
MAN UTD	v	Derby (h)	514
MAN UTD	v	Wimbledon (h)	495
MAN UTD	v	Tottenham (a)	493

MOST OFFSIDES IN ONE GAME

TEAM		OPPONENTS	OFFSIDES
EVERTON	v	Bradford (h)	13
COVENTRY	v	Newcastle (a)	12
MIDDLESBRO	v	Wimbledon (a)	11
COVENTRY	v	Derby (h)	11
LIVERPOOL	v	Derby (a)	11

Everton's players strayed offside 179 times overall in the 1999–2000 Premiership, more often than any of their rivals. At home to Bradford City they were at their worst, with an offside flag raised 13 times against the Toffees during the 90 minutes.

Coventry also had difficulties timing their runs on occasion. Away at Newcastle, seven different players strayed beyond the last defender for a combined total of 12 offsides, while Noel Whelan was flagged a league-high eight times at home to Derby.

MOST FOULS IN ONE GAME

Although Chelsea and Newcastle committed 28 fouls apiece in their matches with Tottenham and Sheffield Wednesday respectively – the most in a single fixture by any side – they collected just seven yellow cards between them from these encounters.

In contrast, West Ham committed one fewer foul in their clash with Arsenal at Upton Park but had six players cautioned and one dismissed.

Meanwhile Liverpool's 26 fouls away to Aston Villa also resulted in six yellow cards and one red.

TEAM		OPPONENTS	FOULS
NEWCASTLE	v	Tottenham (a)	28
CHELSEA	v	Sheff Wed (a)	28
WEST HAM	v	Arsenal (a)	27
LIVERPOOL	v	Aston Villa (a)	26
SUNDERLAND	v	Derby (a)	26

NUMBER OF MATCHES LOST AFTER LEADING

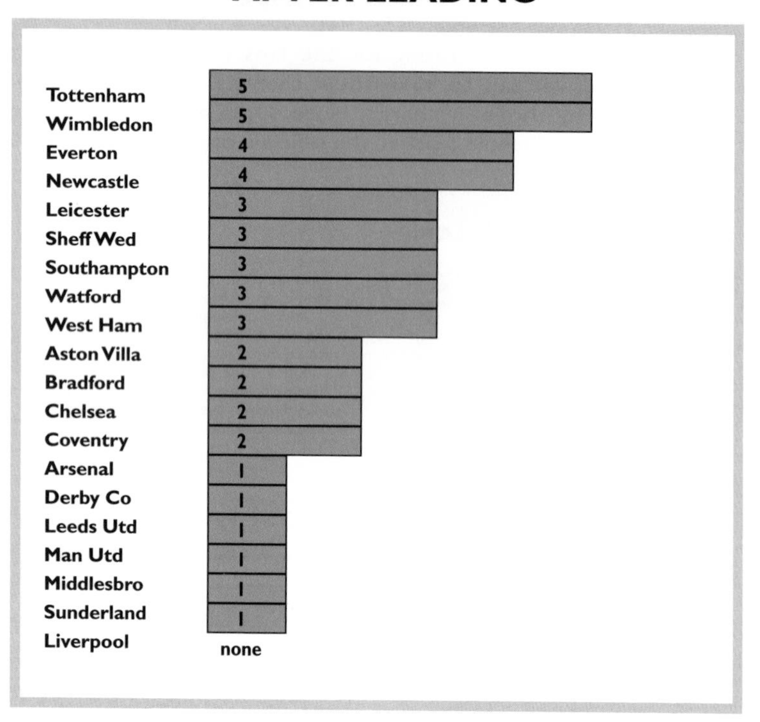

For sheer unpredictability, White Hart Lane was the best place to watch Premiership football during 1999–2000.

Eight of the 19 league matches played at the home of Tottenham Hotspur saw one side take the lead, only for the other to come back and beat them. This worked in Tottenham's favour on four occasions, but against Leeds United, Leicester, Middlesbrough and Aston Villa, Spurs took the lead only to squander it and ultimately lose the match.

George Graham's side also succumbed to a fightback by Middlesbrough at The Riverside Stadium, and along with Wimbledon they head the table for teams who lost the most matches after being in front at one stage.

The Dons will rue the fact that they were guilty of letting an advantage slip five times during the campaign – if they had held on for victory in just one of those matches they would be playing Premiership football in 2000–01.

Ruud Gullit's departure from St James's Park was precipitated by Newcastle's indifferent form in the early stages of the 1999–2000 campaign. In the five matches that Gullit oversaw, The Magpies lost three times after taking a lead, including a four-goal demolition in only 20 minutes at the hands of Southampton, and the 2–1 reverse against bitter rivals Sunderland was the result that led to the Dutchman leaving Newcastle.

Under Bobby Robson, the Geordies found much-needed stability, and lost only once more from a winning position throughout the rest of the season.

Although Liverpool lost their way towards the end of the campaign, they were tough opponents to face. The Reds were the only side not to lose a match after taking the lead, while six teams, including Leeds, Arsenal and Manchester United lost just once after being in front.

0 Liverpool were the only team not to lose a

NUMBER OF MATCHES WON AFTER BEING BEHIND

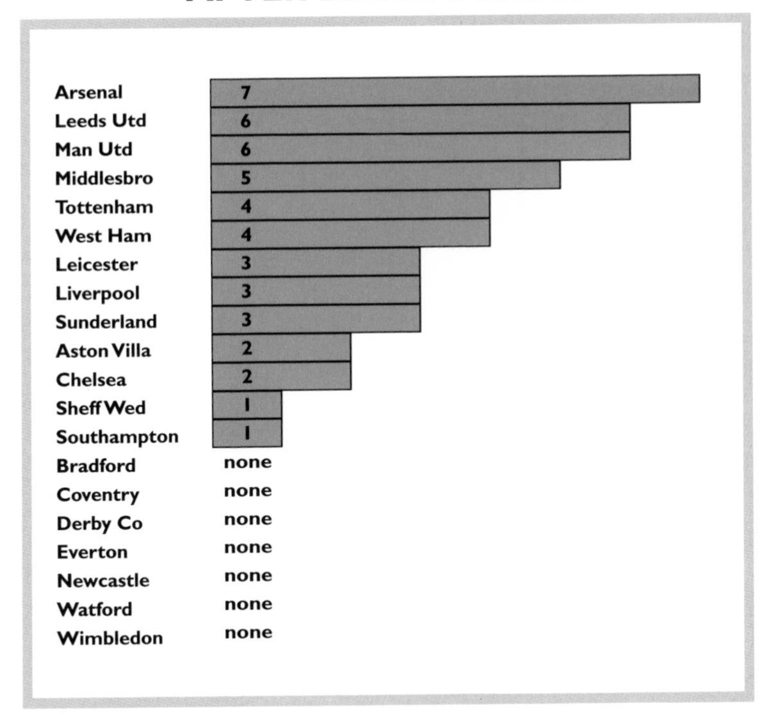

Arsenal were the comeback kings of the 1999–2000 Premiership. On seven occasions during the season, the north Londoners fell behind in a match only to come back and claim all three league points.

There was arguably no more dramatic comeback throughout the campaign than Arsenal's Kanu-inspired reversal at Stamford Bridge, when the African star thumped home three goals in the final 16 minutes of their match with Chelsea, to turn a two-goal deficit around to a 3–2 Gunners' victory.

Kanu also scored twice away to Wimbledon to help Arsenal to a 3–1 victory, while a late strike after coming on as a substitute at home to Aston Villa helped wrap up another three points for the Gunners after they had fallen behind to the visitors.

Generally the more successful teams in the 1999–2000 Premiership were those who responded most positively to going a goal behind in a match – as is certainly the case with England's trio of Champions League qualifiers.

Leeds United and Manchester United managed six wins from a losing position, and along with Arsenal they make up the top three for sides who most frequently reversed a scoreline.

Bryan Robson's Middlesbrough also made a habit of fighting back from a goal down to win.

Boro did so five times during the season and were the only team to inflict a "double" on any of their rivals when coming from behind to beat Tottenham both at home and away.

Only four teams – Arsenal, Aston Vila, Southampton and West Ham – managed to turn a two-goal deficit into a victory, while seven sides, including relegated Watford and Wimbledon, never won a match after going a goal down.

Premiership game after taking the lead

FOUR OR MORE GOALS SCORED IN A MATCH

Team	Matches
Man Utd	10
Everton	7
Arsenal	4
Coventry	4
Leeds Utd	3
Sunderland	3
West Ham	3
Derby Co	3
Aston Villa	3
Chelsea	3
Newcastle	3
Bradford	2
Tottenham	2
Sheff Wed	2
Leicester	1
Liverpool	1
Southampton	1
Wimbledon	1
Middlesbro	none
Watford	none

Runaway league winners Manchester United clocked up a record 97 Premiership goals during the 1999–2000 campaign, netting an average of 2.55 goals per game.

Their biggest victory came when they walloped West Ham 7–1 in the midst of a run that saw them score at least four goals in four consecutive league matches.

In total, Alex Ferguson's side scored more than three goals in a match 10 times throughout the 1999–2000 season, with West Ham and Bradford City conceding at least four strikes in both their league matches against the Champions. Indeed, it is testament to United's killer instinct that they kept on piling forward in search of goals even if a game was clearly won.

Furthermore, four of the 13 hat-tricks netted during the league campaign were by United players – more than any other side – with a different player claiming the match ball each time.

Only Walter Smith's Everton came close to United's tally, with the Merseysiders scoring more than three goals in a match on seven occasions. Everton finished as the third-highest scoring side of 1999–2000 with 59 strikes to their name, but inconsistent form saw them finish a disappointing 13th in spite of their occasional excellence in front of goal.

The league's second highest scorers Arsenal bagged more than three goals in a game four times, as did Coventry City. Not surprisingly for a side that scored only nine away from home, City's four-goal shows were all at Highfield Road.

Only two sides failed to register more than three goals in a game at least once. Neither Middlesbrough nor the Premiership's lowest scorers Watford were able to muster four strikes in a match throughout the season, while although Bradford managed this feat twice, they did not win on either occasion.

FOUR OR MORE GOALS CONCEDED IN A MATCH

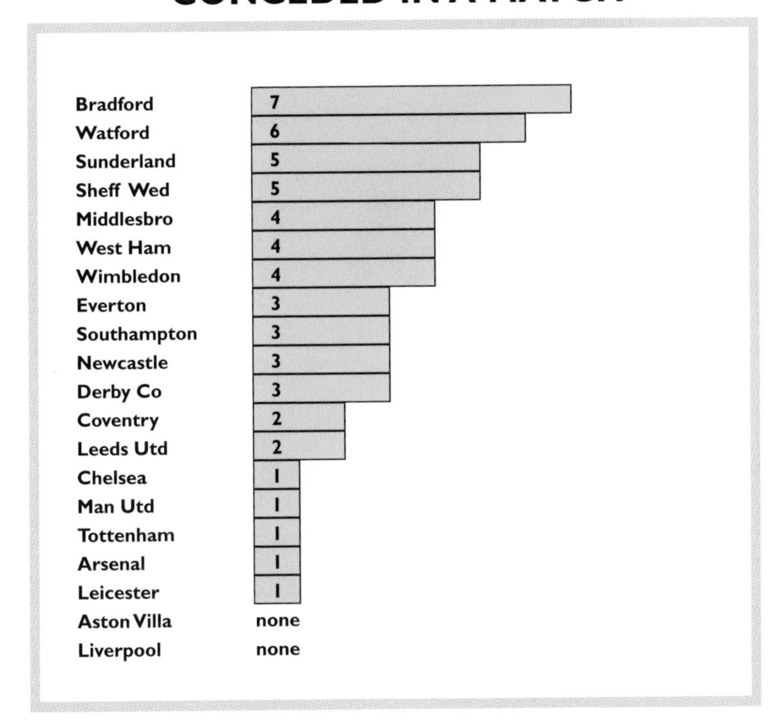

Ultimately it was a run of three wins in their last four matches – helped by a trio of clean sheets in these fixtures – that saved Bradford City from relegation in the 1999–2000 Premiership.

But coming into the final three weeks of the campaign, things were not looking good for the Bantams. Paul Jewell's side had conceded 20 goals in the six matches prior to their excellent victory away to Sunderland in April, with their opponents putting four goals past them in four of those matches.

No Premiership side shipped more than three goals in a match more often than Bradford, and five of their 20 losses were by a scoreline of 4–0 – the most frequent margin of defeat for the Bantams.

Graham Taylor's Watford conceded more goals than any other top-flight side during their Premiership campaign, and were involved in six matches that saw the opposition score at least four times.

The Hornets started the season well, however, and conceded only 11 goals in their opening 10 league fixtures before they were stung 4–1 by Manchester United at Old Trafford.

Despite finishing a highly-creditable seventh in the league, Peter Reid's Sunderland faltered on occasions, conceding four or more goals to five different sides during the campaign. The Black Cats can take some satisfaction, however, from the fact that not one of those five sides managed to achieve a win "double" over the Wearsiders.

Liverpool had the meanest defence throughout the season and were one of only two teams, along with Aston Villa, not to concede more than three goals in a single match. Indeed, such was Liverpool's overall strength at the back that only one opponent – Manchester United – scored more than twice against them in a single game.

WHERE GOALS SCORED

Team	Goals from outside box	Outside box (set-pieces)	Inside box (penalties)
Chelsea	5.7%	3 (0)	50 (1)
Everton	6.8%	4 (1)	55 (6)
Watford	8.6%	3 (0)	32 (2)
Wimbledon	8.7%	4 (1)	42 (1)
Tottenham	10.5%	6 (0)	51 (1)
Leicester	10.9%	6 (1)	49 (3)
Newcastle	11.1%	7 (1)	56 (6)
West Ham	11.5%	6 (1)	46 (2)
Coventry	12.8%	6 (1)	41 (5)
Man Utd	14.4%	14 (3)	83 (3)
Sheff Wed	15.8%	6 (0)	32 (4)
Sunderland	15.8%	9 (1)	48 (6)
Aston Villa	17.4%	8 (0)	38 (1)
Arsenal	17.8%	13 (0)	60 (3)
Middlesbro	19.6%	9 (2)	37 (6)
Bradford	21.1%	8 (1)	30 (5)
Derby Co	22.7%	10 (3)	34 (2)
Leeds Utd	24.1%	14 (3)	44 (4)
Liverpool	27.5%	14 (3)	37 (3)
Southampton	28.9%	13 (1)	32 (1)

KEY: Inside box (penalties) / Outside box (set-pieces)

Teams in the 1999–2000 Premiership scored 101 more goals than in the previous season, and notched a higher ratio of their strikes with efforts from inside the opponent's area.

Shooting accuracy from inside the area increased from 50.1% in 1998–99 to 52.1% a year later, as nearly 85% of goals scored in 1999–2000 were from shots within 18 yards of the goal – a rise of 1.6 percentage points on 1998–99.

Interestingly, there were an identical number of goals scored with shots struck from outside the area in 1999–2000 as in the previous year, with long-range efforts accounting for 163 goals in both seasons. There were 14 more penalties scored in 1999–2000 compared to 1998–99, with Bradford scoring 13% of all goals thus – the highest ratio in the league.

Southampton were the most accurate team in terms of close-range shooting in the 1999–2000 Premiership, but ironically they scored the lowest percentage of their goals from inside the area, with almost 30% coming from shots outside the box.

Leeds United had more long-range strikes at goal than any other side, with Liverpool their closest rivals, and both teams scored 14 times with shots from outside the area – a total matched only by Manchester United. Liverpool were the only team apart from Southampton to notch more than a quarter of all goals from distance, while 24.1% of Leeds' strikes were from outside the area.

Despite having excellent strikers of the ball like Gianfranco Zola and Frank Leboeuf at the club, Chelsea scored the lowest ratio of their goals from outside the area, and none direct from set pieces. Everton, Watford and Wimbledon scored less than 10% of goals from distance, with the Dons and the Toffees recording the worst and second-worst long-range shooting accuracy respectively.

WHERE GOALS CONCEDED

Team	Goals from outside box	Outside box (set-pieces)	Inside box (penalties)
Wimbledon	8.1%	6 (2)	68 (8)
Sheff Wed	10.0%	7 (0)	63 (4)
Derby Co	10.5%	6 (1)	51 (4)
Aston Villa	11.4%	4 (0)	31 (2)
Leeds Utd	11.6%	5 (0)	38 (2)
Leicester	12.7%	7 (1)	48 (3)
Coventry	14.8%	8 (0)	46 (4)
Man Utd	15.6%	7 (1)	38 (0)
Sunderland	16.1%	9 (1)	47 (4)
Tottenham	16.3%	8 (1)	41 (6)
Newcastle	16.7%	9 (2)	45 (1)
Watford	16.9%	13 (3)	64 (6)
West Ham	17.0%	9 (1)	44 (3)
Middlesbro	17.3%	9 (0)	43 (0)
Bradford	17.6%	12 (1)	56 (9)
Chelsea	17.6%	6 (1)	28 (2)
Southampton	19.4%	12 (2)	50 (4)
Liverpool	20.0%	6 (0)	24 (1)
Everton	20.4%	10 (2)	39 (2)
Arsenal	23.3%	10 (4)	33 (0)

KEY: Inside box (penalties) | Outside box (set-pieces)

As Opta's goals conceded table shows, the defensive shortcomings of Sheffield Wednesday and Wimbledon – and, crucially, their weakness inside the penalty area – played a major part in their relegation.

The Dons were the only top-flight side in the 1999–2000 Premiership to concede more than 90% of all goals from shots struck inside the area, and their cause was not helped by a league-high total of eight penalties beating Neil Sullivan. The Wimbledon 'keeper had to deal with 176 close-range shots on target – the most in the top flight.

Meanwhile nine out of every 10 goals conceded by the Owls came from efforts struck less than 18 yards out, with Kevin Pressman's saves-to-shots ratio from close-range shots of 50% the worst of any regular 'keeper.

In 1998–99, Derby protected their area effectively and conceded only 77.8% of all goals from shots struck inside the box, but this increased to 89.5% in 1999–2000 as they slumped to 16th in the league.

Aston Villa and Leeds also conceded the vast majority of goals from close-range efforts, thanks largely to the excellent way that David James and Nigel Martyn respectively coped with long-distance shots – conceding just eight such goals between them.

For the second season running, Arsenal conceded the highest ratio of goals from long-range efforts in the league. But rather than indicating their defensive strength inside the box, this points more to the difficulty David Seaman and Alex Manninger had in dealing with shots struck from distance. Their combined saves-to-shots ratio from long-range efforts of 74.3% was the lowest recorded at any club.

Liverpool restricted their opponents to just 24 goals from shots inside the box.

number of goals scored in a Premiership season

HOW GOALS WERE SCORED

	TOTAL GOALS	Headers	Own goals	Left foot	Right foot
Aston Villa	46	17	1	5	23
Wimbledon	46	16	3	9	18
Chelsea	53	17	5	6	25
Newcastle	63	19	4	9	31
Tottenham	57	16	3	5	33
Bradford	38	10	1	8	19
Leicester	55	14	3	9	29
Derby Co	44	10	1	7	26
Sunderland	57	10		10	37
Middlesbro	46	8	2	12	24
Watford	35	6		9	20
Everton	59	10	2	17	30
Sheff Wed	38	6	2	12	18
Man Utd	97	15	3	18	61
West Ham	52	8	1	15	28
Coventry	47	6	1	9	31
Liverpool	51	6	1	19	25
Southampton	45	5	2	16	22
Leeds Utd	58	4	1	27	26
Arsenal	73	5	3	24	41

KEY: Headers, Own goals, Left foot, Right foot

In the 1999–2000 Premiership, teams fired over more crosses, with greater accuracy, than they did in 1998–99. As a result, there were significantly more headers netted in 1999–2000, with headed efforts making up 19.6% of the total goals count, compared to 18.1% the previous season.

The four sides which scored the most headed goals all fielded strikers with recognized aerial ability. Dion Dublin led Aston Villa's front line for most of the season and scored four headed goals as Villa notched the highest ratio of headers in the Premiership – a league-high 11 different players nodding in goals.

Wimbledon were the only side other than Villa to score more than a third of all goals with headers, with Chelsea just below them.

Newcastle headed more goals than any of their top-flight rivals, thanks largely to Alan Shearer, Duncan Ferguson and Gary Speed, the latter notching five headers from midfield.

Arsenal again showed their lack of aerial strength in attack. Just 6.8% of all Gunners' goals came via headers in 1999–2000 as they recorded the lowest ratio in the league for headed goals for the second consecutive season.

The only other side to score less than 10% of goals with their heads were Leeds United, who preferred to rely on their long-range shooting skills. With the likes of Harry Kewell and Ian Harte in the team, Leeds were in fact the only side to score more goals with left-footed efforts than they did with the right.

Southampton went from first in this table in 1998–99 to 18th in 1999–2000. With Matt Le Tissier largely absent, their crossing dropped in accuracy over this period, while they also missed the aerial strength of Egil Ostenstad and the injury-prone James Beattie.

2 Chelsea conceded the fewest headed goals

HOW GOALS WERE CONCEDED

	TOTAL GOALS	Headers	Own goals	Left foot	Right foot
Liverpool	30	10	3	4	13
Newcastle	54	16		11	27
Aston Villa	35	10	4	6	15
Sheff Wed	70	17	1	19	33
Arsenal	43	10		9	24
Leeds Utd	43	10	1	7	25
Middlesbro	52	12	4	9	27
Tottenham	49	11	2	12	24
Wimbledon	74	15		14	45
Leicester	55	11	3	16	25
Derby Co	57	11	2	17	27
Man Utd	45	8	4	9	24
Bradford	68	12	3	20	33
Everton	49	8	1	11	29
Watford	77	12	2	20	43
West Ham	53	8	1	15	29
Coventry	54	8	1	15	30
Southampton	62	9	6	10	37
Sunderland	56	8	1	11	36
Chelsea	34	2		11	21

KEY: Headers, Own goals, Left foot, Right foot

Aside from a rise in the number of headed goals conceded, the more direct style of attack employed by teams in the 1999–2000 Premiership had further repercussions for top-flight defences.

The increased volume of crosses in 1999–2000 put more pressure on defenders and led to players putting through their own net 39 times – more than twice as often as in 1998–99 – with Southampton the biggest culprits.

Despite the formidable presence of Sami Hyypia, Liverpool went one worse than 1998–99 by conceding the highest ratio of headed goals than any 1999–2000 Premiership side. Sander Westerveld may be a top shot-stopper but he struggled at times with crosses, failing to claim seven – the second most during 1999–2000.

Newcastle's central defence was unsettled throughout 1999–2000 and they subsequently suffered at the back, conceding 16 headers in total.

Along with Newcastle and Liverpool, Aston Villa were the only other side to concede more than a quarter of all goals via headers.

Thanks in particular to Marcel Desailly, Frank Leboeuf and Emerson Thome, Chelsea were phenomenal when defending the high ball and conceded a measly two headed goals all season – just 5.9% of all strikes. Incredibly, every other Premiership side conceded at least four times as many headers as the Blues – which meant that for the second consecutive season they were the best side in the league at dealing with crosses.

Chelsea also avoided scoring any own-goals, while profiting from a season's-best five themselves.

Sunderland and Southampton came closest to matching Chelsea for preventing headed goals, with Paul Butler and Dean Richards both making more than 300 headed clearances.

for the second season in a row

WHEN GOALS WERE SCORED

	FIRST HALF GOALS %	0-15mins	16-30 mins	31-45 mins	46-60 mins	61-75 mins	76-90 mins	SECOND HALF GOALS %
Southampton	26.7%	3	4	5	11	11	11	73.3%
Aston Villa	30.4%	4	2	8	10	17	5	69.6%
Sheff Wed	34.2%	2	6	5	10	8	7	65.8%
Chelsea	37.7%	6	7	7	13	4	16	62.3%
Sunderland	38.6%	7	10	5	9	9	17	61.4%
Derby Co	38.6%	10	1	6	7	8	12	61.4%
Watford	40.0%	2	4	8	10	6	5	60.0%
Man Utd	43.3%	12	12	18	13	24	18	56.7%
Middlesbro	43.5%	8	8	4	5	10	11	56.5%
Arsenal	43.8%	6	9	17	10	10	21	56.2%
Liverpool	45.1%	3	9	11	5	12	11	54.9%
Wimbledon	45.7%	8	7	6	2	15	8	54.3%
Bradford	47.4%	6	4	8	8	4	8	52.6%
Leeds Utd	48.3%	9	10	9	10	11	9	51.7%
Coventry	48.9%	9	6	8	5	10	9	51.1%
West Ham	50.0%	9	6	11	9	7	10	50.0%
Newcastle	50.8%	11	14	7	12	5	14	49.2%
Everton	54.2%	12	12	8	9	11	7	45.8%
Leicester	56.4%	10	9	12	13	4	7	43.6%
Tottenham	59.6%	6	11	17	5	5	13	40.4%

KEY 0-15mins 16-30 mins 31-45 mins 46-60 mins 61-75 mins 76-90 mins

A higher ratio of goals was scored in the first 15 minutes and a lower percentage in the final quarter hour of matches in 1999–2000 than in 1998–99.

Sluggish Southampton never really got going until the second half of their 1999–2000 league matches, and their 4–2 turnover of Newcastle in August illustrates this point perfectly.

The Saints did themselves no favours in the early stages of fixtures, scoring nearly three times as many goals in the second 45 minutes of games as they did in the opening half.

Aston Villa and Sheffield Wednesday were also particularly slow off the mark. Villa bagged just 30.4% of goals in the first half, but noticeably found a second wind between 61 and 75 minutes, when they bagged 37% of their strikes – the highest ratio by any team in any given interval. Meanwhile Wednesday scored just 5% of all league goals in the opening 15 minutes of matches.

Bizarrely, half of Derby's strikes came in the opening and closing quarter-hour intervals of matches combined.

Manchester United were consistently dangerous throughout matches, reaching double figures for each 15-minute period and peaking in the often crucial 15 minutes after the hour mark.

Four sides scored more goals in the first half of matches than they did in the second. Newcastle, Leicester, Everton and Tottenham all scoring more than 30 goals overall before the break, while no team notched more goals than Walter Smith's side in the first quarter-hour of matches.

George Graham may have been too easy on his players at half-time. They bagged a Premiership-high 30% of goals in the 15 minutes before the break, but just 9% in the quarter-hour after the interval. If matches had finished at half-time Spurs would have qualified for the UEFA Cup.

WHEN GOALS WERE CONCEDED

	FIRST HALF GOALS %	0-15mins	16-30 mins	31-45 mins	46-60 mins	61-75 mins	76-90 mins	SECOND HALF GOALS %
Wimbledon	33.8%	5	10	10	13	15	21	66.2%
Newcastle	35.2%	7	5	7	10	12	13	64.8%
Coventry	37.0%	7	4	9	11	8	15	63.0%
Aston Villa	37.1%	3	4	6	7	6	9	62.9%
West Ham	39.6%	7	8	6	11	15	6	60.4%
Sheff Wed	40.0%	8	9	10	9	15	23	60.0%
Derby Co	43.9%	6	4	8	10	6	8	56.1%
Chelsea	44.1%	6	3	6	5	6	8	55.9%
Arsenal	44.2%	8	5	6	13	8	3	55.8%
Sunderland	44.6%	8	11	6	9	9	13	55.4%
Everton	44.9%	8	7	7	11	5	11	55.1%
Bradford	45.6%	12	7	12	9	12	16	54.4%
Middlesbro	46.2%	10	5	9	9	10	9	53.8%
Leeds Utd	48.8%	5	7	9	7	6	7	51.2%
Watford	49.4%	9	11	18	13	15	11	50.6%
Leicester	50.9%	6	10	12	11	6	10	49.1%
Tottenham	51.0%	3	11	11	5	11	8	49.0%
Man Utd	51.1%	7	10	6	4	7	11	48.9%
Southampton	53.2%	8	12	13	6	9	14	46.8%
Liverpool	63.3%	10	4	5	4	5	3	36.7%

KEY 0-15mins 16-30 mins 31-45 mins 46-60 mins 61-75 mins 76-90 mins

There were 32 more goals conceded in the opening 15 minutes of matches in 1999–2000 than there were in the previous campaign – and the worst affected side were Gerard Houllier's Liverpool.

The Reds were caught cold too often for their liking in the first quarter-hour of matches, conceding 33% of all goals in this period – the highest ratio of strikes in any given interval.

Liverpool conceded just 11 second-half goals all season, with Chelsea the only Premiership side not to ship at least double this amount in the corresponding period. If Houllier's side had shown the same discipline before the break that they did after the interval, they would surely have claimed a Champions League spot.

Tottenham were one of four other teams who conceded more goals in the first half than in the second, even though just 6% of their opponents' strikes came in the first 15 minutes of matches.

Wimbledon were the weakest side in the league in the second half of matches. Nearly two thirds of the 74 goals they conceded arrived after the interval, with 21 coming in the final quarter-hour.

Newcastle also lacked resolve in the second 45 minutes. The Magpies recorded single figures for goals conceded in each 15-minute period in the first half of matches, but were into double figures for the three quarter-hour intervals after the half-time break.

Fall guys Sheffield Wednesday were the league's weakest side in the final 15 minutes of matches, conceding 23 goals in this timeframe, while Arsenal were the strongest letting in just three.

The Gunners' opponents put just 7% of all strikes past them in the final 15 minutes of matches – in stark contrast to the 1998–99 season when a staggering 41% of goals against Arsenal came between 76 and 90 minutes of play.

WHO SCORED THE "GOALS FOR"

Team	% Goals by Attackers	Attack	Midfield	Defence	Own Goals
Sunderland	78.9%	45	10	2	
Wimbledon	67.4%	31	11	1	3
Watford	65.7%	23	8	4	
Arsenal	58.9%	43	20	7	3
Man Utd	57.7%	56	34	4	3
West Ham	57.7%	30	19	2	1
Middlesbro	56.5%	26	8	10	2
Bradford	52.6%	20	13	4	1
Sheff Wed	52.6%	20	14	2	3
Tottenham	52.6%	30	19	5	3
Liverpool	51.0%	26	21	3	1
Aston Villa	50.0%	23	16	6	1
Derby Co	50.0%	22	18	3	1
Newcastle	49.2%	31	17	11	4
Coventry	48.9%	23	22	1	1
Southampton	46.7%	21	15	7	2
Everton	44.1%	26	21	10	2
Leicester	43.6%	24	13	15	3
Leeds Utd	43.1%	25	23	9	1
Chelsea	34.0%	18	23	7	5

KEY: Attack, Midfield, Defence, Own Goals

Sunderland's fantastic first season back in the Premiership owed much to their strike partnership of Kevin Phillips and Niall Quinn.

The two scored 77% of the Black Cats' goals, helping Sunderland's strikers as a whole to score 79% of the team's tally of 57 – the highest ratio in the Premiership.

While the goalscoring exploits of Quinn and Phillips ensured a successful season for Peter Reid's side, Wimbledon and Watford were not so fortunate.

Their strikers' ratios were the next highest, but relegation proved that if you are going to rely on your front men alone, you have to be able to create chances for them, and they have to be able to put them away.

Chelsea's strikers endured a miserable time in front of goal, scoring just 34% of their side's goals.

Chris Sutton and Gianfranco Zola managed just five goals between them, and while Tore Andre Flo found the back of the net 10 times, Chelsea's disappointing 1999–2000 Premiership campaign can in some part be attributed to the low returns from the forwards.

Coventry City relied most heavily on their midfield, with 47% of the Sky Blues' goals being scored by midfielders.

Gary McAllister finished the campaign as the Premiership's highest scoring midfielder, and despite the £6m signing of Robbie Keane, Coventry were most reliant on their central players.

Leicester seemed to perfect the art of turning defenders into attackers, playing Matt Elliott up front on occasions, something that the Scotland international took to with some aplomb.

Hardly surprising, then, that the 27% of Foxes goals that were scored by defenders was the highest ratio in the Premiership – maybe the sale of Emile Heskey will not be such a huge loss at Filbert Street after all!

WHO SCORED THE "GOALS AGAINST"

	% GOALS BY ATTACKERS	Attack	Midfield	Defence	Own Goals
Chelsea	70.6%	24	8	2	
Coventry	64.8%	35	11	7	1
Derby Co	61.4%	35	16	4	2
Arsenal	60.5%	26	15	2	
Southampton	59.7%	37	14	5	6
Middlesbro	57.7%	30	13	5	4
Aston Villa	57.1%	20	8	3	4
Liverpool	56.7%	17	8	2	3
Leeds Utd	55.8%	24	11	7	1
Wimbledon	54.1%	40	26	8	
Newcastle	53.7%	29	20	5	
Man Utd	51.1%	23	16	2	4
Everton	51.0%	25	15	8	1
Leicester	50.9%	28	21	3	3
Bradford	48.5%	33	26	6	3
Watford	48.1%	37	28	10	2
West Ham	45.3%	24	23	5	1
Sunderland	44.6%	25	22	8	1
Sheff Wed	44.3%	31	29	9	1
Tottenham	40.8%	20	15	12	2

KEY: Attack, Midfield, Defence, Own Goals

While Chelsea's strikers were struggling in front of goal (see table on page opposite), front men from opposition sides were having far more luck against the Blues.

The Blues conceded a greater percentage of goals to strikers in 1999–2000 than any other Premiership team, 70.6% to be exact, showing that while Chelsea's defence coped well with set-pieces, they were not nearly as comfortable from open play.

Coventry conceded the second highest ratio of goals by attackers, with front men finding the net with nearly two thirds of all the goals City conceded.

Meanwhile, Tottenham conceded just 40.8% of their goals to strikers, and alarmingly they let in 12 goals to defenders, more than any other team.

Susceptibility to set-pieces may be partly responsible, with the 24.5% ratio of goals conceded to defenders also the highest of any Premiership team in the 1999–2000 campaign.

Champions Manchester United only conceded 4.4% of their 45 goals to defenders, no doubt because opposing centre-backs and full-backs were fully occupied in trying to cope with United's incessant attacks.

West Ham United conceded the highest percentage of goals to midfielders, with four of the five goalkeepers used by the Hammers in 1999–2000 conceding a goal to a midfielder.

The 1999–2000 season seemed to go own-goal crazy, with players putting through their own net 39 times, 20 more than in 1998–99.

Most unfortunate were Southampton, who gifted goals to the opposition via their own players on six occasions, while only Arsenal, Chelsea, Newcastle United and Wimbledon avoided scoring in their own net.

than any other team

THE PLAYERS

The top scorer is easy enough for anyone to monitor – but who was the top tackler, the best passer, the best crosser or the best shot-stopper? And which players had the best and worst disciplinary records in the league?

The answers to these and many more questions are contained in this section – and only Opta can provide this information, because of the unique way in which they monitor every single touch of the ball.

But it is not just quantity that counts – it is quality too. So, although many of the categories are sorted on total number of successful outcomes, you can also see percentage completion rates to judge for yourself how good players really are.

The bar charts show several pieces of information. For example, in the chart on page 642 that shows which player had the most shots in total, you will also be able to see the player who had the most shots on target, plus the figure shown alongside the bars which indicates how accurate their shooting was.

There is an explanation beneath each of the charts showing how the ranking is calculated and how to access the information.

The Golden Boot was won by Kevin Phillips, who finished the season with 30 Premiership goals – a magnificent achievement for a player who was playing for one of the sides promoted the previous season, and one that saw him runner-up to Roy Keane in both the Players' Player of the Year and Football Writers' Footballer of the Year awards.

Alan Shearer netted 23 times after a difficult start to the campaign, while Dwight Yorke, Andy Cole and Michael Bridges all scored more goals than the Golden Boot winners of the two previous seasons who had finished with 18 Premiership goals apiece.

PLAYERS RECORDS – SHOTS, PASSES, FOULS, SAVES

A manager can give a pre-match talk until he is hoarse, but once the players go out on to the pitch, it is up to them how they perform. Here are those individual performances in 1999–2000 that either left fans singing the player's name, or pulling their hair out in sheer frustration.

MOST SHOTS IN ONE GAME

PLAYER	MATCH	SHOTS ATTEMPTED (ON TARGET)	GOALS
F Kanouté	v Wimbledon (h)	11 (7)	1
T Andre Flo	v Bradford (a)	9 (6)	0
H Helguson	v Coventry (h)	9 (4)	1
F Lampard	v Sunderland (h)	9 (4)	0
N Kanu	v Watford (h)	9 (2)	1

Frederic Kanouté certainly made a splash on his West Ham debut. The on-loan striker fired in 11 shots – seven on target – as Wimbledon's defence struggled to stem the tide of the Frenchman's goal efforts.

Tore Andre Flo had six shots saved and hit another three wide as Chelsea drew 1–1 at Bradford. Heidar Helguson's last-day exertions earned him a goal and Watford three points against Coventry, while Kanu snatched a late winner against the Hornets with one of only two shots on target in nine.

MOST PASSES IN ONE GAME

No player came close to Roy Keane in terms of passes completed in the 1999–2000 Premiership, and the United captain features three times in the top five for most passes in a game.

He connected with an unsurpassed 105 against Everton and ran the show at home to Bradford and away to Tottenham – although he could not prevent United's 3–1 defeat at Spurs.

Similarly, David Batty's probing for Leeds did not stop Wimbledon beating them, while Didier Deschamps was pivotal to Chelsea's 5–0 win against Keane's United.

PLAYER	MATCH	PASSES COMPLETED
Roy Keane	v Everton (a)	105
Roy Keane	v Bradford (h)	90
David Batty	v Wimbledon (a)	83
Roy Keane	v Tottenham (a)	80
Didier Deschamps	v Man Utd (h)	78

MOST FOULS IN ONE GAME

PLAYER	MATCH	FOULS CONCEDED
Paulo Wanchope	v Chelsea (a)	11
Alan Quinn	v Leicester (h)	9
Michael Duberry	v Everton (a)	8
Marc-Vivien Foe	v Arsenal (a)	8
Mark Hughes	v Newcastle (a)	8

Unorthodox striker Paulo Wanchope committed more fouls than any other Premiership player in 1999–2000, and reached double figures for illegal challenges away to Chelsea.

Alan Quinn was penalised nine times in Sheffield Wednesday's final match of the season against Leicester but, like Wanchope, escaped without a booking.

Michael Duberry did not get a chance to make any more than eight fouls against Everton after being sent off in the 55th minute, while Marc-Vivien Foe went the same way against Arsenal.

MOST SAVES IN ONE GAME

Kevin Pressman pulled off a season's-best 14 saves away to West Ham but despite his heroics the Owls still ran out 4–3 losers.

Meanwhile Mark Schwarzer will relish the chance to fit in some quality beach time in his native Australia this summer, after making more saves than any other Premiership 'keeper in 1999–2000.

Schwarzer made 13 stops against Leeds and 10 against West Ham. Pegguy Arphexad and Thomas Sorensen experienced something similar against Leeds and West Ham respectively.

PLAYER	MATCH	SAVES MADE
Kevin Pressman	v West Ham (a)	14
Mark Schwarzer	v Leeds (h)	13
Thomas Sorensen	v West Ham (h)	11
Pegguy Arphexad	v Leeds Utd (h)	11
Mark Schwarzer	v West Ham (h)	10

PENALTIES, SET PIECES, HEADED GOALS, GOALS FROM OUTSIDE THE BOX

Scoring goals is a profession, and those who can find the back of the net in different ways are at the top of the class. Opta show here which players were able to use their head, power home from long range, hold their nerve from the penalty spot, and show precision from set pieces.

PENALTIES

A total of 85 penalties were awarded in the 1999–2000 Premiership campaign with 65 scored, 16 saved and four missed, making the penalty success rate 76.4%.

Kevin Phillips scored the most, with six of his 30 strikes coming from the spot. Valley Parade witnessed more penalties than any other ground and Bradford's Peter Beagrie notched five from the spot to help keep the Bantams in the top flight. Alan Shearer and David Unsworth equalled this total, while Gary McAllister hammered home four.

PLAYER	PENALTY GOALS
Kevin Phillips	6
Peter Beagrie	5
David Unsworth	5
Alan Shearer	5
Gary McAllister	4

SET PIECES

PLAYER	SET-PIECE GOALS
Patrik Berger	3
David Beckham	3
Branko Strupar	2
Christian Ziege	2

Spectacular free-kick goals were hard to come by in the 1999–2000 campaign with only 23 of the Premiership's 1,060 goals coming from set pieces.

David Beckham kept up his reputation as the best striker of a dead ball in the English game by scoring from three free-kicks, a total equalled by Patrik Berger.

Derby's Branko Strupar and Middlesbrough's Christian Ziege both had two free-kick successes, but no other Premiership player was able to net more than one from a set piece.

HEADED GOALS

Of the 1,060 goals scored, 208 were headers, but the 1999–2000 Premiership campaign demonstrated that it is not just strapping 6'4" strikers that are successful in the air, with those scoring headed goals making up for their lack of inches with style, technique and good-quality service.

Eight of Dwight Yorke's 20 goals came from his head, giving him the highest tally in the league, with Newcastle skipper Alan Shearer just behind him on six. Five other players managed to net five times with their heads.

PLAYER	HEADED GOALS
Dwight Yorke	8
Alan Shearer	6
Andy Cole	5
Steffen Iversen	5
Kevin Phillips	5
Gustavo Poyet	5
Gary Speed	5

GOALS FROM OUTSIDE THE BOX

PLAYER	LONG-RANGE GOALS
Kevin Phillips	6
Harry Kewell	6
David Beckham	5
Titi Camara	5
Patrik Berger	5

The Premiership's Golden Boot winner, Kevin Phillips, proved that he is more than just a penalty-box poacher by also topping the goals from outside the box chart with six strikes.

He shares this honour with Leeds' Harry Kewell, as half a dozen of the Australian's 10 goals in 1999–2000 came from outside the area.

Five of David Beckham's six goals were from outside the 18-yard box and Liverpool pair Titi Camara and Patrik Berger also scored five times with long-range strikes.

FASTEST GOALS IN 1999–2000 PREMIERSHIP

	PLAYER	MATCH	TIME MINS	SECS
1	Rory Delap	Bradford v DERBY	0	20
2	Gustavo Poyet	CHELSEA v Man Utd	0	28
3	Gary McAllister	Bradford v COVENTRY	0	38
4	David Hopkin	Sheff Wed v LEEDS	0	39
5	Niall Quinn	SUNDERLAND v Chelsea	0	45

During the 1999–2000 Premiership, the team conceding the first goal of the game went on to win in only 12.4% of matches.

In the games that saw the five quickest goals of the campaign, the side scoring first never lost, while an early strike was usually a precursor to plenty of additional goals, with 23 coming in the five matches featured in the table.

Derby County hold the distinction of scoring both the quickest and the latest goals of the 1999–2000 Premiership. While Mikkel Beck left it until the 95th minute to make his mark, Rory Delap's lightning strike after just 20 seconds against Bradford proved the spark in a remarkable 4–4 draw.

No team conceded more than the 12 goals Paul Jewell's side shipped in the opening 15 minutes of matches, and the Bantams were on the receiving end of two of the three fastest goals during the season. But as they did against Derby, Bradford picked themselves up after Gary McAllister had put Coventry one-up inside 40 seconds in November, coming back to gain a point.

None of the other three sides in the table which conceded a goal managed to claw their way back into their matches.

Gustavo Poyet's 28-second header against Manchester United got Chelsea off to a perfect start against the Champions, and after Nicky Butt was dismissed 21 minutes later Chelsea had the perfect platform for victory.

Some tardy Leeds United fans probably missed David Hopkin's solitary goal of the campaign, with the Scottish international netting after only 39 seconds against Sheffield Wednesday to set up a 3–0 victory for United.

And Sunderland exacted revenge for a heavy opening-day defeat on Chelsea in some style, battering the Blues 4–1 after Niall Quinn got them off to a flying start after just 45 seconds.

12 Bradford conceded the highest number of

LATEST GOALS IN 1999–2000 PREMIERSHIP

	PLAYER	MATCH	TIME MINS	SECS
1	Mikkel Beck	Southampton v DERBY	94	31
2	Ian Harte	Derby v LEEDS UTD	93	41
3	Stuart McCall	BRADFORD v Tottenham	93	22
4	Emmanuel Petit	ARSENAL v West Ham	92	43
5	Trevor Sinclair	Aston Villa v WEST HAM	92	41

Derby County had a knack of leaving it late to score in the 1999–2000 Premiership. The Rams notched seven last-minute goals in the league – more than any other top-flight side – including one from Mikkel Beck which was four minutes and 31 seconds into stoppage time.

No player scored at a later point in a match in the 1999–2000 Premiership than Beck did against Southampton, and his strike snatched a point for the Rams after they had been 3–1 down.

Derby dealt Sheffield Wednesday an even bigger blow towards the end of the season when two 90th-minute goals turned what should have been three points into just one for the Owls. Wednesday never fully recovered from this result as they went spiralling towards Division One.

The Rams also suffered late heartbreak during the season. Ian Harte tucked away a contentious penalty at Pride Park, after Horacio Carbonari was deemed to have fouled Harry Kewell, to claim a 1–0 victory for his side.

In what was a fiercely-contested derby, Emmanuel Petit's late strike gave Arsenal a 2–1 win over West Ham and robbed the Hammers of their unbeaten record against London sides in 1999–2000.

Stuart McCall's 94th-minute goal at home to Tottenham was Bradford's third goal of the 1999–2000 campaign – and neither of the previous two had come before the 89th-minute of matches. McCall's strike gave the Bantams a draw, while Dean Saunders's late goal away to Middlesbrough proved to be the winner – the four points these strikes earned proved crucial in the final shake-up.

Meanwhile, Trevor Sinclair's cool finish in the dying seconds away to Aston Villa snatched a point for West Ham – meaning that each of the five latest strikes in the 1999–2000 Premiership had a significant bearing on the final outcome of their particular match.

GOALSCORING

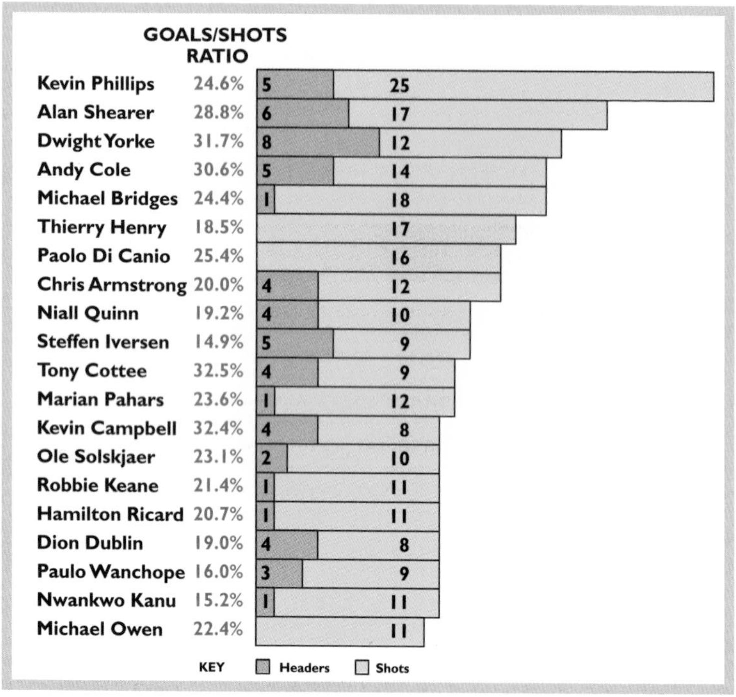

	GOALS/SHOTS RATIO	Headers	Shots
Kevin Phillips	24.6%	5	25
Alan Shearer	28.8%	6	17
Dwight Yorke	31.7%	8	12
Andy Cole	30.6%	5	14
Michael Bridges	24.4%	1	18
Thierry Henry	18.5%		17
Paolo Di Canio	25.4%		16
Chris Armstrong	20.0%	4	12
Niall Quinn	19.2%	4	10
Steffen Iversen	14.9%	5	9
Tony Cottee	32.5%	4	9
Marian Pahars	23.6%	1	12
Kevin Campbell	32.4%	4	8
Ole Solskjaer	23.1%	2	10
Robbie Keane	21.4%	1	11
Hamilton Ricard	20.7%	1	11
Dion Dublin	19.0%	4	8
Paulo Wanchope	16.0%	3	9
Nwankwo Kanu	15.2%	1	11
Michael Owen	22.4%		11

KEY: Headers, Shots

Despite all the multi-million pound strikers that grace the English Premiership, it was Sunderland's bargain buy from Watford, Kevin Phillips, who took the Golden Boot honours with 30 league goals in his first season in the top flight.

"Super Kev" scored a goal with nearly every four shots that he attempted and, despite not being the tallest of players, he showed good aerial ability with five headed goals during the campaign.

Manchester United's calypso kid Dwight Yorke used his head more than most to bag eight goals in the air. Yorke, like Phillips, is not the biggest of players but his own aerial ability, coupled with the quality of service he received, allowed him to net the hightest tally of headed goals.

Similarly Phillips's north-east rival Alan Shearer put the quality crosses he received to good use, with six of his 23 efforts coming from his head.

Two of the Premiership's most exciting foreigners finished high up in the scoring charts, but Thierry Henry and Paolo Di Canio were clearly happier to let their feet do the talking, failing to score any headers during the course of the campaign.

There is no substitute for experience, and veteran Tony Cottee proved this by being the most economical of the top 20 goalscorers. The Leicester striker bagged a goal with 32.5% of his strikes, while 1998–99's most clinical striker Kevin Campbell showed he has not lost his touch with a goals-to-shots ratio of 32.4% – just behind Cottee.

With Manchester United enjoying a record-breaking season for goalscoring, it is no surprise to see both main strikers high up in the scoring charts, with Andy Cole's 19 goals putting him just behind his partner Yorke.

8 Dwight Yorke scored the most

MINUTES PER GOAL

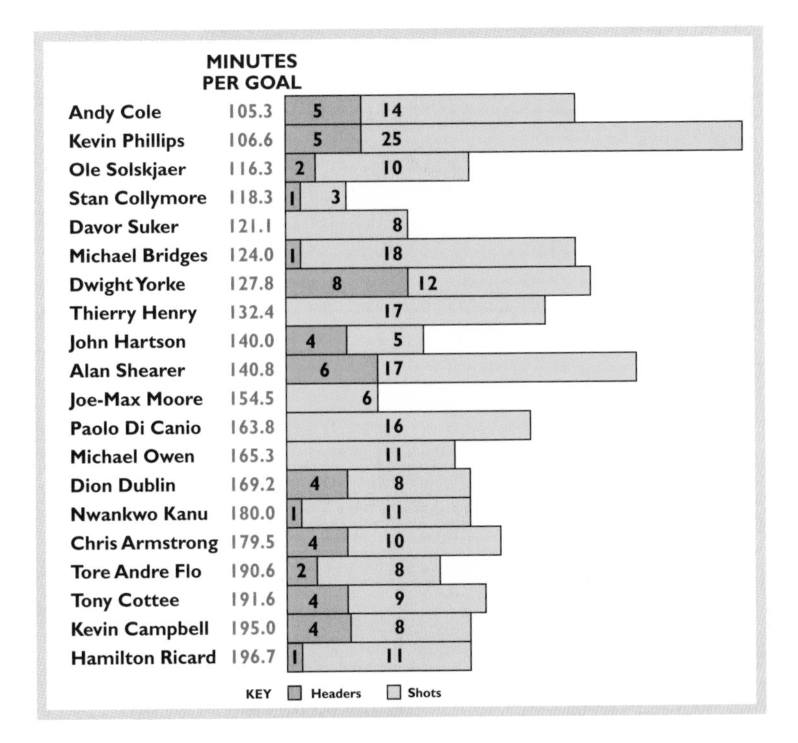

While Kevin Phillips was the most prolific striker in the 1999–2000 Premiership, the player who scored most frequently was Andy Cole.

With Sir Alex Ferguson rotating his strikers throughout the season Cole's appearances were more limited than those of the Sunderland hitman, but he made the most of his opportunities when selected, scoring a goal every 105.3 minutes – the most frequent in the Premiership of all players who spent at least 450 minutes on the pitch.

Cole's United team-mate Ole Gunnar Solskjaer was the third most frequent scorer. In 1998–99 the Norwegian international was top of the list when he averaged a goal every 71.1 minutes, and in 1999–2000 he remained one of the most frequent hitmen in the top flight.

It was Davor Suker's first and only season at Highbury, but he certainly showed the form that won him the 1998 World Cup Golden Boot, scoring a goal every 121.1 minutes, despite not being a first-choice striker.

Manchester United and Arsenal are represented by three strikers apiece in the top 20, highlighting not only the two teams' wealth of striking ability, but also their penchant for creating goalscoring opportunities.

Stan Collymore was fully justifying Martin O'Neill's faith in him before a broken leg cut short his season. He found time to score four goals in 473 minutes, including a hat-trick against Sunderland, to show that perhaps there is still time for him to fulfil his potential.

Collymore's new team-mate Tony Cottee is also worthy of mention. The 34-year-old showed he still has what it takes to play in the top flight, ending the season as Leicester City's top scorer with 13 goals, averaging a goal every 191.6 minutes he played.

headed goals in the Premiership

SHOOTING

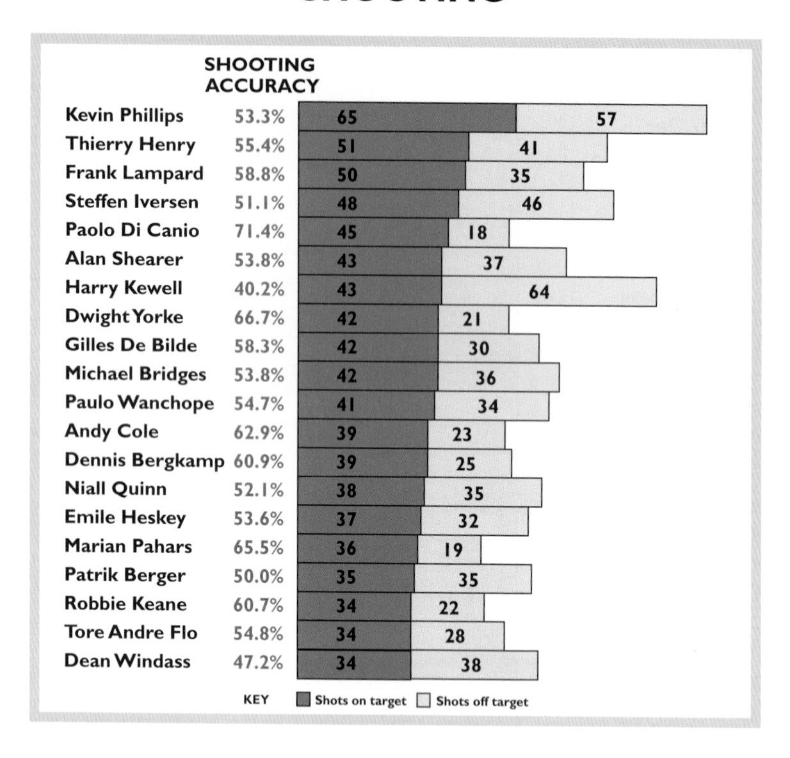

Not surprisingly, given that he scored 30 goals, Sunderland's Kevin Phillips attempted more shots than any other player during the 1999–2000 Premiership season. The England striker fired in a total of 112 efforts on goal, and the 65 that were on target were far and away more than any other player in the top flight.

Arsenal managed more shots than any other team, and it was their French fancy Thierry Henry who managed the second-highest number of shots on target, behind Phillips. The youngster had a slow start to the season, but if he can maintain his form since the turn of the year, it bodes well for the Gunners.

Frank Lampard was the Premiership's sharpest-shooting midfielder with 50 of his 85 attempts being on target, although of these shots only seven ended up in the back of the net.

Lampard's team-mate Paolo Di Canio was easily the most accurate of all the strikers, with 71.4% of all his shots testing the 'keeper. Dwight Yorke was able to help the Champions clock up a record goals total with 66.7% of his shots being on target, while Southampton's Marian Pahars showed that he clearly knows where the goal is, with 65.5% of his efforts hitting the target.

The West Yorkshire version of the Wizard of Oz, Harry Kewell, proved to be the most wayward of the top 20 shooters. His low shooting accuracy reflects the fact that 64 of his 107 attempted shots were off target, which helped restrict him to a haul of 10 goals for Leeds.

Alan Shearer also put a bad start to the campaign behind him to finish as the Premiership's second-hightest scorer. His 23 league goals came from 43 attempts on target and took his carreer tally to an impressive 300.

71.4% Paolo Di Canio had the highest shooting accuracy

GOAL ASSISTS

Player	From open play	From set-pieces
David Beckham	11	4
Nolberto Solano	9	6
Paolo Di Canio	10	3
Ryan Giggs	12	
Dennis Bergkamp	8	1
Gianfranco Zola	6	3
Thierry Henry	8	
Niall Quinn	8	
Marc Overmars	8	
David Ginola	8	
Trevor Sinclair	8	
Nick Barmby	7	1
Wim Jonk	6	2
Paul Merson	5	3
Steffen Iversen	7	
Alan Shearer	7	
Moustapha Hadji	7	
Ole Solskjaer	7	
Kevin Campbell	7	
Emmanuel Petit	6	1

KEY From open play From set-pieces

Manchester United's fantastic achievement in scoring 97 goals in the 1999–2000 season is thanks in part to their world-class wide wonders.

David Beckham, who set up more goals than any other player in 1998–99 with 14 assists, went one better in 1999–2000 and shared top spot with Newcastle United's Peruvian winger Nolberto Solano.

Beckham's team-mate Ryan Giggs set up more goals from open play than any other Premiership player, and no defence in the top flight had an answer to the United wide men, as the pair created chance after chance for the likes of Andy Cole and Dwight Yorke.

Top striker in the assists table was the Opta 1999–2000 Player of the Year, Paolo Di Canio.

When not scoring one of his 16 league goals, Di Canio was setting up his team-mates, with a further 13 Hammers goals being created by the maverick Italian.

Kevin Phillips has his strike partner Niall Quinn to thank for many of his 30 goals, with the Republic of Ireland international setting up eight goals to add to the 14 he scored himself.

Nick Barmby's eight assists helped him force his way back into the England reckoning, while his Everton team-mate Kevin Campbell still made the top 20 despite missing nearly a third of the season through injury.

Wim Jonk is the highest-ranked central midfielder in the table, and his number of assists is even more admirable considering what a disappointing season Sheffield Wednesday had, culminating in their relegation to Nationwide League Division One.

Paul Merson celebrated a return to form with a player of the month award and an FA Cup final. He also created eight Premiership goals for Villa.

among players with more than 30 shots

PASSING IN OPPOSITION HALF

	PASSING ACCURACY	PASSES IN OPPOSITION HALF
Dwight Yorke	84.3%	1,003
Kieron Dyer	82.7%	738
Roy Keane	79.9%	1,047
Neil Lennon	79.4%	1,085
Paul Scholes	77.8%	964
John Collins	76.6%	979
Robert Lee	76.4%	957
Dennis Wise	75.0%	1,042
Dietmar Hamann	74.2%	764
Patrick Vieira	74.0%	963
Stephen McPhail	73.7%	753
Phil Neville	73.7%	843
Didier Deschamps	73.4%	813
Gary Speed	73.0%	1,160
Denis Irwin	72.1%	763
Gianfranco Zola	71.9%	761
Chris Makin	71.6%	774
Muzzy Izzet	71.3%	814
Nolberto Solano	70.4%	919
Paolo Di Canio	70.0%	966

He may make his name by scoring goals, but Dwight Yorke can pass the ball brilliantly as well.

He was the most accurate passer in the opposition half in 1999–2000, and is one of only three strikers to feature in the top 20 list, which is quite an achievement.

Yorke was also one of three Manchester United players in the top five and, to highlight the champions' dominance of the season, two of the three full-backs in the list are also United players.

Top midfielder in the table, for which players must have attempted at least 700 passes in the opposition half to qualify, was Newcastle United's Kieron Dyer, who forced his way into the Euro 2000 reckoning, and along with his team-mates, benefited greatly from the arrival of Bobby Robson.

Dyer's colleagues Robert Lee – a Ruud Gullit outcast at the start of the season – Gary Speed and Nolberto Solano featured in seventh, 14th and 19th places respectively.

Newcastle finished the campaign as the third-most accurate passing side in the opposition half, behind Chelsea and Manchester United, so it is hardly surprising that players from these sides represent 60% of the list.

These sides based their excellent passing game around players on the list, and it is little surprise to see them among the Premiership's elite.

The youngest player in the table is Leeds United's Stephen McPhail. The 20-year-old started 23 of Leeds' Premiership matches, and his fine form during the 1999–2000 campaign only confirmed what many around Elland Road knew already – that the Irishman has a big future ahead of him.

Denis Irwin and Chris Makin were the only two defenders in the top 20 most accurate passers in opposition territory.

1,160 Gary Speed made the highest number

CROSSING

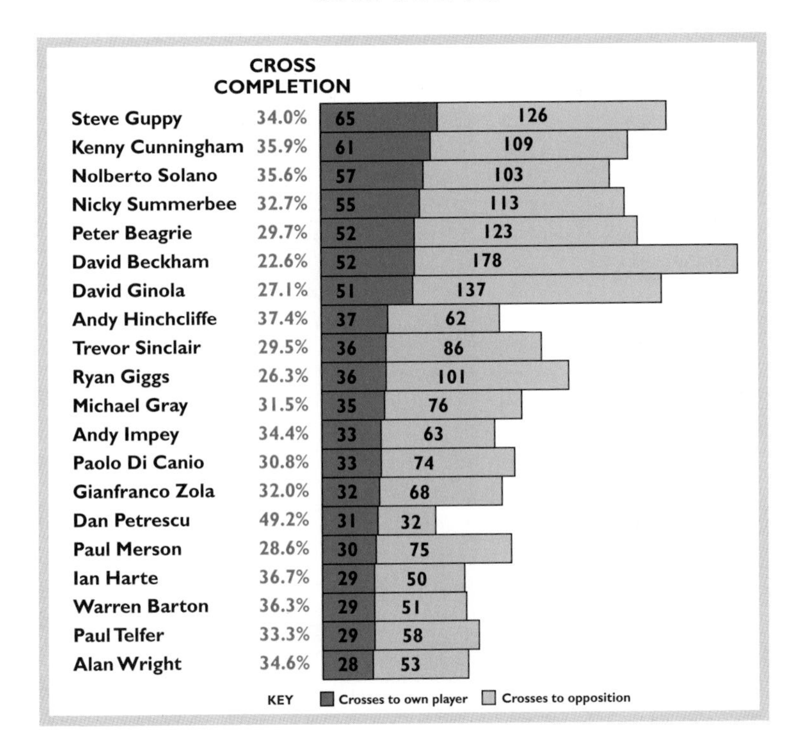

Despite there being so few left-sided English players in the top flight, one of them made the highest number of accurate crosses in the 1999–2000 campaign. Leicester's Steve Guppy caught Kevin Keegan's eye earlier on in the season and he was the top crosser of the ball in the Premiership, with 65 centres being delivered to a team-mate.

Wimbledon captain and full-back Kenny Cunningham was, surprisingly, Guppy's nearest challenger with just four fewer accurate crosses. The hard-working Irish defender tried to provide the ammunition to keep his side out of the relegation zone. Peruvian Nolberto Solano was third after enjoying a season feeding Newcastle's awesome strikeforce of Alan Shearer and Duncan Ferguson.

The 1998–99 top crosser, David Beckham, found himself pushed down the pecking order, making 52 accurate crosses. However, the Manchester United wide man set up the joint-highest number of goals in 1999–2000, with Newcastle's Nolberto Solano and actually attempted more crosses than anyone else.

Beckham's team-mate Ryan Giggs saw a great improvement in his form from the 1998–99 season, completing 36 crosses compared to just 19 successful centres during the previous campaign.

Romanian international Dan Petrescu was easily the most accurate crosser with a very high cross completion rate of 49.2%, after 31 of his 63 centres found a team-mate. Two left-backs were also very accurate, with Sheffield Wednesday's Andy Hinchcliffe and Leeds' Ian Harte hitting the target with 37.4% and 36.7% of crosses respectively.

Naturally, the majority of the players performed in wide positions but three more central players also made it into the top 20 in the form of Paolo Di Canio, Gianfranco Zola and Paul Merson.

of passes in the opposition half

DRIBBLING

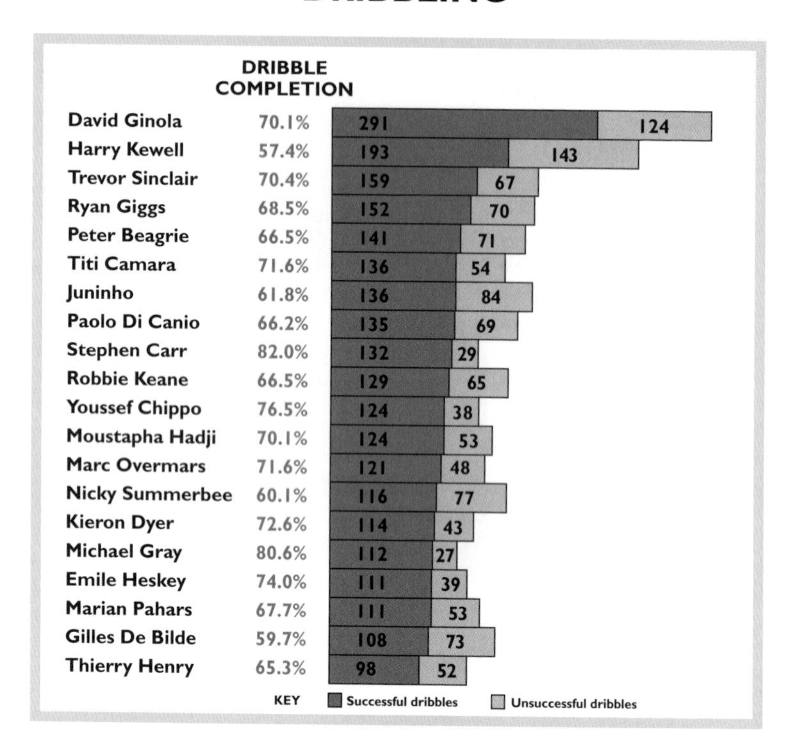

DRIBBLE COMPLETION
David Ginola 70.1% 291 124
Harry Kewell 57.4% 193 143
Trevor Sinclair 70.4% 159 67
Ryan Giggs 68.5% 152 70
Peter Beagrie 66.5% 141 71
Titi Camara 71.6% 136 54
Juninho 61.8% 136 84
Paolo Di Canio 66.2% 135 69
Stephen Carr 82.0% 132 29
Robbie Keane 66.5% 129 65
Youssef Chippo 76.5% 124 38
Moustapha Hadji 70.1% 124 53
Marc Overmars 71.6% 121 48
Nicky Summerbee 60.1% 116 77
Kieron Dyer 72.6% 114 43
Michael Gray 80.6% 112 27
Emile Heskey 74.0% 111 39
Marian Pahars 67.7% 111 53
Gilles De Bilde 59.7% 108 73
Thierry Henry 65.3% 98 52
KEY
Successful dribbles
Unsuccessful dribbles

For the second season running, the Gallic flair of David Ginola saw him finish as the runaway leader at the top of Opta's Premiership dribblers chart. He made almost 100 more successful dribbles than his nearest rival.

North London's best-known shampoo salesman showed Premiership defences a pair of heels that were as clean as his hair by making 291 successful dribbles – 98 more than second-placed Harry Kewell – and the Frenchman managed an overall success rate of 70.1%.

Kewell is arguably the most exciting player among Leeds' crop of talented youngsters and, like Ginola, he has repeated his impressive dribbling performance of the 1998–99 season. The Australian international made 193 successful dribbles during the Yorkshire club's eventful season and will be looking forward to showing his skills in the 2000–01 Champions League.

The most successful English dribbler was West Ham's Trevor Sinclair, who completed 159 of his 226 attempted dribbles. The England "B" international also scored seven and created eight in a successful season at Upton Park.

Tottenham right-back Stephen Carr eclipsed his team-mate Ginola as the most successful dribbler of the 20 most prolific runners with the ball, completing 82% of his 161 attempted dribbles. He was closely followed by Sunderland's Michael Gray, who completed 80.6% of his dribbles. Carr and Gray were the only two defenders who made it into the top 20.

But the list is mainly full of tricky wingers who on their day can turn the course of a game with their ability to take on and beat their man – the kind of players that can infuriate one day and excite the next.

143 Harry Kewell made the most unsuccessful

TACKLES

	TACKLES WON %	Tackles won	Tackles lost
John Collins	60.8%	107	69
Neil Lennon	69.8%	104	45
Patrick Vieira	67.7%	88	42
Muzzy Izzet	68.4%	78	36
Robbie Savage	53.4%	78	68
Paul Ince	61.6%	77	48
Chris Perry	51.7%	75	70
Sol Campbell	60.2%	74	70
Andy O'Brien	57.0%	73	55
Stuart McCall	53.3%	73	64
Youssef Chippo	49.0%	72	75
George Boateng	56.3%	71	55
Emerson Thome	58.6%	68	48
Stefan Schwarz	59.8%	67	45
Nicky Butt	55.4%	67	54
Frank Sinclair	54.5%	66	55
Mickael Silvestre	51.6%	66	62
Jonathon Woodgate	56.0%	65	51
Jason Euell	55.6%	65	52
Lucas Radebe	60.4%	64	42

KEY: Tackles won / Tackles lost

After a very good season with Everton, during which he played in central midfield, left midfield and even briefly at right-back, John Collins ended 1999–2000 having won more tackles than any other Premiership player.

But the top five was dominated by the Leicester City midfield, with Neil Lennon, Muzzy Izzet and Robbie Savage having won 260 tackles between them.

Lennon and Izzet also had the highest tackle success rates of all the players in the list, closely followed by Arsenal's Patrick Vieira.

Martin O'Neill's side may not have been the most cultured, but they were certainly one of the most hard-working, as is proven here.

Vieira is the only Gunner to appear on the list, despite Arsenal finishing the 1999–2000 season with the highest tackle success rate and indeed the most successful tackles.

Top Englishman was Paul Ince who, after playing consistently well for Middlesbrough, was rewarded with a place in the England squad for Euro 2000.

The two centre-backs who made the most successful tackles were Spurs duo Chris Perry and Sol Campbell.

Spurs conceded a total of 49 goals in 1999–2000, but it clearly could have been worse for George Graham's side had it not been for the two defensive stalwarts at the heart of the Tottenham rearguard.

The only striker in the chart was Wimbledon striker Jason Euell, who played most of the season in midfield under Egil Olsen's system, and clearly had to do more than his fair share of defensive work as the Dons came under more pressure than most in a season that ended in relegation from the top flight.

One surprise is the absence of Roy Keane, whose team-mate Nicky Butt does feature in the top 20.

THE DIRTIEST

Player	Disciplinary points	Fouls committed (1pt)	Yellow card (3pts)	Red card (6pts)
Paulo Wanchope	140	119	7	
Niall Quinn	120	102	6	
Mark Hughes	117	87	10	
Robert Page	107	71	12	
Hamilton Ricard	105	84	7	
Youssef Chippo	101	68	9	1
Chris Sutton	99	78	7	
Patrick Vieira	96	63	9	1
Don Hutchison	96	69	7	1
Lee Bowyer	94	55	13	
Marc-Vivien Foe	91	61	6	2
Alan Shearer	91	79	2	1
Brian Deane	91	73	6	
Dean Windass	90	72	6	
Emile Heskey	90	75	5	
Chris Makin	89	50	11	1
Dennis Wise	89	62	7	1
Seth Johnson	86	47	13	
George Boateng	85	58	9	
Chris Armstrong	84	72	4	

KEY Fouls committed = 1pt Yellow card = 3pts Red card = 6pts

Half of the top 20 serial foulers in 1999–2000 were strikers, with a keenness to get the ball and frustration both playing their part.

Paulo Wanchope was the biggest offender; in 1998–99 he committed 117 fouls to be the third-dirtiest player, while for the 1999–2000 campaign he went two better on both counts, topping the list with 119 fouls.

Of these misdemeanours, 18 were handballs, the most in the Premiership and twice as many as his nearest rival.

Only two defenders featured in the list, with Welsh international Robert Page the fourth dirtiest player for the season, while Sunderland's Chris Makin also featured.

Page was Watford's captain during the campaign, and he and Chelsea skipper Dennis Wise were hardly leading by example when it came to discipline.

Of the five dirtiest teams in the Premiership for 1999–2000, only eight players from the list of 20 represent them.

However, Middlesbrough were the only team to have both first-choice strikers in the list, with Hamilton Ricard and Brian Deane having accumulated 105 and 91 Opta points respectively.

Seven Premiership players were sent off twice but of those, only Marc-Vivien Foe was persistent enough to feature, with Nicky Butt, Richard Dunne, John Hartson, Frank Leboeuf, Alex Rae and Stefan Schnoor all seeing red twice but not on the list, due mainly to squad rotations and suspensions.

Lee Bowyer and Seth Johnson received the joint-highest number of yellow cards in the 1999–2000 Premiership season, and feature 10th and 18th respectively.

Chris Sutton featured on the list despite spending less than 31 hours on the pitch. The Blues striker suffered from just that, earning an Opta disciplinary point every 18.7 minutes on average.

10 The number of players in the top 20

THE CLEANEST

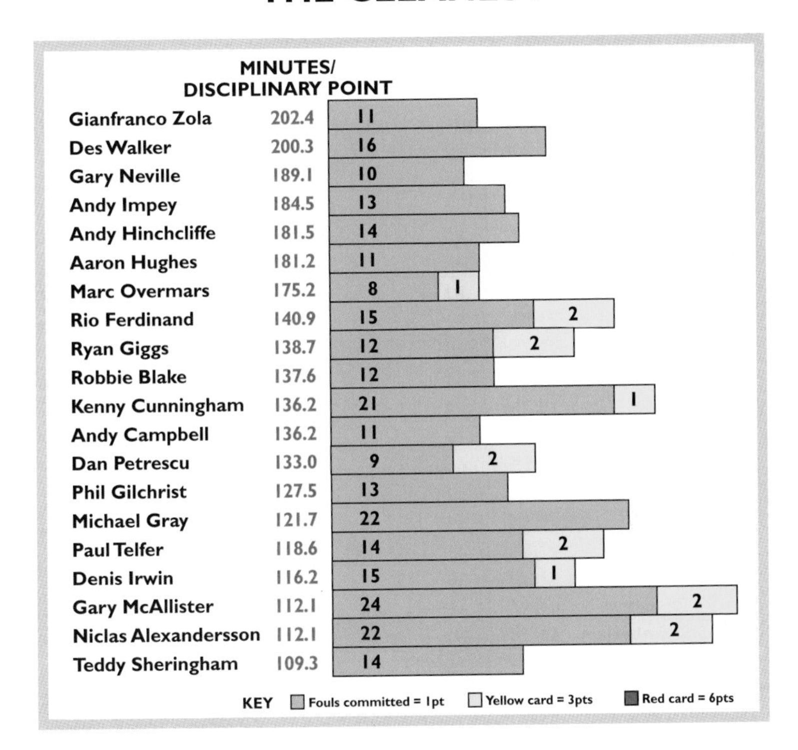

With refereeing decisions falling under much greater scrutiny from the media these days, a great deal of attention lands on those players who lose their discipline, resulting in a flurry of red and yellow cards.

Little mention is ever given to those who steer clear of trouble and avoid the wrath of the Premiership referees. The cleanest players have been calculated on an average of minutes played per disciplinary point, to give some credit to the Premiership's good guys.

Chelsea's pint-sized striker Gianfranco Zola was the cleanest of them all after committing just 11 fouls in the 2,226 minutes he was on the pitch during 1999–2000. None of these infringements was deemed worthy of a caution, and the squeaky-clean Italian was one of just four strikers in the top 20 clean players.

Despite Sheffield Wednesday coming under such pressure in 1999–2000, the experienced Des Walker once again showed himself to be a model professional. The former England star committed just 16 fouls all season. The Owls were one of the cleanest sides overall, with three of their players represented in the top 20, although their fans would have gladly exchanged this record for Premiership survial.

Champions Manchester United had the best disciplinary record, so it was no surprise to see four of their players among the top 20, Gary Neville having the best record of all the Red Devils with just 10 fouls all season.

The centre of midfield is always the most competitive of areas and only one central midfielder managed to make it as one of the league's cleanest players. Coventry City skipper Gary McAllister was an ever-present for the Sky Blues but committed only 24 fouls during the whole campaign.

SAVES

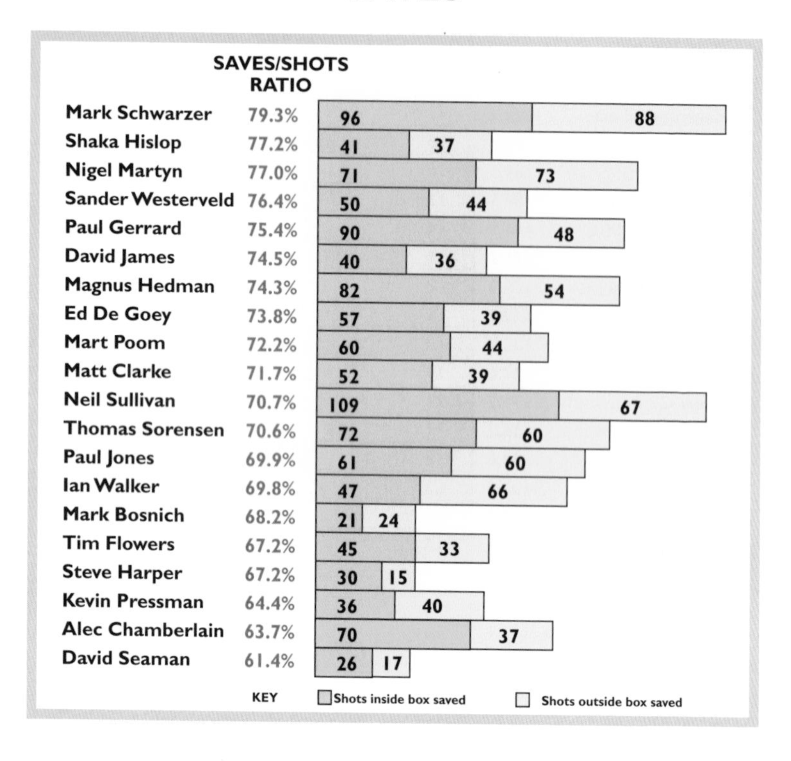

Middlesbrough's big Australian Mark Schwarzer stood head and shoulders above all other Premiership 'keepers as the number one shot-stopper.

The former Bradford player has been at The Riverside since February 1997 and his commanding displays quickly established him as Boro's first choice. In 1999–2000 he was in fine form, making more saves than any other Premiership 'keeper, easily recording the best saves-to-shots ratio in the league and the most saves as well.

Behind Schwarzer was West Ham's Shaka Hislop, who was in sparkling form before his season was cruelly cut short by a broken leg in February. Up until then the Hammer had made 78 saves with an impressive saves-to-shots ratio of 77.2% which was instrumental in West Ham's promising start to the season.

Nigel Martyn is more commonly referred to as "England's Number One" by the Elland Road faithful and Opta's evidence appears to support this theory. The former Palace man saved 77% of all the shots he faced, giving him the highest average of any homegrown shot-stopper in the Premiership.

Liverpool splashed out £4 million in the summer of 1999 for Vitesse Arnhem 'keeper Sander Westerveld and he repaid some of this investment by conceding only 29 goals during the campaign. He made 94 saves as he helped Liverpool achieve the best defensive record in the Premiership in 1999–2000.

At the other end of the table, England international David Seaman will be disappointed with his form that showed him registering the worst saves-to-shots ratio of any first-choice Premiership 'keeper. Although just 27 goals were put past him, Seaman saved just 61.4% of the shots he faced – a very poor return for an international 'keeper.

109 New Spurs recruit Neil Sullivan made the most

SAVES INSIDE

	SAVES/SHOTS RATIO	SHOTS INSIDE BOX SAVED
Paul Gerrard	70.9%	90
Mark Schwarzer	70.6%	96
Sander Westerveld	68.5%	50
Magnus Hedman	67.2%	82
Shaka Hislop	67.2%	41
Ed De Goey	67.1%	57
Nigel Martyn	65.1%	71
Matt Clarke	64.2%	52
David James	63.5%	40
Mart Poom	63.2%	60

Injury to Thomas Myhre at the start of the 1999–2000 gave Paul Gerrard an opportunity – and he never looked back, with his saves-to-shots ratio from efforts struck inside the area the best in the whole Premiership.

Middlesbrough's Mark Schwarzer was a busy man in 1999–2000, but played his part in his side's excellent end-of-season run when they lost just two of their last 14 matches. And Sander Westerveld impressed for Liverpool.

SAVES OUTSIDE

	SAVES/SHOTS RATIO	SHOTS OUTSIDE BOX SAVED
Nigel Martyn	93.6%	73
Shaka Hislop	92.5%	37
David James	92.3%	36
Neil Sullivan	91.8%	67
Mark Schwarzer	91.7%	88
Mart Poom	89.8%	44
Ian Walker	89.2%	66
Magnus Hedman	88.5%	54
Sander Westerveld	88.0%	44
Thomas Sorensen	87.0%	60

England goalkeeper Nigel Martyn left long-range hopefuls smarting by keeping out a greater percentage of efforts struck from outside the area than any other Premiership stopper in the 1999–2000 season.

He was followed by Shaka Hislop, who saved 92.5% of shots faced from outside the area before injury ended his season.

No fewer than eight nationalities were represented in the top 10, with Martyn and David James the only two Englishmen.

saves from shots hit inside the box in 1999–2000

GOALS CONCEDED

	MINUTES/GOAL CONCEDED	CLEAN SHEETS
Sander Westerveld	111.2	14
David James	98.6	11
Ed De Goey	97.9	16
Mark Bosnich	89.3	9
Nigel Martyn	79.5	13
David Seaman	78.3	5
Shaka Hislop	76.8	5
Steve Harper	73.6	4
Ian Walker	69.8	8
Mark Schwarzer	69.4	9
Magnus Hedman	67.0	9
Paul Gerrard	66.2	9
Tim Flowers	64.4	4
Mart Poom	63.0	9
Thomas Sorensen	60.5	9
Matt Clarke	52.1	5
Paul Jones	51.7	8
Neil Sullivan	45.6	5
Kevin Pressman	40.0	3

Dutch goalkeeper Sander Westerveld had an excellent first season in English football, and heads the "minutes per goal conceded" chart for the 1999–2000 campaign.

Liverpool conceded fewer goals than any other team, and while Sami Hyypia and Stephane Henchoz played their part, the 'keeper was instrumental in that fine record.

It was very much a case of "Double Dutch", with Westerveld's 14 clean sheets for the season bettered only by Ed De Goey, and a continuation of this form could see the Liverpool 'keeper become his country's number one.

As for De Goey, he broke Peter Bonetti's record of 22 clean sheets in all competitions in a single season, shutting out opposing attackers on 27 occasions.

Like his fellow-Dutchman, De Goey had an excellent defence to help him, with the likes of Marcel Desailly, Frank Leboeuf and Albert Ferrer usually very solid.

Sandwiched between the two in terms of minutes per goal conceded was David James, whose impressive season won him a place in the 28-man provisional England squad for the European Championships.

England 'keeper Nigel Martyn features in fifth position, just above his rival for England, David Seaman.

Some may be surprised to see Manchester United 'keeper Mark Bosnich at number four. The former Villa stopper struggled to live up to the legacy left by Old Trafford hero Peter Schmeichel.

The Aussie started 23 Premiership matches, although he only finished 20 of them, and despite the fact that United let in 45 goals, Bosnich conceded only every 89.3 minutes on average.

Considering that in 1998–99, Schmeichel conceded roughly every 86 minutes, perhaps Bosnich has not been as poor a replacement as many of his critics have claimed.

CATCHING

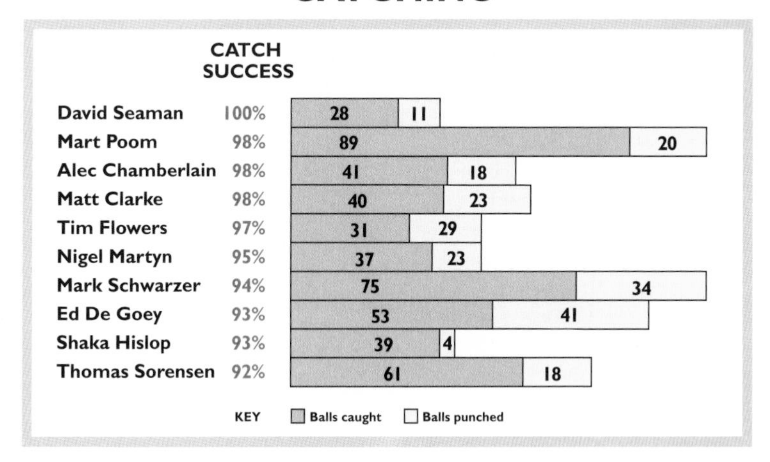

Despite a below-par season for England 'keeper David Seaman, he had the best catching record in the Premiership, with a perfect success rate.

The pressure of Derby's struggle at the foot of the table did not affect the performance of 1998–99's top catcher Mart Poom, who caught the ball more times than any other stopper.

Alec Chamberlain and Matt Clarke also had to keep goal for struggling sides and managed an impressive record of catches.

DISTRIBUTION

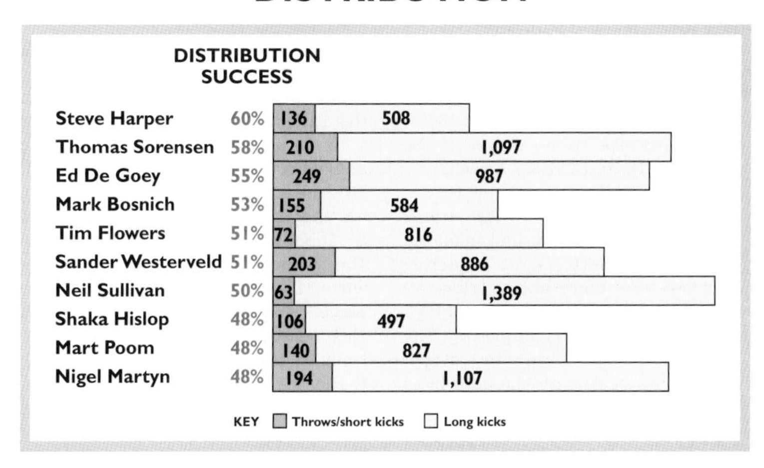

There was much competition for goalkeeping places at Newcastle during the 1999–2000 season, with four different 'keepers having appeared in the first team. But Steve Harper did himself no harm by recording the highest distribution success rate in the Premiership at 60%.

His north-east rival Thomas Sorensen was close behind with 58%, followed by Chelsea's Ed De Goey, who made more throws and short kicks than any other 'keeper in the top flight.

than any of his Premiership rivals

OPTA PLAYER OF THE SEASON

END OF SEASON REPORT: THE GOOD, BAD AND THE UGLY

Stat'll do nicely for top Paolo

Sunday Mirror 21 May 2000

Who is the best player in the Carling Premiership? Who is the best player in his particular position? Who makes the biggest contribution match-by-match? This section details Opta's answers to those questions.

Roy Keane was chosen by the players as the PFA Player of the Year and by the media as the Football Writers' Footballer of the Year. The PFA Young Player of the Year was Leeds United's Harry Kewell.

But do these choices match up to the facts and figures? The Opta Index monitors each touch of the ball made by every player and offers a more objective viewpoint on the contribution that all players make on the pitch.

You may find the results surprising. The Index is only a guide to player performance and deals with the data in as objective a way as possible. Opta do not make subjective judgements on the quality of goals, the importance of winning strikes or the fact that successful dribbles by David Ginola are usually more pleasing on the eye than those by Tony Adams.

For an in-depth explanation of the Index see page 12.

Opta's player of the 1999–2000 season was Paolo Di Canio of West Ham United. The Italian striker had a fantastic campaign at Upton Park, culminating in him captaining West Ham in the final few matches of the season.

His renaissance has been remarkable and Di Canio has fully repaid the faith shown in him by Harry Redknapp, making the £1.5 million transfer fee look a snip.

Di Canio scored 16 Premiership goals and directly set up 13 for team-mates. This means he was involved in 56% of all his team's goals, and only Kevin Phillips of Sunderland can boast a higher ratio. The former Celtic striker hit the target with 71% of his attempts at goal and no player who fired in more than 20 shots this season had a superior accuracy in front of goal. And one in four of his shots found the back of the net.

When the Sunday Mirror asked Di Canio for his reaction to being Opta's player of the season, he said: "I am really happy to hear the news that I am the top striker in England. This award is as much for the fans who love me, the coaching staff at the club who have worked with me and especially for Harry who believed in me after what happened at Sheffield Wednesday."

GOALKEEPERS

PLAYER NAME	TEAM	OPTA POINTS
Mark Schwarzer	Middlesbro	1,047
Neil Sullivan	Wimbledon	862
Matt Clarke	Bradford	843
Pavel Srnicek	Sheff Wed	836
Paul Gerrard	Everton	785
Mart Poom	Derby Co	783
Shaka Hislop	West Ham	777
Nigel Martyn	Leeds Utd	748
Magnus Hedman	Coventry	739
Thomas Sorensen	Sunderland	719
Paul Jones	Southampton	698
David James	Aston Villa	660
Ed De Goey	Chelsea	655
Sander Westerveld	Liverpool	655
Ian Walker	Tottenham	629
Steve Harper	Newcastle	555*
Tim Flowers	Leicester	529
Mark Bosnich	Man Utd	500
Alec Chamberlain	Watford	439
David Seaman	Arsenal	294

The goalkeeping Index is often the position that throws up the most controversial ranking. Opta are not suggesting that the list is a definitive guide to the quality of individual players – after all few people would agree that Matt Clarke should be in the England team ahead of David Seaman – but the Index does convey an average contribution over the course of a season.

Of course, goalkeepers in those sides struggling at the bottom of the table often have far more shots to save, higher numbers of crosses to deal with and plenty of possession too.

Since every action earns or loses points, the busier 'keepers will often earn more points especially if they can concede as few goals as possible.

However, that does not mean that the Index cannot be used as a guide to form.

Top of the stops for 1999–2000 was Mark Schwarzer, who also finished with the best saves-to-shots ratio of all Premiership goalkeepers. He saved a greater proportion of shots than anyone, which helped him to top the Index.

At the other end of the scale, David Seaman had the worst saves-to-shots ratio of any top-flight 'keeper and the fact that he had relatively little to do as well means that he ranks last of all the first-choice Premiership shot-stoppers in 1999–2000.

Mark Schwarzer made a total of 184 saves – more than any other 'keeper - whereas Seaman faced only 70 shots all season and conceded 23 times.

Neil Sullivan finished second in the Index and will be a valuable asset to his new club, while Matt Clarke's performances certainly contributed to keeping the Bantams in the top flight.

DEFENDERS

PLAYER NAME	TEAM	OPTA POINTS
Sami Hyypia	Liverpool	1,039
Sol Campbell	Tottenham	1,034
Denis Irwin	Man Utd	1,030
Gary Pallister	Middlesbro	1,012
Stephen Carr	Tottenham	1,004
Lucas Radebe	Leeds Utd	996
Albert Ferrer	Chelsea	979
Ian Harte	Leeds Utd	979
Gerry Taggart	Leicester	978
Christian Ziege	Middlesbro	971
Richard Gough	Everton	970
David Wetherall	Bradford	968
Jaap Stam	Man Utd	967
Silvinho	Arsenal	961
Paul Williams	Coventry	957
Philip Neville	Man Utd	955
Tony Adams	Arsenal	949
Emerson Thome	Chelsea	927
David Weir	Everton	927
Mickael Silvestre	Man Utd	925

It is rare that one player can have such a marked impact in his first season in a new team and in a foreign country, changing an aspect of his team's performance that was considered their key weakness and turning it into major strengths one of the club's major strengths.

But in 1999–2000, Sami Hyypia was the catalyst behind turning Liverpool's aerially-suspect defence, with its "Keystone Kops" image, into the tightest rearguard in the land.

Liverpool conceded just 30 goals all season and Hyypia was at the heart of the Reds' new-found parsimony, completing 538 clearances – only David Wetherall of beleaguered Bradford made more in the Premiership – and 61 tackles, the highest number made by any Liverpool player.

Sol Campbell was again the target for some of Europe's top clubs, including Manchester United, and his awesome presence continues to be a key factor for Spurs and England. Only Chris Perry among the top-flight defenders made more interceptions or successful tackles, as George Graham continued creating another solid defence.

And Denis Irwin showed that the key to scoring highly in the Index is consistency, with his collection of solid displays earning a new contract at Manchester United, despite the pressure from younger players such as Phil Neville and Mickael Silvestre.

Arsenal's indifferent season is summed up by the fact that stalwart Tony Adams only just made the top 20, while the Gunners' top defender was newcomer Silvinho, who looked more comfortable going forward than defending.

Finally, the top right-back was Stephen Carr, who was not only superb in defence, but scored a couple of brilliant goals, including a cracking shot against Manchester United and a delicate chip versus Sunderland on the last day.

MIDFIELDERS

PLAYER NAME	TEAM	OPTA POINTS
Roy Keane	Man Utd	1,252
Neil Lennon	Leicester	1,177
Emmanuel Petit	Arsenal	1,122
Muzzy Izzet	Leicester	1,115
John Collins	Everton	1,105
Frank Lampard	West Ham	1,040
Tim Sherwood	Tottenham	977
Patrick Vieira	Arsenal	973
Gary McAllister	Coventry	971
Dennis Wise	Chelsea	968
Paul Ince	Middlesbro	937
Didier Deschamps	Chelsea	932
Don Hutchison	Everton	930
Steve Lomas	West Ham	923
Steven Gerrard	Liverpool	891
Wim Jonk	Sheff Wed	865
Dietmar Hamann	Liverpool	852
Lee Bowyer	Leeds Utd	811
Robert Lee	Newcastle	804
Stuart McCall	Bradford	783

There is little doubt that Roy Keane was a deserving winner of both the player of the season and Footballer of the Year awards.

The Manchester United skipper is arguably the most important player to any side in English football. With his combination of tigerish tackling and accurate link play, he is the fulcrum of the Red Devils' side.

Keane made more passes (1,919) than any other player in the Premiership and completed a staggering 85% of them. That passing success rate was the second best in the Premiership behind his United team-mate Jaap Stam, who of course played the vast majority of his distribution in his own half.

The Irishman also weighed in with five goals, including two vital strikes in a 2–1 away win against Arsenal – United's closest rivals – showing once more that he is the man for the big occasion. It is no wonder, then, that United broke their pay structure to keep Keane at Old Trafford.

Leicester City's success has been built on their industrious midfield. Neil Lennon and Muzzy Izzet feature in second and fourth places in the Index respectively. Only Keane completed more passes than Lennon's 1,494 and the Northern Irishman also made the second highest number of successful challenges (104) during the course of the campaign. Meanwhile, Izzet scored eight goals and earned a call-up to the Turkish squad for Euro 2000.

Emmanuel Petit finished between Lennon and Izzet in third place, despite an inconsistent campaign. On their day, any midfield in Europe would struggle against the Petit-Vieira axis, but there were not quite enough of those days to compete with Manchester United. John Collins, who won more tackles than any other player, finished fifth, while Frank Lampard was the highest-rated Englishman.

ATTACKING MIDFIELDERS

PLAYER NAME	TEAM	OPTA POINTS
Paul Scholes	Man Utd	1,219
David Beckham	Man Utd	1,137
Nolberto Solano	Newcastle	1,093
Gustavo Poyet	Chelsea	1,043
Trevor Sinclair	West Ham	967
Gary Speed	Newcastle	958
Patrik Berger	Liverpool	954
Darren Anderton	Tottenham	946
Kieron Dyer	Newcastle	941
Harry Kewell	Leeds Utd	919
Juninho	Middlesbro	918
Ryan Giggs	Man Utd	913
David Ginola	Tottenham	911
Rory Delap	Derby Co	901
Nick Barmby	Everton	895
Peter Beagrie	Bradford	856
Niclas Alexandersson	Sheff Wed	849
Paul Merson	Aston Villa	845
Moustapha Hadji	Coventry	821
Youssef Chippo	Coventry	791

As they say at Old Trafford: "Paul Scholes – he scores goals." And what goals! The feisty midfielder weighed in with nine strikes during 1999–2000 and some, like the stunning volley against Bradford City or the stinging drive against Middlesbrough, were simply breathtaking.

Not only was he one of four different United players to net a hat-trick during the campaign, but Scholes was also superb in other areas, completing 82% of his passes and setting up five goals for team-mates.

David Beckham finished second in the attacking midfielders Index, claiming 15 goal assists – the joint highest number in 1999–2000 and one more than his season-high 14 in 1998–99. He also discovered his goalscoring touch after having his hair cut. The highest-profile player in England netted six times, with five bulging Premiership nets post-salon appointment.

Nolberto Solano of Newcastle was a target for Real Madrid for most of the campaign, and it was clear that his 15 assists delighted the likes of Alan Shearer and Duncan Ferguson.

Gustavo Poyet would have enjoyed being on the end of the service from Beckham and Solano but he fared well for the Blues, scoring some stunning goals including a sublime volley on the opening day against Sunderland.

But one surprise is that PFA Young Player of the Year Harry Kewell finished only 10th in the Opta Index. While much of his play was eye-catching, the reason why the Australian was ranked that low was due to the effectiveness of his overall game. He completed just 66% of his passes, fired in more shots off target than any player over the 1999–2000 campaign and lost possession of the ball on more dribbles than any other top-flight player.

STRIKERS

PLAYER NAME	TEAM	OPTA POINTS
Paolo Di Canio	West Ham	1,290
Dwight Yorke	Man Utd	1,283
Thierry Henry	Arsenal	1,133
Kevin Phillips	Sunderland	1,034
Steffen Iversen	Tottenham	906
Michael Bridges	Leeds Utd	902
Emile Heskey	Liverpool	888
Alan Shearer	Newcastle	851
Kevin Campbell	Everton	822
Robbie Keane	Coventry	812
Paulo Wanchope	West Ham	811
Gilles De Bilde	Sheff Wed	807
Dean Windass	Bradford	801
Niall Quinn	Sunderland	795
Dion Dublin	Aston Villa	749
Marian Pahars	Southampton	749
Carl Cort	Wimbledon	747
Brian Deane	Middlesbro	718
Hamilton Ricard	Middlesbro	681
Tony Cottee	Leicester	621

Ten years ago, it would have been difficult to imagine the strains of Verdi's La Traviata floating across Upton Park. But Hammers fans have been brushing up on their opera to serenade a new hero at the Boleyn.

Paolo Di Canio is not the first rogue to enjoy cult status down in the East End, but his popularity has burgeoned as Harry Redknapp has sought to fill his dressing-room with more characters than a certain local soap opera.

Di Canio scored 16 Premiership goals in 1999–2000 and directly set up 13 for team-mates. This means he was involved in 56% of all his team's goals, and only Kevin Phillips of Sunderland could boast a higher ratio.

Just behind Di Canio was Dwight Yorke who, despite claims that he was not as good as he was in 1998–99, broke United's long-standing hoodoo of the 20 league goal barrier. Yorke became the first player to achieve this tally since Brian McClair, but also completed a higher proportion of passes in the opposition half than any Premiership player – an astonishing feat for a forward.

Arsenal's Thierry Henry took time to settle, but banished the memory of sulky Nicolas Anelka by matching his predecessor's 17-goal haul and equalled the Premiership record by scoring in seven consecutive games. Indeed, he has a chance to break the record in his first Premiership fixture in 2000–01.

In fourth was Kevin Phillips, who won the Golden Boot and scored 30 league goals. This was a truly phenomenal achievement given that the top scorers in the previous two seasons had managed just 18 strikes, and considering he was playing in one of the promoted sides.

Steffen Iversen laid a claim to be Sergei Rebrov's partner at White Hart Lane by finishing sixth.

TEAMS OF THE SEASON

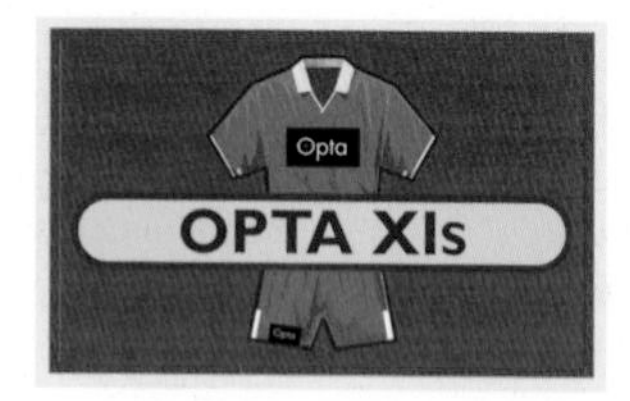

Every week, in most newspapers, there is a team of the week picked by the journalists or their suggestion to the England manager about which players should feature in the latest squad.

And in every pub, school and office, a favourite pastime is picking a personal England team, an all-star team or a World XI of superstars.

This section is a definitive guide to the teams of the 1999–2000 season. There are the top scorers, the most accurate marksmen, the best passers and the best- and worst-behaved player. Plus there is an England XI, an overseas team and an Under-21 side all based on the Opta Index.

Each team is laid out in a 4–4–2 formation graphic like the one shown below. Each player is selected based on being the best (or worst) in his particular position and will be shown as indicated. For example, Gary Neville will always feature as a right-back, Paul Scholes as a central midfield player and Alan Shearer as a striker. However, there are occasions where a versatile player like Kieron Dyer may feature in different positions for different teams in this section.

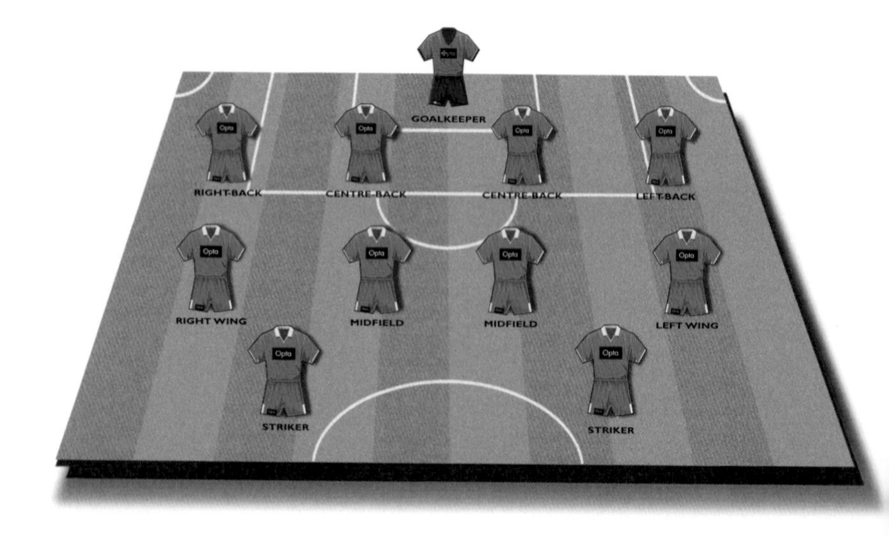

TEAM OF THE SEASON

Manchester United's record-breaking Premiership campaign is reflected in Opta's team of the season. No fewer than five Red Devils make the side, led by inspirational skipper Roy Keane.

The Irishman recorded the best overall pass completion rate in the 1999–2000 season – apart from Jaap Stam – and found a team-mate with more passes than any other player over the course of the entire campaign.

David Beckham and Paul Scholes were a constant threat from midfield, with the former setting up 15 goals and the latter finding the net nine times, including a hat-trick in the 7–1 demolition of West Ham.

Denis Irwin was the model of consistency once again and Dwight Yorke became the first Manchester United player since Brian McClair to net 20 times in a single league campaign. The Tobagan also recorded the best passing accuracy in the opposition half – an outstanding achievement for a forward with almost every pass made under pressure.

The second highest representation came from Tottenham Hotspur, where Sol Campbell and Stephen Carr both had solid seasons as George Graham continues the task of re-establishing the north London club as a major force in English football.

Liverpool's Finnish man-mountain, Sami Hyypia, was a rock at the heart of Gerard Houllier's new-look defence and was rightly nominated by his peers in the Player of the Year awards.

Mark Schwarzer recorded a 79% saves-to-shots ratio – the best in the top flight – as well as making more saves than any other 'keeper.

But all of these players followed in the wake of Opta's player of the season, Paolo Di Canio. The Italian forward put his bad boy history behind him to enthral and enchant crowds up and down the country with a series of virtuoso performances and a range of outstanding goals. He scored 16 in total, including a goal of the season contender against Wimbledon.

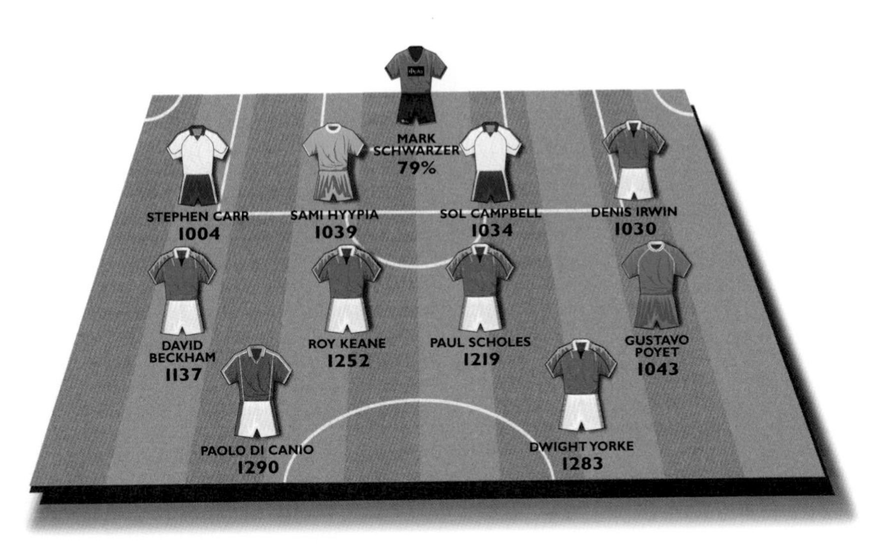

goals than those of any other team

GOALSCORERS

After a disastrous start that almost saw Alan Shearer walk away from his beloved Newcastle, the England captain finished the campaign with a flourish and the 300th goal of his glittering career. His deflected strike against Arsenal was his 23rd Premiership goal of a difficult season, that saw him end his international career after the Euro 2000 tournament.

But, his goalscoring prowess was overshadowed during 1999–2000 by the prolific form of Premiership newcomer Kevin Phillips.

The former Watford striker blitzed Premiership defences by netting 30 league goals and winning the Golden Boot.

In midfield, the top-scoring player was Gary McAllister, though four of his 11 strikes came from the penalty spot. He narrowly pipped Leeds' young Australian Harry Kewell and Uruguayan Guatavo Poyet, who both finished the season with 10 goals. The other midfield slot was grabbed by Paul Scholes, who scored nine of Manchester United's record-breaking tally of 97 goals.

The top-scoring defender actually played some of the 1999–2000 season in midfield, but Rory Delap's eight strikes made him worthy of a place in the team.

The other three defenders all netted six times. Christian Ziege, too, played some matches in midfield, but was a particular threat from set-pieces, scoring twice from dead-ball situations. David Unsworth and Gerry Taggart make up the central defensive partnership as they fired in their six goals in less time on the pitch than Matt Elliott, who deputised up front for Leicester when Martin O'Neill was short of strikers.

Between the sticks for the team was Sander Westerveld, who helped Liverpool concede the fewest goals in the top flight. The Dutchman picked the ball out of the net on just 29 occasions in an impressive first campaign.

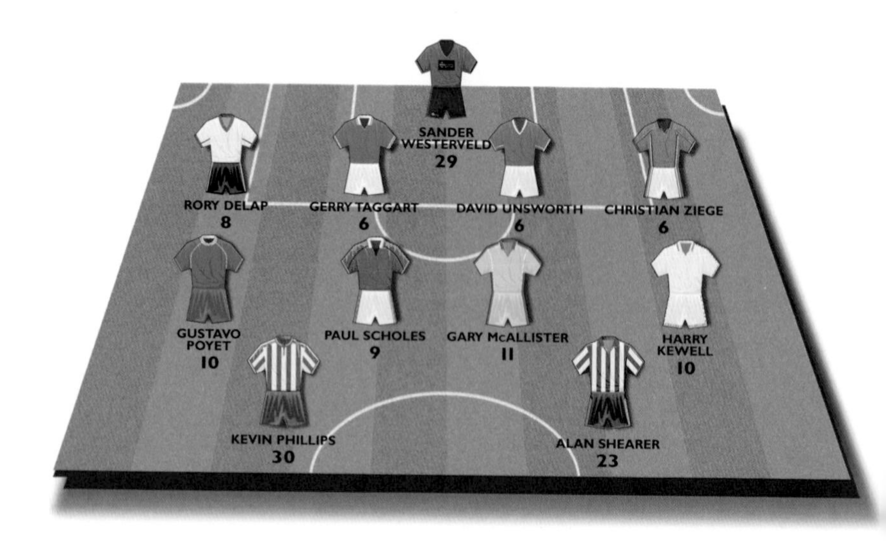

6 Kevin Phillips scored more penalties than

BEST PERFORMANCES

Not only did Paolo Di Canio register the highest average Index score over the course of the season, he recorded the highest points total by an individual in a single game.

The Italian's majestic display in the 5–0 drubbing of Coventry saw him score twice and set up the other three goals.

Mark Schwarzer turned in the next best performance, according to Opta. The big 'keeper made an incredible 13 saves during the 0–0 draw with Leeds at The Riverside.

Top defensive performances saw Danny Mills score Leeds' winner in their 2–1 win over Sunderland and record a pass completion rate of 77%. Greek defender Nikos Dabizas scored the winner against Spurs at St James's Park, while defensively he registered more clearances than any other player on the pitch.

Newcastle left-back Didier Domi scored against Coventry and made 17 blocks, clearances and interceptions, while Sol Campbell ended the season in style when Spurs beat Sunderland. The England centre-back made a colossal 23 clearances and nine blocks.

Midfielder Muzzy Izzet scored to rescue a point for Leicester against Liverpool after setting up Tony Cottee for his team's opening goal. Newcastle's Gary Speed was superb against Sheffield Wednesday, scoring a goal and making 58 successful passes with a completion rate of 91%.

Gustavo Poyet netted twice from four efforts at goal, all of which were on target, against Sunderland on the opening day, while David Beckham's late winner capped a superb display as Manchester United beat Middlesbrough 1–0 at Old Trafford.

The second best striking performance of the season saw Alan Shearer fire in five goals and help Newcastle to an outstanding 8–0 victory against Sheffield Wednesday. Shearer's five goals came from just five attempts in the whole match. That game proved to be the season's turning point for Shearer and Newcastle.

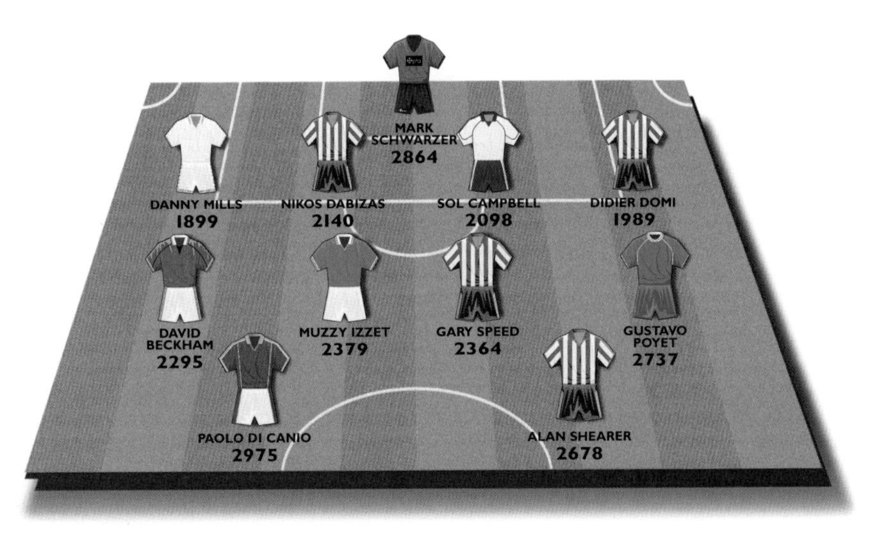

any other player in 1999–2000

BEST PASSING

Manchester United made more passes than any other team in the 1999–2000 season and also recorded the best completion rate. It is no surprise, therefore, that four of the Red Devils feature in Opta's team of best passers.

Jaap Stam recorded the best overall pass completion rate, Dwight Yorke the best rate in the opposition half and nobody made more successful passes than Roy Keane's tally of 1,919. They are joined by utility man Phil Neville, who made Kevin Keegan's Euro 2000 squad, despite failing to hold down a regular spot in United's first team.

The second most accurate passing team were Chelsea. Marcel Desailly and Celestine Babayaro imbue all the qualities required to play Gianluca Vialli's possession game alongside Frank Leboeuf, who made more long passes than any other player in 1999–2000.

The Blues were one of only two sides other than Manchester United to have more than one player in the team of top passers. Ironically, the team Chelsea chairman Ken Bates accused of employing "kick and rush" tactics, Leicester City, also had two players, with Neil Lennon impressing in the heart of Martin O'Neill's industrious midfield and Tony Cottee ranking as the second most accurate striker when it came to distribution.

Kieron Dyer of Newcastle shone in his first Premiership campaign, recording the second best pass completion rate in the opposition half of 83% – just behind Yorke – and Mark Pembridge did an effective job for Walter Smith down Everton's left flank or in the centre of the Toffees' midfield.

The goalkeeper with the most accurate distribution was Thomas Sorensen. But, this statistic needs to be assessed in context as he had the advantage of aiming for Niall Quinn, who won more headed flick-ons than any other player in the top flight.

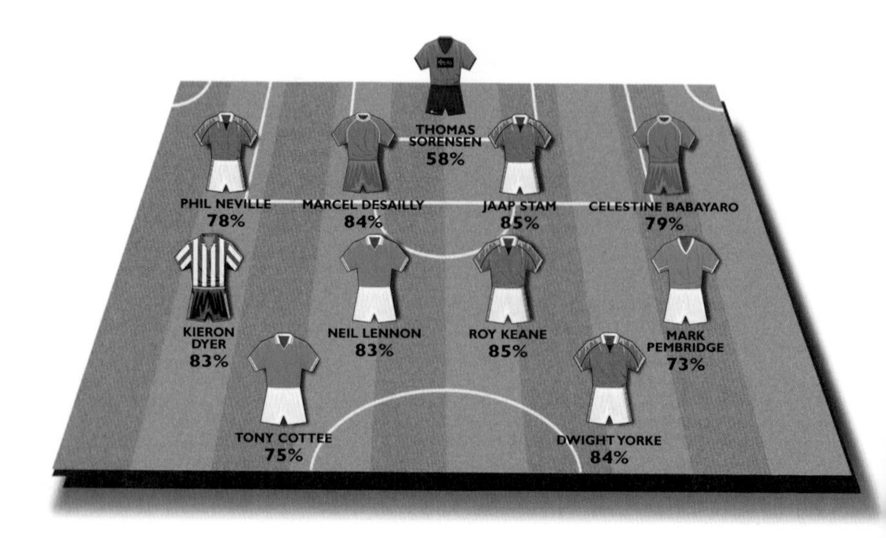

BEST TACKLERS

Everton may have shaken off their "dogs of war" tag with the addition of cultured passers to their squad such as John Collins and Stephen Hughes, but they rarely shirked a challenge.

Collins actually contested more tackles than any other player in 1999–2000, winning a staggering 107 challenges.

The Scot was closely followed by Neil Lennon of Leicester City with 104 successful tackles, in arguably the most combative midfield in the top flight alongside Muzzy Izzet and Robbie Savage.

Stefan Schwarz reminded Premiership observers of his tough tackling, making 67 successful challenges for the Mackems before being sidelined through injury, while Youssef Chippo of Coventry City is the only player in the XI who actually failed to win the ball more often than he won it – earning an A for effort, but only C+ for effectiveness.

Dean Windass and Paulo Wanchope proved to be the most willing forwards in the Premiership, winning 73 tackles between them over the course of the season, although the Bradford man's tally was enhanced by occasional outings in midfield and Wanchope's timing was often awry, as he committed more fouls than any other player.

The three relegated sides also have one player apiece in the team of top tacklers after having plenty of work to do. Peter Atherton was effective at right-back, centre-back and in a holding role in midfield, while Paul Robinson weighed in with 55 successful challenges on Watford's left flank. And completing the trio from doomed sides, Neil Sullivan smothered the ball at the feet of various forwards on a total of 25 occasions.

Finally, all that work that George Graham made his players do at the training ground has clearly paid off. Sol Campbell and Chris Perry of Spurs made the two highest tallies of successful tackles by central defenders.

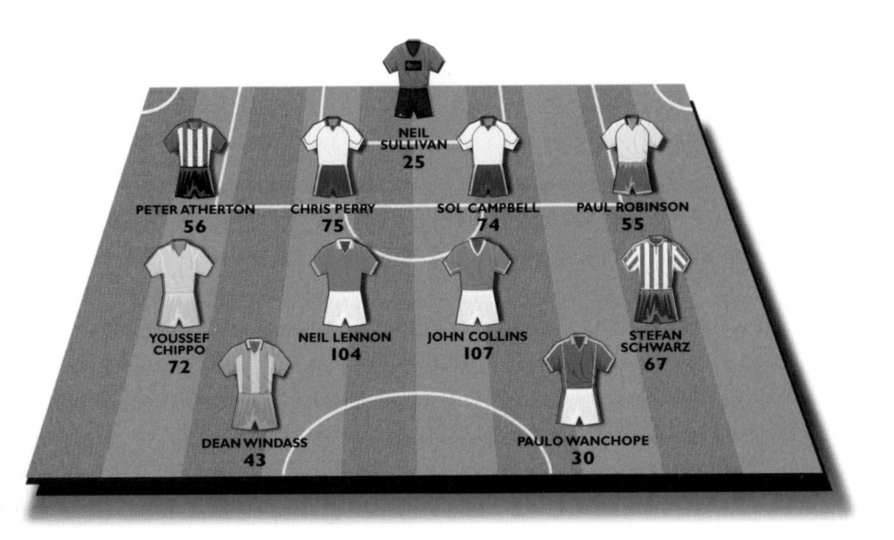

than any other player in 1999–2000

ENGLAND XI

Ossie Ardiles once commented: "As manager of the national team, you know that, apart from the Chancellor, you will probably be the most hated man in the country."

Kevin Keegan currently holds the hopes of millions of England fans in his hands, but despite the difficulty of the job, few would turn down the role, if offered.

Opta has its own way of selecting the best players for the England team – the Index. This objective ranking system shows the average contribution of players over 90 minutes.

Up front, two former team-mates, who both had excellent seasons, line up together. Kevin Phillips scored 30 goals and was involved in 59% of Sunderland's 57 strikes. Michael Bridges netted 19 times for Leeds and drew comparisons with Dennis Bergkamp for his deft style of play.

In midfield, three of Keegan's favourites feature prominently, with David Beckham supplying the ammunition from the right, Dennis Wise reverting to the left-sided role he occasionally plays for the Blues and Paul Scholes arriving from deep positions to score goals. The one surprise is perhaps Frank Lampard, but the young Hammer could become a regular at international level on current form.

Kieron Dyer occupies the right-back berth after a scintillating debut against Luxembourg, while one of Keegan's favourite players, Phil Neville, fills the problem left-back role. In the centre of defence Sol Campbell is a certain starter, while Opta recognise the continued consistency of Gary Pallister.

The goalkeeping slot would be taken by Nigel Martyn who recorded the best saves-to-shots ratio of any England 'keeper.

Notable absentees include Andy Cole, who did not play enough games to qualify for the Index and England stalwarts such as Tony Adams and Alan Shearer, who had indifferent spells over the course of the season for a variety of reasons.

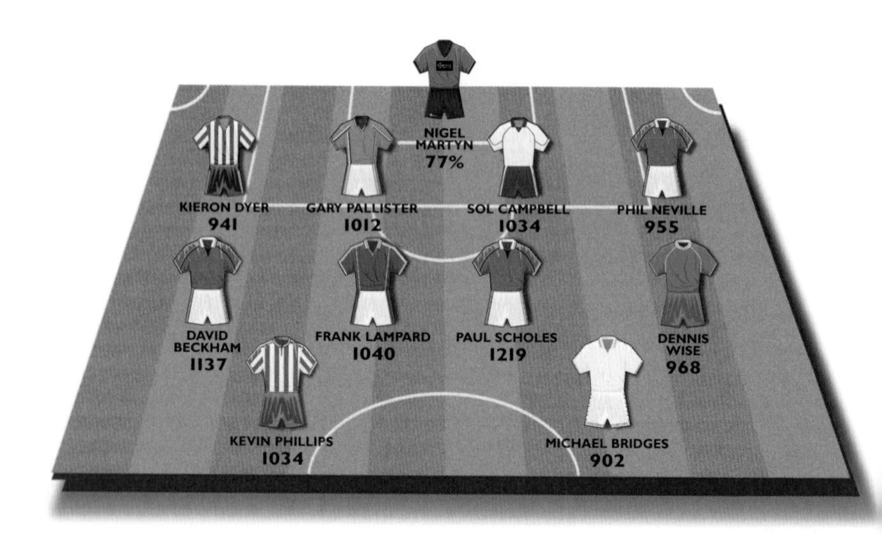

BRITISH ISLES XI

Cut-price overseas imports have somewhat stemmed the flow of players from all parts of the British Isles into the Premiership. But there are still plenty of talented players from Wales, Scotland, Northern Ireland and the Republic plying their trade in the English Premiership.

The Opta line-up contains six players from Mick McCarthy's Irish squad. Robbie Keane brought a breath of fresh air to Coventry City when he joined from Wolverhampton Wanderers in August and repaid Gordon Strachan's faith with 12 goals, while international strike partner Niall Quinn scored 14 and created eight more in Sunderland's excellent first season back in the top flight.

Stephen Carr scored some cracking goals for Spurs and was rated as the best right-back in the Premiership, while Rory Delap showed his versatility by playing in several positions on the right-hand side of the pitch and scoring eight goals for the Rams.

Roy Keane was outstanding for Manchester United, scoring five times, including a vital brace to secure victory at Arsenal and Denis Irwin was the model of consistency for United once again.

Also in the Manchester United line-up and Opta's British Isles team is Ryan Giggs. The Welshman improved his consistency and set up more goals from open play than any other player. He also helped himself to six goals in United's avalanche of 97 strikes.

At the heart of the defence are Northern Irishman Gerry Taggart who scored six goals for the Foxes and Scotsman Richard Gough who proved that, even at 38, he is still a difficult opponent.

And a second Scot completes the team. Neil Sullivan went some way to dispelling the traditional image of Scottish 'keepers by making the second highest number of saves during the 1999–2000 season, although he was unable to save Wimbledon's porous defence every time.

any other England player at Euro 2000

OVERSEAS XI

There were more than 50 nationalities represented in the Premiership over the course of the 1999–2000 season. Such is the cosmopolitan nature of the English Premiership that Opta's Overseas XI actually contains 11 players, all with different nationalities – and selected from six different continents.

South America is represented by Nolberto Solano of Peru, who created 15 goals for Newcastle team-mates – the joint-highest tally in the top flight – and Uruguayan Gustavo Poyet who scored 10 goals in the Blues' Premiership campaign.

Concacaf contribute Dwight Yorke. The United forward missed several games playing for Trinidad and Tobago, but still had time to help his side to a sixth title in eight seasons, by scoring 20 Premiership goals.

Africa is represented by Lucas Radebe. No Leeds United player contributed more defensive clearances, or made more interceptions and he earned just two yellow cards. Radebe was a vital source of experience in Leeds' youthful squad that qualified for the Champions League.

Australasia provides the goalkeeper, with Mark Schwarzer recording the best saves-to-shots ratio of all first-choice number ones and also making more saves than any 'keeper in the top flight.

Asia has one representative, thanks to Kevin Keegan not fancying Muzzy Izzet. The Leicester midfield player qualifies through his father to play for Turkey, although, of course, the national team plays in European competition.

And the other five representatives in Opta's overseas team come from Europe. Finn Sami Hyypia made more defensive clearances than all but David Wetherall; marauding German wing-back Christian Ziege scored two set-piece goals; Frenchman Emmanuel Petit created more goalscoring opportunities than any other Gunner; Spaniard Albert Ferrer made more interceptions than any other Chelsea player; and Italian Paolo Di Canio was Opta's player of the season, making or scoring 29 of the Hammers' 52 goals.

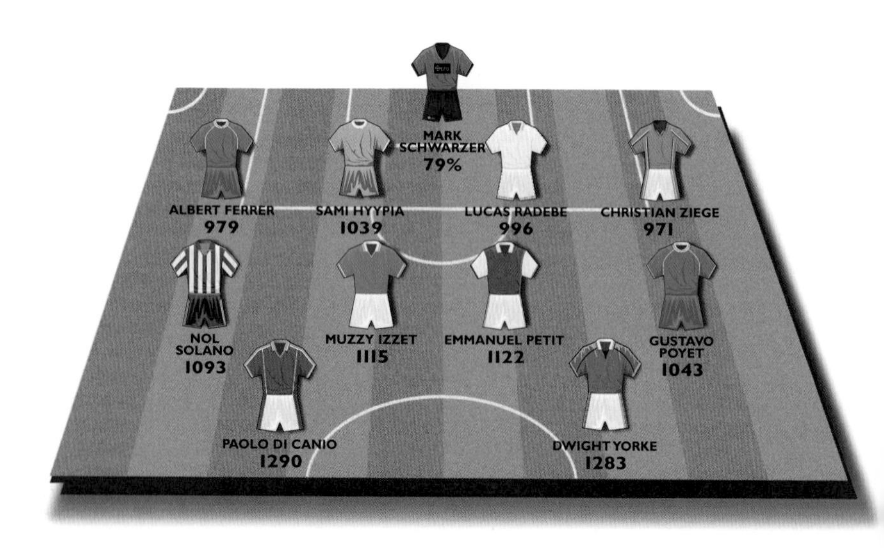

UNDER-21 XI

The 1999-2000 Premiership season brought forth a multitude of new footballing stars to the public's attention. Naturally, Leeds' youthful team grabbed the majority of the headlines as they pushed for Championship glory. But there was still plenty of room for other talented young players to make their impact.

West Ham 'keeper Stephen Bywater had a shaky game against Bradford, after injury to Shaka Hislop forced him into the first team ahead of schedule, but recovered to make a few more outings.

And he is joined by team-mate and England under-21 skipper Frank Lampard, who had another excellent season, firing 50 shots on target – the third-highest total in the Premiership. The Hammer is joined in central midfield by Liverpool's Steven Gerrard, in a partnership that could soon be recreated at international level.

Carl Cort demonstrated great versatility in a struggling Wimbledon side and joins Leeds' Harry Kewell to complete the midfield. The Australian was successful with 193 dribbles – the second-highest total in the division – and was named PFA Young Player of the Year.

Kieron Dyer took the right-back position after his outstanding performance on his England debut against Luxembourg. But he also demonstrated his attacking instincts in the league, completing 80% of his passes in the opposition half – the second best rating in the Premiership. He is joined in defence by cultured central defenders Jonathon Woodgate of Leeds and Mickael Silvestre of Manchester United. With the left-back slot going to Ian Harte – the joint-highest scoring defender in the top flight.

Up front, Michael Bridges surprised most pundits by ending up as the Premiership's fourth-highest scorer. And, after a slow start to his Highbury career, Thierry Henry proved himself to be a more than capable replacement for Nicolas Anelka, scoring in seven successive league games and equalling the Premiership record.

DIRTY DOZEN

Opta's Dirty Dozen team is based on the average number of minutes it takes a player to accumulate disciplinary points with one point per foul conceded, three per yellow card and six for each dismissal.

Chris Sutton had a miserable first season for Chelsea, scoring just one league goal. The £10-million man also earned an average of one point for every 18.7 minutes of league football played, making him the dirtiest player in the top flight for the second season running.

Not far behind was Paulo Wanchope who committed more fouls than any other Premiership player, with a grand total of 185 misdemeanours.

Mark Hughes racked up the third most disciplinary points, but earned only 10 yellow cards in 1999–2000, compared to the 14 he picked up in the previous foul-strewn campaign.

Marc-Vivien Foe was one of seven players dismissed on two occasions. The Cameroon international was one of four West Ham players in the team, being joined by Igor Stimac and John Moncur as the Hammers picked up eight dismissals – more than any other team.

Chris Makin and Gavin McCann of Sunderland featured, with the Wearsiders being ranked as the dirtiest team in the 1999–2000 season. The full-back was cautioned 11 times and dismissed once, while McCann earned eight bookings in a campaign curtailed by injury.

Mark Williams of Watford picked up eight yellow cards and saw red once as Watford sank back into Nationwide Division One, while Stefan Schnoor was sent off twice for Derby County.

Paul Gerrard was the goalkeeper with the worst disciplinary record. Although he committed just four fouls, he was cautioned on three occasions.

Making up the dozen was Leeds' Alan Smith. The feisty youngster has already built a reputation and earned five yellows and one red card, despite his limited appearances during 1999–2000.

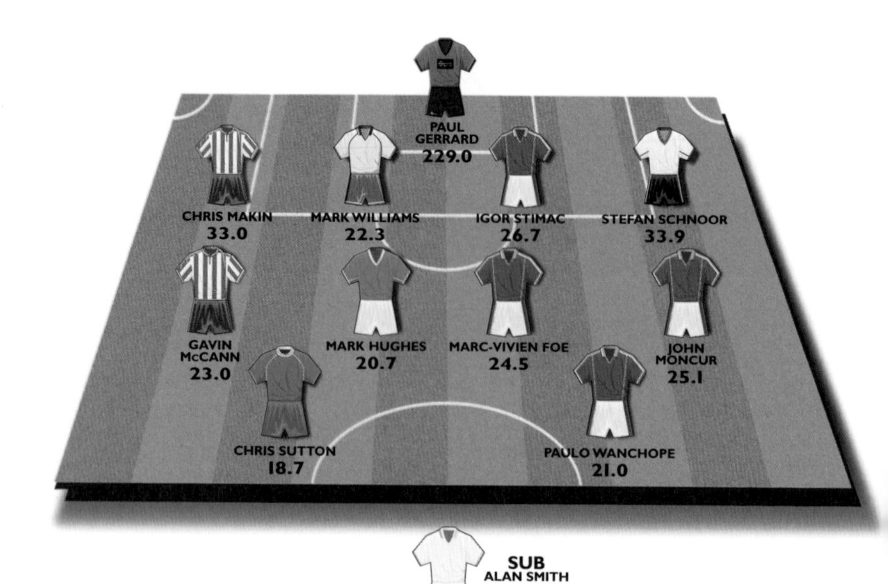

8 West Ham had more players sent off than

CLEAN XI

Opta's clean team is based on the average number of minutes it takes a player to accumulate disciplinary points with one point per foul conceded, three per yellow card and six for each dismissal.

Gianfranco Zola was the player least likely to incur the wrath of a Premiership referee during the 1999–2000 campaign. On average he earned one disciplinary point every 202.4 minutes. A diminutive striker, though, might not be expected to be put in too many positions where he might make fouls or earn bookings.

That is what makes the performances of the clean team's back four so impressive. They all earned fewer than one disciplinary point per two games played. Des Walker topped the list, going on average 200 minutes between fouls and not getting booked all season.

In fact Andy Hinchcliffe, Aaron Hughes and Gary Neville all managed to navigate the campaign without finding themselves in the referee's notebook.

Another surprising entry into the clean team was Watford's Steve Palmer. The burly defensive midfielder earned less than one disciplinary point per game on average. He, too, avoided the referee's notebook, despite playing in the hurly-burly of midfield.

Gary McAllister, on the other hand, was booked on two occasions, but still recorded a better average than Palmer, earning one point every 112 minutes.

The wide positions were occupied by two of the game's creative players who are less than enthused by the physical aspect of the sport. Marc Overmars made the team for the second year in a row, committing just eight fouls, while Dan Petrescu made only nine. The Romanian also racked up one more yellow card than the solitary caution earned by Overmars.

Watford's second representative in the team was Alec Chamberlain, who did not earn a single point in 2,430 minutes of Premiership football – a longer period than any other player.

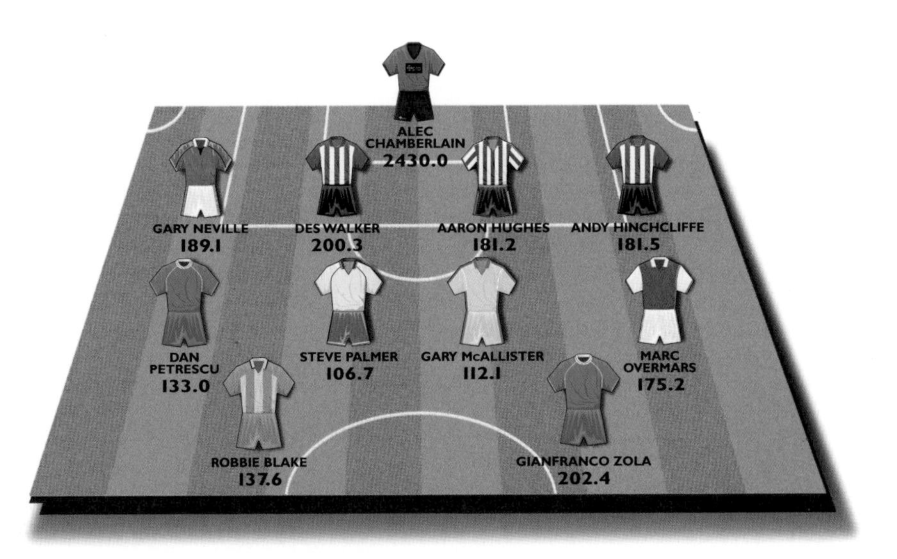

any other team in the 1999–2000 season

Can you remember a positive headline about referees in the 1999-2000 season? No? Now try to think of a negative incident. That's a much easier task, isn't it?

From the moment Uriah Rennie dismissed Alan Shearer in the opening game of the season to the final week, when Andy D'Urso caused uproar by booking five players and sending three more off when Everton visited Leeds United, the majority of times referees got a mention were for negative reasons.

The standard of refereeing has been called into question more and more in recent seasons, but it is no surprise that criticism has become more commonplace as greater coverage is given to the game.

The media spotlight has intensified to such an extent that virtually every decision is scrutinised in painstaking detail, with any number of pundits willing to offer their "expert" opinion.

Referees' Officer Philip Don claimed: "Referees are on a hiding to nothing. When was the last time you read a report which said the referee had a good game? It's always one incident that gets highlighted when a performance should be judged over 90 minutes."

The situation is not helped because managers and players are often outspoken after a match about the performance of a referee and, like the media, rarely praise the officials.

Don said: "Managers are entitled to their opinion, but they do have a responsibility, as what they say often influences the fans and media."

Of course, the referees' performances are judged by a team of assessors and at the end of 1999-2000, Uriah Rennie and Paul Alcock were removed from the Premiership list and will be officiating in the Nationwide League in 2000-01.

Opta's unique referees section highlights the number of fouls awarded, including penalties and the number of yellow and red cards issued, but clearly this is not the whole story. The statistics bear a direct relation to the behaviour of the players involved in the matches as much as a particular referee's interpretation of events on the field.

Also, there is no view within these figures about the severity of punishment or the level of offence committed.

OVERALL RECORD

REFEREE NAME	MATCHES	YELLOW CARDS	RED CARDS	FOULS	PENALTIES	AVERAGE POINTS
Harris	17	62	2	577	1	45.76
Reed	19	78	7	560	4	44.63
Poll	21	75	2	679	4	44.19
D'Urso	20	69	7	591	3	42.45
Rennie	18	58	8	528	4	42.33
Elleray	17.83	59	3	530	3	41.17
Barber	20	68	4	589	2	41.15
Lodge	20	71	6	551	4	40.60
Bennett	12	37	1	341	8	40.17
Jones	20	61	2	602	2	40.15
Riley	16	49	5	447	3	39.56
Durkin	20.17	60	2	579	6	39.12
Barry	20	71	2	529	8	38.90
Winter	21	65	4	568	7	38.48
Dunn	20	66	3	544	3	38.45
Wiley	21	63	1	592	3	37.90
Knight	12	46	1	303	2	37.75
Halsey	13	44	4	321	2	37.15
Wilkie	16	58	3	381	6	36.94
Alcock	19	57	2	493	8	36.84
Gallagher	17	52	1	444	2	36.00
Totals	380	1269	70	10749	85	40.08

Opta's unique blow-by-blow analysis offers the most detailed analysis of referees' performances currently available. Every foul, penalty or card has been logged to offer a fascinating overview of the officials for the 1999-2000 season.

In Opta's unique comparative table, each foul is awarded one point, each penalty or yellow card three points and each red card six points. The final total of disciplinary points for each referee is then divided by the number of games officiated to provide an average on which the referees are sorted in the table above.

While the actions of the players obviously have a bearing on the number of each of these events, the scoring system does provide a snapshot of the strictness of the various officials vis-à-vis their peers in the 1999-2000 campaign.

Last year's strictest officials, Mike Reed and Rob Harris, switch positions from their final placings in 1998-99. Harris officiated at fewer games in 1999-2000, partly because he was banned for several weeks after the Tranmere v Sunderland FA Cup tie fiasco, when he dismissed Clint Hill but then did not notice that the side from the Wirral had brought on a substitute without taking anyone off.

And the fact that he was the strictest referee proved something of a surprise, given that he awarded the fewest penalties and only four officials handed out fewer red cards. Again, this was surprising, as Harris dismissed more players than any other referee in the 1998-99 season.

Just as the strictest referees are still at the top, so 1998-99's most lenient officials remain at the bottom of the table. Dermot Gallagher recorded 1999-2000's lowest average points score, swapping positions with Paul Alcock among those referees still officiating during 1999-2000. But even he could not win, as he was criticised for being too lenient at times.

Alcock's position is strange, in that he awarded the joint-highest number of penalties along with Neale Barry and Steve Bennett.

than any other Premiership referee

HOME TEAMS

REFEREE NAME	GAMES	FOULS	PENALTIES	YELLOW CARDS	RED CARDS	POINTS	POINTS/ GAME
Rennie	18	269	2	27	5	386	21.44
Poll	21	347	1	31	1	449	21.38
Reed	19	262	0	38	3	394	20.74
Barber	20	307	2	29	1	406	20.30
Knight	12	157	2	24	0	235	19.58
Bennett	12	165	4	17	1	234	19.50
Harris	17	261	1	22	0	330	19.41
Halsey	13	177	1	22	1	252	19.38
Riley	16	217	0	25	2	304	19.00
D'Urso	20	278	1	29	1	374	18.70
Elleray	17.83	250	2	25	0	331	18.56
Wiley	21	296	0	31	0	389	18.52
Lodge	20	262	0	32	1	364	18.20
Barry	20	259	2	33	0	364	18.20
Dunn	20	269	2	25	2	362	18.10
Durkin	20.17	271	1	26	1	358	17.75
Winter	21	285	0	25	1	366	17.43
Wilkie	16	169	4	26	1	265	16.56
Gallagher	17	206	1	21	0	272	16.00
Jones	20	266	0	17	0	317	15.85
Alcock	19	232	4	16	1	298	15.68
Total	38	5205	30	541	22	7050	18.55

AWAY TEAMS

REFEREE NAME	GAMES	FOULS	PENALTIES	YELLOW CARDS	RED CARDS	POINTS	POINTS/ GAME
Harris	17	316	0	40	2	448	26.35
Jones	20	336	2	44	2	486	24.30
Reed	19	298	4	40	4	454	23.89
D'Urso	20	313	2	40	6	475	23.75
Poll	21	332	3	44	1	479	22.81
Elleray	17.83	280	1	34	3	403	22.60
Lodge	20	289	4	39	5	448	22.40
Durkin	20.17	308	5	34	1	431	21.37
Alcock	19	261	4	41	1	402	21.16
Winter	21	283	7	40	3	442	21.05
Rennie	18	259	2	31	3	376	20.89
Barber	20	282	0	39	3	417	20.85
Barry	20	270	6	38	2	414	20.70
Bennett	12	176	4	20	0	248	20.67
Riley	16	230	3	24	3	329	20.56
Wilkie	16	212	2	32	2	326	20.38
Dunn	20	275	1	41	1	407	20.35
Gallagher	17	238	1	31	1	340	20.00
Wiley	21	296	3	32	1	407	19.38
Knight	12	146	0	22	1	218	18.17
Halsey	13	144	1	22	3	231	17.77
Total	38	5544	55	728	48	8181	21.53

7 All seven penalties awarded by

HOME AND AWAY

A virtually unheard-of event happened at Old Trafford on 29 January 2000. Referee Andy D'Urso awarded a penalty kick to the opposition!

The incident was significant for two reasons. It was the first penalty awarded against Manchester United at Old Trafford in the league since December 1993, when Norwich City were the beneficiaries, and the disgraceful scenes of dissent which followed sparked a swift and strong reaction from Lancaster Gate.

Andy D'Urso was chased around the penalty area and had to backtrack all the way to the corner flag to avoid being knocked over by a posse of United players vehemently contesting the decision. The FA announced a crackdown on mass protesting against officials' decisions, and indeed several clubs found themselves in the dock by the end of the 1999-2000 campaign.

Philip Don claimed: "That incident was the watershed, and from that point attitudes began to change. I thought he handled it well, although he may have shown a card earlier."

However, one aspect that it showed was the difficulty referees experience when awarding controversial decisions against the home side. And it is interesting to compare the 1998-99 season with the figures from the 1999-2000 campaign.

Quite clearly, away sides were punished more harshly than their home opponents, and it is fascinating to note that for fouls, yellow cards and penalties, the percentage figures are almost identical season-on-season.

Against away side	1998–99	1999–2000
Fouls	52%	52%
Yellow cards	57%	57%
Penalties	64%	65%
Red cards	61%	69%

It is important to look beyond the figures to assess the situation. In the modern game, the onus appears to be very much on the home side to attack and secure three points, with a draw being viewed as a valuable point gained by many visiting teams. This is especially so when playing away at the top sides. Teams defend and play on the counter-attack, which means that they are likely to commit more fouls and earn more cards. Also, because the home side often enjoys territorial advantage, there is a greater chance of a foul being committed in the penalty area.

But certain referees could be considered to be swayed by the home crowd, while others perhaps go the other way.

Jeff Winter were for the home team

REFEREES – CARDS PER GAME

REFEREE	CARDS PER GAME
Reed	4.84
D'Urso	4.15
Lodge	4.15
Rennie	4.11
Knight	4.00
Halsey	4.00
Wilkie	4.00
Harris	3.88
Barber	3.80
Poll	3.76
Barry	3.75
Riley	3.69
Elleray	3.65
Dunn	3.60
Winter	3.48
Bennett	3.25
Jones	3.25
Alcock	3.21
Gallagher	3.18
Durkin	3.17
Wiley	3.10

While the general perception was that referees were stricter in 1999-2000 than in previous seasons, there were actually two fewer red cards than in 1998-99 and 135 fewer cautions.

The campaign opened with much criticism about the number of bookings being made. As a result, a letter was sent to all Premiership referees midway through the season, and this precipitated a reduction in the number of cards. Philip Don remarked: "At the start of the season, refs applied the law but didn't use their discretion as much as they could. This caused outcry, and in January we wrote saying to use more discretion and not be so trigger-happy."

The statistics clearly show the new lenient approach. There were just 21 red cards in the second half of the season compared with 49 up to Boxing Day. There were also 520 yellow cards compared with 749, reducing the average from 4.02 cautions per game to 2.68.

Strictest with regard to cautioning players was Mike Reed, who booked an average of 4.84 players per game, while Alan Wiley was the least likely to flourish a card.

REFEREES – FOULS PER CARD

While referees were instructed that they were able to use their discretion to a greater extent after Christmas, that did not stop players taking advantage of the "amnesty".

Philip Don claimed: "Referees played their part, but I don't think managers and players accepted their responsibility."

In fact, players committed as many fouls as ever, but got away without being cautioned as often, depending on which referee was in charge of a particular game.

Despite being the third most lenient referee over the course of the campaign, Alan Wilkie showed the greatest propensity for issuing cards. He was the only official who allowed on average fewer than six fouls before showing a card, even beating Mike Reed into second place.

The most lenient referee was Peter Jones, who allowed on average more than nine fouls to pass before brandishing a card although, as highlighted earlier, he was far more likely to show one sooner if the player was from the away team. And Alan Wiley was the second most forgiving referee in this category.

REFEREE	FOULS PER CARD
Wilkie	5.95
Reed	6.09
Halsey	6.17
Knight	6.31
Lodge	6.64
Barry	7.05
D'Urso	7.12
Rennie	7.14
Dunn	7.56
Riley	7.58
Barber	7.75
Winter	7.78
Alcock	8.08
Elleray	8.15
Gallagher	8.22
Poll	8.59
Harris	8.74
Bennett	8.74
Durkin	9.05
Wiley	9.11
Jones	9.26

1 Rob Harris – the Premiership's strictest referee –

REFEREES – GAMES PER RED CARD

There was an air of disbelief at St James's Park on the opening day of the 1999-2000 season as Uriah Rennie sent Alan Shearer off for what appeared to be a minor indiscretion.

Shearer was actually sent off for persistent misconduct, but Rennie was also persistently in the news for his decisions.

When Leicester met Liverpool, Rennie dismissed both Frank Sinclair and David Thompson for two bookable offences, but ignored a forearm smash by Matt Elliott on Michael Owen that later earned the Scot a ban after video evidence was reviewed

Not far behind Rennie were Mike Reed – who was rebuked for celebrating a good advantage that led to a goal for Liverpool – and Andy D'Urso, who averaged a red card every 2.7 and 2.9 games respectively.

Reed's most controversial match was West Ham v Arsenal in which he sent off Patrick Vieira, precipitating the infamous spitting incident. D'Urso was notable for dismissing six players from away teams – more than any other referee in the Premiership.

REFEREE	GAMES PER RED
Rennie	2.3
Reed	2.7
D'Urso	2.9
Riley	3.2
Halsey	3.3
Lodge	3.3
Barber	5.0
Winter	5.3
Wilkie	5.3
Elleray	5.9
Dunn	6.7
Harris	8.5
Alcock	9.5
Jones	10.0
Barry	10.0
Durkin	10.1
Poll	10.5
Bennett	12.0
Knight	12.0
Gallagher	17.0
Wiley	21.0

REFEREES – PAYING THE PENALTY

REFEREE	PENALTIES
Bennett	8
Alcock	8
Barry	8
Winter	7
Wilkie	6
Durkin	6
Rennie	4
Reed	4
Lodge	4
Poll	4
Riley	3
Elleray	3
D'Urso	3
Dunn	3
Wiley	3
Knight	2
Halsey	2
Gallagher	2
Barber	2
Jones	2
Harris	1

There were 12 more penalties in the 1999-2000 season than in the previous campaign, and roughly the same proportion of approximately two spot-kicks being awarded to the home side for each one earned by the away team.

Jeff Winter produced the biggest differential, awarding all seven of his spot-kicks to home sides, including an extremely controversial one against Ben Thatcher when Bradford met Wimbledon at Valley Parade.

Strangely, the strictest referee in the top flight awarded just one penalty all season and in fact was the last official to break his spot-kick duck by awarding one to Aston Villa at White Hart Lane in April.

Three refs shared the role of awarding the highest number of penalties, with Paul Alcock, Neale Barry and Steve Bennett all pointing to the spot on eight occasions.

Alan Wilkie officiated at Bradford City v Derby County – one of the most exciting games of the season – and added to the entertainment value by awarding four penalties in the one match which finished 4-4.

awarded the fewest penalties in 1999–2000

THE FA CARLING PREMIERSHIP 2000–01

One of the best parts of being a football supporter is savouring the prospect of a game. The anticipation often surpasses the actual event itself and for many is usually better than the feeling after the match, should a team fall to an ignominious defeat.

And this feeling of anticipation is never stronger than the day that the fixtures are published. There is renewed hope for supporters that this will be their team's year; a new and testing challenge for fans of the promoted sides and the desire for trophy-winners to emulate previous achievements all linger until the first ball is kicked.

Manchester United are seeking a good start to the 2000–01 campaign and have a few added incentives. A title win would see them achieve a hat-trick of league Championships, something that only three teams – Huddersfield Town, Arsenal and Liverpool – have ever achieved.

The Red Devils finished the 1999–2000 season winning 11 Premiership matches in a row, setting a new record for consecutive victories and will be looking to extend that further against Newcastle United. Of course, there is the added element of revenge as the Magpies were the last team to beat the Champions in the Premiership.

Arsenal's Thierry Henry will be looking to set a record himself at the Stadium of Light. The Frenchman scored in seven league matches in a row at the end of 1999–2000 and a goal in his first game of 2000–01 would mean he breaks the record currently held jointly by Mark Stein and Alan Shearer.

Charlton Athletic and Manchester City go head-to-head at The Valley, possibly a case of "better the devil you know" for them, but Ipswich Town have a daunting trip to White Hart Lane to play Spurs and they will have to face new signing Sergei Rebrov who will be looking to impress on his debut for the Lilywhites.

Chelsea and West Ham meet in a London derby, while Bradford renew acquaintances with Liverpool – the team they beat to stay up on the final day of 1999–2000.

There are three sets of fixtures in the first week, with the pick perhaps being Arsenal versus Liverpool, when Arsene Wenger will be looking to record a first-ever win over the Reds. But Ipswich's first home match sees them entertain Manchester United, Bradford continue their tough start by hosting Chelsea and George Graham will take his side north, hoping to exact revenge for the 6–1 FA Cup drubbing by Newcastle United.

The fixtures are printed in chronological order with the league result from each of the previous three seasons printed alongside each match.

All fixtures printed on the following pages are printed courtesy of the FA Premier League and are, of course, subject to change.

19–20 August 2000			1999–2000	1998–99	1997–98
Charlton Athletic	v	Manchester City	0–1	n/a	2–1
Chelsea	v	West Ham United	0–0	0–1	2–1
Coventry City	v	Middlesbrough	2–1	1–2	n/a
Derby County	v	Southampton	2–0	0–0	4–0
Leeds United	v	Everton	1–1	1–0	0–0
Leicester City	v	Aston Villa	3–1	2–2	1–0
Liverpool	v	Bradford City	3–1	n/a	n/a
Manchester United	v	Newcastle United	5–1	0–0	1–1
Sunderland	v	Arsenal	0–0	n/a	n/a
Tottenham Hotspur	v	Ipswich Town	n/a	n/a	n/a

22–23 August 2000			1999–2000	1998–99	1997–98
Arsenal	v	Liverpool	0–1	0–0	0–1
Aston Villa	v	Leeds United	1–0	1–2	1–0
Bradford City	v	Chelsea	1–1	n/a	n/a
Everton	v	Charlton Athletic	n/a	4–1	n/a
Ipswich Town	v	Manchester United	n/a	n/a	n/a
Manchester City	v	Sunderland	n/a	n/a	0–1
Middlesbrough	v	Tottenham Hotspur	2–1	0–0	n/a
Newcastle United	v	Derby County	2–0	2–1	0–0
Southampton	v	Coventry City	0–0	2–1	1–2
West Ham United	v	Leicester City	2–1	3–2	4–3

26–28 August 2000			1999–2000	1998–99	1997–98
Arsenal	v	Charlton Athletic	n/a	0–0	n/a
Aston Villa	v	Chelsea	0–0	0–3	0–2
Bradford City	v	Leicester City	3–1	n/a	n/a
Everton	v	Derby County	2–1	0–0	1–2
Ipswich Town	v	Sunderland	n/a	0–2	2–0
Manchester City	v	Coventry City	n/a	n/a	n/a
Middlesbrough	v	Leeds United	0–0	0–0	n/a
Newcastle United	v	Tottenham Hotspur	2–1	1–1	1–0
Southampton	v	Liverpool	1–1	1–2	1–1
West Ham United	v	Manchester United	2–4	0–0	1–1

5–6 September 2000			1999–2000	1998–99	1997–98
Charlton Athletic	v	Southampton	n/a	5–0	n/a
Chelsea	v	Arsenal	2–3	0–0	2–3
Coventry City	v	Newcastle United	4–1	1–5	2–2
Derby County	v	Middlesbrough	1–3	2–1	n/a
Leeds United	v	Manchester City	n/a	n/a	n/a
Leicester City	v	Ipswich Town	n/a	n/a	n/a
Liverpool	v	Aston Villa	0–0	0–1	3–0
Manchester United	v	Bradford City	4–0	n/a	n/a
Sunderland	v	West Ham United	1–0	n/a	n/a
Tottenham Hotspur	v	Everton	3–2	4–1	1–1

9–10 September 2000			1999–2000	1998–99	1997–98
Bradford City	v	Arsenal	2–1	n/a	n/a
Coventry City	v	Leeds United	3–4	2–2	0–0
Derby County	v	Charlton Athletic	n/a	0–2	n/a
Ipswich Town	v	Aston Villa	n/a	n/a	n/a
Leicester City	v	Southampton	2–1	2–0	3–3
Liverpool	v	Manchester City	n/a	n/a	n/a
Manchester United	v	Sunderland	4–0	n/a	n/a
Middlesbrough	v	Everton	2–1	2–2	n/a
Newcastle United	v	Chelsea	0–1	0–1	3–1
Tottenham Hotspur	v	West Ham United	0–0	1–2	1–0

16–18 September 2000			1999–2000	1998–99	1997–98
Arsenal	v	Coventry City	3–0	2–0	2–0
Aston Villa	v	Bradford City	1–0	n/a	n/a
Charlton Athletic	v	Tottenham Hotspur	n/a	1–4	n/a
Chelsea	v	Leicester City	1–1	2–2	1–0
Everton	v	Manchester United	1–1	1–4	0–2
Leeds United	v	Ipswich Town	n/a	n/a	n/a
Manchester City	v	Middlesbrough	n/a	n/a	2–0
Southampton	v	Newcastle United	4–2	2–1	2–1
Sunderland	v	Derby County	1–1	n/a	n/a
West Ham United	v	Liverpool	1–0	2–1	2–1

23–25 September 2000			1999–2000	1998–99	1997–98
Bradford City	v	Southampton	1–2	n/a	n/a
Coventry City	v	West Ham United	1–0	0–0	1–1
Derby County	v	Leeds United	0–1	2–2	0–5
Ipswich Town	v	Arsenal	n/a	n/a	n/a
Leicester City	v	Everton	1–1	2–0	0–1
Liverpool	v	Sunderland	1–1	n/a	n/a
Manchester United	v	Chelsea	3–2	1–1	2–2
Middlesbrough	v	Aston Villa	0–4	0–0	n/a
Newcastle United	v	Charlton Athletic	n/a	0–0	n/a
Tottenham Hotspur	v	Manchester City	n/a	n/a	n/a

30 September – 2 October 2000			1999–2000	1998–99	1997–98
Arsenal	v	Manchester United	1–2	3–0	3–2
Aston Villa	v	Derby County	2–0	1–0	2–1
Charlton Athletic	v	Coventry City	n/a	1–1	n/a
Chelsea	v	Liverpool	2–0	2–1	4–1
Everton	v	Ipswich Town	n/a	n/a	n/a
Leeds United	v	Tottenham Hotspur	1–0	2–0	1–0
Manchester City	v	Newcastle United	n/a	n/a	n/a
Southampton	v	Middlesbrough	1–1	3–3	n/a
Sunderland	v	Leicester City	2–0	n/a	n/a
West Ham United	v	Bradford City	5–4	n/a	n/a

14–16 October 2000			1999–2000	1998–99	1997–98
Arsenal	v	Aston Villa	3–1	1–0	0–0
Coventry City	v	Tottenham Hotspur	0–1	1–1	4–0
Derby County	v	Liverpool	0–2	3–2	1–0
Everton	v	Southampton	4–1	0–1	0–2
Ipswich Town	v	West Ham United	n/a	n/a	n/a
Leeds United	v	Charlton Athletic	n/a	4–1	n/a
Leicester City	v	Manchester United	0–2	2–6	0–0
Manchester City	v	Bradford City	n/a	n/a	1–0
Middlesbrough	v	Newcastle United	2–2	2–2	n/a
Sunderland	v	Chelsea	4–1	n/a	n/a

21–23 October 2000			1999–2000	1998–99	1997–98
Aston Villa	v	Sunderland	1–1	n/a	n/a
Bradford City	v	Ipswich Town	n/a	0–0	2–1
Charlton Athletic	v	Middlesbrough	n/a	1–1	3–0
Chelsea	v	Coventry City	2–1	2–1	3–1
Liverpool	v	Leicester City	0–2	0–1	1–2
Manchester United	v	Leeds United	2–0	3–2	3–0
Newcastle United	v	Everton	1–1	1–3	1–0
Southampton	v	Manchester City	n/a	n/a	n/a
Tottenham Hotspur	v	Derby County	1–1	1–1	1–0
West Ham United	v	Arsenal	2–1	0–4	0–0

28–30 October 2000			1999–2000	1998–99	1997–98
Arsenal	v	Manchester City	n/a	n/a	n/a
Aston Villa	v	Charlton Athletic	n/a	3–4	n/a
Bradford City	v	Leeds United	1–2	n/a	n/a
Chelsea	v	Tottenham Hotspur	1–0	2–0	2–0
Ipswich Town	v	Middlesbrough	n/a	n/a	1–1
Leicester City	v	Derby County	0–1	1–2	1–2
Liverpool	v	Everton	0–1	3–2	1–1
Manchester United	v	Southampton	3–3	2–1	1–0
Sunderland	v	Coventry City	1–1	n/a	n/a
West Ham United	v	Newcastle United	2–1	2–0	0–1

4–6 November 2000			1999–2000	1998–99	1997–98
Charlton Athletic	v	Bradford City	n/a	n/a	4–1
Coventry City	v	Manchester United	1–2	0–1	3–2
Derby County	v	West Ham United	1–2	0–2	2–0
Everton	v	Aston Villa	0–0	0–0	1–4
Leeds United	v	Liverpool	1–2	0–0	0–2
Manchester City	v	Leicester City	n/a	n/a	n/a
Middlesbrough	v	Arsenal	2–1	1–6	n/a
Newcastle United	v	Ipswich Town	n/a	n/a	n/a
Southampton	v	Chelsea	1–2	0–2	1–0
Tottenham Hotspur	v	Sunderland	3–1	n/a	n/a

11–13 November 2000			1999–2000	1998–99	1997–98
Arsenal	v	Derby County	2–1	1–0	1–0
Aston Villa	v	Tottenham Hotspur	1–1	3–2	4–1
Bradford City	v	Everton	0–0	n/a	n/a
Chelsea	v	Leeds United	0–2	1–0	0–0
Ipswich Town	v	Charlton Athletic	4–2	n/a	3–1
Leicester City	v	Newcastle United	1–2	2–0	0–0
Liverpool	v	Coventry City	2–0	2–0	1–0
Manchester United	v	Middlesbrough	1–0	2–3	n/a
Sunderland	v	Southampton	2–0	n/a	n/a
West Ham United	v	Manchester City	n/a	n/a	n/a

18–20 November 2000			1999–2000	1998–99	1997–98
Charlton Athletic	v	Chelsea	n/a	0–1	n/a
Coventry City	v	Ipswich Town	n/a	n/a	n/a
Derby County	v	Bradford City	0–1	n/a	n/a
Everton	v	Arsenal	0–1	0–2	2–2
Leeds United	v	West Ham United	1–0	4–0	3–1
Manchester City	v	Manchester United	n/a	n/a	n/a
Middlesbrough	v	Leicester City	0–3	0–0	n/a
Newcastle United	v	Sunderland	1–2	n/a	n/a
Southampton	v	Aston Villa	2–0	1–4	1–2
Tottenham Hotspur	v	Liverpool	1–0	2–1	3–3

25–27 November 2000			1999–2000	1998–99	1997–98
Charlton Athletic	v	Sunderland	n/a	n/a	1–1
Coventry City	v	Aston Villa	2–1	1–2	1–2
Derby County	v	Manchester United	1–2	1–1	2–2
Everton	v	Chelsea	1–1	0–0	3–1
Leeds United	v	Arsenal	0–4	1–0	1–1
Manchester City	v	Ipswich Town	1–0	n/a	1–2
Middlesbrough	v	Bradford City	0–1	n/a	1–0
Newcastle United	v	Liverpool	2–2	1–4	1–2
Southampton	v	West Ham United	2–1	1–0	3–0
Tottenham Hotspur	v	Leicester City	2–3	0–2	1–1

2–4 December 2000			1999–2000	1998–99	1997–98
Arsenal	v	Southampton	3–1	1–1	3–0
Aston Villa	v	Newcastle United	0–1	1–0	0–1
Bradford City	v	Coventry City	1–1	n/a	n/a
Chelsea	v	Manchester City	n/a	n/a	n/a
Ipswich Town	v	Derby County	n/a	n/a	n/a
Leicester City	v	Leeds United	2–1	1–2	1–0
Liverpool	v	Charlton Athletic	n/a	3–3	n/a
Manchester United	v	Tottenham Hotspur	3–1	2–1	2–0
Sunderland	v	Everton	2–1	n/a	n/a
West Ham United	v	Middlesbrough	0–1	4–0	n/a

9–11 December 2000			1999–2000	1998–99	1997–98
Arsenal	v	Newcastle United	0–0	3–0	3–1
Bradford City	v	Tottenham Hotspur	1–1	n/a	n/a
Charlton Athletic	v	Manchester United	n/a	0–1	n/a
Chelsea	v	Derby County	4–0	2–1	4–0
Coventry City	v	Leicester City	0–1	1–1	0–2
Liverpool	v	Ipswich Town	n/a	n/a	n/a
Manchester City	v	Everton	n/a	n/a	n/a
Southampton	v	Leeds United	0–3	3–0	0–2
Sunderland	v	Middlesbrough	1–1	n/a	1–2
West Ham United	v	Aston Villa	1–1	0–0	2–1

16–18 December 2000			1999–2000	1998–99	1997–98
Aston Villa	v	Manchester City	n/a	n/a	n/a
Derby County	v	Coventry City	0–0	0–0	3–1
Everton	v	West Ham United	1–0	6–0	2–1
Ipswich Town	v	Southampton	n/a	n/a	n/a
Leeds United	v	Sunderland	2–1	n/a	n/a
Leicester City	v	Charlton Athletic	n/a	1–1	n/a
Manchester United	v	Liverpool	1–1	2–0	1–1
Middlesbrough	v	Chelsea	0–1	0–0	n/a
Newcastle United	v	Bradford City	2–0	n/a	n/a
Tottenham Hotspur	v	Arsenal	2–1	1–3	1–1

23 December 2000			1999–2000	1998–99	1997–98
Charlton Athletic	v	Everton	n/a	1–2	n/a
Chelsea	v	Bradford City	1–0	n/a	n/a
Coventry City	v	Southampton	0–1	1–0	1–0
Derby County	v	Newcastle United	0–0	3–4	1–0
Leeds United	v	Aston Villa	1–2	0–0	1–1
Leicester City	v	West Ham United	1–3	0–0	2–1
Liverpool	v	Arsenal	2–0	0–0	4–0
Manchester United	v	Ipswich Town	n/a	n/a	n/a
Sunderland	v	Manchester City	n/a	n/a	3–1
Tottenham Hotspur	v	Middlesbrough	2–3	0–3	n/a

26 December 2000			1999–2000	1998–99	1997–98
Arsenal	v	Leicester City	2–1	5–0	2–1
Aston Villa	v	Manchester United	0–1	1–1	0–2
Bradford City	v	Sunderland	0–4	0–1	0–4
Everton	v	Coventry City	1–1	2–0	1–1
Ipswich Town	v	Chelsea	n/a	n/a	n/a
Manchester City	v	Derby County	n/a	n/a	n/a
Middlesbrough	v	Liverpool	1–0	1–3	n/a
Newcastle United	v	Leeds United	2–2	0–3	1–1
Southampton	v	Tottenham Hotspur	0–1	1–1	3–2
West Ham United	v	Charlton Athletic	n/a	0–1	n/a

30 December 2000			1999–2000	1998–99	1997–98
Arsenal	v	Sunderland	4–1	n/a	n/a
Aston Villa	v	Leicester City	2–2	1–1	1–1
Bradford City	v	Liverpool	1–0	n/a	n/a
Everton	v	Leeds United	4–4	0–0	2–0
Ipswich Town	v	Tottenham Hotspur	n/a	n/a	n/a
Manchester City	v	Charlton Athletic	1–1	n/a	2–2
Middlesbrough	v	Coventry City	2–0	2–0	n/a
Newcastle United	v	Manchester United	3–0	1–2	0–1
Southampton	v	Derby County	3–3	0–1	0–2
West Ham United	v	Chelsea	0–0	1–1	2–1

1–2 January 2001			1999–2000	1998–99	1997–98
Charlton Athletic	v	Arsenal	n/a	0–1	n/a
Chelsea	v	Aston Villa	1–0	2–1	0–1
Coventry City	v	Manchester City	n/a	n/a	n/a
Derby County	v	Everton	1–0	2–1	3–1
Leeds United	v	Middlesbrough	2–0	2–0	n/a
Leicester City	v	Bradford City	3–0	n/a	n/a
Liverpool	v	Southampton	0–0	7–1	2–3
Manchester United	v	West Ham United	7–1	4–1	2–1
Sunderland	v	Ipswich Town	n/a	2–1	2–2
Tottenham Hotspur	v	Newcastle United	3–1	2–0	2–0

13–15 January 2001			1999–2000	1998–99	1997–98
Arsenal	v	Chelsea	2–1	1–0	2–0
Aston Villa	v	Liverpool	0–0	2–4	2–1
Bradford City	v	Manchester United	0–4	n/a	n/a
Everton	v	Tottenham Hotspur	2–2	0–1	0–2
Ipswich Town	v	Leicester City	n/a	n/a	n/a
Manchester City	v	Leeds United	n/a	n/a	n/a
Middlesbrough	v	Derby County	1–4	1–1	n/a
Newcastle United	v	Coventry City	2–0	4–1	0–0
Southampton	v	Charlton Athletic	n/a	3–1	n/a
West Ham United	v	Sunderland	1–1	n/a	n/a

20–22 January 2001			1999–2000	1998–99	1997–98
Charlton Athletic	v	West Ham United	n/a	4–2	n/a
Chelsea	v	Ipswich Town	n/a	n/a	n/a
Coventry City	v	Everton	1–0	3–0	0–0
Derby County	v	Manchester City	n/a	n/a	n/a
Leeds United	v	Newcastle United	3–2	0–1	4–1
Leicester City	v	Arsenal	0–3	1–1	3–3
Liverpool	v	Middlesbrough	0–0	3–1	n/a
Manchester United	v	Aston Villa	3–0	2–1	1–0
Sunderland	v	Bradford City	0–1	0–0	n/a
Tottenham Hotspur	v	Southampton	7–2	3–0	1–1

30–31 January 2001			1999–2000	1998–99	1997–98
Arsenal	v	Bradford City	2–0	n/a	n/a
Aston Villa	v	Ipswich Town	n/a	n/a	n/a
Charlton Athletic	v	Derby County	n/a	1–2	n/a
Chelsea	v	Newcastle United	1–0	1–1	1–0
Everton	v	Middlesbrough	0–2	5–0	n/a
Leeds United	v	Coventry City	3–0	2–0	3–3
Manchester City	v	Liverpool	n/a	n/a	n/a
Southampton	v	Leicester City	1–2	2–1	2–1
Sunderland	v	Manchester United	2–2	n/a	n/a
West Ham United	v	Tottenham Hotspur	1–0	2–1	2–1

3–5 February 2001			1999–2000	1998–99	1997–98
Bradford City	v	Aston Villa	1–1	n/a	n/a
Coventry City	v	Arsenal	3–2	0–1	2–2
Derby County	v	Sunderland	0–5	n/a	n/a
Ipswich Town	v	Leeds United	n/a	n/a	n/a
Leicester City	v	Chelsea	2–2	2–4	2–0
Liverpool	v	West Ham United	1–0	2–2	5–0
Manchester United	v	Everton	5–1	3–1	2–0
Middlesbrough	v	Manchester City	n/a	n/a	1–0
Newcastle United	v	Southampton	5–0	4–0	2–1
Tottenham Hotspur	v	Charlton Athletic	n/a	2–2	n/a

10–12 February 2001			1999–2000	1998–99	1997–98
Arsenal	v	Ipswich Town	n/a	n/a	n/a
Aston Villa	v	Middlesbrough	1–0	3–1	n/a
Charlton Athletic	v	Newcastle United	n/a	2–2	n/a
Chelsea	v	Manchester United	5–0	0–0	0–1
Everton	v	Leicester City	2–2	0–0	1–1
Leeds United	v	Derby County	0–0	4–1	4–3
Manchester City	v	Tottenham Hotspur	n/a	n/a	n/a
Southampton	v	Bradford City	1–0	n/a	n/a
Sunderland	v	Liverpool	0–2	n/a	n/a
West Ham United	v	Coventry City	5–0	2–0	1–0

24–26 February 2001			1999–2000	1998–99	1997–98
Bradford City	v	West Ham United	0–3	n/a	n/a
Coventry City	v	Charlton Athletic	n/a	2–1	n/a
Derby County	v	Aston Villa	0–2	2–1	0–1
Ipswich Town	v	Everton	n/a	n/a	n/a
Leicester City	v	Sunderland	5–2	n/a	n/a
Liverpool	v	Chelsea	1–0	1–1	4–2
Manchester United	v	Arsenal	1–1	1–1	0–1
Middlesbrough	v	Southampton	3–2	3–0	n/a
Newcastle United	v	Manchester City	n/a	n/a	n/a
Tottenham Hotspur	v	Leeds United	1–2	3–3	0–1

3–5 March 2001			1999–2000	1998–99	1997–98
Arsenal	v	West Ham United	2–1	1–0	4–0
Coventry City	v	Chelsea	2–2	2–1	3–2
Derby County	v	Tottenham Hotspur	0–1	0–1	2–1
Everton	v	Newcastle United	0–2	1–0	0–0
Ipswich Town	v	Bradford City	n/a	3–0	2–1
Leeds United	v	Manchester United	0–1	1–1	1–0
Leicester City	v	Liverpool	2–2	1–0	0–0
Manchester City	v	Southampton	n/a	n/a	n/a
Middlesbrough	v	Charlton Athletic	n/a	2–0	2–1
Sunderland	v	Aston Villa	2–1	n/a	n/a

17–19 March 2001			1999–2000	1998–99	1997–98
Aston Villa	v	Arsenal	1–1	3–2	1–0
Bradford City	v	Manchester City	n/a	n/a	2–1
Charlton Athletic	v	Leeds United	n/a	1–1	n/a
Chelsea	v	Sunderland	4–0	n/a	n/a
Liverpool	v	Derby County	2–0	1–2	4–0
Manchester United	v	Leicester City	2–0	2–2	0–1
Newcastle United	v	Middlesbrough	2–1	1–1	n/a
Southampton	v	Everton	2–0	2–0	2–1
Tottenham Hotspur	v	Coventry City	3–2	0–0	1–1
West Ham United	v	Ipswich Town	n/a	n/a	n/a

31 March – 2 April 2001			1999–2000	1998–99	1997–98
Arsenal	v	Tottenham Hotspur	2–1	0–0	0–0
Bradford City	v	Newcastle United	2–0	n/a	n/a
Charlton Athletic	v	Leicester City	n/a	0–0	n/a
Chelsea	v	Middlesbrough	1–1	2–0	n/a
Coventry City	v	Derby County	2–0	1–1	1–0
Liverpool	v	Manchester United	2–3	2–2	1–3
Manchester City	v	Aston Villa	n/a	n/a	n/a
Southampton	v	Ipswich Town	n/a	n/a	n/a
Sunderland	v	Leeds United	1–2	n/a	n/a
West Ham United	v	Everton	0–4	2–1	2–2

7–9 April 2001			1999–2000	1998–99	1997–98
Aston Villa	v	West Ham United	2–2	0–0	2–0
Derby County	v	Chelsea	3–1	2–2	0–1
Everton	v	Manchester City	n/a	n/a	n/a
Ipswich Town	v	Liverpool	n/a	n/a	n/a
Leeds United	v	Southampton	1–0	3–0	0–1
Leicester City	v	Coventry City	1–0	1–0	1–1
Manchester United	v	Charlton Athletic	n/a	4–1	n/a
Middlesbrough	v	Sunderland	1–1	n/a	3–1
Newcastle United	v	Arsenal	4–2	1–1	0–1
Tottenham Hotspur	v	Bradford City	1–1	n/a	n/a

14 April 2001			1999–2000	1998–99	1997–98
Arsenal	v	Middlesbrough	5–1	1–1	n/a
Aston Villa	v	Everton	3–0	3–0	2–1
Bradford City	v	Charlton Athletic	n/a	n/a	1–0
Chelsea	v	Southampton	1–1	1–0	4–2
Ipswich Town	v	Newcastle United	n/a	n/a	n/a
Leicester City	v	Manchester City	n/a	n/a	n/a
Liverpool	v	Leeds United	3–1	1–3	3–1
Manchester United	v	Coventry City	3–2	2–0	3–0
Sunderland	v	Tottenham Hotspur	2–1	n/a	n/a
West Ham United	v	Derby County	1–1	5–1	0–0

16 April 2001			1999–2000	1998–99	1997–98
Charlton Athletic	v	Aston Villa	n/a	0–1	n/a
Coventry City	v	Sunderland	3–2	n/a	n/a
Derby County	v	Leicester City	3–0	2–0	0–4
Everton	v	Liverpool	0–0	0–0	2–0
Leeds United	v	Bradford City	2–1	n/a	n/a
Manchester City	v	Arsenal	n/a	n/a	n/a
Middlesbrough	v	Ipswich Town	n/a	n/a	1–1
Newcastle United	v	West Ham United	2–2	0–3	0–1
Southampton	v	Manchester United	1–3	0–3	1–0
Tottenham Hotspur	v	Chelsea	0–1	2–2	1–6

21–23 April 2001			1999–2000	1998–99	1997–98
Arsenal	v	Everton	4–1	1–0	4–0
Aston Villa	v	Southampton	0–1	3–0	1–1
Bradford City	v	Derby County	4–4	n/a	n/a
Chelsea	v	Charlton Athletic	n/a	2–1	n/a
Ipswich Town	v	Coventry City	n/a	n/a	n/a
Leicester City	v	Middlesbrough	2–1	0–1	n/a
Liverpool	v	Tottenham Hotspur	2–0	3–2	4–0
Manchester United	v	Manchester City	n/a	n/a	n/a
Sunderland	v	Newcastle United	2–2	n/a	n/a
West Ham United	v	Leeds United	0–0	1–5	3–0

28–30 April 2001			1999–2000	1998–99	1997–98
Charlton Athletic	v	Ipswich Town	1–3	n/a	3–0
Coventry City	v	Liverpool	0–3	2–1	1–1
Derby County	v	Arsenal	1–2	0–0	3–0
Everton	v	Bradford City	4–0	n/a	n/a
Leeds United	v	Chelsea	0–1	0–0	3–1
Manchester City	v	West Ham United	n/a	n/a	n/a
Middlesbrough	v	Manchester United	3–4	0–1	n/a
Newcastle United	v	Leicester City	0–2	1–0	3–3
Southampton	v	Sunderland	1–2	n/a	n/a
Tottenham Hotspur	v	Aston Villa	2–4	1–0	3–2

5–7 May 2001			1999–2000	1998–99	1997–98
Arsenal	v	Leeds United	2–0	3–1	2–1
Aston Villa	v	Coventry City	1–0	1–4	3–0
Bradford City	v	Middlesbrough	1–1	n/a	2–2
Chelsea	v	Everton	1–1	3–1	2–0
Ipswich Town	v	Manchester City	2–1	n/a	1–0
Leicester City	v	Tottenham Hotspur	0–1	2–1	3–0
Liverpool	v	Newcastle United	2–1	4–2	1–0
Manchester United	v	Derby County	3–1	1–0	2–0
Sunderland	v	Charlton Athletic	n/a	n/a	0–0
West Ham United	v	Southampton	2–0	1–0	2–4

19 May 2001			1999–2000	1998–99	1997–98
Charlton Athletic	v	Liverpool	n/a	1–0	n/a
Coventry City	v	Bradford City	4–0	n/a	n/a
Derby County	v	Ipswich Town	n/a	n/a	n/a
Everton	v	Sunderland	5–0	n/a	n/a
Leeds United	v	Leicester City	2–1	0–1	0–1
Manchester City	v	Chelsea	n/a	n/a	n/a
Middlesbrough	v	West Ham United	2–0	1–0	n/a
Newcastle United	v	Aston Villa	0–1	2–1	1–0
Southampton	v	Arsenal	0–1	0–0	1–3
Tottenham Hotspur	v	Manchester United	3–1	2–2	0–2